Randy J. Larsen
WASHINGTON UNIVERSITY IN ST. LOUIS
David M. Buss
UNIVERSITY OF TEXAS AT AUSTIN

Personality Psychology

Eighth Edition

DOMAINS

OF

KNOWLEDGE

ABOUT

HUMAN

NATURE

Mc
Graw
Hill

PERSONALITY PSYCHOLOGY: DOMAINS OF KNOWLEDGE ABOUT HUMAN NATURE, EIGHTH EDITION

Published by McGraw Hill LLC, 1325 Avenue of the Americas, New York, NY 10019. Copyright ©2024 by McGraw Hill LLC. All rights reserved. Printed in the United States of America. Previous editions ©2021, 2018, and 2014. No part of this publication may be reproduced or distributed in any form or by any means, or stored in a database or retrieval system, without the prior written consent of McGraw Hill LLC, including, but not limited to, in any network or other electronic storage or transmission, or broadcast for distance learning.

Some ancillaries, including electronic and print components, may not be available to customers outside the United States.

This book is printed on acid-free paper.

1 2 3 4 5 6 7 8 9 LWI 28 27 26 25 24 23

ISBN 978-1-264-53186-8 (bound edition)
MHID 1-264-53186-9 (bound edition)
ISBN 978-1-266-17485-8 (loose-leaf edition)
MHID 1-266-17485-0 (loose-leaf edition)

Portfolio Manager: *Sarah Remington*
Product Developer: *Elisa Odoard*
Marketing Manager: *Olivia Kaiser*
Content Project Managers: *Lisa Bruflodt*
Manufacturing Project Manager: *Rachel Hirschfield*
Content Licensing Specialist: *Gina Oberbroeckling*
Cover Image: *Tavis Wright/Image Source, Lightspring/Shutterstock, Svisio/Getty Images, Science Photo Library RF/Getty Images, Lightspring/Shutterstock, Athanasia Nomikou/Shutterstock*
Compositor: *Straive*

All credits appearing on page or at the end of the book are considered to be an extension of the copyright page.

Library of Congress Cataloging-in-Publication Data

Names: Larsen, Randy J., author. | Buss, David M., author.
Title: Personality psychology : domains of knowledge about human nature / Randy J. Larsen, David M. Buss.
Description: Eighth edition. | New York, NY : McGraw Hill, [2024] | Includes bibliographical references and index.
Identifiers: LCCN 2022048326 (print) | LCCN 2022048327 (ebook) | ISBN 9781264531868 (paperback) | ISBN 9781266183867 (ebook)
Subjects: LCSH: Personality.
Classification: LCC BF698 .L3723 2024 (print) | LCC BF698 (ebook) | DDC 155.2–dc23/eng/20221017
LC record available at https://lccn.loc.gov/2022048326
LC ebook record available at https://lccn.loc.gov/2022048327

The Internet addresses listed in the text were accurate at the time of publication. The inclusion of a website does not indicate an endorsement by the authors or McGraw Hill LLC, and McGraw Hill LLC does not guarantee the accuracy of the information presented at these sites.

mheducation.com/highered

Dedication

To all my students of personality, especially Tim Bono, who is applying this knowledge to improve the lives of others.

RL

To my father Arnold H. Buss.

DB

Brief Contents

Contents

*Top Left: Tavis Wright/Image
Source; Top Right: Svisio/Getty
Images; Middle Left: Science Photo
Library RF/Getty Images; Middle
Right: Lightspring/Shutterstock;
Bottom Left: Arthimedes/
Shutterstock; Bottom Right:
Athanasia Nomikou/Shutterstock*

PART I

The Dispositional Domain

HOWARD BARTROP/
Image Source

Chapter 3

Traits and Trait Taxonomies 56

Chapter 4

Theoretical and Measurement Issues in Trait Psychology 86

Chapter 5

Personality Dispositions over Time: Stability, Coherence, and Change   122

PART II

The Biological Domain

Svisio/Getty Images

Chapter 6

Genetics and Personality   154

Chapter 7

Physiological Approaches to Personality   184

Chapter 8
Evolutionary Perspectives on Personality   222

PART III
The Intrapsychic Domain

Chapter 9
Psychoanalytic Approaches to Personality   260

Science Photo Library RF/Getty Images

Chapter 10
Psychoanalytic Approaches: Contemporary Issues   296

Chapter 11
Motives and Personality   330

Contents   xi

PART IV

The Cognitive/Experiential Domain

Chapter 12

Cognitive Topics in Personality   368

Lightspring/Shutterstock

Chapter 13

Emotion and Personality   400

Lightspring/Shutterstock

Chapter 17
Culture and Personality   524

PART VI
The Adjustment Domain

Chapter 18
Stress, Coping, Adjustment, and Health   554

Athanasia Nomikou/Shutterstock

Chapter 19
Disorders of Personality   584

Chapter 20
Summary and Future Directions   624

About the Authors

Randy J. Larsen received his MA in Clinical Psychology from Duquesne University and his PhD in Personality Psychology from the University of Illinois at Champaign-Urbana. Over the years, his clinical experiences include adolescent therapist (Illinois Department of Children and Family Services), prison psychologist (Pennsylvania Department of Corrections), police psychologist (Steel Valley Council of Governments), and prison educator (Missouri Eastern Correctional Center). As a college professor, he has served on the faculty of Purdue University, the University of Michigan (where he met David Buss and began collaborating on this book), and Washington University in St. Louis. His research awards include a Distinguished Scientific

Courtesy of Randy J. Larsen

Achievement Award for Early Career Contributions to Personality Psychology from the American Psychological Association and a Research Scientist Development Award from the National Institute of Mental Health. He has been an associate editor at the *Journal of Personality and Social Psychology, Cognition and Emotion,* and the *Personality and Social Psychology Bulletin* and has been on the editorial boards of the *Journal of Research in Personality, Review of General Psychology,* and the *Journal of Personality.* He has authored over 150 scientific papers and book chapters in personality psychology and is on the Institute of Scientific Information's list of the top 25 most cited scientists in his discipline. His books include *The Science of Subjective Well-Being* (with Michael Eid; Guilford Press), *Taking Sides in Personality Psychology* (with Laurel Newman; McGraw-Hill), and *Handbook of Personality Processes and Individual Differences* (with Lynne Cooper; APA Press). Randy Larsen has served on several Scientific Review Groups for the National Institutes of Health and the National Research Council. His research on personality has been supported by the National Institute of Mental Health, the National Science Foundation, the National Institute of Aging, the National Institute of General Medical Sciences, the McDonnell Foundation for Cognitive Neuroscience, and the Solon Summerfield Foundation. Currently Randy Larsen is the William R. Stuckenberg Professor of Human Values and Moral Development at Washington University in St. Louis. His recent classes there include personality psychology, positive psychology, introductory psychology, and ethics for scientists. He lives in St. Louis with his wife, and their two children are currently in college.

David M. Buss

David M. Buss received his PhD from the University of California at Berkeley. He served on the faculties of Harvard University and the University of Michigan before accepting a professorship at the University of Texas at Austin, where he currently teaches. Buss received the American Psychological Association (APA) Distinguished Scientific Award for Early Career Contribution to Personality Psychology, the APA G. Stanley Hall Award, and the APA Distinguished Scientist Lecturer Award. Books by David Buss include *The Evolution of Desire: Strategies of Human Mating* (Revised Edition) (Basic Books, 2016), which has been translated into 10 languages; *Evolutionary Psychology: The New Science of the Mind* (6th ed.) (Taylor & Francis, 2019), which was presented with the Robert W. Hamilton Book Award; *The Dangerous Passion: Why Jealousy Is as Necessary as Love and Sex* (Free Press, 2000), which has been translated into 13 languages; and two editions of *The Handbook of Evolutionary Psychology* (Wiley, 2005, 2016). Buss has authored more than 300 scientific publications and has also written articles for *The New York Times* and the *Times Higher Education Supplement.* He appears in the ISI List of Most Highly Cited Psychologists Worldwide, has been cited as one of the most eminent psychologists of the modern era, and has been cited as one of the 30 most influential living psychologists. The American Psychological Society (APS) awarded David Buss the Mentor Award for Lifetime Achievement in 2017. He lectures widely throughout the United States and abroad and has extensive cross-cultural research collaborations. David Buss greatly enjoys teaching and had the honor of winning the President's Teaching Excellence Award at the University of Texas.

Preface

We have devoted our lives to the scientific study of personality. We believe this sub-discipline, the scientific study of what it means to be a person, is one of the most exciting parts of psychology. Thus we were enormously gratified to see the volume of e-mails, letters, and comments from satisfied consumers of our first through seventh editions. At the same time, preparing the eighth edition proved to be a humbling experience. The cascade of exciting findings in the field of personality is formidable, requiring not merely updating but also the addition of major sections of new material. Moreover, in important ways, our first edition proved prescient in terms of changes in how the field is organized and taught.

Rather than organize our text around the traditional grand theories of personality, we devised a framework of six important domains of knowledge about personality functioning. These six domains are the *dispositional domain* (traits, trait taxonomies, and personality dispositions over time), the *biological domain* (physiology, genetics, evolution), the *intrapsychic domain* (psychodynamics, motives), the *cognitive-experiential domain* (cognition, emotion, and the self), the *social and cultural domain* (social interaction, gender, and culture), and the *adjustment domain* (stress, coping, health, and personality disorders). We believed these domains of knowledge best represented the state of affairs in personality psychology in the year 2000, as we were writing the first edition of this text. Progress in the field since then has continued to bear out that belief as new knowledge has accumulated in each of these domains.

In addition to major organizing themes (the six domains), our previous editions also differed from other personality texts in the importance placed on *culture, gender,* and *biology,* and these areas of personality have shown substantial growth in recent years. But we have also been fascinated to witness and describe growth in *each* of the six major domains of personality that form the organizational core of the book.

We have always envisioned our text as a reflection of the contemporary personality psychology. Our desire is to capture the excitement of what the science of personality is all about. For the eighth edition, we did our best to remain true to that vision. We believe that the field of personality psychology has entered a golden age, and we hope that the changes we've made to the eighth edition convey a discipline that is vibrant in a way it never has been before. After all, no other field is devoted to the study of all that it means to be human.

For this edition, each chapter has been streamlined through judicious trimming. This provided room for discussing new research conducted within the past three years, making length of this edition similar to the previous. Significant additions to the seventh edition are described below.

Chapter 1: Introduction to Personality Psychology
- Editing to streamline the writing and update the goals of personality research.

Chapter 2: Personality Assessment, Measurement, and Research Design
- Experience sampling used to identify the negative effects of being indoors and computer screen time usage on loneliness during the COVID-19 pandemic.
- A spouse or lover has access to privileged information often inaccessible through other sources, such as their sexual behavior.
- Even the facial expressions displayed during these laboratory conflicts predict subsequent marital outcomes.

- T-data enable experimenters to *test specific hypotheses,* such as the predicted effect of Extraversion on social decision making.
- Actometer measures have been used to assess hyperactivity and ADHD in children.
- Traits such as Narcissism and Psychopathy are positively correlated with pornography consumption.
- Sensation seeking successfully predicted a variety of gambling behaviors, such as playing the lottery, betting on sporting events, playing video poker, using slot machines, and addiction to cocaine.

Chapter 3: Traits and Trait Taxonomies
- Frequency of suicidal ideation, for example, is a good predictor of depressive symptoms.
- One study found as many as eight factors from an analysis of personality nouns, including Dummy (twit, trash), Doll (beauty, sweetie), Philosopher (bookworm, nonconformist), Goof (joker, clown), Chatterbox (flirt, loudmouth), and Ladies' man (stud, hunk).
- New exercise assessing the degree to which people are currently seeking short-term mating (casual sex) versus long-term committed mating relationships.
- New book recommendation on the strengths of introverts: Cain, S. (2013). *Quiet: The power of introverts in a world that can't stop talking.* Broadway Books.
- High-N scorers tend to express more dissatisfaction with their romantic relationships.
- Introverts also seem to cope better with being alone during the COVID-19 pandemic, cope better with chronic pain, and suffer fewer sleep disturbances compared to extraverts.
- A recent review of 152 studies found that the HEXACO model provided broader coverage of the personality domain compared to the five-factor model.

Chapter 4: Theoretical and Measurement Issues in Trait Psychology
- Updated information and links on dating sites that use personality testing to match people
- Clarified how personality tests can be used in selection settings, and how measurement accuracy (reliability and validity) can influence success in selection efforts.
- Improved description of how a few primary traits can combine to create unique personalities.
- Introduce how a high test-retest correlation does not mean people did not change between testing, instead it confirms that people maintained their rank order over time.
- Include recent references to person–situation interaction.
- Since Walter Michel and Seymour Epstein recently passed away, reference to their important work and ideas is now described in the past tense.
- Clarified the concept of "aggregation" and added it as a key term in this edition.
- More detail provided on Barnum statements in personality feedback, using astrology and Bradley Cooper's "mentalist" character in the movie "Nightmare Alley" as examples of how overly general statements can be believable.
- Provide a link to a Big Five assessment site where students can take the questionnaire and obtain personal testing feedback that is quantitative, specific, and based on empirical research.

- Updated research on the female underprediction effect with a report by the College Board (2019) on their SAT underpredicting college GPA for women compared to men.
- Material on using personality tests to select police officers is updated with reference to the George Floyd murder, plus newer references to specific scales in the 16PF that are used in police screening tests is provided.

Chapter 5: Personality Dispositions over Time: Stability, Coherence, and Change
- Cohort changes in sex ratio: In the United States, more than 56 percent of college students are women.
- Subsequent studies confirm that neuroticism predicts divorce.
- High conscientiousness is linked to later income and net worth.
- A study of 272 Japanese centenarians found that these long-lived individuals score high on extraversion and low on neuroticism.
- High conscientiousness and low neuroticism are linked to better coping with anxiety surrounding COVID-19.
- New section reporting research designed to effectively change personality traits, such as increasing one's level of extraversion and decreasing one's level of neuroticism, in desired directions.

Chapter 6: Genetics and Personality
- Many would-be parents are very interested in findings from genetic research. Some express a desire not to have children if they knew they would carry a genetic disposition for a mental disorder.
- A study of 12,117 dogs found that they differed greatly in boldness versus timidness, with bolder dogs exploring more, positively approaching unfamiliar people, and showing low levels of fear.
- A large-scale study of the HEXACO personality traits, which includes the Honest-Humility factor, found heritabilities ranging from 34 to 58 percent.
- Genotype–environment correlations are becoming increasingly important in understanding the complex processes of how personality and social environments are connected.
- A recent study implicated DRD2, DRD4, and two other genes linked to sensation seeking among adolescents.

Chapter 7: Physiological Approaches to Personality
- Reference to some of Damasio's recent work on the mind–body connection.
- New details on the case of Phineas Gage and the 2009 discovery of his photo with the iron rod that inflicted his head wound.
- Discussion of "wearable" technology sensors (e.g., watches, rings, micro-recorders) that can monitor several physiological and behavioral systems, and their recent inclusion in personality research.
- Cautionary note attached to discussion of digit ratio, advising that empirical research published in peer-reviewed research should be weighted more heavily when evaluating results.
- New research on skin conductance and neuroticism.
- New material on heart rate variability (HRV) in section on cardiac measures, and the meaning of heart rate variability for research on stress and personality.
- New citations to studies on brain structure (volume) and personality as well as with intelligence.

- Update on the Human Connectome Project and its role in facilitating research on personality and brain connections between regions.
- New references to extraversion research and to MAO and sensation seeking.
- New example of a computer game to illustrate approach motivation by reward and avoidance motivation by punishment.
- Review of research on coping with the COVID-19 pandemic, with emphasis on punishment sensitivity relating to avoiding risks (e.g., not taking public transportation) and reward sensitivity relating to a reluctance to socially distance or isolate.
- Reference to studies on going against one's chronotype (morningness or eveningness), and now have "chronotype" as a key term.

Chapter 8: Evolutionary Perspectives on Personality
- Characteristics that were probably adaptive in ancestral environments—such as *xenophobia,* or fear of strangers—are not necessarily adaptive in modern environments. This is an example of an *evolutionary mismatch,* a feature adaptive in the past that is no longer adaptive in the modern world.
- The need to belong theory has been used to explain a wide range of phenomena, including cheering for sports teams, joining religious groups, forming online gaming communities, conformity to the group, social identity, reputation management, creating political coalitions, and even the increased political polarization currently witnessed in some countries.
- Humans, of course, help people who are not close kin. We form friendships with non-kin, which sometimes can last a lifetime. We help friends who are in need, and they in turn help us when we are in need. This is the defining feature of *reciprocal altruism*—incurring costs to self to deliver benefits to other with the expectation that those benefits will be reciprocated or returned now or at some future time. The personality trait Agreeableness has been linked with a strong proclivity to be a good reciprocal altruist.
- A recent test of the universality of emotion expression examined the facial expressions of 63 sculptures created in the Americas dating back to 1500 BCE prior to any contact with Western civilization. The authors conclude that modern Westerners share with ancient pre-contact peoples the links between facial expression of emotion and the social contexts in which these expressions commonly occur.
- Emotions can also be expressed by nonverbal body language. A prime example is the emotion of *pride.* When people win an athletic contest, for example, they commonly thrust both arms in the air, forming a V, perhaps symbolic for victory. The nonverbal expression of triumph appears to be recognized across cultures. The nonverbal V is also displayed by congenitally blind individuals who win athletic contests.
- Individual differences in the *fearfulness* facet of neuroticism are predicted by physical strength. Weaker people are more fearful, presumably because they are more vulnerable to threats and fear motivates them to avoid social confrontations.

Chapter 9: Psychoanalytic Approaches to Personality
- Update on the case of Ross Cheit described in chapter opening.
- Updated description of, and references to, research on blindsight and deliberation outside of awareness.
- New material on the scientific status of the ego depletion concept, including several preregistered multi-site experiments that support the basic idea.

- Introduce a fourth form of anxiety, introduced by students of Freud, called self-esteem anxiety, and include this as a new key term.
- Moved some material around to improve the flow of the chapter.

Chapter 10: Psychoanalytic Approaches: Contemporary Issues
- Update on the Holly Ramona case.
- New material on, and link to, the False Memory Syndrome Foundation, and its role in helping patients, families, and legal teams dealing with potentially false memories of abuse.
- New references to Loftus' recent work on false memories (imagination inflation effect) as well as the effects of misinformation on beliefs in conspiracy theories.
- Include links to examples of subliminal advertisements.
- Reference to new work by Jonathon Bargh on unconscious priming effects.
- Report on a meta-analysis on narcissism and high levels of interpersonal conflict.
- Update on Kamala Harris, who is now the first female Vice President of the United States.
- More clear description of what are the "objects" in object relations theory.
- Include several new links to sites where students can take an assessment of their adult attachment style.
- Mention family separations in the current Ukraine conflict as an example of adult attachment disruption.
- "Caregiver" now used, along with mother or parent, in discussing childhood attachment.
- Clarify the connection between childhood separation anxiety and adult relationship disruption, and provide the example of couples in the current Ukraine conflict having to split up, with mothers (and children) leaving the country while fathers stay behind.
- More discussion of the possibility of change in adult attachment styles, with reference to current research.

Chapter 11: Motives and Personality
- Link to videos of Michael Johnson setting the 200-meter world record.
- New citation to definition of motives.
- Updated research on implicit and explicit motives.
- Include replication studies on gender differences in need for intimacy motive.
- Include research on Vladimir Putin's high level of need for power, and suggest this motive may underly his 2022 war on Ukraine, and include studies that use politician's motive scores from speeches to predict the start or end of wars.
- Update on Pete Buttigieg as an example of a high need for achievement person.
- Updated TAT references.
- New research on need for achievement and children's beliefs that intelligence is fixed or malleable (from Carol Dweck's theory).
- Mention social media use, instant messaging, and e-mail behaviors that relate to need for intimacy.
- Update research on Kenrick's re-interpretation of Maslow's need hierarchy.

Chapter 12: Cognitive Topics in Personality
- Updated research on racial bias and lethal force errors among police officers.
- Newer research on Field Dependence/Independence described.
- Reducer/augmenter section has three new studies cited.
- Current research linking locus of control to the COVID-19 pandemic (internals report less stress, more compliance with mitigation guidelines, and more likely to take the vaccine).

- Explicitly distinguish locus of control (pertains to positive/rewarding events) and attributional style (pertains to negative events).
- Newer citations for attributional style.
- Update on personal projects analysis and introduce the concept of well-doing.
- Newer studies establishing the Flynn Effect in college students, and another documenting that this trend has reversed (called the negative Flynn Effect) in the past two decades.
- Added birth and death dates for major figures in this area, and in other chapters as well.

Chapter 13: Emotion and Personality
- Newer citations for measuring positive emotions.
- Update with latest (2022) United Nations survey data on world happiness.
- New key term: eudaimonia—the view that happiness is attained by living a life of meaning and purpose.
- Numerous updates to happiness research.
- Several link errors fixed.
- New research presented on positive illusions.
- New research on personality trait predictors of happiness, plus the role of pro-social behaviors.
- New research on treating depression with exercise.
- New research on the relation between violence and brain abnormalities, with new citations to work of Jonathan Pincus and Adrian Raine.

Chapter 14: Approaches to the Self
- Self-esteem is now a key term.
- Use of social media acronyms (e.g., IRL for In Real Life, FOMO for Fear of Missing Out).
- Several references to the COVID-19 pandemic in examples.
- New studies on social comparison as the toxic element of problematic social media use.
- New research on "helicopter parenting" and its effects on adolescent self-esteem.
- New "Application" on an Asian elephant in the Bronx Zoo who passed the dot-and-mirror test of self-awareness.
- New studies on self-complexity, defensive pessimism, self-handicapping, self-esteem variability, and domain-specific self-esteem.
- Updated links within the chapter.
- Connected self-schema to the concept of associative networks in memory first introduced in Chapter 10.
- Link the topic of social identity to the concept of "reputation."
- Mention studies that question the concept of implicit self-esteem.
- Since Jerome Kagan passed away in 2021, reference to his work changed to past tense.

Chapter 15: Personality and Social Interaction
- Personality also influences our selection of friends. People high on extraversion and agreeableness, for example, tend to choose a larger number of friends on social networking sites compared to more introverted and disagreeable people.
- Vulnerable narcissists, who have somewhat shaky self-esteem, are especially prone to the hostile attribution bias.

- When marital conflicts arise, emotionally unstable partners tend to use *avoidance rather than compromise* to deal with it, thus perpetuating the conflict.
- The link between agreeableness and social likability has been documented as early as adolescence.
- People sometimes try to manipulate their prospective in-laws for the goal of help in solidifying their mateship with their offspring.
- Dark Triad men are apt to use coercion as a tactic of manipulation to obtain sex from reluctant or unwilling women.

Chapter 16: Sex, Gender, and Personality
- Gender differences in emotional stability are especially important because they are linked with important life outcomes such as risk of eating disorders such as binging and purging, which are much more common in females.
- Low self-esteem in women predicts vulnerability to depression in adolescents and college students.
- Although the sexes differ overall in sexual aggression, it really appears to be limited to a subset of men—those who are high on Dark Triad traits, lack empathy, and display hostile masculinity, especially if they also pursue a short-term mating strategy.
- Gender differences in empathizing, in turn, are linked to altruistic behavior such as helping those in need and sharing their belongings.
- Women score higher than men on *objectified body consciousness,* which involves becoming observers and critics of their bodies and feeling shame when their bodies to not match up with cultural idealized body standards.
- The current movement toward using gender-neutral pronouns such as *they, them,* and *theirs,* or novel ones such as *ze* and *xe,* reflect people who do not identify with the gender binary.
- Most reviews conclude that gender stereotypes are well-calibrated to actual gender differences and are not exaggerated.
- Fetal exposure to hormones can have lasting effects on gender-linked interests and abilities.

Chapter 17: Culture and Personality
- A cultural perspective on personality is critical for testing the generalizability of both findings and theories of personality functioning.
- Cultural variation in the number of children a woman has appears to be evoked partly as a consequence of the cultural level of economic development and the cultural level of social support provided to women.
- A longitudinal study found that Australian children who experienced harsher and more unpredictable cultural environments engaged in more and earlier sexual activity.
- Experiments conducted in China and Canada show that when the threat of disease is made salient to people, they are more likely to conform on experimental tasks.
- Self-enhancement, which is culturally variable, shows up in considering oneself "better than average" and over-claiming credit for successful group outcomes.
- Higher exposure to culturally credible cues of religious commitment in others increases religious beliefs—an illustration of transmitted culture.
- A study in Spain concluded that beliefs about the traits of men being more *agentic* and the traits of women being more *communal* show remarkable stability over more than three decades, from 1985 to 2018.

Chapter 18: Stress, Coping, Adjustment, and Health
- COVID-19 is used to illustrate that, while many diseases are caused by microbes, their transmission is often through specific behaviors that can be modified.
- We streamlined content throughout in order to make room for a new section on personality and the COVID-19 pandemic. We now illustrate how the five models of the personality–illness link have been applied to the COVID-19 pandemic as well as to the restrictions recommended by public health officials.
- New key term: Allostatic Load, which refers to the total accumulated "wear and tear" on the body produced by stress over time.
- Covered new research on optimistic attributional style as a mediator of the effects of character strengths on risk for depression.
- Added a link to Carver and Scheier's optimism questionnaire.
- Discuss research that separates the presence of optimism from the absence of pessimism to examine their separate effects on health.
- Describe an application of the Pennebaker expressive writing paradigm applied to college students' personal struggles with the COVID-19 pandemic.
- Shortened the Closer Look on the role of positive emotions in coping with stress.
- Added a new study on Type A illustrating how this individual difference conforms more to a dimension (normally distributed) than to a true typology.
- Cite CDC data showing that heart disease remains the number one cause of death in the United States (though in 2022 COVID-19 was a close second).

Chapter 19: Disorders of Personality
- Update to the case of Kody Scott, which opens this chapter. Mr. Scott passed away from natural causes in 2021, a few months after release from a prison sentence following a 2017 assault conviction. While he had several opportunities to change his life of violence, his repeated convictions throughout his life illustrate that, for most people with a personality disorder, change is difficult and unlikely.
- Updated research on a dimensional (versus categorical) model of personality disorders.
- Description of the minor update to the DSM, which is now titled DSM 5-TR (for Text Revision).
- While the DSM 5-TR continues the categorical approach to personality disorders, we now describe the World Health Organization's (WHO) International Classification of Diseases (ICD) system. In 2022 the ICD fully adopted a dimensional approach to personality disorders. The ICD was ratified by all 193 member nations of the WHO, whereas the DSM is a product mainly of one country—the United States. For now, the DSM 5-TR is the standard for diagnosis in the United States, and so we present this approach to personality disorders. However, we wanted students to be aware of the alternative—the ICD—which is in use in most other developed countries around the world.
- Added detail to Table 19.11 describing the self-concept, emotional, behavioral, and social relationship disturbances associated with the 10 DSM 5-TR personality disorders.

Chapter 20: Summary and Future Directions
- Understanding the role of situations will generate efforts to form a taxonomy of situations, similar to how the field has developed a taxonomy of traits.
- Genetics of personality turning out to be more complex than initially envisioned.
- Progress in linking the six domains of human nature to each other via research collaborations.

Acknowledgments

We would like to thank our own mentors and colleagues who, over the years, generated in us a profound interest in psychology. These include Arnold Buss, Joe Horn, Devendra Singh, and Lee Willerman (*University of Texas*); Jack Block, Ken Craik, Harrison Gough, Jerry Mendelsohn, and Richard Lazarus (*University of California, Berkeley*); Roy Baumeister (*Florida State University, Tallahassee*); Brian Little, Harry Murray, and David McClelland (*Harvard University*); Sam Gosling, Bob Josephs, Jamie Pennebaker, and Bill Swann (now at *University of Texas*); Ed Diener (*University of Illinois*); Gerry Clore (*University of Virginia*); Chris Peterson (*University of Michigan*); Hans Eysenck and Ray Cattell (both deceased); Tom Oltmanns, Roddy Roediger, and Mike Strube (*Washington University*); Alice Eagly (*Northwestern University*); Janet Hyde (*University of Wisconsin*); and Robert Plomin (*King's College London*), Lew Goldberg (*Oregon Research Institute*), and Jerry Wiggins (formerly *University of British Columbia*) as mentors from afar. Special thanks go to Bill Graziano and Ken Thompson, LtCol, USMC (retired), for helpful comments on the text. We would also like to thank our team at McGraw-Hill, including Product Developer Francesca King, Content Project Manager Lisa Bruflodt, Content Licensing Specialist Gina Oberbroeckling, Rights and Permissions Manager Janet Robbins, Project Manager Leslie Lahr, and the entire resource development team.

Finally, RL would like to acknowledge family members who supported him and tolerated his neglect while he concentrated on this book, including his wife, Zvjezdana, and his children, Tommy and Ana. DB would like to thank his ".50" genetic relatives: his parents Arnold and Edith Buss; his siblings Arnie and Laura Buss; and his children Ryan and Tara Buss.

A project of this scope and magnitude requires the efforts of many people. We are greatly indebted to our colleagues who reviewed this manuscript in its various stages. We sincerely appreciate the time and effort that the following instructors gave in this regard:

Jonathon D. Brown
University of Washington

Juliana Lasser
Southern Connecticut State University

Anse Daniel
Miami Dade College

Kenneth Locke
University of Idaho

Matthew Eisenhard
Rowan University

Lynda Mae
Arizona State University

Jessica Fede
Johnson & Wales University

Damian Murray
Tulane University

We also continue to be grateful to the reviewers of our previous editions for their valuable comments.

Alan J. Lambert
Washington University

Bill E. Peterson
Smith College

Alan Roberts
Indiana University

Brian Little
Harvard University

Alisha Janowsky
University of Central Florida

Carolin Keutzer
University of Oregon

Barbara Woike
Barnard College

Charles Mahone
Texas Tech University

Barry Fritz
Quinnipiac University

Christopher Hopwood
Michigan State University

Christopher Leone
  University of North Florida
Christopher VerWys
  Rensselaer Polytechnic Institute
David Harold Zald
  Vanderbilt University
David Pincus
  Chapman University
Eros DeSouza
  Illinois State University
Evan Harrington
  John Jay College of Criminal Justice
Forrest B. Tyler
  *University of Maryland at College
  Park*
Fred B. Bryant
  Loyola University Chicago
Gail A. Hinesley
  Chadron State College
Gerald A. Mendelsohn
  University of California at Berkeley
Gerald Matthews
  University of Cincinnati
Glenn Geher
  *State University of New York–New
  Paltz*
Irene Frieze
  University of Pittsburgh
Jane E. Gordon
  *The McGregor School of Antioch
  College*
Jeff Conte
  San Diego State University
Jeff Conte
  San Diego State University
Jeff Simpson
  Texas A&M University
Jennifer R. Daniels
  Lyon College
Jennifer Wartella
  Virginia Commonwealth University
Jill C. Keogh
  University of Missouri–Columbia
Joan Cannon
  University of Massachusetts at Lowell
John E. Kurtz
  Villanova University
Jonathan C. Smith
  Roosevelt University
Jovan Hernandez
  Metropolitan State University of Denver

Julie K. Norem
  Wellesley College
Justin W. Peer
  University of Michigan–Dearborn
Katherine Ellison
  Montclair State University
Katherine Lau
  SUNY Oneonta
Kathryn Erk
  Fort Hays State University
Kenneth Locke
  University of Idaho
Kristy Thacker
  University at Albany
Lani Fujitsubo
  Southern Oregon State College
Laura A. King
  Southern Methodist University
Len B. Lecci
  *University of North Carolina at
  Wilmington*
Lisa Rapalyea
  University of California–Davis
Lynda Mae
  Arizona State University
Lyra Stein
  Rutgers University
Marcellus Merritt
  University of Wisconsin–Milwaukee
Marjorie Hanft-Martone
  Eastern Illinois University
Mark E. Sibicky
  Marietta College
Mark R. Leary
  Wake Forest University
Mark S. Chapell
  Rowan University
Marvin W. Kahn
  University of Arizona
Michael Ashton
  Brock University
Michael D. Botwin
  California State University–Fresno
Michael J. Lambert
  Brigham Young University
Nicole E. Barenbaum
  University of the South
Richard Ely
  Boston University
Robert M. Stelmack
  University of Ottawa

Sarah Wood
  University of Wisconsin–Stout
Scott J. Dickman
  University of Massachusetts at Dartmouth
Stephanie Sogg
  Massachusetts General Hospital; Harvard Bipolar Research Program
Stephen G. Flanagan
  University of North Carolina
Stephen J. Owens
  Ohio University
Steven C. Funk
  Northern Arizona University
Steven Kent Sutton
  University of Miami
Susan B. Goldstein
  University of Redlands

Tammy Crow
  Southeastern Oklahoma State University
Tammy Crow
  Southeastern Oklahoma State University
Timothy Atchison
  West Texas A&M University
Todd Nelson
  California State University–Stanislaus
Tracy Richards
  Colorado State University
Vetta L. Sanders Thompson
  University of Missouri at St. Louis
Wayne A. Dixon
  Southwestern Oklahoma State University
William Pavot
  Southwest Minnesota State University

The eighth edition of *Personality Psychology* is available online with Connect, McGraw-Hill Education's integrated assignment and assessment platform. Connect also offers SmartBook for the new edition, which is the first adaptive reading experience proven to improve grades and help students study more effectively. All of the title's website and ancillary content is also available through Connect, including:

- An Instructor's Manual for each chapter with chapter outlines, lecture topics and suggestions, ideas for classroom activities and demonstrations, questions for us in classroom discussions, ideas for student research papers, and lists of current research articles.
- A full Test Bank of multiple-choice questions that test students on central concepts and ideas in each chapter.
- PowerPoint Lecture Slides for instructor use in class.

Test Builder in Connect

Available within Connect, Test Builder is a cloud-based tool that enables instructors to format tests that can be printed, administered within a Learning Management System, or exported as a Word document. Test Builder offers a modern, streamlined interface for easy content configuration that matches course needs, without requiring a download.
  Test Builder allows you to:

- Access all test bank content from a particular title.
- Easily pinpoint the most relevant content through robust filtering options.
- Manipulate the order of questions or scramble questions and/or answers.
- Pin questions to a specific location within a test.
- Determine your preferred treatment of algorithmic questions.
- Choose the layout and spacing.
- Add instructions and configure default settings.

  Test Builder provides a secure interface for better protection of content and allows for just-in-time updates to flow directly into assessments.

Instructors
The Power of Connections

A complete course platform

Connect enables you to build deeper connections with your students through cohesive digital content and tools, creating engaging learning experiences. We are committed to providing you with the right resources and tools to support all your students along their personal learning journeys.

65%
Less Time Grading

Laptop: Getty Images; Woman/dog: George Doyle/Getty Images

Every learner is unique

In Connect, instructors can assign an adaptive reading experience with SmartBook® 2.0. Rooted in advanced learning science principles, SmartBook 2.0 delivers each student a personalized experience, focusing students on their learning gaps, ensuring that the time they spend studying is time well-spent.
mheducation.com/highered/connect/smartbook

Affordable solutions, added value

Make technology work for you with LMS integration for single sign-on access, mobile access to the digital textbook, and reports to quickly show you how each of your students is doing. And with our Inclusive Access program, you can provide all these tools at the lowest available market price to your students. Ask your McGraw Hill representative for more information.

Solutions for your challenges

A product isn't a solution. Real solutions are affordable, reliable, and come with training and ongoing support when you need it and how you want it. Visit **supportateverystep.com** for videos and resources both you and your students can use throughout the term.

Students
Get Learning that Fits You

Effective tools for efficient studying

Connect is designed to help you be more productive with simple, flexible, intuitive tools that maximize your study time and meet your individual learning needs. Get learning that works for you with Connect.

Study anytime, anywhere

Download the free ReadAnywhere® app and access your online eBook, SmartBook® 2.0, or Adaptive Learning Assignments when it's convenient, even if you're offline. And since the app automatically syncs with your Connect account, all of your work is available every time you open it. Find out more at **mheducation.com/readanywhere**

"I really liked this app—it made it easy to study when you don't have your text-book in front of you."

- Jordan Cunningham, Eastern Washington University

iPhone: Getty Images

Everything you need in one place

Your Connect course has everything you need—whether reading your digital eBook or completing assignments for class—Connect makes it easy to get your work done.

Learning for everyone

McGraw Hill works directly with Accessibility Services Departments and faculty to meet the learning needs of all students. Please contact your Accessibility Services Office and ask them to email accessibility@mheducation.com, or visit **mheducation.com/about/accessibility** for more information.

Personality Psychology

Top Left: Tavis Wright/Image
Source; Top Right: Svisio/Getty
Images; Middle Left: Science Photo
Library RF/Getty Images; Middle
Right: Lightspring/Shutterstock;
Bottom Left: Arthimedes/
Shutterstock; Bottom Right:
Athanasia Nomikou/Shutterstock

Introduction to Personality Psychology

1

2

INTRODUCTION

Each person is, in certain respects, like all other persons, like some other persons, and like no other person.
Ingram Publishing/SuperStock

Those who carry humor to excess are thought to be vulgar buffoons, striving after humor at all costs, not caring about pain to the object of their fun; . . . while those who can neither make a joke themselves nor put up with those who do are thought to be boorish and unpolished. But those who joke in a tasteful way are called ready-witted and tactful . . . and it is the mark of a tactful person to say and listen to such things as befit a good and well-bred person.

Source: *Aristotle, The Nicomachean Ethics of Aristotle.* K. Paul, Trench, Trubner & Company, Limited, 1893.

Aristotle, in *The Nicomachean Ethics,* expressed these wise observations on the subject of humor and the ways in which people do or do not express it. In this quote, we see Aristotle behaving much as a personality psychologist. Aristotle is analyzing the characteristics of persons who have an appropriate sense of humor. He is providing some details about what features are associated with a sense of humor. Aristotle adds to this description by comparing people who are extreme, having either too much or too little sense of humor. In his book on ethics, Aristotle analyzed many personality characteristics, including truthfulness, courage, intelligence, self-indulgence, anger-proneness, and friendliness.

We might conclude that Aristotle was an amateur personality psychologist. But aren't we all amateur personality psychologists to some extent? Aren't we all curious about the characteristics people possess, including our own? Don't we all use personality characteristics in describing people? And haven't we all used personality terms to explain behavior, either our own or others'?

When we say that our friend goes to a lot of parties because she is extraverted, we are using personality to summarize and explain her behavior. When we refer to another friend as conscientious and reliable, we are describing features of his personality. When we characterize ourselves as thoughtful, intelligent, and ambitious, we are describing features of our personalities.

Features of personality make people different from one another, and these features usually take the form of adjectives, such as John is lazy, Mary is optimistic, and Fred is anxious. *Adjectives that can be used to describe characteristics of people are called* **trait-descriptive adjectives.** There are nearly 20,000 such trait-descriptive adjectives in the English language. This astonishing fact alone tells us that, in everyday life, there are compelling reasons for trying to understand and describe those we interact with, as well as ourselves.

Notice that the adjectives describing personality refer to several very different aspects of people. Words such as *thoughtful* refer to inner qualities of mind. Words such as *charming* and *humorous* refer to the effects a person has on other people. Words such as *domineering* are relational and signify a person's position, or stance, toward others. Words such as *ambitious* refer to the intensity of desire to reach our goals. Words such as *creative* refer both to a quality of mind and to the nature of the products we produce. Words such as *deceitful* refer to the strategies a person uses to attain his or her goals. All of these features describe aspects of personality.

Exercise

Think of someone you know well—say, a friend, family member, or roommate. Consider the many characteristics that make this person unique. List the five adjectives you think best capture this person's personality. For example, if you were to describe this person to someone, what five adjectives would you use? Now, ask your target person to list the five adjectives *he or she* thinks best describe himself or herself. Compare your lists.

Personality Defined

Establishing a definition for something as complex as human personality is difficult. The authors of the first textbooks on personality—Gordon Allport (1937) and Henry Murray (1938)—struggled with the definition. The problem is how to establish a definition that is sufficiently comprehensive to include all of the aspects mentioned earlier, including inner features, social effects, qualities of the mind, qualities of the body, relations to others, and inner goals. Because of these complexities, some textbooks on personality omit a formal definition entirely. Nonetheless, the following definition captures the essential elements of personality: **Personality** *is the set of psychological traits and mechanisms within the individual that are organized and relatively enduring and that influence their interactions with, and adaptations to, the intrapsychic, physical, and social environments.* Let's examine the elements of this definition more closely.

Personality Is the Set of Psychological Traits...

Psychological traits are characteristics that describe ways in which people are different from each other. Saying that someone is *shy* is to mention one way in which he or she differs from others who are more outgoing. Traits also define ways in which people are *similar* to some others. For example, people who are shy are similar to each other in that they are anxious in social situations and perhaps blush easily, particularly when there is an audience focusing attention on them.

Consider another example— the trait of talkativeness. This characteristic can be meaningfully applied to people and describes a dimension

People are different from each other in many ways. The science of personality psychology provides an understanding of the psychological ways that people differ from one another.
Rawpixel.com/Shutterstock

of difference among them. Typically, a talkative person is that way from day to day, from week to week, and from year to year. Certainly, even the most talkative person can have quiet moments, quiet days, or even quiet weeks. Over time, however, those with the trait of talkativeness tend to emit verbal behavior with greater frequency than those who are low on talkativeness. In this sense, traits describe the **average tendencies** of a person. On average, a high-talkative person starts more conversations than a low-talkative person.

Research on personality traits asks four kinds of questions:

* How many traits are there?
* How are the traits organized?
* What are the origins of traits?
* What are the correlations and consequences of traits?

One primary question is *how many* fundamental traits there are. Are there dozens or hundreds of traits, or merely a few? The second research question pertains to the *organization,* or structure, of traits. For example, how is talkativeness related to other traits, such as impulsivity and extraversion? A third research question concerns the *origins* of traits—where they come from and how they develop. Does heredity, our genetic makeup, influence talkativeness? What sorts of cultural and child-rearing practices affect the development of traits such as talkativeness? A fourth key question pertains to the *correlations and consequences* of traits for the experiences we have, the behavior we engage in, and the life outcomes we achieve or fail to achieve. Do talkative persons have many friends? Do they have a more extended social network to draw upon in times of trouble? Do they annoy people who are trying to study?

The four research questions constitute the core of the research program of many personality psychologists. Psychological traits are useful for at least three reasons. First, they help to *describe* people and help to understand the dimensions of difference among people. Second, traits are useful because they help *explain* behavior. The reasons people

Courage is an example of a trait that is activated and reveals itself only in specific situations. The current president of Ukraine, Volodymyr Zelensky, was an actor and comedian prior to his election as his country's president. His high level of courage only became apparent when his country responded to widespread attacks by its neighbor, Russia.
Geopix/Alamy Stock Photo

act may be partly a function of their personality traits. Third, traits are useful because they can help *predict* future behavior—for example, the sorts of careers individuals will find satisfying, who will tolerate stress better, and who is likely to get along well with others. Thus, personality is useful in *describing, explaining,* and *predicting* differences among individuals. All good scientific theories enable researchers to describe, explain, and predict in their domains. Just as an economic theory might be useful in describing, explaining, and predicting fluctuations in spending habits or the broader economy, personality traits describe, explain, and predict differences among persons.

And Mechanisms . . .

Psychological mechanisms are like traits, except that the term *mechanisms* refers more to the processes of personality. For example, most psychological mechanisms involve an information-processing activity. Someone who is extraverted, for example, may look for and notice opportunities to interact with other people, such as in elevators or coffee shops. That is, an extraverted person is prepared to notice and act on certain kinds of social information.

Most psychological mechanisms have three essential ingredients: *inputs, decision rules,* and *outputs.* A psychological mechanism may make people more sensitive to certain kinds of information from the environment (input), may make them more likely to think about specific options (decision rules), and may guide their behavior toward certain categories of action (outputs). For example, an extraverted person may look for opportunities to be with other people, may consider in each situation the possibilities for human contact and interaction, and may encourage others to interact with him or her. Our personalities contain many psychological mechanisms of this sort—information-processing procedures that have the key elements of inputs, decision rules, and outputs (see Figure 1.1).

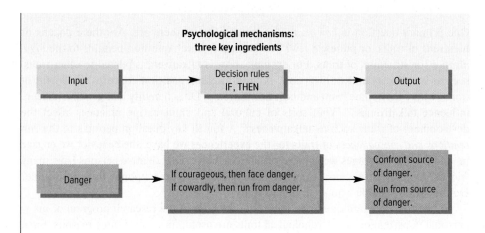

Figure 1.1

Psychological mechanisms have three essential ingredients. Our personalities contain many such mechanisms.

This does not mean that all of our traits and psychological mechanisms are activated at all times. In fact, at any point in time, only a few are activated. Consider the trait of courageousness. This trait is activated only under particular conditions, such as when people face serious dangers and threats to their lives or the lives of others in their group. Some people are more courageous than others, but we will never know which people are courageous unless and until the right situation presents itself. Look around next time you are in class: Who do you think has the trait of courageousness? You won't know until you are in a situation that provides the potential for courageous behavior.

Within the Individual...

Within the individual means that personality is something a person carries with them over time and from one situation to the next. Typically, we feel that we are today the same people we were last week, last month, and last year. We also feel that we will continue to have these personalities in the coming months and years. And, although our personalities are certainly influenced by our environments, and especially by the significant others in our lives, we feel that we carry with us the same personalities from situation to situation in our lives. The definition of personality stresses that the important sources of personality reside within the individual. Hence, they are at least somewhat stable over time and somewhat consistent over situations, issues we will examine empirically in subsequent chapters.

That Are Organized and Relatively Enduring...

Organized means that the psychological traits and mechanisms for a given person are not simply a random collection of elements. Rather, personality is organized because the mechanisms and traits are linked to one another in a coherent fashion. Imagine the simple case of two desires—a desire for food and a desire for intimacy. If you have not eaten for a while and are experiencing hunger pangs, then your desire for food might override your desire for intimacy. On the other hand, if you have already eaten, then your desire for food may temporarily subside, allowing you to pursue intimacy. Our personalities are organized in the sense that they contain decision rules that govern which needs or motives are activated, depending on the circumstances.

Psychological traits are also relatively **enduring** over time, particularly in adulthood, and are somewhat consistent over situations. To say that someone is angry at this moment is not saying anything about a trait. A person may be angry now, but not tomorrow or may be angry in one situation, but not in others. Anger is more of a *state* than a trait. To say that someone is anger prone or generally hot tempered, however, is to describe a psychological trait. Someone who is anger prone is *frequently* angry, relative to others, and shows this proneness time and time again in many different situations. For example, the person might be argumentative at work, hostile and aggressive while playing team sports for recreation, and quarrelsome with family members.

There may be some occasions when this generalization about the consistency of personality from situation to situation does not hold. Some situations may be overpowering and suppress the expression of psychological traits. People who are generally talkative, for example, may remain quiet during a lecture, at the movies, or in an elevator—although you undoubtedly have experienced someone who would not keep quiet in any of these circumstances!

The debate about whether people are consistent across situations in their lives has a long history in personality psychology. Some psychologists have argued that the evidence for consistency is weak (Mischel, 1968). For example, honesty measured in one situation (say, cheating on a test) may not correlate very highly with honesty measured in another situation (say, cheating on income taxes). We will explore this debate more fully later in the book. For now, we will simply say that most personality psychologists maintain that although people are not perfectly consistent, there is enough consistency to warrant including this characteristic in a definition of personality.

The fact that personality includes relatively enduring psychological traits and mechanisms does not preclude change over time. Indeed, describing precisely the ways in which we change over time is one goal of personality psychologists.

And That Influence . . .

In the definition of personality, an emphasis on the **influential forces** of personality means that personality traits and mechanisms can have an effect on people's lives. Personality influences how we act, how we view ourselves, how we think about the world, how we interact with others, how we feel, how we select our environments (particularly our social environments), what goals and desires we pursue in life, and how we react to our circumstances. People are not passive creatures merely responding to external forces. Rather, personality plays a key role in affecting how people shape their lives. It is in this sense that personality traits are forces that *influence* how we think, act, and feel.

Their Interactions with . . .

This feature of personality is perhaps the most difficult to describe, because the nature of **person–environment interaction** is complex. In Chapter 15, we examine interactionism in greater detail. For now, however, it is sufficient to note that interactions with situations include perceptions, selections, evocations, and manipulations. *Perceptions* refer to how we "see," or interpret, an environment. Two people may be exposed to the same objective event, yet what they pay attention to and how they interpret the event may be very different. And this difference is a function of their personalities. For example, two people can look at an inkblot, yet one person sees two cannibals cooking a human over a fire, whereas the other perceives a smiling clown waving hello. As another example, a stranger may smile at someone on the street; one person might perceive the smile as a smirk, whereas another person might perceive the smile as a friendly gesture. It is the same smile, just as it is the same inkblot, yet how people interpret these situations can be determined by their personalities.

Selection describes the manner in which we choose situations to enter—how we choose our friends, romantic partners, hobbies, college classes, and careers. How we go about making these selections is, at least in part, a reflection of our personalities. How we use our free time is especially a reflection of our traits. One person may take up the hobby of parachute jumping, whereas another may prefer to spend time quietly listening to a podcast alone. We select from what life offers us, and these choices are partly a function of personality.

Evocations are the reactions we produce in others, often quite unintentionally. To some extent, we create the social environment that we inhabit. A child with a high activity level, for example, may evoke in parents' attempts to constrain the child, even though these attempts are not intended or desired by the child. A person who is physically large may evoke feelings of intimidation in others, even if intimidation is not the goal. Our evocative interactions are also essential features of our personalities.

Manipulations are the ways in which we intentionally attempt to influence others. Someone who is anxious or frightened easily may try to influence their group to avoid scary movies or risky activities. Someone who is highly conscientious may insist that everyone follow the rules. Or, someone who is very neat and orderly may insist that their spouse pick up their messy things. The ways in which we attempt to manipulate the behavior, thoughts, and feelings of others are essential features of our personalities. All of these forms of interaction—perceptions, selections, evocations, and manipulations—are central to understanding the connections between the personalities of people and the environments they inhabit.

And Adaptations to . . .

An emphasis on **adaptation** conveys the notion that a central feature of personality concerns adaptive functioning—accomplishing goals, coping, adjusting, and dealing with the challenges and problems we face as we go through life. Few things are more obvious about human behavior than the fact that it is goal directed, functional, and purposeful. Even behavior that does not appear functional—neurotic behavior such as excessive worrying, for example—may, in fact, be functional. For example, people who worry a lot may be better at detecting social signs of danger and correctly anticipating ways to cope with threat. Consequently, what appears on the surface to be maladaptive (excessive worrying) may, in fact, have some adaptive functions. In addition, some aspects of personality processes represent deficits in normal adaptations, such as breakdowns in the ability to cope with stress, to regulate one's social behavior, or to manage one's emotions. Although psychologists' knowledge of the adaptive functions of personality traits and mechanisms is currently limited, it remains an indispensable key to understanding the nature of human personality.

The Environment

The physical **environment** often poses challenges for people. Some of these are direct threats to survival. For example, food shortages create the problem of securing adequate nutrients for survival. Extremes of temperature pose the problem of maintaining thermal homeostasis or body temperature. Heights, snakes, spiders, and strangers can all pose threats to survival. Human beings, like other animals, have evolved solutions to these adaptive problems. Hunger pangs motivate us to seek food, and taste preferences guide our choices of which foods to consume. Shivering mechanisms help combat the cold, and sweat glands help fight the sweltering heat. At a psychological level, our fears of heights, snakes, spiders, and strangers—the most common human fears—help us avoid or safely interact with these environmental threats to our survival.

Our social environment also poses adaptive challenges. We may desire the prestige of a good job, but there are many other people competing for the same positions. We may desire interesting friends and mates, but there are many others competing for them. We may desire greater emotional closeness with others, but may not know how to achieve closeness. The ways in which we cope with our social environment—the challenges we encounter in our struggle for belongingness, love, and esteem—are central to an understanding of personality.

Personality partly determines the particular aspects of the environment that are important at any moment in time. A person who is talkative, for example, will notice more opportunities in the social environment to strike up conversations than will someone who is low on talkativeness. A person who is disagreeable, because they sometimes antagonize other people, will occupy a social environment where people frequently argue with them or avoid them. A person for whom status is very important will pay close attention to the relative hierarchical positions of others—who is up, who is down, who is ascending, and who is sliding. In short, among the potentially infinite dimensions of the environments we inhabit, our "effective environment" represents only the small subset of features that our psychological mechanisms direct us to attend and respond to.

In addition to our physical and social environments, we have an intrapsychic environment. *Intrapsychic* means "within the mind." We all have memories, dreams, desires, fantasies, and a collection of private experiences that we live with each day. This intrapsychic environment, although not as objectively verifiable as our social or physical environment, is nevertheless real to each of us and makes up an important part of our psychological reality. For example, our self-esteem—how good or bad we feel about ourselves at any given moment—may depend on our assessment of the degree to which we are succeeding in attaining our goals. Success at work and success at friendship may provide two different forms of success experience and, hence, form different intrapsychic memories. We are influenced by our memories of these experiences whenever we think about our own self-worth. Our intrapsychic environment, as much as our physical and social environments, provides a critical context for understanding human personality.

Exercise

Write a one-page essay about a good friend, someone you know well, in which you describe what is characteristic, enduring, and functional about that person. Include in this description those elements of the ways in which they interact with, or adapt to, the physical, social, and intrapsychic environments.

Three Levels of Personality Analysis

Although the definition of personality used in this book is quite broad and encompassing, personality can be analyzed at three levels. These three levels are well summarized by Kluckhohn and Murray, in their 1948 book on culture and personality, in which they state that every human being is, in certain respects,

1. Like all others (the human nature level),
2. Like some others (the level of individual and group differences), and
3. Like no others (the individual uniqueness level).

Another way to think of these distinctions is that the first level refers to "universals" (the ways in which we are all alike), the middle level refers to "particulars" (the ways in which we are like some people but unlike others), and the third level refers to "uniqueness" (the ways in which we are unlike any other person) (see Table 1.1).

Table 1.1 Three Levels of Personality Analysis

Level of Analysis	Examples
Human nature	Need to belong
	Capacity for love
Individual and group differences	Variation in need to belong (individual difference)
	Men more physically aggressive than women (group difference)
Individual uniqueness	Letisha's unique way of expressing her love
	John's unique way of expressing aggression

Human Nature

The first level of personality analysis describes **human nature** in general—the traits and mechanisms of personality that are typical of our species and are possessed by everyone or nearly everyone. For example, nearly all humans have language skills, which allow them to learn and use a language. People in all cultures on earth speak a language, so spoken language is part of the universal human nature. At a psychological level, all humans possess fundamental psychological mechanisms—for example, the desire to live with others and belong to social groups—and these mechanisms are part of general human nature. There are many ways in which each person is like most or all other people, and by understanding those ways we may achieve an understanding of the general principles of human nature.

Individual and Group Differences

The second level of personality analysis pertains to individual and group differences. Some people are gregarious and love parties; others prefer a quiet evening's reading. Some people take great physical risks by jumping out of airplanes, riding motorcycles, and driving fast cars; others shun physical risks. Some people enjoy high self-esteem and live life relatively free from anxiety; others worry constantly and are plagued by self-doubt. These are dimensions of **individual differences,** ways in which each person is like *some* other people (e.g., extraverts, sensation seekers) and unlike others.

Personality can also be observed by studying **differences among groups.** That is, people in one group may have certain personality features in common, and these common features make that group of people different from other groups. Examples of groups studied by personality psychologists include different cultures, different age groups, different political parties, and groups from different socioeconomic backgrounds. Another important set of differences studied by personality psychologists concerns those between men and women. Although many traits and mechanisms of humans are common to both genders, a few are different for men and women. For example, there is accumulated evidence that, across cultures, men are typically more

Personality psychologists sometimes study group differences, such as differences between men and women.
Prostock-studio/Alamy Stock Photo

physically aggressive than women. Men are responsible for most of the violence the world over. One goal of personality psychology is to understand why certain aspects of personality differ among groups, such as understanding how and why women are different from men (on average) and why people from one culture differ from those from another culture (on average).

Individual Uniqueness

No two individuals, not even identical twins raised by the same parents in the same home in the same culture, have exactly the same personalities. Every individual has personal qualities not shared by any other person in the world. One of the goals of personality psychology is to allow for individual uniqueness and to develop ways to capture the richness of unique individual lives.

One debate in the field focuses on whether individuals should be studied *nomothetically*—that is, as individual instances of general characteristics that are distributed in the population—or should be studied *idiographically,* as single, unique cases. **Nomothetic** research typically involves statistical comparisons of individuals or groups, requiring samples of participants on which to conduct research. Nomothetic research is typically applied to identify universal human characteristics and dimensions of individual or group differences. **Idiographic** (translated literally as "the description of one") research typically focuses on a single person, trying to observe general principles that are manifest in a single life over time. Often, idiographic research results in case studies or the psychological biography of a single person (Runyon, 1983). Sigmund Freud, for example, wrote a psychobiography of Leonardo da Vinci (1916/1947). An example of another version of idiographic research is provided by Rosenzweig (1986, 1997), in which he proposes to analyze people in terms of the sequence of events in their lives, trying to understand critical life events within each person's own history. A more recent example is a personality analysis of President Donald Trump (McAdams, 2020).

The important point is that personality psychologists have been concerned with all three levels of analysis: the universal level, the level of individual and group differences, and the level of individual uniqueness. Each level contributes valuable knowledge to the total understanding of the nature of personality.

A Fissure in the Field

Different personality psychologists focus on different levels of analysis. And there is a gap within the field that has not yet been successfully bridged. It is the gap between the human nature level of analysis and the analysis of group and individual differences. Many psychologists have theorized about what human nature is like in general. However, when doing research, psychologists most often focus on individual and group differences in personality. As a consequence, there is a fissure or gap between the grand theories of personality and contemporary research in personality.

Grand Theories of Personality

Most of the grand theories of personality address the human nature level of analysis. These theories attempt to provide a universal account of the fundamental psychological processes and characteristics of our species. Sigmund Freud (1915/1957), for example, emphasized universal instincts of sex and aggression; a universal psychic structure of the id, ego, and superego; and universal stages of psychosexual development (oral, anal, phallic, latency, and genital). Statements about the universal core of human nature lie at the center of grand theories of personality.

Some of the textbooks used in teaching college courses in personality psychology are structured around grand theories. These books have been criticized, however, because many of those theories are primarily of historical interest. Only parts of them have stood the test of time and guide personality research today. Although the grand theories are an important part of the history of personality psychology, there is much interesting personality research going on today that is not directly relevant to the historical grand theories.

Contemporary Research in Personality

Most of the empirical research in contemporary personality addresses the ways in which individuals and groups differ. For example, the extensive research literature on extraversion and introversion, on anxiety and neuroticism, and on self-esteem all focuses on the ways in which people differ from one another. The extensive research on masculinity and femininity deals with the psychological ways in which men and women differ (on average) and the ways in which people acquire sex-typed social roles. Cultural research shows that one major dimension of difference concerns whether individuals endorse a collectivistic versus an individualistic attitude. Eastern Asian cultures, for example, tend to be more collectivistic and Western cultures tend to be more individualistic (see Chapter 17).

One way to examine personality psychology would be to pick a dozen or so current research topics and explore what psychologists have learned about each. For example, a lot of research has been done on self-esteem—what it is, how it develops, how people maintain high self-esteem, and how it influences social relationships. There are many other interesting topics in contemporary personality psychology—shyness, aggression, trust, dominance, hypnotic susceptibility, depression, intelligence, attributional style, goal setting, anxiety, temperament, sex roles, self-monitoring, extraversion, sensation seeking, agreeableness, impulsivity, sociopathic tendencies, morality, locus of control, optimism, creativity, leadership, prejudice, and narcissism.

A course that just surveys current topics in personality research seems unsatisfactory. It would be like going to an auction and bidding on everything—soon you would be overwhelmed. Just picking topics to cover would not result in an understanding of the connections among the aspects of personality. Indeed, the field of personality has been criticized for containing too many independent areas of investigation, with no sense of the whole person behind the separate topics of investigation. What holds personality together as a coherent field would be missing in such an approach.

You have probably heard the ancient legend of the three visually impaired men who were presented with an elephant. They tried to figure out what the whole elephant was like. The first visually impaired man approached cautiously; walking up to the elephant and putting his hands and then arms around the animal's leg, he proclaimed, "Why, the whole elephant is much like a tree, slender and tall." The second man grasped the trunk of the elephant and exclaimed, "No, the whole elephant is more like a large snake." The third visually impaired man grasped the ear of the elephant and stated, "You are both wrong; the whole elephant more closely resembles a fan." The three visually impaired men proceeded to argue with one another, each insisting that his opinion of the whole elephant was the correct one. In a sense, each visually impaired man had a piece of the truth, yet each failed to recognize that his perceptions of the elephant captured only a narrow part of the truth. Each failed to grasp the whole elephant. Working together, however, the visually impaired men could have assembled a deeper understanding of the whole elephant.

The topic of personality is like the elephant, and personality psychologists are somewhat like the visually impaired people examining only one perspective at a time. For example, some psychologists study the biological aspects of personality. Others study the ways in which culture promotes personality differences among people and among groups. Still other psychologists study how various aspects of the mind interact and work together to produce personality. And others study relationships among people and believe that social interaction is where personality manifests its most important effects. Each of these perspectives on personality captures elements of truth, yet each alone is inadequate to describe the entire realm of human personality—the whole elephant, so to speak.

Six Domains of Knowledge About Human Nature

The various views of researchers in personality stem *not* from the fact that one perspective is right and the others wrong, but rather from the fact that they are studying different domains of knowledge. A **domain of knowledge** is a specialty area of science and scholarship in which psychologists have focused on learning about some specific and limited aspects of human nature. A domain of knowledge delineates the boundaries of researchers' knowledge, expertise, and interests.

This degree of specialization is reasonable. Indeed, specialization characterizes many scientific fields. The field of medicine, for example, has heart specialists, skin specialists (dermatologists), and brain specialists, focusing in great detail on their own domains. It is likewise reasonable for the field of personality psychology to have intrapsychic specialists, trait origins specialists, cultural specialists, and personality and social interaction specialists. Each of these domains of personality has accumulated its own base of knowledge. Nonetheless, it is desirable to integrate these diverse domains to see how they all fit together.

The whole personality, like the whole elephant, is the sum of the various parts and the connections among them. For personality, each part is a domain of knowledge representing a collection of knowledge about certain aspects of personality. How are the domains of knowledge defined? For the most part, natural boundaries have developed in the field of personality psychology. That is, researchers have formed natural clusters of topics that fit together and are distinct from other clusters of knowledge. Within these identifiable domains, researchers have developed common *methods for asking questions,* have accumulated a foundation of *known facts,* and have developed *theoretical explanations* that account for what is known about personality from the perspective of each domain.

The field of personality can be cleaved into six distinct domains of knowledge about human nature: personality is influenced by traits the person is born with and how they develop over time (*dispositional domain*); by biological events (*biological domain*); by processes within the person's own mind (*intrapsychic domain*); by personal and private thoughts, feelings, desires, beliefs, and other subjective experiences (*cognitive-experiential domain*); by social, cultural, and gendered positions in the world (*social and cultural domain*); and by the adjustments or adaptations that people make to the inevitable challenges of life (*adjustment domain*).

Personality psychologists working within each domain often use different theoretical perspectives and focus on different facts. As a consequence, psychologists from different domains can sometimes appear to contradict one another. The psychoanalytic perspective of Sigmund Freud, for example, views the personality as consisting of irrational sexual and aggressive instincts that motivate human activity. The cognitive perspective on personality, in contrast, views humans as rational "scientists," calmly trying to anticipate, predict, and control the events that occur in their worlds.

On the surface, these perspectives appear incompatible. How can humans be both irrational and rational? How can humans be driven by desire yet be cool and detached in their quest for accurate prediction? On deeper examination, the contradictions may be more apparent than real. It is entirely possible, for example, that humans have both powerful sexual and aggressive motivations and cognitive mechanisms designed to perceive and predict events accurately. It is entirely possible that sometimes basic emotions and motivations are activated and at other times the cool cognitive mechanisms are activated. And it is possible that the two sets of mechanisms sometimes become linked with one another, such as when the rational mechanisms are used in the service of fulfilling fundamental desires. In short, although each theoretical perspective may be focused on a critically important part of human psychological functioning, each perspective by itself does not capture the *whole* person.

This book is organized around the six domains of personality functioning—dispositional, biological, intrapsychic, cognitive-experiential, social and cultural, and adjustment. Within each of these domains of personality, we focus on two key elements: (1) the *theories* that have been proposed within each domain, including the basic assumptions about human nature, and (2) the *empirical research* that has been accumulating within each of these domains. In an attempt to bridge the gap between theory and research in personality, we focus primarily on the theories that have received the greatest research attention and the topics within each domain for which there is the greatest cumulative knowledge base.

Dispositional Domain

The **dispositional domain** deals centrally with the ways in which individuals differ from one another. As such, the dispositional domain cuts across all the other domains. The reason is that individuals can differ in their habitual emotions, their enduring concepts of self, their physiological propensities, and even their intrapsychic mechanisms. However, what distinguishes the dispositional domain is an interest in the number, nature, and consequences of fundamental dispositions. The central goal of personality psychologists working in the dispositional domain is to identify and measure the most important ways in which individuals differ from one another. They are also interested in the origins of the important individual differences and in how they develop and are maintained.

Identical twins Alvin (left) and Calvin (right) Harrison, age 26, celebrate their first and second place finishes in the 400-meter race in Brisbane, Australia, August 8, 2000. Psychologists are studying twins to determine whether some aspects of personality are influenced by genetics.
Comstock Images/SuperStock

Biological Domain

The core assumption within the **biological domain** is that humans are, first and foremost, collections of biological systems, and these systems provide the building blocks for behavior, thought, and emotion. As personality psychologists use the term, *biological* *approaches* typically refers to three areas of research within this general domain: genetics, psychophysiology, and evolution.

The first area of research consists of the genetics of personality. Because of advances in behavioral genetic research, a fair amount is known about the genetics of personality. Some questions this research addresses include the following: Are identical twins more alike than fraternal twins in their personalities? What happens to identical twins when they are reared apart versus when they are reared together? Can we identify the specific genes underlying traits using molecular genetic methods? How do genetic and environmental influences interact with each other? Behavioral genetic research permits us to ask and provisionally answer these questions.

The second biological approach is best described as the psychophysiology of personality. Within this domain, researchers summarize what is known about the basis of personality in terms of nervous system functioning. Examples of such topics include cortical arousal and neurotransmitters, cardiac reactivity, strength of the nervous system, pain tolerance, circadian rhythms (whether you are a morning or night person), and the links between hormones, such as testosterone and estrogen, and personality.

The third component of the biological approach concerns how evolution may have shaped human psychological functioning. This approach assumes that the psychological mechanisms that constitute human personality have evolved over thousands of years because they were effective in solving adaptive problems linked to survival and reproduction. An evolutionary perspective sheds light on the functional aspects of personality, and research in this domain has mushroomed over the past decade (e.g., Buss, 2019). We also highlight some fascinating research on personality in nonhuman animals (Sih et al., 2015; Vazire & Gosling, 2003; White, Pascall, & Wilson, 2020).

Intrapsychic Domain

The **intrapsychic domain** deals with mental mechanisms of personality, many of which operate outside of conscious awareness. The dominant theory in this domain is Freud's theory of psychoanalysis. This theory begins with fundamental assumptions about the instinctual system—the sexual and aggressive forces that are presumed to drive and energize much of human activity. Considerable research reveals that sexual and aggressive motives are indeed powerful, and their manifestations in actual behavior can be studied empirically. The intrapsychic domain also includes defense mechanisms, such as repression, denial, and projection—some of which have been examined in laboratory studies. Although the intrapsychic domain is most closely linked with the psychoanalytic theory of Sigmund Freud, there are modern versions as well. For example, much of the research on the power motives, achievement motives, and intimacy motives is based on a key intrapsychic assumption—that these forces often operate outside the realm of consciousness.

Cognitive-Experiential Domain

The **cognitive-experiential domain** focuses on thought processes and subjective experience, such as conscious ideas, feelings, beliefs, and desires about oneself and others. The psychological mechanisms involved in subjective experience differ, however, in form and content from one another. One important element of our experience entails the self and self-concept. Descriptive aspects of the self organize how we view ourselves: knowledge of ourselves, images of past selves, and images of possible future selves. Do we see ourselves as good or as evil? Are our past successes or past failures prominent in our self-views? Do we envision ourselves in the future as married with children or as successful in a career? How we evaluate ourselves—our self-esteem—is another facet of the cognitive-experiential domain.

A somewhat different aspect of this domain pertains to the goals we strive for. Some personality psychologists, for example, view human nature as inherently goal-directed, stressing the organizing influence of fundamental needs or strivings, such as the need for affiliation and the striving for status. Research within this tradition includes approaching personality through the personal projects, that is the tasks that individuals are trying to accomplish in their daily lives. These can range from the commonplace, such as getting a date for Saturday night, to the grandiose, such as changing global social injustice.

Another important aspect of subjective experience entails our emotions. Are we happy or sad? What makes us angry or fearful? Do we keep our emotions bottled up inside, or do we express them at the drop of a hat? Joy, sadness, feelings of triumph, and feelings of despair all are essential elements in our subjective experience and are subsumed by the cognitive-experiential domain.

Social and Cultural Domain

One of the special features of this book is an emphasis on the **social and cultural domain** of personality. The assumption is that personality is not something that merely resides within the heads, nervous systems, and genes of individuals. Rather, personality affects, and is affected by, the social and cultural context.

At a cultural level, it is clear that groups differ tremendously from one another. Cultures such as the Yanomamö of Venezuela are somewhat aggressive; indeed, historically a Yanomamö man would not achieve full status as a man until he had killed another man. In contrast, cultures such as the !Kung San of Botswana are relatively peaceful and agreeable. Overt displays of aggression are discouraged and bring social shame on the perpetrator. Personality differences among these groups are most likely due to cultural influences. In other words, different cultures may bring out different facets of our personalities in manifest behavior. Everyone may have the capacity to be peaceful as well as the capacity to be aggressive, as documented by the dramatic changes in violence and peacefulness over time (Pinker, 2012). Which one of these capacities we display may depend on what is acceptable in, and encouraged by, the culture?

By studying people in different cultures, psychologists are learning how society shapes personality by encouraging or discouraging specific behaviors. An indigenous man along the Amazon River, near Iquitos, Peru.
hadynyah/Vetta/Getty Images

At the level of individual differences within cultures, personality plays itself out in the social sphere. Whether we are dominant or submissive affects such diverse parts of our lives as the conflicts we get into with our partners and the tactics we use to manipulate others. Whether we tend to be anxious and depressed or buoyant and optimistic affects the likelihood of social outcomes, such as marital stability and divorce. Whether we are introverted or extraverted affects how many friends we will have and our popularity within the group. Many important individual differences are played out in the interpersonal sphere.

One important social sphere concerns relationships between men and women. At the level of differences between the genders, personality may operate differently for men than for women. Gender is often, although not always, an important part of our identities.

Adjustment Domain

The **adjustment domain** refers to the fact that personality plays a key role in how we cope, adapt, and adjust to the ebb and flow of events in our day-to-day lives. Evidence, for example, shows that personality is linked with important health outcomes, such as heart disease. Personality is also linked with health-related behaviors, such as smoking, drinking, illegal drug-taking, and risk-taking. Some research has even demonstrated that personality is linked with how long we live.

In addition to health, many important problems in coping and adjustment can be traced to personality. In this domain, certain personality features are related to poor adjustment and have been designated as personality disorders. Chapter 19 is devoted to the personality disorders, such as narcissistic personality disorder, antisocial personality disorder, and avoidant personality disorder. An understanding of "normal" personality functioning can be deepened by examining the disorders of personality, much as in the field of medicine, in which an understanding of normal physiological functioning is often illuminated by the study of disease.

Personality relates to health by influencing health-related behaviors, such as smoking.

Martin Novak/Alamy Stock Photo

Exercise

Think of a behavior pattern or characteristic that you find interesting in yourself or someone you know. Characteristics such as procrastination, narcissism, and perfectionism are good examples, but any personality characteristic that catches your interest is good. Then write six sentences about this characteristic, one to represent each of the six domains: dispositional, biological, intrapsychic, cognitive-experiential, social and cultural, and adjustment. Each sentence should make a statement or ask a question about the characteristic from the perspective of a particular domain.

The Role of Personality Theory

One of the central aims of this book is to highlight the interplay between personality theory and research. In each domain of knowledge, there are some prevailing theories, so we close this chapter with a discussion of theories. Theories are essential in all scientific endeavors, and they serve several useful purposes. A **good theory** is one that fulfills three purposes in science:

- Provides a guide for researchers,
- Organizes and explains known findings, and
- Makes predictions.

One of the most important purposes of theories is that they serve as a *guide for researchers,* directing them to important questions within an area of research.

A second useful function of theories is to *organize and explain known findings.* In physics, for example, there is a bewildering array of events—apples fall from trees, planets exert attraction on each other, black holes suck down light. The theory of gravity neatly and powerfully accounts for all these observations. By accounting for and explaining known findings, theories bring both coherence and understanding to the known world. The same applies to personality theories. Theories are viewed as powerful if they succeed in accounting for known findings, in addition to guiding psychologists to important domains of inquiry.

A third purpose of theories is to *make predictions* about behavior and psychological phenomena that no one has yet documented or observed. Einstein's theory of relativity, for example, predicted that light will bend around large stars long before we had the technology to test this prediction. When researchers finally confirmed that light does, indeed, bend when going around stars such as our sun, that finding confirmed the power of Einstein's theory in predicting outcomes.

Finally, we need to distinguish between scientific **theories** and **beliefs.** For example, astrology is a collection of beliefs about the relationship between personality and the position of the stars at birth. Some people hold that such relationships are true, even in the absence of supporting evidence. To date, psychologists have not found reliable factual support, using standard research methods and systematic observations, for the idea that the positions of the stars at a person's birth influence personality. As such, astrology remains a *belief,* not a scientific theory. Beliefs are often personally useful and crucially important to some people, but they are based on faith, not on reliable facts and systematic observations. Theories, on the other hand, are tested by systematic observations that can be repeated by other researchers who attempt to replicate the findings (sometimes successfully, sometimes not).

In sum, three key criteria of personality theories highlight the interplay of theory and research. They guide researchers to important domains of inquiry, explain and account for known findings, and make predictions about new phenomena.

Standards for Evaluating Personality Theories

As we explore each of the six domains, it will be useful to bear in mind five **scientific standards for evaluating personality theories:**

- Comprehensiveness
- Heuristic value
- Testability
- Parsimony
- Compatibility and integration across domains and levels

The first standard is **comprehensiveness**—does the theory do a good job of explaining all of the facts and observations within its domain? Theories that explain more empirical findings are generally superior to those that explain fewer findings.

A second evaluative standard is **heuristic value**—does the theory provide a guide to important new discoveries about personality that were not known before? Theories that steer scientists to making these discoveries are generally superior to theories that fail to provide this guidance. Plate tectonic theory in geology, for example, guided researchers to discover regions of volcanic activity that were unknown prior to the theory. Similarly, a good personality theory will guide personality researchers to make discoveries that were previously unknown.

A third important standard for evaluating theories is **testability**—does the theory provide precise predictions that can be tested empirically? Some theories—for example, certain aspects of Freud's theory of intrapsychic conflict—have been criticized on the grounds that they are difficult or impossible to test; other aspects of Freud's theory are testable (see Chapters 9 and 10). As a general rule, the testability of a theory rests with the precision of its predictions. Precise theoretical predictions aid progress in the science because they allow inadequate theories to be discarded (those whose predictions are falsified) and good theories to be retained (those whose predictions are empirically confirmed). If a theory does not lend itself to being tested empirically, it is generally judged to be a poor theory.

A fourth standard for evaluating personality theories is **parsimony**—does the theory contain few premises and assumptions (parsimony) or many premises and assumptions (lack of parsimony)? As a general rule, theories that require many premises and assumptions to explain a given set of findings are judged to be poorer than theories that can explain the same findings with fewer premises and assumptions. Although parsimony is important, bear in mind that this does not mean that simple theories are always better than complex theories. Indeed, simple theories often crash and burn because they fail to meet one or more of the other five standards described here; for example, they may fail to be comprehensive because they explain so little. It is our view that human personality is genuinely complex, and so a complex theory—one containing many premises—may ultimately be necessary.

A fifth standard is **compatibility and integration across domains and levels.** A theory of cosmology in astronomy that violated known laws of physics, for example, would be incompatible across levels and hence judged to be fundamentally flawed. A theory of biology that violated known principles of chemistry similarly would be judged to be fatally flawed. In the same way, a personality theory in one domain that violated well-established principles in another domain would be judged highly problematic. For example, a theory of the development of personality dispositions that was inconsistent with well-established knowledge in physiology and genetics would be judged to be problematic. Similarly, a theory of evolutionary influences on personality that contradicted what is known about cultural influences, or vice versa, would be problematic. Although the criterion of *compatibility and integration across domains and levels* is a well-established principle in most sciences (Tooby & Cosmides, 1992), it has rarely been used to evaluate the adequacy of personality theories. We believe that the "domains" approach taken in this book highlights the importance of the evaluative criterion of compatibility across levels of personality analysis.

In sum, as you progress through the six domains of personality functioning, keep in mind the five standards by which theories within each domain can be evaluated—comprehensiveness, heuristic value, testability, parsimony, and cross-domain compatibility (see Table 1.2).

Table 1.2 Five Standards for Evaluating Personality Theories

Standard	Definition
Comprehensiveness	Explains most or all known facts.
Heuristic value	Guides researchers to important new discoveries.
Testability	Makes precise predictions that can be empirically tested.
Parsimony	Contains few premises or assumptions.
Compatibility and integration	Consistent with what is known in other domains; can be coordinated with other branches of scientific knowledge.

Is There a Grand Ultimate and True Theory of Personality?

The field of biology contains a grand unifying theory—the theory of evolution by natural selection, originally proposed by Darwin (1859) and further refined in its neo-Darwinian form as inclusive fitness theory (Hamilton, 1964). This theory is comprehensive, guides biologists to new discoveries, has led to thousands of empirical tests, is highly parsimonious, and is compatible with known laws in adjacent scientific disciplines. Evolutionary theory provides the grand unifying framework within which most biologists conduct their work. Ideally, the field of personality psychology would also contain such a grand unifying theory. Alas, at the current time, it does not.

Perhaps Sigmund Freud, the inventor of psychoanalytic theory, provided the most ambitious attempt at a grand unifying theory of personality (see Chapter 9). And many grand theories have followed Freud's. But over the past several decades, most personality researchers have come to the realization that the field currently lacks a grand unifying theory. Instead, most have focused on more specific domains of functioning. It is precisely for this reason that our book is organized around the six domains—these represent the domains in which progress, scientific findings, and new discoveries are being made.

In our view, an ultimate grand theory of personality psychology will have to unify all six domains. It will have to explain personality characteristics and how they develop over time (dispositional domain). It will have to explain evolutionary, genetic, and physiological underpinnings of personality (biological domain). It will have to explain deeply rooted motives and dynamic intrapsychic processes (intrapsychic domain). It will have to explain how people experience the world and process information about it (cognitive-experiential domain). It will have to explain how personality affects, and is affected by, the social and cultural context in which people conduct their lives (social and cultural domains). And it will have to explain how people cope and function—as well as how adjustment fails—as they encounter the numerous adaptive challenges they face over the sometimes bumpy course of their lives (the adjustment domain).

Although the field of personality psychology currently lacks a grand theory, we believe that work in these six domains will ultimately provide the foundations on which such a unified personality theory will be built. We are excited to report that there have been tremendous developments and discoveries in all six domains. We hope you share our excitement about discovering these domains of human personality.

KEY TERMS

trait-descriptive adjectives 4
personality 4
psychological traits 5
average tendencies 5
psychological mechanisms 6
within the individual 7
organized 7
enduring 7
influential forces 8
person–environment interaction 8
adaptation 9
environment 9

human nature 11
individual differences 11
differences among groups 11
nomothetic 12
idiographic 12
domain of knowledge 14
dispositional domain 15
biological domain 15
intrapsychic domain 16
cognitive-experiential domain 16
social and cultural domain 17
adjustment domain 18

good theory 18
theories 19
beliefs 19
scientific standards for evaluating
    personality theories 19
comprehensiveness 19
heuristic value 19
testability 20
parsimony 20
compatibility and integration across
    domains and levels 20

Personality Assessment, Measurement, and Research Design

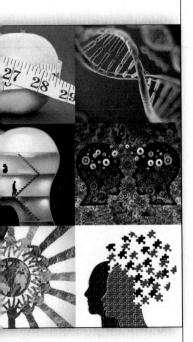

2

INTRODUCTION

Much of the discussion surrounding political candidates involves their personalities.
Left: Action Sports Photography/ Shutterstock; Right: Matt Smith Photographer/Shutterstock

Imagine that a presidential election is looming. You are faced with a choice between two candidates. The personalities of the candidates may prove to be critical to your decision. How will they hold up under stress? What are their attitudes toward abortion or gun control? Will they stand tough in negotiating with leaders from other countries? This chapter focuses on the means by which we gain information about other people's personalities—the sources from which we gather personality data and the research designs we use in the scientific study of personality.

When deliberating between the two presidential candidates, you might want to know what they say about their values and attitudes—through a *self-report*. You might want to know what others say about their strengths in dealing with foreign leaders—through an *observer report*. You also might want to place the candidates in a more controlled situation, such as a debate, and see how each performs—to acquire *test data* (T-data). Furthermore, you might want to know about certain events in their lives, such as whether they have ever used illegal drugs, been arrested, dodged the draft, been divorced, filed for bankruptcy, or been caught in an embarrassing sexual scandal—*life history data.*

Each of these sources of data reveals something about the personalities of the presidential candidates, yet each alone is incomplete and may be biased. (For fascinating personality analyses of presidential candidates, see Immelman, 2002; O'Donnell & Rutherford, 2016; Post, 2003; and Renshon, 1998, 2005.) The candidate may self-report a grandiose record of successful business dealings, for example, but then the actual records show a history of bankruptcy filings and unpaid bills. Observers may report that the candidate is honest, yet be unaware of lies the candidate has told. A debate may show one candidate in a positive light, but perhaps the other candidate had a cold that day. And the public record of serving in the military reserve may not reveal the family connections that enabled the candidate to avoid combat. Each source of data provides important information. But each source, by itself, is of limited value, an incomplete picture.

This chapter covers three topics related to personality assessment and research. The first concerns where we get our information—the sources of personality data and the actual measures that personality psychologists use. The second topic is how we evaluate the quality of those measures. The third topic pertains to how we use these measures in actual research designs to study personality.

Sources of Personality Data

Self-Report Data (S-Data)

Perhaps the most obvious source of information about a person is **self-report data (S-data)**–the information a person reveals. Clearly, individuals may not always provide accurate information about themselves for a variety of reasons, such as the desire to present themselves in a positive light. Nevertheless, the journals that publish the latest research in personality reveal that self-report is the most common method for measuring personality (Connelly & Ones, 2010).

Self-report data can be obtained through a variety of means, including interviews that pose questions to a person, periodic reports by a person to record the events as they happen, and questionnaires. The questionnaire method, in which individuals respond to a series of items that request information about them, is by far the most commonly used self-report assessment procedure.

There are good reasons for using self-report. The most obvious is that individuals have access to a wealth of information about themselves that is inaccessible to anyone else, such as their habitual level of anxiety (e.g., Vazire, 2010). Individuals can report about their feelings, emotions, desires, beliefs, and private experiences. They can report about their self-esteem. They can report about their innermost fears and fantasies. And they can report about immediate and long-term goals. Because of this potential wealth of information, self-report is an indispensable source of personality data.

Self-report can take a variety of forms, ranging from open-ended "fill in the blanks" to forced-choice true-or-false questions. Sometimes these are referred to as **unstructured** (open-ended, such as "Tell me about the parties you like the most") and **structured** ("I like loud and crowded parties"–answer "true" or "false") personality tests. A prime example of the open-ended form of self-report is called the Twenty Statements Test (TST) (see A Closer Look for more information). In this test, a participant receives a sheet of paper that is essentially blank, except for the words "I am" repeated 20 times. There is a space after each of these partial statements, and participants are asked to complete them. For example, a person might say, in this order: *I am a woman; I am 19 years old; I am shy; I am intelligent; I am someone who likes quiet nights at home; I am introverted;* and so on. Personality instruments that use open-ended formats require coding schemes for classifying the responses they obtain. In other words, psychologists must devise a way to score or interpret the participant's open-ended responses. To get an idea of how outgoing the woman in our example is, the psychologist might count how many statements refer to social characteristics.

More common than open-ended questionnaires are structured personality questionnaires, in which the response options are provided. The simplest form of the structured self-report questionnaire involves a series of trait-descriptive adjectives, such as *active, ambitious, anxious, arrogant, artistic, generous, gregarious, greedy, good-natured, xenophobic,* and *zany.* Individuals indicate whether each adjective describes them. The simplest format for presenting these terms is a checklist, such as the Adjective Check List (ACL) (Gough, 1980). In completing the ACL, the individuals place a check beside adjectives that they feel accurately describe them and leave blank items that don't describe them. A more complex method involves requesting participants to indicate in numerical form the degree to which each trait term characterizes them, say on a 7-point rating scale of 1 (least characteristic) to 7 (most characteristic). This is called

A Closer Look   Who Am I?

The TST was published by a pair of sociologists. Manford Kuhn and Thomas McPartland were interested in attitudes people had toward themselves. In 1954, they published the "Who am I?" test. This test asked the participant to simply answer this question by completing the phrase "I am ____" 20 times. Kuhn and McPartland developed a way of scoring the test by analyzing the content of the person's responses. The order of each response was thought to be significant (e.g., something mentioned earlier might be more important to the self-definition than something mentioned later).

In early use by psychologists, the TST was applied mainly to clinical and personality research questions. For example, one study used the TST to see if the self-concepts of persons in "unadjusted" marriages differed from the self-concepts of persons in "well-adjusted" marriages (Buerkle, 1960). People in adjusted marriages tended to mention their partner, their marriage, and their family more often in their self-definitions than those in unadjusted marriages. This finding implies that part of a successful marriage is incorporating the marriage role into one's definition of oneself.

In the 1970s, researchers turned a more critical eye on the TST. It is an open-ended questionnaire, so people with low verbal ability do not complete it as quickly or as thoroughly as persons with high verbal ability, leading the test scores to be biased by intelligence differences in participants (Nudelman, 1973). However, if people are given enough time to complete the 20 questions—at least 15 minutes—then the intelligence bias is eliminated. The TST survived and emerged as a measure that the field deemed useful for assessing how people defined themselves.

In the 1980s, the TST was used in the study of timely personality topics, such as the influence of gender and other social roles in people's self-definitions. For example, one study compared married and single women (Gigy, 1980). Married women tended to respond to the "Who am I?" question by mentioning relationships (*I am a mother, I am a wife*), acquired roles in family life (*I am the one who feeds the children*), and household activities (*I am the one who buys groceries*). Clearly, marriage can mean a large change in self-concept.

Culture and ethnicity are sometime important in self-definitions (Bochner, 1994). One cross-cultural study using the TST compared people from Kenya with people from the United States. Several groups were compared on the percentage of responses that included references to social group categories (e.g., *I am a member of the local school board* or *I am a player on the local softball team*). U.S. college students mentioned social groups in their self-definitions 12 percent of the time. In Kenya, university students mentioned social groups 17 percent of the time. However, for traditional rural Kenyan citizens, results were quite different. Massai tribespersons in Kenya mentioned social groups 80 percent of the time in their responses, and Samburu tribespersons mentioned social groups 84 percent of the time in their TST responses (Ma & Schoeneman, 1997). Results such as these show how culture may influence how we view ourselves. The TST has proven especially effective at identifying the most important components of a person's identity—the ingredients that provide a person with a sense of self-esteem, meaning in life, and sense of belonging in the world of other people (Liquete, Dekoninck, & Wisker, 2021; Vignoles et al., 2006).

---

a **Likert rating scale** (after the person who invented it). It is simply a way for someone to express with numbers the degree to which a particular trait describes him or her. A typical Likert rating scale looks like this:

ENERGETIC

1	2	3	4	5	6	7
Least characteristic					Most characteristic	

Most commonly, a *personality scale* consists of summing the scores on a series of individual rating scales. A personality scale for activity level, for example, might consist of summing up scores from rating scales on *energetic, active,* and *vigorous.*

Exercise

DIRECTIONS: This list contains a series of adjectives. Please read them quickly and put an X in the box beside each one you consider to be self-descriptive. Try to be honest and accurate.

___ absent-minded	___ cheerful	___ dependent
___ active	___ civilized	___ despondent
___ adaptable	___ clear-thinking	___ determined
___ adventurous	___ clever	___ dignified
___ affected	___ coarse	___ discreet
___ affectionate	___ cold	___ disorderly
___ soft-hearted	___ touchy	___ zany

More common than adjective checklists, however, are self-report questionnaires in the form of statements. Examples of widely used self-report inventories are the NEO Personality Inventory (Costa & McCrae, 2005) and the California Psychological Inventory (CPI) (Gough, 1957/1987). Sample items from the CPI are *I enjoy social gatherings just to be with people; I looked up to my father as an ideal man; A person needs to "show off" a little now and then; I have a very strong desire to be a success in the world; I am very slow in making up my mind.* Participants read each statement and then indicate whether they agree with the statement and feel that it is true of them or disagree with the statement and feel that it is false about them. Sample items from the NEO Personality Inventory are *I like most people I meet; I laugh easily; I often get disgusted with people I have to deal with.* Participants indicate the degree to which they agree the item describes them, using a 1–5 Likert scale, with 1 anchored with the phrase *strongly disagree* and 5 anchored with *strongly agree.*

Exercise

Pick a personality characteristic you would like to measure. Start by writing down a clear definition of that characteristic. For example, you might choose characteristics such as friendly, conscientious, anxious, or narcissistic. Then write a short questionnaire, about five items long, to measure this characteristic. Your items can be statements or adjectives, and they can be open-ended, true–false, or on a Likert response scale. Then give your questionnaire to other people. How easy was it to write items? Do you think your measure accurately assesses the trait?

Self-report measures, like all methods, have limitations and weaknesses. For the self-report method to be effective, respondents must be both willing and able to answer the questions put to them. Yet people are not always honest, especially when asked about unconventional experiences, such as unusual desires, unconventional sex practices, and undesirable traits. Some people may lack accurate self-knowledge. Because of these limitations, personality psychologists often use sources of data that do not rely on the honesty or insight of the participant. One of those sources is observers.

Application

Experience sampling—a wrinkle in self-report. One source of data in personality research is called **experience sampling** (e.g., Barrantes-Vidal & Kwapil, 2014; Hormuth, 1986; Larsen, 1989; Mehl & Pennebaker, 2003). In this method, people answer some questions, perhaps about their moods or physical symptoms, every day for several weeks or longer. People are usually contacted electronically one or more times a day at random intervals to complete the measures. In one study, 74 college students reported on their moods every day for 84 consecutive days (Larsen & Kasimatis, 1990). The investigators were interested in discovering the links between the day of the week and mood. They found a strong weekly cycle in the moods of the college students. Positive moods peaked on Friday and Saturday and negative moods peaked on Tuesday and Wednesday (Monday was not the worst day of the week). The introverts turned out to have a much more regular weekly mood cycle than extraverts. That is, the moods of the introverts were more predictable from this 7-day rhythm than the moods of the extraverts. This difference was probably due to the fact that extraverts are less likely to wait for the weekend to do things that put them in a good mood—partying, socializing, or going out for a special meal with friends. Extraverts typically avoid routine in their daily lives, and introverts typically lead more predictable lives. Experience sampling has also been used to identify the negative effects of being indoors and computer screen time usage on loneliness during the Covid pandemic (Stieger, Lewetz, & Swami, 2021).

Although experience sampling uses self-report as the data source, it differs from more traditional self-report methods in being able to detect patterns of behavior over time. Thus, experience sampling provides information not readily available using questionnaires taken at just one point in time. It's an excellent method, for example, for obtaining information about how a person's self-esteem may go up and down over time or how a person reacts to the stress of life day after day. Experience sampling is increasingly being used in personality research using technologies such as smartphones, Facebook, Twitter, and Instagram postings, and even Fitbit records. One study in Korea, for example, found that people high on narcissism posted more selfies and updated their profile pictures more often than those low on narcissism (e.g., Moon et al., 2016).

Observer-Report Data (O-Data)

In everyday life, we form impressions of others with whom we come into contact. For each individual, there are typically dozens of observers who form impressions. Our friends, families, teachers, and casual acquaintances are all potential sources of information about our personalities. **Observer-report data (O-data)** capitalizes on these sources for gathering information about a person's personality.

Observer reports offer both advantages and disadvantages as sources of personality data. One advantage is that observers may have access to information not attainable through other sources. For example, observers can report about the impressions people make on others, their social reputation, whether interactions with others are smooth or conflict-ridden, and their status within the group hierarchy. Indeed, one study found that altruistic traits can be identified by observers with some accuracy by a mere 20-second exposure (Fetchenhauer, Groothuis, & Pradel, 2010). As noted by Santayana (1905/1980), "[The observer] sometimes reaches truths about people's character and destiny which they are far from divining" (p. 154).

A second advantage of observer-reports is that multiple observers can be used to assess each individual, whereas in self-report only one person provides information (Connelly & Ones, 2010; Paunonen & O'Neill, 2010). The use of multiple observers allows investigators to evaluate the degree of agreement among observers—also known as **inter-rater reliability**. Furthermore, statistical procedures, such as averaging the assessments of multiple observers, have the advantage of reducing the idiosyncratic features and biases of single observers. A more valid and reliable assessment of personality typically can be achieved using multiple observers.

Observer reports can be used as one source of personality information.
Bananastock/AGE Fotostock

Selection of Observers

A key decision point that researchers face when using observers is how to select them. Personality researchers have developed two strategies. One strategy is to use professional personality assessors who do not know the participant in advance. The other strategy is to use individuals who actually know the target participants.

One setting in which professional observers are used is the Institute for Personality and Social Research (IPSR) at the University of California at Berkeley. Participants go to the institute for periods of time ranging from one to five days so that a wide variety of in-depth personality assessments can take place. One study contacted a set of architects who were judged by their peers to be highly creative, to determine the personality predictors of creativity. Another study looked at novelists judged to be creative. A third assessed graduate students in an MBA program to determine the personality predictors of success in business. During studies at the IPSR, trained personality assessors observe the participants in many contexts. Subsequently, each observer provides an independent personality description of the participants.

A second strategy for obtaining observational data is to use individuals who actually know the target participants. For example, close friends, spouses, mothers, and roommates have all been used to provide personality data on participants (e.g., Buss, 1984; Connelly & Ones, 2010; Vazire & Mehl, 2008). The use of observers who have existing relationships with a person has advantages and disadvantages when compared with professional assessors. One advantage is that such observers are in a better position to observe the target's natural behavior. In the relatively public context of an IPSR assessment, in contrast, professional observers cannot witness the more private actions of a person and must settle for observing public actions. A spouse or lover has access to privileged information often inaccessible through other sources, such as their sexual behavior (Meston et al., 2020).

A second advantage of using intimate observers is that **multiple social personalities** can be assessed (Craik, 1986, 2008). Each of us displays different sides of ourselves to different people—we may be kind to friends, ruthless to enemies, loving to a spouse, and conflicted toward parents. Our personalities can vary from one social setting to another, depending on the nature of relationships we have with other individuals (Lukaszewski &

Roney, 2010). The use of multiple observers provides a method for assessing the many aspects of an individual's personality (Sun, Harris, & Vazire, 2020).

Although there are advantages in using intimate observers in personality assessment, there are also drawbacks (Vazire, 2010). Because intimate observers have relationships with the target person, they may be biased in certain ways. A participant's mother, for example, may overlook the negative and emphasize the positive features of her child.

Naturalistic Versus Artificial Observation

In addition to deciding the type of observers to use, personality researchers must determine whether the observation occurs in a natural or an artificial setting. In **naturalistic observation**, observers witness and record events that occur in the normal course of the lives of their participants. For example, a child might be followed throughout an entire day, or an observer may sit in a participant's home. In contrast, observation can take place in artificial settings, such as occur at the IPSR. Experimenters can instruct participants to perform a task, such as participation in a group discussion, and then observe how individuals behave in these constructed settings. For example, psychologists John Gottman and Robert Levenson have had married couples come to their laboratories and discuss a topic on which they disagree. The psychologists then observe the couple having a small argument. The way in which a couple conducts an argument can predict the likelihood that the couple will remain together or get divorced (Gottman, 1994). Even the facial expressions displayed during these laboratory conflicts predict subsequent marital outcomes (Coan & Gottman, 2007; Gottman, Levenson, & Woodin, 2001; Otero et al., 2020).

Naturalistic observation offers researchers the ability to secure information in the realistic context of a person's everyday life, but at the cost of not being able to control the events and behavioral samples witnessed. Studies are being conducted by observing people's behavior on the internet (Gosling & Mason, 2015). One study, for example, found that extraverts tend to engage in more cyberbullying on the internet than do introverts (Semerci, 2017). Observation in experimenter-generated situations has the advantage of controlling conditions and eliciting the relevant behavior. But this advantage comes at a cost—sacrificing the realism of everyday life.

In summary, there are many dimensions along which O-data differ, such as decisions about whether to use (1) professional assessors or intimate observers and (2) a naturalistic or an artificial setting. The strengths and weaknesses of the options must be evaluated with the goals of the investigation in mind. No single method is ideally suited for all assessment purposes.

Test Data (T-Data)

Beyond self-report and O-data, a third common source of personality-relevant information comes from standardized tests—**test data (T-data)**. Participants are placed in a standardized testing situation. The idea is to see if different people react differently to an identical situation. The situation is designed to elicit behaviors that serve as indicators of personality variables (Block, 1977). An interesting example is the bridge-building test found in Henry Murray's (1948) classic book *The Assessment of Men*. In this test, the person being assessed is given two assistants and a collection of wood, rope, and tools, and they have to build a bridge over a small creek. The person being assessed cannot do the work alone, but must instruct the two assistants on how to build the bridge. Unbeknownst to the person being assessed, the two assistants are role-playing: One is has trouble understanding instructions; the other is a "know-it-all," who has their own ideas about how the bridge should be built and often contradicts the person being assessed. These two "helpers" actually are there to frustrate the person being assessed. Although the person being assessed thinks he or she is being observed on leadership skills, the person is actually being evaluated on tolerance of frustration and performance under adversity.

One fascinating example of the use of T-data is Edwin Megargee's (1969) study of manifestations of *dominance.* Megargee wanted to devise a laboratory test situation to examine the effect of dominance on leadership. He first administered the California Psychological Inventory Dominance scale to a large group of men and women. He then selected only men and women who scored either very high or very low on dominance. Megargee then took pairs of individuals into the laboratory, in each case pairing a high-dominant participant with a low-dominant participant. He created four conditions: (1) a high-dominant man with a low-dominant man, (2) a high-dominant woman with a low-dominant woman, (3) a high-dominant man with a low-dominant woman, and (4) a high-dominant woman with a low-dominant man.

Megargee then presented each pair with a large box containing many red, yellow, and green nuts, bolts, and levers. Participants were told that the purpose of the study was to explore the relationship between personality and leadership under stress. Each pair had to work as a team of troubleshooters to repair the box as fast as possible—by removing nuts and bolts with certain colors and replacing them with other colors. They were told that one person from the team had to be the *leader,* a position which entailed giving instructions. The second person was to be the *follower,* who had to go inside the box and carry out the menial tasks requested by the leader. The experimenter then told the participants that it was up to them to decide who would be the leader and who would be the follower.

Who takes the leadership role when people work together is often a function of personality.

Sam Edwards/AGE Fotostock

The key variable of interest for Megargee was who would become the leader and who would become the follower. He simply recorded the percentage of high-dominant participants within each condition who became leaders. He found that 75 percent of the high-dominant men and 70 percent of the high-dominant women took the leadership role in the same-sex pairs. When high-dominant men were paired with low-dominant women, however, 90 percent of the men became leaders. But the most startling result occurred when the woman was high in dominance and the man was low in dominance. In this condition, only 20 percent of the high-dominant women assumed the leadership role.

Megargee tape-recorded the conversations while they were deciding who would be the leader. When he analyzed these tapes, he made a startling finding: the high-dominant women were *appointing* their low-dominant partners to the leadership position. In fact, the high-dominant women actually made the final decision about the roles 91 percent of the time. This finding suggests that women were *expressing* their dominance in a different manner than the men in the mixed-sex condition.

Megargee's study highlights several key points about laboratory studies. First, it shows that it is possible to set up conditions to reveal key indicators of personality. Second, it suggests that laboratory experimenters should be sensitive to manifestations of personality that occur in incidental parts of the experiment, such as the discussions among the participants. And, third, there are often interesting links between S-data obtained through questionnaires and T-data obtained through controlled testing conditions. Such links help to establish the validity of both the questionnaire and the laboratory test of dominance.

Like all data sources, T-data have limitations. First, some participants might try to guess what trait is being measured and then alter their responses to create a specific impression of themselves. A second challenge is the difficulty in verifying that the research participants define the testing situation in the same way as the experimenter. An experiment designed to test for "obedience to authority" might be misinterpreted as a test for "intelligence," perhaps raising anxiety in ways that distort subsequent responses. Failure to confirm the correspondence between the conceptions of experimenters and those of participants may introduce error.

A third caution in the use of T-data is that these situations are inherently *interpersonal,* and a researcher may inadvertently influence how the participants behave. A researcher with an outgoing and friendly personality, for example, may elicit more cooperation from participants than a cold or aloof experimenter (see Kintz et al., 1965). The choice of who runs the experiment, including the personality of the experimenter, may inadvertently introduce effects that alter the obtained results.

Despite these limitations, T-data remain a valuable and irreplaceable source of personality information. Procedures used to obtain T-data can be designed to *elicit behavior* difficult to observe in everyday life. They allow investigators to *control the context* and to eliminate extraneous sources of influence. And they enable experimenters to *test specific hypotheses,* such as the predicted effect of extraversion on social decision making (Tolnai, 2021). For these reasons, T-data procedures remain an indispensable set of tools for the personality researcher (Elfenbein et al., 2008).

Mechanical Recording Devices

Personality psychologists have been enterprising in adapting technological innovations. An example is the use of the "actometer" to assess personality differences in activity or energy level. The actometer is essentially a modified self-winding watch, which can be strapped to the arms or legs of participants (typically, children). Movement activates the winding mechanism, registering the person's activity on the hands of the dial. Of course, day-to-day and even hour-to-hour fluctuations in mood, physiology, and setting limit the usefulness of any single sample of activity level. However, several samples can be recorded on different days to generate composite scores, reflecting, for each person, whether he or she is hyperactive, normally active, or sedentary (Buss, Block, & Block, 1980).

Preschool children ages 3 and 4 wore actometers on the wrist of the nonfavored hand for approximately two hours (Buss, Block, & Block, 1980). The dial of each actometer was covered with tape, so the children would not be distracted. Indeed, in pretesting, the children who could observe the dial became preoccupied with it—sitting in one spot, shaking the device back and forth—a practice that interfered with the usefulness of the measure. Several separate recording sessions were held, and the actometer readings were aggregated to obtain a more reliable index of each child's activity level.

The experimenters then sought answers to three questions: (1) Does activity level measured with the actometer yield the same results as activity level measured through observation? (2) To what extent is activity level stable over time? and (3) Do activity level measurements using this mechanical recording device relate to observer-based judgments of personality functioning? To answer these questions, the children's teachers provided observer evaluations using the children's version of the California Q-Sort—an instrument designed to produce a wide-ranging description of children's personality characteristics (Block & Block, 1980). Examples of items on the Q-Sort include *is a talkative individual; behaves in a giving way toward others; is basically submissive; is guileful and deceitful, manipulative, opportunistic; has a high energy level.*

Activity level is stable over time and correlates with teacher ratings of vital, energetic, and active.

FatCamera/iStock/Getty Images Plus/Getty Images

These observations were made when the children were 3, 4, and 7 years old, whereas the actometer measures were recorded at ages 3 and 4.

There was a strong correspondence between actometer measures of activity level and the observer-based measures. Activity level also is moderately stable over time. For example, actometer measures at age 3 showed a moderate correspondence with actometer measures at age 4. Is there any relationship between actometer measurements of activity level and observer-based judgments of personality? The highly active children, as assessed with the actometer, were judged by their teachers to be vital, energetic, and active. Highly active children also were judged to be restless and fidgety. Teachers saw the active children as uninhibited, assertive, competitive, aggressive physically and verbally, attention-getting, and manipulative of others. Thus, actometer-based activity scores are linked to *other* personality characteristics, traits that have important consequences for social interaction. Actometer measures have also been used to assess hyperactivity and ADHD in children (Dekkers et al., 2021).

In sum, some aspects of personality can be assessed through mechanical recording devices, such as the actometer (Dekkers et al., 2021). These forms of T-data have several advantages and disadvantages. They provide a mechanical means of assessing personality, unhampered by the biases that might be introduced when a human observer is involved. A second advantage is that they can be obtained in relatively naturalistic settings—such as a children's playground. Their primary disadvantage is that few personality dispositions lend themselves to being assessed by mechanical devices. There are no mechanical devices, for example, to directly measure introversion or conscientiousness.

Electronic and Internet Recording Devices

Electronic recording devices are increasingly being used in personality assessment. These include monitoring through smartphones, Instagram, Facebook, Twitter, and fitness devices such as Fitbit. One study using the Electronic Activated Recorder found that moral behavior, as indicated by showing sympathy and gratitude, was highly stable over time (Bollich et al., 2016). Another found that people high on narcissism updated their Instagram profile pictures with great regularity (Moon et al., 2016).

Electronic and internet recordings cut across the categories of T-data, S-data, and O-data. For example, experimenters can introduce an experimental manipulation (T-data), such as prompting participants to discuss a traumatic experience and compare that group with a control group simply asked to write about their day, and then compare the two groups on subsequent physical and psychological health (e.g., Pennebaker & Chung, 2011). Or researchers can ask participants to self-report what they are doing when prompted (S-data) or simply observe behavior such as number of selfies and correlate those with self-reported narcissism (O-data).

Electronic recording devices have the strong advantages in that they can assess naturally occurring behavior in ways not obtainable through laboratory or self-report methods. Nonetheless, because participants are aware that they are being monitored electronically, their behavior may still be sensitive to what they think experimenters want to see, and so act in ways they think are socially desirable.

Physiological Data

A critical source of personality data is physiological measurement. Physiological measures can provide information about a person's level of arousal, reactivity to various stimuli, and the speed at which he or she takes in new information—all potential indicators of personality. Sensors can be placed on different parts of a person's body, for example, to measure sympathetic nervous system activity, blood pressure, heart rate, and muscle contraction. Brain waves, such as reactivity to stimuli, also can be assessed. And even physiological changes associated with sexual arousal can be measured via instruments such as a penile strain gauge (Geer & Head, 1990) or a vaginal bloodflow meter (Handy, Freihart, & Meston, 2020).

In Chapter 7, we go into some detail on physiological measures. For our purposes here—examining alternative ways of measuring personality—we look at only one example of using physiological data as a source of personality information. Psychologist Christopher Patrick (1994, 2005) has been studying psychopaths, particularly men in prison who have committed serious crimes against other people. One theory about psychopaths is that they do not have the normal fear or anxiety response that most people have. Things that might make most people anxious may not make the psychopath anxious. To test this idea, Patrick used a technique called the "eyeblink startle reflex," which had previously been used in studies of fear.

When people are startled by a loud noise, they show the startle reflex, which consists of blinking their eyes, lowering the chin toward the chest, and inhaling suddenly. If people are already anxious, they exhibit the startle reflex faster than when feeling normal. It makes adaptive sense that they will be prepared to have a faster defensive startle if they are already in a fearful or anxious state. You can demonstrate this by showing people pictures of frightening or unpleasant scenes, such as a snake, a vicious dog, or spiders, which most people find make them a little anxious. If they are startled while looking at these scenes, they will startle faster than when looking at nonfeared objects, such as a house, a tree, or a table. Interestingly, Patrick found that psychopaths who were in prison for violent crimes did not exhibit the faster eyeblink response while viewing the anxiety-producing photographs. Psychopaths may commit their crimes because they don't have the normal level of anxiety or guilt that prevents most of us from doing anything wrong. This is a good example of how physiological measures can be used to examine and understand various personality characteristics.

A more recent physiological data source comes from **functional magnetic resonance imaging (fMRI)**, a technique used to identify the areas of the brain that "light up" when performing certain tasks such as verbal problems or spatial navigation problems. It works by gauging the amount of oxygen brought to particular places in the brain. When a certain part of the brain is highly activated, it draws large amounts of blood. the oxygen carried by the blood accumulates in that region of the brain. The fMRI is able to detect concentrations of iron carried by the oxygen contained in the red blood cells and thus determine the part of the brain that is used in performing certain tasks. The colorful images that emerge from fMRI brain scans are often quite dramatic.

In principle, fMRI provides a physiological data source that can be linked with personality dispositions, intelligence, or psychopathology. In practice, however, the method has limitations. Because fMRI must compare the "activated" state with a "resting" state, it becomes critical to know what the resting state really is. If men's resting state turns more to sports and women's resting state turns more to social interactions, for example, it is possible that a comparison of a task such as looking at faces to the resting state would suggest that men and women are performing the task differently, when in fact the

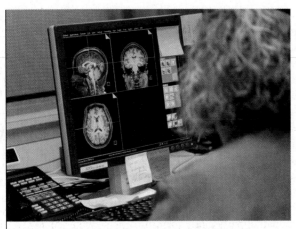

Measures of physiological responses, such as these fMRI brain scans, are a source of data in personality research.

NIH-National Institute on Drug Abuse

difference is due entirely to a sex difference in the resting state (Kosslyn & Rosenberg, 2004).

One of the key benefits of physiological data is that it is difficult for participants to fake responses, particularly on measures of arousal or reflexive responses, such as the eyeblink startle reflex. Nonetheless, physiological recording procedures share most of the same limitations as other laboratory T-data. In particular, recording is typically constrained by a relatively artificial laboratory situation.

Projective Techniques

Another type of T-data is **projective techniques**, in which the person is given a standard stimulus and asked what they see. The most famous projective technique for assessing personality is the set of inkblots developed by Hermann Rorschach. The hallmark of any projective technique is that the person is presented with an ambiguous stimulus, such as an inkblot, and then asked to impose structure on this stimulus by describing what they see—for example, what is in the inkblot. The idea behind projective techniques is that what the person sees in the stimulus reveals something about his or her personality. Presumably, people "project" their concerns, conflicts, traits, and ways of seeing or dealing with the world onto the ambiguous stimulus.

Projective techniques are considered T-data because all people are presented with a standard testing situation, all are given the same instructions, and the test situation elicits behaviors that are thought to reveal personality.

A person interpreting an inkblot may project his or her personality into what is "seen" in the image.

Andrey_Popov/Shutterstock

To the psychologist interpreting responses to the inkblots, the content of those responses is important. Someone with a "dependent personality," for example, might produce a high frequency of responses such as food, food providers, passively being fed, nurturers, oral activity, passivity, helplessness, and "baby talk"(Bornstein, 2005).

In sum, all projective measures present participants with ambiguous stimuli, asking them to provide structure by interpreting, drawing, or telling a story about the stimuli. Psychologists who advocate projective measures argue that they are useful for getting at wishes, desires, fantasies, and conflicts that the participants themselves may be unaware of and so could not report on a questionnaire. Others are critical of projectives, questioning their validity and reliability as accurate measures of personality (Areh, Verkampt, & Allan, 2021; Wood, Nezworski, & Stejskal, 1996).

Life-Outcome Data (L-Data)

Life-outcome data (L-data) refers to information that can be gleaned from the events, activities, and outcomes in a person's life that are available to public scrutiny. For example, marriages and divorces are a matter of public record. Personality psychologists can sometimes secure information about the clubs a person joins, how many speeding tickets a person has received, and whether he or she owns a handgun. Whether a person gets arrested for a violent or white-collar crime is a matter of public record. Success at one's job, whether one is upwardly or downwardly mobile, and the creative products one produces, such

The tendency to have frequent temper outbursts in childhood has been linked with negative adult outcomes, such as increased likelihood of divorce.
Chris Knapton/Alamy Stock Photo

as books published and music recorded, are often important outcomes in a person's life. These can all serve as important sources of information about personality.

Personality psychologists often use S-data and O-data to predict L-data. An example that illustrates how O-data can be used to predict important life events is provided by Avshalom Caspi and his colleagues (Caspi, Elder, & Bem, 1987). Based on clinical interviews with mothers of children aged 8, 9, and 10, researchers created two personality scales to measure ill-temperedness. One was based on the *severity* of temper tantrums; it noted physical behaviors such as biting, kicking, striking, and throwing things and verbal expressions such as swearing, screaming, and shouting. The other scale assessed the *frequency* of these temper tantrums. Caspi and his colleagues summed these two scales to create a single measure of temper tantrums. This measure represents O-data because it is based on the mothers' actual observations. Then, in adulthood, when the participants were 30–40 years old, the researchers gathered information about life outcomes, such as education, work, marriage, and parenthood. They examined whether ill-temperedness, measured in childhood as O-data, predicted significant life outcomes two to three decades later, measured as L-data.

The results proved to be remarkable. For the men, early temper tantrums were linked with many negative outcomes in adult life. The men who had exhibited temper tantrums in childhood achieved significantly lower rank in their military service. They tended to have erratic work lives—changing jobs more frequently and experiencing more unemployment than those who had not been judged to be ill-tempered as children. Furthermore, such men were less likely than their even-tempered counterparts to have a satisfying marriage. Fully 46 percent of the ill-tempered men were divorced by age 40, whereas only 22 percent of the men in the low-temper-tantrum category were divorced by the age of 40.

For the women, early temper tantrums did not have a bearing on their work lives, in contrast to the men. However, the women who had temper tantrums as children tended to marry men who were significantly lower than themselves in occupational status; fully 40 percent of the women who had showed temper tantrums as children "married down," compared with only 24 percent of the women who had been even-tempered as children. As with the men, childhood temper tantrums were linked with frequency of divorce for the women. Roughly 26 percent of the women who had childhood tantrums were divorced by age 40, whereas only 12 percent of the even-tempered women were divorced by that age.

In addition to empirical studies that predict marriage and divorce outcomes, life-outcome data are used in other ways that affect our everyday lives. Our driving records, including speeding tickets and traffic accidents, are used by insurance companies to determine how much we pay for car insurance. Our histories of credit card usage are sometimes tracked by businesses to determine our behavioral preferences, which influence the advertisements we get exposed to on social network sites such as Facebook. Advertisers sometimes track the websites we visit and use e-mail "spam" and pop-up advertisements based on our patterns of internet surfing. Indeed, even a person's e-mail address can reveal personality. People who adopt e-mail addresses such as honey.bunny77@hotmail.com tend to be somewhat more extraverted than those who adopt blander e-mail addresses (Back, Schmukle, & Egloff, 2008). Driving records, credit card usage, and patterns of internet usage are modern sources of L-data. Do you think we can predict these patterns of publicly traceable data from personality variables, such as impulsivity (more driving accidents), status striving (credit card purchase of prestige possessions), and sex drive (more frequent visiting of pornography websites)? Indeed, traits such as Narcissism and Psychopathy are positively correlated with pornography consumption (Burtaverde et al., 2021).

In sum, L-data can serve as an important source of real-life information about personality. Personality characteristics measured early in life are often linked to important life outcomes several decades later. In this sense, life outcomes, such as work, marriage, and divorce, are, in part, manifestations of personality. Nonetheless, it must be recognized that life outcomes are caused by a variety of factors, including gender, culture, economic status, and ethnicity and the opportunities to which one happens to be exposed. Personality characteristics represent only one set of causes of these life outcomes.

Exercise

Think of a personality characteristic that you find interesting. For example, you might consider such characteristics as activity level, risk taking, temper, or cooperativeness. Using the four main data sources, think of ways that you might gather information on this characteristic. Give specific examples of how you could assess this characteristic using S-, O-, T-, and L-data as sources of information on people's level of this characteristic. Be specific in providing examples of how and what you might do to assess your chosen personality characteristic.

Issues in Personality Assessment

Now that we have outlined the basic data sources, it is useful to take a step back and consider two broader issues in personality assessment. The first issue involves using two or more data sources within a single personality study. What are the links among the various sources of personality data? The second issue involves the fallibility of personality measurement and how the use of multiple data sources can correct some of the problems associated with single data sources.

Links Among Various Data Sources

A key issue that personality psychologists must address is how closely the findings obtained from one data source correspond to findings from another data source. If, for example, a person rates herself as dominant, do observers, such as her friends and spouse, also view her as dominant? Do findings obtained from electronic recording devices, such as Facebook or Instagram, correspond to data obtained from observer reports or self-reports of narcissism?

Depending on the personality variable under consideration, agreement across data sources tends to range from low to moderate. Ozer and Buss (1991) examined the relationships between self-report and spouse report for eight dimensions of personality. They found that the degree of agreement varied depending on the particular trait and on the observability of the trait. Traits such as extraversion showed moderate agreement across data sources. The trait of "calculating," on the other hand, showed low self-spouse agreement. Traits that are easily observable (such as extraversion) show a higher degree of self-observer agreement than do traits (such as calculating) that are difficult to observe and require inferences about internal mental states (see Vazire, 2010).

One of the central advantages of using multiple measures is that each measure has unique idiosyncrasies that have nothing to do with the underlying construct of interest. By using multiple measures from various data sources, researchers are able to average out these idiosyncrasies and home in on the key variable under study.

A major issue in evaluating linkages among the sources of personality data is whether the sources are viewed as alternative measures of the same construct or as assessments of different phenomena. A person self-reporting about her relative dominance, for example, has access to a wealth of information—namely, her interactions with dozens of other people in her social environment. Any particular observer—a close friend, for example—has access to only a limited and selective sample of relevant behavior. Thus, if the friend rates a woman as highly dominant, whereas the woman rates herself as only moderately dominant, the disagreement may be due entirely to the different behavioral samples on which each person is basing the ratings. Thus, lack of agreement does not *necessarily* signify an error of measurement (although it might).

In summary, the interpretation of links among the sources of personality data depends heavily on the research question being posed. Strong agreement between two sources of data leads researchers to be confident that their alternative measures are tapping into the same personality phenomenon, as proves true with extraversion and activity level. Lack of strong agreement, on the other hand, may mean that the different data sources are assessing different phenomena, or it may indicate that one or more data sources have problems—an issue to which we now turn.

The Fallibility of Personality Measurement

Each data source has problems and pitfalls that limit its utility. This is true of all methods in science. Even so-called objective scientific instruments, such as telescopes, are less than perfect because minor flaws, such as a slight warping in the lens, may introduce errors into the observations. The fallible nature of scientific measures is no less true in personality research.

One powerful strategy of personality assessment, therefore, is to examine results that transcend data sources—a procedure sometimes referred to as *triangulation*. If a particular effect is found—for example, the influence of dominance on the assumption of leadership—does the effect occur when dominance is measured with self-report as well as with observer reports? If extraverts are more easily bored than introverts, does this show up when boredom is assessed with physiological recording devices as well as via self-report? Throughout this book, we pay special attention to findings that transcend the limitations of single-data-source assessment.

Evaluation of Personality Measures

Once personality measures have been identified, the next task is scientific scrutiny to determine how good the measures are. In general, three standards are used to evaluate personality measures: reliability, validity, and generalizability. Although these three standards are discussed here in the context of evaluating personality questionnaires, these standards are applicable to all measurement methods within personality research, not merely to those involving self-report personality questionnaires.

Reliability

Reliability can be defined as the degree to which an obtained measure represents the true level of the trait being measured. Assume for a moment that each person has some true amount of the trait you wish to measure and that you could know this true level. If your measure is reliable, then it will correlate with the true level. For example, if a person has a true IQ of 115, then a perfectly reliable measure of IQ will yield a score of 115 for that person. Moreover, a reliable measure of IQ will yield the same score of 115 each time it is administered to the person. A less reliable measure would yield a score, say, in a range of 112–118. An even less reliable measure would yield a score in an even broader range, between 100 (which is average) and 130 (which is borderline genius). Personality psychologists prefer reliable measures, so that the scores accurately reflect each person's true level of the personality characteristic.

There are several ways to estimate reliability. One is through **repeated measurement**. There are different forms of repeated measurement. A common procedure is to repeat a measurement over time—for example, at intervals of one month—for the same people. If the two tests are highly correlated, yielding similar scores for most people, the resulting measure is said to have high *test-retest reliability.*

A second way to gauge reliability is to examine the relationships among the items themselves at a single point in time. If the items within a test—viewed as a form of repeated measurement—all correlate well with each other, then the scale is said to have high *internal consistency reliability.* The reliability is internal because it is assessed within the test itself. The rationale for using internal consistency as an index of reliability is that psychologists constructing various measures assume that all items on a scale are measuring the same characteristic. If they are, then the items should correlate positively with each other.

A third way to measure reliability—applicable only to observer-based personality measures—is to obtain measurements from multiple observers. When different observers agree with each other, the measure is said to have high *inter-rater reliability.* When different raters fail to agree, the measure has low inter-rater reliability.

It is important to demonstrate that a personality measure is reliable, whether through test-retest, internal consistency, or inter-rater reliability. One factor that can reduce measurement reliability, especially for self-report questionnaires, is response sets, to which we now turn.

Response Sets

When participants answer questions, psychologists typically assume that they are responding to the content of the questions. For example, when people are confronted with the item "I have never felt like smashing things," psychologists assume that participants think of all the times when they were angry and then recall whether on those occasions they have ever felt like smashing something. Psychologists also assume that participants make a deliberate and conscious effort to consider the content of the question and then answer "True" or "False" to honestly reflect their behavior. This assumption may sometimes be incorrect.

The concept of **response sets** refers to the tendency of some people to respond to the questions on a basis that is unrelated to the question content. Sometimes this is also referred to as **noncontent responding**. One example is the response set of **acquiescence**, or yea saying. This is the tendency to simply agree with the questionnaire items, regardless of the content of those items. Psychologists counteract acquiescence by intentionally reverse-scoring some of the questionnaire items, such as an extraversion item that states, "I frequently prefer to be alone." **Extreme responding** is another response set, which refers to the tendency to give endpoint responses, such as "strongly agree" or "strongly disagree" and to avoid the middle part of response scales, such as "slightly agree" or "slightly disagree."

Personality psychologists worry about the effects of response sets on the reliability of measurement. Response sets may invalidate self-report measures of personality, so psychologists have looked for ways to detect and counteract their effects.

The response set known as **social desirability** has received the greatest amount of research by personality psychologists. Socially desirable responding is the tendency to answer items in such a way as to come across as socially attractive or likable. People responding in this manner want to make a good impression, to appear to be well adjusted, to be good citizens. For example, imagine being asked to answer "True" or "False" to the statement "Most of the time I am happy." A person might actually be happy only 45 percent of the time yet answer "True" because this is the well-adjusted thing to say in our culture. People like happy people, so the socially desirable response is "Yes, I am happy most of the time." This is an example of responding not to the content of the item but to the kind of impression a "True" or "False" answer would create, and it represents a response set. An interesting study found that highly religious individuals were more prone to exaggerate their level of agreeableness, in part because they saw agreeableness as a highly desirable trait (Ludeke & Carey, 2015).

There are two views regarding the interpretation of social desirability. One is that it represents distortion and should be eliminated

Some rare individuals, like the late Mother Teresa of Calcutta, might score high on social desirability because they are in fact truly good, not because they want to create a good impression of themselves by lying on a personality questionnaire.
David Bagnall/Alamy Stock Photo

Table 2.1 Crowne/Marlowe Scale for Measuring Social Desirability

Instructions: Listed below are a number of statements concerning personal attitudes and traits. Read each item and decide whether the statement is true or false as it pertains to you personally.

	True	False
1. I'm always willing to admit it when I make a mistake.	____	____
2. I always try to practice what I preach.	____	____
3. I never resent being asked to return a favor.	____	____
4. I have never been irked when people expressed ideas very different from my own.	____	____
5. I have never deliberately said something that hurt someone's feelings.	____	____
6. I like to gossip at times.	____	____

Source: Crowne & Marlowe, 1964.

or minimized. The other view is that social desirability is a valid part of other desirable personality traits, such as happiness, conscientiousness, or agreeableness.

Viewing social desirability as distortion does not assume that the person is consciously trying to create a positive impression. A social desirability response set may not actually be an outright effort to distort responses and, so, is different from faking or lying. Some people may have a distorted view of themselves or have a strong need to have others like them. For these reasons, most psychologists have resisted calling this response set "lying" or "faking" (cf. Eysenck & Eysenck, 1972, for a different opinion). Nevertheless, many personality psychologists believe that socially desirable responding introduces inaccuracies into test scores and should be eliminated or controlled.

One approach to the problem of socially desirable responses is to assume that they are erroneous or deceptive, to measure this tendency, and to remove it statistically from the other questionnaire responses. There are several social desirability measures available. Items from a popular measure developed by Crowne and Marlowe (1964) are shown in Table 2.1. Crowne and Marlowe thought of social desirability as reflecting a need for approval, and they published the social desirability scale in their book *The Approval Motive.* Looking at the items on their scale, you can see that they typically refer to minor transgressions that most of us have committed or inadequacies that many of us suffer from. In addition, some items refer to almost saintlike behavior. To the extent that a person denies common faults and problems and endorses a lot of perfect and well-adjusted behaviors, they will get a high score on social desirability. A person's score on social desirability can be used to statistically adjust his or her scores on other questionnaires, thereby controlling for this response set.

A second way to deal with the problem of social desirability is by developing questionnaires that are less susceptible to this type of responding. For example, in choosing questions to put on a questionnaire, the researcher may select only the items that have been found *not* to correlate with social desirability.

A third approach to minimizing the effects of socially desirable responding is to use a **forced-choice questionnaire** format. In this format, test takers are confronted with pairs of statements and are asked to indicate which statement in each pair is more true of them. Each statement in the pair is selected to be similar to the other in social desirability, forcing participants to choose among statements that are equally socially desirable (or undesirable). The following items from the Vando Reducer Augmenter Scale (Vando, 1974) illustrate the forced-choice format: Which would you most prefer (a or b)?

1. **a.** To read the book
   b. To see the movie
2. **a.** Eat soft food
   b. Eat crunchy food
3. **a.** Continuous anesthesia
   b. Continuous hallucinations
4. **a.** A job that requires concentration
   b. A job that requires travel

If one answers all *b*s, this scale measures the preference for arousing or strong stimulation. The two choices presented in each item are of approximately the same value in terms of social desirability. Consequently, participants must decide on an answer based on something other than social desirability. They should respond to the *content* of the item and hence provide accurate information about their personalities.

Although many psychologists view socially desirable responding as error to be eliminated, others see it as an important trait, one that is correlated with positive traits such as happiness, adjustment, and conscientiousness. These psychologists suggest that being mentally healthy may, in fact, entail possessing an overly positive view of oneself and one's abilities. In her book *Positive Illusions,* social psychologist Shelly Taylor (1989) summarizes much research suggesting that self-enhancing illusions about oneself, the world, and one's future can promote psychological adjustment and mental health. Indeed, research finds that unrealistic beliefs about the self (positive illusions) are related to better physical health, such as slower progression of disease in men infected with HIV. If psychologists were to measure such positive illusions in the form of social desirability and remove them from other personality measures, they might, in effect, be throwing the baby out with the bathwater. That is, social desirability may be part of being high on adjustment and positive mental health.

Work on social desirability has attempted to disentangle self-deceptive optimism from impression management. Psychologist Delroy Paulhus has developed a social desirability inventory called the Balanced Inventory of Desirable Responding, which contains two separate subscales (Paulhus, 1984, 1990). The Self-Deceptive Enhancement subscale was designed to tap self-deceptive overconfidence and contains items such as "My first impressions of other people are always right." The Impression Management subscale was designed to measure the tendency to present oneself favorably, as in the distortion interpretation of social desirability, and contains items such as "I don't gossip about other people's business." This subscale was intended to be sensitive to self-presentation motives, such as those that lead someone to want to create a good impression in others.

To the extent that response sets, such as social desirability, are considered error, they can reduce measurement reliability (Paulhus & Vazire, 2007). That is, a personality questionnaire that is influenced by response sets would not reflect the true level of the trait being measured. Personality psychologists worry about response sets for this reason, especially for self-report questionnaires. Indeed, new measures of personality are often designed in ways that minimize participants' efforts to fake or present themselves in a socially desirable light (e.g., McDaniel et al., 2009). Response sets also can influence a measure's validity, a topic to which we now turn.

Validity

Validity refers to the extent to which a test measures what it claims to measure (Cronbach & Meehl, 1955; Wiggins, 2003). Establishing whether a test actually measures what it is designed to measure is a complex and challenging task. There are five types of validity: face validity, predictive validity, convergent validity, discriminant validity, and construct validity. The simplest type of validity is **face validity**, which refers to whether the test, on the surface, appears to measure what it is supposed to measure. For example, a scale measuring manipulativeness might include the following face-valid items: *I made a friend just to obtain a favor; I tricked a friend into giving me personal information; I managed to get my way by appearing cooperative; I pretended that I was hurt to get someone to do me a favor.* Because most people agree that these acts are manipulative, the scale containing them is highly face valid.

A more important component of validity is **predictive validity**, which refers to whether the test predicts criteria external to the test (thus it is sometimes called **criterion validity**). A scale intended to measure sensation seeking, for example, should predict which individuals actually take risks to obtain thrills and excitement, such as parachute jumping or motorcycle riding. One study, for example, found that a measure of sensation seeking successfully predicted a variety of gambling behaviors, such as playing the lottery, betting on sporting events, playing video poker, using slot machines, and even addiction to cocaine (O'Connor, Aston-Jones, & James, 2021)—attesting to the predictive validity of the sensation-seeking measure (McDaniel & Zuckerman, 2003). A scale created to measure conscientiousness should predict which people actually show up on time for meetings and follow rules. Scales that successfully predict what they should predict have high predictive validity.

A third aspect of validity, **convergent validity**, refers to whether a test correlates with other measures that it should correlate with. For example, if a self-report measure of tolerance corresponds well with peer judgments of tolerance, then the scale is said to have high convergent validity. Early in this chapter, we described a study of "activity level," in which mechanical recordings of activity level correlated highly with observer-based judgments of activity level—another example of convergent validity. Convergent validity is high to the degree that alternative measures of the same construct correlate or converge with the target measure.

A fourth kind of validity, called **discriminant validity**, is often evaluated simultaneously with convergent validity. Whereas *convergent validity* refers to what a measure *should* correlate with, *discriminant validity* refers to what a measure *should not* correlate with. For example, a psychologist might develop a measure of life satisfaction, the tendency to believe one's life is happy, worthwhile, and satisfying. However, there is another trait called social desirability, the tendency to say nice things about oneself; thus the psychologist might be concerned with the discriminant validity of his or her life-satisfaction measure and try to show that this measure is different from measures of social desirability. Part of knowing what a measure actually measures consists of knowing what it does not measure.

A final type of validity is **construct validity**, defined as a test that measures what it claims to measure, correlates with what it is supposed to correlate with, and does not correlate with what it is not supposed to correlate with. Construct validity is the broadest type of validity, subsuming face, predictive, convergent, and discriminant validity. This form of validity is called construct validity because it is based on the notion that personality variables are **theoretical constructs**. If asked to "show your intelligence" or "show your extraversion," you would be hard-pressed to respond. That is because there is not any one thing you can produce and say, "This is my intelligence" or "This is my extraversion." Intelligence and extraversion, like almost all personality variables, are abstractions. Nevertheless, these theoretical constructs are useful to psychologists in describing and explaining differences among people. Determining whether actual measures can claim to be valid ways of assessing the constructs is the essence of construct validity.

How do we know if a measure has construct validity? If a measure converges with other measures of the same construct, if it relates to other variables that a theory of the construct says it should, and if it does *not* relate to phenomena that the theory says it should not relate to, then we have the beginnings of construct validity. For example, say that a researcher has developed a questionnaire measure of creativity. Do the questionnaire scores correlate with other measures of creativity gathered on the same sample, such as ratings of creativity provided by friends (convergent validity), or awards or grades obtained in fine arts classes (predictive validity)? Do the results correlate with behavioral tests in which participants are asked to name creative uses for common objects, such as a hammer and string?

Finally, if creativity is hypothesized to be different from intelligence, it will be important to prove that the measure of creativity does *not* correlate with measures of intelligence (discriminant validity). When a large number of known relations are built up around a measure, then we begin to believe that the measure is credible as a measure of a specific personality construct.

Generalizability

A third criterion for evaluating personality measures is **generalizability** (Cronbach & Gleser, 1965; Wiggins, 1973). Generalizability is the degree to which the measure retains its validity across various contexts. One context of interest might be different groups of *persons.* A personality psychologist, for example, might be interested in whether a questionnaire retains its predictive validity across age groups, genders, cultures, or ethnic groups. Is a particular scale equally valid when used on men versus women? Is a test equally valid for African Americans and European Americans? Is it equally valid among Japanese and Javanese? Does the scale measure the same trait or quality among college students as among middle-aged adults? If the scale is widely applicable across these person and cultural contexts, then the scale is said to have high generalizability across populations of people.

Another facet of generalizability refers to *different conditions.* Does a dominance scale, for example, predict who becomes the leader in business settings as well as in informal, after-work settings? Does a scale designed to measure conscientiousness predict who will show up for class on time, as well as who will keep their bedrooms tidy? Scales have high generalizability to the degree that they apply widely over different persons, situations, cultures, and times.

Research Designs in Personality

In this chapter, we have examined the *types of personality measures* and the *means for evaluating the quality* of those measures. The next step in personality research is to use these measures in actual *research designs.* Although the variations are nearly infinite, there are three basic research designs in the field of personality psychology: experimental, correlational, and case study. Each has strengths and weaknesses. Each provides information that complements the information provided by the others.

Experimental Methods

Experimental methods are typically used to determine causality—that is, to find out whether one variable *influences* another variable. A *variable* is simply a quality that can take different values for different people. Height, for example, is a variable because individuals differ in height. Aggressiveness is a variable because individuals differ in their levels of aggressiveness. Personality characteristics, such as extraversion and agreeableness, are other examples of variables. In order to establish the influence of one variable on another, two key requirements of good experimental design must be met: (1) **manipulation** of one or more variables and (2) ensuring that participants in each experimental condition *are equivalent to each other at the beginning of the study.*

In the first requirement, manipulation, the variable thought to be the influence is manipulated as part of the experiment. For example, if a drug is hypothesized to influence memory, then some participants get the drug and other participants get pills containing no active substances; then all participants have their memories tested. The second requirement, equivalence, is accomplished in one of two ways. If the experiment has manipulation among groups, then the **random assignment** of participants to experimental groups is a procedure that helps ensure that all groups are the same at the beginning of the study. However, in some experiments, manipulation is within each single group. For example, in the memory experiment, participants might get the drug and have their memories tested, then later take the blank pills and have their memories tested again. In this case, each participant is in both conditions. In this kind of experiment (called a within-participant design), equivalence is obtained by **counterbalancing** the order of the conditions, with half of the participants getting the drug first and blank pill second, and the other half getting the blank pill first and the drug second.

The meaning of each of these features will become clear through an example of a personality experiment. Perhaps you are curious about why some people like to study with music or a TV on, whereas others need total silence for studying. A personality theory predicts that extraverts prefer lots of stimulation and introverts prefer very little. Imagine being interested in testing the hypothesis that extraverts function best under conditions of high external stimulation, whereas introverts function best under conditions of low stimulation. To test this hypothesis, you could first give a group of participants a self-report questionnaire that measures extraversion–introversion. Then you could select only those who score at either extremes—as very introverted or very extraverted—to participate in your experiment. Next you would take these participants into the laboratory and have them work on math and sentence comprehension problems under two different conditions—in one condition, a radio would be blaring in the background, and in the other there would be total silence. Half of each group (i.e., half of the extraverts and half of the introverts) should be randomly placed in the noisy condition first and the quiet condition second. The other half should be placed in the quiet condition first and the noisy condition second. Then, you would measure the number of errors each group makes under each of the two conditions. If the personality theory you are testing is correct, you should get a pattern of results like that in Figure 2.1. The hypothetical results in Figure 2.1 show that the extraverts made few errors in the noisy condition and more errors when it was quiet. The introverts showed the opposite pattern—noise hurt their performance, whereas they functioned best under conditions of silence.

This study, although hypothetical, highlights the key features of good experimental design. The first is manipulation. The external condition (the *independent variable*) was manipulated—whether there was a lot of or a little ambient noise in the laboratory. The second feature is counterbalancing—half of the participants received the noisy condition first, and the other half received the quiet condition first. Counterbalancing is critical because there might be *order effects* as a consequence of being exposed to one condition first. Counterbalancing allows the experimenter to rule out order effects as an explanation for the results. The third feature is random assignment—all people have an equal chance of being selected for a given condition. Randomization can occur by flipping a coin or, more commonly, by the use of a table of random numbers. Randomization ensures that there are no predetermined patterns linked with condition assignment that could account for the final results.

In experimental designs, it is desirable to establish whether the groups in the different conditions are *significantly* different. In the introversion–extraversion example, we want to know if the performance of introverts and extraverts in the noisy condition is significantly different. Is the performance of the introverts significantly different from that of the extraverts in the quiet condition? To answer these questions, we need to know five things: the sample size, the mean, the standard deviation, the *t*-test, and the *p*-value (significance of the differences among the conditions).

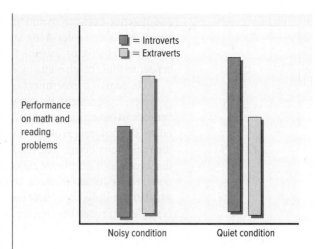

Figure 2.1
Performance on math and reading problems.

The *mean* refers to the average—in this case, the average number of errors within each condition. The *standard deviation* is a measure of variability within each condition. Because not all participants make the same average number of errors, we need a way to estimate how much participants within each condition vary; this estimate is the standard deviation. Using these numbers, we can use a statistical formula—called the *t-test*—to calculate the difference between two means.

The next step is to see whether the difference is large enough to be called a statistically significant difference (the *p*-value). Although "large enough" is a somewhat arbitrary concept, psychologists have adopted the following convention: If the difference between the means would be likely to occur *by chance alone* (i.e., due to random fluctuations in the data) only one time out of 20 or less, then the difference is **statistically significant** at the $p < .05$ level (the .05 refers to 5 percent chance level, or one time in 20).

People who study alone in a library are likely to be introverted, whereas those who do their studying in groups tend to be extraverted.
Left: Stockbroker/Purestock/SuperStock; Right: Leah Warkentin/Design Pics

A difference between means that is significant at the .05 level implies that the finding would be likely to occur by chance alone only five times out of 100. Another way to think about this is to imagine that, if the experiment were repeated 100 times, we would expect to find these results by chance alone only five times.

In sum, the experimental method is effective at demonstrating *relationships among variables*. Experiments similar to the one described, for example, have established a link between extraversion–introversion and performance under conditions of high versus low noise. The procedures of manipulating the conditions, counterbalancing the order in which the conditions occur, and randomly assigning participants to conditions help to ensure that extraneous factors are canceled out. Then, after calculating means and standard deviations, *t*-tests (or other more complicated statistics) and *p*-values are used to determine whether the differences between the groups in the two conditions are statistically significant. These procedures determine whether personality influences how people perform.

Correlational Studies

A second major type of research design in personality is the correlational study. In the **correlational method**, a statistical procedure is used for determining whether there is a relationship between two variables. For example, do people with a high need for achievement in college go on to earn higher salaries in adulthood than people lower on need for achievement? Correlational research designs attempt to identify the relationships between two or more variables, without imposing the sorts of manipulations seen in experimental designs. Correlational designs typically try to determine what goes with what in nature. We might be interested, for example, in the relationship between self-esteem, as assessed through S-data, and the esteem in which a person is held by others, as assessed through O-data. Or we might be interested in how achievement motivation relates to grade point average. A major advantage of correlational studies is that they allow us to identify relationships among variables as they occur naturally. To continue the example of extraversion–introversion and performance under noise conditions, we might measure people's preferences for studying with or without music in real life, and then see whether there is a correlation with their scores on a measure of introversion–extraversion.

The most common statistical procedure for gauging relationships between variables is the **correlation coefficient**. Consider the relationship between height and weight. We can take a sample of 100 college students and measure their height and weight. If we chart the results on a scatterplot, we see that people who are tall also tend to be relatively heavy and that people who are short tend to be less heavy. But there are exceptions, as you can see in Figure 2.2.

Correlation coefficients can range from +1.00 through 0.00 to −1.00. That is, the variables of interest can be positively related to each other (+.01 to +1.00), unrelated to each other (0.00), or negatively related to each other (−.01 to −1.00). Height and weight happen to be strongly positively correlated with each other—with a calculated correlation coefficient of +.60, for the data shown in Figure 2.2.

Consider a more psychological example. Suppose we are interested in the relationship between people's self-esteem and the amount of time they are unhappy. We might see a scatterplot as depicted in Figure 2.3. This scatterplot was obtained from a sample of college students using a standard questionnaire measure of self-esteem. As the second variable, a measure of unhappiness, the participants were asked to keep a diary for two months, noting for each day whether that day was generally good (felt happy) or generally bad (felt unhappy). Then we calculated the percentage of days for each participant

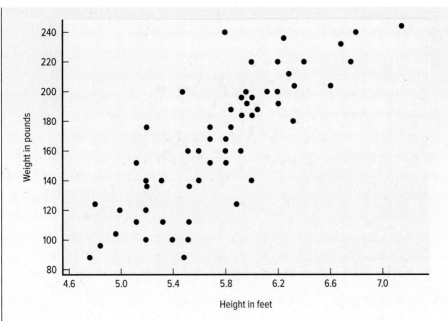

Figure 2.2

Fifty-five cases plotted, showing a strong positive correlation between height and weight. Each symbol
(·) represents one person who was measured on both height and weight. Heavier people tend to be taller;
lighter persons tend to be shorter.

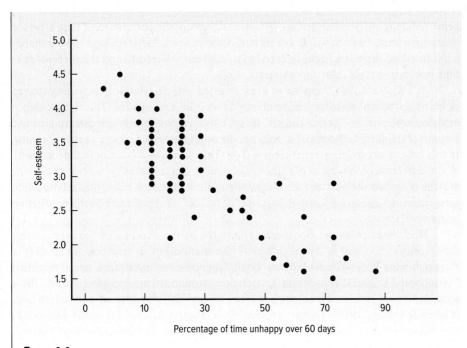

Figure 2.3

Fifty-eight cases plotted to illustrate the negative correlation between self-esteem and the percentage of
time reported as being unhappy over two months. The correlation is −.60, indicating that people with
higher self-esteem tend to be less unhappy than people with low self-esteem.

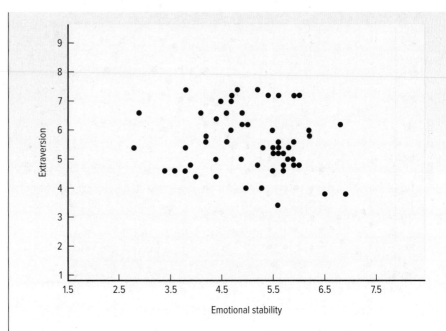

Figure 2.4

Fifty-seven cases plotted to show the relationship between emotional stability and extraversion. The correlation between these two variables is essentially 0.00, meaning that there is no relationship. Consequently, in the scatterplot, people fall fairly equally in all sections of the plot, with no clear pattern.

being unhappy. As you can see, as self-esteem goes up, the percentage of time a person is unhappy tends to go down. In contrast, those with low self-esteem tend to be unhappy a lot. In short, there is a negative correlation between self-esteem and the percentage of time unhappy—in this case, approximately −.60.

As a final example, suppose we are interested in the relationship between extraversion and emotional stability (the tendency to be calm and secure). The relationship is depicted in Figure 2.4. As you can see, there is no relationship between extraversion and emotional stability; as one variable goes up, the other may go up, down, or stay the same. In this case, the correlation coefficient is 0.00. This means that you can find people with all the different combinations of extraversion and emotional stability, such as those who are outgoing and sociable but also highly neurotic and unstable. In sum, relationships between variables can be positive, negative, or neither, as signified by positive, negative, or zero correlations.

Most researchers are not merely interested in the *direction* of the relationship; they are also interested in the *magnitude* of the relationship, or how large or small it is. Although what is considered large or small depends on many factors, social scientists have adopted a general convention. Correlations around .10 are considered small; those around .30 are considered medium; and those around .50 or greater are considered large (Cohen & Cohen, 1975). Using the examples in Figures 2.2 and 2.3, the +.60 correlation between height and weight is considered large, as is the −.60 correlation between self-esteem and percentage of time unhappy. These correlations have the same magnitude but are different in sign.

The concept of statistical significance can also be applied to correlation values. This is basically part of the statistical calculation, and it results in a numerical statement about how likely you are to find a correlation this size by chance, given the variables measured and the size of the sample. Here psychologists also require a probability of .05 or less before referring to a correlation as statistically significant.

It is important to keep in mind that one cannot infer causation from correlations. There are at least two reasons correlations can never prove causality. One is called the **directionality problem**. If *A* and *B* are correlated, we do not know if *A* is the cause of *B* or if *B* is the cause of *A*. For example, we know there is a correlation between extraversion and happiness. From this fact alone, we do not know if being extraverted causes people to be happy or if being happy causes people to be extraverted.

The second reason that correlations can never prove causality is the **third variable problem**. Two variables might be correlated because a third, unknown variable is causing both. For example, the amount of ice cream sold on any given day may be correlated with the number of people who drown on that particular day. Does this mean eating ice cream causes drowning? Not necessarily, because there is most likely a third variable at work: hot weather. On very hot days, many people eat ice cream. Also, on very hot days many people go swimming who otherwise don't swim very much, so more are likely to drown. Drowning has nothing to do with eating ice cream; rather, these two variables are likely to be caused by a third variable: hot weather.

Case Studies

Sometimes a personality researcher is interested in examining the life of one person in-depth as a case study. There are advantages to the **case study method**. Researchers can find out about personality in great detail, which rarely can be achieved if the study includes large samples. Case studies can give researchers insights into personality that can then be used to formulate a more general theory to be tested on a larger population. They can provide in-depth knowledge of particularly outstanding individuals, such as Mahatma Gandhi or Martin Luther King. Case studies also can be useful in studying rare phenomena, such as a person with a photographic memory or a person with multiple personalities.

One case study occupied an entire issue of the *Journal of Personality* (Nasby & Read, 1997), the case of Dodge Morgan, who, at the age of 54, completed a non-stop solo circumnavigation of the earth by a small boat. The case study is a highly readable account of this interesting man undertaking an almost impossible task. The focus is on how Morgan's early life experiences formed a particular adult personality, which led him to undertake the extreme act of going around the world alone in a small boat. The psychologists used Morgan's voyage log book, autobiographical material, interviews, and even standard personality questionnaires in conducting their case study. The report is noteworthy in that the psychologists also discussed the strengths and weaknesses of the case study method for advancing the science of personality psychology. The authors concluded that personality theories provide a language for discussing individual lives; analysis of individual lives, in turn, provides a means for evaluating personality theories on how they help us understand specific individuals.

Dodge Morgan was 54 when he completed a nonstop, solo circumnavigation of the earth in his boat American Promise. *An extensive case study of this fascinating man was conducted by psychologists William Nasby and Nancy Read and reported in their paper "The Voyage and the Voyager" published in the* Journal of Personality, *1997, volume 65, pages 823–852.*

Portland Press Herald/Getty Images

Case study design can use a wide array of tools. One can develop coding systems to be applied to written texts, such as personal letters and correspondence. One can interview dozens of people who know the individual. One can interview the participant for hours and at great depth. One can follow the person around with a video camera and record, with sound and image, the actions in his or her everyday life.

Case Study: An Attention-Seeking Boy

One of the strongest advocates of the case study method was Gordon Allport, one of the founders of the field of modern personality psychology. Allport firmly believed that important hypotheses about personality could come from examining single individuals in great depth. He also believed that one could test hypotheses about the underlying personality characteristics of a single individual using case study methods. The following example illustrates this sort of hypothesis formation and testing:

> *A certain boy at school showed exemplary conduct; he was orderly, industrious, and attentive. But at home he was noisy, unruly, and a bully toward the younger children . . . .*
>
> *Now the psychologist might create the hypothesis: This boy's central disposition is a craving for attention. He finds that he gains attention best at school by conforming to the rules; at home, by disobeying them.*
>
> *Having made this hypothesis, the psychologist could then actually count the boy's acts during the day (being checked by some independent observer) to see how many of them were "functionally equivalent," i.e., manifested a clear bid for attention. If the proportion is high, we can regard the hypothesis as confirmed, and the p.d. [personality disposition] as established. (Allport, 1961, p. 368)*

Source: Allport, G. Pattern and Growth in Personality, 1961.

Case Study: The Serial Killer Ted Bundy

Although Ted Bundy was convicted of killing three women, he was suspected of raping and killing as many as 36 women during his half-decade murder spree in the states of Oregon, Washington, Colorado, and Florida in the 1970s (Rule, 2000). Case studies have been devoted to explaining what drove Bundy to rape and kill. Some traced it back to the fact that he was adopted and felt a burning shame over the fact that he never knew his biological parents. Some tied it to his failed aspirations as a lawyer—where a status-striving motive was frustrated. Some traced it to the fact that he developed a deep-seated hostility toward women after being rejected by his fiancée—a woman who was considerably higher than he in socioeconomic status and who he felt was impossible to replace. All case studies of Bundy revealed, however, that he shared many traits with other serial killers. He had a "classic" sociopathic personality—characterized by grandiosity, extreme sense of entitlement, preoccupation with unrealistic fantasies of success and power, lack of empathy for other people, a long history of deceitfulness, repeated failures to meet normally expected obligations of school and work, and high levels of interpersonal exploitativeness. Furthermore, Ted Bundy showed early behavior and personality dispositions that are known to be associated with serial killers, the so-called serial killer triad: (1) torturing animals while young, (2) starting destructive fires, and (3) bedwetting

Ted Bundy, a convicted serial killer, showed the personality characteristics of a classic sociopath.
Bill Frakes/The LIFE Images Collection/Getty Images

(although this third element has recently been called into question because it is not characteristic of all serial killers). Case studies such as those of Ted Bundy can reveal unique aspects of his life (e.g., being rejected by a higher status fiancée, failure to achieve status as an attorney), as well as the common personality dispositions that are often linked with serial killers (e.g., torturing animals, setting fires; see also the case of Keith Hunter Jesperson, who confessed to raping and killing eight women, in Olson, 2002).

Despite the strengths of the in-depth case study method, it has some critical limitations. The most important one is that findings based on one individual cannot be generalized to other people. A case study is to the other research designs what a study of the planet Mars is to the study of planetary systems. We may find out a great deal about Mars (or a particular person), but what we find out may not be applicable to other planets (or other people). For this reason, case studies are most often used as a *source of hypotheses* and as a *means to illustrate* a principle by bringing it to life.

When to Use Experimental, Correlational, and Case Study Designs

Each of the three major types of research designs has strengths and weaknesses or, more precisely, questions that each is good at answering and questions that each is poor at answering. The experimental method is ideally suited for establishing causal relationships among variables. For example, it can be used to determine whether noisy conditions hamper the performance of introverts, but not of extraverts. On the other hand, the experimental method is poor at identifying the relationships among variables as they occur naturally in everyday life. Moreover, it may be impractical or unethical to use the experimental method for some questions. For example, if a researcher is interested in the role of nutrition in the development of intelligence, it is unethical to conduct an experiment in which half of the participants are put on a starvation diet for several years as children to see if it affects their IQs as adults.

Exercise

Think of a question about one aspect of personality. Most questions take the form of "Is variable *A* related to or caused by variable *B*?" For example, are extraverted persons better than introverts at coping with stress? Are people with high self-esteem more likely to be successful than people with low self-esteem? Do narcissistic persons have problems getting along with others? Write down your question about personality. Now think about how you might approach your question using an experiment, using the correlational method, and doing a case study. Briefly describe how you would use each of these three research designs to try to answer your question.

However, there are people who, for whatever unfortunate circumstances, have had several years of very poor nutrition. Thus a correlational study could be done on whether level of nutrition is related to the development of intelligence. The weakness of the experimental research design is precisely the strength of the correlational design. Correlational designs are ideally suited for establishing the relationships between two or more variables that occur in everyday life, such as between height and dominance, conscientiousness and grade point average, or anxiety and frequency of illness. But correlational designs are poor at establishing causality.

Case studies are ideally suited for generating hypotheses that can be tested subsequently using correlational or experimental methods. Case studies can be used to identify patterns in individual psychological functioning that might be missed by the more rigorous but artificial experimental approach and the limited correlational designs. Furthermore, case studies are wonderful in depicting the richness and complexity of human experience. Despite these strengths, case studies cannot establish causality, as can experimental methods, nor can they identify patterns of covariation across individuals as they occur in nature. Case studies also cannot be generalized to anyone beyond the single individual being studied. Together, all three designs provide complementary methods for exploring human personality.

SUMMARY AND EVALUATION

Personality assessment and measurement start with identifying the sources of personality data—the places from which we obtain information about personality. The four major sources of personality data are self-report (S-data), observer report (O-data), laboratory tests (T-data), and life history outcomes (L-data). Each of these data sources has strengths and weaknesses. In self-report, for example, participants might fake or lie. Observers in the O-data mode may lack access to the relevant information. Observational studies of people's behavior on the internet, however, are creating new research opportunities, such as predicting Facebook or Instagram postings or cyberbullying from personality traits. Laboratory tests may be inadequate for identifying patterns that occur naturally in everyday life. Each source of personality data is extremely valuable, however, and each provides information not attainable through the other sources. Furthermore, new measurement techniques continue to be invented and explored; recent examples include assessments through electronic and internet technologies such as smartphones, Instagram, and Facebook.

Once sources of data have been selected for measuring personality, the researcher then evaluates their quality. Personality measures, ideally, should be reliable in the sense of attaining the same scores through repeated measurement. They should be valid, measuring what they are supposed to measure. And researchers should establish how generalizable their measures are—determining the people, settings, and cultures to which the measure is most applicable. Scales applicable only to college students in the United States, for example, are less generalizable than scales applicable to people of differing ages, economic brackets, ethnic groups, and cultures.

The next step in personality research involves selecting a particular research design within which to use the measures. There are three basic types of research designs. The first, the experimental research design, which involves controlling or manipulating the variables of interest, is best suited to determining causality between two variables. The second, correlational research design, is best for identifying relationships between naturally occurring variables but is poorly suited to determining causality. The third is the case study method, which is well suited to generating new hypotheses about personality and to understanding single individuals.

Perhaps the most important principle of personality assessment and measurement is that the decisions about data source and research design depend heavily on the purpose of the investigation. There are no perfect methods; there are no perfect designs. But there are data sources and methods that are better suited for some purposes than for others.

KEY TERMS

self-report data (S-data) 24

unstructured 24

structured 24

Likert rating scale 25

experience sampling 27

observer-report data (O-data) 27

inter-rater reliability 28

multiple social personalities 28

naturalistic observation 29

test data (T-data) 29

functional magnetic resonance imaging
   (fMRI) 33

projective techniques 34

life-outcome data (L-data) 35

reliability 38

repeated measurement 38

response sets 39

noncontent responding 39

acquiescence 39

extreme responding 39

social desirability 39

forced-choice questionnaire 40

validity 42

face validity 42

predictive validity 42

criterion validity 42

convergent validity 42

discriminant validity 42

construct validity 42

theoretical constructs 42

generalizability 43

experimental methods 44

manipulation 44

random assignment 44

counterbalancing 44

statistically significant 45

correlational method 46

correlation coefficient 46

directionality problem 49

third variable problem 49

case study method 49

The Dispositional Domain

PART ONE

Tavis Wright/Image Source

The dispositional domain focuses on aspects of personality that are stable over time, are relatively consistent over situations, and make people different from each other. For example, some people are outgoing and talkative; others are introverted and shy. The introverted and shy person tends to be that way most of the time (is stable over time) and tends to be introverted and shy at work, at play, and at school (is consistent over situations).

The study of traits makes up the dispositional domain. The term *disposition* is used because it refers to an inherent tendency to behave in a specific way. The term *trait* is used interchangeably with the term *disposition.* The major questions for psychologists working in the dispositional domain are these: How many personality traits exist? What is the best taxonomy, or classification system, for traits? How can we best discover and measure these traits?

How do personality traits develop? How do traits interact with situations to produce behaviors?

In this domain, traits are seen as the building blocks of personality. A person's personality is viewed as being built out of a set of common traits. Psychologists try to identify the most important traits, the ones out of which all differences among people can be formed.

The next step is to develop taxonomies, or classification systems. Taxonomies are very useful in all areas of science. Currently, the most popular taxonomy of personality has five fundamental traits: extraversion, neuroticism, agreeableness, conscientiousness, and openness to experience.

In the dispositional domain, there is a unique conception of how people change yet remain stable at the same time. We will discuss how the traits that underlie behavior can remain stable, yet how the traits expressed in behavior can change over a person's life span. Consider the trait of dominance. Suppose that a child who is dominant at age 8 grows into an adult who is dominant at age 20. As an 8-year-old, this person might display her high level of dominance by showing a readiness for rough-and-tumble play, referring to less dominant peers as sissies, and insisting on monopolizing whatever interesting toys are available. By age 20, however, they manifest dominance in quite different behaviors, perhaps by persuading others to accept their views in political discussions, boldly asking others out on dates, and deciding on the restaurants they will go to on these dates. Consequently, trait levels can stay the same over long time periods, yet the behaviors expressing those traits can change as the person ages.

We will discuss the ways in which personality psychologists have studied the development of dispositions as well as studies of how dispositions can change across the life span.

Tavis Wright/Image Source

Traits and Trait Taxonomies

3

THE DISPOSITIONAL DOMAIN

People readily form impressions of others that can be described using a few traits of personality, such as whether the person is friendly, generous, and poised. Portrait of large group of students cheering at college sporting event.
Hero Images/Hero Images/Corbis

Suppose that you walk into a party with a friend, who introduces you to the host, an acquaintance of theirs. The three of you chat for 10 minutes, and then you mingle with the other guests. Later, as you leave the party with your friend, they ask what you thought of the host. As you mull over the 10-minute interaction, what springs to mind? Perhaps you describe the host as *friendly* (smiled a lot), *generous* (told you to help yourself to the bountiful spread of food), and *poised* (was able to juggle the many demands of guests as they came and went). These words are all examples of *trait-descriptive adjectives*—words that describe *traits, attributes* of a person that are reasonably *characteristic* of the person and perhaps *enduring* over time. Just as you might describe a glass as *brittle* or a car as *reliable* (enduring characteristics of the glass and the car), trait-descriptive adjectives imply consistent and stable characteristics. For much of the past century, psychologists have focused on identifying the basic traits that make up personality and identifying the nature and origins of those traits.

Most personality psychologists hypothesize that traits (also called *dispositions*) are reasonably stable over time and at least somewhat consistent over situations. The host of the party just described, for example, might be friendly, generous, and poised at other parties later on—illustrating stability over time. And they might also show these traits in other situations—perhaps showing friendliness by smiling at people on elevators, generosity by giving homeless people money, and poised by maintaining her composure when called on in class. However, the actual degree to which traits show stability over time and consistency across situations has been the subject of considerable debate and empirical research.

Three fundamental questions guide those who study personality traits: The first question is "How should we *conceptualize* traits?" Every field needs to define its key terms explicitly. In biology, for example, *species* is a key concept, so the concept of species is defined explicitly (i.e., a group of organisms capable of reproducing with each other). In physics, the basic concepts of mass, weight, force, and gravity are defined explicitly. Because traits are central concepts in personality psychology, they, too, must be precisely formulated.

The second question is "How can we identify which traits are the *most important* traits from among the thousands of ways in which individuals differ?" Individuals differ in many ways that are both characteristic and enduring. Some individuals are extremely extraverted, enjoying loud and crowded parties; others are introverted, preferring quiet evenings spent reading. Some like rock music, whereas others like rap music. A crucial goal of personality psychology is to identify the most important ways in which individuals differ.

The third question is "How can we formulate a *comprehensive taxonomy* of traits—a system that includes within it *all* of the major traits of personality?" Once the important traits have been identified, the next step is to formulate an organized scheme—a *taxonomy*—within which to assemble the individual traits. The periodic table of elements, for example, is not merely a random list of all the physical elements that have been discovered. Rather, it is a taxonomy that organizes the elements using a coherent principle—the elements are arranged according to their atomic numbers (which refer to the number of protons in the nucleus of a given atom). Within biology, to use another example, the field would be hopelessly lost if biologists were to merely list all of the thousands of species that exist, without relying on an underlying organizational framework. Thus, the individual species are organized into a taxonomy—all the species of plants, animals, and microbial species are linked systematically through a single tree of descent. Likewise, a central goal of personality psychology is to formulate a comprehensive taxonomy of all important traits. This chapter describes how personality psychologists have addressed these three fundamental questions of trait psychology.

What Is a Trait? Two Basic Formulations

When you describe someone as *impulsive, unreliable,* and *lazy,* what specifically are you referring to? Personality psychologists differ in their formulations of what these traits mean. Some personality psychologists view these traits as *internal* (or hidden) *properties* of persons that *cause* their behavior. Other personality psychologists make no assumptions about causality and simply use these trait terms to *describe* the enduring aspects of a person's behavior.

Traits as Internal Causal Properties

When we say that Dierdre has a *desire* for material things, that Dan has a *need* for stimulation, or that Dominick *wants* power over others, we are referring to something inside of each that causes them to act in particular ways. These traits are presumed to be *internal* in the sense that individuals carry their desires, needs, and wants from one situation to the next (e.g., Alston, 1975). Furthermore, these desires and needs are assumed to be *causal* in the sense that they *explain* the behavior of the individuals who possess them. Dierdre's desire for material things, for example, might cause her to spend a lot of time at the shopping mall, work extra hard to earn more money, and acquire many household possessions. Internal desire *influences* her external behavior, causing her to act in certain ways.

Psychologists who view traits as internal dispositions do not equate traits with the external behavior in question. This distinction is most easily explained using a food example. Harry may have a strong desire for a large hamburger and french fries. However, because he is trying to lose weight, he refrains from expressing his desire in behavior—he looks at the food hungrily but resists the temptation to eat it. Similarly, Dominick may have a desire to take charge in most social situations, even if he does not always express this desire. For example, some situations may have an already identified leader, such as in a class discussion with his psychology professor. Note that this formulation assumes that we can measure Dominick's need for power independently of measuring Dominick's actual behavioral expressions.

These examples are analogous to that of a glass, which has the trait of being brittle. Even if a particular glass never shatters (i.e., expresses its brittleness), it still possesses the trait of being brittle. In sum, psychologists who view traits as internal dispositions believe that traits can lie dormant in the sense that the *capacities* remain present even when particular behaviors are not actually expressed. Traits—in the sense of internal needs, drives, desires, and so on—are assumed to exist, even in the absence of observable behavioral expressions.

The scientific usefulness of viewing traits as causes of behavior lies in ruling out other causes. When we say that Joan goes to lots of parties *because* she is extraverted, we are implicitly ruling out other potential reasons for her behavior (e.g., that she might be going to a lot of parties simply because her boyfriend drags her to them, rather than because she herself is extraverted). The formulation of traits as internal causal properties differs radically from an alternative formulation that considers traits as merely descriptive summaries of actual behavior.

Traits as Purely Descriptive Summaries

Proponents of this alternative formulation define traits simply as *descriptive summaries* of attributes of persons; they make no assumptions about internality or causality (Chapman & Goldberg, 2017; Hampshire, 1953; Saucier & Goldberg, 2001). Consider an example in which we ascribe the trait of *jealousy* to a young man named George. According to the descriptive summary view, this trait merely describes George's *expressed behavior*. For example, George might glare at other men who talk to his girlfriend, insist that she wear his ring, and require her to spend all of her free time with him. The trait of jealousy accurately *summarizes* the general trend in George's behavior, yet no assumptions are made about what causes George's behavior.

Although it is possible that George's jealousy stems from an internal cause, perhaps deeply rooted feelings of insecurity, his jealousy might instead be due to *social situations*. George's expressions of jealousy might be caused by the fact that other men are flirting with his girlfriend and she is responding to them (a situational cause), rather than because George is intrinsically a jealous person. The important point is that those who view traits as descriptive summaries do not prejudge the cause of someone's behavior. They merely use traits to describe, in summary fashion, the trend in a person's behavior. Personality psychologists of this persuasion (e.g., Chapman & Goldberg, 2017; Saucier & Goldberg, 1998; Wiggins, 1979) argue that we must first identify and describe the important individual differences among people, then subsequently develop causal theories to explain them.

The Act Frequency Formulation of Traits—An Illustration of the Descriptive Summary Formulation

A number of psychologists who endorse the descriptive summary formulation of traits have explored the implications of this formulation in a program of research called the "act frequency approach" (Amelang, Herboth, & Oefner, 1991; Angleiter, Buss, & Demtröder, 1990; Buss & Craik, 1983; Chapman & Goldberg, 2017; Church et al., 2007; Jackson et al., 2010; Romero et al., 1994).

The act frequency approach starts with the notion that *traits are categories of acts.* Just as the category "birds" has specific birds as members of the category (e.g., robins, sparrows), trait categories such as "dominance" or "impulsivity" have specific acts as members. The category of dominance, for example, might include specific acts such as the following:

They issued orders that got the group organized.
They managed to control the outcome of the meeting without the others being
      aware of it.
They assigned roles and got the game going.
They decided which programs they would watch on TV.

Dominance is a trait category with these and hundreds of acts as members. A dominant person, according to the act frequency approach, is someone who performs a large number of dominant acts relative to others. For example, if we videotaped Mary and a dozen of her friends over a period of three months and then counted up how many times each person performed dominant acts, Mary would be considered dominant if she performed more dominant acts than her friends. Thus, in the act frequency formulation, a trait such as dominance is a descriptive summary of the general trend in a person's behavior—a trend that consists of performing a large number of acts within a category relative to other persons.

Act Frequency Research Program

The act frequency approach to traits involves three key elements: act nomination, proto-typicality judgment, and the recording of act performance.

Act Nomination

Act nomination is a procedure designed to identify which acts belong in which trait categories. Consider the category of "impulsive." Now think of someone you know who is impulsive. Then list the specific acts or behaviors this person has performed that exemplify his or her impulsivity. You might say, "He decided to go out with friends on the spur of the moment, even though he had to study," "He immediately accepted the dare to do something dangerous, without thinking about the consequences," or "He blurted out his anger before he had time to reflect on the situation." Through act nomination procedures such as this one, researchers can identify dozens or hundreds of acts belonging to various trait categories.

Prototypicality Judgment

The second step involves identifying which acts are most central to, or *prototypical* of, each trait category. Consider the category of "bird." When you think of this category, which

Table 3.1 Self-Report of Creative Acts

Instructions. Following is a list of acts. Read each act and circle the response that most accurately indicates how often you typically perform each act. Circle "0" if you never perform the act; circle "1" if you occasionally perform the act; circle "2" if you perform the act with moderate frequency; and circle "3" if you perform the act very frequently.

Circle	Acts	
0 1 2 3	1.	I came up with a funny nickname for someone.
0 1 2 3	2.	I sat down and drew or painted from my imagination.
0 1 2 3	3.	I took photos just for fun.
0 1 2 3	4.	I carried a sketchpad all day long.
0 1 2 3	5.	I listened to a great variety of musical styles.
0 1 2 3	6.	I wrote a song.
0 1 2 3	7.	I made a card for someone.
0 1 2 3	8.	I kept a journal of thoughts and turned them into poems.
0 1 2 3	9.	I told a joke that made people laugh.
0 1 2 3	10.	I gave self-made drawings as presents for people's birthdays.

Source: Adapted from Ivcevic, 2007. From among the most prototypical everyday and artistic creative acts. Items 1, 3, 5, 7, and 9 are prototypical everyday creative acts. Items 2, 4, 6, 8, and 10 are artistic creative acts. According to the act frequency approach, you would be judged to be "creative" if you performed a high overall frequency of these creative acts, relative to your peer group.

birds come to your mind first? Most people think of birds such as *robins* and *sparrows.* They do not think of *turkeys* and *penguins.* Even though penguins and turkeys are members of the category bird, robins and sparrows are considered to be more prototypical of the category—they are better examples, more central to what most people mean by "bird" (Rosch, 1975).

In a similar way, acts within trait categories differ in their prototypicality of the trait. Panels of raters judge how prototypical each act is as an example of a particular concept. For example, raters find the acts *She controlled the outcome of the meeting without the others being aware of it* and *She took charge after the accident* to be more prototypically dominant than the act *She deliberately arrived late for the meeting.*

Recording Act Performance

The third and final step in the research program consists of securing information on the actual performance of individuals in their daily lives. As you might imagine, obtaining information about a person's daily conduct is difficult. Most researchers have used self-reports of act performance or reports from close friends or spouses. As shown in Table 3.1, you can provide your own responses to this measure of everyday and artistic creative acts. Similar measures have been developed for conscientious acts (Jackson et al., 2010) and extraverted acts (Rauthmann & Denissen, 2011). In the same way, observational measures of dominant acts have been developed in the context of face-to-face groups (Anderson & Kilduff, 2009). Interestingly, traditional trait measures do a moderately good job of predicting manifest behavior in everyday life (Fleeson & Gallagher, 2009). The act frequency approach has also been applied to thought frequencies. Frequency of suicidal ideation, for example, is a good predictor of depressive symptoms (Chang & Chang, 2016).

Evaluation of the Act Frequency Formulation

The formulation of traits as purely descriptive summaries, as in the act frequency approach, has been criticized on several grounds (see Angleitner & Demtroder, 1988; Block, 1989). Most of the criticisms have been aimed at the technical implementation of the approach. For example, the act frequency approach does not specify how much context should be included in the description of a trait-relevant act. Consider the following dominant act: *He insisted that the others go to his favorite restaurant.* To understand this act as a dominant act, we might need to know (1) the relationships among the people involved, (2) the occasion for going out to eat, (3) the history of restaurant going for these people, and (4) who is paying for the dinner. How much context is needed to identify the act as a dominant act?

Another criticism of the approach is that it seems applicable to overt actions, but what about *failures* to act and covert acts that are not directly observable? For example, a person may be very courageous, but we will never know this under ordinary life circumstances in which people have no need to display courageousness.

Despite these limitations, the act frequency approach has produced some noteworthy accomplishments. It has been especially helpful in making explicit the *behavioral phenomena* to which most trait terms refer—after all, the primary way that we know about traits is through their expressions in actual behavior. As noted by several prominent personality researchers, "Behavioral acts constitute the building blocks of interpersonal perception and the basis for inferences about personality traits" (Gosling et al., 1998). Thus, the study of behavioral manifestations of personality remains an essential and indispensable part of the agenda for the field, despite the difficulties entailed by their study (Furr, 2009). The act frequency approach is also helpful in identifying behavioral regularities—phenomena that must be explained by any comprehensive personality theory (Furr, 2009). And it has been helpful in exploring the *meaning* of some traits that have proven difficult to study, such as impulsivity (Romero et al., 1994), conscientiousness (Jackson et al., 2010), and creativity (Amelang et al., 1991). It has also proven useful in identifying cultural similarities and differences in the behavioral manifestation of traits (Church et al., 2007). Initiating a conversation with a shy person, for example, is a greater reflection of extraversion in the Philippines than in the United States, whereas smiling at a stranger is a greater reflection of extraversion in the United States than in the Philippines.

Explorations of the act frequency approach have helped to identify the domains in which it provides insight into personality. One study, for example, examined the relationship between self-reported act performance and observer codings of the individual's actual behavior (Gosling et al., 1998). Some acts showed high levels of self-observer agreement, such as "Told a joke to lighten a tense moment," "Made a humorous remark," and "Took charge of things at the meeting." Acts that reflect the traits of extraversion and conscientiousness tend to show high levels of self–observer agreement. Acts that reflect the trait of agreeableness, on the other hand, tend to show lower levels of self-observer agreement. The more observable the actions, the higher the agreement between self-report and observer codings.

Other research has demonstrated that the act frequency approach can be used to predict important outcomes in everyday life such as job success, salary, and how rapidly individuals are promoted within business organizations (Kyl-Heku & Buss, 1996; Lund et al., 2006). Others have used the act frequency approach to explore topics such as *acts of deception* in social interaction (Tooke & Camire, 1991) and acts of *"mate guarding"* that predict violence in dating and marital relationships (Shackelford et al., 2005).

In sum, there are two major formulations of traits. The first considers traits to be internal causal properties of persons that affect overt behavior. The second considers traits to be descriptive summaries of overt behavior, with the causes of those trends in conduct to be determined subsequently. However, traits are formulated, all personality psychologists must confront the next vexing challenge—identifying the most important traits.

Identification of the Most Important Traits

Three fundamental approaches have been used to identify important traits. The first is the **lexical approach.** According to this approach, all traits listed and defined in the dictionary form the basis of describing differences among people (Allport & Odbert, 1936). The logical starting point for the lexical strategy is the natural language. The second method of identifying important traits is the **statistical approach.** This approach uses factor analysis, or similar statistical procedures, to identify major personality traits. The third method is the **theoretical approach** in which researchers rely on theories to identify important traits.

Lexical Approach

The lexical approach to identifying important personality traits starts with the **lexical hypothesis:** *All important individual differences have become encoded within the natural language.* Over time, differences among people that are important are noticed, and words are invented to talk about those differences. People invent words such as *dominant, creative, reliable, cooperative, hot-tempered,* or *self-centered* to describe these differences. People find these trait terms helpful in describing people and for communicating information about them. And so, usage of these trait terms spreads and becomes common within the group. Trait terms not useful to people in describing and communicating with others fail to become encoded within the natural language.

If we consider the English language, we find an abundance of trait terms codified as adjectives, such as *manipulative, arrogant, slothful,* and *warm.* A perusal of the dictionary yields about 18,000 trait-descriptive adjectives (Norman, 1967). The key implication of this finding, according to the lexical approach, is clear: trait terms are extraordinarily important for people in communicating with others.

The lexical approach yields two criteria for identifying important traits—**synonym frequency** and **cross-cultural universality.** The criterion of synonym frequency means that if an attribute has not merely one or two trait adjectives to describe it but rather many words, then it is a more important dimension of individual difference. "The more important is such an attribute, the more synonyms and subtly distinctive facets of the attribute will be found within any one language" (Saucier & Goldberg, 1996, p. 24). Consider individual differences in "dominance." There are many terms to describe it: *dominant, bossy, assertive, powerful, pushy, forceful, leaderlike, domineering, influential, ascendant, authoritative,* and *arrogant.* The prevalence of many synonyms, each term conveying a subtle difference in dominance, suggests that dominance is an important trait and that different shades of dominance are important in social communication. In short, synonym frequency provides one criterion of importance (see Wood, 2015, for a contrary position).

Cross-cultural universality is the second key criterion of importance within the lexical approach: "The more important is an individual difference in human transactions, the more languages will have a term for it" (Goldberg, 1981, p. 142). The logic is that if a trait is sufficiently important in all cultures that its members have codified terms to describe the trait, then the trait must be universally important in human affairs. In contrast, if a trait term exists in only one or a few languages, then it may be of only local or limited relevance. Such a term is unlikely to be a candidate for a universal taxonomy of personality traits (McCrae & Costa, 1997).

The Yanomamö Indians of Venezuela, for example, have the words *unokai* and *"non-unokai,"* which mean, roughly, "a man who has achieved manhood by the killing of another man" (*unokai*) and "a man who has not achieved manhood status by the killing of another man" (*non-unokai*) (Chagnon, 1983). In Yanomamö culture, this individual difference is of critical importance. The unokai have elevated status, are widely feared, have more wives, and assume leadership. In mainstream American culture, by contrast, there is the generic *killer,* but there is no single word that has the specific connotations of *unokai.* Thus, although this individual difference is important to the Yanomamö, it is unlikely to be part of a universal taxonomy of personality traits.

One problem with the lexical strategy concerns the fact that personality is conveyed through different parts of speech, including adjectives, nouns, and adverbs. For example, there are dozens of noun terms encoded within the English language to describe someone who is not too smart: *birdbrain, blockhead, bonehead, chucklehead, cretin, deadhead, dimwit, dolt, dope, dullard, dumbbell, dummy, dunce, jughead, lunkhead, moron, peabrain, pinhead, softhead, thickhead,* and *woodenhead.* One study found as many as eight factors from an analysis of personality nouns, including Dummy (twit, trash), Doll (beauty, sweetie), Philosopher (bookworm, nonconformist), Goof (joker, clown), Chatterbox (flirt, loudmouth), and Ladies' man (stud, hunk) (Saucier, 2003). Personality nouns remain a viable source of potential information about important dimensions of individual differences.

The lexical strategy has proven to be a remarkably generative starting point for identifying important individual differences (Ashton & Lee, 2005). To discard this information "would require us needlessly to separate ourselves from the vast sources of knowledge gained in the course of human history" (Kelley, 1992, p. 22). Two other commonly used approaches are the statistical and theoretical strategies.

Statistical Approach

The statistical approach to identifying important traits starts with a pool of personality items. These can be trait words or questions about behavior, experience, or emotion. Most researchers using the lexical approach turn to the statistical approach to group trait adjectives into basic categories of personality traits. However, the starting point can also be self-ratings on a large collection of personality-relevant sentences (e.g., *I find that I am easily able to persuade people to my point of view*). Once a large and diverse pool of items is assembled, the statistical approach is applied. It consists of having people rate themselves (or others) on the items, then using a statistical procedure to identify groups or clusters of items. The goal of the statistical approach is to identify the major dimensions, or "coordinates," of the personality map, much the way latitude and longitude provide the coordinates of the map of Earth.

The most commonly used statistical procedure is **factor analysis.** Although the complex mathematical procedures underlying factor analysis are beyond the scope of this text, the essential logic is simple. Factor analysis identifies groups of items that *covary* (i.e., go together) but tend not to covary with other groups of items. Consider, as a spatial metaphor, the office locations of physicists, psychologists, and sociologists on your campus. Although these may be spread out, in general the offices of the psychologists tend to be closer to one another than they are to the offices of the physicists or sociologists. The physicists are closer to one another than they are to the sociologists or psychologists. A factor analysis reveals three clusters of professors.

Table 3.2 A Sample Factor Analysis of Personality Adjective Ratings

Adjective Rating	Factor 1 (Extraversion)	Factor 2 (Ambition)	Factor 3 (Creativity)
Humorous	**.66**	.06	.19
Amusing	**.65**	.23	.02
Popular	**.57**	.13	.22
Hard-working	.05	**.63**	.01
Productive	.04	**.52**	.19
Determined	.23	**.52**	.08
Imaginative	.01	.09	**.62**
Original	.13	.05	**.53**
Inventive	.06	.26	**.47**

Note: The numbers refer to factor loadings, which indicate the degree to which an item correlates with the underlying factor (see text).
Source: Adapted from Matthews & Oddy, 1993.

Similarly, a major advantage of identifying clusters of personality items that covary is that it provides a means for determining which personality variables have some common property. Factor analysis can also be useful in reducing the large array of diverse personality traits into a smaller and more useful set of underlying factors. It provides a means for organizing the thousands of personality traits.

Let's examine how factor analysis works in an example shown in Table 3.2. This table summarizes the data obtained from a sample of 1,210 subjects who rated themselves on a series of trait-descriptive adjectives. Among the adjectives rated were *humorous, amusing, popular, hard-working, productive, determined, imaginative, original,* and *inventive.*

The numbers in Table 3.2 are called **factor loadings,** indexes of how much of the variation in an item is "explained" by the factor. Factor loadings indicate the degree to which the item correlates with, or "loads on," the underlying factor. In this example, three clear factors emerge. The first is an "extraversion" factor, with high loadings on *humorous, amusing,* and *popular.* The second is an "ambition" factor: *hard-working, productive,* and *determined.* The third is a "creativity" factor, with high loadings on *imaginative, inventive,* and *original.* Factor analysis is quite useful in identifying three distinct groups of trait terms that covary with each other but are relatively independent of (tend not to covary with) other groups. Without this statistical procedure, a researcher might be forced to consider the nine traits as all separate from each other. Factor analysis tells us that *hard-working, productive,* and *determined* all covary sufficiently that they can be considered a single trait, rather than three separate traits.

Here is a cautionary note about using the statistical approach for identifying important traits: you get out of it only what you put into it. If an important personality trait happens to be left out of a factor analysis, it will not show up in the subsequent results. Thus, it is critical that researchers pay close attention to their initial selection of items.

Factor analysis and similar statistical procedures have been extremely valuable to personality researchers. Perhaps their most important contribution has been the ability to reduce a large, cumbersome array of diverse personality items into a smaller, more meaningful set of broad, basic factors.

Theoretical Approach

The theoretical approach to identifying important dimensions of individual differences starts with a theory that determines which variables are important. In contrast to the statistical strategy, which can be described as atheoretical in the sense that there is no prejudgment about which variables are important, the theoretical strategy dictates which variables are important to measure.

To a Freudian, for example, it is critical to measure "the oral personality" and "the anal personality" because these represent important, theory-driven constructs. Or, to a self-actualization theorist such as Maslow (1968), it is critical to measure individual differences in the degree to which people are motivated to self-actualize (see Williams & Page, 1989, for one such measure). The theory, in short, strictly determines which variables are important.

As an example of the theoretical strategy, consider the theory of **sociosexual orientation** (Simpson & Gangestad, 1991; Penke & Asendorph, 2008a). According to the theory, men and women will pursue one of two alternative sexual relationship strategies. The first entails seeking a single committed relationship characterized by monogamy and tremendous investment in children. The second sexual strategy is characterized by a greater degree of promiscuity, more partner switching, and less investment in children. (When applied to men, one easy way to remember these two strategies is to label them as "dads" and "cads.") Because the theory of sociosexual orientation dictates that the mating strategy one pursues is a critical individual difference, Gangestad and Simpson have developed a measure of sociosexual orientation (see the following Exercise).

Exercise

Please use the following rating scales to record your answers.
To what degree are you currently seeking short-term mates (i.e., casual sex partners):

| Very little | 1 | 2 | 3 | 4 | 5 | 6 | 7 | A lot |

To what degree are you currently seeking, or are currently in, a committed romantic relationship:

| Very little | 1 | 2 | 3 | 4 | 5 | 6 | 7 | A lot |

Source: Buss, D.M. (2022). Unpublished research.

Evaluating the Approaches for Identifying Important Traits

In sum, the theoretical approach lets the theory determine which dimensions of individual differences are important. Like all approaches, the theoretical approach has strengths and limitations. Its strengths coincide with the strengths of the theory. If we have a powerful theory that tells us which variables are important, then it saves us from wandering aimlessly like a sailor without a map or compass. A theory charts the course to take. At the same time, its weaknesses coincide with the weaknesses of the theory. To the extent that the theory contains gaps or biases, the subsequent identification of important individual differences will reflect omissions and distortions.

The current state of the field of personality trait psychology is best characterized as "letting a thousand flowers bloom." Some researchers start with a theory and let their measurement of individual differences follow from that theory. Others believe that factor analysis is the only sensible way to identify important individual differences. Still other researchers believe that the lexical strategy, by capitalizing on the collective wisdom of people over the ages, is the best method of ensuring that important individual differences are captured.

In practice, many personality researchers use a combination of the three strategies. Norman (1963), Goldberg (1990), and Saucier (2009), for example, started with the lexical strategy to identify their first set of variables for inclusion. They then applied factor analysis to this initial selection of traits to reduce the set to a smaller, more manageable number (five or six). This solved two problems that are central to the science of personality (Saucier & Goldberg, 1996): the problem of identifying the domains of individual differences and the problem of figuring out a method for describing structure that exists among the individual differences identified. The lexical strategy can be used to sample trait terms, and then factor analysis supplies a powerful statistical approach to providing structure and order to those trait terms.

Taxonomies of Personality

Over the past century, dozens of taxonomies of personality traits have been proposed. Many have been merely lists of traits, often based on the intuitions of personality psychologists. As personality psychologist Robert Hogan observed, "The history of personality theory consists of people who assert that their private demons are public afflictions" (Hogan, 1983). Indeed, two editors of a book on personality traits (London & Exner, 1978) expressed despair at the lack of agreement about a taxonomy of traits, so they simply listed the traits alphabetically. Clearly, we can develop a firmer basis for organizing personality traits. The taxonomies of traits presented in the rest of this chapter are not random samplings from the dozens available. Rather, they represent taxonomies that have solid empirical and theoretical justification.

Hans Eysenck at his London office.
Courtesy of Randy J. Larsen

Eysenck's Hierarchical Model of Personality

Of all the taxonomies of personality, the model of Hans Eysenck, born in 1916, is most strongly rooted in biology. Eysenck was raised in Germany at the time when Hitler was rising to power. Eysenck showed an intense dislike for the Nazi regime, so at age 18 he migrated to England. Although intending to study physics, Eysenck lacked the needed prerequisites, so almost by chance he began to study psychology at the University of London. He received his PhD in 1940 and after World War II became director of the psychology department at the Maudsley Hospital's new Institute of Psychiatry in London. Eysenck's subsequent productivity was enormous, with more than 40 books and 700 articles. Eysenck was the most cited living psychologist until he died in 1998.

Eysenck developed a model of personality based on traits that he believed were highly heritable (see Chapter 6) and had a likely psychophysiological foundation. The three main traits that met these criteria, according to Eysenck, were *extraversion-introversion* (E), *neuroticism-emotional stability* (N), and *psychoticism* (P). Together, they can be easily remembered by the acronym PEN.

Description

Let us begin by describing these three broad traits. Eysenck conceptualizes each of them as sitting at the top of its own hierarchy, as shown in Figure 3.1. *Extraversion,* for example, subsumes a large number of narrow traits—sociable, active, lively, venturesome, dominant, and so forth. These narrow traits are all subsumed by the broader trait of extraversion because they all covary sufficiently to load on the same large factor. Extraverts typically like parties, have many friends, and like having people around them to talk to (Eysenck & Eysenck, 1975). Many extraverts love playing practical jokes on people. They display a carefree and easy manner. They also tend to have a high activity level.

Introverts, in contrast, like to spend more time alone. They prefer quiet time and pursuits such as reading. Introverts are sometimes seen as aloof and distant, but they often have a small number of intimate friends. Introverts tend to be more serious than extraverts and to prefer a more moderate pace. They tend to be well organized, and they prefer a routine, predictable lifestyle (Larsen & Kasimatis, 1990). For a superb book on the nature and strengths of introverts, see Cain (2013). *Quiet: The power of introverts in a world that can't stop talking.* Broadway Books.

The trait of *neuroticism* (N) consists of a cluster of more specific traits, including anxious, irritable, guilty, lacking self-esteem, tense, shy, and moody. Conceptually, narrow traits such as anxious and irritable might be viewed as very different from each other. Empirically, however, men and women who feel anxious also tend to get easily irritated. Thus, factor analysis has proven to be a valuable tool in showing that these two narrow traits are actually linked together, tending to co-occur in people.

The typical high scorer on neuroticism (N) tends to be a worrier. Frequently anxious and depressed, the high-N scorer has trouble sleeping and experiences a wide array of psychosomatic symptoms. A study of 5,847 individuals found that those high on neuroticism tend to be especially prone to the disorders of depression and anxiety (Weinstock & Whisman, 2006). One of the hallmarks of the high-N scorer is overreactivity on the negative emotions. The high-N scorer experiences more arousal than the low-N scorer in response to the normal stresses of everyday life. They have more trouble returning to an even keel after an emotionally arousing event. Those high on neuroticism also stay angry longer after a perceived transgression and are less likely to forgive someone who they perceived has violated them (Maltby et al., 2008). They are more likely to be vigilant to threats, particularly social threats such as being socially excluded (Denissen & Penke, 2008b; Tamir, Robinson, & Solberg, 2006). High-N scorers tend to express more dissatisfaction with their romantic relationships (Kruezer & Gollwitzer, 2021). The low-N scorer is emotionally stable, even-tempered, calm, slower to react to stressful events, returns to his or her normal self quickly after an upsetting event, and expresses more satisfaction with their romantic relationships.

The third large trait in Eysenck's taxonomy is *psychoticism* (P). As shown in Figure 3.1, P consists of the constellation of narrower traits that includes aggressive, egocentric, creative, impulsive, lacking empathy, and antisocial. Factor analysis proves valuable in grouping together narrower traits. Factor analyses show, for example, that impulsivity and lack of empathy tend to co-occur in individuals. That is, people who tend to act without thinking (impulsivity) also tend to lack the ability to see situations from other people's perspectives (lack of empathy).

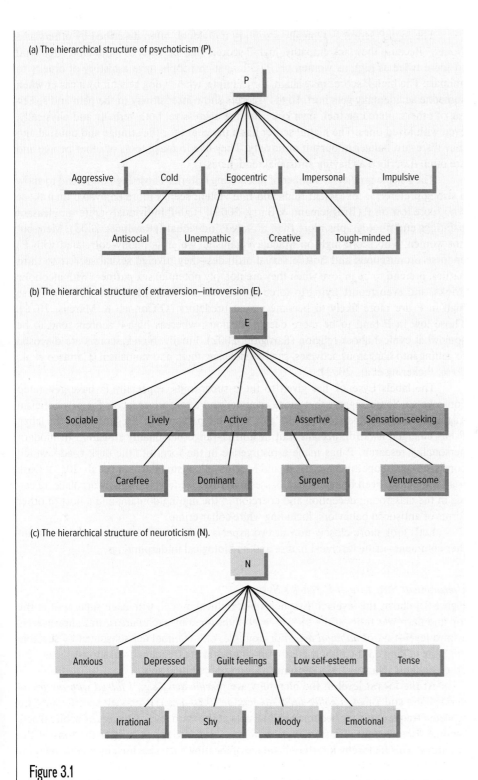

(a) The hierarchical structure of psychoticism (P).

(b) The hierarchical structure of extraversion–introversion (E).

(c) The hierarchical structure of neuroticism (N).

Figure 3.1

Eysenck's hierarchical structure of major personality traits. Each "super-trait" (P, E, and N) occupies the
highest level in the hierarchy, representing broad personality traits. Each of these broad traits subsumes
more narrower traits in the hierarchy. (a) The hierarchical structure of psychoticism (P); (b) the hierarchical
structure of extraversion–introversion (E); (c) the hierarchical structure of neuroticism–emotional stability (N).

The high-P scorer is typically a solitary individual, often described by others as a "loner." Because they lack empathy, high-P scorers may be cruel or inhumane. Men tend to score twice as high as women on P. Often, such people have a history of cruelty to animals. The high-P scorer may laugh, for example, when a dog gets hit by a car or when someone accidentally gets hurt. High-P scorers show insensitivity to the pain and suffering of others, including their own kin. They are aggressive, both verbally and physically, even with loved ones. The high-P scorer has a penchant for the strange and unusual and may disregard danger in pursuit of novelty. They like to make fools of other people and are often described as having antisocial tendencies.

The P-scale predicts a number of fascinating criteria. Those high on P tend to show a strong preference for violent films and rate violent scenes more enjoyable than those who score low on P (Bruggemann & Barry, 2002). High-P individuals prefer unpleasant paintings and photographs more than do low-P individuals (Rawlings, 2003). Men, but not women, who score high on Machiavellianism (which is highly correlated with P) endorse promiscuous and hostile sexual attitudes—they divulge sexual secrets to third parties, pretend to be in love when they are not, ply potential sex partners with alcoholic drinks, and even report trying to force others into sex acts (McHoskey, 2001). Those high in P are more likely to become sexual predators (O'Connell & Marcus, 2016). Those low in P tend to be more deeply religious, whereas high-P scorers tend to be somewhat cynical about religion (Saroglou, 2002). Finally, high-P scorers are disposed to getting into dangerous activities, such as violence, theft, and vandalism (Carrasco et al., 2006; Pickering et al., 2003).

The labels Eysenck has given to these super-traits, especially P, have generated controversy. Some suggest that more accurate and appropriate labels for psychoticism might be "antisocial personality" or "psychopathic personality." Regardless of the label, P has emerged as an important trait in normal-range personality research. In modern personality research, P has made a resurgence in the form of "the dark triad," which consists of psychopathy, narcissism, and Machiavellianism (Furnham et al., 2013). Dark triad traits have been linked to bad bosses and toxic leadership in the workplace; cheating in the classroom; deception and coercion in the mating domain; and a host of other forms of antisocial behaviors, including white-collar crime.

Let's look more closely now at two aspects of Eysenck's system that warrant further comment—its hierarchical nature and its biological underpinnings.

Hierarchical Structure of Eysenck's System

Figure 3.1 shows the levels in Eysenck's hierarchical model, with each super-trait at the top and narrower traits at the second level. Subsumed by each narrow trait, however, is a third level—that of *habitual acts*. For example, one habitual act subsumed by sociable might be talking on the phone; another might be taking frequent breaks to socialize with other students. Narrow traits subsume a variety of habitual acts.

At the lowest level in the hierarchy are *specific acts* (e.g., *I talked with my friend during class* and *I took a coffee break to chat at 10:30 a.m.*). If enough specific acts are repeated frequently, they become habitual acts at the third level. Clusters of habitual acts become narrow traits. Clusters of narrow traits become super-traits at the tops of the hierarchy. This hierarchy has the advantage of locating each specific personality-relevant act within a precise nested system. Thus, the fourth-level act *I danced wildly at the party* can be described as extraverted at the highest level, sociable at the second level, and part of a regular habit of party-going behavior at the third level.

Biological Underpinnings

There are two aspects of the biological underpinnings of Eysenck's personality system: *heritability* and *identifiable physiological substrate.* For Eysenck, a key criterion for a "basic" dimension of personality is that it has reasonably high heritability. The behavioral genetic evidence confirms that all three super-traits in Eysenck's taxonomy—P, E, and N—do have moderate heritabilities, although this is also true of many personality traits (see Chapter 6).

The second biological criterion is that basic personality traits should have an identifiable physiological substrate—properties in the brain and central nervous system that are presumed to be part of the causal chain that produces personality traits. In Eysenck's formulation, extraversion is supposed to be linked with central nervous system arousal or reactivity. Eysenck predicted that introverts would be more easily aroused (and be more autonomically reactive) than extraverts (see Chapter 7). In contrast, he proposed that neuroticism was linked with the degree of *lability* (changeability) of the autonomic nervous system. Finally, high-P scorers were predicted to be high in testosterone levels and low in levels of MAO, a neurotransmitter inhibitor.

In sum, Eysenck's personality taxonomy has many distinct features. It is hierarchical, starting with broad traits, which subsume narrower traits, which subsume specific actions. The broad traits show moderately heritability. And Eysenck has attempted to link these traits with physiological functioning—adding an important level of analysis not included in most personality taxonomies.

Despite these admirable qualities, Eysenck's personality taxonomy has several limitations. One is that many other personality traits also show moderate heritability, not just extraversion, neuroticism, and psychoticism. A second limitation is that Eysenck may have missed some important traits in his taxonomy—a point argued by other personality psychologists, such as Raymond B. Cattell, and more recently by authors such as Lewis Goldberg, Paul Costa, and Robert McCrae. Nonetheless, Eysenck's taxonomy continues to be used in modern personality testing that includes the development of new assessment questionnaires that are superior to previous ones (Ruch et al., 2021).

Circumplex Taxonomies of Personality

People have been fascinated with circles for centuries. They have no beginning and no end, and they symbolize wholeness and unity. Circles have also fascinated personality psychologists as representations of the personality sphere.

In the twentieth century, the two most prominent advocates of circular representations of personality were Timothy Leary (also known for his LSD experiments at Harvard) and Jerry Wiggins, who formalized the circular model with modern statistical techniques. (Circumplex is simply a fancy name for circle.)

Wiggins (1979) started with the lexical assumption—the idea that all important individual differences are encoded within the natural language. But he went further in his efforts at taxonomy by arguing that trait terms specify different *kinds* of ways in which individuals differ. One kind of individual difference pertains to what people do to and with each other—**interpersonal traits.**

Other kinds of individual differences are specified by the following types of traits: *temperament* traits, such as nervous, gloomy, sluggish, and excitable; *character* traits, such as moral, principled, and dishonest; *material* traits, such as miserly and stingy; *attitude* traits, such as pious and spiritual; *mental* traits, such as clever, logical, and perceptive; and *physical* traits, such as healthy and tough.

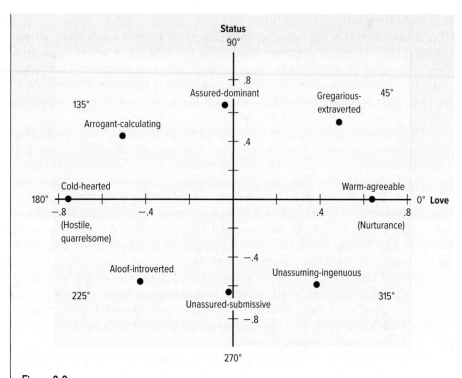

Figure 3.2

The circumplex model of personality.

Source: Adapted from "Circular Reasoning About Interpersonal Behavior," by J. S. Wiggins, N. Phillips, and P. Trapnell, 1989, *Journal of Personality & Social Psychology,* 56, p. 297. Copyright 1989 by the American Psychological Association. Reprinted with permission.

Because Wiggins was concerned primarily with *interpersonal* traits, he carefully separated these from the other categories of traits. Then, based on the earlier theorizing of Foa and Foa (1974), he defined *interpersonal* as interactions among people involving exchanges. The two resources that define social exchange are *love* and *status:* "interpersonal events may be defined as *dyadic interactions that have relatively clear-cut social (status) and emotional (love) consequences for both participants*" (Wiggins, 1979, p. 398, italics original). Hence, the dimensions of status and love define the two major axes of the Wiggins circumplex, as shown in Figure 3.2.

There are three clear advantages to the Wiggins circumplex. First, it provides an *explicit definition* of interpersonal behavior. It should be possible to locate any transaction in which the resources of status or love are exchanged within a specific area of the circumplex pie. These include not just giving love (e.g., giving a friend a hug) or granting status (e.g., showing respect or honor to a parent). They also include denying love (e.g., yelling at a boyfriend) and denying status (e.g., dismissing someone as too inconsequential to talk to). The Wiggins circumplex model has the advantage of providing an explicit and precise definition of interpersonal transactions.

The second advantage is that the circumplex *specifies the relationships between each trait and every other trait within the model.* There are basically three types of relationships specified by the model. The first is **adjacency,** or how close the traits are to each other in the circumplex. The variables that are adjacent, or next, to each other within the model are positively correlated. Thus, gregarious-extraverted is correlated with warm-agreeable. Arrogant-calculating is correlated with hostile-quarrelsome.

The second type of relationship is **bipolarity.** Traits that are bipolar are located at opposite sides of the circle and are negatively correlated with each other. Dominant is the opposite of submissive, so the two are negatively correlated. Cold is the opposite of warm, so they are negatively correlated. Specifying this bipolarity is useful because nearly every interpersonal trait has another trait that is its opposite.

The third type of relationship is **orthogonality,** which specifies that traits that are perpendicular to each other on the model (at 90° of separation, or at right angles to each other) are entirely unrelated to each other. In other words, there is a zero correlation between such traits. Dominance, for example, is orthogonal to agreeableness, so the two are uncorrelated. This means that dominance can be expressed in a quarrelsome manner (e.g., *I yelled in order to get my way*) or in an agreeable manner (e.g., *I organized the group in order to get help for my friend*). Similarly, aggression (quarrelsome) can be expressed in an active/dominant manner (e.g., *I used my position of authority to punish my enemies*) or in an unassured/submissive way (e.g., *I gave him the silent treatment when I was upset*). Orthogonality allows one to specify with greater precision the different ways in which traits are expressed in actual behavior.

The third key advantage of the circumplex model is that it *alerts investigators to gaps* in investigations of interpersonal behavior. For example, whereas there have been many studies of dominance and aggression, personality psychologists have paid little attention to traits such as unassuming and calculating. The circumplex model, by providing a map of the interpersonal terrain, directs researchers to these neglected areas of psychological functioning.

In sum, the Wiggins circumplex model provides an elegant map of major individual differences in the social domain. The circumplex structure of interpersonal traits has been discovered in children as well as adults (Di Blas, 2007). It has been used to discover interpersonal sensitivities (Hopwood et al., 2011). For example, people tend to find others unpleasant who have personalities that are the polar opposite of their own. And it has been used to identify some maladaptive aspects of interpersonal functioning: Those who are submissive and agreeable, for example, may be overly accommodating (e.g., allowing themselves to be shortchanged at the store without saying anything) or passively aggressive (e.g., giving others the "silent treatment") (Hennig & Walker, 2008). Despite these positive qualities, the circumplex also has some limitations. The most important limitation is that the interpersonal map is limited to two dimensions. Other traits, not captured by these two dimensions, also have important interpersonal consequences. The trait of conscientiousness, for example, is interpersonal in that persons high on this trait are very dependable in their social obligations to friends, mates, and children. Even a trait such as neuroticism or emotional stability may show up most strongly in interpersonal transactions with others (e.g., *He overreacted to a subtle interpersonal slight when the host took too long to acknowledge his presence* and *He insisted that he and his partner leave the party*). A more comprehensive taxonomy of personality that includes these dimensions is known as the five-factor model.

Five-Factor Model

In the past few decades, the taxonomy of personality traits that has received the most attention and support from personality researchers has been the **five-factor model**—variously labeled the five-factor model, the Big Five, and even in a humorous vein The

High Five (Costa & McCrae, 1995; Goldberg, 1981; McCrae & John, 1992; Saucier & Goldberg, 1996). The broad traits composing the Big Five have been provisionally named (I) *surgency* or *extraversion,* (II) *agreeableness,* (III) *conscientiousness,* (IV) *emotional stability,* and (V) *openness-intellect.* This five-dimensional taxonomy of personality traits has accrued some persuasive advocates (e.g., John, 1990; McCrae & John, 1992; Rammstetd, Goldberg, & Borg, 2010; Saucier & Goldberg, 1998; Wiggins, 1996), as well as some strong critics (e.g., Block, 1995; McAdams, 1992).

The five-factor model was originally based on a combination of the lexical approach and statistical approaches. The lexical approach started in the 1930s, with the pioneering work of Allport and Odbert (1936), who laboriously combed the English dictionary and identified 17,953 trait terms. Allport and Odbert then divided the trait terms into four lists: (1) *stable traits* (e.g., secure, intelligent); (2) *temporary states, moods, and activities* (e.g., agitated, excited); (3) *social evaluations* (e.g., charming, irritating); and (4) *metaphorical, physical, and doubtful terms* (e.g., prolific, lean).

The terms from the first category, 4,500 presumably stable traits, were subsequently used by Cattell (1943) as a starting point for his lexical analysis of personality traits. Because of the limited power of computers at the time, however, Cattell could not subject this list to a factor analysis. Instead, he reduced the list to a smaller set of 171 clusters (groups of traits) by eliminating some and lumping together others. He ended up with a smaller set of 35 clusters of personality traits.

Fiske (1949) then took a subset of 22 of Cattell's 35 clusters and discovered, through factor analysis, a five-factor solution. However, this single study of relatively small sample size was hardly a robust foundation for a comprehensive taxonomy of personality traits. In historical treatments of the five-factor model, therefore, Fiske is noted as the first person to discover a version of the five-factor model, but he is not credited with having identified its precise structure.

Tupes and Christal (1961) made the next major contribution to the five-factor taxonomy. They examined the factor structure of the 22 simplified descriptions in eight samples and emerged with the five-factor model: *surgency, agreeableness, conscientiousness, emotional stability,* and *culture.* This factor structure was subsequently replicated by Norman (1963), then by a host of other researchers (e.g., Botwin & Buss, 1989; Digman & Inouye, 1986; Goldberg, 1981; Costa & McCrae, 1985; Rammstetd et al., 2010). The key markers that define the Big Five, as determined by Norman (1963), are shown in Table 3.3.

The past 30 years have witnessed an explosion of research on the Big Five. Indeed, the Big Five taxonomy has achieved a greater degree of consensus than any other trait taxonomy in the history of personality trait psychology. But it has also generated some controversy. We consider three key issues: (1) What is the empirical evidence for the five-factor taxonomy of personality? (2) What is the identity of the fifth factor? (3) Is the Big Five taxonomy really comprehensive, or are there major trait dimensions that lie beyond the Big Five?

What Is the Empirical Evidence for the Five-Factor Model?

The five-factor model has proven to be astonishingly replicable in studies using English-language trait words as items (Goldberg, 1981, 1990; McCrae & Costa, 2008). The five factors have been found by dozens of researchers using different samples. This model has been replicated in every decade for the past half-century. It has been replicated in different languages and in different item formats (Rammstetd et al., 2010). These replications include many countries, such as Belgium, Brazil, China, France, Germany, India, Indonesia, Italy,

Table 3.3 Norman's Markers for the Big Five

I. Extraversion or Surgency
Talkative–silent
Sociable–reclusive
Adventurous–cautious
Open–secretive

II. Agreeableness
Good-natured–irritable
Cooperative–negativistic
Mild/gentle–headstrong
Not jealous–jealous

III. Conscientiousness
Responsible–undependable
Scrupulous–unscrupulous
Persevering–quitting
Fussy/tidy–careless

IV. Emotional stability
Calm–anxious
Composed–excitable
Not hypochondriacal–hypochondriacal
Poised–nervous/tense

V. Culture—Intellect, Openness
Intellectual–unreflective/narrow
Artistic–non-artistic
Imaginative–simple/direct
Polished/refined–crude/boorish

Source: Norman, 1963.

Japan, Korea, Mexico, Nigeria, the Philippines, Russia, Thailand, Turkey, the United Kingdom, the United States, and Vietnam (Minkov, van de Vijver, & Schachnerf, 2019).

In its modern form, the Big Five taxonomy has been measured in two major ways. One way is based on self-ratings of single-word trait adjectives, such as *talkative, warm, organized, moody,* and *imaginative* (Goldberg, 1990), and one way is based on self-ratings of sentence items, such as "*My life is fast-paced*" (McCrae & Costa, 1999). We will discuss these in turn.

Lewis R. Goldberg has done the most systematic research on the Big Five using single-word trait adjectives. According to Goldberg (1990), key adjective markers of the Big Five are as follows:

1. Surgency or extraversion: *talkative, extraverted, assertive, forward, outspoken* versus *shy, quiet, introverted, bashful, inhibited.*
2. Agreeableness: *sympathetic, kind, warm, understanding, sincere* versus *unsympathetic, unkind, harsh, cruel.*
3. Conscientiousness: *organized, neat, orderly, practical, prompt, meticulous* versus *disorganized, disorderly, careless, sloppy, impractical.*
4. Emotional stability: *calm, relaxed, stable* versus *moody, anxious, insecure.*
5. Intellect or imagination: *creative, imaginative, intellectual* versus *uncreative, unimaginative, unintellectual.*

In addition to measures that use single-trait words as items, the most widely used measure using a sentence-length item format has been developed by Paul T. Costa and Robert R. McCrae. It's called the NEO-PI-3: the neuroticism-extraversion-openness (NEO) Personality Inventory (PI) Revised (R) (McCrae, Costa, & Martin, 2005). Sample items from the NEO-PI-3 are neuroticism (N): *I have frequent mood swings;* extraversion (E): *I don't find it easy to take charge of a situation* (reverse scored); openness (O): *I enjoy trying new and foreign foods;* agreeableness (A): *Most people I know like me;* and conscientiousness (C): *I keep my belongings neat and clean.*

Exercise

Your job is to develop a way to measure the Big Five traits in someone you know, such as a friend, a roommate, or a family member. Read the adjectives in Table 3.3 carefully until you have an understanding of each of the Big Five traits. Then, consider the different sources of personality data described in Chapter 2:

1. Self-report—typically, asking questions on a questionnaire.
2. Observer-report—typically, asking someone who knows the subject to report what the subject is like.
3. Test data—typically, objective tasks, situations, or physiological recordings that get at manifestations of the trait in question.
4. Life-outcome data—aspects of the person's life that may reveal a trait, such as introverted people selecting careers in which there is little contact with others.

	Very low	Somewhat low	Average	Somewhat high	Very high
Extraversion					
Agreeableness					
Conscientiousness					
Emotional stability					
Openness–intellect					

Source: Exercise original, created for this book.

Your job is to assess your target person on each of the Big Five traits, using a combination of data sources. You should first list, for each of the five traits, the way you measured that trait, such as the items on your questionnaire or interview or the life-outcome data. Then, in the second part of your report, indicate how high or low you think your examinee is on each of the five traits.

You might be thinking at this point that five factors may be too few to capture all of the fascinating complexity of personality. And you may be right. But consider this. Each of the five global personality factors has a host of specific "facets," which provide a lot of subtlety and nuance. The global trait of conscientiousness, for example, includes these six facets: competence, order, dutifulness, achievement striving, self-discipline, and delibera-tion. The global trait of neuroticism has these six facets: anxiety, angry hostility, depres-sion, self-consciousness, impulsivity, and vulnerability. These facets of each global factor go a long way toward adding richness, complexity, and nuance to personality description.

Although the NEO-PI-3 traits are presented in a different order (N, E, O, A, and C) than the Goldberg order, and in a few cases the traits are given different names, the underlying personality traits being measured are nearly identical to those found by Goldberg. This convergence between the factor structures of single-trait item formats and sentence-length item formats provides support for the robustness and replicability of the five-factor model (Rammstedt et al., 2010).

What Is the Identity of the Fifth Factor?

Although the five-factor model has achieved impressive replicability across samples, investigators, and item formats, there is some disagreement about the content and replicability of the fifth factor. Different researchers have variously labeled this fifth factor as *culture, intellect, intellectance, imagination, openness, openness to experience,* and even *fluid intelligence* and *tender-mindedness* (see Brand & Egan, 1989; De Raad, 1998). A major cause of these differences is that different researchers start with different item pools to factor analyze. Those who start with the lexical strategy and use adjectives as items typically endorse *intellect* as the meaning and label of the fifth factor (Saucier & Goldberg, 1996). In contrast, those who use questionnaire items tend to prefer *openness* or *openness to experience* because this label better reflects the content of those items (McCrae & Costa, 1997, 1999, 2008).

One way to resolve these differences is to go back to the lexical rationale to begin with and to look *across cultures* and *across languages.* According to the lexical approach, traits that emerge universally in different languages and cultures are more important than those that lack cross-cultural universality. What do the cross-cultural data show? In a study conducted in Turkey, a clear fifth factor emerged that is best described as *openness* (Somer & Goldberg, 1999). A different Dutch study found a fifth factor marked by *progressive* at one end and *conservative* at the other (De Raad et al., 1998). In German, the fifth factor represents *intelligence, talents,* and *abilities* (Ostendorf, 1990). In Italian, the fifth factor is *conventionality,* marked by the items *rebellious* and *critical* (Caprara & Perugini, 1994). Looking across all these studies, the fifth factor has proven difficult to pin down, although *openness* and *intellect* best describe the most common content (John & Naumann, 2010).

In summary, although the first four factors are highly replicable across cultures and languages, there is uncertainty about the content, naming, and replicability of the fifth factor (De Raad et al., 2010). Perhaps some individual differences are more relevant to some cultures than to others—intellect in some cultures, conventionality in other cultures, and openness in yet other cultures. Clearly, more extensive cross-cultural work is needed, particularly in African cultures and in more traditional cultures that are minimally influenced by Western culture.

What Are the Empirical Correlates of the Five Factors?

Over the past 20 years, a tremendous volume of research has been conducted on the empirical correlates of each of the five factors. This section summarizes some of the most recent interesting findings.

Extraversion. Extraverts love to party—they engage in frequent social interaction, take the lead in livening up dull gatherings, and enjoy talking a lot. Indeed, evidence suggests that **social attention** is the cardinal feature of extraversion (Ashton, Lee, & Paunonen, 2002). From the perspective of the extravert, "the more the merrier." Extraverts have a greater impact on their social environment, often assuming leadership positions, whereas introverts tend to be more like wallflowers (Jensen-Campbell & Graziano, 2001). Extraverted men are more likely to be bold with women they don't know, whereas introverted men tend to be shy with women (Berry & Miller, 2001). This may explain why introverts are more likely than extraverts to meet their romantic partners online, a context in which their interpersonal shyness is less of a handicap (Danielsbacka, Tanskanen, & Billari, 2019).

Extraverts tend to be happier, and this positive affect is experienced most intensely when a person acts in an extraverted manner with other people (Fleeson, Malanos, & Achille, 2002; Oelermns & Bakker, 2014). Extraversion also has an impact in the workplace. Extraverts tend to be more involved and enjoy their work (Burke, Mattheiesen, & Pallesen, 2006) and show more commitment to their work organization (Erdheim, Wang, & Zickar, 2006). Extraverts are more cooperative than introverts (Hirsh & Peterson, 2009), which might contribute to their positive work experiences. Extraverts tend to be physically stronger than introverts, in part because they engage in more vigorous and frequent physical activity (Fink et al., 2016; Tolea et al., 2012). But there are also downsides—extraverts like to drive fast and listen to music while driving, and as a consequence, tend to get into more car accidents, and even road fatalities, than their more introverted peers (Lajunen, 2001). They are less likely than introverts to save money for retirement (Hirsh, 2015). When given a choice, extraverts prefer to spend leisure time on beaches and near oceans, whereas introverts enjoy the solitude of mountains (Oishi, Talhelm, & Lee, 2015). Introverts also seem to cope better with being alone during the Covid-19 pandemic, cope better with chronic pain, and suffer fewer sleep disturbances compared to extraverts (Flowers et al., 2021).

Agreeableness. Whereas the motto of the extravert might be "let's liven things up," the motto of the highly agreeable person might be "let's all get along." Those who score high on agreeableness favor using negotiation to resolve conflicts; low-agreeable persons try to assert their power to resolve social conflicts (Graziano & Tobin, 2002; Jensen-Campbell & Graziano, 2001). The agreeable person is also more likely to withdraw from social conflict. Agreeable individuals like harmonious social interaction and cooperative family life. They are also highly prosocial and empathic and enjoy helping others in need (Caprara et al., 2010). They value prosocial behaviors in others, but at the same time tend to judge harshly those who commit antisocial acts (Kammrath & Scholer, 2011). Agreeable children tend to be less often victimized by bullies during early adolescence (Jensen-Campbell et al., 2002). As you might suspect, politicians, at least in Italy, tend to score high on scales of agreeableness (Caprara et al., 2003). Those high on agreeableness seem to be good at reading other people's minds (Nettle & Liddle, 2008), an empathic ability that leads to more forgiveness of the transgressions of other people (Strelan, 2007).

At the other end of the scale of agreeableness lies aggressiveness. Wu and Clark (2003) found that aggressiveness was strongly linked to many everyday behaviors. Examples include hitting someone else in anger, blowing up when things don't work properly, slamming doors, yelling, getting into arguments, clenching fists, raising voices, being intentionally rude, damaging someone's property, pushing and hitting others, and slamming down the phone. So the next time you think about getting into an argument with someone, you might want to find out where they are on the agreeable–aggressiveness disposition.

Agreeable individuals, in short, get along well with others, are well liked, avoid conflict, strive for harmonious family lives, and may selectively prefer professions in which their likeability is an asset. Disagreeable individuals are aggressive and seem to get themselves into a lot of social conflict.

Conscientiousness. If extraverts party up and agreeable people get along, then conscientious individuals are industrious and get ahead. The hard work, punctuality, and reliable behavior exhibited by conscientious individuals result in a host of life outcomes such as a higher grade point average (Conrad, 2006; Noftle & Robins, 2007; Poropat, 2009), greater job satisfaction, greater job security, and more positive and committed social relationships (Langford, 2003). Highly conscientious individuals are also more likely to delay gratification, save money, and invest their money wisely over their life spans (Furnham & Cheng, 2019a, 2019b). Those who score low on conscientiousness, in contrast, are likely to perform more poorly at school and at work. The fact that highly conscientious individuals succeed in the work domain is likely due to three key corre- lates. They do not procrastinate, in contrast to their low-conscious peers whose motto might be "never put off until tomorrow what you can put off until the day after tomor- row" (Lee, Kelly, & Edwards, 2006). Second, they tend to be perfectionists, setting high standards for themselves (Cruce et al., 2012; Stoeber, Otto, & Dalbert, 2009) and score high on achievement motivation (Richardson & Abraham, 2009). And those high in conscientiousness are exceptionally industrious, putting in the long hours of diligent hard work needed to get ahead (Lund et al., 2006). Those high on conscientiousness are more likely to stick with good plans for physical exercise (Bogg, 2008) and consequently are less likely to gain weight when they reach middle age (Brummett et al., 2006). High scorers on conscientiousness also display more passion and perseverance for long-term goals (Duckworth et al., 2007). They are more likely to do volunteer work when they retire from their jobs (Mike, Jackson, & Oltmanns, 2014). Having a romantic partner who is highly conscientious is linked with being more physically healthy (Williams et al., 2019).

Low C is linked with risky sexual behaviors, such as failing to use condoms (Trobst et al., 2002) and being more responsive to other potential partners while already in an existing romantic relationship (Schmitt & Buss, 2001). Among a sample of prison- ers, low-C scorers tend to have frequent arrests (Clower & Bothwell, 2001). The high-C individual, in sum, tends to perform well in school and work, avoids breaking the rules, and has a more stable and secure romantic relationship. But there does appear to be at least one downside to being highly conscientious—high scorers, compared to low scorers, experience a more substantial drop in psychological well-being when they are unem- ployed for extended periods of time (Boyce, Wood, & Brown, 2010).

Emotional stability. Life poses stresses and hurdles that everyone must confront. The dimension of emotional stability taps into the way people cope with these stresses. Emotionally stable individuals are like boats that remain on course through choppy waters. Emotionally unstable people get buffeted about by the waves and are more likely to get knocked off course. The hallmark of emotional instability, or neuroticism, is vari- ability of moods over time—such people swing up and down more than emotionally sta- ble individuals (Murray, Allen, & Trinder, 2002).

Emotionally unstable individuals experience more fatigue over the course of the day (De Vries & Van Heck, 2002) and experience more grief and depression after the death of a loved one (Winjgaards-de Meij et al., 2007). Psychologically, emotionally unstable individuals are more likely to have dissociate experiences such as an inability to recall important life events, feeling disconnected from life and other people, and feel- ing like they've woken up in a strange or unfamiliar place (Kwapil, Wrobel, & Pope, 2002). Those high on neuroticism also tend to have more frequent thoughts of suicide (Chioqueta & Stiles, 2005; Stewart et al., 2008). Those high on neuroticism report poorer physical health, more physical symptoms, and fewer attempts to engage in health- promoting behaviors (Williams, O'Brien, & Colder, 2004). They also engage in health- impairing behaviors, such as drinking alcohol as a means of coping with their problems (Theakston et al., 2004).

Personality characteristics predict who will climb mountains, literally and metaphorically.
OJO Images/Getty Images

Interpersonally, those high on emotional instability have more ups and downs in their social relationships. In the sexual domain, for example, emotionally unstable individuals experience more sexual anxiety (e.g., worry about performance) as well as a greater fear of engaging in sex (Heaven et al., 2003; Shafer, 2001). And with highly stressful events, such as an unwanted loss of a pregnancy, emotionally unstable individuals are more likely to develop "posttraumatic stress disorder," in which the psychological trauma of the loss is experienced profoundly and for a long time (Engelhard, van den Hout, & Kindt, 2003).

Emotional instability augers poorly for professional success. This may be partly due to the fact that emotionally unstable people are thrown off track by the everyday stresses and strains that we all go through. It may be partly due to their experience of greater fatigue. But it may also be attributable to the fact that they engage in a lot of "self-handicapping" (Ross, Canada, & Rausch, 2002). Self-handicapping is defined as a tendency to "create obstacles to successful achievement in performance or competitive situations in order to protect one's self-esteem" (Ross et al., 2002, p. 2). One such obstacle might be problematic alcohol consumption, which is linked with emotional instability in young adults (Pocuca et al., 2019). Emotionally unstable individuals are also more likely to choke under pressure, such as a time deadline to complete a task (Byrne, Silasi-Mansat, & Worthy, 2015). Nonetheless, those high on neuroticism actually outperform their more emotionally stable counterparts in an office setting when changes in the work needs create an unusually busy work environment (Smillie et al., 2006). In sum, the affective volatility that comes with being low on emotional stability affects many spheres of life, from sexuality to achievement.

Intellect-openness. Would you agree or disagree with the following? "Upon awakening during the night, I am unsure whether I actually experienced something or only dreamed about it," "I am aware that I am dreaming, even as I dream," "I am able to control or direct the content of my dreams," "A dream helped me to solve a current problem or concern" (Watson, 2003). If you tend to agree, you probably score high on openness. Those high on openness tend to remember their dreams more, and have more waking dreams, more vivid dreams, more prophetic dreams (dreaming about something that later happens), and more problem-solving dreams (Watson, 2003).

Openness has been linked to experimentation with new foods, a liking for novel experiences, and even "openness" to having extramarital affairs (Buss, 1993). One possible cause of openness may lie in individual differences in the processing of information. Those high in openness have more difficulty ignoring previously experienced stimuli (Peterson, Smith, & Carson, 2002). It's as though the perceptual and information processing "gates" of highly open people are literally more "open" to receiving information coming at them from a variety of sources. Perhaps that is why high openness is linked with measures of creativity (Nusbaum & Silva, 2011). Less-open people have more tunnel vision and find it easier to ignore competing stimuli. Those high in openness exhibit less prejudice against minority groups and are less likely to hold negative racial stereotypes (Flynn, 2005). They also are more likely to get tattoos and body piercings (Nathanson, Paulhus, & Williams, 2006; Tate & Shelton, 2008). Highly open people tend to be more politically liberal, especially when there is an external threat such as terrorism (Sibley, Osborne, & Duckitt, 2012). They excel in achievement in the arts (Kaufman et al., 2016) and show higher levels of musical sophistication (Greenberg et al., 2015). Openness also predicts more cross-sex friendships on social networks such as Facebook (Lönnqvist et al., 2014). In sum, openness has been correlated with a host of other fascinating variables from intrusive stimuli to possible alternative sex partners.

Combinations of Big Five variables. Many life outcomes, of course, are better predicted by combinations of personality dispositions than by single personality dispositions. Here are a few examples.

- *Good grades* are best predicted by Conscientiousness (high) and Emotional Stability (high) (Chamorro-Premuzic & Furnham, 2003a, 2003b). One reason might be that emotionally stable and conscientious people are less likely to procrastinate (Watson, 2001).
- *Academic dishonesty* is more likely among those low in Conscientiousness and low in Agreeableness (Giluk & Postlethwaite, 2015).
- *What makes a good computer wiz?* High Conscientiousness, high Openness, and Introversion (Gnambs, 2015).
- *Obedience to authority* in a Milgram-like experiment is more likely among people high in Conscientiousness and high in Agreeableness (Bègue et al., 2014).
- *Educational attainment and earnings* are predicted by high Emotional Stability, Openness, and Conscientiousness (O'Connell & Sheikh, 2011).
- *Risky sexual behaviors,* such has having many sex partners and not using condoms, are best predicted by high Extraversion, high Neuroticism, low Conscientiousness, and low Agreeableness (Miller et al., 2004; Trobst et al., 2002).
- While *frequency of sexual intercourse per week* is best predicted by extraversion in women, for men the combined traits of extraversion, emotional stability, and low agreeableness best predict sexual frequency (Whyte et al., 2019).
- *Alcohol consumption* is best predicted by high Extraversion and low Conscientiousness (Hong & Paunonen, 2009; Paunonen, 2003). A study of more than 5,000 workers in Finland found that low Conscientiousness also predicts *increases* in alcohol consumption over time, that is, who ends up becoming a heavy drinker (Grano et al., 2004).

- *Substance abuse disorders,* such as illegal drug abuse, are linked to high Neuroticism and low Conscientiousness (Kotov et al., 2010).
- *Pathological gambling* is best predicted by a combination of high Neuroticism and low Conscientiousness (MacLaren et al., 2011; Myrseth et al., 2009).
- *Aggression* against other people when angry is well predicted by Neuroticism, but being high on Agreeableness appears to cool the tempers that these emotionally unstable people sometimes experience (Ode, Robinson, & Wilkowski, 2008).
- *Violent criminals* tend to be low on Agreeableness and high on Extraversion (Shimotsukasa et al., 2019).
- *Mount Everest mountain climbers* tend to be extraverted, emotionally stable, and high on Psychoticism (Egan & Stelmack, 2003).
- *Happiness* and experiencing positive affect in everyday life are best predicted by high Extraversion and low Neuroticism (Cheng & Furnham, 2003; Steel & Ones, 2002; Stewart, Ebmeier, & Deary, 2005; Yik & Russell, 2001).
- *Proclivity to engage in volunteer work,* such as community services, is best predicted by a combination of high Agreeableness and high Extraversion (Carlo et al., 2005).
- *Forgiveness,* the proclivity to forgive those who have committed some wrong, characterizes individuals who are high on Agreeableness and high on Emotional Stability (Brose et al., 2005; Steiner, Allemand, & McCullough, 2012).
- *Leadership effectiveness* in business settings is best predicted by high Extraversion, high Agreeableness, high Conscientiousness, and high Emotional Stability (Silverthorne, 2001).
- *Propensity to migrate* within and among states within the United States is predicted by high Openness and low Agreeableness (Jokela, 2009), although some studies show that high Openness combined with high Extraversion predicts intentions to emigrate to a new country (Canache et al., 2013).
- *Propensity to have children* is predicted by high Extraversion (sociability) and high Emotional Stability (Jokela et al., 2009).
- *Favorable attitudes toward being touched by an intimate partner* are most strongly felt by those high in Agreeableness and Openness (Dorros, Hanzel, & Segrin, 2008).

We should not be surprised that combinations of personality variables often do better than single variables in predicting important life outcomes, and we can expect future research to focus increasingly on these combinations.

Is the Five-Factor Model Comprehensive?

Critics of the five-factor model argue that it leaves out important aspects of personality. Almagor, Tellegen, and Waller (1995), for example, present evidence for seven factors. Their results suggest the addition of two factors: *positive evaluation* (e.g., *outstanding* vs. *ordinary*) and *negative evaluation* (e.g., *awful* vs. *decent*). Goldberg, one of the proponents of the five-factor model, has discovered that factors such as *religiosity* and *spirituality* sometimes emerge as separate factors, although these are smaller in size (accounting for less variance) than those of the Big Five (Saucier & Goldberg, 1998).

   Lanning (1994), using items from the California Adult Q-Sort, has found a replicable sixth factor, which he labels *attractiveness,* including the items *physically attractive, sees self as attractive,* and *charming.* Schmitt & Buss (2000) have found reliable individual differences in the sexual sphere, such as *sexiness* (e.g., sexy, stunning, attractive, alluring, sensual, and seductive) and *faithfulness* (e.g., faithful, monogamous, devoted). These individual difference dimensions are correlated with the five factors: *Sexiness* is positively correlated with *Extraversion,* and *faithfulness* is positively correlated with both *Agreeableness* and *Conscientiousness.* But these correlations leave much of the individual variation unaccounted for, suggesting that these individual differences in sexuality are not completely subsumed by the five-factor model.

Paunonen and colleagues have identified 10 personality traits that appear to fall outside of the five-factor model: Conventionality, Seductiveness, Manipulativeness, Thriftiness, Humorousness, Integrity, Femininity, Religiosity, Risk Taking, and Egotism (Paunonen, 2002, 2003). Other researchers have confirmed that these traits are not highly correlated with the Big Five and that they highlight many interesting facets of personality at a more specific level than the "global" factors represented by the five-factor model (Lee, Ogunfowora, & Ashton, 2005).

Proponents of the five-factor model are typically open-minded about the potential inclusion of factors beyond the five factors, if and when the empirical evidence warrants it (Costa & McCrae, 1995; Goldberg & Saucier, 1995). Nonetheless, these researchers have not found the evidence for additional factors beyond the Big Five to be compelling. *Positive* and *negative evaluation,* some have argued, are not really separate factors but, rather, false factors that emerge simply because raters tend to evaluate all things as either good or bad (McCrae & John, 1992). With respect to the *attractiveness* factor found by Lanning (1994), Costa & McCrae (1995) argue that *attractiveness* is not ordinarily considered to be a personality trait, although the *charming* item that loads on this factor surely would be considered part of personality.

One approach to personality factors beyond the Big Five has been to explore **personality-descriptive nouns** rather than adjectives. Saucier (2003) has discovered eight fascinating factors within the domain of personality nouns such as: *Dumbbell* (e.g., dummy, moron, twit), *Babe/Cutie* (e.g., beauty, darling, doll), *Philosopher* (e.g., genius, artist, individualist), *Lawbreaker* (e.g., pothead, drunk, rebel), *Joker* (e.g., clown, goof, comedian), and *Jock* (e.g., sportsman, tough, machine). As Saucier concludes, "Personality taxonomies based on adjectives are unlikely to be comprehensive, because type-nouns have different content emphases" (Saucier, 2003, p. 695).

The HEXACO Model

Another approach to personality factors beyond the Big Five has been to go back to the lexical approach, focusing on large pools of trait adjectives in different languages (De Raad & Barelds, 2008). In an exciting development, several studies have converged on six rather than five factors. One study of seven languages (Dutch, French, German, Hungarian, Italian, Korean, and Polish) found variants of the Big Five, plus a sixth factor, **Honesty–Humility** (Ashton, Lee, & de Vries, 2014). At one end of the Honesty-Humility factor lie trait adjectives such as honest, sincere, trustworthy, and unselfish; the other end is anchored by adjectives such as arrogant, conceited, greedy, pompous, self-important, and egotistical. Independent investigators have found this sixth factor in Greece (Saucier et al., 2005) and Italy (Di Blas, 2005).

So much evidence has accumulated that some argue that the most comprehensive cross-language taxonomy of personality is best captured by the **HEXACO model**: Humility-Honesty (H), Emotionality (E), Extraversion (X), Agreeableness (A), Conscientiousness (C), and Openness to Experience (O) (Ashton et al., 2014). In this model, five of the six factors are very close to those of the Big Five, although there are subtle differences. The largest difference, of course, is the addition of the Honesty-Humility factor. This six-factor taxonomy has emerged in lexical-based studies of the major world languages, the most recent emerging from Poland (Gorbaniuk et al., 2013) and among Portuguese Brazilians (Costa et al., 2019). The Honesty–Humility factor has also accrued strong construct validity. High scorers are more likely to offer sincere and humble apologies (Dunlop et al., 2015), even though they are less likely to violate social rules. It predicts cooperation in experimental games (Ashton et al., 2014). Those high on Honesty–Humility are more likely to be sincerely religious (Silvia, Nusbaum, & Beaty, 2014) and more easily show sexual and moral disgust (Tybur & de Vries, 2013). High scorers are also more likely to pursue what is called a slow life-history mating strategy marked by long-term commitment to one partner and high investment in children (Davis et al., 2019).

Those low on Honesty–Humility tend to be interpersonally exploitative, are more likely to sabotage others in their work environment, and are even more likely to engage in criminal activity (Johnson, Rowatt, & Petrini, 2011; Zettler & Hilbig, 2010). They are more likely to violate social contracts and cheat in games (Fiddick et al., 2016). They are more boastful (Hilbig, Heydasch, & Zettler, 2014). Moreover, be wary of romantically rejecting someone low on Honesty–Humility; such people are more likely to seek revenge against their former romantic partner (Sheppard & Boon, 2012).

The low end of Honesty–Humility captures several unpleasant interpersonal traits, including egotism, narcissism, and an exploitative interpersonal style. This cluster, sometimes called "the dark triad" (narcissism, Machiavellianism, and psychopathy), increasingly appears to be an important dispositional domain beyond that captured by the five-factor model (Paulhus & Williams, 2002; Veselka, Schermer, & Vernon, 2012). These findings point to an expansion of the basic factors of personality within the dispositional domain (Lee & Ashton, 2008, 2010; Lee & Ashton, 2008).

The expansion of the five-factor model to the six-factor HEXACO model is an exciting new development in personality psychology and is being validated in many different cultures. Evidence continues to accumulate that Honesty–Humility is not well captured by the five-factor model (Ashton, Lee, & Visser, 2019). A recent review of 152 studies found that the HEXACO model provided broader coverage of the personality domain compared to the five-factor model (Thielmann et al., 2021). This illustrates important progress in the vibrant science of personality psychology.

SUMMARY AND EVALUATION

This chapter focused on three fundamental issues for a personality psychology based on traits: how to conceptualize traits, how to identify the most important traits, and how to formulate a comprehensive taxonomy of traits.

There are two basic conceptualizations of traits. The first views traits as the internal properties of persons that cause behavior. In this conception, traits cause the outward behavioral manifestations. The second conceptualization views traits as descriptive summaries of overt behavior. The summary view does not assume that traits cause behavior; rather, it treats the issue of cause separately, to be examined after the behavioral summaries are identified.

There have been three major approaches to identifying the most important traits. The first is the lexical approach, which views all the important traits as captured by the natural language. The lexical approach uses synonym frequency and cross-cultural universality as criteria for identifying important traits. The second approach, the statistical approach, adopts statistical procedures, such as factor analysis, and attempts to identify clusters of traits that covary. The third approach, the theoretical approach, uses an existing theory of personality to determine which traits are important. In practice, personality psychologists use blends of these three approaches—for example, by using the lexical approach to identify the universe of traits and then applying statistical procedures to identify groups of traits that covary and form larger factors.

The third fundamental issue—formulating an overarching taxonomy of personality traits—has yielded several solutions. Eysenck developed a hierarchical model in which the broad traits *extraversion, neuroticism,* and *psychoticism* subsume more narrow traits, such as activity level, moodiness, and egocentricity. Eysenck's taxonomy is based on a factor analysis but is also anchored in biological underpinnings—a heritable basis for the traits and the identification of the underlying physiological basis for the traits.

Circumplex taxonomies of personality have been more narrowly targeted toward the domain of interpersonal traits as opposed to the entire personality sphere. Circumplex models are circular arrangements of traits organized around two key dimensions—status (dominance) and love (agreeableness).

The five-factor model of personality is a taxonomy that subsumes the circumplex in that the first two traits in the model—*extraversion* and *agreeableness*—are roughly the same as the circumplex dimensions of *dominance* and *agreeableness*. In addition, however, the five-factor model includes *conscientiousness, emotional stability,* and *openness-intellect*. The five-factor model has been criticized for not being comprehensive and for being inadequate for understanding underlying psychological processes. Recent evidence points to the exciting discovery of a sixth factor—*honesty-humility*—that necessitates an expansion of the Big Five. Some now argue for the cross-cultural robustness of a six-factor personality structure, the HEXACO Model: Honesty-Humility (H), Emotionality (E), Extraversion (X), Agreeableness (A), Conscientiousness (C), and Openness to Experience (O). This development is likely the most important advance in personality taxonomy in the past 25 years.

KEY TERMS

lexical approach 63
statistical approach 63
theoretical approach 63
lexical hypothesis 63
synonym frequency 63
cross-cultural universality 63
factor analysis 64
factor loadings 65

sociosexual orientation 66
interpersonal traits 71
adjacency 72
bipolarity 73
orthogonality 73
five-factor model 73
extraversion 77
social attention 77

agreeableness 78
conscientiousness 78
emotional stability 79
intellect-openness 80
combinations of Big Five variables 81
personality-descriptive nouns 83
honesty-humility 83
HEXACO model 83

Tavis Wright/Image Source

Theoretical and Measurement Issues in Trait Psychology

4

Theoretical Issues
Meaningful Differences Among Individuals
Stability over Time
Consistency Across Situations
Person–Situation Interaction
Aggregation

Measurement Issues
Carelessness
Faking on Questionnaires
Beware of Barnum Statements in Personality Test Interpretations

Personality and Prediction
Applications of Personality Testing in the Workplace
Legal Issues in Personality Testing in Employment Settings
Personnel Selection—Choosing the Right Person for the Job
Selection in Business Settings—The Myers–Briggs Type Indicator: A Worst-Case Example
Selection in Business Settings—The Hogan Personality Inventory: A Best-Case Example

SUMMARY AND EVALUATION

KEY TERMS

Sarah was a senior in college with a double major in math and computer science. She was a bit shy, especially with men her own age. Although she wanted to date more, she was very particular about the characteristics she looked for in a partner. She decided that a Web-based dating service might be an efficient way to find someone to date. She signed up with an internet dating service and discovered that the first step was to complete an extensive personality questionnaire. She answered a lot of questions about her likes and dislikes, her habits, traits, and what others thought of her. She even answered questions about the kind of car she owned and her driving style. After this, the site returned the personality profiles of a few men who, the site claimed, would be good matches for her. One looked particularly interesting, so she spent a couple of hours with him online. Sarah decided to call him a couple of times on the phone. They had a lot in common, and Sarah found it easy to talk to him. She enjoyed the conversations, as did he, so they decided to take the next step and meet in person for a dinner date. When they made arrangements to meet, she was surprised to learn that they lived in the same apartment complex and that they had probably already seen one another, perhaps had even spoken to one another. But it took an internet dating service, using a program that matches people according to personality, for them to actually find each other.

A key task for a first date is determining what you have in common with the other person—that is, how similar your personalities are.

monkeybusinessimages/iStock /Getty Images Plus

There are many internet-based dating services, and many of these use personality questionnaires to help them do a better job of matching people. The dating site EliteSingles.com uses a version of the Big Five trait inventory by Costa and McCrae (1995) that we discussed in the previous chapter. This dating site uses an algorithm that matches people on their five personality trait scores. SoSyncd.com (www.sosyncd.com) is a dating site that matches people according to their scores on the Myers–Briggs Type Indicator, a personality measure that we review later in this chapter. Other internet dating services, such as Chemistry.com, eHarmony.com, and okcupid.com also gather personality data and employ sophisticated matching algorithms. Personality psychologists have been accumulating evidence over the past half-century that personality similarity is a significant predictor of whether people will be attracted to each other (see Chapter 15) and whether they will be satisfied with their relationship once it is established (Decuyper, De Bolle, & De Fruyt, 2012).

Matching on personality traits sounds like a great idea, but it works only to the extent that the personality measures are valid. Not answering the questions honestly can invalidate the measure. A person might, for example, try to cover up an aggressive, abusive personality. A person might lie about other characteristics as well, such as saying he is single when in fact he is married, or saying she is 5′ 11″ when in fact she is 5′ 5″. A study by the Pew Research Center found that, among users of dating sites, 54 percent felt that someone else had misrepresented themselves online. Someone who misrepresents themselves online is commonly called a "catfish" (UrbanDictionary.com), and dating sites often try to remove the "catfish" from their "pool" of users. Consequently, some sites use techniques developed by personality psychologists for detecting impression management efforts on questionnaires. For example, some sites ask about common faults or minor misbehaviors that practically everyone would endorse, such as "I have, on occasion, told a white lie." People who deny a lot of these common faults raise a red flag because they are probably misrepresenting themselves on their other answers as well.

This use of testing brings into focus several questions about the measurement of personality traits. Do traits represent consistent behavior patterns, such that we could make accurate predictions about a person's *future* behavior based on her or his trait standings? How do personality traits interact with situations, particularly social situations? Are there ways to detect that someone is not telling the truth on a personality questionnaire? Are some people motivated to fake good or to fake bad on questionnaires?

Choosing a dating partner is one example of personality in a selection context. Personality measures are also used in other selection settings, such as for jobs or for prison parole or for placement within an organization. What are some of the legal issues in using personality measures to make such consequential decisions? Are there some common problems with selection procedures? Can an employer use a measure of "integrity" to screen out potentially dishonest employees? What about selecting people for admission into college, law school, or medical school on the basis of personal characteristics?

Although many of these questions seem abstract, they are important for how we think about personality traits. They are important for understanding controversial issues, such as the use of personality measures in business, industry, and education for the selection, training, and promotion of candidates.

Theoretical Issues

Trait theories of personality offer a collection of viewpoints about the fundamental building blocks of human nature. As we saw in Chapter 3, there are differences among the various theories concerning what constitutes a trait, how many traits exist, and what are the best methods for discovering basic traits. Despite their differences, trait theories share three important assumptions about personality traits. These assumptions go beyond any one theory or taxonomy of personality traits and, so, form the basic foundation for trait psychology. These three important assumptions are

- meaningful individual differences,
- stability over time, and
- consistency across situations.

Meaningful Differences Among Individuals

Trait psychologists are primarily interested in determining the ways in which people are *different from each other.* Any meaningful way in which people differ from each other may potentially be identified as a personality trait. Some people like to talk a lot; others don't. Some people are active; others are couch potatoes. Some people enjoy working on difficult puzzles; others avoid mental challenges. Because of its emphasis on the study of differences among people, trait psychology has sometimes been called **differential psychology** in the interest of distinguishing this field from other branches of personality psychology (Anastasi, 1976). Differential psychology includes the study of other forms of individual differences in addition to personality traits, such as abilities, aptitudes, and intelligence. In this chapter, however, we focus mainly on personality traits.

The trait perspective historically has been concerned with accurate measurement. It takes a quantitative approach, which emphasizes *how much* a given individual differs from the average person. Of all the perspectives and strategies for studying personality, the trait approach is the most mathematically and statistically oriented due to its emphasis on amount (Paunonen & Hong, 2015).

You might be wondering how the many differences among people could be captured and represented by a few key personality traits. How is it that the uniqueness of every individual can be portrayed by just a few traits? Trait psychologists are somewhat like chemists in this regard. They argue that by combining a few primary traits in various amounts, they can recreate the unique personalities of every individual. This process is analogous to that of combining the three primary colors. Every visible color in the spectrum, from dusty mauve to burnt umber, is created through various combinations of the three primary colors: red, green, and blue. According to trait psychologists, every unique personality, no matter how complex or unusual, can be thought of as the product of a particular combination of a few basic or primary traits.

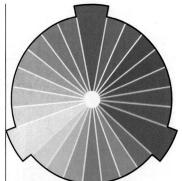

The Color Wheel. The infinite hues of color are created from a combination of three primary colors. Similarly, trait psychologists hold that the infinite variety of personalities is created from a combination of a few primary traits.

Stability over Time

The second assumption made by all trait theories is that there is a degree of stability in personality over time. If someone is highly extraverted during one period of observation, trait psychologists tend to assume that he or she will be extraverted tomorrow, next week, a year from now, or even decades from now. The view that many broad-based personality traits show considerable stability over time has been supported by a large number of research studies, which we review in Chapter 5. Traits such as intelligence, emotional reactivity, impulsiveness, shyness, and aggression show high test-retest correlations, even with years or decades between measurement occasions. Personality traits that are thought to have a biological basis, such as extraversion, sensation seeking, activity level, and shyness, also show remarkable consistency over time. Attitudes, however, are much less stable over time, as are interests and opinions (Conley, 1984a, 1984b). Of course, people do change in important behavioral ways throughout adulthood, especially after encountering some important life "turning point," such as serving in the military. For example, Jackson and colleagues (2012) showed that people lower in agreeableness and openness in high school were more likely to enter the military upon graduation. After training, the military recruits were even lower on agreeableness, and this low agreeableness persisted at least five years after training, when most of the recruits were no longer in the military and had either started college or entered the labor force. However, in the absence of major life "turning points," when it comes to broad personality traits, stability over time is more often the rule than the exception (Allemand, Gomez, & Jackson, 2010).

Although a trait might be stable over time, the way in which it manifests itself in actual behavior might change substantially. Consider the trait of disagreeableness. As a child, a highly disagreeable person might be prone to temper tantrums and fits of breath holding, fist pounding, and undirected rage. As an adult, a disagreeable person might be difficult to get along with and hence might have trouble sustaining personal relationships or holding down a job. Researchers have found, for example, a correlation of −.45 between throwing temper tantrums in childhood and being able to hold a job as an adult 20 years later (Caspi, Elder, & Bem, 1987). This finding is evidence of stability in the underlying trait (disagreeableness), even though the *manifestation* of that trait changes over time.

The Hartshorne and May (1928) study examined cross-situational consistency in academic and play situations in children. While they found little evidence for cross-situational consistency in such traits as honesty, the study has been criticized for measuring behavior on one occasion in each situation. Studies that aggregate measurements over several occasions in each situation find much higher levels of cross-situational consistency.
Left: Oksana Kuzmina/Shutterstock; Right: Africa Studio/Shutterstock

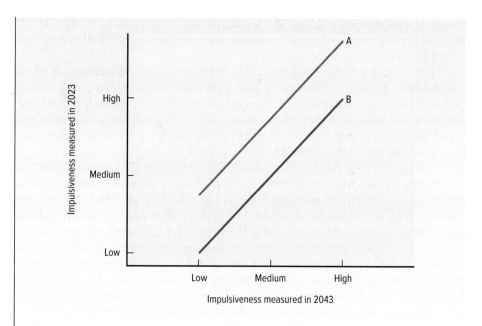

Figure 4.1

Hypothetical regression lines between impulsiveness measured 20 years apart. Line A represents an age change in impulsiveness, with all persons scoring as less impulsive in later life (e.g., those scoring "medium" in 2023 score as "low" 20 years later). Line B represents no change in impulsiveness over 20 years (e.g., those scoring "low" in 2023 also score "low" in 2043). Both lines represent rank-order stability, however, and thus high test-retest correlations across 20 years would be found for both group A and group B.

What about traits that decrease in intensity with age, such as activity level, impulsiveness, or sociopathy? For example, criminal tendencies usually decrease with age, so a 20-year-old sociopath becomes much less dangerous to society as he or she ages. The answer to this question lies in the concept of **rank-order stability**. If all people show a decrease in a particular trait at the same rate over time, they could still maintain the same rank order relative to each other. Accounting for general change with age can be compared to subtracting or adding a constant to each participant's score on the trait measure. Figure 4.1 illustrates how a general decrease in impulsiveness with age might have no real effect on the correlation between measures obtained 20 years apart. People in general can show a decrease in impulsiveness as they get older, yet those individuals who were the *most* impulsive at an earlier age are still the ones who are *most* impulsive at a later age, even as everyone declined on impulsiveness as they grew older. We revisit the idea of rank-order stability, as well as the whole notion of stability and change, in Chapter 5.

Consistency Across Situations

The third assumption made by trait psychologists is that traits will exhibit some **consistency** across situations. Although the evidence for stability in traits *over time* is substantial, the question of consistency in traits *from situation to situation* has been more hotly debated (for a review, see Leikas, Lonnqvist, & Verkasalo, 2012). Trait psychologists have traditionally believed that people's personalities show consistency from situation to situation. For example, if a young man is "really friendly," he is expected to be friendly at work, friendly at school, and friendly during recreation activities. This person might be friendly toward strangers, toward people of different ages and ethnicities, and toward professors or supervisors at work.

Even though someone is "really friendly," there are, of course, situations in which the individual will not act friendly. Perhaps a particular situation exerts an influence on how friendly most people will be. For example, people are more likely to start conversations with strangers if they are at a party than if they are at a library. If situations largely control how people behave, then the idea that traits are consistent across situations holds less promise in explaining their behavior.

The issue of cross-situational consistency has a long history in personality psychology. Hartshorne and May (1928) studied a large group of elementary school students at summer camp, focusing especially on the trait of honesty. They observed honest and dishonest behavior in several situations. For example, they observed which children cheated while playing field games at summer camp and, again, which children cheated during some written exams in school. The correlation between honesty measured in each of these two situations was rather low. Knowing that a child cheated one night while playing kick-the-can at summer camp tells us very little about whether this child is likely to copy from a neighbor during a test at school. Hartshorne and May reported similar low cross-situational correlations for the traits of helpfulness and self-control.

Forty years later, in 1968, Walter Mischel (1930–2018) published an influential book entitled *Personality and Assessment.* In it, he summarized the results of the Hartshorne and May study, as well as the results of many other studies reporting low correlations between similar behaviors measured in different situations. After reviewing many such findings, Mischel concluded that "behavioral consistencies have not been demonstrated, and the concept of personality traits as broad predispositions is thus untenable" (p. 140).

Mischel's 1968 book became a classic because it questioned the very foundation of personality traits—the notion that people are consistent from situation to situation. He suggested that personality psychologists should abandon their efforts to explain behavior in terms of personality traits and recommended that they shift their focus to situations. If behavior differs from situation to situation, then it must be situational differences, rather than underlying personality differences, that determine behavior. This position, called **situationism**, can be illustrated with the following examples. A young woman may be friendly at school with people she knows but reserved with strangers. Or a young man may want to achieve good grades at school but may not care whether he excels in sports (see the Closer Look box on "Situationism Today").

Mischel's challenge to the trait approach preoccupied the field of trait psychology for the 30 years following publication of his 1968 book. Many researchers felt that Mischel was wrong about personality traits, yet data supporting cross-situational consistency was difficult to find. As such, they began formulating new theoretical perspectives and gathering new data designed to rescue the idea of traits (e.g., Buss, 1989; Endler & Magnusson, 1976). Mischel, in turn, countered with new ideas and new data of his own, intended to reinforce his position that the trait concept was limited in its usefulness (e.g., Mischel, 1984, 1990; Mischel & Peake, 1982).

Although the dust is still settling from this long-running debate (for a recent summary, see Benet-Martinez et al., 2015), it is safe to say that both trait psychologists *and* Mischel modified their views as a result of these efforts. Mischel tempered his position, saying that situations are *not always* the strongest determinants of behavior. However, he maintained that trait psychologists overstated the importance of broad traits (Mischel & Shoda, 2010). Prior to Mischel's critique, it was common for trait psychologists to make broad statements about the predictability of people's behavior from their scores on personality tests. Mischel pointed out that psychologists simply are not very good at predicting how *an individual* will behave *in particular situations.* Trait psychologists, too, have modified their views. Two of the most lasting changes that trait psychologists have embraced as a result of Mischel's critique have been the notion of **person–situation interaction** and the practice of **aggregation**, or averaging, as a tool for assessing personality traits.

A Closer Look

Situationism Today

The popular science writer Malcolm Gladwell (author of *The Tipping Point* and *Blink, and other books*) came out with a book in 2008, titled *Outliers*. (The term *outlier* comes from statistics and refers to an individual in a sample who is markedly different from all others in that sample.) In this book, Gladwell tackles the issue of being exceptional: Why some people are exceedingly successful in some areas of life, such as sports, science, or business, whereas most others are only mediocre. This question embodies the very concept of individual differences and lies at the heart of personality psychology. It also is a useful example to illustrate the extreme situational perspective.

Gladwell takes the position that most exceptional people get that way because of special opportunities or life situations that give them some advantage. His view is that the successful among us were presented with a beneficial life situation and ran with it. For example, the founders of many major computer companies (e.g., Microsoft, Apple, Sun Microsystems) were all born between 1953 and 1956 and therefore were exposed to early prototype computers when they were geeky teenage boys with lots of time on their hands. They all spent countless hours with these early prototypes and grew up to be exceptionally successful in the computing industry.

Gladwell presents case after case like this, arguing that exposure to critical life situations, at the right time, is what matters most in understanding why some people are

so successful. This is an entirely situational explanation, in that the cause of the success lies not in the person but in the situations to which she or he was exposed. In Gladwell's view, success is all about opportunity, timing, luck, and hard work. It has nothing to do with traits within the person, such as aptitude, intelligence, interest, motivation, or personality. Gladwell is a modern situationist, presenting a one-sided perspective on understanding exceptional success.

The authors of the book you are presently reading were also both born between 1953 and 1956, just like Bill Gates, Steve Jobs, and Bill Joy. We also were exposed to primitive computers when we were geeky teenager boys with lots of discretionary time on our hands. However, neither of us grew up to be corporate giants in the computing industry, even though we were exposed to the same kinds of life situations Gladwell argues were responsible for the exceptional success of these computing magnates. What explains this discrepancy? Well, we are both extremely interested in people, and we both were motivated to learn as much as we could about human nature when we were growing up. We must have had some innate ability in this field because we both went on to earn PhDs in psychology and to conduct award-winning research in the field of personality. Clearly, our interests, motivations, abilities, and personalities are very different from those of Bill Gates and Steve Jobs, even though we experienced many of the same life situations. We might argue that it is precisely

these personal characteristics that determined why we became personality psychologists and why Jobs and Gates became computing tycoons. This would be a strictly personality position, arguing that personal characteristics—ability, intelligence, interest, personality—entirely determine life outcomes. Books presenting this perspective, which are as one-sided as Gladwell's, have also been written by nonscientists (e.g., *The Personality Code,* by Travis Bradberry, Putnam Press, 2007).

The real answer to understanding most life outcomes can be found in the *interaction* between personal characteristics and life situations: Exceptional life outcomes happen when chance situations meet the prepared person. If someone had all the personal characteristics of Bill Gates or Steve Jobs, yet was from a poor, inner-city school that did not get those early prototype computers, he or she would most likely not go into this career. However, if someone had the exact same life experiences as Jobs and Gates, yet differed from them in basic interests, aptitudes, and personality (like us), then it is also likely that he or she would not go into computing as a career. It takes the right situations happening to people with the right personal characteristics to produce the exceptional outcome. Gladwell's book tells only half of the story, the situational half. The whole story is more complicated—and more interesting—than he portrays. For an integrated perspective on person–situation interaction, see Funder (2006).

Person–Situation Interaction

We first looked at the topic of person–situation interaction in Chapter 1. In this section, we examine this topic in a bit more detail, focusing on interactionism as a response to Mischel's challenge to trait consistency. As Mischel's debate with trait psychologists made clear, there are two possible explanations for behavior, or why people do what they do in any given situation:

1. Behavior is a function of personality traits, $B = f(P)$.
2. Behavior is a function of situational forces, $B = f(S)$.

Clearly, there is some truth in both of these statements. For example, people behave differently at funerals than they do at sporting events, illustrating that situational forces direct behavior in certain ways, as Mischel emphasized. Some people, however, are consistently quiet, even at sporting events, whereas other people are talkative and sociable, even at funerals. These examples lend support to the trait position, which stresses that personality determines why people do what they do.

The obvious way to integrate these two points of view is to declare that both personality and situations interact to produce behavior, or

$$B = f(P \times S)$$

This formula suggests that behavior is a function of the *interaction* between personality traits and situational forces. Consider, for example, the trait of having a hot temper, a tendency to respond aggressively to minor frustrations. Acquaintances of a person high on this trait might be unaware of her short temper as long as they did not encounter her having to deal with a frustrating situation. The trait of having a short temper might be expressed only under the right situational conditions, such as in frustrating situations. If a person is frustrated by a situation (e.g., a vending machine takes the person's money but does not give him or her the product) *and* the person happens to have a quick temper (personality forces), then he or she will become upset and perhaps strike out at the source of the frustration (e.g., kick the vending machine repeatedly while cursing loudly). Any explanation of why such people get so upset would have to take into account both particular situations (e.g., frustration) and personality traits (e.g., hot temper). This point of view is called person–situation interaction, and it has become a fairly standard view in modern trait theory. Another way to view this is in the form of "If . . . , if . . . , then . . . ." statements (Shoda, Mischel, & Wright, 1994). For example, "**If** the situation is frustrating, and **if** the person has a hot temper, **then** aggression will be the result."

In the interactional view, differences among people are understood to make a difference only under the right circumstances. Some traits are specific to certain situations. Consider the trait of test anxiety. A young man might be generally easygoing and confident. However, under a set of *very specific* situational conditions, such as when he has to take an important exam, he becomes very anxious. In these particular circumstances, someone who is otherwise easygoing might become distressed, anxious, and quite upset. This example illustrates how certain very specific situations can provoke behavior that is otherwise out of character for the individual. This is referred to as **situational specificity**, in which a person acts in a specific way under particular circumstances implying that his or her behavior is caused by the situation.

Some trait–situation interactions are rare because the kinds of situations that elicit specific behaviors are themselves rare. For example, you would find it difficult to identify which of your classmates were high in courageousness. It would take a certain kind of *situation,* such as an earthquake, tornado, or an active shooter situation at your school, for you to find out just who is courageous and who is not.

The point is that personality traits interact with situational forces to produce behavior. Personality psychologists have given up the hope of predicting "all of the people all of the time" and have settled on the idea that they can predict "some of the people some of the time." For example, given the trait of anxiety, we might be able to predict who is likely to be anxious in some situations (e.g., evaluation situations, such as tests) but not anxious in other situations (e.g., when relaxed at home with family).

An interesting example of person X situation interaction is provided in a study by Debbie Moskowitz (1993). It has long been thought that the personality traits of dominance (the disposition to try to influence others) and friendliness (the degree to which a person is cordial and congenial) show large gender differences, with men being more dominant than women, and women being more friendly than men (Eagly, 1987). However, the study by Moskowitz showed that these traits interact with situation variables. Specifically, a person's level of dominance or friendliness may depend on who he or she is interacting with at the time, for example, whether the individual is interacting with a same-sex or opposite-sex person, and whether that person is someone known or a stranger. Moskowitz's (1993) study showed that women are more friendly than men, but only when they are interacting with other women; when interacting with opposite-sex strangers, women were not more friendly than men. As for dominance, the men were more dominant than women, but only when interacting with a same-sex friend; when interacting with opposite-sex strangers, the men were not more dominant than women. This study shows that who a person is interacting with will influence the expression of the personality traits of dominance and friendliness, and that this expression may or may not differ for men and women, depending on the social setting. A summary of her research on person–situation interaction, along with additional examples, can be found in Moskowitz and Fournier (2015).

Some situations are so strong, however, that nearly everyone behaves or reacts in similar ways. For example, in a study of emotional reactions to life events, Larsen, Diener, and Emmons (1986) were interested in finding out who tended to overreact emotionally to everyday events. Participants in this study kept a daily diary of life events for two months. They also rated their emotions each day. Based on a trait measure of emotional reactivity, these researchers were able to predict who would overreact to a minor or moderately stressful event, such as getting a flat tire, being stood up for a date, or having an outdoor event gets rained out. When *really* bad things happened, such as the death of a pet or loosing valuable possessions, virtually everyone reacted with strong emotions. Researchers have coined the term **strong situation** to refer to situations in which nearly all people react in similar ways.

Certain strong situations, such as funerals, religious services, and crowded elevators, seem to pull for uniformity of behavior. By contrast, when situations are weak or ambiguous, personality has its strongest influence on behavior. The Rorschach inkblot cards are a classic example of a weak or ambiguous situation. A person being asked to interpret these inkblots is, in effect, being asked to provide structure by describing what he or she sees in the inkblot. Many situations in real life are also somewhat ambiguous. When a stranger smiles at you, is it a friendly smile or is there a bit of a sneer in the smile? When a stranger looks you right in the eye and holds the stare for a bit too long, what does it mean? Many social situations, like these two, require us to interpret the actions, motives, and intentions of others. As with interpretations of inkblots, how we interpret social situations may reveal our personalities. For example, people with a Machiavellian character (e.g., the tendency to use others, to be manipulative and

Personality plays a role in determining which situations a person chooses to enter. For example, whether one chooses team activities for recreation, such as playing on a soccer team, or individual activities, such as long-distance running, is a function of one's level of extraversion. Studies show that extraverts prefer team activities and introverts prefer solitary activities for recreation.

Left: Peathegee Inc/Blend Images LLC; Right: Paolo Bona/Shutterstock

calculating) often think others are out to get them (Golding, 1978). Especially in ambiguous social interactions, Machiavellian persons are likely to be suspicious of others. This is a rather straightforward version of P × S interaction; not all people react the same to a given situation. Kihlstrom (2013) called this the static version of interaction, where personality traits and situational characteristics are thought of as separate influences that, when acting together, explain more than either situations or personality considered separately (i.e., the interaction of P × S is more than the sum of its parts).

Situational Selection

There are, however, more dynamic forms of P × S interaction, where the situation is not really separate from personality (Kihlstrom, 2013). In these dynamic versions, personality plays a role in constructing the situations that people find themselves in. We call this "dynamic" because the causal effects between personality and situations run in both directions. That is, situations are, in part, a function of personality just as much as personality is, in part, a function of situations.

There are at least three distinct kinds of dynamic P × S interactions, and they each refer to different ways that personality affects situations. These concepts come up in later chapters, so we'll spend some time on them now. The first form of dynamic interactionism is **situational selection,** the tendency to choose the situations in which one finds oneself (Ickes, Snyder, & Garcia, 1997; Snyder & Gangestad, 1982). In other words, people typically do not find themselves in random situations. Instead, they select the situations in which they will spend their time. Snyder (1983) states this idea concisely: "Quite possibly, one's choice of the settings in which to live one's life may reflect features of one's personality; an individual may choose to live his or her life in serious, reserved, and intellectual situations precisely because he or she is a serious, reserved, and thoughtful individual" (p. 510).

Some personality questionnaires assess personality by inquiring about the situations a person frequently selects; "Do you frequently attend crowded social events like parties or sporting events?" Researchers have examined whether specific personality traits predict how often people enter into specific situations (Diener, Larsen, & Emmons, 1984). These researchers had participants wear pagers so that the participants could be signaled electronically throughout the day for six weeks. They were paged twice each day, resulting in a sample of 84 occasions for each participant. Each time the pager went off, the participants had to complete a brief questionnaire. One question inquired about the kind of situation each participant was in when the pager went off. Over the 84 times when the participants were "caught," the researchers predicted that certain personality traits would predict how many times they were caught in certain situations. For example, the researchers found that the trait of need for achievement correlated with spending more time in work situations, the need for order with spending time in more familiar situations, and extraversion with choosing social forms of recreation (e.g., team sports, such as baseball or volleyball) more often than solitary sports, (e.g., long-distance running or swimming).

The idea that personality influences the kinds of situations in which people spend their time suggests that we can investigate personality by studying the choices people make in life. When given a choice, people typically choose situations that fit their personalities (Snyder & Gangestad, 1982). The personality effect does not have to be large to result in substantial life-outcome differences. For example, choosing to enter into work situations just 10 percent more of the time (e.g., studying 10 percent longer, or working 10 percent more hours) may result in very large differences in real-life outcomes, such as achieving better grades, a higher salary, or faster promotions. Think, for example, about how you choose to spend your free time and about whether your choices reflect your own personality, to a degree.

The relationship between persons and situations goes in both directions. So far, we have been emphasizing how personality affects situational selection. However, once in the situation, that situation can affect the person's personality. A study by psychologist Will Fleeson and colleagues (Fleeson, Malanos, & Achille, 2002) illustrates how situations can influence personality. It has long been known that the trait of extraversion is related to positive emotions. We discuss this more in Chapter 13, but for now it is important simply to know that a strong correlation exists between extraversion and frequently feeling high levels of positive emotions. In their study, Fleeson and colleagues had subjects come to the lab in groups of three to participate in a group discussion. They were randomly assigned to an "introverted" or an "extraverted" condition. Instructions for the extraverted condition emphasized that they should behave in a talkative, bold, and energetic manner for the group discussion. Instructions for the introverted condition emphasized that they should behave in a reserved, compliant, and unadventurous manner for the group discussion. They were then asked to have a discussion of either the 10 most important items needed after an airplane crash or to come up with 10 possible solutions to the parking problem on their campus.

During the discussion, observers rated how positive each participant appeared. Also, following the discussion, each participant self-reported how positive he or she felt during the discussion. For both of these variables—observed positivity and self-reported positive feelings—the participants assigned to the extraverted condition were substantially higher than those assigned to the introverted condition. Moreover, this effect did not depend on the person's actual levels of trait extraversion. This study shows that being in an extraverted situation (being with a group of energetic, talkative people) can raise a person's level of positive affect. The study clearly illustrates that, when it comes to person × situation interactions, situations can influence persons just as much as persons can influence situations.

Evocation

The second form of dynamic person–situation interaction is **evocation**, the idea that certain personality traits may evoke specific responses from the environment. For example, people who are disagreeable and manipulative may evoke certain reactions in others, such as hostility and avoidance. In other words, people may evoke or create their own environments by eliciting certain responses from others. Consider the case of a male patient who had trouble sustaining relationships with women, such that he was divorced three times (Wachtel, 1973). He complained to his therapist that every woman with whom he became involved turned out to be bad-tempered, vicious, and spiteful. He complained that his relationships started out satisfying but always ended with the women becoming angry and leaving him. Wachtel (1973) speculated that the *man* must have been doing something to *evoke* this response from the women in his life.

The idea of evocation is similar to the idea of transference, to be discussed in Chapter 9 on psychoanalysis. Transference occurs when a patient in psychoanalysis recreates, with the analyst, the interpersonal problems he or she is having with significant others. In doing so, the patient may evoke in the therapist the reactions and feelings that he or she typically evokes in other persons. Malcolm (1981) reported on a male psychoanalyst who found one female patient to be particularly boring. The analyst could hardly stay awake during the therapy sessions because the patient and her problems seemed so dull and trivial to him. After experiencing this reaction for a few weeks, however, the analyst realized that the patient was making him feel bored, just as she made other men in her life feel bored. She made herself dull, he concluded, to avoid the attentions of men and drive them away. However, she was in therapy, in part, because she complained of being lonely.! This case illustrates how people can evoke reactions in others—creating and re-creating certain kinds of social situations over and over again in their everyday lives.

Manipulation

A third form of dynamic person–situation interaction is **manipulation,** which can be defined as the various means by which people influence the behavior of others. Manipulation is the intentional use of certain tactics to coerce, influence, or change others. Manipulation changes the social situation. Manipulation differs from selection in that selection involves choosing existing environments, whereas manipulation entails altering those environments already inhabited. Individuals differ in the tactics of manipulation they use. Researchers have found, for example, that some individuals use a charm tactic—complimenting others, acting warm and caring, and doing favors to influence others. Other people use a manipulation tactic sometimes referred to as the silent treatment, ignoring or failing to respond to the other person. A third tactic is coercion, which consists of making demands, yelling, criticizing, cursing, and threatening the other to get what one wants (Buss et al., 1987). We discuss the interpersonal aspects of manipulation tactics in more detail in Chapter 15.

Aggregation

We've seen how their debate with Mischel led trait psychologists to appreciate that behavior is an outcome of the interaction between personality traits and situations. Another important lesson learned by trait psychologists is the value of aggregation when it comes to measuring personality traits. **Aggregation** is the process of adding up, or averaging, several single observations, resulting in a better (i.e., more reliable) measure of a personality trait than a single observation of behavior. This approach usually provides psychologists with a better measure of a personality trait than does using a single observation. Consider the concept of batting average, which is seen as a measure of a baseball player's batting ability (a trait). It turns out that batting average is not a very good predictor of whether or not a player will get a hit during any *single* time at bat. In fact, psychologist Abelson (1985) analyzed single batting occasions over the whole season. He found that batting average accounted for only .3 percent of the variance in getting a hit. This is a remarkably poor relationship, so why do people pay such close attention to batting average, and why do players with a good batting average earn so much more money? Because what matters is how a player performs *over the long run,* over an entire season. This is the principle of aggregation in action.

To draw another analogy, let's say you decide to marry someone, in part, because of that person's cheerful disposition. Clearly, there will be days when your partner is not going to be cheerful. However, what matters to you is your partner's behavior *over the long term* (i.e., how cheerful your spouse will be in general) and not his or her mood on any given day or occasion.

As another example of aggregation, imagine taking an intelligence test that has only one item. Do you think this one-item test would be a good measure of your overall intelligence? You would be right if you concluded that a single question was probably not a very accurate or fair measure of overall intelligence. A related example might be if the instructor in your personality course were to decide that your entire grade for a course would be determined by asking you only one question on the final exam. Surely one question could not possibly measure your breadth of knowledge of the course material. Single questions or single observations are rarely good measures of anything. This is really worth repeating: Single questions or single observations of behavior are rarely good measures of any personality trait or ability.

Recall the Hartshorne and May (1928) study in which the researchers measured honesty by assessing whether or not a child cheated during a game on one occasion during summer camp. Do you think this one-item measure of honesty was an accurate reflection of the participants' true levels of honesty? It probably was not. This is likely the main reason why Hartshorne and May found such small correlations among their various measures of honesty (i.e., because they were all based on single observations).

Personality psychologist Seymour Epstein (1924-2016) published a series of papers (1979, 1980, 1983) showing that aggregating several questions or observations results in better trait measures. Longer tests (or multiple observations) are more reliable than shorter ones (reliability was introduced in Chapter 2) and hence are better measures of traits. If we want to know how conscientious a person is, we should observe many conscientious-related behaviors (e.g., how neat he or she is, how punctual they are, whether they use a calendar to schedule their life) on many occasions and aggregate, or average, the observations. Any single behavior on any single occasion may be influenced by all sorts of extenuating circumstances unrelated to personality. But the average, or trend, of the person's behavior may be the best indicator of his or her personality. Most personality psychologists today view traits as average tendencies.

Imagine that a trait psychologist is developing a questionnaire to measure how helpful, caring, and conscientious respondents are. She includes the following item on the questionnaire: "How often in the past few years have you stopped to help a person whose car was stuck in the snow?" Imagine further that you live in a place where it rarely snows. You answer "never," even though you are generally a helpful person. Now imagine being asked a whole set of questions, such as how often you donate money to charity, participate in blood donation programs, and do volunteer work in your community. Your answers to that whole series of questions provide a better indicator of your true level of helpfulness than your answer to any single question. This is why aggregation is important.

Psychologists "rediscovered" aggregation in the 1980s. Charles Spearman (1863-1945), an influential British psychologist, published a paperback in 1910, explaining that tests with more items are generally more reliable than tests with fewer items.

Spearman provided a formula—now called the Spearman-Brown prophesy formula—for determining precisely how much a test's reliability would increase as it was made longer. Although this formula appeared in all the major textbooks on measurement and statistics, personality psychologists seemed to have forgotten about the principle of aggregation until Epstein (1980, 1983) published his reminders in the early 1980s. Since then, other researchers have provided ample demonstrations of how the principle of aggregation works to increase the strength of correlations between measures of personality and measures of behavior. For example, according to a study by Diener and Larsen (1984), measures of activity level on one day correlated with activity level on another day at a correlation of only .08. However, when activity level was averaged over a three-week period and then correlated with activity level averaged over another three-week period, that correlation went up to .66. Clearly, aggregation provides a more stable and reliable measure of a person's average standing on a trait than any single observation can.

Besides being an important measurement principle, the notion of aggregation has profound implications for how we conceptualize personality traits and their effects in our daily lives. The biggest implication is that traits are really about averages, not about what a person does at any given point in time. In other words, traits are best at predicting trends or averages, and will never be good at predicting single behaviors on single occasions. If we say a person is punctual, for example, it means they are usually on time when they have an appointment. However, from time to time they might show up late (e.g., if they got a flat tire on the way to the appointment). We will never know ahead of time if they will be on time for the appointment tomorrow (on one occasion), but our best guess, knowing they are a punctual person, would be to predict that they will be on time. We would be wrong on those occasions when something happens to disrupt their schedule. Nevertheless, what matters most is a person's average tendency. When we are writing a letter of recommendation, for example, we might say that this person is highly reliable and punctual, ignoring the few occasions they showed up late through no fault of their own. Traits are about average tendencies, not about what happens on any given occasion.

The notion of traits as **density distributions of states** was developed by psychologist Will Fleeson (e.g., 2001, 2004) to understand the implications of aggregation for how we think about personality traits. Take the trait of extraversion, for example, which is associated with frequently engaging in specific behaviors like talking a lot, acting vigorously, being enthusiastic, etc. Focus on one of those behaviors, say talking, and imagine measuring that by outfitting 100 people with wearable micro-recorders that assesses how much each person talked during each waking hour for a month straight. For each person, you could count how many words they spoke each hour, and plot a frequency distribution of their talking behavior. Figure 4.2 illustrates two hypothetical density distributions of talking behavior from such a study. Person A's distribution in this figure has a lower mean level of talking behavior than Person B's, so we say that Person B is likely higher on the trait of extraversion (they talk more, and more frequently). However, Person A has some hours during this period when they actually talked quite a bit, even more than Person B's mean level. In other words, viewing each persons' talking behavior as a distribution illustrates that people vary quite a bit over time; sometimes a person is talkative, sometimes they are not. But what *really* matters is their mean level, how much they talk on average. Implicit in this is the acknowledgment that a person will sometimes behave below, and sometimes above, their own mean level on any given trait. Situations likely explain much of this within-person variability around their own mean level, whereas personality traits likely determine a person's mean level over time (Fleeson & Law, 2015). Viewing traits as density distributions of states over time in a person's daily life acknowledges that in real-life people are variable, their behavior varies from moment to moment, hour to hour, and day to day. Nevertheless, within this variability is the person's true mean, his or her average tendency, and the trait

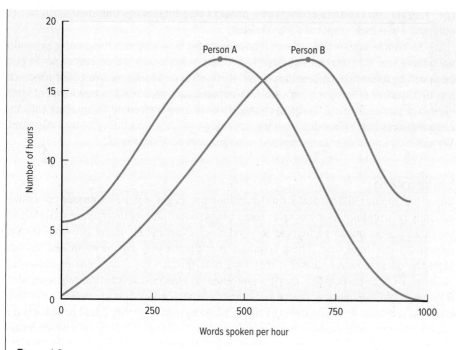

Figure 4.2

Two hypothetical density distributions of talking behavior showing differences in mean level. Note, however, a great deal of overlap, with the more talkative person (B) sometimes talking less than the less talkative person's (A) mean level, and vice versa.

conception is really about average tendencies. This is similar to the set-point concept in body weight; a person's weight fluctuates day to day, but it fluctuates around their set-point, or average level, to which he or she typically returns.

Measurement Issues

More than any other approach to personality, the trait approach relies on self-report questionnaires to measure personality. Although trait psychologists can use other measurement methods (e.g., reports from peers, behavioral observation), self-report questionnaires are the most frequently used method for measuring traits (Craik, 1986). Personality psychologists assume that people differ from each other in the *amounts* of various traits they possess, so the key measurement issue is determining *how much* of a particular trait a person possesses.

Traits are represented as dimensions along which people differ from each other. One of the most efficient ways to assess people's standing on any personality trait dimension is simply to ask them several questions about their behaviors, thoughts, and emotions. If the right questions are asked, as the trait view holds, an accurate

Personality tests are frequently administered in large group settings. In such settings, some people may be careless or even fake their responses. Psychologists have developed ways of detecting faking and carelessness in the answers from individual test takers.

Hero Images/Getty Images

(i.e., reliable and valid) assessment of a person's standing on the trait dimension will be obtained when their responses are averaged.

As compelling as this view of trait assessment is, it assumes that people generally are willing and able to report accurately on their behavior. However, some people may be unwilling to disclose information about themselves or may be motivated for some reason to distort or otherwise falsify their self-reports, such as during an employment interview or a parole hearing. Trait psychologists have long concerned themselves with the circumstances that affect the accuracy, reliability, validity, and utility of trait measures. We will now consider some important measurement considerations.

Carelessness

Some participants filling out a trait questionnaire might not be motivated to answer carefully or truthfully. For example, some colleges and universities require introductory psychology students to participate in psychology experiments, many of which involve personality questionnaires. These volunteer participants may not be motivated to complete the questionnaires carefully; they may rush through the questionnaire, answering randomly. Other participants may be motivated to answer correctly but might accidentally invalidate their answer sheets. For example, when participants are asked to put their answers on optical scanning sheets by filling in circles with a number 2 lead pencil, it is not uncommon for participants to inadvertently neglect to fill in a circle or two, which means that all subsequent answers are then out of order. Another problem arises when, for some reason, the participant is not reading the questions carefully but is nevertheless providing answers. Perhaps the participant has difficulty reading, is tired, or even is hallucinating.

A common method for detecting these problems is to embed an **infrequency scale** within the set of questionnaire items. An infrequency scale contains items that all or almost all people will answer in a particular way. Using such items, if a person endorses more than one or two of these items in the "wrong" direction, then his or her test is flagged as suspicious. For example, on the Personality Research Form (Jackson & Messick, 1967), the infrequency scale contains items such as the following: "I do not believe that wood really burns," "I make all my own clothes and shoes," and "Whenever I walk up stairs, I always do so on my hands." These questions are answered "False" by over 95 percent of the people in samples from the United States and Canada. If a participant answers more than one or two of these items as "True," we may begin to suspect that *none* of his or her other answers are believable.

Another technique used to detect carelessness is to include duplicate questions spaced far apart in the questionnaire. The psychologist can then determine the number of times the participant answered identical questions with different responses. If this happens often, the psychologist might suspect carelessness or another problem that invalidates the person's answers.

Faking on Questionnaires

Faking involves the motivated distortion of answers on a questionnaire. When personality questionnaires are used to make important decisions about people's lives (e.g., hire them for a job, promote them, decide that they are not guilty by reason of insanity, or allow prisoners to be paroled), then there is always the possibility of faking. Some people may be motivated to "fake good" in order to appear to be better off or better adjusted than they really are. Others may be motivated to "fake bad" in order to appear to be worse off or more maladjusted than they really are. For example, a worker suing a

	The person being tested really is being . . .	
	Honest	Dishonest
Honest	Correct	False positive "incorrect"
Dishonest	False negative "incorrect"	Correct

The psychologist concludes he or she is . . .

Two ways to make a mistake when deciding whether a person was faking his or her responses to a personality questionnaire.

company for mental anguish caused by a poor working conditions might be motivated to appear very distressed to the court-appointed psychologist.

Questionnaire developers have devised ways to detect faking good and faking bad. In constructing the 16 Personality Factor questionnaire, for example, Cattell, Eber, and Tatsouoka (1970) had groups of participants complete the questionnaire under specific instructions. One group of participants was instructed to fake good, to appear to be as well-adjusted as possible. Another group of participants was instructed to fake bad, to try to appear as maladjusted as possible. The data for these two groups were then used to generate a "faking good profile" and a "faking bad profile." The data from real participants can then be compared with those in these two faking profiles, and the psychologist can calculate just how much a person's responses fit the profile of the groups asked to fake their answers. This approach offers psychologists an imperfect but nevertheless empirical method for determining the likelihood that a person is faking his or her responses to the questionnaire.

A study of military cadets applying for pilot training clearly illustrates that, when an important outcome is based on personality scores, people are motivated to "fake good" while answering the questions (Galic, Jerneic, & Kovacic, 2012). These researchers showed in samples of military cadets applying to pilot school, that the applicant's scores were similar to scores obtained by persons who were instructed to fake the most desirable responses. These authors warn that whenever important decisions are based on responses to questionnaires, care must be taken to account for desirable responding, or "faking good," on the part of the test takers.

There are two ways for psychologists to make a mistake when seeking to distinguish between genuine and faked responses. They may conclude that a truthful person was faking and reject that person's data (called a **false negative**). Or they may decide that a person who was faking was actually telling the truth (called a **false positive**). Psychologists do not know for certain how well their faking scales perform when it comes to minimizing the percentages of false positives and false negatives. Because of this problem of undetected faking, many psychologists are suspicious of results based solely on self-report questionnaire measures of personality.

Beware of Barnum Statements in Personality Test Interpretations

"We have something for everyone."

–P. T. Barnum

Barnum statements are generalities—statements that could apply to anyone. In the 2021 movie "Nightmare Alley" Bradley Cooper plays a carnival mentalist who convinces people he knows them personally by using what we would call Barnum statements (e.g., "you are comfortable being alone, but also enjoy socializing with your friends.") When Barnum statements appear in personality testing feedback (e.g., "you value your friends") people tend to accept such statements as applying to them personally and hence are believable. Barnum statements can account for the popularity and believability of astrology predictions, which are very popular online (e.g., Horoscope.com). For example, one of the authors recently received the following horoscope: "You sometimes have doubts about whether you have done the right thing" and "Although you are able to deal with confrontation in a pinch, you typically like to avoid it if you can." While these statements appeared believable to the author, they are nevertheless Barnum statements because they apply to just about anyone. People read such general statements and think, "Yes, that's me all right," when in fact such general statements really could apply to most people. Such overly general statements don't really provide specific information about *this* person.

Personality test interpreters also sometimes offer interpretations that consist of Barnum statements. To illustrate this, one of the authors of this textbook completed an online version of the Meyers-Briggs Type Indicator (MBTI), a very popular personality questionnaire. He then submitted his answers to two different online interpretation services to get feedback about his personality. Reading the results of the first interpretation, he felt it had him right: "You advance toward good and retreat from evil; you hate to miss out on what is going on around you; you always try to tell the truth to those around you; you strive to be authentic and genuine, and you communicate well with others." The second interpretation also sounded accurate: "You want to be liked and admired by others; you are interested in new ideas; at times your attention span can be short; you dislike bureaucracy."

These two interpretations sounded personally relevant and accurate to the author who took the test. The only problem was that he filled in his answers to the questionnaire at random. That is, the author of this book did not read the questions, but merely clicked "true" or "false" randomly while taking the MBTI. How then did these test interpretations seem to apply so personally and directly to him? Read the interpretations again and you will see that they are Barnum statements. They could apply to just about anyone.

This example is not meant to suggest that the MBTI is not a good test. Recall that these interpretations were obtained from free online services. So this example could also be an illustration of the advice "you get what you pay for." Most reliable test interpretation services charge a fee for this service.

Reliable test interpretation services typically make statements that are quantitative and/or that provide information about a person's standing on a trait relative to others. So, for example, an interpretation might state: "Your scores on extraversion put you in the highest, or most extraverted, 10% of the population." Or the statement might refer to research results on the correlates of extraversion score, such as: "Persons with extraversion scores such as yours are found to be extremely satisfied in careers that involved frequent social contacts, such as salespersons, teachers, or public relations work." To see what specific and quantitative feedback on a personality questionnaire looks like, you can take a version of Big Five questionnaire online, and receive feedback on your results for each of the five traits.

Reliable test interpretation services also typically include checks for careless responding, as discussed earlier in this chapter. They typically provide an assessment of how suspicious one should be regarding the validity of a person's answers to the questions. Neither of the free test interpretation services used in the above MBTI example provided such checks, and so did not detect that the answers submitted were random. A few repeated items or some **infrequency scale** items would have quickly detected and flagged the author's random answers as suspicious.

So far we have discussed some of the theoretical and measurement issues in trait psychology. Trait psychologists do not only concern themselves with these somewhat abstract issues. Trait psychology also has some real-world applications. We turn now to a consideration of the practical uses to which personality trait measures have been put.

Personality and Prediction

Personality measures have a long history of use in industry and government. They are used in the federal and state prison systems to make decisions about inmates. They are also widely used in industry to match people with particular jobs, to help screen people for employment, and to select people for promotion. An employer may feel that emotional stability is a requirement for a specific job (e.g., firefighter) or that the personality trait of honesty is especially important (e.g., for a clerk in a jewelry store or for a driver of a money delivery truck). Other jobs may require strong organizational skills, the ability to work in a distracting environment, or to be a cooperative team member. Whether someone does well in employment settings may be determined, in part, by whether the individual's personality traits mesh with the job requirements. In short, personality traits may *predict* who is likely to do well in a particular job.

Applications of Personality Testing in the Workplace

In an increasingly competitive business environment, many employers resort to employment testing to improve their workforce. The majority of the Fortune 100 companies use some form of employment selection that includes psychological testing. A survey by the American Management Association revealed that 44 percent of its responding members used testing to screen or select employees. Although cognitive ability testing (e.g., comprehension, reading speed) is the most commonly used form of psychological testing in the workplace, personality tests are being used more and more frequently.

Personality measures are useful in work settings to the degree that they predict performance at, or satisfaction with, a particular job. For example, Harris (2019) reports that sales managers with higher scores on the trait of assertiveness achieved an average of 35% more sales growth than managers who were less assertive. In addition to using personality in screening and selecting employees for specific jobs, personality is starting to be used in organizations in efforts to change corporate culture, build inclusiveness, in coaching employees, and in leadership development and work-life balance programs.

In the last few decades, the major uses of personality assessment in the workplace fall into three main categories: personnel selection, integrity testing, and concerns over negligent hiring.

Personnel Selection

Employers use personality tests to select people especially suitable for a specific job. For example, an insurance company might use a measure of extraversion–introversion to select applicants high on extraversion for a sales job so that their characteristics match successful incumbents in their sales department. Alternatively, the employer may want to use personality assessments to deselect, or screen out, people with specific traits. For example, a police department might use the MMPI or a similar test to screen out applicants who have high levels of emotional instability or psychopathology. A number of personality tests and applications can aid employers in **personnel selection.**

Integrity Testing

Personality tests that assess honesty or integrity are the most widely used form of personality assessment in the business world today. They are commonly used in the retail and financial services industries in selecting people for entry-level jobs where the employee handles money or merchandise in an unsupervised setting. You might think a lie detector test would be useful, but these can no longer be used in the private-sector workplace (see the Closer Look box on "Lying, Lie Detection, and Integrity Testing"). Self-report questionnaires measuring integrity are used instead.

A Closer Look   Lying, Lie Detection, and Integrity Testing

Throughout history, employers have been concerned about employee theft. Such thefts could be avoided or at least minimized if there were a way to tell whether a person was generally honest or dishonest before hiring him or her. Over two centuries ago, the Chinese developed a test to determine whether a person was dishonest. The test consisted of asking the suspect a question, waiting for the answer, and then placing rice powder in the suspect's mouth. If the suspect could not swallow the rice powder, it was viewed as a sure sign that he or she was lying. This may sound like superstition, but if you think of the dry mouth that usually accompanies nervousness, then there might be some face validity to this early lie detection technique.

The modern lie detector, a polygraph, is a mechanical device that relies on psychophysiological measures, such as heart rate, respiration, and skin conductance (see Chapter 7). The use of physiological measures for lie detection started early in the 1900s in the United States. The idea behind this approach is that physiological measures

may be useful in detecting the nervous arousal (e.g., guilt and anxiety) that often accompanies lying. The origin of the modern lie detection machine is shrouded in mystery. Some attribute it to a police officer from Berkeley, California, named Larson, who constructed the prototype of the multichannel polygraph between 1917 and 1921 and also published a manual on how to use the machine. Others trace the idea of using psychophysiological recordings—in particular, systolic blood pressure—to measure

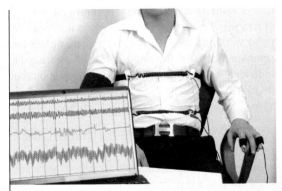

Polygraph exams were widely used in employment screening until they were banned by Congress in 1988 from use in private-sector employment settings. The government, however, still uses polygraphs in employment screening as well as periodic honesty verification of persons in sensitive positions. In fact, the U.S. government runs several training institutes that certify persons to administer standard polygraph exams.
Andrey Burmakin/Shutterstock

deception in laboratory and legal settings to William Moulton Marston, who worked on this problem while he was a graduate student at Harvard University from 1915 to 1921. The lie detector gained widespread attention

in the 1930s when it was introduced in the trial of Bruno Hauptman, who was accused of murdering the Lindbergh baby. Businesses began using the polygraph widely in the 1970s.

The polygraph was originally designed to detect guilt reactions that arise from denying specific criminal acts. However, many employers began to use polygraph and other so-called lie detector tests to screen potential employees for general *honesty*. That is, the original purpose was to assess a state (guilt), whereas the polygraph was often pressed into usage to assess a trait (honesty). At any rate, participants were connected to these devices and asked various incriminating questions, such as whether they had ever taken anything that did not belong to them. If they showed any signs of nervousness or arousal (e.g., increased heart rate or shallower breathing), they might not have been hired. Employers also routinely used lie detector tests to question employees who were already on the job. Fast-food chains were among the largest users of polygraph tests in employment settings during this era (1970–88). Managers hired polygraphers to connect employees to these devices, then ask questions such as whether they had taken any hamburgers or money in the past few months. If the polygraphs indicated any signs of nervousness, the employee might have been fired.

Through the 1970s and 1980s, more than 3 million polygraph tests were administered each year in the United States alone (Murphy, 1995). If you went into a large class of college students in the 1980s and asked if anyone had ever taken a polygraph exam, it was common to see at least a couple of hands go up for every hundred or so persons. Most said that they took the polygraph test as part of an employment screening procedure, often when applying for jobs in fast-food outlets.

A scientific evaluation of the polygraph as a lie detector was undertaken in 1983 by the U.S. federal government's Office of Technology Assessment. Its report concluded that there was no such device as a lie detector. Technically, this is true, as the polygraph detects physiological arousal, and sometimes lying is not accompanied by physiological arousal. In addition, sometimes physiological arousal is not accompanied by lying. The government evaluators also concluded that none of the methods used for lie detection were foolproof and that there were several effective ways to beat the device. Moreover, the polygraph's use in employment settings to screen for honesty may have resulted more in employment discrimination than in honesty detection.

In 1988, the U.S. Congress banned the use of the polygraph for most employment purposes in the private sector. Interestingly, the government still uses polygraphs for employee selection in several government service branches, such as the Secret Service, the CIA, the FBI, the DEA, Customs, and even the Postal Service. The government also maintains several polygraph schools, where people go to be trained in the use of the polygraph. In the private sector, however, the use of the polygraph in employment settings is highly restricted at this time.

This leaves the private-sector employer with no mechanical means for detecting whether potential employees are honest. However, since the ban on polygraphs, many personality test publishing companies have developed and promoted questionnaire measures to use in place of the polygraph (DeAngelis, 1991). These questionnaires, called **integrity tests**, are designed to assess whether a person is generally honest, trustworthy, reliable, helpful, and dependable. Many of these tests are reliable and valid and so may be legally used for employment screening (DeAngelis, 1991).

One review of integrity questionnaires (Ones & Viswesvaran, 1998) concluded that the measures can predict the following negative workplace criteria: (1) supervisors' ratings of employees' dishonesty, (2) applicants who are likely to get caught stealing once hired, (3) applicants who have a criminal history, and (4) applicants who are likely to commit theft in an anonymous testing situation. Another review examined 28 studies on workplace absenteeism and found that personality-based integrity tests reliably predicted higher rates of absenteeism, and therefore could be used to screen out job applicants who might have more unexcused absences from work (Ones, Viswesvaran, & Schmidt, 2003). A more recent review (Van Iddekinge et al., 2012) found that integrity tests (reverse scored, so high scores mean less integrity) correlated in the range of .26 to .32 with counterproductive work behaviors such as stealing from the workplace, harassing co-workers, and loafing. Because Integrity tests are widely used in industry, the professional Society for Industrial and Organizational Psychology contains useful information about these tests on their website.

Annual economic losses to American business from counterproductive work behaviors (e.g., theft, loafing, harassment) are estimated at between $15 billion and $25 billion per year. Because of this, many employers are interested in any technique that could detect those job candidates low on integrity during preemployment screening. There are two kinds of integrity tests—**overt and covert integrity tests.** Both are based on self-report. Overt measures ask about past counterproductive workplace behaviors, such as theft and absenteeism, as well as general criminal history, childhood delinquency, or school disciplinary problems. They are called overt measures because they ask directly about bad behaviors. Covert measures, on the other hand, do not directly ask about counterproductive behaviors (hence are covert), but rather assess personality traits that are correlated with counterproductive work behaviors. Of the Big Five traits, conscientiousness has the strongest correlations (negatively) with workplace problems (Berry, Sackett, & Wiemann, 2007), and so covert integrity measures will include many conscientiousness items. Agreeableness and Emotional Stability are also correlated (again negatively) with workplace problems (Viswesvaran & Ones, 2016), and so covert integrity tests also include items about getting along with others (agreeableness) and not being irritable and anxiety- or anger-prone (emotional stability). In U.S. corporations, today there is a growing emphasis on integrity and ethics in the workplace, and using integrity tests to help make hiring decisions is one way personality psychology is having an impact on society.

Concerns over Negligent Hiring

A third reason some employers use personality testing arises from the fact that should an employee assault a customer or another coworker on the job, the employer may be held accountable in a court case. In such a case, the employer could be charged with **negligent hiring,** that is, when an employer fails to verify that a candidate employee may represent a danger in the workplace, that is, unstable or prone to violence. With cases of negligent hiring now being tried in the courts of most states, employers are defending themselves against a growing number of suits seeking compensation for crimes committed by their employees. Such cases hinge on whether the employer should have reasonably discovered dangerousness ahead of time, before hiring such a person into a position where he or she posed a threat to others. Personality testing may provide evidence that the employer did in fact try to reasonably investigate an applicant's fitness for the workplace, and thus lessen the employer's exposure to a negligent hiring charge.

Legal Issues in Personality Testing in Employment Settings

Legal issues surrounding the use of personality and other tests in employment settings can be traced to the Civil Rights Act of 1964, which barred racial discrimination in public places, including theaters, restaurants, hotels, and polling places. **Title VII of the Civil Rights Act of 1964** also required employers to provide equal employment opportunities to all persons. The first test of the Civil Rights Act in employment law occurred in the case of *Griggs v. Duke Power.* Prior to 1964, the Duke Power Company had used clearly discriminatory practices in hiring and work assignment, including barring Blacks from certain jobs. After passage of the Civil Rights Act, Duke Power instituted various requirements for such jobs, including passing certain aptitude tests. The effect was to perpetuate discrimination. In 1971 the Supreme Court ruled that the seemingly neutral testing "aptitude" practices used by Duke Power were unacceptable because they operated to maintain discrimination. Moreover, the court ruled that any selection procedure could not produce disparate impact for a group protected by the act (e.g., racial groups, women). This Supreme Court decision put the burden of proof on the employer to demonstrate that selection procedures, including aptitude and personality measures, were not discriminatory, that is, did not produce disparate impact on specific groups.

The next major event in employee selection occurred in 1978 when the Department of Labor released the **Uniform Guidelines on Employee Selection Procedures.** These guidelines were widely adopted and are still in use today by the Department of Justice. The purpose of the guidelines is to provide a set of principles for employee selection that meet the requirements of all federal laws, especially those that prohibit discrimination on the basis of race, color, religion, gender, sexual orientation, or national origin. They provide details on the proper use of personality tests and other selection procedures in employment settings. The guidelines define discrimination and adverse impact, describe how to evaluate and document the validity evidence for tests, and instruct employers on what records to keep.

Another important legal case in employment law is that of **Ward's Cove Packing Co. v. Atonio**. Ward's Cove Packing Co. was a salmon cannery operating in Alaska. Production line jobs at the cannery were filled predominantly by non-Whites, whereas administrative, or white-collar, jobs were filled predominantly with White workers. Virtually all of the administrative jobs paid more than cannery line positions. In 1974 the non-White cannery workers started legal action against the company, alleging that a variety of the company's hiring and promotion practices—for example, nepotism, a rehire preference, a lack of objective hiring criteria, and separate hiring channels—were responsible for the racial stratification of the workforce. The claim was advanced under the disparate impact portion of Title VII of the Civil Rights Act. In 1989 the Supreme Court decided that employees filing discrimination lawsuits must expose specific hiring practices that led to disparities in the workplace. However, the Court also decided that even if the employees can prove discrimination, the hiring practices may still be considered legal if they serve "legitimate business goals of the employer."

The *Ward's Cove* case watered down the effects of the *Griggs* decision and allowed companies a loophole to continue with discriminatory employment practices, as long as they could prove such practices served the needs of the company. For example, if a test excluded most Black applicants, yet the company could prove that the test was job-relevant, then the company could continue using this test. This situation prompted Congress to pass the Civil Rights Act of 1991, which contained several important modifications to Title VII of the original act. The 1991 act expanded protected groups to include those based on race, color, religion, gender, or national origin. The new act also prohibited the use of different cutoff scores based on race or gender in employment tests (see the A Closer Look box titled "The Female Underprediction Effect"). Most important, however, the new act shifted the burden of proof onto the employer by requiring that it must prove a close connection between disparate impact and the ability to actually perform the job in question.

Another important case, one with clear personality connections, was the case of **Price Waterhouse v. Hopkins,** also decided in 1989 by the Supreme Court. Ann Hopkins was a senior manager at an accounting firm, who was being considered for promotion to partner. Following its usual promotion practice, the firm asked each existing partner to evaluate Ms. Hopkins. Many of the evaluations came in as negative, criticizing her interpersonal skills and accusing her of being abrasive and too masculine for a woman (they felt she needed to wear more makeup, to walk and talk more femininely). She sued the company, charging that it had discriminated against her on the basis of sex, on the theory that her evaluations had been based on sexual stereotyping. The case eventually rose to the Supreme Court. Price Waterhouse acknowledged discrimination but maintained that sexual stereotypes were just one factor and argued that there were other reasons to deny partnership to Hopkins. They argued that even without any sex discrimination, Hopkins still would have been passed over.

The other legal issue, the one that won the case for Hopkins, was that she had been passed over for partner because of gender stereotyping within the company. In essence, she argued, the voting partners compared her to a cultural stereotype of how a woman is supposed to behave in the workplace, and they decided that Hopkins did not fit that image. The American Psychological Association joined the case and provided

A Closer Look

Conscientiousness Explains the Female Underprediction Effect

If you are reading this book for a college course, then a selection situation you are familiar with is selection into college. Most colleges and universities select students for admission based, in part, on entrance exam scores, typically the SAT or ACT. These tests are thought to predict performance in college and so colleges and universities believe they are useful for selecting students who will likely to do well if admitted.

College entrance exams typically predict college grade point average (GPA) in the range of .30 to .45 correlations between SAT scores and college grade point average or GPA (College Board Online, 2009; Dahlke, Sackett, & Kuncel, 2019). In a recent analysis of students at Washington University in St. Louis, for example, one of the authors found that SAT scores correlated .33 with first-semester GPA among freshmen. Hence, we conclude that SAT scores do have a modest degree of predictive validity when it comes to forecasting grades in college.

However, the prediction of college GPA from admissions test scores works a bit differently for women than for men. It turns out that admissions scores underpredict GPA for women relative to men. That is, women tend to attain higher college GPAs than men with the same admissions tests scores. This has been known for over 30 years and has come to be called the **female underprediction effect** (Hyde & Kling, 2001). A review of research studies found this underprediction effect for women in 130 separate samples containing approximately 500,000 college students

(Fischer, Schult, & Hell, 2013). On average, women earned GPAs that were .24 points higher (on the standard 4-point GPA scale) than men with the same admissions test scores. Other studies also show that the validity of the SAT to predict college grades is different for men and women (Dahlke et al., 2019). A 2019 report by the College Board (publisher of the SAT) also highlights how its own test underpredicts college GPA for women compared to men.

Does the female underprediction effect mean that entrance exams are biased? Not necessarily. It may mean that some other variable, other than what is measured by the SAT/ACT, is contributing to women generally outperforming men with the same SAT/ACT scores in college. Any variable that women score higher on, and that also predicts college grades, could account for the underprediction effect. Researchers have identified conscientiousness as a likely candidate, because it significantly predicts college GPA, independent of what is measured by SAT/ACT, and is a trait that is higher in women than men (Noftle & Robins, 2007).

The personality trait of conscientiousness refers to being industrious, organized, diligent, thorough, and self-disciplined. Moreover, in college age samples, women are slightly higher on conscientiousness than men. Does this slight edge in conscientiousness account for women doing better than men in college, better than one would expect from their entrance exams alone? Several large and well-done studies now provide strong evidence that the female underprediction effect is accounted

for, in large part, by the personality trait of conscientiousness.

One study (Kling, Noftle, & Robins, 2013) examined three large samples of college students and found the female underprediction effect in each. When the researchers then entered students' scores on conscientiousness into the prediction equation, those scores mediated the link between gender and the underprediction of college grades. Another study (Keiser et al., 2016) reported similar results in two large samples of college students; the female underprediction effect is reduced substantially when conscientiousness is included in prediction of college GPA. These studies show that: (1) women are higher in conscientiousness than men, (2) students who are more conscientious earn higher grades in college, and (3) the higher conscientiousness of women account, in part, for why they do better in college than expected based on their entrance exam scores alone.

This research clearly shows that academic outcomes (i.e., GPA) are influenced by cognitive factors *and* personality factors. This is why universities and colleges consider a wide array of information about each applicant, in addition to his or her ACT or SAT test scores. For example, many colleges consider letters of reference, personal statements, extracurricular activities, leadership positions, and pro-social activities. It may well be that these other pieces of information reflect, in part, an applicant's personality, especially his or her level of conscientiousness.

expert evidence that such stereotypes do exist and that women who deviate from the cultural expectations are often penalized for violating these standards. The Supreme Court accepted the argument that gender stereotyping does exist and that it can create a bias against women in the workplace that is not permissible. By court order, Ann Hopkins was made a full partner in her accounting firm. She went on to describe her long court case, both from a legal and personal perspective, in a book titled *So Ordered: Making Partner the Hard Way* by Ann Branigar Hopkins (Amherst: University of Massachusetts Press, 1996).

Disparate Impact

To prove a case of **disparate impact,** a plaintiff must show that an employment practice disadvantages people from a protected group. The Supreme Court has not defined the size of the disparity necessary to prove disparate impact. Most courts define disparate impact as a difference that is sufficiently large that it is unlikely to have occurred by chance. Tests of statistical significance are generally used to establish this. Some courts, however, have preferred the 80 percent rule contained in the Uniform Guidelines on Employee Selection Procedures. Under this rule, adverse impact is established if the selection rate for any race, sex, ethnic group, or any other protected class of people is less than four-fifths (or 80 percent) of the rate for the group with the highest selection rate.

Once the court accepts that disparate impact has occurred, the burden shifts to the employer to prove that the selection practice is job-related and consistent with business necessity. The Uniform Guidelines suggest three methods by which an employer can show job-relatedness: content validity, criterion validity, and construct validity. Content validity is used when the test closely approximates the job, as in a typing exam for a typist position. This form of validation is not generally applicable to personality testing because such tests measure general personality traits not specific abilities. Criterion validity compares performance on the test with performance on critical or important job behaviors. It is the preferred method of validation under the Uniform Guidelines but is not always technically feasible. Construct validity establishes relationships between aspects of satisfactory job performance and a specific trait, then measures of that trait are used for selection. For example, the job of a customer service representative may require a specific interpersonal style to function effectively. This form of validation is the most appropriate for personality testing because it focuses on the link between a particular trait and different aspects of job performance. If a test is job-related and satisfies the validity requirements of the Uniform Guidelines, then, in most cases the disparate impact claim is dropped by the court.

There have been relatively few disparate impact cases involving personality tests because such tests generally do not disadvantage any protected group. Integrity tests may have the best record of any selection technique in demonstrating freedom from disparate impact. Moreover, integrity test publishers typically have extensive statistical evidence demonstrating the validity of integrity tests in predicting theft and job-relevant counterproductive behavior, which would satisfy the employer's burden. Similar data supporting the job relevance for other personality tests also exist. In some cases, however, an employer may need to perform its own validity studies.

Race or Gender Norming

The Civil Rights Act of 1991 forbids employers from using different norms or cutoff scores for different groups of people. For example, it would be illegal for a company to set a higher threshold for women than men on their selection test. A few personality test publishers, including versions of the MBTI, recommend different scoring practices based on **race or gender norming.** This practice is clearly illegal, and employers should avoid tests of this sort in employee selection settings, in favor of personality tests with standard norms applied equally to all applicants.

Americans with Disabilities Act

The **Americans with Disabilities Act (ADA)** states that an employer cannot conduct a medical examination, or even make inquiries as to whether an applicant has a disability, during the selection process. Moreover, even if a disability is obvious, the employer cannot ask about the nature or severity of that disability. Consequently, employers should be careful when they administer psychological testing to job applicants to make sure that the testing is not a medical examination. Psychological testing can be considered a medical examination if it provides evidence that would lead to a diagnosis or the identification of mental disorder or impairment.

Consider the following example: A psychological test (like the MMPI) is constructed to diagnose mental illnesses, but a particular employer says she does not use the test to disclose mental illness. Instead, the employer says she uses the test to disclose preferences and habits of job applicants. However, the test also is interpreted by a psychologist working for the company. In addition, the test is routinely used in clinical settings to provide evidence that would lead to a diagnosis of a mental disorder or impairment (e.g., whether a person has paranoid tendencies or is depressed). Under these conditions, this test might be considered a medical examination and hence violate the ADA laws.

Right to Privacy

Perhaps the largest issue of legal concern for employers using personality testing is privacy. The **right to privacy** in employment settings grows out of the broader concept of the right to privacy. In general, cases that charge an invasion-of-privacy claim against an employer can be based on the federal constitution, state constitutions and statutes, and common law.

In the case of *McKenna v. Fargo,* a federal district court in New Jersey upheld the right of a city fire department to use personality testing to select applicants for the position of firefighter. The case was based on an invasion-of-privacy claim. The court determined that, although the test did infringe on the applicant's right to privacy, the city's interest in screening out applicants who would be unstable under the pressures of the job was sufficient to justify the intrusion. The *McKenna* ruling establishes that personality test questions that inquire about an applicant's sexual, religious, or political attitudes may intrude on an applicant's right to privacy. However, the ruling also recognizes that a government can justify this intrusion if it has a compelling need, such as the need for firefighters who can protect the safety of the public.

In another case, a California Court of Appeals found that certain items on a personality test administered to security guard applicants violated the state constitutional right to privacy. In *Saroka v. Dayton Hudson,* the plaintiff had applied for a security guard position with the Target Stores chain and was required to complete both the MMPI and the California Psychological Inventory (CPI). The two tests are widely used to assess personality traits and adjustment, and they contain items asking about very personal topics such as religion, sexual behavior, and political beliefs. The plaintiff argued that the questions required him to reveal very private thoughts and highly personal behaviors and were not job-related. The court agreed. Target tried to mount a defense by arguing that they had a compelling business interest in the outcome of the selection process. The court ruled that Target did not show how questions about an applicant's religious beliefs or sexual orientation would have any bearing on his or her emotional stability. Because Target Stores could not provide evidence on the construct or criterion validity of the specific items in question, they lost the case.

Exercise

Think of a job or career where personality might play a role in how well a person does in that job, or how satisfied they would be in that career. It can be any job or career—investment banking, programming, car salesperson—just pick one for this exercise. Now, think about the requirements for doing well in this career or job and make a list of two or three key requirements. This step is called **job analysis,** and in it you try to identify the key requirements associated with a particular job. For example, social skills might be a key part of being a car salesperson. Now take each of the key requirements and see if you can identify a personality or ability trait that might contribute to that job requirement. For example, look over the material on selecting police officers in the section on "Personnel Selection." If you can link the key requirements identified in your job analysis with specific personality traits, then there is a good chance the personality measures would be useful in selecting employees for that job. This exercise is one of the real-world applications that personality psychologists working in industry do all the time.

Personnel Selection—Choosing the Right Person for the Job

The job of a police officer can illustrate the importance of selecting the right person for the job. Recent high-profile deaths of unarmed suspects by police, such as the George Floyd killing in May of 2020, highlight the importance of selecting the right persons for the occupation of police officer (or equally important, screening the wrong ones out). According to data assembled by the Mapping Police Violence project, with 2 weeks left in the 2021 calendar year, police in the United States were involved in the deaths of 1,033 people this year, a rate that has been this high for the past several years. Selecting the right persons for the job of police officer is literally a life-or-death decision for people in the community. Personality tests are frequently used to screen out the wrong individuals from the pool of applicants for police officers. One of the most frequently given tests is the revised Minnesota Multiphasic Personality Inventory (MMPI II). The MMPI II has 550 items, and its primary use is to identify persons with significant psychological, social, and adjustment problems. Individuals with elevated scores indicating mental or emotional difficulties, or aggression and impulse control problems, can be screened out of the pool of potential officers (Barrick & Mount, 1991).

Little was known about which personality traits contribute to the successful performance of the job of police officers until Hargrave and Hiatt (1989) examined the California Psychological Inventory (CPI) in relation to police officer performance. In their study, they found that 13 percent of the cadets in training were found to be "unsuitable" by their instructors. Moreover, these unsuitable cadets differed from the "suitable" group on 9 scales of the CPI, including the conformity and social presence scales. In another sample of 45 officers on the job who were having serious problems, Hargrave and Hiatt (1989) found that the CPI also discriminated this group from other police officers who were not having problems. These findings provided evidence that the CPI is useful in the selection of police officers, and it, as well as other personality questionnaires, are being used for this purpose (e.g., Black, 2000; Coutts, 1990; Grant & Grant, 1996; Lowry, 1997; Mufson & Mufson, 1998).

The 16 Personality Factor (16 PF) questionnaire, described in Chapter 3, is also being used in vocational advising and selection. The 16 PF profile that best matches police officers is one that emphasizes boldness and self-confidence, qualities that facilitate one's abilities to direct or control others and to achieve goals (Institute for Personality and

Ability Testing, 2015). A heightened need for adventure and a strong need to influence others are linked with the enjoyment of careers that provide challenge and opportunities to take charge. The police officer personality profile is low on the need for support from others, which suggests a very self-assured personality. In terms of the Big 5 personality traits, norms for police officers are high levels of Conscientiousness and Extraversion, and low levels of Neuroticism (Detrick & Chibnall, 2013).

Selection in Business Settings—The Myers–Briggs Type Indicator: A Worst-Case Example

Businesses confront critical decisions, especially hiring decisions, on which their success depends. Different jobs pose different demands, and it's likely that personality plays a critical role in determining success in different positions. According to recent estimates (e.g., Emre, 2018), personality testing is a two-billion dollar business in the United States. One of the most widely used personality tests is the **Myers–Briggs Type Indicator (MBTI)** (Myers et al., 1998). The test was developed by a mother-daughter team, Katherine Briggs and Isabel Myers, who were fascinated with Jungian concepts (see Chapter 10). Neither mother nor daughter had any training in psychology or statistics or measurement. Instead, thinking up questions to get at different personality types was a hobby for them, something they enjoyed doing together. The interesting history of how the MBTI went from a "home-cooked" set of questions (Menand, 2018) to one of the most widely used personality tests today is presented by Merve Emre (2018). We present the MBTI in some detail here as a worst-case example. The test has a number of serious problems that severely limit its usefulness for selection purposes. Understanding these problems should help students recognize better tests, and we present a best-case example in the section following our critique of the MBTI.

The 16PF personality profile that characterizes police officers emphasizes boldness and self-confidence (qualities that facilitate the direction or control of others), a heightened need for adventure, and a low need for support from others (suggestive of self-assurance). The personality traits associated with being a good police officer are distributed equally among men and women (Krug, 1981).

David Hiller/Getty Images

The MBTI provides information about personality by testing for eight fundamental preferences. A sample item: "Do you usually value sentiment more than logic, or value logic more than sentiment?" This type of item is an example of a "forced-choice" format, in which individuals must respond in one way or another, even if they feel that their preferences might be somewhere in the middle. The eight fundamental preferences are shown in Table 4.1.

These eight preferences reduce to four scores—you are either extraverted OR introverted; sensing OR intuitive; thinking OR feeling; judging OR perceiving. These four scores are then combined to yield 16 *types*. Indeed, each person is placed into one of the 16 types yielded by his or her four scores. For example, you could be an *ESTP* type: Extraverted, Sensing, Thinking, and Perceiving. This type, according to the MBTI authors, has a distinctive leadership style in business settings. She likes to take charge when a crisis occurs; she's good at persuading others to adopt her point of view; she is assertive and leads the group to the most direct route to the goal; and she wants to see immediate results.

Contrast this with another type, an *INFJ:* Introverted, Intuitive, Feeling, and Judging. This type, according to the authors of the instrument, has a fundamentally different leadership style. Rather than take charge and assert, INFJs are more likely

Table 4.1   Eight Fundamental Preferences Measured by the Myers–Briggs Type Indicator

Extraversion Draws energy from the outside; involved with people; likes action and activity	**Introversion** Draws energy from internal world of thoughts and ideas
Sensing Prefers taking in information through all five senses; attends to what actually exists	**Intuition** Prefers information derived from a "sixth sense"; notices what's possible rather than what is
Thinking Prefers logic, organization, and clean objective structure	**Feeling** Prefers a person- and value-oriented way of processing information
Judging Prefers living a well-ordered and controlled life	**Perceiving** Prefers to live spontaneously, with room for flexible spur-of-the-moment activities

Source: Myers et al. (1998); Hirsh & Kummerow (1990).

to develop a *vision* for the organization; get others to cooperate rather than demand cooperation; work to inspire others rather than command others; and work solidly and with integrity and consistency to achieve business goals. One can readily imagine that different types of business leaders would be better in different organizational settings. In a time of crisis, for example, an ESTP might be better at organizing others to deal with immediate threats. On a plateau in business, an INFJ might be better at pausing to reflect on a long-term vision for the organization.

By some estimates, between two to three million people a year take the MBTI (Gardner & Martinko, 1996; Vox, 2015). Although it was developed for applications in education, counseling, career guidance, and workplace team-building, it is also used in personnel selection settings (Pittenger, 2005). Its wide use most likely comes from its intuitive appeal; people can readily understand the relevance of the personality traits supposedly measured by this test.

There are, however, several problems with the MBTI. The first problem is that the theory on which it is based—Jung's theory of **psychological types**—is not widely endorsed by academic or research-oriented psychologists. For one thing, people don't come in "types," such as extraverted types and introverted types. Instead, most personality traits are normally distributed. Figure 4.3 illustrates the difference between data that would support a type model of introversion–extraversion (called a bimodal distribution) and the real data on introversion–extraversion, which is normally distributed according to a bell-shaped curve. Very few characteristics of persons follow a typological or bimodal distribution. Biological sex is one characteristic that does conform to a bimodal distribution; there are many female-type people, as well as many male-type people, and fewer (though not zero) people in between. The distribution of extraversion–introversion is not like a type distribution at all; it has only one peak, right in the middle, suggesting that the majority of people are neither purely introverted nor purely extraverted, but are somewhere in between. Virtually, all personality traits follow this normal distribution, so the concept of personality "types" is simply not justified when it comes to personality.

One consequence of forcing a typology onto a trait that is normally distributed concerns the importance of cutoff scores for classifying people into one category or the other (e.g., as introverted or extraverted). Most users of the MBTI use the median score (the score at which 50 percent fall above and 50 percent fall below) from some

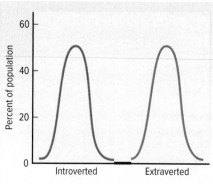

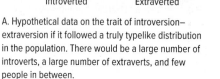

A. Hypothetical data on the trait of introversion–extraversion if it followed a truly typelike distribution in the population. There would be a large number of introverts, a large number of extraverts, and few people in between.

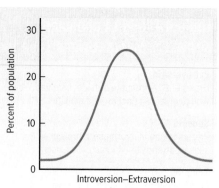

B. Typical data on the trait of introversion–extraversion, which follows a bell curve or normal distribution in the population. There are a large number of people in between the relatively rare extreme introverts and extreme extraverts.

Figure 4.3

Examples illustrating what the trait of introversion–extraversion would look like in terms of distributions in the population if it followed a type model (Panel A) or a normal distribution model (Panel B). Real data support the normal distribution model, not the type model.

standardization sample as the cutoff. The problem lies in the fact that a large percentage of people in any sample will be clustered right around the median score. If that median score moves a point or two in either direction, because of differences in sample characteristics used to determine the cutoff score, a very large number of people will be reclassified into their opposite category. In fact, a person with an introversion–extraversion score of 20 might be classified as an introvert in one sample (if it had a median of 21) and classified as an extravert in another sample (if it had a median of 19). So, the same individual score (a 20) will be interpreted very differently depending on the median used to perform the cutoff for classification. Despite this problem with cutoff scores and typologies, the majority of users of the MBTI continue to follow the scoring system that classifies persons into letter category groups, a practice that has been soundly criticized in the professional consulting literature (e.g., Pittenger, 2005).

A related consequence of using a typology scheme for scoring the MBTI is that the scores will be unreliable. Reliability is often estimated by testing a group of people twice, separated by a period of time. With the MBTI, because cutoff scores are used to categorize people into groups, and because many people are very close to the cutoff scores, slight changes in people's raw scores on retesting can result in a large percentage being reclassified into different personality types. Indeed, a study of the test-retest reliability of the MBTI (McCarley & Clarskadon, 1983) showed that, across a five-week test-retest interval, 50 percent of the participants received a different classification on one or more of the type categories. Other researchers find a similar lack of validity and reliability findings (Stein & Swan, 2019). These results are not surprising, and this is one reason most scientific personality psychologists do not recommend using typological scoring systems for any personality measure.

Another problem with typological scoring systems is that it assumes large between-category differences, and no within-category differences, among people. For example, all extraverted types are assumed to be alike, and introverted types are assumed to be very different from extraverted types. This, however, is not necessarily the case. Imagine two people who score as extraverted types, yet one of these is just one point above the median and the other is 31 points above the median. These two extraverted types are likely to be very different from each other (they differ by 30 points on the scale yet are given the same type category). Now imagine an introverted type who scored one point below the median, and an extraverted type who scored one point above the median. This introvert and this extravert are likely to be indistinguishable from each other (they differ by only 2 points on the scale yet are given different type categories). This is another reason psychologists who know about measurement issues avoid using type scoring systems for any personality test.

Dozens of validity studies of the MBTI have been published, mostly relating type categories to occupational preferences. These studies have been criticized, however, because most fail to report statistical details necessary to determine whether the differences are significant. For example, Gardner and Martinko (1996) review 13 studies that examined the distribution of MBTI types in managerial professions. All of these studies reported the frequencies of types in different categories, yet none reported scale score means that would have allowed strong statistical tests of mean personality differences among the different managerial categories. Moreover, other reviewers (e.g., Hunsley, Lee, & Wood, 2003) point out that no adequate tests have been done on the predictive validity of the MBTI (e.g., that the MBTI can predict *future* career choices or job satisfaction). Also, a recent study examining the incremental validity of the MBTI (e.g., whether the MBTI can add meaningfully to the prediction of career choice or job satisfaction above and beyond that obtained with more traditional personality measures) showed that the MBTI added no predictive power beyond that obtained with a more traditional personality measure (the Strong Interest Inventory; Pulver & Kelly, 2008).

Every few years psychologists take a fresh look at the evidence for the MBTI and summarize what they find. In 1991, Bjork and Druckman reviewed the evidence and concluded: "At this time, there is not sufficient, well-designed research to justify the use of the MBTI in career counseling programs" (p. 99). A few years later, Boyle (1995) also reviewed the literature and found no strong scientific evidence supporting the utility of the MBTI. In 2003, Hunsley, Lee, and Wood reviewed the accumulated evidence and summarized their findings: "One can only conclude that the MBTI is insufficient as a contemporary measure of personality" (pp. 63–4). And in a more recent review paper, Pittenger (2005) evaluated all of the scientific literature on the MBTI and concluded: "Using the MBTI to select employees, to assign employees to work groups or assignments, or for other forms of employment evaluation are [sic]not justified for the simple reason that there are no available data to recommend such decisions" (p. 219). A recent article in a mainstream personality science journal suggests that the best use of the MBTI is to educate students and the public about flaws in personality tests (Stein & Swan, 2019), which is exactly how we are discussing the MBTI here.

Given the highly negative reviews on the scientific merit of the MBTI, why does it continue to be a hugely popular tool in consulting and career counseling? There are probably several reasons. First, the popularity of the MBTI may reflect the success of the publisher's marketing campaign (Emre, 2018). In addition, the test comes with rather simple scoring and interpretation instructions, making it usable and understandable by people without advanced training. Moreover, the interpretations the test offers are readily translated into seemingly sensible predictions about work and interpersonal relations. Like the popularity of horoscopes, people like hearing about themselves and their futures, even if little or no scientific evidence exists for those descriptions and predictions.

Is there any legitimate use for the MBTI? Although it should definitely not be used as the single piece of evidence on which to base employment selections or career decisions, it may have a role in such areas as team-building, career exploration, or relationship counseling. The test can get people thinking about differences among people.

People with vastly different personalities see the world differently, and if the test fosters an appreciation for this diversity, then it may be useful. The test might also be useful if it gets people thinking about the relationship between personality and behavior. If we understand that how we act toward others, and they toward us, is influenced in part by our personalities, then this increases our ability to understand and relate well to others. For example, if teachers take the MBTI as part of a "teacher development workshop," they may think about their own teaching style or may gain an awareness that not all pupils are alike in how they relate to teachers. So the test may indeed have some utility for getting people to think about personality, even though the test does not appear adequate as an instrument for selection.

Selection in Business Settings—The Hogan Personality Inventory: A Best-Case Example

If the MBTI is not useful for selection, which tests are good alternatives? There are literally thousands of published personality tests (Spies & Plake, 2005) and hundreds of companies that use personality tests to help other companies select employees. We have chosen one of these companies and one of their personality tests to describe here, mainly because the procedures this company uses are based on a solid scientific foundation. The company is called Hogan Assessment Systems, and its main personality test is called the Hogan Personality Inventory.

The founder of this assessment company, Robert Hogan, was a professor of psychology at the University of Tulsa for many years. He had been teaching and doing research in personality psychology through the 1970s and 1980s, even becoming the head editor of the most prestigious scientific journal in personality psychology, the *Journal of Personality and Social Psychology.* During this time, Hogan's own research concerned efforts to identify aspects of personality important in contemporary business settings. He started with the Big Five model of personality but focused on how these traits might work in the business world. He developed a theory about the social aspects of personality that are important to business and concluded that the dominant themes in social life are the motive to get along with others and the motive to get ahead of others.

In most business settings, people work in groups, and every group has a status hierarchy. Hogan's theory states that, within such groups, people want three things: (1) acceptance, including respect and approval; (2) status and the control of resources; and (3) predictability (Hogan, 2005). Some of Hogan's research showed that business problems often occur when a manager violates one or more of these motives within a work group, for example, by treating staff with disrespect, by micromanaging in a way that takes away the staff's sense of control, or by not communicating or providing feedback, thereby making the workplace unpredictable.

Hogan developed a questionnaire measure of personality, called the **Hogan Personality Inventory (HPI)**, that measures aspects of the Big Five traits that are relevant to the above three motives important to business. For the details on why and how this inventory was developed, see Hogan and Hogan (2002) or visit the company's website (www.hoganassessments.com). The traits this inventory measures are described in Table 4.2. Hogan and his wife, Joyce Hogan, also a research psychologist, started using this inventory in research on the effectiveness of people working in a variety of businesses. They began to look at how specific job requirements fit with specific combinations of these personality traits. Soon they were doing validity studies, exploring how the personality test predicted how well people fit into specific business cultures. They also conducted outcome studies to see how well the personality inventory predicted

Table 4.2   The Hogan Personality Inventory (HPI) Contains Seven Primary Scales and Six Occupational Scale

Primary Scales	Occupational Scales
Adjustment—self-confidence, self-esteem, and composure under pressure. The opposite of neuroticism.	*Service Orientation*—being attentive, pleasant, and courteous to customers.
Ambition—initiative, competitiveness, and the desire for leadership roles.	*Stress Tolerance*—being able to handle stress, remaining even-tempered and calm under fire.
Sociability—extraversion, gregariousness, and a need for social interaction.	*Reliability*—honesty, integrity, and positive organizational citizenship.
Interpersonal Sensitivity—warmth, charm, and the ability to maintain good relationships.	*Clerical Potential*—following directions, attending to detail, and communicating clearly.
Prudence—self-discipline, responsibility, and conscientiousness.	*Sales Potential*—energy, social skills, and the ability to solve customers' problems.
Inquisitiveness—imagination, curiosity, vision, and creative potential.	*Managerial Potential*—leadership ability, planning, and decision-making skills.
Learning Approach—enjoying learning, and staying current on business and technical matters.	

occupational performance in a wide variety of jobs. Across a large number of studies, the test achieved high levels of reliability and validity, predicting a number of important occupational outcomes, including organizational fit and performance. Joyce Hogan and J. Holland (2003) provide a meta-analysis of 28 validity studies on the Hogan Personality Inventory, the results of which strongly support the validity of the personality scales for predicting several important job-relevant criteria.

In 1987, Robert and Joyce Hogan started their company, Hogan Assessment Systems, to consult with businesses that wanted to use personality measures to select employees. Soon afterward, Robert Hogan left his position at the University of Tulsa to devote his full effort toward helping companies successfully use personality measures in business applications. The Hogans continue to use a scientific approach to improve and validate the use of their personality inventory in the business community. For a recent review of predicting career success from personality, with an interesting discussion of how some traits predict getting a job whereas other traits predict keeping a job, see Hogan and Chamorro-Premuzic (2015).

Why is the Hogan Personality Inventory (HPI) a better choice than the MBTI when it comes to employee selection? First, the HPI is based on theoretically agreed-upon model of personality, the Big Five trait model, which enjoys a great deal of consensus in personality science today. The construction and development of the HPI followed standard statistical procedures, resulting in an inventory with a high level of measurement reliability (test–retest correlations range from .74 to .86). To date, there have been more than 500 validity studies of the HPI. These studies have examined the ability of the test to predict a wide variety of important business outcomes in a large number of job categories, such as employee turnover, absenteeism, improved sales performance, customer service, employee satisfaction, customer satisfaction, and overall business performance. The test has been able to predict occupational success in a wide variety of job categories. Personality profiles on the HPI are available for more than 200 different work categories that span the range of jobs in the U.S. economy. The company maintains a database from over a million people who have taken the HPI. It meets all the measurement and statistical standards held by the **American Psychological Association** and the **Society for Organizational and Industrial Psychologists**, whereas the MBTI does not.

The HPI itself consists of true–false items and takes about 20 minutes to administer. None of the items are invasive or intrusive, and none of the scales show adverse impact on the basis of gender, race, or ethnicity. Hogan Assessment Systems maintains a research archive and record-keeping practice that scrupulously follows the procedures outlined by the Uniform Guidelines on Employee Selection Procedures discussed earlier. If a company using the HPI is sued by a job applicant, Hogan Assessment Systems will provide reports and records on test development and validity necessary to defend the case in court. In over 30 years of use in business, personality assessments done with Hogan systems have never been successfully challenged in court.

While Hogan Assessment Systems provides other services, such as employee development, we will describe one case example of the use of the HPI in a specific employee selection application. A leading financial services company approached Hogan Assessment Systems to develop a preemployment assessment procedure to select financial consultants. The job requirements were analyzed and compared to known validity research on performance in related jobs, and a personality selection profile was determined. After new people were hired and on the job for a few years, the company evaluated the effectiveness of the selection procedure by comparing the performance of financial consultants hired before and after the selection procedure went into effect. They found that those financial consultants hired on the basis of their personality profiles earned 20 percent more in commissions annually, conducted 32 percent more volume in dollar terms annually, and made 42 percent more trades annually. Obviously, selecting those applicants with the "right stuff" was beneficial to this company. Other business examples of the use of the HPI in selecting employees can be found at www.hoganassessments.com.

It is clear that personality factors can play an important role in predicting who does well in specific employment settings. When it comes to using personality tests to select employees for specific positions, one should realize that not all personality tests do the job equally well. Clearly, those assessment systems with a strong scientific base, grounded in an accepted theory of personality, with acceptable reliability and strong evidence of validity relative to the needs of the company will have the best potential for helping business users achieve positive results.

SUMMARY AND EVALUATION

This chapter described some important issues and concepts that the various trait theories have in common. The hallmark of the trait perspective is an emphasis on differences among people. Trait psychology focuses on the study and measurement of differences between people, as well as the consequences of these differences in real life. Trait psychology assumes that people will be relatively consistent over time in their behavior because of the various traits they possess. Trait psychologists also assume a degree of cross-situational consistency for traits. Nevertheless, some situations are very strong in terms of their influence on behavior. Some situations are so strong that they overpower the influence of personality traits. One important lesson is that traits are more likely to influence a person's behavior when situations are weak and ambiguous and don't push for conformity from all people.

Most trait psychologists agree that personality trait scores refer primarily to average tendencies in behavior. A score on a trait measure refers to how a person is likely to behave, on average, over a number of occasions and situations. Trait psychologists are better at predicting average tendencies in behavior than specific acts on specific occasions. For example, from a person's high score on a measure of trait hostility, a personality psychologist could not predict whether this person is likely to get into a fight tomorrow. However, the psychologist could confidently predict that such a person is more likely to be in more fights in the next few years than a person with a lower score on hostility. Traits represent average tendencies in behavior.

Trait psychologists are also interested in the accuracy of measurement. More than any other personality perspective, trait psychology has occupied itself with efforts to improve measurement, particularly through self-report questionnaire measures. Psychologists who devise questionnaires work hard at making them less susceptible to lying, faking, and careless responding and more valid in terms of predicting real-world outcomes.

A particularly important measurement issue is social desirability, or the tendency to exaggerate the positivity of one's personality. Currently, trait psychologists hold that one motive for socially desirable responding is impression management, akin to lying. However, another view on social desirability is that socially desirable responding is a valid response by some people who simply view themselves as better or more desirable than most, or who actually have deceived themselves into thinking they are better off psychologically than they probably are. As is typical, trait psychologists have devised measures to identify and distinguish between these two types of socially desirable responding.

Finally, their interest in measurement and prediction has led trait psychologists to apply these skills to the selection and screening of job applicants and other real-world applications of personality. There are legal issues employers must keep in mind when using trait measures as a basis for making important hiring or promotion decisions. For example, tests must not discriminate unfairly against protected groups, such as women and certain minorities. In addition, the tests must be shown to be related to important real-life variables, such as job performance. We considered a number of important legal cases in employment law that are relevant to personality testing. We also considered two specific personality questionnaires that are popular in employment selection settings. One instrument, the MBTI, is widely used but also widely criticized in the scientific literature for its low levels of measurement reliability and unproven validity. The other instrument, the Hogan Personality Inventory, can be considered a "best practice" case when it comes to the use of personality in employee selection.

KEY TERMS

differential psychology 89
rank-order stability 91
consistency 91
situationism 92
person–situation interaction 93
aggregation 93
situational specificity 94
strong situation 95
situational selection 96
evocation 97
manipulation 98
Aggregation 98
density distributions of states 100

infrequency scale 102
faking 102
false negative 103
false positive 103
Barnum statements 104
personnel selection 106
integrity tests 107
overt and covert integrity tests. 107
negligent hiring 108
Title VII of the Civil Rights Act of 1964 108
Griggs v. Duke Power 108
Uniform Guidelines on Employee Selection Procedures 108

Ward's Cove Packing Co. v. Atonio 109
Price Waterhouse v. Hopkins 109
female underprediction effect 110
disparate impact 111
race or gender norming 111
Americans with Disabilities Act (ADA) 112
right to privacy 112
job analysis 113
Myers–Briggs Type Indicator (MBTI) 114
psychological types 115
Hogan Personality Inventory (HPI) 118

Tavis Wright/Image Source

Personality Disposition over Time: Stability, Coherence, and Change

5

THE DISPOSITIONAL DOMAIN

Even though people change and develop as they age, each person still has a sense of self as the same person from year to year. As we see in this chapter on development, when it comes to personality, some things change and some things stay the same.
Rawpixel.com/Shutterstock

Think back to your days in middle school. Can you remember what you were like then? Try to recall what you were most interested in, how you spent your time, what things were important to you. If you are like most people, you probably feel that, in many ways, you are a different person now than you were in middle school. Your interests have probably changed somewhat. Different things may be important to you. Your attitudes about school, family, and relationships have probably all changed at least a bit. Perhaps now you are more mature and have a more experienced view of the world.

As you think about what you were like then and what you are like now, you probably also feel that there is a core of "you" that is essentially the same over the years. If you are like most people, you have a sense of an enduring part of you, a feeling that you are "really" the same person now as then. Certain inner qualities seem the same over these several years.

In this chapter, we explore the psychological continuities and changes over time, which define the topic of personality development. When it comes to personality, "Some things change; some things stay the same." In this chapter, we discuss how psychologists think about personality development, with a primary focus on personality traits or dispositions.

Conceptual Issues: Personality Development, Stability, Coherence, and Change

This section defines personality development, examines the major ways of thinking about personality stability over time, and explores what it means to say that personality has changed. The study of personality development has attracted a lot of research attention, with two entire scientific journals devoting special issues to the topic, one in the *Journal of Personality* (Graziano, 2003) and one in the *European Journal of Personality* (Denissen, 2014; Specht et al., 2014).

What Is Personality Development?

Personality development is defined as the continuities, consistencies, and stabilities in people over time *and* the ways in which people change over time. Each of these two facets—stability and change—requires definitions and qualifications. There are many forms of personality stability and many forms of personality change. The three most important forms of stability are rank order stability, mean level stability, and personality coherence. We discuss each of these. Then we examine personality change.

Rank Order Stability

Rank order stability is the maintenance of individual position within a group. Between ages 14 and 20, most people become taller, but the rank order of heights tends to remain fairly stable because this form of development affects all people pretty much the same, adding a few inches to everyone. The tall people at age 14 fall generally toward the tall end of the distribution at age 20. The same can apply to personality traits. If people tend to

Exercise

To illustrate the phrase "Some things change; some things stay the same," consider the period just before high school (your middle school years) and compare that with the period just after high school—typically, your college years. Identify three characteristics that have changed noticeably during that period. These characteristics might be your interests, your attitudes, your values, and what you like to do with your time. Then list three characteristics about you that have not changed. Again, these characteristics could reflect certain traits of your personality, your interests, your values, or even your attitudes about various topics. Write them down in the following format:

	What I was like in middle school:	What I was like after high school:
Characteristics that have changed	1. _____ 2. _____ 3. _____	1. _____ 2. _____ 3. _____
Characteristics that have not changed		1. _____ 2. _____ 3. _____

maintain their positions on dominance or extraversion relative to the others over time, then there is high rank order stability to those personality characteristics. Conversely, if people fail to maintain their rank order—if the submissive people rise up and put down the dominants, for example—then the group is displaying rank order instability, or rank order change.

Mean Level Stability

Another kind of personality stability is constancy of level, or **mean level stability**. Consider political orientation. If the average level of liberalism or conservatism in a group remains the same over time, the group exhibits high mean level stability. If the average degree of political orientation changes—for example, if people tend to get more conservative as they get older—then that population shows **mean level change**.

Personality Coherence

A more complex form of personality development involves changes in the *manifestations* of a trait. Consider the trait of dominance. Suppose that the people who are dominant at age 8 are the same people who are dominant at age 20. The 8-year-old boys, however, manifest their dominance by showing toughness in rough-and-tumble play, calling their rivals "sissies," and insisting on monopolizing the computer games. At the age of 20, they manifest their dominance by persuading others to accept their views in political discussions, boldly asking someone out on a date, and insisting on the restaurant at which the group will eat.

This form of personality development—maintaining rank order in relation to other individuals but changing the manifestations of the trait—is called **personality coherence**. Notice that this form of personality coherence does not require that the precise behavioral manifestations of a trait remain the same. Indeed, the manifestations may be so different that there is literally no overlap between age 8 and age 20. The act manifestations

The manifestation of disagreeableness may differ across the life span, ranging from temper tantrums in infancy to being argumentative and having a short temper in adulthood. Even though the behaviors are different at the different ages, they nevertheless express the same underlying trait. This kind of consistency is called personality coherence.
Left: Kristy-Anne Glubish/Design Pics; Right: Chris Ryan/OJO Images/age fotostock

A Closer Look   A Case of Personal Stability

Mohandas Karamchand Gandhi was born in 1869 to a family of modest means in India. His mother was devoutly religious, and she impressed young Mohandas with her beliefs and practices. The Gandhi family practiced traditional Hinduism, but also practiced Buddhist chants, read from the Koran, and sang traditional Christian hymns. Mohandas developed a personal philosophy that led him to renounce all personal desires and to devote himself to the service of his fellow human beings.

After studying law in England, and practicing for a few years in South Africa, Gandhi returned to India. At that time, India was under British rule, and most Indians resented the oppression of their colonial rulers. Gandhi devoted himself to the ideal of Indian self-rule and to freedom from British oppression. When the British decided to fingerprint all Indians, for example, Gandhi came up with an idea he called passive resistance—he encouraged all Indians to simply refuse to go in for fingerprinting. During the period of 1919–1922, Gandhi led widespread but nonviolent strikes and boycotts throughout India. He coordinated campaigns of peaceful noncooperation with anything British—he urged Indians not to send their children to the British-run schools, not to participate in the courts, even not to adopt the English language. In their frustration, British soldiers sometimes attacked crowds of boycotting or striking Indians, and many were killed. The people of India loved Gandhi. They followed him in droves, recording everything he did and said. He became a living legend, and the people referred to him as Maha Atma, or the Great Soul. We know him today as Mahatma Gandhi.

In 1930, Gandhi led the people in nonviolent defiance of the British law forbidding Indians from making their own salt. He started out with a few of his followers on a march to the coast of India, intending to make salt from seawater. By the time Gandhi had reached the sea, several thousand people had joined him in this act of civil disobedience. By this time, the British had jailed more than 60,000 Indians for disobedience to British law. The jails of India were bursting with native people put there by foreign rulers for breaking foreign laws. The British rulers were finally coming to some sense of embarrassment and shame for this situation. In the eyes of the world, this frail man Gandhi and his nonviolent followers were shaking the foundation of the British Empire in India.

Gandhi was not an official of the Indian government. Nevertheless, the British began negotiations with him to free India from British rule. During negotiations, the British played tough and put Gandhi in jail. The Indian people demonstrated and nearly a thousand of them were killed by the British, bringing shame on the colonial rulers in the eyes of the world. Gandhi was finally freed. A few years later, in 1947, Britain handed India its independence.

Gandhi negotiated a mostly peaceful transition from British rule to self-rule for the people of India. In his lifetime, he was one of the most influential leaders in the world. His ideas have influenced the struggles of many oppressed groups since.

In 1948, an assassin fired three bullets into Gandhi at point-blank range. The assassin was a Hindu fanatic who believed that Gandhi should have used his position to preach hatred of the Muslims of India. Gandhi instead preached tolerance and trust, urging Muslims and Hindus to participate together in the new nation of India.

Mahatma Gandhi lived in a tumultuous period and led one of the largest social revolutions in human history. Despite the changing conditions of his life, his personality remained remarkably stable. For example, he practiced self-denial and self-sufficiency throughout his adult life, preferring a simple loincloth and shawl to the suit and tie worn by most leaders of the world's great nations.
Dinodia Photos/Alamy Stock Photo

This most nonviolent and tolerant man became a victim of violence.

Even though Gandhi became the "Father of India," he remained essentially the same person throughout his adult life. Each day of his life, he washed himself in ashes instead of expensive soap, and he shaved with an old, dull straight razor rather than with expensive blades. He cleaned his own house and swept his yard daily. Each afternoon he spun thread on a hand-wheel for an hour or two. He made cloth for his own clothes and for those of his followers. He practiced the self-denial and self-sufficiency he learned early in his life. In most ways, his personality was remarkably stable over his life, even though he was at the center of one of the most tumultuous social revolutions in history.

have all changed, but something critical has remained the same—the overall level of dominant acts relative to others of the same age. Thus, personality coherence includes both elements of continuity and elements of change—continuity in the underlying trait but change in the outward manifestation of that trait.

Personality Change

The notion of personality development in the sense of change over time also requires elaboration. To start with, not all change qualifies as development. For instance, if you walk from one classroom to another, your relationship to your surroundings has changed. But we do not speak of your "development" in this case because the change is external to you and not enduring.

And not all internal changes can properly be considered development. When you get sick, for example, your body undergoes important changes: your temperature may rise, your nose may run, and your head may ache. But these changes do not constitute development because the changes do not last—you soon get healthy, your nose stops running, and you spring back into action. In the same way, temporary changes in personality—due to taking alcohol or drugs, for example—do not constitute personality development unless they produce more enduring changes in personality.

If you become consistently more conscientious or responsible as you aged, however, this would be a form of personality development. If you become gradually less energetic as you aged, this also would be a form of personality development.

In sum, personality change has two defining qualities. First, the changes are typically *internal* to the person, not merely changes in the external surroundings, such as walking into another room. Second, the changes are relatively *enduring* over time, rather than being merely temporary.

Three Levels of Analysis

We can examine personality over time at three levels of analysis: the population as a whole, group differences within the population, and individual differences within groups. As we examine the empirical research on personality development, it is useful to keep these three levels in mind.

Population Level

Several personality psychologists have theorized about the changes that we all go through in navigating from infancy to adulthood. Freud's theory of psychosexual development, for example, contained a conception of personality development that was assumed to apply to *everyone* on the planet. All people, according to Freud, go through an invariant stage sequence, starting with the oral stage and ending with the mature genital stage of psychosexual development (see Chapter 9).

This level of personality development deals with the changes and constancies that apply more or less to everyone. For example, almost everyone in the population tends to increase in sexual motivation at puberty. Similarly, there is a general increase in impulsive and risk-taking behaviors as people enter the teen years. This is why auto insurance rates go down as people age—because a typical 30-year-old is less likely than a typical 16-year-old to drive dangerously. This change in impulsivity is part of the population level of personality change.

Group Differences Level

Some changes over time affect different groups of people differently. Sex differences are one type of group differences. In the realm of physical development, for example, females go through puberty, on average, two years earlier than males. At the other end of life, men in the United States tend to die five to seven years earlier than women. These are sex differences in development.

Analogous sex differences can occur in the realm of personality development. As a group, men and women suddenly develop differently from one another during adolescence in their average levels of risk taking (men become more risk taking). Men and women also develop differently in empathy toward others (women develop a stronger awareness and understanding of others' feelings). These forms of personality development are properly located at the group differences level of personality analysis.

Other group differences include cultural or ethnic group differences. For example, in the United States, there is a large difference in body image satisfaction between European American women and African American women. European American women tend, as a group, to be less satisfied with their bodies than are African American women with theirs. Consequently, European American women are much more at risk for developing eating disturbances, such as anorexia or bulimia, compared with women in other groups. This group difference emerges primarily around puberty.

Individual Differences Level

Personality psychologists also focus on individual differences in personality development. For example, can we predict which individuals will go through a midlife crisis? Can we predict who will be at risk for a psychological disturbance later in life based on early personality? Can we predict who will change over time and who will remain the same? These issues focus on individual differences in personality.

Some changes affect different groups of people differently. For example, European American women tend to be, as a group, less satisfied with their bodies than are African American women with theirs. Consequently, European American women have a higher risk for developing eating disorders, such as anorexia or bulimia, compared with women in other groups.

Left: wavebreakmedia/Shutterstock; Right: Sam Edwards/Glow Images

Personality Stability over Time

This section examines the research on the stability of personality over the lifetime. We first examine stability in infancy, then explore stability during childhood, and finally look at stability during the decades of adulthood.

Stability of Temperament During Infancy

Many parents with two or more children will tell you that their children had distinctly different personalities from the day they were born. For example, Albert Einstein, the Nobel Prize–winning father of modern physics, had two sons with his first wife. These two boys were quite different. The older boy, Hans, was fascinated with puzzles as a child and had a gift for math. He went on to become a distinguished professor of hydraulics. The younger son, Eduard, enjoyed music and literature. As a young adult, however, he ended up in a Swiss psychiatric hospital, where he died. Although this is an extreme example, many parents notice differences among their children, even as infants. Do the intuitions of parents square with the scientific evidence?

By far the most commonly studied personality characteristics in infancy and childhood fall under the category of temperament. Although there is some disagreement about what the term means, most researchers define **temperament** as the individual differences that emerge very early in life, are likely to have a heritable basis (see Chapter 6), and are often involved with emotionality or arousability.

Mary Rothbart (1981, 1986; Rothbart & Hwang, 2005) studied infants at different ages, starting at three months of age. She examined six factors of temperament, using ratings completed by the caregivers:

1. *Activity level:* the infant's overall motor activity, including arm and leg movements.
2. *Smiling and laughter:* How much does the infant smile or laugh?
3. *Fear:* the infant's distress and reluctance to approach novel stimuli.
4. *Distress to limitations:* the child's distress at being refused food, being dressed, being confined, or being prevented access to a desired object.
5. *Soothability:* the degree to which the child reduces stress, or calms down, as a result of being soothed.
6. *Duration of orienting:* the degree to which the child sustains attention to objects in the absence of sudden changes.

The caregivers, mostly mothers, completed observer-based scales designed to measure these six aspects of temperament. Table 5.1 shows the cross-time correlations over different time intervals. If you scan the correlations in the table, you will notice first that they are all positive. This means that infants who tend to score high at one time period on activity level, smiling and laughter, and the other personality traits, also tend to score high on these traits at later time periods.

Next, the correlations in the top two rows of Table 5.1 tend to be higher than those in the bottom four rows. This means that activity level and smiling and laughter tend to show higher levels of stability over time than the other personality traits.

Now notice that the correlations in the right-most two columns are generally higher than those in the left-most columns. This suggests that personality traits tend to become more stable toward the end of infancy (from 9 to 12 months), compared with the earlier stages of infancy (from 3 to 6 months).

Table 5.1 Stability Correlations for Temperament Scales

Scale	MONTHS					
	3–6	3–9	3–12	6–9	6–12	9–12
AL—activity level	0.58	0.48	0.48	0.56	0.60	0.68
SL—smiling and laughter	0.55	0.55	0.57	0.67	0.72	0.72
FR—fear	0.27	0.15	0.06	0.43	0.37	0.61
DL—distress to limitations	0.23	0.18	0.25	0.57	0.61	0.65
SO—soothability	0.30*	0.37*	0.41	0.50	0.39	0.29
DO—duration of orienting	0.36*	0.35*	0.11	0.62	0.34	0.64

Source: Adapted from Rothbart, 1981.
*Correlations based on only one cohort.

Like all studies, this one has limitations. Perhaps most important, the infants' caregivers may have developed certain conceptions of their infants, and it may be their conceptions rather than the infants' behaviors that show stability over time. Nonetheless, these findings reveal four important points. First, stable individual differences appear to emerge very early in life, when they can be assessed by observers. Second, for most temperament variables, there are moderate levels of stability over time during the first year of life. Third, the stability of temperament tends to be higher over short intervals of time than over long intervals of time—a finding that occurs in adulthood as well. And, fourth, the level of stability of temperament tends to increase as infants mature (Goldsmith & Rothbart, 1991; Rothbart & Hwang, 2005).

Stability During Childhood

Longitudinal studies, which examine the same groups of individuals over time, are costly and difficult to conduct. As a result, there are few studies to draw on. A major exception is the Block and Block Longitudinal Study, which initiated the testing of a sample of more than 100 children from the Berkeley-Oakland area of California when the children were 3 years old (see, e.g., Block & Robbins, 1993). Since that time, the sample has been followed and repeatedly tested at ages 4, 5, 7, 11, and into adulthood.

One of the first publications from this project focused on individual differences in activity level (Buss, Block, & Block, 1980). When the children were 3 years old, and then again at 4, their activity levels were assessed in two ways. The first was through the use of an **actometer**, a recording device attached to the wrists of the children during several play periods. Motoric movement activated the recording device—essentially a self-winding wristwatch. Independently, the children's teachers completed ratings of their behavior and personalities. The behavioral measure of activity level contained three items directly relevant: "is physically active," "is vital, energetic, active," and "has a rapid personal tempo." These items were summed to form a total measure of teacher-observed activity level. This observer-based measure was obtained when the children were 3 and 4 and then again when they reached age 7.

Table 5.2 shows the correlations among the activity level measures, both at the same ages and across time to assess the stability of activity level during childhood. The correlations between the same measures obtained at two different points in time are

Table 5.2   Intercorrelations Among Activity Measures

	ACTOMETER		JUDGE-BASED		
	Age 3	Age 4	Age 3	Age 4	Age 7
Actometer:					
Age 3	. . .	.44*	.61***	.56***	.19
Age 4	.43**	. . .	.66***	.53***	.38**
Judge-based:					
Age 3	.50***	.36**	. . .	.75***	.48***
Age 4	.34*	.48***	.51***	. . .	.38**
Age 7	.35*	.28*	.33*	.50***	. . .

Source: Buss, Block, & Block, 1980.

*p < .05. **p < .01. ***p < .001 (two-tailed). Correlations above the ellipses (. . .) are based on boys' data, those below the ellipses (. . .) are based on girls' data.

called **stability coefficients** (these are also sometimes called test-retest reliability coefficients). The correlations between different measures of the same trait obtained at the same time are called **validity coefficients**.

Several key conclusions about validity and stability can be drawn from these findings. First, the actometer-based measurements of activity level have significant positive validity coefficients with the judge-based measurements of activity level. Activity level in childhood can be validly assessed through both observational judgments and activity recordings from the actometers. The two measures are moderately correlated at each age, providing cross-validation of each type of measure.

Second, notice that the correlations of the activity level measurements are all positively correlated with measurements of activity level taken at later ages. Activity level shows moderate stability during childhood. Children highly active at age 3 are also likely to be active at ages 4 and 7. Their less active peers at age 3 are likely to remain less active at ages 4 and 7. A 21-year study tracking physical activity of Finish boys and girls found that this level of moderate stability carries throughout childhood and into adulthood (Telama et al., 2005).

Finally, the size of the correlations tends to decrease as the time interval between the different testings increases. As a general rule, the longer the time between testings, the lower the stability coefficients. Measures taken early in life can predict personality later in life, but the predictability decreases over time.

These general conclusions apply to other personality characteristics as well. Aggression and violence have long been a key concern of our society from school shootings to suicide bombers. What causes some children to act so aggressively?

As it turns out, numerous studies of childhood aggression have been conducted by personality psychologists. Olweus (1979) reviewed 16 longitudinal studies of aggression during childhood. The studies varied widely on many aspects, such as age at which the children were first tested (2–18), length interval between first testing and final testing (half a year to 18 years), and the specific measures of aggression used (e.g., teacher ratings, direct observation, and peer ratings).

Figure 5.1 shows a summary graph of the results of all these studies. The graph depicts the stability coefficients for aggression as a function of the interval between first

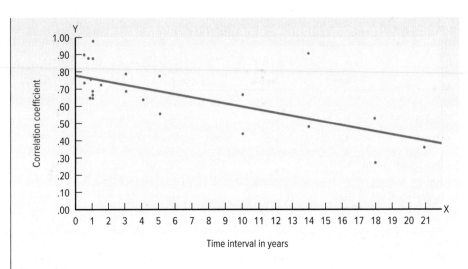

Figure 5.1

The figure shows the stability of aggression in males over different time intervals. Aggression shows the highest levels of stability over short time intervals such as from one year to the next. As the time interval between testings increases, however, the correlation coefficients decline, suggesting that aggressiveness changes more over long time intervals than over short time intervals.

Source: Olweus, 1979.

and final testing. Marked individual differences in aggression emerge very early in life, certainly by the age of 3 (Olweus, 1979). Individuals retain their rank order stability on aggression to a substantial degree over the years. Moderate levels of rank order stability have also been documented for major personality traits from early childhood to adolescence (Hampson et al., 2007), from middle childhood to adolescence (Tackett et al., 2008), and from adolescence to early adulthood (Blonigen et al., 2008). Longitudinal studies of aggression continue to support the conclusion of moderate levels of stability (Piquero et al., 2012). And, as we have seen with infant temperament and childhood activity level, the stability coefficients tend to decline as the interval between the two times of measurement increases.

In sum, we can conclude that individual differences in personality emerge very early in life—most likely in infancy for some traits and by early childhood for other traits, such as aggression. These individual differences tend to be moderately stable over time, so that people who are high on a particular trait tend to remain high. Indeed, childhood personality at age 3 turns out to be a good predictor of adult personality at age 26 (Caspi et al., 2003). Finally, the stability coefficients gradually decline over time as the distance between testings increases.

Rank Order Stability in Adulthood

Many studies have been conducted on the stability of adult personality. Longitudinal studies span as many as four decades of life. Furthermore, many age brackets have been examined, from age 18 through older cohorts ranging up to age 84.

A summary of these data is shown in Table 5.4, assembled by Costa and McCrae (1994; see also McCrae & Costa, 2008). This table categorizes the measures of personality into the five-factor model of traits, described in Chapter 3. The time intervals between the first and last personality assessments for each sample range from a low of three years

A Closer Look

Bullies and Whipping Boys from Childhood to Adulthood

The individual differences that emerge early in life sometimes have profound consequences, both for the life outcomes of individuals and for the impact on the social world. Norwegian psychologist Dan Olweus has conducted longitudinal studies of "bullies" and "whipping boys" (Olweus, 1978, 1979, 2001). The meanings of these terms are precisely what they sound like. Bullies pick on and victimize other children. They trip victims in the hallway, push them into lockers, elbow them in the stomach, demand their lunch money, and call them names.

Although the victims, or "whipping boys," do not have many external characteristics that appear to set them apart, they do have certain psychological characteristics. Most commonly, victims tend to be anxious, fearful, insecure, and lacking in social skills. They are emotionally vulnerable and may be physically weak as well, making them easy targets who don't fight back. The victims suffer from low self-esteem, lose interest in school, and often show difficulties establishing or maintaining friendships. They seem to lack social support that might buffer them against bullies. It has been estimated that 10 percent of all schoolchildren are afraid of bullies during the school day, and most children have been victimized by bullies at least once (Brody, 1996).

In one longitudinal study, bullies and victims were identified through teacher nominations in Grade 6. A year later, the children attended different schools in different settings, having made the transition from elementary school to junior high school. At this different setting during Grade 7, a different set of teachers categorized the boys on whether they were bullies, victims, or neither. The results are shown in Table 5.3. As you can see from looking at the circled numbers in the diagonal in Table 5.3, the vast majority of the boys received similar classifications a year later, despite the different school, different setting, and different teachers doing the categorizing.

The bullying, however, does not appear to stop in childhood. When Olweus followed thousands of boys from grade school to adulthood, he found marked continuities. The bullies in childhood were more likely to become juvenile delinquents in adolescence and criminals in adulthood. An astonishing 65 percent of the boys who were classified by their Grade 6 teachers as bullies ended up having felony convictions by the time they were 24 years old (Brody, 1996). Many of the bullies apparently remained bullies throughout their lives. Unfortunately, we don't know the fate of the victims, other than that they tended not to get involved in criminal activities.

A study of 228 children, ranging in age from 6 to 16, found several fascinating personality and family relationship correlates of bullying (Connolly & O'Moore, 2003). A total of 115 children were classified as "bullies" based on both their own self-ratings and on the basis of at least two of their classmates categorizing them as bullies. These were then compared with 113 control children, who both did not nominate themselves as bullies and were not categorized as bullies by any of their classmates. The bullies scored higher on the Eysenck scales of Extraversion, Neuroticism, and Psychoticism (see Chapter 3). Bullies, in short, tended to be more outgoing and gregarious (extraversion); emotionally volatile and anxious (neuroticism); and impulsive and lacking in empathy (psychoticism). In addition, the bullies, relative to the controls, expressed more ambivalence and conflict with their family members, including their brothers, sisters, and parents. Conflicts in the home, in short, appear to be linked to conflicts these children get into during school, pointing to a degree of consistency across situations.

The good news is that anti-bullying intervention programs work to curtail bullying (Fraguas et al., 2021). These work by first recognizing the problem via surveys of students and teachers. The second step involves classroom training in which teachers educate students about a zero-tolerance policy for any form of victimization. The third step involves educating all adults in schools, from cafeteria workers to bus drivers, about how to spot bullying and. how to report it. These intervention programs, developed by Dan Olweus himself and implemented in many schools in Europe and North America, dramatically reduce bullying rates and the harmful consequences of bullying (Fraguas et al., 2021).

Table 5.3 Longitudinal Classification of Boys in Aggressive Behaviors

Grade 6	GRADE 7		
	Bully	**Neither**	**Victim**
Bully	(24)	9	2
Neither	9	(200)	15
Victim	1	10	(16)

to a high of 30 years. The results yield a strong general conclusion: across self-report measures of personality, conducted by different investigators and over differing time intervals of adulthood, the traits of Neuroticism, Extraversion, Openness, Agreeableness, and Conscientiousness all show moderate to high levels of stability. The average correlation across these traits, scales, and time intervals is roughly +.65. These basic findings have been replicated recently in a large British sample (Furnham & Cheng, 2019c).

These studies all rely on self-report. What are the stability coefficients when other data sources are used? In one six-year longitudinal study of adults using spouse ratings,

Table 5.4 Stability Coefficients for Selected Personality Scales in Adult Samples

Factor/Scale	Interval	r
Neuroticism		
NEO-PI N	6	.83
16PF Q4: Tense	10	.67
ACL Adapted Child	16	.66
Neuroticism	18	.46
GZTS Emotional Stability (low)	24	.62
MMPI Factor	30	.56
	Median:	.64
Extraversion		
NEO-PI E	6	.82
16PF H: Adventurous	10	.74
ACL Self-Confidence	16	.60
Social Extraversion	18	.57
GZTS Sociability	24	.68
MMPI Factor	30	.56
	Median:	.64
Openness		
NEO-PI O	6	.83
16PF I: Tender-Minded	10	.54
GZTS Thoughtfulness	24	.66
MMPI Intellectual Interests	30	.62
	Median:	.64
Agreeableness		
NEO-PI A	3	.63
Agreeableness	18	.46
GZTS Friendliness	24	.65
MMPI Cynicism (low)	30	.65
	Median:	.64
Conscientiousness		
NEO-PI C	3	.79
16PF G: Conscientious	10	.48
ACL Endurance	16	.67
Impulse Control	18	.46
GZTS Restraint	24	.64
	Median:	.67

Note: Interval is given in years; all retest correlations are significant at *p* < .01. NEO-PI = NEO Personality Inventory, ACL = Adjective Check List, GZTS = Guilford Zimmerman Temperament Survey, MMPI = Minnesota Multiphasic Personality Inventory.

Source: Costa & McCrae, 1994. These stability coefficients are similar to those of all subsequent studies. A longitudinal study in Finland, for example, found that the five factors showed adult rank order stability ranging from .65 to .97 (Rantanen et al., 2007).

stability coefficients were +.83 for Neuroticism, +.77 for Extraversion, and +.80 for Openness (Costa & McCrae, 1988). Another study used peer ratings of personality to study stability over a seven-year interval. Stability coefficients ranged from +.63 to +.81 for the five-factor taxonomy of personality (Costa & McCrae, 1992). In sum, moderate to high levels of personality stability, in the individual differences sense, are found whether the data source is self-report, spouse-report, or peer-report.

Studies continue to confirm the rank order stability of personality during the adult years. In one study, Robins and his colleagues (Robins et al., 2001) studied 275 college students during their freshman year, and then again in their senior year. Across the four years of college, the rank order stability obtained was .63 for Extraversion, .60 for Agreeableness, .59 for Conscientiousness, .53 for Neuroticism, and .70 for Openness. A study of 2,141 German students tested over a two-year period from college to employment found stabilities of .70 for Extraversion, .65 for Agreeableness, .69 for Conscientiousness, .65 for Neuroticism, and .75 for Openness (Ludtke, Trautwein, & Husemann, 2009). In sum, the moderate levels of rank order stability of the Big Five are highly replicable across different populations and investigators.

Similar findings emerge for personality dispositions that are not strictly subsumed by the Big Five. In a massive meta-analytic study of the stability of self-esteem—how good people feel about themselves—Trzesniewski, Donnellan, and Robins (2003) found high levels of continuity over time. Summarizing 50 published studies involving 29,839 individuals and four large national studies involving 74,381 individuals, they found stability correlations ranging from the .50s to the .70s. How people feel about themselves—their level of self-confidence—appears very consistent over time. Similar findings have been obtained with measures of prosocial orientation and interpersonal empathy (Eisenberg et al., 2002). In sum, personality dispositions, whether the standard Big Five or other dispositions, show moderate to considerable rank order stability over time in adulthood.

Researchers have posed an intriguing question about rank order personality stability in the individual differences sense: When does personality consistency peak? That is, is there a point in life when people's personality traits become so firm that they don't change much relative to those of other people? To address this question, Roberts and DelVecchio (2000) conducted a meta-analysis of 152 longitudinal studies of personality. The key variable they examined was personality consistency, defined as the correlation between Time 1 and Time 2 measures of personality (e.g., the correlation between a personality trait at age 15 and the same trait at age 18).

Roberts and DelVecchio (2000) found two key results. First, personality consistency tends to increase with increasing age. For example, the average personality consistency during the teenage years was +.47. This jumped to +.57 during the decade of the twenties and +.62 during the thirties (see Vaidya et al., 2008, for similar results). Personality consistency peaked during the decade of the fifties at +.75. As the authors conclude, "trait consistency increases in a linear fashion from infancy to middle age where it then reaches its peak after age 50" (p. 3). As people age, personality appears to become more and more "set."

Mean Level Stability and Change in Adulthood

The five-factor model of personality also shows fairly consistent mean level stability over time, as shown in Figure 5.2. Especially after age 50, there is little change in the average level of stability in Openness, Extraversion, Neuroticism, Conscientiousness, and Agreeableness.

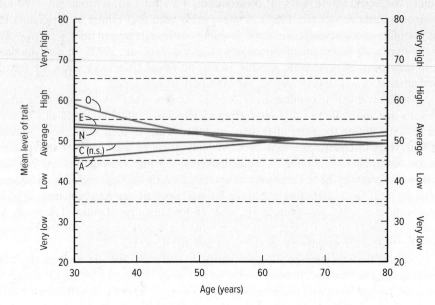

N = Neuroticism, E = Extraversion, O = Openness, A = Agreeableness, C = Conscientiousness

Figure 5.2

The figure shows the mean level of five traits over the life span. Although the average scores on each trait are quite stable over time, Openness, Extraversion, and Neuroticism show a gradual decline from age 30 to 50. In contrast, Agreeableness shows a gradual increase over these ages.

Source: Costa & McCrae, 1994.

Little change, however, does not mean no change. In fact, there are small but consistent changes in these personality traits, especially during the decade of the twenties. As you can see in Figure 5.2, there is a tendency for Openness, Extraversion, and Neuroticism to gradually decline with increasing age until around age 50. At the same time, Conscientiousness and Agreeableness show a gradual increase over time—effects found in Switzerland, Germany, as well as in the United States (Anusic, Lucas, & Donnellan, 2012; Specht, Egloff, & Schmukle, 2011). The magnitude of these age effects is not large.

Studies confirm that mean level personality traits change in slight, but nonetheless important, ways during adulthood. By far the most consistent change is a good one—people score lower on Neuroticism or Negative Affect as they grow older. From freshman to senior years in college, for example, students show a decrease in Neuroticism corresponding to roughly half a standard deviation ($d = -.49$) (Robins et al., 2001). Students reported experiencing less negative affect and more positive affect over time (Vaidya et al., 2002). A study from adolescence to midlife also found a decrease in the experience of Negative Affect—individuals feel less anxious, less distressed, and less irritable as they move into midlife (McCrae et al., 2002). Emotional stability even increases from middle adulthood (ages 42-46) to older age (ages 60-64) (Alleman, Zimprich, & Hertzog, 2007). Similar findings were obtained in a longitudinal study of 2,804 individuals over a 23-year time span—Negative Affect decreased consistently as the participants got older (Charles, Reynolds, & Gatz, 2001).

A meta-analysis of 92 different samples found that both women and men gradually become more emotionally stable as they grow older, with the largest changes occurring between the ages of 22 and 40 (Roberts, Walton, & Viechtbauer, 2006). Increases in emotional stability (or decreases in Neuroticism) with age also have been found in Germany (Lehmann et al., 2013) and Japan (Kawamoto, 2016). A study of 1,600 men found that those who got married showed above-average increases in emotional stability compared to their bachelor peers (Mroczek & Spiro, 2003). In sum, most people become less emotionally volatile, less anxious, and generally less neurotic as they mature—a nice thing to look forward to for people whose current lives contain a lot of emotional turmoil.

Some people, however, change more than others (Johnson et al., 2007; Neyer, 2006; Vaidya et al., 2008). People who experience very few stressful life events show the largest decreases in Neuroticism over time (Jeronimus et al., 2014). In contrast, those who experience a lot of stressful life events tend to increase in Neuroticism over time. Being high on Neuroticism seems to cause people to get themselves into stressful life events. So the link between Neuroticism and stress seems to be bidirectional. Entering into a stable romantic relationship, transitioning to becoming a parent, and investing heavily in work all seem to have the effect of increasing levels of Conscientiousness compared to those who do not enter into these adult roles (Bleidorn, 2012; Hudson & Roberts, 2016; van Scheppingen et al., 2016; Wagner, Lüdtke, & Trautwein, 2015).

While Neuroticism and Negative Affect decline with age, people score higher on Agreeableness and Conscientiousness as they grow older. One study found an increase in Agreeableness of nearly half a standard deviation ($d = +.44$), and Conscientiousness increased roughly one-quarter of a standard deviation ($d = +.27$) (Robins et al., 2001). The facets of Conscientiousness that increase most with age are industriousness (working hard), impulse control, and reliability (Jackson et al., 2009). Similar findings have been discovered by other researchers: College students become more agreeable, extraverted, and conscientious from freshman year to two and a half years later (Vaidya et al., 2002); Agreeableness and Conscientiousness increase throughout early and middle adulthood (Srivastava et al., 2003); Positive Affect increases from the late teen years through the early fifties (Charles et al., 2001). Increases in Agreeableness over the course of adulthood have been found in Germany and Japan (Lehmann et al., 2013; Kawamoto, 2016). Some studies find increases in the trait of Openness with age, although these are less robust than changes in traits such as emotional stability. One study found an increase in Openness from adolescence to young adulthood (Pullman, Raudsepp, & Allik, 2006), whereas another study found this Openness increase in a similar age group only for women (Branje, van Lieshout, & Geris, 2006). Perhaps a good summary of the mean level personality changes comes directly from the longitudinal researchers: "The personality changes that did take place from adolescence to adulthood reflected growth in the direction of greater maturity; many adolescents became more controlled and socially more confident and less angry and alienated" (Roberts, Caspi, & Moffitt, 2001, p. 670). These personality changes have been dubbed the *maturity principle* (Caspi, Roberts, & Shiner, 2005).

Finally, the Big Five personality dispositions may be changeable through therapy. Piedmont (2001) evaluated the effects of an outpatient drug rehabilitation program on personality dispositions, as indexed by the Big Five. The therapy, administered to 82 men and 50 women over a six-week period, revealed fascinating findings. Those who went through the program showed a decrease in Neuroticism and increases in Agreeableness and Conscientiousness ($d = .38$). These personality changes were largely maintained in a follow-up assessment 15 months later, although not quite as dramatically ($d = 28$). Programs to help people change their personality traits when they want change, notably to become lower on Neuroticism, have met with some success (Hudson & Fraley, 2015).

In sum, although personality dispositions generally show high levels of mean stability over time, predictable changes occur with age and perhaps also with therapy—lower Neuroticism and Negative Affect, higher Agreeableness, higher Conscientiousness.

Exercise

Each person's personality is, in some ways, stable over time; however, in other ways, it changes over time. In this exercise, you can evaluate yourself in terms of what describes you now and how you think you will be in the future (Markus & Nurius, 1986). Following is a list of items. For each one, simply rate it on a 1–7 scale, with 1 meaning "does not describe me at all" to 7 meaning "is a highly accurate description of me." Give a rating for each of two questions: (1) Does this describe me now? and (2) Will this describe me in the future?

Items	Describes Me Now	Will Describe Me in the Future
Happy		
Confident		
Depressed		
Lazy		
Travels widely		
Has lots of friends		
Destitute (poor)		
Sexy		
In good shape		
Speaks well in public		
Makes own decisions		
Manipulates people		
Powerful		
Unimportant		

Compare your answers to the two questions. Items you gave the same answers to indicate that you believe this attribute will remain stable over time. The items that change, however, may reflect the ways in which your personality will change over time.

You can view your possible self in a number of ways, but two are especially important. The first pertains to the *desired self*—the person you wish to become. Some people wish to become happier, more powerful, or in better physical shape. The second pertains to your *feared self*—the sort of person you do not wish to become, such as poor or rigid. Which aspects of your possible self do you desire? Which aspects do you fear?

Personality Change

Global measures of personality traits, such as the five-factor model, give us hints that personality can change over time. But researchers who have focused heavily on personality stability have not explicitly designed studies to assess personality change. It is important to remember that knowledge about personality change is sparse.

One reason for the relative lack of knowledge about change is that there might be a bias among researchers against even looking for personality change (Helson & Stewart, 1994). As Block (1971) notes, even the terms used to describe stability and change are laden with evaluative meaning. Terms that refer to absence of change tend to be positive: *consistency, stability, continuity,* and *constancy* all seem like good things to have. On the other hand, *inconsistency, instability, discontinuity,* and *inconstancy* all seem undesirable or unpredictable.

Changes in Self-Esteem from Adolescence to Adulthood

In a unique longitudinal study, Block and Robbins (1993) examined self-esteem and the personality characteristics associated with those whose self-esteem had changed over time. **Self-esteem** was defined as "the extent to which one perceives oneself as relatively close to being the person one wants to be and/or as relatively distant from being the kind of person one does not want to be, with respect to person-qualities one positively and negatively values" (Block & Robbins, 1993, p. 911). Self-esteem was measured by use of an overall difference between a *current* self-description and an *ideal* self-description: the researchers hypothesized that the smaller the discrepancy, the higher the self-esteem. Conversely, the larger the discrepancy between current and ideal selves, the lower the self-esteem.

The participants were first assessed on self-esteem at age 14, roughly the first year of high school. They were assessed again at age 23, roughly five years after high school.

For the sample as a whole, there was no change in self-esteem with increasing age. However, when males and females were examined separately, a startling trend emerged. Over time, the genders departed from each other, with men's self-esteem tending to increase and women's self-esteem tending to decrease. The males tended, on average, to increase in self-esteem by roughly a fifth of a standard deviation, whereas the females tended, on average, to decrease in self-esteem by roughly a standard deviation. This is an example of personality change at the group level—the two subgroups (females and males) changed in different directions over time.

In sum, the transition from early adolescence to early adulthood appears to be harder on women than on men, at least in terms of self-esteem. As a whole, females tend to decrease in self-esteem, an increasing gap between their current self-conceptions and their ideal selves. Males tend to show a smaller discrepancy between their real and ideal selves over the same time period.

Autonomy, Dominance, Leadership, and Ambition

Another longitudinal study examined 266 male managerial candidates at the business AT&T (Howard & Bray, 1988). The researchers first tested these men when they were in their twenties (in the late 1950s) and then followed them up periodically over a 20-year time span when they were in their forties (in the late 1970s).

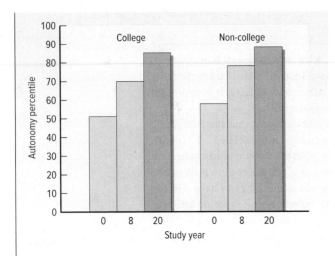

Figure 5.3

The figure shows change with age in autonomy scores of men in the AT&T study. Both college-educated and non-college-educated men tend to become more autonomous or independent as they grow older.

Several dramatic personality changes were observed. The most startling change was a steep drop in the *ambition* score. This drop was steepest during the first eight years but continued to drop over the next 12 years. The drop was steepest for the college men, less so for the non-college men, although note that the college men started out higher on ambition than did the non-college men. Supplementary interview data suggested that the men had become more realistic about their limited possibilities for promotion in the company. It is not that these men lost interest in their jobs or became less effective. Indeed, their scores on *autonomy, leadership motivation, achievement,* and *dominance* all increased over time (see Figure 5.3).

Sensation Seeking

Conventional wisdom suggests that people become more cautious and conservative with age. Studies of sensation seeking confirm this. The Sensation-Seeking Scale (SSS) contains four subscales, each containing items as a forced-choice between two distinct options. First is *thrill and adventure seeking,* with items such as "I would like to try parachute jumping" versus "I would never want to try jumping out of a plane, with or without a parachute." The other scales are *experience seeking* (e.g., "I am not interested in experience for its own sake" versus "I like to have new and exciting experiences and sensations even if they are a little frightening, unconventional, or illegal"); *disinhibition* (e.g., "I like wild, uninhibited parties" versus "I prefer quiet parties with good conversation"); and *boredom susceptibility* (e.g., "I get bored seeing the same old faces" versus "I like the comfortable familiarity of everyday friends").

Sensation seeking increases with age from childhood to adolescence and peaks in late adolescence around 18–20; then it falls as people get older (Zuckerman, 1974). This age trend of sensation seeking has been replicated within the United States and across many cultures (Chan et al., 2012; Steinberg et al., 2008). Parachute jumping and wild, uninhibited parties seem to be less appealing to older folks.

Femininity

In a study of women from Mills College in the San Francisco bay area, Helson and Wink (1992) examined changes in personality between the early forties and early fifties. They used the California Psychological Inventory at both time periods. The most dramatic change occurred on the *femininity* scale (now called the femininity/masculinity scale). High scorers on femininity are described by observers as dependent, emotional, feminine, gentle, high-strung, mild, nervous, sensitive, sentimental, submissive, sympathetic, and worrying (Gough, 1996). Low scorers (i.e., those who score in the masculine direction) tend to be described as aggressive, assertive, boastful, confident, determined, forceful, independent, masculine, self-confident, strong, and tough. In terms of acts performed (recall the act frequency approach from Chapter 3), as reported by the spouses of these women, high scorers on the femininity scale tend

A Closer Look   Day-to-Day Changes in Self-Esteem

Most personality psychologists who study self-esteem focus on a person's average level, whether the person is generally high, low, or average in their self-esteem. A few studies have examined changes in self-esteem over long time spans in people's lives—for example, in the years from adolescence to adulthood. However, with some reflection, most of us would realize that we often change from day to day in how we feel about ourselves. Some days are better than other days when it comes to self-esteem. Some days we feel incompetent, that things are out of our control, and that we even feel a little worthless. Other days we feel satisfied with ourselves, that we are particularly strong or competent, and that we are satisfied with who we are and what we can become. Feelings of self-esteem can change not just from year to year but also from day to day.

Psychologist Michael Kernis studied how changeable or variable people are in their self-esteem in terms of day-to-day fluctuations. *Self-esteem variability* is the magnitude of short-term changes in ongoing self-esteem (Kernis, Grannemann, & Mathis, 1991). Variability is measured by having people keep records of how they feel about themselves for several consecutive days, sometimes for weeks or months. From these daily records, the researchers can determine just how much each person fluctuates, as well as their average level of self-esteem.

Researchers make a distinction between level and variability of self-esteem. These two aspects of self-esteem turn out to be unrelated to each other and are hypothesized to interact in predicting important life outcomes, such as depression (Kernis, Grannemann, & Barclay, 1992). For example, variability in self-esteem is an indicator that the person's self-esteem, even if high, is fragile, and the person is vulnerable to stress. Consequently, we can think of level and variability as defining two qualities of self-esteem as in the figure below.

Kernis and colleagues (1991, 1992) have suggested that self-esteem variability is related to how much one's self-view is influenced by events, particularly social events. Some people's self-esteem is pushed and pulled by the happenings of life more than other people's. For example, for some people, self-esteem might soar with a compliment and plummet with a social slight. Others, who can better roll with the punches of life, might be more stable in their self-esteem, weathering both the downs and ups of life without much change in their self-view.

Several studies have examined whether self-esteem variability predicts life outcomes, such as depressive reactions to stress. In one study (Kernis et al., 1991), self-esteem level was related to depression, but this relation was much stronger for those higher in self-esteem variability than for those lower in self-esteem variability.

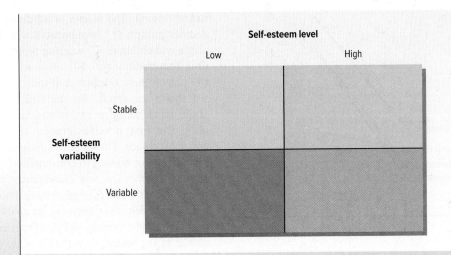

Level of self-esteem (whether one is high or low) and variability in self-esteem (whether one is stable or variable from day to day) are unrelated to each other. This makes it possible to find people with different combinations, such as a person who has a high level of self-esteem but is also variable.

(Continued)

A Closer Look (*Continued*)

In other words, at all levels of self-esteem, the participants who were low in variability showed less of a relation between self-esteem and depression than did the participants who were high in variability. Similar results were obtained by Butler, Hokanson, and Flynn (1994), who showed that self-esteem variability is a good predictor of who would become depressed six months later, especially when there was life stress in the intervening months. Variability indicates that the person may have a fragile sense of self-value and that, with stress, he or she may become more chronically depressed than someone whose self-esteem is more stable.

Researchers have come to view self-esteem variability as a vulnerability to stressful life events (Roberts & Monroe, 1992). That is, variability is thought to result from a particular sensitivity in one's sense of self-worth. Psychologists Ryan & Deci (2000) have suggested that variable individuals are dependent for their self-worth on the approval of others. They are very sensitive to social feedback, and they judge themselves through the eyes of others. High-variability individuals show (1) an enhanced sensitivity to evaluative events, (2) an increased concern about their self-concept, (3) an over-reliance on social sources for self-evaluation, and (4) anger and hostility when things don't go their way.

to do such things as send cards to friends on holidays and remember an acquaintance's birthday. Low scorers tend to take charge of committee meetings and take initiative in sexual encounters (Gough, 1996).

A fascinating change occurred in this sample of educated women—they showed a consistent drop in femininity as they moved from their early forties to their early fifties—a group level change in this personality variable. Women who choose not to have children also score lower in femininity than women who do have children, although this may not reflect change so much as choices made based on this preexisting personality dimension (Newton & Stewart, 2013).

Independence and Traditional Roles

The longitudinal study of Mills College women (Helson & Picano, 1990) yielded another fascinating finding. The women were divided into four distinct groups: (1) homemakers with intact marriages and children, (2) working mothers with children (neotraditionals), (3) divorced mothers, and (4) non-mothers (Helson & Picano, 1990). Figure 5.4 shows the results for the CPI Independence scale, which measures two related facets of personality. The first is self-assurance, resourcefulness, and competence. The second is distancing self from others and not bowing to conventional demands of society. The act frequency correlates of this scale reflect these themes (Gough, 1996). Those high on the Independence scale tend to set goals for groups they are in, talk to many people at parties, and take charge of the group when the situation calls for it. High scorers also tend to interrupt conversations and do not always follow instructions from those who are in a position to lead (hence, distancing themselves from others in these ways).

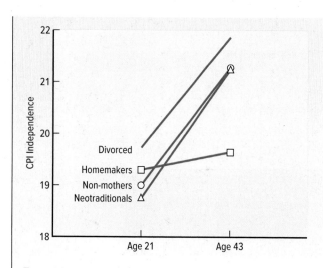

Figure 5.4

Means on the CPI Independence scale at ages 21 and 43 for homemakers (*n* = 17) and three groups of women with less traditional role paths: neotraditional, *n* = 35; divorced, *n* = 26; and non-mothers, *n* = 26.

For the divorced mothers, non-mothers, and working mothers, independence scores increased significantly over time. Only the traditional homemakers showed no increase in independence over time. These data, of course, are correlational, so we cannot infer causation. It is possible that something about the roles affected the degree to which the women became more independent. It is also possible that the women who were less likely to increase in independence were happy to remain in the traditional homemaking role. Regardless of the interpretation, this study illustrates the utility of examining subgroups within the population.

In sum, there are enough empirical clues to suggest that personality traits show some predictable changes with age. First, impulsivity and sensation seeking show predictable declines with age. Second, men tend to become somewhat less ambitious with age. There are indications that both men and women become somewhat more competent and independent with increasing age. Finally, there are hints that changes in independence are linked with the role and lifestyle adopted, with traditional homemaking women increasing less on independence than women who get divorced or pursue work and careers.

Personality Changes Across Cohorts: Assertiveness and Narcissism

One interest issue in exploring personality change over time is determining whether the changes observed are due to true personal change that all people undergo as they age or, conversely, changes in the **cohort effects**—the social times in which they lived. Jean Twenge (2000, 2001a, 2001b) has been at the forefront in exploring personality change that is likely to be caused by cohort effects. She argues that American society has changed dramatically over the past nine decades. One of the most dramatic changes centers on women's status and roles. During the depression era of the 1930s, for example, women were expected to be self-sufficient, but during the 1950s and 1960s, women assumed a more domestic role. Then from 1968 through 1993, women surged into the workforce and American society increasingly adopted norms of sexual equality. For example, from 1950 to 1993, the number of women obtaining bachelor's degrees doubled roughly from 25 to 50 percent. And the number of women obtaining PhDs, medical degrees, and law degrees all more than tripled. As of 2021, women now outnumber men in attending college in many countries. In the United Kingdom, to take one example, 36 percent more women than men apply to universities (Bilton, 2018), and women tend to be more qualified for entrance than men, based on their superior grades. In the United States, more than 56 percent of college students are women (Renn & Reason, 2021). Have these societal changes impacted women's personality?

Twenge (2001a) discovered that women's trait scores on *assertiveness* rose and fell dramatically, depending on the cohort in which the woman was raised. Women's assertiveness scores generally rose half a standard deviation from 1931 to 1945; fell by roughly that amount from 1951 to 1967; and then rose again from 1968 to 1993. On measures such as the California

Women's assertiveness scores rose from 1968 to 1993, pointing to a cohort effect.

Tetra Images/Corbis

Psychological Inventory scale of Dominance, for example, women increased +.31 of a standard deviation from 1968 to 1993. Men, in contrast, did not show significant cohort differences in their levels of assertiveness or dominance. Twenge (2001a) concludes that "social change truly becomes internalized with the individual . . . girls absorb the cultural messages they received from the world around them, and their personalities are molded by these messages" (p. 142).

Older people sometimes complain that the younger generation is too self-centered ("The kids these days!"). Is there any truth to these laments? Twenge et al., (2008) explored this issue by analyzing the personality syndrome labeled *narcissism*—those who tend to be self-centered, exhibitionistic, self-aggrandizing, interpersonally exploitative, grandiose, lacking empathy, and having an undue sense of entitlement (Buss & Chiodo, 1991). Twenge et al., (2008) found that scores on narcissism increased by about a third of standard deviation between 1982 and 2006. Based on a study of 30,073 individuals, critics of this analysis concluded that the evidence for major cohort changes in narcissism is actually weak (ranging from +.02 to +.04) and that there is little evidence for "an emerging epidemic of narcissism" (Donnallan, Trzesniewski, & Robins, 2009). Similar debates occur in studies of narcissism in China. One study found that younger Chinese individuals were more narcissistic than older cohorts, and children from single-child families were slightly more narcissistic than children from multiple-child families (Cai, Kwan, & Sedikedes, 2012). In contrast, a recent meta-analysis of multiple studies published from 2008 to 2017 concluded that younger Chinese were actually slightly less narcissistic than older Chinese (Gao et al., 2019). Although the debate about narcissism continues, cautious readers may wish to wait for further evidence before concluding that today's youth are truly more self-centered than their elders.

Can You Intentionally Change Your Personality?

A fascinating question is whether people can actively and intentionally change their personality traits in the directions they desire in order to promote positive life outcomes. To address this question, researchers designed a three-month-long digital intervention using a Smartphone application (Steiger, Lewetz, & Swami, 2021). They described for participants each of the Big Five personality traits, and asked them to pick one for which they desired change. For example, if the goal was to increase Extraversion: *"I want to be more extraverted, which means to be more sociable; to have more energy and zest for action; to be less quiet; to be more active and enterprising; to take the lead more often"* (Steiger, Lewetz, & Swami, 2021, p. 8). The interventions consisted of a set of tools on the Smartphone app, including a daily diary, reminders of their implementation goals, educational video clips, and two active contacts from per day for three months.

Compared to a control group who did not receive the active intervention, those who did succeeded in changing some personality traits over the course of three months. Those who desired to increase their extraversion, agreeableness, and conscientiousness succeeded in doing so over the course of three months. Perhaps even more impressive, people who desired to decrease their level of neuroticism also succeeded in doing so. Because these traits are linked with important life outcomes, such as success in the workplace, successful mateships, and overall life satisfaction, changing traits in directions desired should increase the odds of these successful life outcomes.

The authors attribute the success of the personality change intervention to several factors: (1) the Smartphone app was specifically designed to provide micro-interventions to achieve the personality change goals each person identified; (2) the app allowed daily contact, which typically cannot be achieved with a live in-person coach; (3) participants were highly motivated to work on the aspects of their personality that they wished to change.

The success of this personality change intervention suggests that personality traits may not be as "set in plaster" as previously thought. At least some personality traits can be actively changed through an intensive digital intervention in the directions people desire to change.

Personality Coherence over Time: Prediction of Socially Relevant Outcomes

The final form of personality development is called personality coherence, defined as predictable changes in the *manifestations* or *outcomes* of personality factors over time, even if the underlying characteristics remain stable. We focus on the consequences of personality for socially relevant outcomes, such as marital stability and divorce; alcoholism, drug use, and emotional disturbance; and job outcomes later in life.

Marital Stability, Marital Satisfaction, and Divorce

In a longitudinal study of unprecedented length, Kelly and Conley (1987) studied a sample of 300 couples from their engagements in the 1930s all the way through their status later in life in the 1980s. At the final testing, the median age of the subjects was 68 years. Within the entire sample of 300 couples, 22 couples broke their engagements and did not get married. Of the 278 couples who did get married, 50 ended up getting divorced sometime between 1935 and 1980.

During the first testing in the 1930s, acquaintances rated each participant's personality on many dimensions. Three aspects of personality proved to be strong predictors of marital dissatisfaction and divorce—the neuroticism of the husband, the lack of impulse control of the husband, and the neuroticism of the wife. High levels of neuroticism proved the strongest. Neuroticism predicted marital dissatisfaction of both the men and the women in the 1930s, again in 1955, and yet again in 1980. Subsequent studies confirm that neuroticism predicts divorce (Spikic & Mortelmans, 2021).

The couples who had a stable and satisfying marriage had neuroticism scores roughly half a standard deviation lower than the couples who subsequently got divorced.

The reasons for divorce themselves appear to be linked to the personality characteristics measured earlier in life. The husbands with low impulse control when first assessed, for example, tended later in life to have extramarital affairs—breaches of the marital vows that loomed large among the major reasons cited for the divorce. The men with higher impulse control appear to have been able to refrain from having sexual flings, which are so detrimental to marriages (Buss, 2016). Another study of Chinese married couples found that the traits of Machiavellianism (high interpersonal exploitativeness) and psychopathy (low empathy) predicted high levels of marital instability (He et al., 2018). Beyond these main effects, *personality similarity* with one's marriage partner is linked with longer and more stable marriages; couples more dissimilar in personality are more likely to break up (Rammstedt et al., 2013).

These results point to an important conclusion about personality coherence. Personality may not be destiny, but it leads to important and predictable life outcomes, such as infidelity, marital unhappiness, and divorce.

Psychologists have identified personality variables that predict whether a marriage will turn out to be happy and satisfying or whether it will end in divorce.
Although personality is not destiny, it does relate to important life outcomes, such as marital unhappiness and divorce.
Left: Ariel Skelley/Blend Images LLC; Right: Image Source/Alamy Stock Photo

Interestingly, neuroticism also plays a role in another important life outcome—resilience after losing a spouse. A fascinating longitudinal study showed that one of the best predictors of coping well with the death of a spouse was the personality disposition of emotional stability (Bonanno et al., 2002). A total of 205 individuals were assessed several years prior to the death of their spouse and again 18 months after their spouse's demise. Those high on emotional stability grieved less, showed less depression, and displayed the quickest psychological recovery. Individuals low on emotional stability (high on neuroticism) were still psychologically anguished a year and a half later. Personality, in short, affects many aspects of romantic life: who is likely to get involved in a successful romantic relationship (Shiner, Masten, & Tellegen, 2002); which marriages remain stable and highly satisfying (Kelly & Conley, 1987); which people are more likely to get divorced (Kelly & Conley, 1987); and how people cope following the loss of a spouse (Bonanno et al., 2002).

Alcoholism, Drug Use, and Emotional Disturbance

Personality also predicts the later development of alcoholism and emotional disturbance (Conley & Angelides, 1984). Of the 233 men in one longitudinal study, 40 were judged to develop a serious emotional problem or alcoholism. These 40 men had earlier been rated by their acquaintances as high on neuroticism. Specifically, they had neuroticism scores roughly three-fourths of a standard deviation higher than men who did not develop alcoholism or a serious emotional disturbance.

Early personality characteristics also were useful in distinguishing between the men who had become alcoholic and those who developed an emotional disturbance. Impulse control was the key factor. The alcoholic men had impulse control scores a full standard deviation lower than those who had an emotional disturbance. Other studies also find that those high on Sensation Seeking and Impulsivity, and low on traits such as Agreeableness and Conscientiousness, tend to abuse alcohol more than their peers (Cooper et al., 2003; Hampson et al., 2001; Markey, Markey, & Tinsley, 2003; Ruchkin et al., 2002). A study of more than 600 women and men found that high levels of impulsivity were linked with over-drinking and problem drinking of alcohol (Aluja et al., 2019). Low levels of Agreeableness and Conscientiousness are also linked to substance abuse (prescription and illegal drugs) in mid-life (Turiano et al., 2012). In sum, neuroticism and impulsivity are coherently linked with socially relevant outcomes later in life.

Religiousness and Spirituality

Another important life outcome pertains to spirituality—the degree to which individuals embrace religion or seek to lead a spiritual life. Personality traits in adolescence predict these outcomes in late adulthood. Adolescents who scored high on conscientiousness and agreeableness were more likely to score high on religiousness later in life (Wink et al., 2007). Openness to experience, in contrast, was the only personality trait in adolescence that predicted spirituality seeking in late life. Personality in youth appears to influence spirituality and religiousness later in life, regardless of the early socialization practices to which people are exposed.

Education, Academic Achievement, and Dropping Out

Impulsivity plays a key role in education and academic achievement. Kipnis (1971) had a group of individuals self-report on their levels of impulsivity. He also obtained their SAT scores, which are regarded as measures of academic achievement and potential. Among those with low SAT scores, there was no link between impulsivity and subsequent grade point average. Among those with high SAT scores, however, impulsive people had consistently lower GPAs than their less impulsive peers. Impulsive individuals were more likely to flunk out of college than were those who were less impulsive. Impulsivity (or lack of self-control) also affects workplace performance. One longitudinal study looked at personality dispositions at age 18 and work-related outcomes at age 26 (Roberts, Caspi, & Moffitt, 2003). They found that those who were high on self-control at age 18 had higher occupational attainment, greater involvement with their work, and more financial security at age 26. Conversely, the impulsive 18-year-olds were less likely to progress in their work, showed less psychological involvement, and experienced lower financial security.

The personality trait of Conscientiousness turns out to be the single best predictor of successful achievement in school and work. High Conscientiousness at age 3 predicts successful academic performance nine years later (Abe, 2005). Observer-based assessment of children's conscientiousness at ages 4–6 predicts school grades nine years later (Asendorpf & Van Aken, 2003). Conscientiousness of children assessed between the ages of 8 and 12 predicts academic attainment two decades later (Shiner, Masten, & Roberts, 2003). Although other personality traits also predict successful academic performance, such as Emotional Stability (Chamorro-Premuzic & Furnham, 2003a, 2003b), and Agreeableness and Openness (Hair & Graziano, 2003), Conscientiousness is the most powerful longitudinal predictor of success in school and work. The predictive power of Conscientiousness on educational outcomes has been replicated in other countries such as Luxembourg (Spengler et al., 2013).

A relatively new and much-hyped personality trait purported to predict education and achievement is *Grit*—defined by both perseverance and passion toward long-term goals (Duckworth et al., 2007). A massive meta-analysis of the Grit literature shows that it is highly correlated with Conscientiousness (Crede et al., 2016). Even after controlling for Conscientiousness, however, the *perseverance* facet of Grit does predict academic success, although the passion for long-term goals facet does not. Persistence seems to pay off more than pure passion when it comes to achievement.

Interestingly, work experiences also have an effect on personality change (Roberts et al., 2001). Those who attain high occupational status at age 26 have become happier, more self-confident, less anxious, and less self-defeating since they were 18 years old. Those who attain high work satisfaction also become less anxious and less prone to stress in their transition from adolescence to young adulthood.

Finally, what about people who attain financial success in the workplace? These individuals not only become less alienated and better able to handle stress, but they also increase their levels of social closeness—they like people more, turn to others for comfort, and like being around people. High conscientiousness continues to predict later income and net worth (Exley, 2021). In sum, just as personality at age 18 predicts work outcomes at age 26 (e.g., self-control and conscientiousness predict income), work outcomes predict personality change over time. We see again that impulsivity is a critical personality factor that is linked in meaningful ways with later life outcomes.

Health, Retirement, and Longevity

How long people live and how healthy or sickly they become during their years of life are exceptionally important developmental outcomes. It may come as a surprise that your personality actually predicts how long you are likely to live. The most important traits conducive to living a long life are *high conscientiousness, positive emotionality (extraversion), low levels of hostility,* and *low levels of neuroticism* (Danner, Snowdon, & Friesen, 2001; Friedman et al., 1995; Miller et al., 1996; Mroczek, Spiro, & Turiano, 2009). Among these, Conscientiousness and Emotional Stability are the strongest predictors of living a long life (Jokela et al., 2019). What about centenarians, those who live to be 100 years or more? A study of 272 Japanese centenarians found that these long-lived individuals score high on extraversion and low on neuroticism (da Rosa et al., 2021). There are several paths through which these personality traits affect longevity (Ozer & Benet-Martinez, 2006).

First, conscientious individuals engage in more health-promoting practices, such as maintaining a good diet and getting regular exercise; they also avoid unhealthy practices such as smoking and becoming a "couch potato." Conscientious children in elementary school, for example, end up smoking less and drinking less alcohol when they are adults fully 40 years later (Hampson et al., 2006). Conscientiousness at age 17 also predicts refraining from engaging in legal (nicotine, alcohol) and illegal drug use three years later (Elkins et al., 2006). Those low on Conscientiousness in adolescence are more likely to get addicted in young adulthood to drugs of all sorts. Moreover, conscientious individuals are more likely to follow doctors' orders and adhere to the treatment plans they recommend. Being low on Conscientiousness (being impulsive or low on self-control) during the preschool years predicts high levels of risk-taking during adolescence (Honomichl & Donnellan, 2012). Being impulsive (undercontrolled) in childhood predicts an increased likelihood of high blood pressure and stroke 40 years later (Chapman & Goldberg, 2011). Being impulsive also predicts unhealthy weight gain and weight fluctuations in later adulthood (Sutin et al., 2011). High conscientiousness and low neuroticism also predict better coping with anxiety surrounding Covid-19 (Nikčević et al., 2021).

Second, extraverts are more likely to have lots of friends, leading to a good social support network—factors linked with positive health outcomes. And third, low levels of hostility, a component of neuroticism, put less stress on the heart and cardiovascular system—a topic explored in greater detail in Chapter 18.

High levels of neuroticism are also linked with poor health behaviors, such as smoking, although neuroticism predicts mortality even after statistically controlling for smoking (Mroczek, Spiro, & Turiano, 2009). Those higher on Neuroticism may also

A Closer Look   Adult Outcomes of Children with Temper Tantrums

In a longitudinal study spanning 40 years, Caspi, Elder, & Bem (1987) explored the implications of childhood personality for adult occupational status and job outcomes. They identified a group of explosive, undercontrolled children, using interviews with their mothers as the data source. When the children were 8, 9, and 11, their mothers rated the frequency and severity of their temper tantrums. Severe tantrums were defined as behaviors involving biting, kicking, striking, throwing things, screaming, and shouting. From the sample, 38 percent of the boys and 29 percent of the girls were classified as having frequent and uncontrolled temper tantrums.

These children were followed throughout life, and the adult manifestations of childhood personality for men were especially striking. The men who as children had frequent and severe temper tantrums achieved lower levels of education in adulthood. The occupational status of their first job was also consistently lower than that of their calmer peers. The explosive children who had come from middle-class backgrounds tended to be downwardly mobile, and by midlife their occupational attainment was indistinguishable from that of their working-class counterparts. Furthermore, they tended to change jobs frequently, showed an erratic work pattern with more frequent breaks from employment, and averaged more months being unemployed.

Because 70 percent of the men in the sample served in the military, their military records could also be examined. The men who as children had been classified as having explosive temper tantrums attained a significantly lower military rank than their peers. Finally, 46 percent of these men were divorced by the age of 40, compared with only 22 percent of the men without a childhood history of temper tantrums. In sum, early childhood personality shows coherent links with important adult social outcomes, such as job attainment, frequency of job switching, unemployment, military attainment, and divorce.

It is easy to imagine why explosive, undercontrolled individuals tend to achieve less and get divorced more. Life consists of many frustrations, and people deal with their frustrations in different ways. Explosive undercontrollers are probably more likely to blow up and yell at the boss, for example, or to quit their jobs during an impulsive moment. Similarly, explosive undercontrollers are probably more likely to vent their frustrations on their spouses or perhaps even to impulsively have an extramarital affair. All of these events are likely to lead to lower levels of job attainment and higher levels of divorce.

be at greater risk of suicide when they perceive they are a burden to others (Hartley et al., 2019). Neuroticism also affects adjustment to retirement from jobs. High scorers on neuroticism experience more adjustment problems in retirement and more difficulty in coping with this critical transition that involves the loss of some social support (Hansson et al., 2019). High childhood intelligence predicts lower mortality risk over 40 years (Wrulich et al., 2015). In sum, the personality traits of conscientiousness, positive emotionality (extraversion), low hostility, and high intelligence predict positive health outcomes and longevity.

Predicting Personality Change

Can we predict who is likely to change in personality and who is not? In a fascinating longitudinal study, Caspi and Herbener (1990) studied middle-aged couples over an 11-year period. The couples were tested twice, once in 1970 and again in 1981. All the subjects had been born in either 1920–1921 or 1928–1929 and were part of a larger longitudinal project.

The key question was this: Is the choice of a marriage partner a cause of personality stability or change? If you marry someone similar to you, do you tend to remain more stable over time than if you marry someone different from you? They reasoned that similarity between spouses would support personality stability, because the couple would tend to reinforce one another on their attitudes, seek similar external sources of stimulation, and participate in the same social networks. Marrying someone who is unlike oneself may create

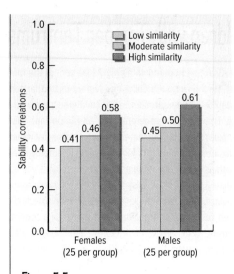

Figure 5.5

The figure shows the stability of personality over time as
a function of the similarity (low, medium, or high) of the
person to their spouse. Those married to someone similar
show the highest levels of personality stability over time.
Source: Caspi & Herbener, 1990.

attitude clashes and exposure to different social and environmental
events, and it may generally create an environment uncomfortable
to maintaining the status quo.

Using personality measures obtained on both husbands
and wives, Caspi and Herbener divided the couples into three
groups: those who were highly similar in personality, those who
were moderately similar in personality, and those who were low
in similarity. Then they examined which individuals showed
stability in personality over the 11-year period of midlife. The
results are shown in Figure 5.5.

Figure 5.5. The people married to spouses highly similar to
themselves showed the most personality stability. Those married
to spouses least similar to themselves showed the most personality change. The moderate group fell in between. This study is
important in pointing to a potential source of personality stability
and change—the selection of spouses. It will be interesting to see
whether future research can document other sources of personality
stability and change—perhaps by examining the selection of similar
or dissimilar friends, or by selecting college or work environments
that show a good "fit" with one's personality traits upon entry into
these environments (Roberts & Robins, 2004).

SUMMARY AND EVALUATION

Personality development includes both the continuities and changes over time. There are
three forms of personality stability: (1) rank order stability is the maintenance of one's
relative position within a group over time; (2) mean level stability is the maintenance of
the average level of a trait or characteristic over time; and (3) personality coherence is
predictable changes in the manifestations of a trait. We can examine personality development at three levels of personality analysis: the population level, the group differences
level, and the individual differences level.

There is strong evidence for personality rank order stability over time. Temperaments
such as activity level and fearfulness show moderate to high levels of stability during infancy.
Activity level and aggression show moderate to high levels of stability during childhood.
Bullies in childhood tend to become juvenile delinquents in adolescence and criminals
in adulthood. Personality traits, such as those of the five-factor model, show moderate to
high levels of stability during adulthood. In general, the stability coefficients decrease as the
length of time between the two periods of testing increases.

Personality also changes in predictable ways over time. On the Big Five, Neuroticism
generally decreases over time; people become a bit more emotionally stable as they age.
Agreeableness and Conscientiousness tend to increase over time. These changes suggest
increased maturity, as the sometimes tumultuous times of adolescence settle out into the maturity of adulthood. Moving into adult roles such as a serious romantic relationship, becoming a
parent, and investing heavily in work appears to increase people's level of Conscientiousness.
From early adolescence to early adulthood, men's self-esteem tends to increase, whereas
women's self-esteem tends to decrease. Sensation seeking declines predictably with age. In
women, femininity tends to decrease over time, notably from the early forties to the early fifties. Several studies suggest that the personality characteristics of autonomy, independence,
and competence tend to increase as people get older, especially among women.

In addition to personality change due to age, there is also evidence that mean personality levels can be affected by the social cohort in which one grows up. Jean Twenge has documented several such effects, most notably on women's levels of assertiveness or dominance. Women's assertiveness levels were high following the 1930s, in which women had to be extremely independent; they fell during the 1950s and 1960s, when women were largely homemakers and fewer became professionals. From 1967 to 1993, however, women's levels of assertiveness increased, corresponding to changes in their social roles and increasing participation in professional occupations. Twenge also presents some evidence for a general increase in narcissism among younger cohorts, although this conclusion has been challenged by others who find no cohort changes in narcissism.

Personality shows evidence of coherence over time. Early measures of personality can be used to predict socially relevant outcomes later in life. High levels of neuroticism in both sexes and impulsivity in men, for example, predict marital dissatisfaction and divorce. Neuroticism early in adulthood is also a good predictor of later alcoholism and the development of emotional problems. Impulsivity plays a key role in the development of alcoholism and the failure to achieve one's academic potential. Highly impulsive individuals tend to get poorer grades and drop out of school more than their less impulsive peers. Children with explosive temper tantrums tend to manifest their personalities as adults through downward occupational mobility, more frequent job switching, lower attainment of rank in the military, and higher frequencies of divorce. People who are impulsive at age 18 tend to do more poorly in the workplace—they attain less occupational success and less financial security. Work experiences, in turn, appear to affect personality change. Those who attain occupational success tend to become happier, more self-confident, and less anxious over time.

What explains these forms of personality stability and coherence over time? One possibility pertains to our choices of romantic partners. People tend to choose those who are similar to themselves in personality, and the more similar our partners, the more stable our personality traits remain over time. Selecting a mate with a similar personality is also linked with experiencing a longer and more stable marriage.

How can we best reconcile the findings of considerable personality stability over time with evidence of important changes? First, longitudinal studies have shown conclusively that personality traits, such as those subsumed by the Big Five, show substantial rank order stability over time. These personality traits also show evidence of coherence over time. Bullies in middle school, for example, tend to become criminals in adulthood. Those with self-control and conscientiousness in adolescence tend to perform well academically and well in the workplace later in life. In the context of these broad patterns of stability, people also show mean level changes with age—as a group people become less neurotic, less anxious, less impulsive, lower in sensation seeking, more agreeable, and more conscientious. Some changes are more pronounced in women—they become less feminine and more competent and autonomous over time. And some personality change affects only some individuals, such as those who succeed in the workplace. In short, although personality dispositions tend to be stable over time, they are not "set in plaster" in the sense that some change occurs in some individuals some of the time.

KEY TERMS

personality development   124
rank order stability   124
mean level stability   125
mean level change   125

personality coherence   125
temperament   129
longitudinal studies   130
actometer   130

stability coefficients   131
validity coefficients   131
self-esteem   139
cohort effects   143

PART TWO

The Biological Domain

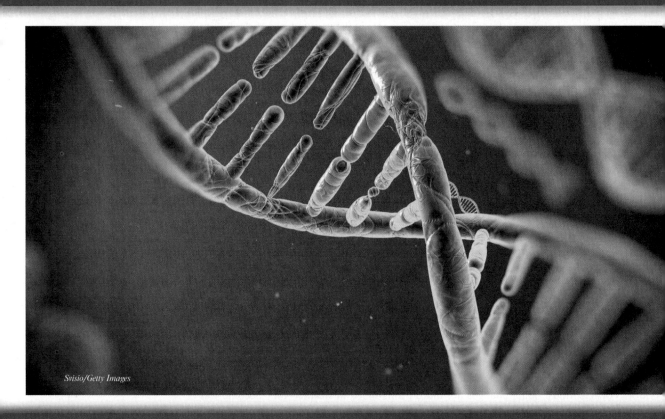

Svisio/Getty Images

The biological domain refers to those physical elements and biological systems within our bodies that influence or are influenced by our behaviors, thoughts, and feelings. For example, one type of physical element within our bodies that may influence our personalities is our genes. Our genetic makeup determines whether our hair is curly or straight; whether our eyes are blue or brown; and whether we have large, heavy bones or a slight build. Our genetic makeup influences how active we are, whether we are hot-tempered and disagreeable, and whether we like to be with others or prefer solitude. Understanding how genes and their interactions with environments contribute to personality falls squarely within the biological domain (see Chapter 6).

Another area in which biology and personality intersect is in physiological systems, such as the brain, where differences among people might contribute to personality differences. For example, some people might have more activity in the right half than in the left half of their brains. Empirically, this imbalance of activation is linked with a tendency to experience distress and other negative emotions more strongly. Here, physical differences among people are associated with differences in emotional style. Because these differences represent enduring and stable ways that people differ from one another, these physiological features represent aspects of personality (see Chapter 7).

The literature contains many examples of physiological measures that are correlates of personality. The finding that shy children show elevated heart rates when in the presence of strangers, compared to non-shy children, is one example (Kagan & Snidman, 1991). Would eliminating the heart rate reactivity make the shy child less shy? Probably not. This is because the physiological response is a *correlate* of the traits in question, rather than an underlying substrate that *produces* or *contributes* to the personality trait.

This is not to say that studying physiological correlates of personality is a worthless endeavor. On the contrary, physiological measures often reveal important *consequences* of personality. For example, the high cardiovascular reactivity of Type A persons may have serious consequences for developing heart disease. For this reason, identifying physiological measures that are correlates of personality is a scientifically useful and important task.

On the other hand, there are several modern theories of personality in which underlying physiology plays a more central role in *generating* or forming the substrate of specific personality differences. In Chapter 7, we consider several of these theories in detail. Each shares the notion that specific personality traits are based on underlying physiological differences. Each theory also assumes that if the underlying physiological substrate is altered, the behavior pattern associated with the trait will be altered as well.

The third biological approach we cover is based on Charles Darwin's theory of evolution. Adaptations that helped individuals to survive and reproduce were passed on as evolved characteristics. For example, primates who could walk upright could colonize open fields, and their hands were freed for using tools. Evidence for the evolution of such physical characteristics is solid.

Psychologists are now considering evidence for the evolution of psychological characteristics. They are taking the principles of evolution, such as natural selection, and applying them to an analysis of psychological traits. For example, natural selection may have operated on our ancestors to select for group cooperation; early humans who were able to cooperate and work in groups were more likely to survive and reproduce; those who preferred not to cooperate were less likely to become an ancestor. Adaptations for cooperation are evolved psychological characteristics that present in modern humans. Evolutionary perspectives on personality are discussed in Chapter 8.

Svisio/Getty Images

Genetics and Personality

6

THE BIOLOGICAL DOMAIN

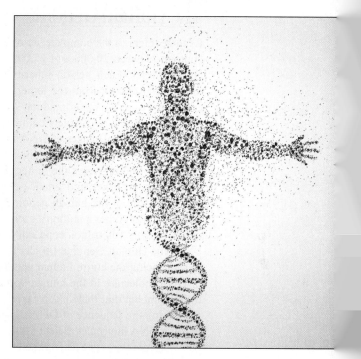

A record of the past is written in the genetic blueprint.
Lonely/Shutterstock

The Jim twins are identical twins separated at birth and raised in different adoptive families. They met for the first time when they were 39 years old, having been apart for their entire lives. One of the twins, Jim Springer, made the first phone call on February 9, 1979, after learning that he had a twin brother, Jim Lewis, who was living in the Midwest. They had an instant connection; three weeks after the phone call, Jim became the best man at his brother's wedding.

When they first met, the Jim twins displayed an astonishing set of similarities. Both weighed 180 pounds. Both were 6 feet tall. They had each been married twice, and in each case their first wives were named Linda and their second wives named Betty. Each had a son named James. Their jobs were also similar—each worked part-time as a sheriff. Both smoked Salem cigarettes and drank Miller Lite beer. Both suffered from the same kind of headache syndrome, and both had a habit of biting their fingernails. Both left love notes for their wives scattered around the house. And both had remarkably similar personality scores on standardized tests (Segal, 1999).

The Jim twins were not identical in all ways, of course. One was a better writer, the other a better speaker. They wore their hair differently; one combed his hair down over his forehead, and the other combed his hair back. But overall, the similarities were striking, especially since they had grown up from infancy in entirely different families. This is a single twin pair, and of course no conclusions can be drawn from one case. But the case of the Jim twins raises the intriguing question, "What is the role of genetics in influencing personality?"

The Human Genome

Genome refers to the complete set of genes an organism possesses. The human genome contains between 20,000 and 25,000 genes. All these genes are located on 23 pairs of chromosomes. Each person inherits one set of each pair of chromosomes from the mother and one set from the father. One way to think about the human genome is to consider it to be a book containing 23 chapters, with each chapter being a chromosome pair. Each one of the chapters contains hundreds or thousands of genes. And each gene consists of long sequences of DNA molecules. One astonishing fact is that the nucleus of each cell within the body contains two complete sets of the human genome, one from the mother and one from the father. The only exceptions are red blood cells, which do not contain any genes, and female egg cells and male sperm cells, each of which contains only one copy of the human genome. Because the body contains roughly 100 trillion cells (a million times a million), each of which is smaller than the head of a pin, each of us has roughly 100 trillion copies of our genome within our bodies.

The Human Genome Project is a multibillion-dollar research endeavor dedicated to sequencing the entire human genome—that is, to identifying the particular sequence of DNA molecules in the human species. On June 26, 2000, scientists made headlines by announcing that they had completed the first draft of the complete human genome. Identifying the sequence of DNA molecules does not mean identifying all the functions of these DNA molecules. Scientists now have the "book" of life, but they must still figure out what role the genes play in the body, mind, and behavior.

Some findings appear to be changing standard assumptions about the human genome. Two findings are especially noteworthy. First, although the number of genes humans possess is similar to the number of genes estimated for mice and worms, the *manner* in which human genes get decoded into proteins turns out to be far more variable than in other species. These alternative forms of decoding create a tremendous variety of proteins—many more than seen in mice or worms—and may account for the complex differences we observe between rodents and humans (Plomin, 2002). Second, these protein-coding genes, making up roughly 2 percent of the human genome, are only part of the story. Many parts of the other 98 percent of the DNA in the human chromosomes used to be viewed as **"genetic junk"** because scientists believed that these parts were functionless residues that served no purposes. Genetic researchers are discovering that this "junk DNA" is not junk at all. Rather, parts of these chunks of DNA have an impact on humans, potentially affecting everything from a person's physical size to personality (Gibbs, 2003; Plomin, 2002). These hidden layers of complexity in the human genome—given names such as "pseudogenes" and "riboswitches"—mean that we have a long way to go before understanding the complex and mysterious links between genes and human behavior.

Most of the genes within the human genome are the same for each person on the planet. That is why all normally developing humans have many of the same characteristics: 2 eyes, 2 legs, 32 teeth, 10 fingers, a heart, a liver, 2 lungs, and so on. A small number of these genes, however, are different for different individuals. Thus, although all humans have two eyes, some people have blue eyes, some have brown eyes, and a few even have violet eyes. Some of the genes that differ from individual to individual influence physical characteristics, such as eye color, height, and bone width. Some genes that differ across individuals influence the behavioral characteristics that define human personality.

Controversy About Genes and Personality

Perhaps no other area of personality psychology has been fraught with as much controversy as the study of behavioral genetics. Researchers in this field attempt to determine the degree to which individual differences in personality are caused by genetic and environmental differences. Scientific reports on behavioral genetic studies often make headlines and cover stories. On January 2, 1996, for example, *The New York Times* caused a stir with reports of a scientific breakthrough: "Variant Gene Is Connected to a Love of the Search for New Thrills." It reported the discovery of a specific gene for novelty seeking—the tendency to be extraverted, impulsive, extravagant, quick-tempered, excitable, and exploratory. A November 5, 2012, news article proclaimed that "Being Perfectionist Lies in Your Genes" (http://www.newstrackindia.com/newsdetails/2012/11/05/161-Being-perfectionist-lies-in-your-genes.html). Some popular media sources are proposing "designer babies," where parents select from a genetic checklist the characteristics they would like in their children. These ideas are controversial because they suggest that genetic differences among individuals, rather than differences in parental socialization or personal experience, are responsible for shaping some core features of human personality.

Part of the reason for the controversy is ideological. Many people worry that findings from behavioral genetics will be used or misused to support particular political agendas. If individual differences in thrill seeking, for example, are caused by specific genes, then does this mean that we should not hold juvenile delinquents responsible for stealing cars for joy rides? If scientists trace a behavior pattern or personality trait to a genetic component, some people worry that such findings might lead to pessimism about the possibilities for change.

Part of the controversy concerns the idea of eugenics. **Eugenics** is the notion that we can design the future of the human species by fostering the reproduction of people with certain traits and by discouraging the reproduction of persons without those traits. Many are concerned that findings from genetic studies might be used to support programs to prevent some individuals from reproducing or, even worse, to bolster the cause of those who would advocate that some people should not reproduce in order to create a "superior human species." On the other hand, many would-be parents are very interested in findings from genetic research, and some express a desire not to have children if they knew they would carry a genetic disposition for a mental disorder and even not choose a mate with such a known genetic proclivity (Morosoli et al., 2021).

However, modern psychologists who study the genetics of personality are typically extremely careful in their attempts to educate others about the use and potential misuse of their findings (Harden, 2021; Plomin et al., 2013). Knowledge is better than ignorance, they argue. If people believe that hyperactivity, for example, is caused by parenting behaviors when in fact hyperactivity turns out to be primarily influenced by genes, then attempts to influence hyperactive behavior by altering parental practices could cause frustration and resentment on the part of the parents. Furthermore, psychologists maintain that genetic findings need not lead to the evil consequences that some worry about. Finding that a personality characteristic has a genetic component, for example, does not mean that the environment is powerless to modify that characteristic. Let's now turn to the field of genetics and personality to discover what lies beneath the swirling controversy.

Goals of Behavioral Genetics

To understand the primary goals of behavioral genetics, let's look at a concrete example—individual differences in height. Some individuals are tall, such as basketball player LeBron James (6 feet, 8 inches). Other individuals are short, such as actor Danny DeVito (around 5 feet). Geneticists focus on the key question, "What causes some individuals to be tall and others to be short?"

In principle, there can be many causes of height differences. Differences in diet while growing up can cause differences in height. Genetic differences can also account for some of the differences in height. One of the central goals of genetic research is to determine the percentage of an individual difference that can be attributed to genetic differences and the percentage due to environmental differences.

In the case of height, both environmental and genetic factors are important. Clearly, children tend to resemble their parents in height—generally, tall parents have taller than average children and short parents have shorter than average children. And genetic research has confirmed that roughly 90 percent of the individual differences in height are indeed due to genetic differences. The environment, which contributes 10 percent to individual differences in height, is far from trivial. In the United States, average adult height has increased in the entire population by roughly 2 inches over the past century, most likely due to increases in the nutritional value of the food eaten by U.S. citizens. This example brings home an important lesson: Even though some observed differences among people can be due to genetic differences, this does not mean that the environment plays no role in modifying the trait.

In determining height, genetics accounts for 90 percent of the variation, and environmental factors, such as diet, account for 10 percent of the variation. The actor Danny DeVito is nearly 2 feet shorter than basketball player LeBron James.

Left: Helga Esteb/Shutterstock; Right: Jason Miller/Getty Images

Exercise

Can you think of some human characteristics that you consider to be mostly under genetic influence? Consider, for example, individual differences in eye color. Can you think of other characteristics that are not very much influenced by genetic factors? Consider, for example, individual differences in eating with forks versus eating with chopsticks. How might you go about testing whether some individual differences are, or are not, influenced by genetic differences?

The methods used by behavioral geneticists examined in this chapter can be applied to any individual difference variable. They can be used to identify the causes of differences in height and weight, differences in intelligence, differences in personality traits, and even differences in attitudes, such as liberalism or conservatism.

Behavioral geneticists sometimes try to figure out the **percentage of variance** due to genetic and environmental causes. *Percentage of variance* refers to the fact that individuals vary, or are different from each other, and this variability can be partitioned into percentages that are due to different causes. Behavioral geneticists also are interested in determining the ways in which genes and the environment interact and correlate with each other. And they are interested in figuring out precisely where in the environment the effects are taking place—in parental socialization practices, for example; in the teachers to whom children are exposed; or even in peer influences (Harris, 2007). We turn to these more complex issues toward the end of this chapter. First, we must examine the fundamentals of behavioral genetics: What is heritability, and what methods do geneticists use to get their answers?

What Is Heritability?

Heritability is a statistic that refers to the proportion of observed variance in a *group* of individuals that can be accounted for by genetic variance (Plomin, 2019). It describes the degree to which genetic differences among individuals cause differences in an observed property, such as height, extraversion, or sensation seeking. Heritability may be one of the most frequently misunderstood concepts in psychology. If precisely defined, however, it provides useful information for identifying the genetic and environmental determinants of personality.

Heritability has a formal definition: *the proportion of phenotypic variance that is attributable to genotypic variance.* **Phenotypic variance** refers to observed individual differences, such as in height, weight, or personality. **Genotypic variance** refers to individual differences in the total collection of genes possessed by each person. Thus a heritability of .50 means that 50 percent of the observed phenotypic variation is attributable to genotypic variation. A heritability of .20 means that only 20 percent of the phenotypic variation is attributable to genotypic variation. In these examples, the environmental component is simply the proportion of phenotypic variance that is *not* attributable to genetic variance. Thus, a heritability of .50 means that the environmental component is .50.

A heritability of .20 means that the environmental component is .80. These examples illustrate the simplest cases and assume that there is no correlation or interaction between genetic and environmental factors.

The environmental contribution is defined in a similar way. Thus, the percentage of observed variance in a *group* of individuals that can be attributed to environmental (nongenetic) differences is called **environmentality**. Generally speaking, the larger the heritability, the smaller the environmentality and vice versa.

Exercise

Discuss the meaning of the following statement: "All normally developing humans have language, but some people speak Chinese, others French, and others English." To what degree is variability in the language spoken due to variability in genes or variability in the environment in which one is raised?

Misconceptions About Heritability

One common misconception about heritability is that it can be applied to a single individual. It can't. It is meaningful to say that individual differences in height are 90 percent heritable, but it makes absolutely no sense to say, "Meredith's height is 90 percent heritable." You cannot say, for example, that the first 63 inches of her height are due to genes and the other 7 inches are due to the environment. For an individual, genes and environment are inextricably intertwined. Both play a role in determining height, and they cannot be separated. Thus, heritability refers only to differences in a sample or population, not to an individual.

Another common misconception about heritability is that it is constant. In fact, it is nothing of the sort. Heritability is a statistic that applies only to a population at one point in time and in a particular array of environments. If the environments change, then heritability can change. For example, in principle, heritability can be high in one population (e.g., among Swedes) but low in another (e.g., among Nigerians). And heritability can be low at one time and high at another time. Heritability always depends on both the range of genetic differences in the population and on the range of environmental differences in that population. To draw on a concept from Chapter 2, heritability does not always generalize across persons and places.

A final common misconception is that heritability is an absolutely precise statistic (Plomin et al., 2001). Nothing could be further from the truth. Error or unreliability of measurement, for example, can distort heritability statistics. And because heritability statistics are typically computed using correlations, which themselves fluctuate from sample to sample, further imprecision creeps in. In sum, heritability is best regarded merely as an *estimate* of the percentage of phenotypic differences due to genetic differences. It is not precise. It does not refer to an individual. And it is not eternally fixed (see Johnson, Penke, & Spinath, 2011, for a more detailed treatment of what heritability means and its limits).

Nature–Nurture Debate Clarified

Clarifying the meaning of the term *heritability*—what it is and what it is not—allows us to think more clearly about the **nature–nurture debate**—the arguments about whether genes or environments are more important determinants of personality. The clarification comes from distinguishing between two levels of analysis: the level of the individual and the level of a population of individuals.

At the level of an individual, there is no nature–nurture debate. Every individual contains a unique constellation of genes. And those genes require environments during one's life to produce a recognizable individual. At this moment, each person reading these pages is the product of an inseparable intertwining of genes and environment. It makes no sense to ask "Which is more important, genes or environment, in accounting for Sally?" At the individual level of analysis, there is simply no issue to debate. As an analogy, consider baking a cake. Each particular cake consists of flour, sugar, eggs, and water. It makes no sense to ask whether the finished cake is "caused" more by the flour or more by the eggs. Both are necessary ingredients, inextricably combined and inseparable in the finished cake. Genes and environment for one individual are like flour and eggs for one cake—both ingredients are necessary, but we cannot logically disentangle them to see which is more important.

At the level of the population, however, we can disentangle the influence of genes and environments. This is the level of analysis at which behavioral geneticists operate. It makes sense to ask, "Which is more important in accounting for individual differences in trait *X*—genetic differences or environmental differences?" At the population level, we can partition the differences into these two sources: differences in genes and differences in environments. And for a particular population at a given point in time, we can make sensible statements about which is more important *in accounting for the differences.* Consider the cake example. If you have 100 cakes, it makes sense to ask whether the differences among the cakes in, say, sweetness is caused more by differences in the amount of flour used or by differences in the amount of sugar used.

Now consider physical differences among people. Individual differences in height, for example, show a heritability of roughly .90. Individual differences in weight show a heritability of roughly .50. And individual differences in mate preferences—the qualities we desire in a marriage partner—show very low heritabilities of roughly .10 (Waller, 1994). Thus, it is meaningful to say that genetic differences are more important than environmental differences for height. Genetic and environmental factors are roughly equal when it comes to weight. And environmental differences are overwhelmingly important for mate preferences.

The next time you get into a debate with someone about the nature-nurture issue, be sure to ask, "Are you asking the question at the level of the individual or at the level of individual differences within a population?" Only when the level of analysis is specified, can the answers make any sense.

Behavioral Genetic Methods

Behavioral geneticists have developed an array of methods for teasing apart the contributions of genes and environments as causes of individual differences. Selective breeding with animals is one method. Family studies provide a second method. A third, and perhaps the most well-known, method is that of twin studies. Adoption studies provide a fourth behavioral genetic method. We briefly discuss the logic of each of these methods, exploring where heritability estimates come from.

Selective Breeding—Studies of Humans' Best Friend

Artificial selection—as occurs when dogs are bred for certain qualities—can take place only if the desired characteristics are under the influence of heredity. **Selective breeding** occurs by identifying the dogs that possess the desired characteristic and having them mate only with other dogs that also possess the characteristic. Dog breeders have been successful precisely because many of the qualities they wish specific dog breeds to have are moderately to highly heritable.

Some of these heritable qualities are physical traits such as size, ear length, wrinkled skin, and coat of hair. Other characteristics are more behavioral and can be considered personality traits (Gosling, Kwan, & John, 2003). Some dogs, such as pit bulls, are, on average, more aggressive than most other dogs. Other breeds, such as the Labrador, are, on average, very sociable and agreeable. And others, such as the Chesapeake Bay retriever, have a strong desire to please their owners by retrieving objects. A recent study of 12,117 dogs found that they differed greatly in boldness versus timidity, with bolder dogs exploring more, positively approaching unfamiliar people, and showing low levels of fear (Svartberg, 2021). All of these traits are characteristics that have been selectively bred.

If the heritability for these personality traits in dog breeds is literally zero, then attempts to breed dogs selectively for such traits will be doomed to fail. On the other hand, if the heritability of these personality traits is high (e.g., >80 percent), then selective breeding will be highly successful and will occur rapidly. The fact that selective breeding has been so successful with dogs tells us that heredity must be a factor in the personality traits, such as boldness, aggressiveness, agreeableness, and desire to please, that were successfully selected. For obvious ethical reasons, we cannot do selective breeding experiments on people. Fortunately, however, there are other methods of behavioral genetics that can be used to study humans.

The Labrador retriever and the Chesapeake Bay retriever have been selectively bred for certain characteristics. Both have webbed feet, for example, which makes them strong swimmers and excellent water retrievers. They have also been selectively bred for certain personality characteristics. The Labrador was bred to be sociable and friendly, whereas the Chesapeake Bay was bred to be loyal to only one owner and suspicious of strangers. Consequently, the Chesapeake Bay retriever makes a good watch dog in addition to its skills as a sporting dog. The Labrador, however, is the most popular family dog in America, most likely due to the friendliness and cheerful disposition of this breed.

Left: Comstock Images/Alamy Stock Photo; Right: Courtesy of Randy J. Larsen

Family Studies

Family studies correlate genetic relatedness among family members with the degree of personality similarity. They capitalize on the fact that there are known degrees of genetic relatedness among family members. Parents are usually not related to each other genetically. However, each parent shares 50 percent of their genes with each of their children. Similarly, siblings share 50 percent of their genes, on average. Grandparents and grandchildren share 25 percent, as do uncles and aunts with their nieces and nephews. First cousins share 12.5 percent of their genes.

If a personality characteristic is heritable, then family members with greater genetic relatedness should be more similar to each other than family members with less genetic relatedness. If a personality characteristic is not at all heritable, then even family members who are closely related genetically, such as siblings, should not be any more similar to each other than those who are less genetically related to each other.

Family members who share the same genes also typically share similar environments. Two members of a family might be similar not because a given personality characteristic is heritable, but rather because of a shared environment. For example, certain brothers and sisters may be similar on shyness not because of shared genes, but because of shared parents. For this reason, results from family studies alone are never definitive. A more compelling behavioral genetic method is that of twin studies.

The family study method assumes that for traits with a large genetic component, the degree of similarity among relatives on that trait will be in proportion to the amount of genetic relatedness or degree of kinship, among them.
John Lund/Tiffany Schoepp/Blend Images LLC

Twin Studies

Twin studies estimate heritability by gauging whether identical twins, who share 100 percent of their genes, are more similar to each other than are fraternal twins, who share only 50 percent of their genes. Twin studies, and especially studies of twins reared apart, have received tremendous media attention. The Jim twins, described earlier, are identical twins given up for adoption at birth. Because they were adopted into different families, they were unaware that they had a twin. When they met for the first time, to everyone's astonishment these men shared many behavioral habits—having the same favorite TV shows, using the same brand of toothpaste, owning a Jack Russell terrier dog, and so on. They also shared many personality traits, such as being highly conscientious and emotionally stable. Is this coincidence? Perhaps, but these coincidences seemed to happen with regularity in studying twins (Segal, 1999).

Twin studies take advantage of a fascinating quirk of nature. Nearly all individuals come from a single fertilized egg, and humans—as contrasted with some other mammals, such as mice—typically give birth to a single child at a time. Occasionally, however, twins are born, occurring only once in 83 births (Knopik et al., 2022). Twins come in two distinct types: identical and fraternal.

Identical twins, technically called **monozygotic (MZ) twins**, come from a single fertilized egg (or zygote—hence, *monozygotic*), which divides into two at some point during

Twins come in two varieties: monozygotic and dizygotic. Can you identify which of these two pairs of twins is more likely to be monozygotic? Which pair is definitely dizygotic? What is the clue that helps you answer these questions?
Left: golf9c9333/Getty Images; Right: Digital Vision/Getty Images

gestation. No one knows why fertilized eggs occasionally divide. They just do. Identical twins are remarkable in that they are genetically identical, like clones, coming from the same single source. They share literally 100 percent of their genes.

The other type of twin is not genetically identical to the co-twin; instead, such twins share only 50 percent of their genes. They are called fraternal twins, or **dizygotic (DZ) twins**, because they come from two eggs that were separately fertilized (*di* means "two," so *dizygotic* means "coming from two fertilized eggs"). DZ twins can be same sex or opposite sex. In contrast, identical twins are always the same sex because they are genetically identical. Dizygotic twins are no more alike than regular siblings in of genetic relatedness. They just share the same womb at the same time and have the same birthday; otherwise, they are no more similar than are ordinary brothers and sisters. Of all the twins born, two-thirds are dizygotic and one-third are monozygotic.

The twin method capitalizes on the fact that some twins are genetically identical, sharing 100 percent of their genes, whereas other twins share only 50 percent of their genes. If fraternal twins are just as similar to each other as identical twins are on a personality characteristic, then we can infer that the characteristic under consideration is not heritable: The greater genetic similarity of identical twins, in this case, is not causing them to be more similar in personality. Conversely, if identical twins are substantially *more similar* to each other than are DZ twins, then this provides evidence that is compatible with a heritability interpretation. In fact, studies have shown that identical twins are more similar than fraternal twins in dominance, height, and the ridge count on their fingertips (Knopik et al., 2022), suggesting that heritability plays a causal role in influencing these individual differences. For dominance, identical twins are correlated $+.57$, whereas fraternal twins are correlated only $+.12$ (Loehlin & Nichols, 1976). For height, identical twins are correlated $+.93$, whereas fraternal twins are correlated only $+.48$ (Mittler, 1971).

There are several formulas for calculating heritability from twin data, each with its own problems and limitations. One simple method, however, is to double the difference between the MZ correlation and DZ correlation:

$$\text{heritability}^2 = 2(r_{mz} - r_{dz})$$

In this formula, r_{mz} refers to the correlation coefficient computed between pairs of monozygotic twins, and r_{dz} refers to the correlation between the dizygotic twins. Plugging in the correlations for height, for example, leads to the following heritability estimate: heritability of height $= 2(.93 - .48) = .90$. Thus, according to this formula, height is 90 percent heritable and 10 percent environmental. The basic logic of this method can be applied to any characteristic: personality traits, attitudes, religious beliefs, sexual orientation, drug use habits, and so on.

We must note an important assumption of the twin method. This assumption is known as the **equal environments assumption**. The twin method assumes that the environments experienced by identical twins are no more similar to each other than are the environments experienced by fraternal twins. If they are more similar, then the greater similarity of the identical twins could be due to the fact that they experience more similar environments rather than the fact that they have more genes in common. If identical twins are treated by their parents as more similar than fraternal twins are treated by their parents—for example, if the parents of identical twins dress them in more similar clothing than do the parents of fraternal twins—then the greater similarity of the identical twins might be due to more similar treatment.

Behavioral geneticists have been worried about the validity of the equal environments assumption and so have designed studies to test it. One approach is to examine twins who have been misdiagnosed as identical or fraternal (Scarr, 1968; Scarr & Carter-Saltzman, 1979). That is, some twins who were believed to be identical by their parents were really just fraternal. And some twins whose parents believed them to be fraternal turned out to be identical. These mistakes in labeling allowed the researchers to examine whether fraternal twins who were *believed* to be identical were in fact more similar to each other than accurately labeled fraternal twins. Similarly, it allowed the researchers to examine whether the identical twins, believed to be fraternal, were in fact less similar to each other than identical twins correctly labeled as identical. The findings on a variety of cognitive and personality tests supported the validity of the equal environments assumption. The parents' beliefs and labeling of the twins did not affect their actual similarity on the personality and cognitive measures. This means that, however twins are labeled, the environments experienced by identical twins do not seem to be functionally more similar to each other than the environments experienced by fraternal twins.

Additional studies over the years have continued to support the equal environments assumption (Knopik et al., 2022). Although identical twins do tend to dress more alike than fraternal twins, spend more time together, and have more friends in common, there is no evidence that these environmental similarities cause them to be any more similar in their personalities than they are to begin with (Plomin et al., 2008).

Adoption Studies

Adoption studies provide one of the most powerful behavioral genetic methods available. In adoption studies, one can examine the correlations between adopted children and their adoptive parents, with whom they share no genes. If one finds a positive correlation between adopted children and their adoptive parents, then this provides evidence for environmental influences on the personality trait in question.

We can also examine the correlations between adopted children and their genetic parents, who had no influence on the children's environments. If we find a zero correlation between adopted children and their genetic parents, this is evidence for a lack of heritable influence on the personality trait in question. Conversely, if we find a positive correlation between parents and their adopted-away children, with whom they have had no contact, then this provides evidence for heritability.

Adoption studies are especially powerful because they allow us to get around the equal environments assumption, which must be made in twin studies. In twin studies, because parents provide both genes and environments to their children, and may provide more similar environments for identical than for fraternal twins, there is a potential compromise of the equal environments assumption. In adoption studies, however, genetic parents provide none of the environmental influences on their children, thus unconfounding genetic and environmental causes.

Adoption studies, however, have potential problems of their own. The most important potential problem is the assumption of representativeness. Adoption studies assume that adopted children, their birth parents, and their adoptive parents are representative of the general population. For example, these studies assume that couples who adopt children are not any different from couples who do not adopt children. Fortunately, the assumption of representativeness can be tested directly. Several studies have confirmed that the assumption of representativeness holds for cognitive abilities, personality, education level, and even socioeconomic status (Plomin & DeFries, 1985; Plomin, DeFries, & Fulker, 1988).

Another potential problem with adoption studies is **selective placement**. If adopted children are placed with adoptive parents who are similar to their birth parents, then this may inflate the correlations between the adopted children and their adoptive parents. Fortunately, there does not seem to be selective placement, so this potential problem is not a real problem in actual studies (Plomin, DeFries, & McClearn, 2008).

One of the most powerful behavioral genetic designs is one that combines the strengths of twin and adoption studies at the same time, by studying twins reared apart. The correlation between identical twins reared apart can be interpreted directly as an index of heritability. If identical twins reared apart show a correlation of $+.65$ for a personality trait, then that means that 65 percent of the individual differences are heritable. Identical twins reared apart are exceedingly rare. Painstaking efforts have been undertaken to find such twins and study them (Segal, 1999). The effort has been well worth it, as such studies have yielded a bounty of fascinating results, to which we now turn. A summary of the traditional behavioral genetic methods, along with their advantages and limitations, is shown in Table 6.1.

Table 6.1　Summary of Traditional Behavioral Genetic Methods

Method	Advantages	Limitations
Selective breeding studies	Can infer heritability if selective breeding works	Are unethical to conduct on humans
Family studies	Provide heritability estimates	Violate equal environments assumption
Twin studies	Provide both heritability and environmentality estimates	Sometimes violate equal environments assumption
Adoption studies	Provide both heritability and environmentality estimates; get around the problem of equal environments assumption	Adopted kids might not be representative of population; problem of selective placement

Major Findings from Behavioral Genetic Research

This section summarizes what is known about the heritability of personality. The results may surprise you.

Personality Traits

The most well-studied personality traits in behavioral genetic designs are Extraversion and Neuroticism. Recall that Extraversion is a dimension comprising people who are outgoing and talkative at one end and people who are quiet and withdrawn at the other (introverted) end. Neuroticism is a dimension with one end characterized by people who are anxious, nervous, and emotionally volatile and at the other end people who are calm and emotionally stable. Henderson (1982) reviewed the literature on more than 25,000 pairs of twins. He found substantial heritability for both traits. In one study involving 4,987 twin pairs in Sweden, for example, the correlations for Extraversion were +.51 for identical twins and +.21 for fraternal twins (Floderus-Myrhed, Pedersen, & Rasmuson, 1980). Using the simple formula of doubling the difference between the two correlations yields a heritability of .60.

The findings for Neuroticism are similar (Floderus-Myrhed et al., 1980). The identical twin correlation for Neuroticism is +.50, whereas the fraternal twin correlation is only +.23. This suggests a heritability of .54. Twin studies have yielded very similar results, suggesting that Extraversion and Neuroticism are traits that are approximately half due to genetics. A large-scale twin study conducted in Australia found a heritability for Neuroticism of 47 percent (Birley et al., 2006). Similar moderate heritabilities continue to be found for Neuroticism and Extraversion in more samples using diverse measurement methods (Loehlin, 2012; Moore et al., 2010). A massive study of 253,015 individuals from 58,645 families from the Netherlands found a heritability of Neuroticism of 47 percent (Boomsma et al., 2018).

The findings for Extraversion and Neuroticism from adoption studies suggest somewhat lower heritabilities. Pedersen (1993), for example, found heritability estimates based on comparisons of adoptees and their biological parents of about 40 percent for Extraversion and about 30 percent for Neuroticism. Correlations between adoptive parents and their adopted children tend to be around zero, suggesting little *direct* environmental influence on these traits.

Individual differences in *activity level* have also been subjected to behavioral genetic analysis. You may recall from Chapter 5 that individual differences in activity level, measured with a mechanical recording device called an actometer, emerge early in life and show stability in children over time. Activity level was assessed in adults from 300 monozygotic and dizygotic twin pairs in Germany (Spinath et al., 2002). The researchers measured the physical energy each individual expended through body movements, recorded mechanically with motion recorders analogous to self-winding wristwatches. Movement of a person's limbs activates the device, which records the frequency and intensity of body activity. Activity level showed a heritability of .40; a moderate proportion of differences in motor energy are due to genetic differences.

The trait of activity level—how vigorous and energetic a person is—shows a moderate degree of heritability.

Maskot/Alamy Stock Photo

Activity level is one among several temperaments that show moderate heritability. A study of 1,555 twins in Poland found 50 percent heritability, on average, for all temperaments, including activity, emotionality, sociability, persistence, fear, and distractibility (Oniszczenko et al., 2003). A study of Dutch twins, at ages 3, 7, and 10, found heritabilities for aggressiveness, from 51 to 72 percent (Hudziak et al., 2003).

Behavioral genetic studies also have examined other personality dispositions. The trait of shyness shows a moderate heritability of 44 percent at age 6, and these genetic factors are largely responsible for the stability of the shyness trait over time (Morneau-Vaillancourt et al., 2019). Using 353 male twins from the Minnesota Twin Registry, researchers explored the heritability of psychopathic personality traits (Blonigen et al., 2003). These include traits such as Machiavellianism (e.g., enjoys manipulating other people), Coldheartedness (e.g., has a callous emotional style), Impulsive Nonconformity (e.g., indifferent to social conventions), Fearlessness (e.g., a risk taker; lacks anticipatory anxiety concerning harm), Blame Externalization (e.g., blames others for one's problems), and Stress Immunity (e.g., lacks anxiety when faced with stressful life events). All of these "psychopathic" personality traits showed moderate to high heritability. For example, for Coldheartedness, the r_{mz} was +.34, whereas the r_{dz} was −.16; for Fearlessness, the r_{mz} was +.54, whereas the r_{dz} was only .03. Using the method of doubling the difference between the MZ and DZ correlations suggests *substantial* heritability to all of these psychopathic-related personality dispositions (Vernon et al., 2008; Niv et al., 2012). The heritability of psychopathic personality traits, which predispose individuals to criminal activity, may be the key reason that a study from Sweden of more than a million individuals showed the heritability of violent crime to be roughly 50 percent (Frisell et al., 2012).

Interestingly, heritability of personality might not be limited to our own species. In a study of chimpanzees, Weiss, King, and Enns (2002) explored the heritability of dominance (high extraversion, low neuroticism) and well-being (e.g., seems happy and contented), as indexed by trained observer judgments. Individual differences in chimpanzee well-being showed a moderate heritability of .40, whereas dominance showed an even stronger heritability of .66. These findings suggest that the importance of genes in influencing personality may extend to other primates.

Behavioral genetic studies using more comprehensive personality inventories have been carried out in many different countries as personality research expands to include more and more cross-cultural work. A study of 296 twin pairs in Japan revealed moderate heritability for Cloninger's seven-factor model of temperament and character, which includes dispositions such as novelty seeking, harm avoidance, reward dependence, and persistence (Ando et al., 2002). A study of twins in Germany, using observational methodology, revealed a 40 percent heritability to markers of the Big Five (Borkenau et al., 2001). Similar findings for the Big Five personality traits have been documented in Canada and Germany using self-report measures (Jang et al., 2002; Moore et al., 2010).

One of the most fascinating studies to examine personality traits is the Minnesota Twin Study (Bouchard & McGue, 1990; Tellegen et al., 1988). This study examined 45 sets of identical twins reared apart and 26 sets of fraternal twins reared apart. The researchers found the correlations shown in Table 6.2 between identical twins reared apart. These findings startled many people. How could traditionalism, for example, which reflects a preference for the established ways of doing things, show such strong heritability? Traits that we intuitively think of as environmentally determined, such as self-esteem, have moderate heritabilities (Kamakura, Ando, & Ono, 2007). Even character traits that we sometimes think of as instilled by parents and teachers—compassion, integrity, courage, and tolerance—turn out to be strongly linked to traditional personality traits and show moderate heritabilities (Steger et al., 2007). And how could neuroticism have such a high

Table 6.2 Correlations Between Identical Twins Reared Apart

Personality Trait	Twin Correlation
Sense of well-being	.49
Social potency	.57
Achievement orientation	.38
Social closeness	.15
Neuroticism	.70
Sense of alienation	.59
Aggression	.67
Inhibited control	.56
Low risk taking	.45
Traditionalism	.59
Absorption or imagination	.74
Average twin correlation	**.54**

Sources: Bouchard & McGue, 1990; Tellegen et al., 1988.

heritability, given the traditional view that it is parents who make their children neurotic by their inconsistency of reinforcement and improper attachment? These behavioral genetic findings caused some researchers to question long-held assumptions about the origins of individual differences, a topic we consider later in this chapter.

Summaries of the behavioral genetic data for many of the major personality traits—Extraversion, Agreeableness, Conscientiousness, Neuroticism, Openness to experience—yield heritability estimates of approximately 50 percent (Bouchard & Loehlin, 2001; Caspi, Roberts, & Shiner, 2005). A large-scale study of the HEXACO personality traits, which includes the Honest-Humility factor, found heritabilities ranging from 34 to 58 percent (de Vries et al., 2021). A meta-analysis of personality traits in more than 100,000 participants revealed a slightly lower heritability of 40 percent (Vukasovic & Bratko, 2015). A different meta-analysis, however, showed heritabilities of 48 percent for Neuroticism and 49 percent for Extraversion (van den Berg et al., 2014). The heritability of personality may be responsible for the fact that personality traits remain fairly stable over time (Blonigen et al., 2006; Briley & Tucker-Drob, 2014; Caspi et al., 2005; Johnson, McGue, & Krueger, 2005; Kamakura, Ando, & Ono, 2007; Kandler et al., 2010; van Beijsterveldt et al., 2003). Overall, major personality traits show a modest degree of heritability. The same studies, however, also suggest that a substantial portion of the variance in personality traits is environmental in origin.

Attitudes and Preferences

Stable attitudes are generally regarded to be part of personality: They show wide individual differences; they tend to be stable over time; and, at least sometimes, they are linked with actual behavior. Behavioral geneticists have examined the heritability of attitudes. The Minnesota Twin Study showed that traditionalism—as evidenced by attitudes favoring conservative values over modern values—showed a heritability of .59.

A longitudinal study of 654 adopted and nonadopted children from the Colorado Adoption Project revealed significant genetic influence on conservative attitudes (Abrahamson, Baker, & Caspi, 2002). Markers of conservative attitudes included whether participants agreed or disagreed with specific words or phrases such as "death penalty," "gay rights," "censorship," and "Republicans." Significant genetic influence emerged as early as 12 years of age in this study. Other studies confirm the moderate heritability of values (Renner et al., 2012). For example, twin studies of 19 measures of political ideologies from five different countries revealed heritabilities ranging between 30 and 60 percent (Hatemi et al., 2014).

Genes also appear to influence occupational preferences. Occupational preferences are not mere whims, but can have important effects on a person's life work, wealth, and eventual social status. In a study of 435 adopted and 10,880 genetic offspring residing in Canada and the United States, Ellis and Bonin (2003) had participants respond to 14 different aspects of prospective jobs, using a scale ranging from 1 (not at all appealing) to 100 (extremely appealing). The 14 job aspects were high income, competition, prestige, envied by others, taking risks, element of danger, controlling others, feared by others, little supervision, independence, job security, part of a team, clear responsibilities, and help others. These occupational preferences were then correlated with seven measures of parental social status, including mother's and father's education level, occupational status, and income. A full 71 percent of the correlations were statistically significant for the genetic children, whereas only 3 percent were significant for the adopted children (suggesting that rearing environment does not create the effect). The authors conclude that "this study not only suggests that the genes influence various preferences related to occupations, but that these preferences have an effect on social status attainment" (p. 929). In short, occupational preferences such as desire for competition and wealth can lead to choosing occupations in which more status and income are actually achieved. The jobs in which we spend a large portion of our lives and the prestige and income that comes from those jobs are at least partly influenced by the genes we inherit from our parents.

Not all attitudes and beliefs show these levels of moderate heritability, however. One study of 400 twin pairs yielded heritabilities of essentially zero for beliefs in God and involvement in religious affairs (Loehlin & Nichols, 1976). A study of adopted and nonadopted children confirmed that there is no evidence of a heritable influence on *religious* attitudes (Abrahamson et al., 2002). Another study also found low heritability (12 percent) for religiousness, measured by items such as "frequency of attending religious services," during adolescence (Koenig et al., 2005). In adulthood (average age of 33), however, the heritability of religiousness had increased to 44 percent. These findings suggest that genes have an increasingly important role in religiousness as people move from adolescence into adulthood (Button et al., 2011).

No one knows why some attitudes appear to be partly heritable. Are there specific genes that predispose people to be more conservative? Or are these heritabilities merely incidental byproducts of genes for other qualities? Future research in behavioral genetics will be able to address these questions and provide an answer to the mystery of why some attitudes appear to be partly heritable.

Drinking and Smoking

Drinking and smoking are often regarded as behavioral manifestations of personality dispositions, such as Sensation seeking (Zuckerman & Kuhlman, 2000), Extraversion (Eysenck, 1981), and Neuroticism (Eysenck, 1981). Individuals differ widely in their smoking and drinking habits, and although consumers sometimes quit for good and

A Closer Look   Sexual Orientation

Sexual orientation refers to the object of a person's sexual desires, whether the person is sexually attracted to those of the same sex or the opposite sex or both. These differences tend to be relatively stable over time. These differences are linked with important life outcomes, such as the social groups one affiliates with, the leisure activities pursued, and the lifestyle adopted. By the definition of personality provided in Chapter 1, sexual orientation clearly falls well within the scope of personality.

Is sexual orientation heritable? Psychologist Michael Bailey has conducted the most extensive studies of this issue. Bailey and his colleagues examined the twin brothers of a sample of homosexuals, as well as the adoptive brothers of another sample of homosexuals. Heritability estimates from all studies ranged from 30 percent to a strikingly high 70 percent. Similar heritabilities were found in a sample of lesbians and their adoptive sisters (Bailey et al., 1993).

These heritability findings came on the heels of another startling discovery, which was published in *Science* magazine (LeVay, 1991). Brain researcher Simon LeVay discovered that homosexual and heterosexual men differ in a specific area of the brain known as the hypothalamus. One area of the hypothalamus, the medial preoptic region, appears to be partially responsible for regulating male-typical sexual behavior (LeVay, 1993, 1996). LeVay obtained the brains of gay men who had died of AIDS and compared them with the brains of heterosexual men who had died of AIDS or other causes. He found that the size of the medial preoptic region of the hypothalamus—the region believed to regulate male-typical sexual behavior—was two to three times *smaller* in the gay men than in heterosexual men. Unfortunately, given the extremely expensive nature of

brain research, the samples in this study were quite small. Moreover, no one has yet replicated these findings.

Behavioral geneticist Dean Hamer has published some evidence that male sexual orientation is influenced by a gene on the X chromosome (Hamer & Copeland, 1994). However, this finding also needs to be replicated, and several researchers have debated its validity (e.g., see Bailey, Dunne, & Martin, 2000).

Obviously, this research area is controversial, and the findings are hotly debated. Moreover, the genetic studies of sexual orientation have attracted their share of critics. The studies have been challenged on the grounds that the samples, which were secured from advertisements in lesbian and gay publications, were unrepresentative (Baron, 1993).

Another weakness in past studies was a neglect of the correlates of sexual orientation. For example, childhood gender nonconformity is strongly related to adult sexual orientation. Gay men as adults recall having been feminine boys, and lesbian women as adults recall being masculine girls. This association has been established with many sources of data (e.g., using peer reports of childhood gender nonconformity). Regarding the importance of gender nonconformity in childhood, a leading researcher has remarked that "it is difficult to think of other individual differences that so reliably and so strongly predict socially significant

Results of more recent, well-controlled studies find concordance rates for homosexual orientation to be about 20 percent, lower than previously thought.
Jakob Helbig/Getty Images

outcomes across the life span, and for both sexes, too" (Bem, 1996, p. 323).

Bailey set out to clear up these weaknesses—unrepresentative samples and lack of accounting for childhood gender nonconformity—by conducting one of the largest twin studies of adult sexual orientation to date (Bailey, Dunne, & Martin, 2000). The participants were from a sample of almost 25,000 twin pairs in Australia, out of which approximately 1,000 MZ and 1,000 DZ twins participated. Their average age at time of participation was 29 years. The participants completed a questionnaire about childhood participation in gender-stereotyped activities and games. They completed a detailed

(Continued)

questionnaire on adult sexual orientation and activity, such as "when you have sexual daydreams, how often is your sexual partner male? how often female?"

Women were more likely than men to have slight homosexual feelings without being exclusively homosexual, whereas men tended to be either exclusively heterosexual or exclusively homosexual. Just over 3 percent of the men, but only 1 percent of the women, were predominantly or exclusively homosexual in sexual attraction and sexual fantasy.

Regarding whether sexual orientation runs in families, this study found lower rates than previous studies, at 20 percent concordance for the identical twin men and

24 percent concordance for the identical twin women. Concordance is the probability that one twin is gay if the other is also gay. Previous studies typically found concordance rates ranging between 40 and 50 percent. Bailey argues that previous studies overestimate genetic contributions due to selecting participants by advertising in gay and lesbian magazines.

In the Bailey, Dunne, & Martin (2000) study, participants were randomly selected from a large pool of twins, so there was no selection bias. It seems likely that the real rate of genetic contribution to sexual orientation is lower than that previously thought. Childhood gender nonconformity did show significant heritability for both men (50

percent heritability) and women (37 percent heritability). This finding provides some support for Bem's (1996) theory that childhood gender nonconformity may be the inherited component of adult sexual orientation.

Recent studies have also discovered a modest heritability to *gender identity*— "A person's deeply-felt, inherent sense of being a boy, a man, or a male; a girl, a woman, or a female; or an alternative gender (e.g., genderqueer, gender nonconforming, gender neutral) that may or may not correspond to a person's sex assigned at birth or to a person's primary or secondary sex characteristics" (American Psychological Association, 2015; Polderman et al., 2018, p. 95).

abstainers sometimes start, these differences tend to be stable over time. Individual differences in drinking and smoking habits also show evidence of heritability. In one study of Australian twins, an MZ twin who smoked was roughly 16 times more likely than an MZ twin who did not smoke to have a twin who also smoked (Hooper et al., 1992). The comparable figures for DZ twins were only a sevenfold increase, suggesting evidence of heritability. Similar findings were obtained in a sample of 1,300 Dutch families of adolescent Dutch twins (Boomsma et al., 1994). These studies also point simultaneously to the importance of environmental factors—a point taken up in the following section.

Heritability studies of alcohol drinking are more mixed. Some studies find heritability for boys, but not for girls (Hooper et al., 1992). Other studies find heritability for girls, but not for boys (Koopmans & Boomsma, 1993). Most studies, however, show moderate heritability for both sexes, ranging from .36 to .56 (Rose, 1995).

Heritability studies of alcoholism, as opposed to everyday drinking habits, show even stronger heritabilities. Indeed, nearly all show heritabilities of .50 or greater (Kendler et al., 1992). In one study, the heritabilities of alcoholism were 67 percent in women and 71 percent in men (Heath et al., 1994). Interestingly, the same study found a genetic linkage between alcoholism and "conduct disorder" (antisocial behavior), suggesting that the genes for both tend to occur in the same individuals. This possibility is also supported by a study finding that the personality traits of impulsivity and sensation seeking predict antisocial behavior, and this link appears to be due to genes that predispose some individuals to these traits (Mann et al., 2017).

Marriage and Satisfaction with Life

Genes can even influence the propensity to marry or stay single (Johnson et al., 2004). The heritability estimate for propensity to marry turned out to be an astonishing 68 percent! One causal path is through personality characteristics. Men who got married, compared to their single peers, scored higher on social potency and achievement—traits linked with upward mobility, success in careers, and financial success. These traits are also highly valued by women in selecting marriage partners (Buss, 2016). Thus, a genetic proclivity to marry occurs, at least in part, through heritable personality traits that are desired by potential marriage partners.

Genes also play an interesting role in marital satisfaction (Beam et al., 2018). First, individual differences in women's marital satisfaction are roughly 50 percent heritable (Spotts et al., 2004; this study could not evaluate the heritability of a husband's marital satisfaction). Second, the personality characteristics of wives, notably dispositional optimism, warmth, and low aggressiveness, accounted for both their own marital satisfaction and their husband's marital satisfaction (Spotts et al., 2005). Thus, the marital satisfaction of both women and men seems partly to depend on the moderately heritable personality dispositions of the wives. Interestingly, husbands' personality did not explain as much of their own or their wives' marital satisfaction. Taken together, these results suggest that genes play a role in the quality of marriages, and even who gets divorced versus staying married (Jerskey et al., 2010), in part through heritable personality characteristics.

If heritable personality contributes to marital satisfaction, what about overall satisfaction with life overall? Heritable personality characteristics play a key role here too (Bartels, 2015). Four moderately heritable personality factors—having a sense of purpose, an orientation toward personal growth, feeling your life is under your own control, and having positive social relationships—predict psychological well-being and overall satisfaction with life (Archontaki, Lewis, & Bates, 2013). Nonetheless, the same studies show that environmental influences also play a key role in life satisfaction (Hahn, Johnson, & Spinath, 2013), a topic to which we now turn.

Shared Versus Nonshared Environmental Influences: A Riddle

With all of the findings on the moderate heritability of so many personality characteristics, it is important not to lose sight of one important fact: The same studies that suggest moderate heritability also provide the best evidence for the importance of environmental influences. If personality characteristics show heritabilities in the range of 30 to 50 percent, this means that the same characteristics show a substantial degree of environmentality—as much as 50 to 70 percent. This conclusion must be tempered, however, by the fact that all measures contain errors of measurement; some of the differences in personality might be attributable to *neither* environmental nor genetic differences, but rather to errors of measurement.

One critical distinction behavioral geneticists make is between **shared** and **nonshared environmental influences**. Consider siblings—brothers and sisters in the same family. Some features of their environment are shared: the number of books in the home; the presence or absence of a TV, DVD player, or computer; the quality and quantity of food in the home; the parents' values and attitudes; and the schools, church, synagogue, or mosque the parents and children attend. All of these are features of the shared environment. On the other hand, the same brothers and sisters do not share *all* features of their environment. Some children might get special treatment from their parents. They might have different groups of friends. They might occupy different rooms in the house. One might go to summer camp, whereas the others stay home each summer. All of these features are called nonshared because they are *experienced differently* by different siblings.

We know that the environment exerts a major influence on personality. But *which* environment matters most—the shared or the nonshared environment? Some behavioral genetic designs allow us to figure out whether the environmental effects come more from

Exercise

shared or from nonshared sources. The details of how this is done are too technical to examine in this book, but, if you are interested, you can check out Plomin et al., (2013) for more details.

The bottom line is this: For most personality variables, the shared environment has either little or no impact. Adoption studies show that the average correlation for personality variables between adopted siblings who share much of their environment, but who share no genes, is only .05. This suggests that even though these siblings grow up together—with the same parents, same schools, same religious training, and so on—whatever is happening in their shared environment (e.g., parenting, rearing practices, values) is not causing them to be similar in personality.

Most environmental causes appear to stem from the aspects of the environment that siblings experience differently. Thus, it's not the number of books in the home. It's not parental values or parental attitudes toward child rearing. In fact, it's not what most psychologists have long believed it is. Rather, the critical environmental influences on personality appear to lie in the unique nonshared experiences of individual children.

Which unique experiences are important? Well, here we run into a brick wall. Most theories of socialization over the decades have focused exclusively on the shared environment, such as poverty and parental attitudes toward child rearing. It is only recently that psychologists have begun to study nonshared environments.

There are two possibilities of what they will find. One possibility is a major breakthrough—a discovery of a critically important environmental variable that has been overlooked by psychologists who for years focused only on the shared environment. Different peer influences may be one good candidate (Golsteyn et al., 2021; Harris, 2007). The other possibility is less satisfying. It is conceivable that there are so many environmental variables that exert an impact on personality that each one alone might account only for a tiny fraction of the variance (Willerman, 1979). If this is the case, then we are stuck with the discovery of many small effects.

Does this mean that the shared environment accounts for nothing? Have psychologists been entirely misguided in their thinking by their focus on shared effects? The answer is no. In some areas, behavioral genetic studies have revealed tremendously important shared environmental influences: attitudes, religious beliefs, political orientations, health behaviors, and to some degree verbal intelligence (Segal, 1999). As an example, adoptive siblings reared together but genetically unrelated are correlated .41 (girls) and .46 (boys) in their patterns of smoking and drinking (Willerman, 1979). Thus, although smoking and drinking have a substantial genetic component, there is also a large shared environmental component.

Another study found that shared environments accounted for several personality clusters in the "adjustment" domain (Loehlin, Neiderhiser, & Reiss, 2003). These include antisocial behavior (e.g., showing behavior problems and breaking rules), depressive symptoms (e.g., moody, withdrawn), and autonomous functioning (e.g., being able to care for self in basic needs and recreational activities). And a study of adult twins using observational measurement—trait ratings of videotaped behaviors—suggests that shared environment might be more important in explaining Big Five personality traits than is typically revealed by studies using self-report (Borkenau et al., 2001). If this study is replicated by future research, it may have the far-reaching consequence of challenging the now-conventional wisdom that shared environments have little effect on personality traits.

In summary, environments shared by siblings are important in some domains. But, for many personality traits, such as extraversion and neuroticism, shared environments do not seem to matter. It is the unique environment experienced by each sibling that carries the causal weight.

Exercise

Discuss what you think might be shared environmental influences contributing to the tendency to smoke. That is, what in the environment might have influenced most people who start to smoke and maintain their smoking habit?

Genes and the Environment

As important as it is to identify sources of environmental and genetic influence on personality, the next step requires an understanding of how genetic and environmental factors interact. More complex forms of behavioral genetic analysis involve the concepts of *genotype-environment interaction* and *genotype-environment correlation.*

Genotype–Environment Interaction

Genotype-environment interaction refers to the differential response of individuals with different genotypes to the same environments. Consider introverts and extraverts, who have somewhat different genotypes. Introverts tend to perform well on cognitive tasks when there is little stimulation in the room, but they do poorly when there are distractions, such as music blaring or people walking around. In contrast, extraverts do just fine with the music blasting, the phone ringing, and people walking in and out. But the same extraverts make a lot of errors in these cognitive tasks when there is little stimulation—when the task they are working on is boring or monotonous.

Extraversion-introversion is a perfect example of genotype-environment interaction, whereby individuals with different genotypes (introverts and extraverts) respond differently to the same environment (e.g., noise in the room). Individual differences *interact* with the environment to affect performance. You may want to take this into consideration when you arrange your studying environment. Before turning on the music, first determine whether you lie on the introverted or extraverted end of the continuum. If you are an introvert, you would likely do better studying in a quiet environment with few interruptions.

Studies have identified other genotype-environment interactions. One examined the effects of abusive parenting on whether children developed antisocial personalities (Caspi et al., 2003). Abused children who had a genotype that produced low levels of the brain neurotransmitter monoamine oxidase A (MAOA) frequently developed conduct disorders, antisocial personalities, and violent dispositions. In contrast, maltreated children who had high levels of MAOA were far less likely to develop aggressive antisocial personalities. This study and replications of it (Kim-Cohen et al., 2006) provide excellent examples of genotype–environment interaction—exposure to the same environment (abusive parenting) produces different effects on personality, depending on the differences in genotype. Interestingly, this suggests that violent parents may create violent children *only* if the children have a genotype marked by low levels of MAOA. Similar genotype–environment interactions have been discovered between the 5-HTT gene and childhood maltreatment in predicting persistent depression later in life. Only individuals with two short 5-HTT forms of the gene who had experienced maltreatment as children developed persistent depression (Uher et al., 2011). The empirical study of genotype–environment interactions represents one of the most exciting developments in the behavior genetics of personality (Jang et al., 2005; Moffitt, 2005); psychological disorders (Bornovalova et al., 2010); depression linked with early puberty in girls, depending on socioeconomic status (Mendle et al., 2016; Johnson, 2007); and the ways in which personality is expressed in satisfied versus dissatisfied romantic relationships (South et al., 2016).

Genotype–Environment Correlation

Just as interesting is the concept of **genotype–environment correlation**, the differential exposure of individuals with different genotypes to different environments. Consider, for example, a child who has a genotype for high verbal ability. Her parents may notice this and provide her with lots of books to read, engage in intellectual discussions with her, and give her word games and crossword puzzles. Parents of children with less verbal skill, who presumably have different genotypes than those with high verbal abilities, may be less inclined to provide this stimulation. This is an example of genotype–environment correlation; individuals with different genotypes (e.g., those with high versus low verbal abilities) are exposed to different environments (e.g., high versus low stimulation). In another example, parents might promote sports activities for athletically inclined children more than for less athletically inclined children.

Plomin, DeFries, and Loehlin (1977) describe three very different kinds of genotype–environment correlation: passive, reactive, and active. **Passive genotype–environment correlation** occurs when parents provide both genes and the environment to children, yet the children do nothing to obtain that environment. Suppose, for example, that parents who are verbally inclined pass on genes to their children that make them verbally inclined. However, because the parents are highly verbal, they buy a lot of books. Thus, there is a correlation between the children's verbal ability and the number of books in their home, but it is passive in the sense that the child has done nothing to cause the books to be there.

In sharp contrast, the **reactive genotype–environment correlation** occurs when parents (or others) respond to children differently, depending on the child's genotypes. A good example is cuddlers versus noncuddlers. Some babies love to be touched—they giggle, smile, laugh, and show great pleasure when they are handled. Other babies are more aloof and simply do not like to be touched very much. Imagine that a mother starts out touching and hugging each of her two children a lot. One child loves it; the other hates it. Over the course of several months, the mother reacts by continuing to hug the cuddler but cuts down on hugging the noncuddler. This example illustrates the reactive genotype–environment correlation, which is achieved because people react to children differently, based in part on the children's heritable dispositions. Another possible example is a study that found that parents who are warm toward their children have children who are higher in Agreeableness (Ayoub et al., 2019). The behavioral genetic design allowed researchers to conclude that the most likely causal pathway was a genetic influence of the children's personality on parental warmth (see Ramos et al., 2019, for a similar demonstration of reactive genotype-environment correlation). In short, it seems like parents react to highly agreeable children with greater warmth—an example of reactive genotype-environment correlation.

Modern views on the nature-nurture debate suggest more complex answers to the question of the origins of personality. One view is that genes and environments interact in determining personality.
Shutterstock

Active genotype-environment correlation occurs when a person with a particular genotype creates or seeks out a particular environment. High sensation seekers, for example, expose themselves to risky environments: skydiving, motorcycle jumping, and drug taking. Highly intellectual individuals are likely to attend lectures, read books, and engage others in verbal discussions. This active creation and selection of environments has also been called "niche picking" (Scarr & McCartney, 1983). Active genotype-environment correlation highlights the fact that we are not passive recipients of our environments; we mold, create, and select the environments we subsequently inhabit, and some of these actions are correlated with our genotypes.

These genotype-environment correlations can be positive or negative. That is, the environment can encourage the expression of the disposition, or it can discourage its expression. Adolescents who have personalities marked by positive emotionality (e.g., an upbeat, optimistic stance) tend to evoke high levels of helpful and affirmative regard from their parents, so that genotypes for positive emotionality are positively correlated with environments of high parental regard (Krueger et al., 2008). The positive link between personality and parenting, in short, is genetically mediated (South et al., 2008). Conversely, parents of highly active children may try to get them to sit still and calm down, and parents of less active children may try to get them to perk up and be more lively. This example illustrates a negative genotype-environment correlation because the parents' behavior opposes the children's expression of traits (Buss, 1981). One meta-analysis found that children showing antisocial behavior, a moderately heritable trait, tend to elicit harsh discipline from parents who attempt to curb their behavior (Avinun & Knafo, 2014). Another example of negative genotype-environment correlation occurs when people who are too arrogant or dominant elicit negative reactions from others, who try to "cut them down" (Cattell, 1973). The key point is that environments can go against a person's genotype, resulting in a negative genotype-environment correlation, or they can facilitate the person's genotype, creating a positive genotype-environment correlation.

A study of 180 twins reared apart points to an intriguing potential example of genotype-environment correlation (Krueger, Markon, & Bouchard, 2003). The study assessed personality traits through the Multidimensional Personality Questionnaire (MPQ), which identifies three major factors of personality: Positive Emotionality (happy, content), Negative Emotionality (anxious, tense), and Constraint (controlled, conscientious). The researchers evaluated each individual's *perceptions* of the family environments in which they were raised, which yielded two main factors: Family

Cohesion (e.g., parental warmth, absence of family conflict) and Family Status (e.g., parents provided intellectual and cultural stimulation, active recreational activities, and financial resources). The intriguing results were that the correlations between personality and perceptions of family environment were genetically mediated. In other words, the perceived environment in which the individuals were raised was largely due to heritable personality traits. Specifically, experiencing a cohesive family was explained by genetic influence on the personality traits of Constraint and lack of Negative Emotionality. In contrast, recalling a family environment high in cultural and intellectual activity was explained by the personality trait of Positive Emotionality.

These results may be subject to several interpretations. One interpretation is that personality affects the subjective manner in which people remember their early environments. Perhaps calm, controlled individuals are more likely to forget about real family conflict that was present during their childhood, and so may simply recall greater family cohesion than actually existed. An alternative interpretation is in terms of genotype-environment correlation: Individuals with calm, controlled personalities (high Constraint, low Negative Emotionality) may actually *promote* cohesion among family members—in essence, creating a family environment that further fosters their calm, controlled personality. Another study found genetic mediation of the link between Neuroticism and perceived environmental stress (Luo et al., 2017). Perhaps those high in Neuroticism create precisely the stressful environments that they then inhabit. Future studies of personality, parenting, and perceived family environments offer the promise of unraveling the complex ways in which genes interact and correlate with environments (Spinath & O'Connor, 2003).

Another promising avenue for exploring genotype-environment correlations is through peers (Burt, 2009; Loehlin, 2010). One study found a GE correlation for adolescent alcohol consumption based on the differential selection of peers, especially for females (Loehlin, 2010). Another found evidence for GE correlation between impulsivity, which leads to mild forms of rule breaking (e.g., drinking, smoking, vandalism), and popularity during adolescence (Burt, 2009). Thus, genes predispose some individuals to break rules, which in turn leads to greater popularity during adolescence—an example of reactive gene-environment correlation. Genes for impulsivity, in short, are correlated with a social environment of being popular—a correlation established, in part, through acts of rule breaking. Genotype-environment correlations are becoming increasingly important in understanding the complex processes of how personality and social environments are connected (Persson, 2020).

Molecular Genetics

The most recent development in the science of behavioral genetics has been the exploration of **molecular genetics**. The methods of molecular genetics are designed to identify the specific genes or combinations of genes associated with personality traits. The details are quite technical, but the most common method, called the association method, is to identify whether individuals with a particular gene (or allele) have higher or lower scores on a particular trait than individuals without the gene (Benjamin et al., 1996; Ebstein et al., 1996).

The most frequently examined is the **DRD4 gene**, located on the short arm of chromosome 11. This gene codes for a protein called a dopamine receptor. The function of this dopamine receptor, as you might guess, is to respond to the presence of dopamine, a neurotransmitter. When the dopamine receptor encounters dopamine from other neurons in the brain, it discharges an electrical signal, activating other neurons.

The most frequently examined association between the DRD4 gene and a personality trait has involved novelty seeking, the tendency to seek out new experiences, especially those considered risky, such as drug experiences, risky sexual experiences, gambling, and high-speed driving (Zuckerman & Kuhlman, 2000). Individuals with so-called long repeat versions of the DRD4 gene are higher on novelty seeking than those with the short repeat versions of this gene (Benjamin et al., 1996). The researchers hypothesized that the reason for this association is that people with long DRD4 genes tend to be relatively unresponsive to dopamine. This causes them to seek out novel experiences that give them a "dopamine buzz." In contrast, those with the short DRD4 genes tend to be highly responsive to whatever dopamine is already present in their brains, so they tend not to seek out novel experiences, which might boost their dopamine to uncomfortable levels.

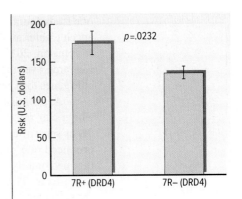

Figure 6.1

Men with DRD4 7R+ invest more money in a financial risk game.

Source: Dreber et al. (2009).

Although the association between DRD4 and novelty seeking has been replicated several times, there have also been several failures to replicate (Plomin & Crabbe, 2000). One study found that high novelty seeking was linked with a different allele of a *different* gene—the A1 allele of the D2 dopamine receptor gene (DRD2) (Berman et al., 2002). A more recent study implicated DRD2, DRD4, and two other genes linked to sensation seeking among adolescents (Aluja et al., 2019).

Part of the problem is that the size of the associations is very small. It has been speculated that there may be 10 other genes that are equally important in novelty seeking. And perhaps there are 500 genes that vary with other aspects of human personality (Knopik et al., 2022; Ridley, 1999). It seems unlikely that any single gene will ever be found to explain more than a small percentage of variation in personality.

As an illustration, one experiment found that men with the 7-repeat (7R) allele of the DRD4 gene were more likely to engage in financial risk taking than men lacking the 7R allele, but the effect size is small, even though statistically significant (Dreber et al., 2009), as shown in Figure 6.1.

Interestingly, the 7R allele of the DRD4 gene occurs at dramatically different rates in different geographical regions. It occurs at higher rates in America than in Asia and has been hypothesized to be favored by evolutionary selection (see Chapter 7) when people migrate to new environments or inhabit resource-rich environments (Chen et al., 1999; Penke, Denissen, & Miller, 2007). Empirical evidence for this hypothesis comes from a study of the migration patterns of 2,320 individuals from 39 groups (Chen et al., 1999). Migratory populations show a higher proportion of the 7R allele of the DRD4 gene than do sedentary populations, which could be caused by selective migration of individuals carrying those genes, selective favoring of those genes in the new environments, or both. Evidence on sedentary and nomadic populations favors the hypothesis that the 7R allele of the DRD4 gene is more advantageous among nomadic than settled populations (Eisenberg et al., 2008). Men with the 7R allele may also have an advantage in highly competitive societies in resource competition and in direct competition for access to mates (Harpending & Cochran, 2002).

As exciting as the results are from these molecular genetic methods, it is important to exercise caution when interpreting them. In several cases, researchers have found an association between a particular gene and personality-related traits, such as anxiety and attention deficit disorder, but subsequent researchers have failed to replicate these associations (Plomin & Crabbe, 2000; Turkheimer, Pettersson, & Horn, 2014). Furthermore, some gene-personality links are found for one gender, but not for the other. For example, one study found that women with one copy of the A allele at OXTR rs2254298 experienced greater attachment anxiety than did women with two copies of the G allele (Chen & Johnson, 2012). Nonetheless, this gene-personality link was not found among men. Research over the next decade or two, however, should reveal the degree to which specific genes for specific personality traits can be found.

A promising method known as genome-wide association studies (GWAS), which can rapidly examine the entire genome for links with personality, may yield faster scientific advances (Turkheimer et al., 2014). A GWAS study of Extraversion produced one promising candidate (van den Berg et al., 2016). But it appears likely that personality traits are linked to a large number of genes, each accounting for only tiny effects. This has led to explorations of measures of *polygenic risk scores,* which are mathematical sums of many genetic variants. As an example, researchers recently discovered that a polygenic risk score could be used to partially predict the so-called well-being spectrum—a triad of traits marked by depression, neuroticism, and a low sense of well-being (Baselmans et al., 2019). People low on this triad experience a lot of loneliness and rate themselves low on physical healthiness. Understanding the full scientific story of the molecular genetics of personality may be possible many years in the future.

Finally, rather than looking for direct links between single genes and personality or behavior, modern research is beginning to explore gene–environment interactions using molecular genetic techniques (e.g., Caspi et al., 2003; South & Krueger, 2008). Stressful life events can cause depressive symptoms but *only* in people who carry the short version of the serotonin transporter (5-HTT) gene (Uher et al., 2011). For those carrying other variants of this gene, stressful life events do *not* produce depressive symptoms. This provides an illustration of the power of combining molecular genetic techniques with the important concept of gene–environment interaction.

Behavioral Genetics, Science, Politics, and Values

The history of behavioral genetic research has taken some fascinating twists and turns, which are worth noting (see Knopik et al., 2022 for an excellent summary of this history). During the past century in the United States, behavioral genetic research received what can be phrased as a "frosty reception." Findings that some personality traits were moderately heritable seemed to violate the dominant paradigm, which was environmentalism (and, especially, behaviorism). The prevailing **environmentalist view** was that personality was determined by socialization practices, such as parenting style. People worried about the potential misuse of findings from behavioral genetics. Images of Nazi Germany sprang to mind, with the evil notions of a master race.

A large part of the controversy over genetic research has centered around studies of intelligence, which has often been considered to be a personality variable. Many people have worried that findings from genetic studies will be misused to label some people intrinsically superior or inferior to others (e.g., see Herrnstein & Murray, 1994). Others worry that findings will be misused to give some people preferential treatment in education or job placement. Still others are concerned that standard tests of intelligence fail to capture many of the multiple facets of intelligence, such as social intelligence, emotional intelligence, and creativity. All of these are legitimate concerns. Findings from behavioral genetics must be viewed with caution and interpreted responsibly in the context of the larger picture of human nature and society.

In the past decade or so, attitudes have shifted, and the field of psychology now considers the findings from behavioral genetics as fairly mainstream. Behavioral genetic studies tend not to generate the intense controversy that they did in prior decades. Indeed, findings from sophisticated behavioral genetic research on personality are now seen as critical in combating important individual and social problems, such as the effects of stressful life events on depression.

The links between science and politics, between knowledge and values, are complex, but they need to be confronted. Because scientific research can be misused for political goals, scientists bear a major responsibility for presenting findings carefully and accurately. Science can be separated from values. Science is a set of methods for discovering what exists. Values are notions of what people *want* to exist—to be desired or sought after. Although scientists clearly can be biased by their values, the virtue of the scientific method is that it is self-correcting. The methods are public, so other scientists can check the findings, discover errors in procedure, and over time correct any biases that creep in. This does not imply that scientists are unbiased. The history of science is filled with cases in which values influenced the nature of the questions posed and the acceptance or rejection of particular findings or theories. Nonetheless, the scientific method provides a system for correcting biases in the long run.

SUMMARY AND EVALUATION

The behavioral genetic study of personality has a fascinating history. Early on, when behavioral genetic methods were being developed, the field of psychology was dominated by the behaviorist paradigm. In this context, findings from behavioral genetic research were not warmly received. Social scientists worried that findings from behavioral genetic research might be misused for ideological purposes.

Over the past few decades, the empirical evidence on heritability has become stronger and stronger, in part because of the convergence of evidence across behavioral genetic methods. There are four traditional behavioral genetic methods: selective breeding studies, family studies, twin studies, and adoption studies. Selective breeding studies cannot be ethically conducted on humans. Family studies are problematic because the genetic and environmental factors are often confounded. Twin studies have potential problems, such as violations of the equal environments assumption (the assumption that identical twins are not treated any more alike than fraternal twins) and the assumption of representativeness (the notion that twins are just like non-twins). Adoption studies also have potential problems, such as the non-random placement of adopted-away children into particular families. Empirical tests of these assumptions suggest that they are not violated much or are violated in ways that do not seem to make much difference. However, the most compelling evidence on the heritability of personality comes from looking across methods that do not share methodological problems. Thus, if the findings from twin studies *and* adoption studies converge on the same results, then we can have more confidence in the findings than we can when only a single method is used.

The study of large samples of twins reared together, the study of smaller samples of identical twins reared apart, and sound adoption studies have added greatly to the credibility of behavioral genetic research. The empirical findings clearly show that personality variables, such as Extraversion and Neuroticism, as well as the other dimensions of the Big Five, have moderate heritability. Perhaps even more striking are the findings that drinking, smoking, attitudes, occupational preferences, and even sexual orientation appear to be somewhat heritable. Equally important, however, is the finding that the same studies provide the best evidence for the importance of environmental influences. Overall, personality characteristics are 30 to 50 percent heritable and 50 to 70 percent environmental.

The environmental causes appear to be mostly of the nonshared variety—that is, the different experiences that siblings have even though they are in the same family. This finding is startling because nearly all theories of environmental influence—such as those that posit the importance of parental values and child-rearing styles—have been of the shared variety. Thus, behavioral genetic research may have provided one of the most important insights into the nature of nurture—the location of the most important environmental influences on personality. The next decade of personality research should witness progress in identifying the precise locations of these nonshared environmental influences. Separating perceived environments from objective environments will be an important part of this research program.

In interpreting the research findings, it is important to keep in mind the meaning of heritability and the meaning of environmentality. Heritability is the proportion of observed individual differences that are linked with genetic differences in a particular population or sample. It does not pertain to an individual; genetic and environmental influences are inextricably interwoven at the individual level and cannot be separated. Heritability does not mean that the environment is powerless to alter the individual differences. And heritability is not a fixed statistic—it can be low in one group and high in another, low at one time and high at another. Environmentality is the proportion of observed individual differences that is caused by environmental differences. Like heritability, environmentality is not a fixed statistic. It, too, can change over time and across situations. The discovery of a powerful environmental intervention, for example, could, in principle, dramatically increase environmentality while lowering heritability. The key point is that neither heritability nor environmentality is fixed in space and time.

Some behavioral genetic research examines the interactions and correlations among genetic and environmental variables. There are three major types of genotype-environment correlations: passive, reactive, and active. *Passive* genotype-environment correlation occurs when parents provide both genes and environment to their children in ways that just happen to be correlated—for example, parents who pass on genes for verbal ability and stock their houses with a lot of books. Books and verbal ability become correlated, but in a passive way because the children did not do anything for the correlation to occur. *Reactive* genotype-environment correlation occurs when parents, teachers, and others respond differently to some children than to others. Parents generally tickle and coo at smiley babies more than at nonsmiley babies, creating a correlation between genotypes for smiling and a cuddly social environment. The correlation occurs because parents react to babies differently. *Active* genotype-environment correlation occurs when individuals with certain genotypes seek out environments nonrandomly. Extraverted individuals might throw a lot of parties, thus surrounding themselves with a different social environment than that of the more reclusive introverts. The correlation occurs because individuals actively create it.

The more complex and interesting behavioral genetic concepts such as genotype-environment correlation have received relatively little research attention. One exception is the fascinating finding that individuals low on Negative Emotionality and high on Constraint recall their early family environment as being extremely cohesive. One interpretation is in terms of genotype-environment correlation: Calm, nonneurotic individuals may promote calmness and cohesion in their families, thus creating an upbringing that further fosters their calm, controlled personality.

Molecular genetics represents the most recent development in the realm of personality psychology. The research techniques attempt to establish an association between specific genes and collections of genes and scores on personality traits. The DRD4 gene, for example, is linked with novelty seeking. One of the most promising new developments is combining molecular genetics with the search for *gene-environment interactions*—the ways in which people with different genes react differently to the same environment. Stressful environments, for example, appear to produce depressive symptoms, but primarily in people with the short version of the serotonin transporter (5-HTT) gene.

KEY TERMS

genome 156
genetic junk 156
eugenics 157
percentage of variance 159
heritability 159
phenotypic variance 159
genotypic variance 159
environmentality 160
nature-nurture debate 161
selective breeding 162
family studies 163

twin studies 163
monozygotic (MZ) twins 163
dizygotic (DZ) twins 164
equal environments assumption 165
adoption studies 165
selective placement 166
shared environmental influences 173
nonshared environmental
     influences 173
genotype-environment interaction 175
genotype-environment correlation 176

passive genotype-environment
     correlation 176
reactive genotype-environment
     correlation 176
active genotype-environment
     correlation 177
molecular genetics 178
DRD4 gene 178
environmentalist view 180

Svisio/Getty Images

Physiological Approaches to Personality

THE BIOLOGICAL DOMAIN

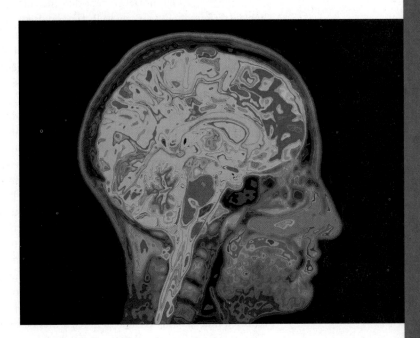

Brain imaging techniques have enabled researchers to learn more about the brain's role in behavior and personality than previously thought possible.
SpeedKingz/Shutterstock

Elliot was a successful businessman, a proud father, and a good husband. At his business firm, he was a role model for his younger colleagues. Personally, he was charming and pleasant. His social skills were such that he often was called on to settle disputes at work. Elliot was respected by others. His position in the community, his satisfying personal life, and his prosperity and professional status were all enviable.

One day Elliot began to have severe headaches. After a few days, he went to his doctor, who suspected a brain tumor. This suspicion was confirmed when a small tumor was found growing not on his brain, but on the lining of tissue that covers the brain. The location was just above his eyes, behind his forehead. The tumor was, however, pushing against his brain and had damaged a small portion of the front of his brain, part of the prefrontal cortex, which had to be removed with the tumor.

The operation went smoothly and Elliot recovered quickly, with no apparent lasting damage, at least none that could be found with standard tests. Elliot's IQ was tested after the operation and was found to be superior, as it was before his operation. His memory was tested and was found to be excellent. His ability to use and understand language was also unaffected by the operation. His ability to do arithmetic, to memorize lists of words, to visualize objects, to make judgments, and to read a map all remained unaffected by the operation. All his cognitive functions remained normal or above normal, completely unaffected by the removal of a small portion of his prefrontal cortex.

Elliot's family, however, reported that his personality had changed. He began to behave differently at work as well. He could not seem to manage his time properly. He needed lots of prompting from his wife to get going in the morning. Once at work, he had problems finishing tasks. If he was interrupted in a task, he had difficulty starting back up where he had left off. Often he would get captivated by one part of a task and get side-tracked for hours. For example, in refiling some books, which should have taken 15 minutes, he stopped to read one of the books and returned to his desk hours later. He knew his job, but just had trouble putting all the actions together in the right order.

Soon Elliot lost his job. He tried various business schemes on his own and finally took his life savings and started an investment management business. He teamed up with a disreputable character, against the advice of many of his friends and family members. This business went bankrupt, and he lost all his savings. To his wife and children, Elliot appeared to be behaving impulsively, and they had trouble coping with all the difficulties he was getting into. A divorce soon followed. Elliot quickly remarried, but to a woman whom none of his friends or family approved. This marriage ended quickly in another divorce. Without a source of income, and without a family to support him, Elliot became a drifter.

Elliot came to the attention of Dr. Antonio Damasio, then a neurologist at the University of Iowa, who later wrote a book about Elliot's condition (Damasio, 1994). It seems that the small bit of brain matter destroyed by Elliot's tumor was essential in transmitting emotional information to the higher reasoning centers of the brain. Elliot reported that the only change in himself that he noticed was that, after his operation, he did not feel any strong emotion, or much of any emotion for that matter.

The case of Elliot shows us that the body and the mind are intimately connected. Indeed, after Elliot's operation, the biggest change in him was in his personality, not in his memory, his reasoning, or his knowledge. Dr. Antonio Damasio discusses Elliot, as well as the brain findings underlying personality change, in several YouTube.com videos. In addition, Dr. Damasio describes other interesting cases of brain damage and personality change in more recent books (e.g., Damasio, 2018, 2021).

Studies have shown that traumatic brain injury can lead to large changes in personality (Edmundson et al., 2015). One of the most common changes in personality following brain injury is a diminished ability to inhibit or control one's impulses. This has been found in children who experienced brain trauma (Gerring & Vasa, 2016), in adults with traumatic brain injuries (Kim, 2002), and in elderly persons whose brains have been injured by stroke (Freshwater & Golden, 2002). This increased impulsivity and lack of self-control is most likely due to disruptions between the frontal lobes, which serve as the executive control center of the brain, and other parts of the brain. As a result, persons with extensive brain injury can retain most of their cognitive abilities, yet lose some degree of self-control (Lowenstein, 2002). Persons with personality changes following traumatic brain injuries often have spontaneous outbursts, sudden changes in mood, and episodes of aggression and can become quite disruptive to their families (Beer & Lombardo, 2007). Indeed, this is the personality profile of one of the most famous brain injury patients, Phineas Gage, who was injured by an iron rod that was blasted through his brain while he was working as a railway builder in the mid-1800s (see A Closer Look).

An advantage of the physiological approach is that physiological characteristics can be measured mechanically and reliably. The term *physiological characteristics* refers to the functioning of organ systems within the body. Examples of **physiological systems** are the nervous system (including the brain and nerves), the cardiac system (including the heart, arteries, and veins), and the musculoskeletal system (including the muscles and bones, which make all movements and behaviors possible). To get an idea of the importance of these physiological systems, imagine the result of removing any one of

A Closer Look   The Brain Injury of Phineas Gage

Phineas Gage (1823–1860) was a nineteenth-century rail worker, serving as foreman on a construction gang preparing the way for the Rutland and Burlington Railroad in Vermont. His work involved blasting large rocks with dynamite, and one day he was injured in a serious accident. Prior to his accident, Phineas was an industrious worker, highly agreeable and conscientious, and seen by his employers as one of their most capable and efficient foremen. On September 13, 1848, he was tamping dynamite into a hole in a rock using an iron rod. The dynamite accidentally ignited and the explosion shot the iron rod out of the hole like a bullet. Phineas was bending over the work area. The iron rod he was working with was 1¼ inches in diameter, was 3 feet, 7 inches long, and weighed almost 14 pounds. It was tapered at one end almost to a point. The heavy iron rod came out of the tamping hole point first. It shot up through Gage's left cheek and passed behind his left eye and exited the top of his skull, landing approximately 75 feet away. Gage was knocked off his feet but did not lose consciousness. The iron rod destroyed a portion of the left frontal part of his brain and blinded his left eye. Remarkably, Gage survived this accident. He spent 10 weeks under a doctor's care, then returned to his home in New Hampshire. Even more remarkably, most of his intellectual functions remained intact. However, his personality changed dramatically. His doctor, John Harlow, described the new Phineas Gage as "obstinate, capricious, and vacillating, devising many plans of future operations which are no sooner arranged than they are abandoned, a child, yet with the passions of a strong man" (cited in Carter, 1999). He lacked the ability to prioritize daily tasks, nor could he devise plans to achieve goals. He was impulsive and aggressive. He started using profane language and disregarded social conventions, behaving impolitely toward those around him. Women were advised to avoid him. He never worked as a foreman again. Instead, he had various farm jobs, mostly caring for horses and cleaning stables. He died on May 21, 1860, almost 12 years after his devastating accident. His skull and the iron rod are on display at Harvard's Countway Library of Medicine. See Macmillan (2000) for a modern perspective on this famous case. The accompanying photo of Phineas Gage was confirmed as him in 2009 when historians were able to digitally magnify the iron rod and

Photo of Phineas Gage. He is holding the iron rod that inflicted the serious head injury described in this Closer Look.

History and Art Collection/Alamy

read the inscription engraved on it, saying it was the rod that inflicted the grave injury on Mr. Gage (Wilgus & Wilgus, 2009).

them. Without a brain, a person could not think or respond to the environment; without the musculoskeletal system, a person could not move or act on the environment; and without a cardiac system, the result is obvious. All of the physiological systems are important to the maintenance of life, and their study has resulted in the fields of medicine, anatomy, and physiology.

From the perspective of personality psychology, physiology is important to the extent that differences in physiology create, contribute to, or indicate differences in personality. For example, people differ from one another in how sensitive their nervous systems are to stimulation. Given exposure to loud noise, for example, your roommate playing loud music while you try to study, some people find it quite distracting and irritating, whereas other people are not bothered at all. A person who is particularly sensitive might frequent quiet environments (e.g., study in the library), avoid crowds (e.g., not go to loud parties), and limit the amount of stimulation in their environments (e.g., never play loud rock-and-roll music). The physiologically oriented personality psychologist would say that this person is introverted (a psychological characteristic) because he or she has an overly sensitive nervous system (a physiological characteristic). Thus, this approach assumes that differences in physiological characteristics are related to differences in important personality characteristics and behavior patterns.

Application

Individual Differences in Digit Ratio

Scholars have speculated on connections between bodily shapes and personality traits for centuries. Most simple theories have been discredited (Stelmack & Stalkas, 1991), such as the system of phrenology that related bumps on the head to aspects of personality. However, one bodily difference that is receiving attention these days is the ratio of the index finger to the ring finger, commonly called the "digit ratio" index. This ratio is easy to calculate by measuring the length of the index finger (2 digit or 2D) and ring finger (digit 4 or 4D, see graphic) and then dividing 2D by 4D. This is called the 2D:4D ratio, and if it is less than 1.0 it means the ring finger is longer than the index finger, and if the 2D:4D ratio is greater than 1.0 the ring finger is shorter than the index finger. People differ from one another in this simple measure, and personality psychologists are curious about whether this measure reflects anything meaningful. To address this question, researchers gather data to see what might correlate with digit ratio.

One common and reliable finding is that women have a higher digit ratio than men. Women tend, on average, to have index fingers that are longer than their ring fingers, resulting in a 2D:4D ratio greater than 1.0, whereas men tend to have index fingers that are shorter than their ring fingers, resulting in a 2D:4D ratio less than 1.0. Why might this be so? Research with humans and animals (those with measurable digits, such as mice and monkeys) has confirmed that digit ratio is determined prior to birth through exposure of the fetus to testosterone in the mother's womb (in utero). Consequently, the digit ratio after birth is thought to be a lifelong indicator of the amount of prenatal testosterone that the fetus was exposed to. The more testosterone exposure, the smaller the index finger relative to the ring finger (i.e., the smaller the digit ratio).

Prenatal testosterone exposure is greater for male fetuses than female fetuses—hence the lifelong difference between the sexes in digit ratio. However, even within a single gender, differences in digit ratio appear related to the kinds of personality traits hypothesized to be related to testosterone. These traits are described by Wilson and Daly (1985) as the "young male syndrome" and include risk taking, assertiveness, and competitiveness. Using terms more connected with personality psychology, some of which are discussed in this chapter, the relevant personality traits would have to do with impulsivity, sensation seeking, and extraversion/assertiveness/social dominance. Although males do score higher on all of these traits, on average, compared to women, research linking digit ratio to these traits is mixed.

A study by Wacker, Mueller, and Stemmler (2012) hypothesized that more specific traits related to aspects of the "young male" syndrome might correlate with digit ratio. Moreover, they thought this relationship might be stronger in males than females. In a study of more than 200 young adult males, they administered a large number of personality scales related to the "young male" syndrome and used factor analysis to distill relatively pure and specific measures of these traits. They found a strong relationship between lower digit ratio and impulsive sensation seeking (men with longer ring fingers relative to their index fingers scored higher in impulsive sensation seeking). This finding is consistent with a number of other studies that found lower digit ratio was associated with risk taking, such as participating in riskier lotteries (Garbarino, Slonim, & Sydnor, 2011), receiving more traffic violations (Schwerdtfeger, Heims, & Heer, 2010), and choosing riskier careers in finance (Sapienza, Zingales, & Maestripieri, 2009). Results with women tend to be less clear, though some studies have reported that, in females, a lower digit ratio (similar to the male digit ratio) is associated with higher levels of risk taking (Honekopp, 2011). In a recent study of more than 1,000 people, Bönte et al. (2017) found that lower digit ratio correlated with competitiveness in both male and female participants. In another study of college female athletes in the United Kingdom, researchers found that having a lower digit ratio correlated with the participant obtaining a higher national ranking in her sport, a finding that also held for male college athletes (Tester & Campbell, 2007). One study of female rhesus macaque monkeys found that females with lower digit ratios achieved a higher dominance status in their group (Nelson et al., 2010).

HOW TO MEASURE YOUR FINGER

☐ With your palm up and fingers straight, measure the base of your index finger to its tip.

☐ Do the same with your ring finger.

To calculate digit ratio, divide index finger length by ring finger length.

Source: Michael Hanlon, "What the Length of Your Index Finger Says About You," Daily Mail, December 3, 2010.

There is a vast amount of information on digit ratio on the internet. Just enter this term in an internet search and you will find many reports and articles. However, much of this information should be viewed skeptically, with an eye toward evaluating the quality of the data, if any, that are reported. Studies that are peer reviewed and published in scientific journals should be given much more weight than the large amount of commentary and quasi- or pre-scientific (not peer reviewed) information found on the web. Looking at the published peer reviewed studies, we conclude that this bodily difference is very likely a lifelong signature of testosterone exposure prenatally and that it does correlate modestly with risk taking and sensation seeking as well as forms of social dominance in adulthood. There is a large gender difference in digit ratio, and within genders the correlates tend to be similar, though somewhat weaker for women. We return to a discussion of testosterone in Chapter 16 when we cover sex and gender in personality psychology.

Another characteristic of the physiological approach to personality is simplicity or parsimony. Physiological theories often propose to explain a good deal of behavior with a few constructs. Often the theories state that a physiological difference results in a given personality difference or a difference in an important behavior pattern. Why, for example, do some people take up skydiving, motorcycle racing, and other high-risk hobbies? One theory (covered later in this chapter) states that they do so because they have a deficiency of a certain chemical in their nervous systems that gives rise to sensation-seeking behavior. Despite the obvious simplicity of theories such as these, human nature is actually more complicated. For example, two people could be equally high on sensation seeking, yet one of them satisfies this need in a socially approved manner (e.g., by becoming an emergency room physician), whereas the other satisfies it in a socially unacceptable manner (e.g., illegal gambling, drug use, reckless driving). Most physiologically oriented psychologists would *not* argue that "physiology is destiny." Most would agree that physiology is only *one* cause among many for explaining behavior.

As you know from Chapter 1, Gordon Allport, who wrote one of the first textbooks on personality (1937), argued that "[t]he organization (of personality) entails the operation of both body and mind, inextricably fused into a personal unity" (p. 48). Because personality consists of both bodily and mental aspects, its study can be approached from either direction. In this chapter, we focus on an approach to personality that focuses on underlying bodily systems.

A Physiological Approach to Personality

Most physiological personality psychologists today focus on measures of distinct physiological systems, such as heart rate or brain activation. The typical research question posed by contemporary psychologists concerns whether some people will exhibit more or less of a specific physiological response than others under certain conditions. For example, people who are introverted may avoid loud parties because they easily become overwhelmed by the social and physical stimulation at such parties. Notice that this statement specifies: (1) which particular environmental conditions (i.e., loud parties) affect (2) which particular personality trait (i.e., introversion) to produce (3) which particular physiological response (i.e., increased heart rate), (4) which then promotes a specific behavioral response (i.e., avoidance). These connections are depicted in Figure 7.1.

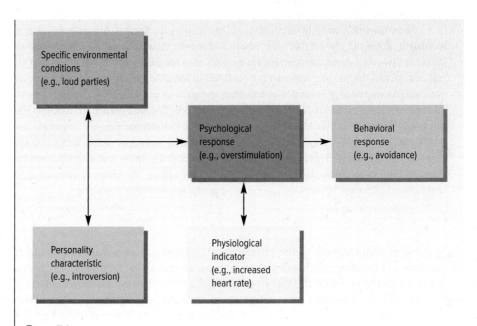

Figure 7.1

Theoretical bridge between personality and physiology: Connections among environmental conditions, personality traits, and responses build a theoretical bridge that links personality to specific situations in terms of evoking a certain psychological response, which can be identified and measured using specific physiological measures. A theory specifies which conditions or stimuli will interact with which personality traits to produce specific responses, which can be observed physiologically.

Specific statements—about which traits are connected to which psychological reactions under which conditions or in response to which stimuli—are now the way personality psychologists talk about physiology. Researchers must be able to build such a **theoretical bridge** between the personality dimension of interest and physiological variables in order to use physiological concepts to help explain personality (Allen & DeYoung, 2017; Levenson, 1983; Yarkoni, 2015). Let's turn now to a brief review of physiological variables, with an emphasis on how they are measured in personality research.

Physiological Measures Commonly Used in Personality Research

Most of the common physiological measures in personality research are obtained from **electrodes**, or sensors placed on the surface of a participant's skin. They are noninvasive in that they do not penetrate the skin, and these electrodes cause practically no discomfort. One drawback to such measures in the past has been that participants are literally wired to the physiological recording machine (often called a polygraph), so movement was constrained. A new generation of sensors has overcome this limitation through the use of **telemetry**, a process whereby physiological data signals are sent from the participant to storage devices through Bluetooth, Wi-Fi, or other radio waves instead of by wires. There are many "wearable" sensors (e.g., watches, rings, audio microphones, one's phone) that are starting to be used in personality research (Ihsan & Furnham, 2018; Mehl & Wrzus, 2021). Wearable sensor technology is a rapidly advancing field, and it will have an impact on personality science as more researchers incorporate this technology into their studies. Three physiological measures of particular interest to personality psychologists are electrodermal activity (skin conductance of electricity), cardiovascular activity, and measures of the brain. We will discuss each of these in turn, though other biological measures, such as the amounts of hormones or neurotransmitters in the blood, are also of interest.

Electrodermal Activity (Skin Conductance)

The skin on the palms of the hands (and the soles of the feet) contains a high concentration of sweat glands. These sweat glands are directly influenced by the **sympathetic nervous system**, the branch of the **autonomic nervous system** that prepares the body for action—that is, the fight-or-flight mechanism. When the sympathetic nervous system is activated (such as during episodes of anxiety, startle, or anger), the sweat glands begin to fill with salty water. If the activation is sufficiently strong or prolonged, the sweat may actually spill out onto the palms of the hands, causing the person to develop sweaty palms. Interestingly, all mammals have a similarly high concentration of sweat glands on the friction surfaces of their hands/paws.

Even before the sweat is visible, however, it can be detected by the clever application of a small amount of electricity because water (i.e., sweat) conducts electricity. The more water present in the skin, the more easily the skin carries, or conducts, electricity. This bioelectric process, known as **electrodermal activity** (*dermal* means "of the skin"), or skin conductance, makes it possible for researchers to indirectly measure sympathetic nervous system activity.

In this technique, two electrodes are placed on the palm of one hand or on a finger. A very low voltage of electricity is then put through one electrode into the skin, and the researcher measures how much electricity is present at the other electrode.

The difference in the amount of electricity passed into the skin at one electrode and the amount detected at the other electrode tells researchers how well the skin is conducting electricity. The more sympathetic nervous system activity there is, the more water is produced by the sweat glands in the skin, and the better the skin conducts the electricity. The levels of electricity involved are so small that the participant does not feel anything. In the past, electrodermal recording required a polygraph that was connected to the research participant with wires. These days, electrodermal activity can be recorded from a wearable ring or sensors attached to a watch, which conveys the data via Wi-Fi or Bluetooth to the internet for recording and analysis.

Electrodermal responses can be elicited by all sorts of stimuli, including sudden noises, emotional images, conditioned stimuli, mental effort, pain, and emotional reactions such as anxiety, fear, and guilt (as in the so-called lie detector test, which uses skin conductance). One phenomenon of interest to personality psychologists is the observation that some people show skin conductance responses in the *absence* of any external stimuli. Imagine a participant sitting quietly in a dimly lit room who is instructed to just relax. Most people in this situation exhibit very little in the way of autonomic nervous system activity. However, some participants in this situation exhibit spontaneous electrodermal responses, even though there is nothing objectively causing these responses. Not surprisingly, the personality trait most consistently associated with nonspecific electrodermal responding is neuroticism (Cruz & Larsen, 1995). Later research showed that neuroticism is associated with larger and longer-lasting electrodermal responses while viewing unpleasant images (Norris, Larsen, & Cacioppo, 2007). A person who is high on neuroticism appears to have a sympathetic nervous system that is in a state of chronic activation and that also exhibits stronger and more prolonged responses to aversive or unpleasant stimuli. That is, part of being a "high-strung" (high on neuroticism) person is to have the flight-or-fight branch of one's nervous system more activated than it is with most other people. This is just one example of how electrodermal measures have been used by personality psychologists to ascertain differences in personality among people.

Cardiovascular Activity

The cardiovascular system involves the heart and associated blood vessels, and examples of measures of cardiovascular activity include blood pressure and heart rate. **Blood pressure** is the pressure exerted by the blood on the inside of the artery walls, and it is typically expressed with two numbers: diastolic and systolic pressure. The systolic pressure is the larger number, and it refers to the maximum pressure within the cardiovascular system produced when the heart muscle contracts. The diastolic pressure is the smaller number, and it refers to the resting pressure inside the system between heart contractions. Blood pressure can increase in a number of ways—for example, the heart may pump with larger strokes generating more volume, or through a narrowing of the artery walls. Blood pressure is responsive to a number of physical (e.g., exercise) and psychological (e.g., stress, fear, mental effort) conditions, and personality researchers have been especially interested in blood pressure response to stress.

Another easily obtained cardiovascular measure is **heart rate**, often expressed in beats-per-minute (BPM). Heart rate can change beat by beat, so a technique with a degree of sophistication is needed to ensure accurate measurement. One approach is to measure the time interval between successive beats. If that interval is exactly one second, then the heart rate is 60 BPM. As the time interval between beats becomes shorter, the heart is beating faster, and vice versa. By measuring the intervals between successive heartbeats, the psychologist can get a readout of heart rate on a beat-by-beat basis. Heart rate is important because as it increases, it indicates that the person's body is preparing for action—to flee or to fight, for example. It tells us that the person is distressed, anxious, fearful, or otherwise more aroused than normal. Heart rate also increases with cognitive effort, as when people try to solve a difficult math problem. People differ from each other in heart rate responses, with some showing large increases and others only minor increases in response to the same stimuli or task.

A cardiovascular measure being used in contemporary research, and available with many wearable sensors, is **heart rate variability (HRV)**. This measure assesses how much ones heart rate differs from beat to beat over a given time period. A healthy and well-rested person, who is not under any stress, will typically show elevated HRV. Higher HRV is normal and occurs when the sympathetic and parasympathetic branches of the nervous system are in balance. Conversely, a person under stress, or who is fatigued or overtrained, will show decreased HRV. Decreased HRV occurs when one of the branches of the nervous system predominates the other (as with sympathetic activation during fight-or-flight reactions) and produces a more steady or unchanging heart rate over time (lower variability). Some research shows that persons experiencing dysregulated emotions, or who are under stress, show decreased HRV. Consequently personality traits associated with stress or emotionality can be negatively correlated with HRV.

Researchers have been interested in what happens to a person's cardiovascular system when he or she is challenged by having to perform a stressful task in front of an audience. Techniques used to induce temporary stress range from having participants sing a song in front of an audience, to having participants perform backward serial subtraction (e.g., "take the number 784 and subtract 7, take the result and subtract 7, and keep doing so until you are told to stop"). Participants report that performing such tasks is stressful and, not surprisingly, everyone's blood pressure and heart rate goes up during these tasks. However, some people show much larger increases in heart rate than others. This phenomenon has been called **cardiac reactivity** and has been associated with the **Type A personality**—a behavior pattern characterized by impatience, competitiveness, and hostility. Evidence suggests that chronic cardiac reactivity contributes to coronary artery disease, which may be why the Type A personality trait is associated with a higher likelihood of heart disease and heart attacks (see Chapter 18). The relation between cardiovascular reactivity and Type A is one example of how physiological measures have been used in the study of personality.

The Brain

The last decade of the last century (1990–1999) was designated the "Decade of the Brain" by then president George H. W. Bush. As a result, research on the brain became a priority at the National Institutes of Health during that decade. This resulted in major advances in the scientific technology for studying the brain as well as increases in our understanding of how the brain works. The field of **neuroscience**, which is the scientific study of the nervous system, particularly the brain, expanded greatly during that decade and after.

From a personality perspective, an important outcome of the Decade of the Brain was to make brain imaging technology more user-friendly, more widely available due to lower costs, as well as improving the speed, resolution, and information value of brain imaging data. This resulted in researchers being able to include brain imaging in studies of very large samples of individuals. Because personality is the study of differences between individuals, large samples sizes are necessary. Scientists are now able to analyze differences in brain measures in sample sizes large enough to focus on reliable

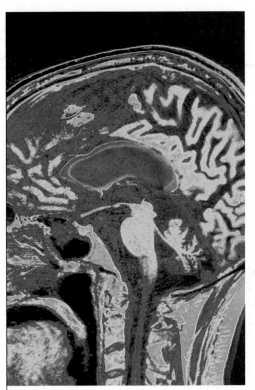

fMRI imagery tracks brain activation by monitoring glucose metabolism in the brain. When an area of the brain is used, it consumes energy in the form of glucose (Beer & Lombardo, 2007).

BSIP/Universal Images Group via Getty Images

differences between individuals. The result has been a very rapid increase in research on individual differences and the creation of a new scientific discipline called "personality neuroscience."

In 2018, a new scientific journal—*Personality Neuroscience*—was created to serve as an outlet for the increasing amount of research on personality and the brain. This journal is open access, meaning that articles published there can be read online for free (https://www.cambridge.org/core/journals/personality-neuroscience). This journal also has a Twitter account (@PNeuroscience) for short updates or breaking news of interest to followers. The fact that the field of personality neuroscience has its own scientific journal indicates that this field has achieved a critical mass of researchers and known findings and indicates scientific maturity (McNaughton, 2020).

In terms of brain measures used in personality research, there are four distinct categories of measures: brain function, brain structure, brain connections, and brain electrical activity. We turn now to a brief introduction to each of these categories.

Brain Function

If someone tells you their phone number, and you hold it in your memory long enough to type it into your phone, the working memory center in your brain will be activated. If you go to put on your shoes, and a large spider jumps out onto your hand, the fear center in your brain will be activated. *Brain function* refers to changes (increases or decreases) in the activation of various regions of the brain in response to specific cognitive activity (like working memory) or environmental events (like a spider scaring you). Scientists can measure these changes in brain activation patterns through the use of imaging techniques.

Two important techniques used to measure brain activation are positron emission tomography (PET) and functional magnetic resonance imaging (fMRI). These powerful imaging tools, which were developed primarily for medical diagnosis, allow physicians and psychologists to look inside the working brains of their patients and subjects. Images show exactly which portions of the brain are active. For example, if we wanted to know what part of the brain is involved in working memory, we would have a sample of people perform a memory task (such as remembering a phone number) while their brains are scanned by fMRI. The fMRI measures activity level in areas of the brain in terms of glucose consumption; more glucose consumption in a region indicates that the neurons there are more active. It provides very fine spatial resolution and is able to pinpoint specific areas of activation that are associated with specific cognitive, motor, or emotional tasks. It turns out, for example, that working memory occurs in the prefrontal cortex, whereas long-term memory is in the hippocampus.

An early study of personality and brain activation was published by Canli, Mangum, and Wells (2001), in which they used fMRI to scan the brains of people as they looked at 20 negative images (e.g., spiders, people crying) and 20 neutral images (a cup, a lamp). Canli and colleagues found that the personality trait of neuroticism correlated with increased frontal brain activation to the negative images. A later review of 18 published studies on the neural correlates of neuroticism (Servaas et al., 2013) found that tasks that evoke anxiety or fear produce more brain activation in the appropriate brain regions in persons high in neuroticism. An important point relevant to these studies—and to all the studies mentioned in this section—is that neuroticism does not correlate with resting brain activity. Rather, personality correlates with brain activation during tasks that involve psychological processes relevant to the trait, consistent with the notion of a "theoretical bridge" mentioned earlier in this chapter. Neuroticism correlates with increased brain activation during fear conditioning, anticipation of an aversive event like punishment, or the processing of negative emotions and images. This illustrates the concept of the theoretical bridge presented in Figure 7.1 earlier in this chapter. Psychologist Colin DeYoung (2015) describes a theoretical bridge for each of the Big Five personality traits, specifying how each trait can be broken down into specific underlying mechanisms that are responsive to specific conditions and can be related to specific brain measures. DeYoung's (2015) proposals are likely to guide neuroscientific research on the Big Five personality traits for several years to come (Allen & DeYoung, 2017; Fajkowska & Kreitler, 2018; McNaughten & Smillie, 2018).

What about brain activation research outside of the Big Five traits? A study (Izuma et al., 2018) examined self-esteem, which concerns differences between people in how positively they feel about themselves, how much they like themselves (see Chapter 14 for more detail on self-esteem). The study by Izuma and colleagues started with the known finding that the reward centers of the brain are activated when people think about or look at something they prefer or like (e.g., their favorite ice cream, money). However, in this experiment, participants' brains were scanned while they looked at various images, some of which were images of themselves. Researchers found that persons with higher self-esteem showed more activation in their brain reward centers while looking at images of themselves than persons lower in self-esteem. Other studies have examined activity in brain centers involved in processing reward and punishment in relation to personality (Standen et al., 2022). Tools that measure brain activation are very likely to revolutionize what we know about the brain and personality over the next few decades, making this a particularly exciting area of research (DeYoung, Grazioplene, & Allen, 2021).

Brain Structure

A relatively newer use of imaging techniques is to assess brain structure instead of function, to see whether personality correlates with the size of various areas of the brain (DeYoung et al., 2010). So, instead of measuring how active a region is, MRI can be used to measure the volume or thickness of various brain areas. In one study, DeYoung and colleagues (2012) used the Big Five model of personality to generate predictions about which areas of the brain would be responsible for generating the behaviors or responses relevant to each trait. They then assessed brain structure in a large (for neuroscience studies; $N = 116$ subjects) sample of healthy young adults. They found support for many of their predictions about the volume of certain brain regions being associated with specific personality traits. For example, extraversion correlated with the volume of medial orbitofrontal cortex, a brain region involved in processing reward information. Neuroticism correlated with the volume of brain regions that have been associated with threat and punishment. Other researchers are reporting robust correlations between extraversion and neuroticism and other measures of brain structures, including cortical surface area (Privado et al., 2017). In a particularly large sample (578 participants), Lewis and colleagues (2018) found that conscientiousness correlated with having a thicker cortex across several brain regions. Even larger studies (over 1,000 participants in each) have shown that all of the big five traits are correlated with the structural volume of various regions, with correlations that range from small to moderate (Hyatt et al., 2021; Owens et al., 2019).

Application

Bigger Is Better?

When Albert Einstein passed away in 1955, the physician Thomas Stoltz Harvey performed an autopsy on his body at Princeton Hospital. During the autopsy, Dr. Harvey removed Einstein's brain. Rumors abounded that Einstein's brain was much larger than average, accounting for his genius. However, the overall weight of Einstein's brain (1230 grams) fell completely within normal limits. After weighing the brain and taking several photos of it from different angles, Harvey dissected Einstein's brain into 240 pieces, which he preserved in formalin. In the accompanying photo, Dr. Harvey displays a jar with portions of Einstein's brain. Harvey and his colleagues were more interested in the cellular level than in overall structure. Consequently, observations about the structure of Einstein's brain made by other physicians and anthropologists were based on the photos, not examination of the whole brain. While it appears that Einstein's brain may have had deeper or more folds in his brain (which would result in larger surface area), making such conclusions without examining the whole brain is unreliable. Other scientists have argued that any conclusions about genius and the structure of the brain require the study of many brains, not just one. This can be done now with neuroimaging of brain structure and does not require an autopsy. One large study (over 7,000 participants) found that total brain volume correlated .28 with general intelligence (after controlling for age and gender differences in brain volume; Cox et al., 2019). Though exploratory, these researchers report even higher correlations with several specific brain regions. Other researchers have found that the degree of interconnectedness between brain regions correlated with intelligence (Krupnik, Yovel, & Assaf, 2021). Another study of specific brain structure and IQ (Grazioplene et al., 2015) found that the volume in a particular part of the brain involved in learning (caudate nucleus) correlates with measured IQ. So, general results suggest that it is not overall brain size, but rather the size of particular portions of the brain involved in learning that is likely to be well developed in people like Einstein. However, what is not known is whether having a larger caudate leads to more learning (and hence higher IQ) or whether more learning leads to a larger caudate.

Medical Pathologist Dr. Thomas Harvey (1912-2007) holds a jar containing portions of Albert Einstein's brain preserved in formalin.
Michael Brenna/Getty Images

Brain Connections

An even newer brain imaging technique is to focus not on the function or structure of brain regions *per se,* but on the connections *between* specific regions. For example, there is a brain region associated with emotion and another region associated with decision making. Researchers are now able to image the circuitry that connects these two regions and measure the size and activation of the connectivity between these regions. These connectivity measures relate to the amount of communication or interaction between two or more brain regions. Personality correlates may be found in the strength of connections between brain areas. For example, some people may have more of a connection between reason and emotion, whereas for others emotion and reason are less connected (i.e., emotions figure very little, if at all, in their decision making). This new approach, focusing on the functional connectivity between brain regions, is an important development in neuroscience and is just now being extended into personality psychology, where the emphasis will be on individual differences in the strength of connections between brain regions.

As an example of one interesting finding emerging from this brain connectivity approach, variation in the default brain network—the background total spontaneous communication between the brain's many regions—has been related to the personality trait of openness to experience (Beaty et al., 2016). This finding suggests that the brains of people high on openness (who tend to be imaginative, creative, and enjoy abstract reasoning) show more total connectivity among all their brain regions than persons low on openness. In a different study, researchers looked at the degree of connectivity linking to the executive control centers and found that conscientiousness correlated with more connectivity (Toschi et al, 2018). This finding is consistent with the observation that conscientious people are reliable and efficient at setting goals, prioritizing, and planning, so it makes sense that their frontal brain areas are more connected to other areas of their brain. Understanding the brain as a network, with a focus on the connections among brain areas, is an exciting new approach within personality neuroscience (Market, Montag, & Reuter, 2018). This new area of research holds much promise for understanding the biological foundation of personality traits (see A Closer Look on The Human Connectome Project).

A Closer Look   The Human Connectome Project

Mapping the human brain has been one of the greatest scientific challenges of this century. Much work has already been done identifying key areas of the brain associated with various functions, such as memory, perception, and emotion. However, mapping the neural pathways that connect these various regions is just getting started. As an analogy, think about the electrical system of a house, where you know about the various electrical devices (e.g., lights, TV, computer, refrigerator, etc.), but the

actual wiring of the house, the connections between devices, remains a mystery to you. Decoding the complex wiring diagram within the human brain is an amazingly challenging task, like determining the wiring diagram for major city.

The Human Connectome Project was started in 2011 as an effort to decode the wiring diagram of the human brain and was initially formed as a consortium of three universities (Washington University, University of Minnesota, and Oxford University). Their

goal was to comprehensively map the human brain circuitry of 1,200 healthy adults and make the data public. After achieving this goal, dozens of other research centers (e.g., University of Southern California) joined the effort, targeting other populations, such as the elderly, infants, children, and persons with mental disorders. The original project team now runs the Connectome Coordinating Facility, which manages an open-source Web-accessible neuroinformatics platform to allow others to access

(Continued)

A Closer Look (*Continued*)

and work with the truly vast amount of data being generated. The goal is not just to have a wiring diagram for the human brain (the structure of circuitry), but to also know the functions of the connections and whether there are meaningful individual differences in those connections.

A large part of the project has been directed at understanding individual differences—that is, understanding that not everyone's brain is wired the same. There is variation from person to person in brain circuitry, and this variation may relate to personality differences or to various medical conditions. Some of the initial publications coming out of this project focus on such individual differences. One important paper (Smith, Williams, & Segerstrom, 2015) assesses the link between positive life outcomes and patterns of brain connectivity in 460 participants between the ages of 22 and 35. The researchers defined positive life outcomes by grouping measures of positive characteristics like vocabulary, intelligence, education, life satisfaction, and financial income and then subtracting negative characteristics like smoking, trait anger, and

self-reports of delinquency or rule breaking. Each subject receives a ranking on this single positive-negative life outcome dimension, with higher rank indicating more positive outcomes in the person's life. They then correlated the strength of connections between various brain regions to this global positive life outcome. They found that the connectivity strength of more than 30 brain circuits correlated with higher rank on the positive life outcome dimension. In general, those persons with stronger or more overall brain connectivity had more positive characteristics, such as larger vocabulary, better memory, higher life satisfaction, larger income, and better education. Conversely, those with weaker network connections in their brains had more of the negative characteristics, such as anger, rule breaking, and substance use.

While these initial results sound promising, we need to remind ourselves that correlation does not establish causation, and it does not prove that the stronger brain connections "cause" the person to be more intelligent, have a better

vocabulary, etc. It could well be that developing a larger vocabulary, or becoming more intelligent by staying in school and learning, causes the brain connections to develop. So there is a lot left to be learned about the development of both brain connectivity and the development of individual differences, and how the two are linked. Nevertheless, this kind of work illustrates the promise of a physiological approach to personality, with the possibility in the future of using brain scans to predict the kinds of skills, abilities, and personalities we might expect from a particular individual. If the causal influences of biology and environment are understood well enough, it may lead to the design of better schools or other interventions to help people change their behavior (and their brains) toward the more positive end of the life-outcome dimension.

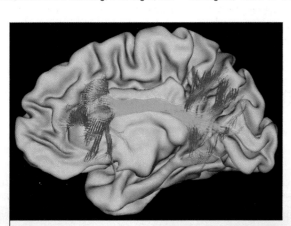

3D probabilistic trajectories of white matter fibers arising from a seed in the left frontal cortex, superimposed on the right cortical gray matter surface for reference. The orientation vectors are color-coded (red: left-right; green: anterior posterior; blue: inferior-superior) and have opacity representative of the underlying number of streamlines that took the particular fiber orientation brain scan.

Source: S. Sotiropoulos and T. E. J. Behrens for the WU-Minn HCP consortium–http://humanconnectome.org

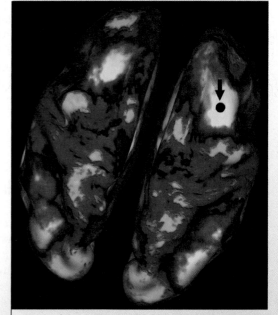

A map of the average "functional connectivity" in the human cerebral cortex collected on healthy subjects while "at rest" in the MRI scanner. Regions in yellow/red are functionally connected to the "seed" location in the right frontal cortex (black circle, arrow), whereas regions in green and blue are weakly connected or not connected at all.

Source: M. F. Glasser and S. M. Smith for the WU-Minn HCP consortium–http://humanconnectome.org

Brain Electrical Activity

It has been known for more than a century that the brain spontaneously produces small amounts of electricity, which can be measured by electrodes placed on the scalp. This measure is called the **electroencephalogram (EEG)**, and EEG recordings can be obtained for various regions of the brain while the participant is asleep, is relaxed but awake, or is doing a task. Such measures of regional brain activity can provide useful information about patterns of activation in various parts of the brain, which may be associated with different types of medical conditions or cognitive tasks (e.g., processing verbal versus spatial information, as in receiving directions from someone verbally or being shown a map of where to go). Personality psychologists have been especially interested in whether different regions of the brain show different patterns of electrical activity for different people. Later in this chapter we review left-right asymmetry in EEG activation as it relates to emotional traits.

Another technique in measuring brain electrical activity is called the evoked potential technique, in which the brain EEG is measured but the participant is given a stimulus, such as a tone or a flash of light, and the researcher assesses the participant's brain responsiveness to that stimulus. As discussed below, researchers have found the traits of extraversion and sensation seeking to be related to diminished reactivity, including diminished evoked potentials using EEG recording.

Other Measures

Although skin conductance, heart rate, and brain assessments are commonly used measures in physiological studies of personality, other biological measures have also proven useful (see Table 7.1). One important class of measures includes biochemical analyses of blood and saliva. For example, from saliva samples, biochemists can extract indicators of how competently a person's immune system is functioning (Miller & Cohen, 2001). The quality of immune system functioning may go up and down with stress or emotions and thereby may relate to personality. Hormones, such as testosterone and oxytocin, play a role in important behaviors and can also be extracted from saliva samples. Testosterone has been linked to uninhibited, aggressive, and risk-taking behavior patterns (Dabbs & Dabbs, 2000). Oxytocin is a hormone related to affiliation and social bonding and has been found to be higher in extraverts than introverts (Andari, 2015). Cortisol, a byproduct of the hormone noradrenaline, can be readily assessed from saliva samples. Researchers have found, for example, that shy children have high levels of cortisol in their systems (Kagan & Snidman, 1991), suggesting that they experience more stress than less shy children. Monoamine oxidase (MAO) is an enzyme found in the blood that is known to regulate neurotransmitters, the chemicals that carry messages between nerve cells. MAO may be a causal factor in the personality trait of sensation seeking. Other theories of personality are based directly on different amounts of neurotransmitters in the nervous system. One particular neurotransmitter—dopamine—plays a role in several neurological functions, one of which is responding to rewarding or pleasurable stimuli and is associated with such psychological states as "liking," "wanting," and "enjoyment" (Smillie & Wacker, 2014) and promotes exploration by prompting the person to seek out rewards and follow cues of rewards (DeYoung, 2013). Evidence is accumulating that the personality trait of extraversion is related to increased dopamine function, with extraversion scores significantly predicting how people respond to drugs that manipulate dopamine levels (Wacker & Smillie, 2015). Researchers have known for some time that extraverts tend to have more positive emotions and are happier than introverts (see Chapter 13 on Emotions and Personality), and this may be due in part to dopamine function in extraverts being different from

Table 7.1 Common Physiological Measures Used in Personality Research

Physiological Measure	Physiological System	Psychological Response System	Examples of Stimuli Used in Research
Electrodermal activity	Sweat gland activity controlled by sympathetic nervous system	Anxiety, startle, guilt, effort, pain	Noise, mental effort, emotional stimuli, painful stimuli
Cardiovascular activity	Blood pressure and heart rate controlled by autonomic nervous system	Flight-or-fight response, mental effort, stress	Stress, social anxiety, effort, high cognitive load
Electroencephalogram (EEG)	Brain's spontaneous electrical activity	Brain activation, alertness	Resting with eyes closed, reading
Evoked EEG	Brain's electrical activity in response to specific stimuli	Attention, recognition, cognitive processing	Brief sensory stimuli, emotional stimuli
Neuroimaging (e.g., fMRI, PET)	Brain's energy metabolism	Specific brain areas responsible for cognitive control, emotion, memory, pain, decision making, sensory processing	Wide variety of tasks that activate these psychological response systems
Antibodies	Immune system	Immune response to infection, stress	Virus, bacteria, stress
Testosterone	Hormone system (steroid)	Aggression, competitiveness, psychological drive and libido, muscle bulk	Tasks involving competition, aggression, attraction
Cortisol	Hormone system (adrenal)	Stress response	Life events, stress, anxiety stimuli
Serotonin, dopamine, MAO, etc.	Neurotransmitters	Transmission of specific nerve signals	Rewarding stimuli, emotions

introverts. A special issue of the journal *Frontiers in Human Neuroscience* (2014, vol. 8) published 16 papers on individual differences in the dopamine system, primarily in reference to the personality trait of extraversion. There are, however, several other physiological theories of extraversion, to which we now turn.

Physiologically Based Theories of Personality

Now that we have covered basic physiological measures used in personality research, we turn to some of the biological theories that have generated interest and attention among personality psychologists. We begin with what is perhaps the most widely studied physiological theory of personality—the theory that proposes a biological explanation for why some people are introverted and others extraverted.

Extraversion–Introversion

Among the people you know, someone probably fits the following description: is talkative and outgoing, likes meeting new people and going new places, is active, is sometimes impulsive and venturesome, gets bored easily, and hates routine and monotony.

Table 7.2 Items from the Eysenck Personality Questionnaire Extraversion Scale

Extraversion Items

For every question, circle just one response.

YES	NO	Are you a talkative person?
YES	NO	Are you rather lively?
YES	NO	Can you usually let yourself go and enjoy yourself at a lively party?
YES	NO	Do you enjoy meeting new people?
YES	NO	Do you tend to keep in the background on social occasions? (reversed)
YES	NO	Do you like going out a lot?
YES	NO	Do you prefer reading to meeting people? (reversed)
YES	NO	Do you have many friends?
YES	NO	Would you call yourself happy-go-lucky?

Scoring directions: Reverse your answers to the items marked "reversed"; then count how many questions you endorsed with a "yes." The average college student scores about 6 on this questionnaire.

Source: Eysenck, Eysenck, and Barrett (1985).

Such a person would score as an extravert on an extraversion–introversion questionnaire. See Table 7.2 for items from a popular extraversion–introversion questionnaire—the Eysenck Personality Inventory.

You probably also know someone who is just the opposite, someone who is quiet and withdrawn, who prefers being alone or with a few friends to being in large crowds, who prefers routines and schedules, and who prefers the familiar to the unexpected. Such a person would score in the introverted direction on an extraversion–introversion questionnaire. If you are wondering *why* introverts and extraverts are so different from each other, physiologically minded personality psychologists have an intriguing explanation: Eysenck's theory.

An early example of a physiologically based theory of personality was put forward by H. J. Eysenck (1916–1997) in his 1967 book *The Biological Basis of Personality.* While we covered Eysenck's descriptive taxonomy of personality traits in Chapter 3, here we go into detail on his biological explanation for individual differences on the dimension that ranges from introversion to extraversion. Eysenck proposed that introverts are characterized by higher levels of activity in the brain's **ascending reticular activating system (ARAS)** than are extraverts. The ARAS is a structure in the brain stem thought to control overall cortical arousal. In the 1960s, the ARAS was thought of as a gateway through which nervous stimulation from the sense organs entered the brain's cortex. If the gate were somewhat closed, then the resting **arousal level** of the cortex would be lower, and if the gate were more open, then the resting arousal level would be higher. Introverts, according to this theory, have higher resting levels of cortical arousal because their ARAS lets in too much stimulation. Introverts engage in introverted behaviors (are quiet and seek low-stimulation settings, such as libraries) because they need to keep their already heightened level of arousal in check. Conversely, extraverts engage in extraverted behaviors because they need to increase their level of arousal (Claridge, Donald, & Birchall, 1981).

Are you a talkative person? Do you like mixing with people? Do you like plenty of bustle and excitement around you? Answering no to such questions suggests an introverted personality.
everst/Shutterstock

Do you like telling jokes and funny stories to your friends? Do you like mixing with people? Can you get a party going? Answering yes to such questions suggests an extraverted personality. Interestingly, Eysenck's extraversion-introversion theory is based not on a need to be with people, but rather on a need for arousal and stimulation.
Rawpixel.com/Shutterstock

Eysenck also incorporated Hebb's (1955) notion of "optimal level of arousal" into his theory. By optimal level of arousal, Hebb meant a level that is just right for any given task. For example, imagine going into a final exam in an underaroused state (e.g., sleepy, tired). Being sleepy and underaroused would be just as bad for your performance as going into the exam in an overaroused state (e.g., extremely anxious and agitated). There is an optimal level of arousal for taking an exam—not too much, not too little—one in which you are focused, alert, and attentive but not aroused to the point of anxiety or panic.

If introverts have a higher baseline level of arousal than extraverts (i.e., level of arousal while at rest), then introverts are above their optimal level of arousal more often than extraverts. According to the theory, the generally overaroused condition of introverts leads them to be more restrained and inhibited. They avoid active social interactions that might aggravate their already overstimulated condition. Extraverts, on the other hand, need to get their arousal level higher and so seek out stimulating activities and engage in more unrestrained behaviors. The qualities that typically characterize introverts (e.g., quiet, withdrawn) and extraverts (e.g., outgoing, engaging) are understood to be attempts to regulate arousal downward (in the case of introverts) or upward (in the case of extraverts) to maintain an optimal level of arousal.

In the decades following publication of Eysenck's theory, many studies were conducted to test it (see reviews by Eysenck, 1991; Matthews & Gilliland, 1999; Stelmack & Rammsayer, 2008). If it is true that introverts are more cortically aroused than extraverts, then introverts should display enhanced responsiveness on measures of cortical activity, such as the electroencephalogram (EEG), as well as on measures of autonomic nervous system activity, such as electrodermal response. Studies designed to test this hypothesis typically have taken the form of comparing introverts with extraverts on physiological measures gathered under conditions of various degrees of stimulation (Gale, 1986). In conditions where participants were presented with either no stimulation or very mild stimulation, differences between introverts and extraverts turned out to be small or nonexistent. However, in studies that looked at nervous system responsiveness to moderate levels of stimulation, introverts showed larger or faster responses than extraverts, as predicted by Eysenck's theory (Bullock & Gilliland, 1993; Gale, 1983).

The fact that introverts and extraverts are not different at resting levels, but *are* different under moderate levels of stimulation, led Eysenck to revise his arousal theory (Eysenck & Eysenck, 1985). When he first stated his theory in 1967, Eysenck did not distinguish between resting, or *baseline,* levels of arousal and arousal *responses* to stimulation. A good deal of evidence now suggests that the real difference between introverts and extraverts lies in their **arousability**, or arousal response, not in their baseline arousal level. Extraverts and introverts do not differ in their level of brain activity while sleeping, for example, or while lying quietly in a darkened room with their eyes shut (Stelmack, 1990). However, when presented with moderate levels of stimulation, introverts show enhanced physiological reactivity compared with extraverts (De Pascalis, 2004; Doucet & Stelmack, 2000; Gale, 1987).

Exercise

The Lemon Juice Demonstration: This demonstration is designed to illustrate that introverts are more reactive to stimulation than extraverts. Although some teachers have tried this in the classroom, it can be a bit messy and so might best be done as a thought experiment. Here is how it would go: Take a double-tipped cotton swab and tie a thread exactly in its center so that it hangs perfectly in balance (i.e., is horizontal). Swallow three times and put one end on your tongue for exactly 20 seconds. After removing the swab, place 4 drops of lemon juice under your tongue. Place the other end of the cotton swab on your tongue for 20 seconds. Remove the swab and let it hang by the thread. If you are an extravert, it is likely that the swab will remain horizontal, indicating that you did not react strongly to the lemon juice by producing more saliva. If you are an introvert, it is likely that the swab will no longer balance horizontally and will instead be heavier on the end placed on the tongue following the lemon juice. This would indicate that you produced more saliva in response to the lemon juice. Eysenck conducted a similar experiment (Eysenck & Eysenck, 1967) as did Corcoran (1964).

An important corollary of the theory is that, when given a choice, extraverts should prefer higher levels of stimulation than do introverts. Indirect evidence supports this prediction. For example, laboratory studies have shown that extraverts will press a button at a higher rate than introverts when the button pressing produces changes in the visual environment (such as change the channel on a TV, change the image in a slide show) (e.g., Brebner & Cooper, 1978). In a more naturalistic study, done in a university library, persons studying in a noisy reading room scored as more extraverted than did students studying in the quieter rooms (Campbell & Hawley, 1982). Findings such as these suggest that, when given a choice, extraverts tend to seek greater levels of stimulation than introverts (Campbell, 1983).

A clever study designed by psychologist Russell Geen (1984) tested the hypothesis that, when allowed to control the noise level during a learning task, extraverts would choose a louder level than introverts. In this experiment, participants were told they would engage in a learning task in a noisy environment (like studying with the TV on). However, they were allowed to control the volume of the noise (though they could not turn it completely off). Extraverts did choose a louder noise level than introverts. In their preferred noise levels (the levels chosen), the performance of extraverts and introverts did not differ. However, in another condition, the introverts were given the higher noise level chosen by the extraverts, and in this condition their performance declined. Similarly, when the extraverts were given the lower noise level chosen by the introverts, their performance also declined. This study shows not only that extraverts prefer more intense stimulation than introverts but also that stimulation outside of their preferred level (higher for introverts, lower for extraverts) resulted in performance declines, supporting the notion of an optimal level of stimulation, which differs for extraverts (where optimal is more intense) and introverts (where optimal is less intense).

Sensitivity to Reward and Punishment

Jeffrey Gray (1934–2004) proposed an influential alternative biological theory of personality (Gray, 1972, 1990), called **reinforcement sensitivity theory**. Based on brain function research with animals, Gray has constructed a model of human personality based on two hypothesized biological systems in the brain. The first is the **behavioral activation system (BAS)**, which is responsive to incentives, such as cues for reward, and regulates approach behavior, most likely through the dopamine system (DeYoung, 2013). When the BAS recognizes a stimulus as potentially rewarding, it triggers approach behavior. For example, in playing an electronic game, a teenager might notice mainly the possible rewards in the game, and focus mainly on working to earn those rewards (approach motivation). The other system in the brain postulated by Gray (1975) is the **behavioral inhibition system (BIS)**, which is responsive to cues for punishment, frustration, and uncertainty. The effect of BIS activation is to cease or inhibit behavior or to bring about avoidance behavior. As an example of this, a different teenager playing the same computer game might notice mainly the potential threats, and focus more on avoiding the threats (avoidance motivation) than earning the rewards. A rough analogy is that the BAS is like an accelerator that motivates approach behavior, whereas the BIS is like brakes that inhibit behavior or help a person avoid threats.

According to Gray, people differ from each other in the relative sensitivity of their BIS or BAS systems. A person with a reactive BIS is especially sensitive to cues of punishment, frustration, and uncertainty. He or she is vulnerable to unpleasant emotions, including anxiety, fear, and sadness. According to Gray, the BIS is responsible for the personality dimension of **anxiety**. A person with a reactive BAS, on the other hand, is especially sensitive to reward cues in the environment. Such a person is predisposed to positive emotions and tends to approach stimuli. The ability of an individual with a reactive BAS to inhibit behavior decreases as he or she approaches a goal. According to Gray, the BAS is responsible for the personality dimension of **impulsivity**, the inability to inhibit behaviors.

Some debate has focused on exactly where to locate BAS (impulsivity) and BIS (anxiety) in existing trait taxonomies, especially that defined by Eysenck's dimensions of extraversion and introversion (see Figure 7.2). In fact, one of the authors of this book has had a series of exchanges with Gray and his colleagues about this issue (Pickering, Corr, & Gray, 1999; Rusting & Larsen, 1997, 1999). It appears that the relation between Gray's constructs and Eysenck's constructs is direct, with BAS being equivalent to extraversion and BIS being equivalent to neuroticism. Many researchers (e.g., Wilt & Revelle, 2017) argue that extraverts (compared to introverts) are more reactive to cues of reward and incentives ("wanting"), not necessarily the consumption of rewards ("liking") and, as such, extraversion and BAS have the same reward-seeking behavior as a main feature. Similarly, neuroticism is thought to overlap with the BIS in that it (neuroticism) includes increased sensitivity to threat, punishment, and uncertainty and a readiness to respond to such stimuli with defensive (flight-or-fight) or stress (cortisol) reactions (Allen & DeYoung, 2017). Many researchers view the BIS and BAS constructs as identical to neuroticism and extraversion in that both refer to dispositional tendencies to withdraw from punishment or to approach reward, respectively (e.g., Davidson et al., 2003; Kosslyn et al.,

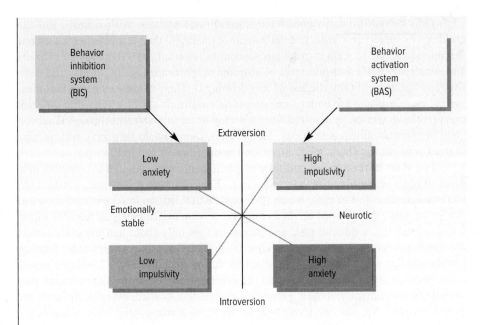

Figure 7.2

Relation between Eysenck's dimensions of extraversion and neuroticism and Gray's dimensions of impulsivity and anxiety.

2002; Knutson & Bhanji, 2006; Sutton, 2002). Gray revised his model to locate BIS much closer to neuroticism and locate BAS much closer to extraversion (Pickering et al., 1999).

Gray believed that differences among people in sensitivity to reward and punishment are responsible for generating wide variety of behaviors and emotions associated approach and avoidance. If we ask why some people are more susceptible than others to anxiety attacks, fears, worry, depressions, phobias, obsessions, or compulsions, Gray would argue that this is due to an overly sensitive behavioral inhibition system. Such people tend to notice and are sensitive to punishment cues and frustration. Moreover, they are distressed by uncertainty and novelty. Then, if we ask why some people are more susceptible than others to positive emotions, to approach behaviors, and to seeking out and interacting with others, Gray would argue that this is due to an overly sensitive behavioral activation system.

Psychologist Charles Carver (1947–2019) and his colleagues (Carver, Sutton, & Scheier, 1999; Carver & White, 1994) developed and validated a questionnaire to measure individual differences in the strength of the BIS and BAS. Other researchers have added to the validity evidence behind this scale. For example, Zelenski and Larsen (1999) found this scale to be one of the best measures of BIS and BAS. Carver, Sutton, and Scheier (1999) reviewed Gray's theory, emphasizing individual differences in approach or incentive motivation (extraversion or impulsivity) and individual differences in withdrawal or aversive motivation (neuroticism or anxiety). They showed how several programs of research can be integrated into the theme that humans appear to possess separate systems for responding to incentives and threats. For example, these systems show reliable individual differences, they relate to major affective dispositions, they may be lateralized in our cerebral architecture, and they may relate differently to learning by punishment and learning by reward. Carver and his colleagues referred to the BIS and BAS as the "Big Two" personality dimensions.

Gray himself primarily conducted research with animals. With animals, you can use drugs or surgery to eliminate certain areas of the brain, then test whether this affects the animal's ability to learn through punishment or reward. Gray's theory relates anxiety and impulsivity to the two principles of learning: reinforcement (both positive and negative) and punishment (and the loss of reinforcement). There is some evidence that these two forms of learning are under separate neural control. It appears likely that different brain mechanisms may be involved when a person or an animal learns through reinforcement or through punishment (Gray, 1991). Thus, there should be people with varying degrees of sensitivity (high, medium, or low) to punishment and to reward.

In a study of reward and punishment, participants were required to complete hundreds of trials of a difficult reaction time task (Larsen, Chen, & Zelenski, 2003). They had to name the colors of color words (the word "RED" written in yellow, also known as the Stroop task) that popped up on a computer screen, as accurately as possible within a half-second. It is a difficult task, and people can get only about half the trials correct given that they have to respond so quickly on each trial. One group was rewarded for each correct and fast response, and they earned $5 during the course of a 20-minute experiment. Another group was punished after incorrect or slow responses, and, although they started the experiment with $10, proceeded to lose $5. As such, everyone finished the experiment with $5, but one group was rewarded on a trial-by-trial basis, whereas the other group was punished on a trial-by-trial basis. It turned out that BAS scores predicted better performance in the reward condition, with high-BAS persons becoming more accurate when they were working for reward. BIS scores, on the other hand, predicted performance in the punishment condition, with high-BIS persons responding with better performance when they were being punished, compared to low-BIS participants.

Much of the work carried out to test Gray's theory has focused on impulsivity (the inability to inhibit responses). Our jails are full of people who are deficient in the ability to control their behavior, especially behavior that may be immediately rewarding. For example, a 17-year-old male sees an expensive sports car parked on the street. As he looks at the car and thinks about how much fun it would be to drive, he notices that the keys are in the ignition. The owner appears nowhere in sight and the street is fairly deserted. He starts to reach for the door handle. The ability to stop this approach behavior, even though it promises a brief but thrilling reward, separates the average person from the impulsive car thief.

Impulsive individuals can be characterized as having stronger approach than avoidance tendencies and are less able to inhibit approach behavior, especially in the presence of desirable goals or rewards. You probably know people who often say things that get them into trouble or who hurt other people's feelings without even thinking. Even though they know they might hurt someone's feelings and feel bad themselves (i.e., are "punished" by feelings of remorse), why can't they control what they do and say?

According to Gray's theory, impulsive people do not learn well from punishment because they have a weak behavioral inhibition system. If this is true, then researchers should be able to demonstrate that in a task that involves learning from punishment, impulsive persons do less well than nonimpulsive persons. Studies have been conducted on impulsive college students, juvenile delinquents, psychopaths, and criminals in jail (Newman, 1987; Newman, Widom, & Nathan, 1985). The typical finding is that such persons are, in fact, deficient in learning through punishment. Impulsive persons, it seems, do not learn as well from punishment as from reward.

The COVID-19 pandemic has brought new threats to consider (situations where transmission is more likely), as well as highlighting rewards that we took for granted (e.g., spontaneous socializing). Researchers have begun to test whether personality relates to how people cope with the pandemic. A recent review of this research (Bacon et., 2021) concluded that fear-driven compliance was correlated with BIS measures, and BAS measures correlated with more difficulty with social isolation and a desire to return toward normality.

Exercise

Think of a situation in which you are trying to teach someone something new. For example, perhaps you want to teach your roommate to keep her part of the room neat and tidy. Think of a way you might use reward to teach her that behavior. For example, every time she picked up her clothes off the floor you compliment her or offer her a piece of candy. Now think of a way you might use mild punishment to teach the same behavior. For example, each time she leaves dirty dishes in the sink, you can try scolding and yelling at her. Which do you think would work better? Do you think she would be more affected by the reward or by the punishment? Could the effectiveness of the reward or the punishment depend on the personality of your roommate?

Sensation Seeking

Sensation seeking is another dimension of personality postulated to have a physiological basis. Sensation seeking is the tendency to seek out thrilling and exciting activities, take risks, and avoid boredom. Research on the need for sensory input grew out of studies on **sensory deprivation**. Let's begin, then, with a description of sensory deprivation research.

Imagine volunteering for a study in which you are put into a small chamber where there is no light, no sound, and only minimal tactile sensations. Imagine further that you agree to do this for 12 hours straight. What would this experience be like? Research suggests that at first you would feel relaxed, then bored, then anxious as you started to have unusual sensory experiences. Deprived of all sensory input, the brain will create its own activation which is experienced as sensory events. Early research by Hebb (1955) showed that in such a situation, college students chose to listen over and over to a taped lecture intended to convince 6-year-olds about the dangers of alcohol. Other participants in those early sensory deprivation experiments who were offered a recording of an old stock market report opted to listen to it over and over again, apparently to avoid the unpleasant consequences of sensory deprivation. Persons in sensory-deprived environments appear motivated to acquire *any* sensory input, even if ordinarily such input would be perceived as boring.

The theory of sensation seeking was proposed to explain why some people routinely seek out thrilling experiences, even though such experiences may come with certain risks.
Glow Images

Hebb's Theory of Optimal Level of Arousal
Hebb developed the theory of **optimal level of arousal**, which was used by Eysenck in his theory of extraversion. Hebb's theory states that people are motivated to reach an optimal level of arousal. If they are underaroused, relative to this level, an increase in arousal is rewarding; conversely, if they are overaroused, a decrease in arousal

is rewarding. For its time, Hebb's theory was controversial because most researchers thought that tension *reduction* was the goal of all motives, yet Hebb was saying that we are motivated to *seek out* tension and stimulation. How else can we explain the fact that people *like* to work on puzzles, enjoy mild frustration, and occasionally take risks or do something to arouse mild fears, such as going on a roller coaster ride or to a scary movie. Hebb's belief that people need stimulation and sensory input is consistent with the results of sensory deprivation research. The nervous system appears to need at least some sensory input.

Sensation Seeking Research Started by Marvin Zuckerman (1928–2018)
Early on in sensory deprivation research, Zuckerman and Haber (1965) noted that some people were not as distressed as others by the sensory deprivation experience. In these early experiments, some people found sensory deprivation extremely unpleasant. These participants requested lots of sensory material (tapes, reading material) during the experiment and quit the experiment relatively early. Zuckerman believed that such persons had a particularly *high need for sensation* because they were the least tolerant of sensory deprivation. He called them sensation seekers because they appeared to seek out stimulation, not just in the sensory deprivation experiment but in their everyday lives as well.

Zuckerman developed a questionnaire designed to measure the extent to which a person needs novel or exciting experiences and enjoys the thrills and excitement associated with them. He called the questionnaire the Sensation-Seeking Scale, and items from it appear in Table 7.3 (Zuckerman & Aluja, 2015).

As it turned out, Zuckerman's questionnaire about preferences for stimulation in everyday life predicted how well people tolerated the sensory deprivation sessions. High sensation seekers found sensory deprivation to be particularly unpleasant, whereas low sensation seekers were able to tolerate it for longer periods of time. In the early 1960s, Zuckerman left the sensory deprivation laboratory and began to study the other unique characteristics associated with the personality dimension of sensation seeking. Notice that this theoretical explanation of sensation seeking is very similar to that Eysenck offered for extraversion. In fact, while the theoretical explanations of Zuckerman and Eysenck differ, there is a moderately strong positive correlation between extraversion and sensation seeking (Zuckerman & Glicksohn, 2016).

Table 7.3 Items from the Sensation-Seeking Scale

There are several aspects of sensation seeking that are reflected in the items on this scale.

Thrill and adventure seeking—reflected in items that ask about desire for outdoor sports or activities involving elements of risk, such as flying, scuba diving, parachute jumping, motorcycle riding, and mountain climbing—for example, "I sometimes like to do things that are a little frightening" (high) versus "A sensible person avoids activities that are dangerous" (low).

Experience seeking—reflected in items that refer to the seeking of new sensory or mental experiences through unconventional or nonconforming lifestyle choices—for example, "I like to have new and exciting experiences and sensations even if they are frightening, unconventional, or illegal" (high) versus "I am not interested in experience for its own sake" (low).

Disinhibition—reflected in items indicating a preference for getting "out of control" or an interest in wild parties, gambling, and sexual variety—for example, "Almost everything enjoyable is illegal or immoral" (high) versus "The most enjoyable things are perfectly legal and moral" (low).

Boredom susceptibility—reflected in items that refer to a dislike for repetition, routine work, monotony, predictable and dull people, and a restlessness when things become unchanging—for example, "I get bored seeing the same old faces" (high) versus "I like the comfortable familiarity of everyday friends" (low).

All of the items on the Sensation-Seeking Scale, as well as scoring instructions, can be found in Zuckerman (1978).

In the 40-plus years that Zuckerman and his colleagues conducted research on sensation seeking, many interesting findings emerged. Police officers who volunteer for riot duty have higher sensation-seeking scores than officers who do not volunteer for riot duty. Skydivers score higher on sensation-seeking measures than non-skydivers. In a study of 550 motorcycle riders, sensation seeking correlated with a tendency to speed and do high-risk stunts (Antoniazzi & Klein, 2019). Among college students who volunteered to be in psychology experiments, the students with high sensation-seeking scores volunteered to participate in the more unusual studies (studies on ESP, hypnosis, or drugs) than in the typical studies (on learning, sleep, or social interaction). In studies of gambling behavior, the participants with high sensation-seeking scores tended to make riskier bets. High sensation seekers also report having a larger number of sex partners, engaging in a wider variety of sex acts, and start having sex at an earlier age than low sensation seekers. The list of correlates of sensation seeking is quite long, and you may consult various reviews to learn more about this personality trait (e.g., Zuckerman, 1978, 1984, 1991b).

According to Zuckerman, there is a physiological basis for sensation-seeking behavior. Zuckerman's more recent work (1991b, 2005, 2006) focused primarily on the role played by neurotransmitters in bringing about differences in sensation seeking. **Neurotransmitters** are chemicals in the nerve cells that are responsible for the transmission of a nerve impulse from one cell to another. As you may recall from your introductory psychology class, nerve cells are separated from one another by a slight gap, called a synapse. A nerve impulse must jump across this gap if it is to continue toward its destination. Neurotransmitters are the chemicals released by the nerves that allow nerve impulses to jump across the synapse and continue on their way.

The neurotransmitter must be broken down after the impulse has passed, or too many nerve transmissions would occur. As an analogy, think of the turnstyle at a sports arena or subway, which lets in one person at a time. If it were left open, many people could run through, allowing too many people in. If it were stuck closed, however, no one could get through. The neurotransmitter system is similar in that the chemical balance in the synapse has to be just right in order for the correct amount of nervous transmission to get through and continue on.

Certain enzymes, particularly **monoamine oxidase (MAO)**, are responsible for maintaining the proper levels of neurotransmitters. MAO works by breaking down the neurotransmitter after it has allowed a nerve impulse to pass. If an excessive amount of MAO were present, it would break down too much of the neurotransmitter, and nerve transmission would be diminished. If there were too little MAO present, an excessive amount of the neurotransmitter would be left in the synapse, allowing for too much nervous transmission to take place. Suppose that you had to do a fine movement with your fingers, such as pick up a dime off a flat surface. With too little MAO in your system, your fingers might be shaking and your movements jerky (too much nervous transmission). With too much MAO, however, your fingers might be clumsy because of dulled sensation and lethargic movement control. When MAO levels are just right, neurotransmitter levels are regulated appropriately, and the nervous system works properly to control the muscles, thoughts, and emotions.

High sensation seekers tend to have low levels of MAO in their bloodstream, compared with low sensation seekers. Across studies, the correlation tends to be small to moderate but is consistently negative (Zuckerman, 1991b, 2005). If high sensation seekers tend to have low MAO levels, and low MAO means more neurotransmitter available in the nerve cells, then perhaps sensation seeking is caused by or is maintained by having high levels of neurotransmitters in the nervous system. A recent review of the research supports this neurotransmitter theory of sensation seeking (Norbury & Husain, 2015).

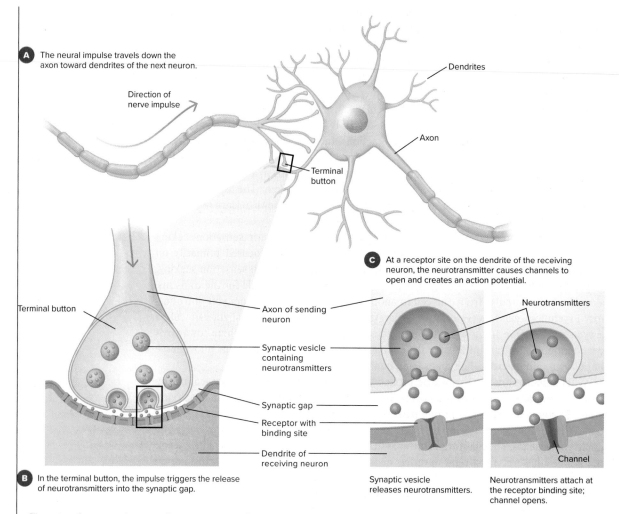

A The neural impulse travels down the axon toward dendrites of the next neuron.

Dendrites

Direction of nerve impulse

Axon

Terminal button

C At a receptor site on the dendrite of the receiving neuron, the neurotransmitter causes channels to open and creates an action potential.

Neurotransmitters

Terminal button

Axon of sending neuron

Synaptic vesicle containing neurotransmitters

Synaptic gap

Receptor with binding site

Dendrite of receiving neuron

Channel

B In the terminal button, the impulse triggers the release of neurotransmitters into the synaptic gap.

Synaptic vesicle releases neurotransmitters.

Neurotransmitters attach at the receptor binding site; channel opens.

Illustration of a synapse, the junction between two nerve cells. Synapses transmit electrical signals from one nerve cell to the next. When an electrical signal reaches a synapse, it triggers the release of chemicals called neurotransmitters (pink) from vesicles (purple). The vesicles burst through the membrane, and neurotransmitters cross a microscopic gap called the synaptic gap and bind to the receptor nerve cell, causing it to propagate an electrical impulse.

One study compared imprisoned violent offenders with a normal community sample, and found the violent offenders scored higher on sensation seeking AND had lower levels of MAO in their blood (Skondras et al., 2004). MAO acts like the brakes of the nervous system by decomposing neurotransmitters in the synapse and thereby inhibiting neurotransmission. With low MAO levels, high sensation seekers have less inhibition in their nervous systems and therefore less control over behavior, thoughts, and emotions. According to Zuckerman's (1991a) theory and research, sensation-seeking behaviors (e.g., illicit sex, drug use, wild parties) are not due so much to seeking an optimal level of arousal, but to having too little of the biochemical brakes in their synapses.

Neurotransmitters and Personality

Whereas Zuckerman's theory concerns levels of MAO, which breaks down neurotransmitters, other researchers hypothesize that levels of neurotransmitters themselves are directly responsible for specific individual differences (Depue, 2006; DeYoung, 2013). One neurotransmitter, **dopamine**, appears to be associated with pleasure and pleasure-seeking behaviors. For example, animals will work to obtain increases in their dopamine levels, much as they would work to obtain food or addictive drugs. As such, dopamine appears to function like a reward system and has even been called the feeling good chemical (Hamer, 1997). Drugs of abuse, such as cocaine, mimic dopamine in the nervous system, which accounts for the pleasure associated with taking them. However, such drugs deplete a person's natural levels of dopamine, leading to unpleasant feelings after the drug leaves the nervous system, creating a drive or urge to obtain more of the drug (i.e., addiction).

A second important neurotransmitter is **serotonin**. Researchers have documented the role of serotonin in depression and other mood disorders, such as anxiety. Specifically, drugs such as Prozac, Zoloft, and Paxil block the reuptake of serotonin, leaving it in the synapse longer, leading depressed persons to feel less depressed. In one study, Prozac was given to nondepressed subjects. Over several weeks of observation, they reported less negative affect and engaged in more outgoing and social behavior than did those in a control group (Knutson et al., 1998). In studies of monkeys, the monkeys that were higher in dominance and that engaged in more grooming had higher levels of serotonin. The monkeys low in serotonin were more fearful (Rogness & McClure, 1996).

A third important neurotransmitter, **norepinephrine**, is involved in activating the sympathetic nervous system for fight-or-flight. Not surprisingly, personality theories have been proposed based on the neurotransmitters dopamine, serotonin, and norepinephrine. Probably the most comprehensive is Cloninger's **tridimensional personality model** (Cloninger, 1986, 1987; Cloninger, Svrakic, & Przybeck, 1993), in which three personality traits are tied to levels of the three neurotransmitters. The first trait, **novelty seeking**, is based on low levels of dopamine. Recall that low levels of dopamine create a drive state to obtain substances or experiences that increase dopamine. Novelty, thrills, and excitement can make up for low levels of dopamine, so novelty-seeking behavior is thought to result from low levels of this neurotransmitter.

The second personality trait identified in Cloninger's model is **harm avoidance**, which he associates with abnormalities in serotonin metabolism. People low in harm avoidance are described as energetic, outgoing, and optimistic, whereas people high in harm avoidance are described as cautious, inhibited, shy, and apprehensive. Although various descriptions of the theory indicate increased or decreased serotonin levels are associated with increased harm avoidance, Cloninger himself (personal communication, October 2003) states that the correlation between harm avoidance and absolute levels of serotonin is not linear (one-to-one). Low levels of serotonin metabolite are associated with depression, but serotonin levels can also be elevated in states of anxiety or stress. The selective serotonin uptake inhibitors (like the antidepressants Prozac, Zoloft, or Paxil) result in increased levels of serotonin at synapses, which may increase anxiety initially but then lead to lowered stress responses, probably by decreasing sensitivity to serotonin when it is released in response to stress.

The third trait in Cloninger's model is **reward dependence**, which Cloninger sees as related to low levels of norepinephrine. People high on this trait are persistent; they continue to act in ways that produce reward. They work long hours, put a lot of effort into their work, and often continue striving after others have given up.

Genes Work Through Neurotransmitter Systems to Influence Personality
Although we discussed behavior genetics in more detail in Chapter 6, it is worth mentioning here that many researchers interested in personality and genetics are focusing on

the genes involved in regulating neurotransmitter systems. For example, if low levels of dopamine are related to novelty seeking, then perhaps the genes involved in dopamine transmission would be a good place to start in the search for the genetic basis of this personality trait. Keltikangas-Järvinen and her colleagues (2003) in Finland found that the type 4 dopamine receptor gene (DRD4) is associated with heightened levels of novelty seeking. An early meta-analysis of genetic studies of novelty seeking has suggested that very specific types of repeated genetic codes on the DRD4 gene (Schinka, Letsch, & Crawford, 2002) are reliably associated with novelty seeking. A later meta-analysis (Munafo et al., 2008) concluded that specific variants of DRD4 are reliably associated with novelty seeking and impulsivity, implying that genetic variations of DRD4 are involved in this personality trait. These findings imply that many genes are involved in the creation of any single personality trait. So, although looking for one gene as the basis of a personality trait is like looking for the proverbial needle in the haystack, the reality is that researchers are now looking for many different—and interacting—needles in the same big haystack. That is, they are looking for multiple genes that interact in complex ways to influence neurotransmitter systems. Personality traits, as well as other individual characteristics such as height and eye color, are likely to be massively polygenic (made up of tens or even hundreds of individual genetic variations). As new technology for analyzing gene sequences is developed, the search for the molecular genetic basis of various personality traits (and other characteristics) will likely become more tractable (Jarnecke & South, 2017). Nevertheless, any answers that are found in the future are likely to reveal complicated and multiple interacting genetic contributions, possibly requiring environmental triggers, for the expression of any biologically based personality trait.

It is probably clear that Cloninger's model has much in common with Gray's, Eysenck's, and Zuckerman's. For example, novelty seeking seems a lot like the reward sensitivity associated with the BAS of Gray's theory. All of these theories have different explanatory bases for the traits (Depue & Collins, 1999). For example, Gray suggests that brain systems involved in learning through reward and punishment are important in determining these traits. Eysenck also implicates the brain and nervous system. Zuckerman focuses on the synapse and the neurochemicals found there. And Cloninger specifies particular neurotransmitters. All are perhaps describing the same behavioral traits but focusing on different levels of explanation within the body, ranging from the synapse to the brain that influences reactivity to various kinds of stimuli.

Let's turn now to a consideration of two other personality dimensions that appear to have a biological base yet are not related to physiological reactivity—morningness–eveningness and brain asymmetry.

Morningness–Eveningness

Perhaps you are the kind of person who likes to sleep late and stay up late each day, saving your important schoolwork for late afternoon or evening, when you are feeling at your peak. Or maybe you are more of a morning person, regularly getting up early without the aid of an alarm clock. Moreover, perhaps you tend to do all your important work early in the day, when you are feeling at your best, and get to sleep fairly early in the evening. Being a morning type or an evening type of person appears to be a stable characteristic. Personality psychologists have become interested in such stable differences among persons in preferences for different times of the day and have coined the term **morningness–eveningness** to refer to this dimension (Horne & Ostberg, 1976).

Differences between morning and evening types of persons, sometimes called "larks" and "owls," appear to be due to differences in underlying biological rhythms.

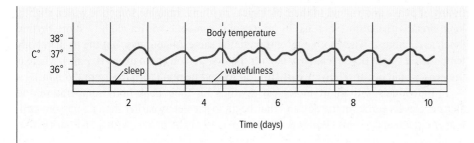

Figure 7.3

Circadian rhythm in body temperature.

Many biological processes have been found to fluctuate around an approximate 24- to 25-hour cycle. These have been called **circadian rhythms** (*circa* means "around," *dia* means "day," or "24 hours"). Of particular interest have been circadian rhythms in body temperature and endocrine secretion rates. For example, on average, body temperature shows a peak around mid-evening (between 8 and 9 p.m.) and a trough in the early morning (around 6 a.m.). Figure 7.3 presents a graph of body temperature by time of day.

Researchers use a temporal-isolation design to study such circadian rhythms. In this design, participants volunteer to live in an environment totally controlled by the experimenter with respect to time cues. There are no windows, so the participants do not know if it is day or night. There are no regularly scheduled meals, so the participants do not know if it is breakfast-, lunch-, or suppertime. Participants are given food whenever they ask for it. There is no access to live internet, TV, or radio. Instead, the participants have a large collection of streaming video or streaming audio for entertainment on demand. Volunteers live in this "time free" environment for several weeks or months. Often, the participants are students who want to use the time in isolation as an opportunity to study for an important exam or who need to write a PhD thesis.

Imagine being a participant in such a study. You would go to sleep whenever you wanted, sleep as long as you wanted, eat whenever you felt like it, work or watch movies as the inclination struck, and so on. This is called **free running** in time, in which there are no time cues to influence your behavior or biology. If you were in such a situation and your temperature were taken every hour, and if you were like the average person, you would find that your temperature followed an approximate 24- to 25-hour cycle, starting to rise before waking up and falling before going to sleep (Aschoff, 1965; Finger, 1982; Wever, 1979).

Note that 24- to 25-hour rhythms are the average; there are wide differences among persons in the actual length of their biological rhythms (Kerkhof, 1985). Circadian rhythms in temporal-isolation studies have been found to be as short as 16 hours in one person and as long as 50 hours in another person (Wehr & Goodwin, 1981). While free running in a temporal-isolation experiment, the first person would complete a sleep-wake cycle every 16 hours, whereas the second person's sleep-wake cycle would last 50 hours. Imagine sleeping for 18 hours straight, then staying awake for 32 hours straight, which is what the person with the 50-hour "day" settled into when there were no external time cues.

Such wide differences among persons are evident only in a temporal isolation situation. In real life, there are time cues all around us that fluctuate in a 24-hour rhythm—most notably, the light-dark cycle. These cues entrain us and make us fit into the 24-hour day. Even though people with short and long biological cycles entrain quite well to the 24-hour cycle, there nevertheless are differences among those people in terms of the timing of peaks and valleys in their biological rhythms. Imagine someone with a slightly long circadian rhythm (such as 26 hours) and someone with a slightly short rhythm (such as 22 hours). They both may entrain to the same 24-hour day, but the peak in body temperature might occur relatively late for the first person (perhaps at 10 p.m.), whereas the peak would occur relatively early for the second person (perhaps around 6 p.m.).

Individuals with short biological rhythms hit their peak body temperature and alertness levels earlier in the day and thus begin to get sleepy earlier than do persons with longer circadian rhythms (Bailey & Heitkemper, 1991). A person with a 26-hour rhythm would have a harder time getting up at 6 in the morning, because his or her 26-hour biological rhythm still has 2 hours to go, even though the 24-hour clock is telling him or her to start a new day. A person with a 22-hour rhythm would have an easier time getting up early because he or she has completed a biological "day" in 22 hours and is ready to start another day even *before* the 24-hour clock is up.

Exercise

Do you know someone who you think is a morning type of person? What specific evidence makes you come to this conclusion? Do you think people with a morning type of rhythm are different in other ways from evening-type people? For example, are there other personality characteristics associated with being a morning type? Benjamin Franklin is quoted as saying that "early to bed, early to rise, makes a person healthy, wealthy, and wise." Do you think it is possible that morning types are actually wiser, or have better grades in college, or that they have better outcomes in life? Do morning people have better financial outcomes than evening people? How would you design a study to test if Benjamin Franklin was correct?

Research on individual differences in circadian rhythms provides the groundwork for understanding why some people are morning types and others are evening types. As you know, those with *shorter* biological rhythms tend to be morning persons, and those with *longer* biological rhythms tend to be evening persons. Horne and Ostberg (1976, 1977) developed a 19-item questionnaire to measure morningness–eveningness (see Table 7.4). The items ask about preferences for activities earlier or later in the day. In a sample of 48 participants, who took their body temperature every hour for several days, the researchers found that the scores on this questionnaire correlated –.51 with time of day that peak body temperature was reached. While the original study was done in Sweden, the negative correlation between self-reported preferences for activities in the morning and timing of peak body temperature has been replicated in the United States (Monk et al., 1983), Italy (Mecacci, Scaglione, & Vitrano, 1991), Spain (Adan, 1991, 1992), Croatia (Vidacek et al., 1988), and Japan (Ishihara, Saitoh, & Miyata, 1983).

These cross-cultural replications are consistent with the idea that preferences for morning or evening activities, and the time of day people are at their best, is a stable disposition with a biological basis. Scores on the Horne and Ostberg measure of morningness–eveningness are stable over time. Croatian researchers tested 90 college students on this measure and then tested them again seven years later, when they had finished college (Sverko & Fabulic, 1985). They found a significant positive correlation, suggesting that the morningness–eveningness characteristic is fairly stable over time. There

Table 7.4   Items from the Morningness–Eveningness Questionnaire

Instructions

Please read each question carefully before answering. Each question should be answered independently of others. Do *not* go back and change or check your answers.

All questions have a selection of answers. For each question, circle the number in front of only one answer. Please answer each question as honestly as possible.

1. Considering only your "feeling best" rhythm, at what time would you get up if you were entirely free to plan your day?
   1. between 11:00 a.m. and noon
   2. between 9:30 a.m. and 11 a.m.
   3. between 7:30 a.m. and 9:30 a.m.
   4. between 6:00 a.m. and 7:30 a.m.
   5. before 6:00 a.m.

2. Considering only your "feeling best" rhythm, at what time would you go to bed if you were entirely free to plan your evening?
   1. after at least 1:30 in the morning
   2. between midnight and 1:30 a.m.
   3. between 10:30 p.m. and midnight
   4. between 9:00 p.m. and 10:30 p.m.
   5. before 9:00 p.m.

3. On the average, how easy do you find getting up in the morning?
   1. not at all easy
   2. not very easy
   3. fairly easy
   4. very easy

4. How alert do you feel during the first half-hour after having awakened in the morning?
   1. not at all alert
   2. not very alert
   3. fairly alert
   4. very alert

5. How is your appetite during the first half-hour after having awakened in the morning?
   1. very poor
   2. fairly poor
   3. fairly good
   4. very good

Source: Adapted from Horne and Ostberg (1976).

was, however, a general shift in the whole sample toward morningness, which might be expected in a group that moves from being college students to persons having jobs. The positive correlation indicates that people maintain their rank order, even as people shift toward morningness with increasing age.

Many studies have been done on the validity of the morningness–eveningness construct. In one study (Larsen, 1985), college students completed a report every day for 84 consecutive days, stating what time they felt at their best each day and what time they got up and went to bed each day. The Horne and Ostberg questionnaire correlated strongly with average rise and retire times, as well as with the time of day the participants reported feeling at their best. The morning persons got up earlier, went to bed earlier, and reportedly felt at their best earlier, on average over the three months, than the evening persons.

Based on research described in the text, many universities take morningness or eveningness preferences into account when matching students up as roommates.

aphrodite74/Getty Images

What would happen if people who had to live together, such as college roommates, were mismatched on morningness–eveningness? One person likes to stay up late and sleep late, whereas the other likes to get up early, even on weekends, as well as go to bed early. How happy do you think these people would be with their rooming situation? This was the topic of a study by Watts (1982), who selected first-year college students living on the campus of Michigan State University. The participants had to have only one roommate. The roommate pairs completed the Morningness–Eveningness Questionnaire (MEQ), and they rated various aspects of their roommate relationship. Watts found that, the greater the difference between the roommates' MEQ scores, the lower ratings they gave to the quality of their relationship. Roommates who were very different on morningness–eveningness said that they did not get along very well with each other, that they did not enjoy their relationship and were not good friends, and that they were unlikely to continue living together. It appears that differences in morningness–eveningness, or **chronotype** incompatibility, create stress for people having to live together. Many colleges and universities now have students consider their level of morningness or eveningness, and communicate about their time preferences, when going through the roommate selection process.

It is not surprising that chronotype compatibility is also found in intimate relationships. Randler and Kretz (2011) studied 84 couples and found a correlation between the couples' scores on a M–E questionnaire, implying that couples pair up on chronotype. This correlation did not change as a function of length of the relationship, implying that selective mating on M–E occurs at the start of the relationship. The authors speculate that, because morning-types and evening-types inhabit different temporal environments, they are likely to meet and mate with others who have similar time-of-day preferences. For example, morning types have been found to start social contact earlier in the day than evening types (Randler & Jankowski, 2014). Who are they likely to find available at that early time of day? Other morning-types, most likely.

Being a morning type or evening type refers to preferences for time of day that may have a biological basis; however, sometimes situations occur that go against such preferences. Imagine a college student who is definitely an evening type, yet a class he or she needs to take is offered only at 8 a.m., or a morning type of person who takes a job in a factory and is assigned to the late shift (4 p.m. to midnight). Going against one's natural circadian preferences is stressful, but not impossible. People can adjust to shift work and changes in sleep-wake schedule, though it is taxing and takes effort (Ishihara et al., 1992). Such disruptions as transmeridian airline flights (which create jet lag) or working all night without sleeping (i.e., pulling an all-nighter) will be experienced as more stressful to some people than others, depending on underlying circadian rhythm length and whether the disruption involves a shortening or lengthening of the day. Several studies have used heart rate variability (HRV) as a measure of biological stress, and found that going against one's chronotype (e.g., an evening type required to get up early for some important task) is associated with greater stress and strain on the HRV measures (i.e., lowered HRV; reviewed by Honkalampi et al., 2021).

In summary, the preference for being active and doing important or demanding work earlier or later in the day may be rooted in the length of a person's inherent biological circadian rhythm length. This is a good example of a physiological approach to personality because it highlights the notion of a consistent behavior pattern (i.e., preference for different times of the day) being based on an underlying physiological mechanism (i.e., circadian rhythms).

Brain Asymmetry and Affective Style

As you are probably aware, the left and right sides of the brain are specialized, with asymmetry in the control of various psychological functions. One type of asymmetry that has received research attention is the relative amount of electrical activity in the front part of the left and right brain hemispheres. As mentioned earlier in this chapter, the recording of such electrical activity is called an **electroencephalograph**, or **EEG**. Moreover, such electrical activity is rhythmic and exhibits waves that are fast or slow, depending on neurological activation in the brain. One particular type of brain wave, called an **alpha wave**, oscillates at 8 to 12 times a second. The amount of alpha wave present in a given time period is an inverse indicator of brain activity during that time period. In other words, alpha waves are given off when a person is calm and relaxed, perhaps feeling a bit sleepy and not attentive to the environment. In a given time period of brain wave recording, the *less* alpha wave activity present, the *more* we can assume that part of the brain was active.

In this research, psychologists focus on the frontal part of the brain, comparing the amount of activation in the right and left frontal hemispheres. Study results suggest that the left hemisphere is relatively more active than the right when a person is experiencing pleasant emotions and vice versa, that the right frontal hemisphere is more active when the person is experiencing unpleasant emotions. For example, in an early study by Davidson and colleagues (1990), they showed film clips to the participants in an attempt to amuse some of the participants and disgust the others. The participants were also videotaped while they watched the funny or disgusting films. EEGs were taken while the participants looked at the films. When the participants were smiling at the amusing films, they had relatively more activation in their left than right frontal hemispheres. Similarly, when the participants were exhibiting a facial expression of disgust (lower lip pulled down, tongue protruding, nose wrinkled) while watching the disgusting film, their brains were more active in the right than left hemispheres.

Similar results have also been obtained in very young children. Instead of using pleasant and unpleasant films, Fox and Davidson (1986) used sweet and bitter solutions placed in the mouths of 10-month-old infants to produce pleasant and unpleasant affective reactions. The infants showed relatively more left- than right-brain activation to the sweet solution and more right- than left-brain activation to the bitter solution. In another study, the infants' mothers left them alone in the testing room, whereupon a stranger entered the room (Fox & Davidson, 1987). In this standard anxiety-producing procedure, some infants become distressed but some do not; some infants cry and fuss but others do not. The researchers divided their sample of infants into those who cried during separation from their mothers and those who did not cry. They found that the criers exhibited more right-brain activation, relative with the left, compared with the noncriers. These results suggest that this tendency to become distressed or not (and the associated brain EEG asymmetry) is a stable characteristic of infants. Fox and colleagues (1992) studied a group of infants at age 7 months and again at age 12 months and found that the EEG measures of hemisphere asymmetry taken at those two time periods were highly correlated, suggesting stability over time in frontal brain asymmetry. Similar results have been found with adults, showing that measures of EEG asymmetry show test-retest correlations in the range of .66 to .73 across studies (Davidson, 1993, 2003). These findings suggest that individual differences in **frontal brain asymmetry** exhibit enough stability and consistency to be considered as indicative of an underlying biological disposition or trait.

Other studies suggest that EEG asymmetry indicates a predisposition to experience pleasant or unpleasant emotional states. Tomarken, Davidson, and Henriques (1990) and Wheeler, Davidson, and Tomarken (1993) examined the relation between individual differences in frontal asymmetry and reactions to affective film clips in normal participants. In these studies, EEG asymmetry was measured while the participants were resting. Then the participants were shown either happy and amusing films or disgusting and fearful films. For the dependent variable, the participants were asked to rate how the films made them feel. The hypothesis was that the participants with greater right-side activation at rest (measured before watching the films) would report more intense *negative* affective reactions to the fear and disgust films, compared with the participants with relatively more left-side activation. The opposite prediction was made for the participants with greater left-side activation—they should report stronger *positive* emotions in response to the happy and amusing films. The predictions were essentially supported, with frontal asymmetry measures taken *before* the films were seen predicting the participants' *subsequent* self-reported affective reactions to the films, with the right-side-dominant participants reporting more distress to the unpleasant films and the left-side-dominant participants reporting more pleasant reactions to the films.

Similar results have also been found with monkeys. Because monkeys cannot answer questions about how positive or negative they are feeling, researchers have used measures of **cortisol** to assess negative emotions. As mentioned earlier in this chapter, cortisol is a stress hormone that prepares the body to fight or flee, and increases in cortisol mean that the animal has recently experienced stress. Davidson and his colleagues (reviewed in Kosslyn et al., 2002) have found that monkeys with greater right-sided activation had higher levels of cortisol. Identical results have been found with 6-month-old children. These researchers induced fear in the infants by having a male stranger enter the room, slowly approach the infant, and stare at the infant for two minutes. Those infants who had greater right-sided activation at baseline showed increased cortisol responses to the stranger. Also, those infants who showed the most right-sided activation during the stranger approach phase also displayed more crying and facial expressions of fear, and tried to escape more, compared to infants with less right-sided activation (Buss et al., 2003).

More than 100 studies of frontal EEG asymmetry have been published to date, most of them treating asymmetry as an individual difference variable related to differences in emotional responding to positive or negative situations or stimuli (e.g., Ma et al., 2021). One useful way to think about frontal asymmetry is as a moderator of the relation between an emotional stimulus and emotional response (Coan & Allen, 2004). A positive stimulus should produce a positive emotional response for most people, but this effect will be especially strong (i.e., produce a higher correlation) for people with a left frontal asymmetry. For example, Wheeler, Davidson, and Tomarken (1993) showed that the correlation between watching happy and amusing video and self-reported positive emotions was much stronger among people with left frontal asymmetry (compared to right frontal asymmetry). Similarly, a negative stimulus should produce a negative emotional response for most people, but this effect will be especially strong for persons with right frontal asymmetry. An example of this is that going away to college for the

Application

Assessing Brain Asymmetry Without an EEG

An EEG is not the only way to obtain an index of asymmetry in brain activation. Research suggests that a person's characteristic level of left- or right-sided activation may be indicated by the direction in which their eyes drift as they concentrate on answering difficult questions. When answering a difficult question (e.g., "Make up a sentence using the words *rhapsody* and *pleasure*"), people's eyes drift one way or the other as they reflect on their answer (Davidson, 1991). Among right-handed persons, eyes drifting to the right signify left-sided activation, and eyes drifting to the left signify right-sided activation. If you ask a person several difficult questions (e.g., "How many turns do you make from your house or apartment to the nearest store?") and note which way his or her eyes usually drift, you may get an indication of whether he or she tends to be right- or left-sided asymmetric. Of course, this quick measure is not as reliable as an EEG. It nevertheless may be a rough gauge of whether a person is left- or right-side asymmetric.

Perhaps you could make some observations of a few friends or acquaintances, asking them several difficult questions and observing which way they move their eyes as they think through their answers. Most people will not show completely consistent patterns of going one way or the other. That is why it is important to ask several questions and see which way they *usually* move their eyes. You will also need to decide whether they are more vulnerable to positive or negative emotions (see Figure 7.4). Persons who glance frequently to the right are more likely to be left-hemisphere dominant and should be more vulnerable to the pleasant emotions (e.g., happiness, joy, enthusiasm). Persons who frequently glance to the left while engaging in reflective thought are more likely to be right-hemisphere dominant and, by implication, should be more vulnerable to the negative emotions (e.g., distress, anxiety, sadness).

Figure 7.4

These gaze patterns illustrate left and right gaze direction, associated with opposite brain hemisphere activation, for use in completing the exercise described in this application.

Mark Dierker

first time often causes the negative emotion of homesickness, and homesickness has been found to be stronger in college freshmen who have more right (compared to left) frontal asymmetry (Steiner & Coan, 2011). The point of this information is that frontal asymmetry, a measure of underlying brain physiology, acts much like a traditional personality trait when it comes to explaining differences in how people respond emotionally to pleasant and unpleasant events in their lives.

The importance of brain asymmetry research is that different portions of the brain may respond with pleasant or unpleasant emotions, given the appropriate affective stimulus. Fox and Calkins (1993) discuss this notion in terms of thresholds for responding. The concept of thresholds implies that persons with a left- or right-sided pattern require less of the affective stimulus to evoke the corresponding emotion. The person who displays a right-frontal-activation pattern may have a lower threshold for responding with negative emotions when an unpleasant event happens. It may take less of a negative event to evoke unpleasant feelings for right-dominant persons. For an individual who displays a left-frontal-activation pattern, the threshold for experiencing pleasant emotions in response to positive events is lowered. A person's affective lifestyle may have its origins in, or at least may be predicted by, his or her pattern of asymmetry in frontal brain activation.

SUMMARY AND EVALUATION

The study of personality can be approached biologically. Theorizing about the biological influences on personality has a long history, and there are two ways to think about how physiological variables can be useful in personality theory and research. One way to view physiological measures is as variables that may be correlated with personality traits. For example, in a sample of college students, there may be a positive correlation between spontaneous skin conductance responses and scores on a neuroticism questionnaire (perhaps due to the heightened level of chronic anxiety associated with neuroticism). Here a physiological variable is seen as a correlate of a personality dimension, as something that is associated with being high on neuroticism. Does elevated skin conductance cause a person to become neurotic? Probably not. Instead, a chronic activation of the fight-or-flight nervous system goes along with, or is a correlate of, being neurotic.

A second way to think about physiological approaches to personality is to view physiological events as contributing to, or providing the physiological substrate for, the personality characteristic. This chapter covered six such examples of theories about the biological underpinnings of specific personality dimensions: extraversion (and nervous system reactivity or arousability), sensitivity to cues of reward and punishment (based on brain circuits of the BIS and BAS systems), sensation seeking (and level of MAO and hormones in the bloodstream), tridimensional personality theory (based on neurotransmitters), morningness–eveningness (and circadian rhythms in body temperature), and affective style (and hemispheric asymmetry in the frontal cortex of the brain). In these theories, the physiological variables are assumed to be more than just correlates of the personality traits; they are assumed to be the biological underpinnings of the those personality traits (see Table 7.5).

Table 7.5 Biological Theories of Specific Personality Traits

RELATED TO PHYSIOLOGICAL REACTIVITY

Personality Trait	Biological Underpinnings
Extraversion–introversion	Arousal level of brain (early theory)
	Arousability of nervous system
Sensitivity to reward and punishment	Behavioral activation system (BAS) responds to incentives and reward
	Behavioral inhibition system (BIS) responds to threat and punishment
Sensation seeking	Optimal arousal level (early theory)
	Monoamine oxidase (MAO) levels
Tridimensional personality model	
Novelty seeking	Dopamine
Harm avoidance	Serotonin
Reward dependence	Norepinephrine

NOT RELATED TO PHYSIOLOGICAL REACTIVITY

Personality Trait	Biological Underpinnings
1. Morningness–eveningness	Length of circadian rhythm
	Shorter = morning type
	Longer = evening type
2. Affective style	Asymmetry in frontal brain activation
	Left = tendency toward positive
	Right = tendency toward negative

KEY TERMS

physiological systems 186
theoretical bridge 191
electrodes 191
telemetry 191
sympathetic nervous system 191
autonomic nervous system 191
electrodermal activity 191
heart rate variability (HRV) 193
cardiac reactivity 193
Type A personality 193
neuroscience 193
electroencephalograph (EEG) 199
ascending reticular activating system (ARAS) 201

arousal level 201
arousability 203
reinforcement sensitivity theory 204
behavioral activation system (BAS) 204
behavioral inhibition system (BIS) 204
anxiety 204
impulsivity 204
sensation seeking 207
sensory deprivation 207
optimal level of arousal 207
neurotransmitters 209
monoamine oxidase (MAO) 209
dopamine 211

serotonin 211
norepinephrine 211
tridimensional personality model 211
novelty seeking 211
harm avoidance 211
reward dependence 211
morningness-eveningness 212
circadian rhythms 213
free running 213
chronotype 216
alpha wave 217
frontal brain asymmetry 218
cortisol 218

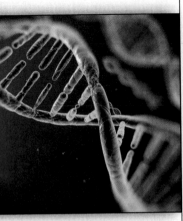

Svisio/Getty Images

Evolutionary Perspectives on Personality

8

THE BIOLOGICAL DOMAIN

I

magine living as our ancestors did a million years ago. You awaken at dawn and shrug off the coldness of night. A few warm embers glow in the fire, so you stoke it with kindling. The others in your group gather around the fire as the sun breaks the horizon. Stomachs start growling. Your thoughts turn to food. Small groups set off in search of berries, nuts, and small game animals.

After a long day of hunting and gathering, the members converge back at their temporary home site. As night begins to fall, the group gathers around the fire. The day's foraging has been successful and the mood is warm and animated. Tales of the hunt are reenacted, the bounty of gathered goods admired. With bellies full, discussion turns to whether the group should move the next day or stay a bit longer. A successful hunter makes eye contact with his young lover, but she shyly looks away. Others notice this flirtation. Mating universally draws interest. As people grow sleepy and children are put to sleep, the young lovers quietly slip away from the group to be alone. Their warm embrace echoes millions of past events as people partake of life's cycle.

Evolutionary psychology is a rapidly growing scientific perspective, and it offers important insights into human personality. In this chapter, we look at some of these insights in three areas: human nature, sex differences, and individual differences. We will see how theories of evolutionary psychology fit with the discoveries of personality psychologists and generate new lines of research. We begin by reviewing some basic information about the theory of evolution.

How much of human nature today is the result of behavior patterns that evolved as our ancestors solved the problems of surviving and reproducing? Prisma/UIG/Getty Images

Evolution and Natural Selection

All of us come from a long and unbroken line of ancestors who accomplished two critical tasks: They survived to reproductive age, and they reproduced. If any one of your ancestors had failed at reproduction, you would not be here today to contemplate their existence. In this sense, every living human is an evolutionary success story. As descendants of successful ancestors, we carry with us the genes for the adaptations that led to their success. From this perspective, our human nature—the collection of adaptations that defines us as human—is the product of the evolutionary process.

Long before Charles Darwin, it was known that change takes place over time in organic structures. The fossil record showed the bones of long extinct dinosaurs, suggesting that not all species in the past are with us today. The paleontological record showed changes in animals' body forms, suggesting that nothing remains static. Moreover, the structures of species seemed extraordinarily well adapted to their environments. The long necks of giraffes enabled them to eat leaves from tall trees. The turtle's shell seemed designed for protection. The beaks of birds seemed well-suited for cracking local nuts to get at their nutritious seeds. What could account for change over time and apparent adaptation to environmental conditions?

Natural Selection

Darwin's contribution was not in observing change over time, nor in noticing the adaptive design of mechanisms. Rather, Darwin proposed a theory of the *process* by which adaptations are created and change takes place over time. He called it the theory of **natural selection.**

Darwin noticed that species seemed to produce many more offspring than could possibly survive and reproduce. He reasoned that changes, or *variants,* that better enabled an organism to survive and reproduce would lead to more descendants. The descendants would inherit the variants that led to their ancestors' survival and reproduction. Through this process, the successful variants were selected and unsuccessful variants weeded out. Natural selection, therefore, results in gradual changes in a species over time, as successful variants increase in frequency and eventually spread throughout the gene pool, replacing the less successful variants. Over time, these successful variants come to characterize the entire species; unsuccessful variants decrease in frequency and vanish from the species.

This process of natural selection, sometimes called *survival selection,* led Darwin to focus on the events that impede survival, which he called the **hostile forces of nature.** These hostile forces included food shortages, diseases, parasites, predators, and extremes of weather. Variants that helped organisms successfully combat these hostile forces of nature led to an increased likelihood of surviving to reproductive age. Food preferences for substances rich in fat, sugar, and protein, for example, helped organisms survive food shortages. An immune system teeming with antibodies helped organisms survive diseases and parasites. The behavioral immune system, including the emotion of disgust, helped to avoid contact with disease-carrying organisms, including other humans (Schaller, 2016). Fear of snakes and spiders helped them to avoid poisonous bites. These mechanisms, resulting from a long and repeated process of natural selection, are called adaptations, inherited solutions to the survival and reproductive problems posed by the hostile forces of nature.

Even after Darwin came up with his theory of natural selection, there remained many mysteries that puzzled him. He noticed that many mechanisms seemed contrary to survival. The elaborate plumage, large antlers, and other conspicuous features displayed by the males of many species seemed costly in terms of survival. He wondered how the brilliant plumage of peacocks could evolve when it posed such an obvious threat to survival, acting as a neon sign to predators advertising fast food. In response to puzzles of this sort, Darwin proposed a second evolutionary theory—the theory of sexual selection.

Sexual Selection

Darwin's answer to the mysteries of the peacock's tail and the stag's antlers was that they evolved because they contributed to an individual's mating success, providing an advantage in the competition for desirable mates. The evolution of characteristics because of their mating benefits, rather than because of their survival benefits, is known as **sexual selection.**

Sexual selection, according to Darwin, takes two forms. In one form, members of the same sex compete with each other, and the outcome of their contest gives the winner greater sexual access to members of the opposite sex. Two stags locking horns in combat is the prototypical image of this **intrasexual competition.** The characteristics that lead to success in contests of this kind, such as greater strength, intelligence, or attractiveness to allies, evolve because the victors are able to mate more often and, hence, pass on their genes.

In the other type of sexual selection—**intersexual selection**—members of one sex choose a mate based on their preferences for particular qualities. These characteristics evolve because those that possess them are chosen more often as mates, and their genes thrive. Animals lacking the desired characteristics fail to mate, and their genes perish.

Success at same-sex competition leads to success at mating; traits that help to win these battles are passed on in greater numbers and hence evolve in the population.

Source: NPS photo by Jeff Foot

Genes and Inclusive Fitness

Genes are packets of DNA that are inherited by children from their parents in distinct chunks. Genes are the smallest discrete units that are inherited by offspring intact, without being broken up. According to modern evolutionary biologists, evolution operates by the process of **differential gene reproduction,** defined by reproductive success relative to others. The genes of organisms that reproduce more than others get passed down to future generations at a greater frequency than do the genes of those that reproduce less. Survival is usually critical for reproductive success, so characteristics that lead to greater survival get passed along. Success in mating is also critical for reproductive success, and the qualities that lead to success in same-sex competition or to success at being chosen as a mate get passed along. Successful survival and successful mate competition, therefore, are both paths to differential gene reproduction. The characteristics that lead to the greater reproduction of genes that code for them are selected and, hence, evolve over time.

Traits for helping can evolve through inclusive fitness.

UpperCut Images/Getty Images

The modern evolutionary theory based on differential gene reproduction is called **inclusive fitness theory** (Hamilton, 1964). The "inclusive" part refers to the fact that the characteristics that facilitate reproduction need not affect the personal production of offspring. They can affect the survival and reproduction of genetic relatives as well. For example, if you take a personal risk to defend or protect your sister or another close relative, then this might enable them to better survive and reproduce. Because you share genes with your kin—50 percent on average in the case of siblings—then helping kin survive and reproduce will also lead to successful gene reproduction.

A critical condition for such helping to evolve is that the cost to your own reproduction as a result of the helping must be less than the benefits to the reproduction of your genes that reside in your relative. If helping your sister survive—for example, by jumping into rushing rapids to save her from drowning—puts your own life at risk, the odds of saving her must exceed twice the odds of your dying in order for evolution to select for mechanisms underlying this helping behavior. Thus, inclusive fitness can be defined as one's personal reproductive success (roughly, the number of children you produce) *plus* the effects you have on the reproduction of your genetic relatives, weighted by the degree of genetic relatedness. Inclusive fitness can lead to adaptations that incline you to take some risk for the welfare of your genetic relatives, but not too great a risk. Inclusive fitness theory, as an expansion and elaboration of Darwin's theory, represented a major advance in understanding human traits, such as some forms of altruism.

Products of the Evolutionary Process

All living humans are products of the evolutionary process, the descendants of a long line of ancestors who succeeded in surviving, reproducing, and helping their genetic relatives. The evolutionary process acts as a series of filters. In each generation, only a small subset of genes passes through the filter. The recurrent filtering process lets only three things pass through: adaptations; byproducts of adaptations; and noise, or random variations.

Adaptations

Adaptations are the primary product of the selective process. An adaptation can be defined as a "reliably developing structure in the organism, which, because it meshes with the recurrent structure of the world, causes the solution to an adaptive problem" (Tooby & Cosmides, 1992, p. 104). Known human adaptations include a taste for sweet and fatty foods, the drive to defend close relatives, and preferences for specific mates, such as those who are healthy.

Let's examine the components of the definition of adaptation. The focus on reliably developing structure means that an adaptation tends to emerge with regularity during the course of a person's life. The mechanisms that allow humans to see, for example, develop reliably. But this does not mean that vision develops invariantly. The development of the eye can be perturbed by genetic anomalies or by environmental trauma. The emphasis on reliable development suggests that evolutionary approaches are *not* forms of "genetic determinism." Environments are always needed for the development of an adaptation, and environmental events can always interfere with or enhance such development.

The emphasis on meshing with recurrent structures of the world means that adaptations emerge from, and are structured by, the selective environment. Features of the environment must be recurrent over time for an adaptation to evolve. The venomous snakes must be recurrently dangerous, ripe fruit must be recurrently nutritious, and enclosed caves must be recurrently protective before adaptations to them can emerge.

Finally, an adaptation must facilitate the solution to an adaptive problem. An **adaptive problem** is anything that impedes survival or reproduction, or anything whose solution increases the odds of survival or reproduction. Stated differently, all adaptations must contribute to fitness during the period of time in which they evolve by helping an organism survive, reproduce, or facilitate the reproductive success of genetic relatives.

The hallmark of adaptation is *special design*. That is, the features of an adaptation are recognized as components of specialized problem-solving machinery. Factors such as *efficiency* in solving a specific adaptive problem, *precision* in solving the adaptive problem, and *reliability* in solving the adaptive problem are key criteria in recognizing the special design of an adaptation. Adaptations are like keys that fit only specific locks. The tines of the key (adaptation) show special design features, which mesh with the specific mirror-image elements within the lock (adaptive problem).

All adaptations are products of a history of selection. In this sense, we live with an ancient brain in a modern world, which is in some ways different from the world in which we evolved. For example, ancestral humans evolved in relatively small groups of 50 to 150, using both hunting and gathering as methods of acquiring food

For most of our evolutionary past, humans lived in small, close-knit groups, usually of perhaps 150 people. This form of group living is relatively rare today.

ranplett/Vetta/Getty Images

(Dunbar, 1993). In the modern world, by contrast, many people live in large cities surrounded by thousands or millions of people. Characteristics that were probably adaptive in ancestral environments—such as **xenophobia,** or fear of strangers—are not necessarily adaptive in modern environments. This is an example of an *evolutionary mismatch*—a feature adaptive in the past that is no longer adaptive in the modern world (Li, van Vugt, & Colarelli, 2018). Some of the personality traits that make up human nature may be vestigial adaptations to an ancestral environment that no longer exists.

Byproducts of Adaptations

The evolutionary process also produces things that are not adaptations—such as **byproducts of adaptations**. Consider the design of a lightbulb. A lightbulb is designed to produce light—that is its function. But it also may produce heat, not because it is designed to produce heat, but rather because heat is an incidental byproduct, which occurs as a consequence of design for light. In the same way, human adaptations can also have **evolutionary byproducts,** or incidental effects that are not properly considered to be adaptations. The human nose, for example, is clearly an adaptation designed for smelling. But the fact that we use our noses to hold up our eyeglasses is an incidental byproduct. The nose was designed for smelling odors, not for holding up glasses. Notice that the hypothesis that something is a byproduct (e.g., by holding up eyeglasses) requires specifying the adaptation (e.g., the nose) of which it is a byproduct. Thus, both sorts of evolutionary hypotheses—adaptation and byproduct hypotheses—require a description of the nature of the adaptation.

Noise, or Random Variations

The third product of the evolutionary process is **evolutionary noise,** or random variations that are neutral with respect to selection. In the design of a lightbulb, for example, there are minor variations in the surface texture of the bulb that do not affect the functioning of the design elements. Neutral variations introduced into the gene pool through mutation, for example, are perpetuated over generations if they do not hinder the functioning of adaptations.

In sum, there are three products of the evolutionary process: adaptations, byproducts, and noise. Adaptations are the primary product of the selective process, so evolutionary psychology is primarily focused on identifying and describing human psychological adaptations. The hypothesis that something is a byproduct requires specifying the adaptation of which it is a byproduct. The analysis of byproducts, therefore, leads us back to the need to describe adaptations. And noise is the residue of nonfunctional variation that is selectively neutral.

Evolutionary Psychology

The basic elements of the evolutionary perspective apply to all forms of life, from insects to people. We turn now to the application of this perspective to human psychology. This branch of psychology is referred to as evolutionary psychology.

Premises of Evolutionary Psychology

Evolutionary psychology involves three key premises: domain specificity, numerousness, and functionality.

Domain Specificity

Most adaptations are hypothesized to be **domain specific** because they are designed by the evolutionary process to solve a particular adaptive problem. Consider the problem of food selection—choosing the right foods to eat from among a large array of possible objects in the world. A general decision rule, such as "eat the first thing you encounter," would be highly maladaptive because it would fail to guide you to choose the small subset of objects that are edible and nutritious. Such a general rule would result in the consumption of poisonous plants, twigs, dirt, or feces, which would interfere with successful survival. The mechanisms favored by the evolutionary process are more specialized. In food selection, functional specificity is seen in our preferences for calorically rich fat and in our evolved sweet tooth, which leads us to foods rich in sugar, such as ripe fruit. General mechanisms cannot guide us to the small islands of successful adaptive solutions that are surrounded by oceans of maladaptive solutions.

Another reason for domain specificity is that different adaptive problems require different sorts of solutions. Our taste preferences, which guide us to successful food choices, do not help us solve the adaptive challenge of choosing high-quality mates. If we were to use our food preferences as a general guide to the choice of mates, we would select strange mates indeed. Successful mate choices require different specialized adaptations. Domain specificity implies that selection tends to fashion at least somewhat specialized mechanisms for each adaptive problem.

Numerousness

Our ancestors faced many sorts of adaptive problems in the course of human evolution, so we have numerous adaptive mechanisms. If you look at a textbook on the body, for example, you will discover a large number of physiological and anatomical mechanisms. We have a heart to pump our blood, a liver to detoxify poisons, a larynx to prevent us from choking, and sweat glands to keep the body thermally regulated.

Evolutionary psychologists suggest that the human mind, our evolved psychology, also contains a large number of mechanisms—psychological adaptations. Consider the most common fears and phobias. We tend to be scared of snakes, heights, darkness, spiders, cliff edges, and strangers. We have a large number of psychological mechanisms because the number of hazardous hostile forces of nature has been so large. We also have psychological adaptations for the selection of mates, the detection of cheaters in social exchanges, the favoring of habitats offering resources and protection, the rearing of children, and the formation of strategic alliances. Evolutionary psychologists expect there to be a large number of psychological adaptations to correspond to the large number of distinct adaptive problems humans have recurrently confronted.

Functionality

The third key premise of evolutionary psychology is **functionality,** the notion that our psychological mechanisms are designed to accomplish particular adaptive tasks. If you were a medical researcher studying the liver, you could not get very far in your understanding unless you understood the functions of the liver (e.g., breaking down toxins). Evolutionary psychologists suggest that understanding adaptive function offers insight into our evolved *psychological* mechanisms. We can't understand our preferences for certain mates, for example, without inquiring about the function of such preferences (e.g., to select a healthy or fertile mate). The search for function involves identifying the specific adaptive problem for which the mechanism is an evolved solution.

Empirical Testing of Evolutionary Hypotheses

To understand how evolutionary psychologists test hypotheses, it is necessary to consider the hierarchy of levels of evolutionary analysis depicted in Figure 8.1. At the top of the hierarchy is evolution by selection. The theory has been tested directly in many cases. New species can be formed in the laboratory by its application, and dogs can be selectively bred using its principles. Because there has never been a single case in which the general theory proved to be incorrect, most scientists take the general theory for granted and proceed with more specific forms of hypothesis testing.

At the next level down are middle-level evolutionary theories, such as the theory of parental investment and sexual selection. According to this theory, the sex (male or female) that invests more in offspring is predicted to be more discriminating or "choosy" about its mating partners. And the sex that invests less in offspring is predicted to be more competitive with members of its own sex for sexual access to the high-investing sex. From these hypotheses, specific predictions can be derived and tested empirically. In the human case, women bear the heavy parental investment

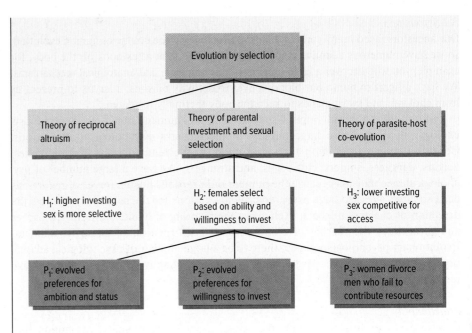

Figure 8.1

The evolutionary analysis hierarchy depicts the conceptual levels of evolutionary analysis. At the top of the hierarchy is natural selection theory. At the next level down are middle-level evolutionary theories from which specific hypotheses and predictions can be derived. Each level of the hierarchy is evaluated by the cumulative weight of the empirical evidence from tests of the predictions derived from it.

Source: Adapted from Buss, 1995a.

burdens of internal fertilization and nine-month pregnancy. Women are the high-investing sex; thus, according to the theory, they should exert more selectivity in their choice of mates than should men, who require only the contribution of sperm in order to reproduce. Two specific predictions can be derived from this hypothesis: (1) Women will choose as mates men who are willing to invest resources in them and their children, and (2) women will divorce or break up with men who fail to continue providing resources to them and their children.

Using this method of deriving specific testable predictions, researchers can carry out the normal scientific business of empirical research. If the findings fail to support the predictions and hypotheses, then the middle-level theory from which they were derived is called into question. If the findings support the predictions and hypotheses, then the middle-level theory from which they were derived increases in credibility.

The **deductive reasoning approach,** or the "top down," theory-driven method of empirical research is one approach to scientific investigation. Another method, which is equally valid, is called the **inductive reasoning approach,** or the "bottom-up," data-driven method of empirical research. In the inductive reasoning approach, a phenomenon is first observed, and then the researchers develop a theory to fit the observations. Just as astronomers observed the galaxies in the universe expanding before they had a theory to explain why, psychologists notice and empirically document a number of phenomena before they have theories to explain them. In the domain of personality, for example, we might notice that men tend to be more physically aggressive than women. Although nothing in the theory of evolution by selection would have predicted this sex difference in advance, it is fair game for subsequent theorizing. The dual inductive and deductive approaches, of course, can apply to all theories in personality psychology, not just evolutionary theories.

Once a theory is proposed to explain the sex difference in aggression, however, we can ask, "If the theory is true, then what *further* predictions follow from it that we have not already observed?" It is in these further predictions that the value and tenability of the theory rest. If the theory generates a wealth of new predictions, which are then confirmed empirically, we know that we are on the right explanatory track. If the theory fails to generate further testable predictions, or if its predictions fail to be confirmed empirically, then the theory is called into question. For example, one theory of sexual aggression against women has proposed that men who have experienced deprivation of sexual access to women are more likely to use aggressive tactics. This has been called the *mate deprivation hypothesis* (Lalumiere et al., 1996). The evidence so far, however, has failed to support this hypothesis—men who have difficulty attracting women are no more likely to use sexual aggression than are men who are highly successful at attracting women. The mate deprivation hypothesis, in short, appears to be false (Buss, 2016, 2021).

Evolutionary hypotheses have sometimes been criticized as being vague, speculative "just-so stories," implying that they are like fairy tales that have little scientific value. Most evolutionary hypotheses have been framed in a precise and testable manner, so this criticism is not valid (Confer et al., 2010; Lewis et al., 2017). Individual scientists bear a responsibility to formulate evolutionary (and nonevolutionary) hypotheses in as precise and testable manner as possible.

With this theoretical background in mind, let's now turn to the implications of an evolutionary perspective for the three key levels of personality analysis: human nature, sex differences, and individual differences.

Human Nature

In the history of psychology, "grand" theories of personality were proposed about the universal contents of human nature. Sigmund Freud's theory of psychoanalysis, for example, proposed that humans had the core motives of sex and aggression. Alfred Adler proposed that humans had the striving for superiority as a core motive. Robert Hogan suggests that humans are driven by the desire for status and acceptance by the group—getting ahead and getting along. Even the most radical behaviorist, B. F. Skinner, had a theory of human nature, consisting of a few domain-general learning mechanisms. Thus, all personality theories attempt to answer the question: If humans have a nature that is different from the nature of gorillas, dogs, rats, or cats, what are its contents and how can we discover them?

The perspective of evolutionary psychology offers a set of tools for discovering the human nature component of personality. From this perspective, human nature is the primary product of the evolutionary process. Psychological mechanisms that are successful in helping humans survive and reproduce tend to out-replicate those that are less successful. Over evolutionary time, these successful mechanisms spread throughout the population and come to characterize a species. Let's examine a few evolutionary hypotheses about the contents of human nature.

Need to Belong

Hogan (1983) argues that the most basic human motivators are status and acceptance by the group. The most important social problems early humans had to solve in order to survive and reproduce involved establishing cooperative relations with other members of the group and climbing status hierarchies. Achieving status and popularity likely conferred many reproductively relevant resources on an individual, including better protection, more food, and more desirable mates.

Being ostracized from a group would have been extremely damaging. Therefore, it can be predicted that humans have evolved psychological adaptations to prevent being excluded. Baumeister and Tice (1990) propose that this is the origin and function of **social anxiety,** defined as distress or worry about being negatively evaluated in social situations. They propose that social anxiety is a species-typical adaptation that prevents social exclusion. People who were indifferent to being excluded by others may have suffered in the currency of survival by lacking the protection of the group. They may also have suffered by failing to find mates. These individuals may have experienced lower reproductive success than those whose maintained inclusion in the group by avoiding doing things that elicit criticism.

If this hypothesis is correct, what testable predictions might follow from it? One set of testable predictions pertains to the *events* that elicit social anxiety (Buss, 1990). Groups shun those who inflict costs on others within the group. Showing cowardice in the face of danger, displaying aggression toward in-group members, trying to lure away the mates of in-group members, and stealing from in-group members would all have inflicted costs on particular members of the group.

Much empirical evidence exists that the need to belong is a central motive of human nature (Allen et al., 2022; Baumeister & Leary, 1995). The group serves several key adaptive functions for individuals. First, groups can share food, information, and other resources. Second, groups can offer protection from external threat, or defense against rival groups. Third, groups contain concentrations of mates, which are needed

Humans evolved to live in groups. Consequently, an individual who is shunned by a group will feel anxious.
SW Productions/Getty Images

for reproduction. And fourth, groups usually contain kin, which provide opportunities to receive altruism and to invest in genetic relatives.

Several lines of empirical research support the theory about the need to belong. First, external threats increase group cohesion (Stein, 1976). In one study, World War II veterans were examined for enduring social ties (Elder & Clipp, 1988). Remarkably, their strongest social ties 40 years after the war were with comrades who had experienced combat together. This effect was intensified among the units in which some comrades had died, suggesting that the more intense the external threat, the greater the social bonding.

Further support for the importance of the need to belong as a fundamental human motive comes from a cross-cultural study on the effects of social interactions on self-esteem (Denissen et al., 2008). Those who spend a lot of time with others enjoy higher self-esteem. Day-to-day fluctuations in self-esteem are linked with quality and quantity of social interactions. And even at the level of nations, countries whose inhabitants frequently interact with friends and relatives enjoy higher self-esteem than countries with less frequent social interactions. These findings point to the notion that self-esteem functions, at least in part, as an internal tracking device that monitors social inclusion (Denissen et al., 2008).

Failure to meet the need to belong can lead to negative health consequences. People who feel rejected or shunned by others experience worse physical health, higher blood pressure, higher levels of perceived stress, and higher cortisol levels (a stress hormone) (Beekman, Stock, & Marcus, 2016; Gere & MacDonald, 2010). Studies of people's life regrets find that most regrets involve social relationships and lack of social connectedness (Morrison, Epstude, & Roese, 2012). Friends provide benefits (Lewis et al., 2011).

Adaptations for the need to belong appear to emerge quite early in life. In a clever laboratory study of children 5 to 6 years old, some were ostracized from a video game that others were apparently playing; another group was socially included in the game (Watson-Jones, Whitehouse, & Legare, 2016). Subsequently, the ostracized children showed more anxiety, conformity, and imitation. These reactions, the authors argue, function to motivate in-group inclusion after being shunned.

The need to belong theory has been used to explain a wide range of phenomena, including cheering for sports teams, joining religious groups, forming online gaming communities, conformity to the group, social identity, reputation management, creating political coalitions, and even the increased political polarization currently witnessed in some countries (Gabriel, 2021).

Researchers have begun to identify the underlying brain circuitry for the pain caused by social exclusion (MacDonald & Leary, 2005; Panksepp, 2005). Social rejection has often been described as literally painful. Brain research suggests that social exclusion is mediated by components of the physical pain system, such as the anterior cingulate cortex. The fact that people use words like *hurt, wounded,* and *damaged* when they are socially excluded may reflect the shared brain circuitry through which physically induced pain and socially induced pain are mediated.

Humans have always been intensely living in groups, and lack of a group almost surely would have meant death in ancestral environments, so it is not surprising that we have a strong need to belong—a part of our human nature.

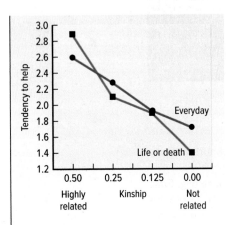

Figure 8.2

Tendency to help kin under life-or-death versus everyday conditions. Genetic overlap predicts the tendency to help, especially under life-or-death conditions.

Source: Adapted from "Some Neo-Darwinian Decision Rules for Altruism: Weighing Cures for Inclusive Fitness as a Function of the Biological Importance of the Decision," by E. Burnstein, C. Crandall, and S. Kitayama, 1994, *Journal of Personality & Social Psychology, 67,* pp. 773–789, Figure 2, p. 778. Copyright © 1994 by the American Psychological Association. Reprinted with permission.

Helping and Altruism

An evolutionary perspective provides a straightforward set of predictions about the human nature of helping and altruism (Burnstein, Crandall, & Kitayama, 1994). Burnstein and colleagues hypothesized that helping others is a direct function of the recipients' ability to enhance the inclusive fitness of the helpers. Helping should decrease, according to this hypothesis, as the degree of genetic relatedness decreases between the helper and the recipient. Thus, you should be more likely to help your sibling, who shares 50 percent of your genes, on average, than your nieces and nephews, who share only 25 percent of your genes, on average. Helping should be lower between individuals who share only 12.5 percent of their genes, such as first cousins. No other theory in psychology generates this precise helping gradient as a function of genetic relatedness or specifies kinship as a key principle for altruism.

Studies in the United States and Japan support these predictions. In one study, participants were asked to imagine different individuals asleep in different rooms of a rapidly burning building. The participants imagined that they had time to rescue only one of them. They circled the target they were most likely to help. As shown in Figure 8.2, the tendency to help is a direct function of the degree of genetic relatedness. This is especially true in a life-or-death context, as confirmed by independent researchers (Fitzgerald & Colarelli, 2009).

Genetic relatedness represents just the start of an evolutionary analysis of the altruistic component of human nature. Burnstein, Crandall, and Kitayama (1994) predicted that people should help younger relatives more than older relatives because helping older kin would have less impact, on average, on their reproductive success than would helping a younger person. Furthermore, individuals of higher reproductive value (ability to produce children) should be helped more than individuals of lower reproductive value.

In one study, 1-year-olds were helped more than 10-year-olds, who in turn were helped more than 45-year-olds (Burnstein, Crandall, & Kitayama, 1994). Least helped were 75-year-old individuals. These findings, replicated across both Japanese and American samples, provide further support for the hypothesis that life-or-death helping decreases as the kin member gets older. Interestingly, these results were strongest in the life-or-death situation, but showed a reversal in a trivial helping condition. For everyday helping, such as running a small errand for someone, the 75-year-olds were helped more than the 45-year-olds (see Figure 8.3).

The tendency to help younger people depended on a critical survival context—famine conditions (Burnstein, Crandall, & Kitayama, 1994). When the participants imagined themselves living in a sub-Saharan African country that suffered widespread famine and disease, they reported a curvilinear relationship between age and helping. Infants in this condition were helped *less* than 10-year-olds, who were helped the most. But then helping began to drop, with the least helped being the 75-year-olds. Another study found that people are willing to endure more physical pain—maintaining a painfully awkward physical position for as long as possible—as a function of closeness of kinship (Madsen et al., 2007). Studies confirm that in real-life situations in which life is in danger, having kin in close proximity literally increases the odds of surviving compared to people in the same situation who lack kin in close proximity (Grayson, 1993; Sear & Mace, 2008). Moreover, people who write wills leave their cash and other assets to close genetic relatives more than to distant ones (Judge & Hrdy, 1992; Elinder et al., 2021).

Humans, of course, help people who are not close kin. We form friendships with non-kin which sometimes can last a lifetime. We help friends who are in need, and they in turn help us when we are in need. This is the defining feature of *reciprocal altruism*—incurring costs to self to deliver benefits to other with the expectation that those benefits will be reciprocated at some future time (Trivers, 1971). The personality trait Agreeableness has been linked with a strong proclivity to be a good reciprocal altruist (Ashton et al., 1998). We select our friends in part based on their potential as cooperative reciprocity partners, and sometimes end friendships then when they fail us in times of need (Apostolou et al., 2021a, 2021b). We also distinguish between "true friends" who stay with us through thick and thin and "fair weather friends" (Apostolou et al., 2021; Tooby & Cosmides, 1996). We even help total strangers sometimes, although this form of helping is sometimes aimed at enhancing our social reputation, which in turn increases our desirability as a friend or coalition partner.

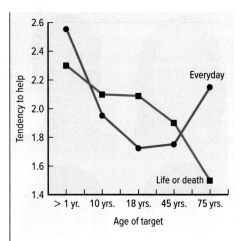

Figure 8.3

Tendency to help as a function of the recipient's age under life-or-death versus everyday conditions. When helping is relatively trivial, people tend to help those most in need, such as the young and the elderly. Under costly forms of help, however, the young are helped more than the old.

Source: Adapted from "Some Neo-Darwinian Decision Rules for Altruism: Weighing Cures for Inclusive Fitness as a Function of the Biological Importance of the Decision," by E. Burnstein, C. Crandall, and S. Kitayama, 1994, *Journal of Personality & Social Psychology, 67,* pp. 773–789, Figure 3, p. 779. Copyright © 1994 by the American Psychological Association. Reprinted with permission.

Images of the seven emotional expressions that are correctly identified by people from many diverse cultures. Can you identify which image is associated with the following emotions: happiness, disgust, anger, fear, surprise, sadness, and contempt?

These studies suggest that a central component of human nature is helping other people, but in highly domain-specific ways. We help friends, who are likely to reciprocate and help us in times of need. And we help close kin. And we help strangers in ways that can enhance our social reputation. The ways in which humans help others—the distribution of helping acts across individuals—is highly predictable from an evolutionary perspective.

Universal Emotions

Evolutionary psychologists have taken three distinct perspectives on the study of emotions, such as fear, rage, and jealousy. One view is to examine whether facial expressions of emotion are interpreted in the same ways across cultures, on the assumption that universality is one criterion for adaptation (Ekman, 1973, 1992a, 1992b). If all humans share an adaptation, such as smiling to express happiness, that adaptation is likely to be a core part of human nature. A second evolutionary view is that emotions are adaptive psychological mechanisms that signal various "fitness affordances" in the social environment (Ketelaar, 1995). According to this perspective, emotions guide the person toward goals that would have conferred fitness in ancestral environments (e.g., the pleasure one feels having one's status rise within a group) or to avoid conditions that would have interfered with fitness (e.g., getting beaten up or abused or ostracized). A third evolutionary perspective on social emotions is the "manipulation hypothesis," which suggests that emotions are designed to exploit the psychological mechanisms of other people. For example, expressions of rage might be designed to make a verbal threat more credible than the same threat made without displaying rage (Sell, Tooby, & Cosmides, 2009).

All these evolutionary perspectives on emotions hinge on the proposition that they are universal and universally recognized in the same way. Ekman (1973, 1992a, 1992b) pioneered the cross-cultural study of emotions. He assembled pictures of several different faces, each of which showed one of seven emotions: happiness, disgust, anger, fear, surprise, sadness, and contempt. When these pictures were shown to subjects in Japan, Chile, Argentina, Brazil, and the United States, all showed tremendous agreement on which emotions corresponded to which face. Subsequent research has confirmed the universal recognition of these emotional expressions in Italy, Scotland, Estonia, Greece, Germany, Hong Kong, Sumatra, and Turkey (Ekman et al., 1987).

Especially impressive is the study of the Fore of New Guinea—a cultural group with practically no contact with outsiders. They spoke no English, had seen no TV or movies, and had never lived with Caucasians. Nonetheless, the Fore also showed the

A Closer Look

The Emotion of Disgust: The Disease-Avoidance Hypothesis

The emotion of disgust is a hypothesized adaptation that serves as a defense against microbial attacks, protecting people from the risk of disease (Curtis, Aunger, & Rabie, 2004; Oaten, Stevenson, & Case, 2009). Disgust is an emotion that involves feelings of revulsion and sometimes nausea. It motivates strong withdrawal from the disgust-producing stimulus. If the emotion of disgust is an evolved defense against disease, several predictions follow. One is that disgust should be evoked most strongly by disease-carrying substances. The second is that these disgust elicitors should be universal across cultures. Empirical research supports both predictions (Curtis & Biran, 2001). People from cultures ranging from the Netherlands to West Africa find foods potentially contaminated by parasites or unhygienic preparation to be exceptionally disgusting. Examples are rotting flesh, dirty food, bad-smelling food, food leftovers, moldy food, dead insects in food, and witnessing food preparation by someone with dirty hands. Foods that have had contact with worms, cockroaches, or feces evoke especially strong disgust reactions. A third prediction is that disgust should activate the immune system. Showing people images of contaminated food actually elevated their body temperature—one of the key features of immune response to disease (Stevenson et al., 2012).

A cross-cultural study asked Americans and Japanese to list things they found most disgusting. Feces and other body wastes were the most frequently mentioned (Rozin, 1996). Feces are known to harbor harmful elements, including parasites and toxins, and are dangerous to humans. Students refuse to drink from a glass that has been thoroughly cleaned and sterilized when told that it once held dog feces (Rozin & Nemeroff, 1990). The facial expression of disgust is universally recognized; it is expressed by people who are blind from birth; and it is interpreted correctly by people who are born deaf (Oaten, Stevenson, & Case, 2009).

Another prediction from the disease-avoidance hypothesis of disgust is a gender difference: Since women typically care for their infants and children, they need to protect them from disease, as well as themselves (Al-Shawaf, Lewis, & Buss, 2018; Crosby et al., 2020). And indeed, women find images depicting disease-carrying objects to be more disgusting than men do, and also perceive that the risk of disease is greater from those objects than men do (Curtis, Aunger, & Rabie, 2004). Individuals differ in disgust sensitivity—a prime candidate for an important personality variable. Individuals who have especially heightened sensitivity to contamination and who were most easily disgusted have significantly fewer infections—a finding that provides evidence for the protective function of disgust (Stevenson et al., 2012). Interestingly, individuals who score high on a measure of pathogen disgust find relatively unattractive faces to be especially unattractive compared with people low on pathogen disgust (Park, van Leeuwen, & Stephen, 2012).

Potential contact with people who have poor hygiene, who appear diseased, or have body boundary violations such as gaping wounds, and who engage in practices such as anal sex—all of which are possible conduits for disease transmission—often evokes disgust (Tyber, Lieberman, & Griskevicius, 2009). Indeed, sexual contact is an important source of disease transmission (Tyber et al., 2013). The mouth, the skin, the anus, and the genitals are all key entry and exit points for microorganisms to move from host to host. Kissing, touching, oral–genital contact, genital–genital contact, and other sexual behaviors put individuals at risk of contracting diseases. Sexual disgust may be a specialized adaptation to avoid potentially infected sex partners, above and beyond the disgust adaptation designed to avoid contaminated food and infectious animals and insects (Al-Shawaf, Lewis, & Buss, 2018; Crosby et al., 2020). Much empirical evidence, in short, supports the disease-avoidance hypothesis of disgust. It is an emotion that evolved to avoid predictable classes of disease conduits that jeopardized survival, and is part of human nature.

universal pairing of emotions and faces. Subsequent research has also shown the universality of the facial expression of contempt (Ekman et al., 1987).

A recent test of the universality of emotion expression examined the facial expressions of 63 sculptures created in the Americas dating back to 1500 BCE prior to any contact with Western civilization (Cowen & Keltner, 2020). Researchers isolated the facial expressions from the social context in which the expressions occurred, and then had Western participants judge the emotion for each. They found strong correspondence between the perceived emotional expression and the social context in which it was expressed. For example, when the judges said that the emotion of "pain" was being expressed, this was linked to the social context of "torture." "Anger" was linked to the social context of "combat." And "sadness" was linked to the social context of "defeat." The authors conclude that modern Westerners share with ancient pre-contact peoples the links between facial expression of emotion and the social contexts in which these expressions commonly occur.

Emotions can also be expressed by nonverbal body language. A prime example is the emotion of *pride*. When people win an athletic contest, for example, they commonly thrust both arms in the air, forming a V, perhaps symbolic for victory (Matsumoto & Hwang, 2012). The nonverbal expression of triumph appears to be recognized across cultures. The nonverbal V is also displayed by congenitally blind individuals who win athletic contests (Tracy & Matsumoto, 2008).

This work suggests that emotions, as central components of personality, are universally expressed and recognized, thus fulfilling an important criterion for adaptation. They are good candidates for evolved components of human nature.

We have reviewed only a few hypotheses about the components of human nature from an evolutionary perspective: the need to belong, social anxiety about ostracism, the urge to help, and the universality of emotions. An evolutionary perspective may shed light on many other components of human nature, such as childhood fears of loud noises, darkness, spiders, and strangers; emotions such as envy, passion, and love; the universality of play among children; retaliation and revenge for perceived personal violations; status striving as a fundamental motive; and many more. Human nature, however, represents only one level of personality analysis. We now turn to the second level—sex differences.

Sex Differences

Evolutionary psychology predicts that males and females will be *the same* or *similar* in domains in which the sexes have faced the same or similar adaptive problems. Both sexes have sweat glands because both sexes have faced the adaptive problem of thermal regulation. Both sexes have similar taste preferences for fat, sugar, and salt because both sexes have faced similar food consumption problems.

In other domains, men and women have faced different adaptive problems over evolutionary history. Women dealt with childbirth; men did not. Women, therefore, have evolved particular adaptations that are lacking in men, such as mechanisms for producing labor contractions through the release of oxytocin into the bloodstream.

Men and women have also faced different *information-processing problems* in some adaptive domains. Because fertilization occurs internally within the woman, for example, men have faced the adaptive problem of uncertainty of paternity in their offspring. Men who failed to solve this problem risked investing resources in children who were not their own. We are all descendants of a long line of ancestral men whose characteristics led them to behave in ways that increased their likelihood of paternity and decreased the odds of investing in children who were presumed to be theirs but whose genetic fathers were other men.

This does not imply that men were or are consciously aware of the problem of compromised paternity. A man does not think, "Oh, if my wife has sex with someone else, then my certainty that I'm the genetic father will be jeopardized, and this will endanger the replication of my genes; I'm really mad." Or if a man's wife is taking birth-control pills, he does not think, "Well, because Joan is taking the pill, it doesn't really matter whether she has sex with other men; after all, my certainty in paternity is secure." Instead, jealousy is a blind passion, just as our hunger for sweets and disgust at contaminated food are blind passions. The "wisdom" of jealousy is passed down to us over millions of years by our successful forebears (Buss, 2000a).

Women faced the problem of securing a reliable or replenishable supply of resources to carry them through pregnancy and lactation, especially when food resources were scarce, such as during droughts and harsh winters. We are all descendants of a long and unbroken line of women who successfully solved this adaptive challenge—for example, by preferring mates who showed the ability to accrue resources and the willingness to channel them toward particular women (Buss, 2016). The women who failed to solve this problem failed to survive, imperiled the survival chances of their children, and hence failed to become our ancestors.

Evolutionary-predicted sex differences hypothesis holds that the sexes will differ in precisely those domains where women and men have faced different sorts of adaptive problems (Buss, 2009a, 2009b). To an evolutionary psychologist, the likelihood that the sexes are psychologically identical in domains in which they have recurrently confronted different adaptive problems over the long expanse of human evolutionary history is essentially zero (Symons, 1992). The key question therefore is not "Are men and women different psychologically?" Rather, the key questions about gender differences, from an evolutionary psychological perspective, are the following:

1. In what *domains* have women and men faced different adaptive problems?
2. What are the *sex-differentiated psychological adaptations* of women and men that have evolved in response to these sex-differentiated challenges?
3. Which social and cultural contexts affect the magnitude of sex differences?

This section reviews some of the key domains in which the sexes have been predicted to differ: aggression, jealousy, desire for sexual variety, and mate preferences.

Sex Differences in Aggression

The earliest known homicide victim was a Neanderthal man who died 50,000 years ago (Trinkaus & Zimmerman, 1982). He was stabbed in the left front of his chest, indicating a right-handed attacker. As paleontological detective work has become increasingly sophisticated, evidence of prehistoric violence among our forebears has mushroomed (Buss, 2005b). Ancient skeletal remains contain cranial and rib fractures that appear inexplicable except by the force of clubs and weapons that stab. Weapon fragments are occasionally found lodged in skeletal rib cages. Humans apparently have a long evolutionary history of violence.

A global study of homicides in 2013 revealed that 95 percent of homicides are committed by males and 70 percent of homicide victims are males (UNODC, 2014). Although the exact percentages vary from culture to culture, cross-cultural homicide statistics reveal strikingly similar findings. In all cultures studied, men are overwhelmingly the killers, and most of their victims are other men. Among chimpanzees, our closest primate cousins, the lethal killing of one chimpanzee by others reveal similar statistics—92 percent of the

Men tend to engage in riskier tactics of competition, such as aggression and violence.
Ollyy/Shutterstock

attackers are male and 73 percent of the victims are male (Wilson et al., 2014). Any complete theory of aggression must explain both facts—why males engage in violent forms of aggression so much more often than females do and why males comprise the majority of their victims.

An evolutionary model of intrasexual competition provides the foundation for the explanation. It starts with the theory of parental investment and sexual selection (Archer, 2009; Trivers, 1972). In species in which females invest more heavily in off-spring than males do, females become the valuable limiting resource on reproduction for males. Males become constrained in their reproduction not so much by their own ability to survive but rather by their ability to gain mating access to the high-investing females. In a species in which females can bear only a small number of offspring, such as humans, females express great care in their choice of mates, and males will be forced to compete with each other for access.

Because female mammals bear the physical burden of gestation and lactation, there is a considerable sex difference in minimum obligatory parental investment. Therefore, males can have many more offspring than females can. Stated differently, the ceiling on reproduction is much higher for males than for females. This difference leads to differences in the *variances* in reproduction between the sexes. The differences between the haves and have-nots become greater for males than for females. Among males, a few males will sire multiple offspring, whereas some will have none at all. This is known as **effective polygyny.**

As a general rule, the greater the variance in reproduction, the more ferocious the competition within the sex that shows higher variance. In an extreme case such as the ele-phant seals off the coast of northern California, 5 percent of the males sire 85 percent of all offspring produced in a given breeding season (Le Boeuf & Reiter, 1988). Species that show high variance in reproduction within one sex tend to be highly **sexually dimorphic,** highly different in size and structure. The more intense the effective polygyny, the more dimorphic the sexes are in size and form (Plavcan, 2012; Trivers, 1985). Elephant seals are highly size dimorphic: males are four times heavier than females (Le Boeuf & Reiter, 1988). Chimpanzees are less sexually dimorphic: males are roughly twice as large as females. Humans are mildly dimorphic, with males roughly 12 percent larger than females, although some specific body components, such as upper body strength, show much larger sexual dimorphism (Lassek & Gaulin, 2009). Within primate species, the greater the effec-tive polygyny, the more the sexual dimorphism and the greater the reproductive variance between the sexes (Alexander et al., 1979; Plavcan, 2012).

Effective polygyny means that some males gain a disproportionate share of copu-lations, whereas other males are shut out entirely, banished from contributing to the ancestry of future generations. Such a system leads to ferocious competition within the high-variance sex. In essence, polygyny selects for risky strategies, including those that lead to violent combat with rivals and those that lead to increased risk taking to acquire the resources needed to attract members of the high-investing sex.

The greater body size and strength in males is also likely due to a long history of females who select as mates males with these qualities (Buss, 2012; Plavcan, 2012). One study found that women who fear crime are especially likely to prefer long-term mates who are aggressive and physically formidable (Snyder et al., 2011). Another study found that men with more muscle mass had a larger number of sex partners and an earlier age of first sexual intercourse (Lassek & Gaulin, 2009). A third study found that men who experienced aggressive victimization in adolescence at the hands of other males have fewer sex partners (Gallup et al., 2009).

This evolutionary account provides an explanation for facts revealed in the cross-cultural homicide record. Males are more often the perpetrators of violence because they are the products of a long history of effective polygyny. Throughout human evolution, male strategies have been characterized by risky intrasexual competition for females or for the social status and resources that attract females. The fact that men die, on average, five to seven years earlier than women is one of the many markers of this aggressive risk-taking intrasexual strategy (Promislow, 2003).

Men are the victims of aggression more than women because men are in competition primarily with other men. Men block other men's access to women. With increased aggression comes a greater likelihood of injury and early death. The patterns of aggression are well predicted by the evolutionary theory of intrasexual competition (Buss & Duntley, 2006; Griskevicius et al., 2009). Even psychologists who argue that most psychological and behavioral sex differences are due to social roles concede that sex differences in aggression are likely caused by a long evolutionary history in which women and men have confronted different adaptive problems in the context of mating and mate competition (Archer, 2009).

Sex Differences in Jealousy

Another difference between the sexes in the nature of the adaptive problems they have faced stems from the fact that fertilization occurs internally and unseen within women. This means that ancestral men have risked investing in children who were not their own. Few women, however, have ever been uncertain about which children were their own. A reproductively damaging act, from an ancestral man's point of view would have been if his mate had a pregnancy from sexual intercourse with another man. That is the act that jeopardized his paternity certainty and hence his reproductive success.

From an ancestral woman's point of view, however, the fact that her mate was having sex with another woman, by itself, would not jeopardize her certainty in that she is the mother of her own children. Such an infidelity, however, could be extremely risky to the woman's reproductive success: she could risk losing her mate's resources, time, commitment, and investment, all of which could be diverted to another woman.

For these reasons, evolutionary psychologists have predicted that men and women should differ in the weighting they give to cues that trigger jealousy. Specifically, men have been predicted to become relatively more jealous than women in response to cues to a sexual infidelity. Women have been predicted to become relatively more jealous than men in response to cues to the long-term diversion of a mate's commitment, such as emotional involvement with someone else. To test these predictions, participants were put in an agonizing dilemma, which you can participate in as well. Take a look at the Exercise that follows.

Exercise

Think of a serious, committed romantic relationship that you had in the past, that you currently have, or that you would like to have. Imagine that you discover that the person with whom you've been seriously involved has become interested in someone else. Of the following, what would distress or upset you more?

1. Imagining your partner forming a deep emotional attachment to that person.
2. Imagining your partner enjoying passionate sexual intercourse with that other person.

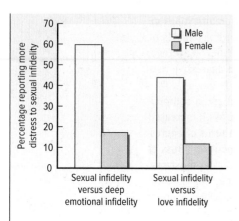

Figure 8.4

Percentage reporting more distress to sexual infidelity than to emotional or love infidelity. A large sex difference is found, with far more men than women reporting more distress to sexual infidelity, and the overwhelming majority of women reporting more distress to emotional or love infidelity.

Source: From "Sex Differences in Jealousy: Evolution, Physiology, and Psychology," by D. M. Buss, R. Larsen, J. Semmelroth, and D. Weston, 1992, *Psychological Science, 3,* pp. 251–255, Figure 1, top panel, p. 252. Copyright © 1992 Association for Psychological Science. Reprinted by permission of SAGE Publications, Inc.

As shown in Figure 8.4, men are far more distressed than women when imagining their partners having sexual intercourse with someone else (Buss et al., 1992). The overwhelming majority of women, in contrast, are more distressed when imagining their partners becoming emotionally involved with someone else. This does not mean that women are indifferent to their partners' sexual infidelities or that men are indifferent to their partners' emotional infidelities— far from it. Both events upset both sexes. However, when forced to choose which one is more upsetting, a large sex difference emerges, precisely as predicted by the evolutionary hypothesis of sex differences in the nature of the adaptive problems. These results also show up in measures of physiological distress (Buss et al., 1992; Pietrzak et al., 2002). When imagining partners having sex with someone else, men's heart rate goes up five beats per minute, which is like drinking three cups of coffee at one time. Their skin conductance increases, and their frown response is visible. Women, in contrast, show greater physiological distress at imagining their partners becoming emotionally involved with someone else.

Are these sex differences found across cultures? Thus far, researchers have replicated these sex differences in Germany, the Netherlands, and Korea (Buunk et al., 1996), as shown in Figure 8.5. Other researchers have replicated these sex differences in Korea and Japan (Buss et al., 1999). The sex differences in jealousy appear to be robust across a range of cultures.

Not every psychologist agrees with the evolutionary explanation. DeSteno and Salovey (1996) have proposed that men and women differ in their "beliefs" about sexual and emotional involvement. When a man thinks that his partner is becoming sexually involved with a rival, for example, he might also think that his partner will be getting emotionally involved—a so-called double shot of infidelity. The reason men get more upset about sexual rather than emotional infidelity, DeSteno and Salovey argue, is not because men are really more jealous about sexual infidelity—it's because men "believe" that a sexual infidelity will result in the double shot of infidelity, which includes emotional infidelity.

Women, DeSteno and Salovey (1996) argue, have different beliefs, although they fail to explain why. Women believe in a reverse double-shot, that if their partners become emotionally involved with a rival, they will also become sexually involved. It's women's beliefs about this double shot of infidelity that upset them, DeSteno and Salovey argue, and not that women really are more upset about an emotional betrayal.

The evolutionary explanation opposes the double-shot explanation. Given the large sex differences stemming from fundamental differences in reproductive biology, according to evolutionary psychologists, it would be unlikely for selection to have failed to produce psychological sex differences about the two forms of infidelity. The hard hand of data, however, usually settles scientific disagreements. Buss and his colleagues (1999) conducted four empirical studies in three different cultures to pit the predictions of evolutionary theory against the predictions of the double-shot hypothesis. One of the studies involved 1,122 participants from a liberal arts college in the southeastern United States. Researchers asked them to imagine their partners becoming interested in someone else: What would upset or distress you more: (1) imagining your partner forming a deep emotional *(but not sexual)* relationship with that person? or (2) imagining your partner enjoying a sexual *(but not emotional)* relationship with that person? Men and women differed

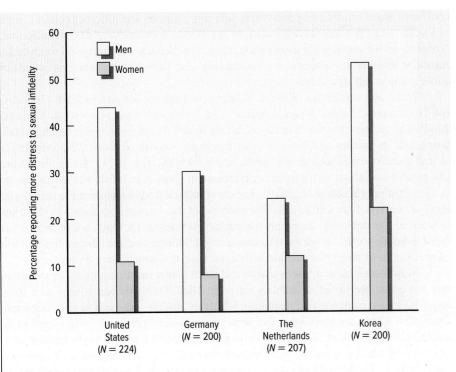

Figure 8.5

Sex differences in jealousy across four cultures. In all four cultures, more men than women are distressed about imagining a partner's sexual infidelity; most women are more distressed by a partner's emotional infidelity.

Source: From "Sex Differences in Jealousy in Evolutionary and Cultural Perspective: Tests from the Netherlands, Germany, and the United States," by A. P. Buunk, A. Angleitner, V. Oubaid, and D. M. Buss, 1996, *Psychological Science, 7,* pp. 359–363, Figure 1, p. 361. Copyright © 1996 Association for Psychological Science. Reprinted by permission of SAGE Publications, Inc.

by 35 percent, as predicted by the evolutionary model. Women continued to express greater upset about a partner's emotional infidelity, even if it did not involve sex. Men continued to show more upset than the women about a partner's sexual infidelity, even if it did not involve emotional involvement. If the double-shot hypothesis were the correct explanation, the sex difference should have disappeared when the sexual and emotional components of infidelity were isolated. It did not.

In a second study of 234 women and men (Buss et al., 1999), the researchers used a different strategy for pitting the competing hypotheses against each other. They asked participants to imagine that their worst nightmare had occurred—that their partners had become both sexually *and* emotionally involved with someone else. They then asked the participants to state *which aspect* they found more upsetting. The results were conclusive. The researchers found large gender differences, precisely as predicted by the evolutionary explanation—63 percent of the men but only 13 percent of the women found the sexual aspect of the infidelity to be more upsetting. In contrast, 87 percent of the women, but only 37 percent of the men, found the emotional aspect of the infidelity to be more upsetting. No matter how the questions were worded, no matter which method was used, the same gender difference emerged in every test. Several other scientists have now confirmed these results using somewhat different methods and different cultures, such as Sweden (e.g., Wiederman & Kendall, 1999). Wiederman and Kendall concluded that, "contrary to the double-shot explanation, choice of scenario was unrelated to attitudes regarding whether the other gender was capable of satisfying sexual relations outside of a love relationship" (p. 121).

These and similar sex differences have now been replicated in China, Germany, the Netherlands, Korea, Japan, England, and Romania (Brase, Caprar, & Voracek, 2004). The gender differences emerge robustly in cultures that are highly sexually egalitarian such as Sweden and Norway (e.g., Bendixen, Kennair, & Buss, 2015), as well is in traditional cultures such as the Himba of Namibia (Scelza, 2014). Scelza also found that men's upset about sexual infidelity increased in cultures in which men invest heavily in their children (Scelza et al., 2019). The cross-cultural findings support the theory that these are universal sex differences. The double-shot theory cannot explain why these sex differences are universal. Based on the available evidence, the double-shot theory has failed to be supported both from the cross-cultural findings and from the studies that test its predictions in direct competition with those from the evolutionary theory.

In an ingenious study, Schutzwohl and Koch (2004) used an entirely new method that has never been used in jealousy research. They had participants listen to a story about their own romantic relationship in which an infidelity was said to have occurred. Embedded within the story were five cues that had been previously determined to be cues highly diagnostic of *sexual infidelity* (e.g., He suddenly has difficulty becoming sexually aroused when you and he want to have sex) and five cues diagnostic of *emotional infidelity* (e.g., He doesn't respond any more when you tell him that you love him). In a surprise recall test a week later, men spontaneously remembered more cues to sexual than to emotional infidelity (42 percent vs. 29 percent), whereas women remembered more cues to emotional than to sexual infidelity (40 percent vs. 24 percent). These findings support the hypothesis that sex differences in jealousy are real and not "experimental artifacts" (Schutzwohl & Koch, 2004).

Other studies have discovered other design features of sex differences in the psychology of jealousy. One found that women experienced more *psychological relief* when they discovered that their partner was not emotionally unfaithful, whereas men experienced greater relief upon the disconfirmation of a partner's sexual infidelity (Schutzwohl, 2008). Women more than men inquire about the emotional nature of a partner's extra-pair relationship, whereas men more than women inquire about the sexual nature of a partner's extra-pair relationship (Kuhle, Smedley, & Schmitt, 2009). And those who are chronically more jealous tend to show even larger sex differences in jealous responses to sexual versus emotional infidelity (Miller & Maner, 2009). This latter finding highlights the importance of integrating stable individual differences with evolutionary theories of sex differences in personality (Miller & Maner, 2009).

The gold standard in science is independent replication, and by this criterion the evolutionary explanation has fared well. After each challenge, additional research by independent scientists has continued to find support for the existence of sex differences in jealousy and the evolutionary explanations for them (e.g., Brase, Caprar, & Voracek, 2004; Buss & Haselton, 2005; Cann, Mangum, & Wells, 2001; Dijkstra & Buunk, 2001; Fenigstein & Pelz, 2002; Geary et al., 2001; Maner & Shackelford, 2008; Murphy et al., 2006; Pietrzak et al., 2002; Sagarin, 2005; Sagarin et al., 2003, 2009; Schutzwohl & Koch, 2004; Shackelford, Buss, & Bennett, 2002; Shackelford et al., 2004; Strout et al., 2005). Indeed, a meta-analysis of 47 independent samples provided strong support for the evolutionarily predicted sex differences across methods, including studies that evaluated reactions to actual infidelities (Sagarin et al., 2012; Zengel, Edlund, & Sagarin, 2013).

Finally, in using a novel method of content coding jealous interrogations of romantic partners, Kuhle (2011) discovered that men tended to interrogate partners more about the sexual aspects ("Did you have sex with him?"), whereas women interrogated partners about the emotional aspects ("Do you love her?") (see Figure 8.6). In sum, the predicted gender differences in jealousy are robust across many methods and many cultures (Buss, 2018; Frederick & Fales, 2016).

Sex Differences in Desire for Sexual Variety

Another gender difference predicted by evolutionary theories is a difference in the desire for sexual variety (Figure 8.7). This prediction stems from parental investment and sexual selection theory. The members of the sex that invests less in offspring are predicted to be less discriminating in their selection of mates and more inclined to seek multiple mates. In ancestral times, men could increase their reproductive success by gaining sexual access to a variety of women.

If you were given your ideal wish, how many sex partners would you like to have in the next month? How about the next year? How about over your entire lifetime? When unmarried college students were asked these questions, the women indicated that they wanted about one in the next month and four or five in their entire lifetimes (Buss & Schmitt, 1993). The men, in contrast, thought that 2 would be about right in the next month, 8 over the next couple of years, and 18 in their lifetimes. In terms of expressed desires, men and women differ in the ways predicted by the evolutionary account.

The sex differences in number of partners desired have been replicated in a cross-cultural study. Schmitt and his colleagues (2003) studied 16,288 individuals from 10 world regions, representing 52 different nations from Argentina to Slovakia to Zimbabwe. They used instruments identical to those used for Figure 8.7, translated into

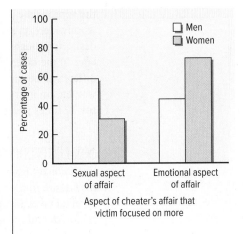

Figure 8.6

Men and women differ in which aspects of their partner's infidelity they focus on more.

Source: Kuhle, 2011.

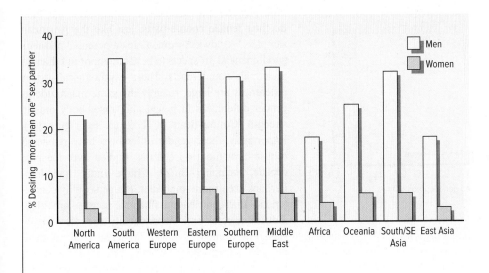

Figure 8.7

"Ideally, how many different sexual partners would you like to have in the next month?" Total sample size 16, 288.

Source: Data from International Sexuality Description Project, courtesy of David P. Schmitt.

the appropriate language for each culture. For the time interval of the next 30 years, men worldwide expressed a desire for roughly 13 sex partners, whereas women expressed a desire for roughly 2.5 partners (see Figure 8.7 for illustrative findings). The sex difference in the desire for sexual variety, in short, appears to be large and universal. The sex difference extends to how often men and women think about sex. One study found that women, on average, think about sex nine times per week; men, on average, think about sex 37 times per week (Regan & Atkins, 2006).

Sex Differences in Mate Preferences

Evolutionary psychologists have also predicted that men and women differ in the qualities they desire in a long-term mate. Because women bear the burden of the heavy obligatory parental investment, they are predicted to place more value on a potential mate's financial resources and the qualities that lead to such resources. Men, in contrast, are predicted to place greater value on a woman's physical appearance, which provides a wealth of observable cues to her fertility. Among college students, men ranked physical attractiveness an average of 4.04, whereas the women ranked it lower, giving it 6.26 (the highest possible rank would be a "1," whereas the lowest possible rank would be "13"). On the dimension of good earning capacity, the women ranked it 8.04, whereas the men ranked it 9.92 (Buss & Barnes, 1986). Thus, it is clear that women and men both place many qualities above looks and resources. In particular, "kind and understanding" (rank: 2.20) and having an "exciting personality" (rank: 3.50) are more valued by both sexes. Interestingly, people prefer the trait of "kindness" in mates when the kindness is directed toward them, but not necessarily when it is directed toward others (Lukaszewski & Roney, 2010). Personality, in short, plays a key role in what people want in a marriage partner.

Nonetheless, in the study, the men and women differed in their rankings of looks and resources in the predicted direction. These sex differences have been found across 37 cultures (Buss, 1989; Kamble et al., 2014; Souza, Conroy-Beam, & Buss, 2016). Zambian, Chinese, Indonesian, Brazilian, Indian, and Norwegian men rank physical attractiveness as more important than do their female counterparts, just like the American samples. Worldwide, women rank a potential partner's good financial prospects to be more important than do their male counterparts. These psychological gender differences are large, roughly the same magnitude as gender differences in height and upper body muscle strength (Conroy-Beam et al., 2015; see Figure 8.8). Importantly, these gender differences have remained robust throughout all cultures studied over the past decade, including Brazil, China, India, and Iran. Perhaps even more important, the personality characteristics that contribute to financial success—ambition, industriousness, and dependability—are also highly valued by women worldwide. Whereas men prioritize physical attractiveness, women prioritize social status as a "necessity" in selecting long-term mates (Li, Valentine, & Patel, 2011).

In summary, personality plays a key role in mate preferences across the globe, and on a few

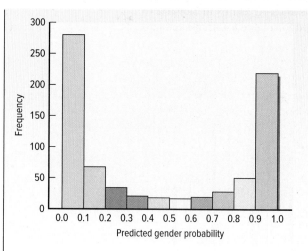

Figure 8.8

We can predict biological sex, whether one is male or female, with 92.4 percent accuracy solely from knowing a person's expressed preferences for good financial prospects, good looks, chastity, ambition, and age in a potential mate.

Source: Findings and graph courtesy of Daniel Conroy-Beam; for more information, see Conroy-Beam, Buss, Pham, & Shackelford, 2015.

A Closer Look

Consenting to Sex with a Stranger

The sex difference in desire for sexual variety shows up in behavioral data. In one study conducted at a university in Florida, experimental confederates approached people of the opposite sex (Clark & Hatfield, 1989). After introducing themselves, they said, "Hi, I've been noticing you around campus lately, and I find you very attractive. Would you go out on a date with me tonight?" A different group was asked, "Would you go back to my apartment with me tonight?" And a third group was asked, "Would you have sex with me tonight?"

Experimenters simply recorded the percentage of people approached who agreed to the request. Of the women who were approached by the male confederate, 55 percent agreed to the date, 6 percent agreed to go back to the man's apartment, and 0 percent agreed to have sex with him. Of the men approached by the female confederate, 50 percent agreed to go out on the date, 69 percent agreed to go back to her apartment, and 75 percent agreed to have sex with her.

The reactions of the two sexes were very different in the sex condition. Women approached for sex often felt insulted; many thought the request was strange. Men, in contrast, were typically flattered.

These studies and many others support the evolutionary hypothesis that men and women differ in their desire for sexual variety. Men tend to have more sexual fantasies than do women, and they engage more often in "partner switching" during the course of those fantasies—they fantasize about two or more sex partners during a single fantasy episode (Buss, 2016). A meta-analysis found that attitudes toward casual sex were one of the largest sex differences sexuality, with men typically much more positive than women about casual sex (Oliver & Hyde, 1993).

Journalist Natalie Angier questions these results, arguing that women would hop into bed as easily as men in these situations but are deterred by a concern for their personal safety (Angier, 1999). Russell Clark explored this possibility (Clark, 1990). First, he replicated the "sex with strangers" study on a different sample in a different part of the country, and the results were virtually identical—more men than women were willing to have sex with a virtual stranger. Second, Clark noted that roughly half of the women in each study were quite willing to go out on a date with the strangers, which seemed puzzling if they were concerned about their safety. Third, when Clark's experimenters asked the participants to describe the reason for their refusal (if they refused), women's and men's answers were nearly identical—both mentioned that they had a boyfriend or girlfriend or that they did not know the person well enough.

Importantly, the gender differences in consenting to sex with strangers have been robustly replicated in other countries, including France, Germany, and Denmark (e.g., Hald & Hogh-Olesen, 2010).

Perhaps a date seems safer than sex, and women really do want sex with strangers, if only they could be assured of their safety. To explore this possibility, Clark (1990) conducted yet another experiment. Men and women were contacted by close personal friends who testified about the integrity and character of the stranger. The participants were assured by their friends that the stranger was warm, sincere, trustworthy, and attractive. The participants were then asked one of two questions: "Would you be willing to go on a date?" or "Would you be willing to go to bed?" After being debriefed, the participants were asked for their reasons for their decisions.

The majority of both sexes agreed to the date—91 percent of the women and 96 percent of the men. In the sex condition, however, a large sex difference emerged—50 percent of the men but only 5 percent of the women agreed. Not a single woman indicated a concern for safety. Clearly, making conditions safer for women increases the odds that they will consent to sex with a stranger—from 0 to 5 percent— so safety concerns are not irrelevant, but the sex difference remains large. Most women agree to date strangers when a close friend vouches for the man's warmth and integrity, but 95 percent still refuse to consent to sex.

It's not that women lack interest in sex. The evidence is compelling, however, that most women are careful about whom they choose to sleep with and for the most part avoid jumping into bed with total strangers. Men are more willing.

These findings have now been replicated in a study involving three countries—Italy, Germany, and the United States (Schutzwohl et al., 2009). The new twist in this study involved varying the attractiveness of the requestor, which increased acceptance rates for both sexes. For the "exceptionally attractive" requestor, 83 percent of the men agreed to sex, whereas 24 percent of the women agreed to sex. So although there are indeed circumstances in which some women consent to sex with strangers, men are still much more likely to do so.

These differences hold with equal force in lust for affairs. In one study by Johnson (1970) of Sacramento State College, 48 percent of American men, but only 5 percent of American women, expressed a desire to engage in extramarital sex. In a classic older study by Terman (1938) of 769 American men and 770 American women, 72 percent of the

(Continued)

men, but only 27 percent of the women, admitted that they sometimes desired sex with someone outside of their marriage. Germans revealed similar tendencies—46 percent of married men but only 6 percent of married women admit that they would take advantage of a casual sexual opportunity with someone else if the chance arose (Sigusch & Schmidt, 1971).

Women, of course, may be more reluctant to confide their sexual desires to a surveyor, so the figures are likely to underestimate women's sexual urges. Nonetheless, the gender difference proves so robust across studies and methods of inquiry that there is no reason to doubt that men and women differ, on average, in desire for a variety of sex partners.

dimensions there are universal gender differences in what people want in a marriage partner. Although the evolutionary hypotheses for these sex differences have so far received support in cross-cultural research, competing hypotheses have been proposed to explain them, and these are currently being tested.

Exercise

Following is a list of characteristics that might be present in a potential mate or marriage partner. Rank them on their desirability in someone you might marry. Give a 1 to the most desirable characteristic in a potential mate, a 2 to the second most desirable characteristic in a potential mate, a 3 to the third most desirable characteristic, and so on down to 13 for the 13th most desirable characteristic in a potential mate.

_____ kind and understanding   _____ good housekeeper   _____ college graduate

_____ religious   _____ intelligent   _____ physically attractive

_____ exciting personality   _____ good earning capacity   _____ healthy

_____ creative and artistic   _____ wants children

_____ easygoing   _____ good heredity

Individual Differences

The study of individual differences has been the most challenging level of analysis for evolutionary psychologists. Unlike sex differences, for which scientists have an impressive conceptual and empirical foundation, there is less of a foundation for adaptive individual differences. Thus, this section must necessarily be more speculative than previous sections.

There are several ways in which individual differences can be explained from the vantage point of evolutionary psychology (Buss, 2009b; Buss & Hawley, 2011; Penke, Denissen, & Miller, 2007). The most common is explaining individual differences as a result of environmental differences acting on species-typical (human nature) psychological mechanisms. An analogy is the phenomenon of calluses that people sometimes develop on their hands and feet. Individual differences in calluses can be explained by proposing that different individuals are exposed to different amounts of repeated friction to their skin. All humans have essentially the same callus-producing mechanisms, so individual differences are the result of the environmental differences that activate the mechanisms to differing degrees. Evolutionary psychologists invoke a similar form of explanation to account for psychological individual differences. Individual differences in jealousy, for example, may be explained by differences in the degree to which individuals are exposed to evoking conditions, such as cues to a partner's infidelity or the presence of "mate poachers" (Buss, 2012).

Second, individual differences can emerge from *contingencies among traits* (Bouchard & Loehlin, 2001). For example, "a hair-trigger temper may be advantageous if one is big and strong but not if one is small and weak" (p. 250). Rather than the trait's expression being contingent on the environment, however, its expression is contingent on other traits the person has—in this case, the size and strength of one's body.

A third source of individual difference stems from *frequency-dependent selection:* the process whereby the reproductive success (fitness) of a trait depends on its frequency relative to other traits in the population. For example, in a large population of people with a cooperative disposition, selection may favor those with a cheating disposition as long as they are not too common. As the frequency of cheaters gets more common, cooperators evolve defenses to punish cheaters, and so the success of cheating goes down. Thus, heritable individual differences can be created through frequency-dependent selection.

A fourth source of individual differences comes from the fact that *the optimum level of a personality trait can vary over time and space.* Consider as an example differences over evolutionary time or space in the abundance of food, perhaps due to droughts or ice ages. In times of food scarcity, selection favors a risk-taking personality trait—one that prompts a person to risk encountering predators in order to venture widely to get food and prevent starvation. In times of food abundance, selection favors a more cautious personality to reduce the risk of venturing widely. These variations in the optimum level of a trait can create heritable individual differences in personality.

In sum, the evolutionary framework identifies several sources of individual differences: (1) those that arise from individuals possessing universal adaptations whose expression is contingent on the environment, (2) those that arise from contingencies with other traits, (3) those due to variation over time and space in the optimum value of a trait, and (4) those due to frequency-dependent selection. Next we explore some examples of these individual differences.

Environmental Triggers of Individual Differences

According to one theory, the critical event of early father presence versus father absence triggers specific sexual strategies in individuals (Belsky, Steinberg, & Draper, 1991). Children who grow up in father-absent homes during the first five years of life, according to this theory, develop expectations that parental resources will not be reliably or predictably provided. These children expect that adult pair bonds will not be enduring. Such individuals cultivate a sexual strategy of early sexual maturation, early sexual initiation, and frequent partner switching—a strategy designed to produce many offspring. An extraverted personality trait may accompany and facilitate this sexual strategy, and there is indeed evidence that extraverted people have more offspring over their lifetimes (Berg et al., 2016).

In contrast, individuals who experience a reliable, investing father during the first five years of life, according to the theory, develop a different set of expectations about the nature and trustworthiness of others. People are seen as reliable and trustworthy, and relationships are expected to be enduring. These early environmental experiences predispose individuals toward a long-term mating strategy, marked by delayed sexual maturation; a later onset of sexual activity; a search for long-term, securely attached adult relationships; and heavy investment in a small number of children.

There is some empirical support for this theory. Children from divorced homes, for example, are more sexually promiscuous than children from intact homes (Belsky, Steinberg, & Draper, 1991). Furthermore, girls from father-absent homes reach menarche (age of first menstruation) earlier than girls from father-present homes (Kim, Smith, & Palermiti, 1997). Nonetheless, these findings are correlational, so causation cannot be inferred. Men or women who are genetically predisposed to pursue a short-term mating strategy may be more likely to get divorced and more likely to pass on to their children genes for that strategy (Bailey et al., 2000). However, despite the current lack of conclusive data (Del Giudice & Belsky, 2011), this theory and modest provisional support for it nicely illustrates one evolutionary approach to the emergence of consistent individual differences—in this case, the effects of different environments on species-typical mechanisms.

According to reactive heritability, a man with a slim, wiry build is less likely than a stocky muscular man to engage in aggressive behavior.

Radius Images/Alamy Stock Photo

Heritable Individual Differences Contingent on Other Traits

Another type of evolutionary analysis of personality involves evaluating one's personal strengths and weaknesses. Suppose, for example, that men could pursue two different strategies in social interaction—an aggressive strategy marked by the use of physical force and a nonaggressive strategy marked by cooperativeness. The success of these strategies, however, hinges on an individual's size, strength, and fighting ability. Those who happen to be muscular in body build can more successfully carry out an aggressive strategy than those who are skinny or chubby. If humans have evolved ways to evaluate themselves on their physical formidability, they can determine which social strategy is the more successful to pursue—an aggressive strategy or a cooperative strategy. Adaptive self-assessments, therefore, can produce stable individual differences in aggression or cooperativeness. In this example, the tendency toward aggression is not directly heritable. Rather, it is **reactively heritable:** It is a secondary consequence of heritable body build (Tooby & Cosmides, 1990).

There is some evidence to support this idea (Ishikawa et al., 2001). Body weight, which is highly correlated with strength, predicts aggression both among pro hockey players and among young men more generally (Archer & Thanzami, 2009; Deaner et al., 2012). Physically stronger males are also quicker to anger and are more likely to believe in the utility of warfare (Sell, Hone, & Pound, 2012). Even more interesting when it comes to personality, the combination of physical strength and physical attractiveness predicted the traits of extraversion, leadership orientation, and amount of bargaining power in social interactions—a prime example of how a personality trait can be contingent on other traits (Lukaszewski, 2013; Lukaszewski & Roney, 2011; von Rueden, Lukaszweski, & Gurven, 2015). These traits, in turn, predict men's (but not women's) proclivity to be oriented toward a short-term mating strategy (Lukaszewski et al., 2014). The notion of self-assessment of heritable qualities remains a fascinating avenue for understanding the adaptive patterning of individual differences, and is now being extended beyond traits like aggressiveness and extraversion to a wider array of condition-dependent models of personality (Lewis, 2015; Lukaszewski et al., 2020). For example, individual differences in the *fearfulness* facet of neuroticism are predicted by physical strength (Rodriguez & Lukaszewski, 2020). Weaker people are more fearful, presumably because they are more vulnerable to threats and fear motivates them to avoid social confrontations.

Frequency–Dependent Strategic Individual Differences

The process of evolution by selection tends to use up heritable variation. Heritable variants that are more successful tend to replace those that are less successful, resulting in species-typical adaptations that show little or no heritable variation.

In some contexts, two or more heritable variants can evolve within a population. The most obvious example is biological sex. Within sexually reproducing species, the two sexes exist in roughly equal numbers because of **frequency–dependent selection.** If one sex becomes rare relative to the other, evolution will produce an increase in the numbers of the rarer sex. Frequency–dependent selection causes the frequency of men and women to remain roughly equal.

Some propose that human individual differences in women's mating strategies have been caused by frequency–dependent selection (Gangestad & Simpson, 1990; Gangestad & Thornhill, 2008). Competition tends to be most intense among individuals who are pursuing the same mating strategy (Maynard Smith, 1982). This lays the groundwork for the evolution of alternative strategies.

According to Gangestad and colleagues, women's mating strategies should center on two key qualities of potential mates: the parental investment a man could provide and the quality of his genes. A man who is able and willing to invest in a woman and her children can be an extraordinarily valuable reproductive asset. Women could also benefit by selecting men who have high-quality genes, which can be passed down to her children. Men may carry genes for good health, physical attractiveness, or sexiness, which are then passed on to the woman's sons or daughters.

There may be a trade-off, however, between selecting a man for his parenting abilities and selecting a man for his genes. Men who are highly attractive to many women, for example, may be reluctant to commit to any one woman. Thus, a woman who is seeking a man for his genes may have to settle for a short-term sexual relationship without parental investment.

These various selection forces, according to theorists, gave rise to two alternative female mating strategies. A woman seeking a high-investing mate would adopt a **restricted sexual strategy** marked by delayed intercourse and prolonged courtship. This would enable her to assess the man's level of commitment, detect the existence of his prior commitments to other women or children, and simultaneously signal to the man her sexual fidelity and hence assure him of his paternity of future offspring.

A woman seeking a man for the quality of his genes, on the other hand, has less reason to delay sexual intercourse. A man's level of commitment to her is irrelevant, so prolonged assessment of his prior commitments is not necessary. This is referred to as an **unrestricted mating strategy.**

According to this theory, the two mating strategies of women—restricted and unrestricted—evolved and are maintained by frequency-dependent selection. As the number of unrestricted females in the population increases, the number of "sexy sons" in the next generation also increases. As the number of sexy sons increases, however, the competition among them also increases. Then, because there are so many sexy sons competing for a limited pool of women, their average success declines.

Now consider what happens when the number of restricted females seeking investing men increases in the population. Because there are now so many women seeking investment, they end up competing with each other for men willing to invest. Therefore, as the number of women seeking investment increases, the average success of their strategy declines. In short, the key idea behind frequency-dependent selection is that the success of each of the two strategies depends on how common each strategy is in the population. As a given strategy becomes more common, it becomes less successful; when it becomes less common, it becomes more successful.

There is some evidence for this theory (Thornhill & Gangestad, 2008). Individual differences in female mating strategy have been shown to be heritable. Women who pursue an unrestricted sexual strategy place more value on qualities of men linked with good genes, such as physical attractiveness and good health (Greiling & Buss, 2000; Thornhill & Gangestad, 2008). Sexual strategies are somewhat flexible and responsive to aspects of the social situation. Thus, people shift in the *restricted* direction of sociosexual desire when they enter a new relationship and become more *unrestricted* again when they break up with an existing romantic partner and enter the mating market (Penke & Asendorpf, 2008a). Nonetheless, the dispositional components of sociosexual desire are reflected in the findings that unrestricted individuals tend to dissolve romantic relationships more quickly, become sexually involved with new partners more readily, and are more likely to be sexually unfaithful within existing mateships (Penke & Asendorpf, 2008a).

Another example of personality differences originating from frequency-dependent selection centers on **psychopathy**—a cluster of personality traits marked by irresponsible and unreliable behavior; egocentrism; impulsivity; an inability to form lasting relationships; superficial social charm; and a deficit in social emotions such as love, shame, guilt, and empathy (Cleckley, 1988; Lalumiere, Harris, & Rice, 2001). Psychopaths pursue a deceptive "cheating" strategy in social interactions. Psychopathy is more common among men than women, but occurs in both sexes (Mealey, 1995). Psychopaths pursue a strategy of exploiting the cooperative proclivities of others. After feigning cooperation, psychopaths typically defect, cheat, or violate the trust. This cheating strategy might be pursued by those who are unlikely to out-compete others in more mainstream or traditional social hierarchies (Mealey, 1995).

According to one evolutionary theory, a psychopathic strategy can be maintained by frequency-dependent selection. As the number of cheaters increases, and hence the average cost to the cooperative hosts increases, adaptations will evolve in cooperators to detect and punish cheating, thus lowering its overall effectiveness (Price, Cosmides, & Tooby, 2002). As psychopaths get detected and punished, the average success of the strategy declines. As long as the frequency of psychopaths is not too large, however, it can be maintained in a population composed primarily of cooperators.

There is some empirical evidence consistent with this theory. First, behavioral genetic studies suggest that psychopathy is moderately heritable (Willerman, Loehlin, & Horn, 1992). Second, psychopaths often pursue an exploitative sexual strategy, which could be the primary route by which genes for psychopathy increase or are maintained (Rowe, 2001). Psychopathic men, for example, tend to be more sexually precocious, have sex with more women, have more illegitimate children, and be more likely to get divorced if they marry other than nonpsychopathic men (Rowe, 2001). This short-term exploitative sexual strategy would increase in populations marked by high geographic mobility, in which the costs to reputation are often avoided (Buss, 2012). This leads to the alarming idea that we may be witnessing an increase in psychopaths in modern times as society becomes increasingly geographically mobile. Evidence supports the frequency-dependent theory of this individual difference cluster—that it is part of normal personality variation and is not due to "pathology" (Lalumiere, Harris, & Rice, 2001). In sum, individual differences in this cluster of personality traits—unreliability, egocentrism, impulsivity, superficial social charm, and a deficit in empathy and other social emotions—may originate evolutionarily from frequency-dependent selection.

The most recent effort to explore individual differences from the perspective of frequency-dependent selection focuses on *life history strategy* (Figueredo et al., 2005a, 2005b, 2012; Gladden, Figueredo, & Jacobs, 2009). According to this approach, individuals have evolved differences in the effort they allocate to reproductively relevant problems, such as survival, mating, and parenting. The core idea is that there are trade-offs among these problems. Effort allocated to mating, for example, is effort taken away from parenting. On one end of the continuum, individuals favor what is called a *K-strategy*—greater effort is allocated to survival and heavy parenting over effort allocated to obtaining many mates (van der Linden, 2012). These high-K individuals are hypothesized to have strong attachments to their biological parents, avoid risk taking that would imperil survival, pursue long-term mating, and invest heavily in children. Low-K individuals are hypothesized to form weaker attachments to their biological parents, have a risk-taking personality, pursue short-term mating, and invest little in their children. Some empirical research supports the hypothesis that these variables do indeed covary or cluster together (Figueredo et al., 2005b; Gladden et al., 2009; Templer, 2008). Others have criticized this theory on conceptual grounds (e.g., Penke et al., 2007). And other researchers have evidence that exposure to harsh environments during childhood is linked with pursuing a fast life history strategy marked by risk taking and short-term mating (Chua et al., 2016).

In sum, we have examined several ways in which evolutionary psychologists study individual differences that might be adaptively patterned. First, different environments can direct individuals into different strategies, as in the case of father absence directing individuals toward a short-term sexual strategy. Second, there can be adaptive self-assessment of heritable traits, as is the case when individuals who are muscular in body build pursue a more aggressive strategy than those who are skinny. Third, two heritable strategies can be supported by frequency-dependent selection.

Fourth, the forces of selection can be different in different places or different times. This can result in evolved individual differences caused by different evolutionary selection pressures in different local ecologies. Although no individual differences in personality have yet been definitively traced to this particular evolutionary source, it remains a viable theoretical possibility in the evolutionary arsenal of explanatory options.

The Big Five, Motivation, and Evolutionarily Relevant Adaptive Problems

Evolutionary psychologists have attempted to understand the importance of the Big Five personality dispositions within an evolutionary framework (Buss, 1991b, 1996; Buss & Greiling, 1999; Denissen & Penke, 2008a; Ellis, Simpson, & Campbell, 2002; Nettle, 2006). One approach views stable individual differences on the five-factor model as individual differences in "motivational reactions," or solutions, to particular classes of adaptive problems (Buss, 2009a; Denissen & Penke, 2008a, 2008b; Ellis, Simpson, & Campbell, 2002; Nettle, 2006). Thus, Agreeableness reflects differences in the proclivity to cooperate versus to act selfishly in conflicts over resources. Emotional Stability reflects differences in sensitivity to the adaptive problem of social exclusion; high neuroticism, for example, can be beneficial in causing increased vigilance to social danger but at a cost of increased stress and depression (Nettle, 2006; Tamir, Robinson, & Solberg, 2006). Extraversion reflects pursuit of a risk-taking social strategy marked by success in short-term mating versus adopting a more stable family life marked by long-term mating (Nettle, 2006). Conscientiousness reflects a long-term strategy of delayed gratification and goal pursuit versus an impulsive strategy marked by grabbing immediate adaptive benefits.

Heritable individual differences on these dimensions can be maintained in the population because different levels are adaptive under different conditions; the optimum level varies over time and space. In technical terms, these personality differences are maintained by **balancing selection** (Penke, Denissen, & Miller, 2007), which occurs when genetic variation is maintained by selection because different levels on a trait dimension are adaptive in different environments.

A complementary evolutionary approach is to conceptualize major factors of personality as clusters of the most important features of the "adaptive landscape" of other people (Buss, 1991b, 2011). Humans, according to this perspective, have evolved "difference-detecting mechanisms" designed to notice and remember individual differences that have the most relevance for solving social adaptive problems. Specifically, the five factors may provide important answers to questions such as these:

- Who is likely to rise in the social hierarchy and hence gain access to status and position in the social hierarchy? *(Dominance, Extraversion)*
- Who is likely to be a good cooperator and reciprocator, and who will be a loyal friend or romantic partner? *(Agreeableness)*
- Who will be reliable and dependable in times of need and work industriously to provide resources? *(Conscientiousness)*
- Who will drain my resources, encumber me with their problems, monopolize my time, and fail to cope well with adversity? *(Emotional Instability)*
- Who can I go to for sage advice? *(Openness, Intellect)*

Ellis, Simpson, and Campbell (2002) developed a theoretical synthesis of the Big Five and evolutionary psychology and conducted studies to see whether positioning on the five factors was correlated with these adaptively relevant individual differences. They included two additional individual differences that are relevant to romantic relationships: physical attractiveness (a sign of health and fertility) and physical prowess (a sign of the ability to protect a friend or romantic partner from danger). Using factor analysis, they discovered that the Big Five were indeed closely linked with solutions to these critical adaptive problems. In romantic relationships, those who were high on Agreeableness, for example, were also judged to be highly cooperative, devoted to their partners, and in love with their partners. Those who were high on Extraversion were also judged to be socially ascendant, taking leadership roles in the group, and showing proclivities to elevate themselves in social hierarchies. People highly responsible and efficient (signs of Conscientiousness) were dependable in times of need, were well organized, and showed good potential for future earning.

This study is just the start of exploring the five-factor model within an evolutionary framework. But it does highlight the important point that individual differences of people who inhabit one's social environment are adaptively consequential. It is reasonable to hypothesize that humans have evolved psychological sensitivities to noticing, detecting, naming, and remembering precisely those individual differences that are most relevant to solving critical social adaptive problems—problems ultimately linked to survival and reproduction.

Limitations of Evolutionary Psychology

Like all approaches to personality, the evolutionary perspective carries a number of important limitations. First, adaptations are forged over the long expanse of thousands or millions of generations, and we cannot go back in time and determine with absolute certainty what the precise selective forces on humans have been. Scientists make inferences about past environments and past selection pressures. Nonetheless, our current mechanisms provide windows for viewing the past. Our fear of snakes and heights, for example, suggests that these were hazards in our evolutionary past. Humans seem to come into the world prepared to learn some things quite easily (e.g., fear of snakes, spiders, and strangers) (Seligman & Hager, 1972). Intense male sexual jealousy suggests that uncertain paternity was an adaptive problem in our evolutionary past. The intense pain we feel on being ostracized from a group suggests that group membership was critical to survival and reproduction in our evolutionary past. Learning more and more about our evolved mechanisms is thus a major tool for overcoming the limitation of sparse knowledge of the environments of our ancestors.

A second limitation is that evolutionary scientists have just scratched the surface of understanding the nature and design features of evolved psychological adaptations. In the case of jealousy, for example, there is a lack of knowledge about the range of cues that trigger it, the precise nature of the thoughts and emotions that are activated when a person is jealous, and the range of behaviors, such as vigilance and violence, that are manifest outcomes. More research will ultimately circumvent this limitation.

A third limitation is that modern conditions differ from ancestral conditions in many respects. What was adaptive in the past might not be adaptive in the present. Ancestral humans lived in small groups of perhaps 50 to 150 in the context of close extended kin (Dunbar, 1993). Today we live in large cities in the context of thousands of strangers. Thus, it's important to keep in mind that selection pressures have changed. In this sense, humans can be said to live in the modern world with an ancient brain.

A fourth limitation is that it is sometimes easy to come up with different and competing evolutionary hypotheses for the same phenomena. To a large extent, this is true of all of science, including personality theories that do not invoke evolutionary explanations. The existence of competing theories is not an embarrassment but rather is an essential element of science. The critical obligation of scientists is to render their hypotheses in a precise manner so that specific empirical predictions can be derived from them.

In this way, the competing theories can be pitted against each other, and the hard hand of empirical evidence can be used to evaluate the competing theories.

Finally, evolutionary hypotheses have sometimes been accused of being untestable and hence unfalsifiable. The specific evolutionary hypotheses on aggression, jealousy, and so on presented in this chapter illustrate that this accusation is certainly false for some of them (see **Buss, 2019**, for others). Nonetheless, some evolutionary hypotheses (like some standard "social" hypotheses) have indeed been framed in ways that are too vague to be of much scientific value. The solution to this problem is to hold the same high scientific standards for all competing theories. To be scientifically useful, theories and hypotheses should be framed as precisely as possible, along with attendant predictions, so that empirical studies can be conducted to test their merits.

SUMMARY AND EVALUATION

Selection is the primary key to evolution, or change in life forms over time. Variants that lead to greater survival, reproduction, or the reproductive success of genetic relatives tend to be preserved and spread through the population.

Evolutionary psychology starts with three fundamental premises. First, adaptations are presumed to be domain specific; they are designed to solve specific adaptive problems. Adaptations good for one adaptive problem, such as food selection, offer little help in solving other adaptive problems, such as mate selection. Second, adaptations are numerous, corresponding to the many adaptive problems humans have faced over evolutionary history. Third, adaptations are functional. We cannot understand them unless we figure out what they were designed to do—the adaptive problems they evolved to solve.

The empirical science of testing evolutionary hypotheses proceeds in two ways. First, middle-level evolutionary theories, such as the theory of parental investment and sexual selection, can be used to derive specific predictions in a top-down method of investigation. Second, we can observe a phenomenon and then develop a theory about its function in a process known as bottom-up investigation. Specific predictions are then derived, based on the hypothesis, about phenomena not yet observed.

Evolutionary psychological analysis can be applied to all three levels of personality analysis: human nature, sex differences, and individual differences. At the level of human nature, there is good evidence that people have evolved the need to belong to groups; to help specific others, such as genetic relatives; and to possess basic emotions, such as happiness, disgust, anger, fear, surprise, sadness, and contempt. Disgust is a universal human emotion that functions to avoid disease vectors, including contaminated food and disease-infected people. At the level of sex differences, men and women diverge only in domains in which they have faced recurrently different adaptive problems over evolutionary history. Examples include proclivities toward violence and aggression, desire for sexual variety, events that trigger jealousy, and specific mate preferences for qualities such as physical appearance and resources.

Individual differences can be understood from an evolutionary perspective using several approaches. First, individual differences can result from different environmental inputs into species-typical mechanisms. Second, individual differences can be contingent on other traits, such as when being large and strong inclines one to an aggressive disposition, whereas being small and weak inclines one to be less aggressive. Third, individual differences can result from frequency-dependent selection. Fourth, individual differences can be caused by variations over time or space in the optimum value for a trait.

The Big Five personality dispositions have begun to be examined through the lens of evolutionary psychology. One approach is to view individual differences as variations in strategic solutions to adaptive problems. Agreeableness, for example, reflects individual differences in adopting a strategy of cooperation versus acting selfishly when there are conflicts over resources. Emotional Instability reflects high levels of vigilance to social threats, which can be adaptive under some circumstances but carries a cost of high levels of stress and fatigue. These adaptive individual differences can be maintained by *balancing selection,* which occurs when genetic variation is maintained by selection because different levels on a trait dimension are adaptive in different environments.

A second approach proposes that evaluating other people on the five factors provides adaptively relevant information to solving key problems of social living: Whom can I trust for cooperation, devotion, and reciprocation (those high on Agreeableness)? Who is likely to ascend social hierarchies (those high on Extraversion)? Who will be likely to work hard, be dependable, and accrue resources over time (those high on Conscientiousness)? Future evolutionary research will undoubtedly explore individual differences in the social adaptive problems humans face in the context of group living.

Evolutionary psychology has several critical limitations at this stage of scientific development. The first is the lack of precise knowledge about the environments in which humans evolved and the selection pressures our ancestors faced. We are also limited in our knowledge about the nature, details, and workings of evolved mechanisms, including the features that trigger their activation and the manifest behavior that they produce as output. Nonetheless, the evolutionary perspective adds a useful set of theoretical tools to the analysis of personality at the levels of human nature, sex differences, and individual differences.

KEY TERMS

natural selection 224
hostile forces of nature 224
sexual selection 225
intrasexual competition 225
intersexual selection 225
genes 226
differential gene reproduction 226
inclusive fitness theory 226
adaptive problem 227
xenophobia 228

byproducts of adaptations 228
evolutionary byproducts 228
evolutionary noise 228
domain specific 229
functionality 229
deductive reasoning approach 231
inductive reasoning approach 231
social anxiety 232
evolutionary-predicted sex
    differences 239

effective polygyny 240
sexually dimorphic 240
reactively heritable 250
frequency-dependent selection 251
restricted sexual strategy 251
unrestricted mating strategy 252
psychopathy 252
balancing selection 254

The Intrapsychic Domain

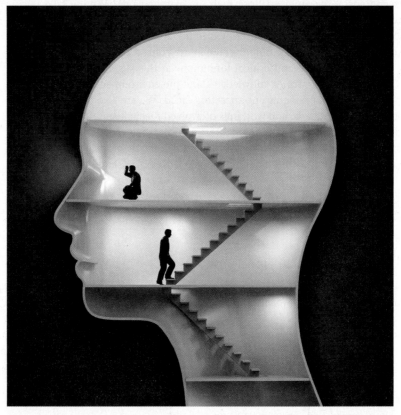

We now turn to the intrapsychic domain. This domain concerns the factors within the mind that influence behavior, thoughts, and feelings. The pioneer of this domain was Sigmund Freud. Freud was a medical doctor and neurologist and was highly influenced by biology. He often applied biological metaphors to the mind—for example, proposing that the mind had separate "organ systems," which operated independently from each other yet that influenced each other. His goal was to analyze the elements within the mind and describe how the elements worked together. He named this enterprise psychoanalysis, which refers both to his intrapsychic theory of personality and his method of helping people change.

In this domain, we devote two chapters to psychoanalysis. In Chapter 9, we cover the foundations

of classical psychoanalysis, primarily in terms of Freud's original ideas and formulations. We will present Freud's most influential contributions including the notion that the human mind is divided into two parts, the part we are aware of (the conscious part) and the part we are not aware of (the unconscious part). Moreover, Freud proposed three forces in the human mind—the id, the ego, and the superego—and these forces were constantly interacting over taming the twin motives of sex and aggression, or the life and death instincts. We also present Freud's ideas on personality development and how he stressed the importance of childhood events in determining the adult personality. Besides introducing a psychoanalytic theory of personality, Freud also developed a system of helping people change their personalities. This form of psychotherapy, called psychoanalysis, is also described in this chapter.

Some of Freud's ideas, such as repression, unconscious processing, and recalled memories, have stood the test of time and are active research topics in personality today. However, many students of Freud have modified some of his ideas, so we devote Chapter 10 to a discussion of contemporary topics in psychoanalytic theory. These include the idea of personality development as continuing through adulthood rather than stopping in childhood as Freud originally proposed. Another key development in contemporary psychoanalysis concerns the importance of a child's attachments to caregivers in influencing his or her subsequent relationships.

The intrapsychic domain differs from all the other domains in that it is concerned with the forces within the mind that work together and interact with each other and the environment. To some extent, this domain is similar

to the biological domain in that the biological domain also emphasizes forces within the person. However, in the intrapsychic domain, the concern is with aspects of *psychic* functioning. In the biological domain, we are concerned with aspects of *physical* functioning, such as the brain, genes, and the chemicals in the bloodstream.

One fundamental assumption of psychologists working in the intrapsychic domain is that there are areas of the mind that are outside awareness. Within each person, there is a part of him- or herself that even he or she does not know about. This is called the unconscious mind. Moreover, according to classical psychoanalysis, the unconscious mind is thought to have a life of its own, with its own motivation, its own will, and its own energy. According to Freud, when people have mental problems like depression or anxiety, the cause can likely be found in their unconscious.

Another assumption within the intrapsychic domain is that most things do not happen by chance. That is, every behavior, every thought, and every experience means something or reveals something about the person's personality. A slip of the tongue, for example, occurs not by accident, but because of an intrapsychic conflict. A person forgets someone's name not by accident, but because of something about the person whose name cannot be remembered. Or a person dreams of flying, not because dreams are random, but because of an unconscious wish or desire being expressed in the dream. Everything a person does, says, or feels has meaning and can be analyzed in terms of intrapsychic elements and forces.

In Chapter 11, we examine work on motivational aspects of personality. Here psychologists emphasize the common motives that most people

have to varying degrees. Individual differences in motives help psychologists answer the question "Why do people want what they want?" The three most common motives studied in this domain are the need to achieve, the need to have close relationships with other people, and the need to have power and influence over others. We present some of the basic findings on each of these three motives, as well as describe a projective technique that has been developed for assessing these needs. We also describe a contemporary notion that suggests that motives can be conscious or unconscious and that unconscious motives affect different kinds of behavior than conscious motives.

Most of the research on motives emphasizes deficit motives—that is, motives that arise because something is lacking. There is, however, the notion that one particular motive is not based on a deficit, but rather is based on growth and change. This motive refers to the more abstract need to become who we are, to actualize our potential as the persons we were meant to be. The need to self-actualize can also operate outside awareness, and we may engage in certain behaviors, not because we have thought everything through, but because it just feels like the right thing to be doing at the moment.

In Part 3 of this book, we explore some of the major ideas and findings from the intrapsychic domain of personality. As you read, it is important to keep in mind that the intrapsychic domain, as well as all the other domains, refers to just one set of factors that influence personality. Personality is determined by many factors; like a jigsaw puzzle, it is made up of many parts. Let's now consider the part that dwells in the deeper reaches of the human mind.

Science Photo Library RF/Getty Images

Psychoanalytic Approaches to Personality

9

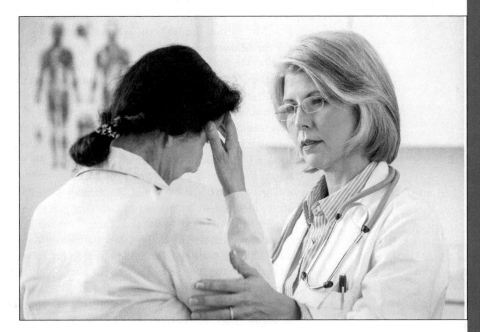

Events from childhood often form the topics for discussion during therapy sessions.
Blend Images/Alamy Stock Photo

The following seven paragraphs describe an incident of childhood sexual abuse.

Dr. Ross Cheit is a professor of political science and international and public affairs at Brown University. In 1992, he received a phone call from his sister, saying that his nephew had joined a boys' choir, just as Professor Cheit had done when he was a boy. Instead of being happy at the news that his nephew was following in his footsteps, Professor Cheit was strangely unhappy. Over the next few weeks, Professor Cheit became increasingly depressed and irritable and began to have marital difficulties. He did not connect any of his troubles to the phone call from his sister.

Shortly thereafter, Professor Cheit recalled a memory of a man he had not seen or thought about for 25 years. The man he remembered was William Farmer. Mr. Farmer had been a staff member at the San Francisco Boys Chorus summer camp, which Professor Cheit had attended between the ages of 10 and 13. Professor Cheit was now 38, and for the first time in 25 years he was recalling how Mr. Farmer would come into his cabin at night, sit on his bed, and begin stroking his chest and then his stomach, and then reach into his pajamas.

Intent on gathering objective information about his abuse, Professor Cheit hired a private investigator. The director of the boys' chorus at the time Professor Cheit was there, Madi Bacon, now 87 years old, was located in Berkeley. When Professor Cheit first talked to her and mentioned Farmer's name, she spontaneously remarked how she had almost had to fire Farmer for "hobnobbing" with the boys. For the first time, Professor Cheit felt that his memory of being molested was authentic. Moreover, after talking with Madi Bacon, he realized that he might not have been the only young boy abused by Farmer.

Using chorus records, Professor Cheit located dozens of the 118 boys who had been at camp with him 25 years earlier. In contacting them, he soon found that others had been molested by Mr. Farmer but had kept quiet. A professor at a university in Michigan, a librarian in the Midwest, and a homeless man living in San Francisco—all had allegedly been abused by Mr. Farmer. The camp nurse at the time recalled catching Mr. Farmer in bed with a sick child in the camp infirmary. The nurse claims to have reported the incident to the camp director, Madi Bacon, who took no action. Professor Cheit obtained documentation that, on at least four occasions, the camp director was informed of molestation of the boys by staff members but took no steps to address the problem.

Now more sure than ever that his memory of abuse was authentic, Professor Cheit wanted to talk directly with Mr. Farmer, who was finally located in the tiny town of Scio, Oregon. Professor Cheit phoned him. Mr. Farmer had no trouble remembering Professor Cheit as one of the boys in summer camp 25 years earlier. "What can I do for you?" Farmer inquired. "You can tell me whether you have any remorse for what you did to me and the other boys at summer camp," replied Professor Cheit. With a tape recorder running, Professor Cheit kept Mr. Farmer on the phone for nearly an hour. Mr. Farmer admitted molesting Professor Cheit in his cabin at night, and he acknowledged that the camp director had known of the abuse but had allowed him to stay on at the camp. He also admitted that he had since lost other jobs for molesting children and conceded that he knew the acts he had committed with children were criminal.

On August 19, 1993, Professor Cheit and his parents filed a lawsuit against the San Francisco Boys Chorus, charging that the chorus had "negligently or intentionally" allowed staff members to molest children in its care. Lawyers for the chorus at first denied the charges. Professor Cheit's lawsuit asked the Boys Chorus to meet three conditions: to apologize, thereby admitting guilt; to institute protective measures for current campers; and to pay $450,000 to Professor Cheit as financial compensation. During the litigation, Professor Cheit produced five corroborating witnesses and the tape-recorded admission from Mr. Farmer himself. Just over a year later, the lawsuit was settled. The boys chorus agreed to apologize to Professor Cheit, to put safeguards in place to protect present chorus members from possible molestation, and to pay Professor Cheit $35,000.

Professor Cheit was fortunate in that the state of California had just changed its statute of limitations laws, allowing for criminal charges of child abuse to be filed any time within three years of the time that the alleged victim *remembered* the abuse, with independent corroboration. On July 12, 1994, Mr. Farmer was arrested at his home, then in Texas, and extradited to Plumas County, California, the site of the Boys Chorus camp. According to the county district attorney, Mr. Farmer was charged with six counts of child molestation involving three boys, including Professor Cheit, in 1967 and 1968. Mr. Farmer was charged with committing crimes over a quarter of a century earlier. He pleaded not guilty. The details of this fascinating case are discussed in several books, including Chu (1998) and Schachter (1997).

Professor Cheit is currently on the faculty at Brown University, where he is a Professor of International and Public Affairs and Political Science. He is also a board director of the Center for Institutional Courage. He maintains various social media accounts. He has authored several important papers and book chapters about childhood sexual abuse (e.g., Cheit, Shavit, & Reiss-Davis, 2010) and motivated forgetting (e.g., DePrince et al., 2012). In 2014 Professor Cheit published a major book about social and legal responses to contested cases of childhood sexual abuse in America.

Is it possible that a person can forget something as traumatic as sexual abuse? Can a forgotten memory lie dormant for years, only to be aroused later by an event, such as a chance phone call? Once aroused, can such a memory cause a person to start having symptoms, such as feelings of depression and irritability, without his or her knowing the cause of those difficulties? Some psychologists believe that people sometimes are unaware of the reasons for their own problematic behaviors. When treating a person for a psychological problem, some therapists believe that the cause of the problem resides in the person's unconscious, the part of the mind outside the person's immediate awareness. They contend that a memory of a past traumatic event can be completely forgotten yet nevertheless cause a psychological problem years later (Bass & Davis, 1988). This reasoning has led many states, such as California, to place the statute of limitations on child abuse at three years from when the abuse is *remembered* by the person. Furthermore, such therapists believe that if they can help make this unconscious memory conscious—that is, if they can help the patient recall a forgotten traumatic memory—they can put the patient on the road to recovery (Baker, 1992).

This perspective on the causes and cures of psychological problems has its origin in a theory of personality developed by Sigmund Freud (1856–1939), commonly called psychoanalysis. In this chapter, we examine the basic elements of classical psychoanalytic theory and explore some of the empirical studies conducted to test certain aspects of the theory. We consider the scientific evidence for the repression of childhood memories, for the concept of unconscious motivation, and for other aspects of psychoanalytic theory. Whereas many of Freud's ideas have not stood the test of time, other ideas are still with us and are topics of contemporary research. Because this theory is so much the result of one person's thinking, let's first look at a brief biographical sketch of Freud.

Sigmund Freud: A Brief Biography

Although Freud was born in 1856 in Freiberg, Moravia (now part of the Czech Republic), his family moved to Vienna when he was 4 years old, and he spent virtually the remainder of his life there. Freud excelled in school and obtained his medical degree from the University of Vienna. Although he started out as a researcher in neurology, he realized that he could make more money to support his wife and growing family if he entered into private medical practice. After studying hypnosis with Jean-Martin Charcot in Paris, Freud returned to Vienna and started a private practice, treating patients with "nervous disorders." During that time, Freud began developing the idea that portions of the human mind were outside conscious awareness. The unconscious is the part of the mind about which the conscious mind has no awareness. Freud sought to explore the implications of the unconscious for understanding people's lives and their problems with living. From his early contact with patients, Freud began to surmise that the unconscious mind operated under its own power, subject to its own motivations and according to its own logic. Freud devoted the rest of his life to exploring the nature and logic of the unconscious mind.

Freud's first solo-authored book, *The Interpretation of Dreams,* was published in 1900. In it, he described how the unconscious mind was expressed in dreams and how dreams contained clues to our innermost secrets, desires, and motives. The analysis of dreams became a cornerstone of his treatment of patients. This book sold poorly at first but nevertheless attracted the attention of other medical doctors seeking to understand psychological problems. By 1902, there was a small group of followers (e.g., Alfred Adler) who met with Freud every Wednesday evening. At these meetings, Freud talked about his theory,

Sigmund Freud at age 82. This photo was taken upon his arrival in London after fleeing from the Nazi invasion of Austria. While he set up an office and began seeing patients in London, he was gravely ill with cancer of the jaw and throat.
Keystone/Getty Images

shared insights, and discussed patients' progress, all the while smoking one of the 20 or so cigars he smoked each day. During this period, Freud was systematically building his theory and testing its acceptance by knowledgeable peers. By 1908, the membership of the Wednesday Psychological Circle had grown significantly, prompting Freud to form the Vienna Psychoanalytic Society (Grosskurth, 1991).

In 1909, Freud made his only visit to the United States, to present a series of lectures on psychoanalysis at the invitation of psychologist G. Stanley Hall, who was then president of Clark University. Rosenzweig (1994) describes Freud's trip to the United States in fascinating detail. In 1910, the International Psychoanalytic Association was formed, and in 1911 the American Psychoanalytic Association was formed, with Freud's support. Freud's theories were gaining recognition around the world and in the United States.

Freud and his work drew both praise and criticism. Whereas some accepted his ideas as brilliant insights into the workings of the human mind, others opposed his views on various scientific and ideological grounds. To some, his treatment approach (the so-called talking cure) was absurd. Freud's theory that the adult personality was a result of how the person as a child coped with his or her sexual and aggressive urges was considered politically incorrect by the standards of Victorian morality. Even some of the founding members of his Vienna Psychoanalytic Society grew to disagree with developments in his theory. Nevertheless, Freud continued to refine and apply his theory, writing 20 books and numerous papers during his career.

Germany invaded Austria in 1938, and the Nazis began their persecution of the Jews there. Freud, who was Jewish, had reasons to fear the Nazis. The Nazi party burned his books and the books of other modern intellectuals. With the assistance of wealthy patrons, Freud, his wife, and their six children fled to London. Freud died the following year after a long, painful, and disfiguring battle with cancer of the jaw and throat.

Freud's London house continued to be occupied by his daughter, Anna Freud, herself a prominent psychoanalyst, until her death in 1982. The house is now part of the Freud Museum in London. Visitors can walk through Freud's library and study, which remain largely as he left them when he died. The study, which is where Freud treated his patients, still contains his celebrated couch, covered with an Oriental rug. It also contains the many ancient artifacts and small statues and icons that seemed to fascinate him and reveal his passion for archeology. Freud has been referred to as an archeologist of the human mind.

Fundamental Assumptions of Psychoanalytic Theory

Freud's model of human nature relied on the notion of **psychic energy** to motivate all human activity. What were the forces that motivated people to do one thing and not another or that motivated people to do anything at all? Freud proposed a source of energy that is within each person and used the term *psychic energy* to refer to this wellspring of motivation. Freud believed that psychic energy operated according to the law of conservation of energy: The amount of psychic energy an individual possessed remained constant throughout his or her lifetime. Personality change was viewed as a redirection of a person's psychic energy.

Basic Instincts: Sex and Aggression

What was the source of all psychic energy? Freud believed that there were strong innate forces that provided *all* the energy in the psychic system. He called these forces **instincts.** Freud's original theory of instincts was profoundly influenced by Darwin's theory of evolution. Darwin had published his book on evolution just a few years after Freud was born. In Freud's initial formulation, there were two fundamental categories of instincts: self-preservation instincts and sexual instincts. Curiously, these corresponded exactly to two major components of Darwin's theory of natural selection: selection by survival and selection by reproduction. Thus Freud's initial classification of instincts could have been borrowed from Darwin's two forms of evolution by selection (Ritvo, 1990).

In his later formulations, however, Freud collapsed the self-preservation and sexual instincts into one, which he called the life instinct. And due in part to his witnessing the horrors of World War I, he developed the idea of a death instinct. Freud postulated that humans had a fundamental instinct toward destruction and that this instinct was often manifest in aggression toward others. The two instincts were usually referred to as **libido** for the life instinct and **thanatos** for the death instinct. Although the libido was generally considered sexual, Freud also used this term to refer to any need-satisfying, life-sustaining, or pleasure-oriented urge. Similarly, thanatos was considered to be the death instinct, but Freud used this term in a broad sense to refer to any urge to destroy, harm, or aggress against others or oneself. Freud wrote more about the libido early in his career, when this issue was perhaps relevant to his own life. Later in his career, Freud wrote more about thanatos, when he faced his own impending death.

Although Freud initially believed that the life and death instincts worked to oppose one another, he later argued that they could combine in various ways. Consider the act of eating. Eating obviously serves the life instinct, entailing the consumption of nutrients necessary for survival. At the same time, eating also involves acts of tearing, biting, and chewing, which Freud thought could be seen as aggressive manifestations of thanatos. As another example, Freud viewed rape as an expression of extreme death instinct, directed toward another person in a manner that is fused with sexual energy. The combination of erotic and aggressive instincts into a single motive is a particularly volatile mixture.

Because each person possesses a fixed amount of psychic energy, according to Freud, the energy used to drive one type of behavior is not available to drive other types of behaviors. The person who directs his or her death instinct into a socially acceptable channel, such as competitive sports, has less energy to expend toward more destructive manifestations of this instinct. Because psychic energy exists in a fixed and limited amount within each person, it can be directed and redirected in various ways. But it is always a zero-sum system, meaning that the more energy used for one behavior, the less available for another behavior.

Unconscious Motivation: Sometimes We Don't Know Why We Do What We Do

According to Freud, the human mind consists of three parts. The **conscious** mind is the part that contains all the thoughts, feelings, and perceptions that you are presently aware of. Whatever you are currently perceiving or thinking about is in your conscious mind. These thoughts represent only a small fraction of the information available to you.

You also have a vast number of memories, ideas, pieces of information, and thoughts that you could easily bring to mind if you so desired. What were you wearing yesterday? What was the name of your best friend in senior year of high school? What is

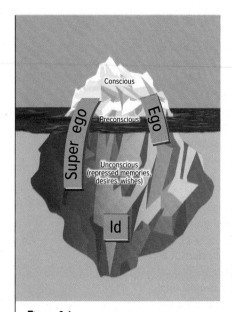

Figure 9.1

The iceberg metaphor of the human mind; the conscious part is what is above the waterline, the preconscious is what is below water but still visible from above, and the unconscious, the largest part, is that part hidden well below the surface.

the earliest memory you have of your mother? This information is stored in the **preconscious** mind. Any piece of information that you are not presently thinking about, but that could be retrieved and made conscious with some effort, is found in the preconscious mind.

The **unconscious** is the third and, according to Freud, largest part of the human mind. Residing in the unconscious mind is unacceptable information hidden from conscious view so well that it cannot even be considered preconscious. A person cannot just bring some unconscious memory into conscious experience. What is stored in the unconscious are secrets that even the person him- or herself cannot access. Those memories, feelings, thoughts, or urges are so troubling or even distasteful or frightening that being aware of them would overwhelm the person. For Freud, the unconscious is the largest and most important part of the human mind. And the form of psychotherapy developed by Freud was a collection of techniques designed to discover what is in the patient's unconscious and help the person cope with that in a mature adult fashion. Many of the cases reported in the psychoanalytic literature involve distressing unconscious themes—such as incest (real or desired); hatred toward siblings, parents, or spouses; and memories of childhood traumas.

The metaphor of an iceberg is often used to describe the topography of the mind according to Freud. The part of the iceberg above the water represents the conscious mind. The part that you can see just below the water surface is the preconscious mind. And the part of the iceberg totally hidden from view (the vast majority of it) represents the unconscious mind. See Figure 9.1.

Society does not allow people to express freely all of their sexual and aggressive instincts. Individuals must learn to control their urges. One way to control these urges, according to Freud, is to keep them from entering conscious awareness in the first place. Consider a child who has gotten extremely angry with a parent. This child might have a fleeting wish that the parents die. Such thoughts would be very distressing to a child—so distressing that they might be held back from conscious awareness and banished instead to the unconscious—the part of the mind holding thoughts and memories about which the person is unaware. All kinds of unacceptable sexual and aggressive urges, thoughts, and feelings might accumulate in the unconscious during the course of a typical childhood.

Exercise

Think back to the first house or apartment you lived in as a child. If you are like most people, you can probably remember as far back as your fourth or fifth year of age. Try to recall the structure of the house or apartment, the location of the rooms relative to each other. Draw a floor plan, starting with the basement if there was one, then the first floor, then the upstairs rooms (if the house had a second floor). On your floor plan, label each room. Now think about each room, letting the memories of events that happened in each of them come back to you. It is likely that you will recall some people and events that you have not thought about for a decade or more. You also might notice that many of your memories have an emotional quality; some memories are pleasant, whereas others are unpleasant. The memories that you can bring to conscious awareness are in your preconscious. You may have memories of events that occurred that do not come back to you during this exercise because they are in your unconscious.

Psychic Determinism: Nothing Happens by Chance

Freud maintained that nothing happens by chance or by accident. There is a reason behind every act, thought, and feeling. Everything we do, think, say, and feel is an expression of the mind—the conscious, preconscious, or unconscious mind. In his 1904 book *The Psychopathology of Everyday Life,* Freud introduced the idea that the little "accidents" of daily life are often expressions of the **motivated unconscious,** such as calling someone by the wrong name, missing an appointment, and breaking something that belongs to another. Slips of the tongue (also known by linguists as parapraxis) were thought by Freud to be examples of the unconscious breaking through into conscious speech. Such verbal blunders, he held, can bring to light some element of the unconscious that they person normally keeps hidden from themselves. Freud analyzed several verbal "mistakes" in his writings, and so today they are sometimes called "Freudian slips." Oftentimes such verbal mistakes are caught and called out by the media. For example, Texas Republican Dick Armey once referred to the openly homosexual congressman from Massachusetts, Barney Frank, as "Barney Fag." Once, a psychology professor referred to Sigmund Freud as "Sigmund Fraud." Another psychology professor, in her introductory lecture, said: "Psychology is the study of the individual orgasm . . ., uh, organism . . . ." Such mix-ups can often be embarrassing, but, according to Freud, they portray the motivated and autonomous activity of the unconscious breaking through. There is a reason for every slip of the tongue, for being late, for forgetting a person's name, and for breaking something that belongs to another. The reasons can be discovered if the contents of the unconscious can be examined.

Freud taught that most symptoms of mental illnesses are also caused by unconscious material. He held that every psychological problem—from depression to obsessions to sexual dysfunction—had as its root cause some form of unconscious motivation. Freud provided detailed case histories of 12 patients, as well as dozens of shorter discussions of specific patients. In these case studies, he found support for his theory that psychological problems were caused by unconscious memories, urges, or desires. For example, Freud wrote about the case of Anna O. Although Freud did not directly treat or even meet Anna O., her physician, Joseph Breuer, consulted with Freud on her treatment.

At the time, Anna O. was a 21-year-old woman who had fallen ill while taking care of her sick father who eventually died of tuberculosis. Anna O.'s illness began with a severe cough and later included the loss of movement in her right side, disturbances of vision and hearing, and the inability to drink liquids. Dr. Breuer diagnosed Anna O.'s illness as hysteria and developed a form of therapy that appeared effective in relieving her symptoms. This form of therapy consisted of Breuer talking with Anna O. about her symptoms and, in particular, about her memories of events that happened before the onset of the symptoms. For example, in talking about her severe cough, they talked about her memories of caring for her father and the severe cough he had from his tuberculosis. As she explored these memories, and especially her feelings toward her father and about his death, her own cough lessened and disappeared. Similarly, when talking about her inability to drink liquids (she had been quenching her thirst with fruit and melons), she suddenly recalled the memory of seeing a dog drink from a woman's glass, an incident that completely disgusted her at the time but about which she had forgotten.

To Breuer, and to Freud, hysterical symptoms did not occur by chance. Rather, they were physical expressions of traumatic experiences that were banished to the unconscious mind and forgotten. However, once in the unconscious such repressed material can come out in the form of symptoms. From the experience treating Anna O., Breuer concluded that the way to cure hysterical symptoms was to help the person recall the

A Closer Look

Examples of the Unconscious: Blindsight and Deliberation-Without-Awareness

Following an injury or stroke that damages the primary vision center in the brain, people will lose their ability to see. In this kind of blindness the eyes still work fine; it is just that the brain center responsible for object recognition fails. People who suffer this kind of "cortical" blindness often display an interesting capacity to make certain judgments about objects that they truly cannot see. This phenomenon is termed **blindsight,** and it has fascinated psychologists since it was first documented in the 1960s (Leopold, 2012). While reports of patients with blindsight increasingly appear in the literature (e.g., Burra et al., 2019; Kletenik et al., 2022), neurologists are still debating the underlying mechanism (Michel & Lau, 2021; Philips, 2021).

Imagine having a person with cortical blindness as a subject. You could hold a red ball in front of her open eyes and ask if she can see it. She would reply no, which is consistent with the fact that she is blind. Now you ask her to point to the red ball (which she has just denied seeing). What happens? She points directly to the red ball even though she does not have the ability to see it!

Blindsight is taken as evidence of the unconscious. One part of the mind knows about something that another part of the mind does not know about. There are many demonstrations of people with blindsight. For example, when an object is placed in front of a person with cortical blindness, that person can guess the color of that object at levels much better than merely by chance. In other words, such a condition illustrates that information that is

unconscious (in this case, the object's color) is actually being processed somewhere in the mind (because the person can guess the color at better than chance levels).

An explanation for such "unconscious" perception has been offered in terms of nerve pathways from the eyes into the brain. The optic nerve carries information from the eye into the brain, and the majority of this information is transferred to the primary visual center in the striate cortex at the back of the brain. However, minor pathways split off of the optic nerve before getting to the visual center and carry some of this visual information to other parts of the brain. These other centers are involved in movement recognition, color recognition, and even emotional evaluation. If the vision center were completely destroyed, the person would not recognize *what* the object was, but the person might know if it was moving, what color it is, or how he or she feels about it.

One of the most interesting and robust examples of blindsight concerns the perception of the emotional significance of something that one does not see. In one study, a person with blindsight underwent a conditioning procedure where a visual cue that the person could not see (a picture of a circle) was accompanied by an unpleasant shock, whereas other visual cues (pictures of squares, rectangles, etc.) were not paired with shock. Following a period of conditioning, the stimuli shapes were later "shown" to the blind subject, and the subject exhibited a fear response (electrodermal response) to the circle but not the squares or rectangles,

even though the subject was blind (Hamm et al., 2003). These researchers argue that emotional conditioning does not require a conscious representation of the feared object in the mind of the subject. Other studies of people with cortical blindness demonstrate that, when "shown" pictures of facial expressions, they can "guess" the emotions expressed in the faces even when they cannot see the faces being presented. Obviously, a lot of emotional processing occurs at some level in the brain that does not involve the primary visual center. People could have feelings about (i.e., like or dislike) something that they are not even aware of.

Another example of the unconscious at work concerns the phenomenon of **deliberation-without-awareness,** or the "let me sleep on it" effect. The notion here is, if a person confronted with a difficult decision can put it out of his or her conscious mind for a period of time, then the unconscious mind will continue to deliberate on it outside of the person's awareness, helping him or her to arrive at a "sudden" and often correct decision sometime later. This is called "unconscious decision making." Banks (2021) provides a modern review of unconscious thought, including deliberation outside of awareness. Other researchers demonstrate unconscious decision making among online e-commerce customers (Shen et al., 2020).

The phenomenon of unconscious decision making was the topic of several clever studies published in the prestigious journal *Science* by a team of Dutch researchers (Dijksterhuis et al., 2006). These researchers

memory of the incident that had originally led to the symptoms. By the patient's recalling the traumatic incident (e.g., her father's death), an emotional catharsis or release can be achieved by having her or him express any feelings associated with that memory. This then removes the cause of the symptom and hence the symptom disappears.

hypothesized that, for simple decisions, conscious deliberation would work best, but when decisions were complex, involving many factors, then unconscious deliberation would work best. They presented subjects with the task of deciding on the best car out of four different cars. Subjects in the simple condition considered 4 attributes of the cars, whereas subjects in the complex condition considered 12 attributes of the cars. In all cases, one car was characterized by 75 percent positive attributes (i.e., the best car), two by 50 percent positive attributes, and one by 25 percent positive attributes. After reading all the information about the cars, half of the subjects were assigned to the conscious deliberation condition and the other half were assigned to the unconscious deliberation condition. In the conscious deliberation condition, subjects were asked to think about the information for four minutes before deciding on the best car. In the unconscious deliberation condition, subjects were distracted for four minutes by being asked to solve anagram puzzles, then immediately asked to decide on the best car.

As shown in Figure 9.2, in the simple decision condition, with only 4 attributes to consider on each car, subjects who consciously deliberated made the best decisions. However, when the decision was complex, involving 12 different attributes of the cars, subjects in the "unconscious" deliberation condition made the best decisions. The authors demonstrate similar effects in three additional studies. Even though the studies concern consumer items (e.g., cars), there is reason to believe that the unconscious deliberation effect might apply to any type of decision (e.g., what career path to pursue, who to vote for, whom to marry, etc.). The authors (Dijksterhuis et al., 2006) argue that, with any decision, it would "benefit the individual to think consciously about simple matters and to delegate thinking about more complex matters to the unconscious" (p. 1007).

A recent review of the unconscious decision-making literature urges caution in interpreting results, and shows how alternative explanations (other than that the unconscious is an intelligent decision maker) can account for some findings (Newell & Shanks, 2014). However, this review leaves out several recent studies that have employed functional brain imaging to investigate unconscious decision making (Brooks & Stein, 2014). For example, one study (Creswell, Bursley, & Satpute, 2013) used brain imaging while half the subjects were consciously deliberating on a decision, and the other half were doing a distractor task and supposedly unconsciously deliberating (since they knew they would have to make a decision when finished with the distractor task). A third group just did the distractor task. When the researchers subtracted out the brain activation pattern identified in the distractor task group, from the distractor task/unconscious deliberation group, they found residual brain activation that matched the deliberation group. In other words, the group that was being distracted so they could not deliberate, nevertheless showed brain activation patterns consistent with the notion that they were in fact deliberating in one part of their brains, while other parts of their brains were occupied with the distractor task.

Research on deliberation without awareness is not without its critics (Newell & Shanks, 2014). Some have argued that the results do not prove that the subjects' "unconscious" actively arrives at the correct decision (Aczel et al., 2011). Others have argued that decisions are memory based and thus offer an explanation for the findings that do not rely on anything like an "unconscious" (Lassiter et al., 2009). As you will see throughout this chapter, much that is connected with psychoanalysis is contentious and a matter of debate. Nevertheless, psychoanalytic ideas are stimulating research into novel and interesting phenomena.

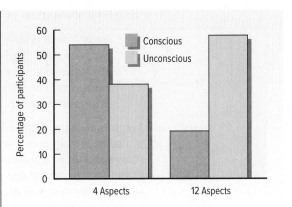

Figure 9.2

Percentage of participants who correctly chose the most desirable car as a function of complexity of decision and mode of thought.

Source: Dijksterhhuis, A., M. W. Bos, L. F. Nordgren, and R. B. van Baaren (2006). On Making the Right Choice: The Deliberation Without-attention Effect. Science, 311, 1005–1007.

Freud adopted and refined the technique developed by Breuer for effecting the "talking cure." Freud believed that for a psychological symptom to be cured, the unconscious cause of the symptom must first be discovered. Often the process involves discovering a hidden memory of an unsettling, disagreeable, or even repulsive experience that has been repressed or pushed into the unconscious (Masson, 1984). Freud always acknowledged the importance of the case of Anna O. on his thinking, and gave credit to the careful observations of Dr. Breuer:

> *If it is a merit to have brought psychoanalysis into being, that merit is not mine. I had no share in its earliest beginnings. I was a student and working for my final examinations at the time when another Viennese physician, Dr. Josef Breuer, first made use of this procedure on a girl who was suffering from hysteria. (From Freud's lectures presented at Clark University in Massachusetts, 1909.)*

Freud is uncharacteristically modest in the preceding quote. He adapted the notions of symptom formation and the talking cure from Breuer and combined these with other ideas about the unconscious, repression, stages of development, and many other notions; from these, he formulated a grand theory of personality that has yet to be rivaled by a single unitary theory of personality.

Structure of Personality

Psychoanalytic personality theory describes how people cope with their sexual and aggressive instincts within the constraints of a civilized society. Sexual and aggressive instincts often lead to drives and urges that conflict with society and with reality. One part of the mind creates these urges, another part has a sense of what civilized society expects, and another part tries to satisfy the urges within the bounds of reality and society. How is it that the mind can have so many parts, and how do these parts work together to form personality?

A metaphor may be helpful in answering this question. Think of the mind as a plumbing system, which contains water under pressure. The pressure is the metaphor for the psychic energy from the sexual and aggressive instincts, which builds up and demands release or redirection. According to Freud's theory, when it comes to this internal pressure, there are three schools of plumbing: one plumber suggests that we open all the valves at the slightest pressure, another offers ways to redirect the pressure so that the strain is relieved without making much of a mess, and the third plumber wants to keep all the valves closed. Let's discuss each of these "psychic plumbers" in some detail, using Freud's terminology.

Id: Reservoir of Psychic Energy

Freud taught in the beginning there was id, the most primitive part of the human mind. Freud saw the **id** (German for "it") as something we are born with and as the source of all drives and urges. As portrayed in Figure 9.1, the location of the id is entirely unconscious. Using the plumbing metaphor, the id is the plumber who wants to let off all pressure at the slightest hint of strain or tension. The id is like a spoiled child—selfish, impulsive, and pleasure-loving. According to Freud, the id operates according to the **pleasure principle,** which is the desire for immediate gratification. The id cannot tolerate any delays in satisfying its urges. During infancy, the id dominates. When an infant sees an attractive toy, it will reach for the toy and will cry and fuss if it cannot get it. Infants can sometimes appear unreasonable in their demands. Because the id operates according to the pleasure principle, it does not listen to reason, does not follow logic, has no values or morals (other than immediate gratification), and has very little patience.

The id also operates with **primary process thinking,** which is thinking without logical rules of conscious thought or an anchor in reality. Dreams and fantasies are examples of primary process thinking. Although primary process thought does not follow the normal rules of reality (e.g., in dreams, people fly and walk through walls), Freud believed that there were principles at work in primary process thought and that these principles could be discovered. If an urge from the id requires an external object or person, and that object or person is not available, the id may create a mental image or fantasy of that object or person to satisfy its needs. Mental energy is invested in that fantasy, and the urge is temporarily satisfied. This process is called **wish fulfillment,** whereby something unavailable is conjured up and the image of it is temporarily satisfying. Someone might be very angry, for example, but the target of the anger is too powerful to attack. In this case, engaging in wish fulfillment might produce an imagined fantasy of revenge for past wrongs. This strategy of wish fulfillment works only temporarily to gratify the id because the need is not satisfied in reality. A person must find other ways to gratify id urges or hold them in check.

Ego: Executive of Personality

The ego is the plumber who works to redirect the pressure produced by the id instincts into acceptable or at least less problematic outlets. The **ego** is the part of the mind that constrains the id to reality. According to Freud, it develops within the first two or three years of life (after the "terrible 2s"). The ego comes with self-awareness and so is located in the conscious and preconscious areas of the mind. The ego operates according to the **reality principle.** Perhaps you have heard the phrase "reality check" which comes from the notion that the ego, while trying to satisfy the id, has to take the reality of the person's situation into account, it cannot just focus on the childlike urges of the id. The ego understands that the urges of the id are often in conflict with social and physical reality. A child

In the psychoanalytic theory of personality, conflicts between children and parents are normal, necessary, and an important part of personality development.

georgerudy/123RF

A Closer Look

The Ego Depletion Controversy: Is Self-Control a Limited Resource?

In Freud's structure of the mind, the ego is that part that must deal with reality by resolving conflicts between inner and outer pressures. For example, a man walking through a "red-light" district in a city might feel the urge of his id to walk over to a prostitute, and he might simultaneously feel the urge from his superego to find a church. It is up to his ego, however, to start him moving in one direction or the other. Freud also taught that the mind is a closed energy system; the more energy used by one self-control activity, the less energy is available for other self-control activities. This implies that the psychic energy used to resolve one conflict would leave less psychic energy available for resolving subsequent conflicts.

Psychologist Baumeister and his colleagues (1998, 2007, 2018) have subjected this basic notion—that psychic energy can be depleted by efforts toward self-control, leaving less energy available for subsequent self-control situations—to a series of experimental tests. There are many studies where the findings are supportive of Freud's basic notion about the ego and psychic energy. However, the scientific literature now contains several significant failures to replicate such ego depletion effects (e.g., Hagger et al., 2016). This has led to controversy surrounding this phenomenon, making it worth a closer look. We begin by reviewing some early studies that established the ego depletion effect.

In one early experiment, participants signed up for a study on taste perception and were asked to skip a meal just prior to their session (to ensure that they would be hungry). Arriving at the laboratory,

participants were left alone in a room; on the table was a bowl of radishes and a stack of freshly baked chocolate chip cookies (Baumeister et al., 1998). One group of participants was instructed to "eat two or three radishes and avoid eating the cookies while waiting for the experiment to start." Another group was instructed to "eat two or three cookies and avoid eating the radishes." And a third group, the control group, was not exposed to any food while waiting. Following this waiting period, where presumably the "radish eating" group would have had to exercise self-control over the immediate gratification of eating some cookies, the participants then were instructed to solve a geometrical puzzle that was, unbeknown to them, impossible to solve. Participants were told that they could quit working on the puzzle at any time. Results showed that participants in the radish condition gave up on the puzzle sooner than participants in either the cookie condition or the noneating control condition. Participants in the radish condition also reported being more tired after the puzzle task than those in the cookie or noneating conditions. These findings are consistent with the psychic energy theory of **ego depletion.** In the radish condition, the participants' exertion of self-control in the face of temptation to eat cookies resulted in a decrease of psychic energy available to work on the difficult puzzle, leading them to give up sooner and report being more tired after the experiment.

Hundreds of studies have been published on ego depletion since these early studies (Baumeister, 2014). Most take the form of breaking research participants into two groups: one group performs a

self-control task, and the second group performs a similar task that does not require self-control. Next, all participants go on to perform a second, unrelated self-control task. If self-control depletes a limited psychic resource, then performing the first self-control task should deplete this groups' psychic energy, leaving less available for the second self-control task (Baumeister, Vohs, & Tice, 2007).

As research accumulated, some failures to find the ego depletion effect came to light. A paper reviewing published and unpublished studies (Carter et al., 2015) found that published studies tended to report an effect, whereas unpublished studies were less likely to find an effect. In 2016 a large replication study was reported (Hagger et al, 2016), in which 23 laboratories around the world conducted the same ego depletion experiment. The depletion manipulation (called the "e" task) was a task where subjects were presented with words on a computer screen in quick succession. Subjects had to press a button as quickly as possible if there was the letter "e" in the word. After they practiced this, the depletion subject's task was made much more difficult; they had to withhold responding to the "e" if it was next to or one letter away from a vowel. It takes a lot of effort to change strategy after a simple task is well learned, so the complicated "e" task was assumed to induce depletion by demanding effortful self-control. The control group continued with the simple "e" detection task. Both did 150 speeded trials of either the simple or complicated "e" task, which took about 7 minutes. Then a subsequent reaction time task, also requiring self-control, was used to measure ego depletion (subjects had to identify specific digits in a string of digits presented on the screen). If subject's self-control was depleted by the complicated "e" task, they should have more lapses of attention on the subsequent digit task, resulting in poorer overall performance. Across the 23 replications of this experiment, involving 2,141 subjects, the average ego depletion effect was trivial and not significantly different from zero. In other words, the experiment failed 23 times.

This significant failure to replicate the ego depletion effect has gotten a lot of attention in the field. On the one hand, it is hard to argue with the evidence; the experiment failed to find an effect 23 times. On the other hand, the replication effort has been criticized in term of procedures (run entirely on computers, using a purely cognitive task) and in terms of results. For example, a Swedish researcher (Dang, 2016) re-analyzed the replication data set (it is publicly available), controlling for how much "effort" subjects reported they put into the complicated "e" task (the depletion phase). For subjects who considered this task to demand a lot of their effort (i.e., who reported exerting a lot of effort in completing that task) an ego depletion effect was found, which is exactly what the theory of ego depletion would predict!

Commenting on the "failure to replicate" controversy, Baumeister, Tice, and Vohs (2018) make the point that laboratory experiments using simple cognitive tasks are different from everyday life, and that ego depletion can be observed outside the laboratory. For example, he cites a study (Sievertsen, Gino, & Piovesan, 2016) showing that schoolchildren's scores on standardized testing are worse if exams are administered later in the day (compared to earlier or after a break). Another

study he sites (Dai et al., 2015) showed that hospital workers were more likely to skip mandatory hand washing later in their 12-hour shifts compared to earlier in their shift. Baumeister, Tice, and Vohs (2018) conclude that ego depletion has been demonstrated enough in the lab and in the field to be taken seriously as a potential explanation for why people have difficulty with effortful self-control under conditions of depletion.

Besides studies using cold cognitive self-control tasks (e.g., letter identification), other studies in the literature have examined self-control of more id-like urges of pleasure, sex (Gailliot & Baumeister, 2007), and aggression (DeWall et al., 2007). After all, the ego's control of id urges was what Freud talked about. In one experiment on aggression, the ego depletion group had to resist the urge to eat tempting food, whereas the control group could eat as much as they wanted. Later, in a second task, the ego depletion group reacted more aggressively to an insult than did the control group (Stucke & Baumeister, 2006). In studies of sexual restraint, ego-depleted subjects were found to be less likely than a group that did not undergo ego depletion to stifle inappropriate sexual thoughts and were more likely to consider engaging in sexual activity with someone other than their primary relationship partner (Gailliot & Baumeister, 2007).

There have now been several multi-laboratory replication studies showing small to moderate effects of various ego depletion tasks (Dang et al., 2021; Vohs et al., 2021). A recent review of the literature (Forestier et al., 2022) summarizes how different laboratory definitions of self-control can lead to differing results. However, studies of real-world self-control situations, such as the online learning burden during COVID (Greene et al., 2022) or

exercise programs in the workplace (ten Brummelhuis et al., 2021), continue to demonstrate the ego depleting effects of self-control efforts.

All of us have to resist unacceptable impulses all the time: resist falling asleep in a boring class, resist eating forbidden foods, playing when we should be working, resting when we should be exercising, saying something that might hurt a relationship partner, engaging in inappropriate aggressive or sexual activities, or any one of a long list of problematic behaviors (such a list of everyday temptations, can be found in Hoffman et al., 2012, and in Hoffman, Vohs, & Baumeister, 2012). To resist these behaviors, we call upon our powers of self-control, which Freud taught was the main function of the ego.

Are we doomed to go through life with a chronically exhausted ego due to the serial temptations we encounter? Baumeister is optimistic about our self-control ability and has introduced a muscle metaphor of ego depletion (e.g., Baumeister, Vohs, & Tice, 2007). In this metaphor, self-control is like a muscle. If it is overused, it can become temporarily weak and unable to respond adequately to self-control challenges. However, like training a muscle, Baumeister believes that self-control can be strengthened over the long term through practice. People who practice mild but regular self-control in one area of life (e.g., dieting) exhibit better self-control in other areas of their lives (e.g., regular exercise). Moreover, Baumeister has identified conditions that can counteract the effects of ego depletion, including states of positive emotion and humor, forming plans for how to behave in tempting situations prior to entering them, and being guided by a strong set of social values. In Table 9.1 we list several of the key variables identified in the research on ego depletion.

(Continued)

A Closer Look (*Continued*)

Table 9.1 Key Variables Identified in Research on Ego Depletion

Responses That Require Self-Control

- Controlling thoughts
- Managing emotions
- Overcoming unwanted impulses
- Controlling attention
- Guiding behavior
- Making many choices

Behaviors That Are Sensitive to Ego Depletion

- Eating among dieters
- Overspending
- Aggression after being provoked
- Sexual thoughts, feelings, behaviors
- Logical and intelligent decision making

Social Behaviors That Demand Self-Control

- Self-presentation for impression management
- Kindness in response to bad behavior
- Dealing with demanding or difficult people
- Interracial interactions

Ways to Counteract the Harmful Effects of Ego Depletion

- Humor and laughter
- Other positive emotions
- Cash incentives
- Implementing intentions to cope with temptations with a specific plan
- Pursuing social values (e.g., wanting to help people, wanting to be a good relationship partner)

cannot just grab a candy bar off the shelf at the grocery store or hit his sister whenever she makes him angry. Although such acts might reduce immediate tension in the child, they conflict with society's and parents' rules about stealing and beating up little sisters. The ego understands that such actions can lead to problems and that *direct* expression of id impulses must therefore be avoided, redirected, or postponed, depending on the situation.

The ego works to postpone the discharge of id urges until an appropriate situation arises. The ego engages in **secondary process thinking,** which is the development of strategies for solving problems and obtaining satisfaction. Often this process involves taking into account the constraints of physical reality about when and how to express a desire or an urge. For example, teasing one's sister is more acceptable than hitting her, and this can perhaps satisfy the id's aggressive urge almost as well. There may be some urges, however, that simply remain unacceptable according to social reality or conventional morality, *regardless* of the situation. The third part of the mind, the superego, is responsible for upholding social values and ideals.

Superego: Upholder of Societal Values and Ideals

Around the age of 5, a child begins to develop the third part of the mind, which Freud called the superego. The **superego** is the part of the mind that internalizes the values, morals, and ideals of society. Usually, these are instilled into the child by society's various socializing agents, such as parents, schools, and organized religions. Freud emphasized the role of parents in particular in children's development of self-control and conscience, suggesting that the development of the superego was closely linked to a child's identification with his or her parents.

To return to the plumbing metaphor, the superego is the plumber who wants to keep the valves closed all the time and even wants to add more valves to keep the pressure under control. The superego is the part of personality that makes us feel guilty, ashamed, or embarrassed when we do something "wrong" and makes us feel pride when we do something "right." The superego sets moral goals and ideals of perfection and so is the source of our judgments that some things are good and some are bad. It is what some refer to as conscience. The main tool of the superego in enforcing right and wrong is the emotion of guilt. As portrayed in Figure 9.1, the superego operates at all levels of the mind; conscious, preconscious, and unconscious.

Like the id, the superego is not bound by reality. It is free to set standards for virtue and for self-worth, even if those standards are perfectionistic, unrealistic, and harsh. Some children develop low moral standards and consequently do not feel guilty when they hurt others. Other children develop very powerful internal standards, due to a superego that demands perfection. The superego burdens them with almost impossibly high standards. Such persons might suffer from a chronic level of shame and guilt because of their continual failures to meet their unrealistic standards.

Interaction of the Id, Ego, and Superego

The three parts of the mind—id, ego, and superego—are in constant interaction. They have different goals, provoking internal conflicts within an individual. Consequently, one part of a person can want one thing, whereas another part wants something else. For example, imagine that a young woman is last in line at a fast-food counter. The man in front of her unknowingly drops a $20 bill from his wallet and does not notice. The woman sees the money on the floor in front of her. The situation sets off a conflict among the three parts of her personality. The id says, "Take it and run! Just grab it; push the person out of the way if you have to." The superego says, "Thou shalt not steal." And the ego is confronted with the reality of the situation as well as the demands from the id and the superego, saying "Did the clerk see the $20 fall? Do any of the other customers see the $20 on the floor? Could I put my foot over it without being noticed? Maybe I should just pick it up and return it to the person; perhaps he will even give me a reward." The young woman in this situation is bound to experience some anxiety. Anxiety is an unpleasant state, which acts as a signal that things are not right and something must be done. It is a signal that the control of the ego is being threatened by reality, by impulses from the id, or by harsh controls exerted by the superego. Such anxiety might be expressed as physical symptoms, such as a rapid heart rate, sweaty palms, and irregular breathing. A person in this state might also feel herself on the verge of panic. Regardless of the symptoms displayed, a person whose desires are in conflict with reality or with internalized morals will appear more anxious in such a situation.

A well-balanced mind, one that is free from anxiety, is achieved by having a strong ego. It is the ego that balances the competing forces of the id, on the one hand, and the superego on the other. If either of these two competing forces overwhelms the ego, then anxiety is the result.

Dynamics of Personality

Because anxiety is an unpleasant experience, people try to resolve the conditions that give rise to anxiety. These efforts to defend oneself from anxiety are called **defense mechanisms,** and they are used to defend against all forms of anxiety.

Types of Anxiety

Freud identified three types of anxiety: objective, neurotic, and moral anxiety.

Objective anxiety is fear. Such anxiety occurs in response to a real, external threat to the person. For example, being confronted by a large, aggressive-looking man with a knife while taking a shortcut through an alley would elicit objective anxiety (fear) in most people. In this case, the control of the ego is being threatened by an external factor rather than by an internal intrapsychic conflict. In the other two types of anxiety, the threat comes from within.

The second type of anxiety, **neurotic anxiety,** occurs when there is a direct conflict between the id and the ego. The danger is that the ego may lose control over an unacceptable urge arising from the id. For example, a woman who becomes anxious whenever she feels sexually attracted to someone—who panics at even the thought of sexual arousal—is experiencing neurotic anxiety. As another example, a man who worries excessively that he might blurt out an unacceptable word or phrase in public is also beset by neurotic anxiety.

The third type of anxiety, **moral anxiety,** is caused by a conflict between the ego and the superego. For example, a person who suffers from chronic shame or feelings of guilt over not living up to "proper" standards, even though such standards might not be attainable, is experiencing moral anxiety. A young woman with bulimia, an eating disorder, might run 3 miles and do 100 sit-ups in order to make up for having eaten a "forbidden" food. People who punish themselves, who have low self-esteem, or who feel worthless and ashamed most of the time are most likely suffering from moral anxiety, from an overly powerful and demanding superego, which constantly challenges the person to live up to higher and higher expectations.

There is a fourth type of anxiety introduced not by Freud but by his followers. A student of Freud's named Fenichel (1945) expanded the types of anxiety to include **self-esteem anxiety.** That is, people have a preferred and generally positive view of themselves, and they will defend against any unflattering blows to that self-view. Obviously, realizing that one has unacceptable sexual or aggressive wishes might be a blow to one's self-view, especially for persons in the Victorian era. However, in today's society there may be other events that threaten self-esteem, such as failure, embarrassment, or being "unfriended" on Facebook. Most modern psychologists believe that people defend themselves against these threats to their self-esteem (Baumeister & Vohs, 2004). Much of the contemporary research on self-esteem maintenance can thus be thought of as having roots in the psychoanalytic concept of anxiety defense (Baumeister, Dale, & Sommer, 1998).

The ego faces a difficult task in attempting to balance the impulses of the id, the demands of the superego, and the realities of the external world. The id, ego, and superego are constantly interacting within each person. The id might be saying, "I want it now!" The superego is saying, "You shall never have it!" And the poor ego is caught in the middle, saying, "Maybe, if I can just work things out." Most of the time, this conversation is going on outside a person's awareness. Sometimes the conflicts among the id, ego, and superego are expressed in a disguised way in various thoughts, feelings, and behaviors. In most cases, such conflicts are accompanied by anxiety, and so we turn now to a discussion of various mechanisms that people use to defend themselves against anxiety.

Defense Mechanisms

In all three types of anxiety, the function of the ego is to cope with threats and to defend against the dangers they pose in order to reduce anxiety. The ego accomplishes this task through the use of various defense mechanisms, which enable the ego to control anxiety, even objective anxiety. Defense mechanisms serve two functions: (1) to protect the ego and (2) to minimize anxiety and distress. Let's turn now to a discussion of one of the defense mechanisms that Freud wrote about extensively and that has received a good deal of attention from researchers in personality psychology.

Repression

Early in his theorizing, Freud used the term **repression** to refer to the process of preventing unacceptable thoughts, feelings, or urges from reaching conscious awareness. Repression is the forerunner of all other forms of defense mechanisms. Repression is defensive in the sense that, through it, a person avoids the anxiety that would arise if unacceptable material were made conscious. From his clinical practice, Freud learned that people often tend to remember the pleasant circumstances surrounding an event more easily than the unpleasant ones, a finding supported by modern researchers finding a positivity bias in memory. What happens to negative memories? Freud concluded that unpleasant memories were often repressed, forgotten, as if they never happened.

Freud first developed the concept of repression as a general strategy that the ego uses to maintain forbidden impulses in the unconscious. The term is still used today to refer to "forgotten" wishes, urges, or events—recall the account of "repressed" traumatic memories with which the chapter opened. Later, Freud articulated several more specific kinds of defense mechanisms. All of these specific forms involved a degree of repression in that some aspect of reality is denied or distorted in the service of reducing anxiety and protecting the control of the ego within the psychic system.

Other Defense Mechanisms

Freud's daughter Anna Freud (1895–1982), herself an accomplished psychoanalyst, played a large role in identifying and describing other mechanisms of defense (Freud, 1936/1992). She believed that the ego could muster some very creative and effective mechanisms to protect against blows to self-esteem and threats to psychic existence. A few of these defense mechanisms will be described in detail in this section.

There is a questionnaire measure of defense mechanisms (Cramer, 1991) and a good deal of empirical research has accumulating on defense mechanisms (Cramer, 2015). For example, people begin using defense mechanisms as early as 6 years of age, and children's self-confidence level is lower if they use denial as a defense mechanism (Cramer, 2018). During adolescence and adulthood, the defense mechanism of denial, covered next, becomes a commonly used defense mechanism (Cramer, 2012).

Denial When the reality of a situation is anxiety provoking, a person may resort to the defense mechanism of **denial.** In contrast to repression, which involves keeping an *experience* out of memory ("It never happened"), a person in denial insists that things are not the way they seem ("It's not what it looks like"). Denial involves refusing to see the facts. A man whose wife has left him might still set a place at the dinner table for her and insist that she is supposed to come home at any time. Playing out this scenario night after night might be more acceptable than acknowledging that she is, in reality, gone. He acknowledges that she is gone, so it is not repression, but he insists she is not gone for good, denying the reality of his situation. Denial can also be less extreme, as when someone reappraises an anxiety-provoking situation so that it seems less threatening. For example, a man might convince himself that his wife *had* to leave him for some reason, that it really was not *her* fault, and that she *would* return if only she could. In this case, he is denying that his wife freely chose to leave him.

A common form of denial is to dismiss unflattering feedback as wrong or irrelevant. When people are given a poor evaluation, say by a supervisor, some will reject the evaluation rather than change their view of themselves. They might blame their difficulties on bad luck or problems with the supervisor, anything but accepting personal responsibility and having to alter their view of themselves. Indeed, the tendency to blame events outside one's control for failure but to accept responsibility for success is so common that psychologists refer to this as the **fundamental attribution error.** It may be interpreted, however, as a specific form of denial.

Health psychologists are also interested in denial. How can a person smoke two packs of cigarettes a day and not worry about his or her health? One answer would be to deny one's personal vulnerability, or to deny the evidence linking smoking to illness, or to deny that one wants to live a long and healthy life. Baumeister and colleagues (1998) review evidence that people often minimize the risks they see in the various unhealthy behaviors that they engage in.

Denial often shows up in daydreams and fantasies. Daydreams are frequently about how things might have been. To some extent, daydreams deny the present situation by focusing on how things could have been otherwise. In doing so, they may lessen or defend against the potentially anxiety-provoking circumstances of one's present situation. For example, a person who has done something embarrassing might daydream about how things might have gone had he or she not done that stupid, embarrassing thing. Like dreaming, daydreams can be based on primary process thinking (see above) and hence don't need to be anchored to reality, and fantasy can replace the reality of some threat to self-esteem, at least temporarily.

Displacement In **displacement,** a threatening or an unacceptable impulse is channeled or redirected from its original source to a nonthreatening target. Consider, for example, a woman who has an argument with her supervisor at work. She is really angry with the supervisor, but her ego keeps her in check because, after all, the supervisor is her boss and can make her work life difficult. So, instead of arguing with her supervisor, she goes home and displaces her anger onto her husband, perhaps yelling and belittling him. Although this approach may contribute to marital problems, it will most likely avoid the difficulties associated with losing one's temper at one's boss. Sometimes displacement has a domino effect, whereby one spouse berates another, who in turn yells at the children, who then abuse the family dog. Moreover, although displacement is often thought of as a defense mechanism involving the redirection of aggressive instincts, it can also involve sexual urges that are redirected from a less acceptable to a more acceptable target. For example, a man may have a strong sexual attraction toward a woman who is subordinate to him at work, but this woman has no interest in him. Rather than make a pass at this woman at work, and risk a harassment complaint, he may redirect his sexual energy toward his wife and rediscover that he is still attracted to her. Freud also noted that sometimes even fears are redirected through displacement and cited as an example the case of a boy who feared his father but who redirected that fear toward horses.

Although these examples seem to involve conscious awareness and a calculating choice of how to express the unacceptable emotion, the process of displacement

A Closer Look   Empirical Studies of Repression

Although psychoanalysts have been interested in repression since Freud introduced the concept, empirical research on this topic has been relatively sparse until the 1990s. Perhaps this has been due to the difficulty of defining repression in such a way that it may actually be measured for research purposes. Researchers have developed questionnaires to identify individuals who typically use repression as a mechanism for coping with threatening, stressful, or anxiety-producing situations.

Freud held that the essential aspect of repression was the motivated unavailability of unpleasant, painful, or disturbing emotions (Bonanno, 1990). He wrote that repression was a process whereby unpleasant emotions are turned away and kept "at a distance from the conscious" (Freud, 1915/1957, p. 147). Almost 65 years later, Weinberger, Schwartz, and Davidson (1979) were the first to propose that repression, as a style of coping with unpleasant emotions, can be measured by examining various combinations of scores on questionnaires of anxiety and defensiveness. These researchers administered a questionnaire measure of anxiety and a questionnaire measure of defensiveness to a group of subjects. The anxiety questionnaire contained items that inquired about whether one has strong symptoms of anxiety (e.g., heart pounding) when engaging in various behaviors, such as public speaking. The defensiveness questionnaire contained items inquiring about common faults, such as whether respondents had ever gossiped, had ever become so angry that they wanted to break something, or had ever resented someone's asking them for a favor. Clearly, almost everyone is guilty of these minor offenses at one time or another. Therefore, subjects who consistently deny engaging in these somewhat undesirable behaviors score high on defensiveness. The researchers combined the subjects' anxiety

and defensiveness scores, which resulted in the fourfold typology portrayed in Figure 9.3. Most of the subsequent research on repression involved comparing the repressor group to the other three groups on a dependent measure.

In the initial study, after subjects had completed the questionnaires, Weinberger, Schwartz, and Davidson (1979) had the subjects engage in a phrase association task in which they match phrases in one list with phrases in another list that have similar meaning; several phrases contained angry and sexual overtones. As the subjects attempted to match the phrases, the researchers measured their physiological reactions. The researchers also measured the subjects' self-reported levels of distress immediately after their performance. They found that the repressors reported the lowest levels of subjective distress yet were found to exhibit the highest levels of physiological arousal (heart rate, skin conductance). In short, repressors *verbally* say they are not distressed yet *physiologically* appear to be very distressed. Other researchers have obtained similar findings (e.g., Asendorpf & Scherer, 1983; Davis & Schwartz, 1987). These experimental results are consistent with Freud's view that repression keeps unpleasant experiences out of conscious awareness. Moreover, the results are consistent with Freud's ideas that such repressed unpleasant experiences still affect the individual, in spite of being outside of awareness (in this case, the repressed experiences affect the person's level of physiological arousal, even though the person is not consciously aware of being anxious).

Another way to examine repression is to ask subjects to recall childhood experiences associated with pleasant and unpleasant

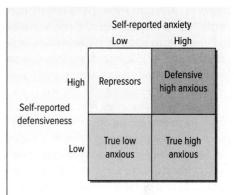

Figure 9.3

Finding repressors by measuring anxiety and defensiveness. The subjects who deny being anxious, but who are high on defensiveness, are most likely repressors.

emotions. This is exactly what psychologists Penelope Davis and Gary Schwartz did in 1987. They asked their subjects to recall and describe childhood experiences that they associated with happiness, sadness, anger, fear, and wonder. The researchers' findings showed that the repressors, defined as high defensive–low anxious persons, did recall fewer negative emotional experiences than the other subjects and that the repressors were substantially older at the time of their earliest negative emotional memories. Somewhat surprisingly, the repressors also had limited access to positive memories. This finding illustrates what may be one of the costs of repression—pleasant as well as unpleasant emotional memories may be diminished or lost to conscious recall.

Davis (1987) expanded on the general idea that repressors have limited access to emotional memories. First, she found that the effect is strongest for memories about the *self*. The repressors in her study had no trouble remembering bad things that had happened to *other* people (e.g., siblings), but they did have limited recollection about unpleasant events that had happened to them. Second, the effects of repression

(Continued)

A Closer Look (*Continued*)

appeared to be strongest for the memories associated with feelings of fear and embarrassment. Although Freud (1915/1957) wrote "the motive and purpose of repression was nothing else than the avoidance of unpleasure" (p. 153), according to Davis, the motive to repress is particularly strong for experiences associated with fear and embarrassment. Why might this be the case? These emotions are often evoked in situations where the focus of attention is on the self in an evaluative or threatening way. In fear, for example, there is a threat to the very existence of the self. In embarrassment, the threat of being negatively evaluated by others looms large, leading a person to feel exposed and vulnerable.

Hansen and Hansen (1988) found that repressors' memories are relatively less elaborate when it comes to emotion than are those of nonrepressors. That is, repressors have memories for emotional events that are less developed, less refined, and less rich than those of nonrepressors. These authors raise the intriguing question of what might account for this impoverished emotional memory on the part of repressors. It could come about in one of two ways. First, repressors may have limited *recall* of their emotional experiences. That is, repressors may have actually *had* varied emotional experiences and those experiences may actually be *in* their memories, but they just have trouble retrieving or recalling them. Alternatively, repressors could actually have blocked certain emotional experiences from entering into their memories in the first place. The effect of repression could have occurred at the *encoding* rather than the recall stage.

Although most studies of repression have examined memory for past events,

a few studies (e.g., Hansen, Hansen, & Shantz, 1992) suggest that the effect of repression may occur not only as diminished *memory* for negative events but also in the person's actual reaction to negative events when they occur. This is what Freud would have predicted, that repressors actually do not experience negative emotions as strongly as nonrepressors do. We can ask whether repressors simply have poor memories for bad events or whether, when bad events happen, they actually experience less negative emotion than nonrepressors do, or both.

In a study by Cutler, Larsen, and Bunce (1996), repressors and nonrepressors kept daily diaries of 40 different emotions for 28 consecutive days. After reporting on their emotions every day for a month, the subjects were then asked to think back over the month and to rate how much of each emotion they recalled experiencing, on average, during the course of that month. The researchers thus had a measure of actual day-to-day emotion, recorded close to the time when the subjects experienced the emotions, as well as a measure of recalled emotion. This approach allowed the researchers to test whether the repressors reported less negative emotion, recalled less negative emotion, or both. The results showed that the repressors, compared with the nonrepressors, actually reported *experiencing* fewer and less intense unpleasant emotions on a day-to-day basis. The repressors' memories for unpleasant emotions, however, were only slightly less accurate than the memories of the nonrepressors. The effect of repression seems to occur during the *experience* of

unpleasant events, whereby repressors somehow dampen their emotional reactions to bad events.

Forty years after Weinberg and colleagues (1979) proposed measuring repression as a combination of high defensiveness and low anxiety, a good amount of empirical research has accumulated validating the concept of repressive coping style (Oskis et al., 2019). Much of it has focused on the negative consequences of this way of coping. More recent research, however, has focused on the potential benefits of repression. For example, a study of rescue workers in Israel, whose work often involves handling human remains after terrorist attacks, found that those workers with a repressive coping style displayed more resilience, and fewer stress symptoms, than workers without a repressive style (Solomon, Berger, & Ginzburg, 2007). Other work has confirmed that the effects of repression occur more at encoding experiences than at recall (Derakshan, Eysenck, & Myers, 2007; Myers, 2010; Myers & Derakshan, 2015), suggesting that repression is not so much about a failure of memory as it is about an inhibited experience of negative emotions in the first place. And finally, researchers are beginning to uncover the brain circuits associated with the trait of repressive coping style (Klucken et al., 2015).

Freud taught that the function of repression was to keep unpleasant experiences out of conscious awareness. We now know more specifically that the blunting effect of repression occurs primarily during the reaction to bad events. Repressors do not have bad memories; rather, somehow they keep unpleasant events from entering into their memories in the first place.

takes place outside of awareness. Recall that the ego spans the preconscious and the unconscious. *Deliberately* redirecting one's anger, for example, is not displacement, even though someone might do this to manage a situation. Real displacement takes place outside of awareness, as a means of avoiding certain inappropriate or unacceptable feelings (e.g., anger or sexual attraction) toward a specific other person or object. Those feelings then are displaced onto another person or object that is more appropriate or acceptable.

Researchers have tried to study the displacement of aggressive impulses. In one study, student participants were frustrated (or not, if they were in the control group) by the experimenter. Later they had the opportunity to act aggressively toward the experimenter, the experimenter's assistant, or another participant. The frustrated participants were more aggressive, but they were equally aggressive toward the experimenter, the assistant, or the other student (Hokanson, Burgess, & Cohen, 1963). The target did not matter. Other studies have replicated this finding. In one study subjects were angered, not by the experimenter, but by another participant, then given an opportunity to act aggressively toward that subject or toward a friend of that participant. Again, angered participants were more aggressive in general, it did not seem to matter who the target was.

Are these results evidence for displacement? Baumeister and colleagues (1998) conclude they are not. Angered people act aggressively, they argue, and there is no evidence that it is defensive. They argue that, although displacement is an interesting dynamic concept, there is little empirical support for the idea that urges are like hydraulic fluid in a closed system being shunted this way or that depending on displacement.

Rationalization   Another common defense mechanism, especially among educated persons, such as college students, is **rationalization.** It involves generating acceptable reasons for outcomes that might otherwise appear socially unacceptable. In rationalization, the goal is to reduce anxiety by coming up with an explanation for an event that is easier to accept than the real reason. For example, a student who receives a failing grade on a term paper might explain it away by insisting that the teacher did not give clear directions for how to write the paper. Or perhaps a woman whose boyfriend has broken up with her explains to her friends that she never really liked him that much to begin with. These reasons are a lot more emotionally acceptable than the alternatives that one is not as smart or as desirable as one thinks.

Reaction Formation   In an attempt to stifle the expression of an unacceptable urge, a person may continually display a flurry of behavior that indicates the opposite impulse. Such a tactic is known as **reaction formation.** For example, imagine the woman who is angry with her supervisor, described in the discussion of displacement. If, instead of displacing her anger, her ego unconsciously resorts to reaction formation, then she might go out of her way to be overly kind to her boss, to show the boss special courtesy and consideration.

An interesting example of reaction formation is provided by Cooper (1998), who discusses the concept of "killing someone with kindness." Consider a man who is angry with his girlfriend, but the anger is not conscious; he is not aware of how angry he really is. It is raining outside so he offers her his umbrella. She refuses to take it, but he insists. She keeps refusing, and he keeps insisting that she take it. Here he is replacing his hostility with apparent kindness. However, his aggression is coming out in his persistent insistence and his ignoring her wishes not to take the umbrella. According to psychoanalysis, this dynamic can often be found when defenses are being used; people may try to cover up their wishes and intention and yet unwittingly express them.

The mechanism of reaction formation makes it possible for psychoanalysts to predict that sometimes people will do exactly the opposite of what you might otherwise think they would do. It also alerts us to be sensitive to instances when a person is doing something in excess, such as when someone is being overly nice to us for no apparent reason. Perhaps in such cases the person really means the opposite of what he or she is doing.

Projection   Another type of defense mechanism, **projection,** is based on the notion that sometimes we see in others the thoughts, feelings, or behaviors we find most upsetting in ourselves. We literally "project" (i.e., attribute) our own unacceptable qualities onto

In projection, we see in others those traits or desires we find most upsetting in ourselves. We can then disparage them for having the undesirable characteristic, without admitting that we have that very characteristic.

Prostock-studio/Shutterstock

others. We can then hate them, instead of hating ourselves, for having those unacceptable qualities. At the same time, we can disparage the tendencies or characteristics in question without admitting that we possess them. Other people become the target by virtue of their having qualities that we intensely dislike in ourselves. For instance, a thief is often worried about the prospect of others stealing from him and claims that others are not to be trusted. Or a woman denies having any interest in sexuality yet insists that all the men she knows "have nothing but sex on their minds." Married men who have affairs are more suspicious than other husbands that their wives are unfaithful. What a person intensely dislikes in or gets upset about with others is often revealing of his or her innermost insecurities and conflicts. A person who always insults others by calling them "stupid" may, in fact, harbor some insecurity about his or her own intelligence.

As another example, consider people who become involved in anti-homosexuality campaigns. Some people publicly express moral outrage towards persons with this sexual orientation. Trent Lott was Senate Majority Leader in June 1998 when he stated on television that homosexuals had an illness similar to alcoholism or kleptomania. At the same time, Christian fundamentalists were airing TV advertisements stating that homosexuality was a disease and that gay persons should be cured. Pat Robertson, a fundamentalist preacher on the Christian Broadcasting Network, said that a hurricane might strike Orlando, Florida, because of a Gay Pride event there. Could it be that homophobic persons are engaging projection as a defense mechanism against their own insecure sexual orientation?

In modern psychological research there is an effect, similar to projection, called the **false consensus effect.** This was first described by Ross, Greene, and House in 1977. It refers to the tendency many people have to assume that others are similar to them. That is, extraverts think many other people are extraverted, and conscientious persons think many other people are conscientious. To think that many other people share your own preferences, motivations, or traits is to display the false consensus effect.

Baumeister and colleagues (1998) argue that having a false consensus about one's unflattering traits could be ego defensive. For example, to be the only person whose credit card is over the limit would imply that one is unique in this moral deficiency. But if one believes that many people are over their credit limits, or close to it, then this false consensus belief might be protective of one's self-concept. The adolescent who explains some misbehavior with the phrase, "Gee, everyone else was doing it," is perhaps engaging in defensive false consensus, essentially saying, "I'm not so bad because everyone is bad too."

Sublimation According to Freud, **sublimation** is the most adaptive defense mechanism. Sublimation is the channeling of unacceptable sexual or aggressive instincts into socially desired activities. A common example is going out to chop wood when you are angry rather than acting on that anger or even engaging in other less adaptive defense mechanisms, such as displacement. Watching Mixed Martial Arts (MMA) fight is more desirable than beating someone up. Mountain climbing or volunteering for combat duty in the army might be forms of sublimating a death wish. Freud, during his only visit to the United States, reportedly remarked about all the sublimated sexual energy that must have gone into building the skyscrapers of New York City. One's choice of occupation (e.g., athlete, mortician, or emergency room nurse) might be interpreted as the sublimation of certain unacceptable urges. The positive feature of sublimation is that it allows for some limited expression of id tendencies, so the ego does not have to invest energy in holding the id in check. Freud maintained that the greatest achievements of civilization were due to the effective sublimation of sexual and aggressive urges.

Defense Mechanisms in Everyday Life

Life provides each of us with plenty of psychological bumps and bruises. We don't get a job we badly wanted; an acquaintance says something hurtful; someone "unfriends" us; another person posts photos that capture you in an unflattering light. In short, we must face unexpected or disappointing events all the time. Defense mechanisms may be useful in coping with these occurrences and the emotions they generate (Larsen, 2000a, 2000b; Larsen & Prizmic, 2004). We all have to deal with stress, and to the extent that defense mechanisms help, so much the better (see Valliant, 1994, for a discussion and an alternative classification system for defense mechanisms).

It is not too difficult, however, to imagine circumstances that are made worse by the use of defense mechanisms (Cramer, 2000, 2002). Others may avoid a person who projects a lot. A person who displaces frequently may have few friends. Moreover, the use of defense mechanisms takes psychic energy that is therefore not available for other pursuits. How do you know when the use of defense mechanisms is becoming a problem? The answer is twofold: You know a behavior is becoming a problem if it begins inhibiting the ability to be *productive* at your work (whatever your work is) or if it begins limiting the ability to *maintain relationships*. If either one of these areas in life is negatively affected—work or relationships—then you could consider the behavior maladaptive. Moreover, there is much to be said in favor of directly confronting difficult issues and taking action directed at solving problems. Saying a person needs a "reality test" is to say that they are doing something that that conflicts with the way things really are. Nevertheless, sometimes problems simply cannot be solved or a person simply does not have the energy or resources to directly confront a problem. Under these temporary circumstances, defense mechanisms may be very useful. When used occasionally, defense mechanisms most likely will not interfere with work or important relationships.

According to Freud, the hallmark of mature adulthood is the ability to work productively and to develop and maintain satisfying relationships. Being well-adjusted, according to Freud, means that the mature person is able to work and to love others. Reaching mature adulthood, however, involves passing through several rocky stages of personality development, a topic to which we now turn.

Psychosexual Stages of Personality Development

Freud believed that all persons passed through a set series of stages in personality development. Each of these stages involves a conflict, and how the person resolves this conflict gives rise to various aspects of his or her personality. So in psychoanalytic theory, the source of individual differences lies in how the child comes to resolve conflicts in each of the stages of development. The positive end result, after going through all the stages, is a fully formed personality, someone who is able to love and to work. Because all of the action happens in childhood, the famous phrase "The child is father to the man" captures a key Freudian idea; the development stages in childhood determine the adult personality.

At each of the first three stages, young children must face and resolve specific conflicts. The conflicts revolve around ways of obtaining a type of sexual gratification.

For this reason, Freud's theory of development is called the **psychosexual stage theory.** According to the theory, children seek sexual gratification at each stage by investing libidinal energy in a specific body part. Each stage in the developmental process is named after the body part in which sexual energy is invested.

If a child fails to fully resolve a conflict at a particular stage of development, he or she may get stuck in that stage, a phenomenon known as **fixation.** Each successive stage represents a more mature mode of obtaining sexual gratification. If a child is fixated at a particular stage, he or she exhibits a less mature approach to obtaining sexual gratification. In the final stage of development, mature adults obtain pleasure from healthy intimate relationships and from work. The road to this final stage, however, is fraught with developmental conflicts and the potential for fixation. Let's examine these stages and the conflicts that arise, as well as the consequences of fixation at each stage.

The first stage, which Freud called the **oral stage,** occurs during the initial 18 months after birth. During this time, the main sources of pleasure and tension reduction are the mouth, lips, and tongue. You don't have to be around many babies to realize how busy they are with their mouths (e.g., whenever they come across something new, such as a rattle or toy, they usually put it into their mouths first). The main conflict during this stage is weaning, withdrawing from the breast or bottle. This conflict has both a biological and a psychological component. From a biological standpoint, the id wants the immediate gratification associated with taking in nourishment and obtaining pleasure through the mouth. From a psychological perspective, the conflict is one of excessive dependency, with the fear of being left to fend for oneself. Sometimes a child has a painful or traumatic experience during the weaning process, resulting in a degree of fixation at the oral stage. Adults who still obtain pleasure from "taking in," especially through the mouth, might be fixated at this stage (e.g., people who overeat or smoke). Problems with nail biting, thumb sucking, or pencil chewing might also occur. At a psychological level, people who are fixated at the oral stage may be overly dependent: they may want to be babied, to be nurtured and taken care of, and thus to have others make decisions for them. Some psychoanalysts also believe that drug addiction (because it involves pleasure from "taking in") is a sign of oral fixation.

There is another possible conflict of the oral stage that is associated with biting. This conflict can occur after the child grows teeth and finds that he or she can obtain pleasure from biting and chewing. Parents typically discourage a child from biting, particularly if the child bites other children or adults. Thus, the child has the conflict between the urge to bite and parental restrictions. People who fixate during this stage might develop adult personalities that are hostile, quarrelsome, or mocking. They continue to draw gratification from being psychologically "biting" and verbally attacking.

The second stage of development is the **anal stage,** which typically occurs between the ages of 18 months and 3 years of age. At this stage, the anal sphincter is the source of sexual pleasure. During this time, the child obtains pleasure from first expelling feces and then, during toilet training, from retaining feces. At first, the id desires immediate tension reduction whenever there is any pressure in the rectum. This is achieved by defecating whenever and wherever the urge arises. Parents, however, work to instill in the child a degree of self-control through the process of toilet training. Many conflicts arise around this issue of the child's ability to achieve some self-control. Some children achieve too little control and grow up to be sloppy and dirty. Other children have the opposite problem: They develop too much self-control and begin to take pleasure in little acts of self-control. Adults who are compulsive, overly neat, rigid, and never messy are, according to psychoanalysts, likely to be fixated at the anal stage. After all, toilet training usually presents a child with the first opportunity to exercise choice and willpower. When a parent puts the child on the potty seat and says, "Now, do your business," the child has the opportunity to say, "No!" and to withhold. This might signal the beginnings of being stingy, holding back, not giving others what they want, and being overly willful and stubborn.

The third stage, which occurs between 3 and 5 years of age, is called the **phallic stage** because the child discovers that he has (or she discovers that she does not have) a penis. In fact, the major event during this stage is children's discovery of their own genitals and the realization that some pleasure can be derived from touching them. This is also the awakening of sexual desire directed outward, and according to Freud, it is first directed toward the parent of the opposite sex. Little boys fall in love with their mothers, and little girls fall in love with their fathers. But children feel more than just parental love, according to Freud's theory. A little boy lusts for his mother and wants to have sex with her. His father is seen as the competitor, as the one who is preventing the little boy from possessing his mother and receiving *all* of her attention. For the boy, the main conflict, which Freud called the **Oedipal conflict,** is the unconscious wish to have his mother all to himself by eliminating the father. (Oedipus is a character in Greek mythology who unknowingly kills his father and marries his mother.) Daddy is the competitor for Mommy's attention, and he should be beaten and driven from the home or killed. But killing or beating Daddy is wrong.

Part of the Oedipal conflict, then, is that the male child loves, yet is competing with, the parent of the same sex. Moreover, the little boy grows to fear his father because surely this big and powerful person could prevent this all from happening. In fact, Freud argued that little boys come to believe that their fathers might make a preemptive strike by taking away the thing that is at the root of the conflict: the boy's penis. This fear of losing his penis, which Freud (incorrectly) called **castration anxiety,** drives the little boy into giving up his sexual desire for Mommy. The boy decides that the best he can do is to become like the guy who has Mommy—in other words, like his father. This process of wanting to become like Daddy, called **identification,** marks the beginning of the resolution of the Oedipal conflict and the successful resolution of the phallic stage of psychosexual development for boys. Freud believed that the resolution of the Oedipal conflict was the beginning of both the superego and morality, as well as the male gender role.

For little girls, the situation is at once similar and different. One similarity is that the conflict centers on the penis, or actually the lack thereof, on the part of the little girl. According to Freud, a little girl blames her mother for the fact that she lacks a penis. She desires her father yet at the same time envies him for his penis. This is called **penis envy,** and it is the counterpart of castration anxiety. Penis envy is different in that the little girl does not necessarily fear the mother, as the boy fears the father. Thus, for girls, there is no strong motivation to give up her desire for her father.

Freud's student Carl Jung termed this stage the **Electra complex,** for girls. Electra was also a character in a Greek myth. Electra convinced her brother to kill their mother after the mother had murdered the father. Freud actually rejected the idea of the Electra complex, and he was vague about how the phallic stage is resolved for girls. He wrote that it drags on later in life for girls and may never fully be resolved. Because successful resolution results in the development of the superego, Freud believed that women must therefore be morally inferior to men. This aspect of Freud's developmental theory is not widely accepted today, and Freud has been strongly criticized for his beliefs about gender differences (e.g., Helson & Picano, 1990).

The next stage of psychosexual development is called the **latency stage.** This stage occurs from around the age of 6 until puberty. Little psychological development is presumed to occur during this time. It is mainly a period when the child is going to school and learning the skills and abilities necessary to take on the role of an adult. Because of the lack of specific sexual conflicts during this time, Freud believed that it was a period of psychological rest, or latency. Subsequent psychoanalysts have argued instead that much development occurs during this time, such as learning to make decisions for oneself, learning to interact and make friends with others, developing an identity, and learning the meaning of work. Because this is a more contemporary modification of Freud's theory, we examine it in Chapter 10.

The latency period ends with the sexual awakening brought about by puberty. If the Oedipus or Electra complex has been resolved, the person goes on to the next and final stage of psychosexual development, the **genital stage.** This stage begins around puberty and lasts through one's adult life. Here the libido is focused on the genitals, but not in the manner of fantasy or self-manipulation associated with the phallic stage. This differs from the earlier stages in that it is not accompanied by a specific conflict. People reach the genital stage only if they have resolved the conflicts at the prior stages. It is in this sense that personality development, according to Freud, is largely complete at around the age of 5 or 6 years.

Freud's psychosexual stage theory is a theory about personality development, both normal and abnormal. In a nutshell, the theory states that we are all born with a drive for sexual pleasure (the id) but that the constraints of civilized society limit the ways we can satisfy that drive. We all go through a series of predictable clashes or conflicts between our desire for pleasure and the demands placed on us by our parents and by society in general. The nature of the conflicts and the stages we go through are universal, but the specific outcomes are each unique. Parts of our personalities are shaped at each stage by the particular ways we resolve the conflict. If, for example, at the oral stage, a person did not receive enough gratification (was weaned early) or received too much gratification (was weaned too late), then he or she might continue to have inappropriate demands for oral gratification throughout the rest of his or her life (perhaps in the form of being a dependent personality or developing an eating disorder or developing an alcohol or drug addiction problem).

Freud developed the metaphor of an army whose troops are called into battle at each stage of psychosexual development. If the resolution of a stage is incomplete, then some soldiers must be left behind to monitor that particular conflict. It is as if some psychic energy must stand guard, lest the psychosexual conflict break out again. The poorer the resolution at a particular stage, the more psychic soldiers have to be left behind. One consequence of this is that less psychic energy is available for the subsequent tasks of maturity. The more soldiers brought forward to the genital stage, the more psychic energy that can be invested in mature intimate and productive relationships and the better the adult personality adjustment. It is interesting to note that neither happiness nor life satisfaction was directly a part of Freud's conception of the mature personality. Successful personality development instead was defined by the ability to be productive (work) and to maintain mature adult relationships (love).

Personality and Psychoanalysis

Psychoanalysis, besides being a theory of personality, is also a method of psychotherapy, a technique for helping individuals who are experiencing a mental disorder or even relatively minor problems with living. Psychoanalysis can be thought of as a method for deliberately restructuring the personality. The connection between the psychoanalytic theory of personality and psychoanalytic therapy is very strong. Principles of psycho-analytic therapy are based directly on the psychoanalytic theory about the structure, development, and functioning of personality. Freud refined his theory of personality while treating patients in therapy. Similarly, many modern psychoanalysts, even those in academic settings, maintain a practice of seeing patients. Most psychoanalysts have themselves undergone psychoanalytic psychotherapy, which Freud held to be a require-ment for becoming a psychoanalyst.

Techniques for Revealing the Unconscious

The goal of psychoanalysis is to make the unconscious conscious. Mental illness, prob-lems with living, and unexplained physical symptoms can all be viewed as the result of unconscious conflicts. Thoughts, feelings, urges, or memories have been forced into the unconscious because of their disturbing or threatening nature. Due to the dynamic nature of the human mind, and the motivated unconscious, these conflicts or repressed urges or emotions may slip out of the unconscious in ways that cause trouble.

The first aim of psychoanalysis is to identify these unconscious thoughts and feelings. Once the patient can be made aware of this material, the second aim is to enable the person to deal with the unconscious urges, memories, or thoughts realisti-cally and maturely. The major challenge facing the psychoanalyst is determining how to penetrate the unconscious mind of the patient. By its very definition, the uncon-scious mind is the part of which the person has no awareness. How can one person (the therapist) come to know something about another person (the patient) which that other person does not even know? Freud and other psychoanalysts have developed a set of standard techniques that can be used to dredge up material from the uncon-scious minds of patients.

Free Association

If you were to relax, to sit back in a comfortable chair, to let your mind wander, and then to say whatever came into your mind, you would be engaging in **free association.** Chances are, you would say some things that would even surprise you, and you might be embar-rassed by what comes out. If you were able to resist the urge to censor your thoughts before speaking, then you would have an idea of how a patient spends much of his or her time in psychoanalysis. The typical psychoanalytic session lasts 50 minutes and may be repeated several times a week; the sessions may continue for months or years.

By relaxing the censor that screens our everyday thoughts, the technique of free association allows potentially important material into conscious awareness. This takes some practice. Patients are encouraged to say whatever comes to mind, no matter how absurd, trifling, or obscene. The technique is a bit like looking for a needle in a haystack in that the psychoanalyst is likely to be subjected to a barrage of trivial material before stumbling on an important clue to an unconscious conflict.

In free association, the psychoanalyst must be able to recognize the subtle signs that something important has just been mentioned—a slight quiver in the way a word is pronounced, a halting sentence, the patient's immediate discounting of what he or she has just said, a false start, a nervous laugh, or a long pause. An effective psychoanalyst will detect such signs and intervene to ask the patient to stick with that topic for a while, to free associate further on that issue. Archeology is a good metaphor for this type of work, as the psychoanalyst is digging through all sorts of ordinary material in search of clues to past conflicts and trauma.

Dreams

Thinkers have always speculated about the meaning of dreams, and it has long been thought that dreams are messages from deep regions of the mind that are not accessible during waking life. In 1900, Freud published his book *The Interpretation of Dreams,* in which he presented his theory of the meaning and purpose of dreaming. He held that the purpose of dreaming was to satisfy urges and to fulfill unconscious wishes and desires, all within the protection of sleep. But aren't most dreams absurd and nonsensical? How, then, can they have anything to do with desires and wishes? For example, a person might have a dream about riding a white horse that suddenly begins to fly. Does this mean the person wishes to have a flying horse? No, Freud would argue, because the dream contains wishes and desires in *disguised* form. **Dream analysis** was a technique Freud taught for uncovering the unconscious material in a dream by *interpreting* the dream's content. Freud maintained that we must distinguish between the **manifest content** of a dream (what the dream actually contains) and the **latent content** (what the elements of the dream represent). He believed that the direct expression of desires and wishes would be so disturbing that it would waken the dreamer. The ego is still somewhat at work during sleep, and it succeeds in disguising the disturbing content of our unconscious. Having a dream about killing one's father, for example, might be so disturbing that it would awaken a young boy who has an Oedipal fixation. However, a dream about a king who has a garden containing a fountain that is disabled by a small animal, so that it no longer shoots its plume of water up into the air, might make the same psychological point yet allow the sleeper to remain asleep.

Thus, although our dreams often appear to be ridiculous and incomprehensible to us, to a psychoanalyst, a dream may contain valuable clues to the unconscious. Freud called dreams "the royal road to the unconscious." The psychoanalyst interprets dreams by deciphering how the unacceptable impulses and urges are transformed by the unconscious into **symbols** in the dream. Parents may be represented as a king and queen. Children may be represented as small animals. Hence, a dream about a king whose fountain is broken by a small animal can be interpreted as wish fulfillment with an Oedipal overtone.

According to Freud, dreaming serves three functions. First, it allows for wish fulfillment and the gratification of desires, even if only in symbolic form. Second, dreams provide a safety valve by allowing a person to release unconscious tension by expressing his or her deepest desires, although in disguised form. And third, dreams are guardians of sleep. Even though a lot is going on in dreams, such as the expression of wishes and desires, the person remains asleep. Although tension is being released, no anxiety is being aroused, and the person sleeps without interruption.

In many of his writings, Freud provided interpretations of common dream symbols. Not surprisingly, most symbols have sexual or aggressive connotations for Freud. This may be because Freud was influenced by the Victorian era in which he lived, when most people were very inhibited about sexual matters. Freud believed that because people repressed their sexual feelings and desires, these inhibited urges came out in symbolic form in dreams.

Projective Techniques

You've undoubtedly seen drawings that can be interpreted in two or more ways (e.g., the picture of a vase that, when looked at differently, looks like two faces). Imagine that you give a person a picture of something totally ambiguous, such as an inkblot, and ask him or her what he or she sees. A person might see all sorts of things in the shapes created

Exercise

For a few days, keep your phone by your bedside. Immediately on awakening each morning, record on your phone anything you can remember about the dreams you had the night before. After a few days, listen to your dream diary and look for themes. Do you see any recurring themes or elements in your collection of dreams? What are some of the common symbols in your dreams, and what do you think they represent? To help you answer these questions, try free associating to your dream content. That is, find a quiet place and relax. Start by describing your dream aloud, and then just keep talking, saying anything that comes to mind, no matter how foolish or trivial. After doing this exercise, have you learned anything about yourself or about what is important to you?

by the ink splatter: two fish swimming, a clown, the male sexual organ, two dead animals run over by cars, etc. The idea that what a person sees in an ambiguous figure, such as an inkblot, reflects his or her personality, is called the **projective hypothesis.** People are thought to *project* their own personalities into what they report seeing in an ambiguous stimulus. A hostile and aggressive person might see teeth, claws, dead animals, or blood in an inkblot. Someone with an oral fixation might see food or people eating. The inkblot technique, developed by Hermann Rorschach (1884–1922), is often criticized by research psychologists for the scant scientific evidence as to its validity or reliability (Wood et al., 2003). While Sigmund Freud and Hermann Rorschach were contemporaries, Freud himself did not use inkblots. Rorschach designed the inkblots in 1921 to diagnose severe mental illnesses, but in the 1940s they were used by psychoanalysts to assess aspects of personality, based mainly on the Freudian projective hypothesis; that what people see in an ambiguous stimulus is a projection of their own personalities—their unconscious motives, desires, and conflicts.

Another class of projective techniques involves asking the person to produce something, such as a drawing of a person or geometric figures, with minimal instruction. What someone draws might be a projection of his or her own conflicts or concerns. Consider a young man who, when asked to draw a person, draws only a head. When asked to draw another person, but this time of someone of the opposite sex, he draws another head. Finally, when asked to draw a picture of himself, he again draws only a head. We might presume that this person has an unconscious conflict about his body image. As with dreams and free association, the goal of projective techniques is to bypass the patient's conscious censor and reveal his or her unconscious conflicts and repressed urges and desires.

The Process of Psychoanalysis

With the help of free association, dream analysis, and projective techniques, the psychoanalyst gradually comes to understand the unconscious source of the patient's problems. The patient must also come to understand the unconscious dynamics of his or her situation. Toward this end, the psychoanalyst offers the patient **interpretations** of the psychodynamic causes of the problems. The patient is led to view problematic thoughts, dreams, behaviors, symptoms, or feelings as all having unconscious roots and as expressions of unconscious conflicts or repressed urges. The psychoanalyst might say, "Could

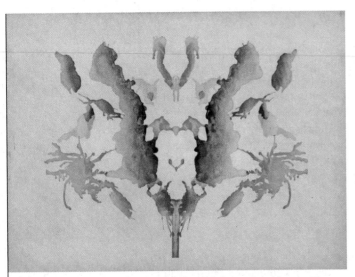

Projective techniques, such as the inkblots developed by the Swiss psychiatrist Hermann Rorschach, are popular methods for assessing unconscious aspects of personality, such as repressed desires, wishes, or conflicts.

zmeel/E+/Getty Images

it be that the reason you feel so sleepy when you go out with your boyfriend is that you are afraid of being sexually attractive to him?" The patient is confronted with an explanation of something she has been keeping from herself. Through many interpretations, the patient is gradually led to an understanding of the unconscious source of her problems. This is the beginning of **insight.** Insight, in psychoanalysis, is more than a simple cognitive understanding of the intrapsychic basis of one's troubles, though this certainly is a part of insight. Insight refers to an intense emotional experience that accompanies the release of repressed material. When this material is integrated into conscious awareness, and the person experiences the emotions associated with that previously repressed material. When the patient uses psychoanalytic interpretations to understand his or her problems, then we say that some degree of insight has been achieved.

As you might imagine, none of this is easy. The patient, or at least the patient's ego, has expended much energy to repress the root of the problem in order to keep anxiety at bay. As the therapist pokes at the unconscious material through free association and dream analysis, and begins to offer interpretations, the patient typically feels threatened. The forces that have worked to repress the disturbing impulse or trauma now work to resist the psychoanalytic process, in a stage of psychoanalysis called **resistance.** As the patient's defenses are threatened by the probing psychoanalyst, the patient may unconsciously set up obstacles to progress. The patient may come up with all sorts of clever ways to misdirect or derail the psychoanalyst. The patient may forget appointments, not pay the analyst's bill, or go very late to a session. Sometimes during a session, a patient in resistance might spend a great deal of time on trivial matters, thereby avoiding important issues. A patient might waste a lot of time recalling the names of and other details about every classmate he or she knew in grade school, a process that could take weeks of session time. Or a patient who is being pressed by the analyst and confronted with interpretations might become angry and insult the analyst.

When an analyst detects a patient's resistance, it is usually a welcome sign that progress is being made. Resistance signifies that important unconscious material is coming to the fore. The resistance itself then becomes an integral part of the interpretations the analyst offers to the patient. For example, the analyst might say, "Perhaps you are insulting me because you want to avoid discussing the various ways in which you have been trying to make yourself sexually unattractive to men. Let's talk some more about what you are trying to avoid by starting an argument with me."

Another important step in most analyses is called **transference.** In this stage, the patient begins reacting to the analyst as if he or she were an important figure from the patient's own life. The patient transfers past or present feelings toward someone from his or her own life onto the analyst. For example, a patient might feel and act toward his analyst the way he felt or acted toward his father. The feelings that the patient transfers onto the analyst can be either positive or negative. For example, a patient may express her admiration for the analyst's powerful intellect and keen mind and offer the sort of adoration that a child is likely to have toward a parent. Old conflicts and old reactions then are played out during the therapy sessions.

The idea behind transference is that the interpersonal problems between a patient and the important people in his or her life will be reenacted in the therapy session with the analyst. Freud called this the **repetition compulsion,** whereby the person reenacts his or her interpersonal problems with new people, including the psychoanalyst. Transference may be one source of clues about the person's unconscious conflicts, and it provides the analyst with opportunities for offering additional interpretations about the patient's behavior.

Exercise

Transference can occur in everyday life as well as in psychoanalysis. The nature of our everyday interactions with others can be influenced by past relationship patterns. For example, a student might work hard on a paper to please a favorite professor. Earning less than a perfect grade on that paper—say, a B+—might cause distress, a tearful scene with the professor, or a temper tantrum. The surprised professor might wonder what this person is really reacting to, since a B+ is actually a pretty good grade. Perhaps the student is replaying a childhood pattern of reacting immaturely whenever he or she disappoints a person from whom he or she desperately seeks approval, such as a demanding parent.

Think of a time when you or someone you know overreacted to an event. Once you have identified such a situation, can you think of any similarities it has to past situations, particularly from childhood? Are there any reasons to suppose that you or someone you know who is overreacting is repeating a conflict from the past?

Movies and other modern media often portray psychoanalysis as resulting in a flash of insight, in which the patient is suddenly and forever cured. Real life is not so simple. A thorough psychoanalysis can take years. The analyst provides interpretation after interpretation, illustrating to the patient the unconscious source of his or her problems. Along the way, the patient may exhibit resistance. Transference also typically becomes an issue for interpretation. Through long and laborious work by both patient and analyst, the patient gradually gains insight. The successfully analyzed patient then has available the psychic energy that his or her ego has formerly been expending in repressing conflicts. This energy may be directed into those twin pursuits Freud said were the hallmarks of adult personality development—to love and to work.

Why Is Psychoanalysis Important?

Throughout much of the twentieth century, Freud's ideas had a profound influence on how the mind was understood to operate. His continuing influence can be seen in several areas. First, psychoanalytic ideas influence the practice of psychotherapy even today. The second largest division of the American Psychological Association is the Division of Psychoanalysis. The basic idea of the "talking cure" can be traced back to Freud.

Even if a psychotherapist does not engage in classic psychoanalysis, many rely on a few psychoanalytic ideas, such as free association (saying whatever comes to mind as a part of therapy) or transference (that the patient will re-create interpersonal problems with the therapist) in their practice of therapy. Despite its limitations (see next section), psychoanalysis has left an important legacy in psychiatry and psychology, which is the importance of listening to the patient and considering their personal life history when forming a diagnosis or treatment plan (Paris, 2017).

Another area of influence concerns the resurgence of interest in some Freudian ideas on the part of research psychologists. Research psychologists are showing a revival of interest in such topics as the unconscious (e.g., Bornstein, 1999), psychic energy (Baumeister, Vohs, & Tice, 2007), and defense mechanisms (Cramer & Davidson, 1998). Although they may not endorse the whole of Freudian theory, such researchers are nevertheless finding empirical support for several of his ideas, either in their original form or as they have been modified by others.

A third area of influence can be found in our popular culture, where many of Freud's ideas have been incorporated into everyday language and the logic of understanding our own and others' behavior. For example, if someone says, "He cannot get along with his teacher because he has a conflict with authority," this comment draws on Freudian ideas. Or if someone explains a person's current problems as being the result of poor parenting, this is a Freudian interpretation. Or if you think a person is avoiding in-person dating and putting all her time Facebook chatting because she is conflicted over sexuality, then you are following a Freudian theme. Many of Freud's ideas have made it into everyday explanations of behavior and everyday forms of speech, such that you probably know more about Freud's theory than you actually realize.

A final reason Freud's ideas are important is that he laid the foundation for many of the topics and questions that psychologists are still addressing. He proposed a developmental sequence in the growth of personality. He devised a method to resolve internal conflicts. He proposed a structure of the basic elements of personality and described what he thought were the main dynamic relationships among these elements. He noted that the mind has regions about which it does not itself have awareness. All these ideas have continued to be areas of inquiry among contemporary psychologists.

Freud started one of the more interesting though controversial approaches to understanding human nature. Consequently, no student of personality should skip over this theory, even if the theory does not play a large role in contemporary studies of personality. Pieces of it have survived and inform various parts of current personality research and theory, so it is worth taking a good look at Freud's classic theory as well as the contemporary modifications of it.

Evaluation of Freud's Contributions

Among contemporary personality psychologists, Freud's theory of personality remains controversial. Some personality psychologists (e.g., Eysenck, 1985; Kihlstrom, 2003b) suggest that psychoanalysis be abandoned. Others contend that psychoanalysis is alive and well (Westen, 1992, 1998; Weinberger, 2003). Opinions among personality psychologists differ dramatically on the accuracy, worth, and importance of psychoanalytic theory, and discussions about the merits of psychoanalysis often provoke passionate debate among those on both sides of the issue (Barron, Eagle, & Wolitsky, 1992).

The controversy surrounding psychoanalysis is covered in *Taking Sides: Clashing Views in Personality Psychology,* by Newman and Larsen (2011). Indeed, that book, or at least Chapter 11 in that book, would make excellent supplementary reading to the current chapter. At one extreme are the critics who hold that psychoanalysis is a stupendous con job by Freud and is totally and completely without merit. At the other extreme are the proponents who argue that it is the most complete theory of human nature to have arisen in recent centuries. Of course, like most controversies, the truth is likely somewhere between these extreme.

Proponents of psychoanalysis point to the major impact that Freud's theory has had on Western thought. Many psychoanalytic terms—id, ego, superego, Oedipal conflict, penis envy, anal character, etc.—have entered our everyday language. In addition to their influence in psychology, Freud's writings have played a significant role in sociology, literature, fine arts, history, anthropology, and medicine, to name only a few disciplines. Within psychology, Freud's works are among the most frequently cited sources in the literature. Many subsequent developments in the discipline of psychology have borrowed or built on the foundation laid by Freud. Freud shaped modern personality psychology and set the course of advancement for perhaps half a century, and Freud's ideas on psychosexual development played a significant role in initiating the field of developmental psychology. His views on anxiety, defense, and the unconscious show up in modified forms across many areas of modern clinical psychology. The psychotherapy techniques he pioneered are frequently practiced, even if sometimes in modified form. Although many modern therapists have done away with the couch, they still inquire about their patients' dreams, ask their patients to free associate, identify and interpret forms of resistance, and work through transference. Moreover, if we think Freud overemphasized sex and aggression, we need merely to look at the popular movies, violent video games, and the proliferation of internet pornography.

Critics of psychoanalysis also have strong arguments (e.g., Kihlstrom, 2003b). They maintain that Freud's theory is primarily of historical value, that it does not inform much of the contemporary research in personality psychology. If you were to look in the pages of mainstream personality journals that publish scientific research, you would find very little that had direct relevance to classical psychoanalysis. Critics insist that without holding psychoanalysis up to scrutiny from outsiders, its merits cannot be fairly evaluated on scientific grounds. Freud himself did not believe in the value of experimentation or hypothesis testing in establishing the validity of psychoanalysis (Rosenzweig, 1994). The scientific method is self-correcting in that experiments are conducted to try to disprove theories. If psychoanalysis is not examined scientifically and is not subjected to tests of disproof, then it is simply not supported by scientific fact. Consequently, in the view of some psychologists, psychoanalysis is more a matter of belief than scientific fact.

Another criticism of psychoanalysis pertains to the nature of the evidence on which it was built. Freud relied primarily on the case study method, and the cases he studied were his patients. Who were his patients? They were primarily wealthy, highly educated, and highly verbal women who had lots of free time to spend in frequent sessions with Freud and

According to classic Freudian theory, human nature is powered by the twin motives of sex and aggression. These two motives are woven throughout much of contemporary literature, movies, video games, and internet content.

Andrey Popov/Shutterstock

lots of disposable income to pay his bills. His observations were made during the therapy sessions only. These are limited observations, obtained on a narrow segment of humanity. However, from these observations, Freud constructed a universal theory of human nature. In his writings, he provided as evidence not original observations, but his *interpretations* of those observations. Scientists provide their *raw observations* (data) so that their conclusions can be verified by others. Freud, however, often provides his *interpretations* of his patients' behavior, rather than reporting raw observations of their behavior per se. If the actual raw observations were made available, it would be interesting to see if other scientists would come to the same conclusions that Freud did. Psychoanalysts today could record therapy sessions for use as evidence. This is rarely done, however, as analysts argue that patients who know they are being recorded do not respond naturally.

There are other specific disagreements with Freudian theory. For example, many believe that Freud's emphasis on sexual drives in his theory of childhood development is inappropriate and perhaps reflects more of a preoccupation of Freud, and the times in which he lived, than an actual topic of childhood development. Others disagree with the notion that personality development pretty much ends at around the age of 5, as Freud held. Those psychologists point to the sometimes profound changes in personality that can occur in adolescence and even throughout adulthood. In Chapter 10, we take up alternative conceptions of personality development that build on, but significantly extend, Freud's ideas. We examine other issues in contemporary psychoanalytic thought as well, including a modern view of the unconscious and the importance of relationships in determining personality development (Kihlstrom, Barnhardt, & Tataryn, 1992).

Some personality psychologists take issue with Freud's generally negative view of human nature. At heart, Freud's theory suggests that human nature is violent, sexual, self-centered, primitive, and impulsive. Freud suggested, in effect, that without the inhibiting influence of society, mediated by the superego, humans would self-destruct. Other personality psychologists suggest a more neutral or even positive core to human nature, which we cover in Chapter 11.

Finally, Freud's view of women, when he wrote about them at all, implied that they were inferior to men (Kofman, 1985). He suggested that women developed weaker superegos than men (making them more primitive, with weaker moral character), that women's problems were more difficult to cure than men's, and even that women universally had an unconscious wish to become like men (the penis envy component of the Electra complex). Karen Horney, an early American psychoanalyst, criticized Freud for neglecting women. Horney (1937, 1939) was among the first to take women's issues seriously from a psychoanalytic perspective. She developed a feminist interpretation of Freud's ideas and was one of the first scholars to distinguish between gender (a social role concept) and biological sex. Other feminist writers have criticized Freud for confusing women's true capacities and potential with the role they were assigned in an oppressive, male-dominated society, an idea we discuss further in Chapter 10. For a strong feminist critique of Freud, see *Feminism and Psychoanalytic Theory* (Chodorow, 1989).

SUMMARY AND EVALUATION

Freud proposed a theory of human nature that has become highly influential. The theory is unique in its emphasis on how the psyche is compartmentalized into conscious and unconscious portions. Freud's theory holds that there are three main forces in the psyche—the id, ego, and superego—which constantly interact in taming the two motives of sex and aggression. These motives may generate urges, thoughts, and memories that arouse so much anxiety that they are banished to the unconscious. Keeping these unacceptable thoughts, desires, and memories out of conscious awareness requires defense mechanisms, such as repression. Several of these defense mechanisms are topics of contemporary research by academic personality psychologists. Freud also theorized about a series of developmental stages that all persons went through, with each stage involving a conflict over expressions of sexuality. How the person resolves these conflicts and learns to satisfy his or her desires within the constraints of a civilized society is the development of personality. That is, adults are different from each other because as children they learned different strategies for dealing with specific kinds of conflicts.

Freud also developed a theory and technique of psychotherapy, also called psychoanalysis. The goals of this form of therapy are to make the patient's unconscious conscious and to help the patient understand the traumatic basis of his or her problems. There has been a lively debate in the field about the value of psychoanalysis. However, as psychoanalytic ideas undergo more scientific examination, and as researchers undertake tests on psychoanalytic hypotheses using controlled laboratory experiments, they will undoubtedly learn more about the value and validity of Freud's theory.

The theory of personality proposed by Freud is one of the most comprehensive views on the working of human nature ever proposed; however, most modern personality psychologists do not totally and uncritically accept the entire theory as it was proposed, word for word, by Freud. Instead, most psychologists accept portions of the theory or agree with modifications to Freud's theory. For example, many psychologists agree that there is an unconscious mind that exists outside awareness, yet many disagree that it is motivated in the way Freud proposed. In Chapter 10, we discuss how this influences the debate over repressed memories.

KEY TERMS

psychic energy 264	defense mechanisms 276	castration anxiety 285
instincts 265	objective anxiety 276	identification 285
libido 265	neurotic anxiety 276	penis envy 285
thanatos 265	moral anxiety 276	Electra complex 285
conscious 265	repression 277	latency stage 285
preconscious 266	denial 277	genital stage 286
unconscious 266	fundamental attribution error 278	psychoanalysis 286
motivated unconscious 267	displacement 278	free association 287
blindsight 268	rationalization 281	dream analysis 288
deliberation-without-awareness 268	reaction formation 281	manifest content 288
id 270	projection 281	latent content 288
pleasure principle 270	false consensus effect 282	symbols 288
primary process thinking 270	sublimation 282	projective hypothesis 289
wish fulfillment 271	psychosexual stage theory 284	interpretations 289
ego 271	fixation 284	insight 290
reality principle 271	oral stage 284	resistance 290
secondary process thinking 274	anal stage 284	transference 290
superego 275	phallic stage 285	repetition compulsion 291
ego depletion 272	Oedipal conflict 285	

Psychoanalytic Approaches: Contemporary Issues

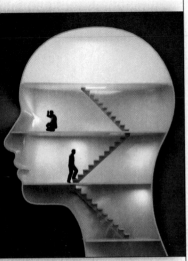

*Science Photo Library RF/
Getty Images*

The Neo-Analytic Movement

Ego Psychology

Object Relations Theory

SUMMARY AND EVALUATION
KEY TERMS

10

Gary Ramona, left, and his attorney walk to Napa County Superior Court on March 24, 1994, for the start of a trial accusing his daughter's therapist of implanting molestation memories using improper suggestion and drugs.
Al Francis/AP Images

The following information is drawn from a case decided in a California court in 1994 (*Ramona v. Isabella,* California Superior Court, Napa, C61898). The case is described in detail in Johnston (1999) and concerns a case of alleged rape and incest.

Holly Ramona was a 23-year-old woman being treated through counseling for bulimia. One of her counselors, Marche Isabella, acknowledges telling Holly Ramona that an overwhelming majority of women with bulimia were sexually abused during childhood. During the course of therapy, which included sessions during which a hypnotic drug (sodium amytal) was administered, Holly Ramona began recalling incidents of sexual abuse that had occurred during her childhood. More specifically, in response to leading questions from her therapists, Holly began "recovering" memories of her father repeatedly raping her between the ages of 5 and 8. The therapist admitted telling Holly that, because sodium amytal is a "truth serum," if she recalled sexual abuse while under its influence, it *must* have really taken place.

Holly's father, Gary Ramona, was severely affected by his daughter's accusations. When Holly went public with the allegations of incest, his wife divorced him, the rest of his family left him, he lost his well-paying job as an executive at a large winery, and his reputation in the community was ruined. Mr. Ramona claimed he was innocent and accused his daughter's therapists of implanting false memories of incest in her mind.

In an unprecedented legal case, Gary Ramona decided to sue the therapists for the damage they had caused him and his family. He charged that his daughter's recovered memories of being raped by him were, in fact, created by the therapists through repeated suggestions that this was the cause of her bulimia and that she wouldn't get better until she actually remembered having been abused. Mr. Ramona held that implanting these false memories was a form of negligence on the part of the therapists, so he filed a malpractice suit against them.

The therapists claimed that Gary Ramona had no legal standing to sue for malpractice because he was not their patient. In an important landmark decision, however, the trial judge held that, as a family member of the patient, and especially as one who had been substantially affected by the therapists' alleged malpractice, Mr. Ramona *did* have the right to file a malpractice suit against the defendants.

During the trial, which lasted seven weeks, Mr. Ramona denied abusing his daughter, whereas Holly repeated her allegations that he had raped her many times during her childhood. It appeared to be a classic case of one person's word against another's. As often happens in such cases, expert witnesses were called in to try to clarify the issues. Psychologist Elizabeth Loftus, a prominent memory researcher, testified during the trial that "there is no support for the idea that you can be raped . . . over a period of years and totally forget about it." A psychiatrist specializing in legal issues, Park Dietz, testified that although Holly Ramona recalled being abused, she could not at first recall who the abuser was. It was only after the sodium amytal session, during which the therapists suggested to Holly that the abuser was her father, that she "remembered" it was her father. Martin Orne, a psychiatrist, psychologist, and authority on hypnosis, also testified that sodium amytal interviews are "inherently untrustworthy and unreliable" and that "Holly Ramona's memory is so distorted that she no longer knows what the truth is." Finally, Harvard psychiatry professor Harrison Pope offered his opinion that Holly Ramona had been "grossly and negligently treated, with catastrophic results."

The jury decided that the therapists were guilty of malpractice and awarded Mr. Ramona $475,000 in damages. The jury foreman was quoted in media sources as having said that the verdict was intended to "send a message about false child abuse memories." Mr. Ramona's attorney saw the verdict as a warning to other therapists, especially to those who believe that adult psychological problems are the result of repressed childhood traumas. Holly Ramona went on to graduate school and is currently a Marriage and Family Therapist, practicing in California under a different name.

Why did this case turn out so differently from the case of Ross Cheit, described at the start of Chapter 9? The major difference between the two cases is that Ross Cheit provided substantial corroborating evidence in support of his recovered memory. Unlike Holly Ramona, Ross Cheit's memory fragment was corroborated by many other persons and even by a tape-recorded confession from the abuser himself.

But what do these cases tell us about the psychoanalytic idea of the motivated unconscious, the idea that the mind can bury memories of horrifying events and then, decades later, accurately retrieve those memories? By themselves, single cases do not prove anything for or against unconsciously motivated repression. People forget all sorts of things. Can you, for example, remember what you ate for dinner last Tuesday?

What is the difference between ordinary forgetting and motivated repression? Is there good scientific evidence for motivated repression? Could people be motivated to "remember" events that did not actually happen, as apparently was the case with Holly Ramona? To answer these questions we examine contemporary revisions to classical psychoanalysis, collectively known as the neo-analytic movement.

The Neo-Analytic Movement

As proposed by Freud, and described in the previous chapter, classical psychoanalysis is a detailed and comprehensive theory, developed in the early 1900s, of the totality of human nature. Many of Freud's ideas are out of date; however, contemporary psychoanalyst Westen (1998) argues that they *should* be out of date; after all, Freud died in 1939 and "he has been slow to undertake further revisions" (p. 333) of his theory. Westen goes on humorously to note that "Freud, like Elvis, has been dead for a number of years but continues to be cited with some regularity" (p. 333). Whereas many of Freud's ideas have not stood the test of time, others have and have been incorporated into a contemporary version of psychoanalysis. Today, psychoanalysis is probably best thought of as a theory containing ideas variously inspired by Sigmund Freud but modified and advanced by others.

Westen (e.g., 1990, 1998) is a proponent of contemporary psychoanalysis. Writing on the legacy of Freud, Westen notes that contemporary psychoanalysts no longer write much about id, superego, and repressed sexuality; nor do they liken treatment to an archeological expedition in search of forgotten memories. Instead, most contemporary psychoanalysts focus their attention on childhood relationships and adult conflicts with others, such as difficulties becoming intimate or readily becoming intimate with the wrong kinds of persons (Greenberg & Mitchell, 1983). Westen (1998) defines contemporary psychoanalysis as being based on the following five postulates:

1. The unconscious still plays a large role in life, although it may not be the autonomous influence that Freud held it was.
2. Behavior often reflects compromises in conflicts among mental processes, such as emotions, motivations, and thoughts (Westen & Gabbard, 2002a).
3. Childhood plays an important part in personality development, particularly in terms of shaping adult relationship styles.
4. Mental representations of the self and relationships developed early in life guide our interactions with others later in life (Westen & Gabbard, 2002b).
5. Personality development involves not just regulating sexual and aggressive feelings but also moving from an immature, socially dependent way of relating to others to a mature, independent relationship style.

This neo-analytic viewpoint has wider appeal and better scientific support, in some cases, than Freud's original ideas. To start our coverage of more contemporary psychoanalysis, we begin with a discussion of repression and memory.

Repression and Contemporary Research on Memory

It is easy to find conflicting opinions among respected psychologists on the issue of motivated repression. One review of the clinical literature on motivated repression concluded "the evidence for repression is overwhelming and obvious" (Erdelyi & Goldberg, 1979, p. 384). Another review of the same literature concluded "the concept of repression has not been validated with experimental research" (Holmes, 1990, p. 97).

Elizabeth Loftus, a professor of psychology and world-renowned memory researcher, has perhaps conducted the most research on the authenticity of recovered memories. Loftus has been the one psychologist most connected to the repressed memory debate, and summarizes the scientific status of the concepts of "repressed" and

Professor Elizabeth Loftus testified in the Ramona trial and has contributed a good deal of scientific information to the debate over repressed memories.
Jodi Hilton/AP Images

"recovered" memories of sexual abuse (Davis & Loftus, 2009). In her article titled "The Reality of Repressed Memories" (1993), Loftus discusses many cases of individuals who suddenly recover memories of important events: some of these turn out to be true memories, whereas others are false or inaccurate accounts, which are later recanted. However, she argues that we should not conclude that *all* recovered memories are **false memories** just because some, such as Holly Ramona's, have turned out to be false. Similarly, we should not assume that *all* recovered memories are true, just because some, such as Ross Cheit's that we explored in Chapter 9, have turned out to be true. Loftus believes that what is important is being aware of the processes that may contribute to the creation of inaccurate or false memories. Loftus (1992, 1993, 2011) suggests that many variables contribute to the construction of false memories.

One factor that might influence people to have false memories is the popular press. Many books purport to be guides for survivors of abuse; these are undoubtedly of some comfort to people who have been living with painful memories of abuse. For those who have no such memories, these books often provide strong suggestions that abuse could have happened, even if there is no memory of the abuse. For example, one book in this category is *The Courage to Heal* (Bass & Davis, 1988), which states:

> *You may think you don't have memories. . . . To say, "I was abused," you don't need the kind of recall that would stand up in a court of law. Often the knowledge that you were abused starts with a tiny feeling, an intuition. . . . Assume your feelings are valid. . . . If you think you were abused and your life shows the symptoms, then you were. (p. 22)*

What are some of the symptoms *The Courage to Heal* suggests indicate a person was abused? The book lists, among other things, low self-esteem, self-destructive thoughts, depression, and sexual dysfunction. This book, and others like it, provides a strong message that even in the absence of a specific memory, many people should conclude that they have been abused. However, there are many causes of low self-esteem, depression, and sexual dysfunction. In addition, these symptoms are associated with many other psychological disorders, such as phobias and anxieties, and these disorders certainly can occur without a history of abuse.

The above quote is also a powerful suggestion that may lead some persons to conclude that they must have been abused. A person who starts with this idea may embellish this suggestion by filling in details to make a convincing or consistent story of abuse. If he or she is led further along these lines by a questioning therapist, his or her false memories may become more and more convincing. Loftus (1993) has demonstrated in the lab that subjects questioned in a leading manner after watching a video of a car accident can be led to conclude that one car ran a stop sign, even though there was no stop sign in the video. And with more leading questioning, subjects increase their confidence that one car is to blame because it ran the stop sign (Bernstein & Loftus, 2009).

Another factor that may contribute to false memories is the behavior of some therapists. Loftus tells of a woman who wrote to her after the woman's therapist had concluded that her depression was caused by childhood sexual abuse. The patient stated that her therapist was certain of that diagnosis, even though the patient had no memory of abuse. The patient further stated that she could not understand how something so terrible could have happened without her being able to remember the event. Loftus tells of another case of a man who went to a therapist because he was distraught over his father's suicide. The patient talked about painful events in his life, but the therapist kept suggesting that there must be something else. Not knowing what this "something else" was, the patient became even more depressed. Then, during a therapy session, the therapist stated that "you display the same kinds of characteristics as some of my patients who are victims of . . . ritualistic abuse" (cited in Loftus, 1993, p. 528).

A variety of techniques are used in therapy that encourages patients to reflect on their childhoods. Hypnosis is one technique used to get patients to recall freely childhood experiences within the protection of a relaxed, suggestion-induced, trancelike state. An extensive scientific literature, however, shows that hypnosis does not improve memory (Nash, 1987, 1988). This explains why hypnotizing witnesses are not allowed in courts of law; hypnotized witnesses do not recall facts with any greater accuracy than non-hypnotized witnesses (Kihlstrom, 2003b; Wagstaff, Vella, & Perfect, 1992). In fact, hypnosis may be associated with increased distortions in memory (Spanos & McLean, 1986). In one case, a highly suggestible man was led under hypnosis to develop "memories" for crimes that had not even been committed (Ofshe, 1992). Under hypnosis, people are often more imaginative, more spontaneous, and more emotional and often report unusual bodily sensations (Nash, 2001). After being taken back to childhood through hypnosis, people have been known to recall being abducted by alien creatures with fantastic spaceships (Loftus, 1993).

Loftus and colleagues have pointed to other techniques in psychotherapy that can contribute to the creation of false memories (Loftus, 2000; Lynn et al., 2003). These include the use of suggestive interviewing, the interpretation of symptoms as signs of past trauma, and pressure from an authority figure (the therapist) to recall trauma. Such practices can be used to foster the recollection of events that did not actually happen (Tsai, Loftus, & Polage, 2000). In laboratory studies, Loftus and colleagues have shown that having persons imagine various events can lead them to later rate those events as more familiar, leading subjects to have a more elaborate memory representation, which in turn leads them to rate those imagined events as likely to have happened (Thomas, Bulevich, & Loftus, 2003). This effect is called the **imagination inflation effect,** and it occurs when a memory is elaborated upon through leading questions, which prompt the person to imagine an event, regardless of whether or not it happened. This can lead the person to confuse the imagined event with events that actually happened. For example, by showing people an advertisement suggesting that they shook hands with Mickey Mouse as a child, those people later had higher confidence that they had personally shaken hands with Mickey as a child. Another study had persons imagining shaking hands with Bugs Bunny and produced a similar effect (Braun, Ellis, & Loftus, 2002). Having persons imagine something, even something as unusual as shaking hands with Bugs Bunny, can lead them to have a false confidence that it actually may have happened. Loftus and others have pointed out the implications of this research for the admissibility of allegedly repressed memories in courts (Hyman & Loftus, 2002; Loftus, 2003). Loftus has also shown that this technique can alter memory for even very personally stressful events (Morgan et al., 2012) and that such false memories were found to persist over a one-and-a-half years later when subjects were followed up (Zhu et al., 2012).

Why would some therapists suggest false memories to their patients? Many therapists believe that effective treatment must lead the patient to recall and maturely process unconscious memories of traumatic events. Therapists, like many other people, can suffer from a **confirmatory bias**—the tendency to look only for evidence that confirms

A Closer Look   So, You Want to Have a False Memory

Imagine you are a subject in a psychology experiment in which you are assigned to listen carefully to a list of 15 words, knowing that you will later be tested on your memory for these words. The words are *bed, rest, awake, tired, dream, wake, snooze, blanket, doze, slumber, snore, nap, peace, yawn,* and *drowsy.* Now cover the list of words you just read, and indicate below whether or not each of the following words was on the list:

	On the List?	
	Yes	No
snooze	——	——
mother	——	——
bed	——	——
television	——	——
sleep	——	——
chair	——	——

If you are like most people, you checked yes following the word *sleep.* Indeed, many people are so certain that *sleep* was on the first list that they argue with the experimenter when they are told that, in fact, it was not. Thus, if you checked yes, indicating that sleep was on the original list during the recall phase of the task, and you really remember seeing the word *sleep,* then you just had a false memory. Approximately 80 percent of normal subjects are induced to have this false memory—that is, they believe that *sleep* was on the original list (Roediger, Balota, & Watson, 2001; Roediger, McDermott, & Robinson, 1998).

The procedure you just completed was developed by psychologists Henry Roediger and Kathleen McDermott (1995). They devised the technique based on the **spreading activation** model of memory. This model of memory holds that mental elements (such as words or images or emotional experiences) are stored in memory along with associations to other elements in memory. For example, *doctor* is associated with *nurse* in most people's memories because of the close connection or similarity between these concepts. The mental association between these two concepts can be demonstrated easily; the speed of deciding that a letter string *(doctor)* is a word or not is faster if it is preceded by an associated concept *(nurse)* relative to an unrelated word *(table).* The explanation is that the activation of *nurse* in your memory spreads through an association network and activates other related concepts, such as *doctor,* allowing them to be recognized faster.

How does this explain the false memory for *sleep* in the exercise? Like any concept, *sleep* is stored in your memory in a network of associations to other words, such as *bed, rest, awake, tired, dream, wake, snooze, blanket,* and *doze.* This network of associations is depicted in Figure 10.1.

Activation from the multiple words on the first list spreads or primes the critical concept on the recall list *(sleep)* in the memory network of the person studying the list. The activation from all the words related to *sleep* (e.g., *bed, rest,* and *tired*) sums up and makes the concept of *sleep* more likely to be recalled or recognized later, even though the actual word *sleep* was not on the original list.

Researchers have also shown that the probability of a false memory in this task is a function of the number of words on the first list that are associated with the critical word (e.g., *sleep*). That is, the sum of the association strength from the list items to the critical item determines false recall of the critical item. Association strength is determined by how frequently the critical word (e.g., *sleep*) is named when people are asked for the first word that comes to mind from some other word (e.g., *bed*). In fact, psychologists have determined lists of common associates to a whole variety of words, and the sum of association strength of the listed items to the critical item is what determines the probability of false recall (Roediger, Balota, & Watson, 2001).

How is this material related to the psychoanalytic idea of false memories? First, this material highlights how most cognitive psychologists, even those with strong scientific values, believe that false memories can occur. It is accepted as fact that humans have a **constructive memory**; that is, the human mind contributes to or influences in various ways (adds to, subtracts from, and so on) what is recalled. Rather than referring to pristine and objective retrieval of facts, human memory is fallible and open to error and corruption. Moreover, the corruption is most likely to occur when elements with strong associations to each other converge repeatedly in experience. In this condition, the person is likely to recognize or recall something associated to those elements, even if that new element never occurred. For example, during interrogation, imagine that a person is repeatedly asked about an event in many different leading ways. After some time, the person is asked something that is new but related to the repeated information. The person may then be more likely to recall this new event as happening, not because it did happen, but because it is associated with the previously presented information. This is how innocent mistakes of recognition on word lists might help us understand the larger and more dramatic false memories that have been documented in certain legal cases, such as that of Holly Ramona.

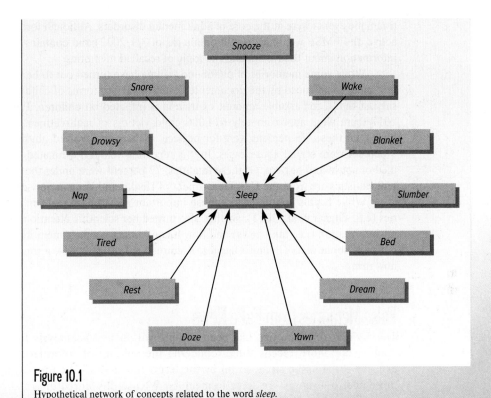

Figure 10.1

Hypothetical network of concepts related to the word *sleep*.

Source: Adapted from Roediger, Balota, & Watson, 2001.

previous beliefs and to not look for evidence that might disconfirm their beliefs. If a therapist believes that childhood trauma is the cause of adult psychological problems, he or she will most likely probe for memories of childhood trauma. Compliant and suggestible patients are then induced to spend long periods of time trying to imagine what events must have happened in their childhoods to produce their current difficulties. Meanwhile, the therapist relates stories of other patients with similar problems who were helped by recalling and coping with memories of childhood abuse. The therapist, as an "authority" on how to get better, stands ready to authenticate any possible memory of trauma that the patient might produce.

Around the time of the Holly Ramona case, a private foundation was formed to gather scientific information on repressed memories. Called the False Memory Syndrome Foundation (FMSF), this organization had a scientific advisory board consisting of the top scientists in the field of memory research, including Elizabeth Loftus. In the decade of the 1990s there was a proliferation of legal cases involving "recalled" memories, many of which devastated many families. The FMSF provided research summaries and expert witnesses to legal teams defending against recalled sex abuse. The foundation also wanted to prevent therapists from unknowingly (or knowingly) implanting false memories in their patients through suggestion, hypnosis, or so-called truth serum therapy. The foundation also worked to assist families who, like Holly Ramona's, were torn apart by false memories. Due to a sharp decline of false memory cases in the 2010s, and a lack of funding, the foundation was closed in 2019 after 27 years of effectively helping to correct the harm being done to patients and families by therapists who insisted that traumatic events were at the core of adult mental disorders. Although formally no longer active, the FMSF web page is still online (as of 3/1/2022) and contains a great deal of information about their work and the topic of recalled memories.

While some memories of childhood trauma have turned out to be false, this position must be balanced by the documented rates of various forms of child abuse. Surveys suggest that a remarkable amount of trauma is inflicted on children. For example, in 2017 there were approximately 674,000 child victims of maltreatment in the United States. Of these, 75 percent were for neglect, 18 percent involved physical abuse, and 9 percent were sexual abuse cases. In this reporting year, an estimated 1,750 children died of abuse and neglect. Of these fatalities, 72 percent were under the age of 3 years! [All statistics are from the U.S. Department of Health and Human Services].

While Loftus continues to publish important research on real versus false memories (e.g., Otgaar et al., 2021), she has also turned her scientific attention to the topic of misinformation (i.e., fake news) and how it can impact people's memories, beliefs, and opinions about facts (Bailey, Olaguez, Klemruss & Loftus, 2021), a topic to which we now turn.

False Memories from Fake News

The validity of memories has been a topic within psychoanalysis for decades. A related, but more recent topic, concerns the validity of information people are exposed to, an issue summed up by the term "fake news." We process information presented to us and store some in memory. We use this stored information to build our beliefs and opinions about events, the world, and other people. Some of our beliefs may be flawed or incorrect because the information they are based on is false. How can psychology help us understand, detect, and potentially counteract the effects of fake news?

Psychology has documented several principles of information processing and memory formation. People who are interested in influencing public opinion can "weaponize" these principles and use them in systematic misinformation campaigns to influence the population. For example, they might want most people in the population to recall some event or information as true, when in fact it is false or never happened. Or they might want to "spin" some event so that most people recall it in a certain way. What are these principles that are "weaponized" by public opinion manipulators to influence what or how people recall specific information?

The construction of a memory takes three steps:

1. *Attend to the information.* This step seems obvious and straightforward—a person must pay attention to information for it to have any chance at all of entering his or her memory. When a grade school teacher says: "Pay attention!" he is trying to get his students to take this first step toward remembering the material being taught. Several psychological factors can influence attention, such as fatigue, interest, cognitive overload, competing demands, or distractions.

2. *Encode the information.* In this step a memory trace is recorded, representing the information being attended to. The mind records, in some fashion and some imperfect form, the information in the brain. Neuroscientists have documented encoding in several areas of the brain but mostly in the hippocampus. There are several factors that influence the likelihood that information will be encoded, and it is mostly these factors that are "weaponized" in misinformation campaigns (elaborated below).

3. *Recall the information.* We know a memory has been successfully made if a person can recall, more or less accurately, the information attended to. Memory is never perfect and is a reconstruction of the original information. Many psychological factors influence recall, including cues, current state, leading questions, length of time since encoding, and the amount of information being recalled.

The step in memory formation that is most often "weaponized" in misinformation campaigns is the encoding step. Here we focus on five factors that influence encoding. These can be used to increase the likelihood that people will encode some bit of information as true, regardless of whether it is true or false.

1. *Repetition.* Every student knows that cramming—repeated exposure to the same information—can increase memory for that information. Skillful manipulators of public opinion also know the power of repetition. Politicians, for example, can repeat an idea over and over, within the same speech, and across speeches. They could also have their surrogates use the same "talking points" so that they all are repeating the same idea. Staying "on message" refers to repeating the key information they want the public to remember. They know that many people, if they hear the same information repeated often enough, will come to remember it as true: "It must have happened that way."

2. *Source expertise.* If the source of the information is seen as an "expert," then that information is more likely to be encoded as true. In the early days of the internet, for example, many people assumed that the internet itself was a form of expertise: "It must be true, I read it on the internet." These days, most people know that the internet contains information from charlatans as well as experts, perhaps more of the former than the latter. Nevertheless, many internet sites strive for an air of expertise or to be seen as legitimate news sites when, in fact, they may be a channel for misinformation. The internet simply is not curated; the information there is not objectively reviewed and corroborated by experts, like it is in scientific publications. Whenever someone is using misinformation to influence public opinion, they often invoke some vague expert as the source. For example, if a politician refers to an ambiguous authority or expert or some hastily assembled committee to back up some bit information, it is wise to check the credentials of those experts. In general, whenever an "expert" is being invoked to back up or endorse some bit of information, it is a good idea to be on guard and to evaluate the claim and the expertise.

3. *Familiarity.* One effect of repetition is to develop a sense of familiarity for a piece of information, "I think I've heard that before, so it must be true" or even "Yes, this just sounds true." Besides repetition, familiarity can also come from the information being similar to something you already know or a possible consequence of what you already know. "I know that X and Y are true, and Z is a likely consequence, so Z must also be true." If it feels familiar enough, through repetition or similarity to existing memories, it will be encoded as true.

4. *Fluency.* This refers to the fact that, other things being equal, the easier it is to process of bit of information, the higher the likelihood it will be encoded. Keep it simple, and people are more likely to remember it. This explains why people who see the movie remember the details better than people who read the book. Movies are more fluent; they take less effort to process than reading a book. This is why "a picture is worth a thousand words." A piece of information that is nuanced, complex, and has several qualifiers (e.g., the Mueller report) will simply not be encoded by most people. However, a very simple bit of information

(e.g., "No collusion!"), especially if repeated over and over, is more likely to be encoded. Some politicians have learned the value of presenting information in small chunks, using simple language, and developing short and catchy slogans.

5. *Consensus.* If people are led to believe that others think some information is true, then they are more likely to encode it as true themselves. When a politician states, "Lots of people are saying . . .," it might be a sign they are employing the consensus effect. If you are being presented with a consensus statement along with some information, you should question the consensus. Where did those observations come from? Who exactly are the people being referred to? Who gathered that information? Often, a consensus statement will be attached to information with no way to verify that consensus. The consensus statement might simply be made up to lend credibility to the information. Questionable consensus statements can come in many forms, but once you see a consensus element attached to some bit of information, you should be on alert for misinformation and question how that consensus might be verified.

The issue of fake news (misinformation) is important in today's society and is relevant to the notion of false memories. Given the proliferation of sources of news and information, as well as the willingness of many influencers to present false or misleading information, it is a challenge to separate factual information from misinformation. Once encoded as true, a bit of false information can contribute to flawed beliefs and misinformed opinions. The phrase, "Once you've seen something, it's hard to un-see it" refers also to encoded misinformation—once information is encoded as true, it goes on to influence beliefs and opinions, an outcome that is difficult to correct.

Contemporary Views on the Unconscious

The idea of a motivated unconscious is at the core of classical psychoanalytic theory. Most contemporary psychologists also believe in the unconscious, although it is a different version of the unconscious than that found in classical psychoanalytic theory. Consider the views of psychologist Bargh (2005), a social psychologist whose research on unconscious processes has had a large impact on psychology: "People are often unaware of the reasons and causes of their own behavior. In fact, recent experimental evidence points to a deep and fundamental dissociation between conscious awareness and the mental processes responsible for one's behavior" (p. 38). This position is summarized in the title of a recent book by Bargh (2017): *Before You Know It: The Unconscious Reasons We Do What We Do.* His view on the unconscious can be illustrated with one of Bargh's own experiments, in which college student subjects took part in what they thought was an experiment on language, where they were presented with many different words. Half of the participants were presented with words synonymous with rudeness; the other half were presented with words synonymous with politeness. After finishing the language experiment, they went to another experiment in another room and encountered a staged situation where it was possible to act in either a rude or polite way. Although the participants showed no awareness of the possible influence of the language experiment, they nevertheless behaved in a manner that was consistent with the kinds of words they were exposed to in the "previous" experiment (Bargh, 2005). Most psychologists believe that the unconscious can influence our behavior, but not all agree with Freud that the unconscious can have its own autonomous motivation (Bargh, 2006, 2008).

We can term these two differing views on the unconscious: the **cognitive unconscious** view and the **motivated unconscious** view. Those with the cognitive unconscious view readily acknowledge that information can get into our memories without our ever being aware of that information (Kihlstrom, 1999). For example, in the phenomenon of **subliminal perception,** some information—such as the phrase "Buy a Coke"—is flashed on a screen so quickly that you don't recognize the actual words. That is, you would say that you had seen a flash but were not able to distinguish what was written. Indeed, you could not even guess that the word *Coke* was presented better than chance compared to guessing that some other non-presented word—say, *House*— was presented. However, if you were asked to judge whether a string of letters is a word or not a word, and the dependent variable was reaction time (how quickly you can make this judgment), then you would judge *Coke* as a word faster than words unrelated to Coke or soft drinks in general. Thus, subliminal information primes associated material in memory. **Priming** makes that associated material in memory more accessible to conscious awareness than comparable material that is not primed. Results such as these clearly demonstrate that information can get into the mind and have some influence, without going through conscious experience. (An online demonstration of priming can be found at https://www.millisecond.com/download/library/.)

If someone were given the subliminal message "Buy a Coke," would they be more likely to spontaneously go out and do so? After all, this is consistent with the psychoanalytic idea of the motivated unconscious—that something in the unconscious can motivate complex behavior. Can advertisers use subliminal messages to unconsciously motivate consumers? Similar questions arise concerning the influence of subliminal rock music messages that supposedly advocate suicide or violence. The vast majority of research on subliminal perception, however, suggests that unconscious information does not influence people's motivations or unleash complex behaviors (Bargh, 2016), like getting up from one's seat, finding a place that sells Coke, and actually purchasing one. Similarly, the average teen exposed to subliminal messages of violence in a rock song is unlikely to go out and commit a violent act.

In the cognitive view of the unconscious, the content of the unconscious mind is assumed to operate just like thoughts in consciousness. Thoughts are unconscious because they are not in conscious awareness, not because they have been repressed or because they represent unacceptable urges or wishes. For example, we might say that buttoning a shirt is unconscious because we can do it without focusing any conscious attention on the act. Typing can also be unconscious for the person who is good at it. Other kinds of mental content, such as beliefs and values, might also be unconscious. Such elements are not in our unconscious because they are threatening; nor do they exert a large influence on our behavior. And although unconscious material can influence subsequent thoughts or behavior, as in the priming examples, these influences are not consistent with the motivated unconscious of classical psychoanalytic theory (Kihlstrom, 2003b; Nash, 1999). As such, the cognitive unconscious as viewed by contemporary psychologists is quite different from the motivated unconscious put forward by Sigmund Freud 120 years ago. According to Freud, the unconscious was a torrid and fuming cauldron of anger and eroticism. It had a life of its own and operated according to its own primitive and irrational rules, and had broad, sweeping influence over our conscious behavior, thoughts, and feelings. In contemporary psychology, the unconscious is peaceful, gentle, and much more rational than Freud's version. Moreover, although the unconscious is still viewed as having an influence on behavior, thoughts, and feelings, that influence is seen as quite limited, rule governed, and specific compared to Freud's version (Bargh & Morsella, 2008, 2010).

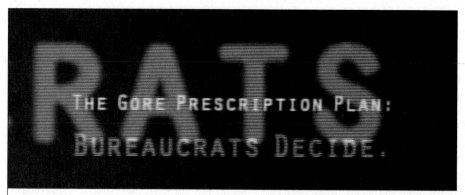

In the 2000 U.S. presidential election campaign, a Republican commercial described some of the questionable fund-raising efforts of Al Gore, the Democratic opponent. During the commercial, the word RATS was subliminally presented, along with information about Gore. After the ensuing outrage, he Bush campaign pulled the commercial. The full commercial, as well as other subliminal advertisements, can be found at: https://www.wordstream.com/ blog/ws/2017/10/24/subliminal-advertising. The fact that both campaign teams believed that such subliminal messages would have an impact on voter motivation shows that many people believe in unconscious motivation. Researchers are debating the power of subliminal political advertisements to influence public opinion (Weinberger & Westen, 2007).

REUTERS TV/REUTERS/Newscom

Ego Psychology

Another major modification to psychoanalysis concerns a shift in focus from id to ego. Freud's version of psychoanalysis focused on the id, especially the twin instincts of sex and aggression, and how the ego responds to the demands of the id. We might characterize Freudian psychoanalysis as **id psychology**. Later psychoanalysts felt that the ego deserved more attention, that it performed many constructive functions. One prominent student of Freud—Erik Erikson (1902–1994)—emphasized the ego as a powerful, independent part of personality. Moreover, Erikson noted that the ego was involved in mastering the environment, achieving one's goals, and hence establishing one's identity. It is no wonder, then, that the approach to psychoanalysis started by Erikson is called **ego psychology**.

Establishing a secure identity is seen as the primary function of the ego. **Identity** can be thought of as an inner sense of who we are, of what makes us unique, and a sense of continuity over time and a feeling of wholeness. You have probably heard the term **identity crisis.** This term comes from Erikson's work, and it refers to the desperation and confusion a person feels when he or she has not developed a strong sense of self. Maybe you have even felt such feelings when you were uncertain about yourself, uncertain about who you were or how you wanted others to view you, what you valued and wanted out of life, and where you were going in terms of the direction of your life. A period of identity crisis is a common experience during adolescence and emerging adulthood. For some people an identity crisis also occurs later in life—the so-called midlife crisis—discussed more in Chapters 11 and 14, (Sheldon & Kasser, 2001).

One of Erikson's lasting contributions was developing the notion of identity as an important developmental achievement in everyone's personality. Identity has been thought of as a story that a person develops about himself or herself (McAdams, 1999, 2008,

A Closer Look

Does Childhood Sexual Abuse Cause Problems in Adulthood? Anatomy of a Controversy Started by a Scientific Paper

In 1998, a scientific paper appeared in the journal *Psychological Bulletin* titled "A Meta-analytic Examination of Assumed Properties of Child Sexual Abuse (CSA) Using College Samples" and authored by psychologists Bruce Rind, Philip Tromovitch, and Robert Bauserman. The authors' goal was to determine whether child sexual abuse (CSA) causes intense or long-term psychological harm for both genders. They reviewed 59 studies on this topic, all conducted on college students. By meta-analyzing these studies, Rind and colleagues found that students with a history of CSA were, on average, slightly less well adjusted than students without a history of CSA. However, poor family environment also correlated with a history of CSA, making it impossible to argue that CSA in itself causes adjustment problems (independent from poor family environment). In general, the authors concluded that CSA does not appear to cause as much intense or long-lasting psychological harm as might be assumed.

This paper ignited a firestorm of controversy that took several years to play out. Most people assume that the sexual abuse of children is bad because of the long-term harm such abuse holds for children. Yet here was a study saying that it was difficult to document any substantial harm over the long run for childhood sexual abuse. Many people entered the debate because they were simply outraged over the conclusions that childhood sexual abuse was not so bad.

Other groups were outraged by the Rind and colleagues paper for other reasons. For example, psychoanalysts have the assumption that psychological problems in adulthood have their roots in

childhood trauma. The Rind and colleagues paper goes against this critical assumption by suggesting that the link between adult difficulties and sexual abuse in childhood is weak to nonexistent.

Organizations that endorse pedophilia (sexual contact between children and adults) applauded the Rind publication on their websites, citing this paper as supporting their moral position that sexual relations between children and adults is acceptable. In 1999 the publisher of the *Psychological Bulletin*—the American Psychological association—issued a statement saying that they do not endorse pedophilia, and that "the sexual abuse of children is wrong and harmful to its victims." In 1999 the U.S. House of Representatives passed a resolution condemning the Rind and colleagues paper, declaring that child–adult sex was inherently "abusive and destructive" and the resolution was passed unanimously in the Senate.

What can we say about this paper in light of the controversy it started? The authors attacked a common assumption that CSA causes harm and leads to long-term problems. Most cultures around the world consider it wrong for adults to have sexual contact with children. However, Rind and colleagues argued that the "wrongfulness" of CSA may be in question because its "harmfulness" is in dispute. In other words, because the act may not produce harmful *consequences,* we might question whether CSA is actually *wrong.*

The rebuttals of the Rind and colleagues paper fall into two categories: methodological and interpretational. On the methodological side, one important

concern is that the data were based on college students. Such a sample would exclude victims of CSA who were so traumatized that they did not go on to attend college. By excluding non-college-attending persons from their research, the authors may have severely underestimated the effect of CSA on adult adjustment. Another methodological concern is the broad definition they used of CSA, which included acts ranging from forced sexual intercourse to being verbally propositioned. By including such "mild" abuses as being verbally propositioned (without sexual contact) in their definition of CSA, it could be that Rind and colleagues diluted the effects of real CSA on adjustment.

A final methodological concern involves the fact that most of the studies analyzed by Rind and colleagues relied completely on retrospective self-report of college students as the only source of data. A much better (though also much more difficult) approach would be a prospective design, where children identified as having been recently abused would be followed over the years until they are adults and then adjustment is assessed and compared with a control group that was not abused.

One can also disagree with how Rind and colleagues interpreted their findings. One issue, for example, concerns the meaning of "small" when the authors describe the relation between CSA and such adjustment outcomes as anxiety, depression, suicide, or divorce. It is true that the effect sizes conform to the statistical definition of small (e.g., effect sizes less than .30). However, even small effects can reflect very important consequences for some

(Continued)

A Closer Look (*Continued*)

people. Moreover, individuals may exhibit elevated levels of one type of symptom, but the symptoms may differ from person to person such that any one symptom may not be very elevated in the CSA population as a whole. In certain ways, statistical effect sizes do not convey the clinical or "real-life" significance of individual suffering and, in this regard, can be misleading.

Another interpretation issue concerns the fact that, because their data suggest that CSA is not related to adult problems, Rind and colleagues (1998) go on to allude that CSA is not, in itself, morally wrong. However, this is a slippery slope. Such a position holds that in order for something to be morally wrong, it must be shown to be harmful. It confuses a moral standard with a scientific standard, and science can only document facts, not decide on right

and wrong. Ultimately, the question boils down to how we decide if something is morally wrong. Legally, the definition of most wrongs is given by society's norms, by what most people feel is wrong or inappropriate. When it comes to children, society generally believes that they are incapable of making rational and informed life decisions. For example, in U.S. society, children are not allowed to enter into financial contracts, to decide whether they want to attend school, or to consent to medical procedures. Add to this list society's belief that children cannot consent to sexual relations. The moral basis is that children cannot consent to sex because they have little knowledge about what is being consented to. Also, when an adult forces the issue, the child may not have the freedom to accept or decline. This position is well summarized in a 1999

public letter written by the then American Psychological Association CEO Raymond Fowler to Congressman Delay, holding "that children cannot consent to sexual activity with adults" and that such activity "should never be considered or labeled as harmless or acceptable" (American Psychological Association, 1999). Because society believes that children lack the maturity to make important life decisions, they need to be protected from those who would exploit their immaturity. In this sense, the data from the Rind and colleagues article are irrelevant to whether CSA is morally wrong. The huge controversy surrounding the article was not so much an attempt to censure unpopular and surprising results. Much of the controversy can be traced to the authors' use of science to replace morality; they confused "harmfulness" with "wrongness."

2011). The story answers the following questions: Who am I? What is my place in the adult world? What are the unifying themes of my life? What is the purpose of my existence? McAdams (e.g., 2016, McAdams & Manczak, 2015) sees identity as a narrative story that a person constructs. Although a person may rearrange and reconstruct the plot of his or her life story, it nevertheless takes on importance as the person's unique story. According to McAdams, once the story has evolved to have coherent themes, the person may make very few changes to his or her story. However, certain events can cause large changes to identity and are incorporated into the narrative, such as graduation, marriage, birth of a child, turning 40, or retirement. Unexpected events can become a part of the story too, such as the death of a marriage partner, loss of a job, or unexpected wealth. A study by Cox and McAdams (2012) showed that even volunteering over spring break to work with people living in poverty can transform the narrative identity that college students write about themselves. McAdams (2008) describes how all of us construct a life story, and that part of becoming an adult is taking ownership of this story:

> People begin to construct narrative identities in adolescence and young adulthood and continue to work on these stories across the adult life course. . . . The stories we construct to make sense of our lives are fundamentally about our struggle to reconcile who we imagine we were, are, and might be in our heads and bodies with who we were, are, and might be in the social contexts of family, community, the workplace, ethnicity, religion, gender, social class, and culture writ large. The self comes to terms with society through narrative identity (pp. 242–243).

Erikson's Eight Stages of Development

Whereas Freud taught that our personalities were formed by around the age of 5 years, Erikson disagreed and felt that important developmental changes occurred throughout the life span, from birth to old age. For example, Freud called the period from age 6 to puberty the latency period because he believed nothing psychologically important was happening. However, Erikson points out that this is a period when children are starting to go to school; they are learning to work and to gain satisfaction from success and from accomplishments; they are learning to be sociable, to share, and to cooperate with peers; and they are learning about social structures, such as the fact that teachers are in charge and represent authorities. Erikson (1963, 1968) argued that much development occurred during the years that Freud called "latency." Indeed, Erikson believed that the development of personality lasted well into adulthood and even into old age (Erikson, 1975). He outlined his theory of personality growth into **eight stages of development** through which people all pass (Figure 10.2).

So Erikson disagreed strongly with Freud about the time span of personality development. In addition, Erikson also disagreed with Freud about the conflict, or crisis, that occurs at each stage. Whereas Freud felt that the crises were inherently

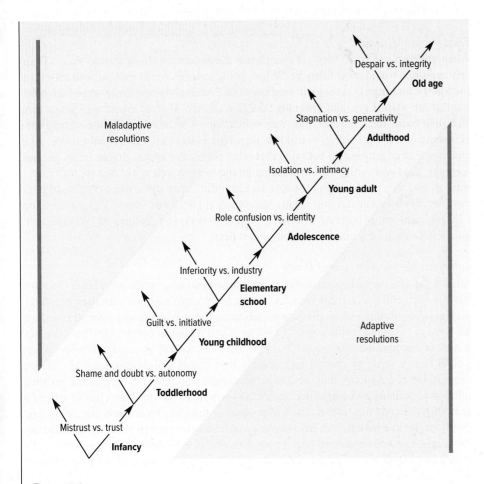

Figure 10.2

Erikson's eight stages of development.

sexual in nature, Erikson believed that the crises were of a social nature. After all, he argued, the persons with whom we have our first social relationships are our parents. Thus, there could be crises of learning to trust our parents, learning to be autonomous from them, learning from them how to act as an adult. Developing children also learn to relate to authority figures (e.g., teachers), to peers in various ways, and develop special bonds of intimacy with one or a few special others. He called these **psycho-social conflicts** rather than the psychosexual conflicts that formed Freud's theory of developmental stages.

Although Erikson disagreed with Freud on these two issues of development (the time frame and the nature of the crises encountered), he did agree with Freud on three general points of development. First, like Freud, Erikson kept a **stage model of development,** implying that people go through the stages in a certain order, at particular time points in life, and that there is a specific issue that characterizes each stage. Secondly, Erikson believed that at each stage the person encountered a specific conflict, a **developmental crisis,** that needed to be resolved in an adaptive way that allowed them to advance to the next stage. Third, Erikson maintained the notion of **fixation**, meaning that if the crisis was not successfully and adaptively resolved, then personality development could become hampered and the person would continue to be preoccupied with issues at that stage of development. Let's now briefly consider each of the eight stages.

Trust Versus Mistrust

When children are born, they are completely dependent on those around them. Their first questions would most likely be "Who's going to take care of me, and will they do a good job? Can I trust that they will feed me when I am hungry, warm me when I am cold, comfort me when I cry, and generally take care of me?" If children are well taken care of, if their basic needs are met, then they will develop a sense of trust in their caregivers. This sense of trust, according to Erikson, forms the basis of all future relationships, with trusting children growing up believing that other people are approachable, trustable, and generally good and loving. However, some infants are not well taken care of, for various reasons, and they never receive the love and care they need and are not trusting of their caregiver. Such infants develop a sense that others are not to be trusted and may develop a lifelong pattern of mistrust in others, suspiciousness, and feelings of estrangement, isolation, or social discomfort when around others.

Autonomy Versus Shame and Doubt

Around the second year, most children are on their feet and on the go. This is the stage many parents call the "terrible twos." Children begin experimenting with their new abilities, including running when the parents tell them to walk, screaming when the parents tell them to "use your inside voice." Children at this stage test parental limits as they try to answer the question "How much of the world do I control?" A good outcome is when a child feels a sense of control and mastery over things and develops self-confidence and a sense of autonomy that lets the child explore and learn. If parents inhibit such autonomy, perhaps by being strict, restrictive, or punishing when the child is independent, then the child may feel shame and doubt over the goals he or she is contemplating. Overly protective parents can also cause problems, according to Erikson, in that they can hinder the child's natural urge to explore and to encounter a wide variety of life events and experiences. For example, parents who prevent their child from rough-and-tumble play with other children may cause their child to grow up doubting his or her physical ability.

Initiative Versus Guilt

Children at this stage—around 3 years of age—often imitate adults, dressing in adult clothes, playing adults, and acting as adults. Children at this stage receive their first practice in adult tasks during play. As adults, we must learn how to work together, to follow leaders, and to resolve disputes. When children play, they practice these skills by organizing games, choosing teams and leaders, and forming goals. Then, during school activities they also take the initiative to accomplish goals and to work with a distinct purpose in mind. If all goes well, children at this stage develop a sense of initiative, which translates into ambition and goal seeking. Such children strive to attain their goals. If things do not go well, children may come to expect they will fail in adult tasks and may feel guilty when they try, or even think of trying, to act like an adult. An adult might scold the child "Who do YOU think you are?" making the child feel guilty over the goals they are contemplating. The child might dampen their initiative and become resigned to feeling guilty over wanting to become an adult.

Industry Versus Inferiority

This stage is about experiencing some success in childhood. Of course, children have limited abilities, and there is a lot of competition in school, in sports, and in most areas of their young lives. Starting around age 4, children begin comparing themselves to each other, especially those their own age, and many (although not all) develop a sense of competence and achievement: "I'm the fastest runner in my class" or "I'm the best speller." If children have enough success experiences, then they believe in their strength and abilities and assume that if they just work hard enough, they can do most things they desire to do. This sense of industry—feeling as if they can work to achieve what they want—sets children on their way to being productive members of society. However, with enough failure experiences, children might develop a sense of inferiority, feeling that they don't have the talent or ability to get ahead in life. If a child believes their efforts don't pay off, that no matter how much they work they don't succeed, then they become pessimistic, anticipating failure and inferior results for their future.

Identity Versus Role Confusion

During adolescence, people go through a whole series of dramatic physical changes that accompany puberty. This can be an especially confusing time of life, in which people emerge from childhood into adulthood, whether they are ready or not. Erikson gave this period special attention in his work, referring to identity achievement as one of the most important goals of development.

At this stage, adolescents begin to ask themselves the questions "Who am I?" and "Do others recognize me for who I think I am?" Many people do a lot of experimentation at this stage, trying on many different identities. One semester, a high school student might try on the role of athlete; the next semester, the role of punk rocker; the next semester, born-again Christian; and the next semester, Goth. Experimenting with identities is common at this time of life, with teenagers searching for identity in all sorts of ways and places. One student said he was going to Hawaii to "find himself." In actuality, no matter where you go, there you are, so the search for identity really has no special place. But many people at this stage join groups; drift around socially; commit themselves to various causes or ideals; or experiment with drugs, politics, or religion—all in an effort to find the true "me." Eventually, most people make some decisions about what is important and what they value and want out of life, and they acquire a sense of "who they are," achieving some degree of consistent self-understanding. People who fail in this stage develop role confusion and enter adulthood without a solid sense of who they are or what they think is the meaning of their lives. Such people bounce around among all sorts of roles and are generally unstable in their relationships, in their jobs, and in their goals and values.

People differ from one another in the extent to which they commit themselves to their values, careers, relationships, and ideologies (Marcia, 2002). Most people will pass through a period of **identity confusion**, which refers to not having a strong sense of who one really is. Some cultures institute a **rite of passage** ritual, usually around adolescence, which typically is a ceremony that initiates a child into adulthood. For example, some southwestern American Indians send adolescent males to be alone in the wilderness, fasting, until they have a vision. After such ceremonies, the adolescent is sometimes given a new name, bestowing a new adult identity. Secular American culture does not provide common rite of passage rituals, though certain religions do, such as the Confirmation ritual in Roman Catholicism or Bar/Bat Mitzvah in Judaism.

In resolving the identity crisis, some persons develop a **negative identity,** an identity founded on undesirable social roles, such as street gang member. Unfortunately, modern culture provides many undesirable role models. Because this is a time of life when youngsters are looking for models, most are very impressionable. This is one reason most states keep their juvenile court system separate from the adult court system, so that young persons do not come into contact with adult criminals to use as role models.

Identity is something that must be achieved. If a person commits to an identity they did not work for or that was handed to them, then that identity is likely to be shallow or changeable (Marcia, 1966). Indeed, Marcia (2002) holds that mature identity development involves going through a crisis and emerging with a firm sense of commitment to one's values, relationships, or career. If a person does not have a crisis, or if he or she forms an identity without exploring alternatives, such as accepting the values of parents, then this is called **identity foreclosure.** People in identity foreclosure are often moralistic and conventional, but when asked to back up their positions, they often cannot provide a good rationale for their beliefs and opinions.

A final concept relevant to identity development, especially to college students, concerns the notion of a **moratorium.** This refers basically to taking time to explore options before making a commitment to an identity. In some ways, college can be thought of as a socially approved period in which a young person is able to explore a variety of roles and responsibilities before taking any one set on "for real." One can change majors, change social groups, explore different relationships, meet people from diverse backgrounds, spend a semester studying abroad, and learn about a variety of fields of study before committing to any ideals and values. Erikson himself emphasized exploring alternatives before making a commitment to a particular identity (1968). He held that only after considering alternatives and spending time "shopping around" was a person ready to make commitments and to spend the rest of his or her life honoring those commitments. This is what it means to say that the development of an identity takes work (Newman & Newman, 1988).

Intimacy Versus Isolation

Connecting with others, both in terms of friendships and intimate relationships, becomes a prime concern toward the latter half of the teenage years. People at this stage appear to have a need to develop relationships that are mutually satisfying and intimate. In such relationships, people grow emotionally and develop into caring, nurturing, and providing adults. For many people, this takes the form of making a commitment to one person

Lee Malvo (Left) and John Muhammad were convicted of the sniper murders of several people in the Washington, D.C., area in 2002. Lee Malvo, who was 17 years old at the time of the crimes, pled that he was so much under the influence of the older man, John Muhammad, that he, Lee Malvo, should not be held responsible for any of the shootings. Malvo was most likely in a period of identity confusion. Malvo was sentenced to, and is currently serving, six consecutive life terms in a Virginia supermax prison without the possibility of parole. The older man with whom Malvo identified—John Muhammad—was executed by lethal injection according to Virginia law on November 10, 2009.

Left: Davis Turner-Pool/Getty Images News/Getty Images; Right: Jahi Chikwendiu-Pool/Getty Images News/Getty Images

through marriage. But many others find intimacy without the social contract of marriage. And of course, marriage is no guarantee of intimacy, as it is certainly possible to have a marriage that is devoid of intimate feelings.

Isolation is the result of a failure to find or maintain intimacy. In the United States, the percentage of married people has dropped, from 72 percent in 1970 to 59 percent in 2000. The total number of divorced persons in the United States was 4.3 million in 1970, but that number had risen to 20 million by 2000. In 2006, the number of never-married persons aged 18 and over reached 55 million. Certainly, being single has its benefits (DePaulo, 2006); however, most people report that a satisfying intimate relationship is something they desire. Failing to achieve this level of relationship is often a serious impairment to one's happiness and life satisfaction (Diener & Biswas-Diener, 2008).

Generativity Versus Stagnation

At this stage, occupying most of the adult years, the main question concerns whether or not the person has generated something that he or she really cares about in life. Often this takes the form of a career that one cares about. Other times, it is a family that has generated children that the parent cares about. Sometimes caring is achieved in a hobby or a volunteer activity that is particularly generative and that gives the person something to care about. The crisis at this stage is that when people step back and look at their adult years, they might get the feeling they are just spinning their wheels, stagnating. In other words, without anything to really care about, people may feel that their lives really don't matter or have any meaning or purpose. Some adults are just "going through the motions," and they really don't care about anything. The people who don't really care about what they are doing, who are just going through the motions, are easily seen as phonies. For example, maybe you've had a teacher who really didn't care about the course material, who just came in, lectured blandly, and left. You have probably also had teachers who cared deeply about their topic, whose lectures were enlivened by their interest and enthusiasm, and who obviously drew satisfaction and meaning from their role as teacher or professor (see Professor Randy Pausch's "Last Lecture" on YouTube). This is the difference between generativity and stagnation.

Integrity Versus Despair

This is the last stage of development, occurring toward the end of life, and even this stage contains a crisis, a final issue, to face. This occurs when we let go of the generative role; maybe we retire from the jobs we loved, maybe the children we loved and raised leave home and start their own lives, or maybe the hobbies or volunteer activities we found so meaningful are no longer possible for us. We start the process of withdrawing from life, pulling back from our adult roles, and preparing to face death. At this stage, we look back on our lives and ask: "Was it all worth doing?" "Did I accomplish most of what I wanted to do in life?" If we can take some satisfaction in our lives, then we can face the inevitability of our passing with a measure of integrity (again, see Professor Randy Pausch's "Last Lecture" on YouTube for an example of integrity at the end of life). However, if we are dissatisfied with our lives, have regrets, if we wish we had more time to make changes or repair relationships, then we experience despair. People who have a lot of regrets at the end of their lives become bitter old people who in despair. On the other hand, if people feel that their one go-around was acceptable, that they pretty much did it all up right and have no regrets, then they face their end with integrity.

Late in life there is still one more developmental stage, one more set of questions to be faced: "Was it all worthwhile? Did I accomplish most of what I wanted out of life?" How one answers these questions determines whether the remaining time is filled with bitterness and despair or satisfaction and integrity.
Ronnie Kaufman/Blend Images LLC

Freidrich Nietzsche (1844–1900), a German philosopher, wrote a story in his book *Thus Spoke Zarathustra* (1891/1969) about a person walking on a mountain trail. Along the trail, a troll suddenly jumps out and kills the person. The person, however, is immediately reborn to the same parents, is given the same name, and lives the same life as before. Then one day, again the person is walking on a mountain trail and a troll suddenly jumps out and slays the person, who is reborn to the same parents, is given the same name as before, and lives the same life. The point, Nietzsche says, concerns what a person would think about this eternal return of the same life. If you would not want to live your life over and over again, then perhaps you should make some changes to it now, as you are living it. The person who says, "Yes, I wouldn't mind another go-around of my life, even if it were all the same," is someone who would go through Erikson's last stage and achieve integrity.

Karen Horney and a Feminist Interpretation of Psychoanalysis

Karen Horney (1885–1952; pronounced Horn-eye) was another early proponent of ego psychology. Like Erikson, she was an American doctor who became strongly influenced by Freud and his theory of personality development and change. Horney was a psychoanalyst at a time when most doctors and practically all psychoanalysts in America were men, practicing from the 1930s up to about 1950. She questioned some of the more paternalistic notions of Freudian psychoanalysis and reformulated some of the ideas to generate a more feminist perspective on personality development. For example, she reacted against Freud's notion of penis envy. Recall that Freud interpreted the phallic stage for women as a sexual conflict, starting when a little girl realizes she does not have a penis. Horney taught that the penis was a symbol of **social power** rather than an organ women actually desired. Horney wrote that girls realize, at an early age, that they are being denied social power because of their gender. She argued that girls did not really have a secret desire to become boys. Rather, she taught, girls desired the social power and preferences given to boys in the culture. **Culture** is a set of shared standards for many behaviors. For example, whether a person should feel ashamed about promiscuous sexual behavior is determined by a cultural norm. Moreover, culture might contain different standards for males and females, such that girls should be ashamed if they engage in promiscuous sex, whereas boys should be proud of such behavior, with it being culturally acceptable at that time in history for them to even brag about such behavior.

Horney was among the first psychoanalysts to stress the cultural and historical determinants of personality, which we explore in more detail in Chapters 16 and 17. Horney noted that many gender roles were defined by culture. For example, she coined the phrase **fear of success** to highlight a gender difference in response to competition and achievement situations. Many women, she argued, felt that if they were to succeed they would lose their friends. Consequently many women, she thought, harbored an unconscious fear of success. She held that men, on the other hand, believed they would actually gain friends by being successful and hence were not at all afraid to strive and pursue achievement. This points to an important cultural influence on gendered behavior.

Horney stressed the point that, although biology determines sex, cultural norms are used to determine what is acceptable for a typical male and female in that culture. Partly because of Horney, today we use the terms **masculine** and **feminine** to refer to traits or roles typically associated with being male or female in a particular culture, and we refer to differences in such culturally ascribed roles and traits as **gender differences,** not *sex differences*. This distinction, important to modern feminism, can be traced back to Karen Horney. It is unfortunate that Horney died in 1952 and did not see the progress made by the women's movement, of which she can truly be counted as an early leader.

Horney had very personal knowledge of the social and cultural forces that oppressed women in her era. Colleagues in the male-dominated profession of psychoanalysis were disapproving of her skeptical attitudes toward classical Freudian ideas. In 1941, the members of

Feminist psychoanalysts recognize that cultural forces, not biology, restrict the social roles that women may fill. Cultural forces can change as the social roles deemed appropriate for women change. One place this is evident is in the role of "Presidential Candidate," a social role traditionally deemed appropriate only for men. In the 2020 U.S. presidential primaries, a record-setting number (6) of women competed for the democratic nomination. Kamala Harris, attorney general for the state of California at the time and depicted here, was one of those women. While the "glass ceiling" was not completely broken in the 2020 presidential election, Kamala Harris was elected Vice President of the United States. She is the first woman to serve in this important and influential social role.

the New York Psychoanalytic Institute voted to remove Horney from her position as instructor there. Horney left immediately and went on to establish her own American Institute for Psychoanalysis, which was very successful. Indeed, she went on to develop a major reconceptualization of psychoanalysis, which stressed social influences over biology and gave special attention to interpersonal processes in the creation and maintenance of mental disorders and other problems with living. Her intriguing theories were laid out in a series of highly readable books (Horney, 1937, 1939, 1945, 1950).

Emphasis on Self and the Notion of Narcissism

Ego psychology generally emphasizes the role of identity, which is experienced by the person as a sense of self. Contemporary psychoanalysts Kernberg (1975) and Kohut (1977) are important contributors to the psychoanalytic conception of the role of the self in normal personality functioning and in disorders. In normal personality functioning, most people develop a stable and relatively high level of self-esteem, they have some pride in what they have so far accomplished, they have realistic ambitions for the future, and they feel that they are getting the attention and affection from others that they deserve. Most of us have a healthy level of self-esteem; we consider ourselves worthwhile, we like ourselves, and we believe that others like us as well. And most of us engage in **self-serving biases,** which refers to the common tendency for people to take credit for successes yet to deny responsibility for failure.

Some take self-esteem too far, however, trying to increase their self-worth in various problematic ways. For example, they may constantly try to appear more powerful than others, more independent, or more liked by others. This style of inflated self-admiration and constant attempts to draw attention to the self and to keep others focused on oneself is called **narcissism.** Sometimes narcissism is carried to extremes and becomes narcissistic personality disorder (see Chapter 19). However, narcissistic tendencies can be found in normal range levels, characterized as an extreme self-focus, a sense of being special, feelings of entitlement (that one deserves treatment without having to earn it), and a constant search for others who will serve as one's private fan club and provide unqualified admiration and praise.

There is a paradox, however, commonly called the **narcissistic paradox:** Although a narcissist appears high in self-esteem, he or she actually has doubts about his or her worth as a person. Although the narcissist appears confident and sure of him-or herself, the person needs constant praise, reassurance, and attention from others. Although the narcissist appears to have a grandiose sense of self-importance, he or she is nevertheless very vulnerable to blows to his or her self-esteem and cannot handle criticism very well. In contemporary psychoanalysis, narcissism is seen as disturbance in the sense of self that has many implications for creating problems with living and relating to others.

An example of one problem associated with narcissism is that when narcissists are criticized or challenged, they may behave aggressively, trying to achieve some respect by attacking or belittling their critics. The *Diagnostic and Statistical Manual V* (APA, 2013) suggests that persons with narcissistic personality disorder can be at risk for violence following blows to their self-esteem, such as getting reprimanded at work or having been left by a spouse. This tendency toward violence in response to criticism was illustrated in a laboratory study conducted by psychologists Bushman and Baumeister (1998). The subjects came to the laboratory and wrote a short essay on a topic given to them. Another person then commented on the essays they had just written, providing strong criticism of the subjects' opinions. Later in the experiment, the subjects were given the opportunity to play a computer game with their critic and were allowed to "blast" their opponent with loud bursts of noise during the game; that is, subjects could distract their opponents with irritating blasts of noise during the competition. The narcissistic subjects who had been insulted blasted the critic much more aggressively than did either the non-narcissistic persons or the narcissistic persons who had not received criticism. This finding suggests that narcissism can lead to vengeful aggression when the narcissist is provoked or criticized. People with secure and normally healthy levels of self-esteem, however, do not become vengeful and aggressive when criticized (Rhodenwalt & Morf, 1998).

Exercise

A questionnaire measure of narcissism. The following items are from the Narcissistic Personality Inventory (NPI) (Raskin & Hall, 1979).

1. I think I am a special person.   True   or   False
2. I expect a great deal from other people.   True   or   False
3. I am envious of other people's good fortune.   True   or   False
4. I will never be satisfied until I get all that I deserve.   True   or   False
5. I really like to be the center of attention.   True   or   False

In one interesting study of narcissism, it was found that the number of first-person pronouns a person used in an essay *(I, mine, me)* was correlated positively with narcissism scores (Emmons, 1987). In another study it was found that when given the opportunity to watch themselves on videotape or to watch a tape of someone else, the narcissists spent more time watching the tape of themselves (Robins & John, 1997). This study also showed that narcissists rate their own performance on the videotape much more positively than it is rated by others, implying an inflated sense of their own abilities.

In sum, narcissism is not the same as having high self-esteem (Brown & Ziegler-Hill, 2004). Studies have confirmed the theoretical notions that narcissists are preoccupied with self, are vulnerable to criticism and blows to their self-worth, and respond to such challenges with anger and aggression. Although narcissists appear to have high self-esteem, their internal or private self-representations are fragile and vulnerable. Clearly, an important notion from contemporary psychoanalytic thought is that one's internal representation of self plays an important role in how one interacts with, and reacts to, the social environment. In the next section, you see how contemporary psychoanalysis also focuses on the internal representation of other persons and how this influences social relationships later in life.

Object Relations Theory

Other changes to Freud's original ideas have been so sweeping that one new approach drops the term "analytic" altogether: object relations theory. Recall that Freud emphasized sexuality in the development of personality. He viewed the adult personality as the result of how people accommodate the inevitable conflicts between their desires for sexual pleasure from various body parts and the constraints of parents, social

In 2019, the U.S. government instituted a policy of separating immigrant families in an effort to deter the flow of migration across the southern U.S. border. Many U.S. citizens were outraged at the images of infants and young children being taken from their parents and put in detention in the United States while the parents were deported. Object relations theory emphasizes the importance of the attachment bond between children and parents and points to the long-term consequences of disrupting that bond along with the separation anxiety it causes the children and their parents.

David J. Phillip/AP Images

institutions, and civilized society. Freud's emphasis on sexuality has been completely rethought by recent generations of psychoanalysts. This new movement—**object relations theory**—emphasizes social relationships and their origins in childhood.

Consider the Phallic phase of development. Freud stressed the sexual attraction for the parent of the opposite sex and the accompanying fear, rage, anger, and jealousy toward the parent of the same sex. Psychoanalysts after Freud looked at the same childhood situation and saw, instead, the importance of forming social relationships to the developing personality. Later analysts emphasized not sexuality but, instead, the development of meaningful social relationships as the task that occurs at this stage of development. After all, the first persons with whom we have meaningful relationships are usually our parents, and in particular the primary caregiver.

Although object relations theory has several versions, which differ from each other in emphasis, all the versions have at their core a set of basic assumptions. One assumption is that the internal wishes, desires, and urges of the child are not as important as his or her developing relationships with significant external others, particularly parents or caregivers. A second important assumption is that the others, particularly the mother, become **internalized** by the child in the form of mental objects. The child creates an unconscious mental representation of the mother. The child, thus, has an unconscious "mother" within, to whom he or she can relate. This allows the child to have a relationship with this internalized object, even in the absence of the real mother—hence the term *object relations* theory.

The relationship object the child internalizes is based on his or her developing relationship with the mother or primary caregiver. If things are going well between the mother and the infant, the infant internalizes a caring, nurturant, trustworthy mother object. This image then forms the fundamentals for how children come to view others with whom they develop subsequent relationships. If the child internalizes a mother object who is not trustworthy, perhaps because the real mother has left the child alone too often or has not fed or soothed the child regularly, then the child might have difficulty learning to trust other people later in life. Children who are traumatically separated from their parents during infancy or early childhood—who experience an attachment disruption—often become adults with distinct personality problems (Malone, Westen, & Levendosky, 2011). The first social attachments that the infant develops form the templates for all meaningful relationships in the future. This is consistent with the classic psychoanalytic idea that the "child is father to the man," in the sense that what develops in childhood determines the outcomes in adulthood. However, in the neo-analytic case, it is early childhood experience with caregivers, especially attachment to the primary caregiver, that determines adult personality.

Early Childhood Attachment

Work on early childhood attachment has drawn on a couple of lines of research in developmental psychology. The first line of research was the work by Harry Harlow (1905–1981) and others on infant monkeys. Harlow's well-known experiments involved taking infant monkeys away from their real mothers and raising them with models of mother monkeys made of wire or cloth. These fake mothers did not provide the grooming, cuddling, holding, or social contact of the real mothers. The infant monkeys raised with the unresponsive fake mothers developed problems in adolescence and adulthood, growing into adults who were socially insecure, were generally anxious, and did not develop normal sexual relations as adults (Harlow, 1958; Harlow & Suomi, 1971; Harlow & Zimmerman, 1959). Moreover, the infant monkeys preferred their real mothers to the fake mothers, and they preferred the cloth mother to the wire mother when given the choice. Harlow concluded that **attachment** between infant and primary caregiver required physical contact with a warm and responsive mother and that it is vitally important to the psychological development of the infant.

Attachment to the mother or caregiver during the first six months of life appears to be crucial to all primates, including humans. Attachment in the human infant begins when he or she develops a preference for people over objects. For example, the child prefers to look at a human face rather than at a toy. Then the preference begins to narrow to familiar persons so that the child prefers to see people he or she has seen before, compared with strangers. And finally the preference narrows even further so that the child prefers the mother or primary caregiver over anyone else.

The ways in which young children develop attachments to their parents and caregivers was the primary topic of research for British psychologist John Bowlby (1907–1990) (1969a, 1969b, 1980, 1988). Bowlby focused on the attachment relationship with the mother

The strong bond between infant and primary caregiver, called attachment, is important in the development of all primates, including humans.
IMPALASTOCK/iStock/Getty Images

and how that relationship meets the needs of the infant for protection, nurturance, and support. Bowlby studied what happens when this attachment relationship is temporarily broken, as when the mother has to leave the infant alone for a short time. He noticed that some infants seem to trust that the mother will return and provide uninterrupted care—these infants are happy when the mother returns. Other infants, in contrast, react negatively to separation and become agitated and distressed when the mother leaves. They can be calmed only by the return of the mother. Bowlby said these infants experience **separation anxiety**. Bowlby also observed a third type of infants, who seem to become depressed when their mothers leave. Even when the mother returns, these infants seem to remain detached from, or angry at, their mothers.

Psychologist Mary Ainsworth (1913–1999) and her colleagues developed a 20-minute procedure for studying separation anxiety—a procedure used for identifying differences among children in how they react to separation from their mothers. This is called the **strange situation procedure**. In this procedure, a mother and her baby enter the laboratory room, which is like a comfortable living room. The mother sits down, and the child is free to explore the toys and other things in the room. After a few minutes, a stranger, an unfamiliar but friendly adult, enters the room. The mother then gets up and leaves the baby alone with this unfamiliar adult. After a few minutes, the mother returns to the room and the stranger leaves. The mother is alone with the baby for several more minutes. All the while, the infant is being videotaped, so that his or her reactions can later be analyzed.

Across many studies, Ainsworth and her colleagues (e.g., Ainsworth, 1979; Ainsworth, Bell, & Stayton, 1972) found essentially the same three patterns of behavior noted by Bowlby. One group of infants, called **securely attached**, stoically endured the separation and went about exploring the room, waiting patiently or even approaching the stranger and sometimes wanting to be held by the stranger. When the mothers returned, these infants were glad to see them, typically interacted with them for a while, then went back to exploring the new environment. These infants seemed confident their mothers would return, hence the term *secure*. This group of infants was the largest of the three (66 percent fell into this securely attached group).

The second group, called the **avoidantly attached** group, consisted of infants who avoided the mothers when they returned. The infants in this group typically seemed unfazed when the mothers left and typically did not give them much attention when they returned, as if aloof from their mothers. Approximately 20 percent of the babies fell into this category.

Ainsworth called the third category of infant response to separation the **ambivalently attached** group. The infants in this group were very anxious about the mothers' leaving. Many started crying and protesting vigorously before the mothers even got out of the room. When the mothers were gone, these infants were difficult to calm. On the mothers' return, however, the infants behaved ambivalently. Their behavior showed both anger and a desire to be close to the mothers; they approached their mothers but then resisted by squirming and fighting against being held.

Mothers of babies in these three groups appear to behave differently. According to subsequent research, reviewed by Ainsworth and Bowlby (1991), mothers of securely attached infants provide more affection and stimulation to their babies, and are generally more responsive, than mothers of infants in the other two groups. These studies have provided clear evidence that a caregiver's responsiveness to infants leads to a more harmonious relationship later in life between the child and parents. For example, in one study, responsiveness to infant crying in the early months of life was associated with less (not more) crying at 1 year of age. Although this finding was greeted with disbelief at first, especially by learning theorists, it eventually influenced recommendations for parenting practices (Bretherton & Main, 2000).

Mothers of babies from both the ambivalent and the avoidant groups tend to be less attentive to their children, less responsive to their needs. Such mothers appear to be less in tune or less engaged with their babies. Some children react to these less responsive mothers by becoming angry themselves (the ambivalent infants) or becoming emotionally detached (the avoidant infants). Fraley, Roisman, and Haltigan (2013) showed that maternal insensitivity assessed when the child was 3 years old was related to lower social competence and academic skills when the child was 15 years old. Although there may be alternative explanations for these findings, they are nevertheless consistent with the notion that the lack of maternal responsiveness can have negative childhood outcomes.

These early experiences and reactions of the infant to the parents, particularly the mother, become what Bowlby called **working models** for later adult relationships. These working models are internalized in the form of unconscious expectations about relationships. If children experience that they are not wanted, or that their mothers cannot be trusted to respond to them, then they may internalize the expectation that probably no one else wants them either, or that no one else can be trusted. On the other hand, if children's needs are met, and they are confident that their parents really love them, then they will expect that others will find them lovable as well (Bowlby, 1988). These expectations about future relationships, which are developed in our first contacts with our caregivers, are thought to become part of our unconscious and thereby exert a powerful influence on our adult relationships.

We might believe that the "strange situation" paradigm is useful only for thinking about how children cope with a temporary separation from their caregivers. However, some researchers are studying an adult analogue of this paradigm, where married couples are temporarily separated by life circumstances (Cafferty et al., 1994). These researchers conducted a longitudinal study on members of the National Guard and other military reserve units who were separated from their spouses and deployed overseas. They found that attachment styles predicted individual differences in emotional reactions to partner separation (securely attached persons were not as distressed) and to post-reunion adjustments (ambivalently attached persons had the most difficulty). When adult marital relationships are temporarily disrupted, it may be that the persons in those relationships will react in ways that resemble how they coped with their earliest attachment separations. In this way the attachment bonds developed in infancy and early childhood may lay the foundation for adult romantic attachment bonds developed decades later.

Adult Relationships

Research on attachment has tested object relations ideas by examining whether the attachment style developed in childhood is related to later adult relationship styles. In 2010, an entire issue of the *Journal of Social and Personal Relationships* was dedicated to research on how childhood attachment styles are related to adolescent and adult relationships (Shaver & Mikulincer, 2010). In a study that started this line of research, psychologists Hazan and Shaver (1987) showed that there are patterns of adult relationships that look similar to the secure, avoidant, and ambivalent childhood attachment patterns. In the adult **secure relationship style**, the person has few problems developing satisfying friendships and relationships. Secure people trust others and develop bonds with them. The adult **avoidant relationship style** is characterized by difficulty in learning to trust others. Avoidant adults remain suspicious of the motives of others, and they are afraid of making commitments. They are afraid of depending on others because they anticipate being disappointed, being abandoned, or being separated. Finally, the adult **ambivalent relationship style** is characterized by vulnerability and uncertainty about relationships. Ambivalent adults become overly dependent and demanding on their partners and friends. They display high levels of neediness in their relationships. They are high maintenance, in the sense that they need constant reassurance and attention.

Psychologist Philip Shaver and his colleagues have shown that there is a positive correlation between the parent–infant attachment style and the later relationship style developed in adulthood. In one study, for example, adults with an avoidant relationship style more frequently reported that their parents had unhappy marriages compared to adults with a secure relationship style (Brennan & Shaver, 1993). The adults with a secure relationship style, on the other hand, tended to report coming from a trusting and supportive family, with parents who were happily married. Those with an avoidant relationship style tended to report that their family members were aloof and distant, and that they did not feel very much warmth or trust either from or toward their parents.

You may recall from Chapter 4, we said that personality dimensions rarely were types; that people do not come in categories, but are best represented by dimensions, usually normal-curve shaped dimensions. Yet in the attachment style area, there are three categories that people are put into: secure, avoidant, ambivalent. Are attachment styles really categories? Recent research shows how attachment style can be better represented by underlying dimensions, for example, degrees of security, degrees of avoidance, degrees of ambivalence (Fraley et al., 2015). Indeed, a measure based on dimensions of attachment styles was a better fit to real data than a measure based on categorical distinctions. This new approach to thinking about and measuring attachment styles as dimensions will likely have a large impact on how research is done, and on how psychologists think about and measure attachment style.

Exercise

Determining which adult attachment style a person has can be accomplished by having them report which style is most like them. Consider the following statements, and choose which is most descriptive of you:

1. I am typically comfortable with others and find it easy to become close friends with people. I can easily come to rely on others and enjoy it when they rely on me. I don't worry about being left out or abandoned and find it easy to let others get close to me.
2. I am sometimes tense when I get too close to others. I don't like to trust other people too much, plus I don't like it when people have to depend on me for something. It makes me anxious when people get close or want me to make an emotional commitment to them. People often want me to be more personal and intimate than I feel like being.
3. In relationships, I often worry that the other person does not really want to stay with me or that he or she doesn't really love me. I often wish that my friends would share more and be more of a confidante than they seem willing to be. Maybe I scare people away with my readiness to become close and make them the center of my world.

The first description is associated with a secure relationship style, the second with an avoidant relationship style, and the third with an ambivalent relationship style. It is possible that you have different styles with different people, or that none of these descriptions applies perfectly to your relationships.

A dominant theme of attachment theory is that a person's romantic attachments in adulthood will be a reflection of his or her attachment patterns in the past, especially with their earliest relationships (for review, see Fraley & Roisman, 2015). Mental representations of the earliest relationships (i.e., the "objects" in Object Relations Theory) can serve as prototypes (or working models) for later relationships, with the early experiences retaining their influential role in attachment behaviors throughout the life span. The psychologist Chris Fraley has published meta-analyses of studies examining the long-term influence of attachment styles (Fraley, 2002a, 2002b). After reviewing a great deal of research, and evaluating different models of change and stability, Fraley concludes that the data are consistent with a moderate degree of stability in attachment security from infancy to adulthood. His best estimate of the correlation between early attachment security and attachment security at any later point in time is approximately .39, which can be described as significantly larger than zero but moderate in magnitude. In a study that followed people for a year and assessed adult attachment style, peoples' attachment style was found to be fairly stable over that time period, about as stable as each of the Big Five personality traits (Fraley et al., 2011). Fraley has published an online quiz that

Object relations theorists believe that the characteristics and quality of adult romantic relationships are determined by, in part, attachment bonds developed in infancy with a primary caregiver.
Left: Purestock/SuperStock; right: Alexander Benz/Purestock/SuperStock

people can take to assess the similarity among their attachment styles with different people in their lives (see www.yourpersonality.net/relstructures/). Another site where you can take a questionnaire and receive feedback on your adult attachment style can be found at: https://www.npr.org/2022/02/09/1079587715/whats-your-attachment-style-quiz, and another at: http://www.web-research-design.net/cgi-bin/crq/crq.pl

Adult relationship styles may be most important for understanding romantic relationships. What do people look for in a romantic relationship? What do people expect from their romantic partners? How do people cope with separation from or abandonment by their romantic partners, either real or imagined? Research suggests that individuals with different attachment styles will answer these questions very differently from each other (e.g., Hazan & Shaver, 1987). Those with an avoidant attachment style tend to shun romance, believing that real love is rare and never lasts. They fear intimacy and rarely develop deep emotional commitments. They tend not to be very supportive of their partners, at least not emotionally, and they expect little support in return.

Adults with an ambivalent attachment style tend to have frequent, but short-lived, romantic relationships. They fall in and out of love easily but rarely say that they are happy with their relationships. They develop a sort of desperation in their adult relationships and show fear of losing their partners. Their focus is often on keeping the other happy, and so they are quick to compromise, to change themselves for the sake of avoiding conflict with the other. As you might guess, ambivalent adults report that being separated from their partners is very stressful.

Adults with a secure attachment style can be separated from their partners without stress, just as securely attached children can remain calm when their mothers leave the room. Secure adults are generally more warm and supportive in their romantic relationships, and their partners report more satisfaction with the relationship than do the partners of avoidant or ambivalent adults (Hazan & Shaver, 1994). Secure adults are also more likely to give emotional support to their partners when it is needed. Secure adults also seek support when they need it more than do ambivalent or avoidant adults. In general, secure adults do a good job of navigating through the treacherous waters of adult romantic relationships. They have a roadmap for satisfying relationships in the mental representation they carry of their childhood attachment bond. A study by Fraley and colleagues (Holland, Fraley, & Roisman, 2012) showed that the effects of attachment style on romantic relationships are more observable after the relationship has been developing for awhile, with stronger effects observed one year into the relationship than at the very start of the relationship. It takes awhile to really get a relationship started and new attachments formed.

An interesting study by psychologist Jeff Simpson illustrates the working of attachment styles in adult relationships (Simpson et al., 2002). In this study heterosexual dating couples served as subjects. The couple was told that the male would undergo a stressful and unpleasant experience as part of the experiment. They were separated and the male was taken to a room where an experimenter recorded his pulse while saying the following:

> *In the next few minutes you are going to be exposed to a situation and set of experimental procedures that arouse considerable anxiety and distress in most people. Due to the nature of these procedures, I cannot tell you any more at this moment. (Simpson, 2012, p. 603)*

Source: Simpson, J. Advances in Experimental Social Psychology. Academic Press, 2012.

The purpose of this statement was to make the male subject anxious. Moreover, he was taken to a darkened, windowless room that contained some polygraphs. The experimenter remarked that the equipment was "not quite ready yet" and that the subject would have to wait a few minutes before the "stress phase" could start. Meanwhile, the female was told that her partner was going to be involved in a "stress and performance session" that would start in 5 or 10 minutes. The couple was brought together to wait, and during this time together, they were unobtrusively videotaped for 5 minutes. After 5 minutes the experimenter entered the room and told the subjects the experiment was over, explained the purpose of the experiment, and told the subjects that they could erase the videotape if they so desired (none did).

The experimenters coded the videotape for a number of behaviors. Mostly they were interested in the degree to which the women offered support to their partners, and the degree to which the men asked for support from their partners. Prior to the start of the experiment, the experimenters used an interview method to assess childhood recollections of experiences with parents and other attachment

Families are currently fleeing from the fierce fighting going on in Ukraine. Most of the fathers, however, once they see their family to the border, are returning to fight in the conflict. This is a real-life example of severe relationship disruption, where each partner will undergo extreme danger and stress while separated from their partner.

Visar Kryeziu/AP Photo

figures. From these interviews the experimenters rated the degree to which each subject was avoidantly or securely attached to his or her primary caregivers in early childhood.

Results showed that women who had avoidant attachment experiences with their parents were significantly less likely to offer support and encouragement to their male partners, even if the male asked for that. The securely attached women did provide support if the partner asked for it but provided less if he did not ask for it. This is a contingent pattern of support, what some researchers consider ideal in relationships (George & Solomon, 1996). Very similar results have been obtained when roles are reversed and the female partner was to undergo stress (Thompson, Simpson, and Berlin, 2022).

The study just described employed an anticipated laboratory stressor, which was not very intense or long-lasting. Studies of real, intense, and chronic stress (persons under missile attacks, persons undergoing combat training) have found that attachment styles do relate to help seeking (Mikulincer, Florian, & Weller, 1993; Mikulincer & Florian, 1995). Specifically, secure men and women seek support from their partners when in distressing conditions, whereas avoidantly attached persons try to distance themselves from others, want to spend time alone when under stress, and distract themselves from the stressors. When stress is severe or chronic, it appears that a person's attachment style might relate to her or his pattern of support seeking.

Individual differences in attachment style may have implications beyond those for romantic relationships. Any area of life that involves closeness, getting along with others, confiding in others, and seeking or giving social support might be negotiated differently by persons with different attachment styles (Elliot & Reis, 2003). Attachment theory has been applied to understanding relationships between twins (Fraley & Tancredy, 2012), relationships with pets (Zilcha-Mano, Mikulincer, & Shaver, 2012), and even one's relationship with one's God (Granqvist et al., 2012). Of particular interest, how one was parented as a child may influence how one, later in life, parents one's own children. Szepsenwol and colleagues (2015) showed that this effect was strongest for men, with men who had an insecure attachment style when they were infants going on to develop a more negative and unsupportive parenting style when they became parents. Karantzas and Simpson (2015) extend the implications of attachment style theory to the situation where adult children become caregivers to their own aging parents, a situation that has been likened to role reversal; the children becoming caregivers to the parents. Any life situation that involves close, caring relationships may be affected by how it went with the very first relationship that was experienced in life.

We want to close this chapter on a hopeful note with the answer to the following question: If a person develops a particular childhood attachment style, is he or she destined to live out the adult version of that style? This important question has been the topic of much theoretical debate and empirical research (Cassidy & Shaver, 1999; Simpson & Rholes, 1998). Attachment theorists believe that even the poorest childhood experiences with relationships can be overcome. Ainsworth and Bowlby (1991) argued that children were not necessarily damaged forever because of unfortunate parenting experiences in infancy. They felt that subsequent positive experiences could compensate for earlier negative relationships. Despite a bad start in life, a person exposed to a loving, nurturant relationship as an adult can revise his or her working model of object relations. While this is difficult, and takes a patient and understanding partner, even insecure childhood attachment can be overcome in adulthood. If the relationship is positive and supportive enough, the person could internalize a new mental version of relationships, one that is more secure and trusting, with positive expectations for relationships (Fraley, 2007; Fraley, Gilath, & Deboeck, 2021).

SUMMARY AND EVALUATION

In this chapter, we explored updated and contemporary versions of some of Freud's original ideas, which can be called the Neo-Analytic movement. We began with an evaluation of repressed memories, examining a case in which the recalled memory turned out to be false, at least as determined in a court of law. This case should not put doubt on the possibility that real trauma can be forgotten or repressed. Indeed, such cases do exist and conform to the notion that traumatic experiences can be pushed out of consciousness. However, the material in this chapter is meant to lead you to a more balanced and skeptical approach to the topic of repressed memories. Although repressed memories *can* occur, some "forgotten" memories are false. Such memories can be implanted by well-meaning therapists and others interrogating a subject about an event. We also discussed how to discriminate real from false memories. The crucial element is corroboration, finding someone who can support the subject's version of the remembered event. We also touched on the topic of fake news and the "weaponization" of memory principles to influence what people come to believe about an event or a person or conspiracy theories.

The view of repressed memories also highlights a more contemporary version of the unconscious. Although most modern cognitive psychologists believe in the unconscious, they do not believe in the motivated version of the unconscious proposed by Freud. Certainly, material can get into the mind without conscious experience, as through subliminal perception or priming, but that material does not have the kind of sweeping motivational effects suggested by Freud.

Another reconstruction of Freud's theory concerns the emphasis on the role of the ego relative to the id. This is in stark contrast to Freud's emphasis on aggressive and sexual id urges as the twin engines powering psychic life. We discussed two proponents of ego psychology. The first, Erik Erikson, was well known for his alternative theory of personality development, which differed from Freud's in two important ways: an emphasis on social tasks and an extension of development through the entire life span. A second important figure in ego psychology was Karen Horney, who was among the first psychoanalysts to consider the role of culture and social roles as central features in personality development. Horney also started a feminist reinterpretation of Freud's theories, which continues to this day. Ego psychology also generated an interest in the development of sense of self, the protection of self, and the paradoxical self-concept in Narcissism.

Object relations theory is another contemporary development in this area, having been called the most important theoretical development in psychoanalysis since Freud's death. The term *object relations* is used to refer to enduring patterns of behavior in relationships with intimate others, as well as to the emotional, cognitive, and motivational processes that generate those patterns of behavior. The theory is about how relationship behaviors are determined by mental representations laid down in childhood through experiences with caregivers. This theory began with studies of attachment between children and primary caregivers—typically, mothers. This bond may set a pattern that continues into adulthood.

Parts and versions of Freud's psychoanalytic theory are alive and well today. However, instead of focusing on unconscious conflicts over id urges, contemporary psychoanalysts are more likely to focus on interpersonal patterns of behavior and the emotions and motives that accompany those. Instead of seeing personality as the result of a sequence of sexual conflicts with the parents, contemporary psychoanalysts are more likely to see personality as the result of solving a series of social crises and the ensuing movement toward increasingly mature forms of relating to others. And, finally, unlike much of classical psychoanalytic theory, which was based on one man's views, much of contemporary psychoanalytic theory is connected to empirical studies and corroborated observations of many persons, including female psychologists, working to improve and expand on some of themes first described by Freud.

KEY TERMS

false memories 306

imagination inflation effect 301

confirmatory bias 301

constructive memory 302

spreading activation 302

cognitive unconscious 307

motivated unconscious 307

subliminal perception 307

priming 307

id psychology 308

ego psychology 308

identity 308

identity crisis 308

Erikson's eight stages of
    development 311

psychosocial conflicts 312

stage model of development 312

developmental crisis 312

fixation 312

identity confusion 314

rite of passage 314

negative identity 314

identity foreclosure 314

moratorium 314

social power 317

culture 317

fear of success 317

masculine 317

feminine 317

gender differences 317

self-serving biases 318

narcissism 318

narcissistic paradox 318

object relations theory 320

internalized 320

attachment 321

separation anxiety 321

strange situation procedure 321

securely attached 322

avoidantly attached 322

ambivalently attached 322

working models 322

secure relationship style 323

avoidant relationship style 323

ambivalent relationship style 323

Science Photo Library RF/
Getty Images

Motives and Personality

11

THE INTRAPSYCHIC DOMAIN

Olympic Gold-medalist Michael Johnson, who used different strategies to motivate himself before a 200-meter race and a 400-meter race. HASLIN Frederic/Corbis via Getty Images

One hot August night in 1996, a gun went off in Atlanta. It started the final of the 200-meter Olympic race. Michael Johnson, who had won a gold medal in the 400-meter race just a few days earlier, exploded from the starting blocks. Would he become the first man in history to win both the 400- and 200-meter races at the Olympics? Michael stumbled slightly at the start of the race but soon assumed the upright style that had come to characterize his running style. As he went around the turn, his trademark golden shoes flashing, it became obvious to the crowd that he was running for more than just the gold medal. As Michael widened his lead over his opponents, people knew they were witnessing something special. Michael finished a full 5 meters ahead of his nearest competitor, and as he crossed the finish line, the timer read 19.32 seconds. People who knew the significance of that time, including Michael himself, gasped in disbelief. He had beaten the previous world record, which he had set earlier, by almost three-tenths of a second, a remarkable gap in short-distance running. You can view this amazing athletic performance at: https://www.youtube.com/watch?v=zOZajO0rCP4

How did Michael motivate himself to set a world record in the 200-meter race and win a gold medal in the 400-meter race? The 400- and 200-meter races are very different, according to runners. In the 400-meter race, the runners can be strategic and take some time to plan a tactic. The 200, on the other hand, demands that the runners run flat-out and aggressive.

Before the 400-meter race, Michael reportedly listens to jazz on his headset; before the 200, he listens to gangsta rap. He tries to make himself feel aggressive before the 200-meter race. He tries to get into what he calls the "danger zone." In warming up for the 200-meter race at Atlanta, Michael pulled on a T-shirt that read DANGER ZONE. "Now I have to think about the 200," he said. "I've got to get into the danger zone. I've got to get more aggressive." He approached the 200-meter race with a fighting instinct, taking the offense by running not just to beat his competitors but to beat them badly. As Michael approached the finish line in the 200-meter race, the aggression could be seen in his face, an expression that looked as if he could assault his opponents. The only thing he assaulted, however, was the world record. He had just motivated himself to run faster than any other living person.[1]

We saw in Chapter 1 that personality psychologists ask, "Why do people do what they do?" Motivational psychologists phrase the question a bit differently—"What do they want?" All personality psychologists seek to explain behavior. Personality psychologists interested in motivation, however, look specifically for a desire or motive that propels people to do the things they do (Winter, 2018).

In this chapter, we cover some of the major theories on human motivation, and we examine some research findings on these theories. Some theories that we will look at are quite different from each other, such as the theories of Henry Murray and Abraham Maslow. In fact, most texts in personality cover these two theories in different chapters. However, all the theories we examine here have two features in common. First, all view personality as consisting of a few general motives, which all people have to various degrees. Second, these motives operate mainly through mental processes, either inside or outside of awareness, generating an intrapsychic influence on a person's behavior (King, 1995).

Basic Concepts

Motives are internal states that arouse and direct behavior toward specific objects or goals. A motive is often caused by a deficit, a lack of something; for example, if a person has not eaten for many hours, he or she is motivated by hunger. Motives differ from each other in both type and amount. Hunger differs from thirst, for example, and both of these differ from the motive to achieve and excel. Motives differ in intensity, depending on the person and his or her circumstances. For example, the strength of the hunger motive varies considerably, depending on whether a person has merely skipped a meal or has not eaten for several days. Also, motives are often based on **needs**, states of tension within a person. As a need is satisfied, the state of tension is reduced. The need to eat creates the motive of hunger. The motive of hunger in turn causes the person to seek out food, to think about food constantly, and perhaps even to see food in objects not normally thought of as food. For example, a hungry person gazing at the sky might exclaim, "Wow, that cloud looks just like a hamburger!" Motives propel people to perceive, think, and act in specific ways that satisfy the need. Figure 11.1 illustrates the relation between needs and motives. Most, though not all, needs are based on deficits, and we begin with those deficit-based needs.

Motives belong in the intrapsychic domain for several reasons. First, researchers who study motives have stressed the importance of *internal* psychological needs and

---

[1]In the 2000 Olympics at Sydney, Michael Johnson again won the gold medal in the 400-meter race but had to drop out of competition in the 200-meter race. Johnson subsequently retired from competition. However, he remains the only male athlete in history to have won both the 200- and 400-meter events at the same Olympics.

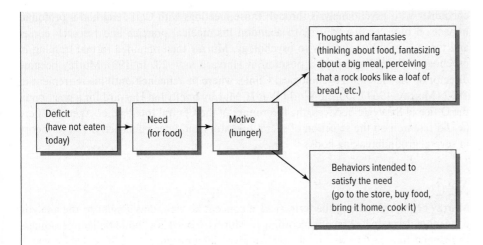

Figure 11.1

Deficits lead to a need, which leads to a motive to satisfy that need, either in reality, by fostering specific actions, or in fantasy, by creating thoughts that are satisfying.

urges that propel people to think, perceive, and act in certain predictable ways. Motives can be unconscious, in the sense that the person does not know explicitly what he or she wants. Just as people may not be fully aware of why they engage in particular fantasies, they may not be consciously aware of what compels them to act in certain ways. This similarity leads to another feature shared by psychologists interested in motives and other intrapsychic constructs—the reliance on projective techniques. Motive psychologists believe that fantasies, free associations, and responses to projective techniques reveal the unconscious motivation behind many thoughts, feelings, and behaviors (Schultheiss & Kollner, 2021).

One of the first researchers to develop a modern theory of human needs was Henry Murray (1893–1988), a psychologist active in research from the 1930s through the 1960s. The path that ultimately led Murray to a career in psychology was quite unique. He went to medical school, became a physician, and interned in surgery. Murray then pursued research in embryology, followed by a PhD in biochemistry from Cambridge University. While studying in England, Murray went to Zurich during spring break in 1925, to visit the famous psychoanalyst Carl Jung (1875–1961); (who learned psychoanalysis directly from Freud and even modified some of Freud's ideas about the unconscious). Murray met with Jung every day for three weeks, meetings from which he "emerged a reborn man" (Murray, reprinted in Shneidman, 1981, p. 54). Murray's

Motive psychologists also share some core ideas with dispositional psychologists, whose work we covered in Part One of this book. Like dispositional psychologists, motive psychologists stress that (1) people differ from one another in the type and strength of their motives; (2) these differences are measurable; (3) these differences cause or are associated with important life outcomes, such as business success or marital satisfaction; (4) differences among people in the relative amounts of various motives are stable over time; and (5) motives may provide one answer to the question, "Why do people do what they do?" The motive approach can be thought of as a halfway point between the intrapsychic domain and the dispositional domain (Winter et al., 1998). We place motives in the intrapsychic domain because of the view that motives exist within the psyche and can operate outside of conscious awareness to affect everyday behaviors, thoughts, and feelings.

encounter with psychoanalysis through those meetings with Carl Jung had a profound impact on him, leading Murray to abandon his medical practice and research career and turn his attention entirely to psychology. Murray then obtained formal training in psychoanalysis and accepted a position at Harvard in 1923. In 1937 Murray became director of the Harvard Psychological Clinic, where he remained until his retirement in 1962 (Murray, 1967). During World War II, Murray briefly left Harvard for a position in the Office of Strategic Services, the forerunner of the Central Intelligence Agency. There he did research on the selection of secret operators and later published his need theory in several groundbreaking books.

Need

Murray began by defining the term *need,* a concept he viewed as similar to the analytic concept of drive. In a nutshell, according to Murray, a need is a "potentiality or readiness to respond in a certain way under certain given circumstances. . . . It is a noun which stands for the fact that a certain trend is apt to recur" (Murray, 1938, p. 124). Needs organize perception, guiding us to see what we want (or need) to see. For example, someone who has a high need for power, a need to influence others, may see even everyday social situations as opportunities to boss others around.

A need also organizes action by compelling a person to do what is necessary to fulfill the need. A person who has a need to achieve, for example, often makes sacrifices and works hard at the task in which he or she wants to excel. Murray believed that needs referred to states of tension and that satisfying the need reduces the tension. According to Murray, however, it was the *process* of reducing tension that the person found satisfying, not the tensionless state per se. Murray believed that people might actually seek to increase tension (e.g., by going on a roller-coaster ride or viewing a horror movie) in order to experience the pleasure of reducing that tension (i.e., to end the roller-coaster ride or the horror movie).

Based on his research with the Office for Strategic Services, Murray proposed a list of fundamental human needs, some of which are described in Table 11.1. Each need is associated with (1) a specific desire or intention, (2) a particular set of emotions, (3) specific action tendencies, and (4) can be described with trait-like names. Consider the need for affiliation, which is the desire to win and maintain associations with people. The primary set of emotions associated with this need are interpersonal warmth, cheerfulness, and cooperativeness, and the associated action tendencies are accepting people, spending time with others, and making efforts to maintain contact with others. The associated traits that characterize people with a strong need for affiliation are attributes such as agreeableness, friendliness, loyalty, and goodwill.

Murray believed that each person had a unique **hierarchy of needs.** An individual's various needs can be thought of as existing at different levels of strength—for instance, a person might have a high need for dominance, an average need for affiliation, and a low need for achievement. Each need interacts with the various other needs within each person. This interaction is what makes the concept of motive **dynamic.** The term *dynamic* is used to refer to the mutual influence of forces within a person—in this case, the interaction of various motives within a person. To return to our person with a high need for dominance, it would make a big difference in her overall behavior if her need for dominance were accompanied with a high or low need for affiliation. If her high need for dominance were coupled with a high need for affiliation (e.g., a strong desire to develop and maintain relationships), then she would most likely develop the social and leadership skills to make others comfortable with her dominance. If her high need for

Table 11.1 A Brief Description of Several of Murray's Needs, Organized into Five Higher-Level Categories

Ambition Needs

- **Achievement:** To master, manipulate, or organize others, objects, or ideas. To accomplish difficult tasks, and to do this as rapidly and independently as possible. To overcome obstacles and excel. To surpass rivals by exercising talent.
- **Exhibition:** To be seen and heard, to be the center of attention. To make an impression on others. To excite, fascinate, entertain, intrigue, amuse, entice, or amaze others.
- **Order:** To put things in orderly arrangement, to desire cleanliness, organization, balance, neatness, and precision.

Needs to Defend Status

- **Dominance:** To seek to influence or direct the behavior of others by persuasion, command, suggestion, or seduction. To control one's environment, particularly the social environment. To restrain or prohibit others.

Needs Related to Social Power

- **Abasement:** To accept injury, criticism, and blame. To submit passively to external force, to resign oneself to fate. To admit inferiority, error, or wrongdoing. To confess and atone and seek pain and misfortune.
- **Aggression:** To overcome opposition forcefully. To avenge an injury. To attack, injure, or kill another. To forcefully punish or oppose another.
- **Autonomy:** To shake off restraint, break out of confines. To get free, to resist coercion and restriction. To avoid being domineered. To be free to act according to one's wishes and to remain unattached.
- **Blame-avoidance:** To avoid humiliation at all costs. To avoid situations that may lead to embarrassment or belittlement. To refrain from action because of fear of failure or worry over the scorn, derision, or indifference from others.

Social Affection Needs

- **Affiliation:** To enjoy cooperation or reciprocal interaction with similar others. To draw near to others. To please and win affection of those you like. To remain loyal to friends.
- **Nurturance:** To take care of others in need, to give sympathy and gratify the needs of helpless others, such as a child, or someone who is weak, disabled, inexperienced, infirm, humiliated, lonely, dejected, or confused. To assist persons in danger. To help, support, console, protect, comfort, nurse, feed, and heal others.
- **Succor:** To receive aid from others. To have one's needs gratified by another, to be nursed, supported, protected, advised, indulged, loved, and consoled. To always have a supporter or a devoted protector.

Source: Adapted from *Explorations in Personality,* by J. H. Murray, New York: Oxford University Press, 1938.

dominance were combined instead with a weak need for affiliation, then she might simply exercise power over others without regard to their feelings. She might impress others as being disagreeable, quarrelsome, or just plain bossy.

Press

Another important contribution of Murray to personality psychology was a specific way of thinking about the environment. For example, a person with a high need for affiliation might be sensitive to the social aspects of his or her environment, such as how many people are present, whether they are interacting, and whether they look approachable and outgoing. Murray used the term **press** to refer to need-relevant aspects of the environment. A person's need for affiliation, for example, won't affect that person's behavior without an appropriate environmental press (such as the presence of friendly people). People with a high need for affiliation would be more likely to notice other people, and to see more opportunities for friendly interaction with others, compared to someone with a low need for affiliation.

Murray also introduced the notion that there is a so-called real environment (which he called **alpha press,** or objective reality) and a perceived environment (called **beta press,** or reality as it is perceived). In any given situation, what one person sees may be different from what other people see. Consider what might happen if two people are walking down the street and a third person approaches and smiles at each of them. One person who is high on the need for affiliation might see the smile as a sign of warmth and openness and a nonverbal invitation to start a conversation. The other person who is low on the need for affiliation might observe the same smile yet see it as a smirk and consequently become suspicious that the stranger is laughing at them. Objectively (alpha press), it was the same smile. Subjectively (beta press), it was a very different event for these two persons, due to their differences in the need for affiliation. Psychologists are more interested in beta press, the subjective experience of a situation by a person.

Apperception and the TAT

Murray held that a person's needs influenced how he or she experiences the environment. In short, needs create beta press, especially when the environment is ambiguous and needs to be interpreted (as when a stranger smiles at the person). The act of interpreting the environment and perceiving the meaning of what is going on in a situation is termed **apperception** (Murray, 1933). Because our needs and motives influence apperception, if we want to know about a person's primary motives, we might ask that individual to interpret what is going on in a variety of situations, especially ambiguous situations.

The simple insight that needs and motives influence how we perceive the world led Murray and his research associate Christiana Morgan to develop a formal technique for assessing needs (Morgan & Murray, 1935). They called this technique the **thematic apperception test** (or TAT, for short). The TAT consists of a set of black-and-white images that are ambiguous. The person being assessed is then asked to make up a story about what is happening in the picture. For example, one TAT image is a drawing of a person on a windowsill. Some people might "see" the person in the drawing as going in (to rob the house?) Others might "see" the person in the drawing as going out (jumping to commit suicide or maybe running away after committing a crime in the house?). A few TAT images contain no people at all, such as a picture of a rowboat on the shore of a small creek. Such pictures are perhaps the most ambiguous: Who put the rowboat there? Are they coming or going? Why did they stop the boat in that particular place? Why are they not in the picture right now? Where are they and what are they doing? It is easy to make up a story because the picture is so ambiguous with respect to what could be happening. The idea is that the story they just make up will contain themes consistent with their own needs and motives.

This photo, obtained from U.S. government archives, was used by Morgan and Murray as one of the TAT pictures. Can you make up a story about the child in this photo? What do you believe he is thinking about? What happens next? What does he go on to do with his life?

Source: Farm Security Administration–Office of War Information Photograph Collection, Library of Congress, LC-USF34-055829-D.

In administering the TAT, a person is shown each picture and told to be creative and make up a short story, interpreting what is happening in each picture. He or she is encouraged to tell a story that has a beginning, a middle, and an end. The psychologist then codes the stories for the presence of various types of imagery associated with particular motives. For example, a subject might write the following about the TAT card of the boat on the shore: "The boat in the picture is being used by a young boy to take produce to market. The boy has stopped to gather some wild berries to take to the market to sell along with his farm produce. This boy works very hard and eventually grows up, puts himself through college, and becomes a famous scientist, specializing in the study of plants, primarily agricultural crops." This story has a lot of achievement imagery, so the subject who wrote it would be seen to have a high need for achievement.

Morgan and Murray published the TAT in 1935. Since then, many researchers have modified its administration (e.g., using fewer cards, selecting other drawings, and using a data projector or computers to display the images to many people at once). Because the pictures in the original TAT are dated (e.g., clothing and hair styles are from the 1930s), newer versions of TAT-type pictures have been developed and found to function similarly to the original set in terms of soliciting need-relevant themes (Schultheiss & Brunstein, 2001). The essential features of the TAT and similar projective techniques are that (1) the subject is given an *ambiguous* stimulus, usually a picture, and (2) he or she is asked to describe and *interpret* what is going on.

Take the need for achievement motive, which can be scored by counting up the number of references in the person's story to wanting to do things better, anticipating success, feeling positive about succeeding, and overcoming obstacles (Schultheiss & Brunstein, 2001; Schultheiss & Pang, 2007). Studies of the TAT suggest that people do respond differentially to the themes of the picture, with, for example, high need for achievement people responding to the achievement pictures differently than low need for achievement people (Kwon, Campbell, & Williams, 2001; Tuerlinckz, De Boeck, & Lens, 2002).

Some personality researchers argue that projective tests in general, and the TAT in particular, are less reliable as measures of personality than other methods, such as self-report questionnaires and informant report. Some even argue that the term *test* should not be used to refer to projective methods (McGrath & Carroll, 2012). Nevertheless, the TAT continues to be used particularly to assess psychoanalytic constructs, such as defense mechanisms (Cramer, 2017; Hibbard et al., 2010), attachment styles (Berant, 2009), and psychosexual stages (Huprich, 2008), as well as for needs and motives. Research shows that, as measures of individual differences in motivation, the TAT (McAdams et al., 1996) and other picture story completion exercises (Schultheiss & Schultheiss, 2014) can be both reliable and valid when scored using specific criteria to identify themes of achievement, power, and intimacy.

We can make a distinction between using the TAT to assess state levels of needs and trait levels of needs. **State levels** of a need refer to a person's momentary amount of a specific need, which can fluctuate with specific circumstances. For example, a person who is failing at a task (e.g., a player on a baseball team that is down 5 to 4 in the ninth inning) might experience a sharp increase in the state of achievement motivation. The TAT has been shown to be sensitive to changes in state levels of various motives, particularly the needs for achievement, power, and intimacy (Moretti & Rossini, 2004). The assessment of **trait levels** of a need refers to measuring a person's average tendency, or their set point or characteristic level, on the specific trait. The idea is that people differ from each other in their typical or average amount of specific needs. Assessing trait levels of needs is the most frequent goal of personality psychologists who use such measures (Schultheiss, Liening, & Schad, 2008).

The TAT remains a useful personality assessment technique among psychologists with a psychoanalytic orientation (e.g., Verdon & Azoulay, 2020), even though some researchers argue that it has low test-retest reliability (see, however, Smith & Atkinson, 1992). In addition, several researchers have reported extremely low correlations between TAT measures of certain needs and questionnaire measures of the same needs, leading them to question whether the TAT is a valid measure. This is the topic of our A Closer Look discussion of the TAT.

The Big Three Motives: Achievement, Power, and Intimacy

Although Murray proposed several dozen motives, researchers have focused most of their attention on a smaller set. These motives are the needs for achievement, power, and intimacy. Let's review what we know about each of these fundamental human motives.

A Closer Look

TAT and Questionnaire Measures of Motives: Do They Measure Different Aspects of Motives?

Psychologist David McClelland (1917–1998) and his colleagues focused primarily on the TAT. Critics have argued that the TAT demonstrates poor test-retest reliability and that responses to one picture may not correlate with responses to other pictures—that is, the TAT has poor internal reliability (Entwisle, 1972). Moreover, when the TAT is used to predict actual motive-related behaviors (such as when TAT need for achievement scores are used to predict overall college grade point averages or performance on an achievement test), the correlations are frequently low and inconsistent (Fineman, 1977). Smith and Atkinson (1992) reviewed the major criticisms of the TAT, as well as responses from its proponents.

These undesirable properties of the TAT have led some researchers to develop questionnaire measures of motives (Jackson, 1967). These questionnaires simply ask people directly about their motives and desires and about whether they engage in the kinds of behaviors that indicate high levels of the motives. These questionnaires turn out to have desirable measurement properties, such as adequate test-retest reliability and predictive validity (Scott & Johnson, 1972). A troubling finding, however, is that TAT measures of motives and questionnaire measures of the same motives are often uncorrelated (Fineman, 1977; for an exception, see Thrash & Elliot, 2002). Many researchers therefore suggest that the TAT measure and other projective measures should be abandoned.

McClelland and his colleagues did not silently accept these criticisms (McClelland, 1985; Weinberger & McClelland, 1990; Winter, 1999). In response, McClelland argued that, when the TAT is properly administered and scored, the motive scores *do* show acceptable test-retest reliability. In addition, he asserted that the TAT predicts long-term real-life outcomes, such as business success, better than questionnaire measures do. He argued that the questionnaire measures are better at predicting short-term behaviors, such as how competitive a person will behave while playing a game in a psychology laboratory. McClelland argued that the TAT measure and the questionnaire measures are uncorrelated because they measure *two different types of motivation*. Let's discuss each in turn.

One type of motive is called **implicit motivation.** These motives are based on needs, such as the need for achievement (nAch), the need for power (nPow), and the need for intimacy (nInt), as they are measured in fantasy-based (i.e., TAT) measures. When the TAT is used to measure these motives, they are called implicit, because the persons writing the stories are not explicitly telling the psychologist about themselves. Instead, they are telling stories about other people. The stories are thought to reflect the *implied* motives of the persons writing the stories—their unconscious motives, their unspoken needs and desires

(Schüler, Sheldon, & Fröhlich, 2010). What people write in response to the TAT pictures is presumed to reflect their real, although unconscious, motivations (Hofer, Bond, & Li, 2010).

The other type of motivation is called explicit, or **self-attributed motivation,** which McClelland argued reflects primarily a person's self-awareness of his or her own conscious motives (McClelland, Koestner, & Weinberger, 1989). These self-attributed motivations, sometimes called explicit motivations, reflect a person's conscious *awareness* about what is important to him or her. As such, they represent part of the individual's conscious self-understanding.

McClelland argued that implicit and self-attributed (explicit) motives represent fundamentally different aspects of motivation and that they should predict different life outcomes. Implicit motives predict long-term, spontaneous behavioral trends over time. For example, compared with questionnaire measures, TAT-assessed need for achievement is the better predictor of long-term entrepreneurial success, and TAT-assessed need for power is the better predictor of long-term success as a business manager (Chen, Su, & Wu, 2012; McAdams, 1990). Self-attributed motives, on the other hand, are better predictors of

responses to immediate and specific situations and to choice behaviors and attitudes (because they measure the person's conscious desires and wants). For example, questionnaire-assessed need for achievement is the better predictor of how hard a person will work to obtain a reward in a psychology experiment, and questionnaire-assessed need for power is the better predictor of a person's self-reported attitudes about social inequality (Koestner & McClelland, 1990; Woike, 1995).

The research literature supports a distinction between implicit and explicit motives, at least for achievement motivation (Spangler, 1992; Thrash & Elliot, 2002). Spangler examined more than 100 studies of need for achievement and performed a meta-analysis of these studies. Half the studies meta-analyzed by Spangler used TAT measures (implicit motives), and the other half used questionnaire measures (self-attributed motives) of the achievement motive. Spangler then looked carefully at the variables being predicted by achievement. He sorted the studies into those that looked at short-term responses to specific tasks (e.g., grades in college courses, performance on ability tests, and performance in laboratory achievement tests) and those that looked at long-term achievements

(e.g., lifetime income, job level attained in an organization, number of publications by research scientists, and participation in community organizations). Spangler found that the TAT-based measure was a better predictor of the long-term outcomes than was the questionnaire measure, whereas the questionnaire was a better predictor of the short-term responses. Understanding the congruence of implicit and explicit measures of motives is receiving a good deal of attention from personality psychologists (e.g., Perugini et al., 2021; Runge et al., 2020; Schultheiss, Wiemers, & Wolf, 2014; Thrash et al., 2019).

Spangler's meta-analysis suggests that both the TAT and questionnaire measures may play important roles in helping psychologists understand the short- and long-term effects of motives. If you want to know how someone will react to achievement demands today or tomorrow, you might be best advised to use a questionnaire or to just ask the person about his or her achievement needs. However, if you want to make a prediction about who in a group of people will earn the largest lifetime income or climb the highest in an organizational setting, you might be better off using the TAT measure of need for achievement.

Need for Achievement

Behavior that is motivated by the need for achievement has long interested psychologists. Because it has received the most research attention, we begin with this motive.

Doing Things Better

Following Murray at Harvard, psychologist David McClelland (1917–1998) carried on the tradition of motive research. McClelland was best known for his research on the **need for achievement (nAch),** defined as the desire to do better, to be successful, and to feel competent. Like all motives, we assume that the need for achievement will energize behavior in certain (achievement-related) situations. It is energized by the incentives of challenge and variety; it is accompanied by feelings of interest and surprise; and it is associated with the subjective state of being curious and exploratory (McClelland, 1985). People motivated by a high nAch obtain satisfaction and pride from accomplishing a task or from the anticipation of accomplishing a task. They cherish the process of being engaged in challenging activities.

As the leader of two successful companies, Apple Computer and Pixar Animation, the late Steve Jobs (1955–2011) was constantly striving to do things better. He is a good example of someone high in achievement motivation.

Anton_Ivanov/Shutterstock

In terms of trait levels, high nAch individuals prefer moderate levels of challenge, neither too high nor too low. This preference makes sense given that the high nAch person is motivated to do better than others. A task that is almost impossible to accomplish will not be attractive because it will not provide the opportunity to do better if everyone does poorly. A task that is too easy will be easy for everyone; the high nAch person will not do better if everyone is successful. Theoretically, we expect high nAch persons to have a preference for *moderately* challenging tasks. Dozens of studies have found support for this idea. One study examined children's preference for challenge in a variety of games (e.g., the ring-toss game, in which children attempt to toss rings around sticks that are placed at varying distances). Children high in nAch preferred a moderate challenge (e.g., tossed their rings at the sticks in the middle), whereas children low in nAch tried either the very easy levels of the games (closer sticks) or the levels at which success was almost impossible (McClelland, 1958). This relationship has also been demonstrated outside the laboratory. Young adults high in nAch have been found to choose college majors that are of intermediate difficulty and to pursue careers that are of moderate difficulty (reviewed in Koestner & McClelland, 1990).

To summarize the characteristics of persons high in nAch from the research literature, (1) they prefer activities that provide some, but not too much, challenge; (2) they enjoy tasks in which they are personally responsible for the outcome; and (3) they prefer tasks for which feedback on their performance is available.

Exercise

Have a look at the TAT picture presented earlier, under Apperception and the TAT. Write a short story about what is happening in this picture. However, instead of writing off the top of your head, try to write a story that would score high on the need for achievement. What themes would you put in such a story? What actions and outcomes might be interpreted as indicating high nAch? What you consciously try to put into such a story are the themes and acts that psychologists look for in the stories of people writing naturally. Some put plenty of such themes and acts into their stories quite naturally and so seem to see achievement-related themes and behaviors all around. Others reveal that their stories and the characters therein act in very non-striving, non-achieving ways. And this comes perfectly naturally to them when they make up a story about the image under Apperception and the TAT.

Increasing the Need for Achievement

Research on the achievement motive typically takes the form of correlating TAT need for achievement (nAch) scores with other measures related to achievement. Demonstrating the relationship between nAch and success in entrepreneurial activities is one example of this type of research. Starting and managing a small business appears to offer a high degree of satisfaction for the person with a strong need to achieve. It provides an opportunity to engage in a challenging pursuit, assume responsibility for making decisions and taking action, and obtain swift and objective feedback about the success of one's performance. Studies in several countries have found that persons with a high nAch are more attracted to business occupations than are their peers who have a low nAch (McClelland, 1965). A study of farmers (who are, in effect, small business operators) showed those with a high need to achieve were more likely than low nAch farmers to adopt innovative farming practices and to show improved rates of production over time (Singh, 1978). A study comparing self-employed entrepreneurs to workers for large corporations found that the self-employed were significantly higher on need for achievement (Lee-Ross, 2015).

Research on entrepreneurial talent has not been limited to business activities. Some studies have examined the work habits of college students. Students with high nAch appear to be more deliberate in their pursuit of good grades: they are more likely to investigate course requirements before enrolling in a class, speak with a professor prior to exams, and contact the professor about the exam after it was given to obtain feedback about their performance (Andrews, 1967). In a very different subject sample, blue-collar workers with high nAch engaged in more problem-solving activities after being laid off than did unemployed workers lower in nAch: they started looking for a new job sooner and used a greater number of job-seeking strategies (Koestner & McClelland, 1990).

More recent studies on entrepreneurial orientation examined achievement motives in a group of students of small business (a major considered to have high entrepreneurial potential) and compared them to a group of students of economics (considered to have much less entrepreneurial potential). Results showed that small business students were significantly higher on achievement motivation than the economics students (Sagie & Elizur, 1999). A study by Langens (2001) also supports the notion that training for high need for achievement can promote success in business. It seems that persons with high achievement motives are drawn to careers that have more potential risk and uncertainty, where success is a matter of personal responsibility and where emergency problem solving is routine.

There are also cultural differences in how the need for achievement is expressed. In the United States, most high-achieving high school students strive for good grades for themselves. Many students, and their parents, go to great lengths to achieve. Cheating can be common, and some students do not view cheating as wrong. The psychologist Demerath (2001) even reports that some parents of high-achieving students sought to have them classified as special-education students, which would entitle them to extra time on standardized tests. When he went to Papua New Guinea, Demerath found a very different norm among students. There, school is seen as a noncompetitive place where it is important for all to do well. Doing well as an individual, especially if it is at the expense of others, is frowned upon. In fact, New Guineans call this "acting extra" and view it as a form of vanity. Given the cultural differences between New Guinea and the United States, such differences in how the need for achievement is expressed make sense. People in Papua, New Guinea, make their living at farming and fishing, and they need to know that if they get sick or something happens and they cannot work their fields or nets, others will pitch in and help. In collectivist cultures, individual achievement is less valued than the person who helps his or her group achieve.

Determining Sex Differences

Much of the research on nAch, particularly that done in the 1950s and 1960s, was conducted on males only. Perhaps this was due to the fact that Harvard (where both Murray and McClelland did much of their research) was primarily a male institution at that time. Or it might have been due to the biased belief of that period that achievement was important only in the lives of men. Whatever the reason, little was known about achievement strivings in women until the 1970s and 1980s. Since then, some similarities and some differences have been found between men and women. Men and women high in nAch are similar in their preference for moderate challenge, personal responsibility for the outcome, and tasks with feedback. The major differences between such men and women occur in two areas: the life outcomes predicted by nAch and childhood experiences. Let's consider each of these in turn.

Research on men has focused primarily on achievement in business as a typical life outcome predicted by nAch. Research on women, however, has identified different "achievement trajectories," depending on whether the women value having a family or value having both family and work goals. Among women who value both work and family, nAch is related more to achieving better grades and to completing college, marrying, and starting a family later than it is among women low in nAch with career and family interests. Among women who are more exclusively focused on family, nAch is seen in the women's investment in activities related to dating and courtship, such as placing greater emphasis on physical appearance and talking with friends about their boyfriends more frequently (Koestner & McClelland, 1990).

Profile in nAch: Pete Buttigieg (born 1982) was valedictorian at his high school and, the year he graduated, he won the JFK Profiles in Courage essay contest. He went on to Harvard and, after graduating with a BA in History and Literature, was awarded a Rhodes Scholarship to attend Oxford, where he obtained a BA degree in Philosophy, Politics, and Economics. He then served 8 years as a Naval Intelligence officer. At age 29 he became the youngest mayor of a large (over 100,000) U.S. city—South Bend, Indiana. He ran for president in 2020 and, while he dropped out during the primary, he was appointed Secretary of Transportation by the winner (Joe Biden). Buttigieg is currently the youngest member of the Presidential Cabinet. This high achieving politician has a bright future in public service.

Scott Olson/Getty Images

The second major difference between men and women has been in the childhood experiences associated with nAch. Among women, nAch is associated with a stressful or difficult early family life. The mothers of girls high in nAch were found to be critical of their daughters and to be aggressive and competitive toward them (Kagan & Moss, 1962). The mothers of high-achieving schoolgirls were also less nurturant and affectionate toward their daughters than the mothers of less academically successful girls (Crandall et al., 1964). In contrast, the early lives of males high in nAch are characterized by parental support and care. An interesting related finding concerns the levels of nAch in children who come from families in which the parents have divorced or separated. A nationally representative study found that women whose parents had divorced or separated when they were children had higher nAch scores than women whose parents had stayed together. The opposite outcome was found for men (Veroff et al., 1960). Living with a single mom may provide an achieving role model for young girls, whereas for boys it may demonstrate that men are unnecessary to family life and perhaps even to be resented.

Several studies have examined gender differences in competitive achievement settings. In one study the researchers had 40 men and 40 women solve simple addition problems as quickly as they could, paying them 50 cents for each correct answer (Niederle & Vesterlund, 2005). In one condition the participants simply played against the clock, trying to solve as many problems as they could. In another condition the game was changed to a tournament, where subjects were divided into teams of two women or two men each, and they played against each other. The winning team received $2.00 for each problem they solved and the losing team received nothing. The researchers found that men and women performed equally well in both conditions: the tournament setting and the individual setting. The experimenters then had a third round, where each person could choose whether he or she wanted to play individually against the clock or in a tournament setting against the other players. Interestingly, only 35 percent of the women chose the tournament setting, whereas 75 percent of the men chose the tournament setting. The authors concluded that even in settings where women perform just as well as men, they are less likely than men to want to engage in direct competition with others. Women may be more selective in how they express their achievement strivings, especially when winning for oneself means that others lose (zero-sum competition).

Promoting Achievement Motivation in Children

Despite the sex differences in childhood antecedents of achievement, McClelland believed that certain parental behaviors could promote high achievement motivation in children. One of these parenting practices is placing an emphasis on **independence training.** Parents can behave in ways that promote autonomy and independence in their children. For example, a young child who is taught to feed him- or herself becomes independent of the parents during meal times; a child who is toilet trained no longer relies on his or her parents for assistance with this task. One longitudinal study found that strict toilet training in early childhood is associated with high need for achievement 26 years later (McClelland & Pilon, 1983). Training a child to be independent in various tasks of life promotes a sense of mastery and confidence in the child. This may be one way that parents can promote a need for achievement in their children.

A second parental practice associated with need for achievement is setting challenging *standards* for the child (Heckhausen, 1982). Parents need to let the child know what is expected of him or her. These expectations should not exceed the child's abilities, however, or else the child may give up. The idea is for parents to provide age-appropriate goals that challenge the child, support the child in working toward these goals, and reward the child when the goal is attained (see Table 11.2). The difficulty of the goals increases with the child's age and growing abilities. Having success experiences in age-appropriate tasks appears to be part of the prescription for developing a heightened need for achievement. For example, learning the ABCs is a challenging task for a 4-year-old; parents might encourage a young child to undertake this task, enthusiastically sing the ABC song with the child, and reward the child with praise and hugs when he or she recites the alphabet independently for the first time. But for

Table 11.2 Raising High Need for Achievement Children

- Set tough but age-appropriate standards.
- Applaud successes and celebrate accomplishments.
- Acknowledge but don't dwell on failures; stress that failures are part of learning.
- Avoid instilling a fear of failure, and instead emphasize the motive to succeed.
- Stress effort over ability: Instead of saying "You can do it because you are smart" say "You can do it if you really try."

a 6-year-old, the challenges should increase, such as learning to read basic words or to add and subtract simple numbers.

A developmental theory of achievement motivation has been proposed by the psychologist Carol Dweck (2002). This theory emphasizes the beliefs that people develop about their abilities and competencies. Briefly, the theory holds that the most adaptive belief system is that abilities are not fixed, but that they are malleable and can be developed through effort. Dweck (2002) argues that sometimes even "smart" people succumb to the belief that their abilities are fixed or given or genetically determined and that truly gifted persons do not need effort to achieve. She argues that this set of beliefs is "dumb" in the sense that people who hold such beliefs will consequently have a low need for achievement. It is more adaptive, Dweck holds, to believe that abilities are changeable, that one's performance is a temporary indicator of where one is, not where one will ultimately be, and that one's true potential will be realized only through sustained effort. This theory is having an impact on schools and other educational settings (Elliot & Dweck, 2005). Dweck (2006) has also written a popular book on how this theory relates to achievement in sports, business, and relationships.

In a large-scale study, Dweck and her colleagues (Paunesku et al., 2015) showed that training students to view intelligence as a malleable and changeable quality, rather than viewing it as fixed or hereditary, leads to measurable increases in grades. We'll have more to say about Dweck's theory in the Chapter 12, when we discuss cognition and personality, but for now we'll simply say that believing one can become smarter with effort appears to be a prerequisite for actually becoming smarter (or at least achieving better grades; Goudeau & Cimpian, 2021).

Need for Power

Another motive of interest to psychologists is based on the need for power—the desire to have an impact on others.

Impact on Others

Although McClelland was known primarily for his studies of the achievement motive, both he and several of his students went on to study other motives. One of his students, David Winter, focused a good deal of his research on the **need for power** (nPow). Winter (1973) defines the need for power as a readiness or preference for having an impact on other people. A more detailed definition is provided by Fodor (2009): persons high on need for power have a need to impress, influence, or control other people and to be recognized by others for their power-oriented actions. They achieve impact on others through various means, but most notably through forceful actions toward or against others, strong efforts to control others, or ostentatious displays of valued personal possessions. They want others to react to them, either with admiration, astonishment, or fear. One study investigated the hypothesis that high nPow individuals would be faster at recognizing facial expressions of emotions in others (Donhauser, Rösch, & Schultheiss, 2015). Because of their desire to impact others, and because this impact often is registered in the faces of those around them, the high need for power person gauges the strength of their dominance by reading the emotions displayed by others. The researchers showed that need for power did correlate with faster recognition of facial expressions of emotions in others. This is most likely how high need for power people monitor whether they are being successful in having an impact: by reading the emotions displayed by those around them. As with the need to achieve, the need for power is assumed to energize and direct behavior when the person is in opportune situations for exerting power. The TAT has likewise been the predominant assessment tool for research on nPow. The subjects' stories are scored for the presence of images related to themes of power. These include descriptions of strong or vigorous actions, behaviors that bring about strong reactions in others, statements that emphasize status or reputation, and displays of desirable possessions (flamboyant jewelry, sports cars, yachts, mansions, etc.).

Research Findings

Many studies have examined the correlates of individual differences in nPow (e.g., Kuhl & Kazén, 2008). The need for power correlates positively with having arguments with others, being elected to student office in college, taking larger risks in gambling situations, behaving assertively and actively in a small-group setting, and acquiring more of what Winter calls "prestige possessions," such as sports cars, credit cards, and nameplates for dormitory doors (Winter, 1973).

It appears that an individual high in nPow is interested in control—control of situations and other people (Assor, 1989). Men high in nPow rate their "ideal wives" as those who are under the men's control and dependent on them, perhaps because such relationships offer them a sense of superiority (Winter, 1973). Men high in nPow are also more likely to abuse their spouses (Mason & Blankenship, 1987). A person with a high need for power prefers as friends people who are not well known or popular, perhaps because such people do not compete for prestige or status (Winter, 1973).

Sex Differences

Research on the power motive has found no sex differences in average levels of nPow or in the kinds of situations that arouse the power motive. Men and women also do not differ in the life outcomes that are associated with nPow, such as having formal social power (e.g., holding office), having power-related careers (e.g., being a manager), or gathering prestige possessions (e.g., sports cars).

The largest and most consistent sex difference is that high nPow men, but not women, perform a wide variety of impulsive and aggressive behaviors. Men high in nPow are more likely than men low in nPow to have dissatisfying dating relationships, arguments with others, and higher divorce rates. Men high in nPow are also more likely to engage in the sexual exploitation, have more frequent sex partners, and engage in sex at an earlier age than do their counterparts who are lower in nPow. Men with a strong need for power also tend to abuse alcohol more than those with a low need for power (feelings of power often increase under the influence of alcohol). None of these correlates have been found for women.

"Profligate impulsive" behaviors (drinking, aggression, and sexual exploitation) are less likely to occur if an individual has had **responsibility training** (Winter & Barenbaum, 1985). Taking care of younger siblings is an example of responsibility training. Having one's own children provides another opportunity to learn to behave responsibly. Among people who have had such responsibility training, nPow is not related to profligate impulsive behavior (Winter, 1988). These findings have led Winter and others (e.g., Jenkins, 1994) to assert that socialization experiences, not biological sex per se, determine whether nPow will be expressed in these maladaptive behaviors.

Health Status and the Need for Power

As you might imagine, people high in nPow do not deal well with frustration and conflict. When high nPow people do not get their way or when their power is challenged or blocked, they are likely to show strong stress responses. McClelland (1982) called such

Speeches delivered by Russian presidents have been analyzed for themes related to achievement, power, and affiliation (Semenova & Winter, 2020). The current (2022) president of Russia—Vladimir Putin—was extremely high on need for power. Research discussed in the text shows that a leader's words are often followed by actions, with the presence of high power imagery in national speeches often being followed by the onset of wars. This is proving to be the case with Putin and his 2022 war on Ukraine

Abaca Press/Alamy Live News

obstacles **power stress** and hypothesized that people high in nPow were vulnerable to various ailments and diseases because of the stresses associated with inhibited power. In a study of college students, when power motives were inhibited or stressed, the subjects' immune function became less efficient, and they reported more frequent illnesses, such as colds and the flu (see McClelland & Jemmott, 1980). A later study of male prisoners found similar results, with prisoners high in nPow showing the highest levels of illness and the lowest levels of immune antibodies (McClelland, Alexander, & Marks, 1982). Other studies have demonstrated that inhibiting the power motive among people high in nPow is linked with high blood pressure. This relationship was also found in a longitudinal study, which revealed that the inhibited power motive measured in men in their early thirties significantly predicted elevated blood pressure and signs of hypertension 20 years later (McClelland, 1979).

An interesting laboratory study induced power stress by having people lead a group discussion without knowing that the group's members were coached ahead of time to disagree with the leader and to display a lot of conflict (Fodor, 1985). The group leader was assessed for muscle tension. Consistent with McClelland's theory, the greatest tension responses were found for those leaders in the group conflict condition who were high in nPow.

War and Peace and Power

In a fascinating line of research, psychologist Winter (1993, 2002) investigated nPow on a national level and related it to the broad areas of war and peace. Traditionally, nPow is measured by evaluating stories written in response to TAT pictures. However, nPow (as well as any motive) can be determined by assessing just about any written document, ranging from children's fairy tales to presidential speeches. Winter analyzed the content of 300 years of State of the Parliament speeches given by the prime ministers of England. Each of the speeches was rated for the presence of power images. He then used these image scores to predict warfare activity in these three centuries of British history. Winter found that wars were started when power imagery in the parliamentary speeches was high. Once under way, wars ended only after the levels of power imagery in the speeches ended. Similar analyses were done on the British–German communications during World War I, as well as on U.S.–Soviet communications during the Cuban missile crisis of the 1960s (Winter, 1993). Similar research coding need for power in the speeches of US senators shows that these scores predict their votes for or against war (Richardson & Winter, 2021). In a similar study, Semenova and Winter (2020) analyzed the speeches of Russian presidents over the past 30 years to code for nPow. In all these cases, increases in power imagery preceded military actions, whereas decreases in power imagery preceded decreases in military threat.

In an extension of this research, Winter and his students examined how power images in communications may lead to escalation in conflict (Peterson, Winter, & Doty, 1994). Subjects were asked to write replies to letters taken from real conflict situations.

The letters the subjects were responding to were altered to create two versions: one with high power imagery and the other with low power imagery. Otherwise, the content of the letters remained the same. The subjects' responses were then analyzed for themes of power. Subjects responded to power imagery with power images of their own. Assuming that the other side would similarly respond with more power images, it is easy to see how conflicts might escalate.

Later studies of communications among governments involved in crises have revealed similar motive patterns (Langner & Winter, 2001). Analyzing official documents during four international crises, Langner and Winter found that making concessions was associated with affiliative motives expressed in the communications, whereas power images were associated with making fewer concessions. In a laboratory study, they found that power or affiliative motives could be primed by having the subjects read different communications from their negotiation partner and that these primed motives predicted the likelihood that they would make a concession during the negotiation. Such personality research may have wide implications for understanding how governments could respond to each other to avoid crises.

To summarize, the need for power is the desire to have an impact on others. It can be measured from the TAT and from other verbal documents, such as speeches and other forms of communication, by looking for themes related to status seeking, concerns about reputation, or attempts to make others do what one wants. For example, Winter (1988) provides an interesting analysis of Richard Nixon's speeches in terms of the needs for achievement, power, and intimacy. Winter (1998) applies a similar analysis to the speeches of former president Bill Clinton, linking Clinton's motives to some of his problems as well as to his popularity. Winter (2018) also analyzed then president Trump's speeches for nPow, finding high levels. Krasno (2015) also analyzed the motives of president Bill Clinton, and found him to be particularly high on both the need for achievement as well as the need for intimacy, a motive to which we now turn.

Need for Intimacy

The last of the "Big Three" motives is based on the desire for warm and fulfilling relationships with others.

Intimacy

The third motive receiving a good deal of research attention is the need for intimacy (nInt). The researcher most closely associated with this motive is Dan McAdams, another McClelland student. McAdams defines the **need for intimacy** as the "recurrent preference or readiness for warm, close, and communicative interaction with others" (McAdams, 1990, p. 198). People high in nInt want more intimacy and meaningful human contact in their day-to-day lives than do those who are low in nInt.

Research Findings

McAdams and others have conducted a number of studies of nInt over the years in an effort to determine how people high and low in nInt differ from each other. As with the other motives, the TAT is often used to measure the strength of the intimacy motive. People high in nInt (compared to those who are low) have been found to (1) spend more time during the day thinking about relationships; (2) report more pleasant emotions when they are around other people; (3) smile, laugh, and make more eye contact; and (4) start up conversations more frequently and write more text messages, e-mails, and social media posts. We might think that the people high in nInt are simply extraverts, but the findings do not support this interpretation. Rather than being the loud, outgoing, life-of-the-party extravert, the person high in nInt is more likely to be someone with a few very good friends, who prefers sincere and meaningful conversations over wild parties. When asked to describe a typical time with a friend, people high in nInt tend to report one-on-one interactions instead of group interactions. When they get together with friends, people high in nInt are likely to listen to their friends and to discuss intimate or personal topics with them, such as their feelings, hopes, beliefs, and desires. Perhaps this is why people who are high in nInt are rated by their peers as especially "sincere," "loving," "not dominant," and "not self-centered" (McAdams, 1990).

A few studies have examined the relationship between nInt and well-being. In a longitudinal study, nInt measured at age 30 in a sample of Harvard graduates was significantly related to overall adjustment (e.g., having a satisfying job and family life, coping well with life's stress, being free from alcohol problems) 17 years later (McAdams & Vaillant, 1982). Other studies have shown that nInt is associated with certain benefits and positive life outcomes for both men and women. Among women, nInt is associated with happiness and satisfaction with life. Among men, nInt is associated with less strain in life. Unlike the motives for power and achievement, for which no sex differences have been found as far as level of need is concerned, there does exist a consistent sex difference in average need for intimacy—women have, on average, a higher level of nInt than men (McAdams, 1990; McAdams & Bryant, 1987).

To summarize, the need for intimacy is the desire for warm and intimate relationships with others. Individuals with a strong nInt enjoy the company of others and are more expressive and communicative toward others compared with people low in nInt. The intimacy motive is distinguished from extraversion in that persons high in nInt prefer having a few close friends to being a member of a rowdy group. In contrast to the need for achievement and power, for which men and women show comparable levels, women's need for intimacy is, on average, higher than men's (Dreschure & Schultheiss, 2016).

The motives we have covered so far—the needs for power, intimacy, and achievement—all fall within the tradition of academic personality psychology. There is, however, another motivational tradition, one that is rooted more in clinical psychology than in academic personality research. This tradition has come to inform the field of personality psychology, and concepts from this tradition are present or implied in several areas of contemporary research. We turn now to the humanistic tradition within personality psychology.

Humanistic Tradition: The Motive to Self-Actualize

In 1995, an American legend passed away—Jerry Garcia, lead guitarist of the Grateful Dead—reportedly of heart failure, at the age of 53. In the many newspaper stories recounting his life and times, reporters often suggested that Garcia lived longer than he should have, given his lifestyle. His band was constantly on the road for three decades, and Garcia was known to have abused a multitude of drugs, including cocaine, heroin, and alcohol, on a regular basis.

Other entertainers from the past have also abused drugs and alcohol—and died as a result—at much younger ages than Garcia, such as John Belushi (died at 33), Kurt Cobain (died at 27), Jimi Hendrix (died at 27), Janis Joplin (died at 27), Jim Morrison (died at 27), Keith Moon (died at 31), Elvis Presley (died at 42), Tupac Shakur (died at 25),

Sid Vicious (died at 21), and Amy Winehouse (died at 27). With each such death, the public engages briefly in an age-old debate about personal responsibility and the self-destructiveness often seen in artists. Some people argue that such artists are victims of their times or their culture. Garcia, for example, was thought to carry the burden of representing the best (and worst) of the 1960s counterculture; he and his band were often viewed as a time capsule from that era.

Another view of the same situation is that Garcia did kill himself, that he slowly self-destructed through harmful life choices. This view implies that Garcia was responsible for his own demise. In an MTV interview the week of Garcia's death, then-President Bill Clinton represented this view: "While he had great talent, he also had a terrible problem [heroin addiction]. . . . You don't have to have a destructive lifestyle to be a genius." The implication is that Garcia's genius and his self-destructive tendencies were two separate parts of his personality and that one did not necessarily produce the other. Garcia killed himself by his own free will, in President Clinton's perspective, and he was responsible for his own death due to the lifestyle choices he had made over the years.

Earlier, in our A Closer Look section, we discussed unconscious (implicit) motives. These are motives that a person is largely unaware of yet guide his or her behavior and life choices. Choices based on unconscious motives are, in most respects, made without free will. The Garcia question really becomes whether or not he was aware of his motives, whether he knew what he was doing when he made his many self-destructive life choices.

An emphasis on conscious awareness of needs, choice, and personal responsibility is one of the characteristics of the **humanistic tradition** approach to motivation. Humanistic psychologists emphasize the role of *choice* in human life, as well as the influence of *responsibility*

Amy Winehouse, who died of alcohol poisoning in 2011 at the age of 27. Some argue she was a victim of the entertainment culture portrayal of her as a "bad girl" star. Others argue that Winehouse was a musical prodigy who also chose to live a destructive lifestyle. The issue of choice and personal responsibility is important in the humanistic approach to motivation.
Rosie Greenway/Getty Images

in creating a meaningful and satisfying life. The meaning of any person's life, according to the humanistic approach, is found in the choices that person makes and the responsibility he or she takes for those choices. In midlife, for example, some people come to realize that they are not exercising much choice in their daily lives, that they have fallen into a rut in their careers, their personal relationships, or both. This is the theme of much of the existential literary tradition, such as the book *The Stranger* by Albert Camus.

A second major characteristic of the humanistic tradition is an emphasis on the human need for growth and the realization of one's full potential. Human nature, according to this view, is positive and life-affirming. This view stands in marked contrast to psychoanalysis, which takes a rather pessimistic view of human nature, one that views humans as seething cauldrons of primitive sexual and aggressive instincts. The humanistic tradition provides an optimistic counterpoint, one that stresses the process of positive growth toward a desired or even an idealized human potential. That human potential is summed up in the concept of the self-actualization motive.

We will define self-actualization shortly. First, we must note a third characteristic of the humanistic tradition that distinguishes it from other motivational approaches. The humanistic tradition views much of motivation as being based in a need to *grow,* to become who one is meant to be. The other traditions, including those of Freud, Murray, and McClelland, view motivation as coming from a specific *deficit,* or lack.

This is a subtle but important distinction, and it represents a historical break in motivation theory and research. All the motives we have discussed—achievement, power, and intimacy—are deficiency motives. In the humanistic tradition, the most human of all motivations—the motive to self-actualize—is seen as *not* based on a deficit of something. Rather, it is a growth-based motive, a motive to develop, to flourish, and to become more and more what one is destined to become. In the words of Maslow (1970), who coined the term in the 1960s, self-actualization is the process of becoming "more and more what one idiosyncratically is, to become everything that one is capable of becoming" (p. 46).

Maslow's Contributions

Any discussion of the motive to self-actualize has to begin with Maslow's contributions (see Maslow & Hoffman, 1996). Several of his ideas form the foundation for theory and research in this area.

Hierarchy of Needs

Maslow (1908–1970) began with the concept of need but defined needs primarily by their goals. Maslow believed that needs were hierarchically organized, with more basic needs found toward the bottom of the hierarchy and the self-actualization need at the top (see Figure 11.2). He divided the hierarchy of needs into five levels.

At the base of Maslow's need hierarchy are the **physiological needs.** These include needs that are of prime importance to the immediate survival of the individual (the need

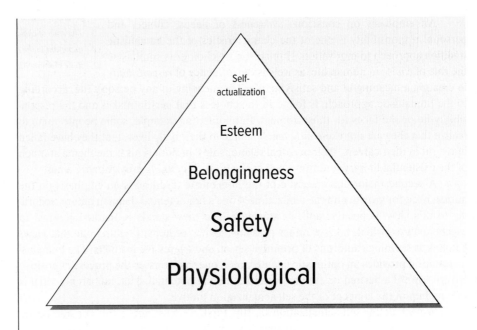

Figure 11.2

Maslow's hierarchy of needs in his theory of motivation. The needs are organized hierarchically into levels. Lower-level needs are more pressing when not satisfied (indicated by larger, bolder fonts) than are higher-level needs.

A Closer Look

A Reinterpretation of Maslow's Hierarchy of Needs: An Evolution-Based Model

Psychologist Doug Kenrick and colleagues (Kenrick et al., 2010) proposed a reinterpretation of Maslow's hierarchical model of fundamental human needs. Because this is the first major overhaul of Maslow's key contribution, we chose it for a closer look. Although this reformulation merges Maslow's ideas with basic concepts from evolutionary psychology (covered in Chapter 8), only time will tell whether it provides a more useful framework for studying human needs and motives.

Maslow published his hierarchy of needs in 1943, and it had a large impact on many subfields of psychology, including personality and developmental psychology. However, today many see it as a quaint bit of armchair theorizing that,

although interesting, is largely disconnected from any contemporary theory. Kenrick and colleagues suggest that it can take on new significance if the hierarchy can be renovated by incorporating theoretical and empirical developments from evolutionary psychology. They propose a new model that retains several of Maslow's key ideas (i.e., it remains a hierarchical model, several original needs are retained, and it presumes a developmental order to the needs). However, what is added is a theoretical explanation for the model that is based on the evolutionary function of each particular need. This model is presented in the accompanying Figure 11.3.

A novel and enduring part of Maslow's model of needs is the idea of a hierarchy,

the notion that certain motives take precedence over others. Hence the needs are arranged in a specific order. Also, the needs lower in the pyramid are, when unsatisfied, are stronger and more persistent than needs higher in the pyramid, presumably because they are more important for survival. Additionally, the needs are also related to development, such that as a person matures, he or she shifts from needs lower to higher in the hierarchy.

All of these elements are retained by Kenrick and colleagues' 2010 reinterpretation. The basic needs related to physiological, safety or self-protection, affiliation, and esteem motives are also retained because they are important to survival, a major evolutionary goal. But, as we learned

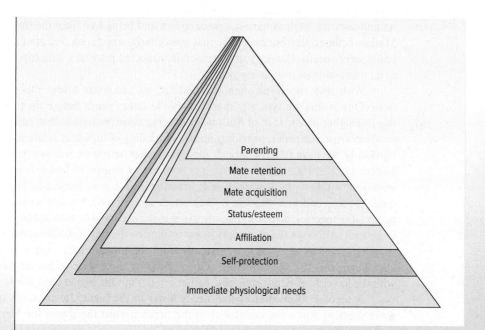

Figure 11.3

An updated hierarchy of fundamental human motives.

Source: "Renovating the Pyramid of Needs: Contemporary Extensions Built upon Ancient Foundations," by D. T. Kenrick et al., *Perspectives on Psychological Science,* 5 (2010), 292–314.

(Continued)

A Closer Look (*Continued*)

in Chapter 8, survival is only part of the evolutionary process. More important is reproduction, since survival without reproduction is an evolutionary dead end. So Kenrick and colleagues add the important needs to find and retain a mate, and to succeed at parenting by raising one's children so that they may, in turn, reproduce, ensuring one's genes into future generations.

Kenrick and colleagues use functional explanations for each need in the hierarchy, with each need fulfilling a particular function with regard to evolution. Maslow's ultimate need—the need to self-actualize—has no apparent function with respect to surviving and reproducing, and so Kenrick and colleagues leave that need out of their model.

The journal that published Kenrick and colleagues' revised model of needs also published four articles critical of this new model. One criticism (Kesebir, Graham, & Oishi, 2010) argued that a theory of human needs should be human-centered, and not animal-centered. After all, the Kenrick and colleagues' model applies to rats and lizards as much as it applies to humans, ignoring what might be distinctively human about human nature. Others argued that self-actualization can be viewed as evolutionarily important and should not be dropped off of the list of fundamental human needs (Peterson & Park, 2010). Others argued that the purpose of life, other than ensuring one's genes into future generations, is missing from the Kenrick

and colleagues' model (Ackerman & Bargh, 2010). Kenrick and colleagues provide a thoughtful reply to these criticisms (Schaller et al., 2013), illustrating why and how evolution can be relevant to our understanding of uniquely human needs and motives.

The Kenrick and colleagues (2010) model of human needs does have a unifying theory it is built upon, something that was lacking in Maslow's version. Also, the theory on which the Kenrick model is based (evolution) has a great deal of empirical support and is almost universally accepted among scientists. Cook, Krems, and Kenrick published a paper in 2021 describing a decade of research testing various aspects of this model. It is turning out to be a useful framework for viewing human motivation.

for food, water, air, and sleep), as well as to the long-term survival of the species (e.g., the need for sex). At the next highest level are the **safety needs.** These have to do with shelter and security, such as having a place to live and being free from the threat of danger. Maslow believed that building a life that was orderly, structured, and predictable also fell under safety needs. Having your automobile inspected prior to a long trip might be seen as an expression of your safety needs.

With only two levels mentioned so far, we can make a few important observations. One is that we typically must satisfy the lower needs before we proceed to satisfy the higher needs. One of Maslow's enduring contributions is that he assembled the needs in a specific order, providing an understanding of how they relate to one another. Obviously, we have to have enough food and water before we will worry about earning esteem and respect from our peers. It is possible, of course, to find examples of people who do not follow the hierarchy (e.g., starving artists, who frequently go without adequate food to continue expressing themselves in their art). Maslow's theory, like most personality theories, is meant to apply to the average person or to describe human nature in general. Although there are always exceptions to the rule, people appear, on average, to work their way up Maslow's hierarchy from the lowest to the highest level. Maslow also taught that the need hierarchy emerges during the course of human development, with the lower-level needs emerging earlier in life than the higher-level needs.

A second observation is that needs lower in the hierarchy are more powerful or more pressing when not satisfied than the needs toward the top of the hierarchy. The higher-level needs are less relevant to survival, so they are less urgent when not satisfied than the lower needs. Another way to put this is that when people are working on satisfying their higher needs, their motivation is weak and easily ignored. Maslow (1968) stated that "this inner tendency [toward self-actualization] is not strong and overpowering and unmistakable like the instincts of animals. It is weak and delicate and subtle and easily overcome by habit, cultural pressures, and wrong attitudes toward it."

People typically work at satisfying multiple needs at the same time. It is easy to find examples of people engaging in a variety of tasks that represent different needs in a given period of time (e.g., eating, installing a new lock on the front door, going to a family reunion, and studying for an exam to earn a better grade). At any given time, however, we can determine the level at which a person is investing *most* of his or her energy. The point is that, even if we are working primarily on self-actualization needs, we need to do certain things (e.g., buy groceries) to make sure the lower needs continue to be satisfied.

In the movie The Edge, the plot involves two high-esteem men who are suddenly knocked several steps down on Maslow's hierarchy of needs by a large and persistent grizzly bear.

United Archives GmbH/Alamy

The plots of many novels and movies, particularly adventure stories, involve people who find themselves in situations that force them to take a step downward on the hierarchy of needs—circumstances that require a sudden shift in focus to safety or even physiological needs. The series of *Alien* and *Die Hard* movies are examples of films that illustrate this phenomenon. In the film *The Edge,* actors Anthony Hopkins and Alec Baldwin take a few steps down the hierarchy of needs when their plane crashes in the wilderness and they are pursued by a large, hungry, and very persistent grizzly bear.

The third level in Maslow's hierarchy consists of **belongingness needs.** Humans are a very social species, and most people possess a strong need to belong to groups (families, sororities/fraternities, churches, clubs, teams, etc.) (Baumeister & Leary, 1995). Being accepted by others and welcomed into a group represents a somewhat more psychological need than the physiological needs or the need for safety. Some observers have argued that modern society provides fewer opportunities for satisfying our need to belong than it did in the past, when ready-made groups existed and people were automatic members (e.g., multigenerational extended families and small towns in which virtually everyone felt like a member of the community). Loneliness is a sign that these needs are not being satisfied; alienation from one's social group or culture is another. The popularity of so-called street gangs is a testament to the strength of belongingness needs. Gang membership can fulfill belongingness needs for people who might otherwise feel alienated or excluded from groups available to members of the dominant culture.

One reason the need to belong is so basic comes from the theory of evolution. In our evolutionary past, belonging to a social group was essential to survival. People hunted in groups, lived in groups, shared food gathered by individuals in the group, and moved around in nomadic groups. Belonging to a group allowed the individual members to share the workload and to protect each other, raise each others' young, and share important resources. Belonging to a group had survival value. Not only was each individual ensuring his or her own survival by living in a group, but all members of the group were invested in each other's survival because each member played an important role in the group. Today it is not necessarily the case that group living fosters survival; nevertheless, modern humans still have a strong desire to belong to groups, such as church groups, work groups, clubs, fraternities and sororities, and various interest groups.

The fourth level of need in Maslow's hierarchy concerns **esteem needs.** There are really two types of esteem—esteem from others and self-esteem, the latter often depending on the former. We want to be seen by others as competent, strong, and able to achieve. We want to be respected by others for our achievements and our abilities. We also want this respect to translate into self-esteem; we want to feel good about ourselves, to feel that we are worthwhile, valuable, and competent. Much of the activity of adult daily life is geared toward achieving recognition and esteem from others and bolstering self-confidence.

The pinnacle of Maslow's need hierarchy is the **self-actualization need,** the need to develop one's potential, to become the person one was meant to be. You might think this is difficult, as it assumes that one must first figure out who one was meant to be. However, self-actualizers seem to just know who they are and have few doubts about the direction their lives should take (Bauer, Schwab, & McAdams, 2011).

Research Findings

Maslow developed his theory based on his ideas and thoughts about motivation, not on empirical research. He never, for example, developed a measure of self-actualization, though others did (Flett, Blankstein, & Hewitt, 1991; Jones & Crandall, 1986). How has his theory fared in the hands of researchers? Although not all the studies support Maslow's theory (e.g., Wahba & Bridwell, 1973), some studies support its main tenets (e.g., Hagerty, 1999). One group of researchers tested the idea that lower-level needs in the hierarchy are stronger than the higher-level needs when deprived (Wicker et al., 1993). These researchers presented subjects with a variety of goals that mapped onto Maslow's theory: having enough to eat and drink, feeling safe and unafraid, being part of a special group, being recognized by others as an outstanding student, and being mentally healthy and making full use of one's capabilities. They then asked subjects several questions about each goal, including "How good would you feel if you attained it?" and "How bad would you feel if you did not attain it?" What the researchers found is that the negative reactions were strongest when subjects thought about not attaining the lower-level goals. Subjects were more upset when they contemplated their safety needs not being met than they were when they thought about not meeting their self-actualization needs. Just the opposite pattern was found for the positive reaction ratings. When subjects were asked about attaining goals, they reported more positive emotions in response to contemplating the attainment of goals higher in the hierarchy. For example, acquiring esteem from others makes one feel better about oneself than having enough to eat and drink. This study supports Maslow's hierarchical arrangement of motives, while highlighting differences in how people react to the attainment or frustration in the various need levels. Maslow's idea that the lower needs are "prepotent"—imperative for sheer survival—and therefore stronger than the higher needs when unfulfilled was supported.

One study compared groups defined in terms of where they stood on Maslow's need hierarchy in terms of overall happiness (Diener, Horowitz, & Emmons, 1985). All the subjects were asked, "What is it that most makes you happy?" The researchers assumed that the answer to this question would reveal each subject's level of need in Maslow's hierarchy. For example, one subject said, "A good meal and the ability to digest it," which was scored as being at the physiological level. The results showed no relationship between level of need and overall happiness (which was gauged in this study by a questionnaire measure). For happiness, it does not appear to matter what level of need a person is working on. People working on self-actualization needs are not any more likely to be happier than people working on other needs. Maslow also notes in his book that happiness does not necessarily come with working on the self-actualizing need.

Given these findings, we might ask, "What *are* the characteristics that distinguish self-actualized persons from others?" Let's turn to a discussion of Maslow's research on the particular traits that best describe self-actualizing persons.

Characteristics of Self-Actualizing Persons

To learn more about self-actualization, Maslow conducted case studies of a number of people who he thought were self-actualizers. Maslow estimated about 1 percent of the population are growth motivated and are working on becoming all that they can become. Maslow's list of self-actualizing people whom he investigated included several living persons whom he kept anonymous. He also studied several historical figures through their writings and other biographical information, including Albert Einstein, Eleanor Roosevelt, and Thomas Jefferson. Maslow then looked for common characteristics that could be identified in this group. From this study, he produced a list of 15 characteristics that he suggested are commonly found among self-actualizers (see Table 11.3). Most of the people Maslow studied were famous, and many had made great contributions to science, politics, or the humanities. When reading over the list of characteristics in Table 11.3, bear in mind that the theory does not say "you must be famous or make great contributions to humanity" to become self-actualized. Students of personality often make this misinterpretation because of the special nature of the people studied by Maslow. It is possible for ordinary, as well as extraordinary, people to achieve self-actualization.

A notion related to self-actualization is the concept of flow, proposed by psychologist Mihaly Csikszentmihalyi (e.g., Csikszentmihalyi, Abuhamdeh, & Nakamura, 2005). **Flow** is defined as a subjective state that people report when they are completely involved in something to the point of forgetting time, fatigue, themselves, and everything else but the activity itself. In states of flow, a person is functioning at his or her fullest capacity. Although flow experiences are somewhat rare, they occur under specific conditions; there is a balance between the person's skills and the challenges of the situation, there is a clear goal, and there is immediate feedback on how one is doing. The experience of flow itself can be a powerful motivating force and can be an indication that, at least for the moment, one is engaging in self-actualization.

Exercise

Think of a person you know or have met who deeply impresses you. Try to identify someone who you think might be a self-actualizer. Review Maslow's list of the 15 characteristics he associated with self-actualized individuals (Table 11.3), and identify the characteristics that the person you've chosen appears to possess. Try to provide concrete examples from the person's life to illustrate the 15 characteristics.

Rogers's Contributions

Maslow focused on the characteristics of self-actualizing individuals, and he taught that only about 1 percent of humanity reached the self-actualizing level of motivation. The psychologist Carl Rogers (1902–1987), on the other hand, focused on ways to foster self-actualization and developed a form of therapy that helped people to move toward self-actualization. During the four decades of his productive career, Rogers developed a theory of personality and a method of psychotherapy (client-centered therapy). Like Maslow, Rogers believed that people were basically good and that human nature was fundamentally benevolent and positive. He felt that the natural human state was to be fully functioning, but under certain conditions people become stalled in their movement

Table 11.3   Characteristics of Self-Actualizers from Maslow's Case Studies

1. *Efficient perception of reality.* They do not let their own wishes and desires color their perceptions. Consequently, they are able to detect the deceitful and the fake.

2. *Acceptance of themselves, others, and nature or fate.* They realize that people, including themselves, make mistakes and have frailties, and they accept this fact. They accept natural events, even disasters, as part of life.

3. *Spontaneity.* Their behavior is marked by simplicity and honest naturalness. They do not put on airs or strain to create an effect. They trust their impulses, their actions are genuine.

4. *Problem focus.* They have an interest in the larger philosophical and ethical problems of their times. Petty issues hold little interest for them.

5. *Affinity for solitude.* They are comfortable with being alone.

6. *Independence from culture and environment.* They do not go in for fads. They prefer to follow their self-determined interests.

7. *Continued freshness of appreciation.* They have a "beginner's mind," for which every event, no matter how common, is experienced as if for the first time. They appreciate the ordinary and find pleasure and awe in the mundane.

8. *More frequent peak experiences.* A peak experience is a momentary feeling of extreme wonder, awe, and vision, sometimes called the "oceanic feeling." These are special experiences that appear to be very meaningful to the person who has one.

9. *Genuine desire to help the human race.* All self-actualizers tend to have a deep and sincere caring for their fellow humans.

10. *Deep ties with relatively few people.* Although they care deeply about others, they have relatively few very good friends. They tend to prefer privacy and allow only a few people to really know them.

11. *Democratic values.* They respect and value all people and are not prejudiced in terms of holding stereotypes about people based on superficial characteristics, such as race, religion, sex, and age. They treat others as individuals, not as members of groups.

12. *Ability to discriminate between means and ends.* They enjoy doing something for its own sake rather than simply doing something for the goals the activity can fulfill.

13. *Philosophical sense of humor.* Most humor is an attempt to make fun of a perceived inferiority of a person or group of people. Self-actualizers do not think such jokes are funny. Instead, what they find funny are examples of human foolishness in general, even their own.

14. *Creativity.* Creativity can be thought of as the ability to see connections among things—connections that no one has seen before. They are more likely to be creative because of their fresh perception of even ordinary things.

15. *Resistance to enculturation.* Cultures tell us how to behave, how to dress, and even how to interact with each other. Self-actualizers remain detached from culture-bound rules. They often appear and act differently from the crowd.

Source: Adapted from Maslow, 1954/1987.

toward self-actualization. His theory explains how people lose their direction. Moreover, he proposed techniques for helping people get back on track toward achieving their potential. His general approach to self-actualization—the person-centered approach—has been expanded and applied to groups, to education, to corporate organizations, and even to government (see Rogers, 2002, for his posthumously published autobiography).

At the core of Rogers's approach is the concept of the **fully functioning person,** the person who is on his or her way toward self-actualization. The fully functioning person may not actually *be* self-actualized yet, but he or she is not blocked or sidetracked in moving toward this goal. Several characteristics describe the fully functioning person. Such persons are open to new experiences, and they enjoy diversity and novelty in their daily lives. Fully functioning individuals are also centered in the present. They do not dwell on the past or their regrets. Neither do they live in the future. Fully functioning individuals also trust themselves, their feelings, and their own judgments. When faced with a decision, they don't automatically look around to others for guidance (e.g., "What would make my parents happy?"). Instead, they trust themselves to do the right thing. Fully functioning individuals are often unconventional, setting their own obligations and accounting to themselves.

How does someone become fully functioning? This is where Rogers's theory of the development of the self comes into play. An entire chapter of this book is devoted to an exploration of the self, and much of the work covered in Chapter 14 can be traced back to Carl Rogers, who strongly believed that there was one primary motive in life—the motive to self-actualize, to develop the self that was meant to be.

Journey into Selfhood: Positive Regard and Conditions of Worth

According to Rogers, all children are born wanting to be loved and accepted by their parents and others. He called this inborn need the desire for **positive regard.** Parents frequently make their positive regard contingent on conditions, such as the conditions expressed in the statements "Show me you are a good child and earn all as on your report card" or "I will really like it if you earn the star role in your school play." In another example, parents push children into sports, and the children might stay in the sports, not because they like sports, but to earn the love and positive regard of their parents. Of course, it is good for parents to have expectations for their children, but not to make their love contingent on the child's meeting those expectations. Parents should love their children unconditionally, but unfortunately many parents implicitly put conditions on their children for earning that love and positive regard.

The requirements set forth by parents or significant others for earning their positive regard are called **conditions of worth.** Children may become preoccupied with living up to these conditions of worth rather than discovering what makes them happy. They behave in specific ways to earn the love, respect, and positive regard of parents and other significant people in their lives. Positive regard, when it must be earned by meeting certain conditions, is called **conditional positive regard.**

Children who experience many conditions of worth may lose touch with their own desires and wants. They begin living their lives in an effort to please others. They become what others want them to become, and their self-understanding contains only qualities that others condone. They are moving away from the ideals of a fully functioning person. What matters most is pleasing others. "What will *they* think?"—not "What do I really want in this situation?"—is a question such people ask themselves repeatedly.

As they reach adulthood, they remain preoccupied with what others think of them. They work primarily for approval from others; they want to accumulate "likes" from important others; they pay attention to what the "influencers" say and do. They lose any sense of self-direction and are directed, instead, by what others want or what they think others want. They act in ways that make everybody, except themselves, happy. They have been working to please others for so long that they have forgotten what they want out of life. They have lost self-direction and are no longer moving toward self-actualization and may not even know it. Some might feel that "likes are not enough" (Bono, 2018), but they don't know what can replace them. Others might feel that their life is somehow inauthentic, that they've lost their way, but they are not sure how to get back to an authentic life.

How can one avoid this outcome? Rogers believed that positive regard from parents and significant others should have no strings attached. It should be given freely and liberally without conditions or contingencies. Rogers called this **unconditional positive regard**—when the parents and significant others accept the child without conditions, communicating that they love and value the child because the child just is. Parents need to show unconditional acceptance of the child, even when providing discipline or guidance. For example, if a child has done something wrong, the parent can still provide correction in combination with unconditional positive regard: "You have done something bad. *You* are not bad, and I still *love* you; it's just that the thing you have done is bad, and I don't want you to do that anymore."

With enough unconditional positive regard, children learn to accept experiences rather than deny them. They don't have to engage in efforts to distort themselves for others or alter their behaviors or experiences to fit a mold or model of what others want. Such persons are free to accept themselves, even their own weaknesses and shortcomings, because they have experienced unconditional **positive self-regard.** They are able to give themselves unconditional positive regard and accept themselves for who they are. They trust themselves, follow their own interests, and rely on their feelings to guide them. In short, they begin to take on the characteristics of a fully functioning person, they begin to actualize the self that they were meant to be.

Promotion of Self-Actualization in Self and Others

People who are not moving forward in terms of self-actualization experience frequent episodes of anxiety. **Anxiety,** according to Rogers, is the result of having an experience that does not fit with one's self-conception. Imagine a young woman who worked hard all through grade school and high school to earn good grades in an effort to make her parents happy. Part of her self-concept is that she "is smart and gets good grades." Then she enters college and obtains some less than perfect grades in some of her courses. This experience is alien; it does not fit with her self-concept as a person who is smart and gets good grades, so it makes her anxious. "What will *they* think," she says to herself, referring to her parents, "when they find out about these grades?" This new experience is a threat to her self-image, and that self-image is vitally important to her because in the past it brought her the positive regard of her parents. Rogers believed that people needed to defend themselves against anxiety, to reduce the discrepancy between their self-concept and their experiences. A fully functioning person could change his or her self-concept to incorporate the experience (e.g., "Perhaps I'm not so smart after all, or perhaps I don't always need to get perfect grades").

A less functional response to anxiety is to alter the experience by using a defense mechanism. Rogers emphasized the defense mechanism of **distortion.** Persons who engage in distortion modify their experience rather than their self-image to reduce the threat. For example, a person might say, "The professors in these classes are unfair," or "The grades really don't reflect how well I did," or in another way distort the experience. Or perhaps the person decides to take only "easy" classes, in which she is likely to earn high grades. Her decisions about which classes to take are based not on her *own* interests and desires (as would be the case for a self-actualizing reason) but on which classes are more likely to result in better grades to make her parents happy (a condition-of-worth reason). Taking classes merely to obtain easy grades is at odds with her self-concept of someone who is smart, and she may become anxious over the fact that so many of her experiences do not fit exactly with the way she would like to see herself.

People may get off the path toward self-actualization, not because they lack IQ or education but because they have gotten out of touch with their own emotions. A study found a relationship between the self-actualizing tendency and emotional intelligence (Bar-On, 2001). **Emotional intelligence** is a relatively new construct that has five components: the ability to know one's own emotions, the ability to regulate those emotions, the ability to motivate oneself, the ability to know how others are feeling, and the ability to influence how others are feeling. This may be an especially adaptive form of intelligence, which we describe in more detail in Chapter 12 on cognitive approaches. In the Bar-On (2001) study, the self-actualizing tendency was defined as working on actualizing one's talents and skills, and it was found that emotional intelligence correlated with this tendency. The author argues that emotional intelligence is more important for fostering self-actualizing than IQ, or cognitive intelligence.

Self-actualizers are in touch with their feelings and use their own emotions to guide their choices and decisions in life. This is positive *self*-regard in action. But many people, once they have gotten off track, have trouble finding their way back to themselves. Rogers designed a form of psychotherapy to help people get their lives back on track toward self-actualization.

Application

Paul Gauguin is most famous for his paintings of South Pacific islanders using lush color, the denial of perspective, and the use of flat, two-dimensional forms. His powerfully expressive yet stylistically simple paintings helped form the basis of modern art. Gauguin was not always an artist, however. In 1872, Gauguin started a very successful career as a stockbroker in Paris. His marriage to his Danish wife Mette produced five children, and they led a content, upper-middle-class life in Paris. Gauguin always wanted to paint, however. He felt he could be a great painter, but his job as a stockbroker consumed all of his time (Hollmann, 2001).

In 1874, Gauguin attended the first Impressionist painting exhibition in Paris. He was entranced with this style of painting. He had a strong desire to become a painter, but instead he put all of his energy into his stockbroker's job and used the proceeds to purchase some paintings by Monet, Pissarro, and Renoir. This was the closest he could come, he felt, to realizing his potential as an artist.

Fortunately or unfortunately, the bank that employed Gauguin began having difficulties in 1884. Gauguin began to take time away from work and started painting. His income went down, and he had to move his family from expensive Paris to the town of Rouen, where the cost of living was lower. As Gauguin devoted more time to painting and less time to stockbrokering, his income went even lower and his marriage started to suffer. Neither Paul nor his wife were happy with their current situation, but for different reasons; Paul wanted more of the new life of painting he was discovering, and his wife wanted more of the old life and for him to return to the Paris life of stockbrokers, banks, and the upper middle class.

After a period of some marital discord, Paul Gauguin left his wife and five children and, with absolute sincerity and clarity of purpose, began to realize his potential as an artist. He fell in with the likes of van Gogh, Degas, and Pissarro, who mentored him in impressionism. In 1891, he decided to flee civilization in search of a new way of life, one that more matched his painting style: primitive, bold, and sincere. He sailed to Tahiti and the islands of the South Pacific, where, except for a brief visit back to France, he remained until his death in 1903 (Gauguin, 1985). In Tahiti, his paintings of indigenous people grew more powerful and distinctive, and on a large scale he achieved his potential as one of the modern world's greatest artists.

The ethical questions in Gauguin's life concern the competing responsibilities that are so evident; he had one life as a responsible banker and stockbroker, complete with a loving

Application (*Continued*)

wife and five dependent children. On the other hand, Gauguin felt (correctly) that he had the potential to become a truly outstanding artist. Should he have been true to this inner calling, or should he have been true to his responsibilities as husband, father, and provider for his family? How should we judge his decision to abandon his family to pursue his self-actualization? What role does his success as an artist have in our judgment? What if, for example, he had abandoned his family then failed miserably as an artist? What should get priority in life when there is a conflict between one's immediate responsibilities and one's inner calling to realize a very different self? These are the difficult ethical questions of choice and responsibility that sometimes come to people on their way toward self-actualization.

A painting by Paul Gauguin titled "Self-Portrait with Yellow Christ" (1890), from a private collection. The life of Paul Gauguin raises several complicated ethical questions about responsibility, choice, and self-actualization.
Paul Gauguin/Art Images/Getty Images

Rogers's form of psychotherapy, sometimes called **client-centered therapy,** is very different from Freudian psychoanalysis. In client-centered therapy, the client (a term Rogers preferred over *patient*) is never given an interpretation of his or her problem. Nor is a client given any direction about what course of action to take to solve the problem. The therapist makes no attempts to change the client directly.

Instead, the therapist tries to create the right conditions in which the client can change him- or herself.

There are three **core conditions** for client-centered therapy (Rogers, 1957). These conditions must be present in the therapy context in order for progress to occur. A film of Carl Rogers conducting a therapy session with "Gloria" is widely available on the internet and is sometimes used in training therapists. In this film, Rogers expertly sets up these three conditions in his conversation with Gloria (see the analysis of this film by Wickman & Campbell, 2003). The first core condition is an atmosphere of *genuine acceptance* on the part of the therapist. The therapist must be genuinely able to accept the client. Second, the therapist must express *unconditional* positive regard for the client. This means that the therapist accepts everything the client says without passing judgment on the client. Clients trust that the therapist will not reject them if they say the "wrong" thing, or if something unflattering comes out in the course of therapy. The atmosphere is safe for clients to begin exploring their concerns.

The third condition for therapeutic progress is *empathic understanding.* The client must feel that the therapist understands him or her. A client-centered therapist attempts to know the client's thoughts and feelings as if they were his or her own. **Empathy** is understanding the other person from his or her point of view (Rogers, 1975). The therapist conveys empathic understanding by restating the content and feelings of what the client has said. Instead of interpreting the meaning behind what the client says (e.g., "You have a harsh superego, which is punishing you for the actions of your id"), the client-centered therapist simply listens to what the client says and reflects it back. It is analogous to looking in a mirror; a good Rogerian therapist reflects back the person's feelings and thoughts, so that the person can examine them in full and undistorted detail. The client comes to understand him- or herself better by making the therapist understand. The therapist expresses this understanding by restating the content ("What I heard you say is . . .") and by reflecting back the person's feelings ("It sounds as if you are feeling . . ."). This may sound simple, but it is a very effective approach to helping people understand themselves and helping them change how they think about themselves.

Exercise

Empathic listening is a technique of conversation that can be rather easily developed. You might practice with a friend. Find someone to role-play with you, and ask the person to start by describing a small problem from his or her life. Your job is to role-play a client-centered approach in the conversation. That is, you will try to do the two activities involved in reflecting back: first, try to just restate the content of what your friend says. That is, paraphrase back what the person has said, exactly as you understand it (e.g., "What I hear you saying is . . ."). The second reflecting-back action is to restate your friend's feelings. That is, take any feelings the friend mentions or implies and state them back to him or her exactly as you understand those feelings (e.g., "It seems you are feeling . . . about this situation"). The friend will correct you or elaborate on the situation or feelings. After a few minutes, switch the roles and have your friend be the empathic listener while you describe a small problem. If done correctly, you should feel that your friend is really understanding you and that you are encouraged to explore your problem situation and your feelings about that situation.

Application

The metaphor of a mirror is a useful one that can help us appreciate how the client-centered techniques work. Imagine that you want to adjust your outward appearance, so you look in a mirror to examine your appearance and see how the adjustment looks. Similarly, if you want to change your inner self, you can use the positive atmosphere and empathic understanding of a client-centered therapist to examine yourself and to contemplate changes. The following example demonstrates the technique of reflecting back:

Client: I just don't know which classes to take next year. I wish someone could make those decisions for me.
Therapist: You are looking for someone to tell you what to do.
Client: Yes, but I know that's impossible [sigh]. Nobody can decide what's right for me if even I don't have a clue.
Therapist: You find it exasperating that you are having so much trouble deciding on a class schedule.
Client: Well, none of my friends have this much trouble making decisions.
Therapist: You feel that your situation is not normal; it's not like the experience of your friends.
Client: Yeah, and it makes me mad. I should just be able to pick four or five courses and stick with my decision, but I can't seem to. I know it's silly.
Therapist: You think it is a trivial thing, yet it makes you angry that you cannot seem to make the decision.
Client: Well, you know, it really is trivial, isn't it? I know I can always change classes if they don't work out. I guess I just need to try them out.
Therapist: You see some options, that you can get out of a class if it isn't right for you.

The therapist never directs the client or offers an interpretation of the problem. This is why Rogerian therapy is sometimes called non-directive therapy—the focus is on the client's understanding of the situation, not the therapist's interpretation. The client works to clarify the therapist's understanding and, in so doing, increases his or her self-understanding. The client may come to accept that he or she has been denying or distorting experiences, such as taking classes for grades rather than for their own intrinsic interest. In helping the therapist understand why she is having so much trouble deciding on a class schedule, the person in the example may come to the realization that she has been taking classes primarily to make her parents happy. In an accepting atmosphere, she may come to this unflattering realization, and she might go on to explore how she can change her self-concept to accept this new understanding.

Ever since Rogers published his classic article describing empathy as one of the necessary conditions for therapeutic change (Rogers, 1957), many psychologists have attempted to understand the nature of empathy. Are some people natural-born empathizers, or is empathy a skill that can be acquired and improved with training? A study of 839 twin pairs suggests that the ability to take the perspective of another person is not significantly heritable (Davis, Luce, & Kraus, 1994). This finding implies that people are not necessarily born with a predisposition to be good at the empathic understanding of others' points of view. Other studies have demonstrated that empathy can be taught effectively. For example, in one study the researchers measured empathic ability both before and after training in peer counseling (Hacher et al., 1994). They found that the training program, which emphasized listening skills (such as those in the previous Exercise and Application), produced significant increases in overall empathy scores. The training especially helped college and high school students improve their abilities to take the perspectives of other people and understand others' concerns. Interestingly, these researchers found that, although college women initially had higher starting levels of empathic ability, men and women were equally teachable.

In another study, empathic ability increased with practice (Marangoni et al., 1995). College students watched videotapes of three individuals undergoing an interview about a personal problem (e.g., a recent divorce or the difficulties of being both a wife and a career woman). The researchers' hypothesis was supported; the subjects with more empathy were more accurate in their hunches about what the videotaped person was thinking and feeling, compared with the subjects who had less empathic ability. Moreover, the more practice the subjects had, the better they became at discerning what the videotaped individual was thinking and feeling. Finally, some subjects were simply better than others at empathic understanding. Even though everyone's performance could improve with practice, some subjects were consistently better than others. Trying to understand the characteristics that make someone particularly adept at empathic understanding is an important topic for future research.

Rogers's theory is important to personality psychology for a number of reasons (Bohart, 2013). His theory concerns the development of the self over the life span and includes specific processes that can interrupt or facilitate that development. He offers a new perspective on the importance of early experiences, similar to secure attachment, but which he calls unconditional positive regard. As in psychoanalysis, he assigns an important role to anxiety as a signal that things are not going well with the psychological system. Also as in classical psychoanalysis, he offers a system of psychotherapy for helping persons overcome personal setbacks on the road toward actualizing their full potential. His work has had a large impact on the practice of psychotherapy over the last half century (see Patterson, 2000).

SUMMARY AND EVALUATION

Motives can be used to explain why people do what they do. Motive explanations are unique in that they imply a goal that pulls people to think, act, and feel in certain ways. Many motives grow out of deficits. For example, someone motivated to achieve must feel that he or she has not yet achieved enough in life. The three motives discussed in detail—achievement, power, and intimacy—are all deficit motives. The fourth major motive—the motive to self-actualize—is not a deficit motive, but rather a growth motive because it refers to the desire to become more and more what one is destined to become.

Henry Murray was among the first to catalog the variety of human needs. He assumed that individuals differed in the strength of these needs and that the intensity of the needs also fluctuated over time and in different situations. Murray's emphasis was on how individuals differ from each other in terms of the basic needs, such as how some people have a more intense and lasting need for achievement than do other people.

Individual differences in the need for achievement have received a good deal of systematic attention from researchers. The need for achievement is the need to do things better and to overcome obstacles in the quest to attain one's goals. Those with high levels of the need for achievement differ from those low in this need in many important ways, such as the preference for moderate levels of challenge, the tendency to do well in situations where they have control and responsibility, and the interest in receiving feedback on their performance.

The need for power, another deficit motive, has also received research attention. This motive is the desire to have an impact on other people, to make other people respond, and to impress and dominate others. Individuals who have a high need for power seek out positions in which they can influence others and acquire possessions that have all the markings of power, such as sports cars and expensive electronic gadgets. They prefer friends who are not particularly powerful or popular. Men with a high need for power may sometimes engage in social influence tactics that are irresponsible, abusive, or unethical.

The need for intimacy is the motive to acquire warm and communicative relationships. People high in this need tend to think about, and spend more time with, other people. Communication and self-disclosure characterize their interactions, and they prefer one-to-one interactions to large group activities.

The TAT is a projective technique for assessing levels of motivation in people. The technique is based on the idea that what people see is influenced by their needs. For example, a lonely person might see all situations as opportunities to be with people. The TAT was validated by showing that arousing a need in a person influences the person to write TAT stories consistent with that aroused need. Recent reviews of the literature suggest that the TAT assesses implicit motives, and it might be best suited for predicting long-term consequences of motives rather than short-term behaviors.

The need to self-actualize represents a distinct tradition in the psychology of motivation, fundamentally different from the tradition that emphasizes deficit motivation. This humanistic approach emphasizes taking responsibility for decisions and making efforts to move and grow in a positive direction. The humanistic tradition assumes that human nature is positive and life-affirming and that most people would become fully functioning human beings if left to their own devices.

Abraham Maslow developed a hierarchical theory of motivation, the pinnacle of which is self-actualization, ranging from lower-level needs (physiological needs and safety needs) to higher-level needs (need for esteem and self-actualization). Maslow also studied the characteristics of self-actualizing persons and developed a list of the traits and behavior patterns that are common among the small percentage of the population working on becoming more of who they were meant to be.

Psychologist Carl Rogers theorized about obstacles to self-actualization and the therapeutic techniques that help people overcome those obstacles. Client-centered therapy is designed to help people regain their potential for growth and positive change. The therapist creates an atmosphere of unconditional positive regard and communicates empathic understanding to the client in order to enhance therapeutic effectiveness. It is clear from research that empathy is a skill that can be learned, supporting Rogers's theory.

KEY TERMS

motives 332
needs 332
hierarchy of needs 334
dynamic 334
press 336
alpha press 336
beta press 336
apperception 336
thematic apperception test 336
state levels 337
trait levels 337
implicit motivation 338
self-attributed motivation 339

need for achievement 339
independence training 343
need for power 344
responsibility training 345
power stress 346
need for intimacy 347
humanistic tradition 349
physiological needs 350
safety needs 352
belongingness needs 353
esteem needs 353
self-actualization need 354
flow 356

fully functioning person 357
positive regard 357
conditions of worth 357
conditional positive regard 357
unconditional positive regard 358
positive self-regard 358
anxiety 358
distortion 358
emotional intelligence 359
client-centered therapy 361
core conditions 361
empathy 361

The Cognitive/Experiential Domain

Part Four covers the cognitive/experiential domain, which emphasizes an understanding of people's perceptions, thoughts, feelings, desires, and other conscious experiences. The focus here is on understanding experience, especially from the person's point of view. However, distinctions can be made in terms of the kinds of experiences that people have.

One kind of experience that people have concerns cognitive experiences; what they perceive and pay attention to, how they interpret the events in their lives, and their goals and strategies and plans for getting what they want in the future.

People differ from each other when it comes to cognitively interpreting or making sense out of life events. We introduce a theory based on the idea that people construct their experiences by applying personal constructs to their sensations. A related theory concerns how people decide on the causes of life events. Often people interpret events by making attributions of responsibility for those events. That is, "Why did this happen?" and "Whose fault is this?" Personality psychologists have extensively studied how people make attributions of responsibility, and how there may be stable individual differences in the tendency to blame oneself or to blame external factors for bad events.

Cognitive experiences can also be studied in terms of the plans and goals that people formulate for themselves and for the strategies they develop for reaching their goals. People anticipate different futures and strive for different goals. Understanding people's goals and how their goals are expressions of personality as well as social standards also forms a part of the cognitive/experiential domain of knowledge about human nature.

A topic related to cognitive experience, and included in this part of the book, is intelligence. There are several controversies about the concept of intelligence. For example, what is the best definition of intelligence—the accumulation of what a person has learned or the ability to learn new information? Is intelligence one quality, or are there several different kinds of intelligence?

A second broad but important category of experience, one that is associated with, but distinct from, cognition, is emotion. Psychology has seen a sharp rise in research on emotion in the past few decades. We can ask a straightforward question about emotional lifestyle: Is a person generally happy or generally sad? What makes a person anxious or fearful? Why is it that some people become enthusiastic so easily? What makes people angry, and why can some people control their anger, whereas others cannot?

Emotional experiences are often thought of as states that come and go; now you are anxious, now you are not, or now you are angry, now you are not. However, emotions can also be thought of as traits, as the frequent experiences of specific states. For example, a person may become anxious frequently or have a lower threshold for experiencing anxiety. And so we might talk of anxiety proneness as a personality trait—the tendency to easily and frequently become anxious.

When it comes to emotions as traits, we can divide the main topics into variables that refer to the content and variables that refer to the style of emotional life. The content of emotional life can be divided into pleasant and unpleasant emotions. In terms of pleasant emotions, the typical personality-relevant trait is happiness. Psychologists have recently become very interested in happiness, part of a general movement, called Positive Psychology, that focuses on the positive features of human nature.

When it comes to unpleasant emotion traits, the research can be divided into three different dispositional emotions: anger, anxiety, and depression. Depression is a syndrome that is experienced by a significant portion of the population, and it is of great importance in terms of public mental health. Trait anxiety has many different names in the personality literature, including neuroticism, negative affectivity, and emotional instability. Anger proneness is also a traitlike tendency, but this one refers to the tendency to easily or frequently become angry, a characteristic personality psychologists are keenly interested in.

People also differ from each other in the style of their emotional lives. Emotional style refers to how their emotions are typically experienced. Some people, for example, tend to experience their emotions at a higher intensity than other persons. For such high affect-intensity persons, a positive event makes them very happy, and a negative event makes them very unhappy. Consequently such people experience wider emotional swings from day to day or even within a day.

A third major category of experience is distinct from cognition and emotion yet is very important to the average person. This category of experience refers to experiences of the self. These experiences are unique in that individuals can focus on themselves as an object, pay attention to themselves, come to know themselves. The experience of self is unlike all of our other experiences, because in the experience of the self the knower and the known are one and the same. Psychologists have paid a great deal of attention to this unique object of our experience, self-knowing, and research and theorizing on the self has a long and rich tradition in personality psychology.

There are some useful distinctions among types of self-experiences. First there are descriptive aspects of the self: Who are we, what are the important images we have of our past self, and what are the images of possible future selves? A second main component of the experience of self is evaluative: Do we like or dislike who we are? This is called self-esteem, and it is a central organizing force in much of what we do. A third component of our self-experience concerns the social roles we inhabit, the social selves we show to others, which we call identity. For example, many college students show one identity to their parents and another identity to their companions at school. And people sometimes go through identity crises, especially during transitions in life, such as starting college, getting married, or starting a new job.

Cognitive Topics in Personality

12

THE COGNITIVE/EXPERIENTIAL DOMAIN

On February 4, 1999, just past midnight, Amadou Diallo, a 22-year-old immigrant from West Africa, was standing on the front stoop of his Bronx home after putting in a full day at work. An unmarked car carrying four plainclothes officers from the NYPD Street Crime Unit cruised by. The police officers were investigating crimes that had plagued that particular area, including a series of gunpoint rapes. This South Bronx neighborhood was one of the most dangerous in New York City. As they passed Mr. Diallo, he backed into a dark doorway. On noticing this, the officer driving put the car into reverse and backed up to a point directly in front of Mr. Diallo's home.

As Mr. Diallo stood in the doorway, the plainclothes officers exited their vehicle, and two approached Mr. Diallo saying, "Police Department. We'd like to have a word with you." At this point, Mr. Diallo backed further into the vestibule and the two officers then added the commands "Stay where you are," and "Keep your hands where we can see them."

Mr. Diallo reached his right hand into his front pocket. He turned toward the officers while pulling a black object out of his pocket and bringing his hands together. One officer yelled, "Gun!" Two officers fired. The closest officer, trying to back away from Mr. Diallo, fell backward down the steps. The other officers thought he had been shot.

In the next four seconds, the police officers fired a total of 41 bullets, 19 of which struck Mr. Diallo, killing him almost instantly. When the officers approached Mr. Diallo's body, they found him holding not a gun, but his wallet.

The details of this tragic case were made public during the subsequent trial of the police officers. Key documents from this trial, as well as news articles on which the above description is based, are available on the web. The jury concluded that what occurred that night was a series of terrible accidents—errors in perception and cognition that had catastrophic results. The officers "saw" a gun, they "thought" one of their own had been shot, and they "thought" Mr. Diallo was returning gunfire, when in fact it was their own ricocheting bullets. Their behavior then followed these cognitive errors. Many police academies now analyze the Diallo case during the training of new officers. Researchers are also trying to learn what factors contribute to such a tragic misperceptions in police officers (e.g., Andersen et al., 2021). The final chapter of the Diallo case closed in January 2004 when the City of New York settled a civil rights lawsuit by paying Mr. Diallo's family $3 million and offering an apology for the tragic misunderstanding.

The case of Mr. Diallo, and many other subsequent and similar cases, illustrates the connection between cognitive factors and behavior. People perceive and think and then act. Sometimes this all happens very quickly, as in the case of police officers making split-second decisions, and sometimes we take our time thinking things through. We are processing information all the time and using this information to guide our actions. Most of the time, our information processing is fairly accurate, resulting in appropriate actions. Occasionally errors of information processing occur, and mistakes are made, sometimes with tragic consequences. Personality psychologists are interested in how people differ from each other in processing information, including errors in perception and interpretation.

The following case illustrates individual differences in perception. It is not as dramatic as the Diallo case, but it nevertheless illustrates how two people can look at the same object and "see" two very different things.

There were several women from the same sorority in one class. The professor had heard that the sorority had adopted a new dog. Curious, he asked one sorority member what kind of dog it was. She said, "He is big and friendly and loves to go for walks and likes to jump up and lick my face. I just love him." The next day, he had an opportunity to ask a different sorority member the same question. She responded, "Our new dog is a 3-year-old male golden retriever. He weighs about 90 pounds, is tall for the breed, and is rusty-red colored." It is interesting that the same question elicited such different information from these two people. The first student offered no information about the breed of dog; instead, she told how she *felt* about the dog. The second student gave factual details about the dog but said nothing about what she thought of the dog. These two women obviously processed quite different information when asked about the new dog. And it is also quite likely that they think very differently from each other about many things in life. Such differences in how people think are the focus of **cognitive approaches** to personality.

Many years ago, a study was done on what people think about when they are exposed to emotion-provoking stimuli (Larsen, Diener, & Cropanzano, 1987). The researchers showed people images of emotion-provoking scenes, then asked the participants what they thought about when they looked at each image (a technique called thought sampling). For example, one image was of a mother holding a child who was bleeding from a severe head wound. In this study, the researchers were interested not in what the participants felt but in what they thought about—in the information that went through their minds—when exposed to such emotional scenes. One participant said, "My brother once had a bad gash on his head just like that, and I remember all the blood, and how upset my mother became, and my brother screaming and my mother trying to stop the bleeding, and me feeling helpless and confused." The next participant looked at the same image and said, "Head wounds bleed quite a bit because, in the head, there is a high concentration of blood vessels close to the surface of the skin. I was thinking about the major artery groups in the head when I looked at that photo." The first person who looked at the emotional image engaged in what is called **personalizing cognition**. That is, the scene prompted him to recall a similar event from his own life. The second subject looked at the same image and engaged in what is called **objectifying cognition**. That is, the scene prompted her to recall objective facts about the distribution of blood vessels in the human head. The difference between these two persons is a difference in cognition.

Cognition is a general term referring to awareness and thinking, as well as to specific mental acts such as perceiving, attending to, interpreting, remembering, believing, judging, deciding, and anticipating. All these mental behaviors add up to what is called **information processing**, or the transformation of sensory input into mental representations and the manipulation of such representations. If you have ever wondered whether other people think about things the same way you do, then you are a budding cognitive personality psychologist. Perhaps you have wondered if other people see colors the same as you do. Is the perception of green, for example, the same for everyone?

In this chapter, we cover three levels of cognition that are of interest to personality psychologists. The first level is **perception,** or the process of imposing order on the information our sense organs take in. You might think that there are few, if any, differences in how people perceive the world because our sensory and perceptual systems are all the same and what we perceive is an accurate representation of what is out there. But this is not true; two people can look at the same situation and actually see very different things.

Consider Figure 12.1. If you look at this illustration, you can see it in three dimensions. That is, instead of being a two-dimensional, flat drawing, you perceive it as having depth, as coming out of the page. This is because your perceptual system interprets cues of depth as representing a three-dimensional object. Another aspect of this figure—known as the Necker Cube—is that you may perceive the cube as extending out and upward to the right of the base, whereas others perceive the cube as extending outward and downward toward the left. Thus, not everyone sees the same object, even though the drawing is objectively the same.

Imagine how people might differ in what they see when they look at the much more complicated social world. Even at the level of perception, what we see in the world can be quite different from person to person. Moreover, these differences in what people see may be related to their personalities. It is this reasoning that underlies the rationale for such projective assessment techniques as the Rorschach inkblots. As we discussed in Chapters 2 and 9, what people see in the inkblots can be a function of their personalities. When looking at the same inkblot, one person might see a family of butterflies landing on a garden of flowers, and another person, looking at the same inkblot, might see a dog that has been hit by a car, with blood splattered all over the street. Do you think these two people might have different personalities?

The second level of cognition of interest to personality psychologists is **interpretation,** or the making sense of, or explaining,

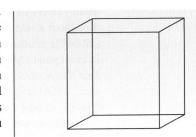

Figure 12.1

The Necker Cube.

various events in the world. Interpretation gives meaning to events. When you are confronted with an event and you are asked, "What does this mean?" or "How did this happen?" and "Whose fault is this?" you are likely to engage in the act of interpretation. For example, suppose you have a small mishap while driving your car, driving up a curb, and scratching your fender. Someone might ask you, "Why did this happen?" You quickly make an interpretation and offer it to your inquisitor as a fact: "The street there is poorly laid out. It's too narrow and the curve is too sharp, and lots of people jump the curb there. It's the fault of the road department." However, maybe you offer a different interpretation, equally certain that it represents a fact: "I'm really a clumsy driver; I just can't handle the car. Maybe I should quit driving."

These are two of many possible interpretations, and which ones people offer may reveal aspects of their personalities. This notion of differences in interpretation underlies the rationale for such projective techniques as the thematic apperception test (TAT), discussed in Chapter 11.

The third level of cognition that is of interest to personality psychologists is people's **conscious goals,** the standards that people develop for evaluating themselves and others. People develop specific beliefs about what is important in life and which tasks they want to pursue. These tasks may be age specific and/or culture specific, such as, in Western cultures, establishing independence from one's family in early adulthood. A final topic in cognitive approaches is intelligence. Because this is a large and controversial topic in psychology, the student of personality should have some grasp of the basic issues and concepts in the area of intelligence.

Personality Revealed Through Perception

Most people assume there is reality out there and that the representation we have of it in our minds is a precise duplicate, a flawless grasp of the facts. This is simply not true; the perceiver contributes to the mental representations such that, even in perception, there are differences among people in what they see when they look at a scene. In this chapter, we expand on this notion and cover two topics that explore individual differences in perception. These topics show how perceptual differences can be stable, consistent, and meaningfully related to other areas of life.

Field Dependence-Independence

Have you ever heard the phrase that someone "can't see the forest for the trees"? This usually refers to the idea that someone cannot look beyond the details to get the big picture about a situation, that he or she is so focused on the specifics they cannot grasp the gist of the situation. Psychologist Herman Witkin (1916–1979) studied such differences in perceptual style for almost 30 years. He came to call this topic *field dependence versus field independence.* Witkin's first book was titled *Personality Through Perception* (Witkin et al., 1954), and this title captures the idea that personality can be revealed through differences in how people perceive their environment.

Witkin was first interested in the cues that people use in judging orientation in space. If you see an object that is tilted, how do you know it is the object, and not your body or the background, that is tilted? To make such judgments, some people rely on cues from the environment surrounding the object (are other things tilted as well?), whereas other people rely more on bodily cues that tell them that *they* are upright and therefore it must be the object that is tilted. To investigate this individual difference, Witkin devised an apparatus called the **rod and frame test (RFT).** Using this apparatus, the participant sits in a darkened room and is instructed to watch a glowing rod surrounded by a square frame, which is also glowing. The experimenter can adjust the tilt of the rod, the frame, and the tilt of the participant's chair. The participant's task is to adjust the rod by turning a dial, so that the rod is perfectly upright. To do this accurately, the participant has to ignore cues in the visual field in which the rod appears (i.e., the square frame surrounding the rod). If the participant adjusts the rod so that it is leaning in the direction of the tilted frame, then that person is said to be dependent on the visual field, or **field dependent.** Other people disregard the external cues (the frame) and, instead, use information from their bodies in adjusting the rod to upright. Such participants are said to be independent of the field, or **field independent;** they appear to rely on their own sensations, not the perception of the field, to make the judgment.

The rod and frame test is a difficult and time-consuming way to measure field dependence/independence, so Witkin sought more efficient ways to measure this perceptual difference (Witkin et al., 1962). One clever way of measuring field dependence/independence is to create a complex figure that contains many simple figures or shapes. You may have seen children's puzzles that consist of a large drawing with several smaller, hidden figures within it. An example of hidden figures is given in Figure 12.2. Witkin devised a similar test, but with geometric figures, called the **embedded figures test (EFT).** Some people, when given the EFT, have trouble locating the simple figures embedded within the more complex surrounding figure, apparently being bound up in the "forest" and unable to see the "trees." These people are said to be field dependent. Other people quickly spot many or all of the embedded figures and, so, are able to disengage from the background. Such people are said to be field independent. Performance on the EFT correlates strongly with performance on the RFT (Witkin, 1973).

Field Dependence/Independence and Life Choices

Just before his death in 1979, Witkin wrote several papers summarizing his research in two broad domains in which field dependence/independence appears to have consequences: education and interpersonal relations. In one large study, 1,548 students were followed from their entry into college until several years after graduation. Choice of major in college was found to be related to field independence/dependence: the field-independent students tended to favor the natural sciences, math, and engineering, whereas the more field-dependent students tended to favor the social sciences and education (Witkin, 1977; Witkin et al., 1977). Field dependence-independence has also been related to career choice, and therefore has some utility in vocational counseling (Guisande, Páramo & Soares, 2007).

A second area of research reviewed by Witkin and Goodenough (1977) concerns the interpersonal correlates of field independence/dependence. Field-dependent people, as might be predicted, tend to rely on social information and frequently ask other people for their opinions. They are attentive to social cues and, in general, are oriented toward other people. They show a strong interest in others, prefer to be physically close to other people, gravitate to social situations, and get along well with others. Field-independent people, on the other hand, function with more autonomy and display a more impersonal or detached orientation toward others. They are not very interested in others' opinions, keep their distance from others, and show a preference for less social situations and activities.

Figure 12.2

An embedded figures test, in which the objective is to find as many of the smaller figures hidden in the larger figure as quickly as possible.

Current Research on Field Dependence/Independence

After Witkin's death in 1979, little research was done on field independence/dependence for about a decade. However, starting in the 1990s, new research began to appear in the literature (Messick, 1994). One new area of research concerns how people react to situations that are rich in sensory stimulation and whether field-independent people can focus on a task and screen out distracting information from the field. For example, one study of police officers examined their ability to disregard noise and distractions in simulated, though naturalistic, shooting situations. Similarities can be drawn between this study and the Diallo case presented at the beginning of this chapter. That night in the Bronx, the officers were trying to focus on Mr. Diallo. However, the light was dim, other people were around, the four officers needed to be aware of each other and aware of the commands being given, and so on. In short, they were in a stimulus-rich environment. Field-independent persons are predicted to be better at ignoring distracting information and focusing on the important details of the event. The researchers conducting the study of 100 police officers in simulated high-stimulation settings (Vrij, van der Steen, & Koppelaar, 1995) made exactly this prediction—that the more field-independent officers would perform better by noticing details more accurately, would be less distracted by the noise and activity, and would be more accurate in deciding when to shoot. Results confirmed predictions, with Field Independent officers performing better under high stimulation conditions. Presumably, the field-independent officers could better focus on the target without being distracted by the noise and activity going on in the field around them. In another study, researchers tracked subjects' eye movements as the subjects scanned visual scenes (Nisiforou & Laghos, 2016). Field dependent subjects displayed more disorganized eye movements, with fixations all around the visual images, compared to field independent persons.

Another area of high stimulation is in hypermedia- and multimedia-based computer instruction, such as educational materials on the World Wide Web, which come with sound and streaming video. Field independence is related to a higher preference for stimulus rich web-based instruction (Clewley, Chen, & Liu, 2011) (see Table 12.1). Field independent subjects also perform better than field dependent subjects in such high stimulation environments as Air Traffic Control simulations (Van Eck, Fu, & Drechsel, 2015) and complex three-dimensional navigational displays (Li, Zhang, Wu & Mei, 2016).

In a study of eighth-graders, researchers found that the field-independent students learned more effectively than the field-dependent subjects in a hypermedia-based instructional environment. Presumably, the field-independent students more easily found the thread that ran through the various media presentations of information. The experimenters concluded that field-independent students are able to get the points embedded within high stimulus media faster and are able to switch between educational media or sensory fields faster, compared with field-dependent students (Weller et al., 1995). Many studies of this perceptual difference suggest that it leads to different styles of learning—for example, field-independent persons are good at selective attention in stimulus-rich environments (at processing specific information while blocking out distractions), whereas field-dependent persons tend to process information in chunks and are good at seeing connections among categories of information (Nicolaou & Xistouri, 2011; Oughton & Reed, 1999; Richardson & Turner, 2000).

Some interesting research has also been done on the relation between field dependence and the ability to "read" or decode facial expressions. On the one hand,

Table 12.1 Summary of research on the personality trait of Field Dependence/Independence

	Field Dependent	Field Independent
Rod and frame test	Influenced by frame	Disregards frame, influenced by body position
Embedded figures test	Slow to locate hidden figures	Quickly locates hidden figures
	Focused on the whole	Focused on the parts
Common college majors	Favors social sciences, education, humanities	Favors natural sciences, engineering, math (STEM)
Social relations	Oriented toward others	More impersonal and detached from others
	Strong social interests and skills	Lower social interests and skills
Simulated shooting studies	Attentive to social context but overloaded in stimulus-rich situations	Can ignore distracting stimuli, focus on the details in stimulus-rich situations
Learning styles	Learns more effectively when info comes in chunks, or in single media or streams	Learns more effectively in multimedia environments
Other observations	Good at seeing the big picture, gets the gist	Good at detecting patterns in visual and auditory stimuli
	Less accuracy using electronic maps	Better at using 3-dimensional navigational displays
	More disorganized eye movements in visual search	Experienced Air Traffic Controllers are more Field Independent
		Faster to learn new languages

Studies have shown that individuals serving in bomb disposal units score higher in field independence than other terrorist response units. The ability to stay focused in a distracting environment would be an asset to a bomb disposal technician.

guvendemir/iStock/Getty Images Plus

because field-dependent people tend to be more socially oriented, we might predict they should do especially well in reading emotional expressions. On the other hand, if we think of facial expressions as complex arrays of information, then maybe the field-independent persons would be better at analyzing facial patterns. In a study on this topic, psychologists Linda Bastone and Heather Wood (1997) had subjects indicate the emotion expressed in 72 different faces. However, to make the task difficult, some emotion displays showed only the eyes, and some showed only the mouth. The field-independent subjects were significantly better at interpreting facial expressions than the field-dependent subjects, but only when the tasks were difficult. This finding reinforces the notion that field-independent persons are good at tasks that require finding patterns in complex displays of information.

Application

The Metaverse Is Coming...

At this point, the Metaverse is more of a concept than a reality. But many computer scientists and corporations are working toward building it, whatever "it" turns out to be. Some have suggested that the 2018 movie *Ready Player One* provides a vision of what the Metaverse may be like. It will be the successor to the mobile Internet and will provide each person with an immersive experience of a graphically rich virtual space. It will likely have high verisimilitude (it will feel quite real). The person won't 'watch' it, but rather they will 'be' in it and have a sense of presence inside the Metaverse. Others will also be there, and interactions with them (or their avatars most likely) will also feel real. It will likely stimulate several senses, including hearing and sight and perhaps touch, taste, and olfaction. If it is anything like *Ready Player One* it will be a world with high information flow and plenty of stimulation and place demands on our information processing capacities.

Virtual reality can provide a stimulus-rich environment for applications in education, science, and elsewhere. It may be that field-independent people are more able to function effectively in stimulus-rich virtual realities.
Andriy Onufriyenko/Moment/Getty Images

Personality psychologists might be interested in whether the trait of Field Dependence versus Independence might play a role in who is attracted to the Metaverse, or who functions well in such high information rate virtual environments. While the exact nature of the Metaverse is yet to be determined (e.g., will it be one world or many worlds, will it be accessed through Virtual Reality or through Augmented Reality, etc.), it is a certainty that the Metaverse is coming.

Is it better to be field independent or field dependent? Like most personality dimensions, there are pros and cons associated with both endpoints (and remember, we are describing points along a continuum, not two categories of people). Field-independent people are skillful at analyzing complex situations and extracting information from the clutter of background distractions. Field-independent people also tend to be more creative (Miller, 2007). However, they are somewhat low on social skills and prefer to keep their distance from others. Field-dependent people, on the other hand, have strong social skills, gravitate toward others, and are more attentive to the social context than are field-independent persons (Tamir & Nadler, 2007). On the downside, field independent people display more disorganized eye movements when searching visual displays. It appears that each of these contrasting perceptual styles is adaptive in particular situations, making it impossible to state which orientation is more valuable (Collins, 1994; Mathes et al., 2011).

Pain Tolerance and Sensation Reducing/Augmenting

The way in which people perceive their surroundings and navigate through information—whether they tend to focus on the whole or tend to notice the particulars—is a perceptual style. What about other individual differences in perception? One perceptual difference among people is in **pain tolerance,** in which people undergo the same physical stimulus (e.g., having to get an injection from the doctor) but react quite differently from each other in terms of the pain they report experiencing. This difference among people in their pain tolerance attracted the interest of psychologist Aneseth Petrie (1914–2001), whose book *Individuality in Pain and Suffering* describes her research on and theory of individual differences in tolerance for sensory stimulation (Petrie, 1967).

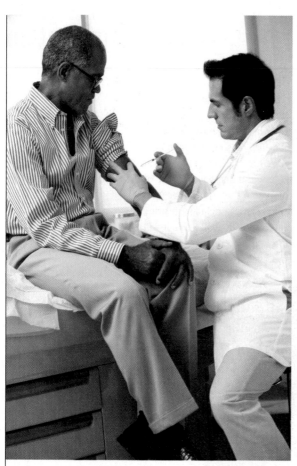

Understanding individual differences in pain tolerance to medical procedures is what led psychologist Aneseth Petrie to develop her theory of sensory reducing/augmenting.

monkeybusinessimages/iStock/Getty Images Plus

Petrie's Research

Petrie studied people in hospitals undergoing painful operations, as well as normal subjects in whom she induced pain—through applying heat or by piling weights on the middle joint of her subjects' fingers. In these studies, she was able to quantify how well each subject could tolerate pain. She developed a theory that people with low pain tolerance had a nervous system that amplified, or augmented, the subjective impact of sensory cues. In contrast, people who could tolerate pain well were thought to have a nervous system that dampened, or reduced, the effects of sensory stimulation. For these reasons, her theory came to be called the **reducer/augmenter theory.** This term refers to the dimension along which people differ in their reaction to sensory stimulation; some appear to reduce sensory stimulation, whereas some appear to augment or amplify stimulation.

Petrie believed that individual differences in pain tolerance originated in the nervous system. A few studies have examined nervous system reactivity directly in relation to augmenting/reducing. For example, researchers reported that reducers show relatively small brain responses to flashes of lights (Spilker & Callaway, 1969) as well as smaller brain responses to bursts of noise (Schwerdtfeger & Baltissen, 1999) in comparison with augmenters. In this last study, conducted in Germany, reducers also reported that the noise was less loud, compared with augmenters, though the noise was, in fact, identical for all the participants.

The brain evoked response increases with increasing stimulus intensity, but the rate of change differs for different individuals, with augmenters showing a steeper rate of change with increasing stimulus intensity (Schwerdtfeger & Baltissen, 2002). Moreover, the brain evoked potential augmenting/reducing measure shows high test-retest reliability, similar to other personality traits (Beauducel et al., 2000). Individual differences in brain augmenting/reducing have also been studied in other animals, including cats and rats (Siegel, 1997). In fact, rats that have been bred to be sensation seeking or sensation avoiding have been shown to display brain evoked responses that indicate reducing and augmenting, respectively (Siegel & Driscoll, 1996). Given that this individual difference in sensory reactivity can be observed in other mammals, it is not surprising that studies also show that this individual differences arises in infancy in humans (Evans, Nelson, & Porter, 2012; Fox & Polak, 2004).

Reducers should be motivated to seek strong stimulation to compensate for their lower sensory reactivity, related to optimal level of arousal, discussed in Chapter 7. Supporting this prediction, reducers have been found to drink more coffee, smoke more, and have a lower threshold for boredom, compared with augmenters (Clapper, 1990, 1992; Larsen & Zarate, 1991). Reducers also have been found to more frequently consume psychoactive drugs and listen to music at a louder level compared to augmenters (Schwerdtfeger, 2007). Several studies replicate the finding that reducers (measured by questionnaire) have a higher tolerance for pain compared to augmenters (e.g., Schwerdtfeger, Gertzmann & Baltissen, 2004).

Exercise

Researchers have developed questionnaire measures to assess people's standing on the reducing/augmenting dimension. One example is the questionnaire developed by Vando (1974) and modified by Clapper (1992), called the Revised Reducer Augmenter Scale (RRAS). This measure is based on the notion that if reducers dampen down stimulation, then they have a relatively high need for stimulation, compared with augmenters. Items on Clapper's RRAS questionnaire present test takers with a choice between a relatively stimulating and a nonstimulating experience. The test taker indicates his or her preference for either the stimulating or the nonstimulating experience. Subjects who prefer many of the stimulating choices are assumed to be reducers. Examples of these items follow. For each pair of activities or events, circle a number that best indicates your preference:

Hard-rock music	1	2	3	4	5	6	Soft pop music
Action movies	1	2	3	4	5	6	Comedy movies
Contact sports	1	2	3	4	5	6	Noncontact sports
A drum solo	1	2	3	4	5	6	A flute solo
Too much exercise	1	2	3	4	5	6	Too little exercise

Many researchers see a strong similarity between the augmenting/reducing construct and other personality constructs related to individual differences in responding to stimulation, such as those covered in Chapter 7 (e.g., sensation seeking), as well as Eysenck's theory of extraversion, covered in Chapters 3 and 7. For our purposes here, the reducer/augmenter research illustrates how personality psychologists have studied individual differences in perception, the most basic form of cognition. Let's turn now to a consideration of how people differ from one another in a higher level of cognition—interpretation.

Personality Revealed Through Interpretation

Trial lawyers are familiar with the fact that two or more people can witness the same event yet offer differing interpretations of that event. Trials often hinge on having the jury arrive at a particular interpretation of the facts, such as whether the suspect *intended* to harm someone, whether the suspect had *planned* the crime ahead of time, or whether the suspect is capable of *appreciating the consequences* of his or her behavior at the time of the criminal act. Many defense lawyers do not dispute that their clients committed their acts, but rather argue that the clients did not possess the required intention to be found guilty of a crime.

Everyday life may not be as dramatic as the cases that make their way into courtrooms. Nevertheless, we often find ourselves interpreting everyday events: Why did I get a poor grade on my test? Can I really do anything to lose weight? Whose fault is it that I can't seem to get along with my girlfriend/boyfriend? Such interpretations often concern responsibility or blame—such as whose fault it is when someone gets a poor grade. Other times, such interpretations inquire about expectations for the future—such as if someone can lose weight. Both of these kinds of interpretations—about *responsibility* and about *expectations* for the future—have been studied by personality psychologists. However, before covering these topics, let's examine the theory that started the cognitive revolution in personality psychology: the work of George Kelly.

Kelly's Personal Construct Theory

Psychologist George Kelly (1905–1967), who spent most of his career at Ohio State University, played an important role in starting the cognitive tradition within personality psychology. Although a clinical psychologist, Kelly believed that all people are motivated to understand their circumstances and to be able to predict what will happen to them in the near future. He viewed psychoanalysis as effective because it provided people with a system for explaining psychological problems (e.g., "You are depressed because you have a hostile and sadistic superego, probably as the result of an improper anal stage resolution"). Kelly believed that the content of explanations was not as important as the fact that people believed them and could use them to understand their circumstances. Kelly felt that a primary motivation for all people was to find meaning in their life circumstances, and to use this meaning to predict their own future, to anticipate what is likely to happen next in their lives (Fransella & Neimeyer, 2003).

Kelly's view of human nature was that of humans as scientists. He felt that, just like scientists, people in general engage in efforts to understand, predict, and control the events in their lives. When people do not know why some event happened (e.g., "Why did my girlfriend break up with me?"), they experience greater distress than if they had an explanation. Thus, people seek explanations for the events in their lives, just the way scientists seek explanations for phenomena in the laboratory.

Scientists employ **constructs** to interpret observations. A construct does not exist in itself; it is a word that summarizes a set of observations and conveys the meaning of those observations. Gravity, for example, is a scientific construct. We cannot show you gravity, but we can demonstrate the effects of gravity by observing other things, such as an apple falling from a tree. There are lots of constructs that could be applied to people: smart, outgoing, arrogant, shy, deviant. Like scientists interpreting the physical world, we use constructs all the time to give meaning to, or to interpret, the social world.

The constructs a person routinely uses to interpret and predict events are called, in Kelly's theory, **personal constructs.** Kelly's idea was that people have a few key constructs that they habitually apply in interpreting their world, particularly the social world. No two people have the same personal construct system and so have their own unique interpretation of the world. For Kelly, personality consisted in differences in the way people construe the world, particularly the social world. These differences were the result of differences in the personal constructs that people habitually employed. What do you tend to notice when you meet a person for the first time? For you, it might be important how athletic versus nonathletic a person is, and this plays a large role in how you first construe the person. Another person, however, might apply the construct of intelligent versus nonintelligent to the same target person. As a result, that person will have a different construal of the target person than you have because you are each viewing the target person through the unique "lens" of your preferred construct systems (Hua & Epley, 2012).

For Kelly all constructs are bipolar. That is, they consist of some characteristic understood against its opposite, or what the person takes to be its opposite. So, a few typical constructs might be smart–not smart, cooperative–uncooperative, tall–short, and boring–interesting. People develop characteristic sets of constructs that they frequently use in interpreting the world. A person might apply smart–not smart to most people they meet and use this construct to parse their social world into groups. Moreover, they then behave differently toward people in the smart category compared to the not-so-smart category. However, it is the person's own construal that puts the acquaintances into those categories to begin with. People create their social world, in part, by applying their personal constructs.

In many ways, Kelly was ahead of his times. He was postmodern before postmodernism became popular. **Postmodernism** is an intellectual position grounded in the notion that reality is constructed, that every person and certainly every culture has a version of reality that is unique, and that no single version of reality is any more privileged than another (Gergen, 1992). Kelly's emphasis on how personal constructs serve to create each person's psychological reality puts him in the postmodern camp (Raskin, 2001).

Kelly presented a highly complex but systematic theory of personality and personal constructs, which the interested student can pursue in Kelly's own work (e.g., 1955) or in summaries of his work (e.g., Fransella, 2003). We present some of the basic ideas here. His most basic idea was the *fundamental postulate,* which refers to the statement that "a person's processes are psychologically channelized by the ways in which he anticipates events" (Kelly, 1955, p. 46). To this fundamental postulate, Kelly added a number of corollaries. For example, if two people have similar construct systems, they would be psychologically similar (the commonality corollary). Some couples might be quite different in many ways, but if their personal construct systems are similar, then they are likely to get along well because they interpret the world similarly.

Like many personality theorists, Kelly also devoted a special place in his theory to the concept of anxiety. For Kelly, anxiety was the result of not being able to understand

and predict life events. In his terms, anxiety is the result of our personal constructs failing to make sense of our circumstances. People are anxious when they don't understand what is happening to them and when they feel that events are unpredictable, outside of their control. How do constructs fail? Sometimes they are too rigid and impermeable to new experiences. Something comes along that they just cannot understand. Imagine a woman who, after raising the children and shipping them off to college, decides she wants to work. Her husband, whose conception of a good marriage is one in which "the wife does not have to work," cannot understand this experience. His construct of good versus bad marriage cannot make sense out of his wife's newfound desire for employment. Another way that constructs fail is if they are too permeable, if the person applies them too liberally. If a person categorizes everyone she encounters as either smart or not smart, and once categorized refuses to change her mind about them, even in the face of contradictory information, then her construct is too rigidly applied. A person knows that her construct system is in trouble when she starts having experiences that she cannot understand ("I just can't understand why you are leaving") or cannot anticipate ("That caught me by surprise").

Kelly's ideas about how people construct their experiences based on construct systems that they "carry" through life were part of a cognitive revolution within personality psychology. Several self-report methods exist for the assessment of a person's personal construct system (e.g., Caputi, 2012; Hardison & Neimeyer, 2012). Another example of this cognitive emphasis can be seen in learning theory at about the same time that Kelly was formulating his theory. We turn now to this other important development in the cognitive approach to personality.

Locus of Control

Locus of control is a concept that describes a person's interpretation of responsibility for the events in his or her life. More specifically, *locus of control* refers to whether people tend to locate that responsibility internally, within themselves, or externally, in fate, luck, or chance. For example, when you see a person who gets good grades, do you think it is because she is just plain lucky or because of her personal efforts? When you see someone in good health, do you think it is because of fate or genes, or is it because she puts effort into living a healthy life? Your answers to such questions may reveal your standing on the personality dimension of locus of control—the tendency to believe that events are or are not under one's personal control and responsibility.

Locus of control research started in the mid-1950s, when psychologist Julian Rotter was developing his social learning theory. Rotter was working within traditional learning theory, which emphasizes that people learn because of reinforcement. Rotter expanded these notions to suggest that learning also depended on the degree to which the person *expected* reinforcement—that obtaining a reward was under his or her control. Some people expect that certain behaviors will result in obtaining a reinforcer. In other words, they believe that they are in control of the positive outcomes of life. Other people fail to see the link between their behavior and reinforcement. This is Rotter's "expectancy model" of learning behavior. Interestingly, the expectation part involves characteristics that the individual brings to each situation. That is, *the expectancy of reinforcement* refers to characteristics that distinguish specific individuals. For example, suppose a person expects that acting in an assertive and demanding manner will get her what she wants. She wants a raise at work, so she expects that if she is assertive and demanding toward her boss, she will get her raise. Another person may have the opposite expectation, that acting in such a manner will be counterproductive, so he believes that being assertive will not produce the desired raise. These two individuals have different *expectations* for the outcome associated with the same assertive behavior pattern. She thinks she can do something to obtain a raise; he thinks he must just wait for the boss to make the decision. Differences in the subsequent behavior of these two people—for example, she is assertive and he is submissive at work—may be due to differences in their expectations of whether a certain behavior (assertiveness) will bring reinforcement (the desired raise).

Rotter published a questionnaire measure of internal versus external locus of control in 1966. Some items from that questionnaire are presented in Table 12.2.

Rotter emphasized that a person's expectations for reinforcement held across a variety of situations, what he called **generalized expectancies** (Rotter, 1971, 1990). When people encounter a new situation, they base their expectancies about what will happen on their generalized expectancies about whether they have the ability to influence events. For example, if a young man generally believes that he can do little to influence events, then in a new situation, such as entering college, he would have a generalized expectancy that things are outside of his control. He may, for example, assume that his grades will be due to luck or chance or fate, not to anything that he can actually control.

Such a generalized expectancy that events are outside of one's control is called an **external locus of control**. An **internal locus of control,** on the other hand, is the generalized expectancy that reinforcing events are under one's control and that one is responsible for the major outcomes in life. The Locus of Control (LOC) construct is really a trait dimension, ranging from people who are more internal at one end to people who are more external at the other end. Every person falls at some point along this LOC dimension. People toward the internal LOC end believe that outcomes depend mainly on their own personal efforts, whereas people more toward the external LOC end believe that outcomes largely depend on forces outside of their personal control. An internal locus of control is, in general, conducive to well-being (Heidemeier & Göritz, 2013).

Internal LOC has been found to be predictive of a variety of real-world outcomes. For example, people who displayed an internal LOC at age 10 were found to have a reduced risk of obesity at age 30 compared to people with an external LOC (Gale, Batty, & Deary, 2008). In another study of college students, those with an internal LOC completed their degrees in a more timely manner than students with an external

Table 12.2 Sample Items from the Locus of Control Scale

Yes	No	
_____	_____	1. Are some people just born lucky?
_____	_____	2. Most of the time do you feel that getting good grades means a great deal to you?
_____	_____	3. Do you believe that if somebody studies hard enough he or she can pass any subject?
_____	_____	4. Do you feel that most of the time it doesn't pay to try hard because things never turn out right anyway?
_____	_____	5. Do you feel that if things start out well in the morning, it's going to be a good day no matter what you do?
_____	_____	6. Do you believe that wishing can make good things happen?

Source: Adapted from Rotter, 1982.

LOC (Hall, Smith, & Chia, 2008). Another interesting study showed that adults with a more internal LOC had higher credit ratings than those with a more external LOC (Perry, 2008). In many ways, internal LOC is associated with a tendency toward feeling more in charge of one's life, ranging from better control over one's weight to better control over one's spending habits and hence credit rating.

Exercise

Can you think of situations in which having an internal LOC is a disadvantage? Under what circumstances would a person with an internal orientation experience relatively more stress than someone with an external orientation? What characteristics or situations would match the expectations of the person with an external LOC? When might it be healthy to have an external LOC?

Some situations are truly beyond our control and cannot be influenced by us, no matter what we do. For example, a loved one may be dying from an incurable disease. This is not anyone's fault, and there is nothing anyone can do to prevent the outcome. However, even in such situations some people, particularly close relatives, can feel that they are somehow to blame. In such situations, an internal locus of control might be a handicap to personal coping with the outcome.

Another example is the "survivor syndrome" often reported by persons who have lived through a tragedy in which many others were severely injured or killed, such as in a terrorist bombing or a mass shooting. Often, survivors report feeling that "if only" they had done something differently, they could have helped others make it to safety. They often report some feelings of personal responsibility for the outcome, even though the event was horrifically outside of their control.

In an interesting case study, a 29-year-old man who sailed around the world solo in 260 days (Kjærgaard, Leone, & Venables, 2015) was found, as you might have guessed, to have a very internal score on an LOC measure, quite literally the captain of his fate. Another activity where people's control over outcomes is sometimes at risk is stage acting, and a study of professional actors found that those with a more external LOC suffered more from stage fright than actors with a more internal LOC (Goodman & Kaufman, 2014).

It is important to remember that historically the LOC concept grew out of learning theory and referred to feeling in control of positive reinforcements. Conceptually, LOC was primarily about expectancies for control over positive outcomes. For example, does a person view positive outcomes, such as good grades, a career promotion, or financial success, as primarily due to fate and luck (an external LOC) or primarily due to one's own efforts and abilities (an internal LOC). While LOC historically referred to control of good outcomes, it has been broadened to refer to feelings of control in general; does one take credit for creating for his or her own life outcomes and hence feels in control of life, or does the person believe that most things in life happens by chance or fate. This focus on positive outcomes and general feelings of control makes LOC different from the topic we take up in the next section—learned helplessness and attributional style—which is primarily about where a person places the blame for bad events and negative outcomes in life.

When it comes to locus of control, the general finding is that an internal style is the more adaptive one, to see oneself as being in control of one's fate. Recently, researchers have examined LOC in relation to the COVID-19 pandemic. Studies show that internal LOC college students cope better, and experience less academic stress, during COVID-19 lockdowns (Ganjoo et al., 2021). Krampe and colleagues (2021) found that internal LOC persons were less likely to report mental distress during the COVID-19 pandemic. In a large (N=341) study of college students, Origlio and Odar Stough (2022) looked at changes in depressive symptoms from pre-pandemic levels. They found that, while depressive symptoms (e.g., feelings of helplessness, lose of interest, sadness) increased overall during the COVID-19 pandemic, the increase was smallest for students with an internal LOC. Another study showed that subjects with an internal LOC were more likely to adhere to COVID-19 mitigation guidelines (e.g., social distancing, mask wearing, hand washing) than those with an external LOC (Deveraux, Miller, & Kirshenbaum, 2021).

Will persons who have an internal locus of control have difficulty getting into the back seat of an autonomous vehicle and turning over complete driving control to a computer? For a thoughtful discussion, pro and con, of autonomous driving vehicles, see Michael Crawford's book Why We Drive.
metamorworks/Getty Images

What about situations that require giving up control? For example, the willingness to use autonomous cars requires that a person give up control of the driving to a machine, to turn over one's fate to a computer. People with a highly internal LOC may be reluctant to try an autonomous car. Researchers have shown that persons with an internal locus of control were more unwilling to try autonomous vehicles than persons with an external locus of control (Choi & Ji, 2015). Like with other personality traits, we can never say that one extreme of the dimension is entirely good or entirely bad; one can always find strengths and weakness associated with either high or low levels of any particular trait. As computers and machines do more and more for us, it may be adaptive to relinquish control for some aspects of our lives, and people with a more external locus of control may be more willing and able to do so.

Learned Helplessness

We now turn to another individual difference in how people interpret the world—**learned helplessness.** Research on this topic also had its start in learning theory, similar to Rotter's start. Work on learned helplessness began when psychologists were studying unconditional punishment and avoidance learning in dogs. The researchers subjected the dogs to foot shocks, by running electricity through the wire floor of their cages. The shocks were intermittent, but the dogs could not escape. During the first few shocks, the dogs would pull at their harnesses, jump and twist, and try to escape from the unpleasant shocks. Eventually, however, the dogs would give up, they seemed to accept the shocks and no longer tried to escape. The dogs, apparently knowing that they could not escape, would passively accept the shocks.

The dogs were then put into a different cage, a cage where they *could* escape the foot shocks by simply jumping over a small barrier into a different part of the cage. However, the dogs that had received inescapable shocks earlier did not even try to escape in this new situation. It was as if they had learned that their situation was hopeless, and they gave up seeking to avoid their painful circumstance. Other dogs that had not been shocked earlier quickly learned to avoid the shocks in the new cage by jumping over the barrier. The researchers were surprised that the learned helplessness dogs did not even try to escape, so they turned off the shock after one minute.

Next, the researchers tried lifting the dogs over the barrier to the safe part of the cage. After being shown how to reach safety, the dogs quickly learned to jump over and avoid the shocks. However, without such coaching, the learned helplessness dogs simply accepted their painful fates without attempting to remove themselves from the unpleasant situation.

Numerous studies document the learned helplessness phenomenon with humans (Seligman, 1992, 1994). Using unpleasant noise rather than shock, researchers set up the following learned helplessness situation. Participants are told that they will be given problems to solve and that they can avoid or turn off the blasts of unpleasant noise by solving the problems (e.g., by pressing buttons in a correct order) (Garber & Seligman, 1980; Hiroto & Seligman, 1975). Some participants (the learned helplessness subjects) are given problems without solutions. Consequently, for these participants, the unpleasant blasts of noise are inescapable—nothing they can do will stop the irritating and aversive blasts of noise. But do these participants generalize their helplessness to new situations?

Participants are then taken to a new situation and given a new set of problems to solve. This time there is no unpleasant noise. The researchers tell the participants that they are simply interested in how the participants will work on these new problems. Participants who were exposed to the learned helplessness condition in the earlier trials usually perform much worse on the subsequent problems. It is as if they are saying, "What's the use in trying to solve these problems? They are too difficult." Such participants appear to generalize their experiences of helplessness from one problem-solving situation to another.

In real life, learned helplessness can result whenever people are stuck in an unpleasant situation that is apparently outside of their control. For example, imagine a woman who tries everything she knows to get her husband to stop abusing her. She tries being nice to him, and it works for a while, but soon he is abusive again. She threatens to leave, and this works for a while, but he starts abusing her again. No matter what she does, nothing seems to solve the problem. A woman in such circumstances may develop learned helplessness. She may give up even trying to solve the problem: "What's the use," she may say, "nothing I do seems to help, so maybe I just have to take it."

However, people in learned helplessness don't have to "take it." They need an outside perspective, like coaching the learned helpless dogs to jump over the barrier to escape. They need someone who can see the situation objectively and who can recommend strategies for solving the problem. Whenever a problem situation looks as if it has no solution or is inescapable, that is the time to ask others for help, to seek an outside opinion (Seligman & Csikszentmihalyi, 2000).

The original model of learned helplessness began with experiments on dogs and was generalized to humans through experimental studies. Humans are more complex than dogs, at least when it comes to thinking about the unpleasant events in their lives and forming expectations. What factors determine whether feelings of helplessness in one situation will spill over to other situations? What cognitive factors influence people to decide that they do or do not have the ability to take control of an unpleasant situation? In seeking answers to these questions, psychologists began to study what was going on in the minds of people who underwent learned helplessness conditioning

(Peterson, Maier, & Seligman, 1993). In the "Closer Look" section that follows, we present the main way that the learned helplessness concept was reformulated to account for distinctively human cognitions. This important development is called *attributional style*, and it has proven to be a useful way to understand human depression (a topic we take up in Chapter 13) and how people respond to stressful events (a topic in Chapter 18). While Attributional Style may at first seem very similar to LOC (as both are about causal interpretations), they are different in that the former (attributional style) is about attributions for negative life events and the latter (LOC) is mostly about causal attributions for positive or rewarding events.

Personality Revealed Through Goals

So far in this chapter, we have considered aspects of personality related to how a person perceives and interprets the world. We turn now to a third aspect of cognition, a person's goals and how these are related to personality. Such goals may range from minor ones, such as buying groceries for the week, to the more lofty, such as reducing world hunger. The focus in this approach is on intention, on *what persons want to happen,* on what they want to achieve in their lives. People differ in their goals, and these differences are part of their personalities.

Different psychologists have offered different terms, such as personal strivings (Emmons, 1989), current concerns (Klinger, 1977a, 1977b), personal projects (Little, 1999), and life tasks (Cantor, 1990). All of these constructs emphasize what people believe is worth pursuing in life, as well as the kinds of goal-directed behaviors they enact to achieve these desires. Other personality theories in this section emphasize self-guides, or the standards that people strive to meet (Higgins, 1996); their understanding of their own abilities and motivations (Dweck, Chiu, & Hong, 1995); or their internal abilities related to goals, including people's expectations, beliefs, plans, and strategies (Mischel, 2004).

Personal Projects Analysis

A **personal project** is a set of relevant actions intended to achieve a goal that a person has selected. Psychologist Brian Little (e.g., Little, 2007, 2011) believes that personal projects make natural units for understanding the workings of personality because they reflect how people face up to the serious business of navigating through daily life. Most people, if asked, are able to make a list of the important projects that they work on in their daily lives, such goals as to lose weight, do homework, make new friends, start and maintain an exercise program, search the web for graduate schools to apply to, develop a better relationship with God, or find some principles to live by. People typically have many goals that come and go in their day-to-day lives—one project is more important today, and a different one is important tomorrow—as well as other projects that are more ongoing.

Little developed the Personal Projects Analysis method for assessing personal projects. Participants first generate a list of their personal projects, as many or as few as they deem relevant. Most college student participants list an average of 15 personal projects that are currently important in their daily lives. Next, participants rate each project on several scales, such as how important the project is to them, how difficult it is, how much they enjoy working on it, how much progress they have made on it, and the negative and positive impacts it has had in their lives (Little & Gee, 2007).

A Closer Look

Reformulated Learned Helplessness: Attributional Style

The reformulation of learned helplessness theory focuses on the cognitions, or thoughts, a person has that may lead to feelings of helplessness. More specifically, the focus is on the *explanations* that people give for events in their lives, particularly the *unpleasant events* (Peterson, Maier, & Seligman, 1993). Imagine that you had submitted a paper in your class and that you received a surprisingly low grade on that paper. A common question you might ask yourself is "What *caused* the low grade on my paper?" Your explanation for the cause of the low grade might reveal something about your explanatory style. When things go wrong, who or what typically gets the blame? Psychologists prefer the term **causal attribution** to refer to a person's explanation of the cause of an event. To what cause would you attribute your paper's low grade? Was it because you happened to be in a rush and submitted a quickly written paper? Was it because you are simply a poor writer? Was it because the professor who graded it was unduly harsh in her grading? Or was it because your dog ate your original paper, so you quickly wrote another, which was not nearly as good as the one your dog ate? All of these explanations are causal attributions for the event.

Psychologists use the term **attributional style** to refer to tendencies some people have to frequently use certain explanations for unpleasant events. Explanations for the causes of events can be broken down along three broad dimensions. First, explanations for events can be either *internal* or *external*. The poor paper grade could be due to something pertaining to *you* (internal, such as your lack of skill) or something pertaining to the *environment* (external, such as the professors being unduly harsh). Some people blame

themselves for all sorts of events and are constantly apologizing for events that are outside their control. The more internal your explanation, the more likely you are to blame yourself for unpleasant events, even those events over which you have little or no control.

A second dimension concerns whether the cause of the event is *stable* or *unstable*. For example, if you were temporarily set back by your dog eating the original version of your paper, then that would be an unstable cause (a one-off event that is unlikely to repeat). However, an explanation that concerns your lack of writing skill is a more or less *permanent,* or stable, characteristic. When bad events happen, some people tend to think that the causes of such situations are long-lasting, that the causes are stable or permanent.

The third important dimension of causal attributions for negative events concerns whether the cause is *global* or *specific*. A specific cause is one that affects only the particular situation (e.g., writing papers), whereas a global cause affects many situations in life (all areas involving intellectual skills). For example, you might have explained the cause of your poor paper grade like this: "I am just unable to write; I can hardly put a noun and a verb together to form a sentence." This is a global explanation and might imply that you would be expected to do poorly in whatever task required writing, not just in writing this specific paper.

Whenever someone offers an explanation for an event, that explanation can be analyzed in terms of the three dimensions: internal–external, stable–unstable, and global–specific. Most people use different combinations of explanations—sometimes blaming themselves, sometimes blaming external causes, sometimes blaming

specific causes, and so forth. However, some people develop a consistent explanatory style. For example, suppose someone consistently blames herself whenever *anything* goes wrong. After arriving at her destination on a plane that was late, the woman apologizes to her friend who picked her up at the airport, saying, "I'm sorry I'm late," when, in fact, *she* was not at all responsible for being late. She might say to her friend instead, "I'm sorry that *the plane I was on was late* and that you had to be inconvenienced. Next time I'll use a different airline." This might be a more appropriate external explanation for the real cause of being late.

The attributional style that most puts a person at risk for feelings of helplessness and poor adjustment is one that emphasizes internal, stable, and global causes for bad events. This has been called the **pessimistic explanatory style.** This style is in contrast to the **optimistic explanatory style,** which emphasizes external, temporary, and specific causes of events. For example, one scenario on the Attributional Style Questionnaire (Peterson, 1991) asks you to imagine being on a date that goes badly, in which both you and your date have a lousy time. You are then asked why this might happen to you. If your explanation involves an external attribution to an unstable and highly specific cause (e.g., "I happened to choose a movie that neither one of us liked, then we went to a restaurant where the service was poor, and afterward my car got stuck in the mud"), then you are scored as more optimistic than someone who offers an internal, stable, and global interpretation (e.g., "I just have trouble relating to people, I cannot keep a conversation going, and I am completely shy when it comes to the opposite sex") (see Figure 12.3).

Is attributional style a stable characteristic? One study examined attributional style over the life span (Burns & Seligman, 1989). A group of participants, whose average age was 72 years, completed a questionnaire on attributional style and provided diaries or letters written in their youth, an average of 52 years earlier. The diaries and letters were content analyzed for attributional style. The correlation between these two measures of attributional style for negative life events that were generated five decades apart was .54, indicating a significant amount of rank order stability in attributional style.

Because an optimistic explanatory style correlates with beneficial effects in many areas of life, including earning better grades in college (Bastounis et al., 2016; Maleva et al., 2014), programs have been developed to train people to have a more optimistic explanatory style. For example, one program for college students (Gerson & Fernandez, 2013) is a three-session program that teaches students to adopt an optimistic explanatory style and has been shown to increase student reports of optimism, resilience, and thriving in college. Another study of college students found that students with an optimistic explanatory style were more likely to use academic resources, such as peer mentoring and attending review sessions (Quinn-Nilas, Kennett, and Maki, 2019). Studies of elementary school children found that an optimistic explanatory style was related to more positive peer relationships and higher levels of psychological well-being (Li, Chu, & Yu, 2017). A study of working adults found that a optimistic explanatory style was related to less burnout in the workplace (Paquet et al., 2021). A large amount of research on explanatory style focuses on how people adapt to traumatic events, with the general finding that an optimistic style is associated with better response. For example, researchers examined survivors of the 2004 tsunami that devastated two-thirds of the coast of Sri Lanka (Levy, Slade, & Ranasinghe, 2009) and found that a pessimistic explanatory style was associated with more symptoms of post-traumatic stress disorder.

An interesting extension of the concept of attributional style is to extend it from individuals to groups. For example, recent studies have examined the attributional style of sports teams (Carron, Shapcott, & Martin, 2014) and the explanatory style of business organizations (Smith, Caputi, & Crittenden, 2013). Results generally mirror those found with individuals, that team optimism was associated with better outcomes (higher percentage of winning, business success).

In Chapter 13, we discuss the role of explanatory style in depression, and in Chapter 18 we return to the topic of explanatory style, again in some detail, with reference to stress and health.

	Internal/external	Stable/unstable	Global/specific
Optimistic style	External: "My girlfriend broke up with me because her parents forced her."	Unstable: "My girlfriend broke up with me because she needs all her time right now to devote to the charity drive, which only lasts one month."	Specific: "My girlfriend broke up with me because she found out I dated Julie last weekend."
Pessimistic style	Internal: "My girlfriend broke up with me because I'm from a low-class family, I'm not going to college, and I have very little ambition in life."	Stable: "My girlfriend broke up with me because I'm shorter than her, and she wants someone who is taller."	Global: "My girlfriend broke up with me because I'm an inconsiderate, two-timing, unfaithful jerk who couldn't keep a relationship going if his life depended on it."

Figure 12.3

The three dimensions underlying attributional style, with their pessimistic and optimistic versions.

Personal Projects Analysis has a number of interesting implications for understanding personality. Researchers have investigated the relation between the Big Five personality traits (discussed in Chapter 3) and aspects of personal projects. For example, people who score high on the trait of neuroticism are also likely to rate their personal projects as stressful, difficult, likely to end in failure, and outside of their control (Little, 1999). Such people are also likely to state that they have made little progress toward achieving their goals. Apparently, part and parcel of being high on the neuroticism dimension is experiencing difficulty and dissatisfaction in accomplishing one's personal projects (Little, Lecci, & Watkinson, 1992).

Researchers have also been interested in which specific aspects of personal projects are most closely related to overall reports of life satisfaction and happiness. Little (1999, 2007) summarizes research suggesting that overall happiness is most related to feeling in control of one's personal projects, feeling unstressed about those projects, and being optimistic that projects will be successful. These aspects of personal projects have also been found to predict well-being in an elderly sample (Lawton et al., 2002). These aspects of Personal Project Analysis (low stress, high control, high optimism) do indeed predict overall levels of happiness and life satisfaction (Palys & Little, 1983). Such findings have led Little to conclude that "bringing our personal projects to successful completion . . . seems to be a pivotal factor in whether we thrive emotionally or lead lives of . . . quiet desperation" (Little, 1999, p. 25). Findings on personal project analyses are presented in an edited volume by Little, Salmela-Aro, and Phillips (2007). A summary of 4 decades of research on personal projects is found in Little and Balsari-Palsule (2021). Professor Brian Little (2020) argues that personal projects are the vehicles through which we give our lives meaning, and he calls this "well-doing" rather than well-being.

Cognitive Social Learning Theory

A number of modern personality theories have expanded on the notion that personality is expressed in goals and in how people think about themselves relative to their goals. Collectively, these theories form what has been called the **cognitive social learning approach** to personality, an approach that emphasizes the cognitive and social processes whereby people learn to value and strive for certain goals over others.

Albert Bandura and the Notion of Self-Efficacy   Albert Bandura (1925–2021) was trained in classical behavioral psychology, popular in the 1940s, which viewed humans, and all organisms, as passive responders to the external environment, completely determined by external reinforcements. Bandura helped change this view by emphasizing the active nature of human behavior. He argued that people have intentions and forethought; they are reflective and can anticipate future events; they monitor their behavior and evaluate their own progress; plus they learn by observing others. Because he expanded on classical learning theory by adding cognitive and social variables, he helped start the cognitive social learning theory approach to personality. Bandura referred to these distinctly human cognitive and social activities under the rubric of the self-system. The self-system exists for the self-regulation of behavior in the pursuit of goals (Bandura, 1997).

In Bandura's theory, one of the most important concepts is that of **self-efficacy,** which refers to the belief that one can execute a specific course of action to achieve a goal. For example, a child learning to bat a baseball may believe she can hit most balls pitched to her. We would say she has high self-efficacy beliefs for batting. A child who doubts his hitting ability, on the other hand, has low self-efficacy beliefs in this area. As it turns out, high self-efficacy beliefs often lead to effort and persistence on tasks, and to setting higher goals, compared to people with low self-efficacy beliefs (Bandura, 1989). As another example, college students who have higher self-efficacy beliefs about their studies are more persistent in their academic work and perform better in their classes than students with lower self-efficacy (Multon, Brown, & Lent, 1991).

Self-efficacy and performance mutually influence one another. Self-efficacy leads to better performance; then better performance leads to further increases in self-efficacy. As such, high self-efficacy is most important when starting out on some particular task. If the task is complex, it can be broken down into parts or subgoals, which can be accomplished. Accomplishing each subgoal along the way can increase overall self-efficacy. Self-efficacy can also be influenced by **modeling,** by seeing others engage in the performance with positive results.

Carol Dweck and the Theory of Mastery Orientation   We introduced the work of psychologist Carol Dweck (1946–) in Chapter 11. Her early research focused on helpless and mastery-oriented behaviors in schoolchildren (Deiner & Dweck, 1978, 1980). She noted that some students persist in the face of failure, whereas others quit as soon as they encounter difficulties or their first failure. She started investigating the cognitive beliefs, particularly beliefs about ability, that lie behind these behavior patterns. For example, she discovered that students' implicit beliefs about the nature of intelligence had a significant impact on the way they approach challenging intellectual tasks: Students who view their intelligence as an unchangeable and fixed internal characteristic (what Dweck calls an "entity theory" of intelligence) tend to shy away from academic challenges, whereas students who believe that their intelligence can be increased through effort and persistence (what Dweck calls an "incremental theory" of intelligence) seek them out (Dweck, 1999a, 2002; Dweck, Chiu, & Hong, 1995).

It may sound like such a small thing, simply believing that intelligence is a fixed trait that cannot change, yet this belief is associated with putting less effort into school, with giving up earlier on academic challenges, and with lower academic success. Dweck's research illustrates the power of this belief in many studies of school children and college students (see review in Dweck, 2009, 2012). Having the opposite mindset—that intelligence is malleable and is something that can be changed with effort—is associated with better academic motivation and higher grades (Romero et al., 2014). Moreover, Dweck and colleagues have designed and tested several school-based interventions to change student's beliefs about their own intelligence, with students who have been trained to view intelligence as malleable subsequently putting more effort into academic performance and doing better in terms of grades (reviewed in Rattan et al., 2015).

Dweck's theory also has implications for how the praise of teachers and parents may unwittingly lead children to accept an entity view of intelligence. Praising a child for his or her intelligence may reinforce the notion that success and failure depend on something beyond the child's control. Comments such as "I'm so happy you got an A+ on your biology test, Mary! You are such a smart girl!" are interpreted by the child as "If good grades means that I'm intelligent, then poor grades must mean I am dumb." Or when trying to comfort a student, a teacher might say, "It's okay—not everyone can be good at math." This can reinforce an entity theory of math ability in the child, leading her to have lower motivation

Research by Carol Dweck and colleagues clearly shows that praising a child for her effort is more effective than praising her for her intelligence. See text for the explanation of this.

Andy Dean Photography/Shutterstock

and lower expectations for her own math performance (Rattan, Good, & Dweck, 2012). When children with an entity view of intelligence do perform well, they have high self-esteem, but self-esteem diminishes as soon as they hit an academic plateau or challenges that make them falter. Children who are admired for their effort are much more likely to view intelligence as changeable, and their self-esteem remains stable regardless of how hard they have to work to succeed. According to Dweck, it is much better to praise children for their effort ("Congratulations, your effort really paid off!") than for their ability ("Congratulations, you are really smart!"). Children who are praised for their effort learn to associate success with effort, not ability.

E. Tory Higgins and the Theory of Regulatory Focus   Psychologist E. Tory Higgins (1946–) has also developed a motivational theory concerning goals, called regulatory focus theory (Higgins, 2012). His theory adds the notion that people regulate their goal-directed behaviors in two distinct ways that serve two different needs. One focus of regulation is called **promotion focus**, in which the person is concerned with advancement, growth, and accomplishments. Behaviors with a promotion focus are characterized by eagerness, approach, and "going for the gold." The other focus of regulation is called **prevention focus,** in which the person is concerned with protection, safety, and the prevention of failure. Working hard to maximize gains (promotion focus) is a very different motivation than working hard to minimize loses (prevention focus). Behaviors with a prevention focus are characterized by vigilance, caution, and attempts to prevent negative outcomes.

When examined from a trait perspective, promotion focus correlates with such traits as extraversion and behavioral activation (which we discussed in Chapter 7). Prevention focus correlates with such traits as neuroticism and harm avoidance and (negatively) with impulsivity (Grant & Higgins, 2003). However, the concepts of prevention and promotion focus are more concerned with motivation and goal behaviors than the standard personality traits with which they correlate.

Walter Mischel and the Cognitive-Affective Personality System (CAPS)   As discussed in Chapter 4, psychologist Walter Mischel (1930–2018) had a huge impact on personality psychology when he wrote a book in 1968, titled *Personality and Assessment,* that was highly critical of the evidence for personality traits. Recall that he argued that people's behavior was more strongly influenced by the situations they were in than by the personality traits they brought to those situations. In more recent years, Mischel and his former student—Youchi Shoda—proposed a theory that personality variables (though not necessarily traits) do have an influence on behavior, mainly by interacting with and modifying the psychological meaning of situations.

In Mischel and Shoda's cognitive-affective personality system (CAPS), they reconceptualize personality not as a collection of traits, but as an organization of cognitive and affective activities that influence how people respond to certain kinds of situations (Mischel, 2000, 2004; Shoda et al., 2013, 2015; Smith & Shoda, 2009). The emphasis is more on personality processes than on static traits. These cognitive and affective processes consist of such mental activities as construals (how one views a situation), goals, expectations, beliefs, and feelings as well as self-regulatory standards, abilities, plans, and strategies. According to this theory, each individual is characterized by a relatively stable network of such mental activities. Individuals acquire their specific set of these mental abilities through their learning history, their particular culture and subculture, their genetic endowment, and their biological history.

The CAPS theory argues that people differ from each other in the distinct organization of their cognitive and affective processes. As people move through the different situations in their lives, different cognitive and affective processes will be activated and mediate the impact of specific situations. For example, if a situation engenders frustration (e.g., being blocked from a goal), and the person has a specific cognitive-affective system (e.g., high expectations for success, the belief that aggression is permissible to obtain what you want), then he or she may respond with hostility. So, it is not the case that aggressive people would be aggressive in all situations (the trait view) but that aggressive people are sensitive to certain kinds of situations (e.g., frustration), and only then will they behave aggressively.

Mischel and Shoda present a contextualized view of personality as expressed in **"if . . . then . . ." propositions:** If situation A, then the person does X; but if situation B, then the person does Y. Personality leaves its signature, Mischel argues, in terms of the specific situational ingredients that prompt behavior from the person. To illustrate his approach, Mischel (2004) presents data gathered at a summer camp for delinquent children. All of the children had impulse control problems and had been aggressive in the past. The children were observed over many days and in many different situations in the summer camp. The researchers were interested in verbal aggression. They broke down the situations into five categories: when the child was "teased by a peer," "warned by an adult," "punished by an adult," "praised by an adult," and "approached by a peer." The children showed distinct profiles of verbal aggression across these different situations. For example, some children were aggressive only after being warned by an adult. Other children were aggressive only when approached by a peer. Mischel points out that verbal aggression was not consistent across all five situations and that specific "if . . . then . . ." profiles could be discerned for each child. These profiles were consistent, however, in the sense that kids who were aggressive when warned by an adult behaved that way repeatedly (Mischel, Shoda, & Mendoza-Denton, 2002).

The CAPS theory offers an important new way to think about personality, a way that emphasizes cognitive and affective processes that influence a person's behaviors relative to specific situational characteristics in terms of "if. . ., then . . ." propositions (for another example, see Smith et al., 2009). We present this theory in the chapter on cognitive approaches because it emphasizes the internal processes that people engage in to regulate their behavior. It is interesting that Mischel first argued that situations exert the most control over people's behavior, but later came to believe that it is the psychological situation—that is, the meaning of the situation from the individual's perspective—that organizes behavior (Mischel, 2004, 2010).

Intelligence

No discussion of individual differences in cognition and information processing would be complete without at least some mention of intelligence. Intelligence has been defined in many ways, and there may be many different kinds of intelligence. One definition of intelligence is associated with educational attainment, how much knowledge a person has acquired relative to others in his or her age cohort. This is an **achievement view of intelligence.** Other definitions view intelligence less as the product of education and more as an ability to become educated, as the ability or aptitude to learn. This is the **aptitude view of intelligence.** Traditional measures of intelligence—so-called IQ tests—often have been used and interpreted as aptitude measures. For much of the past century, IQ tests were used to predict school performance and to select persons for educational opportunities. They are still used in this aptitude fashion today. For example, one study on college undergraduates found that general intelligence predicted 16 percent of the variability in grades, which translates into a correlation of about .40 between IQ and grades. Interestingly, need for achievement, which we discussed in Chapter 11, accounted for 11 percent of the variability in grades, beyond the variability accounted for by IQ (Lounsbury et al., 2003).

Early in the study of intelligence, most psychologists thought of this characteristic in trait-like terms, as a property of the individual. And individuals were thought to differ from each other in amount, in how much intelligence they possessed. Moreover, intelligence was thought of as a single broad factor—often called *g* for **general intelligence.** As tests were developed, however, researchers began to identify separate abilities—such as verbal ability, memory ability, perceptual ability, and arithmetic ability. The Scholastic Aptitude Test (SAT) and the American College Test (ACT) are examples that most college students are familiar with because they have taken one or both of these tests. The SAT and ACT each give multiple scores for example, English, Math, Reading, Science, Writing, Reasoning— and thus are both examples of the separate abilities notion. Also, as their names imply, many believe the SAT and ACT are aptitude measures, that they measure the ability to learn and acquire new information. This is why they have been used to select applicants for admission to higher educational institutions. However, the makers of the SAT and ACT hold that the tests are really measures of achievement, how much the test takers have learned in their lives so far. Certainly the SAT and ACT contain questions that only persons with an already thorough high school education can answer, and so, many argue, they are achievement tests. In use, however, the SAT and ACT both predict future college grade point average, so they are used as ability tests. In general, ACT and SAT scores correlate with college GPA in the range of .30 correlations, and thus have some validity as aptitude measures. Moreover, studies that have used general intelligence measures and correlated them with ACT or SAT scores typically find those correlations in the range of .48 to .82 (depending on what IQ measure was used), suggesting that ACT and SAT test performance relates fairly strongly to general intelligence (e.g., Frey & Detterman, 2003). In response to the COVID-19 pandemic, many colleges have made the ACT/SAT optional in applying for admission, though it is unknown if that change will be permanent.

Like the SAT and ACT, most intelligence tests yield multiple scores. For example, the Wechsler Intelligence Scale for Children—Revised (revised in 1991, originally published by Wechsler, 1949) yields 11 subtest scores, six of which require or depend on verbal ability and five of which are nonverbal, such as finding missing elements in a picture and assembling a puzzle. Also, the test yields two broad scores to represent verbal and performance intelligence. Psychologists use the multiple scores to evaluate a person's strengths and weaknesses, as well as to understand how the individual uniquely approaches and solves problems.

A widely accepted definition of intelligence, proposed by Gardner (1983), is that it is the application of cognitive skill and knowledge to solve problems, learn, and achieve goals that are valued by the individual and the culture. With intelligence defined this broadly, it is obvious that there are many kinds of intelligence, perhaps several more beyond the traditional verbal, mathematical, and performance distinctions. Howard Gardner has proposed a theory of **multiple intelligences,** which includes seven forms, such as interpersonal intelligence (social skills, ability to communicate, and get along with others) and intrapersonal intelligence (insight into oneself, one's emotions, and one's motives). Gardner also includes kinesthetic intelligence—describing the abilities of athletes, dancers, and acrobats—and musical intelligence (Gardner, 1999). Other experts are adding to the growing list of forms of intelligence, such as the concept of emotional intelligence, proposed by psychologists Peter Salovey and Jack Mayer (1990) and popularized by journalist Dan Goleman (1995). The concept of emotional intelligence is also receiving a great deal of attention from researchers (see Zeidner et al., 2003, for a general review of emotional intelligence; and Miao, Humphrey, & Qian, 2017, and O'Boyle et al., 2011, for a review of emotional intelligence related to job performance and career satisfaction).

Exercise

The concept of emotional intelligence has been proposed to explain why some people with a lot of academic intelligence do not appear to have a lot of practical intelligence, people skills, or what might be called street smarts. Goleman (1995), in his highly readable book *Emotional Intelligence,* presents many cases of people who have high levels of traditional intelligence yet fail in various areas of their lives, such as in relationships. Goleman also reviews the psychological literature and comes to the conclusion that traditional measures of intelligence, although predicting school performance fairly well, actually do a rather poor job of predicting later life outcomes, such as occupational attainment, salary, professional status, and quality of marriage (e.g., Vaillant, 1977). *Emotional intelligence,* Goleman argues, is more strongly predictive of these life outcomes. Emotional intelligence is proposed as a set of five specific abilities:

- Awareness of one's own feelings and bodily signals and an ability to identify one's own emotions and to make distinctions (such as realizing the fear that lies behind anger).
- Ability to manage and regulate emotions, especially negative emotions, and to manage stress.
- Control of one's impulses—directing one's attention and effort, delaying gratification, and staying on task toward goals.
- Ability to decode the social and emotional cues of others, to listen, and to take the perspective of others (empathy).
- Leadership, the ability to influence and guide others without their becoming angry or resentful, the ability to elicit cooperation, and skill in negotiation and conflict resolution.

It is easy to see how these skills and abilities relate to positive life outcomes and how they are so different from traditional concepts of intelligence, such as scholastic achievement and scholastic ability. Can you think of someone you know who is very high on scholastic ability yet deficient in one or more of the aspects of emotional intelligence? Such a person might be successful in school yet have problems in other areas of life, such as making friends or becoming independent from his or her family. Alternatively, can you think of someone you know who is high on emotional intelligence yet low on scholastic ability?

Gardner's concept of multiple intelligences is controversial. Some intelligence researchers feel that these separate abilities are correlated enough with each other (implying that they tend to co-occur in the same persons) to justify thinking of intelligence as g, a general factor (e.g., Herrnstein & Murray, 1994; Petrill, 2002; Rammsayer & Brandler, 2002). Other experts acknowledge a few broad distinctions, such as the verbal and mathematical intelligences that are so much a part of school systems in the United States. Other experts, including many educators, are examining the implications of the multiple intelligences notion. Some universities are considering using "noncognitive" measures of personality characteristics, like persistence, initiative, and conscientiousness, in addition to the traditional SAT scores, to inform admissions decisions (Hoover, 2013). Some schools are making curriculum changes designed to develop and strengthen various forms of intelligence in their students. For example, some schools are teaching units in emotional intelligence. Other schools offer classes for those high on nonverbal intelligence. Other schools are fostering character education, which can be thought of as a form of civic intelligence. These modern educational efforts are the direct outcomes of research being conducted by personality psychologists exploring the basic nature of intelligence.

We cannot leave the concept of intelligence without looking at the **cultural context of intelligence.** What is defined as "intelligent behavior" will obviously differ across cultures. For example, among the people who live on the islands of Micronesia, the ability to navigate the ocean and other maritime skills are considered superior forms of intelligence. Among Inuit who hunt along the shores in their kayaks, the ability to develop a cognitive map of the complex shoreline in Alaska is a valued ability. Many psychologists define culture, in part, as the shared notions about what counts as efficient problem solving (Wertsch & Kanner, 1992). These skills then become part of the way successful people think in that culture. Western cultures, for example, emphasize verbal skills, both written and oral, as well as the mathematical and spatial skills necessary in a technologically advanced culture. Other cultures, however, might guide their members to develop different problem-solving skills, such as developing a sense of direction, knowledge of animal behavior, or emphasis on a team approach to problem solving.

Because of these cultural considerations, we should always view intelligence as comprised of the skills valued in a particular culture. However, Western culture—along with its economic, social, and political systems—is proliferating into countries around the world. This proliferation of Western culture is sometimes called "globalization," and some thinkers worry that globalization will erase cultural distinctiveness. Will the world become a monoculture? If so, will there become one form of intelligence, which is universally valued? Or will cultures maintain separate identities and define differences in what counts as intelligent behavior? For example, currently most people in Europe speak more than one language, and many speak three or more because of the problem-solving advantage a multilingual person has in Europe. Many Europeans consider Americans to be linguistically challenged or, less charitably, verbally unintelligent because most Americans know only one language.

Interestingly, average IQ scores around the world have risen steadily the past several decades, at the rate of approximately one IQ point every four of five years within populations (Flynn, 2007, 2012). This rise in population IQ scores is known as the *Flynn effect,* named after the person who first documented this observation (Flynn, 1984), though many other researchers have confirmed this observation (Shakeel & Peterson, 2022). Various explanations have been put forward for rising world population IQ scores, such as better nutrition around the world. Flynn's own explanation (2007, 2012) focuses on access to, and improvements in, quality of education around the world over those decades. However, despite steady increases in average IQ over the last half of the twentieth century, psychologists have since observed a steady decline in population IQ scores over the last 20 years, starting around 1998, in specific countries (Teasdale & Owen, 2008) as well as worldwide (Lynn & Harvey, 2008, Dutton, van der Linden, & Flynn, 2016), a phenomenon called the *reverse* or *negative Flynn effect.*

This decline in world population IQ over the past two decades worries intelligence researchers because the average IQ in a country is correlated with many indicators of national well-being, including gross domestic product, which measures the wealth of the nation (Gelade, 2008; Hunt & Wittmann, 2008); educational attainment; and technological advancements (Rindermann, 2008). Lower population IQ within countries has also been associated with the prevalence of juvenile delinquency, adult crime, single parenthood, and poverty (Gordon, 1997). Each decline of one IQ point is associated with a reduction of income of about $425 per year (Zagorsky, 2007). Lynn and Harvey (2008) attribute this decline in national IQ scores around the world to increasing fertility rates, generalizing from the often-replicated observation that IQ and fertility are negatively correlated (i.e., people with lower IQ scores tend to produce more offspring than people with higher IQ scores) (Shatz, 2008; Vining, 1982).

One behavioral variable in intelligence research is called **inspection time,** which refers to the time it takes a person to make a simple discrimination decision regarding two displayed objects. For example, two lines appear on a computer screen and the subject's task is to simply decide which one is longer. The time it takes the subject to inspect the two lines, measured in milliseconds (thousandths of a second), before making the decision is the measure of inspection time. This variable is highly related to standard measures of general intelligence (Osmon & Jackson, 2002). Inspection time correlates with other measures of perceptual speed and reaction time to make decisions (Jensen, 2011), and these mental speed abilities appear to contribute to higher IQ scores (Johnson & Deary, 2011). Inspection time is also a sensitive leading indicator of the normal cognitive decline that occurs with old age for most people (Gregory et al., 2008). Another similar measure is the ability to discriminate auditory intervals that differ only by a few milliseconds, which also is related to general intelligence (Rammsayer & Brandler, 2002). A review of 172 studies of the relationship between IQ and speed of information processing (Sheppard & Vernon, 2008) concluded that measures of intelligence are correlated with mental speed, with smarter people being generally faster on a wide variety of mental tasks. Findings such as these suggest that brain mechanisms specifically involved in information processing are more efficient in persons scoring high on general intelligence measures.

There are many interesting debates about intelligence that are beyond the scope of an introductory personality text. If you are interested, you can go to advanced sources, such as the journal *Intelligence,* or to books, such as Neisser's (1998) or Herrnstein and Murray's controversial *The Bell Curve* (1994) and the direct responses to the controversy created by *The Bell Curve*—such as Fraser (1995), Jacoby and Glauberman (1995), and Lynn (2008). Other alternatives to the Herrnstein and Murray position include works by Sternberg (1985), Gardner (1983), and Simonton (1991). You should know that there are several current debates about intelligence, including whether it can be measured accurately, whether measures of intelligence are biased to favor persons from the dominant majority group in the culture, the extent to which intelligence is heritable and the implications of heritability, whether different racial groups differ with respect to intelligence, and whether race differences should be interpreted as social class or economic differences. These issues are politicized and have many implications for social and government policy, and so generate heated debate. Personality psychologists are playing an important role by doing the research necessary to provide a scientific approach to these socially important issues.

SUMMARY AND EVALUATION

Cognitive topics in personality psychology are a broad class of subject matter. People differ from each other in many ways, in how they think as well as in how they perceive, interpret, remember, want, and anticipate the events in their lives. In this chapter, we organized the coverage into four broad categories: perception, interpretation, goals, and intelligence.

We began by examining some ways in which personality is related to perceptual differences among people. Field independence/dependence concerns the ability to see the trees despite the forest, to see the specifics or patterns within a complex field of stimuli. This individual difference in perceptual style has to do with the ability to focus on the details despite the clutter of background information. This style of perceiving may have important implications for learning styles, career choices, and perhaps how people will respond to the Metaverse when it arrives.

The second perceptual difference we discussed was sensory reducing/augmenting. This dimension originally referred to the tendency to reduce or augment painful stimuli and was first related to individual differences in pain tolerance. It is now more generally used to refer to individual differences in sensitivity to sensory stimulation, with some individuals (augmenters) being more sensitive than others (reducers). This individual difference may have important implications for the development of problem behaviors associated with seeking stimulation, such as smoking or other forms of drug abuse.

Another aspect of cognition is how people interpret events in their lives. This approach to personality has its roots in the work of George Kelly. His personal construct theory emphasizes how people construct their experiences by using their constructs to make sense out of the world. Another general difference among people is in locus of control, the tendency to interpret events either as under one's control or as not under one's control. The locus of control construct began as control over rewards and positive outcomes but is now expanded to control over one's life in general. This makes it different from learned helplessness and attributional style, which refers specifically to negative events and unpleasant outcomes.

Learned helplessness is the feeling engendered when a person experiences an inescapable aversive or punishing situation. The feeling of helplessness may also generalize to new situations so that the person continues to act helplessly and fails to seek solutions to his or her new problems. The theory of learned helplessness was reformulated to incorporate how people think about the causes of negative events in their lives, an individual difference construct called attributional style. Psychologists have focused on specific dimensions of people's attributions for negative events, such as whether the cause of the negative event is internal or external to the person, whether it is stable or unstable, and whether it is global or specific. A pessimistic explanatory style is internal, stable, and global, and an optimistic explanatory style is just the opposite: external, temporary, and specific.

Personality can also be revealed by how people select projects and tasks to pursue in life. If you know what a person really wants out of life, then you probably know that person fairly well. Our goals define us, and the strategies with which we pursue those desires illustrate the active aspects of personality in our daily lives.

Cognitive social learning theory was introduced and several specific examples of this approach were described. All of the example theories incorporate the concept of goals and related cognitive activities, such as expectancies, strategies, and beliefs about one's abilities. These theories are important additions to the psychology of personality because they emphasize how the psychological situation is a function of characteristics of the person (e.g., their self-efficacy beliefs).

Intelligence was also discussed in this chapter, along with different views on intelligence (as academic achievement versus an aptitude for learning). We reviewed the historical development of intelligence as starting with the view of this as a single and general trait up to today's trend toward a multiple intelligences view. We also noted that culture influences which skills and achievements contribute toward intelligence and presented some results on a biological interpretation of intelligence. We touched on the concept of emotional intelligence, which has turned out to be a better predictor than IQ for some positive life outcomes, like having satisfying relationships. In addition, we briefly reviewed some of the controversies that are being debated in the area of intelligence.

KEY TERMS

cognitive approaches 370
personalizing cognition 371
objectifying cognition 371
cognition 371
information processing 371
perception 371
interpretation 371
conscious goals 372
rod and frame test (RFT) 373
field dependent 373
field independent 373
embedded figures test (EFT) 373
pain tolerance 378

reducer/augmenter theory 378
constructs 381
personal constructs 381
postmodernism 381
locus of control 382
generalized expectancies 383
external locus of control 383
internal locus of control 383
learned helplessness 385
causal attribution 388
attributional style 388
pessimistic explanatory style 388
optimistic explanatory style 388

personal project 387
cognitive social learning approach 390
self-efficacy 390
modeling 391
promotion focus 392
prevention focus 392
"if . . . then . . ." propositions 393
achievement view of intelligence 393
aptitude view of intelligence 393
general intelligence 394
multiple intelligences 394
cultural context of intelligence 396
inspection time 397

Emotion and Personality

Issues in Emotion Research

Emotional States Versus Emotional Traits

Categorical Versus Dimensional Approach to Emotion

Content Versus Style of Emotional Life

Content of Emotional Life

Style of Emotional Life

Interaction of Content and Style in Emotional Life

SUMMARY AND EVALUATION

KEY TERMS

13

THE COGNITIVE/EXPERIENTIAL DOMAIN

I magine you are traveling to visit a friend in a city to which you've never been before. You've taken a train to this city and are walking to your friend's apartment. You arrived in the evening, so it is dark as you begin to make your way in the unfamiliar neighborhood. You are using Google Maps on your phone to find your way, and it tells you to turn into a darkened street, which looks more like an alley. The alley is dark, but short, and it may take you to your friend's place faster, so you start down the alley. You are alert and a bit on edge. You look over your shoulder and notice that someone has followed you down the alley. Your heart is pounding. You turn and look ahead, and you see that someone else has entered the alley in front of you as well. You suddenly feel trapped and you freeze. You are in a real predicament, your way is blocked in both directions. Your breathing is rapid and you feel light-headed. Your mind is racing, but you are not sure what to do as the two people close in on you from both directions. Your palms are sweating and you feel the tension in your neck and throat, as if you might scream at any second. The two people are getting closer and closer. You feel nervousness in your stomach as you look first in front, then behind. You want to run but cannot decide which way to go. You are paralyzed with fear; you stand there, trembling, not knowing whether you can run away or whether you will have to fight for your life. Suddenly, one of the persons calls out your name.

The emotion of fear is characterized by a distinct facial expression. Fear also has a distinctly unpleasant subjective feeling. There are also the associated changes in physiology, such as heart rate increases and increases in blood flow to the large muscles of the legs and arms. These changes prepare the frightened person for the intense action tendency associated with fear—to flee or to fight.
PeopleImages/Getty Images

You realize it is your friend, who has come with his roommate to look for you between the train station and the apartment. You breathe a sigh of relief, and quickly your state of fear subsides, your body calms, your mind clears, and you greet your friend with an enthusiastic, "Am I glad to see you!"

In this example, you experienced the emotion of fear. You also experienced the emotion of relief, and perhaps even elation, at being rescued by your friend. **Emotions** can be defined by their three components. First, emotions have distinct subjective feelings, or affects, associated with them. Second, emotions are accompanied by bodily changes, mostly in the nervous system, and these produce associated changes in breathing, heart rate, muscle tension, blood chemistry, and facial and bodily expressions. And third, emotions are accompanied by distinct **action tendencies**, or increases in the probabilities of certain behaviors. With the emotional feeling of fear, there are subjective feelings of anxiety, confusion, and panic. There are also associated changes in bodily function, such as increased heart rate, decreased blood flow to the digestive system (making for stomach queasiness), and increased blood flow to the large muscles of the legs and arms. These changes prepare you for the intense activity sometimes associated with fear. The activity, or action tendency, associated with fear is to flee or to fight.

Why are personality psychologists interested in emotions? People differ from each other in their emotional reactions, even to the same events, so emotions are useful in distinguishing among persons. For example, imagine losing your wallet, which contains a large sum of money, your credit card, and all your identification, including your driver's license. What emotions do you think you would feel—anger, embarrassment, hopelessness, frustration, panic, fear, shame, guilt? Different people would have different emotional reactions to this life event, and understanding how and why people differ in their emotional reactions is part of understanding personality.

Other theories of emotion emphasize the functions that emotions play, such as generating short-term adaptive actions that help us survive. For example, the emotion of disgust has the adaptive value of prompting us to quickly spit out something that is not good for us. Interestingly, the expression of disgust, even when the feeling is evoked by a thought or something that is only psychologically distasteful, is to wrinkle the nose, open the mouth, and protrude one's tongue as if spitting something out.

In his 1872 book *The Expression of the Emotions in Man and Animals,* Charles Darwin proposed a **functional analysis** of emotions and emotional expressions. His analysis focuses on the "why" of emotions and expressions, in particular in terms of whether they increase the fitness of individuals (see Chapter 8 of this text). How do emotions increase evolutionary fitness? Darwin concluded that emotional expressions rapidly communicate information from one animal to another about what is likely to happen. The dog baring its teeth and bristling the hair on its back is communicating to others that he is likely to attack. If others recognize this communication, they may choose to back away, thereby avoiding the attack. Many modern emotion theorists accept this functional emphasis, but most personality psychologists approach emotion with an interest in how people differ from each other in terms of emotions.

Issues in Emotion Research

Several major issues divide the field of emotion research (Davidson, Scherer, & Goldsmith, 2003). Psychologists typically hold an opinion on each of these issues. We consider two of these issues, beginning with the distinction between emotional states and emotional traits.

Emotional States Versus Emotional Traits

We typically think of emotions as states that come and go (similar to motives, as we saw in Chapter 11). A person gets angry, then gets over it. A person becomes sad, then snaps out of it. **Emotional states** are *transitory.* Moreover, emotional states depend more on the situation a person is in than on the specific person. A man is angry *because* he was unfairly treated. A woman is sad *because* her bicycle was stolen. Most people would be angry or sad in these situations. Emotions as states are transitory; they have a specific cause, and that cause typically originates outside of the person (something happens in the environment).

We can also think of emotions as dispositions, or traits. For example, we often characterize people by stating what emotions they *frequently* experience or express: "Mary is cheerful and enthusiastic," or "John is frequently angry and often loses his temper." Here we are using emotions to describe dispositions, characteristic emotional traits. Emotional traits are consistencies in a person's emotional life. Traits, as you'll recall from Chapter 3, are patterns in a person's behavior or experience that are at least somewhat consistent from situation to situation and that are at least somewhat stable over time. Thus, an **emotional trait** is a pattern of emotional reactions that a person consistently experiences across a variety of life situations.

Categorical Versus Dimensional Approach to Emotion

Emotion researchers can be divided into two camps based on their answers to the following question: What is the best way to think about emotions? Some suggest emotions are best thought of as a small number of primary and distinct emotions (anger, joy, anxiety, sadness). Others suggest that emotions are best thought of as broad dimensions of experience (e.g., a dimension ranging from pleasant to unpleasant). Those who think that primary emotions are the key are said to take the **categorical approach**. Hundreds of terms describe different categories of emotions. Averill (1975), for example, compiled a list of 550 terms that describe different feeling states. This is similar to the situation with basic trait terms, in which psychologists started with thousands of trait adjectives and searched for the fundamental factors that underlie those many variations, concluding that there are probably about five primary personality traits that underlie the huge list of trait adjectives.

Emotion researchers who take the categorical approach have tried to reduce the complexity of emotions by searching for the primary emotions that underlie the great variety of emotional terms (Levenson, 2003). They have not reached the kind of consensus that is found in the personality trait domain, however. The lack of consensus found in this area of psychology results from different criteria that researchers use for defining emotion as primary. Ekman (1992a), for example, requires that a primary emotion has a distinct facial expression that is recognized across cultures. The experience of sadness is accompanied by frowning and knitting the brow. This facial expression is universally recognized as depicting the emotion of sadness. Similarly, clenching and baring the teeth is associated with anger and is universally recognized as anger. In fact, people who are blind from birth frown when sad, clench and bare their teeth when angry, and smile when they are happy. Because persons blind from birth have never seen the facial expressions of sadness, anger, or joy, it is not likely that they learned these expressions. Rather, it seems likely that the expressions are part of human nature. Based on these criteria of distinct and universal facial expressions, Ekman's list of primary emotions contains disgust, sadness, joy, surprise, anger, and fear.

Happiness can be thought of as a state or as a trait. People high in trait happiness experience frequent happiness states, or have a lower threshold for becoming happy. Moreover, happiness is recognized around the world through the expression of smiling. People from all cultures smile when they are happy.
Ollyy/Shutterstock

Other researchers hold different criteria for counting emotions as primary. For example, Izard (1977) suggests that the primary emotions are distinguished by their unique motivational properties. That is, emotions are understood to guide behaviors by motivating a person to take specific adaptive actions. Fear is included as a primary emotion on Izard's list because it motivates a person to avoid danger and seek safety. Interest is similarly a fundamental emotion because it motivates a person to learn and acquire new skills. Izard's criteria result in a list of 10 primary emotions. In Table 13.1, various lists of primary emotions are based on various criteria.

Another approach to understanding emotion has been based on empirical research rather than on theoretical criteria. In this **dimensional approach**, researchers gather data by having subjects rate themselves on a wide variety of emotions, then apply statistical techniques (usually some form of factor analysis) to identify the basic dimensions underlying the ratings.

There is a remarkable consensus among researchers on the basic dimensions that underlie self-ratings of affect (Judge & Larsen, 2001; Larsen & Diener, 1992; Watson, 2000). Most of the studies suggest that people categorize emotions using just two primary dimensions: how pleasant or unpleasant the emotion is and how high or low on arousal the emotion is. When these two dimensions are arrayed as axes in a two-dimensional coordinate system, the adjectives that describe emotions fall in a circle around the two dimensions, as shown in Figure 13.1.

This model of emotion suggests that every feeling state can be described as a combination of pleasantness/unpleasantness and arousal. For example, a person can feel unpleasant feelings in a very high-arousal way (nervous, anxious, terrified) or in a very low-arousal way (bored, fatigued, tired). Similarly, a person can feel pleasant feelings in a high-arousal way (excited, enthusiastic, elated) or in a low-arousal way (calm, relaxed). Thus the two dimensions of pleasantness and arousal are seen as fundamental dimensions of emotion.

The dimensional view of emotion is based on research studies in which subjects rate their emotional experiences. Emotions that occur together, which are experienced as similar to each other, are understood as defining a common dimension. For example, the emotions of distress, anxiety, annoyance, and hostility are very similar in terms of

Table 13.1 A Selection of Theorists Who Provide Lists of Primary Emotions

Theorists	Basic Emotions	Criteria
Ekman, Friesen, and Ellsworth (1972)	Anger, disgust, fear, joy, sadness, surprise	Universal facial expression
Frijda (1986)	Desire, happiness, interest, surprise, wonder, sorrow	Motivation to take specific actions
Gray (1982)	Rage, terror, anxiety, joy	Brain circuits
Izard (1977)	Anger, contempt, disgust, distress, fear, guilt, interest, joy, shame, surprise	Motivation to take specific actions
James (1884)	Fear, grief, love, rage	Bodily involvement
Mower (1960)	Pain, pleasure	Unlearned emotional states
Oatley and Johnson-Laird (1987)	Anger, disgust, anxiety, happiness, sadness	Little cognitive involvement
Plutchik (1980)	Anger, acceptance, joy, anticipation, fear, disgust, sadness, surprise	Evolved biological processes
Tomkins (2008)	Anger, interest, contempt, disgust, fear, joy, shame, surprise	Density of neural firing

Source: Adapted from Ortony and Turner (1990).

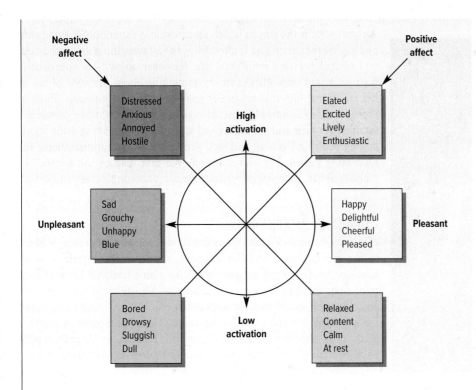

Figure 13.1

The dimensional approach to emotion, showing two primary dimensions: high to low activation and pleasantness to unpleasantness with emotions falling in a circular array. This is sometimes called the circumplex model of emotion.

experience and thus seem to anchor one end of a dimension of high-arousal negative affect. The dimensional approach to emotion refers more to how people *experience* their emotions compared to how researchers *think* about emotions. The dimensional approach suggests that what we experience as emotions are various degrees of pleasantness and arousal and that every emotion we are capable of experiencing can be described as a combination of pleasantness and arousal (Larsen & Fredrickson, 1999; Larsen & Prizmic, 2006).

Some researchers prefer the categorical perspective, finding it useful to think about emotions as distinct categories rather than dimensions. For example, the emotions of anger and anxiety, although similar in terms of being high-arousal negative emotions, are nevertheless associated with distinctly different facial expressions, different subjective feelings, and different action tendencies. There are also personality psychologists who prefer to think about how people differ with respect to the primary dimensions of emotion. For example, who are the people who have a good deal of pleasantness in their lives? Who are the people who have frequent bouts of high-arousal unpleasant emotions? In this chapter, we cover the research and findings from both of these perspectives.

Content Versus Style of Emotional Life

Another distinction that is useful to personality psychologists is between the content of a person's emotional life and the style with which that person experiences and expresses emotion. **Content** refers to the specific kinds of emotions that a person experiences, whereas **style** is the way in which an emotion is experienced. For example, saying that someone is cheerful is to say something about the content of that person's emotional life. However, to say that someone is high on mood variability is to say something about the style of his or her emotional life—that his or her emotions change frequently. Each of these facets of emotion—content and style—exhibits traitlike properties (stable over time and situations and meaningful for making distinctions among people). Content and style provide an organizational theme for discussing personality and emotion. We first discuss the content of emotional life, focusing on various pleasant and unpleasant emotions.

Content of Emotional Life

Content of emotional life means the typical emotions a person is likely to experience over time. For example, someone characterized as an angry or hot-tempered person should have an emotional life that contains frequent bouts of anger, irritability, and hostility. Someone whose emotional life contains a lot of pleasant emotions we might characterize as happy, cheerful, and enthusiastic. Thus, the notion of content leads us to consider the *kinds* of emotions a person is likely to experience over time and across situations in their lives. We begin with a discussion of the pleasant emotional dispositions.

Aristotle wrote that happiness resulted from living a virtuous life. Modern theories that emphasize that living a life of meaning and purpose leads to happiness are following Aristotle's tradition.
Dimitris Tavlikos/Alamy Stock Photo

Pleasant Emotions

In lists of primary emotions, happiness or joy is typically the only pleasant emotions mentioned (though some theorists include interest as a pleasant emotion). In trait approaches to emotion, the major pleasant disposition is happiness and the associated feelings of being satisfied with one's life. We begin with these concepts.

Definitions of Happiness and Life Satisfaction   Over 2,000 years ago, the Greek philosopher Aristotle wrote that happiness was the supreme good and that the goal of life was to attain happiness. Moreover, he taught that happiness was attained by living a virtuous life and being a morally good person. Some modern researchers similarly emphasize **eudaimonia**, the creation of a life of meaning and purpose, as the route to happiness (e.g., King & Hicks, 2012). Other scholars and philosophers have offered other theories on the sources of human happiness. For example, unlike Aristotle, eighteenth-century French philosopher Jean-Jacques Rousseau speculated that the road to happiness lies in the satisfaction of one's desires and the hedonistic pursuit of pleasure. In the late nineteenth century, the founder of psychology in America, William James, taught that happiness was the ratio of one's accomplishments to one's aspirations. One could achieve happiness, James thought, in one of two ways: by accomplishing more in life or by lowering one's aspirations.

Although philosophers have speculated about the roots of happiness for centuries, the scientific study of happiness by psychologists is relatively recent (see Eid & Larsen, 2008, for a review). Psychologists began the serious study of happiness (also called subjective well-being) in the mid-1970s. Since then, scientific research on the topic has grown by leaps and bounds. In recent years, hundreds of scientific articles on happiness have been published annually in the psychological literature (Diener & Seligman, 2002). Indeed, a new journal started in the year 2000, titled *Journal of Happiness Research,* and publishes six volumes a year dedicated to the science of happiness. Another journal, the *Journal of Positive Psychology,* also publishes many scientific studies on happiness.

One way to define **happiness** is to examine how researchers measure it. Several questionnaire measures are widely used in surveys and other research. Because happiness is a subjective quality—it depends on an individual's own judgment of his or her life—researchers *have* to rely on self-report, mainly through questionnaires. Some of these questionnaires focus on judgments about one's life, such as "How satisfied are you with your life as a whole these days?" Other questionnaires focus on emotion, particularly on the balance between pleasant and unpleasant emotions in a person's life. An example of this type of questioning was developed and published by Fordyce (1978), in which the subject is asked the following questions "Over the past six months:"

What percent of the time were you happy?	_____
What percent of the time were you neutral?	_____
What percent of the time were you unhappy?	_____
Make sure your percents add up to:	100 percent

Among college students, data indicate that the average person reports being happy about 65 percent of the time, neutral 15 percent, and unhappy 20 percent (Larsen & Diener, 1985). The percent happy scale is one of the better measures of happiness in terms of construct validity (see Chapter 2). For example, it predicts a wide range of other happiness-related aspects of a person's personality, such as day-to-day moods and peer reports of overall happiness (Tay, Diener, Lucas, & Larsen, 2019).

Researchers conceive of happiness as having two complementary components. One is more cognitive and consists of judgments that one's life has purpose and meaning and has been called the life-satisfaction component. The other component is affective and consists of the ratio of a person's positive emotions to his or her negative emotions averaged over time. This has been called the hedonic component and really refers to the balance of positive to negative emotions in a person's life over time. The two components—life satisfaction and hedonic balance—tend to be highly correlated. Although we can think of cases where a person could be high on one and low on the other (e.g., a starving artist who feels her life has a great deal of purpose and meaning, yet is suffering greatly day to day to produce her art), the fact is that most people who have a life of meaning and purpose also have more positive than negative emotions in their life. Consequently, most psychologists refer to the general construct of happiness to talk about this characteristic.

Can it be that happy people are just deluding themselves and others by denying negative feelings when they report on their emotional lives? This is the idea of social desirability, as discussed in Chapter 4. It turns out that measures of happiness *do* correlate with social desirability scores. In other words, people who score high on self-reported happiness measures also score high on social desirability scales. Moreover, social desirability measures also correlate with non-self-report happiness scores, such as peer reports of happiness. This finding suggests that having a positive view of oneself is part of being a happy person. Said differently, part of being happy is to have **positive illusions** about the self, an inflated view of one's own characteristics as a good, able, and desirable person (Taylor, 1989; Taylor et al., 2000). Research is showing that, while some positive illusions about the self can contribute to happiness (through interpersonal appeal and self-fulfilling prophecies), too much self-deception can lead to negative effects (Schutz & Baumeister, 2017).

Despite the correlation of self-report measures of happiness with social desirability, other findings suggest that these happiness measures are valid (Diener, Oishi, & Lucas, 2003). These findings concern the positive correlations found between self-report and non-self-report measures of happiness. People who report that they are happy tend to have friends and family members who agree (Sandvik, Diener, & Seidlitz, 1993). In addition, studies of the daily diaries of happy people find that they report many more pleasant experiences than unhappy people (Larsen & Diener, 1985). When different clinical psychologists interview a sample of people, the psychologists tend to agree strongly about which are happy and satisfied and which are not (Diener, 2000). And, in an interesting experiment, Seidlitz and Diener (1993) gave the participants five minutes to recall as many happy events in their lives as possible and then gave them five minutes to recall as many unhappy events in their lives as possible. They found that the happy people recalled more pleasant events, and fewer unpleasant events, than did the unhappy people.

Questionnaire measures of happiness and well-being also predict other aspects of people's lives that we would expect to relate to happiness (Diener, Lucas, & Larsen, 2003), implying that measures of happiness have good construct validity (see Chapter 4). For example, compared with unhappy people, happy people are less abusive and hostile, are less self-focused, and report fewer instances of disease. They also are more helpful and cooperative, have more social skills, are more creative and energetic, are more forgiving, and are more trusting (Myers, 1993, 2000; Myers & Diener, 1995; Veenhoven, 1988). In summary, self-reports of happiness appear to be valid and trustworthy (Larsen & Prizmic, 2006). After all, who but the persons themselves are the best judge of their subjective well-being? See Table 13.2 for a sample "life satisfaction" questionnaire.

What Good Is Happiness?   It has long been known that happiness correlates with many positive outcomes in life, such as marriage quality, longevity, self-esteem, and satisfaction with one's job (Diener & Tay, 2015; Myers & Diener, 2018). These correlations between desirable outcomes in life and happiness are often interpreted to mean

Table 13.2 Satisfaction with Life Scale

Below are five statements with which you may agree or disagree. Using the scale below, indicate your agreement with each item by placing the appropriate number on the line preceding that item. Please be open and honest in your responses.

Strong Disagreement 1	Moderate Disagreement 2	Slight Disagreement 3	Slight Agreement 4	Moderate Agreement 5	Strong Agreement 6

1. _____ In most ways, my life is close to my ideal.

2. _____ If I could live my life over, I would change almost nothing.

3. _____ I am satisfied with my life.

4. _____ So far I have gotten the important things I want in life.

5. _____ The conditions of my life are excellent.

Source: Diener et al., 1985.

that success in some area of life (e.g., a good marriage) will make a person happy. As another example, the small correlation between personal wealth and happiness is often interpreted as meaning that having money can make one (slightly more) happy. The majority of researchers in this area have gone on the assumption that successful outcomes foster happiness and that the causal direction goes from being successful leading to increased happiness.

However, a group of researchers (Lyubomirsky, King, & Diener, 2005) questioned this assumption about the causal direction going from success to happiness. They suggested that there may be areas of life where the causality goes in the opposite direction, from happiness to success. For example, it could be that being happy leads one to get married, or to have a better marriage, instead of having a good marriage leading one to become happy.

In an extremely large meta-analysis of the happiness and well-being literature, Lyubomirsky and colleagues (2005) reviewed many studies that might be used to disentangle the causal direction between happiness and several different outcomes. Two kinds of studies are most useful in assessing causal direction. One type of study is longitudinal, in which people are measured on at least two occasions separated in time. If happiness precedes success in life, then we have some evidence that the causal direction might go from happiness to the outcome. The second type of study is experimental, in which happiness is manipulated (people are put in a good mood) for half the sample (the other half is the control group), and some outcome is measured. If the outcome is higher in the group undergoing the happiness induction than in the control group, then we have some evidence that the causal direction might go from happiness to the outcome.

Lyubomirsky and colleagues (2005) found that longitudinal studies provided evidence that happiness leads to, or at least comes before, positive outcomes in many areas of life, including fulfilling and productive work, satisfying relationships, and better mental and physical health and longevity. Experimental studies also provide evidence that happiness can lead to several positive outcomes, including being more helpful and altruistic, wanting to be with others, increases in self-esteem and liking of others, a better functioning immune system, and more effective conflict resolution.

Although happiness has been shown to lead to many positive outcomes in life, the situation with some outcomes might be more complex and involve **reciprocal causality**,

Does having a positive relationship cause a person to be happy? Or, does being happy cause one to have positive relationships?

Antonio Guillem/Shutterstock

which refers to the idea that causality can flow in both directions. For example, we know that happy people are more likely to help others who are in need. Also, from the experimental literature, we know that helping someone in need can lead to increase in happiness. This kind of reciprocal causality may apply to many areas of life, including having a satisfying marriage or intimate relationship, having a fulfilling job, or having high self-esteem.

What Is Known About Happy People   In recent decades, many scientists have asked and answered basic questions about the differences between happy and unhappy people (e.g., Eid & Larsen, 2008). For example, are women happier than men, or are men the happier gender? Haring, Stock, and Okun (1984) analyzed 146 studies on global well-being and found that gender accounted for less than 1 percent of the variation in people's happiness. This finding of minuscule differences between men and women appears across cultures and countries as well. Michalos (1991) obtained data on 18,032 university students from 39 countries. He found that roughly equal proportions of men and women rated themselves as being satisfied with their lives. Diener (2000) also reports gender equality in overall happiness.

Is happiness more likely among young, middle-aged, or older people? We often think that certain age periods of life are more stressful than others, such as the midlife crisis or the stress of adolescence. This might lead us to believe that certain times of life are happier than others. Inglehart (1990) addressed this question in a study of 169,776 people from 16 nations. He found that the circumstances that make people happy change with age. For example, financial security and health are important for happiness later in life, whereas, for younger adults, success at school or work and satisfying intimate relationships are important for happiness. Also, there is some evidence that older people, as long as they remain healthy, report lower levels of negative emotions than younger people (Carstensen et al., 2011). This may be due to older people having developed better coping or emotion management skills. Nevertheless, in looking at overall levels of happiness, many researchers (e.g., Inglehart, 1990) conclude that there is little evidence to suggest that any one time of life is happier than any other.

Is ethnicity related to happiness? Are some ethnic groups happier than others? Many surveys have included questions about ethnic identity, so a wealth of data exists on this question. Summarizing many such studies, Myers and Diener (1995, 2018) conclude that ethnic group membership is unrelated to subjective well-being. For example, African Americans report roughly the same amount of happiness as European Americans and in fact have slightly lower rates of depression (Diener et al., 1993). Crocker and Major (1989) suggest that people from disadvantaged social groups maintain their happiness by valuing the activities they are good at and by comparing themselves with members of their own group.

What about national differences in well-being? Are people from certain nations happier than people from other nations? The answer here seems to be yes. The happiness levels in countries around the world have been tracked by the United Nations (UN) for the past 20 years. In Table 13.3, we present some of the results from their 2022 report and list the 20 most happy and the 20 least happy countries. Looking at the rankings, what do you think might account for the differences among the countries that are high compared to low on well-being?

While nations may move a few ranks up or down from year to year, the constant finding over the years, which you see in Table 13.3, is that people in countries with a higher standard of living (and wealth) are happier than the people from countries with a lower standard of living. Diener and colleagues (1995) statistically analyzed similar international data on the wealth of nations in relation to the mean happiness of the population and concluded that differences in the economic development of nations may be a source of differences in the subjective well-being of nations. Researchers who conducted similar but smaller-scale national surveys have offered similar findings (Easterlin, 1974; Veenhoven, 1991a, 1991b).

Such findings might lead us to think that money or income makes people happy. People often think that if they had a bit more money or if they had a few more material goods, they would be happier. Some believe that if they win the lottery they will be happy for the rest of their lives. Researchers have found that there is no simple answer to the question about whether money makes people happy (Diener & Biswas-Diener, 2002, 2008). We present some of the complexity in A Closer Look: Does Money Make People Happy?

Instead of looking at national mean levels of happiness, where it seems richer countries are happier, if we look within a country at individual levels of happiness and personal income or wealth, the association between happiness and money practically disappears. In fact, research on the objective circumstances of a person's life— age, sex, ethnicity, income, and so on—shows that these matter very little to overall happiness. Yet we know that people differ from each other and that, even through life's struggles and disappointments, some people are consistently happier than others. Costa, McCrae, and Zonderman (1987) found, in a study of 5,000 adults, that the people who were happy in 1973 were also happy 10 years later, in spite of undergoing many changes in life. What else might explain why some people are consistently happier than others?

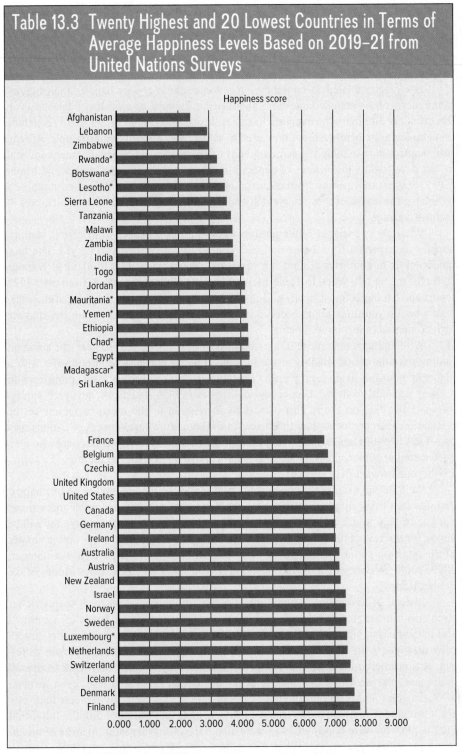

Table 13.3   Twenty Highest and 20 Lowest Countries in Terms of Average Happiness Levels Based on 2019–21 from United Nations Surveys

Source: United Nations World Happiness Report, 2019.

A Closer Look

Does Money Make People Happy?

Pop singer Madonna, also known as "the Material Girl," has sung the praises of materialism. Americans are often thought of as materialistic. In fact, in surveys, the goal of being very well off financially is often rated as the top goal in life by first-year college students, surpassing other goals, such as being helpful to others, realizing potential as a person, and raising a family (Myers, 2000). This attitude is summarized by a bumper sticker seen on an expensive car towing a large boat, which read, "When the game is over, the person with the most toys wins." Does having more make one a winner? Does money lead to happiness?

Looking at in terms of national data, as in Table 13.3, the answer seems to be that wealthier countries do indeed have higher average levels of life satisfaction than poorer countries. Myers and Diener (1995) report that the correlation between a nation's well-being score and its gross national product (adjusted for population size) is +.67. However, national wealth is confounded with many other variables that influence well-being, such as health care services, civil rights, women's rights, care for the elderly, and education. This is a classic example of how potential third variables might explain why two variables are correlated (see discussion of this problem in Chapter 2). For example, wealthier countries may have higher well-being *because* they also provide better health care for their citizens.

To counteract this research problem, we must look at the relationship between income and happiness within specific countries. Diener and Diener (1995) report that, in very poor countries, such as Bangladesh and India, financial status is a moderately good predictor of well-being. However, once people can afford life's basic necessities, it appears that increasing one's financial status matters very little to one's well-being. In countries that have a higher standard of living, where most people have

their basic needs met (such as in Europe or the United States), income "has a surprisingly weak (virtually negligible) effect on happiness" (Inglehart, 1990, p. 242).

What if we were to look within a country and examine changes in affluence over time, within a single economy, to see if people become happier as the country becomes more affluent? The United States, for example, has undergone huge increases in national wealth, income, and affluence over the past half-century. For example, from 1957 to the late 1990s, the average person's after-tax income more than doubled, going from $8,000 to $20,000 annually (after-tax income expressed in constant 1990 dollars). Are Americans happier today than they were in 1957? Myers (2000) reports that Americans were *not* any happier in 2000 than they were in 1957. This is illustrated in Figure 13.2, which shows that the percentage of Americans who describe themselves as very happy has stayed fairly constant over the decades, fluctuating right around 30 percent. This constant rate of personal happiness stands in contrast to the corresponding large increase in personal income experienced during those decades.

Data like that portrayed in Figure 13.2, showing no relation between personal income and national happiness, stands in contrast to Table 13.3, which shows that richer countries have higher happiness. This was first pointed out by Richard Easterlin (1974), and has come to be called the **Easterlin paradox**: At any point in time, happiness varies with income across nations, but over time within a country, happiness does not trend upward with increases in income.

While many theories have been proposed to explain the Easterlin paradox, the simplest is that, at an individual level, increasing wealth (income, living standard) does not have an impact on happiness. Indeed, in the United States over the past 20 years, we have seen a continued upswing in average

income (at a slower rate, but still income has been trending upward), but there has been a significant decrease in average happiness in the United States. This can be seen in the last 10 years (since 2012) of UN World Happiness Reports. In 2019, the UN World Report on Happiness included two papers offering potential explanations for declining happiness in the United States (one implicating digital media, the other citing high rates of addiction). At any rate, this declining level of happiness in the face of improving economic conditions reinforces the notion that wealth, in itself, is mostly unrelated to happiness. The 2022 UN world happiness report shows that the correlation between income and happiness was .11; not exactly zero, but very small.

This finding of a tiny relationship between wealth and happiness contradicts the views of many politicians, economists, and policymakers. For example, people in the lowest levels of the economy have the highest rates of depression (McLoyd, 1998). Economic hardship takes a toll on people, increasing stress and conflict in people's lives (Kushlev, Dunn, & Lucas, 2015). Poverty is associated with elevations in a variety of negative life outcomes, ranging from infant mortality to increased violent crimes, such as homicide (Belle et al., 2000). How can poverty be associated with such unfortunate circumstances, yet income not be related to happiness? The answer, in part, lies in the notion of a threshold of income, below which a person is very unlikely to be happy. Once a person is above this threshold, however, the notion that having more money would make one happier does not seem to hold (Diener & Biswas-Diener, 2002).

Myers and Diener (2018) make the analogy between wealth and health: the absence of either health or wealth can bring misery, but their presence is no guarantee that happiness will follow. An interesting thought experiment would be to consider

(Continued)

A Closer Look (*Continued*)

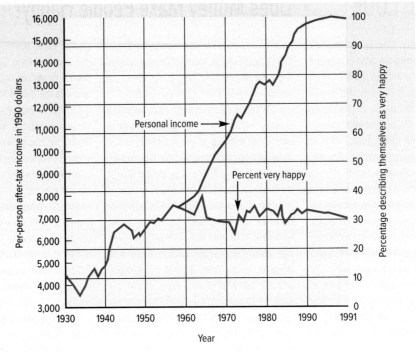

Figure 13.2

Has the large growth in average income been accompanied by an increase in average happiness within the United States? Keep in mind that the income data is averaged, and we know that there is great income inequality in the U.S. population.

Source: Adapted from "The Funds, Friends, and Faith of Happy People," by D. G. Myers, 2000, *American Psychologist,* 55, pp. 56–67, Figure 5.

whether giving random people huge sums of money—millions of dollars—would make them happier. This study is actually run hundreds of times each year in the United States. With the advent of state lotteries in the United States, many people become millionaires overnight. Brickman, Coates, and Janoff-Bulman (1978) conducted a study of lottery winners, comparing their happiness levels with those of people from similar backgrounds who had not won large amounts of money. Within six months of winning, the newly rich lottery winners were found to be no more happy than the subjects in the control group. Apparently, winning the lottery is not as good as it sounds, at least not in terms of making a person permanently happy. External life circumstances have a surprisingly small effect on happiness and subjective well-being (Lucas, 2007).

What can we conclude about money and happiness? Probably the most reasonable conclusion is that below a very low-income level, a person is very unlikely to be happy. Being able to meet the basic needs of life (e.g., the needs on Maslow's hierarchy that are discussed in Chapter 11, including food, shelter, and security) appears crucial. However, once those needs are met, research suggests that there is little to the notion that further wealth will bring increased happiness. Support for this idea is provided in a study by Diener and colleagues (2010) that is based on a very large sample representative of almost everyone on planet Earth. These researchers found that the correlation between personal income and happiness is +.12 in the United States. In a German sample, that correlation was found to be .20 (Lucas & Schimmack, 2009). Fischer (2008) reports a correlation

of .19 between median hourly wage and happiness in U.S. data between 1972 and 2004. Although these correlations, like that reported the 2022 UN data (.11), are not zero, they are hardly large enough to think that having a huge income, in itself, will make you happy. What wealthy people choose to do with their money has more to do with their happiness than does the mere fact of having a lot of money. For example, Dunn, Aknin, and Norton (2008) have shown that spending money on others can have a larger positive impact on happiness than spending the same amount on oneself. Across three separate studies, using data from 136 countries, Aknin et al. (2013) and Kushlev, Radosic, and Diener (2021) showed that using one's money to help others (called pro-social spending) may be a universally rewarding experience that contributes to the buyer's personal happiness.

Personality and Well-Being   In 1980, psychologists Paul Costa and Robert McCrae concluded that demographic variables, such as gender, age, ethnicity, and income, accounted for only about 10–15 percent of the variation in happiness, an estimate more recently confirmed by others (Lucas & Diener, 2021; Lyubomirski, 2007). This leaves a lot of the variance in subjective well-being unaccounted for. Costa and McCrae (1980) proposed that personality traits might have something to do with disposing certain people to be happy and so looked into that research. The few studies existing at that time suggested that happy people were outgoing and sociable (Smith, 1979), emotionally stable, and low on neuroticism (Wessman & Ricks, 1966).

Exercise

Recall and describe in writing a recent time when you purchased something for someone else. After writing a brief description of this, think of a time when you spent an equivalent amount of money on something for yourself. Now consider which of these two events produced the higher level of happiness in you? If you are like the participants in research reported in *Science* by Dunn, Aknin, and Norton (2008), you will find that spending one's money on other people has a larger effect on happiness than spending money on oneself. Why do you think this might be so? The effect is so reliable that these authors even found that participants randomly assigned to spend money on others experienced greater happiness than participants randomly assigned to spend money on themselves.

Costa and McCrae used such information to theorize that there may be two personality traits, out of the Big 5, that influence happiness: extraversion (positively) and neuroticism (negatively). Their idea was both simple and elegant. They began with the notion that happiness was the presence of relatively high levels of positive affect, and relatively low levels of negative affect, in a person's life over time. Extraversion, they held, was associated with more frequent positive emotions, whereas emotional stability (the opposite of neuroticism) was associated with less frequent negative emotions.

Costa and McCrae (1980; McCrae & Costa, 1991) found that their model was supported by research. Extraversion and neuroticism predicted the amounts of positive and negative emotions in people's lives and hence correlated with subjective well-being. In fact, extraversion and neuroticism accounted for up to *three times* as much of the variation in happiness among people compared with *all* of the common demographic variables (e.g., age, income, gender, education, ethnicity, religion) put together. It appears that having the right combination of personality traits (high extraversion and low neuroticism) contributes much more to happiness than gender, ethnicity, age, and all the other demographic characteristics taken together. Their model of well-being is portrayed in Figure 13.3.

Since Costa and McCrae's original study in 1980, dozens of published studies have replicated the finding that extraversion and neuroticism are strong personality correlates of well-being (summarized in Lucas & Diener, 2021 and Rusting & Larsen, 1998b). All of these studies have been correlational, however, usually taking the form of administering personality and well-being questionnaires, then examining the correlations (Lucas & Dyrenforth, 2008).

Correlational studies cannot determine whether there is a direct causal connection between personality and well-being, or whether personality leads one to live a certain lifestyle

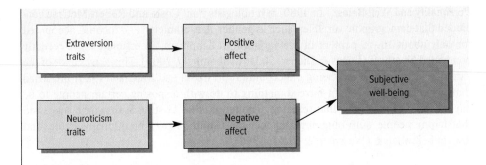

Figure 13.3

The influence of extraversion and neuroticism on subjective well-being by making a person susceptible to positive and negative affect.

Source: Adapted from Costa and McCrae, 1980.

and that lifestyle in turn makes one happy. For example, being neurotic may lead one to be a worrier and complainer. Other people dislike being around someone who worries a lot and is always complaining, so people may avoid the person who is high on neuroticism. Consequently, that person may be lonely and unhappy; however, that unhappiness may be due to the fact that the person drives people away by complaining all the time. The person's neuroticism leads him or her to create certain life situations, such as making others uncomfortable, and these situations in turn make the person unhappy (Hotard et al., 1989).

We can contrast this with a different view of the causal relation between personality and well-being, in which personality is viewed as directly causing people to react to the same situations with different amounts of positive or negative emotions, hence directly influencing their well-being. A neurotic person may respond with more negative emotion, even to the identical situation, compared to a person low in neuroticism. These two different models of the relation between personality and well-being—the direct and the indirect models—are portrayed in Figure 13.4. In the indirect model (Panel b), personality causes the person to create a certain lifestyle, and the lifestyle, in turn, causes the emotional reaction. In the direct model (Panel a), even when exposed to identical situations, certain people respond with more positive or negative emotions, depending on their level of extraversion and neuroticism.

Larsen and his colleagues (e.g., Larsen, 2000a; Larsen & Ketelaar, 1989, 1991; Rusting & Larsen, 1998b; Zelenski & Larsen, 1999) have conducted several studies on whether the personality traits of extraversion and neuroticism have a direct effect on emotional responding. In these studies, the participants underwent a **mood induction** in the laboratory. In one study, the subjects listened to guided images of very pleasant scenes (a walk on the beach) or very unpleasant scenes (having a friend dying of an incurable disease). In other studies, the participants' emotions were manipulated by having them look at pleasant or unpleasant images. Prior to the laboratory session, their personality scores on extraversion and neuroticism were obtained by questionnaire, and mood was measured before and after the mood induction. The researchers were then able to determine if extraversion and neuroticism scores predicted responses to the laboratory mood inductions. Across several studies, the best predictor of responsiveness to the positive mood induction was the personality variable of extraversion. The best predictor of responses to the negative mood induction was neuroticism. It seems that it is easy to put an extravert into a good mood, and easy to put a high-neuroticism person into a bad mood. Moreover, these laboratory studies suggest that personality acts as an amplifier of life events, with

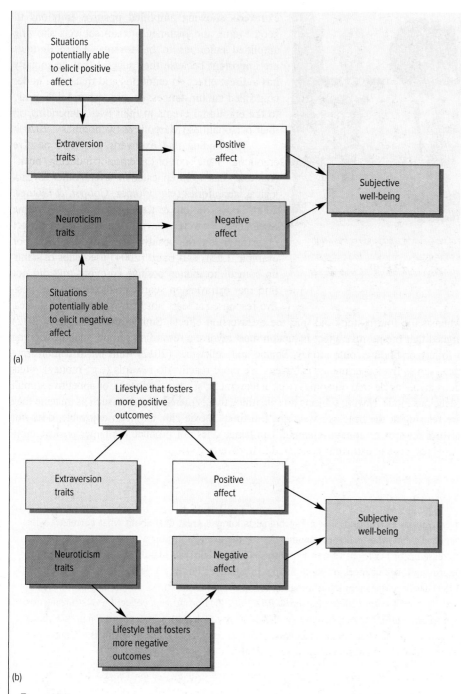

(a)

(b)

Figure 13.4

Two models of the relationship between personality variables and subjective well-being. Panel a: Model showing a direct effect of personality on emotional life, where life events are amplified by the personality traits, resulting in stronger positive or negative emotions for high extraversion or neuroticism subjects, respectively. Panel b: Model of the indirect relation between personality and emotional life. Here personality causes one to develop a lifestyle, and that lifestyle in turn fosters positive or negative affect for the high extraversion or neuroticism persons, respectively.

People high on the personality trait of neuroticism tend to worry frequently. They may worry about their health, their social interactions, their work, their future, or just about anything. Worrying and complaining takes up a great proportion of their time.

Steve Prezant/Image Source

extraverts showing amplified positive emotions to good events and high-neuroticism subjects showing amplified emotions to bad events. These findings are important because they suggest that personality has a direct effect on emotions and that, even under controlled circumstances, people respond differently to the emotional events in their lives, depending on their personalities (Margolis & Lyubomirsky, 2020).

The finding that extraverts get more positive emotional "bang" out of the emotion-inducing "buck" (or event) has been replicated in several other psychological laboratories (e.g., Gomez, Cooper, & Gomez, 2000; Gross, Sutton, & Ketelaar et al., 1998). Some researchers, however, have failed to find the effect of extraversion on positive affective reactivity. For example, Lucas and Baird (2004) used clips of stand-up comedy to induce positive emotions and did not find that extraversion scores predicted a larger positive response (at least not in two out of four studies, whereas the fourth study did find the extraversion effect). Smillie and colleagues (2012) argued that the positive affect induction must involve a rewarding stimuli, such as winning a lottery or finding some money. Smillie and colleagues (2012) went on to demonstrate that, across five experiments, extraverts are more reactive to rewards (e.g., money), situations involving desired outcomes (e.g., achievement, success feedback), or appetitive stimuli (delicious food). Having subjects do something that is merely pleasant, such as imagine they are relaxing at the beach or watch a "feel-good" movie clip, although enjoyable, does not involve rewards or appetitive stimuli and hence does not produce the larger positive emotional response in extraverts compared to introverts.

Application

A program to increase happiness. Psychologists know a great deal about what correlates with happiness, but what can they recommend for the average person who wants to maintain or increase his or her levels of trait happiness? Buss (2000b) has identified several strategies for improving one's chances of being happy. In addition, Fordyce (1988) (see also Swanbrow, 1989) has developed a practical program for applying what is known about happiness in everyday life. And Larsen (2000a; Larsen & Prizmic, 2004) proposes a collection of strategies for coping and improving one's emotional life. Most psychologists believe that happiness is something that people must work at (Kennon & Lyubomirsky, 2021). The following is a summary of much of the advice given by these psychologists:

1. *Spend time with other people, particularly friends, family, and loved ones.* The one characteristic common to most happy people is a disposition to be sociable, to draw satisfaction from being with other people. Cultivate an interest in other people. Go out of your way to spend time with friends and loved ones. Try to get to know those around you.

2. *Seek challenge and meaning in work.* If satisfying relationships are the first priority, the second is having work that you find enjoyable. Happy people enjoy their work and work hard at what they do. If you do not find your current work (or college major) rewarding, then consider switching to something that you find more worthwhile. Work that is challenging, but within your skill level, is usually the most satisfying.

3. *Look for ways to be helpful to others.* Helping others can make you feel good about yourself and give you the feeling that your life is meaningful. Helping others thereby provides a boost in self-esteem. Helping has a second benefit as well; helping someone else can take your mind off your own problems or can make your problems seem little by comparison. There are plenty of worthy causes and plenty of organizations that welcome volunteers.

4. *Take time out for yourself; enjoy the activities that give you pleasure.* Don't wait to find time for your favorite hobby or activity. Instead, make time. Many people learn to keep a calendar while in college to schedule work and other obligations. Use it to schedule fun things as well. Set aside time to read a book, take in a movie, exercise regularly, or do whatever else you enjoy. Think about what gives you pleasure, and build time into your busy schedule for those activities.

5. *Stay in shape.* Exercise is positively associated with emotional well-being. Exercise need not be intense or all that frequent to provide the emotional benefit. Playing on team sports, dancing, biking, swimming, gardening, or even walking, if done at a brisk pace, is about all it takes. It doesn't seem to matter what the activity is, as long as you move around enough to keep in shape.

6. *Have a plan, but be open to new experiences.* Having an organized life allows a person to accomplish much. However, sometimes the most fun moments in life are unplanned. Be open to trying different things or having different experiences—try going somewhere you have never been, try doing a routine activity a little differently, or try doing something on the spur of the moment. Be flexible, rather than rigid, and try to avoid getting stuck in any ruts.

7. *Be optimistic.* Put on a smiling face, whistle a happy tune, look for the silver lining in every cloud. Sure, it sounds too good to be true, but acting happy and trying to look on the bright side of things can go a long way toward making you feel happy. Try to avoid negative thinking. Don't make pessimistic statements, even to yourself. Convince yourself that the cup *really is* half full.

8. *Don't let things get blown out of proportion.* Sometimes when something bad happens, it seems like the end of the world. Happy people have the ability to step back and see things in perspective. Happy people think about their options and about the other things in their lives that *are* going well. They think about what they can do to work on their problems or what to avoid in the future. But they *don't* think it is the end of the world. Often asking yourself "What's the worst that can come of this?" will help put things in perspective.

Just wishing for happiness is not likely to make it so. Psychologists agree that people have to work at being happy; they have to work at overcoming the unpleasant events of life, the losses and failures that happen to everyone. The strategies in the previous list can be thought of as a personal program for working on happiness.

Unpleasant Emotions

Unlike pleasant emotions, the unpleasant emotions come in several distinct varieties. We discuss three important unpleasant emotions that are viewed by psychologists as having dispositional characteristics: anxiety, depression, and anger.

Trait Anxiety and Neuroticism   Recall that people who exhibit the trait of neuroticism are vulnerable to negative emotions. **Neuroticism** is one of the Big Five dimensions of personality, and it is present, in some form, in every major trait theory of personality.

Different researchers have used different terms for neuroticism, such as emotional instability, anxiety-proneness, and negative affectivity (Watson & Clark, 1984). Adjectives useful for describing persons high on the trait of neuroticism include moody, touchy, irritable, anxious, unstable, pessimistic, and complaining. Hans Eysenck (1967, 1990; Eysenck & Eysenck, 1985) suggested that individuals high on the neuroticism dimension tend to overreact to unpleasant events, such as frustrations or problems, and that they take longer to return to a normal state after being upset. They are easily irritated, worry about many things, and seem to be constantly complaining. You may have heard the phrase "She is not happy unless she has something to worry about." Well, it is unlikely that worrying actually makes a person happy. But the fact that some people worry almost all the time suggests that worrying is a characteristic of their personalities. Some people worry about their health ("Is this nagging cough really a sign that I have lung cancer? Could this headache really be a brain tumor?"). Others worry about their social interactions, ruminating after every conversation. And still, others worry about their work.

In addition to worry and anxiety, the person high on the neuroticism dimension frequently experiences episodes of irritation. An interesting way to illustrate this is to ask people to list all the things that have irritated them in the past week. Perhaps seeing someone spit in public is irritating to many people. Or seeing someone with a pierced nose and eyebrows might be mentioned as irritating. Or seeing a couple kissing in public might be mentioned. If people were to write down all the things that irritated them, you would find that people high on neuroticism would have much longer lists than people low on neuroticism.

Eysenck's biological theory   As discussed in Chapter 3, Eysenck (1967, 1990) argued that neuroticism has a biological basis. In his theory of personality, neuroticism is due primarily to a tendency of the **limbic system** in the brain to become easily activated. The limbic system is the part of the brain responsible for emotion and the fight-or-flight reaction. If someone has a limbic system that is easily activated, then that person probably has frequent episodes of emotions associated with flight (such as anxiety, fear, and worry) or with fight (such as anger, irritation, and annoyance). High-neuroticism persons are anxious, irritated, and easily upset, so the theory goes, because their limbic systems are more easily aroused to produce such emotions.

Because the limbic system is located deep within the brain, its activity is not easily measured by EEG electrodes placed on the surface of the scalp. Newer brain imaging technologies, such as MRI or PET, are allowing personality researchers to test this theory directly (DeYoung, 2010). Eysenck (1990) made several logical arguments in favor of a biological basis for neuroticism. First, many studies have shown a remarkable level of stability in neuroticism. For example, Conley (1984a, 1984b, 1985) found that neuroticism showed a high test-retest correlation even after a period of 45 years. Although this does not prove a biological basis for neuroticism, stability is nevertheless consistent with a biological explanation. A second argument is that neuroticism is a major dimension of personality that is found in many different kinds of data sets (e.g., self-report, peer report) in many different cultures and environments by many different investigators. Again, although this ubiquity does not prove a biological basis, the fact that neuroticism is so widely found across cultures and data sources is consistent with a biological explanation. And the third argument in favor of a biological explanation is that many genetic studies find that neuroticism shows one of the higher heritability values. Trait negative affect shows relatively high levels of heritability, whereas trait positive affect shows a significant shared environment component (Goldsmith, Aksan, & Essex, 2001). A predisposition to be neurotic appears to be modestly heritable. Most behavior geneticists believe that what is heritable in emotional traits is individual differences in neurotransmitter function, such as dopamine transport or serotonin reuptake (Canli, 2008).

Other biologically based research on emotion traits examines which areas of the brain are active when processing emotion information, such as looking at sad pictures or thinking about something that makes one anxious or angry (Sutton, 2002). Most of the studies reveal that emotion is associated with an increased activation of the anterior cingulate cortex (Bush, Luu, & Posner, 2000; Whalen, Bush, & McNally, 1998). The **anterior cingulate** is the portion of the brain located deep inside toward the center of the brain, and it most likely evolved early in the evolution of the nervous system. DeYoung and colleagues (2010) measured the volume of brain tissue in different regions of the brain. Neuroticism was correlated with the volume of brain regions associated with the evaluation of threat and punishment and the production of negative emotions. Other studies of neuroticism and brain structure find it associated with larger (Kapogiannis et al., 2013) and thicker (Wright et al., 2006) prefrontal cortex regions, areas that are involved in the regulation of negative emotions and impulses. A meta-analysis of brain imaging studies and neuroticism (Servaas et al., 2013) concluded that neuroticism is associated with differences in brain activation during fear learning, anticipation of aversive events (e.g., shocks), and during the processing of unpleasant information (e.g., images).

Other researchers have focused on the biological basis of the self-regulation of negative emotions. For example, Levesque, Fanny, and Joanette (2003) had subjects watch a sad film. Half of them were told to do whatever they could to stop or prevent the sad feelings and to not show any emotional reactions during the film. Subjects who were successful at inhibiting their negative emotions showed increased activity in the right ventral medial **prefrontal cortex**, part of the so-called executive control center of the brain. Other studies also have identified this area as highly active in the control of emotion (Beauregard, Levesque, & Bourgouin, 2001). When specifically told to try to dampen their emotional responses to unpleasant images, the amount of activity in the prefrontal area correlated positively with neuroticism. This suggests that the high-neuroticism persons were putting in extra effort to regulate their negative emotions (Harenski, Kim, & Hamann, 2009). Schuyler et al. (2014) looked at recovery time in amygdala activation following exposure to unpleasant images. Subjects higher in neuroticism showed slower amygdala recovery, implying that, at least at the level of amygdala activity, negative emotions last longer for high-neuroticism individuals.

Cognitive theories   Another way to think about neuroticism is as a cognitive phenomenon. Some personality psychologists have argued that trait neuroticism is caused by certain styles of information processing (such as attending, thinking, and remembering). Lishman (1972), for example, was among the first to show that high-N (neuroticism) subjects were more likely to recall unpleasant information than were low-N subjects. There was no relation between neuroticism and the recall of pleasant information. After studying lists of pleasant and unpleasant words, high-N subjects also recalled the unpleasant words *faster* than the pleasant words. Martin, Ward, and Clark (1983) had subjects study information about themselves and about others. When asked to recall that information, the high-N subjects recalled more of the negative information about themselves but did not recall more negative information about others. There appear to be a very specific information-processing characteristics associated with neuroticism: it appears to relate to the preferential processing of negative (but not positive) information about the self (but not about others). Martin and colleagues (1983) state that "high-N scorers recall more self-negative words than low-N scorers because memory traces for self-negative words are stronger in the high-N scorers" (p. 500).

As a related explanation for the relation between neuroticism and selective memory for unpleasant information, researchers use a version of the spreading activation concept, which was discussed in Chapter 10. Recall that this notion suggests that material is stored in memory by being linked with other, similar pieces of material.

Many psychologists hold that emotional experiences are also stored in memory. Moreover, some individuals—those high in neuroticism—have richer networks of association surrounding memories of negative emotion. Consequently, for them, unpleasant material is more accessible, leading them to have higher rates of recall for unpleasant information.

One type of unpleasant information in memory concerns memory for illnesses, injuries, and physical symptoms. If high-N subjects have a richer network of associations surrounding unpleasant information in memories, then they are also likely to recall more instances of illness and bodily complaints. Try asking a high-N person the following question: "So, what's your health been like the past few months?" Be prepared for a long answer, with a litany of complaints and many details about specific symptoms. Study after study has established a link between neuroticism and self-reported health complaints. For example, Smith and colleagues (1989) asked subjects to recall whether they had experienced each of 90 symptoms within the past three weeks. Neuroticism correlated with the self-reported frequencies of symptoms, usually in the range of $r = .4$ to $.5$. This means that roughly 16–25 percent of the variation in self-reported health symptoms could be attributed to the personality trait of neuroticism.

Larsen (1992) examined the sources of bias in neurotics' reports of physical illnesses. He asked participants to report every day on whether they experienced any physical symptoms, such as a runny nose, cough, sore throat, backache, stomachache, sore muscles, headache, and loss of appetite. The participants made daily health reports for two months, providing the researcher with detailed day-by-day running reports of physical symptoms. After the daily report phase was complete, Larsen then asked the participants to recall, as accurately as they could, how many times they reported each symptom during the two months of daily reporting. This unusual research design allowed the researcher to calculate the subjects' "true" total number of symptoms, as reported on a daily basis, as well as their remembered number of symptoms. It turned out that both of these scores were related to neuroticism. That is, the high-N participants reported more daily symptoms, *and* they recalled more symptoms, than did the stable low-N subjects. Moreover, even when controlling for the number of day-to-day symptoms reported, neuroticism was *still* related to elevated levels of recalled symptoms.

High-neuroticism persons recall and self-report more symptoms, but are they more likely than stable low-N individuals to actually *have* more physical illnesses? This is a tricky question to address, as even medical doctors rely on a person's self-reports of symptoms to establish the presence of physical disease. The answer is to look at objective indicators of illness and disease and to see if those are related to neuroticism. Major disease categories, such as coronary disease, cancer, or premature death, appear to have little, if any, relation to neuroticism (Watson & Pennebaker, 1989). Costa and McCrae (1985) reviewed this literature and concluded that "neuroticism influences perceptions of health, but not health itself" (p. 24). Similar conclusions were reached by Holroyd and Coyne (1987), who wrote that neuroticism reflects "a biased style of perceiving physiological experiences" (p. 372).

Research on the immune system, however, is showing that neuroticism does appear to be related to diminished immune function during stress (Herbert & Cohen, 1993). In a fascinating study by Marsland and colleagues (2001), subjects underwent vaccination for hepatitis B, and their antibody response to the injection was measured (this is a measure of how well the immune system responds to antigens in a vaccine). It was found that the subjects low in neuroticism mounted and maintained the strongest immune response to the vaccine. This finding suggests that persons high in neuroticism may, in fact, be more susceptible to immune-mediated diseases.

The immune system plays a role in many diseases (see Chapter 18), suggesting that neuroticism may affect health through compromising the body's ability to fight off foreign cells. In a study of neuroticism and lung cancer, Augustine and colleagues (2008) found that age of onset of lung cancer was negatively related to neuroticism. This finding held even after statistically controlling for the age of subjects when they started smoking and the number of cigarettes smoked per day prior to contracting lung cancer. Smoking history and amount smoked were strongly related to earlier onset of lung cancer, but neuroticism was an additional and independent risk factor for earlier onset of this disease. Examining differences between persons one standard deviation above and below the mean on neuroticism showed that the high-N subjects contracted lung cancer an average of 4.33 years earlier than the low-N subjects. The authors speculate that neuroticism is related to the speed of cancer progression due to its impact on the immune system. The chronic stress associated with neuroticism can lead to depletion of the immune system (Irwin, 2002), which in turn can make a person less able to fight off the progression of cancer.

Psychologists have proposed a theory that high-neuroticism subjects pay more attention to threats and unpleasant information in their environment (e.g., Dalgleish, 1995; Matthews, 2000; Matthews, Derryberry, & Siegle, 2000). High-N subjects are thought to have a stronger behavioral inhibition system, compared to low-N persons, making them particularly vulnerable to cues of punishment and frustration and prompting them to be vigilant for signs of threat. These researchers argue that high-N subjects are on the lookout for threatening information in their environment, constantly scanning for anything that might be menacing, unsafe, or negative. This is called an attentional bias to threatening information.

Researchers have incorporated a version of the Stroop effect into investigations of attentional bias and neuroticism. The Stroop effect (Stroop, 1935) describes the increased time it takes to name the color in which a word is written when that word names a different color, relative to when it is a matching color word or a patch of color. For example, if the word *blue* is written in red ink, then it takes longer to name the color of the ink (red) than it would take if the word *red* were written in red ink. Researchers agree that the relevant dimension (color of ink) and the irrelevant dimension (name of the word) produce a conflict within the attentional system. If a person's attentional system can efficiently suppress the irrelevant dimension (the word), then he or she should be faster in naming the color than someone who cannot suppress the word information.

The Stroop task has been modified to study individual differences in attention to emotion words. In the so-called emotional Stroop task, the content of the words is typically anxiety- or threat-related, such as *fear, disease, cancer, germs, vomit, death, failure, grief,* or *coffin* (Larsen, Mercer, & Balota, 2006). The words are written in colored ink, and the subject is asked to name the color of the ink and ignore the content of the words. Attentional bias is confirmed when the time it takes to name the colors of the threat words is longer than the time it takes to name the colors of neutral words (Algom, Chajut, & Lev, 2004). Applied to neuroticism, the idea is that high-N persons have an attentional bias such that certain stimuli (the threat words) are more salient, or attention-grabbing. The threat words should be more difficult for them to ignore when naming the color. Therefore, neuroticism should correlate with longer response times to name the colors when the words refer to threat (e.g., *disease, failure*).

A thorough review of this literature was published by Williams, Mathews, and MacLeod (1996). These researchers reviewed more than 50 experiments that used a version of the emotional Stroop task. Many of the studies show that high-N groups (or participants with anxiety disorder) are often slower to name colors of anxiety- and threat-related words, compared with the color naming of control, nonemotion words. The explanation given for this effect is that the threatening words capture the attention of the high-N participants, but not of the low-N participants.

In summary, neuroticism is a trait that relates to a variety of negative emotions, including anxiety, fear, worry, annoyance, irritation, and distress. Persons high in neuroticism are unstable in their moods, are easily upset, and take longer to recover after being upset. There are both biological and cognitive theories about the causes of negative emotions in neuroticism, and each has some supportive evidence in the scientific literature. One particularly well-known finding concerns the tendency of persons high in neuroticism to complain of health problems. In addition, high-N persons are thought to be on the lookout for threatening information; they pay more attention to negative cues and events in life, however minor, compared with more emotionally stable persons.

Depression   **Depression** is another traitlike dimension. In this chapter, we cover only a small part of what is known about depression. There is a huge body of literature on the topic of depression, as is befitting a psychological disorder that is estimated to strike 20 percent of the people in the United States at some time in their lives (American Psychiatric Association, 1994). There are entire books on depression, graduate courses devoted to this topic, and clinicians who specialize primarily in the treatment of depression. There are thought to be several distinct varieties of depression (e.g., Rusting & Larsen, 1998a). For example, most depressed persons have sleep disturbance; some have difficulty falling asleep (initial insomnia) whereas others have trouble staying asleep (waken early and cannot fall back to sleep, called terminal insomnia). This may suggest different types of depression. See Table 13.4 for a list of symptoms that define depression.

Diathesis-stress model   One way to view depression is through a **diathesis-stress model**. This model suggests that there is a preexisting vulnerability, or diathesis, that is present among people who later become depressed. In addition to this vulnerability, a stressful life event must occur in order to trigger the depression, such as the loss of a loved one, a career failure, or another major negative life event. Neither element alone—the diathesis or the stress—is sufficient to trigger depression. Rather, they must occur together in order for depression to result.

Beck's cognitive theory   Many researchers have emphasized certain cognitive styles as one type of diathesis that makes people vulnerable to depression (Larsen & Cowan, 1988). One of these researchers is Aaron Beck (1921–2021), who has written extensively on his cognitive theory of depression. He suggests that the vulnerability lies in a particular **cognitive schema**, or way of looking at the world. A cognitive schema is a way of processing incoming information, a way of organizing and interpreting the events of daily life.

Table 13.4 Signs of Depression

The signs of depression include having five or more of the following symptoms during the same two-week period:

- Depressed mood most of the day, nearly every day
- Diminished interest or pleasure in most activities
- Change in weight: significant weight loss when not dieting or a weight gain
- Change in sleep pattern: insomnia or sleeping much more than usual
- Change in movements: restlessness and agitation or feeling slowed down
- Fatigue or loss of energy nearly every day
- Feelings of worthlessness or guilt nearly every day
- Diminished ability to concentrate or make decisions nearly every day
- Recurrent thoughts of death or suicide

Source: Adapted from American Psychiatric Association (2013).

The cognitive schema involved in depression, according to Beck, distorts the incoming information in a negative way, a way that makes the person vulnerable to depression.

According to Beck, three important areas of life are most influenced by the depressive cognitive schema. This **cognitive triad** includes information about the self, the world, and the future. Information about these important aspects of life is distorted in specific ways by the depressive cognitive schema. For example, after doing poorly on a practice exam, a depressive person might say to himself, "I am a total failure." This is an example of the *overgeneralizing* distortion applied to the self. Overgeneralizing is taking one instance and generalizing to many or all other instances. The lay term for this is "blowing things out of proportion." The person might have failed at one exam, but that does not mean he is a total failure. The same overgeneralizing style can be applied to the world ("If anything can go wrong, it will.") and the future ("Why bother trying, when everything I do is doomed to fail?"). In Beck's (1976) theory, there are many other cognitive distortions, such as making *arbitrary inferences* (jumping to a negative conclusion, even when the evidence does not support it), *personalizing* (assuming that everything is your fault), and *catastrophizing* (thinking that the worst will always happen). These cognitive elements are portrayed in Figure 13.5.

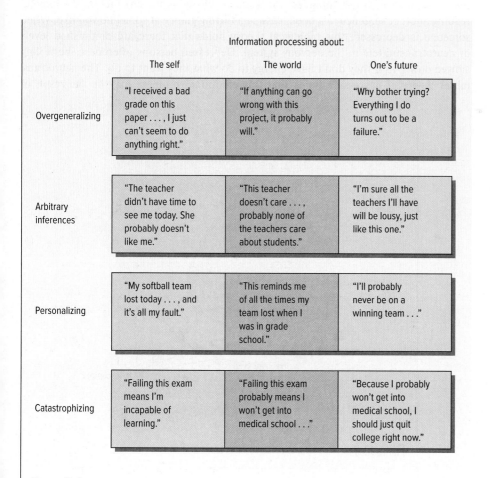

	Information processing about:		
	The self	The world	One's future
Overgeneralizing	"I received a bad grade on this paper . . . , I just can't seem to do anything right."	"If anything can go wrong with this project, it probably will."	"Why bother trying? Everything I do turns out to be a failure."
Arbitrary inferences	"The teacher didn't have time to see me today. She probably doesn't like me."	"This teacher doesn't care . . . , probably none of the teachers care about students."	"I'm sure all the teachers I'll have will be lousy, just like this one."
Personalizing	"My softball team lost today . . . , and it's all my fault."	"This reminds me of all the times my team lost when I was in grade school."	"I'll probably never be on a winning team . . ."
Catastrophizing	"Failing this exam means I'm incapable of learning."	"Failing this exam probably means I won't get into medical school . . ."	"Because I probably won't get into medical school, I should just quit college right now."

Figure 13.5

Beck's cognitive model of depression, showing how distortions are applied to processing information about the self, the world, and one's future. These cognitive distortions can make one vulnerable to becoming depressed.

According to Beck's influential theory, depression is the result of applying these cognitive distortions to the information from daily life. These distortions are applied quickly and outside of immediate awareness, resulting in a stream of automatic negative thoughts, which deeply affect how the person feels and acts ("I'm no good. The world is against me. My future is bleak."). The person who thinks he is a total failure will often act like a total failure and may even give up trying to do better, creating a **self-fulfilling prophecy**. Moreover, depressive feelings lead to more distortions, which in turn lead to more bad feelings, and so on, in a self-perpetuating cycle. Beck devised a form of therapy for changing people's cognitive distortions. In a nutshell, this involves challenging the person's distortions, such as by asking, "Does it really mean that you are a *total failure* because you flunked just this one exam?"

Biology of Depression   Nerve cells in the body communicate with each other by way of chemical messengers called neurotransmitters (Chapter 7). These neurotransmitters are delivered from one neuron across a gap—called the synapse—to another neuron (Figure 13.6). The first neuron is called the presynaptic neuron, and the second neuron is called the postsynaptic neuron. If the neurotransmitter reaches the postsynaptic neuron in sufficient strength, the nerve signal continues on its way toward completing the action for which it is intended, for instance, changing the channel on the remote, reading another sentence in a book, casting a flirting glance at someone you like. When someone is depressed, this biological theory holds that there are diminished levels of neurotransmitters in the nervous system. Depressed persons often describe feeling slowed down, as if they don't have energy to do what they want to do. The **neurotransmitter theory of depression** holds that this emotional problem may be the result of

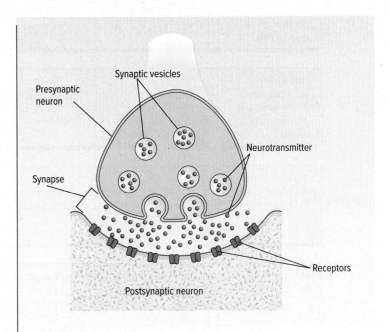

Figure 13.6

Diagram of synapse between two neurons, illustrating how neurotransmitters must be released, cross the synapse, and bond with the receptors on the postsynaptic neuron in order for a nerve impulse to pass on its way to completion.

neurotransmitter imbalance at the synapses of the nervous system. The neurotransmitters thought to be most involved in depression include norepinephrine (also called noradrenaline), serotonin, and, to a lesser degree, dopamine. Many of the drugs used to treat depression target exactly these neurotransmitters. For example, Prozac, Zoloft, and Paxil inhibit the reuptake of serotonin in the synapse, resulting in increased levels of this neurotransmitter in the synapses, facilitating nerve transmission. The medication Tofranil works to maintain a better balance between levels of both serotonin and norepinephrine. While helpful to many people, not all persons with depression are successfully treated with these kinds of medications, suggesting again that there may be varieties of depression, some more biologically based, others more related to stress or cognitively biases.

Studies suggest that exercise might also be usefully applied to the treatment of depression, at least for some persons (Dubbert, 2002). In his 1996 annual report, Surgeon General of the United States David Satcher documented the benefits of exercise for health promotion and disease prevention—including depression prevention. The use of exercise in counseling people with depression is described by Dixon, Mauzey, and Hall (2003). A meta-analysis published in 2016 showed that exercise produced a reduction in depression that was of a similar magnitude to that found for antidepressant medications

Anger Proneness and Potential for Hostility Another important negative emotion is anger and feelings of hostility. Psychologists have long been interested in what makes people hostile and aggressive. Social psychologists, for example, have examined conditions under which the average person will become aggressive (Baron, 1977). One finding is that most people are willing to strike out against someone who has treated them unfairly. Here the emphasis is on how certain situations, such as being treated unfairly, are likely to evoke aggression in *most* people. Personality psychologists agree that some circumstances tend to make most people angry, but their interest is more in terms of individual differences in anger proneness. Two people, for example, are fired (perhaps unjustly) from their jobs; one accepts it and plans a job search strategy, and the other flies into a rage at the workplace or in the community. Personality psychologists begin with the position that some people are characteristically more hostile than others in response to the same kinds of situations, such as frustration. **Hostility** is defined as a tendency to respond to everyday frustrations with anger and aggression, become irritable easily, feel frequent resentment, and act in a rude, critical, antagonistic, and uncooperative manner in everyday interactions (Dembrowski & Costa, 1987).

The scientific objectives, from the personality psychologist's perspective, are (1) to understand how hostile people became that way, what keeps them that way, and in what other ways they differ from nonhostile people and (2) to examine the consequences of hostility in terms of important life outcomes.

One consequence of hostility is its relation to coronary heart disease. We cover this topic in more detail in Chapter 18 on Type A behavior and health. It turns out that chronic hostility is the component of the Type A behavior pattern that most contributes to heart disease. Hostility as a personality trait can be measured with questionnaires that ask about the frequency and duration of anger episodes, whether anger is triggered by minor events (e.g., having to wait in line), or how easily one is bothered or irritated in everyday life (Siegel, 1986). For most people, even those high on the hostility dimension, the trait produces feelings and urges that are uncomfortable and that create a negativistic and brooding outlook. For some, these urges spill over into acts of aggression. Many of the mass shootings in the United States, such as the one in

Would a person with a long history of extreme violence be able to change completely into a gentle, loving father and pillar of his community?

Twin Design/Shutterstock

Uvalde, Texas, in May of 2022, were done by young adult males whose level of anger proneness prompted them to unimaginable acts of aggression, killing and wounding large numbers of bystanders.

Anger is an emotion that causes some people to lose control. Most of the violent inmates in our prisons have trouble with the self-regulation of this potent emotion. Researchers have long speculated that there may be biological differences, particularly in brain function, between violent and nonviolent persons. The psychologist Adrian Raine has spent many years examining some of the most violent and aggressive members of our society (e.g., Raine, 2002; Brennan & Raine, 1997). He has focused on the brain structures associated with individual differences in violence and aggression, and has started a field called "neurocriminology" (Glenn & Raine, 2014; Wagels, Habel, Raine, and Clemens, 2022). In one study of especially violent murderers, Raine, Meloy, and Bihrle (1998) found that these persons showed decreased activity in the prefrontal areas of their brains, those areas mentioned earlier that are associated with normal emotional regulation. Psychologist Jonathan Pincus has also specialized in the study of violent criminals. In his book *Base Instincts: What Makes Killers Kill,* Pincus (2001) presents information on the lives of numerous serial killers, and in virtually all cases, these murderers suffered from some damage to their brains, through violence, accidental injuries, or excessive drug or alcohol abuse. In addition, practically all of these murderers came from severely abusive families. Pincus (1999) presents data that the presence of brain damage in violent criminals is most often in the prefrontal areas. Again, these are the areas involved in self-control (Denson et al., 2009). Interestingly, this is the area that was severely damaged in the case of Phineas Gage, discussed in Chapter 6.

In large studies, not every violent or sadistic person is found to have brain abnormalities. However, the rates of brain abnormalities are much higher in violent persons than in those persons without a history of violence. For example, in a study of 62 criminals in Japan, the researchers divided the inmates into those convicted of murder and those convicted of nonviolent offenses. Brain abnormalities were much more frequent among the murderers than among the nonviolent offenders (Sakuta & Fukushima, 1998). In a study done in Austria, a group of high-violence offenders was were compared to a group of low-violence offenders. In the high-violence group, 66 percent were found to have brain abnormalities, whereas in the low-violence group only 17 percent were found to have the same brain abnormalities (Aigner et al., 2000). In a study of sexual offenders, criminals were divided into those who physically harmed their victims (e.g., raped and/or murdered) and those who did not physically harm their victims (e.g., exposed themselves). In the group of violent sex offenders, 41 percent were found to have brain abnormalities, a rate significantly higher than in the nonviolent sex offenders (Langevin et al., 1988). In a particularly strong longitudinal study, a group of 110 hyperactive and 76 normal boys had their brain activity assessed when they were between 6 and 12 years of age. They were followed up between the ages of 14 and 20 years, with special attention to arrest records. Those adolescent boys with a history of delinquency turned out to have had unusual brain patterns in childhood compared to those adolescents without subsequent delinquency (Satterfield & Schell, 1984).

More recent studies (e.g., Hawes et al., 2016) document the trajectory of having poor anger management in childhood, leading to higher rates of violence and aggression in adulthood. Such findings highlight the importance of developing anger control strategies which, for most people, naturally develop in childhood. Could it be that the brain abnormalities often seen in violent adults involve those brain regions that are responsible for self-control and the management of emotions, especially anger?

The kind of brain damage most often observed in hostile aggressive persons involves areas in the frontal lobe and, to a lesser extent, the temporal lobe. These areas are important in regulating impulses, particularly aggressive impulses, and fear conditioning. The damage may be developmentally caused or caused by injury. For example, sniffing glue or inhaling butane gas, which can induce intoxication similar to alcohol, can cause the kind of brain damage that has been related to antisocial behavior (Jung, Lee, & Cho, 2004). Another example is a case report where a man developed a cyst in his brain. Prior to this development, he was not a violent person. However, after the cyst grew, and presumably caused damage to his brain, he strangled his wife to death after she scratched his face (Paradis et al., 1994). A similar case is reported in Glenn and Raine (2014), along with actual brain scans, of a 40-year-old man who, with no prior history, suddenly became sexually aggressive and was arrested. He was found to have a large tumor in his prefrontal cortex and, when it was removed, his behavior returned to normal, with none of the sexual inappropriateness that got him into trouble with the police. The kind of brain abnormalities found in violent and aggressive persons appears to involve decrements in the person's ability to inhibit or control aggressive impulses.

Style of Emotional Life

So far in this chapter, we have discussed people's emotional lives in terms of emotional content, or the various characteristic emotions that define how one person is different from others. We examined four emotional traits: happiness, anxiety, depression, and anger. Now we turn to a discussion of emotional style. As a quick distinction, we might say that content is the *what* of a person's emotional life, whereas style is the *how* of that emotional life.

Affect Intensity as an Emotional Style

When we think about how emotions are experienced, probably the major stylistic distinction is one of intensity. You know from experience with your own emotional reactions that emotions can vary greatly in terms of magnitude. Emotions can be weak and mild, or strong and almost uncontrollable. To characterize a person's emotional style, we must inquire about the typical intensity of his or her emotional experiences. For emotional intensity to be useful to personality theory, we must establish that it describes a stable characteristic useful for making distinctions among persons.

Affect intensity can be defined by a description of persons who are either high or low on this dimension. Larsen (2009) describes *high affect intensity* individuals as people who typically experience their emotions strongly and are emotionally reactive and variable. High affect intensity subjects typically go way up when they are feeling up and go way down when they are feeling down. They also alternate between these extremes more frequently and rapidly than do low affect intensity individuals. Low affect intensity individuals, on the other hand, typically experience their emotions only mildly and with only gradual fluctuations and minor reactions. Such persons are stable and calm and usually do not suffer the troughs of negative emotions. But they also tend not to experience the peaks of enthusiasm, joy, and other strong positive emotions.

Note that these descriptions of high and low affect intensity persons make use of the qualifying terms *typically* and *usually*. This is because certain life events can make even the lowest affect intensity person experience relatively strong emotions. For example, being accepted into one's first choice of schools can cause elation in almost anyone. Similarly, the death of a loved pet can cause strong sadness in almost everyone. However, because such events are fairly rare, we want to know what people are usually or typically like: how they characteristically react to the normal sorts of everyday positive and negative life events.

Figure 13.7 presents daily mood data for two subjects from a study by Larsen and Diener (1985). These subjects kept daily records of their moods for 84 consecutive days. Note that Subject A's emotions were fairly stable and did not depart too far from his baseline level of mood over the entire three-month reporting period. Actually, he had a bad week at the beginning of the semester, which is denoted by the several low points at the left side of the graph. Otherwise, things were pretty stable for this subject.

Subject B, on the other hand, exhibited extreme changes in mood over time. This subject was hardly ever near his baseline level of mood. Instead, Subject B appears to have experienced both strong positive and strong negative affect frequently and to alternate between these extremes frequently and rapidly. In other words, this high affect intensity person exhibited a good deal of variability in his daily moods, fluctuating back and forth between positive and negative affect from day to day.

Assessment of Affect Intensity and Mood Variability

In early studies of affect intensity (e.g., Diener, Larsen, et al., 1985), this characteristic of emotional life was assessed using a daily experiential sampling method. That is, data were gathered much like that presented in Figure 13.7, panels a and b. Researchers would then compute a total score for each subject to represent how intense or variable that person was over the time period.

This longitudinal method of measuring affect intensity is straightforward and face valid, and it represents the construct of affect intensity quite well. However, it takes several weeks or longer of daily mood reporting to generate a reliable composite affect intensity score for each individual. Consequently, a questionnaire measure of affect intensity has been developed that allows a relatively quick assessment of a person's emotional style in terms of intensity. Table 13.5 lists 10 items from this questionnaire, called the Affect Intensity Measure (AIM) (Larsen & Diener, 1987).

An important aspect of the affect intensity trait is that we cannot really say whether it is bad or good to be low or high on this trait. Both positive and negative consequences are related to scoring either high or low. High-scoring persons, for example, get a lot of zest out of life, enjoying peaks of enthusiasm, joy, and positive emotional involvement. On the other hand, when things are not going well, high-scoring persons are prone to strong negative emotional reactions, such as sadness, guilt, and anxiety. In addition, because high-scoring persons have frequent experiences of extreme emotions (both positive and negative), they tend to suffer the physical consequences of this emotional involvement. Emotions activate the sympathetic nervous system, making the person aroused. Even strong *positive* emotions activate the sympathetic nervous system and produce wear and tear on the nervous system. High-scoring persons tend to exhibit physical symptoms that result from their chronic emotional lifestyles, such as muscle tension, stomachaches, headaches, and fatigue. An interesting finding is that, even though they report more of these physical symptoms, high-scoring persons are not particularly unhappy or upset by them (Larsen, Billings, & Cutler, 1996). Interviews with high-scoring persons usually show that they have no desire to change their level of emotional intensity. They seem to

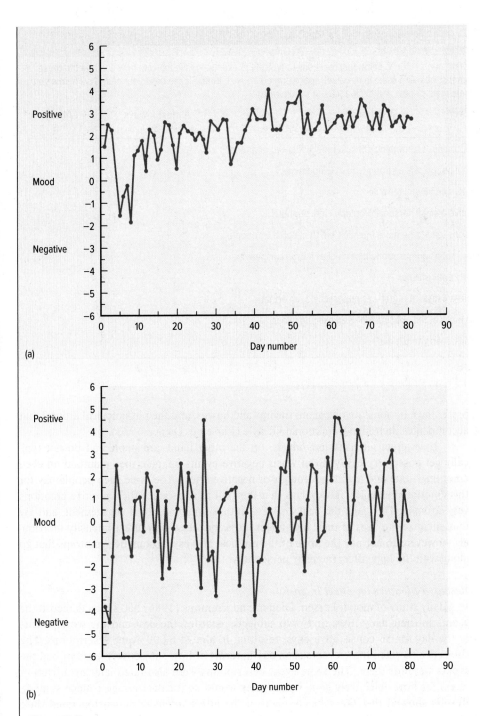

(a)

(b)

Figure 13.7

Data from individual subjects who kept a mood diary every day for three consecutive months. (a) Data from subject A. (b) Data from Subject B, who has much more intense moods and larger day-to-day mood swings than Subject A.

Source: Adapted from Larsen 1991.

Table 13.5 AIM Questionnaire

INSTRUCTIONS: The following statements refer to emotional reactions to typical life events. Please indicate how *you* react to these events by placing a number from the following scale in the blank space preceding each item. Please base your answers on how *you* react, *not* on how you think others react or how you think a person should react.

Never	Almost Never	Occasionally	Usually	Almost Always	Always
1	2	3	4	5	6

1. _____ When I accomplish something difficult, I feel delighted or elated.

2. _____ When I feel happy, it is a strong type of exuberance.

3. _____ I feel pretty bad when I tell a lie.

4. _____ When I solve a small personal problem, I feel euphoric.

5. _____ My emotions tend to be more intense than those of most people.

6. _____ My happy moods are so strong that I feel as if I were in heaven.

7. _____ I get overly enthusiastic.

8. _____ If I complete a task I thought was impossible, I am ecstatic.

9. _____ My heart races at the anticipation of an exciting event.

10. _____ Sad movies deeply touch me.

Source: Copyright 1984, Randy J. Larsen, PhD.

prefer the emotional involvement, the ups and downs, and the physiological arousal that accompanies their highly emotional lifestyle (Larsen & Diener, 1987).

Low affect intensity individuals, on the other hand, are stable and do not typically get upset very easily. Even when negative events happen, they maintain an even emotional state and avoid the troughs of negative affect. The price such people pay for this emotional stability, however, is that they fail to experience their positive emotions very strongly. They lack the peaks of zest, enthusiasm, emotional engagement, and joy that energize the lives of their high-affect intensity peers. Low affect intensity individuals, however, do not pay the price of the physical and psychosomatic symptoms that go along with the high affect intensity personality.

Research Findings on Affect Intensity

In a daily study of mood, Larsen, Diener, and Emmons (1986) had subjects record the events in their daily lives. Sixty-two subjects recorded the best and the worst events of the day for 56 consecutive days, resulting in almost 6,000 event descriptions. The subjects also rated these events each day in terms of how subjectively good or bad the events were for them. The same event descriptions were also rated later by a team of raters for how objectively good or bad they would be for the average college student. Results showed that the subjects high on the affect intensity dimension rated their life events as significantly *more severe* than did the low affect intensity subjects. That is, events that were rated as only "moderately good" by the objective raters (such as receiving a compliment from a professor) were rated as "very good" by the high affect intensity subjects. Similarly, events that were rated as only "moderately bad" by the objective raters (such as losing a favorite pen) tended to be rated as "very bad" by the high affect intensity subjects. Thus, the high affect intensity subjects tended to evaluate the events in their lives—both good and bad events—as having significantly more emotional impact than did the low affect intensity subjects. High affect intensity individuals are thus more emotionally reactive to common emotion-provoking events in their lives, both the good and the bad events.

An aspect of these findings worth emphasizing is that high affect intensity individuals are more reactive to *both* positive and negative events in their lives. Consequently, high affect intensity individuals should exhibit more **mood variability**, or more frequent fluctuations in their emotional lives over time. Larsen (1987) found that individuals high on the affect intensity dimension do, in fact, exhibit more frequent changes in their moods and that these changes tend to be larger in magnitude than are the mood changes of low affect intensity individuals.

During an interview, a high affect intensity subject reported that, to her, the worst thing in life was to be bored. She reported that she often did things to liven up her life, such as playing practical jokes on her roommates. Although such activities sometimes backfired and got her into trouble, she felt that it was worth it to obtain the stimulation. Another high affect intensity subject described himself as an "intensity junkie," hooked on the need for an emotionally stimulating lifestyle. A review of what else is known about individual differences in affect intensity can be found in Larsen (2009).

Interaction of Content and Style in Emotional Life

People differ from each other in terms of the relative amounts of positive and negative emotional *content* in their lives over time, as well as in terms of the *stylistic* intensity of their emotional experiences. In trying to understand emotional life as an aspect of personality, it appears that the hedonic balance—the ratio of pleasant to unpleasant emotions in a person's life over time—represents the content of emotional life. For example, Larsen (2000b) reported that the average college student had a positive hedonic balance on 7 out of 10 days. That is, out of every 10 days, 7 of them contained predominantly positive emotions, and 3 of them contained a predominance of negative emotions. However, there were wide individual differences, so that some people had as few as 20 percent positive days, whereas others had as many as 95 percent positive days. This hedonic balance between positive and negative affect, between the good and bad days in a person's life over time, represents the hedonic content of emotional life (Zelenski & Larsen, 2000).

Affect intensity represents the style of emotional life and refers to the magnitude of a person's typical emotional reactions. Together, these two characteristics—content and style—provide a good deal of descriptive and explanatory power. An interesting aspect of these two dimensions is that hedonic balance and affect intensity are unrelated to each other (Larsen & Diener, 1985). This means that there are people who have frequent positive affect of low intensity and others who have frequent positive affect of high intensity. Similarly, there are people who have frequent negative affect of low intensity and others who have frequent negative affect of high intensity. In other words, hedonic balance interacts with affect intensity to produce specific types of emotional lives that may characterize different personalities. The effects of this interaction of hedonic balance and affect intensity in creating emotional life are illustrated in Figure 13.8.

In Figure 13.8, you can see that individuals high and low on the affect intensity dimension typically experience the content of their emotional lives in very different ways. A person low in affect intensity has an emotional life that is characterized by its enduringness, evenness, and lack of fluctuation. If such a person also happens to be a happy person (more positive than negative emotional content in life), then he or she experiences this happiness as a tranquil sort of enduring contentment. If he or she happens to

	Low affect intensity	High affect intensity
Frequent positive affect	Emotional life experienced as contentment, easygoing composure, serenity, and tranquil calmness	Emotional life experienced as exuberance, animated joyfulness, and zestful enthusiasm
Frequent negative affect	Emotional life experienced as chronic melancholia, mild but persistent unhappiness, dejection, and discontentment	Emotional life experienced as acute and agitated negative affect, distress, aggravation, depression, and episodes of strong anxiety

Figure 13.8

Quality of emotional life as a function of content (hedonic balance) and style (affect intensity).

be an unhappy person (less positive than negative emotional content in life), then his or her emotional life consists of a chronic and somewhat annoying or irritating level of negative affect over time. On the other hand, a person high on the affect intensity dimension has an emotional life characterized by abruptness, changeableness, and volatility. If this kind of person also happens to be a happy person, then he or she experiences this happiness as enlivened and animated spikes of enthusiasm and exhilaration. If this high affect intensity person is, instead, an unhappy person, then he or she experiences troughs of a variety of strong negative emotions, such as anxiety, guilt, depression, and loneliness.

SUMMARY AND EVALUATION

Emotions can be thought of either as states or as traits, and both of these are patterns of experience, physiological changes, and changes in behavior, or action tendencies. Emotional states are short-lived and are typically caused by an event in the environment. As traits, however, emotions are consistent and stable patterns of experience in a person's life, where these patterns are due mostly to the person's personality. In this chapter, we looked at emotions as traits. For example, people differ from each other in how often they are angry, happy, or depressed. Such differences can be useful in describing aspects of personality.

Emotional content is the type of emotional experience that a person is likely to have. If we know, for example, the typical content of a person's emotional life, then we know the kinds of emotions he or she is likely to experience over time.

Emotional content can be broadly divided into the pleasant and the unpleasant emotions. In the pleasant emotion category, are happiness and the associated judgment of life satisfaction. On most people's lists of primary emotions, there is only one major pleasant emotion, whereas there are many varieties of unpleasant emotions. From a trait perspective, under pleasant emotions, we discussed dispositional happiness. Some people are happier than others, and psychologists are developing theories and gathering data to understand why people differ on happiness and how people might increase their level of trait happiness.

In terms of dispositional negative emotions, we discussed three emotion traits: anxiety, depression, and anger. Trait anxiety has many names in the personality literature, including neuroticism and negative affectivity. This trait appears to have distinct cognitive components and is related to ongoing health, especially self-reported health. Depression is another emotional trait that is also defined as a syndrome of associated experiences and behaviors, and we examined several cognitive theories of depression, as well as a neurotransmitter theory of depression. Anger proneness and aggression were also discussed as trait affects, and we examined brain abnormalities associated with this disposition. Anxiety, depression, and anger are currently topics of intense interest for neuroscientists, and data are accumulating on the brain centers involved in the experience, as well as the regulation, of each of these emotions.

Emotional style is the typical way in which a person experiences emotions. We focused on the stylistic component of affect intensity, or the typical magnitude with which people experience emotions. Persons who score high on the affect intensity dimension have larger emotional reactions to the events in their lives, are reactive to both pleasant and unpleasant events, and are more variable in their day-to-day moods. Content and style interact within persons to produce distinct varieties of emotional lives.

KEY TERMS

emotions 402
action tendencies 402
functional analysis 402
emotional states 403
emotional traits 403
categorical approach 403
dimensional approach 404
content 406
style 406
happiness 407

positive illusions 408
reciprocal causality 409
Easterlin paradox 413
mood induction 416
neuroticism 419
limbic system 420
anterior cingulate 421
prefrontal cortex 421
depression 424
diathesis-stress model 404

cognitive schema 425
cognitive triad 425
self-fulfilling prophecy 426
neurotransmitter theory of depression 427
hostility 427
affect intensity 430
mood variability 433

Lightspring/Shutterstock

Approaches to the Self

14

THE COGNITIVE/EXPERIENTIAL DOMAIN

There are many aspects to the self: the way we see and define ourselves, or our self-concept; the evaluation we make of that self-concept, which is called self-esteem; and our social identities, which are the outward reflections we show other people.
B2M Productions/Getty Images

"Know thyself!" was the advice given by the Greek Oracle at Delphi. Do you know yourself? Who are you? How would you answer this question? Would you define yourself first as a student, as a son or daughter, or as someone's spouse or boy- or girlfriend? Or would you define yourself by listing your various characteristics: "I am smart, optimistic, and confident"? Or would you instead give a physical description: "I am a male, 6 feet 6 inches tall, about 200 pounds, with red hair and a ruddy complexion"? No matter how you respond to this question, your answer is an important part of your **self-concept**, and your understanding of yourself. Moreover, some people are satisfied with who they are, whereas others are dissatisfied with their self-concept. How you *feel* about who you are is your **self-esteem**. On top of this, you have a **social identity** as you present yourself to others. Sometimes social identity does not match our self-concept, and the selves we present to others are not the selves we know ourselves to be, leading some of us to feel false or phony in our relationships.

In this chapter, we explore how psychologists have approached the notion of the self. We do this by considering the three main components of the self: self-concept, self-esteem, and social identity.

Why might we want to learn about the self? To most people, their sense of self is their anchor, their frame of reference for interpreting everything around them. For example, when you look at a group photo on a friend's Facebook page, whom in the group do you look at first? If you are like most people, you will say that you look at yourself first. And when looking at the photo of yourself, you immediately engage in an evaluation. You might think the picture is not a good representation, that it does not show you in the best light. Maybe you think that you have a nicer smile than that and that you are, in fact, a happier person than this picture portrays. Or you might think that you have put on a few pounds during the COVID pandemic, that you are heavier than your friends in the photo. Maybe you dislike the fact that you have gotten heavier, and a small blow to your self-esteem occurs when you look at the photo. Or maybe you wonder how certain other people would view this photo of you. Would your parents like to see you this way? A potential employer?

Our sense of self is changing all the time. In infancy, we first distinguished ourselves from the world around us and began the lifelong process of constructing, evaluating, and presenting to others our sense of who we are. During this process, we constantly undergo challenges and changes to our self-concept. For example, in high school, a young man might try out for the basketball team and do poorly. His sense of himself as an athlete is challenged by this experience of failure. He will have to search for other ways of defining himself. Maybe he will dye his hair purple and start wearing a trench coat to school, beginning to define himself in terms of an alternative teen lifestyle. High school and college are years in which many people struggle with defining their self-concept, and it is a time when people are especially sensitive to events that challenge their sense of self.

Once people have a fairly stable sense of themselves, they begin to use that to evaluate events and objects in the world. For example, when something happens to a person, such as a young woman's breakup with a boyfriend, she evaluates that event from the perspective of her self-concept and whether the event is good or bad for who she thinks she is. If having this boyfriend was an important part of her self-concept ("I'm nothing without him.") (Aron et al., 2004), then she evaluates the breakup as devastating. On the other hand, if the young woman has a sense of herself that is rooted in other areas of her life (e.g., academics, friendships, sports) that are mostly independent of her relationship with the young man, then the breakup is less devastating.

Our sense of who we are leads us to evaluate events in the world in certain ways. Only events that are important to our sense of self will have any strong impact either way, as very good or very bad. For example, if doing well in school is not part of your self-concept (maybe you are in college for other reasons), then doing poorly on an academic assignment will not affect you much.

People do not always like or value what they see when they turn inward and evaluate (like–dislike) their self-concept. Liking one's self-concept is high self-esteem. For example, two people may both tend to save money rather than spend it, to not leave tips at restaurants, and to always buy the cheapest things. One of these persons views herself as frugal and conservative, and she evaluates this self-as-thrifty to be a positive characteristic. She has positive self-esteem, at least as far as these attributes go. The second person may see himself as stingy, ungenerous, and without compassion. He views these characteristics as negative. Consequently, he has low self-esteem, at least as far as these attributes go. Both have the same self-concept, of being thrifty and hoarding their money, but differ in how they evaluate those characteristics and hence in their self-esteem.

Finally, social identity is the self that is shown to other people. This is the relatively enduring part of ourselves that we use to create an impression, to let other people know who we are and what can be expected from us. For instance, your driver's license, which is often used for social identification purposes, contains information about your social identity: your family name; your first name; your gender and racial identity; your date of birth; your address; your physical description, such as height, weight, and eye color. These characteristics differentiate you from other people and form some of the more visible and socially available aspects of your social identity. Other, less available aspects of your social identity include how you are perceived by others, your social reputation, and the impression that others have of your personality. Maybe you are the kind of person who wants to be taken seriously, so it is important for you to have a very businesslike social identity. Maybe you are the kind of person who wants to be liked by most people, so you strive to have a social identity as a friendly and agreeable person.

The three components of the self—self-concept, self-esteem, and social identity—are all vitally important in our day-to-day lives. Personality psychologists have studied these aspects of the self and have generated a good deal of knowledge about them. We begin this chapter with a focus on the descriptive component of the self—the self-concept.

Descriptive Component of the Self: Self-Concept

Knowledge of the self does not happen all at once. It develops over years, starting in infancy, accelerating in adolescence, and reaching completion in old age. The self-concept is the basis for self-understanding, and it forms the answer to the question "Who am I?"

Development of the Self-Concept

The first glimmer of a self-concept occurs in infancy, when the child learns that some things are always there (e.g., its body) and some things are there only sometimes (e.g., the mother's breast). The child makes a distinction between its own body and everything else: It discovers that boundaries exist between what is "me" and what is "not me." Gradually, the infant comes to realize that it is distinct from the rest of the world. This distinction forms the rudimentary sense of self, and awareness of one's body.

Have you ever seen a dog bark at its own reflection in a mirror? The dog barks because it does not recognize that the image is a reflection of itself. Dogs soon get bored with mirrors and ignore their reflections. Humans, some primates, and at least one elephant (see Application) do recognize that the mirror is a self-reflection. Psychologists have devised a clever technique for studying whether a human or animal recognizes its own reflection. It is called the "dot and mirror" test. They place a small mark on the face that cannot be seen without a mirror, such as a dot on the forehead. Then, when faced with the mirror, the psychologists look to see if the human or animal uses the reflection to touch the mark on its own face. Chimpanzees and orangutans do exhibit self-recognition with the dot and mirror test and will find the mark after about two to three days with the mirror (Gallup, 1977a). Studies of lower primates, such as the macaque, do not find that they exhibit self-recognition with mirrors, even after 2,400 hours of exposure to the mirror (Gallup, 1977b). Animals that have passed the dot and mirror test of self-recognition include all of the great apes (bonobos, chimpanzees, gorillas, orangutans, and humans), and at least one elephant. Researchers using a modified version of the dot and mirror test argue that bottlenose dolphins, orcas, and one species of magpie demonstrate self-recognition (Prior, Schwarz, & Güntürkün, 2008).

In normal children, self-recognition with the dot and mirror test occurs on average at the age of 18 months (Lewis & Ramsay, 2004). There is, however, some variability in the age of onset of self-recognition, with 15 months being the earliest documented case, and age 24 months being the point at which all or almost all children demonstrate self-recognition. Interestingly, pretend play appears to require self-recognition (Lewis & Ramsay, 2004). A child pretending to feed a doll imaginary food or a child drinking an imaginary liquid from a cup must know that what he or she is doing is not real. Pretending behavior requires that the child distinguish "this is what I pretend to be doing" from "this is what I actually am doing." In a study of children aged 15-21 months, only those children who exhibited self-recognition to a mirror were capable of pretend play (Lewis & Ramsay, 2004). Moreover, children do not begin using personal pronouns (I, me, mine) until they gain self-recognition abilities in the mirror test. Self-recognition is therefore an important cognitive developmental achievement that allows the child to go on to more complex manifestations of self-awareness, such as engaging in pretend play and representing the self in language with personal pronouns.

Application

Happy, an Asian Elephant who passed the dot and mirror test

Happy is a female Asian elephant at the Bronx Zoo. In 2005 scientists set up a camera overlooking the elephant pen there to conduct the dot-test for self-recognition. Happy and two of her pen-mates—Maxine and Patty, also Asian elephants—were in the pen and participated in the testing. The scientists bolted a large mirror to the wall and gave the elephants time to get used to it. After that, they painted a large white X on the right forehead of each elephant. When they next faced the mirror, neither Patty nor Maxine seemed to notice. Happy, on the other hand, did. She paused to look at herself several times in the mirror. She then repeatedly touched the X on her right forehead with her trunk. Happy returned to the mirror many times. In all, she touched the mark on her forehead 12 times that day. This made Happy the first elephant to clearly pass this self-recognition test.

Happy was back in the news in 2022 (see *The New Yorker,* March 7, 2022). Lawyers for the Nonhuman Rights Project filed a suit on her behalf, saying that she should have the right not to be illegally detained by the Zoo. Known as a writ of habeas corpus—the right not to be illegally detained—it has only been applied to persons in the United States. The lawyers argued, in part, that Happy clearly has the human-like capacity for self-recognition, and therefore, she should have the same rights as a person, at least the right not to be detained. Basically, they were making the case that Happy should be considered, in the eyes of the legal system, a person. While the lawyers filing her case ultimately lost, the ruling judge did agree that "Happy is more than just a legal 'thing,' or property." And while the judge agreed that Happy is smart and self-aware and should be treated with respect and dignity, she (the judge) concluded that "Happy is not a 'person,' and is not being illegally imprisoned" by the Bronx Zoo.

Photo of Happy, an Asian elephant in the Bronx zoo, who has passed a test of self-recognition.
Bebeto Matthews/AP Photo

Although very young children are fascinated with their reflections, it takes a while for a child to be able to recognize photographs of him- or herself in a group. A child needs to be about 2 years old before he or she can pick his or her picture out of a crowd (Baumeister, 1991). Around this time, the second year of life, children begin to grasp the idea that other people have expectations for them. For example, this is about the time when children can follow rules set up by parents. Children learn that some behaviors are good and other behaviors are bad, and they evaluate their own behavior against these standards. They will smile when they do something good and frown when something bad occurs. They clearly are developing a sense of themselves relative to standards. This is the beginning of self-esteem as well as the beginnings of a conscience (sense of right and wrong).

Among the first aspects of the self that people learn to identify and associate with themselves are sex and age. This typically occurs between 2 and 3 years of age, when a child begins to call himself a boy or herself a girl and to refer to other children as boys or girls. A rudimentary knowledge of age also develops, with a child often learning to hold up the number of fingers that designate age. Children at this age also expand their self-concept to include references to a family. "I'm Sarah's brother," a child might say, implying that part of his self-concept includes being in the same family as Sarah.

From age 3 to about 12, children's self-concepts are based mainly on developing talents and skills. The child thinks of him- or herself as someone who can do this or cannot do that, such as reciting the alphabet, tying his own shoes, reading, walking to school by herself, telling time, or writing in cursive handwriting. At this age, the self-concept is defined mainly in terms of sex, age, family of origin, and what the child believes he or she can or cannot do.

Starting with the school years, ages 5 or 6 onward, children increasingly begin to compare their skills and abilities with those of others. They are now either better than or worse than other children. This is the beginning of **social comparison**, which most people engage into varying degrees for the rest of their lives (Baumeister, 1997). Social comparison is the evaluation of oneself or one's performance in terms of a comparison with a reference group. "Am I faster, smarter, more popular, more attractive, and so on than my friends?" is the question that children repeatedly ask themselves during this period of development.

Also during this time, children learn that they can lie and keep secrets. This is based on the realization that there is a hidden side to the self, a side that includes private attributes, such as thoughts, feelings, and desires. The realization that "Mommy doesn't know everything about me" is a big step. The development of an inner, **private self-concept** is a major but often difficult development in the growth of the self-concept. It may start out with children developing an imaginary friend, someone only they can see or hear. This imaginary friend may actually be the children's first attempt to communicate to their parents that they know there is a secret part, an inner part, to their understanding of the self. Later, children develop the full realization that only they have access to their own thoughts, feelings, and desires and that no one else can know this part of themselves unless the child chooses to tell others. Because they now know that some information is private, not known by others, they have the newly acquired ability to lie or hide information. Telling their first lie is a big step forward in the development of a child's self-concept.

As children grow from childhood to adolescence, their self-concept changes from one based on such concrete characteristics as physical appearance, abilities, and family relationships to one that is based on more abstract psychological terms. We illustrate this below with examples drawn from Montemayor and Eisen (1977). The statements are from children of different ages all answering the question "Who am I?"

The following is from a 9-year-old boy in the 4th grade. Notice how concrete his description is and that he uses mostly tangible concepts such as age, sex, name, address, and other aspects of his physical self:

> *My name is Bruce. I have brown eyes and brown hair. And I have brown eyebrows. I am nine years old. I LOVE sports. I have seven people in my family. I have great eyesight and I have lots of friends. I will be 10 in September. I live at 1923 Pinecrest. I am a boy. I have an uncle that is almost 7 feet tall. My school is Pinecrest and my teacher is Mrs V. I play Hockey.*

The next statement is from a girl aged 11½ in the 6th grade. Notice that she frequently refers to her likes and also emphasizes more abstract personality and social characteristics:

> *My name is Alice. I am a human being. I am a girl. I am a truthful person. I am not pretty. I do so-so in my studies. I am a very good cellist and a very good pianist. I am a little bit tall for my age. I like several boys and girls. I am old-fashioned. I play tennis and am a very good swimmer. I try to be helpful. I am always ready to be friends with anybody. Mostly I am good, but I lose my temper. I am not well-liked by some girls. I don't know if I'm liked by boys or not.*

The final example is from a 17-year-old girl in the 12th grade. Notice how she emphasizes interpersonal characteristics, her typical mood states, and several ideological and belief references in her self-description:

> *I am a human being. I am a girl. I am an individual. I don't know who I am. I am a Pisces. I am a moody person. I am an indecisive person. I am an ambitious person. I am a very curious person. I am not an individual. I am a loner. I am an American (God help me). I am a Democrat. I am a liberal person. I am a radical. I am a conservative. I am a pseudoliberal. I am an atheist. I am not a classifiable person (i.e., I don't want to be classified).*

A final unfolding of the self-concept, during the teen years, involves **perspective taking:** the ability to take the perspectives of others, or to see oneself as others do, to step outside of oneself and imagine how one appears to other people. This is why many teenagers go through a period of extreme self-consciousness during adolescence, focusing much of their concerns on how they appear to others. You might vividly recall this period of your life, the strong emotions involved in episodes of **objective self-awareness,** of seeing yourself as an object of others' attention. Remember going to gym class in your funny gym uniform or that first trip to the beach in your new swimsuit? Often, objective self-awareness is experienced as shyness, and for some people this is a chronic problem.

Because shyness is such a common problem, especially during the adolescent years, we added A Closer Look on this topic. We will mention here that, because shy people are anxious about interacting with others, they often avoid opportunities to socialize. One way to avoid face-to-face interaction is to socialize online, where the interaction is more controllable, proceeds more slowly, and provides limited information exchange (e.g., no nonverbal information). Also, when with others, one way to avoid having to interact with them is to take out your cell phone and give the device all your attention. Researchers have found that young adults with social anxiety (shyness) are more likely to use the internet excessively (Weinstein et al., 2015). In fact, internet use can reach problematic proportions for shy individuals, such that they can appear "addicted" to their smartphones (Bian & Leung, 2015)—that is, they become preoccupied and have trouble controlling their phone use, experience productivity loss, feel anxiety or "lost" without their phone, and report FOMO (Fear of Missing Out). Other studies of young adults focused on excessive use of Facebook (to the point of interfering with school work) and found that social anxiety was correlated with problematic Facebook usage (Lee-Won, Herzog, & Park, 2015). Other researchers have examined excessive online gaming and again found that persons high in social anxiety spent more hours gaming per week than persons without social anxiety (Lee & Leeson, 2015). Several recent studies show that the strongest personality predictor of problematic internet use is shyness or social anxiety (e.g., Carli & Durkee, 2016; Huan et al., 2014). While there are certainly socially beneficial ways to use the internet (for communication, to stay in

In the development of the self, children learn to compare themselves to others. "I'm faster than you" is a phrase commonly heard whenever a group of young children gather. This is the beginning of social comparison, whereby people define and evaluate themselves in comparison to others.
Sergey Novikov/Shutterstock

touch, to gather information), we all have had the experience of being socially ignored by someone preoccupied with their smartphone. Shy persons are at risk for developing these preoccupations, presumably because it gives them a means to avoid IRL (In Real Life) socializing, the very behavior they should work on increasing.

In summary, the self-concept is a distinct knowledge structure made up of many different elements and stored in our memories much as we might store a cognitive map of our hometown. Part of developing a sense of self lies in being able to see yourself through the eyes of others and, while this perspective can be a valuable skill to have, it can sometimes make a person feel uncomfortable and produce shyness.

Self-Schemata: Possible Selves, Ought Selves, and Undesired Selves

So far, we have considered some of the main steps in the development of a self-concept. Once formed, the self-concept provides a person with a sense of continuity and a framework for understanding the past and present and for guiding future behavior.

The self-concept is a network of information in our memories (similar to the network model of memory introduced in Chapter 10), which organizes and provides coherence to the ways in which we experience the self (Markus, 1983). The self-concept also guides how each person processes information about him- or herself (Markus & Nurius, 1986). For example, people more easily process information that is consistent with their self-concepts; if you see yourself as highly masculine, then you will quickly agree with statements such as the following: "I am assertive" and "I am strong."

The term **self-schema** (*schema* is singular; *schemata* is plural) refers to the specific knowledge structure, or cognitive representation, of the self-concept. For example, a person might have a schema about

One way some people avoid social interaction is by directing all their attention to their smartphone. Studies show that shyness is often associated with smartphone "addiction."
DisobeyArt/Shutterstock

A Closer Look

Shyness: When Objective Self-Awareness Becomes Chronic

Garrison Keillor, the popular host of the *Prairie Home Companion* radio show, suffers from acute shyness and has openly discussed this in articles and in interviews. He says that when shy persons have to be in an interaction, they just want to become invisible. They dislike conversation because they lack social confidence, are made terribly anxious by the interaction, and are not good at promoting themselves. Because of these feelings, the shy person withdraws from social interaction.

Many accomplished people are shy, including singers Barbra Streisand and Lady GaGa and writer J.K. Rowling. Abraham Lincoln was said to be painfully shy. What shy persons have in common is that they desire friendships and social interactions but are held back by their insecurities and fears. Consequently, they avoid the

spotlight; avoid face-to-face interaction; and ruminate excessively after conversations, worrying about whether they said the right things, made a good impression, or sounded stupid. The inner experience of a shy person in an interaction is quite different from that of someone else in the same interaction who is not shy.

Shy people are not necessarily introverts (Cheek, 1989). Introverts prefer to be alone; they enjoy the peace and quiet of solitude. Shy people, on the other hand, want to have contact with others, to be socially involved, and to have friends and be part of the group. But shy persons' self-doubt and self-consciousness prompt them to pass up opportunities to socialize (Henderson & Zimbardo, 2001a, 2001b; see www.shyness.com). They handicap themselves; by not entering groups, not

speaking to unfamiliar people, and not approaching others, they deny themselves the opportunities to learn and practice the very social skills they need to overcome their shyness (see Table 14.1).

Psychologist Jerome Kagan (1929–2021) was a psychologist at Harvard who studied shyness for several decades (Kagan, 1981, 1994, 1999). In his studies of infants, he found that about 20 percent of 4-month-old babies exhibit signs of shyness—they flail their arms and legs and cry when presented with an unfamiliar object or person. Following up these infants for several years, Kagan found that most of them exhibited signs of shyness as young children. For example, in play situations, they often did not move very far from their parents, and some even clung to their parents, not leaving their sides at all when

Table 14.1 Example Items from the Henderson/Zimbardo Shyness Questionnaire

INSTRUCTIONS: Rate each item using a number from the following scale to indicate how characteristic that statement is of you.

Not at all Characteristic 1	Somewhat Characteristic 2	Often Characteristic 3	Very Characteristic 4	Extremely Characteristic 5

1. I am afraid of looking foolish in social situations.

2. I often feel insecure in social situations.

3. Other people appear to have more fun in social situations than I do.

4. If someone rejects me I assume that I have done something wrong.

5. It is hard for me to approach people who are having a conversation.

6. I feel lonely a good deal of the time.

7. I tend to be more critical of other people than I appear to be.

8. It is hard for me to say "no" to unreasonable requests.

9. I do more than my share on projects because I can't say no.

10. I find it easy to ask for what I want from other people.

Source: Adapted from "The Henderson Zimbardo Shyness Questionnaire: A New Scale to Measure Chronic Shyness," by L. Henderson and P. Zimbardo, 2000, The Shyness Institute, 644 Cragmont Ave., Berkeley, CA 94708. Copyright 2000 by The Shyness Institute. All rights reserved. Reprinted with permission of The Shyness Institute.

there were unfamiliar children around. Following them for a few more years, Kagan found that roughly half of the shy children were transformed and were no longer shy in later childhood. In looking at parenting practices, Kagan found that the parents of these formerly shy children had encouraged their children to socialize. That is, these parents often pushed their children to join groups and to talk to other children, and they had given their children lots of praise for socializing. Kagan referred to this as "tough love," in that the parents had to push the reluctant and complaining children to play with peers. However, a few years later, the result was children who were much less shy. The parents of the children who remained shy often had given in to the children's reluctance to join groups. That is, when the children complained or resisted joining a group, the parents typically gave in, not pushing the children to socialize. As a result, such children never learned that they could overcome their self-doubt and lack of social confidence (Kagan, 1999).

Other research has shown that parents who are too controlling and protective toward their children often have children who are shy and anxious (Wood et al., 2003). Being over-protective is captured by the phrase "helicopter" parenting or "battleship" parenting (parents who pro-actively remove all obstacles for their children). A recent study of "helicopter" parents has shown that, while such parents think protecting their children from the challenges of childhood is good, ultimately children of such parents often develop social difficulties in adolescence, such as shyness and social anxiety (Srivastav & Mathur, 2020).

Psychologists studying shyness sometimes prefer the term *social anxiety*, which is defined as discomfort related to social interactions, or even to the anticipation of social interactions (Chavira, Stein, & Malcarne, 2002). Adults with social anxiety report that they are nervous or that they feel awkward when talking to others, especially people with whom they are unfamiliar (Cheek & Buss, 1981). Socially anxious persons appear to be overly concerned about what others will think. After a conversation, they often conclude that they said something wrong, sounded foolish, or looked stupid (Ritts & Patterson, 1996). Sometimes the social anxiety is so strong that it shows in various outward signs, such as a trembling voice or jittery movements. Other people interacting with a socially anxious person often interpret their behavior as unfriendliness, rather than as shyness (Cheek & Buss, 1981). Sometimes shy persons are so overcome with anxiety that it hinders their ability to carry on a conversation. They may spend time staring at their shoes, rather than talking, because they cannot think of a thing to say.

In an interesting study, researchers asked participants to work on a unique task, one that could not be completed without having to ask another person for help (DePaulo et al., 1989). The researchers deliberately created this task so they could investigate whether shy persons would reach out to others when they really needed to. They found that the socially anxious participants were reluctant to ask for help from another person, presumably because the shy person is anxious that the other may rebuff a request for help.

Shy people also tend to interpret social interactions negatively; they are more likely to interpret a comment as a criticism than as a helpful suggestion. For example, DePaulo et al. (1987) had students work in groups, then write reports on each other's performance. They were then individually interviewed about what they thought the others had said about them. It turns out that the shy participants thought that the others liked them less and that the others thought they were less competent. It seems that shy people also expect that others will dislike them. These expectations may lead them to avoid interactions or cut conversations short, losing the very opportunities they need to overcome their shyness.

What makes shy people so socially anxious? Kagan held that some of it is due to genetics. After all, shyness shows up in some infants very early in life. However, some of this social anxiety must also be learned. What most researchers believe is that shy persons have learned to put too much stock in other people's judgments of them. This is called evaluation apprehension, the idea that shy persons are apprehensive about being evaluated by others. As a consequence, just the thought of going out on stage or leading a group meeting fills them with dread. And so they avoid such situations. When forced into interaction, they try to limit it or cut it short. They avoid eye contact, which indicates to others that they prefer to end the conversation. When forced into conversation, they try to keep it impersonal and nonthreatening. They do a lot of agreeing, nodding their heads, without getting too involved in the conversation. In sum, researchers believe that at the root of shyness is a fear of being evaluated negatively by others (Leary & Kowalski, 1995), which translates into a lack of confidence in social interactions and feeling that they lack the social skills necessary to navigate social situations (Cheek & Melchior, 1990).

Recent surveys estimate that 7–13 percent of persons in Western countries will experience social phobia, or extreme shyness, during their lifetime (Furmark, 2002). This suggests that shyness is not uncommon in the general population. Schmidt and Fox (2002) provide a review of the developmental course of shyness, as well as the varieties of shyness. For example, some shy persons are high in sociability and are distinguished by being especially anxious and fearful. Another type is shy persons who are low in sociability, who simply avoid others because of their excessive self-consciousness (Cheek & Krasnoperova, 1999). Empirically, however, it is difficult to distinguish owing to the overlap in the

(Continued)

A Closer Look (*Continued*)

characteristics. Self-reports of shyness do correlate strongly with peer reports of shyness, suggesting that this characteristic is visible to others (Zarevski et al., 2002).

Psychologists studying the brain have suggested that shy persons have a more reactive **amygdala,** which is a section of the limbic or emotional system of the brain that is most responsible for fear. A study by Kagan and colleagues followed up a group of adults who, at age 2 years, had been assessed for shyness. They found that the adults who were shy as children showed a greater fMRI response within the amygdala to novel versus familiar faces, compared to the nonshy adults (Schwartz et al., 2003). In another interesting study, researchers assessed cortisol (the stress hormone described in Chapter 7) on the first and fifth days of school among 35 first-graders (Bruce, Davis, & Gunnar, 2002). They found that most children showed an elevated cortisol response on the first day of school. However, the shy children showed an elevated and extended cortisol response even on the fifth day of school.

Whatever its causes, shyness can have problematic social implications for the shy person. Several studies have examined how shy persons use the internet to avoid face-to-face social interaction (e.g., Caplan, 2002). One study found that shy persons were more likely to use the internet for recreation rather than interact with others IRL (In Real Life) (Scealy, Phillips, & Stevenson, 2002).

Stocker (1997) reviewed much of what is known about helping shy persons overcome their difficulties. She offers seven concrete steps a shy person can take:

1. *Show up.* Shy persons want to avoid the situations that make them anxious. However, if you really want to overcome shyness, you've got to enter those uncomfortable situations: Go to a party or strike up a conversation with a stranger. Often, shy persons overestimate how uncomfortable they will feel; however, once they engage in an interaction, they find that it is not as bad as they had expected.

2. *Give yourself credit.* Stop being your own worst critic. In scorning or deriding their own social performance after the fact, shy persons are often very hard on themselves. If they make one little social faux pas, they often blow that misstep out of proportion, ignoring the fact that 99 percent of the interaction went well.

3. *Take baby steps.* It is useful to take big goals and break them into smaller steps. Instead of wanting to "become an engaging conversationalist," maybe try to set some smaller goals, such as going to a meeting of a group you've been wanting to join. The first time, you don't have to talk; just go and listen. The second time, maybe your goal will be to talk, not during the meeting but maybe to someone after the meeting is over. At the third

meeting, try to ask a question during the actual meeting by speaking up. The point is to set small goals and experience some small successes along the way.

4. *Give unto others.* Shy people, because they are nervous, are focused on themselves during conversations. Shift your attention to others; look at them when they talk, listen carefully to what they say, try to find something interesting and connect to that, ask questions, and give a compliment or a word of support. Paying attention outwardly toward other people will also get your attention off yourself and your own nervousness.

5. *Exude warmth.* The nervousness that shy people feel is often interpreted by others as unfriendliness or tension. Try to create a more positive nonverbal impression by smiling, making eye contact, and staying relaxed.

6. *Anticipate failure.* Overcoming shyness is a learning process. It will take practice, and small failures are inevitable. If you say something wrong in a conversation, chalk it up to the learning process, and get on with more practice.

7. *Join the crowd.* Nobody is perfect all the time. There are lots of people who are not perfect conversationalists. Also, you might think that making small talk is a big deal. However, when you really listen to other people's small talk, you'll realize that it really is just that—small talk, nothing more.

what it means to be masculine, and this schema might include such attributes as assertiveness, strength, and independence. As such, self-schemata are cognitive networks of associations that are built on past experiences and that guide the processing of information about the self.

Self-schemata usually refer to past and current aspects of the self. However, there are also schemata for future selves, which people are able to imagine. The term **possible selves** describe the many ideas people have about who they might become, who they hope to become, or who they fear they will become (Markus & Nurius, 1987). People often have specific desires, anxieties, fantasies, fears, hopes, and expectations about their own future selves (Oyserman, Destin, & Novin, 2015). Although possible selves are not based on actual past experiences, they nevertheless are part of the overall self-concept.

For example, are you the kind of person who could envision yourself becoming a scientist—that is, is this a possible self for you? Buday, Stake, and Petersen (2012) showed that possessing such a possible self as a scientist in high school predicted whether the participants were actually in a science career 10 years later. Other researchers have shown that future career selves in college predicted proactive career behaviors (e.g., visiting the job center on campus, signing up early for career fairs, and so forth; Strauss, Griffin, & Parker, 2012). One's future work self can be a strong motivating force for engaging in behaviors that prepare one for specific careers. Even older persons who are retired can have possible selves, such as future images of themselves as healthier, slimmer, and with several new and satisfying hobbies (Bolkan, Hooker, & Coehlo, 2015).

Because they play a role in defining the self-concept, possible selves may influence a person's behavior in certain ways. For example, a high-school student may have no idea what it would be like to be an astronaut. Nevertheless, because this is one of her possible selves, she has many thoughts and feelings about this image of herself as an astronaut. Information about astronauts, the space agency, aviation science, and so forth has personal significance for her, and she seeks it out every chance she gets. Thus, this possible self will influence her here and now in terms of her current decisions (e.g., to take an extra math course). Possible selves are like bridges between our present and our future; they are our working models of ourselves in the future (Oyserman & Markus, 1990). Such a working model might lead to problem behaviors, however, as when the possible self is a poor role model. In studying a group of juvenile delinquents, Oyserman and Saltz (1993) found that a high proportion had a possible self of *criminal,* and relatively few had such conventional possible selves as *having a job* or *getting along well in school.* A study of 8th graders found that those who could imagine themselves as problem drinkers (i.e., had a "problem drinker" possible self) were more likely, as 9th graders, to have experienced problematic alcohol use (Lee et al., 2015).

Possible selves allow us to stay on schedule, and to work toward self-improvement. Behaviors that stem from possible selves (desired or undesired) can activate a host of intense feelings and emotions. For example, to a person who does not have a possible self with coronary artery disease, missing a few weeks of an exercise program will not be as distressing as it is to a person who has such a possible self.

Psychologist Tory Higgins (1987, 1997, 1999) has elaborated on the possible selves notion by distinguishing the **ideal self**, which is what persons themselves want to be, from the **ought self**, which is persons' understanding of what others want them to be. The ought self is built on what people take as their responsibilities and commitments to others—what they ought to do. It is related to Carl Rogers' notion of conditions of worth, which we covered in Chapter 11. The ideal self is built on one's own desires and goals—what one wants to become. Higgins refers to the ought and the ideal selves as **self-guides,** standards that one uses to organize information and motivate appropriate behavior. The self-guides get their motivating properties from emotions. Higgins argues that these two types of possible selves are at the root of different emotions. If one's real self does not fit one's ideal self, then one will feel sad, despondent, and disappointed. If, on the other hand, one's real self does not fit one's ought self, then one will feel guilty, distressed, or embarrassed.

To summarize, self-schemata are cognitive networks of association built around elements of the self-concept. These include past, present, and future aspects of the self. The self-concept is the sum of people's self-schemata, what they know and believe and associate with themselves. One part of the self-concept concerns possible selves, future selves that people strive to attain or avoid. Who have I been, what am I like now, and what do I want to be like in the future—the answers to these questions define the self-concept.

Evaluative Component of the Self: Self-Esteem

The first glimmer of self-esteem occurs when children identify standards or expectations for behavior and live up to them. For example, parents have expectations for toilet training. When children finally master these expectations, it is a source of pride and self-esteem, at least until more demanding expectations and responsibilities are encountered. In later childhood, the next shift in the source of self-esteem occurs when children begin to engage in social comparison; children compare themselves to others, and if they are doing better than others, then they feel good about themselves. And later, people develop a set of internal standards, part of what they hold to be important to their self-concept. Behavior or experiences inconsistent with these internal standards can lead to decreases in self-esteem. In all cases, self-esteem results from an evaluation of oneself and one's behavior.

Evaluation of Oneself

Self-esteem is a general evaluation of self-concept elements along with a good–bad or like–dislike dimension: Do you generally like yourself and feel that you are a worthwhile, good person? Do you feel that others respect you? Do you feel that you are basically a decent, fair person? Do you take pride and satisfaction in what you have done, in who you are, and in who you would like to become? Self-esteem is the sum of your positive and negative evaluations of all the aspects of your self-concept.

Most of us have a mixed reaction to ourselves; we have to take the bad with the good, and we acknowledge that we have both strengths and weaknesses. How we feel about ourselves can change from day to day and even from hour to hour. When we do something that is not consistent with our self-concept, such as hurt someone's feelings, then we may experience a dip in self-esteem. Such fluctuations, however, occur around our average level of self-esteem. Most personality psychologists are interested in self-esteem in terms of a person's average level. Average levels of self-esteem do fluctuate across the lifespan in predictable ways. The average low point in self-esteem usually occurs in adolescence, followed by a gradual rise through midlife for most people (Donnellan et al., 2012; Wagner et al., 2013). Increases in self-esteem over time tend to accompany other positive life events, such as the development of intimate relationships, educational achievements, and career success (Wagner et al., 2013).

Personality researchers have begun to acknowledge that people can evaluate themselves positively or negatively in different areas of their lives. For example, you may feel pretty good about your intellectual and academic abilities, but perhaps you are shy with members of the opposite sex. Consequently, you may have high academic self-esteem but lower self-esteem when it comes to dating or feeling attractive to others. Global self-esteem may be a composite of several individual areas of self-evaluation. Each of these subareas can be assessed separately, and researchers can examine self-esteem about various domains of the self-concept. For example, there is a scale for measuring three aspects of self-esteem: performance self-esteem, appearance self-esteem, and social self-esteem (Rentzch & Schroeder-Abe, 2022).

Although there are distinct areas of life in which people can feel more or less confident of themselves—such as friendships, finances, academics, and appearance—self-esteem measures of these content areas are moderately correlated. This means that people who tend to have high self-esteem in one area also tend to have high self-esteem in the other areas. Sometimes researchers find it useful to examine specific areas of self-esteem,

Table 14.2 Items in a Global Self-Esteem Questionnaire

1.	True	False	I feel good about myself.
2.	True	False	I feel I am a person of worth, the equal of other people.
3.	True	False	I am able to do things as well as most other people.
4.	True	False	On the whole, I am satisfied with myself.
5.	True	False	I certainly feel useless at times.
6.	True	False	At times I think I am no good at all.
7.	True	False	I feel I do not have much to be proud of.

Source: Adapted from Marsh, 1996.

such as appearance self-esteem in persons at risk for eating disorders. However, the majority of researchers find it useful to think of self-esteem as the person's global or average evaluation of their whole self-concept. Table 14.2 shows a global self-esteem questionnaire that is widely used by researchers in this area. This measure assesses a person's overall self-esteem, and by reading and answering the items for yourself you will get an idea of what self-esteem means in terms of the measures used to assess this construct. High scores on self-esteem are obtained by answering items 1–4 as "True" and items 5–7 as "False."

Research on Self-Esteem

Much of the research on self-esteem concerns how people respond to evaluation. Being evaluated is a very common occurrence, especially during the high-school and college years. Homework is evaluated, tests are given, and students receive regular reports on their performance. Even outside school, a lot of play also involves evaluation, such as occurs with competitive games. In adulthood, the games change but the evaluation continues. At most jobs, there is usually some form of evaluation done on a regular basis, and employees receive regular feedback on their performance. There is also competition and evaluation in many other areas of adult life, such as finances, marriage, and children, where people often compare how they are doing with their peers and neighbors (i.e., keeping up with the Jonses). Because self-esteem is linked to evaluation and social comparison, much of the research on this topic concerns how people react to criticism and judging themselves relative to others.

Reactions to Criticism and Failure Feedback

Many laboratory studies have been conducted on how people high and low on self-esteem react to failure and criticism. In general, participants are taken into the laboratory and instructed to complete an important task. For example, they may be given an intelligence test and told that norms are being developed and that they should try to do the very best they can. Usually, this gets the participants very involved and motivates them to want to perform well. The researcher then "scores" the test when the subjects are finished, and the researcher is critical of the participants' performance, saying that they did very poorly. The research question is "How are high and low self-esteem persons affected by this criticism and personal failure?" The research has looked mainly at how

A Closer Look

"But How Do You Really Feel?" Measuring Implicit Self-Esteem

Recall the Closer Look from Chapter 11 on implicit motivation and research that compares peoples' explicit and implicit levels on particular motives. Implicit motivation was used to refer to the person's unconscious desires and aspirations, their unspoken needs and wants. A similar situation has arisen in the literature on self-esteem, with researchers developing an implicit measure of self-esteem to get at a person's unconscious view of their self-worth and to contrast this to the explicit level he or she reports on a questionnaire measure of self-esteem.

Greenwald and Farnham developed an implicit measure of self-esteem in 2000. It consists of a task done on the computer and does not rely on self-reports of how positively people see themselves. Instead, the task, called the Self-Esteem Implicit Association Test (SE-IAT), measures how quickly and consistently people associate positive words to themselves compared to how quickly and consistently they associate negative words to themselves. The task is described in detail in Greenwald and Farnham (2000).

Before actually undertaking the task, the participant is asked to generate 18 "me-type" items and 18 "not-me-type" items. Me-type items are things such as first and last name, phone number, birth month, birth year, and the zip code in which one lives. Not-me-type items are things like a state where one does not live, a street name that one does not live on, and so forth. The researcher also has two lists of words; one list contains positive words (e.g., smart, nice, joy, lucky) and the other list contains unpleasant words (e.g., stupid, despised, filth, poison).

When the task begins, the researcher presents pairs of words on the computer screen, with each pair containing either a me-type item or a not-me-type item paired with either a positive or a negative word.

The participant is instructed to categorize each pair, as quickly as he or she can, according to some rules, such as "If a me item is paired with a positive word, press the left key, and if a not-me item is paired with a positive word, press the right key." Participants are presented with many pairs of words and categorize each pair as quickly as they can according to the rule. The time it takes them to perform the categorization is measured by the computer in milliseconds.

An implicit self-esteem score is calculated by taking the average time it takes to categorize me-pleasant word pairs and subtracting the average time it takes to categorize me-unpleasant word pairs. A person with a small number is someone who is fast at categorizing me with pleasant words and relatively slow at categorizing me with unpleasant words, and we say that he or she has high implicit self-esteem. Such persons easily associate positive attributes to themselves. We say the measure is "implicit" because it does not rely on some conscious evaluation of themselves.

Studies have established that this implicit self-esteem measure has some degree of construct validity. For example, Izuma and colleagues (2018) conducted a study based on the idea that self-esteem is a positive attitude toward the self. Moreover, neuroscientists have shown that the reward centers in the brain are activated when a person views an image of an object they feel positively toward. Izuma and colleagues hypothesized that implicit self-esteem should correlate with reward center activation when people are viewing an image of their own face compared to viewing a stranger's face. This is exactly what the researchers found.

Other researchers have compared people's level of implicit to their level of explicit self-esteem. Explicit measures are questionnaires, such as that presented in Table 14.2. One particularly interesting line of research examines individuals who have high explicit self-esteem (they say they feel pretty good about themselves) yet have a low level of implicit self-esteem (they more quickly associate negative than positive words to themselves). This discrepancy in how one "really" feels about him- or herself is correlated with narcissism (Jordan et al., 2003). That is, on the outside, narcissists appear to have high self-esteem, but on the inside, they are insecure about their self-esteem. While some researchers have replicated these findings (e.g., Gregg & Sedikides, 2018), others have failed to find that narcissists have low implicit self-esteem (Mota et al., 2019). Further research is clearly needed to more fully understand the self-esteem dynamics of narcissists.

Other studies have examined discrepancies where explicit self-esteem is low (the person says they don't feel very good about themselves) yet implicit levels remain high (unconsciously they remain positive). This kind of discrepancy is associated with emotional problems, such as depression and feeling worthless (Leeuwis et al., 2015). Not all predicted effects for implicit self-esteem are found, however (e.g., Hawkins, Lesick & Zell, 2021), leading some researchers to question how this construct is conceptualized and measured (Jusepeitis & Rothermund, 2022).

As research accumulates on implicit and explicit self-esteem, and the discrepancies between the two, we will gain a better understanding of the dynamics of inner and outer manifestations of how people feel about themselves. Starting with a measure of some new concept, and then proceeding to ask questions about that new concept (and measure), is exactly how science progresses in personality psychology.

failure feedback affects subsequent performance on similar tasks, and whether failure affects high and low self-esteem persons differently (Brown & Dutton, 1995; Stake, Huff, & Zand, 1995). The findings suggest that, following failure, low self-esteem persons are more likely to give up earlier on subsequent tasks. For high self-esteem persons, on the other hand, failure feedback seems to spur them into action on subsequent tasks, and they are less likely to give up and more likely to work just as hard or harder on the second task as they did on the first (Brown & Dutton, 1995).

Why is it that failure seems to incapacitate low self-esteem persons but seems to encourage high self-esteem persons into renewed effort? Researchers think that people readily accept feedback that is consistent with their self-concept, so for low self-esteem persons, failure feedback on the first task is consistent with their self-concept, and it confirms their views that they are the kind of people who fail more than succeed. And so, when confronted with the second task, low self-esteem persons, who have just had their negative self-view confirmed with failing on the first task, believe they will also fail on the second task, and so do not try so hard or just give up. For high self-esteem persons, however, failure is not consistent with their existing self-concept, so they are more likely *not* to accept this feedback. Also, it is likely that they will discount the feedback, perhaps thinking that failure on the first task must have been an accident or a mistake. Consequently, they are motivated to try just as hard the second time, and not to give up, because they do not see their self-concept as the kind of people who fail. Psychologist Roy Baumeister and his colleagues (e.g., Baumeister, Tice, & Hutton, 1989) argue that high self-esteem persons are concerned with projecting a successful, prosperous, and thriving self-image. Low self-esteem persons, on the other hand, are most concerned with avoiding failure. It is a difference of emphasis: high self-esteem persons fear not succeeding; low self-esteem persons fear failure.

Self-Esteem and Social Media Use: Social Comparison

One type of feedback results from social comparison, a process whereby a person compares his or her standing on some characteristic to that of relevant others, and judges himself or herself based on how that comparison turns out. Social media gives us access to a vast amount of information on relevant others. It thereby creates almost unlimited opportunities to engage in social comparison. A person looking through the weekend posts from friends can hardly resist comparing what they did this weekend with what their friends did. And because people usually post only their best experiences, only their most flattering information, someone else who is making social comparisons is very likely to come to a negative judgment of themselves: "My weekend was pretty lame, compared to my friends who went to that awesome music festival."

Facebook started in 2004. A year later, in 2005, approximately 5 percent of Americans reported using social media. By 2021 that percentage had exploded to 72 percent of Americans reporting regular social media use (Pew Research Center, 2021). Age of user is a large factor; among Americans aged 18–29 years, 84 percent are regular social media users, with that percentage dropping with increasing age (81 percent for ages 30–49, 73 percent for ages 50–64, and 45 percent for ages 65 and up). Studies that focus on the under 30 age group typically report that social comparisons were a frequent outcome of social media use, and that such social comparisons result in declines in self-esteem, mood, and life satisfaction (Midgley et al., 2021). These researchers also showed that social comparisons occur much more frequently online than they do in face-to-face interaction. While numerous studies report that frequent use of social media is correlated with negative outcomes (e.g., lower self-esteem, lower well-being; Miljeteig & von Soest, 2022), many studies document that the toxic ingredient in social media use is upward social comparison (Wirtz et al., 2021). The list of life domains about which one might engage in online social comparison is almost limitless, including: one's appearance, popularity, romantic relationships, athletics, social activities, grades, friendships, finances, career, and more. Because people post information on all these life domains, others viewing those posts might naturally compare themselves to relevant others on these domains. Before social media, we rarely had this much information on this many relevant others. With social media, people have a flood of social comparison opportunities every time they sign onto social media. Social media use, especially for social comparison purposes, is related to lower self-esteem, effects that are especially strong for women (Barthorpe et al., 2020).

Studies on self-esteem and social media use make two additional points. The first point is that using social media for social comparison is almost automatic, occurring in a high percentage of social media use sessions (Faelens et al., 2019). Social media "influencers," for example, invite users to engage in social comparison and allow themselves (and perhaps their self-esteem) to be influenced by the "influencer." People can certainly use social media to gather information or to learn something and not engage in social comparison at all. However, studies suggest that social media seems to "pull" for social comparison, triggering an almost automatic natural tendency to compare ourselves to others. And because social media is available 24/7/365, and is so easy to access, a person can engage in social comparison self-judgments hundreds of times a day.

The second main research finding is that frequent social media use for social comparison self-judgments is associated with (Verduyn et al., 2017), or causes (Verduyn et al., 2015), lowered self-esteem. Studies of Facebook use (e.g., Hanna et al., 2017), Instagram use (Stapelton, Lutz, & Chatwin, 2017), and social networking site use (e.g., LinkedIn; Wang et al., 2017) all confirm that using social media sites frequently for social comparison purposes does bring about a negative impact on self-esteem and lowers other aspects of psychological well-being. Clearly, there are beneficial ways to use online social media (to gather information, to learn new things, to check on something like an order or if a request is being acted on, and to check hours or read reviews of a business). However, to use social media habitually to make social comparison judgments of oneself is not beneficial. Resisting and overcoming the "pull" of social comparison when using social media will be a challenge for many people. [See "When Likes Are Not Enough" by Tim Bono (2018) for way to adaptively use social media.]

Self-Esteem and Coping with Negative Events

Other research on high self-esteem persons has examined the strategies these people use to get through life. Unpleasant events happen to everyone. High self-esteem persons appear to maintain their positive evaluation through the ups and downs of everyday life. Have high self-esteem persons somehow figured out how to cope more effectively with these challenges of life? How do high self-esteem persons overcome the disappointments, shortcomings, losses, and failures that are a normal part of being human?

One strategy identified by Brown and Smart (1991) is that, following failure in one area of life, the high self-esteem person often will focus on other areas of life in which things are going well. Larsen (2000a; Larsen & Prizmic, 2004) identifies this strategy as one of the most effective strategies for overcoming feelings of failure. For example, imagine you are a research psychologist and you are evaluated in this job by the number of research articles you publish each year. Imagine then that one of your articles is rejected by a publisher. This represents a small failure in your life. If you were a low self-esteem person, this failure would have a large effect, confirming your view that you are generally a failure in most things that you do, that this is just one more instance of how you are unworthy and inadequate. On the other hand, if you were a high self-esteem person, you would likely remind yourself that you are still a good teacher, a good faculty member at your university, a good spouse, and a good parent to your children; that you still play a good game of squash; and that your dog still loves you. Larsen and Prizmic (2004) have suggested that in order to cope with such failures, people should make a list of all the things in their lives that are going well and that they keep this list on their phones. Then, if a failure occurs in one area of life—for instance, at work—they can pull up this list and review it, just as a high self-esteem person might do naturally. This can help people cope with the inevitable bumps, bruises, and failures of everyday life.

This idea of compartmentalizing the self is consistent with the research on **self-complexity** started by psychologist Patricia Linville (1987). She holds the view that we have many roles and many aspects to our self-concept. However, for some of us, our self-concept is rather simple, being made up of just one or two categories, such as when a man says, "I am nothing without her," meaning that his whole self-concept is wrapped up in this one relationship. Or someone else might have her or his self-concept wrapped up by her or his career. Other people may have a more complex, or differentiated, self-concept. Such a person would say he or she has many parts to his or her self-concept: relationships, family, career, hobbies, friends, sports, and so forth. For people with high self-complexity, a failure in any one aspect of the self (such as a failure on some job-related task or a breakup in a relationship) is buffered because there are many other aspects of the self that are unaffected by that event. However, if a person is low in self-complexity, the same event might be seen as devastating because the person defines him- or herself mainly in terms of this one aspect. The relationship between having a complex self-concept and fairing better in the face of negative life events has been replicated by many researchers (e.g., Banas & Smyth, 2021; Martins & Calheiros, 2012; McConnell et al., 2009). Some researchers have proposed programs for expanding the self-concept with the goal of improving a person's functioning in the face to threats to self-esteem, such as failures or losses (Walton, Paunesku, & Dweck, 2012). The old phrase "Don't put all your eggs into one basket" seems to apply to the self-concept; don't view yourself only in terms of one dimension. A meta-analysis and review of the self-complexity research (Rafaeli-Mor & Steinberg, 2002) concluded that under conditions of objective and identifiable stress, higher self-complexity is associated with better well-being, including higher overall self-esteem.

Protecting Versus Enhancing the Self

Imagine you are a graduating college senior; you have majored in computer science and have a lot of expertise in web-based programming. You are being recruited by a hot internet start-up company for a job managing its information technology department. You know there is a lot of potential for you in this company. In fact, it could make you a millionaire within a few years if the company were to go public. However, you also know that it will be a lot of hard work. You will have to put in lots of hours and dedicate yourself almost entirely to the company for several years. You know you will also need to have some luck to get the right team together, to have some successes on your first few projects. It is a high-stakes but also a high-risk position. Would you take this job?

A Closer Look   The Six Myths of Self-Esteem

Most people naturally try to enhance and protect their self-esteem, believing that it is important to psychological health. In America in the past decade, there has been a growing national concern with developing self-esteem, believing it is related to all manner of good things in life. For example, the State of California set up a task force on self-esteem, which ultimately produced a report titled "The Social Importance of Self-Esteem." In it the task force argued that "many if not most of the major problems plaguing society have roots in the low self-esteem of many of the people who make up society" (Smelser, 2004). As a result, self-esteem courses found their way into the grade schools and high schools around the country, fostering a "feel-good" version of self-esteem (e.g., feel good about yourself).

The Association of Psychological Science set up a task force charged with reviewing the scientific literature on self-esteem, particularly with respect to objective behaviors and outcomes. The report was published in 2003 (Baumeister et al., 2003). We have taken this report and distilled the findings into a series of myths about self-esteem that are not supported by scientific research.

Myth One: High self-esteem is correlated with all manner of positive characteristics, such as being physically attractive, smart, kind, and generous. It is true that, for example, when both self-esteem and physical attractiveness are assessed using self-report (e.g., rate how attractive you are, rate your self-esteem), then strong correlations are typically found. However, when objective measures of attractiveness are used, such as having raters rate photographs of people in terms of attractiveness, then the correlation between self-reported

self-esteem and other-rated physical attractiveness drops to zero. Those with high self-esteem may be gorgeous in their own eyes, but they are not necessarily gorgeous in the eyes of others. These kinds of findings are also obtained with a variety of other positive characteristics. For example, high self-esteem people may rate themselves as smart or high in kindness or generosity as well, yet others do not necessarily see them as being this way. In a sense, persons high in self-esteem may have an inflated or unrealistic view of their positive characteristics, a view that is not necessarily supported by those who know the person well.

Myth Two: High self-esteem promotes success in school. The issue here is really one of causality and causal direction; does self-esteem cause people to achieve success or does achieving success lead to self-esteem? Many of the educational movements imply that if only we could raise children's self-esteem then we would help them on their way to achieving success in life. Consequently, teachers are sometimes taught to praise students all the time, even if they are not successful. However, there is very little empirical science to support the idea that self-esteem leads to academic success. For example, Baumeister and colleagues (2003) review a study that tested more than 23,000 high school students, first in the 10th grade, then again in the 12th grade. They found that self-esteem in the 10th grade only weakly predicted academic achievement in the 12th grade. Academic achievement in the 10th grade correlated higher with self-esteem in the 12th grade. Thus, these results suggest that success causes increases in self-esteem, not the other way around. Many studies show similar

results, and none of them indicate that improving self-esteem offers students much benefit. In fact, some studies show that artificially boosting self-esteem (e.g., through unconditional praise) may actually lower subsequent performance (Baumeister et al., 2003).

Myth Three: High self-esteem promotes success on the job. The same basic issues about causality apply here: Does self-esteem promote success on the job, or vice versa? When people rate their own job performance, there is often a modest correlation with self-esteem, but when job performance is assessed objectively (e.g., supervisor ratings), the correlations drop to close to zero.

Myth Four: High self-esteem makes a person likable. Again, if we use self-reports of popularity (e.g., How much do other people like you?), then these self-ratings of likability do correlate with self-esteem (i.e., high self-esteem persons regard themselves as being popular and believe they have many friends). However, these self-perceptions do not reflect reality. Baumeister and colleagues (2003) report on a study of high-school students who were asked to nominate their most-liked peers. The person in the class receiving the most votes was ranked as most popular, the person with the second-most votes was ranked as second-most popular, and so on. When self-esteem scores were correlated with the objective peer-ranking of popularity, that correlation was approximately zero. Similar findings have been found in college students. In another study reported by Baumeister and colleagues (2003), college students self-reported their own interpersonal skills in several domains (e.g., initiating relationships, self-disclosure, being assertive when necessary, providing emotional support to their friends, and managing interpersonal conflict). The researchers also had the subject's roommates report what the subject was like on each of the above interpersonal skill domains. Although the subject's self-esteem scores correlated with all of the self-reported interpersonal skill domains, the correlations between self-esteem and the roommates' ratings were essentially zero for four out of five of the interpersonal skills. The only interpersonal skill area that the roommates noticed that was associated with self-esteem was the subject's ability to initiate new social contacts and friendships. This does seem to be the one area in which the confidence associated with self-esteem really matters. People who think that they are desirable and attractive should be good at striking up conversations with strangers. Persons with low self-esteem may shy away from trying to make new friends, perhaps fearing rejection. In most other areas of interpersonal skills, however, self-esteem is not associated with having an advantage over other people.

Myth Five: Low self-esteem puts a person at risk for drug and alcohol abuse and premature sexual activity. The scientific studies reviewed by Baumeister and colleagues (2003) do not support the idea that low self-esteem predisposes young people to more or earlier sexual activity. If anything, persons with high self-esteem are less inhibited, more willing to disregard risks, and more prone to engage in sex. There is, however, evidence that unpleasant sexual experiences and unwanted pregnancies appear to lower self-esteem. As for alcohol and illicit drugs, preventing these behaviors has been a major rationale for those calling for programs to promote self-esteem. The data, however, do not conclusively show that low self-esteem causes, or even

correlates with, the abuse of illicit drugs or alcohol. For example, in a longitudinal study, no correlation was found between self-esteem at age 13 and drinking or drug abuse at age 15. A few other studies have found small correlations between low self-esteem and drinking, but other studies have found the opposite. All in all, the results are not conclusive to make any statements about self-esteem protecting people from the dangers of drug and alcohol use or risky sexual behavior.

Myth Six: Only low self-esteem people are aggressive. For decades many psychologists thought that low self-esteem was an important factor underlying aggressive behavior. Under their tough exteriors, aggressive people were thought to suffer from insecurities and self-doubt. However, recent research has shown that aggressive persons often have quite favorable views of themselves. In fact, extremely high self-esteem can blend into narcissism, which has been associated with bouts of anger and aggression when the narcissist does not get his or her way. If self-esteem is threatened or disputed by someone or some event, especially among high self-esteem persons, then they may react with hostility or violence. People with a highly inflated view of their own superiority, those with narcissistic tendencies, may be the most prone to violent reactions. After a challenge to self-esteem (e.g., getting beaten at a game), people might protect their self-concept by directing their anger outward, attacking the victor. Baumeister and colleagues (2003) review the literature on bullying and conclude that bullies are often very self-confident and less socially anxious than average. The general pattern in these studies and those on adults is that even high self-esteem, especially when it blends into narcissism, can be associated with interpersonal aggression.

In several empirical studies, Baumeister, Bushman, and colleagues have demonstrated that, when their self-esteem is threatened, persons who are narcissistic are more likely to retaliate or aggress against the source of the threat (e.g., Baumeister, Bushman, & Campbell, 2000; Bushman & Baumeister, 1998). In a study of men in prison, Bushman and Baumeister (2002) found that those prisoners who had a history of violent offenses were significantly higher on narcissism than those prisoners with no history of violence. All of these findings run counter to the notion that low self-esteem causes aggression and instead point to the counterintuitive notion that threatened egotism is a likely cause of aggression and violence.

After crushing these myths about self-esteem, we can ask the question: So, what good is self-esteem? As described elsewhere in this chapter, self-esteem improves persistence in the face of failure. Persons high in self-esteem perform better in groups than those with low self-esteem. Also, having a poor self-image is a risk factor for developing certain eating disorders, especially bulimia. Low self-esteem is also related to depression, with evidence suggesting that low self-esteem can lead to depression rather than the other way around (Sowislo & Orth, 2013). High self-esteem also is related to social confidence and taking the initiative in making new friends. It is most likely the case that successes in academics, in the interpersonal domain or in one's career, lead to both happiness and self-esteem. Consequently, efforts to artificially boost children's self-esteem (e.g., through unconditional praise) might fail. Rather, we should encourage and praise children when they put effort into learning or achieving the skills necessary to succeed in the various areas of life.

Some people may decline this opportunity to try for a big success because they are motivated to protect their self-esteem. That is, they are concerned with *not failing,* and, in situations in which failure is a possibility, they prefer not to take the risk. In other words, for some people, not failing is much more important than succeeding wildly. It turns out that people low in self-esteem are like this, in that they are motivated to protect their self-concept by avoiding failure much more than they are motivated to enhance it with success (Tice, 1991, 1993).

Low self-esteem persons sometimes put a lot of energy into evading any new negative information about themselves. One strategy is to simply expect to fail; then, when it happens, it is not anything new. **Defensive pessimism** is a strategy in which a person facing a challenge, such as an upcoming test, expects to do poorly. Defensive pessimists are motivated by their fear of failure, but they take this gloomy outlook because the impact of failure can be lessened if it is expected in advance. For example, a little boy who strikes out at bat is not so upset with himself if he expects to strike out in the first place. Psychologist Julie Norem, who has done most of the research on defensive pessimism, sees a positive side to this characteristic: defensive pessimists use their worry and pessimism in a constructive way, to motivate themselves to work on the thing they are pessimistic about. She gives the example of a man who must give a public speech (Norem, 1995). Even though he has done a lot of public speaking, and all his speeches have gone well, he nevertheless is anxious and convinces himself that this time he is surely going to make a fool of himself. Thus, he decides to work extra hard on this speech; he rehearses and rehearses, and prepares and prepares. When it comes time to give the speech, he does great, as usual. By reflecting on the worst outcome, defensive pessimists work through ways to keep that worst case from happening. The downside to defensive pessimism is that the negativity of defensive pessimists annoys others (Norem, 1998, 2001). Defensive pessimism is strongly correlated with neuroticism (Bajcar & Babiek, 2020) as well as with trait anxiety, pessimism, and frequent negative affect (Ramirez-Maestre et al., 2020).

Sometimes people go to great lengths to set up their own failure. This is called self-handicapping (e.g., Tice & Baumeister, 1990). **Self-handicapping** is a process in which a person deliberately does things that increase the probability that he or she will fail (Tice & Bratslavsky, 2000). For example, a young woman may have a pessimistic attitude toward her upcoming exam, so she uses this as an excuse for not studying. However, not studying for the exam provides a handicap, an excuse for failure. By not studying, she increases the chances that she will fail, but it also gives her an excuse for that failure. When she fails, she can then say that she was simply unprepared, not that she is unintelligent or lacks the ability to do well in her classes. For low self-esteem persons, failing is bad, but failing without an excuse is worse. Other researchers have shown that self-handicapping is correlated with low conscientiousness and high neuroticism (Schwinger et al., 2021), with worse performance on academic tests (Putwain, 2019), and that in the workplace it predicts lower performance ratings from supervisors (Bakker & Wang, 2020).

Self-Esteem Variability

Most of the research on self-esteem concerns the average level, or what people's evaluations of themselves are like on average. But we also know from Chapter 5 that people fluctuate on their self-esteem from day to day and even from hour to hour. **Self-esteem variability** is an individual difference characteristic; it is the magnitude of short-term fluctuations in ongoing self-esteem (Kernis, Grannemann, & Mathis, 1991). In this section, we stress two main points. First, researchers make a distinction between level and variability of self-esteem. These two aspects of self-esteem are unrelated to each other. Moreover, level and variability in self-esteem are hypothesized to be based on different psychological mechanisms and are often found to interact in predicting important life outcomes (Kernis, Grannemann, & Barclay, 1992).

A second point is that self-esteem variability is related to the extent to which one's self-evaluation is changeable. That is, some people's self-esteem is pushed and pulled by the events of life much more than other people's self-esteem. Studies have shown that people whose self-esteem hinges on the feedback they receive from others show higher levels of self-esteem variability (Leitner et al., 2014). Trying to make other people happy, as Carl Rogers said (see Chapter 11), can interfere with one's self-development. When one's self-esteem is contingent on positive feedback from others, that self-esteem can be fragile and variable. Psychologist Michael Kernis, who has written extensively about this characteristic (Kernis, 2006; Kernis & Lakey, 2008), believes that self-esteem variability is high in some people because they:

- have an enhanced sensitivity to social evaluation.
- have an increased concern about their self-view.
- over-rely on social sources of evaluation.
- react negatively to social evaluation and become defensive easily.

Several studies have been conducted to examine whether self-esteem variability moderates the relation between self-esteem level and other variables, such as depression (Gable & Nezlak, 1998). In several study (Kernis et al., 1991; Kernis, 2006), self-esteem level was related to depression, but this relation was much stronger for persons higher in self-esteem variability. Based on such findings, researchers have come to view variability as a vulnerability (or diathesis) to depression (Roberts & Monroe, 1992). Women tend to have higher self-esteem variability than men, and they have higher rates of depression than men (Wagner, Ludtke, & Trautwein, 2015), a finding discussed in Chapter 13.

Other studies are exploring the health correlates of chronic self-esteem variability, and typically finding that this characteristic is associated with various health risk factors (Ross et al., 2013; Geukes et al., 2017). All in all, variability in self-esteem is turning out to be as consequential as level of self-esteem.

Social Component of the Self: Social Identity

Social identity is the self that is shown to other people. This is the part of ourselves that we use to create an impression, to let other people know who we are and what they can expect from us. Social identity is different from self-concept because identity contains elements that are socially observable, publicly available outward expressions of the self. Gender and ethnicity are aspects of social identity. This may or may not figure into a person's self-concept, but gender and ethnicity are parts of one's social self, one's identity that is available to others.

Identity has an element of continuity because many of its aspects, such as gender and ethnicity, are constant. People are recognized as being the same from day to day, week to week, and year to year. If you were asked for your "identification," you might produce a passport or a driver's license. These documents contain socially available facts about you, such as your height, weight, age, and eye color. They also contain your family name and your address. All of these pieces of information are aspects of your identity, and they provide others with a brief sketch of who you are. Identity also contains your reputation, and what other people know about you.

The Nature of Identity

Identity has two important features: continuity and contrast. **Continuity** means that people can count on you to be the same person tomorrow as you are today. Obviously, people change in various ways, but many important aspects of social identity remain relatively stable, such as gender, surname (though some women elect to change this when they marry), language, ethnicity, socioeconomic status, and reputation.

Other aspects of identity can change but do so gradually, lending some sense of continuity (e.g., education, occupation, and marital status). Other aspects of identity refer to behavior patterns that are public, such as being an athlete, a delinquent, or a "party animal," which also contribute to a sense of continuity in one's reputation (Baumeister & Muraven, 1996).

Contrast means that your social identity differentiates you from other people. An identity is what makes you unique in the eyes of others. The combination of characteristics that make up your identity differentiates you from everyone else. For example, there may be other students who speak the way you do and work where you do, but you are the only one who likes a particular type of music and has your ethnic background and eye color. Some characteristics are more important to social identity for some people than others. We now turn to how people develop identity by selecting what they choose to emphasize about themselves in their social identities.

Identity Development

Although anything that provides a sense of continuity and contrast can potentially become part of identity, people have some latitude to choose what they want to be known for (or not known for). For example, a student may try out for the swimming team, thereby choosing the identity of an athlete. Another might break a lot of rules, thereby choosing the identity of a delinquent. One person might choose to "come out," making their gay sexual orientation a part of their public social identity, whereas another gay person might choose to "stay in the closet" and not have their sexual orientation part of their public identity. People also differ from each other in the strength of their identities. Some people feel a strong sense of reputation, whereas others feel adrift in their social relations, not knowing who they are expected to be. In fact, most people go through a period, usually in high school or college, in which they experiment with various identities. For many people, this is an uncomfortable time. They may feel socially insecure or sensitive while developing their social identity.

As mentioned in Chapter 10, the term *identity* was popularized in the 1960s by the psychoanalyst Erik Erikson (1968). He believed that identity resulted from efforts to separate oneself from one's parents, to stop relying on one's parents to make decisions about what values to hold and what goals to pursue in life. Erikson believed that achieving an identity took effort and work and that there was always a risk that an identity achieved could come undone, resulting in what he called role confusion. People need to continually work on achieving and maintaining their identity, Erikson taught.

Identity can be achieved in several ways, according to Erikson (1968). Many people struggle with identities, particularly during late adolescence and early adulthood. Experimenting with various identities can be compared to trying on different hats to see which one fits. In trying on identities, a young man in college might one semester be an athlete and the next semester join the debate and chess clubs; the following semester, he gets a tattoo, has some body parts pierced, and starts hanging with a crowd of similarly pierced and tattooed persons. People actively struggle to find a social identity that fits, one they are comfortable with. Usually, after a period of experimentation, most people settle into a comfortable social identity and attain some stability.

Application

Identity Theft: The Case of Martin Guerre

The true story of Martin Guerre is so interesting that several film depictions have been made based on this story. In the real story, which took place in the late middle ages in France, a peasant, Martin Guerre, leaves his wife to fight in the "Hundred Years War." His wife waits patiently for him, but after nine years without a word, she presumes that Martin is dead. Believing herself a widow, she is astonished when Martin returns suddenly after being away so long. Although the neighbors have a big homecoming celebration for Martin, several are suspicious that the man who has returned is an impostor, that he is not really Martin, but someone who knew Martin well enough to steal his identity. To the lonely wife, however, he looks like her Martin, sounds like her Martin, and has a working knowledge of the intimate details of their prior relationship. In addition, the man in her house now is nicer, gentler, more loving, and more attentive than the man who went to war almost a decade earlier. And so she very much wants this man to be her Martin.

Telltale signs of a forged identity emerge bit by bit and unravel the clever facade around Martin's social self. The neighbors get the local magistrate involved. His wife tries to defend Martin as her husband, and even if he is not, she wants him to stay anyway. Nevertheless, the case is made that he is an impostor, that this Martin is not really Martin Guerre. The impostor is believed to have forced the real Martin to reveal details of his self-concept and social identity and then to have used this knowledge to create a social identity so similar to Martin's that he fooled even Martin's wife into believing he was truly her returning husband. The magistrate, convinced that this is not the "real" Martin, charges the impostor with adultery, a crime punishable by death. Martin's wife is not similarly charged because she believed this was her husband.

The 1993 French film based on this story, *The Return of Martin Guerre*, starring Gerard Depardieu, won three French Academy Awards. It is a stunningly filmed study in the portrayal of the self and social identity. In it, we see the small details that go into making a social identity. It shows how people form expectations for social behavior from others based on identity and how small violations of those expectations can create doubts and suspicions.

*The French movie **The Return of Martin Guerre**, starring Gerard Depardieu, portrays a true story from medieval times about the theft of social identity. The scene here shows the "new" Martin, who has just returned from a nine-year absence, embracing the "old" Martin's wife. The film won three French Academy Awards.*
Jacky Coolen/Gamma-Rapho/Getty Images

For other people, the route to identity is not through experimentation. Instead, some people attain an identity by accepting and adopting ready-made social roles. Typically, such people adopt an identity that is practiced and provided by their parents or significant others. For example, they may take over the family business, buy a house in their hometown, and join the same church or synagogue as their parents. Such people appear stable and mature in their identities and have mature values, plans, and objectives even when they are teenagers. Another identity adoption example is arranged marriages, in which the parents decide whom their children will marry and the children accept this decision willingly, a practice still found in India today.

These kinds of instant identity adoptions can be risky, however, as they may be achieved with a certain amount of rigidity, making the person closed to new ideas or life-styles. Such people may be inflexible and stubborn in their social roles, especially when they are under stress. For some, the decision to adopt a ready-made identity is fragile, not based on careful consideration of alternatives, and can fall apart when challenged. Nevertheless, for many people, this route to identity can be an acceptable and reasonable alternative, one that can provide an identity for life.

Identity Crises

A person's identity is challenged from time to time. The answer to the question "Who do others think I am?" can change. For example, when a woman gets divorced, her social identity changes from "I am married" to "I am divorced and newly single." Or a man gives up a career as a business executive to pursue a vocation in small-scale farming, so his identity changes from "I am an executive" to "I am a farmer." Other challenges to identity would be events that change one's reputation, change one's family life, or change one's economic status.

Erikson (1968) coined the phrase identity crisis (see Chapter 10), meaning the feelings of anxiety that accompany efforts to define or redefine one's own individuality and social reputation. For most people, the process of going through an identity crisis is an important and memorable phase of life. Sometimes it happens early, in adolescence; sometimes it happens later, in midlife. And some people have identity crises multiple times in their lives. Psychologist Roy Baumeister suggests that there are two distinct types of identity crises: identity deficit and identity conflict (Baumeister, 1986, 1997).

Identity Deficit

An **identity deficit** arises when a person has not formed an adequate identity and thus has trouble making major decisions: Should I go to college or not? If I go to college, what major should I choose? Should I join the military service? Should I get married? A person without a secure, established identity would have trouble making such major decisions because he or she has no inner foundation. When facing a tough decision, many people turn inward to find the answer. In doing so, many people arrive at a course of action right away, because they know their own values and preferences very well; they know what "a person like me" would do in such situations. When people who have an identity deficit turn inward, however, they find little in the way of a foundation on which to base such life choices.

Identity deficits often occur when a person discards old values or goals. For example, college students often reject old opinions in favor of new ideas and new values to which they are exposed in college. In fact, some college courses are designed to encourage students to doubt or challenge their previous assumptions about themselves or the world. A popular bumper sticker, often seen on college campuses, is "Question Authority." But questioning authority by rejecting old beliefs and assumptions can create an identity deficit, which is accompanied by feelings of emptiness and uncertainty. Such feelings prompt people to search for new beliefs, for new values and goals. People who are trying to fill this identity deficit may try on new belief systems, explore new relationships, and investigate new ideas and values.

People with identity deficits are particularly vulnerable to the propaganda of various groups. They are often very curious about other belief systems, so they are vulnerable to influence by cults or conspiracy theories. Because of their feelings of emptiness and their search for new values and ideas, they tend to be very persuadable during this period. Current research on conspiracy theories shows that many people who believe in such questionable theories are themselves in a period of identity deficit (Robertson et al., 2022).

Identity Conflict

An **identity conflict** involves an incompatibility between two or more aspects of identity. This kind of crisis often occurs when a person is forced to make an important and difficult life decision. For example, a person who immigrates to the United States may have an identity conflict between wanting to assimilate into the majority culture and wanting to maintain his or her ethnic identity. A similar identity conflict arises in working persons who also want to have a family. A person with a strong commitment to building a family might experience an identity conflict if he or she were offered a promotion at work that involved longer hours or frequent out-of-town travel. Whenever two or more aspects of identity clash (such as being both a high-power career woman and a dedicated mother of multiple children), there is a potential for an identity conflict crisis. Some people, however, are able to balance the demands of different identity components, achieving an integration that is recognized and admired by others.

Identity conflicts are "approach–approach" conflicts, in that the person wants to reach two goals that appear to be in conflict. Although these conflicts involve wanting two desirable identities, not much pleasure is experienced during identity conflicts. Identity conflicts usually involve intense feelings of guilt or remorse over perceived unfaithfulness to an important aspect of the person's identity. People in an identity conflict may feel as if they are letting themselves and others down.

Overcoming an identity conflict is often a difficult and painful process. One course of action is to modify a part of one's identity, to revise a formerly important aspect of the self. This may allow them to better balance the components of their identity. For example, a college professor may accept a lighter teaching load (and hence less pay) to have more time with his children; a business executive may telecommute to her job two days a week in order to spend more time with her children. Some people partition their lives in ways that prevent such conflicts from arising. For example, some people keep their work lives and their private lives entirely separate.

Resolution of Identity Crises

Identity crises—both deficits and conflicts—commonly occur during adolescence, though not all adolescents experience identity crises. Those who do find that resolution involves two steps (Baumeister, 1997). First, they decide which values are most important to them. Second, they transform these abstract values into desires and actual behaviors. For example, a person might arrive at the conclusion that what is really important is to have a family. The second step is to translate this value into actions, such as finding the right spouse, someone who also wants a family; working hard to maintain this relationship; preparing a career with which to support a family; and so forth. As the person begins working toward these goals, he or she assumes a secure identity and is unlikely to experience an identity crisis, at least during this phase of life.

Application

The movie character Lester, played by Kevin Spacey in the Oscar-winning film *American Beauty,* undergoes an acute midlife identity crisis. In fact, the movie is about the havoc Lester wreaks on his family, neighbors, and co-workers during his identity crisis. Lester goes from being a complacent husband, a neglecting but "good-enough" father, and a submissive worker to someone who wants things his own way at home and at work. One day, Lester decides that he does not like what he has become and decides to make drastic changes in his life. During his transformation, Lester ruins his marriage, drives his daughter to contemplate running away, loses his job, experiments with drugs, pushes an unstable neighbor over the brink, and contributes to the delinquency of two minor children. Clearly, Lester's attempts to redefine himself are adolescent and dysfunctional throughout most of the movie. However, toward the end, Lester appears to be starting on the right track; he has finally found some integrity and is heading in a positive direction. It is the scene in which Lester decides not to have sex with his daughter's teenage girlfriend that we learn that his new identity will at least be that of a mature adult.

*In the Oscar-winning movie **American Beauty,** actor Kevin Spacey plays Lester, a man undergoing a severe midlife identity crisis. In his effort to transform his social identity, Lester changes the way he interacts with his wife, his boss, his child, and even his neighbors. Although he makes some rash decisions along the way, toward the end of the movie we get a sense that Lester is finally forming a positive new identity.*
TM & DREAMWORKS/SEBASTIAN, LOREY/Album/Alamy

A second phase of life in which identity crises commonly occur is during middle age. For some people, this is a period in which they experience dissatisfaction with their existing identities, perhaps at work or in a marriage. Whatever the reason, people undergoing a midlife identity crisis begin to feel that things are not working out as they wished. They may feel that their lives are inauthentic. People in the midlife identity crisis begin to doubt that they made the right choices early in life, and they reconsider those commitments: "If only I had done . . ." is a frequent complaint. It is a period of regret over time spent pursuing goals that turned out to be unsatisfying or impossible. Many people in this predicament decide to abandon their goals and experience an identity deficit because they give up the principles that have guided their lives so far.

People who undergo midlife crises often act as adolescents again. That is, an identity crisis often looks the same, whether it occurs at adolescence or at midlife: the person experiments with alternative lifestyles, forms new relationships and abandons old ones, and gives up previous ambitions and responsibilities. In midlife crises, people often change their careers, change their spouses, change their religions, change where they live, or do various combinations of these. Sometimes they simply change their priorities—for example, a woman might keep her job and her spouse but decide to spend more time with her spouse and less time working. A midlife identity crisis can be just as much of an emotional roller-coaster ride as an adolescent identity crisis.

To summarize, a social identity consists of the social or public aspects of yourself, the impression that you typically create in others. Many of your more visible characteristics—such as gender, ethnicity, and occupation—contribute to your identity. Other characteristics, including those that make up reputation, also go into the formation of identity. Your identity is what gives you and others a sense of continuity, of being the same person tomorrow as today. It also makes you unique in the eyes of others.

SUMMARY AND EVALUATION

This chapter presented an outline of what personality psychologists know about the self. This knowledge is neatly divided into three broad areas: self-concept, self-esteem, and social identity. These aspects of the self are important to understanding personality. The notion of a self makes sense in terms of our everyday lives and our experience. We frequently use terms such as *selfish, self-worship, selfless, self-conscious,* and *self-esteem* in everyday life. In the evolution of language, we developed a rich vocabulary for talking about the self. This reflects people's general preoccupation with themselves. Another reason psychologists are interested in the self is that it plays an important role in organizing a person's experiences of the world. What a person deems important, for example, are the things that are relevant to his or her self-concept. Moreover, people behave differently when they are self-involved than when they are not, so the concept of the self is important for understanding how people construe their world, their experiences, their priorities, and their future. The self is a major organizing force within the person.

Self-concept is a person's self-understanding—his or her own story. The self-concept has its start in infancy, when the child first makes a distinction between its body and everything else. This glimmer of self-concept goes on to develop, through repeated experiences of self-awareness, into a collection of characteristics that the child uses for self-definition, such as gender, age, and membership in a particular family. Children acquire skills and talents and start comparing themselves with others. This is the beginning of social comparison and is an activity that most people engage in, to various degrees, throughout their lives. They also develop a sense of privacy and the ability to keep secrets. They develop a private self-concept, things they know about themselves that no one else knows. For the first time, they are able to tell a lie or misrepresent facts. Cognitive schemata then develop around aspects of the self; these knowledge structures are collections of characteristics associated with the self-concept. People also develop views of themselves in the future, their possible selves, which include both desirable (ideal self) and undesirable features. All in all, the self-concept is the person's answer to the questions "Who have I been, what am I like now, and who do I want to be in the future?"

Self-esteem is the evaluation a person makes of his or her self-concept along a good–bad dimension. People differ from each other in terms of whether they see themselves as worthwhile, valuable, and good. Research on self-esteem has emphasized how people respond to failure, and findings suggest that high self-esteem persons persevere in the face of failure, whereas low self-esteem persons often give up following failure. High self-esteem people seem particularly good at deflecting the bumps and bruises of everyday life. One strategy they seem particularly adept in using is, when something bad happens in one area of their lives, to remind themselves that other areas in their lives are going well. This puts negative events in perspective and helps them cope. We reviewed social comparison as a self-esteem strategy but noted that it often results in negative outcome (there are always people who have more friends, who are better looking, and who have more money, on any characteristic you can think of). We also noted that social media use can result in lowered self-esteem, but mainly when social media is used for social comparison purposes.

Extremely high self-esteem, associated with narcissistic tendencies, can sometimes result in aggressive responses to threats to that self-esteem. Researchers have shown that narcissistic persons often retaliate following negative feedback. Another clinical problem associated with self-esteem is extreme shyness. Shyness does have some biological correlates, but it is also associated with an over-controlling parenting style. Shyness can often be changed through treatment efforts. Another area of research shows that high self-esteem people are often concerned with enhancing their self-concept (focus on success), whereas low self-esteem persons are often concerned with protecting their self-concept from harm (focus on avoiding failure). Finally, in terms of self-esteem variability, variable persons seem especially sensitive to evaluative life events, such as social slights and public failures.

The final aspect of the self-discussed in this chapter was social identity, as a person's outward manifestation or the impression he or she gives others. Identity develops over time through relations with others. For many people, the development of an identity follows a period of experimentation, but for others it happens more easily by adopting ready-made social roles. There are periods in life when some people undergo identity crises and have to redefine their social identities. Developing an identity is a lifelong task, as identity changes with the changing social roles that come with age.

Erikson coined the term *identity crisis* to refer to the anxiety that comes with having to redefine one's social reputation. There are two kinds of crises: identity deficit, not forming an adequate identity; and identity conflict, in which two or more aspects of identity come into conflict. Despite crises and challenges, most people develop a solid identity, and other people know them for their unique characteristics.

KEY TERMS

self-concept 437
social identity 437
self-esteem 437
social comparison 441
private self-concept 441
perspective taking 442
objective self-awareness 442

self-schema 443
amygdala 445
possible selves 446
ideal self 447
ought self 447
self-guides 447
self-complexity 453

defensive pessimism 456
self-handicapping 456
self-esteem variability 456
continuity 458
contrast 458
identity deficit 460
identity conflict 461

PART FIVE

The Social and Cultural Domain

Lightspring/Shutterstock

In the social and cultural domain, the emphasis is on personality as it is affected by and expressed through social institutions, social roles and expectations, and relationships with other people in our lives.

We saw in Chapter 3 that several taxonomies of traits emphasize interpersonal traits, such as dominance versus submissiveness or love versus hate. Many trait adjectives in language are important for describing how people behave with other people. Interpersonal traits have long-term outcomes in our lives. For example, whether a person is controlling or easy-going affects such different aspects of life as conflicts with spouse and work partners and the strategies used to achieve goals. Whether a person tends to be nervous or optimistic affects the likelihood of diverse social outcomes, such as divorce or success

V

in a sales career. Many of the most important individual differences and personality traits are played out in our interpersonal relationships.

We describe three key processes whereby personality affects social interactions. The first process is through *selection,* in which people may choose specific social environments according to their personalities. A second process is *evocation.* We examine how people evoke distress, as well as positive feelings, in others. A final process whereby personality affects social interactions is through *manipulations* for influencing others. What are the strategies that people use to get what they want from others?

One important interpersonal context concerns relationships between men and women. An essential part of our social identity is our gender. Differences between men and women in personality have long been of interest to personality psychology. Some researchers prefer to minimize the differences between men and women, emphasizing that gender differences are small and that the variability within a sex exceeds the variability between the

sexes. Other researchers focus on the differences between the sexes and emphasize that some are large and are found in different cultures. Men tend to score higher on aggressiveness, whereas women tend to score higher on empathy. Where do these sex differences come from?

Some of what we call gender may have its origins in culture—that is, in how society makes up different rules and expectations for men and women. Other theories emphasize differences between men and women that may be due to hormones. Testosterone levels, for example, differ greatly between men and women, and testosterone has been reliably associated with the personality traits of dominance, aggression, and sexuality.

Another theory is evolutionary and suggests that men and women faced different challenges and have evolved solutions to these different challenges. Whatever their origins, gender differences have long been of interest to personality psychologists and are clearly part of the social and cultural domain because they refer to and are played out in interpersonal relations.

Another socially important difference among people derives from their culture, the system of social rules, expectations, and rituals in which a person is raised. For example, in one culture it might be expected that a crying baby is always picked up and comforted by its parents, whereas in another culture crying babies are left to cry. Could it be that being raised in these two different cultures results in differences in adult personality? Do people in different cultures have different personalities?

An important goal of personality psychology is to understand how cultures shape personality and how specific cultures differ from each other. Cultural personality psychologists have also looked for similarities among cultures. One example of a cultural universal appears to be the expression of specific emotions. Another aspect of personality that may show cultural universality is described by the five-factor model of traits.

In this part of the book, we focus on the broader social-interpersonal, gendered, and cultural aspects of personality.

Lightspring/Shutterstock

Personality and Social Interaction

Selection

Evocation

Manipulation: Social Influence Tactics

Panning Back: An Overview of Personality and Social Interaction

SUMMARY AND EVALUATION

KEY TERMS

15

Sue and Joan sipped coffee while discussing their dates from the previous evening. "Michael seemed like a nice guy, at least at first," Sue noted. "He was polite, asked me what kind of food I liked, and seemed genuinely interested in knowing me as a person. But I was a little turned off by the rude way he talked to the waitress. He also insisted in choosing the food for me and selected a pork dish I didn't like. Over dinner, he talked about himself the whole time. At the end of the evening, he tried to invite himself back to my room, but I told him that I was tired and wanted to call it a night." "Did you kiss him?" asked Joan. "Well, yes, I started to give him a good-night kiss, but he began to get really aggressive with me, and I had to push him away. All the politeness disappeared, and he stormed off angry. I guess he wasn't such a nice guy after all. How did your date go?"

In the course of this conversation, Sue revealed a treasure trove of information about her date, Michael—information that figures prominently in the social decisions we make. Michael displayed aggressiveness, both toward the waitress and toward Sue during the good-night kiss. He displayed self-centeredness, focusing on himself during the course of the dinner. He showed a lack of empathy, as illustrated by his uncaring attitude toward the feelings of the waitress and his abrupt sexual aggressiveness. The thin veneer of politeness quickly gave way over the evening, revealing an abrasive interpersonal disposition that turned Sue off.

This episode illustrates several key ways in which personality influences social interaction. Personality interacts with situations in three ways: through selection, evocation, and manipulation of the situation. These three mechanisms can be applied to an understanding of how personality affects interpersonal situations. First, the personality characteristics of others influence whether we *select* them as our dates, friends, and even marriage partners. In this episode, Sue was turned off by Michael's aggressive and self-centered personality characteristics. People's personality characteristics also play a role in the kinds of interpersonal situations they select to enter and stay in. For example, someone with a personality different from Sue's might actually be attracted to a guy like Michael and could put up with his self-centeredness.

Second, the personality qualities of others *evoke* certain responses in us. Michael's aggressiveness upset Sue, evoking an emotional response that would not have been evoked if he had been kinder and more caring. Behaviors related to personality can evoke many responses in others, ranging from aggression to social support, and from marital satisfaction to marital infidelity.

Third, personality affects the tactics people use to *influence* or *manipulate* others. Michael first tried the charm tactic. Then he pulled out the boasting tactic. Finally, he used coercion, trying to force himself on Sue. A man with a different personality would use different tactics, such as reason or reward.

These three processes—selection, evocation, and manipulation—are key ways in which personality interacts with the social environment. Individuals in everyday life are not exposed to all possible social situations; individuals with certain personality dispositions seek out and avoid social situations selectively. Personality also influences how we evoke different reactions from other people and how others in turn evoke different responses from us, sometimes quite unintentionally. And personality affects how we purposefully influence, change, exploit, and manipulate the others with whom we have chosen to be associated.

Selection

In everyday life, people choose to enter some situations and avoid other situations. These forms of situation selection can hinge on personality dispositions and how we view ourselves. The following story illustrates the process of selection. In this example, a couple inadvertently entered a situation and then chose a rapid exit from it.

> *Chip and Priscilla, a Yuppie couple from Chicago, have just moved to Dallas and are sampling some of the trendier nightspots on Lower Greenville Avenue. As they push through the swinging doors of what appears to be a quaint little Western saloon right out of the TV series Gunsmoke, they are confronted by six huge bikers from the motorcycle gang, who turn on their barstools to glare at them. The bikers have an average of more than two tattoos and three missing teeth. The fumes they emit smell flammable. Two of them stare with contempt at Chip, and one leers evilly at Priscilla. "This doesn't look like our kind of place," Chip says to Priscilla, as they prepare to beat a hasty retreat. (Ickes, Snyder, & Garcia, 1997, p. 165)*

Social selections permeate daily life. Choices range from the seemingly trivial ("Should I attend this party tonight?") to the profound ("Should I select this person as my marriage partner?"). Social selections are decision points that direct us to choose one path and avoid others. These decisions, which determine the nature of our social environments and social worlds, are often based on the personality characteristics of the selector. Extraverts choose to spend more time in social situations, whereas highly conscientious people select more work-related activities—choices that continue from adolescence through young adulthood (Wrzus, Wagner, & Riediger, 2016). Agreeable people choose to spend more time looking at photos and media depicting positive images; disagreeable people expose themselves to more negative photos and media images (Bresin & Robinson, 2015). People high in Dark Triad traits, particularly psychopathy, gravitate toward the bright lights of big cities—geographical preferences that influence environments people subsequently inhabit (Jonason, 2018).

Mate choice provides an especially dramatic example of the mechanism of selection. When you select a long-term mate, you place yourself into close and prolonged contact with one particular person. This alters the social environment to which you are exposed and in which you will reside. By selecting a mate, you are selecting the social acts you will experience and a network of friends and family.

Which personality characteristics do people seek as potential mates? Are there traits that are highly desired by everyone? Do we look for potential mates who have personalities similar to our own or different from our own? And how is the choice of a mate linked to the likelihood that a couple will stay together over time?

Personality Characteristics Desired in a Marriage Partner

What do people want in a long-term partner? This was the focus of an international investigation of 10,047 individuals located on six continents and five islands from around the world (Buss et al., 1990). A total of 37 samples were chosen from 33 countries, representing every major racial group, religious group, and political system. Samples ranged from the coastal-dwelling Australians to the South African Zulus. The economic status of the samples varied from middle- and upper-middle-class college students to lower socioeconomic groups, such as the Gujarati Indians and Estonians. Fifty researchers collected data. Standard questionnaires were translated into the language of each culture and then administered by native residents of each culture. This study, the largest conducted on what people want in a long-term mate, revealed that personality characteristics play a central role in mate selection. In the Exercise below, you can complete this questionnaire yourself and see how your selection preferences compare with those of the worldwide sample.

As you can see in Table 15.1, mutual attraction or love was the most favored characteristic, viewed as indispensable by almost everyone in the world. It turns out that feeling loved is linked to personality traits. People who feel loved tend to be higher on Extraversion and lower on Neuroticism, as well as scoring higher on a general sense of well-being (Oravecz et al., 2020). After mutual attraction or love, personality characteristics loom large in people's mate selection preferences—dependable character, emotional stability, and pleasing disposition. You may recall that these are quite close to the labels

Exercise

INSTRUCTIONS: Evaluate the following factors in choosing a mate or marriage partner. If you consider the factor to be

indispensable, give it	3 points
important, but not indispensable, give it	2 points
desirable, but not very important, give it	1 point
irrelevant or unimportant, give it	0 points

Exercise (*Continued*)

—— 1. Good cook and housekeeper		—— 10. Desire for home and children
—— 2. Pleasing disposition		—— 11. Favorable social status
—— 3. Sociability		—— 12. Good looks
—— 4. Similar educational background		—— 13. Similar religious background
—— 5. Refinement, neatness		—— 14. Ambition and industriousness
—— 6. Good financial prospect		—— 15. Similar political background
—— 7. Chastity (no prior intercourse)		—— 16. Mutual attraction or love
—— 8. Dependable character		—— 17. Good health
—— 9. Emotional stability		—— 18. Education and intelligence

Now compare your ratings with the ratings given by the international sample of 10,047 men and women, shown in Table 15.1.

Table 15.1 Summary of Ratings by Sex Using Entire International Sample

	RATINGS BY MALES			RATINGS BY FEMALES		
Ranked Value	Variable Name	Mean	Std. Dev.	Variable Name	Mean	Std. Dev.
1.	Mutual attraction or love	2.81	0.16	Mutual attraction or love	2.87	0.12
2.	Dependable character	2.50	0.46	Dependable character	2.69	0.31
3.	Emotional stability and maturity	2.47	0.20	Emotional stability and maturity	2.68	0.20
4.	Pleasing disposition	2.44	0.29	Pleasing disposition	2.52	0.30
5.	Good health	2.31	0.33	Education and intelligence	2.45	0.25
6.	Education and intelligence	2.27	0.19	Sociability	2.30	0.28
7.	Sociability	2.15	0.28	Good health	2.28	0.30
8.	Desire for home and children	2.09	0.50	Desire for home and children	2.21	0.44
9.	Refinement, neatness	2.03	0.48	Ambition and industriousness	2.15	0.35
10.	Good looks	1.91	0.26	Refinement, neatness	1.98	0.49
11.	Ambition and industriousness	1.85	0.35	Similar education	1.84	0.47
12.	Good cook and housekeeper	1.80	0.48	Good financial prospect	1.76	0.38
13.	Good financial prospect	1.51	0.42	Good looks	1.46	0.28
14.	Similar education	1.50	0.37	Favorable social status or rating	1.46	0.39
15.	Favorable social status or rating	1.16	0.28	Good cook and housekeeper	1.28	0.27
16.	Chastity (no previous experience in sexual intercourse)	1.06	0.69	Similar religious background	1.21	0.56
17.	Similar religious background	0.98	0.48	Similar political background	1.03	0.35
18.	Similar political background	0.92	0.36	Chastity (no previous experience in sexual intercourse)	0.75	0.66

Source: Adapted from Buss et al. (1990), p. 19, Table 4.

given to three of the factors in the five-factor model of personality (see Chapter 3). Dependability is close to Conscientiousness. Emotional stability is identical to the fourth factor on the five-factor model. And pleasing disposition is quite close to Agreeableness. Other personality factors rated highly include sociability, refinement and neatness, and ambition and industriousness.

Note that the respondents' top choices, except for love, were personality characteristics. Thus, personality factors play a central role in what people worldwide are looking for in a long-term mate—findings that have now been documented over many decades of research (e.g., Fletcher et al., 2004; Kamble et al., 2014; Lei et al., 2011; Souza, Conroy-Beam, & Buss, 2016). The priority placed on personality traits such as Agreeableness, Conscientiousness, and Emotional Stability occurs regardless of sexual orientation; they are as strong among nonheterosexual men and women as they are among heterosexual men and women (Valentova et al., 2016). Low scores on these personality traits tend to be relationship "deal-breakers" (Jonason et al., 2015). Other research has confirmed that people who score higher on Conscientiousness, both women and men, tend to be higher in overall mate value or desirability on the mating market (Strouts, Brase, & Dillon, 2017).

These strong effects of personality apply primarily to traits people seek in a long-term mate. When it comes to short-term mating, the traits of high Extraversion is linked with frequency of sex and number of different sex partners (Whyte et al., 2019).

Assortative Mating for Personality: The Search for the Similar

Over the past century, two fundamentally competing scientific theories have been advanced for who is attracted to whom. **Complementary needs theory** postulates that people are attracted to those who have different personality dispositions than they have (Murstein, 1976; Winch, 1954). People who are dominant, for example, might have a need for someone whom they can control and dominate. People who are submissive, according to complementary needs theory, choose a mate who can dominate and control them. One easy way to think about complementary needs theory is with the phrase "opposites attract."

In contrast, **attraction similarity theory** postulates that people are attracted to those who have similar personality characteristics. People who are dominant might be attracted to those who are also dominant because they like someone who "pushes back." People who are extraverted might like partners who are also extraverted so that they can party together. One easy way to remember this theory is with the phrase "birds of a feather flock together." Although there have been many proponents of both theories over the past century, the results are now in. They provide overwhelming support for the attraction similarity theory and no support for the complementary needs theory (Buss, 2016). The only characteristic on which "opposites attract" that has been reliably documented is biological sex: Men tend to be attracted to women and women tend to be attracted to men, although of course there are individual differences in sexual orientation. The research shows that people are generally drawn to those who share their personalities.

People often are attracted to others who are similar to themselves. This refers to the concept of assortative mating.

Andrew Rich/Vetta/Getty Images

One common finding in mate selection—that people are married to people who are similar to themselves—is a phenomenon known as **assortative mating.** For nearly every variable that has been examined—from single actions to ethnic status—people seem to select mates who are similar to themselves. Even for physical characteristics such as height, weight, and, astonishingly, nose breadth and earlobe length, couples show positive correlations. Couples who have been together the longest appeared most similar in personality, a finding that results from the initial selection process and from dissimilar couples breaking up more often (e.g., Humbad et al., 2010).

But are these positive correlations caused by the active selection of mates who are similar? Or are these positive correlations merely byproducts of other causal processes? Sheer proximity, for example, could, in principle, account for some of the positive correlations. It is known that people tend to marry those who are close by. Notions of romantic love aside, the "one and only" often lives within driving distance, although internet dating sites have reduced this effect. And because people in close proximity may have certain common characteristics, the positive correlations found between married couples may be merely a side effect of mating with those who are close by rather than the active selection of partners who are similar. Cultural institutions, such as colleges and universities, may promote assortative mating by preferentially admitting those who are similar with respect to certain variables, such as intelligence, motivation, and social skills.

To test these competing predictions, Botwin, Buss, and Shackleford studied two samples of subjects: dating couples and newlywed couples (Botwin, Buss, & Shackleford, 1997). The participants expressed their preferences for the personality characteristics in a potential mate on 40 rating scales, which were scored on five dimensions of personality: Extraversion, Agreeableness, Conscientiousness, Emotional Stability, and Intellect–Openness. The next step was to assess personality dispositions on these dimensions, using the same 40 rating scales. Three data sources were used for this second stage: self-reports; reports by their partners; and independent reports by interviewers. Correlations with mate preferences were computed between two sets of personality ratings: the ones made by the participant (self) and the average of the peer and interviewer ratings of the participant (aggregate).

As shown in Table 15.2, these correlations were consistently positive. People scoring high on Extraversion wanted to select an extraverted person as a mate. Those who scored high on Conscientiousness desired a conscientious mate. The conclusions from this study, of course, must be qualified by one important consideration—perhaps the preferences people express for the personalities of their ideal mates might be influenced by

Table 15.2 Personality Correlated with Mate Preferences

| | DATING COUPLES | | | | MARRIED COUPLES | | | |
| | MEN | | WOMEN | | MEN | | WOMEN | |
Trait	Self	Aggregate	Self	Aggregate	Self	Aggregate	Self	Aggregate
Extraversion	.33*	.42**	.59***	.35**	.20*	.15	.30**	.25**
Agreeableness	.37*	.17	.44***	.46***	.30**	.12	.44***	.31**
Conscientiousness	.34**	.45***	.59***	.53***	.53***	.49***	.61***	.53***
Emotional Stability	.29*	.36**	.52***	.30*	.27**	.21*	.32***	.27**
Intellect–Openness	.56***	.54***	.63***	.50***	.24*	.31**	.48***	.52****

*$p < .05$
**$p < .01$
***$p < .001$

Note: Each correlation in the table refers to the relationship between the personality trait of the individual and the corresponding personality trait desired in a mate. Thus, under Men, Self-Report column, the .33* indicates that men who are highly extraverted tend to prefer mates who are also extraverted. The fact that all the correlations in the table are positive, many significantly so, indicates that people generally want mates who are similar to themselves in personality.

Source: Botwin, Buss, & Shackleford (1997).

the mates they already have. If an emotionally stable person is already mated to an emotionally stable person, perhaps the choice is justified by claiming that he or she is truly attracted to the person chosen. This could result in positive correlations between one's own personality and the personality people express for a desired mate. Studies of individuals who are not mated already find the same pattern of results—people prefer those who are similar to themselves (e.g., Buss, 2012), supporting the attraction similarity theory.

These data provide evidence that positive correlations on personality variables between husbands and wives are due, at least in part, to social preferences based on the personality characteristics of those doing the selecting. Subsequent studies have confirmed that people actively prefer romantic partners who are similar to themselves on Extraversion, Agreeableness, Conscientiousness, Emotional Stability, and Intellect–Openness. However, most people consider the "ideal" romantic partner personality to be someone who is slightly higher on Extraversion, Conscientiousness, Agreeableness, and Emotional Stability than they are (Figueredo, Sefcek, & Jones, 2006). In sum, personality characteristics appear to play a pivotal role in the social mechanism of selection.

Do People Get the Mates They Want? And Are They Happy?

People do not always get what we want, and this is true of mate selection. You may want a mate who is kind, understanding, dependable, emotionally stable, and intelligent, but these desirable mates are always in short supply compared with the numbers of people who seek them. Many people end up mated with individuals who fall short of their ideals. Are people whose mates differ from their ideal mates less satisfied than those whose mates embody their desires?

Table 15.3 shows the correlations between the preferences that individuals express for the ideal personality characteristics of their mates and the actual personality characteristics of their obtained mates (Botwin, Buss, & Shackelford, 1997, p. 127). Across three of the four subsamples—women who are dating, women who are married, and men who are married—there are modest but consistently positive correlations between the personality desired in a partner and the actual personality characteristics displayed by

Table 15.3 Personality Mate Preferences and Personality of Partner Obtained

| Partner's Personality | DATING COUPLES | | | | MARRIED COUPLES | | | |
| | WOMEN'S PREFERENCES | | MEN'S PREFERENCES | | MEN'S PREFERENCES | | WOMEN'S PREFERENCES | |
	Self	Aggregate	Self	Aggregate	Self	Aggregate	Self	Aggregate
Extraversion	.25	.39**	.28*	.24	.39***	.49***	.31***	.32**
Agreeableness	.28*	.32	.24	.02	.20*	.40***	.03	.25
Conscientiousness	.28*	.29*	.24	.26	.36***	.46***	.13	.24
Emotional Stability	.36**	.12	.40**	.10	.27**	.37**	.07	.12
Intellect–Openness	.33**	.41**	.40**	.11	.24**	.39***	.14	.39****

*p < .05
**p < .01
***p < .001
Source: Botwin, Buss, & Shackelford (1997).

the partner. The correspondence between what one wants and what one gets is especially strong for Extraversion and Intellect-Openness. In sum, as a general rule, people seem to get the mates they want in terms of personality.

Are people who get what they want happier with their marriages than people who do not? To examine this issue, Botwin, Buss, and Shackelford (1997) created difference scores between the preferences expressed for the ideal personality of a mate and assessments of the spouse's actual personality. These difference scores were then used to predict satisfaction with the marriage, after first controlling for the main effects of the spouse's personality. The results were consistent—one's partner's personality had a substantial effect on marital satisfaction. People were especially happy with their relationships if they were married to partners who were high on Agreeableness, Emotional Stability, and Intellect-Openness. But the difference scores between the partner's personality and one's ideal for that personality did *not* predict marital satisfaction. In other words, the key to marital happiness is having a partner who is agreeable, emotionally stable, and open, regardless of whether the partner departs in specific ways from what one wants (Luo et al., 2008).

The correlations between the participants' marital satisfaction scores and the partners' personality scores, obtained through the partners' self-reports, are shown in Table 15.4. Having a partner who is *agreeable* is an especially strong predictor of being happy with one's marriage for both men and women. People married to agreeable partners are more satisfied with their sex lives and view their spouses as more loving and affectionate, a source of shared laughter, and a source of stimulating conversation. People married to disagreeable partners are the most unhappy with the marriage and perhaps are most at risk of getting divorced.

The other personality factors that are consistently linked with marital satisfaction are Conscientiousness, Emotional Stability, and Intellect-Openness. Men whose wives score high on Conscientiousness are significantly more sexually satisfied with the marriage than are other husbands. Women whose husbands score high on Conscientiousness are generally more satisfied and happier with their spouses as sources of stimulating conversation—a finding replicated in a study of 125 long-wed couples (Claxton et al., 2011). People whose spouses score high on Emotional Stability are more satisfied, view their spouses as sources of encouragement and support, and enjoy spending time with their partners. Low emotional stability scores are linked with relationship dissatisfaction among dating college students and among older adults in committed relationships (Slatcher & Vazire, 2009). A meta-analysis of 19 samples found that emotional stability and agreeableness were the strongest predictors of satisfaction in intimate romantic relationships (Malouff et al., 2010). High neuroticism in one or both members of the couple leads to relationship dissatisfaction (Schaffhuser, Allemand, & Martin, 2014). On a positive note for those married to individuals low on emotional stability, one study found that having frequent sexual intercourse seems to protect couples from the negative marital consequences of neuroticism (Russell & McNulty, 2011).

Another link between personality and marital satisfaction emerges over the years following the newlywed year of marriage. As a general rule, in the newlywed year, people rate their spouses high on Agreeableness, Conscientiousness, Extraversion, and Intellect-Openness (Watson & Humrichouse, 2006). Over the ensuing two years, however, ratings of spouse's personalities become increasingly negative on these dimensions, illustrating a "honeymoon effect." And those who show the most marked negative ratings of their spouse's personality over time show the largest decreases in marital happiness. One speculation is that spouses in progressively unhappy marriages actually display progressively more unpleasant personalities, such as lower levels of Agreeableness, but only

Table 15.4 Facet of Marital Satisfaction and Spouse's Self-Reported Trait Ratings

Marital Satisfaction	SPOUSE'S SELF-REPORTED TRAIT RATINGS				
	E	A	C	ES	I–O
Husband's marital satisfaction					
General	.12	.32***	.06	.27**	.29**
Spouse as someone to confide in	−.05	.27**	.07	.11	.05
Sexual	−.08	.31**	.32***	.25**	.04
Spouse as source of encouragement and support	.03	.29**	.11	.26**	.18
Love and affection expressed	.07	.31**	.14	.21*	.26**
Enjoyment of time spent with spouse	.11	.30**	.13	.28**	.08
Frequency of laughing with spouse	.19*	.23*	.19	.11	.24**
Spouse as source of stimulating conversation	.06	.12	−.04	.21*	.17
Wife's marital satisfaction					
General	.07	.37***	.20*	.23*	.31***
Spouse as someone to confide in	.06	.25**	.15	.24**	.27**
Sexual	.08	.19*	.14	.09	.13
Spouse as source of encouragement and support	.04	.47***	.06	.20*	.31***
Love and affection expressed	−.04	.29**	.14	.28**	.33***
Enjoyment of time spent with spouse	.06	.27**	.06	.33***	.18
Frequency of laughing with spouse	−.02	.27**	−.02	.10	.08
Spouse as source of stimulating conversation	.23*	.24**	.25**	.18	.45***

Note: E = Extraversion; A = Agreeableness; C = Conscientiousness; ES = Emotional Stability; I–O = Intellect–Openness.
* $p < .05$
** $p < .01$
*** $p < .001$
Source: Botwin, Buss, & Shackelford (1997).

within the marital context itself. Those who maintain positive illusions about their partner's personality, in contrast, maintain high levels of satisfaction (Barelds & Dijkstra, 2011). Another key predictor of marital satisfaction is mate value—whether one succeeds in selecting a mate whose personality embodies qualities most people want. Those mated with high mate value individuals tend to be happier in their relationship than those mated with lower mate value individuals (Conroy-Beam, Goetz, & Buss, 2016).

In summary, the personality of one's spouse plays an important role in marital satisfaction. Those who select mates high on Agreeableness, Conscientiousness, Emotional Stability, and Intellect–Openness show the greatest happiness with their marriages. These are qualities linked with high mate value, since most people desire them. Those who select mates low on these personality factors are the most unhappy with their marriages. Differences from each person's individual ideal, however, do not appear to contribute to marital satisfaction.

Personality and the Selective Breakup of Couples

We have examined two ways in which personality plays a role in the mate selection process. First, there appear to be universal selection preferences—personality characteristics that everyone desires in a potential mate, such as dependability and emotional stability. Second, beyond the desires shared by everyone, people prefer partners who are similar to themselves in personality—dominant people prefer other dominant people, conscientious people prefer other conscientious people, and so on. But there is a third role that personality plays in the process of selection—its role in the selective breakup of marriages.

According to one theory of conflict between the sexes, breakups should occur more when one's desires are violated than when they are fulfilled (Buss, 2016). Following the **violation of desire** theory, we would predict that people married to others who lack desired characteristics, such as dependability and emotional stability, will more frequently dissolve the marriage. We would also predict that couples who are dissimilar on personality will break up more often than those who fulfill desires for similarity. Are these predictions borne out in the research findings?

Across a wide variety of studies, *emotional instability* has been the most consistent personality predictor of marital instability and divorce, emerging as a significant predictor in nearly every study that has included a measure of it (Kelly & Conley, 1987; Solomon & Jackson, 2014). One reason is that emotionally unstable individuals display high levels of jealousy—they worry more about a partner's infidelity, try to prevent social contact between their partner and others, and react more explosively when their partner does in fact have sex with others (Dijkstra & Barelds, 2008). Those high on Neuroticism also create more conflict and disagreement and their emotional upset after a fight tends to last longer (Solomon & Jackson, 2014). Low impulse control, or low conscientiousness (i.e., being impulsive and unreliable), particularly as exhibited by husbands, also emerges as a good predictor of divorce (Bentler & Newcomb, 1978; Kelly & Conley, 1987). Low agreeableness predicts marital dissatisfaction and divorce, although this result is less consistent and less powerful than that found for emotional instability and low conscientiousness (Burgess & Wallin, 1953; Kelly & Conley, 1987). One reason for these breakups may be found in another link between personality and social behavior. A study of 52 nations found that the personality traits of low agreeableness and low conscientiousness (high impulsivity) were linked with higher rates of sexual infidelity in romantic relationships (Schmitt, 2004). Interestingly, extraversion and dominance are linked with higher levels of sexual promiscuity (Markey & Markey, 2007; Schmitt, 2004), although these personality traits are *not* related to marital satisfaction or breakups. A study of 8,206 individuals found that high Openness also predicted relationship breakups (Solomon & Jackson, 2014). High Openness may lead to "a wandering eye," more sexual openness to others, and greater boredom with the relationship.

Being married to someone who lacks the personality characteristics that most people desire—dependability, emotional stability, and pleasing disposition—puts one most at risk for breakup. People actively seek mates who are dependable and emotionally stable, and those who fail to choose such mates are more at risk for divorce.

Another study examined the fate of 203 dating couples over the course of two years (Hill, Rubin, & Peplau, 1976). Over that time, roughly half of the couples broke up and half stayed together. Similarity in personality and values predicted staying together. Those who were most *dissimilar* were more likely to break up.

In summary, personality plays key roles in mate selection. First, as part of the initial selection process, it determines the mates to whom we are attracted and the mates whom we desire. Second, personality affects satisfaction with one's mate and therefore influences the selective breakup of couples. Those who fail to select partners who are similar, agreeable, conscientious, and emotionally stable tend to break up more often than those who succeed in selecting such mates.

Shyness and the Selection of Risky Situations

Several other domains of selection have also been explored. One pertains to the effects of the personality disposition of shyness. **Shyness** is defined as a tendency to feel tense, worried, or anxious during social interactions (Addison & Schmidt, 1999). Shyness is a common phenomenon; more than 90 percent of the population experience shyness at some point during their lives (Zimbardo, 1977). Some people, however, seem to be dispositionally shy—they tend to feel awkward in many social situations and so tend to avoid situations in which they will be forced to interact with people.

The effects of shyness on the selection of situations have been well documented. During high school and early adulthood, shy individuals tend to avoid social situations, resulting in some isolation (Schmidt & Fox, 1995). Shy women are more likely to avoid going to the doctor for gynecological exams, putting themselves at greater health risk (Kowalski & Brown, 1994). They are less likely to bring up contraception with their partners before sexual intercourse, and so put themselves in potentially dangerous sexual situations (Bruch & Hynes, 1987).

Shyness also affects willingness to select risky situations in the form of gambles (Addison & Schmidt, 1999). In one experiment, shy people were identified through the Cheek (1983) shyness scale, which contains items such as "I find it hard to talk to strangers" and "I feel inhibited in social situations." On entry into the laboratory, each participant received the following instructions: "During this part of the experiment, you have a chance to win some money by picking a poker chip out of this container. There are 100 poker chips in this box that are numbered from 1 to 100. . . ." The participants

Shy individuals often feel tense or anxious in social situations and avoid entering situations in which they would be forced to interact with others.

4774344sean/Wavebreakmedia/iStockphoto/Getty Images

were given a choice to pick a gamble that they would most likely win (95 percent odds of winning) but from which they would receive only a small amount of money (e.g., 25¢), or to pick a riskier gamble, perhaps with only a 5 percent chance of winning but from which, if they won, they would receive $4.75. The experimenters also recorded the heart rate of the participants during their choice of gambles.

Shy women differed substantially from their non-shy counterparts in choosing the smaller bets that were linked with a higher likelihood of winning. The non-shy women, in contrast, chose the riskier bets with a lower likelihood of winning but with a larger payoff if they did win. During the task, the shy participants showed a larger increase in heart rate, suggesting that fearfulness might have led them to avoid the risky gambles.

These studies illustrate the importance of the personality disposition of shyness in the selection of, or avoidance of, certain situations. Shy women tend to avoid others, creating social isolation, and to avoid choosing risky gambles. They also avoid going to the doctor for gynecological exams and avoid obtaining condoms, thus putting them at greater health risk than less shy women. Shyness, in short, appears to have an impact on the selective entry into, or avoidance of, situations.

Personality Traits and the Selection of Friends and Situations

Personality also influences our selection of friends. People high on extraversion and agreeableness, for example, tend to choose a larger number of friends on social networking sites compared to more introverted and disagreeable people (Zhou et al., 2021).

Other personality traits have been shown to affect selective entry into, or avoidance of, certain situations (Ickes, Snyder, & Garcia, 1997). Those who are more empathic are more likely to enter situations such as volunteering for community activities (Davis et al., 1999). Those high on psychoticism choose volatile and spontaneous situations more than formal or stable ones (Furnham, 1982). Those high on **Machiavellianism** prefer face-to-face situations, perhaps because these offer a better chance to ply their social manipulative skills to exploit others (Geis & Moon, 1981). People high on Extraversion tend to select more friends; however, people high on Agreeableness tend to be selected more often by others as friends (Selfhout et al., 2010).

High sensation seekers are more likely to volunteer for unusual experiments, such as studies involving drugs or sex (Zuckerman, 1978). High sensation seekers more frequently choose to enter risky situations (Donohew et al., 2000). High school students high in sensation seeking more frequently attend parties where alcohol or marijuana is available to be consumed. They also more often have unwanted sex when drunk. Those who are high in sensation seeking also tend to select social situations characterized by high-risk sexual behavior (McCoul & Haslam, 2001). In a study of 112 heterosexual men, those who scored high on sensation seeking were more likely than their low-scoring peers to have unprotected sex more frequently. High sensation seekers have sexual intercourse with many more different partners than low sensation seekers. Those high on sensation seeking gravitate toward risky gambling bets and risky sexual situations (Webster & Crysel, 2012). Personality, in sum, affects the situations to which people are exposed through their selective entry into, or avoidance of, certain kinds of activities.

Evocation

Once we select others to occupy our social environment, a second process is set into motion—the evocation of reactions from others. **Evocation** may be defined as the ways in which features of personality elicit reactions from others. Recall from Chapter 3 the study of highly active children. Compared with their less active peers, highly active children tend to elicit hostility and competitiveness from others. Parents and teachers tend to get into power struggles with these active children. The social interactions of less active children are more peaceful and harmonious. This is a perfect example of the process of evocation at work—a personality characteristic (in this case, activity level) evokes a predictable set of social responses from others (hostility and power struggles). Another example comes from the evocation of trust and cooperativeness by those high on Honesty-Humility (Thielmann & Hilbig, 2014). Perhaps because high scorers tend to trust others, they evoke trustworthy expectations in others.

Aggression and the Evocation of Hostility

It is well known that aggressive people evoke hostility from others (Dodge & Coie, 1987). People who are aggressive expect that others will be hostile toward them. One study found that aggressive people chronically interpret ambiguous behavior from others, such as being bumped into, as intentionally hostile (Dill et al., 1999). This is called a **hostile attributional bias**, the tendency to infer hostile intent on the part of others in the face of ambiguous behavior from them. Vulnerable narcissists, who have somewhat shaky self-esteem, are also prone to the hostile attribution bias (Hansen-Brown & Freis, 2021).

Because they expect others to be hostile, aggressive people tend to treat others in an aggressive manner. People who are treated in an aggressive manner often aggress back. In this case, the aggressive reactions of others confirm what the aggressive person suspected all along—that others have hostility toward them. What the aggressive person fails to realize is that the hostility from others is a product of their own making—the aggressor evokes it from others by inferring hostile intent in others.

Evocation of Anger and Upset in Partners

There are at least two ways in which personality can play a role in evoking conflict in close relationships. First, a person can perform actions that cause an emotional response in a partner. A dominant person, for example, might act in a condescending manner, habitually evoking upset in the partner. Or a husband low in conscientiousness might neglect personal grooming and throw clothes on the floor, which might upset his wife. In short, personality characteristics can *evoke emotions* in others through the actions performed.

A second form of evocation occurs when a person elicits actions from another that in turn upsets the original elicitor. An aggressive man, for example, might elicit the silent treatment from his mate, which in turn upsets him because she won't speak to him. A condescending wife might undermine the self-esteem of her husband and then become angry because he lacks self-confidence. In sum, people's personality characteristics can upset others either directly by influencing how they act toward others or indirectly by eliciting actions from others that are upsetting.

Research on these forms of evocation requires studies that assess the personality characteristics of both persons involved. In one study, the personality characteristics of both husbands and wives were assessed through three data sources: self-report, spouse-report, and independent reports by two interviewers (Buss, 1991a). An instrument assessed multiple sources of anger and upset in close relationships (Buss, 1989). A short version of this instrument is shown in the following Exercise.

Statistical analyses determined personality traits that predicted spouse upset. The results were similar for men and women, so for economy of presentation we will use men's personality traits that upset women to highlight the results.

Exercise

INSTRUCTIONS: We all do things that upset or anger other people from time to time. Think of a close romantic partner or close friend with whom you have been involved. Following is a list of things this person might have done that evoked anger or upset in you. Read the list, and place a check by the things your partner or close friend has done in the past year that have irritated, angered, annoyed, or upset you.

_____   1. He/she treated me as if I were stupid or inferior.

_____   2. He/she demanded too much of my time.

_____   3. He/she ignored my feelings.

_____   4. He/she slapped me.

_____   5. He/she saw someone else intimately.

_____   6. He/she did not help clean up.

_____   7. He/she fussed too much with his/her appearance.

_____   8. He/she acted too moody.

_____   9. He/she refused to have sex with me.

_____ 10. He/she talked about members of the opposite sex as if they were sex objects.

_____ 11. He/she got drunk.

_____ 12. He/she did not dress well or appropriately for a social gathering.

_____ 13. He/she told me that I was ugly.

_____ 14. He/she tried to use me for sexual purposes.

_____ 15. He/she acted selfishly.

These acts represent items from the larger instrument of 147 acts that one can do to upset or anger a member of the opposite sex. The acts correspond to the following factors: (1) condescending, (2) possessive/jealous, (3) neglecting/rejecting, (4) abusive, (5) unfaithful, (6) inconsiderate, (7) physically self-absorbed, (8) moody, (9) sexually withholding, (10) sexualizing of others, (11) abusive of alcohol, (12) disheveled, (13) insulting of partner's appearance, (14) sexually aggressive, and (15) self-centered. It turns out that the personality of the person we are close to is a reasonably good predictor of whether that person will perform these upsetting acts.

Source: Buss (1991a).

Men high on dominance tended to upset their partners by being condescending—treating their wives' opinions as stupid or inferior and placing more value on their own opinions. The husbands who scored low on conscientiousness, in contrast, tended to upset their partners by having extramarital affairs—seeing someone else intimately or having sex with another. Husbands low on openness tended to evoke upset in their wives by acting rejecting (ignoring the wife's feelings), abusive (slapping or hitting the wife), physically self-absorbed (focusing too much on his face and hair), sexually withholding (refusing the wife's sexual advances), and abusing alcohol (getting drunk).

By far the strongest predictors of evoked anger and upset, however, were the personality characteristics of disagreeableness and emotional instability. Disagreeable husbands evoked anger and upset in their wives in the following ways: being condescending, such as treating them as if they were inferior; neglecting and rejecting them, such as failing to spend enough time with them and ignoring their feelings; abusing them,

The strongest predictors of a wife's anger and dissatisfaction with marriage are the personality traits of disagreeableness and emotional instability on the part of the husband.

Stuart Jenner/iStockphoto/Getty Images

such as slapping, hitting, or spitting; committing infidelity; abusing alcohol; insulting their appearance, such as calling them ugly; and exhibiting self-centeredness. Low agreeableness was a better predictor of evoking upset in the wife than any other personality variable in the study. Low agreeable individuals, because of their anger, jealousy, and antisocial behavior, tend to evoke much relationship conflict (Lemay & Dobush, 2015).

The emotionally unstable husbands also evoked anger and upset in their wives. In addition to being condescending, abusive, unfaithful, inconsiderate, and abusing alcohol, these husbands also upset their wives by being moody (acting irritable) as well as jealous and possessive. For example, the emotionally unstable men tended to upset their wives by demanding too much attention, monopolizing the wife's time, being too dependent, and flying into jealous rages. Moreover, when marital conflicts arise, emotionally unstable partners tend to use *avoidance rather than compromise* to deal with it, thus perpetuating the conflict (Delatorre et al., 2021).

In another study that used both hypothetical and daily diary assessments of conflict, those high in agreeableness tended to evoke less interpersonal conflict (Jensen-Campbell & Graziano, 2001). Highly agreeable individuals tend to use *compromise* in dealing with conflict, whereas those low in agreeableness are less willing to compromise and are more likely to use verbal insults and physical force to deal with conflict. Married couples with highly agreeable wives tend to have more frequent sex, perhaps because they are receptive to, or evoke more, sexual overtures (Meltzer & McNulty, 2016). The role of low agreeableness in evoking conflict extends to a variety of interpersonal relationships, including those in the workplace (Bono et al., 2002).

These links between personality and conflict show up at least as early as adolescence—young teenagers low in agreeableness not only evoke more conflict, but also are more likely to become victimized by their peers in high school (Jensen-Campbell et al., 2002).

Agreeable individuals tend to use effective conflict resolution tactics, a path leading to harmonious social interactions (Jensen-Campbell et al., 2003). Agreeable people evoke trust and cooperation in laboratory-based economic games (Zhao & Smillie, 2016). Those high in negative emotionality (high neuroticism) were also likely to experience greater conflict in all their relationships, whereas those high in positive emotionality (a close cousin of agreeableness) experienced less conflict in all of their relationships (Robins, Caspi, & Moffitt, 2002). Studies from the United States, Australia, the Netherlands, and Germany reveal that *agreeableness* and *emotional stability* are the traits that most consistently evoke satisfaction in relationships (Barelds, 2005; Donnellan, Larsen-Rife, & Conger, 2005; Heaven et al., 2003; Neyer & Voigt, 2004; White, Hendrick, & Hendrick, 2004).

Within romantic relationships, one tactic of manipulation that evokes a strong emotion is jealousy induction, such as intentionally flirting with someone else in order to make one's partner jealous or upset. Those high on the dark triad traits of narcissism and psychopathy are especially prone to using jealousy induction (Massar et al., 2017; Tortoriello et al., 2017). They do so with the goals of gaining control over the partner or extracting revenge on them. So the next time you experience jealousy in your romantic relationship, you may wonder whether your romantic partner is intentionally evoking it in you.

In summary, personality plays a key role in the process of evocation—in this case, the evocation of anger and upset. By far, the strongest predictors of this upset are low agreeableness and emotional instability. It would be premature to conclude that this provides a recipe for choosing whom not to marry or whom not to choose as a close friend (in other words, avoid emotionally unstable and disagreeable people). But it does suggest that if you marry or befriend someone with these personality attributes, they will be likely to behave in anger-evoking ways.

Application

Psychologist John Gottman has been conducting research on married people for three decades. His main question has been "What distinguishes the happily married couple from the dissatisfied, unhappy couple?" After studying thousands of marital pairs, some of whom have been happily married for years and others of whom were applying for divorce, he has found many ways that the happy and unhappy couples differ. He distilled his research findings in an applied book on how to make marriage work (Gottman & Silver, 1999). His seven principles of positive relationships are summarized below. Several of these principles concern behaviors related to evoking responses in the partner.

1. Develop an empathic understanding of your partner (see Chapter 11 for a discussion of empathy). Get to know their "world," their preferences, and the important events in their life. As an example, once a day try to find out one important or significant event for your partner: what they are looking forward to or what important event happened to them. Trivial as it sounds, try asking, "How was your day?" each day.

2. Remain fond of each other and try to nurture your affection for your partner. Remember why you like this person, and tell her about it. As an example, keep a photo album together and go over it once in a while, reminding yourself of the fun times you had together and how much you enjoy being with this special person.

3. In times of stress, turn toward, rather than away, from each other. During the good times, do things together. Don't take your partner for granted, and never ignore him, even in day-to-day life. Pay attention, stay connected, touch each other, and talk frequently.

4. Share power, even if you think you are the expert. Let your partner influence you. Ask them for help once in a while. Ask for their opinion. Let them know that their views matter to you.

5. You will undoubtedly have arguments. However, try to argue only about the solvable problems. When arguing:
   • Start gently.
   • Proceed with respect.
   • If feelings get hurt, stop and try to repair those hurt feelings.
   • Be willing to compromise.

6. Realize that some problems may never be solved. For example, perhaps one of you is religious and the other is not, and both intend to stay this way. Avoid gridlock on unsolvable problems and don't let them become permanent arguments. Agree to disagree sometimes.

7. Become a "we" instead of "I" and "I." Make the relationship important. Think about what is best for "us" rather than only what is best for "me."

Source: Adapted from Gottman & Silver, 1999.

Evocation of Likability, Pleasure, and Pain

One of the most important effects a person can have on the social world is the evocation of likability. Being liked by others is linked with higher levels of adjustment, mental health, and even academic performance (Wortman & Wood, 2011). Some personality traits consistently evoke likability in others—those linked with agreeableness, the sociable component of extraversion, and the honesty–humility factor (Wortman & Wood, 2011). The link between agreeableness and social likability has been documented as early as adolescence (de Vries et al., 2020). People with these qualities evoke pleasure in others, leading to their liking (Saucier, 2010). Being extraverted increases likability in online social networks (Stopfer et al., 2013). People low on agreeableness and honesty–humility evoke pain in others. They cause others to be offended, annoyed, irritated, and even intimidated. Personality, in short, creates a footprint on one's social world by evoking liking, pleasure, or pain in other people.

Evocation Through Expectancy Confirmation

Expectancy confirmation is a phenomenon whereby people's beliefs about the personality characteristics of others cause them to evoke in others actions that are consistent with the initial beliefs. The phenomenon of expectancy confirmation has also been called self-fulfilling prophecy. Can mere beliefs have such a powerful role in evoking behavior from others?

In a study of expectancy confirmation, Snyder and Swann (1978) led individuals to believe that they would be dealing with a hostile and aggressive individual and then introduced the two individuals. They found that people's beliefs led them to act in an aggressive manner toward the unsuspecting target. Then the behavior of the unsuspecting target was examined. The intriguing finding was that the unsuspecting target actually acted in a more hostile manner, behavior that was evoked by the person who was led to expect hostility. Beliefs about the personality of the other actually created the behavior that confirmed those initial beliefs (Snyder & Cantor, 1998).

Expectancies about personality have widespread evocation effects in everyday life. After all, we often hear information about a person's reputation prior to actual encounters with the person. We hear that a person is smart, socially skilled, egocentric, a player, or manipulative. Beliefs about the personality characteristics of others may have far-reaching effects on evoking behavior that confirm our initial beliefs. It is sometimes said that, in order to change your personality, you must move to a place where people don't already know you. Through the process of expectancy confirmation, people who already know you may unwittingly evoke in you behavior that confirms their beliefs, thereby constraining your ability to change.

Manipulation: Social Influence Tactics

Manipulation, or social influence, includes all the ways in which people intentionally try to change the behavior of others. No malicious intent need be implied by the term *manipulation*, although such intent is not excluded either. A parent might influence a child not to cross between parked cars, but we would not call this behavior malicious. Indeed, part of social living is that we influence others all the time. The term *manipulation* is used here descriptively, with no negative connotation.

From an evolutionary perspective (see Chapter 8), natural selection favors people who successfully manipulate objects in their environment. Some manipulable objects are inanimate, such as the raw materials used to build shelters, tools, clothing, and weapons. Other manipulable objects are alive, including predators and prey of different species and mates, parents, children, rivals, and allies of the same species. The manipulation of other people can be summarized as the various means by which we influence the psychology and behavior of other people.

The process of manipulation can be examined from two perspectives within personality psychology. First, we can ask, "Are some individuals consistently more manipulative than others?" Second, we can ask, "Given that all people attempt to influence others, do stable personality characteristics predict the sorts of tactics that are used?" Do extraverted people, for example, more often use the charm tactic, whereas introverts use the silent treatment tactic?

A Taxonomy of Eleven Tactics of Manipulation

A **taxonomy** is simply a classification scheme—the identification and naming of groups within a particular subject field. Taxonomies of plants and animals, for example, have been developed to identify and name all the major plant and animal groups. The periodic table is a taxonomy of elements in the known universe. The Big Five personality traits that we examined in Chapter 3 are a taxonomy of major dimensions of personality. In this section, we look at the development of a taxonomy of tactics of manipulation—an attempt to identify and name the major ways in which people try to influence others in their social world.

A taxonomy of tactics of manipulation was developed through a two-step procedure: (1) nominations of acts of influence and (2) factor analysis of self-reports and observer-reports of the previously nominated acts (Buss, 1992; Buss et al., 1987). The act nomination procedure (see Chapter 2) was as follows: "We are interested in the things that people do to influence others in order to get what they want. Please think of your [romantic partner, close friend, mother, father, etc.]. How do you get this person to do something? What do you do? Please write down specific behaviors or acts that you perform in order to get this person to do things. List as many different sorts of acts as you can."

Researchers then converted the nominations into a questionnaire administered via self-report or observer report. You can see for yourself how this was done by taking the test in the following Exercise to find out what tactics of social influence you use.

Exercise

INSTRUCTIONS: When you want your partner to do something for you, what are you likely to do? Look at each of the following items and *rate how likely you are to do each when you are trying to get your partner to do something.* None of them will apply to all situations in which you want your partner to do something, so rate how likely you are, in general, to do what is described. If you are extremely likely to do it, write a "7" in the blank next to the item. If you are not at all likely to do it, write a "1" in the blank next to the item. If you are somewhat likely to do it, write a "4" in the blank. Give intermediate ratings for intermediate likelihood of performing the behaviors.

—— 1. I compliment her/him so that she/he will do it.

—— 2. I act charming so she/he will do it.

—— 3. I try to be loving and romantic when I ask her/him.

—— 4. I give her/him a small gift or card before I ask.

—— 5. I don't respond to her/him until she/he does it.

—— 6. I ignore her/him until she/he does it.

—— 7. I am silent until she/he does it.

—— 8. I refuse to do something she/he likes until she/he does it.

—— 9. I demand that she/he do it.

—— 10. I yell at her/him until she/he does it.

—— 11. I criticize her/him for not doing it.

—— 12. I threaten her/him with something if she/he does not do it.

—— 13. I give her/him reasons she/he should do it.

—— 14. I point out all the good things that will come from doing it.

—— 15. I explain why I want her/him to do it.

—— 16. I show her/him that I would be willing to do it for her/him.

—— 17. I pout until she/he does it.

—— 18. I sulk until she/he does it.

—— 19. I whine until she/he does it.

—— 20. I cry until she/he does it.

—— 21. I allow myself to be debased so that she/he will do it.

—— 22. I lower myself so that she/he will do it.

—— 23. I act humble so that she/he will do it.

—— 24. I act submissive so that she/he will do it.

You can find out your scores by simply adding up your scores in clusters of four: items 1–4 5 charm tactic; items 5–8 5 silent treatment tactic; items 9–12 5 coercion tactic; items 13–16 5 reason tactic; items 17–20 5 regression tactic; items 21–24 5 self-abasement tactic. The tactics you tend to use the most are those with the highest sums. The tactics you use the least are those with the lowest sums. This is an abbreviated version of the instrument used in the studies by Buss (1992).

A large number of participants completed versions of an expanded instrument, consisting of 83 acts of influence. Factor analysis was then used to identify clusters of acts of influence, or tactics. In all, 11 tactics were discovered through this procedure, as shown in Table 15.5. Although this taxonomy identifies manipulation tactics used across many contexts, it is important to remember that some tactics will depend on the goal of the tactician. For example, parents sometimes try to manipulate the mate choices of their sons and daughters, and use tactics specific to that context such as "chaperoning," for example, sticking around when the daughter or son is with a potential mate (Apostolou & Papageorgi, 2014). And people sometimes try to manipulate their prospective in-laws for the goal of help in solidifying their mateship with their offspring (Apostolou, 2017).

Sex Differences in Tactics of Manipulation

Do men and women differ in their usage of tactics of manipulations? Buss (1992) found that, by and large, the answer is no. Women and men equally performed almost all of the tactics of social influence. There was only one small exception: the regression tactic. In samples of dating couples and married couples, women more than men reported more frequent use of the regression tactic, including crying, whining, pouting, and sulking to get their way. The difference was quite small, supporting the overall conclusion that men and women, in general, are similar in their performance of tactics of manipulation. Parents also use somewhat different tactics of manipulation with regard to the mate choices of their sons and daughters. They are more likely to monitor their daughters, control the clothing choices of their daughters, and prevent their daughters from seeing a potential mate the parents do not like (Apostolou & Papageorgi, 2014; Perilloux, Fleischman, & Buss, 2008).

Personality Predictors of Tactics of Manipulation

Are people with certain personality traits are more likely to use certain tactics of manipulation? A sample of more than 200 participants rated each act of influence on the degree to which they used it in each of four relationships: spouse, friend, mother, and father

Table 15.5 Taxonomy of Eleven Tactics of Manipulation

Tactic	Sample Act
Charm	I try to be loving when I ask her to do it.
Coercion	I yell at him until he does it.
Silent treatment	I don't respond to her until she does it.
Reason	I explain why I want him to do it.
Regression	I whine until she does it.
Self-abasement	I act submissive so that he will do it.
Responsibility invocation	I get her to make a commitment to doing it.
Hardball	I hit him so that he will do it.
Pleasure induction	I show her how much fun it will be to do it.
Social comparison	I tell him that everyone else is doing it.
Monetary reward	I offer her money so that she will do it.

Note: These tactics then formed the basis for subsequent analyses, such as whether there are sex differences in the tactics of manipulation and whether personality traits are associated with the tactics of manipulation that people use.

A Closer Look

The Machiavellian Personality

The term *Machiavellian* originates from an Italian diplomat, Niccolo Machiavelli, who wrote a classic treatise, *The Prince,* in 1513 (Machiavelli, 1513/1966). Machiavelli observed, in his diplomatic role, that leaders come and go, rising and falling as they gain and lose power. *The Prince* is a book of advice on acquiring and maintaining power, which Machiavelli wrote to ingratiate himself with a new ruler after the one that he had served had been overthrown. The advice is based on tactics for manipulating others and is entirely lacking in traditional values, such as trust, honor, and decency. One passage in the book, for example, notes that "men are so simple and so much inclined to obey immediate needs that a deceiver will never lack for victims for his deceptions" (p. 63). Machiavellianism eventually came to be associated with a manipulative strategy of social interaction and with a personality style that uses other people as tools for personal gain.

Niccolo Machiavelli, after whom the trait of Machiavellianism was named, wrote a book on strategies for manipulating others.
G. NIMATALLAH/De Agostini Picture Library/ Getty Images Plus

Two psychologists—Richard Christie and Florence Geis—developed a self-report scale to measure individual differences in Machiavellianism (Christie & Geis, 1970). The following are some sample items from the test, with the Machiavellian direction noted in parentheses:

- *The best way to handle people is to tell them what they want to hear (true).*
- *Anyone who completely trusts anyone else is asking for trouble (true).*
- *Honesty is the best policy in all cases (false).*
- *Never tell anyone the real reason you did something unless it is useful to do so (true).*
- *Most people who get ahead in the world lead clean, moral lives (false).*
- *The biggest difference between most criminals and other people is that criminals are stupid enough to get caught (true).*
- *It is wise to flatter important people (true).*

As you can see, the high scorer on the Machiavellianism scale (called a "high Mach") is manipulative, has a cynical worldview, treats other people as tools to be used for personal ends, does not trust other people, and lacks empathy. The low scorer on the Machiavellianism scale (called a "low Mach") is trusting, empathic, believes that things are clearly either right or wrong, and views human nature as basically good.

High and low scorers represent two alternative strategies of social conduct (Wilson, Near, & Miller, 1996). The high Mach represents an exploitative social strategy—one that betrays friendship and uses other people opportunistically. For example, high Machs are especially likely to undermine their coworkers in order to boost their own status in the workplace, often to the detriment the organization they work for (Castille, Kuyumcu, & Bennett, 2017). Theoretically, this strategy works

best in social situations when there is room for innovation, rather than those that are highly constrained by rules. Political consulting or the world of an independent entrepreneur might be relatively unconstrained, allowing much latitude for the high Mach to operate. The more structured world of universities, on the other hand, might allow fewer opportunities for the high Machs to ply their skills.

The low Mach pursues a strategy of cooperation, sometimes called tit-for-tat. This strategy is based on reciprocity—you help me, and I'll help you in return, and we will both be better off as a result. This is a long-term win–win social strategy, in contrast to the short-term strategy of the high Mach.

The success of the high Mach depends on the context. One study examined a real-world setting by studying the sales performance of stockbrokers from two different organizational contexts (Shultz, 1993). One organizational context, the NYNEX, is a highly structured stock brokerage and rule bound, with little room for the salespeople to innovate or improvise. Employees are required to follow a two-volume manual of rules. The second organizational context, represented by stock brokerages such as Merrill Lynch, is more loosely structured and allows more opportunities for wheeling and dealing.

The sales success of stockbrokers was evaluated by the size of the commissions earned by the individuals in the two organizational contexts. In the loosely structured organizations, such as Merrill Lynch, the high Machs had more clients and earned fully twice as many commissions as the low Machs. However, in the more tightly structured organizations, the low Machs earned twice as much money on commissions as the high Machs. This study illustrates a key point about the Machiavellian social strategy of influence—its success is highly

(*Continued*)

A Closer Look (*Continued*)

context-dependent. Machiavellianism is not a social strategy that works all the time. Social situations with lots of rules do not allow high Machs to con others, tell lies, and betray those who trust them with impunity. In these situations, the high Machs get caught, sustain damage to their reputations, and often are fired. In more fluid occupational contexts, high Machs succeed because they can wheel and deal, move quickly from one situation to another, and exploit the opportunities available in these less rule-bound settings.

Machiavellianism is a social strategy in which practitioners are quick to betray others (Wilson, Near, & Miller, 1996). In one laboratory study, participants were given an opportunity to steal money in a worker–supervisor situation (Harrell & Hartnagel, 1976). The participants played the role of workers. They were supervised by a person who acted trusting, stating that he or she did not need to monitor the workers closely. A full 81 percent of the high Machs stole money, as contrasted with only 24 percent of the low Machs. The high Machs who did steal took a larger amount of money than those few low Machs who stole, they tended to conceal their theft, and they lied more often to the supervisor when questioned about the theft.

Not only do high Machs lie and betray others' trust more than low Machs, but there is also evidence that they make more believable liars (Exline et al., 1970; Geis & Moon, 1981). In one study, high and low Machs were instructed to cheat on a task and then to lie to the experimenter about having cheated (Exline et al., 1970). The experimenter then became increasingly suspicious and questioned the participants about whether they had cheated. The high Machs were able to maintain greater eye contact than the low Machs. Fewer of the high Machs than the low Machs confessed. Finally, the high Machs were judged to be better liars than the low Machs.

The manipulative tactics used by the high Machs extend to the romantic and sexual domains. High Machs, compared to their low Mach peers, are more likely to feign love in order to get sex (e.g., "I sometimes say 'I love you' when I don't really mean it to get someone to have sex with me"), get a partner drunk in order to induce the partner to have sex, and express a willingness to use force to achieve sex with an unwilling partner (McHoskey, 2001). Women high in Machiavellianism are prone to faking sexual orgasm in order to manipulate or deceive their partner (Brewer, Abell, & Lyons, 2016). They are more prone to committing sexual harassment (Zeigler-Hill, Myers, & Clark, 2016). They tend to maliciously gossip about their mating rivals (Goncalves & Campbell, 2014; Lyons & Hughs, 2015). High Machs are more likely to cheat on their romantic partner and to be sexually unfaithful with other people (Jones & Weiser, 2014). Interestingly, these links between Machiavellianism and specific tactics of manipulation are stronger for the male than for the female sample.

The Machiavellian strategy has many advantages, but it also has costs. By betraying, cheating, and lying, the high Mach runs the risk of retaliation and revenge by those who were exploited. The high Mach is more likely to incur damage to his or her reputation. Once people acquire reputations as exploitative, other people are more likely to avoid them and refuse to interact with them.

This discussion of the Machiavellian strategy also illustrates the three key processes by which personality affects social interaction, bringing us back full circle to the three central processes of personality and social interaction. First, the high Mach tends to *select* situations that are loosely structured, untethered by rules that would restrict the deployment of an exploitative strategy. Second, the high Mach tends to *evoke* specific reactions from others, such as anger and retaliation for having been exploited. Third, the high Mach tends to *manipulate* other people in predictable ways, using tactics that are exploitative, self-serving, and deceptive.

(Buss, 1992). Correlations were computed between the personality traits of the participants and their use of each tactic of manipulation.

Those scoring relatively high in dominance (extraversion) tended to use coercion, such as demanding, threatening, cursing, and criticizing, in order to get their way. Highly dominant people also tended to use responsibility invocation, getting others to commit to a course of action and saying that it was their duty to do it.

Those low in dominance (relatively submissive individuals) used the self-abasement tactic as a means of influencing others. They lowered themselves, for example, or tried to look weak or sickly to get others to do what they wanted. Interestingly, these submissive individuals also tended to use the hardball tactic—deception, lying, degradation, and even violence—more often than their dominant counterparts.

The two main tactics of influence used by highly agreeable people are pleasure induction and reason. Agreeable individuals show others how enjoyable the activity will be, explain the rationale for wanting others to do it, and point out all the good things that will come from doing it. A study of how children manipulate their parents on their choice mates revealed that highly agreeable children used the reason tactic, convincing their parents to trust them (Apostolou, Zacharia, & Frantzides, 2015).

Those who are disagreeable, in contrast, frequently use coercion and the silent treatment—results also found in a Croatia (Butkovic & Bratko, 2007). Not only do they threaten, criticize, yell, and scream in order to get their way, they also give the stony silent look and refuse to speak to the other until he or she complies. Low-agreeable individuals are also likely to seek revenge on people

The "silent treatment" is a manipulation strategy often employed by persons high on the trait of disagreeableness.
Wavebreak Media ltd/Alamy Stock Pho

they perceive have wronged them; they use cost-inflicting rather than benefit-bestowing tactics of manipulation (McCullough et al., 2001). Low-agreeable individuals tend to be more selfish in their use of collective resources, whereas high-agreeable individuals exercise more self-restraint when the group's resources are scarce or threatened (Koole et al., 2001).

Conscientiousness is associated with reason. Conscientious individuals explain why they want the other person to do something and provide logical explanations for wanting it done. Low-conscientious individuals are more likely to use criminal strategies in gaining resources, as indicated by arrest records and recidivism (being rearrested after being let out of prison) (Clower & Bothwell, 2001).

Emotionally unstable individuals use a wide variety of tactics to manipulate others—hardball and coercion, but also reason and monetary reward. The tactic most commonly used by emotionally unstable people, however, is regression. These people pout, sulk, whine, and cry to get their way (see Butkovic & Bratko, 2007). This kind of behavior comes close to the core definition of emotional instability—the display of volatile emotions, some positive and some negative. Emotional volatility seems strategically motivated—it is used to influence others to get what they want.

Which tactics do people high on Intellect–Openness use? Not surprisingly, these smart and perceptive people tend to use reason above all other tactics. They also use pleasure induction and responsibility invocation, however—findings not as intuitively obvious. Can you guess which tactic those *low* on Intellect–Openness use? They use social comparison—saying that everyone else is doing it and comparing the partner with someone else who would do it.

The Dark Triad personality traits (narcissism, psychopathy, and Machiavellianism) are linked with tactics of social influence (Jonason & Webster, 2012). Those scoring high on these dark traits tended to manipulate others through a wide variety of tactics—coercion, hardball, reciprocity, social comparison, monetary reward, and even charm. High Dark Triad scorers favor the hardball tactic; they tend to bully other people (Baughman et al., 2012). Those high on Dark Triad traits engage in stronger and more varied forms of mate retention, including providing benefits and inflicting costs to keep their partner (Chegeni, Pirklani, & Dehshiri, 2018). And Dark Triad men are apt to use coercion as a tactic of manipulation to obtain sex from reluctant or unwilling women (Prusik et al., 2021).

In summary, these results provide strong evidence that personality dispositions are not static entities residing passively in the heads of people. They have profound implications for social interaction—in this case, for the tactics people use to manipulate others in their social environment.

Panning Back: An Overview of Personality and Social Interaction

The important message from this chapter is that personality does not reside passively within individuals, but rather profoundly affects each person's social environment. The three processes by which personality can influence an individual's social environment—selection, evocation, and manipulation—are highlighted in Table 15.6.

These fundamental mechanisms operate in the physical as well as the social environment. Let's consider selection first. In the physical domain, an introvert is more likely to choose to live in a rural habitat, whereas an extravert is more likely to choose city living with all the opportunities for social interaction urban life provides. In the social domain, an extravert is more likely to select an extraverted mate; an introvert is more likely to choose an introverted mate so that they can read books quietly side by side.

For the process of evocation, a loud, heavy person who treads clumsily is more likely to evoke an avalanche while climbing a snowy mountain. In the social domain, narcissistic people evoke admiration from followers and contempt from those who dislike their unbridled self-centeredness. For the process of manipulation, personality affects how people modify the rooms in which they live (Gosling et al., 2002). Conscientious individuals, for example, keep their rooms tidy, neat, and free of clutter. Those low on Conscientiousness have more messiness in their rooms. Those high in Intellect–Openness decorate their rooms with stylish and unconventional objects and have many books that are highly varied in genre. Those low on Intellect–Openness have fewer and more conventional decorations, a narrower range of books, and a narrower collection of music. In the social domain, disagreeable individuals are more likely than stable individuals to use "the silent treatment" as a tactic of manipulation. Those high in Intellect–Openness tend to use reason and rationality to get their way. And narcissists try to transfer blame for their failures onto others.

Table 15.6   Causal Mechanisms That Create Links Between Personality and Environment: Examples from the Physical and Social Domains

Mechanism	Physical Environment	Social Environment
Selection	Introvert selects rural habitat	Extravert chooses extraverted mate
	Avoidance of cold climates	Emotionally stable person chooses stable roommate
Evocation	Person who treads heavily elicits an avalanche	Disagreeable people evoke relationship conflict
	Clumsy person creates, elicits more noise and clatter	Narcissistic people evoke admiration from followers
Manipulation	Conscientious person creates clean and neat room	Disagreeable person uses "the silent treatment"
	Person high on openness creates stylish, colorful room with varied art and books	Narcissists transfer blame to others

A Closer Look   Narcissism and Social Interaction

Narcissism is a personality dimension that involves, at the upper end, high levels of self-absorption and conceitedness, placing one's own wants and needs above those of others, displaying unusual grandiosity, showing a profound sense of entitlement, and lacking empathy for other people's feelings, needs, and desires (see Chapters 10 and 14; Raskin & Terry, 1988). Those high on narcissism tend to be *exhibition-istic* (e.g., flaunting money to impress others), *grandiose* (e.g., talking about how great they are), *self-centered* (e.g., taking the best piece of food for themselves), and *interpersonally exploitative* (e.g., using others for selfish ends) (Buss & Chiodo, 1991). Interestingly, celebrities such as women on reality TV shows tend to be more narcissistic than average (Young & Pinsky, 2006). Nonetheless, it is also true that narcissistic individuals think they are hot (good looking), but empirical evidence suggests that they are only slightly more attractive than average (Bleske-Rechek, Remicker, & Baker, 2008; Holtzman & Strube, 2010). Personality psychologists have documented the impact of narcissism on social interaction, providing a fascinating illustration of the influence of personality on social selection, evocation, and manipulation.

In terms of *selection,* narcissists tend to choose people who admire them, who will reflect the positive view they hold about themselves. They don't want people around who will view them as anything other than as extraordinary, beautiful, or brilliant. Because narcissists view themselves as exceptional, they tend to select social situations in which they perceive that their "opportunity for glory" will be enhanced, and avoid situations in which their self-perceived magnificence will not be noticed by others (Wallace & Baumeister, 2002). Although they tend to appoint themselves to positions of power, they avoid social situations that don't afford the chance to show off their brilliance (Wallace & Baumeister, 2002). Life,

however, sometimes has a way of crashing in, and narcissists are sometimes rejected. When they are rejected, narcissists tend to lash out with great anger at those they perceive to have wronged them (Carpenter, 2012; Horton & Sedikides, 2009; Jones & Paulhus, 2010), perhaps because their self-esteem is a bit fragile in response to failure (Zeigler-Hill, Myers, & Clark, 2010). Interestingly, narcissists are highly selective in their social perceptions—they view themselves as victims of interpersonal transgressions far more frequently than those low on narcissism (McCullough et al., 2003).

In the mating domain, narcissists tend to be low on commitment to their partner, perhaps because they view themselves as better or more desirable than their partner (Campbell & Foster, 2002; Campbell, Rudich, & Sedikedes, 2002). Because they chose mates who admire them, narcissists do not doubt the commitment of their romantic partners (Foster & Campbell, 2005). When asked in an experiment to list possible reasons why their current romantic partner might be less committed than they are to the relationship, narcissists had great difficulty even completing the task! After the task, narcissists (compared with those low on narcissism) indicated substantially lower levels of their own commitment to their romantic partner and a greater willingness to accept a dating invitation from someone else. Narcissistic entitlement has also been linked to *an inability to forgive others,* a quality that could also impair the functioning of romantic relationships (Exline et al., 2004).

Narcissists also *evoke* predictable responses from others. Because they are exhibitionistic and thrust themselves into the center of attention, narcissists sometimes split people in their evocations—some view them as brilliant, entertaining, and "not boring," whereas others view them as selfish and boorish (Campbell, Rudich, & Sedikides, 2002). They sometimes evoke anger in others because of their self-aggrandizing actions, such as pulling rank

on others to make a point. Narcissists also evoke reactions from others through their behavior and dress. They tend to create Facebook pages that are more self-promoting (Buffardi & Campbell, 2008; Ong et al., 2011), including posting sexy images of themselves (DeWall et al., 2011) and sharing sexy photos of their attractive partners (Seidman, Roberts, & Zeigler-Hill, 2019). Narcissists post more "selfies," update their online profile photos more often, and spend more time on Instagram (Marshall, Lefringhausen, & Ferenczi, 2015; Moon et al., 2016; Sorokowski et al., 2015; Weiser, 2015). They are more likely to wear expensive and flashy clothes; if they are female, they wear more makeup and show more cleavage—actions that may evoke sexual overtures in others (Vazire et al., 2008).

Narcissists also use predictable tactics of *manipulation.* They are exploitative of others and would be described as "users." They use friends for their wealth or connections. When in positions of power, they use their positions to exploit subordinates and show no hesitation in pulling rank to humiliate someone else in front of others. They react to failure by derogating other people, possibly to transfer the blame for their failure onto others (Park & Colvin, 2015; South, Oltmanns, & Turkheimer, 2003). In mating, they engage in manipulative game-playing and are more likely to use sexually coercive and aggressive tactics (Blinkhorn, Lyons, & Almond, 2015; Haslam & Montrose, 2015; Lamarche & Seery, 2019). They also lash out in anger and aggression against others when confronted with their own failure. The entitlement and exploitativeness components of narcissism are especially good predictors of aggression (Reidy et al., 2008). In sum, the personality dimension of narcissism shows many links to the social selections they make, the reactions they evoke from others, and the tactics of manipulation they use to enhance their self-centered goals.

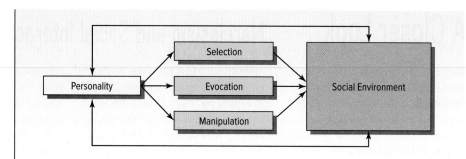

Figure 15.1
Personality and social interaction.

Personality, in short, affects the mates and friends a person chooses and the environments a person decides to enter or avoid (selection), the reactions elicited from others and from the physical environment (evocation), and the ways in which one's physical and social environments are altered once inhabited (manipulation). These three processes are shown in Figure 15.1.

Further research is needed to determine whether the causal arrows in Figure 15.1 run in both directions. Does the choice of a mate who is similar in personality, for example, create a social environment that reinforces that personality and makes it more stable over time (Neyer & Lehnart, 2007)? Does the conflict evoked by disagreeable people create a social environment in which they receive a lot of negative feedback, hence maintaining their disagreeable personality? Does the wide variety of manipulative tactics used by emotionally unstable individuals—from hardball to threats to sulking, whining, and pouting—create a social environment that is indeed rocked with turmoil, thus maintaining the personality disposition of neuroticism? Research within the next decade will undoubtedly answer these questions.

SUMMARY AND EVALUATION

The personality characteristics we carry with us affect how we interact with other people occupying our social world. The reciprocal influences of personality and social interactions have brought the fields of personality psychology and social psychology closer together (Swann & Selye, 2005).

This chapter described three key processes by which personality affects social interaction. First, we *select* people and environments, choosing the social situations to which we expose ourselves. In selecting a mate, people worldwide look for mates who are dependable, are emotionally stable, and have a pleasing disposition. We tend to select mates who are similar in personality to ourselves, a process known as assortative mating. Complementary needs theory—the idea that opposites attract when it comes to human mating—has received no empirical support. Those who fail to get what they want—for example, ending up with mates who are emotionally unstable or disagreeable—tend to be unhappy with their marriages and tend to divorce more often than those who succeed in choosing what they want.

The process of selection extends beyond the choice of romantic partners. The personality trait of shyness, for example, is linked with avoiding gynecological exams, entering risky sexual situations by failing to bring up the topic of contraception, and avoiding risky situations that involve gambling money. Similarly, high sensation-seeking heterosexual males tend to choose risky sexual situations, such as having unprotected sex and sex with a larger number of partners.

Second, we *evoke* emotions and actions in others. These evocations are based, in part, on our personality characteristics. The strongest predictors of angering and upsetting a partner are low Agreeableness and low Emotional Stability. Those low on Agreeableness, for example, tend to create a lot of conflict in their social situations, including with friends and romantic partners, and they tend to be socially victimized during their high school years. In a phenomenon known as expectancy confirmation, our beliefs about the personality characteristics of others sometimes evoke in others precisely the behaviors we expect. A belief that someone is hostile, for example, tends to elicit hostile behavior from that person.

Manipulation is the third process—defined as the ways in which people intentionally influence and exploit others. Humans use many tactics for influencing others, including charm, silent treatment, coercion, reason, regression, and self-abasement. Men and women use these tactics approximately equally, with the exception of regression, which is used slightly more often by women. Personality characteristics play a key role in which tactics we use to influence others. Emotionally unstable people, for example, tend to use regression and the silent treatment. They also tend to use reason and monetary reward, though, suggesting some nonintuitive links between personality and tactics of manipulation. People high on Intellect–Openness tend to use reason; those low on this dimension tend to use the social comparison tactic.

One personality trait linked with manipulation tactics is Machiavellianism. The high Machs tend to tell people what they want to hear, use flattery to get what they want, and frequently lie and deceive. In mating, for example, high Machs are more likely to feign love in order to get sex, use drugs and alcohol to render a potential sex partner more vulnerable, and even express a willingness to use force to get sex. High Machs also betray the trust of others, sometimes feigning cooperation before defecting. They are also more likely than low Machs to steal and then to lie about stealing when they are caught. The success of the high Mach depends heavily on context. In loosely structured social situations and work organizations, high Machs can wheel and deal, using their manipulative, conning strategies to great effect. In more tightly structured, rule-bound situations, however, low Machs outperform high Machs.

All three processes have been documented with the personality disposition of narcissism. Narcissists tend to select others who admire them and avoid those who are skeptical of their claims of greatness. They selectively enter social situations in which there are opportunities for glory and avoid situations in which their brilliance will not be seen by others. Narcissists evoke admiration and respect from those who fawn over them, while evoking anger from those who are victims of their scorn and conceit. In terms of manipulation, narcissists are interpersonally exploitative, using friends for wealth or connections and blaming others when things go wrong. Examining all these processes with respect to narcissists highlights the ways in which personality is connected with the social interactions we create and the environments we inhabit.

In summary, personality is predictably and systematically linked with social interaction through the ways in which we select our partners and social worlds, the ways in which we evoke responses from people we have initially chosen, and the ways in which we influence those people to attain our desired ends.

KEY TERMS

complementary needs theory 473
attraction similarity theory 473
assortative mating 473
violation of desire 478

shyness 479
Machiavellianism 480
evocation 480
hostile attributional bias 481

expectancy confirmation 485
taxonomy 486

Lightspring/Shutterstock

Sex, Gender, and Personality

16

THE SOCIAL AND CULTURAL DOMAIN

Some differences in personality between adult men and women are hypothesized to result from environmental events that occur during adolescence.
Monashee Frantz/AGE Fotostock

"**D**espite the advances of feminism, escalating levels of sexism and violence—from undervalued intelligence to sexual harassment in elementary school—cause girls to stifle their creative spirit and natural impulses, which ultimately destroys their self-esteem" (Pipher, 1994, bookjacket). This is a quotation from the book *Reviving Ophelia,* which remained on the best-seller list for an astonishing 135 weeks (Kling et al., 1999). The sentiment expresses widespread belief that women suffer lower self-esteem than men do and that this difference in adult personality is caused by destructive events during development.

Although we cannot know with certainty why *Reviving Ophelia* remained popular for so long, several possibilities warrant consideration. First, people are intrinsically fascinated with psychological **sex differences:** average differences between women and men in personality or behavior. Second, many people are concerned with the political implications of findings of sex differences. Will such findings be used to foster gender stereotypes? Will findings be used to oppress women? Third, people are concerned with the practical implications of sex differences for their everyday lives. Will knowledge of sex differences help people to communicate better and reduce conflict between genders?

This chapter focuses centrally on the scientific issues, but it also discusses the broader debate about the scientific findings. Are women and men basically different or basically the same when it comes to personality? Have the differences been exaggerated because of stereotypes people have about what women and men are like? Which theories provide compelling explanations for sex-linked features of personality? As used in this text, the phrase *sex differences* simply refers to an average difference between women and men on certain characteristics, such as height, body fat distribution, or personality characteristics, with no prejudgment about the cause of the difference.

We begin by briefly sketching the history of the study of sex differences in personality. This background information will show how complex this topic is: We will see that the definition of **gender,** or social interpretations of what it means to be a man or a woman, can change over time. Next, we look at some of the techniques psychologists use to identify sex differences from research data. We examine sex differences in traits such as assertiveness, criminality, and sexuality, and use these differences to explore the fascinating topic of **gender stereotypes:** beliefs about how men and women differ or are supposed to differ, in contrast to what the actual differences are. Finally, we explore theories that attempt to explain the origins of these sex differences.

The Science and Politics of Studying Sex and Gender

"Few topics in psychology can rival sex differences in their power to stir controversy and captivate both scientists and the public" (Del Guidice, 2019). Some worry, for example, that findings of sex differences might be used to support certain political agendas, such as excluding women from leadership or work roles. Some argue that findings of sex differences merely reflect gender stereotypes rather than real differences. Some argue that any discovery of sex differences merely reflects the biases of the scientists and are not objective descriptions of reality. Roy Baumeister, for example, advocated stopping research on sex differences entirely because findings of sex differences might conflict with ideals of egalitarianism (Baumeister, 1988), although he has since reversed his views on this (personal communication, May 17, 2006) and has published several key articles on sex differences in the domain of sexuality (e.g., Baumeister, Catanese, & Vohs, 2001).

Others argue, however, that both scientific psychology and social change will be impossible without coming to terms with the real sex differences that exist. Feminist psychologist Alice Eagly (1995), for example, argues that sex differences exist, they are consistent across studies, and they should not be ignored merely because they are perceived to conflict with certain political agendas. Indeed, Eagly argues that feminists who try to minimize these differences or pretend that they do not exist hamper the feminist agenda by presenting a dogma that is out of touch with reality. Still others, such as Janet Hyde, argue that sex differences have been exaggerated, that there is so much overlap between the sexes on most personality traits, and that the actual differences are minimal (Hyde, 2005; Hyde & Plant, 1995). In contrast, recent studies using sophisticated multivariate statistical techniques find that sex differences in personality are considerably larger than previous reviews concluded that relied solely on considering one personality trait at a time (Kaiser et al., 2020). We will examine these contrasting positions in more detail.

History of the Study of Sex Differences

Before 1973, relatively little attention was paid to sex differences. Indeed, in psychology research, it was common practice to use participants of only one sex, most often males. And even when both men and women were studied, few articles actually analyzed or reported whether the effects differed for men and women.

All of this changed in the early 1970s (Eagly, 1995; Hoyenga & Hoyenga, 1993). In 1974, Eleanor Maccoby and Carol Jacklyn published a now-classic book, *The Psychology of Sex Differences,* in which they reviewed hundreds of studies and drew several key conclusions about how men and women differed. They concluded that women were slightly better than men at verbal ability. Men were slightly better than women in mathematical ability (e.g., geometry, algebra) and spatial ability (e.g., ability to visualize what a three-dimensional object would look like if it were rotated in space by 90 degrees). In terms of *personality* characteristics, they concluded that only one sex difference existed: Men were more aggressive than women. With other aspects of personality and social behavior, they concluded that there was not enough evidence to determine whether men and women differed. Overall, they concluded that sex differences were few in number and trivial in importance.

The Psychology of Sex Differences set off an avalanche of research. The book itself was criticized on various grounds. Some argued that many more sex differences existed than were portrayed by Maccoby and Jacklyn (Block, 1983). Others challenged the conclusion that men were more aggressive than women (Frodi, Macauley, & Thome, 1977). Furthermore, the methods by which the authors drew their conclusions, although standard practice at that time, were crude by today's standards.

Following the publication of *The Psychology of Sex Differences,* psychology journals changed their reporting practices. They started to require authors to calculate and report sex differences. Claims that many of the findings in psychology were based primarily on studies of men led to calls for the greater inclusion of women as participants. There followed an explosion of research on sex differences. Literally thousands of studies were conducted on the ways in which men and women did or did not differ. By 1992, the federal government of the United States required both sexes to be represented in federally funded research (unless there was a legitimate reason to limit the research to one sex, such as studies of ovarian or prostate cancer).

Since Maccoby and Jacklyn's early work, researchers have developed more precise quantitative procedures for examining conclusions across studies and thus for determining sex differences, called meta-analyses. Recall that meta-analysis is a statistical method for summarizing the findings of large numbers of individual studies. Meta-analysis allows researchers to calculate with greater objectivity whether a particular difference is consistent across studies. Furthermore, it allows researchers to estimate how large the difference actually is—called the **effect size.**

Calculation of Effect Size: How Large Are the Sex Differences?

The most commonly used statistic in meta-analysis is the effect size, or d statistic. The d statistic is used to express a difference in standard deviation units (see Chapter 2). A d of 0.50 means that the average difference between two groups is half a standard deviation. A d of 1.00 means that the difference between the groups is one full standard deviation. A d of 0.25 means that the difference between the groups is one-quarter of a standard deviation. An effect size can be calculated for each study of sex differences and then averaged across studies to give a more precise and objective assessment of whether the sexes differ and, if so, by how much.

Most meta-analyses have adopted a convention for interpreting effect sizes (Cohen, 1977):

d Score	Meaning
0.20 or −0.20	Small difference
0.50 or −0.50	Medium difference
0.80 or −0.80	Large difference

When comparing men to women, assume that positive d scores, such as 0.20 or 0.50, indicate that men score higher than women. Negative d scores, such as −0.20 or −0.50, indicate that women score higher than men. For example, a d score of −0.85 means that women score much higher on a particular trait.

When it comes to who can throw a ball farther, the effect size for the difference between men and women is 2.00, in favor of the men. Although this is a large difference in average ability, there will nevertheless be some women who can throw farther than most men because the distributions still overlap.

Carson Granci/Design Pics/SuperStock

To get a feel for effect sizes, let's examine a few findings outside the realm of personality. Which sex can throw a ball farther, men or women? Although there are great individual differences within each sex, it is clear that men can, on average, throw farther than women. The d is approximately 2.00 (Ashmore, 1990). This means that the sexes differ, on average, by two full standard deviations, which is quite large. Which sex has a higher grade point average in college? The d for grade point average is −0.04, which is very close to zero. This means that men and women are essentially the same in their grade point average, although women have a very slight advantage.

Which sex scores higher in verbal ability? It turns out that women are slightly better than men, but the d is only −0.11. Are men better at math? The d here also turns out to be quite small, only 0.15. These findings are in line with a vast literature that now documents that men and women are essentially the same (or do not differ by much) on most measures of cognitive ability (Hyde, 2005, 2014). About the only well-documented exception pertains to spatial rotation ability, such as the spatial ability involved in throwing a spear (or football) so that it correctly anticipates the trajectory of a moving object, such as an animal or a receiver. The d for this sort of spatial ability is 0.73, which comes close to the standard for "large" (Ashmore, 1990).

Even large effect sizes for average sex differences do not necessarily have implications for any particular individual. Even with a d of 2.00 for throwing distance, some women can throw much farther than the average man, and some men cannot throw as far as the average woman. This overlap in the distributions of the sexes must be kept in mind when evaluating effect sizes (see Figure 16.1).

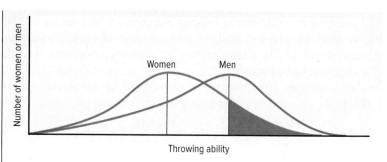

Figure 16.1

Overlap between the sexes in context of a mean difference. Even when one sex greatly exceeds the other in a particular ability, there is a large area of overlap. Women whose throwing ability falls in the shaded area exceed the throwing ability of the average man.

Minimalists and Maximalists

One focus of the debate on sex differences centers on effect sizes—on whether sex differences are small and relatively inconsequential or substantial and important. Those who describe sex differences as small and inconsequential take the **minimalist** position and offer two arguments. The first is that, empirically, most findings of sex differences show small magnitudes of effect (Deaux, 1984; Hyde, 2005, 2014; Hyde & Plant, 1995). Minimalists tend to emphasize that the distributions of men and women on any given personality variable show tremendous overlap, which reflect their small magnitude of effect (see Figure 16.1 for an example of distribution overlap). A second argument advanced by minimalists is that whatever differences exist do not have much practical importance for behavior in everyday life. If the sex differences are small and don't have consequences for people's lives, then perhaps we should concentrate on other psychological issues that are more important.

In contrast, those who take the **maximalist** position tend to argue that the magnitude of sex differences is comparable to the size to many other effects in psychology and should not be trivialized (Eagly, 1995). Some sex differences tend to be small in magnitude, others are large in magnitude, and some are in the moderate range, according to this view. Eagly also notes that even small sex differences can have large practical importance. A small sex difference in helping behavior, for example, could result in a large sex difference in the number of lives women and men aid over the long run. As you read this chapter, keep in mind the range of positions psychologists have taken on sex differences, from the minimalist stance to the maximalist stance.

Sex Differences in Personality

We begin by examining sex differences in temperament in children. The five-factor model of personality provides a convenient framework for organizing a number of findings about sex differences (see Table 16.1). Then we discuss sex differences in other domains such as sexuality, criminality and physical aggression, depression and psychopathy, and the interaction patterns of men and women in groups.

Temperament in Children

The importance of sex differences in temperament is aptly summarized by the authors of a meta-analysis: "The question of gender differences in temperament is arguably one of the most fundamental questions in gender differences research in the areas of personality and social behavior. Temperament reflects biologically based emotional and behavioral consistencies that appear early in life and predict—often in conjunction with other factors—patterns and outcomes in numerous other domains such as psychopathology and personality" (Else-Quest et al., 2006, p. 33). These authors conducted the most massive meta-analysis ever undertaken of sex differences in temperament in children ranging in age from 3 to 13.

The sex differences they discovered ranged from substantial to negligible. **Inhibitory control** showed the largest sex difference, with a $d = -0.41$, which is considered in the moderate range. Inhibitory control refers to the ability to control inappropriate responses or behaviors. One study found very large gender differences on the trait of impulsivity, with boys being less able to control their impulses ($d = -0.72$) (Olino et al., 2013).

Table 16.1 Effect Sizes for Gender Differences in Facets of Personality within the Five Factor Model

Dimension	Effect Size
Extraversion	
Gregariousness	−0.26
Warmth	−0.29
Assertiveness	0.24
Activity	0.09
Excitement Seeking	0.25
Agreeableness	
Trust	−0.25
Tender-mindedness	−0.97
Modesty	−0.26
Aggressive Ideation	0.84
Conscientiousness	
Order	−0.24
Emotional Stability	
Anxiety	−0.54
Fearfulness	−1.04
Intellect-Openness	
Ideas	0.03
Fantasy	−0.31
Feelings	−0.42

Note: Positive numbers indicate that men score higher than women; negative numbers indicate that women score higher than men.

As the authors summarize, "these findings may represent an overall better ability of girls to regulate or allocate their attention" and suppress socially undesirable behavior (Else-Quest et al., 2006, p. 61). **Perceptual sensitivity**–the ability to detect subtle stimuli from the environment–also showed a sex difference favoring girls ($d = -0.38$). Girls, on average, appear to be more sensitive than boys to subtle and low-intensity signals from their external world. Inhibitory control is related to the later development of Conscientiousness. Interestingly, the sex difference appears to fade, because adult men and women do not differ much in conscientiousness.

Surgency, a cluster including approach behavior, high activity, and impulsivity, showed a sex difference ($d = 0.38$), with boys scoring higher than girls. Perhaps the combination of high surgency and low inhibitory control accounts for the fact that boys tend to get into more disciplinary difficulties in school in the early years of their lives. Some subcomponents of surgency showed slightly smaller sex differences, such as activity level ($d = 0.33$) and high-intensity pleasure ($d = 0.30$), which is consistent with the finding that boys more than girls engage in rough-and-tumble play.

The combination of low inhibitory control and high surgency may account for another reliable gender difference–a difference in the domain of *physical aggressiveness.* Using an act frequency measure based on codings of actual behavior, Zakriski, Wright, and Underwood (2005) found a $d = 0.60$, indicating that boys were more physically aggressive than girls (approximate age 13). Boys hit other kids more than girls do.

Girls and boys showed virtually no difference in a summary variable called **negative affectivity,** which includes components such as anger, difficulty, amount of distress, and sadness. A more fine-grained analysis of negative emotions, however, reveals that girls are slightly higher on fearfulness ($d = -0.34$), whereas boys are slightly higher on anger expression ($d = -0.34$) (Olino et al., 2013).

In summary, meta-analysis of temperament in children between the ages of 3 and 13 suggests a few sex differences of small to moderate magnitude. Girls show more inhibitory control and higher fearfulness. Boys show higher surgency, higher levels of activity, more impulsivity, and more anger in emotional expression. These are average sex differences, however, which means that the distributions overlap considerably.

Five-Factor Model

The five-factor model provides a broad set of personality traits within which we can examine whether women and men differ.

Extraversion

Three facets of extraversion have been examined for sex differences: gregariousness, assertiveness, and activity. Women score slightly higher on gregariousness than men, but the difference is quite small. Similarly, men score slightly higher on activity level. A study of personality in 50 different cultures revealed a relatively small gender difference ($d = 0.15$) on extraversion (McCrae et al., 2005b). A facet analysis of gender differences in extraversion reveals a more interesting picture (De Bolle et al., 2015). Women score higher on the facets of Warmth ($d = -0.29$) and Gregariousness ($d = -0.26$), whereas men score higher on Assertiveness ($d = 0.24$) and Excitement Seeking ($d = 0.25$). A related finding, emerging from a study of 127 samples in 70 countries ($N = 77,528$), is that men place a greater importance on the *value of power* than do women (Schwartz & Rubel, 2005). That is, men tend to value social status and dominance over other people more than women.

The medium-size sex difference in assertiveness may show up in social behavior in group contexts. Men interrupt others in conversation more than women do in mixed-sex groups (Hoyenga & Hoyenga, 1993). An important source of conflict between the sexes—unwanted interruptions of dialogue—may stem from this moderate sex difference in assertiveness.

Agreeableness

A study of 50 cultures revealed a small to medium gender difference ($d = -0.32$) on Agreeableness, indicating that women score higher than men (McCrae et al., 2005b; Schmitt et al., 2008). Older adults ranging in age from 65 to 98 also show a gender difference in Agreeableness ($d = -0.35$), with women scoring higher than men (Chapman et al., 2007; Wood, Nye, & Saucier, 2010). Two facets of agreeableness have been examined: trust and tender-mindedness. **Trust** is the proclivity to cooperate with others, giving others the benefit of the doubt, and viewing one's fellow human beings as basically good at heart. **Tender-mindedness** is a nurturant proclivity—having empathy for others and being sympathetic with those who are disadvantaged. As you can see in Table 16.1, women score as more trusting than men. Women are also substantially more tender-minded and compassionate than men

Studies show that women naturally smile more than men. Researchers disagree, however, on what this sex difference means; some suggest smiling is a sign of agreeableness, whereas others hold that smiling is a form of submissiveness or a way to ease tension in social situations.
Realistic Reflections

(e.g., caring, giving), with an effect size of −0.97, which is large (León et al., 2017). Another facet of Agreeableness is Modesty; women are more modest than men in general ($d = -0.26$) (De Bolle et al., 2015). Some research has focused on the context-specificity of these sex differences. Women seem to be more cooperative than men in mixed-sex social interactions (Balliet et al., 2011). In contrast, men are slightly more cooperative than women in same-sex social interactions (Balliet et al., 2011).

Another finding related to Agreeableness pertains to *smiling.* Meta-analyses show that women smile more often than men, with an effect size of −0.60 (Hall, 1984). If smiling reflects an agreeable personality disposition, we can conclude that women are more agreeable than men. However, some researchers view smiling as a sign of submissiveness rather than agreeableness (Eagly, 1995). Furthermore, some argue that it is low-status people who do a lot of smiling. It's possible that smiling reflects agreeableness in some contexts and submissiveness in other contexts.

It will not surprise you that men are more physically aggressive than women. This shows up in personality tests, in aggressive fantasies, and in actual measures of behavior (Hyde, 1986). In general, the effect sizes for aggression are largest for projective tests, such as the TAT ($d = 0.86$), the next largest for peer report measures of aggression ($d = 0.63$), and the smallest for self-report measures of aggression ($d = 0.40$). Fantasy measures of aggression, which assess how often people imagine aggressing against others, show large sex differences, with an effect size of 0.84.

Worldwide, men commit roughly 90 percent of all homicides, and most of the victims of these homicides are other men (Buss, 2005b; Daly & Wilson, 1988). Furthermore, men commit more violent crimes of all sorts, ranging from assaults to gang wars. Figure 16.2 shows the arrest rate for violent crimes within the United States as a function of age and sex. The sex differences show up just after puberty, peaking in adolescence and

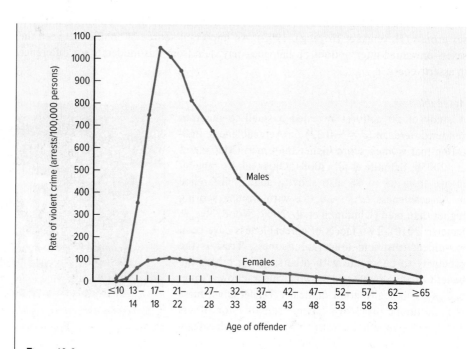

Figure 16.2

Arrest rates for violent crime in the United States as a function of age and gender.

the early 20s. After age 50, violent crimes start to decline, and men and women become much more similar to each other in criminal aggressiveness.

In all cultures for which there are data, the vast majority of killings and other violent crimes are committed by young men (Daly & Wilson, 1988; Pinker, 2012). Psychologically, a key reason for the gender difference is that women are much more sensitive than men to punishment ($d = -.33$), whereas men seem more inclined to take risks, oblivious to the punishments they may receive (Cross, Copping, & Campbell, 2011). Another psychological contributor to men's aggression is men's low level of empathy compared to women (Dryburgh & Vashon, 2019). Men are less likely to put themselves in the shoes of the victim and experience the pain that victims of aggression suffer. These culturally universal findings lend credence to theories that offer evolutionary explanations for some of the sex differences (see Chapter 8). It is important to keep in mind that these forms of aggression refer to physical violence. Other forms of aggression, such as *relational aggression* (verbal insults and gossip about others), show either no gender differences or a slight tendency for women to score higher (e.g., Hess et al., 2010; Ostrov & Godleski, 2010).

Conscientiousness

The 50-culture study revealed a negligible sex difference ($d = -0.14$) on overall levels of Conscientiousness (McCrae et al., 2005b). Only one facet of Conscientiousness has been scrutinized for sex differences—order. Women score slightly higher than men on order, with an effect size of -0.13, although a larger cross-cultural study revealed a slightly larger gender difference in order ($d = -0.24$) (De Bolle et al., 2015). This is small enough to conclude that men and women are essentially the same on this dimension. Nonetheless, even very small effects can sometimes have large cumulative effects over time. For example, a small difference in order between marriage partners may result in many arguments about housecleaning over the course of a year.

Emotional Stability

Emotional Stability may be the most value-laden dimension of the five-factor model. As you will recall from Chapter 3, at one end of the dimension are those who are steady, calm, and stable, the "emotionally stable" end. The opposite end is characterized by volatility and changeability of mood. Although many have labeled this end of the dimension "emotionally unstable" or "neurotic," one could just as easily label it as "emotionally expressive."

The 50-culture study revealed that Emotional Stability shows the largest sex difference ($d = -0.49$) in the five-factor model, indicating that women are moderately lower than men (McCrae et al., 2005b; see also Schmitt et al., 2008). A study of 10 Arab countries—Kuwait, Saudi Arabia, Emirates, Oman, Egypt, Syria, Lebanon, Palestine (Nablus and Gaza), Jordan, and Iraq—found similar sex differences using a measure of anxiety (Abdel-Khalek & Alansari, 2004). Older adults ranging in age from 65 to 98 also show a mean sex difference in Emotional Stability ($d = -0.52$), with women scoring lower than men (Chapman et al., 2007). The Anxiety facet of this factor shows the largest gender difference across cultures, with women scoring more in the anxious direction ($d = -0.54$) (De Bolle et al., 2015). And more detailed measures show that women are especially high on fearfulness ($d = -1.04$) (Campbell et al., 2016) and feelings of vulnerability (Kajonius & Johnson, 2018). Sex differences in emotional stability are especially important because they are linked with important life outcomes such as risk of eating disorders such as binging and purging, which are much more common in females (Brown, Hochman, & Micali, 2020).

Intellect-Openness to Experience

The 50-culture study revealed essentially no sex differences ($d = -0.07$) in Intellect-Openness to experience (McCrae et al., 2005b), similar to a 55-culture study that found a $d = -0.05$ (Schmitt et al., 2008). Botwin, Buss, and Shackelford (1997) examined sex differences in Intellect-Openness to experience using three data sources: self-report, spouse-report, and independent interviewer reports (one male and one female interviewer). Analyses of these three data sources yielded no sex differences in Openness-Intellect. A cross-cultural study of adolescents, college students, and adults reveals essentially no gender differences in Openness to Experience at the global trait level. Nonetheless, a facet analysis reveals that women score higher on two facets of Openness—Fantasy and especially Ideas (De Bolle et al., 2015).

Table 16.1 summarizes the key findings of gender differences in the key facets of the five factor model of personality. Recent studies using multivariate statistics, that is examining gender differences in multiple personality traits simultaneously, conclude that the differences are considerably larger overall than when considering single traits one at a time (Kaiser et al., 2020). A good analogy is studying male and female facial features one at a time (e.g., nose breadth, eye spacing, chin size) versus studying overall faces. It is relatively easy to glance at a face and determine with 95 percent accuracy whether it is a man or woman, but it would be difficult to make this classification by examining only one feature of the face at a time (Kaiser et al., 2019). When it comes to sex differences across multiple traits, one can determine with 85 percent accuracy whether the personality profile comes from a man or a woman (Del Guidice, 2019; Kaiser et al., 2019).

Basic Emotions: Frequency and Intensity

Emotions are central to personality, so much so that we devoted an entire chapter to them (Chapter 13). Cross-cultural research has revealed precisely where the sexes differ in their experiences of emotions and where the sexes are similar. One study examined 2,199 Australians and an international sample of 6,868 participants drawn from 41 different countries (Brebner, 2003). Eight emotions were examined, four "positive" emotions (Affection, Joy, Contentment, Pride) and four "negative" emotions (Fear, Anger, Sadness, Guilt). Participants rated (1) how frequently they experienced each emotion and (2) the intensity with which they experienced each emotion. The basic findings are summarized in Table 16.2.

There are small, but statistically significant differences in the experience of emotions in this international sample. All point to women experiencing both positive emotions *and* negative emotions more frequently and intensely than do men. In the positive domain, affection and joy show the largest sex differences. Pride, in contrast, shows no sex difference in either frequency or intensity. In the negative domain, women experience fear and sadness more than men, especially in the reported intensity of the experience. They also experience the emotion of disgust more than men (Al-Shawaf, Lewis, & Buss, 2018). Guilt, in contrast, shows a minimal gender difference in intensity and no difference in frequency—perhaps contradicting the stereotype that women are more guilt prone than men. These results must be qualified in two ways. First, the effect sizes are generally small. Second, other research has documented that more specialized explorations of emotions reveal some reversals of these sex differences, such as women experiencing more intense jealousy in response to the emotional infidelity of a partner (see Chapter 8).

One of the most common complaints that women express about men is that they don't express their emotions enough (Buss, 2016). Men, in contrast, often complain that women are too emotional. The results point to one possible reason for these

Table 16.2 Sex Differences in Experience of Emotions

Emotion	Frequency	Intensity
Positive Emotions	−0.20	−0.23
Affection	−0.30	−0.25
Joy	−0.16	−0.26
Contentment	−0.13	−0.18
Pride	ns	ns
Negative Emotions	−0.14	−0.25
Fear	−0.17	−0.26
Anger	−0.05	−0.14
Sadness	−0.16	−0.28
Guilt	ns	0.07

Note: Entries in the table are effect sizes (*d*). The designation "ns" indicates that the sex difference was not significant. Negative values indicate that women report experiencing the emotion more frequently or intensely than do men.

Source: Brebner (2003).

complaints—perhaps men don't *express* their emotions because they literally don't *experience* emotions as frequently or as intensely as do women.

Other Dimensions of Personality

Several dimensions of personality are related to, but not directly subsumed by, the five-factor model of personality. We will examine three: self-esteem, sexuality and mating, and the people–things dimension.

Self-Esteem

A topic of major interest to women and men is self-esteem, or how good we feel about ourselves. This is reflected in the many popular books on the topic, such as *10 Simple Solutions for Building Self-Esteem* (Schiraldi, 2007). Although researchers have explored many facets of self-esteem, such as esteem of one's athletic abilities and esteem of one's social skills, by far the most frequently measured component is **global self-esteem,** defined as "the level of global regard that one has for the self as a person" (Harter, 1993, p. 88). Global self-esteem can range from highly positive to highly negative and reflects an overall evaluation of the self (Kling et al., 1999).

Global self-esteem is linked with many aspects of functioning and is central to mental health. Those with high self-esteem cope better with the stresses and strains of daily life. In laboratory studies, when faced with negative feedback about one's performance, those with high self-esteem perform better on cognitive tasks. Those with high self-esteem tend to take credit for their successes but deny responsibility for their failures (Kling et al., 1999).

Meta-analyses yield an interesting pattern of sex differences (Feingold, 1994; Kling et al., 1999). The overall effect size is relatively small ($d = 0.21$), with males scoring slightly higher than females in self-esteem (Kling et al., 1999). The fascinating finding, however, emerged when the researchers analyzed sex differences in self-esteem according to the age of the participants. Young children (ages 7–10) showed only a slight sex difference in self-esteem ($d = 0.16$). As the children approached adolescence, however, the gap

When it comes to attitudes about casual sex, men tend to be more interested in women than women are in men, on average.
Dmytro Zinkevych/Shutterstock

between the sexes widened. At ages 11–14, d was 0.23. And the sex difference peaked during the ages of 15–18 ($d = 0.33$). Females seem to suffer from lower self-esteem than males as they hit their mid- to late teens. The good news is that in adulthood the self-esteem gap starts to close. During the ages of 19–22, the effect size shrinks to 0.18. During the ages of 23–59, the sexes come even closer, with a d of 0.10. And during older age, from 60 on up, the d is only -0.03, which means that the males and females are virtually identical in self-esteem.

The magnitudes of all these effects are relatively small, even during adolescence, when the gap between the sexes is the widest. The widespread fear that women's self-esteem is permanently damaged seems somewhat exaggerated in light of this empirical evidence. Nonetheless, even small differences in self-esteem can be extremely important to day-to-day well-being. For example, low self-esteem in women predicts vulnerability to depression in adolescents and college students (Gao et al., 2022). It is important for researchers to explore why females lose self-esteem relative to males in adolescence and whether programs that attempt to raise self-esteem are successful.

Sexuality, Emotional Investment, and Mating

As we saw in Chapter 3, individual differences in sexuality show some overlap with the five-factor model of personality, but not perfect overlap (Schmitt & Buss, 2000). Two reviews concluded that there exist large sex differences in the desire for sexual variety (Schmitt et al., 2012; Petersen & Hyde, 2010). Men are more likely to have more permissive attitudes toward casual sex ($d = .45$) and view pornography more often ($d = .63$)—sex differences that seem to remain stable over generations (e.g., Wright & Vangeel, 2019). Men more than women also desire a larger number of sex partners, have more frequent sexual fantasies, and are more willing to accept offers of sex from a stranger (Hald & Hogh-Olesen, 2010).

Can men and women be "just friends"? Men have more difficulty in being friends with the opposite sex. Men are more likely than women to initiate friendship with someone of the opposite sex because they are attracted to them, are more likely to become sexually attracted to their opposite-sex friends, and are more likely to dissolve such friendships if their attraction is not reciprocated (Bleske-Rechek & Buss, 2001).

Men are more likely to be sexually aggressive in the sense of trying to force someone to have sex when that person expresses an unwillingness to have sex (Buss, 2016). Not all men are sexually aggressive. Men high on "hostile masculinity" (domineering and degrading attitudes toward women), men high on Dark Triad traits, and men low on empathy are most likely to report using sexual aggression (Jonason, Girgis, & Milne-Home, 2017; Wheeler, George, & Dahl, 2002). Furthermore, men who are narcissistic are especially likely to express rape-supportive beliefs and to lack empathy for rape victims (Bushman et al., 2003). So, although the sexes differ overall in sexual aggression, it really appears to be limited to a subset of men—those who are high on Dark Triad traits, lack empathy, and display hostile masculinity, especially if they also pursue a short-term mating strategy (Buss, 2021).

If men score higher in desire for sexual variety, women typically score higher in "emotional investment," a cluster of items including *loving, lovable, romantic, affectionate, cuddlesome, compassionate,* and *passionate* (Schmitt & Buss, 2000). A study of 48 nations found an average effect size of $-.39$ (Schmitt et al., 2009). This sex difference may stem from the evolution of sex differences in attachment: women show higher levels of emotional attachment both to children and to romantic partners (Schmitt et al., 2009). Women between the ages of 18 and 39 also report greater life longings for family and romantic partners (Kotter-Gruhn et al., 2009).

People-Things Dimension

Another dimension of personality has been labeled the **people-things dimension** (Lippa, 1998; Little, 1972a, 1972b). This refers to the nature of vocational interests. People who score toward the "things" end of the dimension prefer vocations that deal with impersonal objects—machines, tools, or materials. Examples include carpenters, auto mechanics, building contractors, tool makers, and farmers. Those scoring toward the "people" end of the dimension prefer social occupations, which involve thinking about others, caring for others, or directing others. Examples include high school teachers, social workers, nurses, and religious counselors.

The sex difference on the people-things dimension is roughly a d of 1.35; men are more likely to score at the things end of the dimension, and women are more likely to score at the people end (Lippa, 1998). A study of more than half a million people found a d of 0.93, which is considered quite large (Su, Rounds, & Armstrong, 2009). Another study of 1,283,110 individuals also found large sex differences, with women preferring people-oriented occupations and men preferring thing-oriented occupations (Morris, 2016). When girls are asked to describe themselves spontaneously, they are more likely than boys to make references to their close relationships. They are more likely to value personal qualities linked to group harmony, such as sensitivity to others. And they are more likely to identify their personal relationships as central to their identity as a person (Gabriel & Gardner, 1999).

The people-thing distinction is similar to the empathizing-systemizing distinction. **Empathizing** refers to tuning in to other people's thoughts and feelings. **Systemizing** is the drive to comprehend how things work, how systems are built, and how inputs produce outputs (Baron-Cohen, 2003). Women score higher on empathizing, men higher on systemizing, which may partially explain gender differences in occupational preferences—women men prefer the teaching and helping professions; men gravitate toward construction and engineering (Wright, Eaton, & Skagerberg, 2015). Gender differences in empathizing are also linked to altruistic behavior such as helping those in need and sharing their belongings (Chaidir et al., 2019).

These results are not surprising; they fit with our stereotypes of women and men. Still, it is interesting that they were correctly identified more than a century ago: ". . . the greatest difference between men and women [occurs] in the relative strength of the interest in things and their mechanisms [stronger in men] and the interest in persons and their feelings [stronger in women]" (Thorndike, 1911, p. 31).

Masculinity, Femininity, Androgyny, and Sex Roles

Women and men differ in a few dimensions: assertiveness, tender-mindedness, and anxiety, as well as in aggression, sexuality, and depression. But do these differences mean that there is such a thing as a masculine or feminine personality? This section explores conceptions of masculinity and femininity and how the treatment of these topics has changed over time.

In the 1930s, personality researchers began to notice that men and women differed in their responses to a number of personality items on large inventories. For example, when asked whether they preferred to take baths or showers, women indicated that they preferred baths, whereas men indicated that they preferred showers. Based on these sex differences, researchers assumed that the differences could be described by a single personality

A Closer Look

Sex Differences in Depression

Depression is marked by low self-esteem, pessimism (expecting the worst to happen), and the perception that one has little control over one's life. It's one of the most common psychological maladies of modern humans, and there is evidence that the rate of depression is increasing. Five studies that comprised 39,000 individuals living in five areas of the world revealed that young people are more likely than older people to have experienced at least one major episode of depression (Nesse & Williams, 1994). Moreover, the incidence of depression appears to be higher in more economically developed cultures (Nesse & Williams, 1994).

Adult men and women differ in the incidence of depression and in the nature of their depressive symptoms, but the sexes don't start out different. In childhood, there are no sex differences in depression. After puberty, however, women show a depression rate roughly twice that of men—a finding replicated in 25 different European countries (Van de Velde, Bracke, & Levecque, 2010). Roughly 25 percent of all women have at least one depressive episode in their lifetimes. In contrast, only 10 percent of all men will have a depressive episode. The largest sex differences in depression show up between the ages of 18 and 44. After that, the sexes start to converge.

The following list contains some of the critical aspects of sex differences in depressive symptoms:

1. Depressed women more than depressed men report excessive eating and weight gain as one of the symptoms (although loss of appetite is the most common symptom of depression in both sexes).
2. Women are more likely to cry when depressed; men are more likely to become aggressive when depressed.
3. Depressed women are more likely than men to seek treatment; depressed men are more likely to miss work.
4. Nervous activity (e.g., fidgeting) is more common in depressed women than in

depressed men; inactivity is more common in depressed men.
5. Among depressed college students, men are more socially withdrawn, and more likely to use drugs; women are more likely to experience hurt feelings and a decline in self-esteem.
6. Men are more likely to commit suicide "successfully," perhaps because men are more likely to use guns as the method; women are more likely to make nonfatal suicide attempts, perhaps because they use less lethal methods, such as overdosing on pills.

One clue to the sex difference in depression comes from a study of 1,100 community-based adults (Nolen-Hoeksema, Larson, & Grayson, 1999). The researchers speculated that women's greater vulnerability to depressive symptoms may stem from factors such as their lower power in the workplace, their relative lack of control over important areas of their lives, work overload, and lower status in heterosexual relationships. Because they are searching for ways to control their lives, women may start to *ruminate*. **Rumination** involves repeatedly focusing on one's symptoms or distress (e.g., "Why do I continue to feel so bad about myself?" or "Why doesn't my boss like me?"). Because their rumination can fail to lead to effective solutions, according to this theory, women continue to ruminate, and rumination is a key contributor to women's greater experience of depressive symptoms. Women ruminate more than men, and rumination in turn contributes to the perseverance of the depressive symptoms. Nonetheless, the gender difference in rumination is small ($d = -0.24$) and so unlikely to provide the whole explanation (Johnson & Whisman, 2013).

Another theory is that women's greater depression is linked with entering mate competition and is caused by dissatisfaction with their physical appearance (Hankin & Abramson, 2001). The onset of women's depression and the emergence of the sex difference appears around the age of 13, when

heterosexual interactions start to increase. And it is well documented that men place a greater value on physical appearance in their mate selections worldwide, suggesting that women are under greater pressure to compete in the realm of attractiveness (Buss, 2016). Body dissatisfaction increases in women around puberty, as does the onset of eating disorders such as binging and purging and dissatisfaction with current weight (Hankin & Abramson, 2001). Moreover, women score higher on *objectified body consciousness,* which involves becoming observers and critics of their bodies and feeling shame when their bodies do not match up with cultural idealized body standards (Hyde & Mezulis, 2020). The final link is that a woman's dissatisfaction with her body and physical appearance is linked with increases in depression. If a woman's self-worth is in part tied up in her physical appearance in the mating market, then women's pubertal onset of depression could stem partly from the intensity of mate competition after women hit puberty.

An evolutionary adaptationist theory proposes that moderate levels of depression send signals of distress to social partners to elicit help or prompt partners to invest more in the relationship (Hagen & Rosenström, 2016). For example, a mother of a newborn baby might experience postpartum depression if she is not receiving as much help as she needs from her husband or kin, inducing these social partners to invest more (Hagen & Rosenström, 2016). The birth of a child is indeed a time in women's lives in which they are most at risk for experiencing depression (Eid, Gobinath, & Galea, 2019). Whereas men are more likely to get angry to induce partners to invest more, women, having generally lower upper body strength to back up anger, are more likely to get depressed as an unconscious bargaining tactic.

Whatever the multiple origins, sex differences in depression represent one of the largest and most consequential differences in personality.

dimension, with *masculinity* at one end and *femininity* at the other end. A person who scored high on masculinity was assumed to score low on femininity, and vice versa. Researchers assumed that all people could be located on this single masculinity–femininity dimension. Items that showed large sex differences, such as "I enjoy reading *Popular Mechanics*" (men scored higher), and "I would enjoy the work of a librarian" (women scored higher), were used to construct a single scale of masculinity-femininity. But does a single scale with masculinity at one end and femininity at the other end really capture the important individual differences? Can't someone be both masculine *and* feminine? This question led to a new conception of sex-linked personality differences–androgyny.

The Search for Androgyny

In the early 1970s, with the rise of the feminist movement, researchers challenged the assumption of a single masculinity–femininity dimension. Masculinity and femininity are independent dimensions. You can be high on both masculinity and femininity, or low on both. Or you can be stereotypically masculine: high on masculinity, low on femininity; or you can be stereotypically feminine: high on femininity, low on masculinity. This shift reconceptualized masculinity, femininity, and sex roles.

Two major personality instruments were published to assess people using this new conception of sex roles (Bem, 1974; Spence, Helmreich, & Stapp, 1974). The **masculinity** dimension contained items reflecting assertiveness, boldness, dominance, self-sufficiency, and instrumentality. Those who agreed with personality trait terms connoting these qualities scored high on masculinity. The **femininity** dimension contained items that reflected nurturance, expression of emotions, and empathy. People agreeing with these personality items scored high on femininity. Those who scored high on both dimensions were labeled **androgynous,** to reflect the notion that a single person could possess both masculine and feminine characteristics. Table 16.3 shows the four possible scores these instruments can yield.

The researchers who developed these questionnaires viewed the androgynous person as the most highly developed. Androgynous persons presumably embody the most valuable elements of both sexes, such as the assertiveness to take positive steps in one's job and interpersonal sensitivity to the feelings of others. Androgynous people were presumed to be liberated from the shackles of traditional notions of sex roles. Before proceeding with our analysis, however, pause briefly to determine where you are located on these measures. To find out, fill out the following Exercise.

The popularity of this new conception of sex roles is a testament to the influence of feminism in America. With the rise of the women's movement, traditional ideas about the roles of men and women were cast aside. Women started entering the workforce in record numbers. Some men opted for more nurturant roles. John Lennon, of former Beatles fame, decided to stay at home and raise his son, Sean, while his wife, Yoko Ono, went to work, overseeing a massive financial empire (Coleman, 1992). Many people applauded Lennon for his new liberated role. This political movement reinforced the idea that men were supposed to become more nurturant, caring, and empathic. At the same time, women were supposed to become more assertive as they entered many professions traditionally reserved for men.

Table 16.3 Conception of Sex Roles Developed in the 1970s		
	Low Masculinity	**High Masculinity**
Low Femininity	Undifferentiated	Masculine
High Femininity	Feminine	Androgynous

Exercise

INSTRUCTIONS: Forty items follow. Each one contains a pair of statements describing contradictory characteristics; that is, you cannot be both at the same time, such as very artistic and not at all artistic. The letters form a scale between the two extremes. Select the letter that describes where you fall on the scale. For example, if you think that you are not at all aggressive, you would choose *A.* If you think you are very aggressive, you would choose *E.* If you are in between, you would choose *C,* or possibly *B* or *D.* Be sure to make a choice for every item. Mark your choice by drawing an *X* through the letter that you select.

1.	Not at all aggressive	A.....B.....C.....D.....E	Very aggressive
2.	Very whiny	A.....B.....C.....D.....E	Not at all whiny
3.	Not at all independent	A.....B.....C.....D.....E	Very independent
4.	Not at all arrogant	A.....B.....C.....D.....E	Very arrogant
5.	Not at all emotional	A.....B.....C.....D.....E	Very emotional
6.	Very submissive	A.....B.....C.....D.....E	Very dominant
7.	Very boastful	A.....B.....C.....D.....E	Not at all boastful
8.	Not at all excitable in a *major* crisis	A.....B.....C.....D.....E	Very excitable in a *major* crisis
9.	Very passive	A.....B.....C.....D.....E	Very active
10.	Not at all egotistical	A.....B.....C.....D.....E	Very egotistical
11.	Not at all able to devote self completely to others	A.....B.....C.....D.....E	Able to devote self completely to others
12.	Not at all spineless	A.....B.....C.....D.....E	Very spineless
13.	Very rough	A.....B.....C.....D.....E	Very gentle
14.	Not at all complaining	A.....B.....C.....D.....E	Very complaining
15.	Not at all helpful to others	A.....B.....C.....D.....E	Very helpful to others
16.	Not at all competitive	A.....B.....C.....D.....E	Very competitive
17.	Subordinates oneself to others	A.....B.....C.....D.....E	Never subordinates oneself to others
18.	Very home-oriented	A.....B.....C.....D.....E	Very worldly
19.	Very greedy	A.....B.....C.....D.....E	Not at all greedy
20.	Not at all kind	A.....B.....C.....D.....E	Very kind
21.	Indifferent to others' approval	A.....B.....C.....D.....E	Highly needful of others' approval
22.	Very dictatorial	A.....B.....C.....D.....E	Not at all dictatorial
23.	Feelings not easily hurt	A.....B.....C.....D.....E	Feelings easily hurt
24.	Doesn't nag	A.....B.....C.....D.....E	Nags a lot
25.	Not at all aware of feelings of others	A.....B.....C.....D.....E	Very aware of feelings of others
26.	Can make decisions easily	A.....B.....C.....D.....E	Has difficulty making decisions
27.	Very fussy	A.....B.....C.....D.....E	Not at all fussy
28.	Gives up very easily	A.....B.....C.....D.....E	Never gives up easily
29.	Very cynical	A.....B.....C.....D.....E	Not at all cynical
30.	Never cries	A.....B.....C.....D.....E	Cries very easily

Exercise (*Continued*)

31. Not at all self-confident	A.....B.....C.....D.....E	Very self-confident
32. Does not look out only for self, principled	A.....B.....C.....D.....E	Looks out only for self, unprincipled
33. Feels very inferior	A.....B.....C.....D.....E	Feels very superior
34. Not at all hostile	A.....B.....C.....D.....E	Very hostile
35. Not at all understanding of others	A.....B.....C.....D.....E	Very understanding of others
36. Very cold in relations with others	A.....B.....C.....D.....E	Very warm in relations with others
37. Very servile	A.....B.....C.....D.....E	Not at all servile
38. Very little need for security	A.....B.....C.....D.....E	Very strong need for security
39. Not at all gullible	A.....B.....C.....D.....E	Very gullible
40. Goes to pieces under pressure	A.....B.....C.....D.....E	Stands up well under pressure

Source: Spence et al. (1974).

The new androgynous conception, however, was not without its critics. One criticism goes to the heart of the androgyny concept. Several studies found that masculinity and femininity indeed consist of a single, bipolar trait. Those who score high on masculinity, for example, tend to score low on femininity. Those who score high on femininity tend to score low on masculinity (e.g., Deaux & Lewis, 1984).

The originators of the new conceptions of sex roles changed their views. Janet Spence, author of one measure, no longer believed that her questionnaire assessed sex roles (Swann, Langlois, & Gilbert, 1999). Instead, she suggested that her scales really measure the personality characteristics of instrumentality and expressiveness. **Instrumentality** consists of personality traits that involve working with objects, getting tasks completed in a direct fashion, showing independence from others, and displaying self-sufficiency. **Expressiveness,** in contrast, is the ease with which one can express emotions, such as crying, showing empathy for the troubles of others, and showing nurturance to those in need.

Sandra Bem also changed her views on sex roles. She considered her measure (the Bem Sex Role Inventory; Bem, 1974) to assess **gender schemata,** or cognitive orientations that lead individuals to process social information on the basis of sex-linked associations (Hoyenga & Hoyenga, 1993). According to this conception, the ideal is not to be androgynous but, rather to be *gender-aschematic.* That is, the ideal is not to use gender at all in one's processing of social information. The current movement toward using gender-neutral pronouns such as *they, them,* and *theirs,* or novel ones such as *ze* and *xe,* reflect people who do not identify with the gender binary (Sun et al., 2021). Sweden has even introduced the gender-neutral pronoun *hen* as a replacement for *hon* (she) and *han* (he) (Gustafsson Sendén, Bäck, & Lindqvist, 2015).

Although most researchers assume that masculinity, femininity, and "gender schema" are personality attributes absorbed from socialization, parents, the media, or the culture, studies have challenged this view. Cleveland, Udry, and Chantala (2001) found that sex-typed behaviors and attitudes themselves tend to show moderate heritability within sex. Among women, for example, 38 percent of the variance in proclivity to engage in

The distinctions between what behavior is appropriate for a woman and what behavior is appropriate for a man in our culture—social roles—have changed dramatically in the past few decades.

Darren Greenwood/Design Pics

sex-typical behaviors such as crying, expressing emotions, sensitivity to the feelings of others, taking risks, and even fighting was explained by genetic differences. Another study found moderate (roughly 50 percent) heritabilities for measures of "gender atypicality" in boys and girls—that is, masculinity in girls and femininity in boys (Knafo, Iervolino, & Plomin, 2005). These findings still leave large room for environmental influences to affect sex roles, but they suggest that genes also play a role, even within each gender, in the degree to which the sex roles are adopted.

Research on masculinity and femininity is moving beyond these issues and beginning to explore the real-life consequences of masculinity and femininity. One study, for example, found that masculine and feminine traits affect sexual behavior and relationships (Udry & Chantala, 2004). Adolescent couples containing a highly masculine male and a highly feminine female tend to have sex sooner than other pairings. Couples in which both members are average for their sex tend to break up compared with other pairings. Future research can be expected to yield more interesting real-life consequences of masculinity and femininity.

Gender Stereotypes

Much of this chapter so far has been concerned with the ways in which men and women differ. An important related topic pertains to the *beliefs* about how the sexes differ, regardless of whether these beliefs are accurate reflections of the sex differences that empirically exist. The beliefs that we hold about men and women are sometimes called gender stereotypes.

Gender stereotypes have three components (Hoyenga & Hoyenga, 1993). The first is *cognitive* and deals with the ways in which we form **social categories.** For example, we may categorize men into "cads" or "dads," those who play around and are reluctant to commit versus those who are faithful and invest heavily in their children. The second component of gender stereotypes is *affective.* You may feel hostile or warm toward someone because you place that person in a particular social category. The third component of gender stereotypes is *behavioral.* You may discriminate against someone simply because they belong in the social category of "woman" or "man." We discuss all three components of gender stereotypes—cognitive, affective, and behavioral—in the following sections, to illuminate how social categorizing shows up in everyday life.

The Content and Accuracy of Gender Stereotypes

Although there are some variations from culture to culture, it is remarkable that the content of gender stereotypes—the attributes that we believe men and women possess—is highly similar across cultures. In the most comprehensive set of studies yet conducted, Williams and Best (1982, 1990) studied gender stereotypes in 30 countries around the world. In all these studies, men, compared with women, were commonly viewed as more aggressive, autonomous, achievement oriented, dominant, exhibitionist, and persevering. Women, compared with men, were commonly seen as more affiliative, deferent, nurturant, and self-abasing. These general gender stereotypes have a common theme. Women in all 30 countries tend to be perceived as more *communal*—oriented toward the group. Men, in contrast, are perceived to be more *instrumental*—asserting their independence from the group.

How accurate are these stereotypes? Gender stereotypes correspond in many ways to the actual sex differences that have been discovered. A study of 26 nations concluded that gender stereotypes are in fact remarkably accurate, based on actual differences between women and men (Löckenhoff et al., 2014). Some scholars speculate that people overestimate sex differences in personality, showing exaggerated beliefs about how large they actually are (Krueger et al., 2003; Wood & Eagly, 2010). Most reviews, however, conclude that gender stereotypes are well-calibrated to actual gender differences and are not exaggerated (e.g., Jussim et al., 2021).

Stereotypic Subtypes of Men and Women

In addition to general gender stereotypes, studies show that most people have more finely differentiated stereotypic views of each sex. Six and Eckes (1991) examined the structure of their participants' cognitive categories of men and women and came up with several subtypes, as shown in Figure 16.3. Men were viewed as falling into five subtypes. The playboy subtype, for example, includes males who are cool, casual, "players," lady killers, and macho. The career man subtype includes men who are social climbers and managers. Stereotypes of women fell into a smaller number of subtypes. One might be called the "classically feminine" subtype, which includes housewives, secretaries, and maternal women. In the modern world, these women might be "soccer moms," highly devoted to their husbands and children. A second subtype is defined by short-term or overt sexuality. This subtype includes sex bombs, tarts, and vamps. These two female subtypes correspond roughly to the "Madonna–whore" dichotomy, which is commonly made in everyday life (Buss, 2016). That is, these two stereotypes correspond to women who would make good mothers and women who exude sexuality.

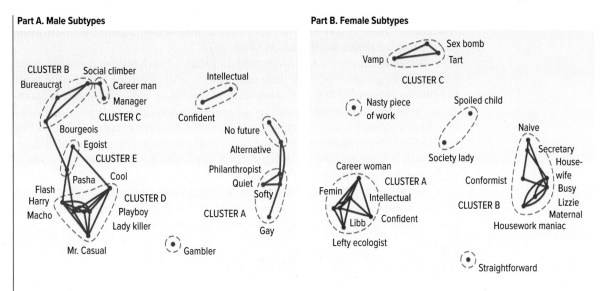

Figure 16.3

The structure of cognitive sexual categories. The structure of cognitive categories of various male and female subtypes, where distance between subtypes on the graphs is assumed to correspond to cognitive "distances" in people's stereotypic concepts. Some subtypes are closely related to each other, as indicated by the dashed lines that surround them to form the various clusters.

Source: Six and Eckes (1991).

Hillary Rodham Clinton illustrates a relatively new
gender stereotype—women who are intellectual,
assertive, liberated, and career-minded.
Airman Devin Doskey/USA

A third stereotype of women, however, involves a subtype that may have emerged relatively recently, perhaps over the past 20 or 30 years—the confident, intellectual, liberated career woman. Hillary Rodham Clinton would be a perfect illustration of this category—she scored at the top of her class in law school and developed an impressive influential career in politics. Also included in this cluster are feminist and lefty ecologists, perhaps suggesting that these political orientations tended to go along with independent, confident career women.

The key point is that, cognitively, most people do not hold only a single gender stereotype. Rather, cognitive categories are differentiated into subtypes of women and subtypes of men. It remains to be seen whether these stereotypical subtypes have any empirical basis. That is, are "playboy" men actually cooler, more casual, and more macho than other men? Are homemakers more naive, busy, and conformist than other women? Answers to these questions must await future research.

Prejudice and Gender Stereotypes

The stereotypes associated with gender are not merely cognitive constructions that rattle around inside people's heads. They have real-world consequences. Prejudiced behavior is one damaging consequence of gender stereotypes. These damaging effects can be found in many important activities: in legal decisions, medical treatment, car purchases, check cashing, and job hunting (Wood & Eagly, 2010).

In wrongful death lawsuits, for example, the families of the victim receive more money if a man was killed than if a woman was killed (Goodman et al., 1991). In medicine, men are more likely to be recommended for coronary bypass surgery than women, even when they show the same amount of heart damage (Khan et al., 1990). A study in which men and women called car dealerships to request prices for particular cars found that the women were quoted higher prices than were the men for exactly the same car (Larrance et al., 1979). Women are subjected to more sexual harassment in the workplace, a form of gender discrimination (Buss, 2016).

Not all sex discrimination favors men. In a study of book reviews published in the journal *Contemporary Psychology,* male authors were at the receiving end of more negative reviews (Moore, 1978). In another study of reviews by men and women of manuscripts submitted to refereed journals for publication, women gave more positive reviews to women authors than to men authors (Lloyd, 1990). Male reviewers did not show this bias. In five hiring experiments of hypothetical faculty applicants in the fields of biology, economics, engineering, and psychology, female applicants were preferred 2:1 over identically qualified male applicants (Williams & Ceci, 2015).

In summary, gender stereotypes can have important consequences for men and women. These consequences can damage people where it counts most—in their health, their jobs, their chances for advancement, and their social reputations.

Theories of Sex Differences

So far in this chapter, we have seen that there are some differences in personality between the sexes but also many similarities. This section examines the major theories that have been proposed for explaining how sex differences arise. These include traditional theories of socialization, theories of social roles, hormonal theories, and theories anchored in evolutionary psychology.

Socialization and Social Roles

Socialization theory—the notion that boys and girls become different because boys are reinforced by parents, teachers, and the media for being "masculine" and girls for being "feminine"—is probably the most widely held theory of sex differences in personality. The theory can be summarized as follows: Boys are given baseball bats and trucks. Girls are given dolls. Boys are praised for engaging in rough-and-tumble play. Girls are praised for being cute and obedient. Boys are punished for crying. Girls are comforted when they cry. Over time, according to socialization theory, children learn behaviors deemed appropriate in their culture for their sex.

Both socialization and social learning theories hold that gender roles have their roots in early sex-differentiated learning experiences—in short, boys are encouraged in one direction, and girls are encouraged in another direction.

RozochkaIvn/Shutterstock

In Bandura's (1977) **social learning theory,** a variant of socialization theory, boys and girls also learn by observing the behaviors of others, called *models,* of their own sex. Boys watch their fathers, male teachers, and male peers. Girls watch their mothers, female teachers, and female peer models. Boys see their fathers work. Girls see their mothers cook. Over time, even in the absence of direct reinforcement, these models provide a guide to behaviors that are masculine or feminine.

Some empirical evidence supports socialization and social learning theories of sex differences. Studies of socialization practices have found that both mothers and fathers encourage dependency more in girls than in boys (Block, 1983). Parents encourage girls to stay close to home, whereas boys are permitted and encouraged to roam. Fathers engage in more physical play with their sons than with their daughters (Fagot & Leinbach, 1987). Parents provide "gendered toys" to their children. Boys generally receive a greater variety of toys, more cars and trucks, more sports equipment, and more tools than girls do (Rheingold & Cook, 1975). Girls receive more dolls, pink clothing and furnishings, strollers, swings, and household appliances. This empirical evidence is consistent with socialization and social learning theories.

Cross-cultural evidence for different treatment of boys and girls exists as well. In many cultures, fathers interact less with their daughters than with their sons (Whiting & Edwards, 1988). Girls in most cultures tend to be assigned more domestic chores than boys. Boys are permitted in most cultures to stray farther from home (Hoyenga & Hoyenga, 1993). Boys in most cultures are socialized to be more competitive than are girls (Low, 1989). In a large study of socialization practices across cultures, Low (1989) found that in 82 percent of the cultures, the girls were trained to be more nurturant than the boys. In the majority of the cultures, the girls were socialized to be more sexually restrained than the boys—the parents tried to teach their daughters to delay having sexual intercourse (Perilloux, Fleischman, & Buss, 2011), whereas the boys were encouraged to have sexual intercourse (Low, 1989). These patterns are also found among modern college populations (Perilloux, Fleischman, & Buss, 2008), explained by what has been called the "daughter-guarding hypothesis."

One potential difficulty pertains to the direction of effects—whether parents are socializing children in sex-linked ways or whether children are eliciting their parents' behavior to correspond to their existing sex-linked preferences (e.g., Scarr & McCartney, 1983). Perhaps the interests of the children drive the parents' behavior rather than the other way around. Parents may start out by giving a variety of toys to their children;

however, if boys show no interest in dolls and girls show no interest in trucks, then over time parents may stop purchasing masculine toys for their daughters and feminine toys for their sons.

Another problem for traditional theories of socialization is that they provide no account of the *origins* of differential parental socialization practices. Why do parents want their boys and girls to grow up differently? Ideally, a comprehensive theory of the origins of sex differences should be able to account for the origins of sex-linked socialization practices. In sum, parents undoubtedly treat boys and girls differently, supporting the theory of sex-linked socialization of personality, but the origins of these practices currently remain a mystery.

Closely related to traditional socialization theories is **social role theory** (Eagly, 1987; Eagly & Wood, 1999; Wood & Eagly, 2010). According to social role theory, sex differences originate because men and women are distributed differently into different occupational and family roles. Men are expected to assume the breadwinning role. Women are expected to assume the homemaker role. Over time, children presumably learn the behaviors that are linked to these roles. Girls learn to be nurturing and emotionally supportive because these qualities are linked with the maternal role. Boys learn to be tough and aggressive, qualities expected of the breadwinner.

There is some evidence supporting social role theory (Eagly, 1987, 1995). Men and women in the United States have assumed different occupation and family roles, with women found more often in domestic and child care roles and men more often in occupational roles. An event-sampling procedure explored how men's and women's behavior varied as a function of the social role to which they were assigned—a supervisor role, a co-worker role, or the role of someone being supervised by someone else. Social role assignment had a large impact on the dominant behaviors that were expressed. Those assigned to the supervisor role displayed more dominance; those assigned the supervisee role displayed significantly more submissiveness (Moskowitz, Suh, & Desaulniers, 1994). When roles were reversed, people who formerly displayed dominance displayed submissiveness when they were put in a supervisee role, whereas the people who formerly were submissive became more dominant.

Like socialization theory, however, social role theory fails to provide an account of the origins of sex-linked roles (Gangestad, Haselton, & Buss, 2006). Who assigns the different roles? Why should men and women passively accept the roles they are assigned? Why don't children follow the role of sitting quietly on airplanes or eating their spinach? Why do women assume domestic roles more than men? Are these roles found in all cultures?

Social role theory, however, is becoming increasingly testable as family and occupational roles change. Women are assuming breadwinning roles more often than in the past, and men are assuming greater responsibility for domestic duties. With these changes, if social role theory is correct, sex differences should diminish as well: "A key prediction of social role theory is that sex differences should shrink as societies adopt more gender egalitarian values and socialization patterns" (Kaiser, 2019, p. 12). Interestingly, the largest test of this prediction, a study of 17,637 individuals in 55 different cultures, has found precisely the opposite pattern (Schmitt et al., 2008). The most sexually egalitarian countries—those with equal access to education, knowledge, and economic wealth—show the largest, not the smallest, sex differences in personality. The findings have been replicated several times (e.g., Schmitt, 2015; Mac Giolla & Kajonius, 2018). This surprising result contradicts the social role theory of sex differences in personality, although future empirical tests are needed.

Hormonal Theories

Hormonal theories propose that men and women differ not because of the external social environment, but rather because they have different hormones (Hooven, 2021). Physiological differences, not differential social treatment, cause boys and girls to diverge in personality. Studies have sought to identify links between hormones such as testosterone (present in greater amounts in men) and sex-linked behavior.

There is some evidence that hormonal influences on sex differences begin in utero. The hormonal bath that the developing fetus is exposed to, for example, might affect both the organization of the brain and consequently the gendered interests and activities of the individual. Some of the best evidence for this comes from a condition called congenital adrenal hyperplasia (CAH), in which the female fetus has an overactive adrenal gland. This results in the female being hormonally masculinized. Young girls with CAH show a marked preference for "male" toys, such as Lincoln logs and trucks (Berenbaum & Beltz, 2011; Berenbaum & Snyder, 1995; Cohen-Bendahan, van de Beek, & Berenbaum, 2005). As adults, CAH females show superiority in traditionally masculine cognitive skills, such as spatial rotation ability and throwing accuracy, as well as preferring traditionally masculine occupations (Kimura, 2002). These findings suggest that fetal exposure to hormones can have lasting effects on gender-linked interests and abilities (Berenbaum & Beltz, 2021).

Testosterone is associated with dominance and aggressiveness, as well as with the massive buildup of muscular tissue. Here, U.S. Olympic weightlifter Tim McRae rejoices after setting a new U.S. record in the snatch of 145 kg, a feat no woman in his weight class is likely to ever match. Olympic athletes are tested to make sure their testosterone levels are within normal ranges for their sex.
Kathy Willens/AP Images

Men and women differ in their levels of circulating hormones. Women's level of circulating testosterone typically falls between 200 and 400 picograms per milliliter of blood at the lowest part of the menstrual cycle and between 285 and 440 at the highest part of the menstrual cycle (just prior to ovulation). Men have circulating testosterone ranging from 5,140 to 6,460 picograms per milliliter of blood. After puberty, there is no overlap between the sexes in their levels of circulating testosterone. Men typically show more than 10 times the level of women.

Sex differences in circulating testosterone are linked with some traditional sex differences in behavior, such as aggression, dominance, and career choice. In women, high levels of testosterone are linked with pursuing a more masculine career and having greater success within the chosen career. Among lesbian women, testosterone has been associated with erotic role identification; more "masculine" lesbian partners having higher levels of testosterone than more "feminine" partners (Singh et al., 1999). Higher testosterone levels are associated with greater dominance and aggressiveness in both sexes. Female prison inmates who had more frequent disciplinary infractions had higher testosterone (Dabbs & Hargrove, 1997). Members of college fraternities who were more rambunctious had higher levels of testosterone than those in fraternities who behaved better (Dabbs, Hargrove, & Heusel, 1996).

Sexual desire is linked to levels of circulating testosterone, but only in women (van Anders, 2012). Women's testosterone levels peak just prior to ovulation, and women report a peak in their sexual desire at precisely the same time. At this peak, women report initiating sexual intercourse and experience more desire for sex (Sherwin, 1988). Just thinking about sex increases testosterone in women, but not in men (Goldey & van Anders, 2012). So the links between hormones and sexuality are more complicated than scientists initially believed (van Anders, 2012).

These findings do not prove that the differences between men and women in sexuality, dominance, aggression, and career choices result from differences in testosterone levels. Correlation does not mean causation. Indeed, there is some evidence in nonhuman primates that rises in testosterone levels *follow* rises in status and dominance within the group rather than leading to them (Sapolsky, 1987). Furthermore, sexual arousal itself can increase in testosterone levels (Hoyenga & Hoyenga, 1993). Sports fans whose team had just won had higher levels of testosterone than fans whose team had lost (Bernhardt et al., 1998). The link between hormones and behavior is bidirectional (Edwards, Wetzel, & Wyner, 2006). Higher testosterone may result from, as well as cause, behavior changes.

An additional limitation of hormonal theories of sex differences in personality is one shared with socialization theories—namely, neither of these theories identifies the *origins* of the differences. Precisely why do men and women differ so dramatically in their levels of circulating testosterone? Is this merely an incidental effect of being male versus being female? Or, is there a systematic process that causes men and women to differ in testosterone precisely because testosterone differences lead to behavioral differences in dominance and sexuality? One theoretical perspective that argues for this possibility is evolutionary psychology.

Evolutionary Psychology Theory

According to the evolutionary psychology perspective (see Chapter 8), men and women differ only in some domains of personality and show large similarities in most domains. The sexes are predicted to be similar in all the domains in which they have faced *similar adaptive problems* over human evolutionary history. The sexes are predicted to differ only in the domains in which men and women have confronted *different adaptive challenges* over human evolutionary history (Buss & Schmitt, 2011).

Adaptive problems are problems that need to be solved in order for an individual to survive and reproduce or whose solution increases overall reproductive success. For example, both sexes have similar taste preferences for sugar, salt, fat, and protein. That's why fast-food restaurants are so popular—they package food with fat and sugar that both men and women desire. Food preferences reflect a solution to an important adaptive problem—getting calories and nutrients to survive.

In the domains of mating and sexuality, according to evolutionary psychologists, men and women have confronted somewhat different adaptive problems (Buss, 1995b). In order to reproduce, women must gestate a fetus for nine months. Men can reproduce through a single act of sex. Women historically faced the adaptive problem of securing resources to carry them through harsh winters or droughts, when resources might be scarce and a woman's mobility might be restricted by pregnancy. The costs of making a poor choice of a mate, according to this logic, would have been more damaging to women than to men. Because of the heavy investment women require for reproduction, women evolved mate preferences for men who showed signals of the ability and willingness to invest in them and their children.

This line of reasoning predicts that men will be more sexually indiscriminate and more aggressive with other men about pursuing opportunities for sex. Because of women's heavy investment, they become the extraordinarily valuable reproductive resource over which men compete. Women are predicted to be more selective about sex partners. A woman who had made a hasty or poor mate choice in the past would have been faced with the difficulties of bearing and raising a child without the help of an investing man. A motivation for casual sex, in short, was more reproductively beneficial to ancestral men than to ancestral women.

Much empirical evidence for sex differences corresponds to these predictions. Men clearly have a greater desire for sexual variety than women do (Buss & Schmitt, 1993, 2011; Symons, 1979). Men desire a larger number of sex partners, seek sex after a shorter time period has elapsed in knowing a potential partner, and have more fantasies about casual sex than do women (Schmitt et al., 2012). Men tend to take more risks to secure the resources and status that women find desirable in mates (e.g., Byrnes, Miller, & Schafer, 1999; Wilson & Daly, 2004). The findings that men are more aggressive, more willing to take physical risks, and more interested in casual sex are precisely the findings predicted by evolutionary psychology (Archer, 2009).

Despite this support, evolutionary psychology theory, like the other theoretical perspectives, leaves unanswered questions: What accounts for individual differences within each sex? Why are some women keenly interested in casual sex? Why are some men meek, dependent, and nurturing, whereas others are callous and aggressive? Some of these questions are beginning to be answered. It turns out, for example, that some women benefit greatly from pursuing a short-term sexual strategy, which can result in obtaining more and better resources, switching to a mate who is better than her regular mate, and possibly securing better genes for her offspring (Buss et al., 2017; Gangestad et al., 2002; Gangestad & Thornhill, 2008). Ultimately, a comprehensive theory of sex differences must account for these differences within each sex, as well as the average differences between the sexes.

An Integrated Theoretical Perspective

The theoretical accounts we have examined seem very different, but they are not necessarily incompatible. Indeed, to some extent, they operate at different levels of analysis. Evolutionary psychology suggests *why* the sexes differ, but it does not always specify *how* they became different. Hormonal and socialization theories specify *how* the sexes became different but do not specify *why* the sexes are different.

An integrated theory would take all of these levels of analysis into account because they may be compatible with each other. Parents, for example, clearly have an interest in socializing boys and girls differently, and these socialization differences are, to some degree, universal (Low, 1989; Perilloux, Fleischman, & Buss, 2008). There is evidence that both men and women change their behavior as a function of the roles they adopt. Both sexes become more dominant when in supervisory roles; both become more submissive when being supervised. Socialization, in short, must play a role in an integrated theory of sex differences, although some evidence contradicts social role theory.

Men and women clearly differ in circulating testosterone levels, and these differences are linked with differences in sexuality, aggression, dominance, and career interests (Edwards et al., 2006; Hoyenga & Hoyenga, 1993). Nonetheless, we cannot ignore the causal possibility, for which there is some evidence, that being in a dominant position actually causes testosterone to rise. Thus, social roles and hormones may be closely linked, and these links may be necessary for an integrated theory of sex differences.

These proximate paths—socialization and hormones—might provide the answers for *how* the sexes differ, whereas evolutionary psychology provides the answers for *why* the sexes differ. Are there evolutionary reasons that parents encourage greater aggressiveness and dominance in boys but more nurturance in girls? Are there evolutionary reasons for surges in testosterone when a person ascends a dominance hierarchy? At this point in the science of sex differences, there are no clear answers to these questions. Nonetheless, it's a good bet that all three levels of analysis—social factors, hormonal and other physiological influences, and evolutionary processes—are needed for a complete understanding of gender and personality.

SUMMARY AND EVALUATION

The study of sex, gender, and personality has provoked heated debate over the past several decades. Perhaps in no other area of personality psychology do politics and values get so intermingled with science. Some researchers, called minimalists, emphasize the great similarities between the sexes, pointing out that the effect size differences are small and the distributions overlapping. Other researchers, called maximalists, emphasize that sex differences are real and replicable and stress the effect size differences rather than the overlap of the distributions.

When we take a step back, it is possible to gain a more accurate understanding of sex, gender, and personality. The past few decades have witnessed an explosion of research on sex differences, along with the development of meta-analytic statistical procedures, which allow for firm conclusions grounded in empirical data.

Some sex differences are real and not artifacts of particular investigators or methods. Some sex differences have remained relatively constant over generations and across cultures. Nonetheless, the magnitudes of sex differences vary tremendously. When questions about sex differences are posed, therefore, we must always ask the questions: In what domains? And how large are the differences?

The domains that show large and small sex differences are now fairly clear. Men score consistently higher on the personality attributes of assertiveness, aggressiveness (especially physical aggressiveness), and casual sexuality. Women consistently score higher on measures of anxiety, trust, and tender-mindedness (nurturance). Women are more likely than men to experience both positive emotions (e.g., affection, joy) and negative emotions (e.g., fear, sadness), although the magnitude of these differences is not large. Men are more likely to be sexually aggressive, trying to force women to have sex, although these findings appear to be limited to a subset of men—those who are narcissistic, psychopathic, lack empathy, and show hostile masculinity. Women tend to score higher on emotional investment—a cultural universal likely linked to attachment and bonding in romantic and other social relationships.

Although no sex differences are reported in depression rates prior to puberty, at around age 13 women tend to show higher rates of depression than do men. This sex difference has been tied to theories suggesting that women ruminate more than men and theories linked to the importance of physical appearance in the domain of mate competition. One adaptationist theory proposes that women's depression signals to social partners that they need help. For example, women are especially vulnerable to depression after they give birth to a child. If she feels like she is not getting enough help from her husband or her relatives, depression may send a signal that these social partners need to pitch in more. No single theory is likely to completely explain the large sex differences in depression found across cultures.

Men score toward the things end of the people–things dimension; women tend to score more toward the people end. Within each of these domains, however, there is overlap. Some women are more assertive, aggressive, and things oriented than the majority of men. Some men are more anxious, tender minded, and people oriented than the majority of women.

In the 1970s, much attention was focused on the concept of androgyny. However, it became clear as more empirical evidence was gathered that masculinity and femininity were not independent, as the androgyny researchers had asserted. Those who score high on masculinity, or instrumentality, tend to score low on femininity, or expressiveness, and vice versa. Many the original androgyny researchers came to believe that these dimensions capture the essence of sex differences. Men tend to be more instrumental. Women tend to be more expressive. Nonetheless, there is much overlap, and many women are highly instrumental and many men are expressive.

Another important topic centers on gender stereotypes, or beliefs that people hold about each sex, regardless of their accuracy. Cross-cultural research has revealed some universality of gender stereotypes. In all cultures, men are believed to be more aggressive, autonomous, dominant, achievement oriented, and exhibitionistic, and women are believed to be more affiliative, deferent, nurturing, and self-abasing. These stereotypes correspond in many ways to the actual sex differences. Although some argue that stereotypes exaggerate the differences, others conclude that people's gender stereotypes are remarkably accurate in corresponding to actual gender differences. People also hold stereotypes about the subtypes within each sex. Men are viewed as playboys, career men, or losers; women as feminists, housewives, or sex bombs.

Traditional theories of sex differences have emphasized social factors—socialization by parents, observational learning from social models, and social roles. They have some support. Cross-cultural studies reveal that boys are universally socialized to be achievement strivers, and girls are universally socialized to be more restrained, especially in the sexual domain. On the other hand, a key prediction from social role theory is that sex differences should shrink in cultures that have become increasingly egalitarian in gender socialization and opportunities. Surprisingly, sex differences in personality appear to be larger, not smaller, in highly gender egalitarian cultures, contradicting this key prediction from social role theory.

Studies of hormones suggest that social factors do not tell the whole story. Testosterone, for example, has been implicated in the personality factors of dominance, aggression, and sexuality. Because men and women differ substantially in their levels of circulating testosterone, it is possible that some of the personality differences are caused by hormonal differences.

According to evolutionary psychologists, men and women differ in domains in which the sexes have faced different adaptive problems over human evolutionary history. In other domains, the sexes are the same or highly similar. Aggression and orientation toward casual sex are two domains in which the sexes differ, according to this theory, and these predictions are empirically supported. What is needed is an integrative theory of sex, gender, and personality that takes into account all of these factors: social factors, physiological factors, and evolutionary factors.

KEY TERMS

sex differences 497
gender 498
gender stereotypes 498
effect size 499
minimalist 501
maximalist 501
inhibitory control 501
perceptual sensitivity 502
surgency 502
negative affectivity 503

trust 503
tender-mindedness 503
global self-esteem 507
people-things dimension 509
empathizing 509
systemizing 509
rumination 510
masculinity 511
femininity 511
androgynous 511

instrumentality 513
expressiveness 513
gender schemata 513
social categories 514
socialization theory 517
social learning theory 517
social role theory 518
hormonal theories 519

Lightspring/Shutterstock

Culture and Personality

Cultural Violations: An Illustration

What Is Cultural Personality Psychology?

Three Major Approaches to Culture
Evoked Culture
Transmitted Culture
Cultural Universals

SUMMARY AND EVALUATION

KEY TERMS

17

THE SOCIAL AND CULTURAL DOMAIN

The Yanomamö Indian tribes are among the last truly traditional societies on earth, living a hunter-gatherer existence in the isolated jungles of Venezuela.
robertharding/Alamy Stock Photo

The Yanomamö Indians of Venezuela set up temporary shelters, from which they forage for food and hunt for game. When these shelters become depleted of food, they push on and settle elsewhere. On one particular day, the men gather at early dawn, preparing to raid a neighboring village. The group is tense. The men in the raiding party risk injury, and a fearful man might turn back, excusing himself from the raid by telling the others that he has a thorn in his foot. Men who do this too often risk damaging their reputation (Chagnon, 1983).

Not all Yanomamö men are the same. There are at least two discernible groups that differ profoundly in personality. The lowland Yanomamö men are highly aggressive. They do not hesitate to hit their wives with sticks for "infractions" as minor as serving tea too slowly. They often challenge other men to club fights or ax fights. And they sometimes declare war on neighboring groups, attempting to kill the enemy men and capture their wives. Yanomamö men shave the tops of their heads to reveal the scars from club fights, sometimes painting the scars red to display them as symbols of courage. Indeed, one is not regarded as a true man until one has killed another man—acquiring the honor of being called an *unokai*. The men who are unokai have the most wives (Chagnon, 1988).

In the highlands reside a different group of Yanomamö. These people are more peaceful and dislike fighting. The high levels of agreeableness can be seen on their faces. These Yanomamö do not raid neighboring villages, do not engage in ax fights, and rarely engage in club fights. They stress the virtues of cooperation. Unfortunately, though, food resources are more plentiful in the lowlands, where the aggressive Yanomamö dominate.

How can we understand cultural differences in personality between the highland and lowland Yanomamö? Did those who were temperamentally more disposed to aggression drive those who were more agreeable up to the highlands and away from the food resources? Or did the two groups start out the same, and only subsequently did cultural values take hold in one group different from those that took hold in the other? These questions form the subject matter of this chapter. What is the effect of culture on personality? What is the effect of personality on culture? And how can we understand patterns of cultural variation amid patterns of human universals?

Personality psychologists explore personality across cultures for several important reasons (Allik & Realo, 2009; Church, 2000; Paunonen & Ashton, 1998). One is to discover whether concepts of personality in one culture, such as American culture, are also applicable in other cultures. A second is to find out whether cultures differ, on average, in the levels of particular personality traits. Are Japanese, for example, really more agreeable than Americans, or is this merely a stereotype? A third reason is to discover whether the factor structure of personality traits varies across cultures or is universal. Will the five-factor model of personality discovered in American samples, for example, be replicated in Holland, Germany, and the Philippines? A fourth reason is to discover whether certain features of personality are universal, corresponding to the human nature level of personality analysis (see Chapter 1).

In this chapter, we explore the features of personality common to everyone but differentially elicited only in some cultures; which features of personality are transmitted so that they become characteristic of some local groups, but not others; and which features of personality are common to everyone in all cultures. We start by examining just how different cultures can be.

Cultural Violations: An Illustration

Consider the following events:

1. One of your family members eats beef regularly. (your beef-eating family member)
2. A young married woman goes alone to see a movie without informing her husband. When she returns home, her husband says, "If you do it again, I will beat you black and blue." She does it again; he beats her black and blue. (the wife-beating husband)
3. A poor man goes to the hospital after being seriously hurt in an accident. The hospital refuses to treat him because he cannot afford to pay. (the refusing hospital)

Now examine each event and decide whether you think the behavior on the part of the person or institution in parentheses is morally wrong. If so, is it a serious violation, a minor offense, or not a violation at all?

If you are a Brahman Hindu, you are likely to believe that the first event—eating beef—is a serious violation but that the second event—the husband beating the wife for disobeying him—is not (Shweder, Mahapatra, & Miller, 1990). If you are an American, however, the odds are that your views are the reverse: Unless you are a vegetarian, you see nothing wrong with eating beef, but you view it as very wrong for the husband to beat his wife. Both Brahman Hindus and Americans, however, agree that the hospital that denies treatment to the badly injured man is committing a serious violation.

This example highlights a fascinating question for personality psychologists. Some aspects of personality (e.g., attitudes, values, self-concepts) are highly variable across cultures. But other aspects of personality are universal—features that are shared by people everywhere. The central questions addressed by this chapter are "How do people from different cultures differ in personality, and how are people from all cultures the same?"

What Is Cultural Personality Psychology?

Before proceeding further, it is useful to briefly define culture. Let's start with an observation: "Humans everywhere show striking patterns of local within-group similarity in their behavior and thought, accompanied by profound intergroup differences" (Tooby & Cosmides, 1992, p. 6). Within-group similarities and between-group differences can be of any sort—physical, psychological, behavioral, or attitudinal. These phenomena are called **cultural variations**.

Consider the example of eating beef. Beef eating is common among Americans but is rare and viewed with abhorrence among Hindus. Among Hindus in India, the values and behaviors are shared for the most part. But they differ from the widely shared American attitudes toward beef eating. This difference—a local within-group similarity and between-group difference—is an example of a cultural variation.

Attaching the label of "culture" or "cultural variation" to phenomena such as these is best treated as a description, not an explanation. Labeling attitudes toward beef eating as "cultural" certainly describes the phenomenon. It tells us that we are dealing with a within-group similarity and a between-group difference. But it doesn't explain what has *caused* the cultural difference or *why* the groups differ. **Cultural personality psychology** generally has three key goals: (1) to discover the principles underlying the cultural diversity, (2) to discover how human psychology shapes culture, and (3) to discover how cultural understandings in turn shape our psychology (Fiske et al., 1997). A cultural perspective on personality is also critical for testing the generalizability of both findings and theories of personality functioning (Oishi, Kushlev, & Benet-Martínez, 2021).

Three Major Approaches to Culture

Certain traits are common to all people, but others display remarkable variation. Cultural variants are the personality attributes that vary from group to group. Psychologists have developed three major approaches to explaining and exploring personality across cultures: evoked culture, transmitted culture, and cultural universals.

Evoked Culture

Evoked culture is defined as cultural differences created by differing environmental conditions activating a predictable set of responses. Consider the physical examples of skin calluses and sweat. There are undoubtedly cultural differences in the thickness and distribution of calluses and in the amount people sweat. The traditional !Kung Bushmen of Botswana, for example, tend to have thicker calluses on their feet than most Americans because they walk around without shoes. These differences are aspects of evoked culture— different environments have different effects on people's callus-producing mechanisms.

People who live near the equator are exposed to more intense heat than those who live in more northern climates, such as Canada. The observation that residents of Zaire sweat more than residents of Canada is properly explained as an environmentally evoked difference that operates on sweat glands, which all humans possess. A behavioral example would be cultural variation in the number of children a woman has, which appears to be evoked partly as a consequence of the cultural level of economic development and the cultural level of social support provided to women (Hyafil & Baumard, 2020).

Note that two ingredients are necessary to explain cultural variations: (1) a universal underlying mechanism (sweat glands possessed by all people; desire for children) and (2) environmental differences in the degree to which the underlying mechanism is activated (differences in ambient temperature; cultural level of economic development). Neither element alone is adequate for a complete explanation.

The same explanatory logic applies to other environmentally triggered phenomena shared by members of one group, but not by other groups. Drought, plentiful game, and poisonous snakes are all environmental events that affect some groups more than others. These events activate mechanisms in some groups that lie dormant in others. In the next section, we discuss several psychological examples of evoked culture and show how they may result in differences in personality traits among groups.

Evoked Cooperation

Whether someone is cooperative or selfish is a central part of personality, but these proclivities may differ from culture to culture. A concrete example of evoked culture

Yanomamö Indians butchering a giant anteater. In their culture, the successful hunter shares his catch with the whole group. The benefits of such cooperative food sharing are high in their environment (Chagnon, 1983).
Claudia Andujar/Science Source

consists of the patterns of cooperative food sharing found among different bands of hunter-gatherer tribes (Cosmides & Tooby, 1992). Different classes of food have different variances in their distribution. High-variance foods differ greatly in their availability from day to day. For example, among the Ache tribe of Paraguay, meat from hunting is a high-variance resource. On any given day, the probability that a hunter will come back with meat is only 60 percent. On any particular day, therefore, one hunter will be successful, whereas another hunter will come back empty-handed. Gathered food, on the other hand, is a lower-variance food resource. The yield from gathering depends more on the skill and effort a person expends than on luck. Under **high-variance conditions**, there are tremendous benefits to sharing. You share your meat today with an unlucky hunter, and next week they will share meat with you. The benefits of engaging in cooperative food sharing increase under conditions of high variance. In this example, the benefits of sharing are increased by the fact that a large game animal contains more meat than one person or family can consume. Some of the meat would spoil if it were not shared with others.

Kaplan and Hill (1985) found that, indeed, within the Ache tribe, meat is communally shared. Hunters deposit their kill with a "distributor," a person who allocates portions to families based on family size. In the same group, gathered food is not shared outside the family. In short, cooperative sharing seems to be evoked by the environmental condition of high food variance.

Halfway around the world, in the Kalahari Desert, Cashden (1980) found that some San groups are more egalitarian than others. The degree of **egalitarianism** is closely correlated with the variance in food supply. The !Kung San's food supply is highly variable, and they share food and express egalitarian beliefs. To be called a "stinge" (stingy) is one of the worst insults, and the group imposes strong social sanctions for stinginess and gives social approval for food sharing. Among the Gana San, in contrast, food variance is low, and they show more economic inequality. Gana San rarely share it outside their extended families.

Environmental conditions can activate some behaviors, such as cooperation and sharing. Everyone has the capacity to share and cooperate, but cultural differences in the degree to which groups do share and cooperate depend, to some extent, on the external environmental conditions, such as variance in the food supply (Henrich & Muthukrishna, 2021).

Early Experience and Evoked Mating Strategies

Another example of evoked culture comes from the work of Jay Belsky and his colleagues (Belsky, 2000; Belsky et al., 2012). They argue that harsh, rejecting, and inconsistent child-rearing practices, erratically provided resources, and marital discord foster a personality of impulsivity and a mating strategy marked by early reproduction. In contrast, sensitive, supportive, and responsive child rearing, combined with reliable resources and spousal harmony, foster a personality of conscientiousness and a mating strategy of commitment, delayed reproduction, and stable marriage. Children in uncertain and unpredictable environments, in short, seem to learn that they cannot rely on a single mate, and so opt for a sexual life that starts early and inclines them to seek multiple mates. In contrast, children growing up in stable homes with parents who predictably invest in their welfare opt for a strategy of long-term mating because they expect to attract a stable, high-investing mate. The evidence from children of divorced homes supports this theory. Such children tend to be more impulsive, tend to reach puberty earlier, engage in sexual intercourse earlier, and have more sex partners than do their peers from intact homes. A longitudinal study found that Australian children who experienced harsher and more unpredictable cultural environments also engaged in more and earlier sexual activity (Maranges & Strickhouser, 2021).

The sensitivity of personality and mating strategies to early experiences may help explain the differences in the value placed on chastity across cultures. In China, for example, marriages are lasting, divorce is rare, and parents invest heavily in their children over extended periods (Lei et al., 2011). In Sweden, many children are born out of wedlock, divorce is common, and fewer fathers invest consistently over time. These cultural experiences may evoke in the two groups different mating strategies, with the Swedes more than the Chinese tending toward short-term mating and more frequent partner switching (Buss, 2016).

Although more evidence is needed to confirm this theory, this example illustrates how a consistent pattern of individual differences can be evoked in different cultures, producing a local pattern of within-group similarities and between-group differences. All humans presumably have within their mating menu a strategy of short-term mating, marked by frequent partner switching, and a strategy of long-term mating, marked by enduring commitment and love (Buss, 2016). These mating strategies may be differentially evoked in different cultures, resulting in enduring cultural differences in mating strategies.

Honors, Insults, and Evoked Aggression

Why are people in some cultures prone to aggression at the slightest provocation, whereas people in other cultures resort to aggression only reluctantly? Why do people in some cultures kill one another at relatively high rates, whereas people in other cultures kill one another at relatively low rates? Nisbett (1993) has proposed a theory to account for these cultural differences—a theory based on the evoked culture.

Nisbett proposed that the economic means of subsistence of a culture affects the degree to which the group develops a **culture of honor.** In cultures of honor, insults are viewed as highly offensive public challenges, which people who are insulted must confront aggressively. The theory is that differences in the degree to which honor becomes a central part of the culture rests ultimately with economics—specifically, the manner in which food is obtained. In herding economies, one's entire stock could be lost suddenly to thieves. Cultivating a reputation as willing to respond with violent force—by physically aggressing when publicly insulted—deters thieves who might steal one's property. In more settled agricultural communities, an aggressive reputation is less important because one's means of subsistence, crops, cannot be easily stolen.

Nisbett tested his theory by using homicide statistics from different regions within the United States and experiments in which subjects from the northern and southern United States were insulted. Southerners (historically using animal herding for subsistence) did not endorse more positive attitudes toward the use of violence in general, compared with the northerners (historically using farming or agriculture for subsistence). The southerners, however, were more likely to endorse violence for the purposes of *protection* and in response to *insults.* Furthermore, the homicide rates in the South were far higher than those in the North, particularly for murders triggered by efforts to defend one's reputation.

Nisbett found a similar pattern in the lab, where the northern and southern participants were insulted by an experimenter. The experimenter intentionally bumped into the participants and then said "asshole." Subsequently, the participants were asked to complete a series of incomplete word stems, such as "h _____." Southerners who had been insulted wrote more aggressive words, such as *hate,* than did the northerners, suggesting that the insults had evoked in the southerners a higher level of anger and aggression. When southerners and northerners were threatened in a laboratory study, southerners had elevated testosterone and responded with greater aggression (Nisbett & Cohen, 1996). Another study found that White populations living in Southern states as well as in Western states (considered to score high in cultures of honor) experienced more school shootings and higher rates of intimate partner violence (Gul, Cross, & Uskul, 2021).

Presumably, all humans have the capacity to develop a high sensitivity to public insults and a capacity to respond with violence. These capacities are evoked in certain cultures, however, and presumably lie dormant in others.

Cultural Differences in Conformity

Pressures to conform with social norms are widespread. Individuals sometimes pay a steep social price for deviating from the group. Children are expected to obey parents and are sometimes punished if they rebel. On the other hand, uniqueness and novelty are sometimes celebrated, and those who resist the tyrannical dictates of a culture are sometimes seen as heroes. Could cultural differences in conformity be an example of evoked culture?

One hypothesis stems from evolutionary psychology and suggests that the prevalence of disease-causing pathogens cause cultural pressure to conform (Murray, Trudeau, & Schaller, 2011). The logic is that infectious diseases historically posed a great threat to human survival. Consequently, humans have evolved defenses to defend against disease-causing pathogens. These include physiological defenses such as the immune system. They also include a *behavioral immune system* that functions to prevent contact with disease-causing agents. This system may include avoiding people with open sores, people who cough, and those who show other signs of disease. When the threat of pathogen infection becomes especially salient, people become more introverted, avoiding contact with other people (Murray, Trudeau, & Schaller, 2011).

Conformity to group norms may also help to avoid diseases. Deviating from cultural norms of food preparation, for example, may increase one's risk of a food-borne disease. In an innovative set of studies, Murray, Trudeau, and Schaller (2011) found that people in cultures with a high prevalence of pathogens tended to be more conformist than those with a lower pathogen prevalence. In cultures with low pathogen prevalence, people expressed greater tolerance for nonconformity. Experiments conducted in China and Canada show that when the threat of disease is made salient to people, they are more likely to conform on experimental tasks (Schaller, Murray, & Hofer, 2021). Differences in conformity may be prime examples of evoked culture—one that rests on a universal psychology that is differentially activated by environmental differences in pathogen prevalence.

The concept of evoked culture provides one model for understanding and explaining cultural variations in personality traits, such as conformity, cooperativeness, or aggression. It rests on the assumption that all humans have the same potentials or capabilities. The aspects of these potentials that get evoked depend on features of the social or physical environment.

Transmitted Culture

Transmitted culture consists of ideas, values, attitudes, and beliefs that exist originally in at least one person's mind that are transmitted to other people's minds through their interaction with the original person (Tooby & Cosmides, 1992; Henrich, 2015). The view that it is wrong to eat beef, for example, is an example of transmitted culture. This value presumably originated in the mind of one person, who then transmitted it to others. Over time, the view that eating beef is a serious violation came to characterize Hindus. Although we do not know much about how culture is transmitted or why certain ideas spread but others do not, the discovery of large cultural differences in seemingly arbitrary values provides evidence for the existence of transmitted culture. People in some cultures view eating beef as wrong; people in other cultures view eating pork as wrong. Others see nothing wrong with eating beef or pork, others eat no meat at all, and others avoid meat and dairy products.

Cultural Differences in Moral Values

Cultures differ in their beliefs about what is morally right and wrong. As an example, consider whether you agree or disagree with the following statement: "It is immoral for adults to disobey their parents" (Rozin, 2003, p. 275). If you are a Hindu Indian, the odds are great that you will agree with this statement (80 percent of the Hindu women and 72 percent of the Hindu men). If you are an American, the odds are that you will disagree (only 13 percent of American women and 19 percent of American men agree).

Views of moral behavior—what is right and what is wrong—are important principles that guide behavior, and they are central to personality. Cultures clearly differ in their views of what is right and wrong, sometimes in seemingly arbitrary ways. Among the Semang of Malaysia, for example, it is considered sinful to comb one's hair during a thunderstorm, to watch dogs mate, to tease a helpless animal, to kill a sacred wasp, to have sexual intercourse during the daytime, to draw water from a fire-blackened vessel, or to act casually or informally with one's mother-in-law (Murdock, 1980).

There may also be universals in what is considered right and wrong. Both Brahman Indians and Americans, for example, agree about the following wrongs: ignoring an accident victim, breaking a promise, kicking a harmless animal, committing brother–sister incest, and stealing flowers (Shweder, Mahapatra, & Miller., 1990). Most cultures consider it wrong to kill without cause. Most cultures consider it wrong to commit incest

A Closer Look

Reaching Across the Great Divide: The Psychology of Cross-Cultural Marriages

What happens when people from different cultures meet and fall in love? We might expect that the more differences between the cultures, the greater the potential difficulties in the marriage. Large cultural differences—those in language, religion, race, politics, and class—may create major divides that may separate a cross-cultural couple.

Sociologists Rosemary Breger and Rosanna Hill (1998) present a detailed look at cross-cultural marriages. Throughout the book, they emphasize how cultural differences create challenges in marriages. For example, many cultural rituals surround food and eating. In some cultures, men are served first and begin eating before women. A man from a different culture might politely wait and not touch his food until his wife begins to eat. If the wife comes from a culture in which men eat first, she might suspect that her husband is dissatisfied with the meal because he is not eating before her. A polite social behavior in one culture can thus be seen as a signal of dissatisfaction in another.

In some cultures, the extended family becomes a part of the couple's life, sometimes sharing sleeping space. In some cultures, you don't just marry the person; you marry their extended family.

According to Larsen and Prizmic-Larsen (1999), one of the largest challenges in cross-cultural marriages results from differences in native languages. They report a case where the wife, who was from Eastern Europe, said to the husband, "You are boring," when her real intent was to ask, "Are you bored?" Good communication is essential to marriage. When one person has to conduct the marriage in a foreign language, there exists potential misunderstandings between the spouses. A heavy accent can lead to verbal misunderstandings. Communicating in a foreign language also takes mental effort and, when tired or angry, one may not be able to communicate very well in a second language.

There are at least two lines of inquiry that interest personality psychologists about cross-cultural marriages. One concerns who is the most likely to marry outside their own culture. Are some personality variables involved in being attracted to those who are different from oneself? A second concerns process. What happens in cross-cultural marriages that might make them different from monocultural marriages? How do two people with cultural differences accommodate and adapt to each other? Are there ways that people can free themselves of cultural bonds and more easily function in a cross-cultural relationship? How do people maintain their identities and sense of self, even when living in a foreign country and conducting their marriage in a foreign language?

Cross-cultural marriages have existed throughout history. In the past, the difficulties were most likely connected with social class differences (e.g., Romeo and Juliet), non-acceptance by one's extended family, religion, or race. Throughout much of the twentieth century, interracial marriage was illegal in many U.S. jurisdictions, but today it is widely regarded as a matter of personal choice and widely accepted.

MinDof/Shutterstock

Darren Greenwood/DesignPics

Relationships that bridge two cultures bring unique challenges, as well as unique opportunities, to the couple.
Don Hammond/Design Pics

Boundaries between cultures are becoming more permeable, especially in the European community. On the other hand, there are many wars and ethnic conflicts based on animosities associated with cultural differences. Those animosities may deter opportunities for certain cultural combinations in marriage. A good example can be found in the countries of former Yugoslavia, where cross-cultural marriages between, say, Muslims and Serbs or between Serbs and Croats were once common and acceptable. However, the conflicts set in motion in 1991 with the breakup of former Yugoslavia, and continuing in Kosovo, Bosnia, and Montenegro, have resulted in a reversal of social diversity. A new term has even entered the English language: **Balkanization,** meaning social resegregation following a time of peaceful integration and social diversity. Balkanization in various countries around the world may make life difficult for cross-cultural marriages.

Former United Nations Secretary General Kofi Annan, born in Ghana, met Swedish attorney Nane Lagergren when they both worked for the U.N. High Commissioner for Refugees. They remained married from 1984 until his death in 2018.

Richard Corkery/NY Daily News Archive via Getty Images

(Lieberman & Lobel, 2012). But even these seeming universals are violated in some cultures. Among certain subcultures, for example, killing is viewed as justified if one has been publicly insulted (Nisbett, 1993). In certain royal dynasties, incest between brother and sister was actively encouraged as a way to preserve the family's wealth and power. Statements about universality are relative in the sense that there are always some cultural or subcultural exceptions.

The key point is that many moral values are specific to particular cultures and are likely to be examples of transmitted culture. They appear to be passed from one generation to the next, not through genes but through the teachings of parents and teachers or through observations of the behavior of others within the culture. Now we turn to another possible example of transmitted culture—the self-concept.

Cultural Differences in Self-Concept

The ways in which we define ourselves—our self-concepts—are the core components of human personality. Self-concepts influence behavior. A person who defines self as conscientious, for example, may take pains to show up for classes on time, return all phone calls from friends, and remember to spell-check her term paper. A person who defines self as agreeable may ensure that the wishes of others are taken into account when deciding where to eat, may give much to charity, and may wait until all others have feasted at the buffet table before serving self. Our self-concepts, in short, affect how we present ourselves to others and how we behave in everyday life. Research shows that self-concepts differ substantially from culture to culture.

Markus and Kitayama (1991, 1994, 1998) propose that each person has two fundamental "cultural tasks," which have to be confronted. The first is communion, collectivism, or **interdependence.** This cultural task involves how you are affiliated with or engaged in the larger group. Interdependence includes your relationships with other members of the group and your embeddedness within the group. The second task—agency, individualism, or **independence**—involves how you differentiate yourself from the group. Independence includes your unique abilities, your personal internal motives and personality dispositions, and the ways you separate yourself from the group.

People from different cultures differ profoundly in how they balance these two tasks. Western cultures, according to this theory, are characterized by independence. Conversations emphasize individual choices (e.g., "Where do you want to eat tonight?"). The system of salaries puts a premium on individual merit—your salary is specifically pegged to *your* performance.

In contrast, many non-Western cultures, such as Japan and China, are characterized by interdependence. These cultures emphasize the fundamental interconnectedness within the group. The self is meaningful only with reference to the larger group of which the person is a part. The major tasks in these cultures are to fit in and to promote harmony and group unity. Personal desires are constrained rather than expressed in a selfish manner (e.g., "Where do *we* want to eat tonight?"). Conversational scripts emphasize sympathy, deference, and kindness. Pay is often determined by seniority rather than by individual performance.

To illustrate the contrasting orientations of independence and interdependence, consider the following descriptions, the first from an American student and the second from a Japanese student, in response to the instruction "describe yourself briefly":

> *I like to live life with a lot of positive energy. I feel like there is so much to do and see and experience. However, I also know the value of relaxation. I love the obscure. I play ultimate Frisbee, juggle, unicycle, and dabble on the recorder and concertina. I have a taste for the unique. I am very friendly and in most situations very self-confident. (Markus & Kitayama, 1998, p. 63)*

> *I cannot decide quickly what I should do, and am often swayed by other people's opinions, and I cannot oppose the opinions of people who are supposed to be respected because of age or status. Even if I have displeasure, I compromise myself to the people around me without getting rid of the displeasure. Also, I am concerned about how other people think about me. (p. 64)*

Notice the different themes that run through the self-descriptions of these individuals. The American tends to use global and largely context-free trait descriptions, such as *friendly, self-confident,* and *happy.* The Japanese tends to use self-descriptions embedded in a social context, such as responding to elders or those higher in status and using the social group as a means of calming down. These illustrate the themes of independence and interdependence. The independence theme is characterized by a self-view as autonomous, stable, coherent, and free from the influences of others. The interdependence theme is characterized by a self-view as connected, interpersonally flexible, and committed to being bound to others (Markus & Kitayama, 1998).

Is there empirical evidence that the way we define ourselves—something fundamental to personality—depends on the culture in which we reside? Using the Twenty Statements Test, researchers found that North Americans tend to describe themselves using abstract internal characteristics, such as *smart, stable, dependable,* and *open-minded* (Rhee et al., 1995). Chinese participants more often describe themselves with social roles, such as "I am a daughter" or "I am Jane's friend" (Ip & Bond, 1995).

Another study administered the Twenty Statements Test to samples of Asians in Seoul, Korea; to Asian Americans in New York City; and to European Americans in New York City (Rhee et al., 1995). It examined cultural differences in self-concept, but with an interesting twist: Do Asians living in New York who self-identify as Asian differ in self-concept from Asians living in the same place who do not self-identify as Asian? Do some people shift their self-concepts and adopt ones similar to those of the adopted culture? The process of adapting to one's new culture is called **acculturation.**

A refugee family from Somalia experiences the Arizona State Fair. After entering a new culture, acculturation is the process of adopting the ways of life and beliefs common in that culture.

Christophe Calais/Contributor/Getty Images

The Asian Americans living in New York who did *not* self-identify as Asian described themselves using highly abstract and autonomous self-statements, similar to the responses of European Americans residing in New York. These Asian Americans used even more trait terms in their self-descriptions (45 percent) than did the European Americans (35 percent).

In contrast, the New York–dwelling Asians who identified themselves as Asian used more socially embedded self-descriptions, much as the Chinese respondents did. They often referred to themselves by describing their role status (e.g., student) and their family status (e.g., son). Moreover, they were more likely to qualify their self-concepts with contextual information. Rather than describing themselves as *reliable,* they described themselves as "reliable when I'm at home."

Another study examined how frequently Japanese and European American students endorsed a variety of attributes as descriptive of themselves (Markus & Kitayama, 1998). A full 84 percent of the Japanese students described themselves as *ordinary,* whereas only 18 percent of the American students used this self-description. Conversely, 96 percent of the Americans described themselves as *special,* whereas only 55 percent of the Japanese described themselves with this term (see Table 17.1).

This theme of standing out versus fitting in and going along with the group is seen in the folk sayings of American and Japanese cultures. In American culture, people sometimes say, "The squeaky wheel gets the grease," signifying that asserting oneself as an individual is the way to pursue one's interests. In Japan, it is sometimes said that "the nail that stands out gets pounded down," which suggests that the American social strategy would fail in Japan. These themes even show up in language usage. Those with an interdependent/collectivist orientation tend to use "we," whereas those with an independent/individualistic orientation tend to use "I" (Na & Choi, 2009).

The trait of narcissism appears to manifest differently depending on culture. One study compared a German sample (independent culture) with Japan (interdependent culture) on expressions of narcissism (Jauk et al., 2021). The German participants scored higher on grandiose narcissism, which involves seeking admiration and

Table 17.1 Most Frequently Endorsed Attributes "I am"

EUROPEAN AMERICANS		JAPANESE	
Attribute	Percentage of Responses	Attribute	Percentage of Responses
Responsible	100%	Happy	94%
Persistent	100	Fun-loving	94
Cooperative	98	Relaxed	92
Special	96	Direct	92
Happy	95	Assertive	90
Unique	95	Laid-back	86
Fun-loving	93	Calm	86
Sympathetic	93	Free-spirited	86
Hardworking	93	Undisciplined	84
Ambitious	93	Ordinary	84
Reliable	93		
Independent	93		

Source: Adapted from Markus and Kitayama (1998), p. 79, Table 1.

displaying exhibitionism—traits that make the self stand out. The Japanese, in contrast, scored higher on vulnerable narcissism, which involves self-construals as more anxious and hypersensitive about the opinions of others.

These cultural differences are linked to how people process information. Japanese tend to explain events **holistically**—with attention to relationships, context, and the links between the focal object and the field as a whole (Nisbett et al., 2001). Americans, in contrast, tend to explain events **analytically**—with the object detached from its context, attributes of people assigned to categories, and a reliance on rules about the categories to explain behavior. When watching animated scenes of fish swimming around, for example, the Japanese made more statements about contextual information, linking the fish's behavior to their surroundings (Masuda & Nisbett, 2001). These cultural differences even show up as differences in neural activity in studies of Western and Eastern cultures, suggesting a brain basis for different forms of processing information (Kim et al., 2021). Thus, the cultural differences in the personality attributes of independence–interdependence may be linked to underlying cognitive proclivities in the ways in which individuals *attend to,* and *explain,* events in their world.

In sum, there is empirical support for the claim that people in different cultures have different self-concepts and process information differently. These differences are culturally transmitted through parents and teachers to children.

Criticisms of the Interdependence–Independence and Collectivist–Individualist Concepts

Several have criticized the Markus–Kitayama theory that Western views of self are independent, whereas Asian views of self are interdependent, both on theoretical and evidentiary grounds. Matsumoto (1999) and Church (2009) contend that the evidence for the theory comes almost exclusively from North America and East Asia (notably, Japan) and may not generalize to other cultures. There is far more overlap in the self-concepts of people from different cultures than Markus and Kitayama imply. Many in collectivist cultures, for example, do use global traits (e.g., *agreeable, fun-loving*) when describing themselves. Many in individualist cultures use relational concepts (e.g., "I am the daughter of . . ."). The cultural differences are more a matter of degree.

On theoretical grounds, Church (2000) notes that "attempts to characterize cultures of individuals in terms of such broad cultural dichotomies may be overly simplistic" (p. 688). Views of self in all cultures incorporate both independent and interdependent self-construals, and self-concepts in all cultures vary somewhat across social contexts.

A meta-analysis of dozens of studies suggests even more caution in generalizing about cultural differences in individualism and collectivism (Oyserman, Coon, & Kemmelmeier, 2002a). It found that although European Americans tended to be somewhat more individualistic (valuing independence) and less collectivistic (valuing interdependence) than those from *some* other cultures, the effect sizes proved to be small and qualified by important exceptions. European Americans were *not* more individualistic than either African Americans or Latinos, for example. Nor were European Americans less collectivistic than Japanese or Koreans—two cultures presumed to anchor one end of the interdependence continuum. The Chinese, rather than the Japanese or Koreans, stand out as being unusually collectivistic and non-individualistic in self-concept. Other studies have found little support for the influence of transmitted culture on self-concept. One study of two presumably individualistic (the United States, Australia) and two presumably collectivistic (Mexico, the Philippines) cultures found that (1) people in all four cultures described themselves in trait terms with a high level of frequency; and (2) people in all four cultures mentioned *personal* rather than *social* or *collective* identity to be more important to their sense of self (del Prado et al., 2007).

Characterizations such as independent–interdependent also have been criticized on the grounds that they are too general (Chen & West, 2008), combining different kinds of social relationships and ignoring the context specificity in which they are expressed (Fiske, 2002). Americans, for example, may be individualistic and independent while playing computer games, but interdependent while with their families or in church.

Despite these criticisms, there are real differences across cultures, and these must be explained. Most researchers have assumed that cultural differences in dimensions such as independence–interdependence are instances of transmitted culture—ideas, attitudes, and self-concepts that are passed from one mind to another within a culture, down through the generations. Others have proposed a different explanation involving evolutionary psychology and evoked culture (Oyserman, Coon, & Kemmelmeier, 2002b). They hypothesize that humans have evolved psychological mechanisms for *both* types of self-concepts and can switch from one mode to another, depending on fitness advantages. Specifically, when one's group is low in mobility, is limited in resources, and has many relatives in close proximity, it has paid survival dividends to be highly collectivistic and interdependent. One's genetic relatives, often the recipients of these collectivist proclivities, tend to benefit. On the other hand, when mobility is high and people move frequently from place to place, when resources are relatively abundant, and when few genetic relatives live close by, it has paid survival dividends to adopt a more individualistic and independent proclivity. This hypothesis is best summed up by its authors: "Thus, an evolutionary perspective suggests both the 'basicness' of independent and interdependent processing as well as the likelihood that all social systems are inhabited by individuals who can do both and draw on one or the other depending on their immediate contexts" (Oyserman, Coon, & Kemmelmeier, 2002b, p. 116). Research is increasingly exploring this fascinating fusion of evolutionary psychology and cultural psychology (e.g., Henrich, 2015).

Toshiyuki Tanaka, a former umpire in the Japanese baseball league, during an interview. In his culture, harmony is valued over conflict. To keep the peace during a heated game, Tanaka often played the role of diplomat. He rarely penalized a team or ejected a player from the game, events common in American baseball. Moreover, Tanaka sometimes admitted it when he made a mistake, which is practically unheard of among American umpires.

Itsuo Inouye/AP Images

Cultural Differences in Self-Enhancement

Self-enhancement is the tendency to present oneself using positive or socially valued attributes, such as *kind, understanding, intelligent,* and *industrious.* Self-enhancement tends to be stable over time (Baumeister, 1997). North Americans tend to maintain a generally positive evaluation of themselves (Fiske et al., 1997). The self-concepts of American adults contain more than four times as many positive attributes as negative ones (Herzog et al., 1995). The Japanese make fewer spontaneous positive statements about themselves. The Japanese score lower than Americans on translations of self-esteem scales (Fiske et al., 1997). Japanese respondents tend to give more negative descriptions of themselves, such as "I think too much" and "I'm a somewhat selfish person" (Yeh, 1995). Even the positive self-descriptions of the Japanese respondents tend to be in the form of negations, such as "I'm not lazy." American respondents would express a similar sentiment with the phrase "I'm a hard worker."

Korean and American respondents also differ (Ryff, Lee, & Na, 1995). Koreans are more likely to endorse negative statements about themselves, whereas American respondents are more likely to endorse positive statements. Differences in self-enhancement also show up in parents' self-descriptions of the quality of their parenting practices (Schmutte, Lee, & Ryff, 1995). American parents describe their parenting practices in generally glowing terms; Korean parents give mostly negative self-evaluations. Another study found that Chinese individuals self-enhance less than U.S. Americans, but only on some traits (Church et al., 2014). Self-enhancement also shows up in considering oneself "better than average" and over-claiming credit for successful group outcomes (Sedikedes & Alicke, 2021).

Cultural differences in self-enhancement extend to evaluations of one's group compared with other groups. Heine and Lehman (1995) asked Japanese and Canadian students to compare their own university with a rival university within their own culture. Among the Canadian respondents, there was a strong tendency toward in-group enhancement, with the rival university evaluated negatively by comparison. Among the Japanese respondents, there was no favoritism in the evaluation of one's own university in comparison with the rival university. Japanese and Asian-Canadians also tend to be more self-critical than Euro-Canadians (Falk et al., 2009), again suggesting cultural differences in self-enhancement.

Psychologists have advanced two explanations for cultural differences in self-enhancement. One is that the Asians are engaging in impression management (see Chapter 4)—deep in their hearts, perhaps, they truly evaluate themselves positively, but to express these views publicly would damage their reputation. A second explanation is that these cultural differences accurately reflect people's deep experiences. Asians, due to profound cultural differences in values, truly evaluate themselves more negatively than do North Americans. There has been only one empirical test of these competing explanations (Fiske et al., 1997). When self-evaluations are made in conditions of total anonymity, where no one would be able to identify the respondent, researchers still found that the self-enhancement commonly seen among Americans does not occur among Asian respondents. This supports the theory that cultural differences reflect the actual subjective experiences and are not merely surface differences due to impression management by Asians.

Cultural differences are matters of degree; people in all cultures appear to display a self-enhancement bias to some extent (Kurman, 2001). In a study of three cultures—Singaporeans, Druze Israelis, and Jewish Israelis—Kurman (2001) asked participants whether they considered themselves below or above average for their sex and age group on six traits: intelligence, health, and sociability (agentic traits) and cooperation, honesty, and generosity (communal traits). Although Singaporeans showed slightly more self-enhancement than the other two cultures, it applied only to the agentic traits, and people in *all* cultures showed a self-enhancement bias. On the communal traits, 85 percent of the participants in all three cultures viewed themselves as "above average" for their age and sex group. On the agentic traits, although the Druze and Jewish Israeli samples showed a self-enhancement level of 90 percent and 87 percent, respectively, the Singaporeans showed a self-enhancement level of nearly 80 percent. Thus, people across cultures show a self-enhancement bias, so the cultural differences must be interpreted within the context of this overall similarity.

Religion—An Example of Transmitted Culture

Religious beliefs vary widely across cultures and change over time, from the polytheistic Greek gods of Zeus, Apollo, and Aphrodite to modern monotheistic religions that follow a Christian God or Islamic Allah. Religious beliefs are examples of transmitted culture—representations in some minds that are transmitted to other minds. The *religious domain* is difficult to define crisply, but it typically contains elements such as *mental representations of unobservable agents* such as gods, ghosts, and souls; *artifacts* linked with unobservable agents such as statues and crosses; *rituals* linked with agents such as prayer and song; *elements of morality* linked to conduct considered to be good or evil; and *coalitional processes* such as identification with a particular religious group, initiation procedures that induct people into the group, and practices aimed at maintaining loyalty and punishing defection (Boyer & Bergstrom, 2008). Given their pervasiveness across cultures (e.g., more than 74 percent of Americans believe in a god or higher spiritual power), religious beliefs are of central importance in our species.

Belief in supernatural agents may seem puzzling. We expect humans to have adaptations that accurately understand the real world in which challenges, such as survival and reproduction, must be solved in real time. Why would people believe in supernatural agents they cannot see, that defy scientific principles of physical causality, and that risk potentially nonadaptive behavior?

Psychologists have advanced two competing theories. One is that there are specialized adaptations for religious phenomena—that they are costly signals of commitment or hard-to-fake signals of altruism (Bulbulia, 2004). By committing to a religious group, individuals gain adaptive benefits of group membership, such as protection, powerful allies, and potential mates. The competing theory is that religious phenomena are not adaptions, but are byproducts of other cognitive adaptations designed for nonreligious functions (Boyer, 1992; Kirkpatrick, 2005; Thompson & Aukofer, 2011).

So what are the cognitive adaptations of which religion is hypothesized to be a byproduct? The first is our *hyperactive agency detection device,* which leads us to infer that unseen forces are human agents (Thompson & Aukofer, 2011). This likely evolved as a protection or precaution adaptation (Boyer, 1992). We mistake a shadow for a burglar but never mistake a burglar for a shadow—a proclivity that helps us to avoid costly errors such as being robbed or mugged. This proclivity leads to misapplied anthropomorphisms, as when we say "the sun is trying to come out" or "the clouds look angry." Clouds and skies, of course, don't have agency, yet we attribute humanlike motivations to them as if they were agents with goals and intentions. It is a small step to infer a god with humanlike agency—a god that wants us to pray to him, worship him, and sacrifice for him and that will punish us if we disobey him. Even children have what is called *promiscuous teleology*—the tendency to attribute purposes to abstract entities such as cultures, mother earth, the universe, and god.

A second class of cognitive mechanisms is *theory of mind adaptations*—we infer unseen beliefs, desires, and intentions in other people. Theory of mind adaptations are extremely useful in predicting the behavior of other people—that is, their proper function. It is a small extrapolation to go from "there are people watching me who have a desire for my well-being" to "there is an all-seeing god watching me who has a desire for my well-being." We imbue these agents with beliefs and desires.

Next comes the *attachment system,* which originally evolved in the context of mother–child bonds for protection and nurturance (Kirkpatrick, 2005). A 2-year-old reaching out to a mother to be soothed bears resemblance to a worshiper reaching out to a god: " . . . we never lose the longing for a caretaker . . . [and] a god is always there for us" (Thompson & Aukofer, 2011, p. 45). Adaptations to form attachments, in short, get transferred to supernatural agents. *Reciprocity adaptations* are also activated, as when we make sacrifices for gods or make covenants with gods and expect that the gods will provide us with benefits in return.

Religions also commonly activate our evolved *kin psychology.* In Catholicism, for example, nuns are "sisters" and priests are "fathers," even though they are not our real genetic relatives. Religious recruiters of some suicide terrorists foment outrage at the terrible treatment of their "brothers" and "sisters." And religions hijack our *mating psychology,* whether in the form of prohibiting adultery, exhorting men not to covet their neighbor's wives, or promising 72 virgins in the afterlife. It comes as no surprise that religious leaders—almost always men—sometimes use their positions to secure mating opportunities with women, who in turn tend to be attracted to men high in status and power (Buss, 2002). Finally, the content of what people the world over pray for is predictable from our evolved psychology: recuperation from illness, triumph in love, a boon for one's business, rain for one's crops, the success of one's children, and bad times to befall one's enemies.

These psychological processes, of course, do not exhaust the list for which religious phenomena are hypothesized to be byproducts. Others include emotionally arousing rituals that get culturally transmitted due to their attention-grabbing nature and group-oriented loyalty that minimizes within-group conflict (Boyer & Bergstrom, 2008; Kirkpatrick, 2005; Legare & Souza, 2012; Thompson & Aukofer, 2011). Some studies find that higher exposure to culturally credible cues of religious commitment in others increases religious beliefs—a perfect illustration of transmitted culture (Gervais, Najile, & Caluori, 2021). Religion, in short, is a collection of diverse phenomena, possibly byproducts of many evolved psychological adaptations.

Religious beliefs are excellent examples of transmitted culture—they are passed down from cultural institutions such as churches or mosques or temples to individuals, from parents to children, from religious leaders to their followers, and from one person's mind to the minds of others. Cultures differ tremendously in their religious views. If you happen to grow up in Brazil, you have a 65 percent probability of being Catholic; in Indonesia, 87 percent are Muslim; in India, 80 percent are Hindu. Religious views, in short, are prime examples of transmitted culture.

Personality traits play a key role in receptivity to culturally transmitted religious beliefs. Among Muslims living in Iran, for example, those high on Conscientiousness and Agreeableness were more likely to hold strong religious beliefs, perform religious rituals, and express gratitude toward God (Aghababaei, 2013). Among Belgians, who are predominantly Christian, Conscientiousness and Agreeableness also were positively linked with religiosity (Saroglou & Fiasse, 2003). Personality, in short, influences receptivity to culturally transmitted religious views.

Do Cultures Have Distinctive Personality Profiles?

People have long been fascinated with the question of whether cultures have distinctive personality profiles. Are people from the Mediterranean region of Europe really more emotionally expressive, or is this merely an incorrect stereotype? Are people from Scandinavia really more calm and stoic, or is this merely an incorrect stereotype? Most studies reveal that stereotypes about national personality rarely correspond to average levels of actual assessed personality (Allik, 2012).

McCrae and 79 colleagues from around the world studied the personality profiles of 51 different cultures, using 12,156 participants (McCrae et al., 2005a). They translated the Revised NEO Personality Inventory into the appropriate language and then examined the aggregate Big Five personality scores for each culture. The largest difference across cultures centered on Extraversion. Americans and Europeans scored higher than Asians and Africans. A few examples will illustrate these differences. With the cross-cultural average set to 50, the average Extraversion score was 52 for Americans, 54 for Australians, 54 for the English, and 52 for Belgians. In contrast, the average Extraversion scores were 47 for Ugandans, Ethiopians, and the People's Republic Chinese. Some have questioned the validity of these findings because they rely exclusively on self-report (Ashton, 2007; Perugini & Richetin, 2007).

Studies confirm personality stereotypes in some domains but not in other domains. For example, stereotypes about gender differences across culture appear to be fairly accurate (Löckenhoff et al., 2014). Women are stereotyped as a bit more agreeable, conscientious, and anxious in a study of 26 cultures, and findings from both self-report and observer-report studies bear this out. On the other hand, many national character stereotypes appear to be inaccurate (McCrae et al., 2013). Some Chinese people stereotype Malays as "friendly, but lazy," but the empirical findings do not support this. The study of 26 countries found little support for national character stereotypes (McCrae et al., 2013). Even when cultural differences in personality are found, they are relatively small. Most of the differences in personality occur *within* cultures, not among cultures. Indeed, the most striking finding is how similar cultures actually are in their overall scores on the five-factor model.

Personality Variations Within Culture

Another dimension of transmitted culture pertains to **within-culture variations,** although these have not received the same degree of attention as cross-cultural variations. Within-culture variations can arise from several sources, including differences in growing up in various socioeconomic classes, differences in historical era, and differences in local evoked or transmitted culture.

There is some evidence that **social class** can have an effect on personality (Kohn et al., 1990). Lower-class parents tend to emphasize the importance of obedience to authority, whereas higher-status parents tend to emphasize self-direction and nonconformity. According to Kohn, these socialization practices stem from the sorts of occupations that parents expect their children to enter. Higher-status jobs (e.g., manager, start-up company founder, doctor, lawyer) often require greater self-direction, whereas lower-status jobs (e.g., factory worker, gas station employee) more often require the need to follow rules and permit less latitude for innovation. In studies of American, Japanese, and Polish men, men from higher social classes in all cultures tended to be more self-directed, showed lower levels of conformity, and had greater intellectual flexibility than men from lower social classes. Interestingly, those from lower classes tend to be more generous and charitable than those in the upper classes, giving more even though they have less (Piff et al., 2010).

These findings are correlational, so direction of effects cannot be assumed. Perhaps people with personalities marked by self-direction and intellectual flexibility gravitate toward the higher social classes. Or perhaps the socialization practices of higher-social-class parents produce children with personalities that are different from the personalities of lower-social-class children. In either case, this example highlights the importance of within-culture differences. Figure 17.1 shows the distribution of individualism–collectivism in two cultures. The shaded part shows the overlap among cultures. Consequently, even though cultures can differ in their average level on a particular trait, many individuals within the one culture can be higher (or lower) than many individuals in the other culture.

Another type of within-culture variation pertains to the **historical era.** People raised in the Great Depression of the 1930s, for example, might be more anxious about job security, adopting a conservative spending style. Those growing up during the sexual revolution of the 1960s and 1970s might show more openness to experimentation. Those growing up during the internet spend more time interacting with others in distant places, expanding social horizons in ways that might influence personality. Many people in modern times find mates through internet dating sites, a phenomenon virtually absent a generation ago (Buss, 2016). Disentangling the effects of historical era on personality is difficult because most currently used personality measures were not used in earlier eras. One exception examined changes in average personality scores over a period of 25 years in the Netherlands (Smits et al., 2011). They found small increases in Extraversion, Agreeableness, and Conscientiousness, and small decreases in Neuroticism over generations.

Cultural Universals

A third approach to culture and personality is to identify features of personality that are universal, or present in most or all human cultures. As described in Chapter 1, these universals constitute the human nature level of analyzing personality.

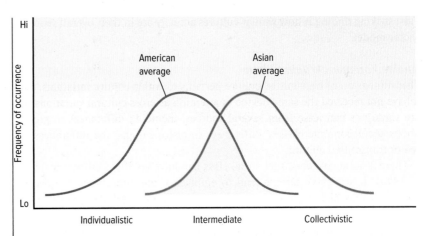

Figure 17.1

Individualism versus collectivism in American and Asian cultures. The distribution of two groups may be significantly different from each other in terms of the group mean yet have much overlap. This means that many individuals from one group are higher (or lower) than many members of the other group, in a pattern opposite that of the mean difference. Asians score higher on collectivism than Americans do, yet there will always be some Americans who score higher than some Asians (those in the shaded area) on this measure.

In the history of the study of personality and culture, the study of **cultural universals** has long been in disfavor. For most of the twentieth century, the focus was almost exclusively on cultural differences. This emphasis was fueled by anthropologists who reported on seemingly exotic cultures. Margaret Mead, for example, purported to discover cultures entirely lacking in sexual jealousy, cultures in which sex roles were reversed and adolescence was not marked with stress and turmoil (Mead, 1928, 1935). On sex roles, for example, Mead presumed to discover "a genuine reversal of the sex-attitudes of our culture, with the woman the dominant, impersonal, managing partner, the man the less responsible and the emotionally dependent person" (Mead, 1935, p. 279). Human nature was assumed to be infinitely variable, infinitely flexible, and not constrained by a universal human nature: "We are forced to conclude that human nature is almost unbelievably malleable, responding accurately and contrastingly to contrasting cultural conditions" (p. 280).

Over the past few decades, the pendulum has swung toward a more moderate view. Anthropologists who visited the islands Mead had visited failed to confirm Mead's findings (e.g., Freeman, 1983). In cultures in which sexual jealousy was presumed to be entirely absent, it turned out that sexual jealousy was the leading cause of spousal battering and spousal homicide. In cultures such as the Chambri, where the sex roles were presumed to be reversed, anthropologists instead found that men were considered to be in charge (Brown, 1991; Gewertz, 1981). Furthermore, the Chambri considered men to be more aggressive than women and women to be more submissive than men. Behavioral observations of social interactions among the Chambri confirmed these conceptions (Gewertz, 1981). All available evidence back to 1850, including some of Mead's recorded observations (as opposed to the inferences she made), suggest that the Chambri's sex roles are, in fact, strikingly similar to those of Western cultures. Brown (1991), Pinker (1997), and Ardila (2021) list practices and attitudes that are good candidates for cultural universals—see Table 17.2.

In this section, we consider three examples of cultural universals: beliefs about the personality characteristics of men and women, the expression of emotion, and the possible universality of the five-factor model of personality traits.

Beliefs About the Personality Characteristics of Men and Women

In the largest study undertaken to examine beliefs about the personality characteristics of men and women, Williams and Best (1990) examined 30 countries over a period of 15 years. These included western European countries such as Germany, the Netherlands,

Table 17.2 Culturally Universal Practices and Attitudes

Incest avoidance

Facial expressions of basic emotions

Favoritism toward in-group members

Favoritism toward kin over non-kin

Collective identities

Division of labor by sex

Revenge and retaliation

Self distinguished from others

Sanctions for crimes against the collectivity

Reciprocity in relationships

Envy, sexual jealousy, and love

Sources: Ardila (2021), Brown (2004), and Pinker (1997).

and Italy; Asian countries such as Japan and India; South American countries such as Venezuela; and African countries such as Nigeria. In each country, university students examined 300 trait adjectives (e.g., *aggressive, emotional, dominant*) and indicated whether each trait is more often linked with men, women, or both sexes. The responses of the subjects within each culture were then summed. The big shock was this: many of the trait adjectives were highly associated with one or the other sex, and there proved to be tremendous consensus across cultures. Table 17.3 shows sample trait adjectives most associated with men and with women across cultures.

How can we summarize and interpret these differences in beliefs about men and women? Williams and Best (1994) scored each of these adjectives on the following dimensions: *favorability* (How desirable is the trait?), *strength* (How much does the trait indicate power?), and *activity* (How much does the trait signify energy?). These dimensions originate from older classical work in the field that discovered three universal semantic dimensions of *evaluation* (good–bad), *potency* (strong–weak), and *activity* (active–passive) (Osgood, Suci, & Tannenbaum, 1957). Overall, the traits ascribed to men and women are equally favorable. Some "masculine" traits, such as *serious* and *inventive,* were viewed as favorable, whereas others, such as *arrogant* and *bossy,* were viewed as unfavorable. Some "feminine" traits, such as *charming* and *appreciative,* were viewed as favorable, whereas others, such as *fearful* and *affected,* were viewed as unfavorable.

How can we interpret these cultural universals in beliefs about the personality characteristics of men and women? One way is that these beliefs represent stereotypes based on the roles men and women assume universally. Williams and Best (1994) argue that society assumes that men are stronger than women and therefore assigns men to roles and occupations such as soldier and construction worker.

A second possibility is that traits ascribed to men and women in all 30 cultures reflect actual observations of real sex differences in personality. Studies of the five-factor model, for example, do find that women score lower on Emotional Stability, suggesting that they are more fearful and emotional. A study in Spain concluded that beliefs about the traits of men being more *agentic* and the traits of women being more *communal* show remarkable stability over more than three decades, from 1985 to 2018 (Moya et al., 2021). And does anyone really doubt that men are, on average, more physically aggressive or violent than women (see Chapter 16)? In short, the universal beliefs about the differences between men and women in personality reflect actual differences in personality (Löckenhoff et al., 2014).

Table 17.3 Pancultural Traits Linked with Men or Women

Traits Associated with Men		Traits Associated with Women	
Active	Loud	Affected	Modest
Adventurous	Obnoxious	Affectionate	Nervous
Aggressive	Opinionated	Appreciative	Patient
Arrogant	Opportunistic	Cautious	Pleasant
Autocratic	Pleasure-seeking	Changeable	Prudish
Bossy	Precise	Charming	Sensitive
Coarse	Quick	Dependent	Sentimental
Conceited	Reckless	Emotional	Softhearted
Enterprising	Show-off	Fearful	Timid
Hardheaded	Tough	Forgiving	Warm

Source: Adapted from Williams and Best (1994). Cross-cultural views of women and men. In W. J. Lonner and R. S. Malpass (Eds.), *Psychology and culture* (1st ed., p. 193), ©1994. Reprinted by permission of Pearson Education, Inc., Upper Saddle River, New Jersey.

Expression of Emotion

It is commonly believed that people in different cultures experience different emotions. As a consequence, personality psychologists have argued that different cultures have different words to describe emotional experience. The Tahitians, some have argued, do not experience grief, longing, or loneliness, so they have no words in their language to express these emotions. For example, when a Tahitian boy dies in combat, according to legends reported by anthropologists, the parents smile and experience no grief, unlike the profound sadness felt by people in the modern Western world who experience similar events. Cultural variability in the presence or absence of emotional words has been interpreted by some personality psychologists to mean that cultures differ in the presence or absence of actual experiences of these emotions.

However, are emotions really this culturally variable? Or are there cultural universals in the experience of emotions? Psychologist Steven Pinker summarizes the evidence in this way: "Cultures surely differ in how often their members express, talk about, and act on various emotions. But that says nothing about what their people feel. The evidence suggests that the emotions of all normal members of our species are played on the same keyboard" (Pinker, 1997, p. 365).

The earliest evidence of cultural universals in emotions came from Charles Darwin. In gathering evidence for his book on emotions, *The Expression of Emotions in Man and Animals,* Darwin (1872/1965) asked anthropologists and travelers who interacted with peoples on five continents to give detailed information about how the natives expressed various emotions, such as grief, contempt, disgust, fear, and jealousy. He summarized the answers he received: "The same state of mind is expressed throughout the world with remarkable uniformity; and this fact is in itself interesting as evidence of the close similarity in bodily structure and mental disposition of all the races of mankind" (Darwin, 1872/1965, pp. 15, 17).

Darwin's methods, of course, were crude by today's scientific standards, but subsequent research has confirmed his basic conclusions. Psychologist Paul Ekman created a set of photographs of people expressing six basic emotions and then showed them to people in various cultures (Ekman, 1973). Some cultures, such as the Fore foragers of New Guinea, had almost no contact with Westerners. The Fore spoke no English, had seen no TV or movies, and had never lived with Caucasians. He also administered the tests to people in Japan, Brazil, Chile, Argentina, and the United States. Ekman asked each subject to label the emotion expressed in each photograph and to make up a story about what the person in the photograph had experienced. The six emotions—happiness, sadness, anger, fear, disgust, and surprise—were universally recognized by people in the various cultures. These findings have been subsequently replicated in other countries, such as Italy, Scotland, Estonia, Greece, Germany, Hong Kong, Sumatra, and Turkey (Ekman et al., 1987). Further research by Ekman and his colleagues has expanded the list of universal emotions to include contempt, embarrassment, and shame (Ekman, 1999).

In addition to finding that people of different cultures effortlessly recognized the emotions expressed on the faces in the photographs, Ekman reversed the procedure. He asked the Fore participants to act out scenarios, such as "Your child has died" and "You are angry and about to fight," and then photographed them. The emotions expressed in these photographs were easily recognized by facial expressions and were strikingly similar to the expressions of the same emotions seen in the photographs of the Caucasian participants. Further evidence for the universality, and possible evolutionary origins, of these basic emotions comes from the finding that children who are blind from birth display the same facial expressions of emotions that those with full sight display (Lazarus, 1991).

Pinker notes that whether a language has a word for a particular emotion or not matters little if the question is whether people *experience* the emotion in the same way: Tahitians

Disgust appears to be an emotion universally experienced by humans.
Tetra Images/Shutterstock

are said not to have a word for grief; however, "when a Tahitian woman says 'My husband died and I feel sick,' her emotional state is hardly mysterious; she is probably not complaining about acid indigestion" (Pinker, 1997, p. 367).

Another example is the German word *Schadenfreude:* "When English-speakers hear the word *Schadenfreude* for the first time, their reaction is not, 'Let me see . . . pleasure in another's misfortunes . . . what could that possibly be? I cannot grasp the concept; my language and culture have not provided me with such a category.' Their reaction is, 'You mean there's a word for it? Cool!'" (Pinker, 1997, p. 367). People universally may experience the emotion of pleasure in an enemy's misfortunes, even if all cultures do not have a single word in their language to capture it.

The view that language is not necessary for people to experience emotions may be contrasted with what has been called the **Whorfian hypothesis of linguistic relativity,** which contends that language *creates* thought and experience. The Whorfian hypothesis argues that ideas that people think and emotions they feel are constrained by the words that happen to exist in their language and culture (Whorf, 1956).

The difference between *experiencing* an emotion and *expressing* that emotion in public may be critical to resolving this debate. Ekman (1973) performed an ingenious experiment to explore the difference between the experience of emotion and its expression in public. He secretly videotaped the facial expressions of Japanese and American students while they watched a graphic film of a primitive puberty rite involving genital mutilation. In one condition, an experimenter wearing a white lab coat was present in the room. In the other condition, the participants were alone. When the experimenter was present (a public context), the Japanese students smiled politely during the film, but the American students expressed horror and disgust. However, when the students were filmed when they were alone in the room watching the film, both the Japanese and American faces expressed equal horror. This suggests that Japanese and American students *experience* this emotion in the same way, even if they differ in their *expression* of it in a more public setting. Higher emotional expression is linked to the personality trait of Extraversion (Matsumoto, 2006). And because Americans are more extraverted than Japanese, these cultural differences in emotional expression may be due to these cultural differences in personality.

Other cross-cultural work has confirmed the universality of some basic forms of emotional expression (e.g., Cowen & Keltner, 2020). One study compared non-verbal emotional vocalizations (e.g., "yuck," "huh") of the "basic emotions" of anger, disgust, fear, joy, sadness, and surprise among Namibian and Western participants (Sauter et al., 2010). These vocal expressions were bi-directionally recognized—Namibians correctly identified the emotion that corresponded with the nonverbal vocalizations uttered by Westerners and vice versa. These findings lend support to the notion that some emotions are universal across cultures, although some researchers question the results of these studies on methodological grounds and argue that emotional expression may be more culturally variable than previously believed (Feldman Barrett, 2021).

Five-Factor Model of Personality

A fascinating question is whether there is a universal structure of personality, such as the five-factor model, or whether different models exist in different cultures. It is helpful to outline the conceptual positions that have been advanced.

According to some, even the concept of personality lacks universality. Hsu, for example, argues that "the concept of personality is an expression of the Western ideal of individualism" (Hsu, 1985, p. 24). Shweder argues that "the data gathered from . . . personality inventories lends illusory support to the mistaken belief that individual differences can be described in language consisting of context-free global traits, factors, or dimensions" (Shweder, 1991, pp. 275–276).

These views have been elaborated on: "Universal [personality] structure does not by itself imply that 'personality' as understood within a European-American framework is a universal aspect of human behavior . . . nor does it imply that the variability that appears as an obvious feature of human life is a function of an internal package of attributes called 'personality'" (Markus & Kitayama, 1998, p. 67). Finally, cultural anthropologist Lawrence Hirschfeld argues that "in many, perhaps most, cultures there is a marked absence of discourse that explains human behavior in terms of trans-situationally stable motivational (or intentional) properties captured by explanations of trait and disposition" (Hirschfeld, 1995, p. 315).

Reflected in these quotations is a fundamental challenge to personality psychology—whether the core concept of traits is universal or, instead, is a local concept applicable only in Western cultures. The most extreme of these perspectives suggests that the very notion of personality, as an internal set of psychological characteristics, is an arbitrary construction of Western culture (Church, 2000). If this extreme position were really true, then any attempt to identify and measure personality traits in non-Western cultures would be doomed to failure (Church, 2000). At the other extreme is the position that personality traits are universal in their applicability and that precisely the same personality structure will emerge across cultures. As two personality researchers noted, "The most important dimensions . . . [of] personality judgment are the most invariant and universal dimensions" (Saucier & Goldberg, 2001, p. 851).

The first source of evidence bearing on this debate pertains to the existence of trait terms in other cultures. Many non-Western psychologists have, in fact, described trait-like concepts that are indigenous to non-Western cultures and that appear strikingly like those that appear in Western cultures. Following are some examples: the Filipino concepts of *pakikiramdam* (sensitivity, empathy) and *pakikisama* (getting along with others); the Korean concept of *chong* (human affection); the Japanese concept of *amae* (indulgent dependence); the Chinese concept of *ren qin* (being relationship oriented); and the Mexican concept of *simpatico* (being harmonious and avoiding conflict) (Church, 2000). Many non-Western cultures, in short, appear to have trait-like concepts embedded in their languages in much the same way that the American culture and English language do.

A second source of evidence bearing on the debate concerns whether the same factor structure of personality traits is found across cultures. Do different cultures have roughly the same broad categories of traits? The trait perspective on personality, of course, does not require the existence of precisely the same traits in all cultures. Indeed, the trait perspective might be extremely useful even if cultures were to differ radically in terms of which trait dimensions they used. Nonetheless, the most powerful support for the trait perspective across cultures would occur if the structure of personality traits were found to be the same across cultures (Church, 2000).

Two approaches have been taken to exploring this issue. In the first approach, which can be labeled the "transport and test" strategy, psychologists have translated existing questionnaires into other languages and then administered them to native residents in other cultures. This strategy has generated some findings supporting the five-factor model. The five-factor model (Extraversion, Agreeableness, Conscientiousness, Emotional Stability, and Intellect–Openness) has now been replicated in France, Holland, and the Philippines and in languages from entirely different language families, such as Sino-Tibetan, Hamito-Semitic, Uralic, and Malayo-Polynesian (McCrae et al., 1998). The five-factor model also has been replicated in Spain (Salgado, Moscoso, & Lado, 2003) and Croatia (Mlacic &

Ostendorf, 2005). A study of 13 different countries—from Japan to Slovakia—also found support for the five-factor model (Hendriks et al., 2003).

Perhaps the most impressive was a massive study of 50 different cultures (McCrae et al., 2005b). This study, involving 11,985 participants, had college-age individuals rate someone they knew well using the Revised NEO Personality Inventory. Factor analyses of observer-based ratings yielded the five-factor model, with only minor variations in factor structure across cultures. This study suggests that cross-cultural evidence for the five-factor model is not limited to self-report data, but extends to observer-based data as well. Using the transport and test strategy, the five-factor structure of personality appears to be general across cultures. Table 17.4, for example, shows the factor structure from a Filipino sample.

A more powerful test of generality, however, would come from studies that start out using indigenous personality dimensions first, then testing whether the five-factor structure still emerges. This approach has been tried in Dutch, German, Hungarian, Italian, Czech, and Polish (De Raad et al., 1998). In each case, the trait terms in the language were identified. The absolute numbers of personality trait terms varied from language to language—Dutch has 8,690 trait terms, whereas Italian has only 1,337 trait terms. But the percentage of words that constituted trait terms was remarkably consistent, averaging 4.4 percent of all dictionary entries. You may recall the lexical hypothesis from Chapter 3, which states that the most important individual differences have been encoded within the natural language.

The next step in the De Raad and colleagues (1998) study was to reduce this list to a manageable number of several hundred trait terms, identified as indigenous to each culture, which could then be tested in each culture. Factor analyses of each sample within each culture showed that there was tremendous replicability of four of the five factors of the five-factor model: Extraversion (*talkative, sociable versus shy, introverted*), Agreeableness (*sympathetic, warm versus unsympathetic, cold*), Conscientiousness (*organized, responsible versus disorganized, careless*), and Emotional Stability (*relaxed, imperturbable versus moody, emotional*).

Despite cross-cultural agreement on these four factors, this study found some differences in what constituted the fifth factor, as noted in Chapter 3. In some cultures, such as Polish and German, the fifth factor resembled the American fifth factor (Intellect–Openness), with *intelligent* and *imaginative* anchoring one end and *dull* and *unimaginative* anchoring the other end. A study in the Philippines also found a replicated five-factor model, including the fifth factor resembling Intellect–Openness, although there are a few indigenous constructs that are less successfully subsumed by the Big Five, such as social curiosity, obedience, and capacity for understanding (Katigbak et al., 2002). Other languages, however, revealed different fifth factors. In Dutch, the fifth factor seemed more like a dimension of political orientation, ranging from *conservative* at one end to *progressive* at the other. In Hungarian, the fifth factor seemed to be one of truthfulness, with *just, truthful,* and *humane* anchoring at one end and *greedy, hypocritical,* and *pretending* at the other (De Raad et al., 1998). The fifth factor, in summary, appeared to be somewhat variable across cultures.

Cross-cultural research using the lexical approach, as you may recall from Chapter 3, has found compelling evidence for *six* factors, rather than five (Ashton, Lee, & de Vries, 2014; Saucier et al., 2005). The new sixth factor—honesty–humility—represents a major discovery across cultures (Ashton & Lee, 2005). By starting with the natural language within each culture, researchers were able to capture an important dimension of personality that was missed using the "transport and test" research strategy.

Clearly, further indigenous tests are needed to determine whether the five-factor or six-factor trait models of personality structure are universal (e.g., Thalmayer et al., 2020). Based on the existing data, however, we can conclude that the truth is somewhere between

Table 17.4 Factor Analysis of the Filipino NEO-PI-R

NEO-PI-R Facet Scale	N	E	O	A	C
N1: Anxiety	**76**	−08	00	00	06
N2: Angry hostility	**67**	−19	01	−44	−10
N3: Depression	**73**	−23	03	−02	−25
N4: Self-consciousness	**68**	−14	−15	22	−04
N5: Impulsiveness	**40**	20	04	−37	−47
N6: Vulnerability	**70**	−22	−23	04	−30
E1: Warmth	−21	**69**	17	28	08
E2: Gregariousness	−29	**65**	−02	07	04
E3: Assertiveness	−28	**42**	23	−29	35
E4: Activity	−15	**51**	10	−24	25
E5: Excitement seeking	−08	**51**	26	−29	−12
E6: Positive emotions	−16	**66**	14	15	01
O1: Fantasy	16	27	**47**	−06	−27
O2: Aesthetics	14	20	**65**	14	22
O3: Feelings	30	32	**53**	03	12
O4: Actions	−39	−03	**46**	01	04
O5: Ideas	−04	−01	**69**	01	30
O6: Values	−13	−06	**62**	−05	−16
A1: Trust	−20	41	09	**52**	−10
A2: Straightforwardness	−03	−22	−02	**57**	10
A3: Altruism	−12	27	13	**65**	31
A4: Compliance	−20	−10	−09	**75**	12
A5: Modesty	18	−27	−03	**55**	−13
A6: Tender-mindedness	22	27	09	**49**	20
C1: Competence	−38	22	16	−10	**69**
C2: Order	−04	−15	−08	10	**73**
C3: Dutifulness	−08	12	07	21	**69**
C4: Achievement striving	−12	06	01	11	**83**
C5: Self-discipline	−24	02	00	07	**81**
C6: Deliberation	−27	−20	03	24	**65**

Note: N = 696. Decimal points are omitted; loadings greater than 40 in absolute magnitude are given in boldface; N = Neuroticism, E = Extraversion, O = Openness, A = Agreeableness, C = Conscientiousness.
Source: McCrae et al. (1998).

the extreme positions outlined at the beginning of this section but closer to those that argue for universality. Trait terms appear to be present in all languages. Factor structures based on instruments developed in the United States, and then translated and transported to other cultures, show great similarity across cultures. Using the more rigorous standard of instruments developed indigenously, four of the five factors emerge consistently across cultures. The fifth factor is somewhat variable across cultures and therefore may reflect an important lack of universality of personality trait structure. And a sixth factor, honesty-humility, has been revealed by at least some studies using the indigenous strategy.

SUMMARY AND EVALUATION

People living in different cultures differ in key personality traits, such as self-concept, the prevailing levels of aggressiveness, and the moral values they hold. The differences are called cultural variations—patterns of local within-group similarity and between-group difference.

There are two major approaches to examining cultural variations. The first, *evoked culture*, involves the capabilities present in all people that are elicited only in some cultural contexts. Evoked cooperation provides one example—people tend to share food when there is high variability in success at obtaining it. Presumably, all people have the capacity to cooperate and share, but these dispositions are evoked only in certain cultural circumstances. Evoked aggression provides a second example of evoked culture. All people have the capacity to be aggressive at times; however, if one grows up in a culture of honor, then aggression is more likely to be evoked in response to public insults.

The second major way of conceptualizing cultural variants is called *transmitted culture*—representations originally in the mind of one or more people that are transmitted to the minds of other people. Four examples of cultural variants that appear to be forms of transmitted culture are differences in moral values, self-concept, levels of self-enhancement, and religious beliefs. Patterns of morality, such as whether it is considered appropriate to disobey one's parents or to eat beef, or wrong for a wife to go to the movies without her husband, are specific to certain cultures. These moral values appear to be transmitted from person to person within the culture. Cultural differences in self-concept are another example of transmitted culture. Many Asian cultures, for example, appear to foster self-concepts that are highly interdependent and contextual, emphasizing the embeddedness of the self within the group. European American culture, in contrast, appears to promote a self-concept that is more independent, stressing the separateness of the person from the group.

Religious beliefs provide another example of transmitted culture. These include beliefs about supernatural agents, rituals, and artifacts linked with those unobservable agents such as statues and crosses. Psychologists have proposed two competing theories to explain religious phenomena—an adaptationist theory and a byproduct theory. The personality traits of Conscientiousness and Agreeableness are linked with higher levels of religiosity, suggesting individual differences in the degree to which this form of transmitted culture is adopted.

Cross-cultural work on interdependence–independence has been criticized on several grounds. First, the magnitudes of effect are sometimes quite small. Second, the dichotomies may be overly simplistic because they ignore context specificity (e.g., Americans might be independent at work and interdependent at home with their families) as well as individual differences within culture (e.g., some Koreans are more individualistic, others more collectivistic). Nonetheless, some cultural differences are real and must be explained. Most researchers have assumed that these differences are instances of transmitted culture. An alternative explanation proposes that all humans have evolved psychological mechanisms capable of acting both individualistically and collectively, as well as a psychology that allows them to switch from one mode to the other, depending on the fitness advantages. This fascinating fusion of evolutionary psychology and cultural psychology holds much promise.

Culture appears to influence our self-concepts. Using the Twenty Statements Test, researchers found that North Americans tend to describe themselves using abstract internal characteristics, such as "I am smart," "I am dependable," and "I am friendly."

Asians, in contrast, tend to define themselves more often using social roles, such as "I am the son of . . ." or "I am Liu's friend." These differences in self-concept appear to be examples of transmitted culture, passed down from person to person through the generations. It's important to keep in mind that these cultural differences are a matter of degree. People in collectivist cultures use some global traits to describe themselves, and people in individualist cultures use some relational terms to describe themselves.

Another reliable cultural difference pertains to self-enhancement, or the tendency to view oneself using positive or socially valued attributes. Korean and Japanese respondents are more likely than American respondents to endorse negative statements about themselves, such as "I am lazy" or "I am a somewhat selfish person." Americans, in contrast, tend to endorse more positive statements about themselves, such as "I'm a hard worker" or "I'm quite creative." Another study found that Chinese individuals tend to be somewhat less self-enhancing than Americans. These differences in self-enhancement also appear to be examples of transmitted culture.

Some elements of personality appear to be culturally universal. One example of a cultural universal is people's beliefs about the personality traits that characterize men and women. Worldwide, people regard men as having personalities that are more active, loud, adventurous, obnoxious, aggressive, opinionated, arrogant, coarse, and conceited. Women are regarded as having personalities that are more affectionate, modest, nervous, appreciative, patient, changeable, charming, fearful, and forgiving. There is some evidence that these cross-cultural gender stereotypes are accurate.

Another cultural universal appears to be the experience and recognition of specific emotional states, such as fear, anger, happiness, sadness, disgust, and surprise. People from Italy to Sumatra recognize and describe these emotions when viewing photographs expressing them, even if the photographs are of people from other cultures. There is also evidence for the cross-cultural recognition of nonverbal vocal expressions of emotions such as anger, disgust, and joy.

Finally, there is some evidence that the structure of personality traits, as represented by the five-factor model of personality, may be universal, at least for four of the five traits—Extraversion, Agreeableness, Conscientiousness, and Emotional Stability. There is evidence for the five-factor model using the "transport and test" strategy model of personality, using observer-based data from 50 cultures. Nonetheless, studies that begin with the natural language within each culture, using the lexical strategy to identify important trait terms, have discovered a six-factor structure. In addition to the five major factors, the new *honesty–humility* factor is in contention for being an important personality factor. This discovery attests to the importance of cross-cultural research, particularly work that uses a strategy that begins *within* each culture.

KEY TERMS

cultural variations 527
cultural personality psychology 527
evoked culture 527
high-variance conditions 528
egalitarianism 528
culture of honor 530
transmitted culture 531

Balkanization 533
interdependence 533
independence 533
acculturation 534
holistic 536
analytic 536
self-enhancement 538

within-culture variations 541
social class 541
historical era 542
cultural universals 542
Whorfian hypothesis of linguistic
   relativity 546

PART SIX

The Adjustment Domain

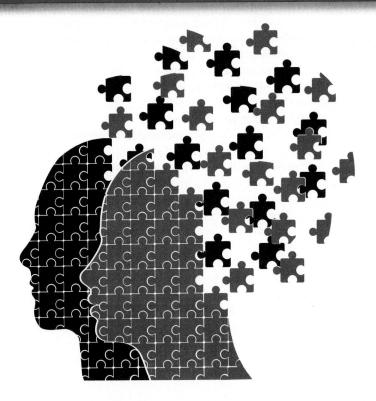

This domain is different from the others discussed in the book so far. The first five domains each referred to a collection of specific explanations of personality. That is, each gave a perspective on, and a collection of knowledge about, the causes of personality and individual differences. In this last domain—the adjustment domain—we examine some of the consequences of personality. We focus on adjustment because, in many ways, personality functions to help us adjust to the challenges and demands of life, albeit in a unique way for each of us. We focus on two important outcomes in this domain: physical health and mental health.

Day by day, all of us are adjusting to the demands of life and reacting to life events. A recent major life event that we all are coping with is the COVID-19 pandemic, plus the many public health efforts to contain the virus. This situation has been stressful for practically everyone. Plus there are other sources of stress in our daily lives. It is important to realize, however, that stress is not "out there" in our life events; rather, stress mostly refers to how we respond to those life events. How we interpret some event determines whether we feel it as stressful. The tendency to interpret events in a way that evokes a stress response is influenced by our personalities. Personality plays a key role in how we appraise and interpret events and cope, adapt, and adjust to the stress in our day-to-day lives. Moreover, some people display patterns of behavior, emotion, and interpersonal relations that create problems for them and for those around them. These problematic personality profiles form the collection of personality disorders. These two areas—coping with stress and disorders of personality—define the adjustment domain because they refer to how effectively people interact with and cope with challenges from the environment.

Considerable evidence has been accumulating that personality is linked with important health outcomes, such as heart disease or early mortality. Psychologists have developed several theories for how and why these relationships exist, as well as have offered ways to change health-harming behavior patterns. Personality is also linked with a variety of health-related behaviors such as smoking, drinking, and risk taking. Some research has even demonstrated that personality is correlated with how long we live (Peterson, 1995, 2000; Strickhouser, Zell, & Krizan, 2017).

We also introduce two important new concepts in the material on health: moderation and mediation. These concepts describe two specific ways that variables work together to produce some effect. Moderation is where two variables are related (e.g., stress and illness) yet the degree of relationship is influenced by a third variable, for example, personality (say, the link between stress and illness is stronger for some people than others). Mediation is where the influence of one variable on another (say, personality and longevity) works by going through a third variable (say, health behaviors, such that personality predicts longevity because personality is associated with behaviors that lead to a longer life, such as exercise and proper diet). While we discuss mediation and moderation within the context of personality and health, these are general ideas that can be found in other areas of personality psychology as well.

In addition to maintaining health and coping with stress, many of the important problems in living can be traced to personality. In this domain of knowledge there is the concept of disorder, the idea that certain personality profiles can be so problematic that they create clear difficulties in the person's life, particularly in terms of work and social relationships. Certain personality features related to poor adjustment and poor outcomes in life are described as personality disorders. We devote an entire chapter to the personality disorders, such as the antisocial personality and the narcissistic personality. We believe that an understanding of "normal" personality functioning can be enhanced by examining what can go wrong with personality. This is similar to the field of medicine, in which an understanding of normal physiological functioning is often illuminated by the study of disorders and disease. We begin our coverage of the adjustment domain with the topics of stress, coping, adjustment, and health.

Athanasia Nomikou/Shutterstock

Stress, Coping, Adjustment, and Health

18

While the pandemic of COVID-19 is caused by a virus, its transmission from person to person is caused by specific behaviors. Psychology can play a role in helping society change those behaviors as well as cope with the social and emotional impact of those changes.
Brian Lawless-PA Images/ Getty Images

For much of history, humans have been battling microbes in an effort to overcome disease and illness. For example, in 1520, the Spanish conquistadors landed in Mexico with several slaves brought from Spanish Cuba. One of the slaves had smallpox. The illness spread to the native Aztec tribes, who had no immunity to smallpox. It quickly killed half of the Aztec people, including their emperor, Cuitlahuac. Aided by the microbe that causes smallpox, the Spanish (who had immunity) had no trouble conquering all of Mexico. The native population of Mexico, estimated at 20 million when the Spaniards arrived, fell to 1.6 million in less than 100 years (Diamond, 1999).

The world is currently experiencing a pandemic of another highly infectious disease: COVID-19. The microbe that causes COVID-19 resides in respiratory fluids, primarily mucus in the mouth and nose. It passes from person to person when mucus from an infected person, even a microscopic amount, gets into the respiratory tract of another. Because this virus was new to humans, there was no immunity to it in the human population when it first appeared in late 2019. Its explosive spread around the world surprised many, except perhaps a few public health experts. We now have a vaccine against the Coronavirus, which limits the severity of the illness. But the main way to stop the spread of this illness is still to lessen or eliminate behaviors that transmit the virus (by practicing social distancing, not gathering in groups, coughing into a tissue or one's elbow, self-isolating if exposure is suspected, and so on).

The world-wide pandemic of COVID-19 illustrates a very important distinction; although its cause is a virus, its transmission is through specific behaviors. For example, gathering with strangers of unknown vaccination status in tightly packed rooms greatly increase the likelihood of transmitting COVID-19. Psychologists can contribute to a discussion of the best ways to change people's behavior, such as practicing social distancing, working from home, and coping with social isolation. The point is that, in the modern approach to health and illness, understanding the role of human behavior can be as important as understanding microbes.

This is only one example of the importance of behavior in understanding illness. Today, many of the leading causes of illness, disability, and death are related not to microbes as much as to lifestyle behaviors, such as smoking, poor diet, inadequate exercise, and stress. Now that we are curing microbial infections, behavioral factors have emerged as important contributors to the development of illness.

The realization that behavioral factors have important health consequences has given rise to the field of **health psychology.** Researchers in this area of psychology study the relationship between the mind and the body, as well as the ways in which these two components respond to challenges from the environment (e.g., stressful events, germs) to produce either illness or health. Many of the psychological variables of interest have to do with stable patterns of behavior—for example, whether a person copes well with stress, exercises some or not at all, sleeps seven to eight hours each night, drinks alcohol only in moderation, routinely wears a seat belt, keeps his or her weight at a desirable level, avoids drugs, practices safe sex, and avoids unnecessary risks. Researchers find that such behaviors, called health behaviors, are correlated with life expectancy. In fact, in the United States, researchers suggest that health behavior deficits contribute to more than half of all premature deaths—that is, death before age 65 (Taylor, 1991).

Personality can have an impact on health in many ways, and personality psychologists are developing new methodological approaches to the study of this link. Current research has led to several detailed models of the mechanisms underlying the links between personality and health (Friedman, 2019; Smith & Spiro, 2002; Smith, Williams, & Segerstrom, 2015). Explaining how personality can influence health is the goal of these models, and we will present five of the models found in the personality and health psychology literature. Each of these models proposes the key variables, and the links between them, in understanding the personality–health association.

Models of the Personality–Illness Connection

Researchers have proposed several ways of thinking about how personality can relate to health. These models can take the form of diagrams of key variables, with the causal relations among those variables depicted by arrows. Models are useful to researchers in guiding their thinking about how those variables influence one another (Smith, 2006; Wiebe & Smith, 1997). In most of the models we will discuss, one variable—stress—will be important. **Stress** is the subjective feeling produced by events that are perceived to be uncontrollable and threatening to one's goals. It is important to realize that stress is a *response* to the perceived demands in some situation. Stress is not in the situation; stress refers to how people respond to a particular situation.

An early model of the personality health relationship, called the **interactional model,** is depicted in Figure 18.1(a). This model suggests that objective events happen to people, but personality factors determine the impact or stressfulness of those

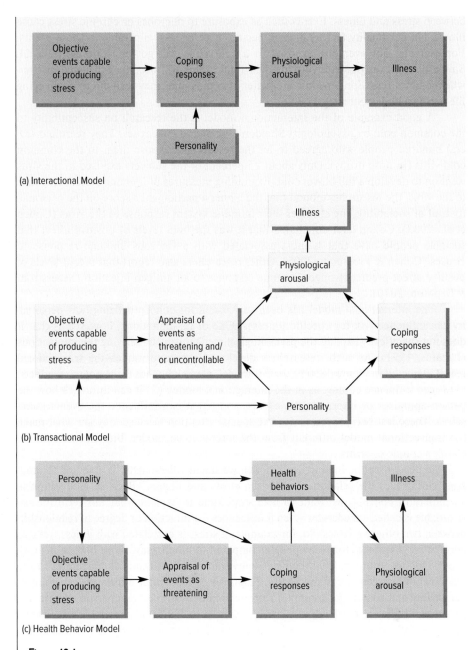

(a) Interactional Model

(b) Transactional Model

(c) Health Behavior Model

Figure 18.1

Three models specifying the role of personality in moderating the effects of stress on illness: (a) the
interactional model, which specifies that personality influences how people cope; (b) the transactional
model, which specifies that personality influences how people cope, as well as how they appraise and
influence situations; and (c) the health behavior model, which specifies that personality influences how
people cope, appraise, and influence situations, as well as the likely health behaviors that people practice.

events by influencing people's ability to cope. In this model, personality has its effects
on coping responses—that is, on how people respond to the event. It is called the interactional model because personality is assumed to moderate (influence) the relationship

between stress and illness. Events such as exposure to microbes or chronic stress cause illness, but personality factors make a person more or less vulnerable to those events. For example, not everyone exposed to a cold virus will go on to develop a cold. Similarly, not everyone studying for their final exams will become exhausted or overwhelmed by stress. Some people are better at coping, and they respond to challenging life events with less stress.

A good example of the interactional model is the research on susceptibility to the common cold by psychologist Sheldon Cohen and colleagues. They recruited several hundred people who agreed to let the researchers expose them to the common cold virus (in nose drops). Only about 25 percent of the subjects exposed to the virus went on to develop a full-blown cold. Examining measures of immune system response to the virus, the researchers found that the higher a participant's score on the personality trait of sociability, the stronger their immune system response to the virus (Cohen et al., 2003). Cohen later concluded that it was the high levels of positive affect that sociable people have that is most associated with a vigorous immune response to viruses (Cohen & Pressman, 2006). Other researchers also report that recent levels of positive affect predict stronger immune response to an antigen injection (Segerstrom & Sephton, 2010).

The interactional model has been very useful for conceptualizing how personality can influence risk for specific illnesses. One of its limitations, however, is that it does not specifically explain the psychological mechanisms underlying the interactions (Lazarus, 1991). As such, researchers developed a second model—the **transactional model,** depicted in Figure 18.1(b). In this model, personality has three potential effects: (1) It can influence coping, as in the interactional model; (2) it can influence how the person appraises or interprets the events; and (3) it can influence the events themselves. These last two processes deserve special attention because they are what make the transactional model different from the interactional model. But first we want to clarify a couple of terms.

In describing the interactional model, we stated; "Personality is assumed to moderate (influence) the relationship between stress and illness." Because moderation is an important concept, we want to take some time to explain what this term means. A variable is called a **moderator** when it influences the direction or degree of relationship between two other variables. So, for example, if stress is correlated with illness, yet this correlation is stronger for some people compared to others (say, those high in neuroticism), then we would say that the personality trait of neuroticism is a moderator of the relationship between stress and illness. Examples of moderator effects are common in personality and health. For example, a strong predictor of whether a person will use illegal drugs is if they have friends who use illegal drugs (self-use and peer use is correlated). However, for people low on the personality trait of sensation seeking, this correlation is not found, so the trait of sensation seeking is said to moderate the relationship between own use and peer use of illegal drugs (Marschall-Lévesque et al., 2014). A moderator is sometimes thought of as a risk multiplier; in this case, the trait of high sensation seeking multiplies the risk of having peers who use drugs on the probability that the person will themselves use drugs. While we introduce the concept of personality as a moderator in the context of health psychology, the concept of moderation is general and can be found in other areas of personality psychology.

In the transactional model, an important component is how the event is appraised, or interpreted, by the person. You will recall from Chapter 12 that interpretation influences behavior. An event, such as getting stuck in traffic on the way to a job interview, can happen to two people, yet the two people can interpret the event differently and thus experience it differently. One person might interpret getting stuck as a major frustration and hence might respond with a great deal of worry, stress, and anxiety. The other person might interpret getting stuck in traffic as an opportunity to relax, enjoy some music on the radio, and use their cell phone to reschedule the job interview.

The third point on the transactional model at which personality can have an impact consists of the events themselves. That is, people don't just respond to situations; they also create situations through their choices and actions, as we discussed in Chapter 4. For example, a disagreeable person may create interpersonal situations in which he or she gets into a lot of arguments. A recent five-year longitudinal study of life events, based on a large and nationally representative sample of young adults, found several "life event selection effects" due to personality (Denissen et al., 2019). That is, some life events (e.g., being fired from a job) were more likely to happen to certain people (e.g., low agreeableness) compared to others.

These two parts of the transactional model—appraisal and the person's influence on events—are why the model is called transactional. These two elements of the model imply that stressful events don't just influence persons; persons also influence events. And this influence comes about through the appraisal of events, as well as the selection and modification of events.

A third model, the **health behavior model,** adds another factor to the transactional model. It is important to realize that so far the two models are simply extensions of the theme that personality influences the stress–illness link. In the third model, which is depicted in Figure 18.1(c), personality does not directly influence the relationship between stress and illness. Instead, in this model, personality affects health indirectly through health-promoting or health-degrading behaviors. Everyone knows that poor health behaviors—such as eating too much fat, smoking, and practicing unsafe sex— increase the risk of developing certain illnesses. This model suggests that personality influences the degree to which a person engages in various health-promoting or health-degrading behaviors. For example, individuals who are low in the trait of conscientiousness engage in a variety of health-damaging behaviors, including smoking, unhealthy eating habits, dangerous driving, and lack of exercise (Bogg & Roberts, 2004).

This brings us to the concept of mediation. **Mediation** is similar to moderation, in that both describe specific ways that three variables are related to one another. Mediation is different, however, in that it specifies that the effect of one variable on another "goes through" a third variable. So, for example, the effect of conscientiousness on longevity goes through, or is due to, specific health behaviors (e.g., regular exercise, frequent doctor exams, etc.). Mediation is a way of understanding the observed relationship (i.e., that conscientiousness is correlated with longevity) by specifying the underlying mechanism or process captured by the mediator variable (i.e., health behavior). This is not just a made up example. Turiano and colleagues (2015) used a national sample of over 6,000 people over a 14-year period and found that Conscientiousness predicted a 13 percent reduction in mortality in the time period. Moreover, when health behaviors were examined as mediators, they found that heavy drinking, smoking, and greater waist circumferences (all negatively related to conscientiousness) significantly mediated the conscientiousness–mortality association. Findings such as these show how mediation can be a powerful way to explain how personality effects might work. Like moderation, mediation is often used in personality and health research, but its application as a way of thinking about how personality might have its effects extends to many other areas of personality psychology.

Conscientiousness is one of the Big Five personality traits that is reliably related to good health (e.g., Hill & Roberts, 2011). In fact, the importance of conscientiousness to health has been described as "indisputable" (Jackson & Hill, 2019). As a personality trait, conscientiousness is manifest in such behaviors as making lists before grocery shopping, keeping a calendar to plan activities, keeping one's work area neat and tidy, using a to-do list, and dressing up for special occasions. A list of several hundred behavioral indicators of conscientiousness can be found in Jackson and colleagues (2010) and also in Stephan and colleagues (2019). Why is it that conscientiousness predicts health and living longer? Researchers conclude that conscientious persons routinely practice good health behaviors. They tend to floss and brush regularly, engage in regular exercise, watch their diets, use a seat belt consistently, and adhere to other behaviors that are linked to better health (see their doctor and dentist regularly). Conscientiousness thus appears to affect health primarily through mediation mechanisms described by the health behavior model.

A fourth model of the link between personality and health, the **predisposition model,** is shown in Figure 18.2(a). The previous three models were all variations on the same theme that personality influences the relationship between stress and illness

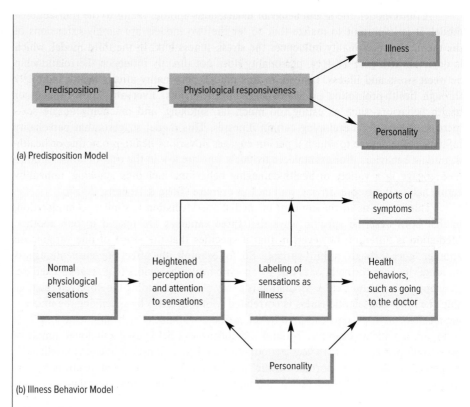

(a) Predisposition Model

(b) Illness Behavior Model

Figure 18.2

Additional models of the relationship between personality and health: (a) the predisposition model, which holds that personality and health are related due to a common predisposition; and (b) the illness behavior model, which specifies how personality might influence whether a person would seek medical attention or report illness symptoms.

either directly (interactional and transactional models) or indirectly (health behavior model). The fourth model is completely different and holds that personality and illness are both expressions of an underlying predisposition. This model is a very simple conception, suggesting that associations might exist between personality and illness because of a third variable, which causes them both. For example, enhanced sympathetic nervous system reactivity may be the cause of subsequent illnesses, *as well as* cause the behaviors and emotions that lead a person to be called "high neuroticism." The predisposition model has not been applied much, though it seems likely that this model may guide future investigators interested in the genetic basis of illnesses. It may well turn out that some genetic predispositions are expressed both in terms of a stable individual difference and in terms of susceptibility to

Conscientiousness has its effects on health through its association with health behaviors, such as brushing and flossing regularly.
Moodboard-Mike Watson Images/Brand X Pictures/Getty Images

specific illnesses (Bouchard & McGue, 1990). For example, some researchers speculate that there is a genetic cause of novelty seeking (a trait like sensation seeking) and that this genetic sequence also causes, or makes a person more likely to develop, addiction to illicit drugs (Cloninger, 1999). Consequently, the correlation between the novelty-seeking personality trait and addiction to illicit drugs (e.g., opioids, cocaine, meth, heroin) may be due to the fact that these two variables (novelty seeking and addiction) are both caused by a third variable—genes. This simple model may be useful as the human genome project (see Chapter 6) progresses toward understanding what specific genes control.

The final model for consideration—called the **illness behavior model**—is not a model of illness per se, but rather a model of illness behavior. Illness itself is defined as the presence of an objectively measurable abnormal physiological process, such as fever, high blood pressure, or a tumor. Illness behavior, on the other hand, refers to actions a person might take when they think they have an illness, such as complaining to others, visiting a doctor, or taking the day off from school or work. Illness behaviors are related to actual illnesses, but not perfectly. Some individuals may tough out an illness, stoically refusing to engage in illness behaviors (e.g., refusing to take the day off from work when ill). Other people engage in all sorts of illness behaviors even in the absence of actual illness.

Figure 18.2(b) portrays the illness behavior model. It suggests that personality influences the degree to which a person perceives and pays attention to bodily sensations and the degree to which the person interprets and labels those sensations as an illness. The way in which a person perceives and labels those sensations, then, influences the person's illness behaviors, such as reporting the symptoms and going to a doctor. As discussed in Chapter 13, the personality trait of neuroticism is associated with a tendency to complain about physical symptoms.

Neuroticism correlates moderately with objective health outcomes (Friedman, 2019; Graham et al., 2017). However, the strongest correlations are with self-reports of health, such as reporting frequencies of different symptoms (Strickhouser, Zell, & Krizan, 2017). This may suggest that high neuroticism persons pay more attention to physical symptoms, or are more likely to interpret bodily sensations as signs of illness, which is consistent with the illness behavior model.

While most of the health associations with neuroticism are negative, there may be some ways that being high on neuroticism might be beneficial. The concept of **healthy neuroticism** (Friedman, 2019; Weston & Jackson, 2016) is a new idea that stresses the possible benefits of neuroticism. For example, being constantly vigilant for threat, on the lookout for things that can go wrong, might prove useful when it comes to threatening health information. A person high on neuroticism might notice symptoms of disease sooner or might interpret them as more serious and take action sooner. Such early action on a disease like cancer can lead to better outcomes. Augustine and colleagues (2008) found that, among a large sample of lung cancer patients, neuroticism correlated with noticing the symptoms sooner and going to the doctor at a younger average age, even after controlling for smoking history. Ristvedt and Trinkaus (2005) found that, in a group of rectal cancer patients, neuroticism predicted a shorter time in going from first noticing symptoms to making an appointment with a doctor. So, while the negative health associations with neuroticism are substantial, there may be some ways, under some conditions, that being a little higher in neuroticism could be beneficial.

It is important to note that these models linking personality to physical health or illness are not mutually exclusive. That is, they may all apply, depending on the personality trait and the illness under consideration. We now illustrate how these models have been applied to understand the role of personality in the COVID-19 pandemic.

COVID-19 and the Five Models of Personality–Illness Connection

COVID-19 is a global health event of unprecedented proportions, disrupting the lives of practically every person on Earth. Efforts to contain the spread of the Coronavirus have also placed unique behavioral and psychological demands on people. Every reader of this textbook has been impacted in some way by COVID-19 and the public health measures it brought about. Consequently, every reader should find some personal relevance in the research examples that follow.

Personality psychologists mobilized their efforts early in the pandemic to examine the role of personality within this global health crisis. As this edition goes to press, we are a little over two years into the pandemic. In this time, almost 600 research studies have been published on personality and various aspects of the COVID-19 pandemic. Summarizing all this research is beyond the scope of an introductory personality textbook. However, this research can be used to illustrate each of the five models of the personality–health connection described above.

The *Interactional Model* emphasizes how personality influences coping with a stressor. Coping with the novel Coronavirus, as well as the many mitigation efforts imposed by public health authorities, has been the topic of much of the COVID-19 research concerning the role of personality. For example, some studies have found that high levels of neuroticism predicted poorer coping during the pandemic (Bacon et al., 2021). In addition, people high on neuroticism worried more about the disease, showed increases in anxiety and loneliness as the pandemic progressed, reported feeling more threatened by the virus, and showed a larger negative impact on mental health and psychological well-being. Persons high in neuroticism paid more attention to COVID-19 news, at times even to the point of being preoccupied with the crisis and ruminating over the various risk factors (Kroencke et al., 2020). In general, the uncertainty of the COVID-19 pandemic, and the shifting demands of guidelines, was more stressful to those higher on neuroticism (compared to those low on neuroticism).

The *Transactional Model* emphasizes how personality can influence people's appraisal or interpretation of stressful events. Many of the studies on personality and the COVID pandemic illustrate this model, especially those examining how people interpret the many mitigation strategies put in place by public health authorities. For example, Bellingtier, Mund, and Wrzus (2021) showed that social distancing and social isolation were perceived as especially stressful by subjects high on the sociability component of extraversion. Research before COVID-19 often found that extraverts coped better with stress by tapping their social support network. However, the unique social isolation demands of the COVID-19 pandemic made it more stressful for people high on sociability. Highly sociable people found social isolation to be more difficult and more stressful, precisely because isolation goes against their natural tendency to want to be with others. Another example of the transactional model can be seen in studies that showed, early in the pandemic, that persons high on neuroticism believe the pandemic will last significantly longer than subjects low on neuroticism (Aschwanden et al., 2020). Subjects high in neuroticism worried more about infection and transmission but were also more likely to take a fatalistic interpretation of the situation, taking fewer precautions and making fewer preparations to get through it. People low on agreeableness were more likely to perceive public health guidelines (e.g., mask wearing) to be restrictions on their personal freedom, and consequently were less likely to comply. Persons high on conscientiousness, on the other hand, were more likely to perceive public health guidelines as consensual norms, believing that most others agree with the guidelines. Conscientious people expressed a greater sense of responsibility toward others and were more likely to report feeling an obligation to help society contain the virus. Many studies show that perceptions matter, and that personality predicts perceptions of responsibility, risk, and the reasonableness of public health guidelines for containing COVID-19.

The *Health Behavior Model* emphasizes how personality can influence specific behaviors that, in turn, directly promote (or impede) healthy outcomes. For example, very specific behaviors (e.g., social distancing, hand washing, mask wearing) are known to lessen the odds of catching and transmitting the Coronavirus. Several studies ask the question of whether personality predicts the likelihood of engaging in these specific behaviors. For example, one study (Bacon et al., 2021) found that, during the high points of the pandemic, high conscientious persons were more likely to avoid crowds, to stay out of restaurants and bars, to practice social distancing and hand washing, and were less likely to engage in panic stockpiling. More conscientious persons were also quicker to transition to online meetings and classes (Audet et al., 2021) and to comply with self-isolation after suspected exposure to the virus. High conscientious persons were also more likely to fact check information and were less likely to pass on or share misinformation about COVID-19 (Lawson & Kakkar, 2021). In the early phase of the pandemic, high conscientious persons took more precautions (e.g., wiping down items brought into the home) and engaged in more preparatory actions (e.g., set up Zoom on their computers, stocked up on necessary supplies). The most consequential single health behavior during the pandemic is, of course, taking the vaccination. Because the public availability of the vaccination is so recent, few studies have been completed comparing vaccinated to unvaccinated groups in terms of personality. Studies have been done on the *intention* to vaccinate and aspects of personality (e.g., greater intention to vaccinate is associated with more internal locus of control, with more empathy toward others, and with more liberal political attitudes).

The *Predisposition Model* emphasizes how personality and illness could both be the result of some third variable. None of the COVID-19 research on personality conforms directly to this model. However, researchers are perplexed by variability in the course of the illness following infection by the Coronavirus; some people have few if any symptoms, whereas others have serious lung disease and become gravely, if not mortally, ill. Predicting the course of COVID-19 continues to be a challenge. Some researchers are looking for a genetic marker or other biological predisposition (e.g., inflammatory response, immune system status) that puts a person at greater risk for serious symptoms. If some personality variable were linked to such a biological predisposition, then this model might prove useful. However, to date, identifying additional biological predispositions to serious symptoms (other than age, vaccination status, and immune system functioning, which are unrelated to personality) has proven elusive.

The *Illness Behavior Model* emphasizes actions people take when they believe they may be sick. Applied to the COVID-19 pandemic, this model might be useful for understanding when people seek out COVID-19 testing, whether they decide to self-isolate or not, or whether and when they seek medical treatment for the illness. At this stage of the pandemic, few researchers have directly applied the Illness Behavior Model to traditional personality traits. Some studies have linked COVID-19 testing to economic status (less available to poor) or racial group (less available to minority groups) or to fear of the disease (fearful persons more likely to seek out testing), but not to traditional measures of personality. Similarly, the decision to self-isolate is associated with greater fear of the virus or a greater concern for the health of others, but has not been related to measures of personality. It is very likely that data on personality and illness behaviors during the COVID-19 pandemic will emerge in future research.

In these examples, the Coronavirus and associated public health demands are viewed as stressful events to which we all must respond. The above models depict how personality may play a role in responding to those contemporary stressors. Because the concept of stress is so important, and so general, we next go into some detail about stress.

The Concept of Stress

Microbes stress the body (usually the immune system), but from a psychological perspective there are many, many other sources of stress. Deadlines that are fast approaching, evaluative tasks that we cannot avoid (like exams), being "unfriended" online, or having to deal with an unpleasant or harassing co-worker; all of these and many more can be sources of psychological stress. Stress is a general feeling of being overwhelmed by events that you cannot control and that threaten a goal that is important to you. Events that cause stress are called **stressors**, and they appear to have these common attributes:

Studying for an exam can be stressful or not, depending on whether the situation controls you or you control the situation. Stress occurs when events seem uncontrollable and threatening to your goals. Taking control by keeping up with homework, planning each day, and preparing in a timely fashion can make studying less stressful.

Tom Merton/Caia Images/Glow Images

1. Stressors are perceived as uncontrollable events, outside our power to influence, such as an exam we cannot avoid or a deadline we cannot change.
2. Stressors threaten an important goal, they call into question something important to us, such as the goal of doing well in a college course or maintaining friendships with important others.
3. Stressors are extreme, in the sense that they produce feelings of being overwhelmed or overloaded or "on the edge."

Stress Response

When a stressor appears, people typically experience a pattern of emotional and physiological reactions. For example, if someone were to startle you by unexpectedly honking an automobile horn as you walked in front of their car, you would experience some startle: Your heart would beat faster and your blood pressure would go up, and your palms and the soles of your feet would begin to sweat. This pattern of reaction has commonly been called the fight-or-flight response. This physiological response is caused by an increase of sympathetic nervous system activity (see Chapter 7 for more details on nervous system responses). The increase in heart rate and blood pressure prepares you for action, such as fighting or fleeing. The sweaty palms and feet are perhaps a preparation for using a weapon or running away. This physiological response is usually very brief, and if the stressor is as minor as someone honking a car horn to see you jump, you will likely glare at the person who startled you, but then return to your normal state in a minute or less.

If, however, a person is exposed to a particular stressor day in and day out, then this physiological fight-or-flight response is just the first step in a chain of events termed the **general adaptation syndrome (GAS)** by Hans Selye (1976), a pioneer in stress research. Selye proposed that the GAS followed a stage model, as depicted in Figure 18.3. The first stage, called the **alarm stage**, consists of the fight-or-flight response of the sympathetic nervous system and the associated peripheral nervous system reactions. These include the release of hormones that prepare the body for challenge. If the stressor continues, then the next stage begins, the **resistance stage**. The body is using its resources at an above average rate, repeatedly activating the fight-or-flight response. At this point, stress is being resisted, but it is taking a lot of effort and energy. If the stressor remains constant, the person eventually enters the third stage, the **exhaustion stage.** Selye felt that this was the stage in which a person is most susceptible to illness and disease, as his or her physiological resources are depleted. Research on stress and the immune system generally supports the GAS stage model (Cohen et al., 2012). A stage model of stress (Cohen, Gianaros, & Manuck, 2016) keeps the basic framework of the GAS, but elaborates on the psychological and biological mechanisms that occur in the resistance stage, and how resistance can transition to the exhaustion stage.

Major Life Events

What are some common stressors, events that are likely to evoke stress in most persons? Holmes and Rahe (1967) studied various **major life events,** those events that require people to make major adjustments in their lives. In their research, Holmes and Rahe wanted to estimate the potential stress value of a wide variety of life events. They started with a long

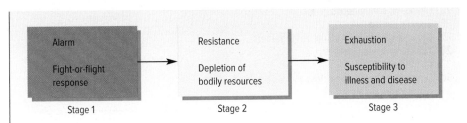

Figure 18.3

The three stages of the general adaptation syndrome proposed by Selye.

list of events such as the death of a family member, loss of a job, or being put in jail. They then had a large number of subjects rate each of the events for how much stress each was likely to provoke. Each event was then assigned stress "points," and by counting up the events a person had experienced and adding up the stress points for all of those events, a good estimate of the total amount of stress experienced by that person could be obtained.

In Table 18.1, we present a student version of the stressful event schedule based on the original Holmes and Rahe research. It has been modified for teaching purposes to apply to college-age adults and should be considered a rough indication of stress levels. In this scale, the number following the event refers to the stress "points" associated

Table 18.1 The Student Stress Test

DIRECTIONS: On the list below, check off each event that has happened to you in the past year. To determine your stress score, add up the number of points corresponding to the events you have experienced in the past year. If your score is 300 or higher, you are at risk for developing a health problem from stress. If your score is between 150 and 300, you have a 50-50 chance of experiencing a health problem in the next few years if the stress persists. If your score is below 150, you have a relatively low risk of a serious health change due to stress (DeMeuse, 1985; Insel & Roth, 1985).

STUDENT STRESS SCALE

1. Death of a close family member	_____	100
2. Death of a close friend	_____	73
3. Divorce between parents	_____	65
4. Jail term	_____	63
5. Major personal injury or illness	_____	63
6. Marriage	_____	58
7. Fired from job	_____	50
8. Failed important course	_____	47
9. Change in health of a family member	_____	45
10. Pregnancy	_____	45
11. Sex problems	_____	44
12. Serious argument with a close friend	_____	40
13. Change in financial status	_____	39
14. Change of major at college	_____	39
15. Trouble with parents	_____	39
16. New girl- or boyfriend	_____	38
17. Increased workload	_____	37
18. Outstanding personal achievement	_____	36
19. First quarter/semester in college	_____	35
20. Change in living conditions	_____	31
21. Serious argument with instructor	_____	30
22. Lower grades than expected	_____	29
23. Change in sleeping habits	_____	29
24. Change in social activities	_____	29
25. Change in eating habits	_____	28
26. Chronic car trouble	_____	26
27. Change in number of family get-togethers	_____	26
28. Too many missed classes	_____	25
29. Change of college	_____	24
30. Dropped more than one class	_____	23
31. Minor traffic violations	_____	20
TOTAL	_____	

Source: Based on "The Social Adjustment Rating Scale," by T. H. Holmes and R. H. Rahe, 1967, *Journal of Psychosomatic Research*, vol. 11, pp. 213–217.

with that event. You can see that death of a close family member, death of a friend, and divorce of parents are the events likely to evoke the most stress. Interestingly, getting married is also likely to be stressful, as are other "positive" events, such as starting college or making some major achievement. This highlights the fact that stress is the *subjective* response to an event and that even though an event is positive, it may have the three characteristics associated with stressors: intensity, threat to a goal, and uncontrollability.

In their initial research, Holmes and Rahe tallied up the stress points that each of the research participants had accumulated in the prior year. They found that the persons with the most stress points were also the most likely to have had a serious illness during that year. This research was among the first systematic demonstrations that elevated stress—a psychological phenomenon—was associated with elevated risk for a number of illnesses. These findings persuaded medical researchers to take seriously the notion that factors other than microbes and organ malfunctions contribute to illness. Researchers following Holmes and Rahe have consistently found linkages between major life events and illness (reviewed in Schwarzer & Luszczynska, 2013).

Other researchers have taken a more experimental approach to see if stress is related to susceptibility to disease. For example, Cohen, Tyrrell, and Smith (1997) obtained reports of stressful life events for a group of volunteers and were able to sum each participants' points for various events. With the permission of the participants, these researchers then tried to infect half the participants with a cold by giving them nose drops containing the cold virus. The other half of the research participants were given saline nose drops; they served as the control group in this experiment. What happened? The participants with more stressful life events in the previous year were more likely to develop a cold after being given the cold virus than were the participants with fewer stressors in their lives. The researchers interpreted this finding as consistent with the general adaptation syndrome: persons under chronic stress eventually deplete bodily resources and become vulnerable to microbial infections.

The relationship between increased stress and lowered resistance to viral and bacterial infection has been demonstrated repeatedly (e.g., Cohen et al., 1995). Currently, most researchers interpret such findings as illustrating the effects of stress on the immune system. That is, stress is thought to lower the functional ability of the immune system to mount an effective response to the presence of microbes, thereby leading to lowered immunity to infection and resulting illness (Marsland et al., 2001; Miller & Cohen, 2001).

Daily Hassles

Major life events are, thankfully, fairly infrequent in our lives. It seems that the major sources of stress in most people's lives are what are termed **daily hassles** (Delongis, Folkman, & Lazarus, 1988; Lazarus, 1991). Although only minor, daily hassles can be chronic and repetitive. Examples of daily hassles are having too much to do all the time, having to fight the crowds while shopping, getting stuck regularly in heavy traffic, having to wait in lines all the time, having an unpleasant boss at work, having a long commute, and having to worry over money. Such daily hassles can be chronically irritating, and can add up to significant stress. The results of research on daily hassles have shown that, similar to major life events, persons with a lot of minor stress in their lives suffer more than expected from psychological and physical symptoms. The top 10 most common daily hassles are listed in Table 18.2.

Table 18.2 The 10 Most Commonly Experienced Daily Hassles

Hassles	Percentage*
Concerns about weight	52%
Health of a family member	48
Rising prices of common goods	43
Home maintenance	43
Too many things to do	39
Misplacing or losing things	38
Yard work or outside home maintenance	38
Property, investment, or taxes	37
Crime	37
Physical appearance	36

*Over a nine-month period, these percentages represent the average percentages of people indicating that the hassle was a significant source of stress in daily life.

Source: Adapted from Kanner et al., 1991.

Varieties of Stress

Stress is a physical and psychological response to perceived demands and pressures. In the stress response, people mobilize physical and emotional resources to cope with the demands and pressures. Psychologists distinguish four varieties of stress:

- **Acute stress** is what most people associate with the term *stress.* Acute stress results from a sudden onset of threat. It produces the flight-or-fight response, which can be experienced as tension, headache, emotional upset, gastrointestinal disturbances, feelings of agitation, and pressure. September 11, 2001, was a day of acute stress for many people. Even for persons not directly involved in the terrible events of that day, many experienced the stress that comes from feeling that events are not under control (Peterson & Seligman, 2003).
- **Chronic stress** can be a serious form of stress. It refers to stress that does not end. Day in and day out, chronic stress grinds us down until our resistance is gone. Serious systemic illnesses, such as those associated with decreased immune system functioning, or cardiovascular disease, can result from chronic stress.
- **Traumatic stress** refers to a massive instance of acute stress, the effects of which can reverberate for years or even a lifetime (e.g., Bunce, Larsen, & Peterson, 1995). Traumatic stress is defined mainly in terms of the symptoms associated with it. That is, we know it is traumatic stress when the person experiences posttraumatic stress symptoms. This collection of symptoms, called **posttraumatic stress disorder (PTSD)**, is a syndrome that occurs in some persons after experiencing or witnessing life-threatening events, such as military combat, natural disasters, terrorist incidents, serious accidents, or violent personal assaults such as rape. Many persons in New York City experienced symptoms of PTSD after the September 11 terrorist tragedy. People who suffer from PTSD often relive the experience through nightmares or intense flashbacks, have difficulty sleeping, have physical complaints, have flattened emotions, and feel detached

or estranged from others. These symptoms can be severe enough and last long enough to significantly impair the person's daily life, such as having trouble with personal relationships or difficulty holding down a job.

Health psychologists believe that stress has **additive effects;** that is, the effects of stress add up and accumulate in a person over time, similar to the concept of aggregation introduced in Chapter 4. Researchers have even coined a word—**allostatic load**—which refers to the cumulative burden of chronic stress over time and involves the physiological consequences of exposure to repeated or prolonged stress. It can be thought of as the total "wear and tear" on one's body from stress, and is assumed to add up over time.

On September 11, 2001, many people in and around the World Trade Center in New York experienced traumatic stress. Many of them went on to develop posttraumatic stress disorder.
Thomas Nilsson/Getty Images

Primary and Secondary Appraisal

Not all people respond to stressors in the same way. Two people can experience the same event, yet one is devastated and completely overwhelmed, whereas the other accepts the event as a challenge and is mobilized into positive action. Differences among people in how they respond to the same event are possible because stress is not "out there" in the environment. Rather, stress is in the *subjective reaction* of the person to potential stressors (Lazarus & Folkman, 1984). This is worth emphasizing, because many people refer to an event as stressful, as if stress were a characteristic of the event. Instead, stress is actually the response to that event. For example, two people are taking the same organic chemistry course; they take the same exam, and they both fail. One person may be very stressed by this event, whereas the other may take it in stride and not feel stressed at all by the failure. How can the same event happen to two people, yet one responds with stress and the other does not?

According to psychologist Richard Lazarus (1922–2002), in order for stress to be evoked in a person, two cognitive events must occur (Lazarus, 1991). The first cognitive event, which Lazarus called **primary appraisal,** is for the person to perceive that the event is a threat to his or her personal goals. The second necessary cognitive event, **secondary appraisal,** is when the person concludes that he or she does not have the resources to cope with the demands of the threatening event. Note that secondary appraisal refers to whether the event is under a person's control, and primary appraisal refers to whether the event is a threat to their goals. If either of these appraisals is absent—if the person does not perceive the event as threatening something important to them, or if the person feels he or she has plenty of resources for coping with the threat—then stress is not evoked. For example, if an event, such as an upcoming exam, is perceived as threatening to someone's goals, yet the person feels he or she has the resources demanded by that event (i.e., the person has been studying and otherwise preparing for the exam), then the person might experience the event more as a challenge than as stress. Alternatively, the person might feel he or she does not have the resources demanded by the event (secondary appraisal) but might not think that the event is important to his or her long-term goals (primary appraisal) and so might not respond with stress.

What might lead some individuals to consistently avoid the stress response? What are some of the strategies that people use to overcome stress and the accompanying anxiety and feelings of being overwhelmed? Next we consider several personality dimensions that have been associated with resistance to stress.

Coping Strategies and Styles

Everyone has unpleasant events happen in their lives. We all have temporary setbacks, losses, and frustrations in our day-to-day lives. However, some people seem better able to cope, to get over stressful events, or to somehow see such events as challenges rather than as sources of stress. One personality dimension that has been studied in relation to stress is attributional style.

Attributional Style

Attributional style is a dispositional way of explaining the causes of bad events. As introduced in Chapter 12, the three important dimensions of attributional style are external versus internal, unstable versus stable, and specific versus global. Various measures have been developed for assessing people's typical attributional style. One such measure is the Attributional Style Questionnaire (ASQ), developed by psychologist Chris Peterson (1950–2012) and his colleagues (1982). However, another very useful technique for scoring attributional style is by analyzing the content of people's written or spoken explanations. People often spontaneously provide explanations for events in their everyday conversations, social media posts, blogs, e-mails, or Twitter posts, It is possible to analyze the explanations a person uses in verbatim material and to rate those explanations along the attributional dimensions of internality, stability, and globality. This technique for measuring attributional style was also developed by Peterson and his colleagues (1992), who called it the Content Analysis of Verbatim Explanations (CAVE).

Exercise

Find an online article, social media post, or twitter thread in which a person is explaining an event—perhaps a story about an accident, an incident with another person, or some sporting event. Analyze their description, paying particular attention to the explanations the person uses (why things happened that way). Next, analyze those explanations in terms of the three dimensions of explanatory style:

- Internal versus external: Was it her or his fault, or due to something beyond his or her control?
- Stable versus unstable: Was the cause something long lasting or temporary?
- Global versus specific: Was the cause something general, affecting a large part of his or her life, or something specific, limited in impact?

Come up with a characterization of the person's style of attribution, how they assign blame for life events. This is essentially what researchers using the CAVE technique do, in a structured way, when they apply the coding system to peoples' explanations.

The CAVE technique has the advantage of assessing attributional style using any material containing causal explanations (Peterson, Seligman, & Vaillant, 1988). For example, presidential speeches, particularly the State of the Union addresses, often contain explanations for a great many events. As another example, movie stars often do interviews that contain explanations for events in their lives. Psychotherapy tapes can be analyzed with CAVE, as they often contain persons' attributions for why things happened to them. Similarly, song lyrics, children's stories, descriptions of sports events, and myths and religious texts all contain explanations for events that can be rated for how internal, stable, and global they are.

Some psychologists, including Chris Peterson, prefer the term **attributional optimism** to refer to a specific combination of attributions (Peterson, 2000). The optimistic person tends to explain bad events as not being due to them, as temporary, and as having a limited impact on their lives. For good events, however, optimists tend to do the opposite, they see the causes as due to themselves, as longer lasting, and as having a larger impact on their lives. So optimism is about specific ways of thinking: expecting good events, taking credit for good events, seeing good events as lasting and having a larger impact, and doing the opposite for negative events.

Like many traits, optimism refers to a bipolar dimension, even though we use only one end of that dimension to refer to it. While optimists are people who score high on this dimension, at the opposite end of the dimension are pessimists. Pessimists engage in the opposite kinds of cognitive activity; they tend to blame themselves when negative events happen and to see negative events as long lasting (expect more negativity in the future) and impactful (blowing negative events out of proportion). Some researchers view attributional optimism as a mediator. For example, Lee and colleagues (2019) found that character strengths (e.g., hope, perseverance) predict a lower likelihood of depression, but that optimistic attributional fully mediates the effects of character strengths.

Much of the early research on attributional optimism and health has been reviewed in detail by Peterson and colleagues (Peterson & Bossio, 1991; Peterson & Seligman, 1987). As a summary, attributional optimism in general has been shown to predict better health as measured by self-report, ratings of general health made by the physicians, fewer visits to the doctor, and living longer. For example, a study by Peterson and colleagues (1998) examined more than 1,000 individuals over a 50-year period. The researchers found that the participants who scored in the more pessimistic direction were more likely to die at an earlier age than the optimistic participants were. When the researchers looked at the causes of death, they found the largest differences between optimists and pessimists in the categories of "accidental death" and "violent death." This result has been replicated, with pessimistic attributional style correlating with the frequency of occurrence of fatal accidents, as well as with other health problems (Peterson & Bossio, 2001).

Because an optimistic attributional style appears to have health benefits, psychologist Marty Seligman and his colleagues developed a training program to increase people's level of attributional optimism (2002; Seligman & Peterson, 2003). In particular, Seligman also introduced a "pessimism prevention" program for use in grade schools, the details of which can be found in Weissberg, Kumpfer, and Seligman (2003) as well as at Dr. Seligman's Authentic Happiness website, hosted by the University of Pennsylvania, http://www.authentichappiness.sas.upenn.edu. The program has been found to be effective at preventing symptoms of depression in low-income minority middle-school students (Cardemil, Reivich, & Seligman, 2002) and mainland Chinese adults (Yu & Seligman, 2002).

Dispositional Optimism

Optimism can have different meanings depending on what the psychologist is emphasizing (Peterson & Chang, 2003). The attributional optimism we just discussed refers to a specific explanatory style for negative events. However, a slightly different definition of optimism is offered by Scheier and Carver (1992; Carver & Scheier, 2000). These researchers use the term **dispositional optimism** as the expectation that good events will be plentiful in the future, and that bad events will be rare in the future. While these two forms of optimism are empirically correlated, they are at least conceptually distinct and each has its own body of research, especially concerning health.

There are several short questionnaire measures of dispositional optimism, with items asking about a person's expectations for good and bad events in his or her future. A widely used 10-item measure of dispositional optimism—the Life Orientation Test (LOT: Scheier & Carver, 1985)—can be found on the web (https://positivepsychology. com/life-orientation-test-revised/). It has proven reliable and valid, and most of the research on disposition optimism is based on this measure.

Scheier and Carver (2018) provide a detailed recent review of this research going back 30 years. The early research—from 1985 to the early 2000s—consisted of mostly small studies establishing a link between optimism and both self-reported and objective measures of health. For example, one study followed people recovering from coronary bypass surgery (Scheier et al., 1999) and found that optimists (assessed by questionnaire) suffered fewer objective complications during recovery from bypass surgery than pessimists. In another study, healthy subjects volunteered to receive a small wound (a 4-mm punch wound similar to a tissue biopsy; Ebrecht et al., 2004). Researchers then assessed the rate of healing from this standardized wound over several weeks time. Subjects were divided into "fast healers" and "slow healers" based on whether they were above or below the median wound healing rate. The researchers found that the fast healers were significantly higher on optimism (measured by questionnaire) than the slow healers. Many similar studies examining disease progression and recovery rates have established that optimists generally have better health outcomes than pessimists across a wide variety of medical conditions (e.g., pregnancy, HIV, stroke, cancer; reviewed in Scheier & Carver, 2018).

Starting in the early 2000s, researchers began conducting large-scale **epidemiological studies** of optimism and health. Epidemiological studies typically enroll a large number of subjects who are initially healthy; then they are followed over time to see who develops specific diseases. For example, Tindle and colleagues (2009) followed over 97,000 working-age adult women over an eight-year period. They found that optimists were less likely than pessimists to develop coronary heart disease during the follow-up period. In fact, optimists were less likely to die from any cause during the eight-year period than pessimists. Taken in combination with the earlier studies, there is a remarkable body of evidence showing that optimism is consistently associated with positive health outcomes.

Given the evidence that optimism and health are related, the next question becomes: How does this relationship come about? How does it work? This is where the personality–health models, introduced at the start of this chapter, are useful. One new approach to optimism research (Scheier et al, 2021) has been to score separately items referring to an optimistic outlook, and items referring to a pessimistic outlook. This allows researchers to test whether effects on health are due to the presence of optimism or the absence of pessimism. Results show that, while both optimism and the absences of pessimism both significantly predict better health, the effects for the absence of pessimism were greater than the presence of optimism. While this is an interesting new development, the vast majority of research on optimism and health uses the total of all the items (i.e., sum of optimism items minus the sum of the pessimism items).

A segment of the research on optimism and health conforms to the "transactional model" (discussed earlier). Optimism is thought to influence how a person appraises stressful events, or copes with stressful events, and thereby lessens the health impact of those adverse events. Such events as starting college, being in high-level athletic competition, caring for a partner with a terminal disease, undergoing a medical procedure such as a bone marrow donation or having major surgery oneself, or being in an active combat zone have all been shown to be stressful for most people. However, research on these events also shows that they are less stressful for optimists than pessimists (reviewed in Scheier & Carver, 2018). The finding that the association between optimism and health is moderated by a diminished stress response among optimists, suggests that the transactional model is one way to understand how optimism works to improve health outcomes.

Another way to understand how optimism works to promote health is through the health behavior model. That is, a number of studies focus on health behavior differences between optimists and pessimists that may have long-term health consequences. Studies have found, for example, that optimists engage in more exercise, are more likely to eat a lower-fat diet, take vitamins more regularly, use less tobacco, use more safe sex practices, consume alcohol in moderation, and seek out knowledge about health risk factors than pessimists (studies reviewed in Scheier & Carver, 2018).

Another health behavior that optimists do more than pessimists is building social support networks. Psychologists have known for quite some time that having a network of others one can go to for support during times of stress has benefits in terms of better health. It turns out that optimists, perhaps due to their upbeat social style, are especially good at building social support networks (Scheier & Carver, 2018). For example, when starting college, optimists have more close friends at the end of their first semester at school than pessimists (Brissette, Scheier, & Carver, 2002). In summary, several studies provide results consistent with the health behavior model of optimism; optimists are more likely to engage in specific health behaviors (e.g., exercise, eat well, make good friends), and these behaviors in turn promote more healthy outcomes over the longer term. The relationship between optimism and health is, at least in part, mediated by specific health behaviors.

The research on optimism provides a window on how personality can relate to, or influence, physical health. There are other personality processes, quite different from optimism, that have also been related to health, and it is to these that we now turn.

Management of Emotions

Sometimes we have emotions, and sometimes emotions have us. Emotions, especially negative ones, can be particularly difficult to control. We can try to inhibit the expression of negative emotions, to keep our feelings under control. Imagine that your school team just lost an important championship, and you are really unhappy, distressed, and in an irritable mood, angry at the referees and disappointed by your team. However, you have an important exam tomorrow, so you must inhibit your distracting unpleasant emotions and concentrate on studying. You can think of similar examples of **emotional inhibition,** such as controlling your anxiety or hiding the fact that you are disappointed.

We all have to cover up or inhibit disappointments once in a while. But what about people who routinely suppress their emotions, who keep everything inside? What are the consequences of chronically inhibiting one's emotions? Some theorists suggest that emotional inhibition leads to undesirable consequences. For example, Sigmund Freud (see Chapter 9) believed that most psychological problems were the result of inhibited (repressed) negative emotions and motivations. Repression, the pushing of unacceptable desires or urges into the unconscious, was thought to be the root of all psychological problems. Psychoanalytic therapy, or the talking cure, was designed to bring inhibited emotion into conscious awareness, so that it could be experienced and expressed and dealt with in a mature manner. Moreover, the therapeutic relationship was seen as a place to experience and express emotions that had long been inhibited. There are other therapies that might be called "expressive therapies" because their goal is to get the person to release inhibited emotions.

Other theorists see emotional inhibition more positively. From a developmental perspective, the ability to inhibit emotions is acquired at an early age, at around 3 years, and is seen as a major developmental achievement. This is when children, though sad, are able to stop themselves from crying or, when angry, can inhibit themselves from striking back (Kopp, 1989; Thompson, 1991). The ability to inhibit negative emotion is seen as a very useful skill to learn in childhood and marks a developmental achievement.

What does the research conclude about the effects of chronically inhibited emotion? Surprisingly, there have been only a few well-done studies that directly address this question. For example, psychologists James Gross and Robert Levenson (1993, 1997; Gross, 2002) designed studies in which some of the participants were asked to suppress the expression of any emotions they were feeling while they watched a video designed to evoke the emotions of happiness (a comedy routine), then sadness (scenes from the funeral of a child, showing a distraught and highly emotional mother). Half of the participants were randomly assigned to the suppression condition, in which they were told, "If you have any feelings as you watch the [video] please try your best not to let those feelings show." The other half of the participants were assigned to the no-suppression condition, in which they were simply told to watch the video and were given no instructions to inhibit their emotions.

While the participants watched the video, the researchers videotaped them to determine how much they expressed their emotions while watching it. The researchers also collected several physiological measures, such as those we discussed in Chapter 7. They also asked the participants to report on their feelings after each segment of the video.

Results showed that the participants who were instructed to suppress their emotions did exactly that; video recordings showed no facial expression of emotion. However, the suppression participants showed heightened physiological activity during the video, indicating increased sympathetic nervous system arousal, compared with the no-suppression participants. The researchers suggested that suppression of emotion takes effort and exerts physiological costs above and beyond the emotional arousal. The participants in the suppression condition showed less *outward* expression of emotion than did the control participants, but they showed more *inward* expression of nervous system activation. Results like these are suggestive that, at least in the short term, keeping one's emotions from showing exerts a physiological cost in terms of increased autonomic nervous system activation. If emotions are chronically suppressed, then the autonomic nervous system, the flight-or-fight response, is also chronically activated, leading to more wear and tear and perhaps more physiological stress.

Which woman is genuinely happy? The woman on the left, Kelli Bradshaw from North Carolina, reacts to hearing her name called as the first runner-up (second place) in the Miss America Pageant in 1998. By implication, the woman on the right, Nicole Johnson from Virginia, simultaneously realizes that she is the next Miss America.

Charles Rex Arbogast/AP Images

Sometimes it is necessary to inhibit feelings. Perhaps you do not want to hurt someone's feelings; perhaps you do not want to antagonize someone in a position of power; or perhaps you do not want to anger someone who is already acting aggressively (Larsen & Prizmic, 2004). For example, your boss may be upset with you for the wrong reason, and you may feel angry toward her. However, you cannot act out that anger because she is your boss and has a lot of power over you in terms of raises, workload, and working conditions. Quite simply, there are some situations in life in which it is wise to choose to hide your feelings.

Problems can arise when emotional inhibition becomes chronic, when a person routinely hides her or his emotions. Someone who characteristically inhibits the free expression of emotion may suffer the effects of chronic sympathetic nervous system arousal. For example, Levy and colleagues (1985) have shown that people who keep their negative emotions to themselves are more likely than expressive persons to have a higher mortality rate, a greater likelihood of recurrence of cancer after treatment, and a suppressed immune system. Cancer patients who express their negative emotions, and who emotionally fight their disease, sometimes live longer than patients who accept their situation, inhibit their emotions, and quietly accept their treatment (Levy, 1990; Levy & Heiden, 1990).

The importance of emotional expression was illustrated in a study done by Noller (1984) on emotional expressiveness in romantic relationships. Noller found that the more people expressed their feelings to their partners, the fewer problems they reported in their relationships. Knowing how your partner feels allows you to adjust your behavior accordingly. If your partner never expresses how he or she feels, then it is difficult to know what makes him or her happy or sad or angry.

Other studies bolster the idea that emotional expressiveness is good for our psychological health. King and Emmons (1990) had participants keep daily records of how they were feeling each day for three consecutive weeks. The participants completed a questionnaire measure of emotional expressiveness. The researchers found that, on days when subjects reported being more emotionally expressive, they also reported higher levels of happiness over the 21 days of the study. A similar study by Katz and Campbell (1994) found that emotional expressiveness was correlated with higher self-esteem.

Disclosure

Related to emotional expressiveness is the topic of **disclosure,** or telling someone about a private aspect of oneself. Many theorists have suggested that keeping things to ourselves, not opening up to other people, may be a source of stress and ultimately may lead to psychological distress and physical disease. These theorists have further argued that being open to others with our feelings may be curative, that talk therapy may work in part because through it we uncover secrets and reveal what we have been keeping to ourselves. Letting that out in a trusting relationship is considered a healthy activity.

Psychologist James Pennebaker has been a pioneer in researching the effects of disclosure. In a typical study, he asks participants to recall an upsetting or traumatic event that has happened to them, something they have not discussed with anyone. He asks them to write down these secrets. People write about many different unpleasant events, such as various embarrassing moments, sexual indiscretions, illegal or immoral behaviors, humiliations, and so on. It is interesting that *all* participants quickly come up with a secret that they have been keeping. This suggests that probably all of us have some secrets.

Early in his research, Pennebaker argued that *not* discussing traumatic, negative, or upsetting events can lead to problems. It takes physical energy, he says, to inhibit the thoughts and feelings associated with such events. In other words, it is not easy to keep a secret to ourselves, and keeping something in, especially if it is a major trauma, is upsetting and takes a lot of energy. Over time, this stress builds and, like all stress, can increase the likelihood of stress-related problems, such as trouble sleeping, irritability, physical symptoms (e.g., stomachaches and headaches), and even illness resulting from lowered immune system functioning. Telling the secret, according to Pennebaker, relieves this stress.

Pennebaker and his colleagues have conducted many studies on the topic of disclosure. In one study (Pennebaker & O'Heeron, 1984), they contacted participants who had lost a spouse through accident or suicide. Clearly, such a sudden and complete loss of a loved one

Research started by psychologist Jamie Pennebaker has repeatedly shown that sharing one's difficulties and traumas with others is better than keeping your problems to yourself.

New Africa/Shutterstock

through an unexpected and traumatic death must have a huge impact on the surviving spouse (recall that death of a spouse was the most stressful life event on the Holmes and Rahe list). The survivors were asked how much they discussed the tragedy with friends, family, or other helping professionals, such as a priest, rabbi, minister, or therapist. The researchers also did a thorough assessment of the participants' health since the death of the spouse. They discovered that the more the participants had talked about the tragedy with others, the better their subsequent health. Of course, this is correlational research, so we cannot know for certain if talking about one's problems causes better health. To pin this down, researchers needed to do experiments where disclosure is randomly assigned in one condition, and in the control condition participants do not disclose their personal reactions (e.g., they may be instructed to talk or write about some neutral topic). We now describe some of these experiments.

In an experimental study on this topic (Pennebaker, 1990), the participants were college students randomly assigned to one of two groups. One group was asked to recall and write about an experience from their past that they found distressing. The other group was asked to write about a trivial topic, such as what they normally ate for breakfast. The students wrote about their assigned topic for 15 minutes each night for four consecutive nights. Six months later, the participants were contacted again and a health history was obtained. Students who had written about a trauma for those four days had fewer illnesses in the subsequent six months, compared with the students who had written about trivial topics. Moreover, student records from the health services showed that the participants who had written about trauma had indeed gone to the campus health center less often than the participants who had written about trivial topics. Interestingly, just the act of writing about an upsetting event, even if no one ever reads the writing, may have a beneficial effect on health.

In another study by Pennebaker, Colder, and Sharp (1990), the participants were also just starting college. For three nights in a row, they were asked to write about their difficulties and their feelings about the challenges of leaving family and friends at home and starting an independent life at college. Other participants (the control group) wrote about trivial topics. Health measures were then obtained after the students had been in college for at least a semester: the students who had written about their feelings and problems had gone to the student health center fewer times during the subsequent semester than had those who had written about trivial topics. A recent experiment (Robinson et al., 2020) mostly replicated this design, but had students write about their personal struggles with the COVID pandemic (or write about everyday events in the control condition), and found that the personal disclosure group reported reduced levels of anxiety during spikes in COVID.

Psychotherapists will sometimes ask their clients, especially those who have experienced a trauma or another extreme event, to talk or write about that trauma. Some psychologists even recommend keeping a diary of the events in one's life and how one is reacting to those events. Such a daily self-disclosure helps put one's feelings into perspective and make some sense out of the events in one's life. The process provides insight into oneself and the events in one's life.

How does disclosure work to promote healthy adjustment? Pennebaker's first theory of the mechanism concerned the relief that results from telling a secret. In other words, keeping the information inside takes effort and is stressful, and disclosing that information removes the strain and relieves the stress (Niederhoffer & Pennebaker, 2002).

Exercise

Try keeping a record of your health every day for two weeks. Record each day whether you have a stomachache, a headache, muscle aches, a sore throat, or a runny nose. After this baseline period of recording your health, start keeping a diary each day for two weeks, writing down and describing the stresses and challenges you experience each day and reflecting on how these make you feel. Pay attention to any difficulties, stress, or even embarrassing or trying moments. When the two weeks are over, stop keeping the diary and begin recording your daily health again. Now compare your health reports before the writing phase with your health reports after the writing phase. Do you see any improvement? While this is not a true experiment (you are both the subject and the experimenter, which is not done in true experiments), you can nevertheless get a feel for how research on this topic is done, and you might see a change in your health for the better as a function of keeping a diary of your personal reactions to challenges and stressors.

More recently, Pennebaker (2003a) put forward a second explanation for how disclosure promotes adjustment. This explanation concerns how writing about an event allows a person to reinterpret and reframe the meaning of that event. In other words, a person writing or talking about a past traumatic event can try to better understand that event, search for some positive meaning in the event (the positive re-appraisal process discussed in the A Closer Look). Both processes—relief from inhibition and reinterpretation of the event—may be occurring, and so both explanations may be correct. Indeed, Pennebaker (2003b) has speculated that this combination may be the basic ingredient that underlies most forms of successful talking therapy.

In summary, research on disclosure suggests that keeping traumatic events and the feelings about those events to ourselves can be stressful. Expressing our emotions in words can, in fact, produce some stress-reducing effects. Moreover, it appears that it does not matter how we put our feelings into words—whether we talk to a trusted friend or relative, go to a caring psychotherapist, go to confession at our church or have a talk with our minister or rabbi, have a discussion with our husband or wife, or write it in a diary. One study, designed to test how little disclosure is necessary to still achieve health benefits, found that two minutes of writing on two consecutive days produced measurable health benefits assessed four to six weeks later (Burton & King, 2008). Whatever form it takes, the disclosure of traumatic events, and our personal reactions to them, is much better for our health than keeping it all to ourselves.

Type A Personality and Cardiovascular Disease

Cardiovascular disease is the number one cause of death the United States today (https://www.cdc.gov/heartdisease/facts.htm, though in 2022 COVID-19 was a very close second to heart disease as the most frequent cause of death). Health professionals have been searching for the factors that put people at risk for this cardiovascular disease. Known risk factors for developing cardiovascular disease include high blood pressure, obesity, smoking, family history of heart disease, inactive lifestyle, and high cholesterol. In the 1970s, physicians began to consider a new risk factor, a specific personality trait. As mentioned in Chapter 13, this grew out of the observation by some physicians that the patients who had heart attacks often behaved differently, and seemed to have different personalities, compared with other patients. Heart attack patients were often

A Closer Look

The Role of Positive Emotions in Coping with Stress

The vast majority of the research on personality and health focuses on negative emotions and how they contribute to stress and illness. However, in recent years, some researchers have taken an interest in the positive emotions and health and coping (for a review, see Tedeschi, Park, & Calhoun, 1998). The general hypothesis is that positive emotions and positive appraisals may lead to a lowered impact of stress on health (Lyubomirsky, 2001).

Several decades ago, Lazarus, Kanner, and Folkman (1980) speculated that positive emotions played three important roles in the stress process: (1) They may sustain coping efforts; (2) they may provide a break from stress; and (3) they may give people time and opportunity to restore depleted resources, including the restoration of social relationships. However, few researchers followed up and gave serious attention to the role of positive emotions in health for almost two decades.

Psychologist Barbara Fredrickson led the way in the search for the effects of positive emotions on stress and illness. She has proposed a **broaden and build model of positive emotions,** suggesting that positive emotions broaden the scope of cognition, and build up resources for coping. The "broaden" part refers to positive emotions helping a person become more creative, which helps the person see more options in stressful situations, and try different ways of coping with the stress. The "build" part of her model suggests that positive emotions help a person build up reserves of energy, as well as build up social resources, especially in terms of building a social support network. She proposes that positive emotions are important in facilitating adaptive coping and adjustment to stress (Fredrickson, 1998, 2000). In experimental research, Fredrickson and Levenson (1998) found

that the experience of positive emotions, following a period of acute stress, facilitated recovery from that stress.

Psychologists Susan Folkman and Judith Moskowitz (2000) built on Fredrickson's ideas and have suggested several important mechanisms in determining whether people will experience positive emotions during periods of severe stress. They give examples of these positive coping mechanisms from their study of gay men who were caregivers of partners dying from AIDS. Caring for someone with a chronic debilitating disease, such as AIDS or Alzheimer's disease, often leads the caregiver to suffer physical costs from the stress and strain. From their study of such caregivers, Folkman and Moskowitz identified three coping mechanisms capable of generating positive emotion during stress.

The first positive emotion coping strategy is called **positive reappraisal,** a cognitive process whereby a person focuses on the good in what is happening or has happened. Forms of positive reappraisal (also called "benefit finding") include seeing opportunities for personal growth and seeing how one's own efforts can benefit other people. In their study of AIDS caregivers, Folkman and Moskowitz found that the caregivers who were able to positively reappraise the situation (e.g., "This illness has brought my partner and I even closer" or "I will emerge from this challenge a stronger and better person") showed better adjustment both during caregiving and after the death of their partners (Moskowitz et al., 1996).

The second positive strategy identified by Folkman and colleagues (1997) is **problem-focused coping,** using thoughts and behaviors to manage or solve the underlying cause of the stress. Folkman and Moskowitz note how this strategy can be useful in situations that, on the surface,

appear uncontrollable. In the AIDS caregiver study, many of the caregivers were caring for partners who were dying, a situation that could not be stopped, reversed, or even slowed at that time. However, even in these seemingly uncontrollable conditions, some caregivers were able to focus on the little things they could control. For example, many created "to-do" lists of little things, such as getting prescriptions filled, administering medications, and changing their partners' bed linens. Keeping such lists, and ticking off the completed items, gave the caregivers opportunities to feel effective and in control in an otherwise overwhelming situation. In short, focusing on solving problems, even little ones, can give a person a positive sense of control.

The third positive strategy is called **creating positive events** and is defined as creating a positive time-out from the stress. This can be done in a number of ways. Often, all it takes is to pause and reflect on something positive, such as a compliment received, a pleasing or humorous memory, or a sunset. Taking time out for a hug has even been shown to help people cope with interpersonal conflict (Murphy, Janicki-Deverts, & Cohen, 2018). These sorts of time-outs can give a person a momentary respite from the chronic stress. Many of the AIDS caregivers took time to reminisce about pleasant times or to plan positive events with their partner, such as taking their partners for scenic drives or planning a time to tell jokes or funny stories each week. Some of the caregivers reported using humor to find some positive relief. It has long been thought that humor can be a tension reducer and that it may contribute to mental and physical health (Menninger, 1963).

This focus on positive emotions and their role in health and illness is new. Many of the early findings are intriguing but also raise new questions for research. For example, do different kinds of positive emotions—such as excitement, happiness, or contentment—play different roles in the stress process? Are the positive emotions most helpful in coping with particular kinds of stress? And, finally, of particular interest to personality psychologists are questions about differences among people in the ability to generate positive emotions while coping with stress (Affleck & Tennen, 1996). Who are the people who can generate humor, for example, during periods of coping? Are specific personality traits, such as extraversion or optimism, uniquely related to positive emotion coping styles? Can psychologists develop brief and targeted interventions to increase positive affect for persons experiencing chronic life stress? Preliminary studies suggest that positive affect interventions are feasible and may be effective at helping people cope with stress (Moskowitz, 2011).

more competitive and aggressive, more active and energetic in their actions and speech, and more ambitious and driven about their careers and other interests (Friedman & Rosenman, 1974). They called this collection of behaviors the Type A personality.

Before examining some of the research findings on Type A, let us look at a few misconceptions. Although researchers often refer to Type A and Type B persons, most psychologists think of it as a dimension, not as a categorical typology. As noted in Chapter 4, few personality variables are truly categorical, whereby people fall into distinct categories. Blood type is an example of a truly categorical variable. However, very few, if any, personality traits are categorical. Instead, most are dimensional, ranging from one extreme to the other, with most people falling somewhere around the middle (i.e., follow a normal bell curve). It is distributed normally, as in Figure 18.4(a), not as a category variable, which would look like Figure 18.4(b). Psychologists frequently describe normally distributed traits by reference to one end (e.g., Type A). A recent study by Wilmot and colleagues (2019) presents strong empirical data that conforms more to a dimension than a true categorical distinction.

Another misconception is that Type A is a single trait; in actuality, Type A is a syndrome of several traits. More specifically, it is a collection of three subtraits, which together make up the Type A dimension. One of these three subtraits is **competitive achievement motivation.** Type A persons like to work hard and achieve goals. They like recognition, power, and the defeat of obstacles. And they feel that they are at their best when competing with others. A person who shows up to a charity bike-a-thon ready for the Tour de France bicycle race is exhibiting competitive achievement motivation. **Time urgency** is the second subtrait of the Type A dimension. Type A persons hate wasting time. They are always in a hurry and feel under pressure to get the most done in the least amount of time. Often, they do two or more things at once, called multi-tasking, such as eating while reading a book. They also hate waiting in line. The third subtrait of Type A is **hostility.** When blocked from attaining one of their goals, which is the definition of **frustration,** Type A persons become frustrated and may react aggressively. They get frustrated easily, and this frustration may propel them to act out their irritation. If the frustrating object is an unresponsive vending machine, for example, they might swear and punch or kick the machine. If the frustrating object is another person, they might behave in an unfriendly, malicious, or even hurtful manner. People who are known to have a "hot temper" usually have this hostility subtrait of this Type A dimension.

Early studies of the Type A personality, mainly conducted by cardiac physicians, found that it was an independent risk factor for developing cardiovascular disease. An **independent risk factor** operates independently from other known risk factors, such as being overweight or smoking. Thus, for example, it is not true that Type A persons just smoke more and that their smoking causes the heart disease. Instead, the Type A personality is independent of smoking, and someone who is Type A *and* smokes is at more of a risk for

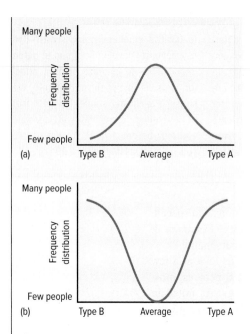

Figure 18.4

Type A and Type B are not really types at all and do not refer to categories of people. Rather, *Type A* refers to a normal distribution of people, anchored at one end by persons showing a lot of Type A behavior and at the other end by persons showing very little (a). Most people, however, are in the middle, or average, range. This is the case with almost all personality traits. A true type, or categorical variable, would be distributed as in (b), with most people at one end or the other and very few people in the middle. This is not the case with the Type A personality.

heart disease than someone who just smokes or who is just Type A. In fact, one study found that the Type A personality was a better predictor of heart disease than the person's history of smoking or the person's cholesterol level (Jenkins, Zyzanski, & Rosenman, 1976).

Physicians conducted most of the early studies of Type A personality, and to measure this personality variable, they developed a structured interview to assess the Type A pattern. Standard questions were asked, and the interviewer noted the participants' answers and how they reacted to the questions. For example, did they frequently interrupt the interviewer or put words in the interviewer's mouth? Did they fidget during the interview? Did they make frequent and vigorous gestures with their hands and heads? Did they disagree or argue with the interviewer? In one part of the interview, the interviewer tries to aggravate the participants by . . . talking . . . . very . . . . . . slowly. Type A people are especially aggravated when other people talk slowly, and they interrupt, talk out of turn, or finish sentences for people in order to speed them up.

As research on Type A personality gained momentum in the 1980s, researchers tried to devise a more efficient measure. Interviews are slow; they can measure only one person at a time, and it takes one interviewer to measure each participant. In short, interviewing is a relatively expensive and time-consuming way to measure any personality trait. Questionnaires are much cheaper because they are generally faster, they can be given to whole groups of participants, and can be administered online and scored automatically. Thus, researchers in this area put some effort into developing a questionnaire measure for Type A personality. One of the most widely used questionnaire measures of Type A personality is the Jenkins Activity Survey. It contains questions that tap into each of the three components of the Type A syndrome—for example, "My work improves as the deadline approaches," "I have been told that I eat too fast," and "I enjoy a good competition."

Early researchers using the structured interview often found a relationship between Type A personality and risk for heart attack, cardiovascular disease, and cardiac complications. Later research, mostly using the Jenkins questionnaire, quite often failed to replicate this finding. This puzzled researchers for several years. Some psychologists began to take a close look at the research, searching for a reason why some studies found a relationship but others didn't. A pattern quickly emerged; studies using the questionnaire measure were less likely to find a relationship between Type A and heart disease than the studies using the structured interview (Suls & Wan, 1989; Suls, Wan, & Costa, 1996). Researchers have concluded that the questionnaire measure taps into, or weights differently, the different subtraits of Type A, compared to the structured interview measures. Apparently, the structured interview gets more at the lethal component of Type A, and so finds an association with heart disease. But which subtrait of the Type A dimension *is* the most toxic, the part that is most related to heart disease?

Hostility: The Lethal Component of the Type A Behavior Pattern

When the interview measures of Type A were developed by physicians, they tended to emphasize the assessment of hostility and aggressiveness. For example, it assessed whether the participants got frustrated when the physicians talked slowly, whether they swore during the interview, or whether they actively gestured or pounded the table. Later, when questionnaire measures were developed, more of an emphasis was placed on the time urgency and achievement components. For example, did the participants say they were always in a hurry, that they worked better as deadlines got closer, or that they achieved more than their peers? Researchers began testing the hypothesis that it was the specific component of hostility, rather than the time urgency or achievement motivation components, that was the specific risk factor for heart disease.

Frequently doing two activities at once is a component of the Type A personality. Time urgency, however, is not the part of Type A that is most associated with heart disease.

Vera Petrunina/Shutterstock

What do researchers mean by the hostility component? People high in hostility are not necessarily violent or outwardly aggressive. They are not necessarily even assertive or demanding of others. Instead, such people are likely to react disagreeably to disappointments, frustrations, and inconveniences. Frustration can be understood as the subjective feeling that comes when you are blocked from attaining a goal. A hostile person reacts to such frustrations, even minor ones, with anger and disagreeable behavior. Hostile people are easily irritated, even by small frustrations, such as when they misplace their car keys or have to wait in a long line at store. In such situations, hostile people can become visibly agitated and upset, sometimes becoming rude, uncooperative, or belligerent.

Several studies have now established that hostility is a strong predictor of cardiovascular disease (see meta-analysis by Chida & Steptoe, 2009). In fact, psychologists Dembrowski and Costa (1987) have demonstrated that even a questionnaire measure of the specific trait of hostility is a better predictor of artery disease than are questionnaire measures of general Type A. Studies have also shown that hostility is associated with systemic inflammation, as indicated by elevated blood **leukocyte** counts, also known as white blood cell counts (Surtees et al., 2003). Hostility has also been associated with elevated biomarkers of systemic inflammation such as C-reactive protein (Toussaint et al., 2018). Physicians have long known that chronic inflammation is related to risk for coronary disease risk, and so have recommended that persons at risk take an aspirin a day to reduce systemic inflammation. Chronic inflammation may be one biological pathway whereby hostility is linked to the health endpoint of cardiovascular disease.

The good news about this research is that not everything about being Type A is bad for the heart and arteries. Given that hostility is apparently the lethal component, can we envision a "healthy" version of the Type A personality? It seems okay to strive for success and achievement, but don't be hostile and aggressive along the way. It's okay to strive to attain goals and even to be a workaholic, but don't get frustrated by the inevitable setbacks that come with everyday life. It's okay to be in a hurry and strive to get as much done as possible, but don't get frustrated and angry when you can't accomplish everything. It's okay to enjoy a competition as long as it's friendly, not hostile. Sometimes it may be good therapy to get into the longest and slowest line at the store and just try to relax, take it easy, and not feel hostile or angry in such situations (Wright, 1988). Davidson and colleagues (2007) estimate that brief hostility-management therapy can result in cost savings for hospitals by reducing hospitalization expenses associated with coronary care.

How the Arteries Are Damaged by Hostile Type A Behavior

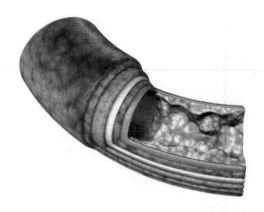

A cross-section of a human coronary artery, the artery that feeds the heart muscle itself, showing extreme arteriosclerosis. Here the artery diameter has narrowed dramatically by the buildup of plaque on the inside artery wall.

MedicalRF.com

How does the hostility component produce its toxic effects on the heart and arteries? Strong feelings of hostility and aggression produce the fight-or-flight response. Part of this response is an increase in blood pressure, accompanied by a constriction of the arteries. The person's body suddenly pumps more blood, but through arteries that are now narrower. This can produce wear and tear on the inside lining of the arteries, causing microscopic tears and abrasions. These tears then become sites at which cholesterol and fat can become attached. In addition to this mechanical wear and tear on the artery walls, stress hormones released into the blood during the fight-or-flight response may lead to artery damage and subsequent buildup of fatty deposits on the artery walls. As these fat molecules build up on the inside of the arteries, the arteries become progressively narrower. This narrowing is permanent and is called **arteriosclerosis**, or hardening or blocking of the arteries. When the arteries that feed the heart muscle itself become blocked, the subsequent shortage of blood to the heart is called a heart attack. Common surgeries to treat heart attacks involve unblocking (with stents or mechanical clearing) or replacing the blocked arteries to the heart muscle.

In summary, research on the Type A personality has taken some interesting twists and turns. It all began with a couple of cardiologists noticing certain personality differences between heart attack patients compared to other medical patients. This led them to define the Type A personality as consisting of three subtraits: competitive achievement motivation, time urgency, and hostility. After several decades of research, psychologists have found that trait hostility is the most toxic component of the Type A personality, and most research on cardiovascular disease and personality today is focusing on this specific trait. Understanding how hostility develops and is maintained, how exactly it damages the arteries, how it is evoked by specific situations, and how it can be overcome or managed are all important questions for future personality researchers.

SUMMARY AND EVALUATION

This chapter focused on the part of personality psychology related to physical well-being and health. We began with several models of the personality and illness link. We also introduced the important concepts of moderation and mediation, which describe specific ways that personality can produce its effects on health and illness. We used recent research on COVID-19 to illustrate each of the five models of the personality–health connection. We then examined the concept of stress as the subjective reaction to events that the person sees as threatening to their goals and as being beyond their control. The stress response comes in three distinct varieties: acute, chronic, and traumatic. Traumatic stress can evolve into a disorder, called posttraumatic stress disorder, in which the person experiences nightmares or flashbacks, difficulties sleeping and other somatic problems, avoidance of similar events, and feelings of being detached from reality or estranged from other people. It is important to realize that stress is not "out there" in the environment but in how one reacts to an event. Two kinds of appraisals of events are important to understanding stress. Primary appraisal concerns an evaluation of how threatening the event is with respect to a person's goals and desires. Secondary appraisal concerns an evaluation of the person's own resources for coping with the threatening event, do they have what it takes to control the event. Both of these appraisals are important for understanding how events come to elicit the stress response. Researchers are also exploring the role of positive emotions in coping with chronic stress, which we summarized in A Closer Look.

Much of the work on personality and stress began with a focus on major life events, such as losing a loved one or getting fired from one's job. Although serious, such events are relatively rare. More insidious are daily hassles, the relatively minor but common frustrations and disappointments of daily life. Stress researchers have also focused on these daily hassles in terms of their impact on health.

Personality psychologists have been concerned with understanding why some people appear more resistant to stress than others. That is, some people appear to take frustration and disappointment more in stride and do not suffer the deleterious health consequences often associated with chronic stress. One personality dimension in this regard is optimism, which has a wealth of findings associating it with stress resistance, good health, competent immune functioning, and longer life expectancy. Psychologists are developing training programs to teach people to become more optimistic. Some related personality processes associated with generally better health prognosis are emotional expressivity and personal disclosure.

This chapter also focused on a specific disease, cardiovascular disease, which is the most common death in the United States. We covered the history of the search for a personality dimension that might be a risk factor for developing heart disease. Type A personality provides an interesting example of progressive research, in which findings are gradually refined until the field becomes more and more certain about a specific effect. In the case of Type A personality, most researchers now agree that the hostility component is most associated with the tendency to develop heart disease. Fortunately, people can be competitive workaholics and strive to do more and more in less and less time, just as long as they do not have the hostile part of the Type A syndrome.

KEY TERMS

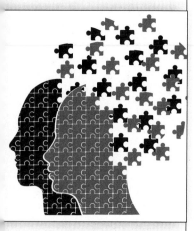

Athanasia Nomikou/Shutterstock

Disorders of Personality

19

Kody Scott, a.k.a. "Monster," in Pelican Bay prison in 1993, photographed through Plexiglas. His autobiography, which he wrote while in solitary confinement, provides a real-life account of the mind of a person with antisocial personality disorder.
Susan Ragan/AP Images

Kody Scott grew up in South Central Los Angeles. When he was 12 years old, he was initiated into the Eight-Tray Gangster CRIPS street gang. He shot his first victim the night he was initiated. He went on to earn the nickname "Monster" for particularly violent beatings he inflicted on people. For example, as a young teenager, Kody severely beat a victim who resisted when Kody attempted to mug him. Kody beat him far beyond what was necessary to make the victim submit. In fact, Kody seemed to enjoy hurting other people.

Kody's biological father was a professional football player with whom his mother had had a brief affair. His mother had an unstable and violent marriage with Kody's stepfather, who left the home for good when Kody was 6 years old. Kody's mother raised her six children in a two-bedroom house in a gang-infested ghetto neighborhood.

Kody was an intelligent and muscular boy who enjoyed thrills and excitement. He might have gone on to become a professional athlete, or he could have succeeded in a career involving adventure and plenty of action, such as a policeman, a soldier, or maybe even an astronaut. Instead, Kody grew up to become Monster, a violent individual who feared nothing, had no feelings of guilt or remorse, and craved excitement.

Kody Scott was one of the most notorious gangbangers in South Central L.A. For the early part of his life, he aspired to be the most feared member of the CRIPS. He was sent to prison in 1993 to serve a seven-year sentence for shooting a drug dealer in the kneecap. In prison, he was classed as a maximum security threat and was housed away from other inmates. He wrote his autobiography, *Monster: The Autobiography of an L.A. Gang Member,* while in solitary confinement in San Quentin prison, under the name Sanyika Shakur (1994), which is also the name of his Facebook page. Even after attaining celebrity status for his book, which sold over 100,000 copies, Kody Scott could not escape the gang culture or his own violent personality. In 2007, already wanted by the L.A. police for parole violations, Scott was arrested again, this time for beating an acquaintance, taking the keys to his Jaguar, and leaving the scene in the victim's vehicle. In May 2008, Kody Scott, age 44, was convicted of carjacking and robbery and sentenced to another six years in Pelican Bay State Prison. He was released two years early, in 2012, and in 2013 published a book of essays. In 2017, however, Kody Scott was again convicted of assault and served his sentence at Centinela State Prison in California. In 2021 he was released from prison. He had plans to write another book and start a series of podcasts. It looked like he might be turning his life around. However, on June 6, 2021, his body was found at a homeless encampment in Oceanside, California. His death was due to natural causes, most likely a stroke. He was 57 years old.

We open this chapter with the case of Kody Scott because he illustrates one of the personality disorders we will cover in this chapter: the antisocial personality disorder. We chose him as a case example because his book "Monster" is a fascinating first-person account into the mind and inner workings of a sociopath. His book confirms that he meets all the criteria for a diagnosis of antisocial personality disorder as well as psychopathy. We have been following him for almost 25 years, throughout all the editions of this textbook. While we hoped he could change and turn his life around, his repeated convictions for violent acts throughout his life illustrates that, for most people with a personality disorder, change is difficult and unlikely. While Kody Scott had several opportunities to leave his life of violence (a best-selling book, work as a motivational speaker, involvement with social justice causes) he could not resist the pull of his antisocial disorder.

The Building Blocks of Personality Disorders

Many of the topics we covered in previous chapters come together to describe and understand the various personality disorders. The symptoms of personality disorders can be seen as maladaptive variations within several of the domains we have covered. These include traits, emotions, cognitions, motives, interpersonal behavior, and self-concepts. The 10 personality disorders we present in this chapter are built on the foundation of these broader concepts, and so we briefly discuss the relevance of each to this chapter.

Traits of personality describe consistencies in behavior, thought, or action and represent meaningful differences among persons, as we described in Chapter 4. Personality disorders can be thought of as maladaptive variations or combinations of normal personality traits. Widiger and colleagues describe how extremes on either end of specific trait dimensions can be associated with personality disorders (Trull & Widiger, 2013; Widiger, Costa, & McCrae, 2002a; Widiger et al., 2002b). For example, a person with extremely low levels of trust and extremely high levels of hostility might be disposed to paranoid personality disorder. A person very low on sociability but very high on anxiety might be prone to avoidant personality disorder. A person with the opposite combination—extremely high on sociability and low on anxiety—might be prone to histrionic personality disorder. Thus, the concept of traits, such as the five-factor model of traits, can be especially useful for describing personality disorders (Trull & McCrae, 2002).

Motivation is another basic building block of personality that is important to understanding personality disorders. Motives describe what people want and why they behave in particular ways. In the intrapsychic domain, Chapters 9 to 11, we discussed several different kinds of motives, ranging from the sexual and aggressive basis of Freud's theory to modern research on the need for intimacy, achievement, and power. A common theme in several personality disorders concerns maladaptive variations on these common motives, especially need for power and need for intimacy. One important variation concerns an extreme lack of motivation for intimacy, which is seen in certain personality disorders. Another theme is an exaggerated need for power over others, which, at an extremely high level, can result in a maladaptive personality disorder. Other motives can be involved in personality disorders, such as the extreme need to be superior and receive the praise of others that is found in narcissistic personality disorder. The person with obsessive-compulsive personality disorder might be seen as having an extremely high motivation for order and detail.

Cognition also provides a building block for understanding personality disorders. As covered in Chapter 12, cognition consists of mental activity involved in perceiving, interpreting, and planning. These processes can become distorted in personality disorders. Some disorders involve routine and consistent misinterpretations of the intentions of others. Personality disorders typically involve an impairment of social judgment, such as when the paranoid thinks others are out to get her or when the histrionic person thinks others actually like being with him. The person with a borderline personality disorder may misinterpret innocent comments as signs of abandonment or criticism or rejection. In various ways, each of the personality disorders involves some distortion in the perception of other persons and altered social cognition.

Emotion is another area that is important to understanding personality disorders. We discussed normal range individual differences in emotion in Chapter 13. With several personality disorders there is extreme variation in experienced emotions. Some disorders involve extreme volatility in emotions (e.g., borderline), whereas other disorders involve extremes of specific emotions, such as anxiety (avoidant personality disorder), fear (paranoid personality disorder), or rage (narcissistic personality disorder). Most personality disorders have an emotional core.

The self-concept is another building block in personality disorders. As described in Chapter 14, the self-concept is the person's own collection of self-knowledge—one's understanding of oneself. With most personality disorders, there is some distortion in the self-concept. Most of us are able to build and maintain a stable and realistic image of ourselves; we know our own opinions, we know what we value, and we know what we want out of life. With many of the disorders, there is a lack of stability in the self-concept, such that the person may feel she or he has no "core" or has trouble making decisions or needs constant reassurance from others. Self-esteem is also an important part of the self, and some disorders are associated with extremely high (e.g., narcissism) or extremely low (e.g., dependent personality disorder) levels of self-esteem. The self provides an important perspective on understanding personality disorders.

Social relationships are frequently disturbed or maladaptive in personality disorders. Thus, the material we covered in the social and cultural domain, Chapters 15 through 17, is important for understanding and describing personality disorders. For example, a mutually satisfying sexually intimate relationship with another person involves knowing when sexual behavior is appropriate and expected and when it is inappropriate and unwanted. Problems with intimacy, either staying too distant from others or becoming too intimate too quickly, are frequent features of several personality disorders. An important element of interpersonal skill involves empathy, knowing how the other person is feeling. Most personality disorders involve a deficit in empathy, such that the disordered person either misinterprets others or does not care about the feelings of others. Many disorders involve what might be called poor social skills, such as the schizoid person who stares at people without starting a conversation, or the histrionic person who behaves in an inappropriately flirtatious manner.

Biology can also form a building block for personality disorders. The material covered in the biological domain, Chapters 6 through 8, is thus relevant. Some of the personality disorders have been found to have a genetic component. Others have been studied via physiological components, such as examining the brain structure or function of antisocial persons. There has even been an evolutionary theory proposed to explain the existence of personality disorders (Millon, 2000a).

Most personality texts do not cover personality disorders. We feel, however, that knowing how normal personality works can inform our understanding of how personality can become broken and disordered. Plus, we believe that the concept of personality disorders really ties together all the different components and domains of personality. As such, it is a fitting topic with which to end this book because it applies much of what has come before to an understanding of how the human personality can become disordered.

The Concept of Disorder

Today, a psychological **disorder** is a pattern of behavior or experience that is distressing and painful to the person or those around him or her; that leads to disability or impairment in important life domains (e.g., problems with work, marriage, or relationship difficulties); and that is associated with increased risk for further suffering, loss of function, death, or confinement (American Psychiatric Association, 2013). The idea that something can go wrong with a person's personality has a long history. Some of the earliest writings in medical psychiatry included classifications and descriptions of personality and mental disorders (e.g., Kraeplin, 1913; Kretschmer, 1925). A very early concept derived by French psychiatrist Philippe Pinel was *manie sans delire,* or madness without loss of reason. This was applied to individuals who demonstrated disordered behavior and emotions but who did not lose contact with reality (Morey, 1997). A related concept, popular in the early 1900s, was called "moral insanity," to emphasize that the person did not suffer any impairment of intellect, but rather was impaired in terms of feelings, temperament, or habits. An influential psychiatrist named Kurt Schneider (1958) proposed the term *psychopathic personality* to refer to behavior patterns that caused the person and the community to suffer. Schneider also emphasized statistical rarity, along with behaviors that have an adverse impact on the person and the community in which that person lives. This definition highlights the notion that all forms of personality disorder involve impaired social relationships; other people suffer as much as or more than the person with the disorder.

A disorder is a conceptual entity that, although abstract, is nevertheless useful. It helps guide thinking about the distinction between what is normal and what is abnormal, or pathological. The field of **abnormal psychology** is the study of the various mental disorders, including thought disorders, emotional disorders, and personality disorders. In this chapter, we focus on disorders of personality and the ways in which they affect functioning.

What Is Abnormal?

There are many ways to define **abnormal.** One simple definition is that whatever is different from normal is abnormal. This is a statistical definition in the sense that researchers can statistically determine how often something occurs and, if it is rare, call it abnormal. In this sense, color blindness or polydactyly (having more than 10 fingers) is considered abnormal. Another definition of abnormal is a social definition based on what society tolerates (Shoben, 1957). If we define the term in this sense, behaviors that society deems unacceptable are labeled as abnormal. In this sense, incest and child abuse are both considered abnormal. Both the statistical and the social definitions of abnormality suffer from changing times and changing social or cultural norms (Millon, 2000a, 2000b). Behaviors deemed offensive or socially inappropriate 20 years ago might be acceptable today. For example, 20 or 30 years ago, homosexuality was considered to be both rare and socially unacceptable, a form of abnormal behavior or even a mental illness. Today, homosexuality is not considered abnormal in itself (American Psychiatric Association, 2013) and is protected under civil rights laws in the United States. Thus, the statistical and social definitions of abnormality are always somewhat tentative because society changes.

Psychologists have consequently looked to other ways of identifying what is abnormal in behavior and experience. They have looked within persons, inquiring about subjective feelings, such as anxiety, depression, dissatisfaction, and feelings of loneliness. They have looked at how people think and experience themselves and their worlds. Psychologists have found that some people have disorganized thoughts, disruptive perceptions, or unusual beliefs and attitudes that do not match their circumstances. They have identified ways in which people fail to get along with one another and ways people have trouble living in the community. They have analyzed patterns of behavior that represent ineffective efforts at coping or that put people at higher risk for other problems, behaviors that harm more than help. From a psychological perspective, any of these may be considered abnormal.

Combining all these approaches to abnormality (statistical, social, and psychological), psychologists and psychiatrists have developed the field of **psychopathology,** or the study of mental disorders. The diagnosis of mental disorders is both a scientific discipline and an important part of the clinical work of many psychiatrists and psychologists. Knowing how to define and how to identify a disorder is the first step in devising treatment or in designing research on that disorder.

The *Diagnostic and Statistical Manual of Mental Disorders*

The most widely used system for diagnosing mental disorders, including personality disorders, is the *Diagnostic and Statistical Manual of Mental Disorders,* published by the American Psychiatric Association (APA) and currently in its fifth edition (called the *DSM-5*). The *DSM-5* sets the standards for diagnoses, and its system is the one taught by almost all psychiatry and psychology doctoral training programs, the system that is used in medical record-keeping, and the diagnostic system most insurance companies require for reimbursement purposes.

Because society standards change over time and because new research accumulates, the *DSM* undergoes revision from time to time. The current version—the *DSM-5*—was published in 2013. The APA began working on this revision a decade earlier and appointed various working groups of experts to assist in each broad area of mental disorders. The personality disorders working group consisted of active personality psychologists and psychiatrists. During the decade they worked on the revision for *DSM-5,* the personality disorders working group considered several broad changes to personality disorders that might be incorporated into *DSM-5.*

One change the personality disorders working group considered was to make diagnosis less categorical and more dimensional. The previous edition—*DSM-IV*—was based on a **categorical view** of personality disorders; a person either had the disorder or did not have the disorder. The categorical view held that there is a qualitative break between people who are, for example, antisocial and people who are not. Categorical thinking was applied to all the personality disorders, viewing disorders as distinct and qualitatively different from normal extremes on each personality trait.

In contrast to this categorical view is the **dimensional view** of personality disorders. In the dimensional view, each disorder is seen as a continuum, ranging from normality at one end to severe disability or disturbance at the other. According to this view, people with and without the disorder differ in degree only. For example, part of being antisocial is disregarding the rights of others. But there are degrees to which this disregard can manifest in behavior. For example, some people might simply be aloof and unconcerned about the feelings of others. Farther out on this dimension, a person might lack a desire to help others, being both aloof and uncaring. Even farther out on this dimension is the person who actively hurts or takes advantage of others. And finally, at the greatest extreme of disregard for others is someone like "Monster," the person introduced at the beginning of this chapter.

The dimensional view implies that certain patterns of behavior, in various amounts, comprise each of the personality disorders. It is only at the extreme ends of the dimensions that the person becomes a problem to themselves and to others. Moreover, extremes of different personality traits can combine in ways that create unique forms of disorder. For example, someone who has an obsessive compulsive personality would score extremely high on the five-factor traits of Conscientiousness and Neuroticism. Modern personality theorists (e.g., Costa & Widiger, 1994; Widiger, 2000) argued that the dimensional view provides a more reliable and meaningful way to describe the personality disorders.

In 2012, a year before the *DSM-5* was published, the well-regarded *Journal of Personality* released a special issue dedicated to the latest research on whether a dimensional view of personality disorders was scientifically valid and clinically useful. Every paper in this special issue provided strong support for the dimensional view. For example, Mullins-Sweatt and Lengel (2012) discussed the clinical utility of a five-factor model view on disorders and concluded that such an approach was more efficient to use, easier to communicate, and provided more specific guidance as to treatment. Similarly, Miller (2012) pointed out the many advantages of using the five-factor model to characterize degrees of personality disorders, as opposed to simply concluding that a person does or does not have a disorder. In various ways, and using a variety of data and argument, every article published in this 2012 special issue pointed to the advantages of applying a dimensional view to personality disorders (see especially Trull, 2012; Widiger & Costa, 2012).

As the *DSM-5* revision work progressed, the personality disorders working group considered this and several other changes to the way personality disorders are defined and diagnosed. The top personality psychologists and psychiatrists were involved, many meetings were held, data were collected, public input was solicited and obtained, and many proposals were written and considered. However, to make a long story very short, the final outcome of the revision effort was the decision, on the part of the APA Board of Trustees, to make no changes to the way personality disorders are defined from the fourth to the fifth edition. The *DSM-5* therefore maintains the categorical model of personality disorders and retains the same criteria for 10 specific personality disorders that were described in the previous edition. The *DSM-5* does contain a section—Section III—that describes which issues need further research. It is in this section—essentially an appendix to the *DSM-5*—where the dimensional model of personality disorders is detailed and a call for further research on the utility of viewing personality disorders as dimensions rather than distinct categories is issued. Later in this chapter, cover the 10 personality disorders that are included in the *DSM-5,* but first we consider the general notion of "disorder."

What Is a Personality Disorder?

A **personality disorder** is an enduring pattern of experience and behavior that differs greatly from the expectations of the individual's culture (*DSM-5*). As discussed in Chapter 3, traits are patterns of experiencing, thinking about, and interacting with oneself and the world. Traits are observed in a wide range of social and personal situations. For example, a person who is high on Conscientiousness is hardworking and persevering. If a trait becomes maladaptive and inflexible and causes significant impairment or distress, then it is considered to be a personality disorder. For example, if someone were so conscientious that he or she checked the locks on the door 10 times each night and checked every appliance in the house 5 times before leaving in the morning, then we might consider the possibility of a disorder.

The essential features of a personality disorder, according to the *DSM-5,* are presented in Table 19.1. A personality disorder is usually manifest in more than one of the following areas: in how people think, in how they feel, in how they get along with others, or in their ability to control their own behavior. The pattern is rigid and is displayed across a variety of situations, leading to distress or problems in important areas in life, such as at work or in relationships. For example, an overly conscientious man might drive his wife crazy with his repeated checking the household appliances. The pattern of behavior that defines a particular personality disorder typically has a long history in the person's life and can often be traced back to manifestations in adolescence or even childhood. To be classed as a personality disorder, the pattern must not result from drug abuse, medication, or a medical condition, such as head trauma.

Culture, Age, and Gender: The Effect of Context

A person's social, cultural, and ethnic background also must be taken into account whenever there is a question about personality disorders. Immigrants, for example, often have problems fitting into a new culture. Persons who originate in a different culture often have customs, habits, expressions, and values that are at odds with, or that create social problems within, a new culture. For example, the U.S. culture is very individualistic, and

Table 19.1 General Criteria for Personality Disorders

1. A personality disorder is an enduring pattern of inner experience and behavior that deviates markedly from the expectations of the individual's culture. This pattern is manifest in two or more of the following areas:
   - Cognition (i.e., ways of perceiving and interpreting the self, others, and events)
   - Affectivity (i.e., the range, intensity, and appropriateness of emotional responses)
   - Interpersonal functioning
   - Impulse control
2. The enduring pattern is inflexible and pervasive across a broad range of personal and social situations.
3. The enduring pattern leads to clinically significant distress or impairment in social, occupational, or other important areas of functioning.
4. The pattern is stable and of long duration, and its onset can be traced back to adolescence or early adulthood.
5. The enduring pattern is not better accounted for as a manifestation or consequence of another mental disorder.
6. The enduring pattern is not due to the direct physiological effects of a substance (e.g., a drug of abuse, a medication) or a general medical condition, such as head trauma.

Source: American Psychiatric Association, 2013.

it values and rewards individuals for standing out from the crowd. To societies that are more collectivistic and value fitting in with the group, efforts to stand out from the crowd might be interpreted as self-centered and individualistic in an unwanted sense. Indeed, the U.S. culture has been called a narcissistic culture; therefore, efforts to draw attention to the self are not socially abnormal in this society.

Before judging that a behavior is a symptom of a personality disorder, we must first become familiar with a person's cultural background, especially if it is different from the majority culture. A study of Third World immigrants to Norway (Sam, 1994) found that many exhibited adjustment problems that might have appeared to be personality disorders. Many young male immigrants, for example, exhibited antisocial behaviors. These behaviors tended to diminish as the immigrants acculturated to their new social environment.

Age also is relevant to judgments about personality disorder. Adolescents, for example, often go through periods of instability that may include identity crises (see Chapter 14), a symptom that is often associated with certain personality disorders. Most adolescents experiment with various identities yet do not have a personality disorder. For this reason, the American Psychiatric Association (1994) cautions against diagnosing personality disorders in persons under age 18. Also, adults who undergo severe loss, such as the death of a spouse or the loss of a job, sometimes undergo periods of instability or impulsive behavior that may look like a personality disorder. For example, a person who loses his job might do some impulsive act, like take off on a cross-country trip without a firm destination, which normally he would never do. So we need to consider the context when evaluating a behavior as a sign of disorder. A person's age and life circumstances must be considered to be sure that the person is not simply going through a phase or reacting to some extreme life event.

Finally, gender is another context in which to frame our understanding of personality disorders. Certain disorders, such as the antisocial personality disorder, are diagnosed much more frequently in men than women. Other personality disorders are diagnosed more frequently in women than men. These gender differences may reflect underlying gender differences in how people cope. For example, in a study of more than 2,000 individuals, Huselid and Cooper (1994) found that males exhibit externalizing problems, such as fighting and vandalism, whereas females tend to exhibit relatively more internalizing problems, such as depression and self-harm. Similar findings were obtained by Kavanagh and Hops (1994). These differences in how men and women cope with problems most likely contribute to gender differences in the behaviors associated with the personality disorders. Psychologists need to be careful not to look for evidence of certain kinds of disorders just because of a person's gender.

Exercise

In this chapter, you will read about specific personality disorders. For each, try to think of examples of how culture, gender, or age might influence whether a person's behavior is seen as evidence of a disorder. For example, are persons from low socioeconomic groups likely to be seen by others as having particular disorders? How does this correspond to the topic of stereotypes and prejudice? How does this fit with the use of "profiles" by police and other law enforcement agencies?

Specific Personality Disorders

The following sections describe specific personality disorders, including the criteria for diagnosing someone with each disorder. The 10 disorders naturally cluster in three categories, and we use a descriptive title for each cluster to capture the characteristics shared across the disorders in each cluster. We also focus this material by giving some real-life examples of each personality disorder.

The Erratic Cluster: Ways of Being Unpredictable, Violent, or Emotional

Persons who are diagnosed with disorders belonging to the erratic group tend to have trouble with emotional control and to have specific difficulties getting along with others. People with disorders in this cluster are unpredictable, their behavior is not guided by social norms or expectations that most people bring to social interaction. This group consists of four disorders: *antisocial, borderline, histrionic,* and *narcissistic* personality disorders.

Antisocial Personality Disorder

The antisocial person shows a general disregard for others and cares very little about the rights, feelings, or happiness of other people. The antisocial person has also been referred to as a sociopath or a psychopath (Zuckerman, 1991a), though we cover the distinction between sociopath and psychopath below. Adults with antisocial disorder typically had a childhood that was fraught with behavioral problems. Such early childhood behavioral problems generally take the form of violating the rights of others (such as minor thefts) and breaking age-related social norms (such as smoking at an early age or fighting with other children). Other common childhood behavioral problems include behaving aggressively or cruelly toward animals, threatening and intimidating younger children, stealing or destroying property, lying, and breaking rules. Behavioral problems in childhood are often first noticed in school, but such children also come to the attention of the police and truant officers. Sometimes even very young children, during an argument with another child, use a weapon that can cause serious physical harm, such as a baseball bat or a knife.

Once childhood behavioral problems become an established pattern, the possibility of an **antisocial personality disorder** becomes more likely (American Psychiatric Association, 1994). As a child with behavioral problems grows up, the problems tend to worsen as the child develops physical strength, cognitive power, and sexual maturity. Minor problems, such as lying, arguing, and petty theft, evolve into more serious ones, such as breaking and entering, assault, and grand theft. Severe aggression, such as rape or cruelty to a mugging victim, might also follow. Some children with these behavioral problems rapidly develop to a level of dangerous and even sadistic behavior. For example, we sometimes hear in the news about preteen children (usually male) who murder other children in cold blood and without remorse. In one study, children who grew into severe delinquency as teenagers were already identifiable by kindergarten teachers' ratings of impulsiveness and antisocial behavior at age 5 (Tremblay et al., 1994). Studies of children ages 6–13 also find that some children exhibit a syndrome of antisocial behaviors, including impulsivity, behavioral problems, callous social attitudes, and lack of feelings for others (Frick et al., 1994).

If a child exhibits no signs of conduct problems by age 16, it is unlikely that he or she will develop an antisocial personality as an adult. Moreover, even among children *with* conduct problems, the majority simply grow out of them by early adulthood

(American Psychiatric Association, 1994). However, a percentage of children with conduct problems go on to develop full-blown antisocial personality disorder in adulthood. Children with earlier-onset conduct problems (e.g., by age 6 or 7) are much more likely to grow into an antisocial personality disorder as an adult than are children who displayed a few conduct problems in high school (Laub & Lauritsen, 1994).

The antisocial adult continues with the same sorts of conduct problems started in childhood, but on a much grander scale. The term *antisocial* implies that the person has a *lack of concern for social norms.* Antisocial persons have very little respect for laws and may repeatedly engage in acts that are grounds for arrest, such as harassing others, fighting, destroying property, and stealing. "Cold-hearted" is a good description of their interactions with others. Antisocial persons may manipulate and deceive others to gain rewards or pleasure (e.g., money, power, social advantage, or sex).

Repeated lying is another feature of the antisocial personality. The pattern of lying starts early in life with minor deceptions and grows into a pattern of deceitfulness. Lying becomes a common part of social interaction for the antisocial personality. Some make a living conning others out of money. "Getting over" on people, especially authorities, through deception may even be pleasurable to the antisocial person.

Another common characteristic of the antisocial personality is *impulsivity,* which is manifest as a failure to plan ahead. The antisocial person might start a chain of behavior without a clear plan or sequence in mind: For example, the person might enter a gas station and decide on the spot to rob the attendant, even though he or she has not planned a getaway. Prisoners with antisocial personalities often complain that their lack of planning led to their arrest, and they are often more remorseful about getting caught than about committing the crime.

A more common form of impulsivity is to simply make everyday decisions without much forethought or without considering consequences. For example, an antisocial man might leave his wife and baby for several days without calling to say where he is. This often results in trouble in relationships and in employment settings. Generally, antisocial persons change jobs often, change relationships often, and move often. This is one reason why the question "How long have you lived at this address" appears on many job applications.

Antisocial persons also tend to be *easily irritated* and to respond to even minor frustrations with aggression. Antisocial persons tend to be *assaultive,* particularly to those around them, such as spouses or children. Fights and physical attacks are common.

Application

Kenneth Lay was the founder and former CEO of Enron, a large energy company that went bankrupt in 2001, creating $60 billion in investment losses and wiping out $2.1 billion in the pension plan of the Enron employees. Lay was charged with 11 counts of conspiracy, insider trading, securities fraud, and lying to auditors. Prosecutors charged that he knew his company was in deep trouble and was aware of fraudulent accounting practices and that he hid losses from investors until the company collapsed. During this time, Lay began dumping his own stock before Enron collapsed, even while encouraging others, including company workers, to buy more. During his trial, Lay claimed he never knew of the accounting fraud. He portrayed himself as a trusting man who was let down by corrupt staff, especially former finance chief

Andrew Fastow, who served over five years in prison for his role in the Enron collapse. At times during his trial, Lay became combative and hostile, insisting that others were responsible. At other times he claimed that the collapse of Enron was the most painful experience of his life, even going so far as to say the experience was equivalent to the death of a loved one. In 2006, he was convicted and might have served up to 45 years in jail if he had not died suddenly of a heart attack before sentencing took place.

Kenneth Lay exhibited several characteristics consistent with the antisocial personality and psychopathy. He was a charming person who could convince others to buy his company's stock, even though he was secretly selling his own shares. Self-assured and confident, he used his personal charisma to dupe others out of billions of dollars. He repeatedly tried to shift the blame for his company's collapse onto others. When faced with evidence of his responsibility, he was easily irritated on the witness stand. He expressed no remorse for destroying the life savings of thousands of Enron workers. And finally, he tried to play the "poor me" card to garner sympathy from the jury by pointing out all the pain and suffering he had endured.

Ron Edmonds/AP Images

Recklessness is another characteristic, with antisocial persons showing little regard for their own safety and that of others. Driving while intoxicated or speeding is indicative of recklessness, as is having unprotected sex with multiple partners.

Irresponsibility is another key feature of the antisocial personality. Antisocial persons get bored easily and find monotony or routine to be unpleasant. An antisocial person may, for example, decide on the spur of the moment to abandon his or her job, with no plan for getting another right away. Repeated unexplained absences from work are a common sign of the antisocial character. Irresponsibility in financial matters is also common, with the antisocial person often running up unpaid debts, or borrowing money from one person to pay a debt owed to another, staying one step ahead of the bill collector. Such a person may squander the money needed to feed his or her children or gamble away the money needed to buy his kids new clothes and shoes.

Lack of remorse and guilt feelings and indifference to the suffering of others are the hallmarks of the antisocial mind. The antisocial person can be ruthless, without normal levels of human compassion, charity, or social concern. See A Closer Look for current theories and research on how people become antisocial and the psychological forces that keep them that way. Table 19.2 summarizes the key characteristics of the antisocial personality disorder. Also included are typical beliefs or thoughts that someone with this disorder might have.

A Closer Look

Theories of the Psychopathic Mind

Here we compare two theories about the origins of psychopathy: a biological explanation and a social learning explanation. Many psychologists have argued that psychopathy is caused by a biological deficit or abnormality (e.g., Cleckley, 1988; Fowles, 1980; Gray, 1987a, 1987b). Research along these lines has focused on the idea that psychopaths are deficient in their ability to experience fear (Lykken, 1982). Being deficient in fear would help explain why psychopaths do not learn as well from punishment as from reward (Newman, 1987). Psychopaths may pursue a career in crime and lawlessness because, in part, they are simply not afraid of the punishment because they are insensitive to fear.

The theory of Jeffrey Gray (1990) has been influential on a number of researchers looking for a biological explanation of psychopathy. Recall from Chapter 7 that Gray proposed a system in the brain that is responsible for inhibiting behavior. The behavioral inhibition system (BIS) acts as a psychological brake, responsible for interrupting ongoing behavior when cues of punishment are present. According to Gray, the BIS is the part of the brain that is especially sensitive to signals of punishment coming from the environment. People who sense that a punishment is likely to occur typically stop what they are doing and look for ways to avoid the punishment.

Researchers are beginning to examine the emotional lives of psychopaths, especially with respect to their experience of fear and its related emotion—anxiety. Psychologist Chris Patrick and his colleagues are following an interesting line of research. One study examined a group of prisoners, all of whom were convicted of sexual offenses (Patrick, Bradley, & Lang, 1993). Even in this group of severe offenders, some individuals were more psychopathic than others, as measured by Hare's Psychopathy Checklist (Hare, Hart, & Harpur, 1991). Patrick and his colleagues had the

prisoners look at unpleasant pictures (e.g., injured people, threatening animals) to try to bring about feelings of anxiety. While they were looking at the pictures, the prisoners were startled by random bursts of a loud noise. People typically blink their eyes when they are startled by a loud noise. Moreover, a person who is in an anxious or fearful state when startled will blink faster and harder than a person in a normal emotional state. This means that eye-blink speed when startled may be an objective physiological measure of how anxious or fearful a person is feeling. That is, the **eye-blink startle method** may allow researchers to measure how anxious persons are without actually having to ask them.

The results from this study of prisoners showed that the more psychopathic offenders displayed *less* of the eye-blink effect when startled, indicating that they were experiencing relatively *less* anxiety to the same unpleasant pictures. However, when *asked* about how distressing the pictures were, both the psychopaths and the nonpsychopaths reported that the pictures were distressing. Overall, these results suggest that psychopaths will say that they are feeling anxious or distressed, yet direct nervous system measures suggest that they are actually *experiencing* less anxiety than nonpsychopaths in the same situation.

In another study, Patrick, Cuthbert, and Lang (1994) again used a group of prisoners who differed from each other in terms of antisocial behaviors. This time, the prisoners were asked to imagine fearful scenes such as having to undergo an operation. The low- and high-antisocial prisoners did

not differ in terms of their self-reports of fear and anxiety—all reported more of these emotions in response to the fear images than in response to neutral images such as walking across the yard. Large differences, however, were found in their *physiological* responses to the fear images. The less antisocial prisoners were more aroused by the fear imagery than were the antisocial subjects. In other words, the antisocial prisoners displayed a deficit in fear responding when their fear responses were assessed with physiological measures, which are less susceptible to being faked than the self-report measures. These results are consistent with the idea that the psychopath is deficient in the ability to experience fear and anxiety. In a review of the literature, Patrick (1994) argued that the core problem with psychopaths is a deficit in the fear response. As a consequence, the psychopath is not motivated to interrupt his or her ongoing behavior to avoid punishment or other unpleasant consequences.

Other researchers have deemphasized biological explanations for psychopathy and argue instead that the emotional unresponsiveness of the psychopath is learned (Levenson, Kiehl, & Fitzpatrick, 1995). The observed fearlessness of the

This is the kind of image used in the study by psychologist Chris Patrick, who found that psychopaths did not exhibit the normal fear response to such threatening stimuli.

Thomas Duerrenberger/Shutterstock.com

psychopath may be the result of a desensitization process. If a person is repeatedly exposed to violence or other antisocial behavior (such as childhood abuse or gang activities), he or she may become desensitized to such behaviors. That is, the callous disregard for others—the hallmark of psychopathy—may result from desensitization, a well-known form of learning. A prospective study of more than 400 victims of childhood abuse found that, compared with a control group, the abused children had significantly higher rates of psychopathy 20 years later (Luntz & Widom, 1994). By being victims of abuse, the argument goes, people learn that abusing others is a means of achieving power and control and obtaining what they want. Many psychopaths are motivated by interpersonal dominance and appear to enjoy having power over others.

This can sometimes be seen in board meetings of corporations, in police stations, in politics, and wherever else one person has an opportunity to bully others. The point of this research, however, is that people who grow up to be bullies were themselves frequently bullied and abused as children.

Levenson (1992) has used results such as these to argue for a social learning model of psychopathy. He holds that at some point people decide to engage in antisocial behavior because they have learned from observing others that this is one way to get what they want.

Psychologists are currently debating the relative merits of viewing psychopathy as biological or as learned. Whatever the cause of psychopathy, the frequency and severity of antisocial behaviors almost always decrease as a person ages. It has been said

that the best therapy for the psychopath is to grow older while in prison. The incidence of antisocial behaviors dramatically decreases in persons age 40 and older (*DSM-5*). It has been widely known that, among criminals, those who make it to their fourth decade are much less likely to be rearrested for antisocial acts than are those in their twenties or thirties. For example, a study of 809 male prison inmates aged 16–69 found that deviant social behaviors, impulsivity, and antisocial acts were much less prevalent in the older prisoners (Harpur & Hare, 1994). There was less of an age decline in antisocial beliefs and callous social attitudes. Thus, although older psychopaths still don't care much about other people or their feelings, they nevertheless are less likely to impulsively act out these beliefs or to engage in actual antisocial behaviors.

Table 19.2   Characteristics of Persons with Antisocial Personality Disorder

Fails to conform to social norms, for example, breaks the law
Repeated lying or conning others for pleasure or profit
Impulsivity
Irritable and aggressive, for example, frequent fights
Reckless disregard for safety of others and self
Irresponsible, for example, truant from school, cannot hold a job
Lack of remorse, for example, indifferent to pain of others, rationalizes having hurt or mistreated others

Typical Thoughts Associated with the Antisocial Personality
"Laws don't apply to me."
"I'll say whatever it takes to get what I want."
"I think I'll skip work today and go to the racetrack."
"That guy I beat up deserved every bit of it."
"She had it coming, she asked for it . . ."
"I'm the one you should feel sorry for here . . ."

A concept related to antisocial personality disorder is **psychopathy,** a term coined in the middle of the twentieth century (Cleckley, 1941) to describe people who are superficially charming and intelligent, but are also deceitful; unable to feel remorse or care for others; impulsive; and lacking in shame, guilt, and fear. Psychopathy and antisocial personality are similar notions, but there are important distinctions so they should not be used interchangeably. The antisocial personality designation places emphasis on *observable behaviors,* such as chronic lying, repeated criminal behavior, and conflicts with authority. The psychopathy designation places emphasis on more *subjective characteristics,* such as the incapacity to feel guilt, a high degree of superficial charm, or having callous social attitudes. The distinction can get blurred because the *DSM*-5 also includes a subjective criterion, "lack of remorse," in its definition of antisocial personality disorder. However, the concept of psychopathy is mainly a research construct, pioneered by the scientific work of psychologist Robert Hare. He developed a measure of the construct called the Psychopathy Checklist, which contains two major clusters of symptoms. One cluster refers to emotional and interpersonal traits, such as incapacity for fear, superficial charm, lack of empathy and care for others, being egocentric, and having callous social attitudes and shallow emotions. The second cluster assesses the social deviance associated with an antisocial lifestyle, such as displaying poor self-control, possessing a high need for excitement, and having early and chronic behavioral problems. The major distinction between psychopathy and antisocial personality disorder mainly lies in the first cluster of emotional and interpersonal traits that define psychopathy. Consequently, most extreme psychopaths would meet criteria for a diagnosis of antisocial personality disorder, but not all people with antisocial personality disorder are psychopaths (if they don't have the subjective characteristics of superficial charm, egocentricity, lack of empathy, and shallow emotions).

One interesting concept is the notion of the "successful" psychopath (Smith, Watts, & Lilienfeld, 2014). Certainly there are some features of psychopathy that may be adaptive in some circumstances, such as interpersonal charm and charisma, fearlessness, and a willingness to take risks. Some psychologists have speculated that these features of psychopathy may facilitate success in certain professions, such as financial consulting, politics, and contact sports. A recent review of research on the "successful" psychopath (Lillenfeld, Watts, & Smith, 2015) concludes that it is a controversial and elusive concept, fought with alternative interpretations, and requires additional research to determine if a positive manifestation of psychopathy can exist without the truly maladaptive and negative elements.

Exercise?

For the next week, read through at least one online news source each day. Look for stories on persons who might be examples of the antisocial personality disorder, for example, white-collar criminals or con artists. Look for background information on the person, and bring it in for discussion. Look for evidence from the person's life and actual behaviors that match up with the characteristics of the antisocial personality listed in Table 19.2.

When evaluating the antisocial personality profile, it is good to keep in mind the social and environmental contexts in which some people live. Psychologists have expressed concern that the *antisocial* label is sometimes applied to people who live in settings where socially undesirable behaviors (such as fighting) are viewed as protective. For example, in a high-crime area, some of the antisocial attitudes may safeguard people against being victimized. Thus, the term *antisocial* should be used only when the behavior pattern is indicative of dysfunction and is not simply a response to the immediate social context. The economic and social contexts must be taken into account when deciding whether undesirable behaviors are signs of dysfunction.

A Closer Look   Fatal Attraction

The thriller *Fatal Attraction* stars Michael Douglas and Glenn Close. Douglas plays Dan, a rich and powerful lawyer who is happily married to a beautiful woman. The couple has a wonderful daughter whom they both love. At a business dinner, Dan meets Glenn Close's character, Alex, who is an attractive, intriguing, single woman who catches Dan's eye. Dan is with his wife, however, and nothing happens with Alex at the dinner. A few weeks later, Dan is on a business trip without his wife one weekend and he sees Alex again. They flirt for some time, and there is definitely some attraction between them. Dan does not know at this point, but it is a fatal attraction. During the weekend, Dan and Alex have sex several times, and they appear to enjoy each other very much. In one scene, Dan and Alex are together in bed after sex, and the camera turns to a pot of coffee that is boiling on the stove. This is a subtle visual hint of the dangerous consequences about to boil over from their adulterous affair.

After this weekend infidelity, Dan returns to his wife. Alex is upset that Dan just seems to want to forget about her. She feels she loves him, yet she hates him at the same time for leaving her. Over the next several weeks, she calls Dan at his home and even stalks him on several occasions. Finally, she confronts Dan and tells him she is pregnant with his baby and feels he should leave his

wife for her. Dan, however, tells Alex to get an abortion and to forget about his ever leaving his wife. He makes it clear that he does not want to be a part of her life. She then alternates between extreme love and extreme hate for him. She wants Dan for herself and decides that the best way to get him is to destroy what is standing between her and Dan, which is his wife and child. The movie becomes a thriller when Alex begins terrorizing Dan and his family.

When this movie first came out, many reviewers referred to the Alex character incorrectly as a "psycho lover" or as "a nutcase." In fact, Alex exhibits several of the symptoms of borderline personality disorder. She exhibits the incredible relationship difficulties that are the hallmark of the borderline style. She vacillates between wanting to have and then wanting to destroy those she loves. She balances on the edge between destroying herself and harming those who are causing her emotional troubles. She becomes progressively angrier during the movie, and we don't know if she will direct this anger toward harming herself or harming others. All of this is triggered by feelings of abandonment, another hallmark of the borderline character. Being left out, left behind, or abandoned is a critical issue for persons with this disorder. Because they often define themselves

solely in terms of their relationships ("I'm nothing without you"), they fear losing those relationships. However, because of their strong and unpredictable emotions, their relationships tend to be unstable and unsatisfying and end prematurely. They bring about that which they fear the most.

In the movie Fatal Attraction, *Glenn Close plays the character Alex, who has many of the characteristics of borderline personality disorder. Entertainment Pictures/Alamy Stock Photo*

Borderline Personality Disorder

The lives of persons with **borderline personality disorder** are marked by *instability*. Their relationships are unstable, their behavior is unstable, their emotions are unstable, and even their images of themselves are unstable. Let's consider each of these, starting with relationships.

The relationships of borderline individuals tend to be intense, emotional, and potentially violent. They suffer from strong fears of abandonment. If such persons sense separation or rejection in an important relationship, profound changes in their self-image and in how they behave may result, such as becoming very angry at other people. Borderline individuals show marked difficulties in their relationships. Sometimes, in their efforts to manipulate people back into their relationships, they engage in *self-mutilating behavior* (burning or cutting themselves) or suicide attempts. A study of 84 hospital patients with a diagnosis of borderline personality disorder found that 72 percent had a history of attempting suicide (Soloff et al., 1994). In fact, among this sample, the average borderline patient had attempted suicide on at least three occasions. The relationships of borderline individuals are unpredictable and intense. They may go from idealizing the other to ridiculing and demeaning the other. They are prone to sudden shifts in their views of relationships, behaving at one time in a caring manner and at another time in a punishing and cruel manner. They may go from being submissive to being an avenger for past wrongs. The movie *Fatal Attraction* contains a character with several features of the borderline personality disorder. See A Closer Look for a discussion of how this personality disorder was portrayed in classic Oscar-nominated movie.

Borderline persons also have *shifting views of themselves.* Their values and goals are shallow and change easily. They base their views more on their impressions than facts. At times, they view themselves as evil or worthless. Self-harming acts can occur and may increase when others threaten to leave them.

Strong emotions are common in the borderline personality, including panic, anger, and despair. Mostly, these emotions are caused by interpersonal events, especially abandonment or neglect. When stressed by others, the borderline person may lash out, becoming bitter, sarcastic, or aggressive. Periods of anger are often followed by shame, guilt, and feelings of being evil or bad. Borderline persons often complain of feeling empty. They also have a way of undermining their own best efforts, such as dropping out of a training program just before finishing or destroying a caring relationship just when it starts going smoothly.

The borderline person is characterized by huge vacillations in both mood and feelings about the self and others. People with borderline personality disorder can shift quickly from loving another to hating that same person. They are very demanding on their friends, relatives, lovers, and therapists. They are also manipulative toward others. For example, they may threaten suicide or self-harm when they don't get their way.

Table 19.3 lists the major features of the borderline personality disorder, along with examples of beliefs and thoughts that persons with this disorder might commonly have. Persons with borderline personality disorder, compared with those without, have a higher incidence rate of childhood physical or sexual abuse, neglect, or early parental loss. Many researchers believe that borderline disorder is caused by an early loss of love from parents, as may happen in parental death, abuse, severe neglect, or parental drug or alcohol abuse (Millon et al., 2000). Early loss may affect a child's capacity to form relationships. Children in such circumstances may come to believe that others are not to be trusted. Although borderline persons have difficulty with relationships, they may form

Table 19.3 Characteristics of Borderline Personality Disorder

Instability of relationships, emotions, and self-image
Fears of abandonment
Aggressiveness
Proneness to self-harm
Strong emotions

Typical Thoughts or Beliefs Associated with the Borderline Personality
"I'm nothing without you."
"I'll just die if you leave me."
"If you go, I'll kill myself."
"I hate you, I hate you, I HATE YOU."
"I love you so much that I'll do anything or be anything for you."
"I feel empty inside, as if I don't know who I am."

stable relationships if given enough structure and support. If they find someone who is accepting and stable, who is very patient, who meets their expectations for commitment, and who is caring and can diffuse trouble as it occurs, then the borderline personality may experience a satisfying relationship.

Histrionic Personality Disorder

The hallmarks of **histrionic personality disorder** are *excessive attention seeking* and *emotionality.* Often such persons are overly dramatic, preferring to be the center of attention. They may appear charming or even flirtatious. Many are inappropriately seductive or provocative. And this *sexually provocative* behavior is often undirected and occurs in inappropriate settings, such as in professional settings. Physical appearance is often very important to histrionic persons, and they work to impress others and obtain compliments. Often, however, they overdo it and appear gaudy or flamboyant.

Histrionic individuals express their opinions frequently and dramatically. However, their *opinions are shallow* and easily changed. Such a person may say, for example, that some political official is a great and wonderful leader yet be unable to give any supporting details or actual examples of leadership. Such persons prefer impressions to facts (Millon et al., 2000). They may *display strong emotions in public,* sometimes to the embarrassment of friends and family. They may throw temper tantrums over minor frustrations or cry uncontrollably over a sentimental little event. To others, their emotions appear insincere and exaggerated, to the point of being theatrical. Histrionic individuals are also highly *suggestible.* Because their opinions are not based on facts, they can be easily swayed.

Socially, histrionic individuals are difficult to get along with, due to their *excessive need for attention.* They may become upset when not given the attention they think they deserve. Such persons may use self-harm to get attention from others. Their seductiveness may put them at risk for sexual victimization. They crave excitement and novelty, and although they may start relationships or projects with great enthusiasm, their interest does not last long. They may forgo long-term gains to make way for short-term excitement. Histrionic traits are maladaptive because they can interfere with relationships and cause difficulties with the individual being a productive member of society.

Table 19.4 lists the main characteristics of histrionic personality disorder, along with typical beliefs and thoughts persons with this disorder might have. As with all personality disorder criteria, the standards for appropriate behavior differ greatly among cultures, generations, and genders. Therefore, we must ask whether specific behaviors

Table 19.4 Characteristics of Histrionic Personality Disorder

Excessive attention seeking
Excessive and strong emotions
Sexual provocativeness
Shallow opinions
Suggestibility
Strong need for attention

Typical Thoughts or Beliefs Associated with the Histrionic Personality
"Hey, look at me!"
"I am happiest when I am the center of attention."
"Boredom is the pits."
"I usually go with my intuition; I don't have to think things through."
"I can amuse, impress, or entertain anyone, mainly because I am so interesting and exciting."
"If I feel like doing something, I go ahead and do it."

Application

A case of histrionic personality disorder. Roxann was a student who also worked in the evenings as a dancer at an adult club. She would tell people that this was temporary and that she was different from the other women who worked there. She readily admitted, however, that the job met her two most important needs: money and attention, "two things I cannot live without." Roxann decided to take some psychology courses for self-improvement. She typically showed up to classes dressed to kill and seemed out of place even among students her own age. Once she went to her professor's office yet did not seem to have any direct questions to discuss. Instead, she seemed just to want to talk about herself and her extracurricular job. After this meeting, she was overheard telling other students that she was on a first-name basis with her professor and that he was actually her good friend. In class, she frequently behaved in ways that drew attention to herself, such as sighing loudly when the professor made a point, or blurting out answers to rhetorical questions. Toward the end of the course, Roxann quit going to class and missed the final exam. She e-mailed the professor, saying that she had been experiencing a debilitating condition and frequently had to lie down to avoid fainting. She said she had been to several doctors, but none were able to find any medical basis for her condition. The professor never heard from her again.

cause social impairment or distress before concluding that those behaviors are signs or symptoms of histrionic personality disorder. For example, behavior that is considered seductive in one culture may be viewed as acceptable behavior in another. A woman from the southern coast of Italy may appear flirtatious in the United States, when, in fact, in her culture people are much more friendly and at ease with each other, and teasing flirtation is a common form of interaction. Consider also the culture of gender. The expression of histrionic personality disorder may depend on gender stereotypes. A male with this personality may behave in a "hyper-macho" fashion and attempt to be the center of attention by boasting of his skills in seduction or how much influence and power he has in his workplace. A woman with the histrionic style may express it with hyperfemininity, seeking to be the center of attention by adorning herself with bright, sexy clothes and wearing lots of gaudy accessories and makeup.

Narcissistic Personality Disorder

The calling cards of **narcissistic personality disorder** are a strong *need to be admired,* a strong sense of *self-importance,* and a *lack of insight into other people's feelings.* Narcissists see themselves in a very favorable light, inflating their accomplishments and undervaluing the work of others. Narcissists daydream about prosperity, victory, influence, adoration from others, and power. They routinely expect adulation from others, believing that homage is generally long overdue. They exhibit feelings of *entitlement,* believing that they should receive special privileges and respect, even though they have done nothing in particular to earn that special treatment.

A sense of *superiority* also pervades the narcissistic personality. They feel that they are special and should associate only with others who are similarly unique or gifted. Such a person may insist on having the best lawyer or attending the best university, viewing him- or herself as unique, different from, and better than everyone else.

People with narcissistic disorder expect a lot from those around them. They must receive regular praise from others and devoted admiration from those close to them. Many narcissistic persons prefer as friends those who are socially weak or unpopular so that they will not compete with the narcissists for attention. The **narcissistic paradox** is that, although narcissists appear to have high self-esteem, their grandiose self-esteem is actually quite fragile. That is, even though they appear self-confident and strong, they need constant admiration and recognition and praise from others. You might think that someone with truly high self-esteem would not have such an unreasonable need for praise and admiration from others. When narcissists show up at a party, they expect to be welcomed with great fanfare. When they go to a restaurant or store, they assume that waiters or clerks will rush to their attention. Narcissists thus depend on others to validate their self-importance.

To say that narcissists' self-esteem is vulnerable does not mean that they are covering up low self-esteem, they have plenty of self-esteem. Rather, they are exquisitely sensitive to criticism, they can fly into a rage when they don't get the praise or recognition that they think they deserve. Their self-esteem is real; narcissists fully expect others to recognize how special, unique, and superior they are, even in the absence of any objective supportive evidence. Their vulnerability is exhibited as a thin-skinned, bristling kind of sensitivity, similar to childish temper tantrums and pouting.

Further making the narcissist socially difficult is an *inability to recognize the needs or desires of others*. In conversation, they tend to talk mostly about themselves—"I" this and "my" that. Narcissists use first-person pronouns (*I, me, mine*) more frequently in everyday conversation than does the average person (Raskin & Shaw, 1987). Psychologists Richard Robins and Oliver John (1997) found that persons scoring high on a narcissism questionnaire evaluate their performances much more positively than those performances are evaluated by others, demonstrating the self-enhancement component of narcissism.

A final social difficulty that creates problems for narcissists is the ease with which they become *envious of others*. When hearing of the success or accomplishment of acquaintances, narcissists may disparage that achievement. They may feel that they deserve the success more than the persons who worked to attain it. Narcissists may disdain others' accomplishments, particularly in public. A veneer of snobbery may hide strong feelings of envy and rage over the successes of others.

Table 19.5 lists the main characteristics of the narcissistic personality disorder, along with examples of some typical beliefs and thoughts persons with this disorder might have. Narcissists sometimes reach positions of high achievement, due primarily to their self-confidence and ambition. Nevertheless, their interpersonal lives are usually fraught with the problems that come with feelings of entitlement, an excessive need for praise and recognition, and an impaired recognition of others' needs. They have difficulty maintaining intimate relationships.

Exercise

Everyone knows someone who is narcissistic, maybe not to the point of a disorder, but nevertheless with several of the characteristics. Think of the most narcissistic person you know. List five of his or her characteristics or behaviors that make you think that this person is a narcissist. How do the acts and characteristics you have listed fit with the symptoms of the narcissistic personality disorder?

Table 19.5 Characteristics of Narcissistic Personality Disorder

Need to be admired
Strong sense of self-importance
Lack of insight into other people's feelings and needs
Sense of entitlement
Sense of superiority
Self-esteem that is strong but paradoxically fragile
Envy of others

Typical Thoughts or Beliefs Associated with the Narcissistic Personality
"I'm special and deserve special treatment."
"The typical rules don't apply to me."
"If others don't give me the praise and recognition I deserve, they should be punished."
"Other people should do my bidding."
"Who are *you* to criticize *me*?"
"I have every reason to expect that I will get the best that life has to offer."

The Eccentric Cluster: Ways of Being Different

A second cluster of personality disorders contains traits that make people ill at ease socially. Other people often see them as odd and unusual. Most of the oddness in these disorders has to do with how the person interacts with others. People with schizoid disorder have no interest in others; people with schizotypal disorder are extremely uncomfortable with others; and people with paranoid personality disorder are suspicious of others. Disorders in this cluster are associated with interpersonal problems, trouble relating to others. They can also impact job performance, or limit the kinds of work a person can do.

   Schizoid and **schizotypal personality disorders** both share their root with the term "schizophrenia," and both of these personality disorders are closely tied to the history of this diagnostic category. *Schizophrenia* literally means cutting the mind off (schism) from itself and from reality. Schizophrenia is a serious mental illness that involves hallucinations, delusions, and perceptual aberrations. The personality disorders of schizoid and schizotypal exhibit some low-grade, non-psychotic symptoms of schizophrenia. For example, the schizotype is eccentric and is interested in odd and unusual beliefs, whereas the schizoid displays extreme social apathy. In the case of schizotypal disorders, persons are likely to possess the genotype that makes them vulnerable to schizophrenia. A large proportion of the family members of persons with schizophrenia exhibit odd and unusual behaviors that would contribute to a diagnosis of schizotypal personality disorder.

Schizoid Personality Disorder

The schizoid personality is *split off* (schism), *or detached, from normal social relations.* The schizoid person simply appears to have no need or desire for intimate relationships or even friendships. Family life usually does not mean much to such people, and they do not obtain satisfaction from being part of a group. They have few or no close friends, and they would rather spend time by themselves than with others. They typically choose hobbies that can be done and appreciated alone, such as stamp collecting. They also typically choose solitary jobs, often with mechanical or abstract tasks, such as machinists or computer programmers. Usually, the schizoid personality experiences *little pleasure* from bodily or sensory experiences, such as eating or having sex. The person's emotional life is typically impoverished, and what emotions they might have are very low intensity.

   At best, the schizoid person appears indifferent to others, neither bothered by criticism nor buoyed by compliments. "Bland" would be one description of such a person's emotional life. Often, the schizoid person does not respond to social cues and so appears *inept* or *socially clumsy*. For example, such a person may walk into a room where there is another person and simply stare at that person, apparently not motivated to start a conversation. Sometimes the schizoid person is *passive* in the face of unpleasant happenings and does not respond effectively to important events. Such a person may appear directionless.

People from some cultures react to stress in a way that looks like schizoid personality disorder. That is, without actually having the disorder, some people under stress may appear socially numb and passive. For example, people who move out of extremely rural environments into large cities may react in a schizoid fashion for several weeks. Such a person, overwhelmed by noise, lights, and overcrowding, may prefer to be alone, have constricted emotions, and manifest other deficits in social skills. Also, people who emigrate from other countries are sometimes seen as cold, reserved, or aloof. For example, people who emigrated from Southeastern Asia during the 1970s and 1980s were sometimes seen as being aloof by people in mainstream urban American culture. These are cultural differences and should not be interpreted as personality disorders.

The famous surrealist painter Salvador Dali displayed many of the characteristics associated with the schizotypal personality disorder.
Slim Aarons/Slim Aarons/Getty Images

Application

The case of Roger, a schizoid research assistant. Roger was an undergraduate who had volunteered to help out in the laboratory of one of his psychology professors. He was responsible, showing up on time and doing the work he was given. However, he seemed detached from the work, never getting too excited or appearing to be even interested, though he volunteered to work for several semesters. Roger often worked in the lab at night. On several occasions, some of the graduate students complained to the professor that Roger was "staring" at them. When pressed for details, these students said that, when they left their office doors open, they would sometimes turn around and find Roger standing in the doorway, looking at them. Several female graduate students complained that he was "creepy" and kept their office doors locked.

Roger lived with his younger brother, who also went to the same university. The brother apparently handled all the daily chores, such as dealing with the landlord, buying groceries, and arranging for utilities. Roger thus had a protected life and spent most of his time studying, reading, or exploring the internet. In class, he never talked or participated in discussion. Outside of class, he appeared to have no friends, nor did he participate in any extracurricular activities. The professor he worked for thought he might be on medication but, after inquiring, learned that Roger took no medication. After graduating with a degree in psychology, Roger returned to live with his parents. He remodeled the space above his parents' garage and was living there rent-free. Every few years, he would e-mail his professor with an update on his rather stable life. However the professor's return e-mails bounced back with the message that "no such e-mail address exists." The professor never knew if Roger did not want to be contacted, or if Roger just had some setting wrong in his e-mail app. After about 10 years Roger stopped e-mailing and the professor lost all contact with him.

Schizotypal Personality Disorder

Whereas the schizoid person is indifferent to social interaction, the schizotypal person is acutely uncomfortable in social relationships. Schizotypes are *anxious in social situations,* especially if those situations involve strangers. Schizotypal persons also feel that they are different from others or that they do not fit in with the group. Interestingly, when such persons have to interact with a group, they do not necessarily become less anxious as they become more familiar with the group. For example, while attending a group function, the schizotype will not become less anxious as time wears on, but instead will become more and more tense. Schizotypes tend to be *aloof from others* and are not prone to trust others or to relax in their presence.

Another characteristic of people with schizotypal personalities is that they are *odd* and *eccentric.* It is not unusual for them to harbor many superstitions such as believing in ESP and many other psychic or paranormal phenomena that are outside of the norms for their culture. They may believe in magic or that they possess some extrasensory or other extraordinary power, such as the ability to control other people or animals with their thoughts. They may have *unusual perceptions* that border on hallucinations, such as feeling that other people are looking at them or claiming to feel energy fields coming from a rock, perceptions that other people do not share.

Because of their social discomfort, and general oddness, schizotypal persons have difficulty with social relationships. They often are at odds with common social conventions, for example, not making eye contact, dressing in unkempt or unusual clothing, or wearing clothing that does not go together. In many ways, the schizotype simply does not fit into the social group.

Because of their similarity in terms of avoiding social relations, the characteristics of schizoid and schizotypal personality disorders are presented together in Table 19.6. Some beliefs and thoughts, mostly concerned with other people, which characterize persons with these disorders, are also listed.

Table 19.6 Characteristics of Schizoid and Schizotypal Personality Disorders

Schizoid
Detached from normal social relationships
Pleasureless life
Inept or socially clumsy
Passive in the face of unpleasant events

Schizotypal
Anxious in social relations and avoids people
"Different" and nonconforming
Suspicious of others
Eccentricity of beliefs, such as in ESP or magic
Unusualness of perceptions and experiences
Disorganized thoughts and speech

Typical Thoughts or Beliefs Associated with the Schizoid and Schizotypal Personalities
"I hate being tied to other people."
"My privacy is more important to me than being close to others."
"It's best not to confide too much in others."
"Relationships are always messy."
"I manage best on my own and set my own standards."
"Intimate relations are unimportant to me."

A Closer Look

The Unabomber: Comorbidity of Personality Disorders

In 1996, Theodore Kaczynski was arrested for murder in a long line of bombings. He had been mailing bombs to unsuspecting university professors and scientists (hence his FBI code name—Unabomber) for 17 years. Many of his targets were computer scientists, but he did injure one psychology professor with a mail bomb (Professor James McConnell at the University of Michigan). Police knew the bombs were all from the same person, but they had no idea of his motives or why he was targeting university professors. After a 17-year period of anonymous killing and maiming from a distance, he decided to make the nature of his grievances clear. He sent several taunting letters to the FBI and a long rambling manifesto to the *Washington Post* and *The New York Times,* which published his diatribe against technology and modern society. This was his undoing. Kaczynski's brother recognized the nature of the complaints in the manifesto and notified the police, who arrested Kaczynski at his isolated 10-by-12-foot shack in Montana.

A reporter—Maggie Scarf—writing in the *New Republic* magazine (June 10, 1996, p. 20), presented her view that Ted Kaczynski most likely had a narcissistic personality disorder. Scarf used the *DSM-IV* description of narcissistic disorder to explain Kaczynski's behavior. For example, as an undergraduate at Harvard, Kaczynski isolated himself so much that his classmates remember very little about him. He saw himself as a misunderstood genius whom the world would one day recognize. As a mathematics graduate student at the University of Michigan, he isolated himself even more. In his isolation he probably nurtured fantasies of prestige and power and revenge on those who refused to praise him. As a promising young professor of mathematics at U.C., Berkeley, he suddenly bolted from his faculty position in 1969. No one, apparently, was recognizing his superiority. People did not realize, as he did, that he possessed a phenomenal intellect and superior vision of how everything worked. His colleagues were fools, he must have concluded, because they could not see his obvious superiority. His students, however, complained loudly about his teaching style. In their course evaluations, they indicated that his lectures were boring and useless and that he ignored questions from the students. They too must be fools, Kaczynski probably concluded.

In her article, Scarf argued that when Kaczynski struck out at society, he was really saying, "I'm special and I deserve your respect" (1996, p. 20). When he began taunting the police to try to capture him, he was really saying, "I am so extraordinary that I operate with impunity; you haven't been able to catch me for 17 years and you never will." Finally, when he gave his manifesto to the world, he was really saying, "You had better realize you are dealing with someone unprecedented in the history of the human race. I am so clever and powerful and smart that I will tell you all the problems with the world and how to fix them, and if you ignore my commands you do so at your own risk" (p. 20). His entire ranting manifesto is easily located on the

Former University of California at Berkeley math professor Theodore Kaczynski was convicted in several of the "Unabomber" attacks, which occurred over a 17-year period. Kaczynski displays characteristics associated with a number of personality disorders.
Ralf-Finn Hestoft/Getty Images

(Continued)

A Closer Look (*Continued*)

World Wide Web by entering "Unabomber" in a search engine.

Scarf is a journalist, not a psychologist, so her diagnosis is based on her speculation. Kaczynski certainly does have some features of the narcissistic personality disorder, but most narcissists are not serial murderers. What other possible clues might we have to his abnormal behavior? It turns out that the entire text of the court-appointed psychiatrist's report on Ted Kaczynski is available on the Web at https://paulcooijmans.com/psychology/unabombreport.html (as of October 2019). This report, prepared by government-appointed psychiatrist Sally Johnson, provides another perspective on Kaczynski. While at Harvard, Kaczynski was involved in a study by Henry Murray, whom we discussed in Chapter 11. Personality test results from his undergraduate days at Harvard indicate that he was extremely introverted and somewhat depressive, even at that early age. During his psychological evaluation 30 years later, the main finding was that he suffered from schizophrenia, paranoid type, which is a severe mental illness. However, he also had an IQ of 136, which puts him in the top 1 percent of the population. As for personality disorders, the psychiatrist concluded that Kaczynski had paranoid personality disorder along with many features of the avoidant and antisocial personality disorders as well. The following is a quote from her official report:

Mr. Kaczynski is also diagnosed as suffering from a Paranoid Personality Disorder with Avoidant and Antisocial Features. Review of his developmental history, adolescence and early adult life draws a picture consistent with the symptomatology associated with this type of personality disorder. Consistent with this type of personality disordered

function, Mr. Kaczynski historically has shown pervasive distrust of others such that their motives are interpreted as malevolent. Symptoms consistent with Paranoid Personality Disorders that are evident in Mr. Kaczynski's presentation include that he suspects, without sufficient basis, that others are exploiting, harming, or deceiving him; that he reads demeaning or threatening meanings into benign remarks or events; that he persistently bears grudges and is unforgiving of insults, injuries or slights; and that he perceives attacks on his character or reputation that are not apparent to others, and is quick to react angrily or to counterattack.

In addition to meeting the criteria for Paranoid Personality Disorder, Mr. Kaczynski also has features of two other personality disorder types. Support for Avoidant Personality Disorder Traits includes that he has demonstrated a pervasive pattern of social inhibition, feelings of inadequacy and hypersensitivity to negative evaluations, beginning in his early life. Consistent with this, he has shown restraint within intimate relationships because of his fear of being shamed or ridiculed; he has been preoccupied with being criticized or rejected in social situations; and is inhibited in new interpersonal situations because of feelings of inadequacy. Consistent with Antisocial Personality Disorder Traits is his pervasive pattern of disregard for and violation of the rights of others. This includes his failure to conform to social norms with respect to lawful behaviors, as indicated by repeatedly performing acts that are

grounds for arrest. This description is based on his own account of his behavior in his writings and interviews. Also consistent with his Antisocial Personality Traits is the characteristic of deceitfulness, as indicated by his persistent and elaborate efforts to conceal his behaviors. He has demonstrated a reckless regard for the safety of others. He demonstrates a lack of remorse as indicated in his writings by being indifferent to having hurt, mistreated, or stolen from others. Mr. Kaczynski falls short of carrying a diagnosis of Antisocial Personality Disorder in that he does not have evidence of a conduct disorder before the age of 15. (Excerpted from the report of Sally C. Johnson, M.D., Chief Psychiatrist, Associate Warden of Health Services, Federal Correctional Institution, Butner, North Carolina, January 1996.)

In 2020 Netflix released a 4-part documentary on the life of Ted Kaczynski titled "Unabomber: In His Own Words." It contains audio of the only interview he has given since his arrest in 1996. It illustrates how features of his antisocial, paranoid, and avoidant disorders can be seen quite early in his life. Kaczynski shows features of at least three different personality disorders, with the prominent one being paranoid personality disorder. This disorder occurred along with paranoid schizophrenia, which involves delusions and elaborate belief systems. The presence of two or more disorders in one person is called comorbidity, which can occur when two or more personality disorders are diagnosed in the same person. Comorbidity is fairly common, and it makes for difficulty in diagnosing disorders (Krueger & Markon, 2006).

Mason, Claridge, and Jackson (1995) published a questionnaire for assessing schizotypal traits and validated it in several British samples. One of the scales contains items that get at the presence of *unusual experiences:* "Are your thoughts sometimes so strong you can almost hear them? Have you sometimes had the feeling of gaining or losing energy when certain people look at you or touch you? Are you so good at controlling others that it sometimes scares you?" Another scale contains items that assess *cognitive disorganization:* "Do you ever feel that your speech is difficult to understand because the words are all mixed up and don't make any sense? Do you frequently have difficulty starting to do things?" Another set of items measures the *tendency to avoid people:* "Are you much too independent to really get involved with people? Can you usually let yourself go and enjoy yourself at a party?" And, finally, there is a scale for assessing the *nonconformity* aspect of schizotypy: "Do you often feel like doing the opposite of what people suggest, even though you know they are right? Would you take drugs that might have strange or dangerous effects?"

Exercise

Many famous persons have been odd or eccentric. Artists (e.g., Salvador Dali, perhaps Van Gogh), writers (e.g., Tennessee Williams, Emily Dickinson), creative entrepreneurs (Howard Hughes, Nikola Tesla), musicians, and film stars have exhibited some fairly eccentric behaviors. Can you think of examples of public figures who have displayed odd beliefs or eccentric actions recently? Would they fit the rest of the characteristics of the schizotypal personality? In what ways might being a little bit schizotypal be beneficial, could there be a form of "healthy" schizotypal personality. Studies often find a correlation between creativity and unconventional thinking and schizotypal tendencies.

Paranoid Personality Disorder

Whereas the schizotype is uncomfortable with others, the paranoid person is extremely *distrustful of others* and sees others as a threat. Such persons assume that others are out to exploit and deceive them, even though there is no good evidence to support this assumption. Paranoid persons feel that they have been unfairly treated by others and are preoccupied with questioning the motives of others.

People with this disorder typically do not reveal personal information to others, preferring to remain private. They often fear that their personal information will be used against them. Their reaction to others is "Mind your own business." Also, the paranoid person often *misinterprets social events.* For example, someone makes an off-hand comment and the paranoid interprets it as a demeaning or threatening remark (e.g., wondering, "What did he mean by *that*?"). Paranoids are reluctant to trust others, and are constantly on the lookout for hidden meanings and disguised motives in the comments and behaviors of others.

The person with a **paranoid personality disorder** often holds *resentments toward others* for slights or perceived insults. Such a person is reluctant to forgive and forget even minor altercations. Paranoid persons often become involved in legal disputes, suing others for the slightest reasons. Sometimes paranoid persons plead with those in power to intervene on their behalf, such as writing to congresspersons or calling the local police over perceived wrongs.

Pathological jealousy is a common manifestation of paranoid personality disorder within relationships. For example, a pathologically jealous woman suspects that her husband or partner is unfaithful, even though there is no objective evidence of infidelity. She may go to great lengths to find support for her jealous beliefs. She may restrict the activities of her partner or constantly question him as to his whereabouts. She might hide an AirTag in his car to track his movements. She likely will not believe her partner's accounts of how he spent his time or believe his claims of faithfulness.

People with paranoid personality disorder are at risk of harming those who they see as threatening. Their *argumentative and hostile nature* may provoke others to a combative response. This hostile response from others, in turn, validates the paranoids' original suspicion that others are out to get them. Their extreme suspiciousness and the unreasonableness of their beliefs make people with this disorder particularly difficult in social relations. Table 19.7 presents the main characteristics of the paranoid personality disorder, along with some examples of beliefs and thoughts commonly found among persons with this disorder.

The Anxious Cluster: Ways of Being Nervous, Fearful, or Distressed

The final cluster of personality traits consists of patterns of behavior that are geared toward avoiding anxiety. The disorders in this cluster, like all the other disorders, illustrate the **neurotic paradox:** Although a particular behavior might make them feel less anxious, it may create another equally or more severe problem. For example, an overly dependent person might make so many demands on their partner that it eventually alienates or drives them away. The paradox is that disordered behavior, while solving one problem, often creates another. This is the logic behind the saying that "Sometimes people are their own worst enemy."

Avoidant Personality Disorder

The major feature of the **avoidant personality disorder** is a pervasive *feeling of inadequacy* and *sensitivity to criticism* from others. Clearly, no one likes to be criticized. However, avoidant persons will go to great lengths to avoid situations in which others may have opportunities to criticize their performance or character, such as in school, at work, or in other group settings. The main reason for this social anxiety is an extreme fear of criticism or rejection from others. Such persons may avoid making new friends or going to new places, due to his

---

Table 19.7 Characteristics of Paranoid Personality Disorder

Is distrustful of others
Misinterprets social events as threatening
Harbors resentments toward others
Is prone to pathological jealousy
Is argumentative and hostile

Typical Thoughts or Beliefs Associated with the Paranoid Personality
"Get them before they get you."
"Other people always have ulterior motives."
"People will say one thing but do another."
"Don't let them get away with anything."
"I have to be on guard all the time."
"When people act friendly toward you, it is probably because they want something. Watch out!"

Application

The case of Ellen, avoidant university student. Ellen was a 21-year-old university student who had gone to the university's psychological clinic with the general complaint that she was uncomfortable in social settings. Because she was so shy and nervous, she kept her contact with others to a minimum. She worried about starting new classes each semester and having to be in rooms with total strangers. She was especially worried about her psychology courses, where "they might find out I am a nutcase." She adds, "They are going to think I am a dysfunctional idiot because I am so shy and I go into a panic at the thought of speaking up in a group of strangers." She adds that she was thinking of switching her major from psychology to computer science. Although she was curious about people, and therefore liked psychology, she nevertheless felt awkward around them. Computers, she thought, were much easier to get along with and did not reject or criticize her.

Ellen reported that, as a child, she was teased mercilessly by the other children in her school. She remembers withdrawing from others at about this time in her life. She says that in grade school she would try to make herself small and inconspicuous, so others would not notice her. As a teenager, she took some jobs babysitting, but she has never held a job working with a team of others. At the university, she apparently has no friends, or at least cannot name any. She says she is afraid others will not like her "when they find out what I am really like," so she avoids social contact. In fact, she never once makes eye contact with the interviewer at the clinic.

At the university, Ellen followed a pattern of letting work pile up, then working hard to get it all done. She tried to do a few errands each day, kept her apartment neat, and went to the grocery store twice a month. She described her life as "not very happy, but at least predictable." She liked exploring the internet on her home computer. She said she enjoys viewing the Facebook pages of others, but the account she set up for herself has no photos and very little information. When pressed on this, she confessed that she just mainly liked to see "what people are up to" but does not enjoy messaging or interacting on these sites. She prefers staying in the background, watching others: "When they don't even know I'm there, then I can be pretty sure they are not laughing at me."

or her fear of criticism or disapproval. Friends may have to plead and promise lots of support and encouragement in order to get them involved in new activities.

Because avoidant persons fear criticism, they may *restrict their activities* to avoid potential embarrassments. For example, an avoidant man may cancel a blind date at the last minute because he can't find just the right clothes to wear. Avoidant individuals cope with anxiety by avoiding the risks of everyday social life. However, by avoiding the anxiety, they create other problems (the neurotic paradox again), often in the form of missed opportunities. In addition, avoidant individuals are typically seen by others as meek, quiet, shy, lonely, and solitary.

Avoidant persons are sensitive to what others think of them. Their feelings are easily hurt, and they appear vulnerable and inhibited in social interactions, withholding their own views, opinions, or feelings out of fear of being ridiculed. They typically have very *low self-esteem* and feel inadequate to many of life's social challenges (e.g., making new friends, joining new groups). Because of their social isolation, they typically do not have many sources of social support. Even though they typically desire to be involved with others, and may even fantasize about relationships, they tend to avoid intimate contact out of their fear of rejection and criticism. The paradox is that, in avoidantly coping with their social anxiety, they shun the supportive relationships with caring others that could actually help boost their self-esteem. Table 19.8 presents the main features of the avoidant personality disorder, along with several examples of thoughts and beliefs that might occur in someone with this disorder.

Dependent Personality Disorder

Whereas the avoidant person avoids others to an extreme, the dependent person seeks out others to an extreme. The hallmark of the **dependent personality disorder** is an *excessive need to be taken care of,* to be nurtured, coddled, and told what to do. Dependent persons act in *submissive* ways so as to encourage others to take care of them or take charge of the situation. Such individuals need lots of encouragement and advice from others and would much rather turn over responsibility for their decisions to someone else. Where should they live, what schools should they attend, what courses should they take, with whom should they make friends? The dependent personality has great difficulty making such decisions and *seeks out reassurance from others.* However, such a person tends to seek advice about even minor decisions, such as whether to carry an umbrella today, what color clothes to wear, and what entrée to order at a restaurant. The dependent person *rarely takes the initiative.* Others might describe them as "needy."

Because of their fear of losing the help and advice of others, dependent persons *avoid disagreements* with those on whom they are dependent. Because of their extreme need for support, dependent personalities might even agree with decisions or opinions that they feel are wrong to avoid angering the persons on whom they depend.

Because of their low self-confidence and need for constant reassurance, dependent persons may *not work well independently.* They may wait for others to start projects or may need direction often during a task. They may demonstrate how inept they are, so as to trick others into assisting them. They may avoid becoming proficient at a task, so as to keep others from seeing that they are competent to work by themselves. Because they rely on others to solve their problems they never learn the skills of living or working independently.

Persons with dependent personalities *may tolerate extreme circumstances to obtain reassurance and support from others.* Such people may submit to unreasonable demands, may tolerate abuse, or may stay in a distorted relationship. People who believe that they are unable to take care of themselves may tolerate a lot of abuse in order to maintain bonds with people who will take care of them. The unfortunate aspect of the dependent personality is that by giving over responsibility and depending on other people,

Table 19.8 Characteristics of Avoidant Personality Disorder

Feelings of inadequacy
Sensitive to criticism
Activities are restricted to avoid embarrassment
Low self-esteem

Typical Thoughts or Beliefs Associated with the Avoidant Personality
"I am socially inept and undesirable."
"I wish you would like me, but I think you really hate me."
"I can't stand being criticized; it makes me feel miserable."
"I must avoid unpleasant situations at all costs."
"I don't want to attract attention to myself."
"I'd much rather be ignored than criticized."

Application

The case of Edward, a dependent personality. Edward was a university professor who had achieved some success in his field. One day, a psychologist friend stopped by his office to invite Edward and his wife to dinner. Edward said he had to call his wife to see if they could go, and his wife agreed and told Edward to invite the friend to stop by their house for a drink before going to dinner. That night, the friend arrived at the house before Edward was ready, and he noticed Edward asked his wife for advice on what to wear. It was raining that night, and Edward asked his wife if he should wear a jacket or a raincoat. He also asked his wife if he should bring an umbrella. At dinner, the friend noticed that Edward asked his wife what he should drink and, as he looked over the menu, Edward asked his wife what he should order for dinner. Edward even asked his wife; "What kind of food do I like?" At this point, the psychologist friend began to think Edward was displaying several diagnostic characteristics of a dependent personality disorder.

dependent persons may never discover that they can take care of themselves. Table 19.9 presents the main characteristics of the dependent personality disorder along with associated beliefs and thoughts that persons with this disorder might have.

Obsessive-Compulsive Personality Disorder

The obsessive-compulsive person is *preoccupied with order* and *strives to be perfect.* The high need for order can manifest itself in the person's attention to details, however trivial, and fondness for rules, rituals, schedules, and procedures. Such persons may, for example, plan out which clothes they will wear every day of the week or clean their apartments every Saturday and Wednesday from 5 until 7 p.m. People with **obsessive-compulsive personality disorder** *hold very high standards for themselves.* However, they may work so hard at being perfect that they are never satisfied with their work. For example, a student might never turn in a research paper because it is never quite perfect enough. The desire for perfection can actually stifle a person's productivity.

Another characteristic is a *devotion to work at the expense of leisure and friendships.* Obsessive-compulsive persons tend to work harder than they need to. They may work at

Table 19.9 Characteristics of Dependent Personality Disorder

Has an excessive need to be taken care of
Is submissive
Seeks reassurance from others
Rarely takes initiative and rarely disagrees with others
Does not work well independently
May tolerate abuse from others to obtain support

Typical Thoughts or Beliefs Associated with the Dependent Personality
"I am weak and need support."
"The worst possible thing would be to be abandoned and left alone."
"I must not offend those on whom I depend."
"I must be submissive to obtain their help."
"I need help making decisions."
"I hope someone will tell me what to do."

night and on weekends and rarely take time off. In his book on adult personality development, George Vaillant (1977) saw it as a sign of positive mental adjustment when his adult subjects reported taking at least a one-week vacation each year. Obsessive-compulsives tend not to meet this criterion for adjustment. When they do take time off for recreation, they prefer serious activities, like chess, sudoku, or cross-word puzzles. For hobbies, they often pick demanding tasks or activities that require great attention to detail, such as cross-stitch sewing or computer programming. Even their play looks a lot like work.

The obsessive-compulsive person may also appear *inflexible* with regard to ethics and morals. Such persons set high principles for themselves and tend to follow the letter of the law. They are highly conscientious and expect others to be that way as well. There is usually only one right way, according to them, to do something—their way. They often have trouble working with others because they are stubborn and reluctant to delegate tasks; "If you want something done right, you have to do it yourself" is a common complaint from obsessive-compulsive persons. They become irritated when others don't take their work as seriously as they do.

A few other unusual characteristics are often present in the obsessive-compulsive person. One is the preference to hang on to worn-out or useless things; many obsessive-compulsive people have trouble throwing things away. Many are *miserly or stingy,* hoarding their money and things. And finally, along with being inflexible, obsessive-compulsives can be frustratingly *stubborn.* They may stubbornly insist, for example, that they cannot complete their work because of the imperfections of others. As you might imagine, they often cause difficulties for others at the workplace. Table 19.10 presents the essential features of obsessive-compulsive personality disorder, along with some typical beliefs and thoughts that characterize persons with this disorder.

There is another disorder—obsessive-compulsive disorder (OCD)—that is often confused with obsessive-compulsive personality disorder (OCPD). OCD is an anxiety disorder that is, in several ways, more serious and debilitating than OCPD. In OCD a pattern of unwanted and intrusive thoughts is recurrent and troubling to the person, such as the persistent thought that he or she may harm someone. In addition, OCD is characterized by the presence of ritualistic behaviors, such as frequent hand washing or the tendency to repeat actions a set number of times (e.g., having to touch an object three times before leaving a room or repeating words to oneself three times). Obsessive-compulsive personality

Table 19.10   Characteristics of Obsessive-Compulsive Personality Disorder

Preoccupied with order
Perfectionistic
Devoted to work, seeking little leisure time or friendship
Frequently miserly or stingy
Rigid and stubborn

Typical Thoughts or Beliefs Associated with the Obsessive-Compulsive Personality
"I believe in order, rules, and high standards."
"Others are irresponsible, casual, and self-indulgent."
"Details are important; flaws and mistakes are intolerable."
"My way is the only right way to do things."
"If you can't do it perfectly, don't do it at all."
"I have only myself to depend on."

disorder, on the other hand, really involves a collection of traits, such as excessive need for order or extremely high conscientiousness. People with OCPD are at risk for developing OCD as well as other kinds of anxiety disorders (Oltmanns & Emery, 2004).

Many of the characteristics of obsessive-compulsive personality, considered one at a time, can be seen as adaptive up to some point. For example, wanting to perform a task as perfectly as possible is, up to a point, desirable and rewarded. Holding one's opinions firm is, up to a point, desirable and indicates character. Keeping everything neat and orderly is, up to a point, useful. How can one tell when such characteristics and behaviors go over the line and indicate an obsessive-compulsive personality? The clearest way to know when obsessiveness is becoming a disorder is when this pattern of behavior starts to interfere with a person's ability to be productive or to maintain satisfying relationships. In the case study of Rita presented here, you'll see that her obsessive and compulsive personality led her to behave in ways that seriously interfered with both of these aspects of her life.

Application

The case of Rita, an obsessive-compulsive personality. Rita was a 39-year-old computer programmer who had been married for 18 years. She was always orderly and kept a very neat house. It was so neat, in fact, that she noticed when the books were in the wrong order on the bookshelves or if a knick-knack had been moved on a table or shelf. She vacuumed the house every day, whether it needed it or not. This resulted in the need for a new vacuum cleaner almost every year. Her husband thought this odd but concluded that she simply had a low threshold for what counted as dirty. She was constantly nagging him or angry at him because he did not seem to care as much as her that things be so neat, clean, and orderly. They did not have children because, according to Rita, children would disrupt the order, predictability, and neatness of her life.

Over the years, Rita added to her list of things she needed to do each day but never took anything off the list. In addition to vacuuming, she added dusting each day. Then she added cleaning the sinks with strong cleaners each day. She had to get up earlier in the mornings to get all of this cleaning done before going to work at her programming job.

Her boss often complained that she was slow. The boss did not appreciate the fact that Rita checked her work over and over again before turning it in. Rita also had difficulties working as part of a team because none of the other programmers met her standards. They did not check their work thoroughly enough, she thought, and were sloppy and imprecise, writing "amateurish" code. Her boss eventually had to isolate her and give her independent work because she could not work well with her co-workers.

Before leaving the house each morning, Rita checked the windows and doors, the gas, the water faucets, and all the light fixtures. After a few months of this, one check was not sufficient, and she began to check everything twice. Her husband complained about this, so she made him wait in the car while she checked each sink, light, door, window, and so on. Her husband dutifully waited each day, but as the months went on, the wait grew longer and longer. He was now sitting in the car for an hour each morning, waiting for Rita to finish checking. One morning, after checking the house thoroughly, she went outside to find that her husband had left without her. That afternoon she received an e-mail from him saying that he could not take it any longer and had decided to divorce her.

Prevalence of Personality Disorders

Figure 19.1 indicates the prevalence rates of the 10 personality disorders in Western cultures. **Prevalence** is a term that refers to the total number of cases that are present within a given sample at a particular point in time. For example, at a particular time, what percent of the people in a sample are diagnosable with paranoid personality disorder? The answer would be the prevalence rate. The data in Figure 19.1 are prevalence rates based on a summary and meta-analysis of nine large adult community samples from the United States, Europe, and Australia (Volkert, Gablonski, & Rabung, 2018). The horizontal bars represent prevalence rates of each disorder in the combined sample (which totaled 113,998 people).

Prevalence data show that obsessive-compulsive personality disorder is the most common, at a 3.2 percent prevalence rate. Certainly orderliness, punctuality, and neatness are often rewarded in Western cultures, so perhaps it should not be surprising that disordered levels of these characteristics form the most common personality disorder. The next most common disorder is antisocial personality disorder, with a 2.76 percent prevalence rate. The least common personality disorders are histrionic, dependent, and narcissistic, each affecting less than 1 percent of the population.

The total prevalence rate for having at least one personality disorder is about 11 percent. That is, at any given time, approximately 11 percent of the population is diagnosable with a personality disorder of one or more types. This brings up the issue of

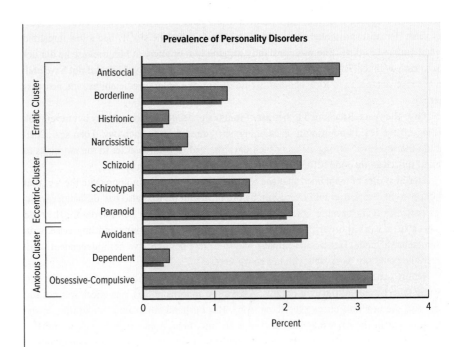

Figure 19.1

Estimates of the Prevalence of Personality Disorders in Western Countries (United States, Australia, Sweden, Germany, United Kingdom, Netherlands).

Source: *Volkert, J., Gablonski, T., and Rabung, S. (2018). Prevalence of personality disorders in the general adult population in Western countries: Systematic review and meta-analysis. British Journal of Psychiatry 213, 709–715.*

comorbidity, which is when two or more disorders occur at the same time in the same person. We also mentioned comorbidity in A Closer Look on the Unabomber. A substantial proportion—between 25 and 50 percent—of the people who meet the criteria for a diagnosis with one personality disorder also meet the criteria for diagnosis on another personality disorder (Volkert, Gablonski, & Rabung, 2018). Many of the personality disorders contain common features. For example, several disorders involve social isolation, including schizotypal, schizoid, and avoidant. Uninhibited and irresponsible behavior is one of the criteria for a diagnosis of borderline, histrionic, and antisocial personality disorders. As such, differential diagnoses are often challenging in personality disorders. A **differential diagnosis** is one in which, out of two or more possible diagnoses, the clinician searches for evidence in support of one diagnostic category over all the others.

Gender Differences in Personality Disorders

The overall prevalence rate for personality disorders is fairly equal in men and women. A few specific disorders, however, show a tendency to be more prevalent in men or in women. The one disorder with the most disparate gender distribution is antisocial personality disorder, which occurs in men with a prevalence rate of about 4.5 percent and in women at only about a 0.8 percent prevalence rate. As such, about one out of every 20 adult men has antisocial personality disorder, whereas it is less than one in 100 for women (Alegria et al., 2013). Studies show that in many ways, female psychopaths are similar to their male counterparts (both show fear, empathy, and remorse deficits; conduct disorder in childhood; history of deceitfulness, impulsivity, recklessness, and irresponsibility). However, female antisocial adults were more likely to have suffered severe physical, emotional, and sexual abuse than male antisocial adults (Alegria et al., 2013).

A few other personality disorders show tendencies to be more common among men or among women. Borderline and dependent personality disorders are somewhat more prevalent in women than men, though the differences are not large. Paranoid and obsessive-compulsive personality disorder may be more common in men than women, but again the differences are not large. One important issue concerns gender biases in diagnoses. For example, in dependent personality disorder, a few of the distinguishing traits might be viewed as traditionally feminine characteristics, such as putting others' needs ahead of one's own or being unassertive. Consequently, if the criteria for this disorder are based on feminine stereotypes, then gender bias may influence this diagnosis, even if a particular woman is not suffering significant impairment from those particular traits. Clinicians need to be aware of how stereotypes affect the ways they diagnose their clients.

A related issue is gender differences in the manifestation of the different disorders. For example, in histrionic personality disorder a main issue concerns excessive attention seeking. A woman might manifest this through hyperfemininity, perhaps being sexually provocative and flirtatious. A male might manifest this disorder through hypermasculinity, including shows of strength and bragging about his assets and accomplishments. Each is engaging in excessive attention seeking but doing it in ways that are gender stereotyped.

Dimensional Model of Personality Disorders

As discussed at the beginning of this chapter, modern theorists are arguing for a dimensional, as opposed to a categorical, view of personality disorders. In the dimensional model of personality, the only distinctions made between normal personality traits and disorders are in terms of extremity, rigidity, and maladaptiveness. For example, Widiger (1997) argues that disorders simply are maladaptive variants and combinations of normal-range personality traits. The personality traits most studied as sources of disorders are the five traits of the five-factor model, which we reviewed in Chapter 3. Costa and Widiger (1994) edited an influential book supporting the idea that the Big Five traits provide a useful framework for understanding disorders. Widiger (1997) presents data arguing that, for example, borderline personality disorder is extreme narcissism, and schizoid disorder is extreme introversion accompanied by low neuroticism (Emotional Stability). Extreme introversion accompanied by extremely high neuroticism can, on the other hand, result in avoidant personality disorder. Histrionic disorder is characterized as extreme extraversion. Obsessive-compulsive disorder is a maladaptive form of extreme conscientiousness. Schizotypal personality disorder is a complex combination of introversion, high neuroticism, low agreeableness, and extreme openness.

The dimensional view is somewhat like chemistry: Add a little of this trait and some of that trait, amplify to extremely high (or low) levels, and the result is a specific disorder. Dimensional models may have certain advantages, such as accounting for why people in the same diagnostic category can be so different from each other in how they express the disorder (because they differ on extremity or in terms of particular combinations of trait dimensions). In addition, the dimensional model allows for a person to have multiple disorders of personality. The dimensional model also explicitly acknowledges that the distinction between what is normal and what is abnormal is more a matter of degree than a clear and qualitative break (Trull & Widiger, 2013). One line of research that is currently active is developing measures of the Five Factor Model that have higher precision at the tails of the distributions; that is, at the extremely high and extremely low ends (Miller & Lynam, 2015; Samuel & Gore, 2012). The original measures of the Five Factor Model were developed with the most precision in the middle of the distribution, which is where most people are (picture a normal curve, with its bell-shaped distribution). However, if one is interested in the extreme on these personality traits, then new measures will need to be developed that have adequate discrimination and accuracy way out on the tails of the distribution, at the extremes. This is currently an active area of research.

As mentioned at the beginning of the chapter, the American Psychiatric Association decided to continue its application of a categorical view in the definition and diagnosis of personality disorders. The decade of work that went into revising the *DSM-IV* into the *DSM-5* has amounted to essentially "no change" to the way we understand personality disorders. The report of the personality disorders working group does, however, appears in Section III of the *DSM-5*.

While the *DSM-5* is the standard developed and adopted in the United States, a different system for diagnosis has been developed and adopted by the World Health Organization (WHO). This system—called the International Classification of Diseases (ICD)—was developed using data from around the world. Its most recent revision in 2022 completely changed the diagnosis of personality disorders from a categorical to a dimensional system. The dimensional approach of the ICD is based on a severity rating for personality disorder, plus includes a descriptive rating on one or more of five personality traits. The dimensional model of the ICD is in alignment with the appendix in the *DSM-5* supporting a dimensional approach. While most countries in the world employ the ICD criteria for mental disorders, psychiatrists and psychologists in the United States mainly employ the *DSM-5* categorical approach to personality disorders. Perhaps the U.S. diagnostic standards will change at some point in the future, for now the consensus in the United States is the categorical model portrayed in the *DSM-5*. As such, we followed the *DSM-5* standards in this chapter, even though we feel the dimensional system of the ICD may prove more useful for clinicians and for researchers.

Causes of Personality Disorders

The material covered in this chapter so far has been mainly descriptive, drawing from and expanding on the diagnostic criteria in the *DSM-5*. Abnormal psychology is a strongly descriptive science, and efforts are mainly to develop classification systems and taxonomies of disorders. This does not mean, however, that there are no attempts to understand how personality disorders develop or what causes one person to have a particular disorder. Researchers generally examine both biological and environmental factors that contribute to the development of personality disorders (Nigg & Goldsmith, 1994). For example, it is clear that persons who suffer with borderline personality disorder frequently experienced poor attachment relationships in childhood (Kernberg, 1975, 1984; Nigg & Goldsmith, 1994) and that many borderline persons were the target of sexual and/or physical abuse in childhood (Westen, 1990). There is abundant evidence that most people with borderline personality disorder grew up in chaotic homes, with a lot of exposure to the behavior of impulsive adults (Millon, 2000b).

It appears that genetic factors play little role in borderline personality disorder. Instead, most of the evidence implicates loss of, or neglect by, the parents in early childhood (Guzder et al., 1996).

When it comes to schizotypal personality disorder, the evidence is more in line with genetic causes. A variety of family, twin, and adoption studies suggest that schizotypal disorder is genetically similar to schizophrenia (Nigg & Goldsmith, 1994). Moreover, the first-degree relatives of persons with schizophrenia are much more likely to exhibit features of schizotypal personality disorder than persons in the general population. However, prevalence rates for paranoid and avoidant personality disorders were also elevated among the relatives of the schizophrenia patients, suggesting that these disorders may be genetically related to schizophrenia (Kendler et al., 1993).

Antisocial personality disorder also has several explanatory theories. For example, many antisocial persons were themselves abused and victimized as children (Pollock et al., 1990), leading to social learning and psychoanalytic theories of the cause of this disorder. A high proportion of antisocial persons also abuse multiple illegal drugs or alcohol, leading some researchers to propose that biological changes associated with drug abuse are responsible for antisocial behavior. There are also clear familial trends suggesting that antisocial personality disorder is due, in part, to genetic causes (Lykken, 1995). Others have proposed learning theories of antisocial personality disorder, due mainly to research showing that such persons are deficient in learning through punishment (e.g., Newman, 1987).

The neurological underpinnings of antisocial and psychopathic traits are also being investigated. A useful model here is the triarchic model, which characterizes psychopaths in terms of three distinguishable components: boldness, meanness, and lack of inhibition (Patrick, Drislane, & Strickland, 2012). A measure of this triarchic model provides better coverage of these three components than previous inventories (Drislane, Patrick, & Arsal, 2014). Moreover, this new measure correlates with neuroscience findings in quite sensible ways. For example, "boldness" is related to an underreactivity in the brain's defensive motivational system. The "lack of inhibition" component is related

Table 19.11 The Personality Disorders Described According to Unique Characteristics Associated with Self-Concept, Emotional Life, Behavior, and Social Relations

Specific Disorders	Self-Concept	Emotion	Behavior	Social Relations
Antisocial Personality	Self as unfettered by rules	Lack of remorse, quick-tempered, easily irritated, aggressive	Reckless, impulsive, irresponsible	Callous and indifferent to rights of others, lacks empathy
Borderline Personality	Self as vague, diffuse, changing, unstable, with no strong feeling of identity	Highly variable, intense, with frequent anger, shame, and guilt	Unpredictable, can be harmful to self or others	Intense, volatile, unstable, fearing abandonment
Histrionic Personality	Self as desirable and charming	Flamboyant in public displays	Attention seeking, extravagant	Attention seeking, demanding, 'high maintenance'
Narcissistic Personality	Self as unique, admirable, special	Feelings of entitlement, vengeful when not recognized	Self-displaying, admiration seeking	Envious, lacking in empathy
Schizoid Personality	Self as loner, without ambition	Bland, taking little pleasure in life	Passive, lack of drive or ambition	Detached, socially inept, having no or few friends
Schizotypal Personality	Self as different, self as outsider	Uncomfortable, high social anxiety	Odd, eccentric with unusual beliefs	Socially anxious, avoiding others
Paranoid Personality	Self as victim	Feels threatened, argumentative, suspicious, jealous	Distrustful, self-protective, resentful	Sensitive, prone to misinterpretations, socially on guard
Avoidant Personality	Self as inadequate	Frequently embarrassed, fearing criticism and rejection	Quiet, shy, solitary	Withdrawing, sensitive to criticism
Dependent Personality	Self as needy, lacking direction	Meek, indecisive, insecure, uncertain	Reassurance seeking, rarely taking initiative	Submissive, needs nurturance, avoids conflict
Obsessive-Compulsive Personality	Self as rigid, with high standards and expectations	Easily irritated, stubborn, without much pleasure	Workaholic, likes repetition, details	No time for friends, others don't meet standards

to deficits in the frontal cortical regions involved in self-regulation, cognitive control, and moral reasoning. Both of these components—boldness and lack of inhibition—are also associated with brain circuits that process rewards (Seara-Cardoso & Viding, 2015). The third component—"meanness"—is thought to be related to dysfunction in brain systems important to empathy, perspective taking, and perhaps even to lower levels of oxytocin, a neurally active hormone related to social bonding.

Explanations of the other personality disorders also follow this pattern. There are biological explanations, learning explanations, psychodynamic explanations, and cultural explanations. There may be some truth to each of these views, that personality disorders, like normal-range personality variables, have multiple causes. Moreover, it is very difficult to separate biology from learning, to separate nature from nurture. For example, an individual's early experiences—such as with an abusive parent—may lead to neurological changes in certain brain centers, such as the abnormalities in the hypothalamus and pituitary functioning (e.g., Mason et al., 1994).

Several large epidemiological and longitudinal studies of personality disorders have been undertaken (e.g., Skodol, 2012). In the decades to come, these studies are likely to pay off with results that improve our understanding of the life course of people with specific disorders. Such results will also suggest likely causal pathways that lead to various disorders.

Most of the research on personality disorders to date is descriptive or correlational. True experiments, where people would be randomly assigned to either have or not have a disorder, are impossible. Because the research is mostly correlational, it cannot pin down the causal direction of relationships that are identified. For example, suppose people with a specific disorder are found to have a high level of a particular neurotransmitter in their system. From these results we know something descriptive, but we don't know whether having a high level of that neurotransmitter causes the disorder, or whether having the disorder causes high levels of the neurotransmitter (or whether a third unknown variable causes both the neurotransmitter changes and the disorder, a problem we discussed in Chapter 2). Longitudinal and epidemiological studies, because they take place over long time periods, can pinpoint which characteristics come before or after other characteristics, and thereby examine one important aspect of causality—temporal order.

Clearly, biology and experience are tightly intermingled, making it difficult to attribute a disorder to only one kind of cause. Efforts to reduce the cause of personality disorders to one factor—say, genetics—are likely to be an oversimplification. Thus, we have to be comfortable with the notion that something as complicated as the human personality—and its disorders—likely has multiple causes. Table 19.11 presents all of the personality disorders along with descriptions of the self-concept, emotional life, behavior, and social relations of persons who have the disorder.

SUMMARY AND EVALUATION

We began this chapter with a discussion of how disorders of personality draw on almost all the other topics studied so far. The concept of disorder relies on making a distinction between what is normal and what is abnormal. There are several definitions of abnormality. One is statistical and relies on how frequently a condition appears among a population of people. Another definition is sociological and has to do with how much a society tolerates particular forms of behavior. A psychological definition emphasizes to what extent a behavior pattern causes distress for the person or for others. The hallmark of the psychological definition of abnormal is anything that prevents a person from having satisfying relationships or from carrying on productive work. Most of the personality disorders result in problems with relationships because they impair the person's ability to get along with others. Many of the disorders also impair the person's ability to engage in productive work. All of the personality disorders refer to symptoms that cause significant problems with relationships or with work, or both.

The study of abnormal psychology, also called psychopathology, has evolved into a distinct discipline within psychology and psychiatry. A major goal of this discipline is to develop reliable taxonomies for mental disorders. The most widely used system for classifying abnormal psychological conditions, at least in the United States, is the *Diagnostic and Statistical Manual of Mental Disorders,* fifth edition (*DSM-5*), published in 2013. In going from the fourth to fifth edition of the DSM, no major changes were made in how personality disorders are defined or diagnosed.

Personality disorders are enduring patterns of experience and behavior that differ greatly from the norm and the expectations of the individual's social group and lead to distress for the person or those around him or her. Disorders typically can be seen in abnormalities in how people think, in how they feel, in how they get along with others, and in their ability to control their own actions. The patterns are typically displayed across a variety of life situations, leading to distress, for either themselves or others, in important areas in life, such as at work or in relationships. Personality disorders typically have a long history in a person's life and can often be traced back to adolescence.

In this chapter, we covered the 10 personality disorders contained in the *DSM-5*. We organized these 10 disorders into three clusters: the erratic cluster (disorders pertaining to ways of being unpredictable), the eccentric cluster (disorders pertaining to ways of being odd), and the anxious cluster (disorders pertaining to ways of being nervous or distressed). Each disorder consists of a unique combination of ways of thinking, experiencing, and acting. Future developments are likely to emphasize the dimensional view of personality disorders, which sees disorders as extreme levels of normal personality traits, or combinations of extreme levels of various traits. This change from categorical to dimensional diagnosis of personality disorders was made in 2022 to the World Health Organization's Internal Classification of Diseases. While this system is used in most countries around the world, the United States and a couple other countries rely on the categorical guidelines promoted by the *DSM-5*. Research on the causes of personality disorders was presented, and an appropriate conclusion is that most personality disorders likely have multiple causes. A more complete causal understanding of personality disorders awaits further epidemiological research.

KEY TERMS

disorder 588
abnormal psychology 588
abnormal 588
psychopathology 597
categorical view 589
dimensional view 590
personality disorder 591
antisocial personality disorder 593
eye-blink startle method 596

psychopathy 597
borderline personality disorder 599
histrionic personality disorder 601
narcissistic personality disorder 602
narcissistic paradox 603
schizoid personality disorder 604
schizotypal personality disorder 604
paranoid personality disorder 609

neurotic paradox 610
avoidant personality disorder 610
dependent personality disorder 612
obsessive-compulsive personality
    disorder 613
prevalence 616
comorbidity 617
differential diagnosis 617

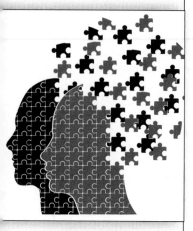

Summary and Future Directions

20

CONCLUSION

Understanding the whole behind all the parts is the ultimate goal of personality psychology.
classicpaintings/Alamy Stock Photo

After reading the first 19 chapters of this book, you should be able to provide answers the next time someone asks, "Why does this person behave that way?" Personality psychology seeks to open this mystery to scientific investigation. If you are fascinated by the variety of human behavior, by the clever or silly things that people do, by the ways people solve or create problems for themselves, or by the variety of potential explanations for people's behavior, then you have something in common with personality psychologists—a deep curiosity about human nature.

Current Status of the Field

This is an exciting time for the field of personality psychology. Advances have led to some consensus regarding the nature, structure, and development of personality, resulting in several decades of sustained growth. The field is thriving. One hallmark that a field is hitting its stride is the existence of a handbook. Personality psychology has several handbooks (e.g., Buss & Hawley, 2011; Corr & Matthews, 2020; DeYoung et al., 2014), as well as handbooks in personality disorders. Another indicator that a field is thriving is the existence of professional societies dedicated to its improvement. In personality psychology there are several societies, including the Society for Personality and Social Psychology, the European Society of Personality Psychology, and the Association for Research in Personality. This latter society, founded in 2001, is devoted to the inter-disciplinary study of personality. It promotes scientific research on personality through an annual conference and through the official scientific journal of the association, the *Journal of Research in Personality.*

Personality psychologists doing research today typically focus on specific components of personality, such as self-esteem; specific traits, such as Extraversion or Agreeableness; or specific processes, such as the unconscious processing of information. This is the direction toward which the field of personality psychology has shifted over the past 100 years. The early personality theorists, such as Sigmund Freud, constructed theories about the whole person. These grand theories focused on universal properties of human nature, such as Freud's theory that all behavior is motivated by sexual or aggressive impulses.

Starting about 60 years ago, personality psychologists began turning away from grand theories of personality. Personality psychologists began constructing mini-theories of specific parts of personality. They began to focus on distinct components of the whole person. This allowed psychologists to focus their research on very specific questions. For example, how do people develop and maintain self-esteem? In what ways do high- and low-self-esteem persons differ from each other? Why do females drop in self-esteem, on average, shortly after puberty? How might a person with low self-esteem increase self-esteem? Certainly, self-esteem is only part of personality. Nevertheless, understanding self-esteem contributes to knowledge about the whole person.

The whole of personality is the sum of its parts and the connections among those parts. Understanding the parts is required for an understanding of the whole. Most research in personality is on specific parts of the proverbial elephant. When these parts are assembled—from the dispositional to the biological, to the intrapsychic, to the cognitive/experiential, to the social and cultural, to the adjustment domains—then we have the foundation for understanding the whole personality.

Understanding the whole elephant requires understanding all of its parts. Then the blind men, working together, begin to assemble a reasonable understanding of the whole elephant. They communicate to each other and work together to build a reasonable understanding of what a whole elephant is like. They use diverse methods and approaches and communicate clearly with each other about how they see the elephant. Personality psychologists are like these blind men. They typically focus only on one domain of personality at a time. However, personality psychologists do an excellent job of working together, and increasingly identifying connections among the different domains. Personality traits, for example, are linked to the cultural transmission of religious beliefs, showing important link between the dispositional domain and the cultural domain. We can get an idea of the whole by knowing the diverse domains of knowledge about human nature and their important connections.

All of the contemporary research and theorizing appears to fit into the six major domains of knowledge. Because they formed the basic structure of this book, let's briefly review each domain that you have read about.

Domains of Knowledge: Where We've Been, Where We're Going

Each of the six domains of knowledge represents a specialty within the field of personality psychology. When any field of knowledge grows large and complex, workers in that field tend to specialize. For example, there once was a time when the field of medicine was more simple and all doctors were general practitioners. The knowledge base of medicine was small enough so that each practitioner could generally master all of it. Today the field of medicine is so large and complicated that no one person can know it all, so most doctors today are specialists. Personality psychology is much the same—a field in which people tend to specialize in one of the six domains of knowledge outlined in this book. In the remainder of this chapter, we review the main features of each of these domains of knowledge, ending with some predictions about likely developments in each domain.

Dispositional Domain

The dispositional domain concerns the aspects of personality that are relatively stable and that make people different from each other. For example, some people are outgoing and talkative; others are introverted and shy. Some are emotionally reactive and moody; others are calm and cool. Some people are conscientious and reliable; others are undependable. There are many ways in which people differ from one another, and many of these differences can be described as personality traits.

Major questions for psychologists working in this domain include: How many personality traits exist? How can we discover and measure them? How do personality traits develop? How do traits interact with situations to produce behaviors?

Trait psychologists will continue to focus on the interaction of persons and situations. Psychologists realize that behaviors always occur within a context. A formulation offered by Shoda and Mischel (1996) is the idea of "if . . . then . . ." relations. Shoda and Mischel argue that personality is a specific pattern of "if . . . then . . ." relationships. For example, if an adolescent is aggressive, it means that certain behaviors (e.g., verbal insults) are likely to occur if certain situations are created (e.g., teased by a peer). Individual persons may be characterized by distinct profiles of "if . . . then . . ." relationships. What are the conditions under which a particular person will become depressed, angry, or frustrated? Each person has a distinct psychological signature in terms of specific "if . . . then . . ." relationships: The person will do behavior A when situation X occurs, but behavior B when situation Z occurs. Two people may be equally high on aggressiveness, but the *situations* that trigger their aggression may differ. Understanding the role of situations will generate efforts to form a taxonomy of situations (Guillaume et al., 2016), similar to how the field has developed a taxonomy of traits.

Personality psychologists will likely refine their understanding of the conditions or situations under which certain behaviors, such as arguing, will be evoked in people with certain traits, such as hostility.
Stuart Jenner/iStockphoto/Getty Images

A major emphasis of the dispositional domain concerns accurate measurement of traits. The dispositional domain emphasizes quantitative techniques for measuring personality. This trend will continue, with trait psychologists developing new methods for efficiently and accurately measuring personality characteristics, as well as new statistics for evaluating personality research. We will likely see an increasing amount of online research activity, allowing for sample sizes of a million or more people in future studies. As more of us spend more of our lives online, validation studies of specific dispositions will likely begin to assess online behaviors, such as how people use social media. Life outcome data (L-data introduced in Chapter 2) will include aspects of our digital or online life outcomes. For example, are people's Facebook or Meta pages a reflection of their personality traits?

Future developments in measurement theory will impact how measures of personality traits are developed and evaluated. For example, efforts are under way to allow test makers to assess the accuracy and validity of individual items on a personality test; in the past this was only done for total test scores. Other statistical developments are enabling personality researchers to examine causal connections between variables, even in the absence of experimental procedures. Statistics are being developed to better capture changes in personality at a population level, as well as to assess changes within individuals. Continued progress in statistics, measurement, and testing will be a key part of the dispositional domain of the future.

Different trait theories are associated with different procedures for identifying the most important individual differences. Some use the lexical strategy—starting with the thousands of trait terms embedded within language. Others use statistical techniques to identify important individual differences. The future will see cooperation among these researchers to test whether specific trait structures are found using different procedures. Indeed, the search will continue for other traits not yet identified by these strategies. For example, in the lexical approach, early researchers deleted adjectives related to sex or that applied to one sex more than to the other. Examples are charming, sexy, coy, chaste, monogamous, and lustful (Schmitt & Buss, 2000). As a consequence of deleting these adjectives, researchers may have missed one or more traits related to sexuality or sex differences. The recent discovery of a sixth factor, *honesty–humility,* obtained from extensive cross-cultural research, represents an exciting new discovery in the dispositional domain (Thielmann et al., 2021).

Trait researchers are also beginning to look for positive aspects to otherwise "negative" traits. The concept of "healthy" neuroticism is one such example, where researchers are identifying the conditions under which it might be beneficial to be above average in neuroticism. In one of the first textbooks in personality psychology, Allport (1937) said that no personality trait was entirely good or entirely bad per se. Other examples of finding positive aspects of otherwise negative traits include the concept of "successful" sociopaths and positive aspects of narcissism (e.g., leadership potential).

Biological Domain

The core assumption of biological approaches to personality is that humans are biological systems. This domain concerns components within the body that influence or are related to personality, as well as the evolutionary causal processes responsible for creating those bodily mechanisms. This domain is not any more fundamental than the other domains, nor is knowledge about this domain any closer to the truth about personality than is the knowledge in other domains. The biological domain simply contains the biological systems that influence or are influenced by behaviors, feelings, and social environments. Biological processes may give rise to observable individual differences, or they may correlate with observable individual differences. Biological differences among people cause personality differences (as in the biological theory of extraversion) or may be the result of personality differences (as in heart disease being the long-term consequence of the hostile Type A personality style).

The advent of "wearables" is also likely to influence biological studies of personality. Wearables are small physiological sensors that a person can wear that produce a continuous record of some underlying physiological process—for example, heart rate, blood pressure, or physical activity. Personality psychologists are just starting to use wearables in research on the biological aspects of personality. More and more of our physiological systems will be measured with wearable devices. Someday it might be possible to assess brain function with a wearable device that resembles headphones rather than the 7- to 9-ton magnets that makes up today's brain imaging devices.

One area of research likely to be active in the future concerns the psychology of approach and avoidance. Many current researchers on biological bases of behavior recognize two tendencies that underlie human behavior and emotion: (1) the tendency to feel positive emotions and to approach and (2) the tendency to feel negative emotions and to avoid or withdraw. Much of the research reviewed in Chapter 7 concerns examples of this theme. Examples include the work on separate brain areas associated with positive and negative emotions, Gray's theory about behavioral approach and behavioral inhibition, and the work on sensitivity to reward and punishment. We predict that the motives to approach and to avoid will continue as one of the prominent themes in personality psychology.

Another major physical element within the body that influences personality is our genes. Our genetic makeup contributes to whether we are tall or short, have blue eyes or brown eyes, or tend toward being skinny or plump. Our genetic makeup influences behavior and personality, such as how active we are, whether we are aggressive, and whether we like to be with others or prefer to spend time by ourselves.

Behavioral genetics research has come a long way from the simple nature versus nurture question. Most of the major personality traits are now known to show some moderate amount of heritability (in the range of .30 to .50). With 30 to 50 percent of the variance in these traits due to genetic differences, that leaves 50 to 70 percent due to either measurement error or the environment. The environment can be broken down into shared and nonshared components. The shared environment is what siblings have in common, such as the same parents, the (presumably) same parental rearing style, the same schools and religious institutions, and so on. The nonshared environment consists of such factors as different friends or peers outside the family, different teachers, different parental treatment, and random factors, such as accidents and illnesses and important but random life events. Researchers are pinpointing shared and nonshared environmental factors that appear important to personality. Thus, we will see the counterintuitive scenario in which genetics researchers will focus on identifying environmental influences.

Other researchers concentrate on genetics at the molecular level. The Human Genome Project, which began in the 1990s, was one of the largest and most expensive scientific projects ever undertaken in the course of human history. The goal was to map the entire human genome, which was accomplished. More recently, genetics research has focused on molecular techniques to learn what every strand of the DNA map is responsible for. Progress will continue to link variation among people (including personality variation) to specific locations in the human genome.

A technician works with DNA sequence information.

Don Farrall/Getty Images

Twin and adoption studies, the primary methods of behavioral genetics, use indirect methods that only estimate the genetic component of traits by assessing the resemblance of relatives. Molecular genetic studies, on the other hand, are able to directly identify the DNA markers of genetic differences among individuals. Already, researchers have begun to focus these molecular techniques on the search for genes related to alcoholism, certain cognitive abilities, criminality, and impulse control. Personality psychologists will team with molecular geneticists to locate specific genes, and especially interactions among genes and interactions between genes and environments, that will relate to personality dimensions (Plomin & Davis, 2009). The genetics of personality is turning out to be much more complicated than initially envisioned. Hundreds of genes appear to each contribute small amounts to explaining any personality dimension, defying simple one-gene-one-disposition explanations. Personality variation will turn out to be interactions between networks of genes that are themselves influenced (i.e., turned off or on) by environmental conditions. A Nobel Prize likely awaits the scientist (or scientists) who solves this puzzle.

The biological domain also includes evolutionary perspectives on personality. From the perspective of evolutionary psychology, personality can be analyzed at three levels: human nature, sex differences, and individual differences. At each of these levels, an evolutionary perspective poses two related questions: What adaptive problems have humans confronted over human evolutionary history? What psychological solutions have evolved in response to solve these adaptive problems?

Because adaptive problems tend to be specific—for example, the problem of food selection differs from the problem of mate selection—the psychological solutions also tend to be specific. Thus, an evolutionary perspective leads us to expect that personality will be quite complex, consisting of a large collection of evolved psychological mechanisms, each corresponding to a specific adaptive challenge. Mate preferences, jealousy, fears and phobias, altruistic feelings, and dozens more all may be parts of evolved psychological mechanisms, according to the evolutionary perspective.

This perspective does not claim that humans are optimally adapted, or even well adapted, to the conditions of modern living. Given the slow pace of evolution, we possess Stone Age brains inhabiting a New Age world of the internet, global travel, and modern medical miracles. Problems can arise when mismatches exist between the ancient world in which our adaptations evolved and the modern world we inhabit.

The evolutionary perspective will continue to gain in importance, although it will not supplant other perspectives (Buss & Hawley, 2011). Instead, evolutionary psychology will add a new layer of questions and hence a necessary set of insights when these questions are answered empirically. Perhaps most critically, an evolutionary perspective asks, "What is the adaptive function of each psychological mechanism?" Posing questions about adaptive function lead to the discovery that human personality is even more complex and contains even more psychological mechanisms about which we are currently unaware. Rather than being motivated merely by sex and aggression, as Freud envisioned, humans will be found to be motivated by a dozen or more drives. But it should not surprise us that human personality will turn out to be so complex. After all, if personality were really simple, consisting of a small number of easily understood psychological mechanisms, then this book would be a lot shorter than it is.

Intrapsychic Domain

The intrapsychic domain concerns factors within the mind that influence behavior, thoughts, and emotions. The pioneer of this domain was Sigmund Freud, though new perspectives have advanced beyond his original ideas. This domain deals with the basic psychological mechanisms of personality, many of which operate outside of conscious awareness. Theories within this domain often start with fundamental assumptions about the motivational system—for example, the sexual and aggressive forces that Freud presumed energized much of human activity. Research has shown that motives, even those outside of awareness, can be powerful and that their manifestations in actual behavior can be studied empirically. The intrapsychic domain also includes defense mechanisms, such as repression, denial, and projection, some of which have been examined in laboratory studies.

The contributions of psychoanalysis can be divided into two areas: classical psychoanalytic theory, as put forward by Freud and his direct disciples; and contemporary psychoanalytic theory, consisting of extensions of and changes to these basic ideas. Newer views emphasize social crises rather than purely sexual conflict in personality development. Modern views also emphasize the importance of internalized representations of important relationships. These views see childhood as crucial to understanding the adult personality, but emphasize relationships, such as the attachment between an infant and the primary caregiver.

A fundamental assumption of psychologists working in the intrapsychic domain is that there are areas of the mind outside awareness. Within each person, there is a part of the mind that even the individual does not know about, the unconscious. In classical psychoanalysis, the unconscious is thought to have a life of its own. It has its own motivation, its own will, and its own energy. It can interfere with the functions of the rest of the mind. It is thought to be the source of all psychological problems. Modern research on motives (e.g., the power motive, achievement motive) also draws on the notion that motive forces can operate outside of conscious awareness.

Psychologists will continue to be interested in unconscious psychological processes. Many psychologists view the unconscious as an automatic information-processing mechanism, which can influence conscious awareness. They also see aspects of everyday behavior as automatic, as outside of conscious control. Impressive methods exist for studying the unconscious (also called the automatic parts of our behavior, thoughts, and emotions), including such techniques as priming and subliminal exposure. We are on the verge of learning much about how cognitive activity occurs outside of awareness and the extent to which unconscious thoughts influence behavior.

Psychoanalysis as a form of personality change and therapy is alive and well, with institutes and centers for psychoanalysis in most major cities in the United States. Despite rumors to the contrary, psychoanalysis as a form of personality change is not dead, and we are likely to see more empirical research evaluating the process and effectiveness of contemporary psychoanalytically inspired forms of therapy. There are even rudimentary apps for smartphones that simulate various forms of therapy, though it is hard to envision how a transference relationship could happen to one's phone!

Cognitive/Experiential Domain

The cognitive/experiential domain centers on subjective experience and other mental processes, such as thoughts, feelings, beliefs, and desires about oneself and others. One central concept in this domain is the self. Some aspects of the self describe how we view ourselves: our knowledge of ourselves, our images of past selves, and our images of

American actor Richard Gere, who often plays violent characters on film, leads a very different private life. As a practicing Buddhist, Gere believes in the principle of nonviolence. He is shown here speaking at an event for the National Day of Action for Tibet, 1998, in Washington, D.C. The development of the self and social identity, especially in complex and contradictory lives, will continue to fascinate personality psychologists.
Tom Williams/CQ Roll Call/Getty Images

possible future selves. Do we see ourselves as good or as evil? Are our past successes or past failures prominent in our self-views? Do we envision ourselves in a positive future? Psychologists will continue to focus their attention on self-concept and identity. It is likely that virtual reality will include virtual selves, and allow people to experience very different self-concepts than their innate self-concept. Indeed, the engineered experiences that make up virtual realities will likely prove useful in studying how personality shapes our experience of reality, virtual or otherwise.

A modern metaphor informing personality psychology is the information-processing, or computer, metaphor. Humans take in sensory information; process it through an elaborate cognitive system, which selects and modifies from the vast array of information available; then store it in memories, which do not bear a one-to-one relationship with the original events. At every step along the way—from attention and perception to memory and recall—there are opportunities for personality to influence the process. Using this information processing framework, personality can be thought of as the consistent errors in information processing that a person makes. For example, one person might consistently see others as more trustworthy than they really are, or another person might consistently over-react to minor life events. Artificial intelligence (AI) systems can process information faster, more accurately, and more reliably than any human. But if you designed an AI system with a personality, what would you add into that system? Would you add in some error or biases to tilt the outcome one way or the other?

A different aspect of the cognitive/experiential domain pertains to the goals people strive for. This tradition views personality through the personal projects of individuals. Goal concepts will continue to be important within personality psychology. Goals are often individual expressions of social or institutional norms or standards, so the goal concept may be one route whereby psychologists can study relationships between individuals and broader social systems such as culture.

Another aspect of subjective experience entails emotions. Is a person habitually happy or sad? What makes a person angry or fearful? Joy, sadness, feelings of triumph, and feelings of despair are all elements in our subjective experience subsumed by the cognitive-experiential domain. If you want to learn what is important to a person, really important, ask about their emotions. When was the last time he or she was angry? What makes him or her sad? What does he or she fear? Emotions are likely to continue to be important concepts in personality. If you designed an AI system, and wanted to give it emotions, what would you program into that system? Would it be possible to give Alexa or Siri emotions? Would it be possible to give Alexa or Siri a self-concept? Personality psychologists will likely play a role in designing more human-like AI systems and digital assistants of the future.

Social and Cultural Domain

One of the novel features of this text is an emphasis on the social and cultural aspects of personality. Personality is not something that merely resides within the heads, nervous systems, and genes of individuals. Rather, personality affects, and is affected by, the significant others in our lives.

Humans are not passive recipients of their environments, and personality plays a key role in social interaction. We selectively enter some interpersonal environments and selectively avoid others. We actively choose our mates and friends. We evoke reactions from others, sometimes quite unintentionally. And we actively influence or manipulate those occupying our social worlds. Personality influences these processes of selection, evocation, and manipulation. Emotionally unstable individuals, for example, tend to choose similarly unstable persons as romantic partners; they evoke predictable forms of anger in those partners through their moodiness; and they more often use the "silent treatment" as a tactic for influencing their partners. Personality, in short, expresses itself through our social selections, evocations, and manipulations.

One important social sphere concerns relations between men and women. Personality may operate differently for men than for women in some domains. An essential part of our identity is gender. Much of what we call gender may have its origins in culture, in how society makes up different rules, roles, and expectations for men and women. Cultural expectations around gender change slowly, but they are changing. One example is the non-binary view, the idea that a person need not feel entirely male or entirely female, or indeed feel that the gender binary does not apply to them at all. As culture changes, people tend to think about themselves and others in entirely new ways.

Other aspects of gender may lie in evolved behavior patterns that represent adaptations to different pressures that faced men and women in the past. Gender differences will continue to be a compelling interest of personality psychologists. In an effort to understand gender differences, it is likely that personality psychologists will enlist the help of specialists from other disciplines, such as anthropologists, animal behaviorists, sociologists, and biologists.

At the cultural level, it is clear that groups differ from one another. Some cultures are individualistic: People prefer to make their own decisions, be responsible primarily for themselves, and emphasize individual rights. Other cultures are more collectivistic or more interdependent. People see themselves as part of a social group and think less of their individual needs and more about their group's needs. Personality differences among these groups may be instances of transmitted culture or evoked culture. Some psychologists assume that such differences are caused by transmitted culture—ideas, values, and representations passed on from parents and socializing agents to children within their culture, down the generations. Other psychologists, however, propose that these are instances of evoked culture. According to this view, everyone may have the evolved capacity to be individualistic and preoccupied with their self. And everyone may also have the evolved capacity to be communal and concerned with the greater good of the group. Which of these capacities any one individual displays may depend on whether one lives in a culture that is highly mobile, with few kin in close proximity (evoking an individualistic proclivity), or highly stable, with many kin in close proximity (evoking a collectivistic proclivity). Environmental variables such as pathogen prevalence may influence an evoked culture of group conformity. This fascinating new direction represents a theoretical fusion of cultural psychology and evolutionary psychology.

The study of culture and cross-cultural differences and similarities will continue to grow in personality psychology. Our world is increasingly becoming a global community. Diversity is a fact of daily life in many nations or in certain areas within a nation. Many of us encounter people from different cultures at our schools, our jobs, our social lives, and in our communities. There is a growing interdependence among people from different backgrounds. An important goal of personality psychology will be to understand how cultures shape personality and how specific cultures are different from, or similar to, each other. This will grow in importance as more and more people from different cultures come into contact with each other.

Interacting with people from different cultures is a fact of daily life in many parts of the world. Understanding how people from different cultures are different from, or similar to, each other will continue to be an important part of personality psychology.

Rawpixel.com/Shutterstock

Adjustment Domain

Personality plays a key role in how we cope, adapt, and adjust to the ebb and flow of events in our lives. Personality is linked with important health outcomes, such as heart disease. Personality is linked to a variety of health-promoting (regular exercise, healthy eating habits, regular medical exams) and health-suppressing (smoking, alcohol abuse, risk taking) behavior. Personality is even linked to how long we live. The role of personality in relation to health and well-being will continue to occupy personality psychologists of the future. There has been a shift toward looking at the role of positive emotions, and this emphasis on the positive in psychology is likely to be a part of personality psychology. In addition, several longitudinal studies were started decades ago in various communities around the United States. Participants in these longitudinal projects are now aging adults, with many experiencing the long-term effects of various health-promoting or health-suppressing behaviors. To the extent that personality influences whether a person engages in those behaviors, research will uncover the long-term health effects of personality.

Another trend in health is the development of "big data," data sets that contain a large amount and variety of information on a large number of persons. For example, Google recently announced "Project Nightingale," an artificial intelligence program that will seek out and harvest extensive medical and lifestyle information on up to 50 million people, a data set that will be both deep (much information) and wide (many people). While many worry about privacy issues regarding their personal medical information, Google argues that its big data approach will make better and more personalized medical care possible. Big data sets can be used to answer questions about personality and health and will be able to detect novel findings or effects that might have been missed by smaller studies. In 2019 Google purchased the company Fitbit, a wearable device maker. It is likely that Google will integrate physical data from connected devices into its big data approach. Other companies with AI plans (e.g., Apple, Amazon) are also moving to a big data to study and understand the factors that influence health, illness, and medical care, including personality factors.

Some important problems in coping and adjustment can be traced to personality disorders. An understanding of "normal" personality functioning can be deepened by examining disorders of personality, and vice versa. Psychologists have applied the trait approach to understanding personality disorders. This will sharpen our descriptive understanding of personality disorders. In terms of causal understanding, we predict the future will likely see breakthroughs in our understanding of the causes of these disorders. This will be made possible by long-term epidemiological studies using extensive data sources, such as whole genome sequencing information and neuroimaging data, along with other life experience and life outcome data.

Integration: Personality in the Twenty-First Century

The six domains of knowledge are complementary, not conflicting. People have many facets, and these facets can be observed and studied from many different perspectives. To say that people have evolved psychological mechanisms to solve social problems does not imply that the principles of psychoanalysis are wrong. Similarly, to say that a portion of the variance in personality traits is due to genetics does not in any way imply that people do not develop or change their personalities in adulthood.

Exciting personality research will occur at the boundaries of domains. Examples include collaborations among brain researchers using functional magnetic resonance imaging (fMRI) technology to conduct brain scans and psychologists studying interpersonal dispositions, collaborations between cultural and evolutionary psychologists to study the causal origins and nature of cultural differences, and collaborations between dispositional researchers and cognitive psychologists to study the information-processing mechanisms underlying stable individual differences. The most interesting efforts involve making to make connections among domains or between personality psychology and other scientific fields.

Progress in this millennium will depend on researchers' willingness and ability to reach across domains. The most exciting progress will occur when researchers, perhaps working on multidisciplinary teams, combine different levels of analysis and different methods in approaching central questions of importance to the field. Building bridges that link domains of knowledge together in new and interesting ways will have the most impact on how we understand human nature.

If we look at the field of personality psychology today, we can find examples of bridges that are already being built among domains. For example, with approach and avoidance motivation, psychologists are studying this phenomenon through brain activity, exploring the developmental course of these motives, examining cultural differences evoked by predictable environmental factors, and delving into how these traits contribute to disorders. It is likely that centers of research will be a model for progress, with groups of diverse scientists—such as trait psychologists, biological psychologists, cultural psychologists, and health psychologists—all working together on questions important to the field of personality psychology. It is not hard to imagine interesting possibilities. For example, it probably won't be long before psychologists interested in repressed memories approach the topic with fMRI brain scans or before psychologists interested in self-esteem begin looking both at neurochemistry and at cultural and evolutionary influences. As we move forward in the twenty-first century, the possibilities for increasing our knowledge of human nature are truly exciting.

Glossary

a

abnormal Broadly defined, the term *abnormal* is based on current levels of societal tolerance. In this sense, behaviors that society deems unacceptable would be labeled as abnormal (e.g., incest and child abuse). Because tolerance levels (e.g., toward homosexuality) can change over time, psychologists have started directing their attention toward people's subjective views and experiences. Anxiety, depression, and feelings of loneliness may be linked to disorganized thought patterns, disruptive perceptions, or unusual beliefs. These may inhibit a person's ability to work or socialize, and may all be considered abnormal.

abnormal psychology The study of the various mental disorders, including thought disorders (such as schizophrenia), emotional disorders (such as depression), and personality disorders (such as the antisocial personality).

acculturation The process of, after arriving in a new culture, adapting to the ways of life and beliefs common in that new culture.

achievement view of intelligence The achievement view of intelligence is associated with educational attainment—how much knowledge a person has acquired relative to others in his or her age cohort.

acquiescence (also known as yea saying) A response set that refers to the tendency to agree with questionnaire items regardless of the content of those items.

action tendencies Increases in the probabilities of certain behaviors that accompany emotions. The activity, or action tendency, associated with fear, for example, is to flee or to fight.

active genotype–environment correlation Occurs when a person with a particular genotype creates or seeks out a particular environment.

actometer A mechanical motion-recording device, often in the form of a watch attached to the wrist. It has been used, for example, in research on the activity level of children during several play periods. Motoric movement activates the recording device.

acute stress Results from the sudden onset of demands or events that seem to be beyond the control of the individual. This type of stress is often experienced as tension headaches, emotional upsets, gastrointestinal disturbances, and feelings of agitation and pressure.

adaptations Inherited solutions to the survival and reproductive problems posed by the hostile forces of nature. Adaptations are the primary product of the selective process. An adaptation is a "reliably developing structure in the organism, which, because it meshes with the recurrent structure of the world, causes the solution to an adaptive problem" (Tooby & Cosmides, 1992, p. 104).

adaptive problem Anything that impedes survival or reproduction. All adaptations must contribute to fitness during the period of time in which they evolve by helping an organism survive, reproduce, or facilitate the reproductive success of genetic relatives. Adaptations emerge from and interact with recurrent structures of the world in a manner that solves adaptive problems and hence aids in reproductive success.

additive effects The effects of different kinds of stress that add up and accumulate in a person over time.

adjacency In Wiggins circumplex model, adjacency indicates how close the traits are to each other on the circumference of the circumplex. Those variables that are adjacent or next to each other within the model are positively correlated.

adjustment domain Personality plays a key role in how we cope, adapt, and adjust to the ebb and flow of events in our day-to-day lives. In addition to health consequences of adjusting to stress, certain personality features are related to poor social or emotional adjustment and have been designated as personality disorders.

adoption studies Studies that examine the correlations between adopted children and their adoptive parents, with whom they share no genes. These correlations are then compared to the correlations between the adopted children and their genetic parents, who had no influence on the environments of the children. Differences in these correlations can indicate the relative magnitude of genetic and environment contributions to personality traits.

affect intensity Larsen and Diener (1987) describe high affect intensity individuals as people who typically experience their emotions strongly and are emotionally reactive and variable. Low affect intensity individuals typically experience their emotions only mildly and with only gradual fluctuations and minor reactions.

aggregation Adding up or averaging several single observations, resulting in a better (i.e., more reliable) measure of a personality trait than a single observation of behavior. This approach implies that personality traits refer to average tendencies in behavior, how people behave on average.

agreeableness Agreeableness is the second of the personality traits in the five-factor model, a model which has proven to be replicable in studies using English-language trait words as items. Some of the key adjective markers for Agreeableness are "good natured," "cooperative," "mild/gentle," "not jealous."

alarm stage The first stage in Selye's general adaptation syndrome (GAS). The alarm stage consists of the flight-or-fight response of the sympathetic nervous system and the associated peripheral nervous system reactions. These include the release of hormones, which prepare our bodies for challenge.

allostatic load Refers to the cumulative burden of chronic stress over time and involves the physiological consequences of exposure to repeated or prolonged stress. It can be thought of as the total "wear and tear" on one's body from stress, and is assumed to add up over time.

alpha and beta press Murray introduced the notion that there is a real environment (what he called alpha press or objective reality) and a perceived environment (called beta press or reality as it is perceived). In any situation, what one person "sees" may be different from what another "sees." If two people walk down a street and a third person smiles at each of them, one person might "see" the smile as a sign of friendliness while the other person might "see" the smile as a smirk. Objectively (alpha press), it is the same smile; subjectively (beta press), it may be a different event for the two people.

alpha wave A particular type of brain wave that oscillates 8 to 12 times a second. The amount of alpha wave present in a given time period is an inverse indicator of brain activity during that time period. The alpha wave is given off when the person is calm and relaxed. In a given time period of brain wave recording, the more alpha wave activity present the more we can assume that part of the brain was less active.

ambivalent relationship style In Hazan and Shaver's ambivalent relationship style, adults are vulnerable and uncertain about relationships. Ambivalent adults become overly dependent and demanding on their partners and friends. They display high levels of neediness in their relationships. They are high maintenance partners in the sense that they need constant reassurance and attention.

ambivalently attached Ambivalently attached infants, as determined by Ainsworth's strange situation paradigm, are very anxious about the mother leaving. They often start crying and protesting vigorously before the mother even gets out of the room. While the mother is gone, these infants are difficult to calm. Upon her return, however, these infants behave ambivalently. Their behavior shows both anger and the desire to be close to the mother; they approach her but then resist by squirming and fighting against being held.

Americans with Disability Act (ADA) The ADA states that an employer cannot conduct a medical examination, or even make inquiries as to whether an applicant has a disability, during the selection process. Moreover, even if a disability is obvious, the employer cannot ask about the nature or severity of that disability.

amygdala A section of the limbic or emotional system of the brain that is responsible for fear.

anal stage The second stage in Freud's psychosexual stages of development. The anal stage typically occurs between the ages of 18 months and three years. At this stage, the anal sphincter is the source of sexual pleasure, and the child obtains pleasure from first expelling feces and then, during toilet training, from retaining feces. Adults who are compulsive, overly neat, rigid, and never messy are, according to psychoanalytic theory, likely to be fixated at the anal stage.

analytic To describe something analytically is to explain the event with the object detached from its context, attributes of objects or people assigned to categories, and a reliance on rules about the categories to explain behavior.

androgynous In certain personality instruments, the masculinity dimension contains items reflecting assertiveness, boldness, dominance, self-sufficiency, and instrumentality. The femininity dimension contains items that reflect nurturance, expression of emotions, and empathy. Those persons who scored high on both dimensions are labeled androgynous, to reflect the notion that a single person can possess both masculine and feminine characteristics.

anterior cingulate Located deep toward the center of the brain, the anterior cingulate cortex most likely evolved early in the evolution of the nervous system. In experiments utilizing fMRI to trace increased activation of parts of the brain, the anterior cingulate cortex seems to be an area of the brain associated with affect, including social rejection.

antisocial personality disorder A person suffering from antisocial personality disorder has a general disregard for others and cares very little about the rights, feelings, or happiness of other people. Also referred to as a sociopath or psychopath, a person suffering from antisocial personality disorder is easily irritated, assaultive, reckless, irresponsible, glib or superficially charming, impulsive, callous, and indifferent to the suffering of others.

anxiety An unpleasant, high-arousal emotional state associated with perceived threat. In the psychoanalytic tradition, anxiety is seen as a signal that the control of the ego is being threatened by reality, impulses from the id, or harsh controls exerted by the superego. Freud identified three different types of anxiety: neurotic anxiety, moral anxiety, and objective anxiety. According to Rogers, the unpleasant emotional state of anxiety is the result of having an experience that does not fit with one's self-conception.

apperception The notion that a person's needs influence how he or she perceives the environment, especially when the environment is ambiguous. The act of interpreting the environment and perceiving the meaning of what is going on in a situation.

aptitude view of intelligence The aptitude view of intelligence sees intelligence less as the product of education and more as an ability to become educated, as the ability or aptitude to learn.

arousal level and arousability In Eysenck's original theory of extraversion, he held that extraverts had lower levels of cortical or brain arousal than introverts. More recent research suggests that the difference between introverts and extraverts lies more in the arousability of their nervous systems, with extraverts showing less arousability or reactivity than introverts to the same levels of sensory stimulation.

arteriosclerosis Hardening or blocking of the arteries. When the arteries that feed the heart muscle itself become blocked, the subsequent shortage of blood to the heart is called a heart attack.

ascending reticular activating system (ARAS) A structure in the brain stem thought to control overall cortical arousal; the structure Eysenck originally thought was responsible for differences between introverts and extraverts.

assortative mating The phenomenon whereby people marry people similar to themselves. In addition to personality, people also show assortative mating on a number of physical characteristics, such as height and weight.

attachment Begins in the human infant when he or she develops a preference for people over objects. Then the preference begins to narrow to familiar persons so that the child prefers to see people he or she has seen before, compared to strangers. Finally, the preference narrows even further so that the child prefers the mother or primary caretaker over anyone else.

attraction similarity theory   States that individuals are attracted to those whose personalities are similar to their own. In other words, "birds of a feather flock together" or "like attracts like." As of 2003, attraction similarity has been proven to be the dominant attraction theory except in biological sex choices (i.e., women tend to be attracted to men and vice versa).

attributional optimism   A specific combination of attributions.

attributional style   Whenever someone offers a cause or explanation for some negative event, that cause can be analyzed in terms of the three categories of attributions: internal–external, stable–unstable, and global–specific. The tendency a person has to employ certain combinations of attributions in explaining events (e.g., internal, stable, and global causes) is called their attributional, or explanatory, style.

autonomic nervous system (ANS)   That part of the peripheral nervous system that connects to vital bodily structures associated with maintaining life and responding to emergencies (e.g., storing and releasing energy), such as the beating of the heart, respiration, and controlling blood pressure. There are two divisions of the ANS: the sympathetic and parasympathetic branches.

average tendencies   Tendency to display a certain psychological trait with regularity. For example, on average, a high-talkative person will start more conversations than a low-talkative person. This idea explains why the principle of aggregation works when measuring personality.

avoidant personality disorder   The major feature is a pervasive feeling of inadequacy and sensitivity to criticism from others. The avoidant personality will go to great lengths to avoid situations in which others may have opportunities to criticize his or her performance or character, such as school or work or other group settings. Such a person may avoid making new friends or going to new places because of fear of criticism or disapproval.

avoidant relationship style   In Hazan and Shaver's avoidant relationship style, the adult has difficulty learning to trust others. Avoidant adults remain suspicious of the motives of others, and they are afraid of making commitments. They are afraid of depending on others because they anticipate being disappointed, let down, abandoned, or separated.

avoidantly attached   Avoidantly attached infants in Ainsworth's strange situation avoided the mother when she returned. Infants in this group typically seemed unfazed when the mother left and did not give her much attention when she returned. Avoidant children seem to be aloof from their mothers. Approximately 20 percent of infants fall into this category.

b

Balancing selection   When genetic variation is maintained by selection because different levels of a personality trait are adaptive in different environments.

Balkanization   Social resegregation following a time of peaceful integration and social diversity. The term is derived from the breakup of Yugoslavia on the Balkan peninsula during the 1990s, in which national groups split apart and resegregated the formerly integrated countries in the Balkans.

Barnum statements   Generalities or statements that could apply to anyone. A good example is the astrology column published in daily newspapers.

behavioral activation system (BAS)   In Gray's reinforcement sensitivity theory, the system that is responsive to incentives, such as cues for reward, and regulates approach behavior. When some stimulus is recognized as potentially rewarding, the BAS triggers approach behavior. This system is highly correlated with the trait of extraversion.

behavioral inhibition system (BIS)   In Gray's reinforcement sensitivity theory, the system responsive to cues for punishment, frustration, and uncertainty. The effect of BIS activation is to cease or inhibit behavior or to bring about avoidance behavior. This system is highly correlated with the trait of neuroticism.

beliefs   See *theories and beliefs.*

belongingness needs   The third level of Maslow's motivation hierarchy. Humans are a very social species, and most people possess a strong need to belong to groups. Being accepted by others and welcomed into a group represents a somewhat more psychological need than the physiological needs or the need for safety.

beta press   See *alpha and beta press.*

biological domain   The core assumption of biological approaches to personality is that humans are, first and foremost, collections of biological systems, and these systems provide the building blocks (e.g., brain, nervous system) for behavior, thought, and emotion. Biological approaches typically refers to three areas of research within this general domain: the genetics of personality, the psychophysiology of personality, and the evolution of personality.

bipolarity   In Wiggins circumplex model, traits located at opposite sides of the circle and negatively correlated with each other. Specifying this bipolarity is useful because nearly every interpersonal trait within the personality sphere has another trait that is its opposite.

blindsight   Following an injury or stroke that damages the primary vision center in the brain, a person may lose some or all of his or her ability to see. In this blindness the eyes still bring information into the brain, but the brain center responsible for object recognition fails. People who suffer this "cortical" blindness often display an interesting capacity to make judgments about objects that they truly cannot see.

blood pressure   The pressure exerted by the blood on the inside of the artery walls, and is typically expressed with two numbers: diastolic and systolic pressure. The systolic pressure is the larger number, and it refers to the maximum pressure within the cardiovascular system produced when the heart muscle contracts. The diastolic pressure is the smaller number, and it refers to the resting pressure inside the system between heart contractions.

borderline personality disorder   The life of the borderline personality is marked by instability. Their relationships are unstable, their emotions are unstable, their behavior is unstable, and even their image of themselves is unstable.

Persons with borderline personality disorder, compared to those without, have a higher incidence rate of childhood physical or sexual abuse, neglect, or early parental loss.

broaden and build model of positive emotions   A model that suggests that positive emotions broaden the scope of cognition, and build up resources for coping.

byproducts of adaptations   Evolutionary mechanisms that are not adaptations, but rather are byproducts of other adaptations. Our nose, for example, is clearly an adaptation designed for smelling. But the fact that we use our nose to hold up our eyeglasses is an incidental byproduct.

C

cardiac reactivity   The increase in blood pressure and heart rate during times of stress. Evidence suggests that chronic cardiac reactivity contributes to coronary artery disease.

case study method   Examining the life of one person in particular depth, which can give researchers insights into personality that can then be used to formulate a more general theory that is tested in a larger population. They can also provide in-depth knowledge of a particularly outstanding individual. Case studies are useful when studying rare phenomena, such as a person with a photographic memory or a person with multiple personalities—cases for which large samples would be difficult or impossible to obtain.

castration anxiety   Freud argued that little boys come to believe that their fathers might make a preemptive Oedipal strike and take away what is at the root of the Oedipal conflict: the boy's penis. This fear of losing his penis is called castration anxiety; it drives the little boy into giving up his sexual desire for his mother.

categorical approach   Researchers who suggest emotions are best thought of as a small number of primary and distinct emotions (anger, joy, anxiety, sadness) are said to take the categorical approach. Emotion researchers who take the categorical approach have tried to reduce the complexity of emotions by searching for the primary emotions that underlie the great variety of emotion

terms. An example of a categorical approach to emotion is that of Paul Ekman, who applies criteria of distinct and universal facial expressions, and whose list of primary emotions contains disgust, sadness, joy, surprise, anger, and fear.

categorical view   In psychiatry and clinical psychology today, the dominant approach to viewing personality disorders in distinct categories. There is a qualitative distinction made in which people who have a disorder are in one category, whereas people who do not have the disorder are in another category.

causal attribution   A person's explanation of the cause of some event.

chronic stress   Stress that does not end, like an abusive relationship that grinds the individual down until his or her resistance is eroded. Chronic stress can result in serious systemic diseases such as diabetes, decreased immune system functioning, or cardiovascular disease.

chronotype   Refers to a person's preference for morningness or eveningness, and is related to that person's underlying circadian rhythm length, with a longer circadian rhythm related to the chronotype of evenineness, and a shorter circadian rhythm related to the chronotype of morningness.

circadian rhythm   Many biological processes fluctuate around an approximate 24- to 25-hour cycle. These are called circadian rhythms (*circa* = around; *dia* = day). Circadian rhythms in temporal isolation studies have been found to be as short as 16 hours in one person, and as long as 50 hours in another person (Wehr & Goodwin, 1981).

client-centered therapy   In Rogers's client-centered therapy, clients are never given interpretations of their problem. Nor are clients given any direction about what course of action to take to solve their problem. The therapist makes no attempts to change the client directly. Instead, the therapist tries to create an atmosphere in which the client may change him- or herself.

cognition   A general term referring to awareness and thinking as well as to specific mental acts such as perceiving, interpreting, remembering, believing, and anticipating.

cognitive approaches   Differences in how people think form the focus of cognitive approaches to personality. Psychologists working in this approach focus on the components of cognition, such as how people perceive, interpret, remember, and plan, in their efforts to understand how and why people are different from each other.

cognitive schema   A schema is a way of processing incoming information and of organizing and interpreting the facts of daily life. The cognitive schema involved in depression, according to Beck, distorts the incoming information in a negative way that makes the person depressed.

cognitive social learning approach   A number of modern personality theories have expanded on the notion that personality is expressed in goals and in how people think about themselves relative to their goals. Collectively these theories form an approach that emphasizes the cognitive and social processes whereby people learn to value and strive for certain goals over others.

cognitive triad   According to Beck, there are three important areas of life that are most influenced by the depressive cognitive schema. This cognitive triad refers to information about the self, about the world, and about the future.

cognitive unconscious   In the cognitive view of the unconscious, the content of the unconscious mind is assumed to operate just like thoughts in consciousness. Thoughts are unconscious because they are not in conscious awareness, not because they have been repressed or because they represent unacceptable urges or wishes.

cognitive-experiential domain   This domain focuses on cognition and subjective experience, such as conscious thoughts, feelings, beliefs, and desires about oneself and others. This domain includes our feelings of self, identity, self-esteem, our goals and plans, and our emotions.

cohort effects   Personality change over time as a reflection of the social times in which an individual or group of individuals live. For example, American women's trait scores on assertiveness have risen and fallen depending on the social and historical cohort in which they have lived. Jean Twenge has posited that individuals internalize social change and absorb the cultural messages they receive from their culture, all of which, in turn, can affect their personalities.

combinations of Big Five variables "Traits" are often examined in combinations. For example, two people high in extraversion would be very different if one was an extraverted neurotic and the other was extraverted but emotionally stable.

comorbidity When two or more disorders occur at the same time in the same person.

compatibility and integration across domains and levels A theory that takes into account the principles and laws of other scientific domains that may affect the study's main subject. For example, a theory of biology that violated known principles of chemistry would be judged fatally flawed.

competitive achievement motivation Also referred to as the need for achievement, it is a subtrait in the Type A behavior pattern. Type A people like to work hard and achieve goals. They like recognition and overcoming obstacles and feel they are at their best when competing with others.

complementary needs theory Theory of attraction that postulates that people are attracted to people whose personality dispositions differ from theirs. In other words, "opposites attract." This is especially true in biological sex choices (i.e., women tend to be attracted to men and vice versa). Other than biological sex choices, the complementary needs theory of attraction has not received any empirical support.

comprehensiveness One of the five scientific standards used in evaluating personality theories. Theories that explain more empirical data within a domain are generally superior to those that explain fewer findings.

conditional positive regard According to Rogers, people behave in specific ways to earn the love and respect and positive regard of parents and other significant people in their lives. Positive regard, when it must be earned by meeting certain conditions, is called conditional positive regard.

conditions of worth According to Rogers, the requirements set forth by parents or significant others for earning their positive regard are called conditions of worth. Children may become preoccupied with living up to these conditions of worth rather than discovering what makes them happy.

confirmatory bias The tendency to look only for evidence that confirms a previous hunch and not to look for evidence that might disconfirm a belief.

conscientiousness The third of the personality traits in the five-factor model, which has proven to be replicable in studies using English-language trait words as items. Some of the key adjective markers for Conscientiousness are "responsible," "scrupulous," "persevering," "fussy/tidy."

conscious goals A person's awareness of what he or she desires and believes is valuable and worth pursuing.

conscious That part of the mind that contains all the thoughts, feelings, and images that a person is presently aware of. Whatever a person is currently thinking about is in his or her conscious mind.

consistency Trait theories assume there is some degree of consistency in personality over time. If someone is highly extraverted during one period of observation, trait psychologists tend to assume that she will be extraverted tomorrow, next week, a year from now, or even decades from now.

construct validity A test that measures what it claims to measure, correlates with what it is supposed to correlate with, and does not correlate with what it is not supposed to correlate with.

construct A concept or provable hypothesis that summarizes a set of observations and conveys the meaning of those observations (e.g., gravity).

constructive memory It is accepted as fact that humans have a constructive memory; that is, memory contributes to or influences in various ways (adds to, subtracts from, etc.) what is recalled. Recalled memories are rarely distortion-free, mirror images of the facts.

content The content of emotional life refers to the characteristic or typical emotions a person is likely to experience over time. Someone whose emotional life contains a lot of pleasant emotions is someone who might be characterized as happy, cheerful, and enthusiastic. Thus, the notion of content leads us to consider the *kinds* of emotions that people are likely to experience over time and across situations in their lives.

continuity Identity has an element of continuity because many of its aspects, such as gender, ethnicity, socioeconomic status, educational level, and occupation, are constant. Having an identity means that others can count on you to be reliable in who you are and how you act.

contrast Identity contrast means that a person's social identity differentiates that person from other people. An identity is the combination of characteristics that makes a person unique in the eyes of others.

convergent validity Whether a test correlates with other measures that it should correlate with.

core conditions According to Carl Rogers, in client-centered therapy three core conditions must be present in order for progress to occur: (1) an atmosphere of genuine acceptance on the part of the therapist, (2) the therapist must express unconditional positive regard for the client, and (3) the client must feel that the therapist understands him or her (empathic understanding).

correlation coefficient (its direction and magnitude) Researchers are interested in the direction (positive or negative) and the magnitude (size) of the correlation coefficient. Correlations around .10 are considered small; those around .30 are considered medium; and those around .50 or greater are considered large (Cohen & Cohen, 1975).

correlational method A statistical procedure for determining whether there is a relationship between two variables. In correlational research designs, the researcher is attempting to directly identify the relationships between two or more variables, without imposing the sorts of manipulations seen in experimental designs.

cortisol A stress hormone that prepares the body to flee or fight. Increases in cortisol in the blood indicate that the animal has recently experienced stress.

counterbalancing In some experiments, manipulation is within a single group. For example, participants might get a drug and have their memory tested, then later take a sugar pill and have their memory tested again. In this kind of experiment, equivalence is obtained by counterbalancing the order of the conditions, with half the participants getting the drug first and sugar pill second, and the other half getting the sugar pill first and the drug second.

creating positive events Creating a positive time-out from stress. Folkman and Moskowitz note that humor can have the added benefit of generating positive emotional moments even during the darkest periods of stress.

criterion validity Whether a test predicts criteria external to the test.

cross-cultural universality In the lexical approach, cross-cultural universality states that if a trait is sufficiently important in all cultures so that its members have codified terms within their own languages to describe the trait, then the trait must be universally important in human affairs. In contrast, if a trait term exists in only one or a few languages but is entirely missing from most, then it may be of only local relevance.

cultural context of intelligence Looks at how the definition of intelligent behavior varies across different cultures. Because of these considerations, intelligence can be viewed as referring to those skills valued in a particular culture.

cultural personality psychology Cultural personality psychology generally has three key goals: (1) to discover the principles underlying the cultural diversity, (2) to discover how human psychology shapes culture, and (3) to discover how cultural understandings in turn shape our psychology (Fiske et al., 1978).

cultural universals Features of personality that are common to everyone in all cultures. These universals constitute the human nature level of analyzing personality and define the elements of personality we share with all or most other people.

cultural variations Within-group similarities and between-group differences can be of any sort—physical, psychological, behavioral, or attitudinal. These phenomena are often referred to as cultural variations. Two ingredients are necessary to explain cultural variations: (1) a universal underlying mechanism and (2) environmental differences in the degree to which the underlying mechanism is activated.

culture of honor Nisbett (1993) proposed that the economic means of subsistence of a culture affects the degree to which the group develops what he calls "a culture of honor." In cultures of honor, insults are viewed as highly offensive public challenges that must be met with direct confrontation and physical aggression. The theory is that differences in the degree to which honor becomes a central part of the culture rests ultimately with economics, and specifically with the manner in which food is obtained.

culture A set of shared standards for many behaviors. It might contain different standards for males and females, such that girls should be ashamed if they engage in promiscuous sex, whereas boys might be proud of such behavior, with it being culturally acceptable for them to even brag about such behavior.

d

daily hassles The major sources of stress in most people's lives. Although minor, daily hassles can be chronic and repetitive, such as having too much to do all the time, having to fight the crowds while shopping, or having to worry over money. Such daily hassles can be chronically irritating though they do not initiate the same general adaptation syndrome evoked by some major life events.

deductive reasoning approach The top-down, theory-driven method of empirical research.

defense mechanisms Strategies for coping with anxiety and threats to self-esteem.

defensive pessimism Individuals who use a defensive pessimism strategy have usually done well on important tasks but lack self-confidence in their ability to handle new challenges. A defensive pessimist controls anxiety by preparing for failure ahead of time; they set low expectations for their performance and often focus on worse-case outcomes. This strategy overcomes anticipatory anxiety and transforms it into motivation.

deliberation-without-awareness The notion that, when confronted with a decision, if a person can put it out of their conscious mind for a period of time, then the "unconscious mind" will continue to deliberate on it, helping the person to arrive at a "sudden" and often correct decision some time later.

denial When the reality of a particular situation is extremely anxiety provoking, a person may resort to the defense mechanism of denial. A person in denial insists that things are not the way they seem. Denial can also be less extreme, as when someone reappraises an anxiety-provoking situation so that it seems less daunting. Denial often shows up in people's daydreams and fantasies.

density distribution of states Refers to the idea that traits are distributions of states in a person's life over time, and the mean of that distribution is the person's level of the trait.

dependent personality disorder The dependent personality seeks out others to an extreme. The hallmark of the dependent personality is an excessive need to be taken care of, to be nurtured, coddled, and told what to do. Dependent persons act in submissive ways so as to encourage others to take care of them or take charge of the situation. Such individuals need lots of encouragement and advice from others and would much rather turn over responsibility for their decisions to someone else.

depression A psychological disorder whose symptoms include a depressed mood most of the day; diminished interest in activities; change in weight, sleep patterns, and movement; fatigue or loss of energy; feelings of worthlessness; inability to concentrate; and recurrent thoughts of death and suicide. It is estimated that 20 percent of Americans are afflicted with depression at some time in their lives (American Psychiatric Association, 2013).

developmental crisis Erikson believed that each stage in personality development represented a conflict, or a developmental crisis, that needed to be resolved before the person advanced to the next stage of development.

diathesis-stress model of depression   Suggests that a preexisting vulnerability, or diathesis, is present among people who become depressed. In addition to this vulnerability, a stressful life event must occur in order to trigger the depression, such as the loss of a loved one or some other major negative life event. The events must occur together—something bad or stressful has to happen to a person who has a particular vulnerability to depression—in order for depression to occur.

differences among groups   See *group differences.*

differential diagnosis   A differential diagnosis is arrived at when, out of two or more possible diagnoses, the clinician searches for evidence in support of one diagnostic category over all the others.

differential gene reproduction   Reproductive success relative to others. The genes of organisms who reproduce more than others get passed down to future generations at a relatively greater frequency than the genes of those who reproduce less. Because survival is usually critical for reproductive success, characteristics that lead to greater survival get passed along. Because success in mate competition is also critical for reproductive success, qualities that lead to success in same-sex competition or to success at being chosen as a mate get passed along. Successful survival and successful mate competition, therefore, are both part of differential gene reproduction.

differential psychology   Due to its emphasis on the study of differences between people, trait psychology has sometimes been called differential psychology in the interest of distinguishing this subfield from other branches of personality psychology (Anastasi, 1976). Differential psychology includes the study of other forms of individual differences in addition to personality traits, such as abilities, aptitudes, and intelligence.

dimensional approach   Researchers gather data by having subjects rate themselves on a wide variety of emotions, then apply statistical techniques (mostly factor analysis) to identify the basic dimensions underlying the ratings. Almost all the studies suggest that subjects categorize emotions using just two primary dimensions: how pleasant or unpleasant the emotion is, and how high or low on arousal the emotion is.

dimensional view   The dimensional view approaches a personality disorder as a continuum that ranges from normality at one end to severe disability and disturbance at the other end. According to this view, people with and without the disorder differ in degree only.

directionality problem   One reason correlations can never prove causality. If A and B are correlated, we do not know if A is the cause of B, or if B is the cause of A, or if some third, unknown variable is causing both B and A.

disclosure   Telling someone about some private aspect of ourselves. Many theorists have suggested that keeping things to ourselves may be a source of stress and ultimately may lead to psychological distress and physical disease.

discriminant validity   What a measure should not correlate with.

disorder   A pattern of behavior or experience that is distressing and painful to the person, leads to some disability or impairment in important life domains (e.g., work, marriage, or relationship difficulties), and is associated with increased risk for further suffering, loss of function, death, or confinement.

disparate impact   Any employment practice that disadvantages people from a protected group. The Supreme Court has not defined the size of the disparity necessary to prove disparate impact. Most courts define disparity as a difference that is sufficiently large that it is unlikely to have occurred by chance. Some courts, however, prefer the 80 percent rule contained in the Uniform Guidelines on Employee Selection Procedures. Under this rule, adverse impact is established if the selection rate for any race, sex, or ethnic group is less than four-fifths (or 80 percent) of the rate for the group with the highest selection rate.

displacement   An unconscious defense mechanism that involves avoiding the recognition that one has certain inappropriate urges or unacceptable feelings (e.g., anger, sexual attraction) toward a specific other. Those feelings then get displaced onto another person or object that is more appropriate or acceptable.

dispositional domain   Deals centrally with the ways in which individuals differ from one another. As such, the dispositional domain connects with all the other domains. In the dispositional domain, psychologists are primarily interested in the number and nature of fundamental dispositions, taxonomies of traits, measurement issues, and questions of stability over time and consistency over situations.

dispositional optimism   The expectation that in the future good events will be plentiful and bad events will be rare.

distortion   A defense mechanism in Roger's theory of personality; distortion refers to modifying the meaning of experiences to make them less threatening to the self-image.

dizygotic twins   (also called fraternal twins) Twins who are not genetically identical. They come from two eggs that were separately fertilized ("di" means two; so dizygotic means "coming from two fertilized eggs"). Such twins share only 50 percent of their genes with their co-twin, the same amount as ordinary brothers and sisters. Fraternal twins can be of the same sex or of the opposite sex.

domain of knowledge   A specialty area of science and scholarship, where psychologists have focused on learning about some specific and limited aspect of human nature, often with preferred tools of investigation.

domain specific   Adaptations are presumed to be domain specific in the sense that they are "designed" by the evolutionary process to solve a specialized adaptive problem. Domain specificity implies that selection tends to fashion specific mechanisms for each specific adaptive problem.

dopamine   A neurotransmitter that appears to be associated with pleasure. Dopamine appears to function something like the "reward system" and has even been called the "feeling good" chemical (Hamer, 1997).

DRD4 gene   A gene located on the short arm of chromosome 11 that codes for a protein called a dopamine receptor. The function of this dopamine receptor is to respond to the presence of dopamine, which is a neurotransmitter. When the dopamine receptor encounters dopamine from other neurons in the brain, it discharges an electrical signal, activating other neurons.

dream analysis   A technique Freud taught for uncovering the unconscious material in a dream by interpreting the content of a dream. Freud called dreams "the royal road to the unconscious."

dynamic   The interaction of forces within a person.

e

Easterlin paradox   At any point in time, happiness varies with income across nations, but over time within a country, happiness does not trend upward with increases in income.

effect size   How large a particular difference is, or how strong a particular correlation is, as averaged over several experiments or studies.

effective polygyny   Because female mammals bear the physical burden of gestation and lactation, there is a considerable sex difference in minimum obligatory parental investment. This difference leads to differences in the variances in reproduction between the sexes: most females will have some offspring, whereas a few males will sire many offspring, and some will have none at all. This is known as effective polygyny.

egalitarianism   How much a particular group displays equal treatment of all individuals within that group.

ego depletion   When exertion of self-control results in a decrease of psychic energy.

ego psychology   Post-Freudian psychoanalysts felt that the ego deserved more attention and that it performed many constructive functions. Erikson emphasized the ego as a powerful and independent part of personality, involved in mastering the environment, achieving one's goals, and hence in establishing one's identity. The approach to psychoanalysis started by Erikson was called ego psychology.

ego   The part of the mind that constrains the id to reality. According to Freud, it develops within the first two or three years of life. The ego operates

according to the reality principle. The ego understands that the urges of the id are often in conflict with social and physical reality, and that direct expression of id impulses must therefore be redirected or postponed.

Electra complex   Within the psychoanalytic theory of personality development, the female counterpart to the Oedipal complex; both refer to the phallic stage of development.

electrode   A sensor usually placed on the surface of the skin and linked to a physiological recording machine (often called a polygraph) to measure physiological variables.

electrodermal activity   (also known as galvanic skin response or skin conductance) Electricity will flow across the skin with less resistance if that skin is made damp with sweat. Sweating on the palms of the hands is activated by the sympathetic nervous system, and so electrodermal activity is a way to directly measure changes in the sympathetic nervous system.

electroencephalogram (EEG)   Refers to recording the minute electrical activity produced by the human brain using electrodes placed on the surface of the scalp. The EEG is useful for diagnosing brain disorders (e.g., epilepsy) but can also be used to identify brain activation patterns associated with psychological states and functions.

electroencephalograph (EEG)   The brain spontaneously produces small amounts of electricity, which can be measured by electrodes placed on the scalp. EEGs can provide useful information about patterns of activation in different regions of the brain that may be associated with different types of information processing tasks.

embedded figures test (EFT)   A method of assessing field dependence/independence by seeing how quickly a person can identify smaller figures hidden inside larger and more complex figures.

emotional inhibition   Suppression of emotional expressions; often thought of as a trait (e.g., some people chronically suppress their emotions).

emotional intelligence   An adaptive form of intelligence consisting of the ability to (1) know one's own emotions, (2) regulate those emotions, (3)

motivate oneself, (4) know how others are feeling, and (5) influence how others are feeling. Goleman posited that emotional intelligence is more strongly predictive of professional status, marital quality, and salary than traditional measures of intelligence and aptitude.

emotional stability   The fourth of the personality traits in the five-factor model, which has proven to be replicable in studies using English-language trait words as items. Some of the key adjective markers for Emotional Stability are "calm," "composed," "not hypochondriacal," "poised."

emotional states   Transitory states that depend more on the situation or circumstances a person is in than on the specific person. Emotions as states have a specific cause, and that cause is typically outside of the person (something happens in the environment).

emotional traits   Stable personality traits that are primarily characterized by specific emotions. For example, the trait of neuroticism is primarily characterized by the emotions of anxiety and worry.

emotions   Emotions can be defined by their three components: (1) Emotions have distinct subjective feelings or affects associated with them; (2) emotions are accompanied by bodily changes, mostly in the nervous system, and these produce associated changes in breathing, heart rate, muscle tension, blood chemistry, and facial and bodily expressions; (3) emotions are accompanied by distinct action tendencies or increases in the probabilities of certain behaviors.

empathizing   Tuning in to other people's thoughts and feelings.

empathy   In Rogers's client-centered therapy, empathy is understanding the person from his or her point of view. Instead of interpreting the meaning behind what the client says (e.g., "You have a harsh superego that is punishing you for the actions of your id."), the client-centered therapist simply listens to what the client says and reflects it back.

enduring   When psychological traits are stable over time.

environment   Environments can be physical, social, and intrapsychic (within the mind). Which aspect of the environment is important at any moment in time is frequently determined by the personality of the person in that environment.

environmentalist view   Environmentalists believe that personality is determined by socialization practices, such as parenting style and other agents of society.

environmentality   The percentage of observed variance in a *group* of individuals that can be attributed to environmental (nongenetic) differences. Generally speaking, the larger the heritability, the smaller the environmentality. And vice versa, the smaller the heritability, the larger the environmentality.

epidemiological studies   Studies that typically enroll a large number of subjects who are initially healthy, then they are followed over time to see who develops specific diseases.

equal environments assumption   The assumption that the environments experienced by identical twins are no more similar to each other than are the environments experienced by fraternal twins. If they are more similar, then the greater similarity of the identical twins could plausibly be due to the fact that they experience more similar environments rather than the fact that they have more genes in common.

Erikson's eight stages of development   According to Erikson, there are eight stages of development: trust versus mistrust, autonomy versus shame and doubt, initiative versus guilt, industry versus inferiority, identity versus role confusion, intimacy versus isolation, generativity versus stagnation, and integrity versus despair.

esteem needs   The fourth level of Maslow's motivation hierarchy. There are two types of esteem: esteem from others and self-esteem, the latter often depending on the former. People want to be seen by others as competent, as strong, and as able to achieve. They want to be respected by others for their achievements or abilities. People also want to feel good about themselves. Much of the activity of adult daily life is geared toward achieving recognition and esteem from others and bolstering one's own self-confidence.

eudaimonia   A philosophical position that holds that living a life of meaning and purpose will lead to happiness

eugenics   The notion that the future of the human race can be influenced by fostering the reproduction of persons with certain traits and discouraging reproduction among persons without those traits or who have undesirable traits.

evocation   A form of person–situation interaction discussed by Buss. It is based on the idea that certain personality traits may evoke consistent responses from the environment, particularly the social environment.

evoked culture   A way of considering culture that concentrates on phenomena that are triggered in different ways by different environmental conditions.

evolutionary byproduct   Incidental effects evolved changes that are not properly considered adaptations. For example, our noses hold up glasses, but that is not what the nose evolved for.

evolutionary noise   Random variations that are neutral with respect to selection.

evolutionary-predicted sex differences   Evolutionary psychology predicts that males and females will be the same or similar in all those domains where the sexes have faced the same or similar adaptive problems (e.g., both sexes have sweat glands because both sexes have faced the adaptive problem of thermal regulation) and different when men and women have faced substantially different adaptive problems (e.g., in the physical realm, women have faced the problem of childbirth and have therefore evolved adaptations that are lacking in men, such as mechanisms for producing labor contractions through the release of oxytocin into the bloodstream).

exhaustion stage   The third stage in Selye's general adaptation syndrome (GAS). Selye felt that this was the stage where we are most susceptible to illness and disease, as our physiological resources are depleted.

expectancy confirmation   A phenomenon whereby people's beliefs about the personality characteristics of others cause them to evoke in others actions that are consistent with the initial beliefs. The phenomenon of expectancy confirmation has also been

called self-fulfilling prophecy and behavioral confirmation.

experience sampling   People answer some questions, for example, about their mood or physical symptoms, every day for several weeks or longer. People are usually contacted electronically ("beeped") one or more times a day at random intervals to complete the measures. Although experience sampling uses self-report as the data source, it differs from more traditional self-report methods in being able to detect patterns of behavior over time.

experimental methods   Typically used to determine causality—to find out whether one variable influences another variable. Experiments involve the manipulation of one variable (the independent variable) and random assignment of subjects to conditions defined by the independent variable.

expressiveness   The ease with which one can express emotions, such as crying, showing empathy for the troubles of others, and showing nurturance to those in need.

external locus of control   Generalized expectancies that events are outside of one's control.

extraversion   The first fundamental personality trait in the five-factor model, a taxonomy which has proven to be replicable in studies using English-language trait words as items. Some of the key adjective markers for Extraversion are "talkative," "extraverted" or "extraverted," "gregarious," "assertive," "adventurous," "open," "sociable," "forward," and "outspoken."

extreme responding   A response set that refers to the tendency to give endpoint responses, such as "strongly agree" or "strongly disagree" and avoid the middle part of response scales, such as "slightly agree," "slightly disagree," or "am indifferent."

eye-blink startle method   People typically blink their eyes when they are startled by a loud noise. Moreover, a person who is in an anxious or fearful state will blink faster and harder when startled than a person in a normal emotional state. This means that eye-blink speed when startled may be an objective physiological measure of how anxious or fearful a person is feeling. The eye-blink startle method may allow researchers to measure how anxious persons are without actually having to ask them.

f

face validity   Whether the test, on the surface, measures what it appears to measure.

factor analysis   A commonly used statistical procedure for identifying underlying structure in personality ratings or items. Factor analysis essentially identifies groups of items that covary (i.e., go together or correlate) with each other, but tend not to covary with other groups of items. This provides a means for determining which personality variables share some common underlying property or belong together within the same group.

factor loadings   Indexes of how much of the variation in an item is "explained" by the factor. Factor loadings indicate the degree to which the item correlates with or "loads on" the underlying factor.

faking   The motivated distortion of answers on a questionnaire. Some people may be motivated to "fake good" in order to appear to be better off or better adjusted than they really are. Others may be motivated to "fake bad" in order to appear to be worse off or more maladjusted than they really are.

false consensus effect   The tendency many people have to assume that others are similar to them (i.e., extraverts think that many other people are as extraverted as they are). Thinking that many other people share your own traits, preferences, or motivations.

false memories   Memories that have been "implanted" by well-meaning therapists or others interrogating a subject about some event.

false negative and false positive   There are two ways for psychologists to make a mistake when making decisions about persons based on personality tests (e.g., when deciding whether or not to hire a person, to parole a person, or that the person was lying). When trying to decide whether a person's answers are genuine or faked, the psychologist might decide that a person who was faking was actually telling the truth (called a false positive). Or they might conclude that a truthful person was faking. This is called a false negative.

family studies   Family studies correlate the degree of genetic overlap among family members with the degree of personality similarity. They capitalize on the fact that there are known degrees of genetic overlap between different members of a family in terms of degree of relationship.

fear of success   Horney coined this phrase to highlight a gender difference in response to competition and achievement situations. Many women, she argued, feel that if they succeed, they will lose their friends. Consequently, many women, she thought, harbor an unconscious fear of success. She held that men, on the other hand, feel that they will actually gain friends by being successful and hence are not at all afraid to strive and pursue achievement.

female underprediction effect   On average, college entrance exam scores underpredict grade point average for women relative to men with the same entrance exam scores. Women tend to do better in college than one would predict from their entrance exam scores alone.

feminine   Traits or roles typically associated with being female in a particular culture.

femininity   A psychological dimension containing traits such as nurturance, empathy, and expression of emotions (e.g., crying when sad). Femininity traits refer to gender roles, as distinct from biological sex.

field dependent and field independent   In Witkin's rod and frame test, if a participant adjusts the rod so that it is leaning in the direction of the tilted frame, that person is said to be dependent of the visual field, or field dependent. If a participant disregards the external cues and instead uses information from his body in adjusting the rod to upright, he is said to be independent of the field, or field independent; appearing to rely on his own sensations, not the perception of the field, to make the judgment. This individual difference may have implications in situations where people must extract information from complex sensory fields, such as in multimedia education.

five-factor model   A trait taxonomy that has its roots in the lexical hypothesis.

The first psychologist to use the terms "five-factor model" and "Big Five" was Warren Norman, based on his replications of the factor structure suggesting the following five traits: Surgency (or extraversion), Neuroticism (or emotional instability), Agreeableness, Conscientiousness, and Intellect-Openness to Experience (or intellect). The model has been criticized by some for not being comprehensive and for failing to provide a theoretical understanding of the underlying psychological processes that generate the five traits. Nonetheless, it remains heavily endorsed by many personality psychologists and continues to be used in a variety of research studies and applied settings.

fixation   A concept found in both Freud's and Erikson's developmental theories, implying that an immature resolution of a developmental crisis results in a portion of a person's psychic energy needing to be used to maintain that resolution, appearing as a preoccupation with that stage, and hence less psychic energy going forward to the next developmental stage.

flow   A subjective state that people report when they are completely involved in an activity to the point of forgetting time, fatigue, and everything else but the activity itself. While flow experiences are somewhat rare, they occur under specific conditions; there is a balance between the person's skills and the challenges of the situation, there is a clear goal, and there is immediate feedback on how one is doing.

forced-choice questionnaire   Test takers are confronted with pairs of statements and are asked to indicate which statement in the pair is more true of them. Each statement in the pair is selected to be similar to the other in social desirability, forcing participants to choose between statements that are equivalently socially desirable (or undesirable), and differ in content.

free association   Patients relax, let their minds wander, and say whatever comes into their minds. Patients often say things that surprise or embarrass them. By relaxing the censor that screens everyday thoughts, free association allows potentially important material into conscious awareness.

free running A condition in studies of circadian rhythms in which participants are deprived from knowing what time it is (e.g., meals are served when the participant asks for them, not at prescheduled times). When a person is free running in time, there are no time cues to influence behavior or biology.

frequency-dependent selection In some contexts, two or more heritable variants can evolve within a population. The most obvious example is biological sex itself. Within sexually reproducing species, the two sexes exist in roughly equal numbers because of frequency-dependent selection. If one sex becomes rare relative to the other, evolution will produce an increase in the numbers of the rarer sex. Frequency-dependent selection, in this example, causes the frequency of men and women to remain roughly equal. Different personality extremes (e.g., introversion and extraversion) may be the result of frequency dependent selection.

frontal brain asymmetry Asymmetry in the amount of activity in the left and right part of the frontal hemispheres of the brain. Studies using EEG measures have linked more relative left brain activity with pleasant emotions and more relative right brain activity with negative emotions.

frustration The high-arousal unpleasant subjective feeling that comes when a person is blocked from attaining an important goal. For example, a thirsty person who just lost his last bit of money in a malfunctioning soda machine would most likely feel frustration.

fully functioning person According to Rogers, a fully functioning person is on his or her way toward self-actualization. Fully functioning persons may not actually *be* self-actualized yet, but they are not blocked or sidetracked in moving toward this goal. Such persons are open to new experiences and are not afraid of new ideas. They embrace life to its fullest. Fully functioning individuals are also centered in the present. They do not dwell on the past or their regrets. Fully functioning individuals also trust themselves, their feelings, and their own judgments.

functional analysis In *The Expression of the Emotions in Man and Animals,* Charles Darwin proposed a functional analysis of emotions and emotional expressions focusing on the "why" of emotions and expressions. Darwin concluded that emotional expressions communicate information from one animal to another about what is likely to happen. For instance, a dog baring its teeth, growling, and bristling the fur on its back is communicating to others that he is likely to attack. If others recognize the dog's communication, they may choose to back away to safety.

functional magnetic resonance imaging (fMRI) A noninvasive imaging technique used to identify specific areas of brain activity. As parts of the brain are stimulated, oxygenated blood rushes to the activated area, resulting in increased iron concentrations in the blood. The fMRI detects these elevated concentrations of iron and prints out colorful images indicating which part of the brain is used to perform certain tasks.

functionality The notion that our psychological mechanisms are designed to accomplish particular adaptive goals.

fundamental attribution error When bad events happen to others, people have a tendency to attribute blame to some characteristic of the person, whereas when bad events happen to oneself, people have the tendency to blame the situation.

g

gender differences The distinction between gender and sex can be traced back to Horney. Horney stressed the point that, while biology determines sex, cultural norms determine what is acceptable for typical males and females in that culture. Today we use the terms *masculine* and *feminine* to refer to traits or roles typically associated with being male or female in a particular culture, and we refer to differences in such culturally ascribed roles and traits as gender differences. Differences that are ascribed to being a man or a woman per se are, however, called sex differences.

gender schemata Cognitive orientations that lead individuals to process social information on the basis of sex-linked associations (Hoyenga & Hoyenga, 1993).

gender stereotypes Beliefs that we hold about how men and women differ or are supposed to differ, which are not necessarily based on reality. Gender stereotypes can have important real-life consequences for men and women. These consequences can damage people where it most counts—in their health, their jobs, their odds of advancement, and their social reputations.

gender Social interpretations of what it means to be a man or a woman.

general adaptation syndrome (GAS) GAS has three stages: When a stressor first appears, people experience the alarm stage. If the stressor continues, the stage of resistance begins. If the stressor remains constant, the person eventually enters the third stage, the stage of exhaustion.

general intelligence Early on in the study of intelligence, many psychologists thought of intelligence in traitlike terms, as a property of the individual. Individuals were thought to differ from each other in how much intelligence they possessed. Moreover, intelligence was thought of as a single broad factor, often called "g" for general intelligence. This stands in contrast to those views of intelligence as consisting of many discrete factors, such as social intelligence, emotional intelligence, and academic intelligence.

generalizability The degree to which a measure retains its validity across different contexts.

generalized expectancies A person's expectations for reinforcement that hold across a variety of situations (Rotter, 1971, 1990). When people encounter a new situation, they base their expectancies about what will happen on their generalized expectancies about whether they have the abilities to influence events.

genes Packets of DNA that are inherited by children from their parents in distinct chunks. They are the smallest discrete unit that is inherited by offspring intact, without being broken up.

genetic junk The 98 percent of the DNA in human chromosomes that are not protein-coding genes; scientists believed that these parts were functionless residue. Recent studies have shown that these portions of DNA may affect everything from a person's physical size to personality, thus adding to the complexity of the human genome.

genital stage The final stage in Freud's psychosexual stage theory of development. This stage begins around age 12 and lasts through one's adult life. Here the libido is focused on the genitals, but not in the manner of self-manipulation associated with the phallic stage. People reach the genital stage with full psychic energy if they have resolved the conflicts at the prior stages.

genome The complete set of genes an organism possesses. The human genome contains somewhere between 20,000 and 30,000 genes.

genotype–environment correlation The differential exposure of individuals with different genotypes to different environments.

genotype–environment interaction The differential response of individuals with different genotypes to the same environments.

genotypic variance Genetic variance that is responsible for individual differences in the phenotypic expression of specific traits.

global self-esteem By far the most frequently measured component of self-esteem; defined as "the level of global regard that one has for the self as a person" (Harter, 1993, p. 88). Global self-esteem can range from highly positive to highly negative, and reflects an overall evaluation of the self at the broadest level (Kling et al., 1999). Global self-esteem is linked with many aspects of functioning and is commonly thought to be central to mental health.

good theory A theory that serves as a useful guide for researchers, organizes known facts, and makes predictions about future observations.

Griggs v. Duke Power Prior to 1964, Duke Power Company had used discriminatory practices in hiring and work assignment, including barring blacks from certain jobs. After passage of the Civil Rights Act of 1964, Duke Power instituted various requirements for such jobs, including passing certain aptitude tests. The effect was to perpetuate discrimination. In 1971 the Supreme Court ruled that the seemingly neutral testing practices used by Duke Power were unacceptable because they operated to maintain discrimination. This was the first legal case where the Supreme Court ruled that any selection procedure could not produce disparate impact for a group protected by the Act (e.g., racial groups, women).

h

happiness Researchers conceive of happiness in two complementary ways: in terms of a judgment that life is satisfying, as well as in terms of the predominance of positive compared to negative, emotions in one's life (Diener, 2000). It turns out, however, that people's emotional lives and their judgments of how satisfied they are with their lives are highly correlated. People who have a lot of pleasant emotions relative to unpleasant emotions in their lives tend also to judge their lives as satisfying, and vice versa.

harm avoidance In Cloninger's tridimensional personality model, the personality trait of harm avoidance is associated with low levels of serotonin. People low in serotonin are sensitive to unpleasant stimuli or to stimuli or events that have been associated with punishment or pain. Consequently, people low in serotonin seem to expect that harmful and unpleasant events will happen to them, and they are constantly vigilant for signs of such threatening events.

health behavior model Personality does not directly influence the relation between stress and illness. Instead, personality affects health indirectly, through health-promoting or health-degrading behaviors. This model suggests that personality influences the degree to which a person engages in various health-promoting or health-demoting behaviors.

health psychology Researchers in the area of health psychology study relations between the mind and the body, and how these two components respond to challenges from the environment (e.g., stressful events, germs) to produce illness or health.

healthy neuroticism A new idea that stresses the possible benefits of neuroticism.

Heart Rate Variability (HRV) Refers to how much heart rate changes on a beat-by-beat basis, with higher HRV being normal and an indicator of balance between the sympathetic and parasympathetic branches of the nervous systems. Lower HRV results when one branch predominates, and is often associated with stress, fatigue, poor sleep, or over-training. HRV assessment is available with several of the popular wearable sensors, including watches and rings.

heart rate Refers to how rapidly the heart is beating, usually expressed in beats per minute. It can be assessed beat by beat by measuring the time interval between successive heart beats and converting that to beats per minute

heritability A statistic that refers to the proportion of observed variance in a group of individuals that can be explained or "accounted for" by genetic variance (Plomin, DeFries, & McClearn, 1990). It describes the degree to which genetic differences between individuals cause differences in some observed property, such as height, extraversion, or sensation seeking. The formal definition of heritability is the proportion of phenotypic variance that is attributable to genotypic variance.

heuristic value An evaluative scientific standard for assessing personality theories. Theories that steer scientists to important new discoveries about personality are superior to those that fail to provide this guidance.

HEXACO model Humility-Honesty (H), Emotionality (E), Extraversion (X), Agreeableness (A), Conscientiousness (C), and Openness to Experience (O).

hierarchy of needs Murray believed that each person has a unique combination of needs. An individual's various needs can be thought of as existing at a different level of strength. A person might have a high need for dominance, an average need for intimacy, and a low need for achievement. High levels of some needs interact with the amounts of various other needs within each person.

high-variance conditions One key variable triggering communal food sharing is the degree of variability in food resources. Specifically, under high-variance conditions, there are substantial benefits to sharing.

historical era One type of intracultural variation pertains to the effects of historical era on personality. (People who grew up during the great economic depression of the 1930s, for example, might be more anxious about job security or adopt a more conservative spending style.) Disentangling the effects of historical era on personality is an extremely difficult endeavor because most current personality measures were not in use in earlier eras.

histrionic personality disorder The hallmark of the histrionic personality is excessive attention seeking and emotionality. Often such persons are overly dramatic and draw attention to themselves, preferring to be the center of attention or the life of the party. They may appear charming or even flirtatious. Often they can be inappropriately seductive or provocative.

Hogan Personality Inventory (HPI) A questionnaire measure of personality based on the Big Five model but modified to emphasize the assessment of traits important in the business world, including the motive to get along with others and the motive to get ahead of others.

holistic A way of processing information that involves attention to relationships, contexts, and links between the focal objects and the field as a whole.

honesty-humility High scorers on Honesty-Humilty are individuals who show a lot of prosocial behavior, treating other people reasonably and fairly, and not being overly concerned with self-promotion.

hormonal theories Hormonal theories of sex differences argue that men and women differ not because of the external social environment but because the sexes have different amounts of specific hormones. It is these physiological differences, not differential social treatment, that causes boys and girls to diverge over development.

hostile attributional bias The tendency to infer hostile intent on the part of others in the face of uncertain or unclear behavior from others. Essentially, people who are aggressive expect that others will be hostile toward them.

hostile forces of nature Hostile forces of nature are what Darwin called any event that impedes survival. Hostile forces of nature include food shortages, diseases, parasites, predators, and extremes of weather.

hostility A tendency to respond to everyday frustrations with anger and aggression, to become irritable easily, to feel frequent resentment, and to act in a rude, critical, antagonistic, and uncooperative manner in everyday interactions (Dembrowski & Costa, 1987). Hostility is a subtrait in the Type A behavior pattern.

human nature The traits and mechanisms of personality that are typical of our species and are possessed by everyone or nearly everyone.

humanistic tradition Humanistic psychologists emphasize the role of choice in human life and the influence of responsibility on creating a meaningful and satisfying life. The meaning of any person's life, according to the humanistic approach, is found in the choices that people make and the responsibility they take for those choices. The humanistic tradition also emphasizes the human need for growth and realizing one's full potential. In the humanistic tradition it is assumed that, if left to their own devices, humans will grow and develop in positive and satisfying directions.

i

id psychology Freud's version of psychoanalysis focused on the id, especially the twin instincts of sex and aggression, and how the ego and superego respond to the demands of the id. Freudian psychoanalysis can thus be called id psychology, to distinguish it from later developments that focused on the functions of the ego.

id The most primitive part of the human mind. Freud saw the id as something we are born with and as the source of all drives and urges. The id is like a spoiled child: selfish, impulsive, and pleasure loving. According to Freud, the id operates strictly according to the pleasure principle, which is the desire for immediate gratification.

ideal self The self that a person wants to be.

identification A developmental process in children. It consists of wanting to become like the same-sex parent. In classic psychoanalysis, it marks the beginning of the resolution of the Oedipal or Electra conflicts and the

successful resolution of the phallic stage of psychosexual development. Freud believed that the resolution of the phallic stage was both the beginning of the superego and morality and the start of the adult gender role.

identity conflict According to Baumeister, an identity conflict involves an incompatibility between two or more aspects of identity. This kind of crisis often occurs when a person is forced to make an important and difficult life decision. Identity conflicts are "approach–approach" conflicts, in that the person wants to reach two mutually contradictory goals. Although these conflicts involve wanting two desirable identities, identity conflicts usually involve intense feelings of guilt or remorse over perceived unfaithfulness to an important aspect of the person's identity.

identity confusion A period when a person does not have a strong sense of who she or he really is in terms of values, careers, relationships, and ideologies.

identity crisis Erikson's term refers to the desperation, anxiety, and confusion a person feels when he or she has not developed a strong sense of identity. A period of identity crisis is a common experience during adolescence, but for some people it occurs later in life, or lasts for a longer period. Baumeister suggests that there are two distinct types of identity crises, which he terms identity deficit and identity conflict.

identity deficit According to Baumeister, an identity deficit arises when a person has not formed an adequate identity and thus has trouble making major decisions. When people who have an identity deficit look toward their social identity for guidance in making decisions (e.g., "What would a person like me do in this situation?"), they find little in the way of a foundation upon which to base such life choices. Identity deficits often occur when a person discards old values or goals.

identity foreclosure A person does not emerge from a crisis with a firm sense of commitment to values, relationships, or career but forms an identity without exploring alternatives. An example would be young people who accept the

identity An inner sense of who we are, of what makes us unique, and a sense of continuity over time and a feeling of wholeness.

idiographic The study of single individuals, with an effort to observe general principles as they are manifest in a single life over time.

"if . . . then . . ." propositions A component of Walter Mischel's theory referring to the notion that, if situation A, the person does X, but if situation B, then the person does Y. Personality leaves its signature, Mischel argues, in terms of the specific situational ingredients that prompt behavior from the person.

illness behavior model Personality influences the degree to which a person perceives and pays attention to bodily sensations, and the degree to which a person will interpret and label those sensations as an illness.

imagination inflation effect A memory is elaborated upon in the imagination, leading the person to confuse the imagined event with events that actually happened.

implicit motivation Motives as they are measured in fantasy-based (i.e., TAT) techniques, as opposed to direct self-report measures. The implied motives of persons scored, for example, from TAT stories, are thought to reveal their unconscious desires and aspirations, their unspoken needs and wants. McClelland has argued that implicit motives predict long-term behavioral trends over time, such as implicit need for achievement predicting long-term business success.

impulsivity A personality trait that refers to lowered self-control, especially in the presence of potentially rewarding activities, the tendency to act before one thinks, and a lowered ability to anticipate the consequences of one's behavior.

inclusive fitness theory Modern evolutionary theory based on differential gene reproduction (Hamilton, 1964). The "inclusive" part refers to the fact that the characteristics that affect reproduction need not affect the personal production of offspring; they can affect the survival and reproduction of genetic relatives as well.

independence training McClelland believes that certain parental behaviors can promote high achievement motivation, autonomy, and independence in their children. One of these parenting practices is placing an emphasis on independence training. Training a child to be independent in different tasks promotes a sense of mastery and confidence in the child.

independence Markus and Kitayama propose that each person has two fundamental "cultural tasks" that have to be confronted. One such task, agency or independence, involves how you differentiate yourself from the larger group. Independence includes your unique abilities, your personal internal motives and personality dispositions, and the ways in which you separate yourself from the larger group.

independent risk factor Operates independently from other known risk factors, such as being overweight or smoking.

individual differences Every individual has personal and unique qualities that make him or her different from others. The study of all the ways in which individuals can differ from others, the number, origin, and meaning of such differences, is the study of individual differences.

inductive reasoning approach The bottom-up, data-driven method of empirical research.

influential forces Personality traits and mechanisms are influential forces in people's lives in that they influence our actions, how we view ourselves, how we think about the world, how we interact with others, how we feel, our selection of environments (particularly our social environment), what goals and desires we pursue in life, and how we react to our circumstances. Other influential forces include sociological and economic influences, as well as physical and biological forces.

information processing The transformation of sensory input into mental representations and the manipulation of such representations.

infrequency scale A common method for detecting measurement technique problems within a set of questionnaire items. The infrequency scale contains

items that most or all people would answer in a particular way. If a participant answered more than one or two of these unlike the rest of the majority of the participants, a researcher could begin to suspect that the participant's answers do not represent valid information. Such a participant may be answering randomly, may have difficulty reading, or may be marking his or her answer sheet incorrectly.

inhibitory control The ability to control inappropriate responses or behaviors.

insight In psychoanalysis, through many interpretations, a patient is gradually led to an understanding of the unconscious source of his or her problems. This understanding is called insight.

inspection time A variable in intelligence research; the time it takes a person to make a simple discrimination between two displayed objects or two auditory intervals that differ by only a few milliseconds. This variable suggests that brain mechanisms specifically involved in discriminations of extremely brief time intervals represent a sensitive indicator of general intelligence.

instincts Freud believed that strong innate forces provided *all* the energy in the psychic system. He called these forces instincts. In Freud's initial formulation there were two fundamental categories of instincts: self-preservation instincts and sexual instincts. In his later formulations, Freud collapsed the self-preservation and sexual instincts into one, which he called the life instinct.

instrumentality Personality traits that involve working with objects, getting tasks completed in a direct fashion, showing independence from others, and displaying self-sufficiency.

integrity tests Because the private sector cannot legally use polygraphs to screen employees, some companies have developed and promoted questionnaire measures to use in place of the polygraph. These questionnaires, called integrity tests, are designed to assess whether a person is generally honest or dishonest.

intellect–openness The fifth personality trait in the five-factor model, which has proven to be replicable in studies using English-language trait words as items. Some of the key adjective markers for Openness are "creative," "imaginative," "intellectual." Those who rate high on Openness tend to remember their dreams more and have vivid, prophetic, or problem-solving dreams.

inter-rater reliability   Multiple observers gather information about a person's personality, then investigators evaluate the degree of consensus among the observers. When different observers agree with one another, the degree of inter-rater reliability increases. When different raters fail to agree, the measure is said to have low inter-rater reliability.

interactional model   Objective events happen to a person, but personality factors determine the impact of those events by influencing the person's ability to cope. This is called the interactional model because personality is assumed to moderate (i.e., influence) the relation between stress and illness.

interdependence   Markus and Kitayama propose that each person has two fundamental "cultural tasks" that have to be confronted. The first is communion or interdependence. This cultural task involves how you are affiliated with, attached to, or engaged in the larger group of which you are a member. Interdependence includes your relationships with other members of the group and your embeddedness within the group.

internal locus of control   The generalized expectancy that reinforcing events are under one's control, and that one is responsible for the major outcomes in life.

internalized   In object relations theory, a child will create an unconscious mental representation of his or her mother. This allows the child to have a relationship with this internalized "object" even in the absence of the "real" mother. The relationship object internalized by the child is based on his or her developing relationship with the mother. This image then forms the fundamentals for how children come to view others with whom they develop subsequent relationships.

interpersonal traits   What people do to and with each other. They include *temperament* traits, such as nervous, gloomy, sluggish, and excitable; *character* traits, such as moral, principled, and dishonest; *material* traits, such as miserly or stingy; *attitude* traits, such as pious or spiritual; *mental* traits, such as clever, logical, and perceptive; and *physical* traits, such as healthy and tough.

interpretation   One of the three levels of cognition that are of interest to personality psychologists. Interpretation is the making sense of, or explaining, various events in the world. Psychoanalysts offer patients interpretations of the psychodynamic causes of their problems. Through many interpretations, patients are gradually led to an understanding of the unconscious source of their problems.

intersexual selection   In Darwin's intersexual selection, members of one sex choose a mate based on their preferences for particular qualities in that mate. These characteristics evolve because animals that possess them are chosen more often as mates, and their genes thrive. Animals that lack the desired characteristics are excluded from mating, and their genes perish.

intrapsychic domain   This domain deals with mental mechanisms of personality, many of which operate outside the realm of conscious awareness. The predominant theory in this domain is Freud's theory of psychoanalysis. This theory begins with fundamental assumptions about the instinctual system—the sexual and aggressive forces that are presumed to drive and energize much of human activity. The intrapsychic domain also includes defense mechanisms such as repression, denial, and projection.

intrasexual competition   In Darwin's intrasexual competition, members of the same sex compete with each other, and the outcome of their contest gives the winner greater sexual access to members of the opposite sex. Two stags locking horns in combat is the prototypical image of this. The characteristics that lead to success in contests of this kind, such as greater strength, intelligence, or attractiveness to allies, evolve because the victors are able to mate more often and hence pass on more genes.

j

job analysis   When assisting a business in hiring for a particular job, a psychologist typically starts by analyzing the requirements of the job. The psychologist might interview employees who work in the job or supervisors who are involved in managing the particular job. The psychologist might observe workers in the job, noting any particular oral, written, performance, or social skills needed. He or she may also take into account both the physical and social aspects of the work environment in an effort to identify any special pressures or responsibilities associated with the job. Based on this job analysis, the psychologist develops some hypotheses about the kinds of abilities and personality traits that might best equip a person to perform well in that job.

l

latency stage   The fourth stage in Freud's psychosexual stages of development. This stage occurs from around the age of six until puberty. Freud believed few specific sexual conflicts existed during this time, and was thus a period of psychological rest or latency. Subsequent psychoanalysts have argued that much development occurs during this time, such as learning to make decisions for oneself, interacting and making friends with others, developing an identity, and learning the meaning of work. The latency period ends with the sexual awakening brought about by puberty.

latent content   The latent content of a dream is, according to Freud, what the elements of the dream actually represent.

learned helplessness   Animals (including humans), when subjected to unpleasant and inescapable circumstances, often become passive and accepting of their situation, in effect learning to be helpless. Researchers surmised that if people were in an unpleasant or painful situation, they would attempt to change the situation. However, if repeated attempts to change the situation failed, they would resign themselves to being helpless. Then, even if the situation did improve so that they could escape the discomfort, they would continue to act helpless.

leukocyte A white blood cell. When there is an infection or injury to the body, or a systematic inflammation of the body occurs, there is an elevation in white blood cell counts. Surtees et al., in a 2003 study, established a direct link between hostility and elevated white blood cell counts.

lexical approach The approach to determining the fundamental personality traits by analyzing language. For example, a trait adjective that has many synonyms probably represents a more fundamental trait than a trait adjective with few synonyms.

lexical hypothesis The lexical hypothesis—on which the lexical approach is based—states that important individual differences have become encoded within the natural language. Over ancestral time, the differences between people that were important were noticed and words were invented to communicate about those differences.

libido Freud postulated that humans have a fundamental instinct toward destruction and that this instinct is often manifest in aggression toward others. The two instincts were usually referred to as libido, for the life instinct, and thanatos, for the death instinct. While the libido was generally considered sexual in nature, Freud also used this term to refer to any need-satisfying, life-sustaining, or pleasure-oriented urge.

life-outcome data (L-data) Information that can be gleaned from the events, activities, and outcomes in a person's life that are available to public scrutiny. For example, marriages and divorces are a matter of public record. Personality psychologists can sometimes secure information about the clubs, if any, a person joins; how many speeding tickets a person has received in the last few years; whether the person owns a handgun. These can all serve as sources of information about personality.

Likert rating scale A common rating scale that provides numbers that are attached to descriptive phrases, such as 0 = disagree strongly, 1 = disagree slightly, 2 = neither agree nor disagree,

3 = agree slightly, and 4 = strongly agree.

limbic system The part of the brain responsible for emotion and the "flight-fight" reaction. If individuals have a limbic system that is easily activated, we might expect them to have frequent episodes of emotion, particularly those emotions associated with flight (such as anxiety, fear, worry) and those associated with fight (such as anger, irritation, annoyance). Eysenck postulated that the limbic system was the source of the trait of neuroticism.

locus of control A person's perception of responsibility for the events in his or her life. It refers to whether people tend to locate that responsibility internally, within themselves, or externally, in fate, luck, or chance. Locus of control research started in the mid-1950s when Rotter was developing his social learning theory.

longitudinal study Examines individuals over time. Longitudinal studies have been conducted that have spanned as many as four and five decades of life and have examined many different age brackets. These studies are costly and difficult to conduct, but the information gained about personality development is valuable.

m

Machiavellianism A manipulative strategy of social interaction referring to the tendency to use other people as tools for personal gain. "High Mach" persons tend to tell people what they want to hear, use flattery to get what they want, and rely heavily on lying and deception to achieve their own ends.

major life events According to Holmes and Rahe, major life events require that people make major adjustments in their lives. Death or loss of a spouse through divorce or separation are the most stressful events, followed closely by being jailed, losing a close family member in death, or being severely injured.

manifest content The manifest content of a dream is, according to Freud, what the dream actually contains.

manipulation Researchers conducting experiments use manipulation in order to evaluate the influence of one variable

(the manipulated or independent variable) on another (the dependent variable).

masculine Traits or roles typically associated with being male in a particular culture.

masculinity Traits that define the cultural roles associated with being male. Two major personality instruments were published in 1974 to assess people using this new conception of gender roles (Bem, 1974; Spence, Helmreich, & Stapp, 1974). The masculinity scales contain items reflecting assertiveness, boldness, dominance, self-sufficiency, and instrumentality. Masculinity traits refer to gender roles, as distinct from biological sex.

maximalist Those who describe sex differences as comparable in magnitude to effect sizes in other areas of psychology, important to consider, and recommend that they should not be trivialized.

mean level change Within a single group that has been tested on two separate occasions, any difference in group averages across the two occasions is considered a mean level change.

mean level stability A population that maintains a consistent average level of a trait or characteristic over time. If the average level of liberalism or conservatism in a population remains the same with increasing age, we say that the population exhibits high mean level stability on that characteristic. If the average degree of political orientation changes, then we say that the population is displaying mean level change.

mediation Describes a situation whereby the effects of one variable on another "go through" a third variable (the mediator). For example, we know that conscientiousness in correlated with longevity. However, it is not conscientiousness in itself that causes a longer life. Instead, researchers have determined that, in this relation to longevity, the effects of conscientiousness go through (are mediated by) various health behaviors such as exercising regularly and eating a sensible diet.

minimalist Those who describe sex differences as small and inconsequential.

modeling   By seeing another person engage in a particular behavior with positive results, the observer is more likely to imitate that behavior. It is a form of learning whereby the consequences for a particular behavior are observed, and thus the new behavior is learned.

moderation   Describes a situation whereby one variable (the moderator) influences the degree or correlation between two other variables. For example, if people high in neuroticism showed a strong correlation between stress and illness, and people low in neuroticism showed a weak or no correlation between stress and illness, then we would say that neuroticism is a moderator of the stress–illness relationship.

molecular genetics   Techniques designed to identify the specific genes associated with specific traits, such as personality traits. The most common method, called the association method, identifies whether individuals with a particular gene (or allele) have higher or lower scores on a particular trait measure.

monoamine oxidase (MAO)   An enzyme found in the blood that is known to regulate neurotransmitters, those chemicals that carry messages between nerve cells. MAO may be a causal factor in the personality trait of sensation seeking.

monozygotic twins   Identical twins that come from a single fertilized egg (or zygote, hence monozygotic) that divides into two at some point during gestation. Identical twins are always the same sex because they are genetically identical.

mood induction   In experimental studies of mood, mood inductions are employed as manipulations in order to determine whether the mood differences (e.g., pleasant versus unpleasant) effect some dependent variable. In studies of personality, mood effects might interact with personality variables. For example, positive mood effects might be stronger for persons high on extraversion, and negative mood effects might be stronger for persons high on neuroticism.

mood variability   Frequent fluctuations in a person's emotional life over time.

moral anxiety   Caused by a conflict between the id or the ego and the superego. For example, a person who

suffers from chronic shame or feelings of guilt over not living up to "proper" standards, even though such standards might not be attainable, is experiencing moral anxiety.

moratorium   The time taken to explore options before making a commitment to an identity. College can be considered a "time out" from life, in which students may explore a variety of roles, relationships, and responsibilities before having to commit to any single life path.

morningness–eveningness   The stable differences between persons in preferences for being active at different times of the day. The term was coined to refer to this dimension (Horne & Osterberg, 1976). Differences between morning and evening types of persons appear to be due to differences in the length of their underlying circadian biological rhythms.

motivated unconscious   The psychoanalytic idea that information that is unconscious (e.g., a repressed wish) can actually motivate or influence subsequent behavior. This notion was promoted by Freud and formed the basis for his ideas about the unconscious sources of mental disorders and other problems with living. Many psychologists agree with the idea of the unconscious, but there is less agreement today about whether information that is unconscious can have much of an influence on actual behavior.

motives   Internal states that arouse and direct behavior toward specific objects or goals. A motive is often caused by a deficit, by the lack of something. Motives differ from each other in type, amount, and intensity, depending on the person and his or her circumstances. Motives are based on needs and propel people to perceive, think, and act in specific ways that serve to satisfy those needs.

multiple intelligences   Howard Gardner's theory of multiple intelligences includes several forms: interpersonal intelligence (social skills, ability to communicate and get along with others), intrapersonal intelligence (insight into oneself, one's emotions and motives), kinesthetic intelligence (the abilities of athletes, dancers, and acrobats), and musical intelligence. There are several other theories proposing multiple forms of

intelligence. This position is in contrast to the theory of "g," or general intelligence, which holds that there is only one form of intelligence.

multiple social personalities   Each of us displays different sides of ourselves to different people—we may be kind to our friends, ruthless to our enemies, loving toward a spouse, and conflicted toward our parents. Our social personalities vary from one setting to another, depending on the nature of relationships we have with other individuals.

Myers–Briggs Type Indicator (MBTI)   One of the most widely used personality tests in the business world. It was developed by a mother-daughter team, Katherine Briggs and Isabel Myers, based on Jungian concepts. The test provides information about personality types by testing for eight fundamental preferences using questions in a "forced-choice" or either/or format. Individuals must respond in one way or another, even if their preferences might be somewhere in the middle. Although the test is not without criticism, it has great intuitive appeal.

n

narcissism   A style of inflated self-admiration and the constant attempt to draw attention to the self and to keep others focused on oneself. Although narcissism can be carried to extremes, narcissistic tendencies can be found in normal range levels.

narcissistic paradox   The fact that, although narcissistic people appear to have high self-esteem, they actually have doubts about their self-worth. While they appear to have a grandiose sense of self-importance, narcissists are nevertheless very fragile and vulnerable to blows to their self-esteem and cannot handle criticism well. They need constant praise, reassurance, and attention from others, whereas a person with truly high self-esteem would not need such constant praise and attention from others.

narcissistic paradox   Although narcissists appear to have high self-esteem, their grandiose self-esteem is actually quite fragile. Even though they appear self-confident and strong, they need constant admiration and recognition and praise from others.

narcissistic personality disorder   The calling card of the narcissistic personality is a strong need to be admired, a strong sense of self-importance, and a lack of insight into other people's feelings. Narcissists see themselves in a very favorable light, inflating their accomplishments and undervaluing the work of others. Narcissists daydream about prosperity, victory, influence, adoration from others, and power. They routinely expect adulation from others, believing that homage is generally long overdue. They exhibit feelings of entitlement, even though they have done nothing in particular to earn that special treatment.

natural selection   Darwin reasoned that variants that better enabled an organism to survive and reproduce would lead to more descendants. The descendants, therefore, would inherit the variants that led to their ancestors' survival and reproduction. Through this process, the successful variants were selected, and unsuccessful variants weeded out. Natural selection, therefore, results in gradual changes in a species over time, as successful variants increase in frequency and eventually spread throughout the gene pool, replacing the less successful variants.

naturalistic observation   Observers witness and record events that occur in the normal course of the lives of their participants. For example, a child might be followed throughout an entire day, or an observer may record behavior in the home of the participant. Naturalistic observation offers researchers the advantage of being able to secure information in the realistic context of a person's everyday life, but at the cost of not being able to control the events and behavioral samples witnessed.

nature–nurture debate   The ongoing debate as to whether genes or environment are more important determinants of personality.

need for achievement   According to McClelland, the desire to do better, to be successful, and to feel competent. People with a high need for achievement obtains satisfaction from accomplishing a task or from the anticipation of accomplishing a task.

They cherish the process of being engaged in a challenging task.

need for intimacy   McAdams defines the need for intimacy as the "recurrent preference or readiness for warm, close, and communicative interaction with others" (1990, p. 198). People with a high need for intimacy want more intimacy and meaningful human contact in their day-to-day lives than do those with a low need for intimacy.

need for power   A preference for having an impact on other people. Individuals with a high need for power are interested in controlling situations and other people.

needs   States of tension within a person; as a need is satisfied, the state of tension is reduced. Usually the state of tension is caused by the lack of something (e.g., a lack of food causes a need to eat).

negative affectivity   Includes components such as anger, sadness, difficulty, and amount of distress.

negative identity   Identities founded on undesirable social roles, such as "gangstas," girlfriends of street toughs, or members of street gangs.

negligent hiring   A charge sometimes brought against an employer for hiring someone who is unstable or prone to violence. Employers are defending themselves against such suits, which often seek compensation for crimes committed by their employees. Such cases hinge on whether the employer should have discovered dangerous traits ahead of time, before hiring such a person into a position where he or she posed a threat to others. Personality testing may provide evidence that the employer did in fact try to reasonably investigate an applicant's fitness for the workplace.

neuroscience   The scientific study of the nervous system.

neurotic anxiety   Occurs when there is a direct conflict between the id and the ego. The danger is that the ego may lose control over some unacceptable desire of the id. For example, a man who worries excessively that he might blurt out some unacceptable thought or desire in public is beset by neurotic anxiety.

neurotic paradox   The fact that people with disorders or other problems with living often exhibit behaviors that exacerbate, rather than lessen, their

problems. For example, borderline personality disordered persons, who are generally concerned with being abandoned by friends and intimate others, may throw temper tantrums or otherwise express anger and rage in a manner that drives people away. The paradox refers to doing behaviors that make their situation worse.

neuroticism   A dimension of personality present, in some form, in every major trait theory of personality. Different researchers have used different terms for neuroticism, such as emotional instability, anxiety-proneness, and negative affectivity. Adjectives useful for describing persons high on the trait of neuroticism include moody, touchy, irritable, anxious, unstable, pessimistic, and complaining.

neurotransmitter theory of depression   According to this theory, an imbalance of the neurotransmitters at the synapses of the nervous system causes depression. Some medications used to treat depression target these specific neurotransmitters. Not all people with depression are treated successfully with drugs. That suggests that there may be varieties of depression; some are biologically based, while others are more reactive to stress, physical exercise, or cognitive therapy.

neurotransmitters   Chemicals in the nerve cells that are responsible for the transmission of a nerve impulse from one cell to another. Some theories of personality are based directly on different amounts of neurotransmitters found in the nervous system.

nomothetic   The study of general characters of people as they are distributed in the population, typically involving statistical comparisons between individuals or groups.

noncontent responding   (also referred to as the concept of response sets) The tendency of some people to respond to the questions on some basis that is unrelated to the question content. One example is the response set of acquiescence or yea saying. This is the tendency to simply agree with the questionnaire items, regardless of the content of those items.

nonshared environmental influences   Features of the environment that siblings do not share. Some children might get special or different treatment from their parents, they might have different groups of friends, they might be sent to different schools, or one might go to summer camp while the other stays home each summer. These features are called "nonshared" because they are experienced differently by different siblings.

norepinephrine   A neurotransmitter involved in activating the sympathetic nervous system for flight or fight.

novelty seeking   In Cloninger's tridimensional personality model, the personality trait of novelty seeking is based on low levels of dopamine. Low levels of dopamine create a drive state to obtain substances or experiences that increase dopamine. Novelty and thrills and excitement can make up for low levels of dopamine, and so novelty-seeking behavior is thought to result from low levels of this neurotransmitter.

O

object relations theory   Places an emphasis on early childhood relationships. While this theory has several versions that differ from each other in emphasis, all the versions have at their core a set of basic assumptions: that the internal wishes, desires, and urges of the child are not as important as his or her developing relationships with significant external others, particularly parents, and that the others, particularly the mother, become internalized by the child in the form of mental objects.

objectifying cognition   Processing information by relating it to objective facts. This style of thinking stands in contrast to personalizing cognitions.

objective anxiety   Fear occurs in response to some real, external threat to the person. For example, being confronted by a large, aggressive-looking man with a knife while taking a shortcut through an alley would elicit objective anxiety (fear) in most people.

objective self-awareness   Seeing oneself as an object of others' attention. Often, objective self-awareness is experienced as shyness, and for some people this is a chronic problem. Although objective self-awareness can lead to periods of social sensitivity, this ability to consider

oneself from an outside perspective is the beginning of a social identity.

observer-report data (O-data)   The impressions and evaluations others make of a person whom they come into contact with. For every individual, there are dozens of observers who form such impressions. Observer-report methods capitalize on these sources and provide tools for gathering information about a person's personality. Observers may have access to information not attainable through other sources, and multiple observers can be used to assess each individual. Typically, a more valid and reliable assessment of personality can be achieved when multiple observers are used.

obsessive-compulsive personality disorder   The obsessive-compulsive personality is preoccupied with order and strives to be perfect. The high need for order can manifest itself in the person's attention to details, however trivial, and fondness for rules, rituals, schedules, and procedures. Another characteristic is a devotion to work at the expense of leisure and friendships. Obsessive-compulsive persons tend to work harder than they need to.

oedipal conflict   For boys, the main conflict in Freud's phallic stage. It is a boy's unconscious wish to have his mother all to himself by eliminating the father. (Oedipus is a character in a Greek myth who unknowingly kills his father and marries his mother.)

optimal level of arousal   Hebb believed that people are motivated to reach an optimal level of arousal. If they are underaroused relative to this level, an increase in arousal is rewarding; conversely, if they are overaroused, a decrease in arousal is rewarding. By optimal level of arousal, Hebb meant a level that is "just right" for any given task.

optimistic explanatory style   A style that emphasizes external, temporary, and specific causes of events.

oral stage   The first stage in Freud's psychosexual stages of development. This stage occurs during the initial 18 months after birth. During this time, the main sources of pleasure and tension reduction are the mouth, lips, and tongue. Adults who still obtain pleasure from "taking in," especially through the mouth (e.g., people who overeat or

smoke or talk too much) might be fixated at this stage.

organized and enduring   "Organized" means that the psychological traits and mechanisms for a given person are not simply a random collection of elements. Rather, personality is coherent because the mechanisms and traits are linked to one another in an organized fashion. "Enduring" means that the psychological traits are generally consistent over time, particularly in adulthood, and over situations.

orthogonality   Discussed in terms of circumplex models, orthogonality specifies that traits that are perpendicular to each other on the model (at 90 degrees of separation, or at right angles to each other) are unrelated to each other. In general, the term "orthogonal" is used to describe a zero correlation between traits.

ought self   A person's understanding of what others want them to be.

overt and covert integrity measures   Both are self-report measures of integrity used in business and industry. Overt measures include questions directly related to past violations of workplace integrity, such as excessive absenteeism or theft. Covert measures include questions that are indirectly related to integrity, such as questions about personality traits that are correlated with workplace integrity, such as conscientiousness.

P

pain tolerance   The degree to which people can tolerate pain, which shows wide differences between persons. Petrie believed that individual differences in pain tolerance originated in the nervous system. She developed a theory that people with low pain tolerance had a nervous system that amplified or augmented the subjective impact of sensory input. In contrast, people who could tolerate pain well were thought to have a nervous system that dampened or reduced the effects of sensory stimulation.

paranoid personality disorder   The paranoid personality is extremely distrustful of others and sees others as a constant threat. Such a person assumes that others are out to exploit and deceive them, even though there is no good evidence to support this assumption. Paranoid personalities feel that they have been injured by other persons and are preoccupied with doubts about the motivations of others. The paranoid personality often misinterprets social events and holds resentments toward others for slights or perceived insults.

parsimony The fewer premises and assumptions a theory contains, the greater its parsimony. This does not mean that simple theories are always better than complex ones. Due to the complexity of the human personality, a complex theory—that is, one containing many premises—may ultimately be necessary for adequate personality theories.

passive genotype-environment correlation Occurs when parents provide both genes and environment to children, yet the children do nothing to obtain that environment.

penis envy The female counterpart of castration anxiety, which occurs during the phallic stage of psychosexual development for girls around 3–5 years of age.

people-things dimension Brian Little's people-things dimension of personality refers to the nature of vocational interests. Those at the "things" end of the dimension like vocations that deal with impersonal tasks—machines, tools, or materials. Examples include carpenter, auto mechanic, building contractor, tool maker, or farmer. Those scoring toward the "people" end of the dimension prefer social occupations that involve thinking about others, caring for others, or directing others. Examples include high school teacher, social worker, or religious counselor.

percentage of variance Individuals vary or are different from each other, and this variability can be partitioned into percentages that are related to separate causes or separate variables. An example is the percentages of variance in some trait that are related to genetics, the shared environment, and the unshared environment. Another example would be the percentage of variance in happiness scores that are related to various demographic variables, such as income, gender, and age.

perception One of the three levels of cognition that are of interest to personality psychologists. Perception is the process of imposing order on the information our sense organs take in. Even at the level of perception, what we "see" in the world can be quite different from person to person.

perceptual sensitivity The ability to detect subtle stimuli from the environment.

personal construct A belief or concept that summarizes a set of observations or version of reality, unique to an individual, which that person routinely uses to interpret and predict events.

personal project A set of relevant actions intended to achieve a goal that a person has selected. Psychologist Brian Little believes that personal projects make natural units for understanding the working of personality, because they reflect how people face up to the serious business of navigating through daily life.

personality coherence Changes in the manifestations of personality variables over time, even as the underlying characteristics remain stable. The notion of personality coherence includes both elements of continuity and elements of change: continuity in the underlying trait but change in the outward manifestation of that trait. For example, an emotionally unstable child might frequently cry and throw temper tantrums, whereas as an adult such a person might frequently worry and complain. The manifestation might change, even though the trait stays stable.

personality development The continuities, consistencies, and stabilities in people over time, and the ways in which people change over time.

personality disorder An enduring pattern of experience and behavior that differs greatly from the expectations of the individual's culture. The disorder is usually manifest in more than one of the following areas: the way a person thinks, feels, gets along with others, or controls personal behavior. To be classed as a personality disorder, the pattern must *not* result from drug abuse, medication, or a medical condition such as head trauma.

personality-descriptive nouns As described by Saucier,

personality-descriptive nouns differ in their content emphases from personality taxonomies based on adjectives and may be more precise. In Saucier's 2003 work on personality nouns, he discovered eight factors, including "Dumbbell," "Babe/Cutie," "Philosopher," "Lawbreaker," "Joker," and "Jock."

personality The set of psychological traits and mechanisms within the individual that are organized and relatively enduring and that influence his or her interactions with, and adaptations to, the environment (including the intrapsychic, physical, and social environment).

personalizing cognition Processing information by relating it to a similar event in your own life. This style of processing information occurs when people interpret a new event in a personally relevant manner. For example, they might see a car accident and start thinking about the time they were in a car accident.

personnel selection Employers sometimes use personality tests to select people especially suitable for a specific job. Alternatively, the employer may want to use personality assessments to deselect, or screen out, people with specific traits. In both cases an employer is concerned with selecting the right person for a specific position from among a pool of applicants.

person-environment interaction A person's interactions with situations include perceptions, selections, evocations, and manipulations. *Perceptions* refer to how we "see" or interpret an environment. *Selection* describes the manner in which we choose situations—such as our friends, our hobbies, our college classes, and our careers. *Evocations* refer to the reactions we produce in others, often quite unintentionally. *Manipulations* refer to the ways in which we attempt to influence others.

person-situation interaction The person-situation interaction trait theory states that one has to take into account both particular situations (e.g., frustration) and personality traits (e.g., hot temper) when understanding a behavior.

perspective taking   A final unfolding of the self-concept during the teen years; the ability to take the perspectives of others, or to see oneself as others do, to step outside of one's self and imagine how one appears to other people. This is why many teenagers go through a period of extreme self-consciousness during this time, focusing much of their energy on how they appear to others.

pessimistic explanatory style   Puts a person at risk for feelings of helplessness and poor adjustment, and emphasizes internal, stable, and global causes for bad events. It is the opposite of optimistic explanatory style.

phallic stage   The third stage in Freud's psychosexual stages of development. It occurs between 3 and 5 years of age, during which time the child discovers that he has (or she discovers that she does not have) a penis. This stage also includes the awakening of sexual desire directed, according to Freud, toward the parent of the opposite sex.

phenotypic variance   Observed individual differences, such as in height, weight, or personality.

physiological needs   The base of Maslow's need hierarchy. These include those needs that are of prime importance to the immediate survival of the individual (the need for food, water, air, sleep) as well as to the long-term survival of the species (the need for sex).

physiological systems   Organ systems within the body; for example, the nervous system (including the brain and nerves), the cardiac system (including the heart, arteries, and veins), and the musculoskeletal system (including the muscles and bones which make all movements and behaviors possible).

pleasure principle   The desire for immediate gratification. The id operates according to the pleasure principle; therefore, it does not listen to reason, does not follow logic, has no values or morals (other than immediate gratification), and has very little patience.

positive illusions   Some researchers believe that part of being happy is to have positive illusions about the self—an inflated view of one's own characteristics as a good, able, and desirable person—as this characteristic

appears to be part of emotional well-being (Taylor, 1989; Taylor et al., 2000).

positive reappraisal   A cognitive process whereby a person focuses on the good in what is happening or has happened to them. Folkman and Moskowitz note that forms of this positive coping strategy include seeing opportunities for personal growth or seeing how one's own efforts can benefit other people.

positive regard   According to Rogers, all children are born wanting to be loved and accepted by their parents and others. He called this inborn need the desire for positive regard.

positive self-regard   According to Rogers, people who have received positive regard from others develop a sense of positive self-regard; they accept themselves, even their own weaknesses and shortcomings. People with high positive self-regard trust themselves, follow their own interests, and rely on their feelings to guide them to do the right thing.

possible selves   The notion of possible selves can be viewed in a number of ways, but two are especially important. The first pertains to the desired self—the person we wish to become. The second pertains to our feared self—the sort of person we do not wish to become.

postmodernism   In personality psychology, the notion that reality is a construct, that every person and culture has its own unique version of reality, and that no single version of reality is more valid or more privileged than another.

posttraumatic stress disorder (PTSD)   A syndrome that occurs in some individuals after experiencing or witnessing life-threatening events, such as military combat, natural disasters, terrorist attacks, serious accidents, or violent personal assaults (e.g., rape). Those who suffer from PTSD often relive the trigger experience for years through nightmares or intense flashbacks; have difficulty sleeping; report physical complaints; have flattened emotions; and feel detached or estranged from others. These symptoms can be severe and last long enough to significantly impair the individual's daily life, health, relationships, and career.

power stress   According to David McClelland, when people do not get their way, or when their power is challenged or blocked, they are likely to show strong stress responses. This stress has been linked to diminished immune function and increased illness in longitudinal studies.

preconscious   Any information that a person is not presently aware of, but that could easily be retrieved and made conscious, is found in the preconscious mind.

predictive validity   Whether a test predicts criteria external to the test (also referred to as criterion validity).

predisposition model   In health psychology, the predisposition model suggests that associations may exist between personality and illness because a third variable is causing them both.

prefrontal cortex   Area of the brain found to be highly active in the control of emotions. Many people who have committed violent acts exhibit a neurological deficit in the frontal areas, portions of the brain assumed to be responsible for regulating negative emotions.

press   Need-relevant aspects of the environment. A person's need for intimacy, for example, won't affect that person's behavior without an appropriate environmental press (such as the presence of friendly people).

prevalence   The total number of cases that are present within a given population during a particular period of time.

prevention focus   One focus of self-regulation where the person is concerned with protection, safety, and the prevention of negative outcomes and failures. Behaviors with a prevention focus are characterized by vigilance, caution, and attempts to prevent negative outcomes.

primary appraisal   According to Lazarus, in order for stress to be evoked for a person, two cognitive events must occur. The first cognitive event, called the primary appraisal, is for the person to perceive that the event is a threat to his or her personal goals. See also *secondary appraisal.*

primary process thinking   Thinking without the logical rules of conscious thought or an anchor in reality. Dreams and fantasies are examples of primary process thinking. Although primary process thought does not follow the normal rules of reality (e.g., in dreams people might fly or walk through walls), Freud believed there were principles at work in primary process thought and that these principles could be discovered.

priming Technique to make associated material more accessible to conscious awareness than material that is not primed. Research using subliminal primes demonstrates that information can get into the mind, and have some influence on it, without going through conscious experience.

Price Waterhouse v. Hopkins A Supreme Court case in which Ann Hopkins sued her employer, Price Waterhouse, claiming that it had discriminated against her on the basis of sex in violation of Title VII of the Civil Rights Act, on the theory that her promotion denial had been based on sexual stereotyping. The Supreme Court accepted the argument that gender stereotyping does exist and that it can create a bias against women in the workplace that is not permissible under Title VII of the Civil Rights Act. By court order Ann Hopkins was made a full partner in her accounting firm.

private self-concept The development of an inner, private self-concept is a major but often difficult development in the growth of the self-concept. It may start out with children developing an imaginary friend, someone only they can see or hear. This imaginary friend may actually be children's first attempt to communicate to their parents that they know there is a secret part, an inner part, to their understanding of their self. Later, children develop the full realization that only they have access to their own thoughts, feelings, and desires, and that no one else can know this part of them unless they choose to tell them.

problem-focused coping Thoughts and behaviors that manage or solve the underlying cause of stress. Folkman and Moskowitz note that focusing on solving problems, even little ones, can give a person a positive sense of control even in the most stressful and uncontrollable circumstances.

projection A defense mechanism based on the notion that sometimes we see in others those traits and desires that we find most upsetting in ourselves. We literally "project" (i.e., attribute) our own unacceptable qualities onto others.

projective hypothesis The idea that what a person "sees" in an ambiguous figure, such as an inkblot, reflects his or her personality. People are thought to project their own personalities into what they report seeing in such an ambiguous stimulus.

projective techniques A person is presented with an ambiguous stimulus and is then asked to impose some order on the stimulus, such as asking what the person sees in an inkblot. What the person sees is interpreted to reveal something about his or her personality. The person presumably "projects" his or her concerns, conflicts, traits, and ways of seeing or dealing with the world onto the ambiguous stimulus. The most famous projective technique for assessing personality is the Rorschach inkblot test.

promotion focus One focus of self-regulation whereby the person is concerned with advancement, growth, and accomplishments. Behaviors with a promotion focus are characterized by eagerness, approach, and "going for the gold."

psychic energy According to Sigmund Freud, a source of energy within each person that motivates him or her to do one thing and not another. In Freud's view, it is this energy that motivates all human activity.

psychoanalysis A theory of personality and a method of psychotherapy (a technique for helping individuals who are experiencing some mental disorder or even relatively minor problems with living). Psychoanalysis can be thought of as a theory about the major components and mechanisms of personality, as well as a method for deliberately restructuring personality.

psychological mechanisms Similar to traits, except that mechanisms refer more to the *processes* of personality. For example, most personality mechanisms involve some information-processing activity. A psychological mechanism may make people more sensitive to certain kinds of information from the environment (input), may make them more likely to think about specific options (decision rules), or may guide their behavior toward certain categories of action (outputs).

psychological traits Characteristics that describe ways in which people are unique or different from or similar to each other. Psychological traits include all sorts of aspects of persons that are psychologically meaningful and are stable and consistent aspects of personality.

psychological types A term growing out of Carl Jung's theory implying that people come in types or distinct categories of personality, such as "extraverted types." This view is not widely endorsed by academic or research-oriented psychologists because most personality traits are normally distributed in the population and are best conceived as dimensions of difference, not categories.

psychopathology The study of mental disorders that combines statistical, social, and psychological approaches to diagnosing individual abnormality.

psychopathy The psychopathy designation places emphasis on more subjective or inner characteristics, such as the incapacity to feel shame, guilt, and fear, a lack of empathy toward others, or having callous social beliefs. In contrast, the sociopathy designation refers more to observable or outward behaviors, such as chronic lying, repeated criminal behavior, and conflicts with authority.

psychosexual stage theory According to Freud, all persons pass through a set series of stages in personality development. At each of the first three stages, young children must face and resolve specific conflicts, which revolve around ways of obtaining a type of sexual gratification. Children seek sexual gratification at each stage by investing libidinal energy in a specific body part. Each stage in the developmental process is named after the body part in which sexual energy is invested.

psychosocial conflicts As posited by Erik Erikson, psychosocial conflicts occur throughout a person's lifetime and contribute to the ongoing development of personality. He defined psychosocial conflicts as the crises of learning to trust our parents, learning to be autonomous from them, and learning from them how to act as an adult.

r

race or gender norming The Civil Rights Act of 1991 forbids employers from using different norms or cutoff scores for different groups of people. For example, it would be illegal for a company to set a higher threshold for women than men on their selection test.

random assignment Assignment in an experiment that is conducted randomly. If an experiment has manipulation between groups, random assignment of participants to experimental groups helps ensure that each group is equivalent.

rank-order stability Maintaining one's relative position within a group over time. Between ages 14 and 20, for example, most people become taller. But the rank order of heights tends to remain fairly stable because this form of development affects all people pretty much the same. The tall people at 14 fall generally toward the tall end of the distribution at age 20. The same can apply to personality traits. If people tend to maintain their position on dominance or extraversion relative to the other members of the group over time, then we say that there is high rank order stability to the personality characteristic. Conversely, if people fail to maintain their rank order, we say that the group has displayed rank order instability or rank order change.

rationalization A defense mechanism that involves generating acceptable reasons for outcomes that might otherwise be unacceptable. The goal is to reduce anxiety by coming up with an explanation for some event that is easier to accept than the "real" reason.

reaction formation A defense mechanism that refers to an attempt to stifle the expression of an unacceptable urge; a person may continually display a flurry of behavior that indicates the opposite impulse. Reaction formation makes it possible for psychoanalysts to predict that sometimes people will do exactly the opposite of what you might otherwise think they would do. It also alerts us to be sensitive to instances when a person is doing something in excess. One of the hallmarks of reaction formation is excessive behavior.

reactive genotype-environment correlation Occurs when parents (or others) respond to children differently depending on their genotype.

reactively heritable Traits that are secondary consequences of heritable traits.

reality principle In psychoanalysis, it is the counterpart of the pleasure principle. It refers to guiding behavior according to the demands of reality and relies on the strengths of the ego to provide such guidance.

reciprocal causality The notion that causality can move in two directions; for example, helping others can lead to happiness, and happiness can lead one to be more helpful to others.

reducer/augmenter theory Petrie's reducer/augmenter theory refers to the dimension along which people differ in their reaction to sensory stimulation; some appear to reduce sensory stimulation, some appear to augment stimulation.

reinforcement sensitivity theory Gray's biological theory of personality. Based on recent brain function research with animals, Gray constructed a model of human personality based on two hypothesized biological systems in the brain: the behavioral activation system (which is responsive to incentives, such as cues for reward, and regulates approach behavior) and the behavioral inhibition system (which is responsive to cues for punishment, frustration, and uncertainty).

reliability The degree to which an obtained measure represents the "true" level of the trait being measured. For example, if a person has a "true" IQ of 115, then a perfectly reliable measure of IQ will yield a score of 115 for that person. Moreover, a truly reliable measure of IQ would yield the same score of 115 each time it was administered to the person. Personality psychologists prefer reliable measures so that the scores accurately reflect each person's true level of the personality characteristic being measured.

repeated measurement A way to estimate the reliability of a measure. There are different forms of repeated measurement, and hence different versions of reliability. A common procedure is to repeat the same measurement over time, say at an interval of a month apart, for the same sample of persons. If the two tests are highly correlated between the first and second testing, yielding similar scores for most people, then the resulting measure is said to have high test-retest reliability.

repetition compulsion The idea that people recreate or repeat their interpersonal problems over and over with different people in their lives. This notion underlies the psychoanalytic transference, wherein the patient recreates the interpersonal difficulties they have in their everyday life with the analyst during the course of their treatment.

repression One of the first defense mechanisms discussed by Freud; refers to the process of preventing unacceptable thoughts, feelings, or urges from reaching conscious awareness.

resistance stage The second stage in Selye's general adaptation syndrome (GAS). Here the body is using its resources at an above-average rate, even though the immediate fight-or-flight response has subsided. Stress is being resisted, but the effort is making demands on the person's resources and energy.

resistance When a patient's defenses are threatened by a probing psychoanalyst, the patient may unconsciously set up obstacles to progress. This stage of psychoanalysis is called resistance. Resistance signifies that important unconscious material is coming to the fore. The resistance itself becomes an integral part of the interpretations the analyst offers to the patient.

response sets The tendency of some people to respond to the questions on some basis that is unrelated to the question content. Sometimes this is referred to as noncontent responding. One example is the response set of acquiescence or yea saying. This is the tendency to simply agree with the questionnaire items, regardless of the content of those items.

responsibility training Life experiences that provide opportunities to learn to behave responsibly, such as having younger siblings to take care of while growing up. Moderates the gender difference in impulsive behaviors associated with need for power.

restricted sexual strategy According to Gangestad and Simpson (1990), a woman seeking a high-investing mate would adopt a restricted sexual strategy marked by delayed intercourse and prolonged courtship. This would enable her to assess the man's level of commitment, detect the existence of prior commitments to other women and/or children, and simultaneously signal to the man the woman's sexual fidelity and, hence, assure him of his paternity of future offspring.

reward dependence In Cloninger's tridimensional personality model, the personality trait of reward dependence is associated with low levels of norepinephrine. People high on this trait are persistent; they continue to act in ways that produced reward. They work long hours, put a lot of effort into their work, and will often continue striving after others have given up.

right to privacy Perhaps the largest issue of legal concern for employers using personality testing is privacy. The right to privacy in employment settings grows out of the broader concept of the right to privacy. Cases that charge an invasion-of-privacy claim against an employer can be based on the federal constitution, state constitutions and statutes, and common law.

rite of passage Some cultures and religions institute a rite of passage ritual, usually around adolescence, which typically is a ceremony that initiates a child into adulthood. After such ceremonies, the adolescent is sometimes given a new name, bestowing a new adult identity.

rod and frame test (RFT) An apparatus to research the cues that people use in judging orientation in space. The participant sits in a darkened room and is instructed to watch a glowing rod surrounded by a glowing square frame. The experimenter can adjust the tilt of the rod, the frame, and the participant's chair. The participant's task is to adjust the rod by turning a dial so that the rod is perfectly upright. To do this accurately, the participant has to ignore cues in the visual field in which the rod appears. This test measures the personality dimension of field dependence–independence.

rumination Repeatedly focusing on one's symptoms or distress (e.g., "Why do I continue to feel so bad about myself?" or "Why doesn't my boss like me?"). Rumination is a key contributor to women's greater experience of depressive symptoms.

S

safety needs The second to lowest level of Maslow's need hierarchy. These needs have to do with shelter and security, such as having a place to live and being free from the threat of danger. Maslow believed that building a life that was orderly, structured, and predictable also fell under safety needs.

schizoid personality disorder The schizoid personality is split off (schism) or detached from normal social relations. The schizoid person simply appears to have no need or desire for intimate relationships or even friendships. Family life usually does not mean much to such people, and they do not obtain satisfaction from being part of a group. They have few or no close friends, and they would rather spend time by themselves than with others.

schizotypal personality disorder Whereas the schizoid person is indifferent to social interaction, the schizotypal personality is acutely uncomfortable in social relationships. Schizotypes are anxious in social situations, especially if those situations involve strangers. Schizotypal persons also feel that they are different from others, or that they do not fit in with the group. They tend to be suspicious of others and are seen as odd and eccentric.

scientific standards for evaluating personality theories The five key standards are comprehensiveness, heuristic value, testability, parsimony, and compatibility and integration across domains and levels.

secondary appraisal According to Lazarus, in order for stress to be evoked for a person, two cognitive events must occur. The second necessary cognitive event, called the secondary appraisal, is when the person concludes that he or she does not have the resources to cope with the demands of the threatening event. See *primary appraisal.*

secondary process thinking The ego engages in secondary process thinking, which refers to the development and devising of strategies for problem solving and obtaining satisfaction. Often this process involves taking into account the constraints of physical reality, about when and how to express some desire or urge. See *primary process thinking.*

secure relationship style In Hazan and Shaver's secure relationship style, the adult has few problems developing satisfying friendships and relationships. Secure people trust others and develop bonds with others.

securely attached Securely attached infants in Ainsworth's strange situation stoically endured the separation and went about exploring the room, waiting patiently, or even approaching the stranger and sometimes wanting to be held by the stranger. When the mother returned, these infants were glad to see her, typically interacted with her for a while, then went back to exploring the new environment. They seemed confident the mother would return. Approximately 66 percent of infants fall into this category.

selective breeding One method of doing behavior genetic research. Researchers might identify a trait and then see if they can selectively breed animals to possess that trait. This can occur only if the trait has a genetic basis. For example, dogs that possess certain desired characteristics, such as a sociable disposition, might be selectively bred to see if this disposition can be increased in frequency among offspring. Traits that are based on learning cannot be selectively bred for.

selective placement If adopted children are placed with adoptive parents who are similar to their birth parents, this may inflate the correlations between the adopted children and their adoptive parents. In this case, the resulting inflated correlations would artificially inflate estimates of environmental influence because the correlation would appear to be due to the environment provided by the adoptive parent. There does not seem to be selective placement, and so this potential problem is not a problem in actual studies (Plomin et al., 1990).

self-actualization need Maslow defines self-actualization as becoming "more and more what one idiosyncratically is, to become everything that one is capable of becoming" (1970, p. 46). The pinnacle of Maslow's need hierarchy is the need for self-actualization. Maslow was concerned with describing self-actualization; the work of Carl Rogers was focused on how people achieve self-actualization.

self-attributed motivation   McClelland argued that self-attributed motivation is primarily a person's self-awareness of his or her own conscious motives. These self-attributed motives reflect a person's conscious awareness about what is important to him or her. As such, they represent part of the individual's conscious self-understanding. McClelland has argued that self-attributed motives predict responses to immediate and specific situations and to choice behaviors and attitudes. See *implicit motivation.*

self-complexity   The view that each of us has many roles and many aspects to our self-concepts. However, for some of us, our self-concepts are rather simple, being made up of just a few large categories. Other people may have a more complex or differentiated self-concept. For people with high self-complexity, a failure in any one aspect of the self (such as a relationship that breaks apart) is buffered because there are many other aspects of the self that are unaffected by that event. However, for persons low in self-complexity, the same event might be seen as devastating because they define themselves mainly in terms of this one aspect.

self-concept   The way a person sees, understands, and defines himself or herself.

self-efficacy   A concept related to optimism and developed by Bandura. The belief that one can behave in ways necessary to achieve some desired outcome. Self-efficacy also refers to the confidence one has in one's ability to perform the actions needed to achieve some specific outcome.

self-enhancement   The tendency to describe and present oneself using positive or socially valued attributes, such as kind, understanding, intelligent, and industrious. Tendencies toward self-enhancement tend to be stable over time, and hence are enduring features of personality (Baumeister, 1997).

self-esteem anxiety   People have a preferred and generally positive view of themselves, and they will defend against any unflattering blows to that self-view to protect their self-esteem.

self-esteem variability   An individual difference characteristic referring to how much a person's self-esteem fluctuates or changes over time. It is uncorrelated with mean level of self-esteem.

self-esteem   "The extent to which one perceives oneself as relatively close to being the person one wants to be and/or as relatively distant from being the kind of person one does not want to be, with respect to person-qualities one positively and negatively values" (Block & Robbins, 1993, p. 911).

self-fulfilling prophecy   The tendency for a belief to become reality. For example, a person who thinks he or she is a "total failure" will often act like a total failure and may even give up trying to do better, thus creating a self-fulfilling prophecy.

self-guides   The ideal self and the ought self-act as self-guides, providing the standards that one uses to organize self-relevant information and motivate appropriate behaviors to bring the self in line with these self-guides.

self-handicapping   Situations in which people deliberately do things that increase the probability that they will fail.

self-report data (S-data)   Information a person verbally reveals about themselves, often based on questionnaire or interview. Self-report data can be obtained through a variety of means, including interviews that pose questions to a person, periodic reports by a person to record the events as they happen, and questionnaires of various sorts.

self-schema   (schemata is plural, schema is singular) The specific knowledge structure, or cognitive representation, of the self-concept. Self-schemas are the network of associated building blocks of the self-concept.

self-serving bias   The common tendency for people to take credit for success yet to deny responsibility for failure.

sensation seeking   A dimension of personality postulated to have a physiological basis. It refers to the tendency to seek out thrilling and exciting activities, to take risks, and to avoid boredom.

sensory deprivation   Often done in a sound-proof chamber containing water in which a person floats, in total darkness, such that sensory input is reduced to a minimum. Researchers use sensory deprivation chambers to see what happens when a person is deprived of sensory input.

separation anxiety   Children experiencing separation anxiety react negatively to separation from their mother (or primary caretaker), becoming agitated and distressed when their mothers leave. Most primates exhibit separation anxiety.

serotonin   A neurotransmitter that plays a role in depression and other mood disorders. Drugs such as Prozac, Zoloft, and Paxil block the reuptake of serotonin, leaving it in the synapse longer, leading depressed persons to feel less depressed.

sex differences   An average difference between women and men on certain characteristics such as height, body fat distribution, or personality characteristics, with no prejudgment about the cause of the difference.

sexual selection   The evolution of characteristics because of their mating benefits rather than because of their survival benefits. According to Darwin, sexual selection takes two forms: intrasexual competition and intersexual selection.

sexually dimorphic   Species that show high variance in reproduction within one sex tend to be highly sexually dimorphic, or highly different in size and structure. The more intense the effective polygyny, the more dimorphic the sexes are in size and form (Trivers, 1985).

shared environmental influences   Features of the environment that siblings share; for example, the number of books in the home, the presence or absence of a TV and VCR, quality and quantity of the food in the home, the values and attitudes of the parent, and the schools, church, synagogue, or temple the parents send the children to.

shyness   A tendency to feel tense, worried, or anxious during social interactions, or even when anticipating a social interaction (Addison & Schmidt, 1999). Shyness is a common phenomenon, and more than 90 percent of the population reports experiencing shyness at some point during their lives (Zimbardo, 1977). Some people, however, seem to be dispositionally shy—they tend to feel awkward in most social situations and so tend to avoid situations in which they will be forced to interact with people.

situational selection   A form of interactionism that refers to the tendency to choose or select the situations in which one finds oneself. In other words, people typically do not find themselves in random situations in their natural lives. Instead, they select or choose the situations in which they will spend their time.

situational specificity   The view that behavior is determined by aspects of the situation, such as reward contingencies.

situationism   A theoretical position in personality psychology that states that situational differences, rather than underlying personality traits, determine behavior. For example, how friendly a person will behave or how much need for achievement a person displays will depend on the situation, not the traits a person possesses.

social and cultural domain   Personality affects, and is affected by, the social and cultural context in which it is found. Different cultures may bring out different facets of our personalities in manifest behavior. The capacities we display may depend to a large extent on what is acceptable in and encouraged by our culture. At the level of individual differences within cultures, personality plays itself out in the social sphere. One important social sphere concerns relations between men and women.

social anxiety   Discomfort related to social interactions, or even to the anticipation of social interactions. Socially anxious persons appear to be overly concerned about what others will think. Baumeister and Tice (1990) propose that social anxiety is a species-typical adaptation that functions to prevent social exclusion.

social attention   The goal and payback for surgent or extraverted behavior. By being the center of attention, the extravert seeks to gain the approval of others and, in many cases, through tacit approval controls or directs others.

social categories   The cognitive component that describes the ways individuals classify other people into groups, such as "cads" and "dads." This cognitive component is one aspect of stereotyping.

social class   Variability between people based primarily on economic, educational, and employment variables. In terms of within-culture variation, social class can have an effect on personality (Kohn et al., 1990). For example, lower-class parents tend to emphasize the importance of obedience to authority, whereas higher-status parents tend to emphasize the importance of self-direction and not conforming to the dictates of others.

social comparison   A process whereby a person compares his or her standing on some characteristic to that of relevant others, and judges himself or herself based on how that comparison turns out.

social desirability   Socially desirable responding refers to the tendency to answer items in such a way as to come across as socially attractive or likable. People responding in this manner want to make a good impression, to appear to be well adjusted, to be a "good citizen."

social identity   Identity refers to the social aspects of the self, that part of ourselves we use to create an impression, to let other people know who we are and what can be expected from us. Identity is different from the self-concept because identity refers mainly to aspects of the self that are socially observable or publicly available outward, such as ethnicity or gender or age. Nevertheless, the social aspects of identity can become important aspects of the self-concept.

social learning theory   A general theoretical view emphasizing the ways in which the presence of others influence people's behavior, thoughts, or feelings. Often combined with learning principles, the emphasis is on how people acquire beliefs, values, skills, attitudes, and patterns of behavior through social experiences.

social power   Horney, in reinterpreting Freud's concept of penis envy, taught that the penis was a symbol of social power rather than some organ that women actually desired. Horney wrote that girls realize, at an early age, that

they are being denied social power because of their gender. She argued that girls did not really have a secret desire to become boys. Rather, she taught, girls desire the social power and preferences given to boys in the culture at that time.

social role theory   According to social role theory, sex differences originate because men and women are distributed differentially into occupational and family roles. Men, for example, are expected to assume the breadwinning role. Women are expected to assume the housewife role. Over time, children presumably learn the behaviors that are linked to these roles.

socialization theory   The notion that boys and girls become different because boys are reinforced by parents, teachers, and the media for being "masculine," and girls for being "feminine." This is probably the most widely held theory of sex differences in personality.

sociosexual orientation   According to Gangestad and Simpson's theory of sociosexual orientation, men and women will pursue one of two alternative sexual relationship strategies. The first mating strategy entails seeking a single committed relationship characterized by monogamy and tremendous investment in children. The second sexual strategy is characterized by a greater degree of promiscuity, more partner switching, and less investment in children.

spreading activation   Roediger and McDermott applied the spreading activation model of memory to account for false memories. This model holds that mental elements (like words or images) are stored in memory along with associations to other elements in memory. For example, *doctor* is associated with *nurse* in most people's memories because of the close connection or similarity between these concepts. Consequently, a person recalling some medical event might falsely recall a nurse rather than a doctor doing something.

stability coefficients   The correlations between the same measures obtained at two different points in time. Stability coefficients are also called test-retest reliability coefficients.

stage model of development   Implies that people go through stages in a certain order, and that a specific issue characterizes each stage.

state levels   A concept that can be applied to motives and emotions, state levels refer to a person's momentary amount of a specific need or emotion, which can fluctuate with specific circumstances.

statistical approach   Having a large number of people rate themselves on certain items, and then employing a statistical procedure to identify groups or clusters of items that go together. The goal of the statistical approach is to identify the major dimensions or "coordinates" of the personality map.

statistically significant   Refers to the probability of finding the results of a research study by chance alone. The generally accepted level of statistical significance is 5 percent, meaning that, if a study were repeated 100 times, the particular result reported would be found by chance only five times.

strange situation procedure   Developed by Ainsworth and her colleagues for studying separation anxiety and for identifying differences between children in how they react to separation from their mothers. In this procedure, a mother and her baby come into a laboratory room. The mother sits down and the child is free to explore the room. After a few minutes an unfamiliar though friendly adult enters the room. The mother gets up and leaves the baby alone with this adult. After a few minutes, the mother comes back into the room and the stranger leaves. The mother is alone with the baby for several more minutes. All the while, the infant is being videotaped so that his or her reactions can later be analyzed.

stress   The subjective feeling that is produced by uncontrollable and threatening events. Events that cause stress are called stressors.

stressors   Events that cause stress. They appear to have several common attributes: (1) stressors are extreme in some manner, in the sense that they produce a state of feeling overwhelmed or overloaded, that one just cannot take it much longer; (2) stressors often produce opposing tendencies in us, such as wanting and not wanting some activity or object, as in wanting to study but also wanting to put it off as long as possible; and (3) stressors are uncontrollable, outside of our power to

influence, such as the exam that we cannot avoid.

strong situation   Certain situations that prompt similar behavior from everyone.

structured and unstructured   Self-report can take a variety of forms, ranging from open-ended questions to forced-choice true-or-false questions. Sometimes these are referred to as *unstructured* (open-ended, such as "Tell me about the parties you like the most") and *structured* ("I like loud and crowded parties"; answer true or false) personality tests.

style of emotional life   How emotions are experienced. For example, saying that someone is high on mood variability is to say something about the style of his or her emotional life, that his or her emotions change frequently. Compare to the content of emotional life.

sublimation   A defense mechanism that refers to the channeling of unacceptable sexual or aggressive instincts into socially desired activities. For Freud, sublimation is the most adaptive defense mechanism. A common example is going out to chop wood when you are angry rather than acting on that anger or even engaging in other less adaptive defense mechanisms such as displacement.

subliminal perception   Perception that bypasses conscious awareness, usually achieved through very brief exposure times, typically less than 30 milliseconds.

superego   That part of personality that internalizes the values, morals, and ideals of society. The superego makes us feel guilty, ashamed, or embarrassed when we do something wrong, and makes us feel pride when we do something right. The superego sets moral goals and ideals of perfection and is the source of our judgments that something is good or bad. It is what some people refer to as conscience. The main tool of the superego in enforcing right and wrong is the emotion of guilt.

surgency   A cluster of behaviors including approach behavior, high activity, and impulsivity.

symbols   Psychoanalysts interpret dreams by deciphering how unacceptable impulses and urges are transformed by the unconscious into symbols in the dream. (For example,

parents may be represented as a king and queen; children may be represented as small animals.)

sympathetic nervous system   That branch of the autonomic nervous system that supports the fight-or-flight response. The sympathetic nervous system is activated when a person feels threatened or experiences strong emotions such as anxiety, guilt, or anger.

synonym frequency   In the lexical approach, synonym frequency means that if an attribute has not merely one or two trait adjectives to describe it, but rather six, eight, or ten words, then it is a more important dimension of individual difference.

Systemizing   The drive to comprehend how things work, how systems are built, and how inputs into systems produce outputs.

t

taxonomy   A technical name given to a classification scheme—the identification and naming of groups within a particular subject field.

telemetry   The process by which electrical signals are sent from electrodes to a polygraph using radio waves instead of wires.

temperament   Individual differences that emerge very early in life, are likely to have a heritable basis, and are often involved in behaviors linked with emotionality or arousability.

tender-mindedness   A nurturant proclivity, having empathy for others, and being sympathetic with those who are downtrodden.

test data (T-data)   A common source of personality-relevant information comes from standardized tests (T-data). In these measures, participants are placed in a standardized testing situation to see if different people react or behave differently to an identical situation. Taking an exam, like the Scholastic Aptitude Test, would be one example of T-data as a measure used to predict success in school.

testability   The capacity to render precise predictions that scientists can test empirically. Generally, the testability of a theory is dependent upon the precision of its predictions. If it is impossible to test a theory empirically, the theory is generally discarded.

thanatos Freud postulated that humans have a fundamental instinct toward destruction and that this instinct is often manifest in aggression toward others. The two instincts were usually referred to as libido, for the life instinct, and thanatos, for the death instinct. While thanatos was considered to be the death instinct, Freud also used this term to refer to any urge to destroy, harm, or aggress against others or oneself.

thematic apperception test Developed by Murray and Morgan, this is a projective assessment technique that consists of a set of black and white ambiguous pictures. The person is shown each picture and is told to write a short story interpreting what is happening in each picture. The psychologist then codes the stories for the presence of imagery associated with particular motives. The TAT remains a popular personality assessment technique today.

theoretical approach The theoretical approach to identifying important dimensions of individual differences starts with a theory, which then determines which variables are important. The theoretical strategy dictates in a specific manner which variables are important to measure.

theoretical bridge The connection between two different variables (e.g., dimensions of personality and physiological variables).

theoretical constructs Hypothetical internal entities useful in describing and explaining differences between people.

theories and beliefs Beliefs are often personally useful and crucially important to some people, but they are based on leaps of faith, not on reliable facts and systematic observations. Theories, on the other hand, are based on systematic observations that can be repeated by others and that yield similar conclusions.

third variable problem One reason correlations can never prove casuality. It could be that two variables are correlated because some third, unknown variable is causing both.

time urgency A subtrait in the Type A personality. Type A persons hate wasting time. They are always in a hurry and feel under pressure to get the most

done in the least amount of time. Often they do two things at once, such as eat while reading a book. Waiting is stressful for them.

Title VII of the Civil Rights Act of 1964 A specific section of the Civil Rights Act of 1964 that requires employers to provide equal employment opportunities to all persons, regardless of sex, race, color, religion, or national origin.

trait levels A concept that can be applied to motives and emotions, trait levels refer to a person's average tendency, or his or her set point, on the specific motive or emotion. The idea is that people differ from each other in their typical or average amount of specific motives or emotions.

trait-descriptive adjectives Words that describe traits, attributes of a person that are reasonably characteristic of the individual and perhaps even enduring over time.

transactional model In the transactional model of personality and health, personality has three potential effects: (1) it can influence coping, as in the interactional model; (2) it can influence how the person appraises or interprets the events; and (3) it can influence exposure to the events themselves.

transference A term from psychoanalytic therapy. It refers to the patient reacting to the analyst as if he or she were an important figure from the patient's own life. The patient displaces past or present (negative and positive) feelings toward someone from his or her own life onto the analyst. The idea behind transference is that the interpersonal problems between a patient and the important people in his or her life will be reenacted in the therapy session with the analyst. This is a specific form of the mechanism of evocation, as described in the material on person-situation interaction.

transmitted culture Representations originally in the mind of one or more persons that are transmitted to the minds of other people. Three examples of cultural variants that appear to be forms of transmitted culture are differences in moral values, self-concept, and levels of self-enhancement. Specific patterns of morality, such as whether it

is considered appropriate to eat beef or wrong for a wife to go to the movies without her husband, are specific to certain cultures. These moral values appear to be transmitted from person to person within the culture.

traumatic stress A massive instance of acute stress, the effects of which can reverberate within an individual for years or even a lifetime. It differs from acute stress mainly in terms of its potential to lead to posttraumatic stress disorder.

tridimensional personality model Cloninger's tridimensional personality model ties three specific personality traits to levels of the three neurotransmitters. The first trait is called novelty seeking and is based on low levels of dopamine. The second personality trait is harm avoidance, which he associates with low levels of serotonin. The third trait is reward dependence, which Cloninger sees as related to low levels of norepinephrine.

trust The proclivity to cooperate with others, giving others the benefit of the doubt, and viewing one's fellow human beings as basically good at heart.

twin studies Twin studies estimate heritability by gauging whether identical twins, who share 100 percent of their genes, are more similar to each other than fraternal twins, who share only 50 percent of their genes. Twin studies, and especially studies of twins reared apart, have received tremendous media attention.

Type A personality In the 1960s, cardiologists Friedman and Rosenman began to notice that many of their coronary heart disease patients had similar personality traits—they were competitive, were aggressive workaholics, were ambitious overachievers, were often hostile, were almost always in a hurry, and rarely relaxed or took it easy. Friedman and Rosenman referred to this as the Type A personality, formally defined as "an action-emotion complex that can be observed in any person who is aggressively involved in a chronic, incessant struggle to achieve more and more in less and less time, and if required to do so, against the opposing efforts of other things or other persons" (1974, p. 37). As assessed by personality psychologists, Type A refers to a syndrome of several traits: (1) achievement motivation and competitiveness, (2) time urgency, and (3) hostility and aggressiveness.

U

unconditional positive regard The receipt of affection, love, or respect without having done anything to earn it. For example, a parent's love for a child should be unconditional.

unconscious The unconscious mind is that part of the mind about which the conscious mind has no awareness.

Uniform Guidelines on Employee Selection Procedures The purpose of the guidelines is to provide a set of principles for employee selection that meet the requirements of all federal laws, especially those that prohibit discrimination on the basis of race, color, religion, sex, or national origin. They provide details on the proper use of personality tests and other selection procedures in employment settings.

unrestricted mating strategy According to Gangestad and Simpson (1990), a woman seeking a man for the quality of his genes is not interested in his level of commitment to her. If the man is pursuing a short-term sexual strategy, any delay on the woman's part may deter him from seeking sexual intercourse with her, thus defeating the main adaptive reason for her mating strategy.

V

validity coefficients The correlations between a trait measure and measures of different criteria that should relate to the trait. An example might be the correlation between a self-report measure of agreeableness and the person's roommate's reports of how agreeable they are.

validity The extent to which a test measures what it claims to measure.

violation of desire According to the violation of desire theory of conflict between the sexes, breakups should occur more frequently when one's desires are violated than when they are fulfilled (Buss, 2003). Following this theory, we would predict that people married to others who lack desired characteristics, such as dependability and emotional stability, will more frequently dissolve the marriage.

W

Ward's Cove Packing Co. v. Atonio Ward's Cove Packing Co. was a salmon cannery operating in Alaska. In 1974 the non-White cannery workers started legal action against the company, alleging that a variety of the company's hiring and promotion practices were responsible for racial stratification in the workplace. The claim was advanced under the disparate impact portion of Title VII of the Civil Rights Act. In 1989 the Supreme Court decided on the case in favor of Ward's Cove. The court decided that, even if employees can prove discrimination, the hiring practices may still be considered legal if they serve "legitimate employment goals of the employer." This decision allowed disparate impact if it was in the service of the company. This case prompted Congress to pass the Civil Rights Act of 1991, which contained several important modifications to Title VII of the original act. Most important, however, the new act shifted the burden of proof onto the employer by requiring that it must prove a close connection between disparate impact and the ability to actually perform the job in question.

Whorfian hypothesis of linguistic relativity In 1956, Whorf proposed the theory that language creates thought and experience. According to this hypothesis, the ideas that people can think and the emotions they feel are constrained by the need locate words that happen to exist in their language and culture and with which they use to express them.

wish fulfillment If an urge from the id requires some external object or person, and that object or person is not available, the id may create a mental image or fantasy of that object or person to satisfy its needs. Mental energy is invested in that fantasy and the urge is temporarily satisfied. This process is called wish fulfillment, whereby something unavailable is conjured up and the image of it is temporarily satisfying.

within the individual The important sources of personality reside within the individual—that is, people carry the sources of their personality inside themselves—and hence are stable over time and consistent over situations.

within-culture variation Variations within a particular culture that can arise from several sources, including differences in growing up in various socioeconomic classes, differences in historical era, or differences in the racial context in which one grows up.

working models Early experiences and reactions of the infant to the parents, particularly the mother, become what Bowlby called "working models" for later adult relationships. These working models are internalized in the form of unconscious expectations about relationships.

X

xenophobia The fear of strangers. Characteristics that were probably adaptive in ancestral environments, such as xenophobia, are not necessarily adaptive in modern environments. Some of the personality traits that make up human nature may be vestigial adaptations to an ancestral environment that no longer exists.

References

Abdel-Khalek, A. M., and Alansari, B. M. (2004). Gender differences in anxiety among undergraduates from ten Arab countries. *Social Behavior and Personality, 32,* 649-656.

Abe, J. A. A. (2005). The predictive validity of the five-factor model of personality with preschool age children: A nine year follow-up study. *Journal of Research in Personality, 39,* 423-442.

Abelson, R. P. (1985). A variance explanation paradox: When a little is a lot. *Psychological Bulletin, 97,* 129-133.

Abrahamson, A. C., Baker, L. A., and Caspi, A. (2002). Rebellious teens? Genetic and environmental influences on the social attitudes of adolescents. *Journal of Personality and Social Psychology, 83*(6), 1392-1408.

Ackerman, J. M., and Bargh, J. A. (2010). The purpose-driven life: Commentary on Kenrick et al. (2010). *Perspectives on Psychological Science, 5,* 323-326.

Aczel, B., Lukacs, B., Komlos, J., and Aitken, M. R. F. (2011). Unconscious intuition or conscious analysis? Critical questions for the deliberation-without-attention paradigm. *Judgment and Decision Making, 6,* 351-358.

Adan, A. (1991). Influence of morningness-eveningness preference in the relationship between body temperature and performance: A diurnal study. *Personality and Individual Differences, 12,* 1159-1169.

Adan, A. (1992). The influence of age, work schedule and personality on morningness dimension. *International Journal of Psychophysiology, 12,* 95-99.

Addison, T. L., and Schmidt, L. A. (1999). Are women who are shy reluctant to take risks? Behavioral and psychophysiological correlates. *Journal of Research in Personality, 33,* 352-357.

Affleck, G., and Tennen, H. (1996). Construing benefits from adversity: Adaptational significance and dispositional underpinnings. *Journal of Personality, 64,* 899-922.

Aghababaei, N. (2013). Between you and God, where is the general factor of personality? Exploring personality-religion relationships in a Muslim context. *Personality and Individual Differences, 55*(2), 196-198.

Aigner, M., Eher, R., Fruenhwald, S., Frottier, P., Gutierrez-Lobos, K., and Dwyer, S. M. (2000). Brain abnormalities and violent behavior. *Journal of Psychology and Human Sexuality, 11,* 57-64.

Ainsworth, M. D. (1979). Infant–mother attachment. *American Psychologist, 34,* 932-937.

Ainsworth, M. D., and Bowlby, J. (1991). An ethological approach to personality development. *American Psychologist, 46,* 333-341.

Ainsworth, M. D., Bell, S. M., and Stayton, D. J. (1972). Individual differences in the development of some attachment behaviors. *Merrill-Palmer Quarterly, 18,* 123-143.

Aknin, L. B., Barrington-Leigh, C. P., Dunn, E. W., Helliwell, J. F., Burns, J., Biswas-Diener, R., and . . . Norton, M. I. (2013). Prosocial spending and well-being: Cross-cultural evidence for a psychological universal. *Journal of Personality and Social Psychology, 104*(4), 635-652.

Alegria, A. A. et al. (2013). Sex differences in antisocial personality disorder: Results from the National Epidemiological Survey on Alcohol and Related Conditions. *Personality Disorders, 4,* 214-222.

Alexander, R. D., Hoodland, J. L., Howard, R. D., Noonan, K. M., and Sherman, P. W. (1979). Sexual dimorphisms and breeding systems in pinnipeds, ungulates, primates, and humans. In N. A. Chagnon and W. Irons (Eds.), *Evolutionary biology and human social behavior.* North Scituate, MA: Duxbury Press.

Algom, D., Chajut, E., and Lev, S. (2004). A rational look at the emotional Stroop phenomenon: A generic slowdown, not a Stroop effect. *Journal of Experimental Psychology: General, 133,* 323-338.

Alleman, M., Zimprich, D., and Hertzon, C. (2007). Cross-sectional age differences and longitudinal age changes in middle adulthood and old age. *Journal of Personality, 75,* 323-358.

Allemand, M., Gomez, V., and Jackson, J. J. (2010). Personality trait development in midlife: Exploring the impact of psychological turning points. *European Journal of Aging, 7,* 147-155.

Allen, K. A., Gray, D. L., Baumeister, R. F., and Leary, M. R. (2022). The need to belong: A deep dive into the origins, implications, and future of a foundational construct. *Educational Psychology Review, 34*(2), 1133-1156.

Allen, T. A., and DeYoung, C. G. (2017). Personality neuroscience and the Five Factor Model. In T. A. Widiger (Ed.), *Oxford Handbook of the Five Factor Model* (pp. 319-349). New York: Oxford University Press.

Allik, J. (2012). National differences in personality. *Personality and Individual Differences, 53,* 114-117.

Allik, J., and Realo, A. (2009). Editorial: Personality and culture. *European Journal of Personality, 23,* 149-152.

Allport, G. W. (1937). *Personality: A psychological interpretation.* New York: Holt, Rinehart and Winston.

Allport, G. W. (1961). *Pattern and growth in personality.* New York: Holt, Rinehart and Winston.

Allport, G. W., and Odbert, H. S. (1936). Trait-names: A psycho-lexical study. *Psychological Monographs, 47* (1, Whole No. 211).

Almagor, M., Tellegen, A., and Waller, N. G. (1995). The big seven model: A cross-cultural replication and further exploration of the basic dimensions of natural language trait descriptors. *Journal of Personality and Social Psychology, 69,* 300-307.

Al-Shawaf, L., Lewis, D. M., and Buss, D. M. (2018). Sex differences in disgust: Why are women more easily disgusted than men?. *Emotion Review, 10*(2), 149-160.

Alston, W. P. (1975). Traits, consistency and conceptual alternatives for personality theory. *Journal for the Theory of Social Behavior, 5,* 17-48.

Aluja, A., Balada, F., Blanco, E., Fibla, J., and Blanch, A. (2019). Twenty candidate genes predicting neuroticism and sensation seeking personality traits: A multivariate analysis association approach. *Personality and Individual Differences, 140,* 90-102.

Aluja, A., Lucas, I., Blanch, A., and Blanco, E. (2019). Personality and disinhibitory psychopathology in alcohol consumption: A study from the biological-factorial personality models of Eysenck, Gray and Zuckerman. *Personality and Individual Differences, 142,* 159-165.

Amelang, M., Herboth, G., and Oefner, I. (1991). A prototype strategy for the construction of a creativity scale. *European Journal of Personality, 5,* 261-285.

American Psychiatric Association. (2013). *Diagnostic and Statistical Manual of Mental Disorders* (5th ed.). Washington, DC: Author.

Anastasi, A. (1976). *Psychological Testing.* New York: Macmillan.

Andari, E. (2015). Editorial: Oxytocin's routes in social behavior: Into the 21st century. *Frontiers in Behavioral Neuroscience, 9,* ArtID: 224

Andersen, J. P., Di Nota, P. M., Boychuk, E. C., Schimmack, U., and Collins, P. I. (2021). Racial bias and lethal force errors among Canadian police officers. *Canadian Journal of Behavioural Science.* https://doi.org/10.1037/cbs0000296.

Anderson, C., and Kilduff, G. J. (2009). Why do dominant personalities attain influence in face-to-face groups? The competence-signaling effects of trait dominance. *Journal of Personality and Social Psychology, 96,* 491-503.

Ando, J., Ono, Y., Yoshimura, K., Onoda, N., Shinohara, M., Kanba, S., and Asai, M. (2002). The genetic structure of Cloninger's seven-factor model of temperament and character in a Japanese sample. *Journal of Personality, 70*(5), 583-610.

Andrews, J. D. W. (1967). The achievement motive in two types of organizations. *Journal of Personality and Social Psychology, 6,* 163-168.

Angier, N. (1999). *Woman: An intimate geography.* Boston: Houghton Mifflin.

Angleitner, A., and Demtroder, A. I. (1988). Acts and dispositions: A reconsideration of the act frequency approach. *European Journal of Psychology, 2,* 121-141.

Angleitner, A., Buss, D., and Demtröder, A. I. (1990). A cross-cultural comparison using the act frequency approach (AFA) in West Germany and the United States. *European Journal of Personality, 4,* 187-207.

Antoniazzi, D., and Klein, R. (2019). Risky riders: A comparison of personality theories on motorcyclist riding behaviour. *Transportation Research Part F: Traffic Psychology and Behaviour, 62,* 33-44.

Anusic, I., Lucas, R. E., and Donnellan, M. B. (2012). Cross-sectional age differences in personality: Evidence from nationally representative samples from Switzerland and the United States. *Journal of Research in Personality, 46,* 116-120.

Apostolou, M. (2017). Stay away, but I may need your help! Mate choice and manipulation of prospective parents-in-law. *Personal Relationships, 24*(2), 323-335.

Apostolou, M., and Keramari, D. (2021b). Why friendships end: An evolutionary examination. *Evolutionary Behavioral Sciences.*

Apostolou, M., and Papageorgi, I. (2014). Parental mate choice manipulation tactics: Exploring prevalence, sex and personality effects. *Evolutionary Psychology, 12,* 588-620.

Apostolou, M., Keramari, D., Kagialis, A., and Sullman, M. (2021). Why people make friends: The nature of friendship. *Personal Relationships, 28*(1), 4-18.

Apostolou, M., Zacharia, M., and Frantzides, N. (2015). Children's tactics of mate choice manipulation: Exploring sex differences and personality effects. *Personality and Individual Differences, 80,* 6-11.

Archer, J. (2009). Does sexual selection explain human sex differences in aggression? *Behavioral and Brain Sciences, 32,* 249-311.

Archer, J., and Thanzami, V. (2009). The relation between mate value, entitlement, physical aggression, size and strength among a sample of young Indian men. *Evolution and Human Behavior, 30,* 315-321.

Archontaki, D., Lewis, G. J., and Bates, T. C. (2013). Genetic influences on psychological well-being: A nationally representative twin study. *Journal of Personality, 81*(2), 221-230.

Ardila, A. (2021). Cultural Universals. *Encyclopedia of Evolutionary Psychological Science,* 1677-1680.

Areh, I., Verkampt, F., and Allan, A. (2021). Critical review of the use of the Rorschach in European courts. *Psychiatry, Psychology and Law,* 1-23.

Aron, A., Aron, E. N., Tudor, M., and Nelson, G. (2004). Close relationships as including other in the self. In H. T. Reis and C. E. Rustbult (Eds.), *Close relationships: Key readings* (pp. 365-379). Philadelphia: Taylor and Francis.

Aschoff, J. (1965). Circadian rhythms in man. *Science, 143,* 1427-1432.

Aschwanden, D., Strickhouser, J. E., Sesker, A. A., Lee, J. H., Luchetti, M., Stephan, Y., Sutin, A. R., and Terracciano, A. (2020). Psychological and behavioural responses to coronavirus disease 2019: The role of personality. *European Journal of Personality.* https://doi-org.libproxy.wustl.edu/10.1002/per.2281

Asendorpf, J. B., and Scherer, K. R. (1983). The discrepant repressor: Differentiation between low anxiety, high anxiety, and repression of anxiety by autonomic-facial-verbal patterns of behavior. *Journal of Personality and Social Psychology, 45,* 1334-1346.

Asendorpf, J. B., and Van Aken, M. A. G. (2003). Validity of five personality judgments in childhood: A 9-year longitudinal study. *European Journal of Personality, 32,* 649-656.

Ashmore, R. D. (1990). Sex, gender, and the individual. In L. A. Pervin (Ed.), *Handbook of personality: Theory and research* (pp. 486-526). New York: Guilford Press.

Ashton, M. C. (2007). Self-reports and stereotypes: A comment on McCrae et al. *European Journal of Personality, 21,* 983-986.

Ashton, M. C., and Lee, K. (2005). A defense of the lexical approach to the study of personality. *European Journal of Personality, 19,* 5-24.

Ashton, M. C., Lee, K., and de Vries, R. E. (2014). The HEXACO honesty-humility, agreeableness, and emotionality factors a review of research and theory. *Personality and Social Psychology Review, 18*(2), 139-152.

Ashton, M. C., Lee, K., and Paunonen, S. V. (2002). What is the central feature of extraversion? Social attention versus reward sensitivity. *Journal of Personality and Social Psychology, 83*(1), 245-252.

Ashton, M. C., Lee, K., and Visser, B. A. (2019). Where's the H? Relations between BFI-2 and HEXACO-60 scales. *Personality and Individual Differences, 137,* 71-75.

Ashton, M. C., Paunonen, S. V., Helmes, E., and Jackson, D. N. (1998). Kin altruism, reciprocal altruism, and the Big Five personality factors. *Evolution and Human Behavior, 19*(4), 243-255.

Assor, A. (1989). The power motive as an influence on the evaluation of high and low status persons. *Journal of Research in Personality, 23,* 55-69.

Audet, É. C., Levine, S. L., Metin, E., Koestner, S., and Barcan, S. (2021). Zooming their way through university: Which Big 5 traits facilitated students' adjustment to online courses during the COVID-19 pandemic. *Personality and Individual Differences, 180.* https://doi-org/10.1016/j.paid.2021.110969

Augustine, A. A., Larsen, R. J., Walker, M. S., and Fisher, E. B. (2008). Personality predictors of the time course for lung cancer onset. *Journal of Research in Personality, 42,* 1448-1455.

Averill, J. R. (1975). A semantic atlas of emotional concepts. *Catalog of Selected Documents in Psychology, 5,* 30.

Avinun, R., and Knafo, A. (2014). Parenting as a reaction evoked by children's genotype a meta-analysis of children-as-twins studies. *Personality and Social Psychology Review, 18,* 87-102.

Ayoub, M., Briley, D. A., Grotzinger, A., Patterson, M. W., Engelhardt, L. E., Tackett, J. L., ... and Tucker-Drob, E. M. (2019). Genetic and environmental associations between child personality and parenting. *Social Psychological and Personality Science, 10*(6), 711-721.

Back, M. D., Schmukle, S. C., and Egloff, B. (2008). How extraverted is honey. bunny77@hotmail.de? Inferring personality from email addresses. *Journal of Research in Personality, 42,* 1116-1122.

Bacon, A. M., Krupić, D., Caki, N., and Corr, P. J. (2021). Emotional and behavioral responses to COVID-19: Explanations from three key models of personality. *European Psychologist, 26,* 334-347. https://doi-org.libproxy.wustl.edu/10.1027/1016-9040/a000461

Bailey, J. M., Dunne, M. P., and Martin, N. G. (2000). Genetic and environmental influences on sexual orientation and its correlates in an Australian twin sample. *Journal of Personality and Social Psychology, 78,* 524-536.

Bailey, J. M., Kirk, K. M., Zhu, G., Dunne, M. P., and Martin, N. G. (2000). Do individual differences in sociosexuality represent genetic or environmentally contingent strategies? Evidence from the Australian Twin Registry. *Journal of Personality and Social Psychology, 78,* 537–545.

Bailey, J. M., Pillard, R. C., Neale, M. C., and Agyei, Y. (1993). Heritable factors influence sexual orientation in women. *Archives of General Psychiatry, 50,* 217–223.

Bailey, N. A., Olaguez, A. P., Klemfuss, J. Z., and Loftus, E. F. (2021). Tactics for increasing resistance to misinformation. *Applied Cognitive Psychology,* Mar 3, 2021, DOI: /10.1002/acp.3812

Bailey, S. L., and Heitkemper, M. M. (1991). Morningness–eveningness and early-morning salivary cortisol levels. *Biological Psychology, 32,* 181–192.

Bajcar, B., and Babiak, J. (2020). Neuroticism and cyberchondria: The mediating role of intolerance of uncertainty and defensive pessimism. *Personality and Individual Differences, 162.* https://doi.org/10.1016/j.paid.2020.110006.

Baker, R. A. (1992). *Hidden memories.* Buffalo, NY: Prometheus Books.

Bakker, A. B., and Wang, Y. (2020). Self-undermining behavior at work: Evidence of construct and predictive validity. *International Journal of Stress Management, 27,* 241–251.

Balliet, D., Li, N. P., Macfarlan, S. J., and Van Vugt, M. (2011). Sex differences in cooperation: A meta-analytic review of social dilemmas. *Psychological Bulletin, 137,* 881–909.

Banas, K., and Smyth, L. (2021). Structure, content and inter-relationships between self-aspects: Integrating findings from the social identity and self-complexity traditions. *European Journal of Social Psychology.* https://doi.org/10.1002/ejsp.2760.

Bandura, A. (1977). *Social learning theory.* Englewood Cliffs, NJ: Prentice Hall.

Bandura, A. (1989). Human agency in social cognitive theory. *American Psychologist, 44,* 1175–1184.

Bandura, A. (1997). Self-efficacy: The exercise of control. W H Freeman/Times Books/ Henry Holt & Co.

Banks, A. P. (2021). Mechanisms of unconscious thought: Capacities and limits. *Journal of Mind and Behavior, 42,* 317–346.

Barelds, D.P.H. (2005). Self and partner personality in intimate relationships. *European Journal of Personality, 19,* 501–518.

Barelds, D.P.H., and Dijkstra, P. (2011). Positive illusions about a partner's personality and relationship quality. *Journal of Research in Personality, 45,* 37–43.

Bargh, (2017). *Before you know it: The unconscious reasons we do what we do.*

Portsmouth, NH: William Heinemann Publishing.

Bargh, J. A. (2005). Bypassing the will: Toward demystifying the nonconscious control of social behavior. In R. R. Hassin, J. S. Uleman, and J. A. Bargh (Eds.), *The new unconscious* (pp. 37–60). New York: Oxford University Press.

Bargh, J. A. (2006). *The new unconscious.* New York: Oxford University Press.

Bargh, J. A. (2008). Free will is un-natural. In J. Baer, J. C. Kaufman, and R. F. Baumeister (Eds.), *Are we free? Psychology and free will* (pp. 128–154). New York: Oxford University Press.

Bargh, J. A. (2016). Awareness of the prime versus awareness of its influence: Implications for the real-world scope of unconscious higher mental processes. *Current Opinion in Psychology, 12,* 49–52.

Bargh, J. A., and Morsella, E. (2008). The unconscious mind. *Perspectives on Psychological Science, 3,* 73–79.

Bargh, J. A., and Morsella, E. (2010). Unconscious behavioral guidance systems. In C. R. Agnew, D. E. Carlston, W. G. Graziano, and J. R. Kelly (Eds.), *Then a miracle occurs: Focusing on behavior in social psychological theory and research* (pp. 89–118). New York: NY: Oxford University Press.

Baron, M. (1993). Genetics and human sexual orientation. *Biological Psychology, 33,* 759–761.

Bar-On, R. (2001). Emotional intelligence and self-actualization. In J. Ciarrochi and J. P. Forgas (Eds.), *Emotional intelligence in everyday life: A scientific inquiry* (pp. 82–97). Philadelphia, PA: Psychology Press.

Baron, R. A. (1977). *Human Aggression.* New York: Plenum Press.

Baron-Cohen, S., Richler, J., Bisarya, D., Gurunathan, N., and Wheelwright, S. (2003). The systemizing quotient: an investigation of adults with Asperger syndrome or high–functioning autism, and normal sex differences. *Philosophical Transactions of the Royal Society of London. Series B: Biological Sciences, 358*(1430), 361–374.

Barrantes-Vidal, N., and Kwapil, T. R. (2014). The application of experience sampling methodology for the study of individual differences in real life. *Personality and Individual Differences, 60,* S6.

Barrick, M. R., and Mount, M. K. (1991). The Big Five personality dimensions and job performance: A meta-analysis. *Personnel Psychology, 44,* 1–25.

Barron, J. W., Eagle, M. N., and Wolitzky, D. L. (1992). *Interface of psychoanalysis and psychology.* Washington, DC: American Psychological Association.

Bartels, M. (2015). Genetics of wellbeing and its components satisfaction with life, happiness, and quality of life: A review

and meta-analysis of heritability studies. *Behavior Genetics, 45*(2), 137–156.

Barthorpe, A., Winstone, L., Mars, B., and Moran, P. (2020). Is social media screen time really associated with poor adolescent mental health? A time use diary study. *Journal of Affective Disorders, 274,* 864–870

Baselmans, B. M. L., van de Weijer, M. P., Abdellaoui, A., Vink, J. M., Hottenga, J. J., Willemsen, G., . . . and Bartels, M. (2019). A genetic investigation of the well-being spectrum. *Behavior Genetics, 49*(3), 286–297.

Bass, E., and Davis, L. (1988). *The courage to heal: A guide for women survivors of child sexual abuse.* New York: Perennial Library/Harper and Row.

Bastone, L. M., and Wood, H. A. (1997). Individual differences in the ability to decode emotional facial expressions. *Psychology: A Journal of Human Behavior, 34,* 32–36.

Bastounis, A., Callaghan, P., Banerjee, A., and Michail, M. (2016). The effectiveness of the Penn Resiliency Program (PRP) and its adapted versions in reducing depression and anxiety and improving explanatory style: A systematic review and meta-analysis. *Journal of Adolescence, 52,* 37–48 .

Bauer, J. J., Schwab, J. R., and McAdams, D. P. (2011). Self-actualizing: Where ego development finally feels good? *The Humanistic Psychologist, 39,* 121–136.

Baughman, H. M., Dearing, S., Giammarco, E., and Vernon, P. A. (2012). Relationship between bullying behaviours and the Dark Triad: A study with adults. *Personality and Individual Differences, 52,* 571–575.

Baumeister, R. F. (1986). *Identity: Cultural Change and the Struggle for Self.* New York: Oxford University Press.

Baumeister, R. F. (1988). Should we stop studying sex differences altogether? *American Psychologist, 43,* 1092–1095.

Baumeister, R. F. (1991). The self against itself: Escape or defeat? In R. C. Curtis (Ed.), *The Relational Self: Theoretical Convergences in Psychoanalysis and Social Psychology* (pp. 238–256). New York: Guilford Press.

Baumeister, R. F. (1997). Identity, self-concept, and self-esteem: The self lost and found. In R. Hogan, J. Johnson, and S. Briggs (Eds.), *Handbook of Personality Psychology* (pp. 681–711). New York: Academic Press.

Baumeister, R. F. (2014). Self-regulation, ego depletion, and inhibition. *Neuropsychologia, 65,* 313–319.

Baumeister, R. F., and Leary, M. R. (1995). The need to belong: Desire for interpersonal attachments as a fundamental human motivation. *Psychological Bulletin, 117,* 497–529.

Baumeister, R. F., and Muraven, M. (1996). Identity as adaptation to social, cultural and historical context. *Journal of Adolescence, 19,* 405–416.

Baumeister, R. F., and Tice, D. M. (1990). Anxiety and social exclusion. *Journal of Social and Clinical Psychology, 9,* 165–195.

Baumeister, R. F., and Vohs, K. (2004). *Handbook of self-regulation.* New York: Guilford Press.

Baumeister, R. F., Bratslavsky, E., Muraven, M., and Tice, D. M. (1998). Ego depletion: Is the active self a limited resource? *Journal of Personality and Social Psychology, 74,* 1252–1265.

Baumeister, R. F., Bushman, B. J., and Campbell, W. K. (2000). Self-esteem, narcissism, and aggression: Does violence result from low self-esteem or from threatened egotism? *Current Directions in Psychological Science, 9,* 26–29.

Baumeister, R. F., Campbell, J. D., Krueger, J. I., and Vohs, K. D. (2003). Does high self-esteem cause better performance, interpersonal success, happiness, or healthier lifestyles? *Psychological Science in the Public Interest, 4,* 1–44.

Baumeister, R. F., Catanese, K. R., and Vohs, K. D. (2001). Is there a gender difference in strength of sex drive? Theoretical views, conceptual distinctions, and a review of relevant evidence. *Personality and Social Psychology Review, 5*(3), 242–273.

Baumeister, R. F., Dale, K., and Sommer, K. L. (1998). Freudian defense mechanisms and empirical findings in modern social psychology: Reaction formation, projection, displacement, undoing, isolation, sublimation, and denial. *Journal of Personality, 66,* 1061–1081.

Baumeister, R. F., Tice, D. M., and Hutton, D. G. (1989). Self-presentational motivations and personality differences in self-esteem. *Journal of Personality, 57,* 547–579.

Baumeister, R. F., Tice, D. M., and Vohs, K. D. (2018). The strength model of self-regulation: Conclusions from the second decade of willpower research. *Perspectives on Psychological Science, 13,* 141–145.

Baumeister, R. F., Vohs, K. D., and Tice, D. M. (2007). The strength model of self-control. *Current Directions in Psychological Science, 16,* 396–403.

Beam, C. R., Marcus, K., Turkheimer, E., and Emery, R. E. (2018). Gender differences in the structure of marital quality. *Behavior Genetics, 48*(3), 209–223.

Beaty, R. E., Kaufman, S. B., Benedek, M., Jung, R. E., Kenett, Y. N., Jauk, E., . . . and Silvia, P. J. (2016). Personality and complex brain networks: The role of openness to experience in default network efficiency. *Human Brain Mapping, 37*(2), 773–779.

Beauducel, A., Debener, S., Brocke, B., and Kayser, J. (2000). On the reliability of augmenting/reducing: Peak amplitudes and principal component analysis of auditory evoked potentials. *Journal of Psychophysiology, 14,* 226–240.

Beauregard, M., Levesque, J., and Bourgouin, P. (2001). Neural correlates of conscious self-regulation of emotion. *Journal of Neuroscience, 21,* RC165 (1–6).

Beck, A. T. (1976). *Cognitive therapy and the emotional disorders.* New York: International Universities Press.

Beekman, J. B., Stock, M. L., and Marcus, T. (2016). Need to belong, not rejection sensitivity, moderates cortisol response, self-reported stress, and negative affect following social exclusion. *Journal of Social Psychology, 156*(2), 131–138.

Beer, J. S., and Lombardo, M. V. (2007). Patient and neuroimaging methods. In R. W. Robins, R. C. Fraley, and R. F. Krueger (Eds.), *Handbook of research methods in personality psychology* (pp. 360–369). New York: Guilford Press.

Bègue, L., Beauvois, J. L., Courbet, D., Oberlé, D., Lepage, J., and Duke, A. A. (2015). Personality predicts obedience in a Milgram paradigm. *Journal of Personality, 83*(3), 299–306.

Belle, D., Doucet, J., Harris, J., Miller, J., and Tan, E. (2000). Who is rich? Who is happy? *American Psychologist, 55,* 116–117.

Bellingtier, J. A., Mund, M., and Wrzus, C. (2021). The role of extraversion and neuroticism for experiencing stress during the third wave of the covid-19 pandemic. *Current Psychology: A Journal for Diverse Perspectives on Diverse Psychological Issues.* https://doi-org.libproxy.wustl.edu/10.1007/s12144-021-02600-y.

Belsky, J. (2000). Conditional and alternative reproductive strategies: Individual differences in susceptibility to rearing experience. In J. Rodgers, D. Rowe, and W. Miller (Eds.), *Genetic influences on human fertility and sexuality: Theoretical and empirical contributions from the biological and behavioral sciences* (pp. 127–146). Boston: Kluwer.

Belsky, J., Schlomer, G. L., and Ellis, B. J. (2012). Beyond cumulative risk: distinguishing harshness and unpredictability as determinants of parenting and early life history strategy. *Developmental Psychology, 48*(3), 662.

Belsky, J., Steinberg, L., and Draper, P. (1991). Childhood experience, interpersonal development, and reproductive strategy: An evolutionary theory of socialization. *Child Development, 62,* 647–670.

Bem, D. J. (1996). Exotic becomes erotic: A developmental theory of sexual orientation. *Psychological Review, 103,* 320–333.

Bem, S. L. (1974). The measurement of psychological androgyny. *Journal of Consulting and Clinical Psychology, 42,* 153–162.

Bendixen, M., Kennair, L. E. O., and Buss, D. M. (2015). Jealousy: Evidence of strong sex differences using both forced choice and continuous measure paradigms. *Personality and Individual Differences, 86,* 212–216.

Benet-Martinez, V., Donnellan, M. B., Fleeson, W., Fraley, R. C., Gosling, S. D., King, L. A., Robins, R. W., and Funder, D. C. (2015). Six visions for the future of personality psychology. In L. Cooper and R. J. Larsen (Eds.), *Handbook of Personality and Social Psychology: Personality Processes and Individual Differences* (pp. 665–690). Washington, DC: American Psychological Association.

Benjamin, J., Li, L., Patterson, C., Greenberg, B. D., Murphy, D. L., and Hamer, D. H. (1996). Population and familial association between the D4 dopamine receptor gene and measures of novelty seeking. *Nature Genetics, 12,* 81–84.

Bentler, P. M., and Newcomb, M. D. (1978). Longitudinal study of marital success and failure. *Journal of Consulting and Clinical Psychology, 46,* 1053–1070.

Berant, E. (2009). Attachment styles, the Rorschach, and the Thematic Apperception Test: Using traditional projective measures to assess aspects of attachment. In J. J. Obegi and E. Berant (Eds.), *Attachment theory and research in clinical work with adults* (pp. 181–206). New York: Guilford Press.

Berenbaum, S. A., and Beltz, A. M. (2011). Sexual differentiation of human behavior: Effects of prenatal and pubertal organizational hormones. *Frontiers in Neuroendocrinology, 32*(2), 183–200.

Berenbaum, S. A., and Beltz, A. M. (2021). Evidence and Implications From a Natural Experiment of Prenatal Androgen Effects on Gendered Behavior. *Current Directions in Psychological Science, 30*(3), 202–210.

Berenbaum, S. A., and Snyder, E. (1995). Early hormonal influences on childhood sex-typed activity and playmate preferences: Implications for the development of sexual orientation. *Developmental Psychology, 31,* 31–42.

Berg, V., Lummaa, V., Rickard, I. J., Silventoinen, K., Kaprio, J., and Jokela, M. (2016). Genetic associations between personality traits and lifetime reproductive success in humans. *Behavior Genetics, 46*(6), 742–753.

Berman, S., Ozkaragoz, T., Yound, R. M., and Noble, E. P. (2002). D2 dopamine receptor gene polymorphism discriminates two kinds of novelty seeking. *Personality and Individual Differences, 33,* 867-882.

Bernhardt, P. C., Dabbs, J. M., Jr., Fielden, J., and Lutter, C. (1998). Testosterone changes during vicarious experiences of winning and losing among fans at sporting events. *Physiology and Behavior, 65,* 59-62.

Bernstein, D. M., and Loftus, E. F. (2009). How to tell if a particular memory is true or false. *Perspectives on Psychological Science, 4,* 370-374.

Berry, C. M., Sackett, P. R., and Wiemann, S. (2007). A review of recent developments in integrity test research. *Personnel Psychology, 60,* 271-301.

Berry, D. S., and Miller, K. M. (2001). When boy meets girl: Attractiveness and the five-factor model in opposite-sex interactions. *Journal of Research in Personality, 35,* 62-77.

Bian, M., and Leung, L. (2015). Linking loneliness, shyness, smartphone addiction symptoms, and patterns of smartphone use to social capital. *Social Science Computer Review, 33*(1), 61-79.

Bilton, I. (2018). https://www.studyinternational.com/news/record-high-numbers-women-outnumbering-men-university-globally/.

Birley, A. J., Gillespie, N. A., Heath, A. C., Sullivan, P. F., Boomsma, D. I., and Martin, N. G. (2006). Heritability and nineteen-year stability of long and short EPQ-R Neuroticism scales. *Personality and Individual Differences, 40,* 737-747.

Black, J. (2000). Personality testing and police selection: Utility of the Big Five. *New Zealand Journal of Psychology, 29,* 2-9.

Bleidorn, W. (2012). Hitting the road to adulthood short-term personality development during a major life transition. *Personality and Social Psychology Bulletin, 38*(12), 1594-1608.

Bleske-Rechek, A. L., and Buss, D. M. (2001). Opposite-sex friendship: Sex differences and similarities in initiation, selection, and dissolution. *Personality and Social Psychology Bulletin, 27,*(10), 1310-1323.

Bleske-Rechek, A., Remiker, M. W., and Baker, J. P. (2008). Narcissistic men and women think they are so hot—But they are not. *Personality and Individual Differences, 45,* 420-424.

Blinkhorn, V., Lyons, M., and Almond, L. (2015). The ultimate femme fatale? Narcissism predicts serious and aggressive sexually coercive behaviour in females. *Personality and Individual Differences, 87,* 219-223.

Block, J. (1971). *Lives through time.* Berkeley, CA: Bancroft Books.

Block, J. (1977). Advancing the psychology of personality: Paradigmatic shift or improving the quality of research. In D. Magnusson and N. S. Endler (Eds.), *Personality at the crossroads* (pp. 37-63). Hillsdale, NJ: Erlbaum.

Block, J. (1989). Critique of the act frequency approach to personality. Journal of personality and social psychology, 56(2), 234-245.

Block, J. (1995). A contrarian view of the five-factor approach to personality description. Psychological bulletin, 117(2), 187-215.

Block, J. H. (1983). Differential premises arising from differential socialization of the sexes: Some conjectures. *Child Development, 54,* 1335-1354.

Block, J. H., and Block, J. (1980). *The California Child Q-Set.* Palo Alto, CA: Consulting Psychologists Press.

Block, J., and Robbins, R. W. (1993). A longitudinal study of consistency and change in self-esteem from early adolescence to early adulthood. *Child Development, 64,* 909-923.

Blonigen, D. M., Carlson, M. D., Hicks, B. M., Kreuger, R. F., and Iacono, W. G. (2008). Stability and change in personality traits from late adolescence to early adulthood: A longitudinal twin study. *Journal of Personality, 76,* 229-266.

Blonigen, D. M., Carlson, S. R., Krueger, R. F., and Patrick, C. J. (2003). A twin study of self-reported psychopathic personality traits. *Personality and Individual Differences, 35,* 179-197.

Blonigen, D. M., Hicks, B. M., Krueger, R. F., Patrick, C. J., and Iacono, W. G. (2006). Continuity and change in psychopathic traits as measured via normal-range personality: A longitudinal-biometric study. *Journal of Abnormal Psychology, 115*(1), 85.

Bochner, S. (1994). Cross-cultural differences in the self-concept: A test of Hofstede's individualism/collectivism distinction. *Journal of Cross-Cultural Psychology, 25,* 273-283.

Bogg, T. (2008). Conscientiousness, the transtheoretical model of change, and exercise: A neo-socioanalytic integration of trait and social-cognitive frameworks in the predictions of behavior. *Journal of Personality, 76,* 775-802.

Bogg, T., and Roberts, B. W. (2004). Conscientiousness and health behaviors: A meta-analysis of the leading behavioral contributors to mortality. *Psychological Bulletin, 130,* 887-919.

Bohart, A. C. (2013). The actualizing person. In M. Cooper, M. O'Hara, P. F. Schmid, A. C. Bohart, M. Cooper, M. O'Hara, . . . and A. C. Bohart (Eds.), *The handbook of person-centred psychotherapy and counselling* (2nd ed., pp. 84-101). New York: Palgrave Macmillan.

Bolkan, C., Hooker, K., and Coehlo, D. (2015). Possible selves and depressive symptoms in later life. *Research On Aging, 37*(1), 41-62.

Bollich, K. L., Doris, J. M., Vazire, S., Raison, C. L., Jackson, J. J., and Mehl, M. R. (2016). Eavesdropping on character: Assessing everyday moral behaviors. *Journal of Research in Personality, 61,* 15-21.

Bonanno, G. A. (1990). Repression, accessibility, and the translation of private experience. *Psychoanalytic Psychology, 7,* 453-473.

Bonanno, G. A., Wortman, C. B., Lehman, D. R., Tweed, R. G., Haring, M., Sonnega, J., Carr, D., and Nesse, R. M. (2002). Resilience to loss and chronic grief: A prospective study from preloss to 18-months postloss. *Journal of Personality and Social Psychology, 83*(5), 1150-1164.

Bono, J. E., Boles, T. L., Judge, T. A., and Lauver, K. J. (2002). The role of personality in task and relationship conflict. *Journal of Personality, 70,* 311-344.

Bono, T. (2018). *When Likes Aren't Enough: A Crash Course in the Science of Happiness.* New York: Grand Central Life & Style.

Bönte, W., Procher, V. D., Urbig, D., and Voracek, M. (2017). Digit ratio (2D:4D) predicts self-reported measures of general competitiveness, but not behavior in economic experiments. *Frontiers in Behavioral Neuroscience, 11,* 238.

Boomsma, D. I., Helmer, Q., Nieuwboer, H. A., Hottenga, J. J., de Moor, M. H., van Den Berg, S. M., . . . and Willemsen, G. (2018). An extended twin-pedigree study of neuroticism in the Netherlands Twin Register. *Behavior Genetics, 48*(1), 1-11.

Boomsma, D. I., Koopmans, J. R., Van Doornen, L. J. P., and Orlebeke, J. M. (1994). Genetic and social influences on starting to smoke: A study of Dutch adolescent twins and their parents. *Addiction, 89,* 219-226.

Borkenau, P., Riemann, R., Angleitner, A., and Spinath, F. M. (2001). Genetic and environmental influences on observed personality: Evidence from the German observational study of adult twins. *Journal of Personality and Social Psychology, 80*(4), 655-668.

Bornovalova, M. A., Hicks, B. M., Iacono, W. G., and McGue, M. (2010). Familial transmission and heritability of childhood disruptive disorders. *American Journal of Psychiatry, 167*(9), 1066-1074.

Bornstein, R. F. (1999). Source amnesia, misattribution, and the power of unconscious perceptions and memories. *Psychoanalytic Psychology, 16,* 155-178.

Bornstein, R. F. (2005). The dependent patient: Diagnosis, assessment, and treatment. *Professional Psychology: Research and Practice, 36,* 82–89.

Botwin, M. D., and Buss, D. M. (1989). Structure of act-report data: Is the five-factor model of personality recaptured? *Journal of Personality and Social Psychology, 56,* 988–1001.

Botwin, M., Buss, D. M., and Shackelford, T. (1997). Personality and mate preferences: Five factors in mate selection and marital satisfaction. *Journal of Personality, 65,* 107–136.

Bouchard, T. J., and Loehlin, J. C. (2001). Genes, evolution, and personality. *Behavior Genetics, 31,* 243–273.

Bouchard, T. J., and McGue, M. (1990). Genetic and rearing environmental influences on adult personality: An analysis of adopted twins reared apart. *Journal of Personality, 58,* 263–292.

Bowlby, J. (1969a). *Attachment and loss: Vol. 1: Attachment.* New York: Basic Books.

Bowlby, J. (1969b). *Attachment and loss: Vol. 2: Separation, anger, and anxiety.* New York: Basic Books.

Bowlby, J. (1980). *Attachment and loss: Vol. 3: Loss, sadness, and depression.* New York: Basic Books.

Bowlby, J. (1988). *A secure base: Parent–child attachment and healthy human development.* New York: Basic Books.

Boyce, C. J., Wood, A. M., and Brown, G.D.A. (2010). The dark side of conscientiousness: Conscientious people experience greater drops in life satisfaction following unemployment. *Journal of Personality, 44,* 535–539.

Boyer, P. (1992). Explaining religious ideas: Elements of a cognitive approach. *Numen, 39*(1), 27–57.

Boyer, P., and Bergstrom, B. (2008). Evolutionary perspectives on religion. *Annual Review of Anthropology, 37,* 111–130.

Brand, C. R., and Egan, V. (1989). The "Big Five" dimensions of personality? Evidence from ipsative, adjectival self-attributions. *Personality and Individual Differences, 10,* 1165–1171.

Branje, S. J. T., van Lieshout, C. F. M., and Geris, J. R. M. (2006). Big Five personality development in adolescence and adulthood. *European Journal of Personality, 21,* 45–62.

Brase, G. L., Caprar, D. V., and Voracek, M. (2004). Sex differences in responses to relationship threats in England and Romania. *Journal of Social and Personal Relationships, 21,* 763–778.

Braun, K. A., Ellis, R., and Loftus, E. F. (2002). Make my memory: How advertising can change our memories of the past. *Psychology and Marketing, 19,* 1–23.

Brebner, J. (2003). Gender and emotions. *Personality and Individual Differences, 34,* 387–394.

Brebner, J., and Cooper, C. (1978). Stimulus- or response-induced excitation: A comparison of the behavior of introverts and extraverts. *Journal of Research in Personality, 12,* 306–311.

Breger, R., and Hill, R. (Eds.). (1998). *Cross-cultural marriage: Identity and choice.* New York: Berg.

Brennan, K. A., and Shaver, P. R. (1993). Attachment styles and parental divorce. *Journal of Divorce and Remarriage, 21,* 161–175.

Brennan, P. A., and Raine, A. (1997). Biosocial bases of antisocial behavior: Psychophysiological, neurological, and cognitive factors. *Clinical Psychology Review Special Issue: Biopsychosocial Conceptualizations of Human Aggression, 17,* 589–604.

Bresin, K., and Robinson, M. D. (2015). You are what you see and choose: Agreeableness and situation selection. *Journal of Personality, 83*(4), 452–463.

Bretherton, I., and Main, M. (2000). Obituary: Mary Dinsmore Salter Ainsworth (1913–1999). *American Psychologist, 55,* 1148–1149.

Brewer, G., Abell, L., and Lyons, M. (2016). Machiavellianism, pretending orgasm, and sexual intimacy. *Personality and Individual Differences, 96,* 155–158.

Brickman, P., Coates, D., and Janoff-Bulman, R. J. (1978). Lottery winners and accident victims: Is happiness relative? *Journal of Personality and Social Psychology, 36,* 917–927.

Briley, D. A., and Tucker-Drob, E. M. (2014). Genetic and environmental continuity in personality development: A meta-analysis. *Psychological Bulletin, 140*(5), 1303–1331.

Brissette, I., Scheier, M. F., and Carver, C. S. (2002). The role of optimism in social network development, coping, and psychological adjustment during a life transition. *Journal of Personality and Social Psychology, 82,* 102–111.

Brody, J. E. (1996, March 27). Personal health. *The New York Times,* Section B.

Brooks, S. J., and Stein, D. J. (2014). Unconscious influences on decision making: Neuroimaging and neuroevolutionary perspectives. *Behavioral and Brain Sciences, 37*(1), 23–24.

Brose, L. A., Rye, M. S., Lutz-Zois, C., and Ross, S. R. (2005). Forgiveness and personality traits. *Personality and Individual Differences, 39,* 35–46.

Brown, D. E. (1991). *Human universals.* New York: McGraw-Hill.

Brown, J. D., and Dutton, K. A. (1995). The thrill of victory, the complexity of defeat: Self-esteem and people's emotional reactions to success and failure. *Journal of Personality and Social Psychology, 68,* 712–722.

Brown, J. D., and Smart, S. A. (1991). The self and social conduct: Linking self-representations to prosocial behavior. *Journal of Personality and Social Psychology, 60,* 368–375.

Brown, M., Hochman, A., and Micali, N. (2020). Emotional instability as a trait risk factor for eating disorder behaviors in adolescents: sex differences in a large-scale prospective study. *Psychological Medicine, 50*(11), 1783–1794.

Brown, R. P., and Zeigler-Hill, V. (2004). Narcissism and the non-equivalence of self-esteem measures: A matter of dominance. *Journal of Research in Personality, 38,* 585–592.

Bruce, J., Davis, E. P., and Gunnar, M. R. (2002). Individual differences in children's cortisol response to the beginning of a new school year. *Psychoneuroendocrinology, 27,* 635–650.

Bruch, M. A., and Hynes, M. J. (1987). Heterosexual anxiety and contraceptive behavior. *Journal of Research in Personality, 21,* 343–360.

Bruggemann, J. M., and Barry, R. J. (2002). Eysenck's P as a modulator of affective and electrodermal responses to violent and comic film. *Personality and Individual Differences, 32,* 1029–1048.

Brummett, B. H., Babyak, M. A., Williams, R. B., Barefoot, J. C., Costa, P. T., and Siegler, I. C. (2006). NEO personality domains and gender predict levels and trends in body mass index over 14 years during midlife. *Journal of Research in Personality, 40,* 222–236.

Buday, S. K., Stake, J. E., and Peterson, Z. D. (2012). Gender and the choice of a science career: The impact of social support and possible selves. *Sex Roles, 66,* 197–209.

Buerkle, J. V. (1960). Self attitudes and marital adjustment. *Merrill-Palmer Quarterly, 6,* 114–124.

Buffardi, L. E., and Campbell, W. K. (2008). Narcissism and social networking web sites. *Personality and Social Psychology Bulletin, 34,* 1303–1314.

Bulbulia, J. (2004). Religious costs as adaptations that signal altruistic intention. *Evolution and Cognition, 10*(1), 19–38.

Bullock, W. A., and Gilliland, K. (1993). Eysenck's arousal theory of introversion-extraversion: A converging measures investigation. *Journal of Personality and Social Psychology, 64,* 113–123.

Bunce, S. C., Larsen, R. J., and Peterson, C. (1995). Life after trauma: Personality and daily life experiences of traumatized persons. *Journal of Personality, 63,* 165–188.

Burgess, E. W., and Wallin, P. (1953). *Engagement and marriage.* New York: Lippincott.

Burke, R. J., Mattheiesen, S. B., and Pallesen, S. (2006). Personality correlates of workaholism. *Personality and Individual Differences, 40,* 1223-1233.

Burns, M. O., and Seligman, M. E. (1989). Explanatory style across the life span: Evidence for stability over 52 years. *Journal of Personality and Social Psychology, 56,* 471-477.

Burnstein, E., Crandall, C., and Kitayama, S. (1994). Some neo-Darwinian decision rules for altruism: Weighing cures for inclusive fitness as a function of the biological importance of the decision. *Journal of Personality and Social Psychology, 67,* 773-789.

Burra, N. D., Hervais-Adelman, A., Celeghin, A., de Gelder, B. and. Pegna, A. J. (2019). Affective blindsight relies on low spatial frequencies. *Neuropsychologia, 128,* 44-49.

Burt, S. A. (2009). A mechanistic explanation of popularity: Genes, rule breaking, and evocative gene-environment correlations. *Journal of Personality and Social Psychology, 96,* 783-794.

Burtăverde, V., Jonason, P. K., Giosan, C., and Ene, C. (2021). Why do people watch porn? An evolutionary perspective on the reasons for pornography consumption. Evolutionary Psychology, 19(2), 14747049211028798.

Burton, C. M., and King, L. A.(2008). Effects of (very) brief writing on health: The two-minute miracle. *British Journal of Health Psychology, 13,* 9-14.

Bush, G., Luu, P., and Posner, M. I. (2000). Cognitive and emotional influences in anterior cingulated cortex. *Trends in Cognitive Sciences, 4,* 215-222.

Bushman, B. J., and Baumeister, R. F. (2002). Does self-love or self-hate lead to violence? *Journal of Research in Personality, 36,* 543-545.

Bushman, B. J., Bonacci, A. M., van Dijk, M., and Baumeister, R. F. (2003). Narcissism, sexual refusal and aggression: Testing a narcissistic reactance model of sexual coercion. *Journal of Personality and Social Psychology, 84*(5), 1027-1040.

Bushman, B., and Baumeister, R. (1998). Threatened egotism, narcissism, self-esteem, and direct and displaced aggression: Does self-love or self-hate lead to violence? *Journal of Personality and Social Psychology, 75,* 219-229.

Buss, A. H. (1989). Personality as traits. *American Psychologist, 44,* 1378-1388.

Buss, D. M. (1981). Predicting parent-child interactions from children's activity level. *Developmental Psychology, 17* 59-65.

Buss, D. M. (1984). Toward a psychology of person-environment (PE) correlation: The role of spouse selection. *Journal of Personality and Social Psychology, 47,* 361-377.

Buss, D. M. (1989). Sex differences in human mate preferences: Evolutionary hypotheses tested in 37 cultures. *Behavioral and Brain Sciences, 12,* 1-49.

Buss, D. M. (1990). The evolution of anxiety and social exclusion. *Journal of Social and Clinical Psychology, 9,* 196-201.

Buss, D. M. (1991a). Conflict in married couples: Personality predictors of anger and upset. *Journal of Personality, 59,* 663-688.

Buss, D. M. (1991b). Evolutionary personality psychology. *Annual Review of Psychology., 42,* 459-491.

Buss, D. M. (1992). Manipulation in close relationships: Five personality factors in interactional context. *Journal of Personality, 60,* 477-499.

Buss, D. M. (1993). Strategic individual differences: The role of personality in creating and solving adaptive problems. In J. Hettema and I. Deary (Eds.), *Social and biological approaches to personality* (pp. 175-189) New York: Wiley.

Buss, D. M. (1995b). Psychological sex differences: Origins through sexual selection. *American Psychologist, 50,* 164-168.

Buss, D. M. (1996). Social adaptation and five major factors of personality. In J. S. Wiggins (Ed.), *The five-factor model of personality: Theoretical perspectives* (pp. 180-207). New York: Guilford Press.

Buss, D. M. (2000a). *The dangerous passion: Why jealousy is as necessary as love and sex.* New York: Free Press.

Buss, D. M. (2000b). The evolution of happiness. *American Psychologist, 55,* 15-23.

Buss, D. M. (2003). *The evolution of desire* (rev. ed.). New York: Basic Books.

Buss, D. M. (2005b). *The murderer next door: Why the mind is designed to kill.* New York: Penguin.

Buss, D. M. (2009a). The great struggles of life: Darwin and the emergence of evolutionary psychology. *American Psychologist, 64,* 140-148.

Buss, D. M. (2009b). How can evolutionary psychology successfully explain personality and individual differences? *Perspectives in Psychological Science, 5.*

Buss, D. M. (2011). Personality and the adaptive landscape: The role of individual differences in creating and solving social adaptive problems. In D.M. Buss and P. Hawley (Eds.), *The evolution of personality and individual differences* (pp. 29-60). New York: Oxford University Press.

Buss, D. M. (2012). *Evolutionary Psychology: The New Science of the Mind* (4th ed.). Boston: Allyn & Bacon.

Buss, D. M. (2016). *The evolution of desire: Strategies of human mating* (Revised and updated ed.). New York: Basic Books.

Buss, D. M. (2018). Sexual and emotional infidelity: Evolved gender differences in jealousy prove robust and replicable. *Perspectives on Psychological Science, 13*(2), 155-160.

Buss, D. M. (2019). *Evolutionary psychology: The new science of the mind (6th ed.).* Routledge.

Buss, D. M., Abbott, M., Angleitner, A., Asherian, A., Biaggio, A., et al. (1990). International preferences in selecting mates: A study of 37 cultures. *Journal of Cross-Cultural Psychology, 21,* 5-47.

Buss, D. M., and Barnes, M. L. (1986). Preferences in human mate selection. *Journal of Personality and Social Psychology, 50,* 559-570.

Buss, D. M., and Chiodo, L. M. (1991). Narcissistic acts in everyday life. *Journal of Personality, 59*(2), 179-215.

Buss, D. M., and Craik, K. H. (1983). The act frequency approach to personality. *Psychological Review, 90,* 105-126.

Buss, D. M., and Duntley, J. D. (2006). The evolution of aggression. In M. Schaller, D. T. Kenrick, and J. A. Simpson (Eds.), *Evolution and social psychology* (pp. 263-286). New York: Psychology Press.

Buss, D. M., and Greiling, H. (1999). Adaptive individual differences. *Journal of Personality, 67,* 209-243.

Buss, D. M., and Haselton, M. G. (2005). The evolution of jealousy. *Trends in Cognitive Science, 9,* 506-507.

Buss, D. M., and Hawley, P. (2011). *The evolution of personality and individual differences.* New York: Oxford University Press.

Buss, D. M., and Schmitt, D. P. (1993). Sexual strategies theory: An evolutionary perspective on human mating. *Psychological Review, 100,* 204-232.

Buss, D. M., and Schmitt, D. P. (2011). Evolutionary psychology and feminism. *Sex Roles, 64,* 768-787.

Buss, D. M., Block, J. H., and Block, J. (1980). Preschool activity level: Personality correlates and developmental implications. *Child Development, 51,* 401-408.

Buss, D. M., Goetz, C., Duntley, J. D., Asao, K., and Conroy-Beam, D. (2017). The mate switching hypothesis. *Personality and Individual Differences, 104,* 143-149.

Buss, D. M., Gomes, M., Higgins, D. S., and Lauterbach, K. (1987). Tactics of manipulation. *Journal of Personality and Social Psychology, 52,* 1219-1229.

Buss, D. M., Larsen, R. J., Semmelroth, J., and Westen, D. (1992). Sex differences in jealousy: Evolution, physiology, and psychology. *Psychological Science, 3,* 251–255.

Buss, D. M., Shackelford, T. K., Kirkpatrick, L. A., Choe, J., Hasegawa, M., Hasegawa, T., and Bennett, K. (1999). Jealousy and the nature of beliefs about infidelity: Tests of competing hypotheses about sex differences in the United States, Korea, and Japan. *Personal Relationships, 6,* 125–150.

Buss, D.M. (2021). When men behave badly: The hidden roots of sexual deception, harassment, and assault. New York: Little Brown Sparks.

Buss, K. A., Schumacher, J. R. M., Dolski, I., Kalin, N. H., Goldsmith, H. H., and Davidson, R. J. (2003). Right frontal brain activity, cortisol, and withdrawal behavior in 6-month-old infants. *Behavioral Neuroscience, 117,* 11–20.

Butkovic, A., and Bratko, D. (2007). Family study of manipulation tactics. *Personality and Individual Differences, 43,* 791–801.

Butler, A. C., Hokanson, J. E., and Flynn, H. A. (1994). A comparison of self-esteem lability and low trait self-esteem as vulnerability factors for depression. *Journal of Personality and Social Psychology, 66,* 166–177.

Button, T. M. M., Stallings, M. C., Rhee, S. H., Corley, R. P., and Hewitt, J. K. (2011). The etiology of stability and change in religious values and religious attendance. *Behavior Genetics, 41,* 201–210.

Buunk, B., Angleitner, A., Oubaid, V., and Buss, D. M. (1996). Sexual and cultural differences in jealousy: Tests from the Netherlands, Germany, and the United States. *Psychological Science, 7,* 359–363.

Byrne, K. A., Silasi-Mansat, C. D., and Worthy, D. A. (2015). Who chokes under pressure? The Big Five personality traits and decision-making under pressure. *Personality and Individual Differences, 74,* 22–28.

Byrnes, J. P., Miller, D. C., and Schafer, W. D. (1999). Gender differences in risk taking: A meta-analysis. *Psychological Bulletin, 125,* 367–383.

Cafferty, T. P., Davis, K. E., Medway, F. J., O'Hearn, R. E., and Chappell, K. D. (1994). Reunion dynamics among couples separated during Operation Desert Storm: An attachment theory analysis. In K. Bartholomew and D. Perlman (Eds.), *Attachment processes in adulthood* (pp. 309–330). Philadelphia, PA: Jessica Kingsley.

Cai, H., Kwan, V. S., and Sedikides, C. (2012). A sociocultural approach to narcissism: The case of modern China.

European Journal of Personality, 26(5), 529–535.

Cain, S. (2013). *Quiet: The power of introverts in a world that can't stop talking.* Broadway Books.

Campbell, A., Coombes, C., David, R., Opre, A., Grayson, L., and Muncer, S. (2016). Sex differences are not attenuated by a sex-invariant measure of fear: The situated fear questionnaire. *Personality and Individual Differences, 97,* 210–219.

Campbell, J. B. (1983). Differential relationships of extraversion, impulsivity, and sociability to study habits. *Journal of Research in Personality, 17,* 308–314.

Campbell, J. B., and Hawley, C. W. (1982). Study habits and Eysenck's theory of extraversion–introversion. *Journal of Research in Personality, 16,* 139–146.

Campbell, W. K., and Foster, C. A. (2002). Narcissism and commitment in romantic relationships: An investment model analysis. *Personality and Social Psychology Bulletin, 28*(4), 484–495.

Campbell, W. K., Rudich, E. A., and Sedikides, C. (2002). Narcissism, self-esteem, and the positivity of self-views: Two portraits of self-love. *Personality and Social Psychology Bulletin, 28*(3) 358–368.

Canache, D., Hayes, M., Mondak, J. J., and Wals, S. C. (2013). Openness, extraversion and the intention to emigrate. *Journal of Research in Personality, 47*(4), 351–355.

Canli, T. (2008). Toward a neurogenetic theory of neuroticism. In D. W. Pfaff and B. L. Kieffer (Eds.), *Molecular and Biophysical Mechanisms of Arousal, Alertness, and Attention* (pp. 153–174). Malden: Blackwell.

Cann, A., Mangum, J. L., and Wells, M. (2001). Distress in response to relationship infidelity: The roles of gender and attitudes about relationships. *Journal of Sex Research, 38,* 185–190.

Cantor, N. (1990). From thought to behavior: "Having" and "doing" in the study of personality and cognition. *American Psychologist, 45,* 735–750.

Caplan, S. E. (2002). Problematic Internet use and psychosocial well-being: Development of a theory-based, cognitive-behavioral measurement instrument. *Computers in Human Behavior, 18,* 553–575.

Caprara, G. V., Alessandri, G., De Giunta, L., Panerai, L., and Eisenberg, N. (2010). The contribution of agreeableness and self-efficacy beliefs to prosociality. *European Journal of Personality, 24,* 36–55.

Caprara, G. V., and Perugini, M. (1994). Personality described by adjectives: Generalizability of the Big Five to the Italian lexical context. *European Journal of Psychology, 8,* 357–369.

Caprara, G. V., Barbaranelli, C., Consiglio, C., Picconi, L., and Zimbardo, P. G. (2003). Personalities of politicians and voters: Unique and synergistic relationships. *Journal of Personality and Social Psychology, 84*(4), 849–856.

Caputi, P. (2012). An introduction to grid-based methods. In P. Caputi, L. L. Viney, B. M. Walker, and N. Crittenden (Eds.), *Personal construct methodology* (pp. 149–158). Hoboken, NJ: John Wiley & Sons.

Cardemil, E. V., Reivich, K. J., and Seligman, M. E. P. (2002). The prevention of depressive symptoms in low-income minority middle school students. *Prevention and Treatment, 5,* np.

Carli, V., and Durkee, T. (2016). Pathological use of the Internet. In D. Mucic, D. M. Hilty, D. Mucic, and D. M. Hilty (Eds.), *e-Mental Health* (pp. 269–288). Cham, Switzerland: Springer International Publishing.

Carlo, G., Okun, M. A., Knight, G. P., and de Guzman, M. R. T. (2005). The interplay of traits and motives on volunteering: Agreeableness, extraversion and prosocial value motivation. *Personality and Individual Differences, 38,* 1293–1305.

Carpenter, C. J. (2012). Narcissism on Facebook: Self-promotional and anti-social behavior. *Personality and Individual Differences, 52,* 482–486.

Carrasco, M., Barker, E. D., Trembley, R. E., and Vitaro, J. (2006). Eysenck's personality dimensions as predictors of male adolescent trajectories of physical aggression, theft, and vandalism. *Personality and Individual Differences, 41,* 1309–1320.

Carron, A. V., Shapcott, K. M., and Martin, L. J. (2014). The relationship between team explanatory style and team success. *International Journal of Sport And Exercise Psychology, 12*(1), 1–9.

Carstensen, L. L., Turan, B., Scheibe, S., Ram, N., Ersner-Hershfield, H., Samanez-Larkin, G. R., . . . Nesselroade, J. R. (2011). Emotional experience improves with age: Evidence based on over 10 years of experience sampling. *Psychology and Aging, 26,* 21–33.

Carter, E. C., Kofler, L. M., Forster, D. E., and McCullough, M. E. (2015). A series of meta-analytic tests of the depletion effect: Self-control does not seem to rely on a limited resource. *Journal of Experimental Psychology: General, 144,* 796–815.

Carter, R. (1999). *Mapping the mind.* Berkeley: University of California Press.

Carver, C. S., and Scheier, M. F. (2000). Autonomy and self regulation. *Psychological Inquiry, 11,* 284–291.

Carver, C. S., and White, T. L. (1994). Behavioral inhibition, behavioral activation, and affective responses to impeding reward and punishments: The BIS/BAS scales. *Journal of Personality and Social Psychology, 67,* 319–333.

Carver, C. S., Sutton, S. K., and Scheier, M. F. (1999). Action, emotion, and personality: Emerging conceptual integration. *Personality and Social Psychology Bulletin, 26,* 741–751.

Cashden, E. (1980). Egalitarianism among hunters and gatherers. *American Anthropologist, 82,* 116–120.

Caspi, A., and Herbener, E. S. (1990). Continuity and change: Assortative mating and the consistency of personality in adulthood. *Journal of Personality and Social Psychology, 58,* 250–258.

Caspi, A., Elder, G. H., Jr., and Bem, D. J. (1987). Moving against the world: Life-course patterns of explosive children. *Developmental Psychology, 23,* 308–313.

Caspi, A., Harrington, H., Milne, B., Amell, J. W., Theodore, R. F., and Moffitt, T. E. (2003). Children's behavioral styles at age 3 are linked to their adult personality traits at age 26. *Journal of Personality, 71,* 495–513.

Caspi, A., Roberts, B. W., and Shiner, R. L. (2005). Personality development: Stability and change. *Annual Review of Psychology, 56,* 453–458.

Caspi, A., Sugden, K., Moffitt, T., Taylor, A., Craig, I. W., Harringon, H., et al. (2003). Influence of life stress on depression: Moderation by a polymorphism in the 5-HTT gene. *Science, 301,* 386–389.

Cassidy, J., and Shaver, P. (1999). *Handbook of attachment: Theory, research, and clinical applications.* New York: Guilford Press.

Castille, C. M., Kuyumcu, D., and Bennett, R. J. (2017). Prevailing to the peers' detriment: Organizational constraints motivate Machiavellians to undermine their peers. *Personality and Individual Differences, 104,* 29–36.

Cattell, R. B. (1943). The description of personality: Basic traits resolved into clusters. *Journal of Abnormal and Social Psychology, 38,* 476–507.

Cattell, R. B. (1973). *Personality and mood by questionnaire.* San Francisco: Jossey-Bass.

Cattell, R. B., Eber, H. W., and Tatsouoka, M. M. (1970). *Handbook for the 16 PF.* Champaign, IL: Institute for Personality and Ability Testing.

Chagnon, N. (1983). *Yanomamö: The fierce people* (3rd Ed.). New York: Holt, Rinehart and Winston.

Chagnon, N. (1988). Life histories, blood revenge, and warfare in a tribal population. *Science, 239,* 985–992.

Chamorro-Premuzic, T., and Furnham, A. (2003a). Personality predicts academic performance: Evidence from two longitudinal university samples. *Journal of Research in Personality, 37,* 319–338.

Chamorro-Premuzic, T., and Furnham, A. (2003b). Personality traits and academic examination performance. *European Journal of Personality, 17,* 237–250.

Chan, W., McCrae, R. R., De Fruyt, F., Jussim, L., Löckenhoff, C. E., De Bolle, M., . . . and Nakazato, K. (2012). Stereotypes of age differences in personality traits: Universal and accurate? *Journal of Personality and Social Psychology, 103,* 1050–1066.

Chang, E. C., and Chang, O. D. (2016). Development of the Frequency of Suicidal Ideation Inventory: Evidence for the validity and reliability of a brief measure of suicidal ideation frequency in a college student population. *Cognitive Therapy and Research, 40*(4), 549–556.

Chapman, B. P., and Goldberg, L. R. (2011). Replicability and 40-year predictive power of childhood ARC types. *Journal of Personality and Social Psychology, 101,* 593–606.

Chapman, B. P., and Goldberg, L. R. (2017). Act-frequency signatures of the Big Five. *Personality and Individual Differences, 116,* 201–205.

Chapman, B. P., Dubestein, P. R., Sorensen, S., and Lyness, J. M. (2007). Gender differences in five factor model of personality traits in an elderly cohort. *Personality and Individual Differences, 43,* 1594–1603.

Charles, S. T., Reynolds, C. A. and Gatz, M. (2001). Age-related differences and change in positive and negative affect over 23 years. *Journal of Personality and Social Psychology, 80*(1), 136–151.

Chavira, D. A., Stein, M. B., and Malcarne, V. L. (2002). Scrutinizing the relationship between shyness and social phobia. *Journal of Anxiety Disorders, 16,* 585–598.

Cheek, J. M. (1983). *The revised Cheek and Buss Shyness Scale.* Unpublished manuscript, Department of Psychology, Wellesley College, Wellesley, MA.

Cheek, J. M. (1989). *Conquering Shyness.* New York: Dell.

Cheek, J. M., and Buss, A. H. (1981). Shyness and sociability. *Journal of Personality and Social Psychology, 41,* 330–339.

Cheek, J. M., and Krasnoperova, E. N. (1999). Varieties of shyness in adolescence and adulthood. In L. A. Schmidt and J. Schulkin (Eds.), *Extreme Fear, Shyness, and Social Phobia: Origins, Biological Mechanisms, and Clinical Outcomes* (pp. 224–250). London: Oxford University Press.

Cheek, J. M., and Melchior, L. A. (1990). Shyness, self-esteem, and self-consciousness. In H. Leitenberg (Ed.), *Handbook of Social and Evaluation Anxiety* (pp. 47–82) New York: Plenum Press.

Chegeni, R., Pirkalani, R. K., and Dehshiri, G. (2018). On love and darkness: The Dark Triad and mate retention behaviors in a non-Western culture. *Personality and Individual Differences, 122,* 43–46.

Cheit, R. (2014). *The Witch-Hunt Narrative: Politics, Psychology, and the Sexual Abuse of Children.* New York: Oxford University Press.

Cheit, R. E., Shavit, Y., and Reisse-Davis, Z. (2010). Magazine coverage of child sexual abuse, 1992–2004. *Journal of Child Sexual Abuse: Research, Treatment, & Program Innovations for Victims, Survivors, and Offenders, 19,* 99–117.

Chen, C., Burton, M., Greenberger, E., and Dmitrieva, J. (1999). Population migration and the variation of dopamine D4 receptor (DRD4) allele frequencies around the globe. *Evolution and Human Behavior, 20,* 309–324.

Chen, F. F., and West, S. G. (2008). Measuring individualism and collectivism: The importance of considering differential components, reference groups, and measurement invariance. *Journal of Research in Personality, 42,* 259–294.

Chen, F. S., and Johnson, S. C. (2012). An oxytocin receptor gene variant predicts attachment anxiety in females and autism-spectrum traits in males. *Social Psychological and Personality Science, 3,* 93–99.

Chen, S., Su, X., and Wu, S. (2012). Need for achievement, education, and entrepreneurial risk-taking behavior. *Social Behavior and Personality, 40,* 1311–1318.

Cheng, H., and Furnham, A. (2003). Personality, self-esteem, and demographic predictions of happiness and depression. *Personality and Individual Differences, 34,* 921–942.

Chida, Y., and Steptoe, A. (2009). The association of anger and hostility with future coronary heart disease: A meta-analytic review of prospective evidence. *Journal of the American College of Cardiology, 53,* 774–778.

Chioqueta, A. P., and Stiles, T. C. (2005). Personality traits and the development of depression, hopelessness, and suicidal ideation. *Personality and Individual Differences, 38,* 1283–1291.

Chodorow, N. J. (1989). *Feminism and psychoanalytic theory.* New Haven, CT: Yale University Press.

Choi, J. K., and Ji, Y. G. (2015). Investigating the importance of trust on adopting an autonomous vehicle. *International Journal of Human–Computer Interaction, 31*(10), 692–702.

Christie, R., and Geis, F. L. (1970). *Studies in Machiavellianism* (pp. 53–76). New York: Academic Press.

Chu, J. A. (1998). *Rebuilding shattered lives: The responsible treatment of complex post-traumatic and dissociative disorders.* New York: Wiley.

Chua, K. J., Lukaszewski, A. W., Grant, D. M., and Sng, O. (2016). Human life history strategies: Calibrated to external or internal cues? *Evolutionary Psychology, 15*(1), 1474704916677342.

Church, A. T. (2000). Culture and personality: Toward an integrated cultural trait psychology. *Journal of Personality, 68,* 651–703.

Church, A. T. (2009). Prospects for an integrated trait and cultural psychology. *European Journal of Personality, 23,* 153–182.

Church, A. T., Katigbak, M. S., Mazuera Arias, R., Rincon, B. C., Vargas-Flores, J. D. J., Ibáñez-Reyes, J., . . . Ortiz, F. A. (2014). A four-culture study of self-enhancement and adjustment using the social relations model: Do alternative conceptualizations and indices make a difference? *Journal of Personality and Social Psychology, 106,* 997–1014.

Church, A. T., Katigbak, M. S., Miramontes, L. G., del Prado, A. M., and Cabrera, H. F. (2007). Culture and the behavioural manifestations of traits: An application of the act frequency approach. *European Journal of Personality, 21,* 389–417.

Clapper, R. L. (1990). Adult and adolescent arousal preferences: The revised reducer augmenter scale. *Personality and Individual Differences, 11,* 1115–1122.

Clapper, R. L. (1992). The reducer-augmenter scale, the revised reducer augmenter scale, and predicting late adolescent substance use. *Personality and Individual Differences, 13,* 813–820.

Claridge, G. S., Donald, J., and Birchall, P. M. (1981). Drug tolerance and personality: Some implications for Eysenck's theory. *Personality and Individual Differences, 2,* 153–166.

Clark, R. D. (1990). The impact of AIDS on gender differences in willingness to engage in casual sex. *Journal of Applied Social Psychology, 20,* 771–782.

Clark, R. D., and Hatfield, E. (1989). Gender differences in receptivity to sexual offers. *Journal of Psychology and Human Sexuality, 2,* 39–55.

Claxton, A., O'Rourke, N., Smith, J. Z., and DeLongis, A. (2011). Personality traits and marital satisfaction within enduring relationships: An intra-couple discrepancy approach. *Journal of Social and Personal Relationships, 29,* 375–396.

Cleckley, H. (1941). *The mask of sanity: An attempt to reinterpret the so-called psychopathic personality.* Oxford, England: Mosby.

Cleckley, H. (1988). *The mask of sanity.* Augusta, GA: Emily S. Cleckley.

Cleveland, H. H., Udry, J. R., and Chantala, K. (2001). Environmental and genetic influences on sex-types behaviors and attitudes of male and female adolescents. *Personality and Social Psychology Bulletin, 27*(12), 1587–1598.

Clewley, N., Chen, S. Y., and Liu, X. (2011). Mining learning preferences in Web-based instruction: Holists vs. serialists. *Journal of Educational Technology and Society, 14,* 266–277.

Cloninger, C. R. (1986). A unified biosocial theory of personality and its role in the development of anxiety states. *Psychiatric Developments, 3,* 167–226.

Cloninger, C. R. (1987). A systematic method for clinical description and classification of personality variants: A proposal. *Archives of General Psychiatry, 44,* 573–588.

Cloninger, C. R. (1999). *Personality and psychopathology.* Washington, DC: American Psychiatric Press.

Cloninger, C. R., Svrakic, D. M., and Przybeck, T. R. (1993). A psychobiological model of temperament and character. *Archives of General Psychiatry, 50,* 975–990.

Clower, C. E., and Bothwell, R. K. (2001). An exploratory study of the relationship between the Big Five and inmate recidivism. *Journal of Research in Personality, 35,* 231–237.

Coan, J. A., and Allen, J. B. (2004). Frontal EEG asymmetry as a moderator and mediator of emotion. *Biological Psychology, 67*(1–2), 7–49.

Coan, J. A., and Gottman, J. M. (2007). Sampling, experimental control, and generalizability in the study of marital process models, *Journal of Marriage and Family, 69,* 73–80.

Cohen, J. (1977). *Statistical power analysis for the behavioral sciences.* San Diego, CA: Academic Press.

Cohen, J., and Cohen, P. (1975). *Applied Multiple Regression/Correlation Analysis for the Behavioral Sciences.* Hillsdale, NJ: Erlbaum.

Cohen, S., Doyle, W. J., Turner, R. B., Alper, C. M., and, Skoner, D. P. (2003). Emotional style and susceptibility to the common cold. *Psychosomatic Medicine, 65,* 652–657.

Cohen, S., and Pressman, S. D. (2006). Positive Affect and Health. *Current Directions in Psychological Science, 15*(3), 122–125.

Cohen, S., Doyle, W. J., Skoner, D. P., Fireman, P., Gwaltney, J. M., Jr., and Newsom, J. T. (1995). State and trait negative affect as predictors of objective and subjective symptoms of respiratory viral infections. *Journal of Personality and Social Psychology, 68,* 159–169.

Cohen, S., Gianaros, P., and Manuck, S. B. (2016). A stage model of stress and disease. *Perspectives in Psychological Science, 11,* 456–463.

Cohen, S., Janicki-Deverts, D., Doyle, W. J., Miller, G. E., Frank, E., Rabin, B. S., and Turner, R. B. (2012). Chronic stress, glucocorticoid receptor resistance, inflammation, and disease risk. *PNAS,* doi/10.1073/pnas.1118355109.

Cohen, S., Tyrrell, D. A. J., and Smith, A. P. (1997). Psychological stress in humans and susceptibility to the common cold. In T. W. Moller (Ed.), *Clinical disorders and stressful life events* (pp. 217–235). Madison, CT: International Universities Press.

Cohen-Bendahan, C. C., van de Beek, C., and Berenbaum, S. A. (2005). Prenatal sex hormone effects on child and adult sex-typed behavior: Methods and findings. *Neuroscience & Biobehavioral Reviews, 29*(2), 353–384.

Coleman, R. (1992). *Lennon: The definitive biography.* New York: Perennial.

College Board Online. (2009). *SAT validity studies.* Retrieved from http://professionals.collegeboard.com/data-reports-research/sat/validity-studies.

Collins, J. N. (1994). Some fundamental questions about scientific thinking. *Research in Science and Technological Education, 12,* 161–173.

Confer, J. C., Easton, J. E., Fleischman, D. S., Goetz, C., Lewis, D. M., Perilloux, C., and Buss, D. M. (2010). Evolutionary psychology: Controversies, questions, prospects, and limitations. *American Psychologist, 65,* 110–126.

Conley, J. J. (1984a). The hierarchy of consistency: A review and model of longitudinal findings on adult individual differences in intelligence, personality, and self-opinion. *Personality and Individual Differences, 5,* 11–25.

Conley, J. J. (1984b). Longitudinal consistency of adult personality: Self-reported psychological characteristics across 45 years. *Journal of Personality and Social Psychology, 47,* 1325–1333.

Conley, J. J. (1985). Longitudinal stability of personality traits: A multitrait-multimethod–multioccasion analysis. *Journal of Personality and Social Psychology, 49,* 1266–1282.

Conley, J. J., and Angelides, M. (1984). *Personality antecedents of emotional disorders and alcohol abuse in men: Results of a forty-five-year prospective study.* Unpublished manuscript: Wesleyan University, Middletown, CT.

Connelly, B. S., and Ones, D. S. (2010). Another perspective on personality: Meta-analytic integration of observers' accuracy and predicative validity. *Psychological Bulletin, 136,* 1092–1122.

Connolly, I., and O'Moore, M. (2003). Personality and family relations of children who bully. *Personality and Individual Differences, 35,* 559–567.

Conrad, M. A. (2006). Aptitude is not enough: How personality and behavior predict academic performances. *Journal of Research in Personality, 40,* 339-346.

Conroy-Beam, D., Buss, D. M., Pham, M. N., and Shackelford, T. K. (2015). How sexually dimorphic are human mate preferences? *Personality and Social Psychology Bulletin, 41,* 1082-1093.

Conroy-Beam, D., Goetz, C. D., and Buss, D. M. (2016). What predicts romantic relationship satisfaction and mate retention intensity: Mate preference fulfillment or mate value discrepancies? *Evolution and Human Behavior, 37,* 440-448.

Cook, C. L., Krems, J. A., and Kenrick, D. T. (2021). Fundamental motives illuminate a broad range of individual and cultural variations in thought and behavior. *Current Directions in Psychological Science, 30,* 242-250.

Cooper, M. L., Wood, P. K., Orcutt, H. K., and Albino, A. (2003). Personality and the predisposition to engage in risky or problem behaviors during adolescence. *Journal of Personality and Social Psychology, 84*(2), 390-410.

Cooper, S. H. (1998). Changing notions of defense within psychoanalytic theory. *Journal of Personality, 66,* 947-965.

Corcoran, D. W. J. (1964). The relation between introversion and salivation. *American Journal of Psychology, 77,* 298-300.

Corr, P. J., and Matthews, G. (Eds.). (2020). *The Cambridge handbook of personality psychology.* Cambridge University Press.

Cosmides, L., and Tooby, J. (1992). Cognitive adaptations for social exchange. In J. Barkow, L. Cosmides, and J. Tooby (Eds.), *The adapted mind* (pp. 163-228). New York: Academic Press.

Costa, A. R. L., Jesuíno, A. D. S. A., de Souza Lima, N. R., and Shu, F. (2019). Adaptation and validation of HEXACO-PI-R to a Brazilian sample adaptation of HEXACO-PI-R to Brazilian sample. *Personality and Individual Differences, 147,* 280-284.

Costa, P. T., and McCrae, R. R. (1980). Influence of extraversion and neuroticism on subjective well-being: Happy and unhappy people. *Journal of Personality and Social Psychology, 38,* 668-678.

Costa, P. T., and McCrae, R. R. (1985). Hypochondriasis, neuroticism, and aging: When are somatic complaints unfounded? *American Psychologist, 40,* 19-28.

Costa, P. T., and Widiger, T. A. (Eds.). (1994). *Personality disorders and the five-factor model of personality.* Washington, DC: American Psychological Association.

Costa, P. T., Jr., and McCrae, R. R. (1988). Personality in adulthood: A six-year longitudinal study of self-reports and spouse ratings on the NEO Personality Inventory. *Journal of Personality and Social Psychology, 54,* 853-863.

Costa, P. T., Jr., and McCrae, R. R. (1992). Trait psychology comes of age. In T. B. Sonderegger (Ed.), *Nebraska symposium on motivation: Psychology and aging* (pp. 169-204). Lincoln: University of Nebraska Press.

Costa, P. T., Jr., and McCrae, R. R. (1994). Set like plaster? Evidence for the stability of adult personality. In T. F. Heatherton and J. L. Weinberger (Eds.), *Can personality change?* Washington, DC: American Psychological Association.

Costa, P. T., Jr., and McCrae, R. R. (1995). Solid ground in the wetlands of personality: A reply to Block. *Psychological Bulletin, 117,* 216-220.

Costa, P. T., Jr., and McCrae, R. R. (1995). Solid ground in the wetlands of personality: A reply to Block. *Psychological Bulletin, 117,* 216-220.

Costa, P. T., Jr., and McCrae, R. R. (2005). The NEO-PI-3: A more readable revised NEO personality inventory. *Journal of Personality, 84,* 261-270.

Costa, P. T., McCrae, R. R., and Zonderman, A. B. (1987). Environmental and dispositional influences on well-being: Longitudinal follow-up of an American national sample. *British Journal of Psychology, 78,* 299-306.

Coutts, L. M. (1990). Police hiring and promotion: Methods and outcomes. *Canadian Police College Journal, 14,* 98-122.

Cowen, A. S., and Keltner, D. (2020). Universal facial expressions uncovered in art of the ancient Americas: A computational approach. *Science Advances, 6*(34), eabb1005.

Cox, K., and McAdams, D. P. (2012). The transforming self: Service narratives and identity change in emerging adulthood. *Journal of Adolescent Research, 27,* 18-43.

Cox, S. R., Ritchie, S. J., Fawns-Ritchie, C., Tucker-Drob, E. M.; Deary, I. J. (2019). Structural brain imaging correlates of general intelligence in UK Biobank. *Intelligence, 76,* ArtID: 101376.

Craik, K. H. (1986). Personality research methods: An historical perspective. *Journal of Personality, 54,* 18-51.

Craik, K. H. (2008). *Reputation: A network analysis.* New York: Oxford University Press.

Cramer, P. (1991). *The development of defense mechanisms: Theory, research, and assessment.* New York: Springer-Verlag.

Cramer, P. (2000). Defense mechanisms in psychology today: Further processes for adaptation. *American Psychologist, 55,* 637-646.

Cramer, P. (2002). Defense mechanisms, behavior, and affect in young adulthood. *Journal of Personality, 70,* 103-126.

Cramer, P. (2012). Psychological maturity and change in adult defense mechanisms. *Journal of Research in Personality, 46,* 306-316.

Cramer, P. (2015). Defense mechanisms: 40 years of empirical research. *Journal of Personality Assessment, 97,* 114-122.

Cramer, P. (2017). Using the TAT to assess the relations between gender identity and the use of defense mechanisms. *Journal of Personality Assessment, 99,* 265-274

Cramer, P. (2018). Change in children's self confidence and the use of defense mechanisms. *Journal of Nervous and Mental Disease, 206,* 593-597.

Cramer, P., and Davidson, K. (1998). Defense mechanisms in contemporary personality research. *Special Issue of the Journal of Personality, 66.*

Crandall, V., Dewey, R., Katkovsky, W., and Preston, A. (1964). Parents' attitudes and behaviors and grade-school children's academic achievements. *Journal of Genetic Psychology, 104,* 53-66.

Crawford, M. B. (2020). *Why we drive: Toward a philosophy of the open road.* New York: William Morrow.

Crede, M., Tynan, M. C., and Harms, P. D. (2016). Much ado about Grit: A meta-analytic synthesis of the Grit literature. *Journal of Personality and Social Psychology.*

Creswell, J. D., Bursley, J. K., and Satpute, A. B. (2013). Neural reactivation links unconscious thought to decision-making performance. *Social Cognitive and Affective Neuroscience, 8*(8), 863-869.

Crocker, J., and Major, B. (1989). Social stigma and self-esteem: The self-protective properties of stigma. *Psychological Review, 96,* 608-630.

Cronbach, L. J., and Gleser, G. C. (1965). *Psychological tests and personnel decisions.* Urbana: University of Illinois Press.

Cronbach, L. J., and Meehl, P. E. (1955). Construct validity in psychological tests. *Psychological Bulletin, 52,* 281-302.

Crosby, C., Durkee, P., Meston, C., and Buss, D. M. (in press). Six dimensions of sexual disgust. *Personality and Individual Differences.*

Cross, C. P., Copping, L. T., and Campbell, A. (2011). Sex differences in impulsivity: A meta-analysis. *Psychological Bulletin, 137,* 97-130.

Crowne, D. P., and Marlowe, D. (1964). *The approval motive: Studies in evaluation dependence.* New York: Wiley.

Cruce, S. E., Pashak, T. J., Handal, P. J., Munz, D. C., and Gfeller, J. D. (2012). Conscientious perfectionism, self-evaluative perfectionism, and the five-factor model of personality traits. *Personality and Individual Differences, 53,* 268-273.

Cruz, M., and Larsen, R. J. (1995). Personality correlates of individual differences in electrodermal lability. *Journal of Social Behavior and Personality, 23,* 93-104.

Csikszentmihalyi, M., Abuhamdeh, S., and Nakamura, J. (2005). Flow. In A. J. Elliot and C. S. Dweck (Eds.), *Handbook of competence and motivation* (pp. 598-608). New York: Guilford Press.

Curtis, V., and Biran, A. (2001). Dirt, disgust, and disease: Is hygiene in our genes? *Perspectives in Biology and Medicine, 44*(1), 17-31.

Curtis, V., Aunger, R., and Rabie, T. (2004). Evidence that disgust evolved to protect from risk of disease. *Proceedings of the Royal Society of London B: Biological Sciences, 271*(Suppl 4), S131-S133.

Cutler, S. S., Larsen, R. J., and Bunce, S. C. (1996). Repressive coping style and the experience and recall of emotion: A naturalistic study of daily affect. *Journal of Personality, 65,* 379-405.

da Rosa, G. D., Martin, P., Kim, J., Russell, D., Abraham, W. T., Gondo, Y., . . . Poon, L. W. (2021). A cultural comparison of personality profiles of US and Japanese centenarians. *The International Journal of Aging and Human Development, 93*(1), 562-583.

Dabbs, J. M., Jr., and Dabbs, M. G. (2000). *Heroes, rogues, and lovers: Testosterone and behavior.* New York: McGraw-Hill.

Dabbs, J. M., Jr., and Hargrove, M. F. (1997). Age, testosterone, and behavior among female prison inmates. *Psychosomatic Medicine, 59,* 477-480.

Dabbs, J. M., Jr., Hargrove, M. F., and Heusel, C. (1996). Testosterone differences among college fraternities: Well-behaved vs. rambunctious. *Personality and Individual Differences, 20,* 157-161.

Dahlke, J. A., Sackett, P. R., and Kuncel, N. R. (2019). Effects of range restriction and criterion contamination on differential validity of the SAT by race/ethnicity and sex. *Journal of Applied Psychology. 104,* 814-831.

Dai, H., Milkman, K. L., Hofmann, D. A., and Staats, B. R. (2015). The impact of time at work and time off from work on rule compliance: The case of hand hygiene in health care. *Journal of Applied Psychology, 100,* 846-862.

Dalgleish, T. (1995). Performance on the emotional Stroop task in groups of anxious, expert, and control subjects: A comparison of computer and card presentation formats. *Cognition and Emotion, 9,* 341-362.

Daly, M., and Wilson, M. (1988). *Homicide.* New York: Aldine de Gruyter.

Damasio, A. (2018). *Feelings and knowing: Making minds conscious.* New York: Pantheon Books.

Damasio, A. (2021). *The strange order of things: Life, feelings, and the making of culture.* New York: Pantheon Books.

Damasio, A. R. (1994). *Descartes' error: Emotion, reason, and the human brain.* New York: Putnam.

Dang, J. (2016). Commentary: A multi-lab preregistered replication of the ego-depletion effect. *Frontiers in Psychology, 7,* 1155.

Dang, J., Barker, P., Baumert, A., Bentvelzen, M., Berkman, E., Buchholz, N. et al. (2021). A multilab replication of the ego depletion effect. *Social Psychological and Personality Science, 12,* 14-24.

Danielsbacka, M., Tanskanen, A. O., and Billari, F. C. (2019). Who meets online? Personality traits and sociodemographic characteristics associated with online partnering in Germany. *Personality and Individual Differences, 143,* 139-144.

Danner, D. D., Snowdon, D. A., and Friesen, W. V. (2001). Positive emotions in early life and longevity: Findings from the nun study. *Journal of Personality and Social Psychology, 80,* 804-813.

Darwin, C. (1859). *The origin of species.* London: Murray.

Darwin, C. (1872/1965). *The expression of the emotions in man and animals.* Chicago: University of Chicago Press.

Davidson, K. W., Gidron, Y., Mostofsky, E., and Trudeau, K. J. (2007). Hospitalization cost offset of a hostility intervention for coronary heart disease patients. *Journal of Consulting and Clinical Psychology, 75,* 657-662.

Davidson, R. J. (1991). Cerebral asymmetry and affective disorders: A developmental approach. In D. Cicchetti and S. L. Toth (Eds.), *Internalizing and externalizing expressions of dysfunction: Rochester symposium and developmental psychopathology* (Vol. 2, pp. 123-154). Hillsdale, NJ: Erlbaum.

Davidson, R. J. (1993). The neuropsychology of emotion and affective style. In M. Lewis and J. M. Haviland (Eds.), *Handbook of emotions* (pp. 143-154). New York: Guilford Press.

Davidson, R. J., Ekman, P., Saron, C. D., Senulis, J. A., and Friesen, W. V. (1990). Approach/withdrawal and cerebral asymmetry: Emotional expression and brain physiology. I. *Journal of Personality and Social Psychology, 58,* 330-341.

Davidson, R. J., Kabat-Zinn, J., Schumacher, J., Rosenkranz, M., Muller, D., Santorelli, S. F., Urbanowski, F., Harrington, A., Bonus, K., and Sheridan, J. F. (2003). Alterations in brain and immune function produced by mindfulness meditation. *Psychosomatic Medicine, 65,* 564-570.

Davidson, R. J., Scherer, K. R., and Goldsmith, H. H. (2003). *Handbook of Affective Sciences.* New York: Oxford University Press.

Davis, A. C., Visser, B., Volk, A. A., Vaillancourt, T., and Arnocky, S. (2019). Life history strategy and the HEXACO model of personality: A facet level examination. *Personality and Individual Differences, 150,* 109471.

Davis, D., and Loftus, E. F. (2009). The scientific status of 'repressed' and 'recovered' memories of sexual abuse. In J. L. Skeem, K. S. Douglas, and S. O. Lilenfeld (Eds), *Psychological Science in the Courtroom: Consensus and Controversy,* pp. 55-79. New York, Guilford Press.

Davis, M. H., Luce, C., and Kraus, S. J. (1994). The heritability of characteristics associated with dispositional empathy. *Journal of Personality, 62,* 369-391.

Davis, M. H., Mitchell, K. V., Hall, J. A., Lothert, J., Snapp, T., and Meyer, M. (1999). Empathy, expectations, and situational preferences: Personality influences on the decision to participate in volunteer helping behaviors. *Journal of Personality, 67,* 469-503.

Davis, P. J. (1987). Repression and the inaccessibility of affective memories. *Journal of Personality and Social Psychology, 53,* 585-593.

Davis, P. J., and Schwartz, G. E. (1987). Repression and the inaccessibility of affective memories. *Journal of Personality and Social Psychology, 52,* 155-162.

De Bolle, M., De Fruyt, F., McCrae, R. R., Löckenhoff, C. E., Costa, Jr, P. T., Aguilar-Vafaie, M. E., . . . Avdeyeva, T. V. (2015). The emergence of sex differences in personality traits in early adolescence: A cross-sectional, cross-cultural study. *Journal of Personality and Social Psychology, 108,* 171-185.

De Pascalis, V. (2004). On the psychophysiology of extraversion. In R. M. Stelmack (Ed), *On the Psychobiology of Personality: Essays in Honor of Marvin Zuckerman.* pp. 295-327; New York: Elsevier.

De Raad, B. (1998). Five big, big five issues: Rationale, content, structure, status, and crosscultural assessment. *European Psychologist, 3,* 113-124.

De Raad, B., and Barelds, D. P. H. (2008). A new taxonomy of Dutch personality traits based on a comprehensive and unrestricted list of descriptors. *Journal of Personality and Social Psychology, 94,* 347-364.

De Raad, B., Barelds, D. P. H., Levert, E., Ostendof, F., Mlacic, B., De Blas, L., Hrebickova, M., et al. (2010). Only three factors of personality description are fully replicable across languages: A comparison of 14 trait taxonomies. *Journal of*

Personality and Social Psychology, 98, 1060-1173.

De Raad, B., Perugini, M., Hrebickova, M., and Szarota, P. (1998). Lingua Franca of personality: Taxonomies and structures based on the psycholexical approach. *Journal of Cross-Cultural Psychology, 29,* 212-232.

De Vries, J., and Van Heck, G. L. (2002). Fatigue: relationships with basic personality and temperament dimensions. Personality and Individual Differences, 33(8), 1311-1324.

de Vries, R. E., Pronk, J., Olthof, T., and Goossens, F. A. (2020). Getting along and/or getting ahead: Differential HEXACO personality correlates of likeability and popularity among adolescents. *European Journal of Personality, 34*(2), 245-261.

de Vries, R. E., Wesseldijk, L. W., Karinen, A. K., Jern, P., and Tybur, J. M. (2021). Relations between HEXACO personality and ideology variables are mostly genetic in nature. *European Journal of Personality,* 08902070211014035.

Deaner, R. O., Goetz, S. M. M., Shattuck, K., and Schnotala, T. (2012). Body weight, not facial width-to-height ratio, predicts aggression in pro hockey players. *Journal of Research in Personality, 46,* 235-238.

DeAngelis, T. (1991). Honesty tests weigh in with improved ratings. *APA Monitor, 22,* 6.

Deaux, K. (1984). From individual differences to social categories: Analysis of a decade's research on gender. *American Psychologist, 39,* 105-116.

Deaux, K., and Lewis, L. L. (1984). Structure of gender stereotypes: Interrelationships among components and gender label. *Journal of Personality and Social Psychology, 46,* 991-1004.

Decuyper, M., De Bolle, M., and De Fruyt, F. (2012). Personality similarity, perceptual accuracy, and relationship satisfaction in dating and married couples. *Personal Relationships, 19,* 128-145.

Deiner, C. I., and Dweck, C. S. (1978). An analysis of learned helplessness: Continuous changes in performance, strategy, and achievement cognitions following failure. *Journal of Personality and Social Psychology, 36,* 451-462.

Deiner, C. I., and Dweck, C. S. (1980). An analysis of learned helplessness (II): The processing of success. *Journal of Personality and Social Psychology, 39,* 940-952.

Dekkers, T. J., Rapport, M. D., Calub, C. A., Eckrich, S. J., and Irurita, C. (2021). ADHD and hyperactivity: The influence of cognitive processing demands on gross motor activity level in children. *Child Neuropsychology, 27*(1), 63-82.

Del Giudice, M. (2019). Measuring sex differences and similarities. *Gender and sexuality development: Contemporary theory and research.* New York: Springer.

Del Giudice, M., and Belsky, J. (2011). The development of life history strategies: Toward a multi-stage theory. In D. M. Buss and P. Hawley (Eds.), *The evolution of personality and individual differences.* New York: Oxford University Press.

del Prado, A. M., Church, A. T., Katigbak, M. S., Miramontes, L. G., Whitty, M. T., Curtis, G. J., et al. (2007). Culture, method, and the content of self-concepts: Testing trait, individual-self primacy, and cultural psychology perspectives. *Journal of Research in Personality, 41,* 1119-1160.

Delatorre, M. Z., Wagner, A., and Bedin, L. M. (2021). Dyadic relationships between personality, social support, conflict resolution, and marital quality. *Personal Relationships.*

Delongis, A., Folkman, S., and Lazarus, R. S. (1988). The impact of daily stress on health and mood: Psychological and social resources as mediators. *Journal of Personality and Social Psychology, 54,* 986-995.

Dembrowski, T. M., and Costa, P. T. (1987). Coronary-prone behavior: Components of the Type A pattern and hostility. *Journal of Personality, 55,* 211-235.

Demerath, P. (2001). The social cost of acting "extra": Students' moral judgments of self, social relations, and academic success in Papua New Guinea. *American Journal of Education, 108,* 3.

DeMeuse, K. (1985). The relationship between life events and indices of classroom performance. *Teaching of Psychology, 12,* 146-149.

Denissen, J. J. (2014). A roadmap for further progress in research on personality development. *European Journal of Personality, 28,* 213-215.

Denissen, J. J. A., and Penke, L. (2008a). Motivational individual reaction norms underlying the five-factor model of personality: First steps toward a theory-based conceptual framework. *Journal of Research in Personality, 42,* 1285-1302.

Denissen, J. J. A., and Penke, L. (2008b). Neuroticism predicts reactions to cues of social exclusion. *European Journal of Personality, 22,* 497-517.

Denissen, J. J. A., Luhmann, M., Chung, J. M., and Bleidorn, W. (2019). Transactions between life events and personality traits across the adult lifespan. *Journal of Personality and Social Psychology, 116,* 612-633.

Denissen, J., Penke, L., Schmitt, D. P., and van Aken, M. (2008). Self-esteem reactions to social interactions: Evidence for

sociometer mechanisms across days, people, and nations. *Journal of Personality and Social Psychology, 95,* 181-196.

Denson, T. F., Pedersen, W. C., Ronquillo, J., and Nandy, A. S. (2009). The angry brain: Neural correlates of anger, angry rumination, and aggressive personality. *Journal of Cognitive Neuroscience, 21,* 734-744.

DePaulo, B. (2006). *Singled out: How singles are stereotyped, stigmatized, and ignored, and still live happily ever after.* New York: St. Martin's Press.

DePaulo, B. M., Dull, W. R., Greenberg, J. M., and Swaim, G. (1989). Are shy people reluctant to ask for help? *Journal of Personality and Social Psychology, 56,* 834-844.

DePaulo, B. M., Kenny, D. A., Hoover, C. W., Webb, W., and Oliver, P. V. (1987). Accuracy of person perception: Do people know what kinds of impressions they convey? *Journal of Personality and Social Psychology, 52*(2), 303-315.

DePrince, A. P., Brown, L. S., Cheit, R. E., Freyd, J. J., Gold, S. N., Pezdek, K., and Quina, K. (2012). Motivated forgetting and misremember: Perspectives from betrayal trauma theory. In R. F. Belli (Ed.), *True and false recovered memories: Toward a reconciliation of the debate* (pp. 193-242). New York: Springer.

Depue, R. A. (2006). Interpersonal behavior and the structure of personality: Neurobehavioral foundations of agentic extraversion and affiliation. In T. Canli (Ed.), *Biology of personality and individual differences* (pp. 60-92). New York: Guilford Press.

Depue, R. A., and Collins, P. F. (1999). Neurobiology of the structure of personality: Dopamine, facilitation of incentive motivation, and extraversion. *Behavioral and Brain Sciences, 22,* 491-517.

Derakshan, N., Eysenck, M. W., and Myers, L. B. (2007). Emotional information processing in repressors: The vigilance-avoidance theory. *Cognition and Emotion, 21*(8), 1585-1614.

DeSteno, D. A., and Salovey, P. (1996). Evolutionary origins of sex differences in jealousy: Questioning the "fitness" of the model. *Psychological Science, 7,* 367-372.

Detrick, P., and Chibnall, J. T. (2013). Revised NEO Personality Inventory normative data for police officer selection. *Psychological Services, 10,* 372-377.

Devereux, P. G.. Miller, M. K.. and Kirshenbaum, J. M. (2021). Moral disengagement, locus of control, and belief in a just world: Individual differences relate to adherence to COVID-19 guidelines. Personality and Individual Differences, 182, Nov, 2021. ArtID: 111069.

DeWall, C. N., Baumeister, R. F., Stillman, T. F., and Gailliot, M. T. (2007). Violence restrained: Effects of self-regulatory capacity and its depletion on aggressive behavior. *Journal of Experimental Social Psychology, 33,* 1547–1558.

DeWall, C. N., Buffardi, L. E., Bosner, I., and Campbell, W. K. (2011). Narcissism and implicit attention seeking: Evidence from linguistic analyses of social networking and online presentation. *Personality and Individual Differences, 51,* 57–62.

DeYoung, C. G. (2010). Personality neuroscience and the biology of traits. *Social and Personality Psychology Compass, 4,* 1165–1180.

DeYoung, C. G. (2013). The neuromodulator of exploration: A unifying theory of the role of dopamine in personality. *Frontiers in Human Neuroscience, 7,* 762.

DeYoung, C. G. (2015b). Cybernetic big five theory. *Journal of Research in Personality, 56,* 33–58.

DeYoung, C. G., Cooper, M. L., and Larsen, R. J. (2014). APA handbook of personality and social psychology: Personality processes and individual differences. Washington, D.C: American Psychological Association Press.

DeYoung, C. G., Grazioplene, R. G., and Allen, T. A. (2021). The neurobiology of personality. In O.P. John and R. W. Robbins (Eds.), *Handbook of personality: Theory and research,* Fourth Edition. New York: Guilford Press.

DeYoung, C. G., Grazioplene, R. G., and Peterson, J. B. (2012). From madness to genius: The openness/intellect trait domain as a paradoxical simplex. *Journal of Research in Personality, 46,* 63–78.

DeYoung, C. G., Hirsh, J. B., Shane, M. S., Rajeevan, N., and Gray, J. R. (2010). Testing predictions from personality neuroscience: Brain structure and the big five. *Psychological Science, 21,* 820–828.

Di Blas, L. (2005). Personality-relevant attribute-nouns: A taxonomic study in the Italian language. *European Journal of Personality, 19,* 537–557.

Di Blas, L. (2007). A circumplex model of interpersonal attributes in middle childhood. *Journal of Personality, 75,* 863–897.

Diamond, J. (1999). *Guns, germs, and steel.* New York: Norton.

Diener, E. (2000). Subjective well-being: The science of happiness and a proposal for a national index. *American Psychologist, 55,* 34–43.

Diener, E., and Biswas-Diener, R. (2002). Will money increase subjective well-being? A literature review and guide to needed research. *Social Indicators Research, 57,* 119–169.

Diener, E., and Biswas-Diener, R. (2008). *Happiness: Unlocking the Mysteries of Psychological Wealth.* Malden, MA: Blackwell.

Diener, E., and Diener, M. (1995). Cross-cultural correlates of life satisfaction and self-esteem. *Journal of Personality and Social Psychology, 68,* 653–663.

Diener, E., and Larsen, R. J. (1984). Temporal stability and cross-situational consistency of affective, behavioral, and cognitive responses. *Journal of Personality and Social Psychology, 47,* 871–883.

Diener, E., and Seligman, M. E. P. (2002). Very happy people. *Psychological Science, 13,* 80–83.

Diener, E., and Tay, L. (2015). Subjective well-being and human welfare around the world as reflected in the Gallup World Poll. *International Journal of Psychology, 50,* 135–149.

Diener, E., Diener, M., and Diener, C. (1995). Factors predicting the subjective well-being of nations. *Journal of Personality and Social Psychology, 69,* 851–864.

Diener, E., Horowitz, J., and Emmons, R. A. (1985). Happiness of the very wealthy. *Social Indicators Research, 16,* 263–274.

Diener, E., Larsen, R. J., and Emmons, R. A. (1984). Person X situation interactions: Choice of situations and congruence response models. *Journal of Personality and Social Psychology, 47,* 580–592.

Diener, E., Larsen, R. J., Levine, S., and Emmons, R. A. (1985). Intensity and frequency: Dimensions underlying positive and negative affect. *Journal of Personality and Social Psychology, 48,* 1253–1265.

Diener, E., Lucas, R. E., and Larsen, R. J. (2003). Measuring positive emotions. In C. R. Snyder, and S. J. Lopez (Eds.), *The Handbook of Positive Psychological Assessment* (pp. 201–218). Washington, DC: American Psychological Association.

Diener, E., Ng, W., Harter, J., and Arora, R. (2010). Wealth and happiness across the world: Material prosperity predicts life evaluation, whereas psychosocial prosperity predicts positive feeling. *Journal of Personality and Social Psychology, 99,* 52–61.

Diener, E., Oishi, S., and Lucas, R. E. (2003). Personality, culture, and subjective well-being: Emotional and cognitive evaluations of life. *Annual Review of Psychology, 54,* 403–425.

Diener, E., Sandvik, E., Seidlitz, L., and Diener, M. (1993). The relationship between income and subjective well-being: Relative or absolute? *Social Indicators Research, 28,* 195–223.

Digman, J. M., and Inouye, J. (1986). Further specification of the five robust factors of personality. *Journal of Personality and Social Psychology, 50,* 116–123.

Dijksterhhuis, A., Bos, M. W., Nordgren, L. F., and van Baaren, R. B. (2006). On making the right choice: The deliberation-without-attention effect. *Science, 311,* 1005–1007.

Dijkstra, P., and Barelds, D. P. H. (2008). Self and partner personality and responses to relationship threat. *Journal of Research in Personality, 42,* 1500–1511.

Dijkstra, P., and Buunk, B. P. (2001). Sex differences in the jealousy-evoking nature of a rival's body build. *Evolution and Human Behavior, 22,* 335–341.

Dill, K. E., Anderson, C. A., Anderson, K. B., and Deuser, W. E. (1999). Effects of aggressive personality on social expectations and social perceptions. *Journal of Research in Personality, 31,* 272–292.

Dixon, W. A., Mauzey, E. D., and Hall, C. R. (2003). Physical activity and exercise: Implications for counselors. *Journal of Counseling and Development, 81,* 502–505.

Dodge, K. A., and Coie, J. D. (1987). Social-information-processing factors in reactive and proactive aggression in children's peer groups. *Journal of Personality and Social Psychology, 53,* 1146–1158.

Donhauser, P. W., Rösch, A. G., and Schultheiss, O. C. (2015). The implicit need for power predicts recognition speed for dynamic changes in facial expressions of emotion. *Motivation and Emotion, 39*(5), 714–721.

Donnellan, M. B., Kenny, D. A., Trzesniewski, K. H., Lucas, R. E., and Conger, R. D. (2012). Using trait-state models to evaluate the longitudinal consistency of global self-esteem from adolescence to adulthood. *Journal of Research in Personality, 46,* 634–645.

Donnellan, M. B., Larsen-Rife, D., and Conger, R. D. (2005). Personality, family history, and competence in early adult romantic relationships. *Journal of Personality and Social Psychology, 88,* 562–576.

Donnellan, M. B., Trzesniewski, K. H., and Robins, R. W. (2009). An emerging epidemic of narcissism or much ado about nothing? *Journal of Research in Personality, 43,* 498–501.

Donohew, L., Zimmerman, R., Cupp, P. S., Novak, S., Colon, S., and Abell, R. (2000). Sensation seeking, impulsive decision-making, and risky sex: Implications for risk-taking and design interventions. *Personality and Individual Differences, 28,* 1079–1091.

Dorros, S., Hanzal, A., and Segrin, C. (2008). The big five personality traits and perceptions of touch to intimate and non-intimate body regions. *Journal of Research in Personality, 42,* 1067–1073.

Doucet, C., and Stelmack, R. M. (2000). An event-related potential analysis of extraversion and individual differences in cognitive processing speed and response execution. *Journal of Personality and Social Psychology, 78,* 956-964.

Dreber, A., Apilcella, C. L., Eisenberg, D. T. A., Garcia, J. R., Zamore, R. S., Lum, J. K., and Campbell, B. (2009). The 7R polymorphism in the dopamine receptor D4 gene (DRD4) is associated with financial risk taking in men. *Evolution and Human Behavior, 30,* 85-92.

Drescher, A., and Schultheiss, O. C. (2016). Meta-analytic evidence for higher implicit affiliation and intimacy motivation scores in women, compared to men. *Journal of Research in Personality, 64,* 1-10.

Drislane, L. E., Patrick, C. J., and Arsal, G. (2014). Clarifying the content coverage of differing psychopathy inventories through reference to the Triarchic Psychopathy Measure. *Psychological Assessment, 26*(2), 350-362.

Dryburgh, N. S., and Vachon, D. D. (2019). Relating sex differences in aggression to three forms of empathy. *Personality and Individual Differences, 151,* 109526.

Dubbert, P. M. (2002). Physical activity and exercise: Recent advances and current challenges. *Journal of Consulting and Clinical Psychology Special Issue: Behavioral Medicine and Clinical Health Psychology, 70,* 526-536.

Duckworth, A. L., Peterson, C., Matthews, M. D., and Kelly, D. R. (2007). Grit: Perseverance and passion for long-term goals. *Journal of Personality and Individual Differences, 92,* 1087-1101.

Dunbar, R. I. M. (1993). Coevolution of neocortical size, group size, and language in humans. *Behavioral and Brain Sciences, 16,* 681-735.

Dunlop, P. D., Lee, K., Ashton, M. C., Butcher, S. B., and Dykstra, A. (2015). Please accept my sincere and humble apologies: The HEXACO model of personality and the proclivity to apologize. *Personality and Individual Differences, 79,* 140-145.

Dunn, E. W., Aknin, L. B., and Norton, M. I. (2008). Spending money on others promotes happiness. *Science, 319,* 1687-1688.

Dutton, E., van der Linden, D., and Lynn, R. (2016). The negative Flynn Effect: A systematic literature review. *Intelligence, 59,* 163-169.

Dweck, C. S. (1999a). Caution—Praise can be dangerous. *American Educator, 23,* 4-9.

Dweck, C. S. (2002). Beliefs that make smart people dumb. In R. J. Sternberg (Ed.), *Why smart people can be so stupid* (pp. 24-41). New Haven, CT: Yale University Press.

Dweck, C. S. (2006). *Mindset.* New York: Random House.

Dweck, C. S. (2012). Mindset: How You Can Fulfill Your Potential. Constable & Robinson Limited.

Dweck, C. S. (2017). From needs to goals and representations: Foundations for a unified theory of motivation, personality, and development. *Psychological Review,* 124(6), 689-719.

Dweck, C. S., Chiu, C., and Hong, Y. (1995). Implicit theories and their role in judgments and reactions: A world from two perspectives. *Psychological Inquiry, 6,* 267-285.

Eagly, A. H. (1987). *Sex Differences in Social Behavior: A Social-Role Interpretation.* Hillsdale, NJ: Erlbaum.

Eagly, A. H. (1995). The science and politics of comparing women and men. *American Psychologist, 50,* 145-158.

Eagly, A., and Wood, W. (1999). A social role interpretation of sex differences in human mate preferences. *American Psychologist, 54,* 408-423.

Easterlin, R. A. (1974). Does economic growth improve the human lot: Some empirical evidence. In P. A. David and W. R. Levin (Eds.), *Nations and Households in Economic Growth* (pp. 98-125). Palo Alto, CA: Stanford University Press.

Ebrecht, M., Hextall, J., Kirtley, L. G., Taylor, A., Dyson, M., and Weinman, J. (2004). Perceived stress and cortisol levels predict speed of wound healing in healthy male adults. *Psychoneuroendocrinology, 29*(6), 798-809.

Ebstein, R., Novick, O., Umansky, R., Priel, B., Osher, Y., Blaine, D., Bennett, E. R., Nemanov, L., Katz, M., and Belmaker, R. H. (1996). Dopamine D4 receptor (D4DR) exon III polymorphism associated with the human personality trait of novelty seeking. *Nature Genetics, 12,* 78-80.

Edmundson, M., Berry, D. R., High, W. M., Shandera-Ochsner, A. L., Harp, J. P., and Koehl, L. M. (2015). A meta-analytic review of Minnesota Multiphasic Personality inventory–2nd edition (mmpi-2) profile elevations following traumatic brain injury. *Psychological Injury and Law, 9,* 121-142.

Edwards, D. A., Wetzel, K., and Wyner, D. R. (2006). Intercollegiate soccer: Saliva cortisol and testosterone are elevated during competition, and testosterone is related to status and social connectedness with teammates. *Physiology and Behavior, 30,* 135-143.

Egan, S., and Stelmack, R. M. (2003). A personality profile of Mount Everest climbers. *Personality and Individual Differences, 34,* 1491-1494.

Eid, M., and Larsen, R. J. (2008). *The Science of Subjective Well-Being.* New York: Guilford Press.

Eid, R. S., Gobinath, A. R., and Galea, L. A. (2019) Sex differences in depression: Insights from clinical and preclinical studies. *Progress in Neurobiology, 176,* 86-102.

Eisenberg, D. T. A., Campbell, B., Gray, P. B., and Soronson, M. D. (2008). Dopamine receptor genetic polymorphisms and body composition in undernourished pastoralists: An exploration of nutrition indices among nomadic and recently settled Ariaal men of northern Kenya. *BMC Evolutionary Biology, 8,* 173.

Eisenberg, N., Guthrie, I. K., Cumberland, A., Murphy, B. C., Shepard, S. A., Zhou, Q., and Carlo, G. (2002). Prosocial development in early adulthood: A longitudinal study. *Journal of Personality and Social Psychology, 82*(6), 993-1006.

Ekman, P. (1973). Cross-cultural studies of facial expression. In P. Ekman (Ed.), *Darwin and facial expression: A century of research in review* (pp. 169-222). New York: Academic Press.

Ekman, P. (1992a). An argument for basic emotions. *Cognition and Emotion, 6,* 169-200.

Ekman, P. (1992b). Facial expressions of emotion: New findings, new questions. *Psychological Science, 3,* 34-38.

Ekman, P., (1999). In T. Dalgleish and M. Power (Eds.), *Handbook of cognition and emotion.* Sussex, U.K: John Wiley & Sons.

Ekman, P., Friesen, W. V., and Ellsworth, P. (1972). *Emotion in the Human Face: Guidelines for Research and an Integration of Findings.* New York: Pergamon Press.

Ekman, P., Friesen, W. V., O'Sullivan, M., Chan, A., Diacoyanni-Tarlatzis, I., Heider, K., Krause, R., et al. (1987). Universals and cultural differences in the judgments of facial expressions of emotions. *Journal of Personality and Social Psychology, 53,* 712-717.

Elder, G. H., and Clipp, E. C. (1988). Wartime losses and social bonding: Influence across 40 years in men's lives. *Psychiatry, 51,* 117-198.

Elfenbein, H. H., Curhan, J. R., Eisenkraft, N., Shirako, A., and Baccaro, L. (2008). Are some negotiators better than others? Individual differences in bargaining outcomes. *Journal of Research in Personality, 42,* 1463-1475.

Elinder, M., Engström, P., and Erixson, O. (2021). The last will: Estate divisions as a testament of to whom altruism is directed. *Plos one, 16*(7), e0254492.

Elkins, I. J., King, S. M., McGue, M., and Iacono, W. G. (2006). Personality traits and the development of nicotine, alcohol, and illicit drug disorders: Prospective links from adolescence to young adulthood. *Journal of Abnormal Psychology, 115,* 26-39.

Elliot, A. J., and Dweck, C. S. (2005). *Handbook of competence and motivation.* New York: Guilford Press.

Elliot, A. J., and Reis, H. T. (2003). Attachment and exploration in adulthood.

Journal of Personality and Social Psychology, 85(2), 317-331.

Ellis, B. J., Simpson, J. A., and Campbell, L. (2002). Trait-specific dependence in romantic relationships. *Journal of Personality, 70,* 611-660.

Ellis, L., and Bonin, S. L. (2003). Genetics and occupation-related preferences. Evidence from adoptive and nonadoptive families. *Personality and Individual Differences, 35,* 929-937.

Else-Quest, N. M., Hyde, J. S., Goldsmith, H. H., and Van Hulle, C. A. (2006). Gender differences in temperament: A meta-analysis. *Psychological Bulletin, 132,* 33-72.

Emmons, R. A. (1987). Narcissism: Theory and measurement. *Journal of Personality and Social Psychology, 52,* 11-17.

Emmons, R. A. (1989). The personal striving approach to personality. In L. Pervin et al. (Eds.), *Goal concepts in personality and social psychology* (pp. 87-126). Hillsdale, NJ: Erlbaum.

Emre, M. (2018). *The Personality Brokers: The Strange History of Myers-Briggs and the Birth of Personality Testing.* New York: Doubleday.

Endler, N. S., and Magnusson, D. (1976). Toward an interactional psychology of personality. *Psychological Bulletin, 83,* 956-974.

Engelhard, I. M., van den Hout, M. A., and Kindt, M. (2003). The relationship between neuroticism, pre-traumatic stress, and post-traumatic stress: A prospective study. *Personality and Individual Differences, 35,* 381-388.

Entwisle, D. R. (1972). To dispel fantasies about fantasy-based measures of achievement motivation. *Psychological Bulletin, 77,* 377-391.

Epstein, S. (1979). The stability of behavior: I. On predicting most of the people much of the time. *Journal of Personality and Psychology, 37,* 1097-1126.

Epstein, S. (1980). The stability of behavior: II. Implications for psychological research. *American Psychologist, 35,* 790-806.

Epstein, S. (1983). Aggregation and beyond: Some basic issues on the prediction of behavior. *Journal of Personality, 51,* 360-392.

Erdelyi, M. H., and Goldberg, B. (1979). Let's not sweep repression under the rug: Toward a cognitive psychology of repression. In J. G. Kihlstrom and F. J. Evans (Eds.), *Functional disorders of memory* (pp. 355-402). Hillsdale, NJ: Erlbaum.

Erdheim, J., Wang, M., and Zickar, M. J. (2006). Linking the Big Five personality constructs to organizational commitment. *Personality and Individual Differences, 41,* 959-970.

Erikson, E. H. (1963). *Childhood and society* (2nd ed.). New York: Norton. (Original work published 1950.)

Erikson, E. H. (1968). *Identity: Youth and Crisis.* New York: Norton.

Erikson, E. H. (1975). *Life history and the historical moment.* New York: Norton.

Evans, C. A., Nelson, L. J., and Porter, C. L. (2012). Making sense of their world: Sensory reactivity and sensory awareness as predictors of social interaction in early childhood. *Infant and Child Development, 21,* 503-520.

Exley, J. (2021). OCEAN: How Does Personality Predict Financial Success? *Journal of Financial Planning.*

Exline, J. J., Baumeister, R. F., Bushman, B. J., Campbell, W. K., and Finkel, E. J. (2004). Too proud to let go: Narcissistic entitlement as a barrier to forgiveness. *Journal of Personality and Social Psychology, 87,* 894-912.

Exline, R. V., Thibaut, J., Hickey, C. B., and Gumpart, P. (1970). Visual interaction in relation to expectations, and situational preferences: Personality influences on the decision to participate in volunteer helping behaviors. *Journal of Personality, 67,* 470-503.

Eysenck, H. J. (1967). *The Biological Basis of Personality.* Springfield, IL: Charles C Thomas.

Eysenck, H. J. (1985). *The decline and fall of the Freudian empire.* London: Viking Press.

Eysenck, H. J. (1990). Biological dimensions of personality. In L. Pervin (Ed.), *Handbook of Personality Theory and Research* (pp. 244-276). New York: Guilford Press.

Eysenck, H. J. (1991). Biological dimensions of personality. In L. A. Pervin (Ed.), *Handbook of personality* (pp. 244-276). New York: Guilford Press.

Eysenck, H. J. (Ed.). (1981). *A model for personality.* Berlin: Springer-Verlag.

Eysenck, H. J., and Eysenck, M. W. (1985). *Personality and Individual Differences: A Natural Science Approach.* New York: Plenum Press.

Eysenck, H. J., and Eysenck, S. B. (1967). On the unitary nature of extraversion. *Acta Psychologica, 26,* 383-390.

Eysenck, H. J., and Eysenck, S. B. G. (1972). *Manual of the Eysenck personality questionnaire.* San Diego: Educational and Industrial Testing Service.

Eysenck, H. J., and Eysenck, S. B. G. (1975). *Eysenck personality questionnaire manual.* San Diego: Educational and Industrial Testing Service.

Faelens, L., Hoorelbeke, K., Fried, E., De Raedt, R., and Koster, E. H. W. (2019). Negative influences of Facebook use through the lens of network analysis. *Computers in Human Behavior, 96,* 13-22.

Fagot, B. I., and Leinbach, M. D. (1987). Socialization of sex roles within the family. In D. B. Carter (Ed.), *Current conceptions of sex roles and sex typing.* New York: Praeger.

Fajkowska, M., and Kreitler, S. (2018). Status of the trait concept in contemporary personality psychology: Are the old questions still the burning questions? *Journal of Personality, 86,* 5-11.

Falk, C. F., Heine, S. J., Yuki, M., and Takemura, K. (2009). Why do Westerners self-enhance more than East Asians? *European Journal of Personality, 23,* 183-203.

Feingold, A. (1994). Gender differences in personality: A meta-analysis. *Psychological Bulletin, 116,* 429-456.

Feldman Barrett, L. (2021, January). AI weighs in on debate about universal facial expressions. *Nature,* 589.

Fenichel, O. (1945). *The psychoanalytic theory of neurosis.* New York: Norton.

Fenigstein, A., and Peltz, R. (2002). Distress over the infidelity of a child's spouse: A crucial test of evolutionary and socialization hypotheses. *Personal Relationships, 9,* 301-312.

Fetchenhauer, D., Groothuis, T., and Pradel, J. (2010). Not only states but traits—Humans can identify permanent altruistic dispositions in 20s. *Evolution and Human Behavior, 31,* 80-86.

Fiddick, L., Brase, G. L., Ho, A. T., Hiraishi, K., Honma, A., and Smith, A. (2016). Major personality traits and regulations of social behavior: Cheaters are not the same as the reckless, and you need to know who you're dealing with. *Journal of Research in Personality, 62,* 6-18.

Figueredo, A. J., de Baca, T. C., and Woodley, M. A. (2012). The measurement of Human Life History strategy. *Personality and Individual Differences, 55,* 251-255.

Figueredo, A. J., Sefcek, J. A., and Jones, D. N. (2006). The ideal romantic personality. *Personality and Individual Differences, 41,* 431-441.

Figueredo, A. J., Sefcek, J. S., Vasquez, G., Brumbach, B. H., King, J. E., and Jacobs, W. J. (2005a). Evolutionary personality psychology. In D. M. Buss (Ed.), *The handbook of evolutionary psychology* (pp. 851-877). New York: Wiley.

Figueredo, A. J., Vasquez, G., Brumbach, B. H., Sefcek, J. A., Kirsner, B. R., and Jacobs, W. J. (2005b). The K-factor: Individual differences in life history strategy. *Personality and Individual Differences, 39,* 1349-1360.

Fineman, S. (1977). The achievement motive and its measurement: Where are we now? *British Journal of Psychology, 68,* 1-22.

Finger, F. W. (1982). Circadian rhythms: Implications for psychology. *New Zealand Psychologist, 11,* 1-12.

Fink, B., Weege, B., Pham, M. N., and Shackelford, T. K. (2016). Handgrip strength and the Big Five personality factors in men and women. *Personality and Individual Differences, 88,* 175–177.

Fischer, C. S. (2008). What wealth-happiness paradox? A short note on the American case. *Journal of Happiness Studies, 9*(2), 219–226.

Fiske, A. P. (2002). Using individualism and collectivism to compare cultures: A critique of the validity and measurement of the constructs. *Psychological Bulletin, 128,* 78–88.

Fiske, A. P., Kitayama, S., Markus, H. R., and Nisbett, R. E. (1998). The cultural matrix of social psychology. In D. Gilbert, S. Fiske, and G. Lindzey (Eds.), Handbook of Social Psychology (pp. 915–981). New York: McGraw-Hill.

Fiske, A. P., Kitayama, S., Markus, H., and Nisbett, R. E. (1997). The cultural matrix of social psychology. In D. Gilbert, S. Fiske, and G. Lindzey (Eds.), *Handbook of social psychology* (3rd ed.). New York: McGraw-Hill.

Fiske, D. W. (1949). Consistency of the factorial structures of personality ratings from different sources. *Journal of Abnormal and Social Psychology, 44,* 329–344.

Fitzgerald, C. J., and Colarelli, S. M. (2009). Altruism and reproductive limitations. *Evolutionary Psychology, 7*(2), 234–252.

Fleeson, W. (2001). Toward a structure- and process-integrated view of personality: Traits as density distributions of states. *Journal of Personality and Social Psychology, 80,* 1011–1027.

Fleeson, W. (2004). Moving personality beyond the person-situation debate: The challenge and the opportunity of within-person variability. *Current Directions, 13,* 83–87.

Fleeson, W., and Gallagher, P. (2009). The implications of Big Five standing for the distribution of trait manifestation in behavior: Fifteen experience-sampling studies and a meta-analysis. *Journal of Personality and Social Psychology, 97,* 1097–1114.

Fleeson, W., and Law, M. K. (2015). Trait enactments as density distributions: The role of actors, situations, and observers in explaining stability and variability. *Journal of Personality and Social Psychology, 109,* 1090–1104.

Fleeson, W., Malanos, A. B., and Achille, N. M. (2002). An intraindividual process approach to the relationship between extraversion and positive affect: Is acting extraverted as "Good" as being extraverted? *Journal of Personality and Social Psychology, 83*(6), 1409–1422.

Fletcher, G. J. O., Tither, J. M., O'Loughlin, C., Friesen, M., and Overall, N. (2004).

Warm and homely or cold and beautiful? Sex differences in trading off traits in mate selection. *Personality and Social Psychology Bulletin, 30,* 659–672.

Flett, G. L., Blankstein, K. R., and Hewitt, P. L. (1991). Factor structure of the Short Index of Self-Actualization. *Journal of Social Behavior and Personality Special Issue: Handbook of self-actualization, 6,* 321–329.

Floderus-Myrhed, B., Pedersen, N., and Rasmuson, I. (1980). Assessment of heritability for personality based on a short form of the Eysenck Personality Inventory: A study of 12,898 twin pairs. *Behavior Genetics, 10,* 153–162.

Flowers, K. M., Colebaugh, C. A., Hruschak, V., Azizoddin, D. R., Meints, S. M., Jamison, R. N., . . . and Schreiber, K. L. (2021). Introversion buffers pandemic-related increases in chronic pain impact. *The Journal of Pain, 22*(5), 611–612.

Flynn, F. J. (2005). Having an open mind: The impact of openness to experience on interracial attitudes and impression formation. *Journal of Personality and Social Psychology, 88,* 816–826.

Flynn, J. R. (1984). The mean IQ of Americans: Massive gains 1932 to 1978. *Psychological Bulletin, 95,* 29–51.

Flynn, J. R. (2007). *What is intelligence? Beyond the Flynn effect.* New York: Cambridge University Press.

Flynn, J. R. (2012). *Are we getting smarter? Rising IQ in the twenty-first century.* New York: Cambridge University Press.

Foa, U. G., and Foa, E. B. (1974). *Societal structures of the mind.* Springfield, IL: Charles C Thomas.

Fodor, E. M. (1985). The power motive, group conflict, and physiological arousal. *Journal of Personality and Social Psychology, 49,* 1408–1415.

Fodor, E. M. (2009). Power motivation. In M. R. Leary, R. H. Hoyle, M. R. Leary, R. H. Hoyle (Eds.), *Handbook of individual differences in social behavior* (pp. 426–440). New York: Guilford Press.

Folkman, S., and Moskowitz, J. T. (2000). Stress, positive emotion, and coping. *Current Directions in Psychological Science, 9,* 115–118.

Folkman, S., Moskowitz, J. T., Ozer, E. M., and Park, C. L. (1997). Positive meaningful events and coping in the context of HIV/AIDS. In B. H. Gottlieb (Ed.), *Coping with chronic stress* (pp. 293–314). New York: Plenum Press.

Fordyce, M. W. (1978). *Prospectus: The self-descriptive inventory* [Unpublished manuscript]. Fort Myers, FL: Edison Community College.

Fordyce, M. W. (1988). A review of results on the happiness measures: A 60-second index of happiness and mental health. *Social Indicators Research, 20,* 355–381.

Forestier, C., de Chanaleilles, M., Boisgontier, M. P., and Chalabaev, A. (2022). From ego depletion to self-control fatigue: A review of criticisms along with new perspectives for the investigation and replication of a multicomponent phenomenon. *Motivation Science, 8,* 19–32.

Foster, J. D., and Campbell, W. K. (2005). Narcissism and resistance to doubts about romantic partners. *Journal of Research in Personality, 39,* 550–557.

Fowles, D. C. (1980). The three arousal model: Implications of Gray's two-factor learning theory for heart rate, electrodermal activity, and psychopathy. *Psychophysiology, 17,* 87–104.

Fox, N. A., and Calkins, S. D. (1993). Multiple-measure approaches to the study of infant emotion. In M. Lewis and J. M. Haviland (Eds.), *Handbook of emotions* (pp. 167–185). New York: Guilford Press.

Fox, N. A., and Davidson, R. J. (1986). Taste-elicited changes in facial signs of emotion and the asymmetry of brain electrical activity in human newborns. *Neuropsychologia, 24,* 417–422.

Fox, N. A., and Davidson, R. J. (1987). Electroencephalogram asymmetry in response to the approach of a stranger and maternal separation. *Developmental Psychology, 23,* 233–240.

Fox, N. A., and Polak, C. P. (2004). The role of sensory reactivity in understanding infant temperament. In R. DelCarmen-Wiggins and A. Carter (Eds.), *Handbook of infant, toddler, and preschool mental health assessment* (pp. 105–119). New York: Oxford University Press.

Fox, N. A., Bell, M. A., and Jones, N. A. (1992). Individual differences in response to stress and cerebral asymmetry. *Developmental Neuropsychology, 8,* 165–184.

Fraguas, D., Díaz-Caneja, C. M., Ayora, M., Durán-Cutilla, M., Abregú-Crespo, R., Ezquiaga-Bravo, I., . . . Arango, C. (2021). Assessment of school anti-bullying interventions: a meta-analysis of randomized clinical trials. *JAMA Pediatrics, 175*(1), 44–55.

Fraley, R. C. (2002a). Attachment stability from infancy to adulthood: Meta-analysis and dynamic modeling of developmental mechanisms. *Personality and Social Psychology Review, 6,* 123–151.

Fraley, R. C. (2002b). Introduction to the special issue: The psychodynamics of adult attachments—Bridging the gap between disparate research traditions. *Attachment and Human Development Special Issue: The Psychodynamics of Adult Attachments—Bridging the Gap Between Disparate Research Traditions, 4,* 131–132.

Fraley, R. C. (2007). A connectionist approach to the organization and continuity of working models of attachment. *Journal of Personality, 75,* 1157-1180.

Fraley, R. C., and Roisman, G. I. (2015). Early attachment experiences and romantic functioning: Developmental pathways, emerging issues, and future directions. In J. A. Simpson, W. S. Rholes, J. A. Simpson, and W. S. Rholes (Eds.), *Attachment theory and research: New directions and emerging themes* (pp. 9-38). New York: Guilford Press.

Fraley, R. C., and Tancredy, C. M. (2012). Twin and sibling attachment in a nationally representative sample. *Personality and Social Psychology Bulletin, 38,* 308-316.

Fraley, R. C., Gilath, O., and Deboeck, P. R. (2021). Do life events lead to enduring changes in adult attachment styles? A naturalistic longitudinal investigation. *Journal of Personality and Social Psychology, 120,* 1567-1606.

Fraley, R. C., Hudson, N. W., Heffernan, M. E., and Segal, N. (2015). Are adult attachment styles categorical or dimensional? A taxometric analysis of general and relationship-specific attachment orientations. *Journal of Personality and Social Psychology, 109*(2), 354-368.

Fraley, R. C., Roisman, G. I., and Haltigan, J. D. (2013). The legacy of early experiences in development: Formalizing alternative models of how early experiences are carried forward over time. *Developmental Psychology, 49,* 109-126.

Fraley, R. C., Vicary, A. M., Brumbaugh, C. C., and Roisman, G. I. (2011). Patterns of stability in adult attachment: An empirical test of two models of continuity and change. *Journal of Personality and Social Psychology, 101,* 974-992.

Fransella, F. (2003). *International handbook of personal construct psychology.* New York: Wiley.

Fraser, S. (1995). *The bell curve wars: Race, intelligence, and the future of America.* New York: Basic Books.

Frederick, D. A., and Fales, M. R. (2016). Upset over sexual versus emotional infidelity among gay, lesbian, bisexual, and heterosexual adults. *Archives of Sexual Behavior, 45*(1), 175-191.

Fredrickson, B. L. (1998). What good are positive emotions? *Review of General Psychology, 2,* 300-319.

Fredrickson, B. L. (2000). Cultivating positive emotions to optimize health and well-being. *Prevention and Treatment* (online), 2. Retrieved from http://journals.apa.org/prevention.

Fredrickson, B. L., and Levenson, R. W. (1998). Positive emotions speed recovery from the cardiovascular sequelae of negative emotions. *Cognition and Emotion, 12,* 191-220.

Freeman, D. (1983). *Margaret Mead and Samoa: The making and unmaking of an anthropological myth.* Cambridge, MA: Harvard University Press.

Freshwater, S. M., and Golden, C. J. (2002). Personality changes associated with localized brain injury in elderly populations. *Journal of Clinical Geropsychology, 8,* 251-277.

Freud, A. (1936/1992). The ego and mechanisms of defense. In Vol. 2 of *The writings of Anna Freud.* New York: International Universities Press.

Freud, S. (1915/1957). The unconscious. In J. Strachey (Ed. and Trans.), *The standard edition of the complete psychological works of Sigmund Freud* (Vol. 14, pp. 166-204). London: Hogarth Press.

Freud, S. (1916/1947). *Leonardo da Vinci, a study in psychosexuality.* New York: Random House.

Frey, M. C. and Detterman, D. K. (2003). Scholastic assessment or g? The relationship between the scholastic assessment test and general cognitive ability. *Psychological Science, 15,* 373-378.

Frick, P. J., O'Brien, B. S., Wootton, J. M., and McBurnett, K. (1994). Psychopathy and conduct problems in children. *Journal of Abnormal Psychology, 103,* 700-707.

Friedman, H. S. (2019). Neuroticism and health as individuals age. *Personality Disorders: Theory, Research, and Treatment, 10,* 25-32.

Friedman, H. S., Tucker, J. S., Schwartz, J. E., Tomlinson-Keasey, C., and Martin, L. R., et al. (1995). Psychosocial and behavioral predictors of longevity. *American Psychologist, 50,* 69-78.

Friedman, M., and Rosenman, R. H. (1974). *Type A behavior and your heart.* New York: Knopf.

Frijda, N. H. (1986). *The emotions.* New York: Cambridge University Press.

Frisell, T., Pawitan, Y., Langstrom, N., and Lichtenstein, P. (2012). Heritability, assortative mating and gender differences in violent crime: Results from a total population sample using twin, adoption, and sibling models. *Behavior Genetics, 42,* 3-18.

Frodi, A., Macauley, J., and Thome, P. R. (1977). Are women always less aggressive than men? A review of the experimental literature. *Psychological Bulletin, 84,* 634-660.

Funder, D. C. (2006). Towards a resolution of the personality triad: Persons, situations, and behaviors. *Journal of Research in Personality, 40,* 21-34.

Furmark, T. (2002). Social phobia: Overview of community surveys. *Acta Psychiatrica Scandinavica, 105,* 84-93.

Furnham, A. (1982). Psychoticism, social desirability, and situation selection.

Personality and Individual Differences, 3, 43-51.

Furnham, A., and Cheng, H. (2019a). Factors influencing adult savings and investment: Findings from a nationally representative sample. Personality and Individual Differences, 151, 109510.

Furnham, A., and Cheng, H. (2019b). The Big-Five personality factors, mental health, and social-demographic indicators as independent predictors of gratification delay. Personality and Individual Differences, 150, 109533.

Furnham, A., and Cheng, H. (2019c). The change and stability of NEO scores over six-years: A British study and a short review. *Personality and Individual Differences, 144,* 105-110.

Furnham, A., Richards, S. C., and Paulhus, D. L. (2013). The Dark Triad of personality: A 10 year review. *Social and Personality Psychology Compass, 7*(3), 199-216.

Furr, R. M. (2009). Personality psychology as a truly behavioural science. *European Journal of Personality, 23,* 369-401.

Gable, S. L., and Nezlak, J. B. (1998). Level and instability of day-to-day psychological well-being and risk for depression. *Journal of Personality and Social Psychology, 74,* 129-138.

Gabriel, S. (2021). Reflections on the 25th anniversary of Baumeister & Leary's seminal paper on the need to belong. *Self and Identity, 20*(1), 1-5.

Gabriel, S., and Gardner, W. L. (1999). Are there "his" and "hers" types of interdependence? The implications of gender differences in collective versus relational interdependence for affect, behavior, and cognition. *Journal of Personality and Social Psychology, 77,* 642-655.

Gailliot, M. T., and Baumeister, R. F. (2007). Self-regulation and sexual restraint: Dispositionally and temporarily poor self-regulatory abilities contribute to failures at restraining sexual behavior. *Personality and Social Psychology Bulletin, 33,* 173-186.

Gale, A. (1983). Electroencephalographic studies of extraversion-introversion: A case study in the psychophysiology of individual differences. *Personality and Individual Differences, 4,* 371-380.

Gale, A. (1986). Extraversion–introversion and spontaneous rhythms of the brain: Retrospect and prospect. In J. Strelau, F. Farley, and A. Gale (Eds.), *The biological basis of personality and behavior* (Vol. 2). Washington, DC: Hemisphere.

Gale, A. (1987). The psychophysiological context. In A. Gale and B. Christie (Eds.), *Psychophysiology and the electronic workplace* (pp. 17-32). Chichester, England, UK: Wiley.

Gale, C. R., Batty, G. D., and Deary, I. J., (2008). Locus of control at age 10 years and health outcomes and behaviors at age 30 years: The 1970 British cohort study. *Psychosomatic Medicine, 70,* 397–403.

Galic, Z., Jerneic, Z., and Kovacic, M. P. (2012). Do applicants fake their personality questionnaire responses and how successful are their attempts? A case of military pilot cadet selection. *International Journal of Selection and Assessment, 20,* 229–241.

Gallup, A. C., O'Brien, D. T., White, D. D., and Wilson, D. S. (2009). Peer victimization in adolescence has different effects on the sexual behavior of male and female college students. *Personality and Individual Differences, 46,* 611–615.

Gallup, G. G. (1977a). Self-recognition in primates: A comparative approach to the bidirectional properties of consciousness. *American Psychologist, 32,* 329–338.

Gallup, G. G. (1977b). Absences of self-recognition in a monkey (*Macaca fascicularis*) following prolonged exposure to a mirror. *Developmental Psychobiology, 10,* 281–284.

Gangestad, S. W., and Simpson, J. A. (1990). Toward an evolutionary history of female sociosexual variation. *Journal of Personality, 58,* 69–96.

Gangestad, S. W., and Thornhill, R. (2008). Human oestrus. *Proceedings of the Royal Society of London, B, 275,* 991–1000.

Gangestad, S. W., Haselton, M. G., and Buss, D. M. (2006). Evolutionary foundations of cultural variation: Evoked culture and mate preferences. *Psychological Inquiry, 17,* 75–95.

Ganjoo, M., Farhadi, A., Baghbani, R., Daneshi, S., and Nemati, R. (2021). Association between health locus of control and perceived stress in college students during the COVID-19 outbreak: A cross sectional study in Iran. *BMC Psychiatry, 21,* Oct 26, 2021. ArtID: 529.

Gao, S., Thomaes, S., Van Den Noortgate, W., Xie, X., Zhang, X., and Wang, S. (2019). Recent changes in narcissism of Chinese youth: A cross-temporal meta-analysis, 2008–2017. *Personality and Individual Differences, 148,* 62–66.

Gao, W., Luo, Y., Cao, X., and Liu, X. (2022). Gender differences in the relationship between self-esteem and depression among college students: A cross-lagged study from China. *Journal of Research in Personality,* 104202.

Garbarino, E., Slonim, R., and Snydor, J. (2011). Digit ratios (2D:4D) as predictors of risky decision making for both sexes. *Journal of Risk and Uncertainty, 42,* 1–26.

Garber, J., and Seligman, M. E. P. (1980). *Human helplessness: Theory and applications.* New York: Academic Press.

Gardner, H. (1983). *Frames of mind: The theory of multiple intelligences.* New York: Basic Books.

Gardner, H. (1999). *Intelligence reframed: Multiple intelligences for the 21st century.* New York: Basic Books.

Gardner, W. I., and Martinko, M. J. (1996). Using the Myers-Briggs Type Indicator to study managers: A literature review and research agenda. *Journal of Management, 22,* 45–83.

Garver, C. E., Gangestad, S. W., Simpson, J. A., Cousins, A. J., and Christensen, P. N. (2002). Women's preferences for male behavioral displays change across the cycle. In Annual Meeting of the Human Behavior and Evolution Society, New Brunswick, New Jersey.

Gauguin, P. (1985). *Noa Noa: The Tahitian Journal.* Mineola, NY: Dover.

Geary, D. C., DeSoto, M. C., Hoard, M. K., Skaggs, S., and Cooper, M. L. (2001). Estrogens and relationship jealousy. *Human Nature, 12,* 299–320.

Geen, R. (1984). Preferred stimulation levels in introverts and extraverts: Effects on arousal and performance. *Journal of Personality and Social Psychology, 46,* 1303–1312.

Geer, J. H., and Head, S. (1990). The sexual response system. In J. T. Cacioppo and L. G. Tassinary (Eds.), *Principles of psychophysiology* (pp. 599–630). Cambridge, England: Cambridge University Press.

Geis, F. L., and Moon, T. H. (1981). Machiavellianism and deception. *Journal of Personality and Social Psychology, 41,* 766–775.

Gelade, G. A. (2008). IQ, cultural values, and the technological achievement of nations. *Intelligence, 36,* 711–718.

George, C., and Solomon, J. (1996). Representational models of relationships: Links between caregiving and attachment. *Infant Mental Health Journal, 17,* 198–216.

Gere, J., and MacDonald, G. (2010). An update of the empirical case for the need to belong. *Journal of Individual Psychology, 66*(1), 93–115.

Gergen, K. J. (1992). Toward a postmodern psychology. In S. Kvale (Ed.), *Psychology and postmodernism* (pp. 17–30). London: Sage.

Gerring, J. P., and Vasa, R. A. (2016). Head injury and externalizing behavior. In T. P. Beauchaine, S. P. Hinshaw, T. P. Beauchaine, S. P. Hinshaw (Eds.), *The Oxford handbook of externalizing spectrum disorders* (pp. 403–415). New York: Oxford University Press.

Gerson, M. W., and Fernandez, N. (2013). PATH: A program to build resilience and thriving in undergraduates. *Journal of Applied Social Psychology, 43*(11), 2169–2184.

Gervais, W. M., Najle, M. B., and Caluori, N. (2021). The origins of religious disbelief: A dual inheritance approach. *Social Psychological and Personality Science, 12*(7), 1369–1379.

Geukes, K., Nestler, S., Hutteman, R. R., Dufner, M., Küfner, A. C. P., Egloff, B., . . . Back, M. D., (2017). Puffed-up but shaky selves: State self-esteem level and variability in narcissists. *Journal of Personality and Social Psychology, 112,* 769–786.

Gewertz, D. (1981). A historical reconsideration of female dominance among the Chambri of Papua New Guinea. *American Ethnologist, 8,* 94–106.

Gibbs, W. (2003). The unseen genome: Gems among the junk. *Scientific American, 289,* 49.

Gigy, L. L. (1980). Self-concept in single women. *Psychology of Women Quarterly, 5,* 321–340.

Giluk, T. L., and Postlethwaite, B. E. (2015). Big Five personality and academic dishonesty: A meta-analytic review. *Personality and Individual Differences, 72,* 59–67.

Gladden, P. R., Figueredo, A. J., and Jacobs, W. J. (2009). Life history strategy, psychopathic attitudes, personality, and general intelligences. *Personality and Individual Differences, 46,* 270–275.

Glenn, A. L., and Raine, A. (2014). Neurocriminology: Implications for the punishment, prediction and prevention of criminal behavior. *Nature Reviews Neuroscience, 15*(1), 54–63.

Gnambs, T. (2015). What makes a computer wiz? Linking personality traits and programming aptitude. *Journal of Research in Personality, 58,* 31–34.

Goldberg, L. R. (1981). Language and individual differences: The search for universals in personality lexicons. In L. Wheeler (Ed.), *Review of personality and social psychology* (Vol. 2, pp. 141–165). Beverly Hills, CA: Sage.

Goldberg, L. R. (1990). An alternative "description of personality": The Big-Five factor structure. *Journal of Personality and Social Psychology, 59,* 1216–1229.

Goldberg, L. R., and Saucier, G. (1995). So what do you propose we use instead? A reply to Block. *Psychological Bulletin, 117,* 221–225.

Goldey, K. L., and van Anders, S. M. (2012). Sexual arousal and desire: Interrelations and responses to three modalities of sexual stimuli. *Journal of Sexual Medicine, 9,* 2315–2329.

Golding, S. L. (1978). Toward a more adequate theory of personality: Psychological organizing principles. In H. London (Ed.), *Personality: A New Look at Metatheories* (pp. 69–96). New York: Wiley.

Goldsmith, H. H., Aksan, N., and Essex, M. (2001). Temperament and socioemotional adjustment to kindergarten: A multi-informant perspective. In T. Wachs and G. A. Kohnstamm (Eds.), *Temperament in Context* (pp. 103-138). Mahwah, NJ: Erlbaum.

Goldsmith, H. H., and Rothbart, M. K. (1991). Contemporary instruments for assessing early temperament by questionnaire and in the laboratory. In J. Strelau and A. Angleitner (Eds.), *Explorations in temperament.* New York: Plenum Press.

Goleman, D. (1995). *Emotional intelligence: Why it can matter more than IQ.* New York: Bantam.

Golsteyn, B. H., Non, A., and Zölitz, U. (2021). The impact of peer personality on academic achievement. *Journal of Political Economy, 129*(4), 1052-1099

Gomez, R., Cooper, A.J., and Gomez, A. (2000). Susceptibility to positive and negative mood states: test of Eysenck's, Gray's and Newman's theories. *Personality and Individual Differences, 29,* 351-365.

Goncalves, M. K., and Campbell, L. (2014). The Dark Triad and the derogation of mating competitors. *Personality and Individual Differences, 67,* 42-46.

Goodman, G., and Kaufman, J. C. (2014). Gremlins in my head: Predicting stage fright in elite actors. *Empirical Studies of the Arts, 32*(2), 133-148.

Goodman, J., Lofts, E. F., Miller, M., and Greene, E. (1991). Money, sex, and death: Gender bias in wrongful death damage awards. *Law and Society Review, 25,* 263-285.

Gorbaniuk, O., Budzińska, A., Owczarek, M., Bożek, E., and Juros, K. (2013). The factor structure of Polish personality-descriptive adjectives: An alternative psycho-lexical study. *European Journal of Personality, 27*(3), 304-318.

Gordon, R. A. (1997). Everyday life as an intelligence test: Effects of intelligence and intelligence context. *Intelligence, 24,* 203-320.

Gosling, S. D., and Mason, W. (2015). Internet research in psychology. *Annual Review of Psychology, 66,* 877-902.

Gosling, S. D., John, O. P., Craik, K. H., and Robins, R. W. (1998). Do people know how they behave? Self-reported act frequencies compared with on-line codings by observers. *Journal of Personality and Social Psychology, 74,* 1337-1349.

Gosling, S. D., Ko, S. J., Mannarelli, T., and Morris, M. E. (2002). A room with a cue: Personality judgments based on offices and bedrooms. *Journal of Personality and Social Psychology, 82,* 379-398.

Gosling, S. D., Kwan, V. S. Y., and John, O. P. (2003). A dog's got personality: A cross-species comparative approach to evaluating personality judgments. *Journal of Personality and Social Psychology, 85,* 1161-1169.

Gottman, J. (1994). *Why marriages succeed or fail.* New York: Simon and Schuster.

Gottman, J. M., and Silver, N. (1999). *The seven principles for making marriage work.* New York: Three Rivers Press.

Gottman, J., Levenson, R., and Woodin, E. (2001). Facial expressions during marital conflict. *Journal of Family Communication, 1,* 37-57.

Goudeau, S., and Cimpian, A. (2021). How do young children explain differences in the classroom? Implications for achievement, motivation, and educational equity *Perspectives on Psychological Science, 16,* 533-552.

Gough, H. G. (1957/1987). *California Psychological Inventory: Administrator's guide.* Palo Alto, CA: Consulting Psychologists Press.

Gough, H. G. (1980). *The Adjective Check List manual.* Palo Alto, CA: Consulting Psychologists Press.

Gough, H. G. (1996). *California psychological inventory manual* (3rd ed.). Palo Alto, CA: Consulting Psychologists Press.

Graham, E. K., Rutsohn, J. P., Turiano, N. A., Bendayan, R., Batterham, P. J., Gerstorf, D., . . . Mroczek, D. K. (2017). Personality predicts mortality risk: An integrative data analysis of 15 international longitudinal studies. *Journal of Research in Personality, 70,* 174-186.

Grano, N., Virtanen, M., Vahtera, J., Elovainio, M., and Kivimaki, M. (2004). Impulsivity as a predictor of smoking and alcohol consumption. *Personality and Individual Differences, 37,* 1693-1700.

Granqvist, P., Mikulincer, M., Gewirtz, V., and Shaver, P. R. (2012). Experimental findings on God as an attachment figure: Normative processes and moderating effects of internal working models. *Journal of Personality and Social Psychology, 103,* 804-818.

Grant, H., and Higgins, E. T. (2003). Optimism, promotion pride, and prevention pride as predictors of quality of life. *Personality and Social Psychology Bulletin, 29,* 1521-1532.

Grant, J. D., and Grant, J. (1996). Officer selection and the prevention of abuse of force. In W. Geller and H. Toch (Eds.), *Police Violence: Understanding and Controlling Police Abuse of Force* (pp. 150-164). New Haven, CT: Yale University Press.

Gray, J. (1990). Brain systems that mediate both emotion and cognition. *Motivation and Emotion, 4,* 269-288.

Gray, J. A. (1972). *The psychology of fear and stress.* New York: McGraw-Hill.

Gray, J. A. (1975). *Elements of a two-process theory of learning.* Oxford, England: Academic Press.

Gray, J. A. (1982). *The Neuropsychology of Anxiety.* Oxford, England: Oxford University Press.

Gray, J. A. (1987a). *The psychology of fear and stress.* Cambridge, England: Cambridge University Press.

Gray, J. A. (1987b). Perspectives on anxiety and impulsivity: A commentary. *Journal of Research in Personality, 21,* 493-509.

Gray, J. A. (1991). The neuropsychology of temperament. In J. Strelau and A. Angleitner (Eds.), *Explorations in temperament: International perspectives on theory and measurement* (pp. 105-128). New York: Plenum Press.

Grayson, D. K. (1993). Differential mortality and the Donner Party disaster. *Evolutionary Anthropology, 2,* 151-159.

Graziano, W. G., (2003). Personality development: An introduction toward process approaches to long-term stability and change in persons. *Journal of Personality, 71,* 893-903.

Graziano, W. G., and Tobin, R. M. (2002). Agreeableness: Dimension of personality or social desirability artifact? *Journal of Personality, 70,* 695-727.

Grazioplene, R. G., Ryman, S. G., Gray, J. R., Rustichini, A., Jung, R. E., and DeYoung, C. G. (2015). Subcortical intelligence: Caudate volume predicts IQ in healthy adults. *Human Brain Mapping, 36,* 1407-1416.

Greenberg, D. M., Müllensiefen, D., Lamb, M. E., and Rentfrow, P. J. (2015). Personality predicts musical sophistication. *Journal of Research in Personality, 58,* 154-158.

Greenberg, J. R., and Mitchell, S. (1983). *Object relations in psychoanalytic theory.* Cambridge, MA: Harvard University Press.

Greene, J. A., Freed, R., Dragnić-Cindrić, D., and Cartiff, B. M. (2022). Effects of an ego-depletion intervention upon online learning. *Computers & Education, 177,* Feb, 2022. ArtID: 104362.

Greenwald, A. G., and Farnham, S .D. (2000). Using the Implicit Association Test to measure self-esteem and self-concept. *Journal of Personality and Social Psychology, 79,* 1022-1038.

Gregg, A. P., and Sedikides, C. (2018). Essential self-evaluation motives: Caring about who we are. In M. van Zomeren and J. F. Dovidio (Eds.), The Oxford Handbook of the Human Essence (pp. 59-70). Oxford University Press.

Gregory, T., Nettelbeck, T., Howard, S., and Wilson, C. (2008). Inspection time: A biomarker for cognitive decline. *Intelligence, 36,* 664-671.

Greiling, H., and Buss, D. M. (2000). Women's sexual strategies: The hidden dimension of extra-pair mating. *Personality and Individual Differences, 28,* 929–963.

Griskevicius, V., Tybur, J. M., Gangestad, S. W., Perea, E. F., Shapiro, J. R., and Kenrick, D. T. (2009). Aggress to impress: Hostility as an evolved context-dependent strategy. *Journal of Personality and Social Psychology, 96,* 980–994.

Gross, J. J. (2002). Emotion regulation: Affective, cognitive, and social consequences. *Psychophysiology, 39,* 281–291.

Gross, J. J., and Levenson, R. W. (1993). Emotional suppression: Physiology, self-report, and expressive behavior. *Journal of Personality and Social Psychology, 64,* 970–986.

Gross, J. J., and Levenson, R. W. (1997). Hiding feelings: The acute effects of inhibiting positive and negative emotions. *Journal of Abnormal Psychology, 106,* 95–103.

Gross, J. J., Sutton, S. K., and Ketelaar, R. (1998). Relations between affect and personality: Support for the affect-level and affective reactivity views. *Personality and Social Psychology Bulletin, 24,* 279–288.

Grosskurth, P. (1991). *The secret ring: Freud's inner circle and the politics of psychoanalysis.* Reading, MA: Addison-Wesley.

Guillaume, E., Baranski, E., Todd, E., Bastian, B., Bronin, I., Ivanova, C., . . . Funder, D. C. (2016). The world at 7: 00: Comparing the experience of situations across 20 countries. *Journal of Personality, 84*(4), 493–509.

Guisande, M. A., Páramo, M. F., and Soares, A. P. (2007). Field-dependence-independence and career counseling: Directions for research. *Perceptual and Motor Skills, 104,* 654–662.

Gul, P., Cross, S. E., and Uskul, A. K. (2021). Implications of culture of honor theory and research for practitioners and prevention researchers. *American Psychologist, 76*(3), 502.

Gustafsson Sendén, M., Bäck, E. A., and Lindqvist, A. (2015). Introducing a gender-neutral pronoun in a natural gender language: The influence of time on attitudes and behavior. *Frontiers in Psychology, 6,* 893.

Guzder, J., Paris, J., Zelkowitz, P., and Marchessault, K. (1996). Risk factors for borderline personality in children. *Journal of the American Academy of Child and Adolescent Psychiatry, 35,* 26–33.

Hacher, S. L., Nadeau, M. S., Walsh, L. K., and Reynolds, M. (1994). The teaching of empathy for high school and college students: Testing Rogerian methods with the Interpersonal Reactivity Index. *Adolescence, 29,* 961–974.

Hagen, E. H., and Rosenström, T. (2016). Explaining the sex difference in depression with a unified bargaining model of anger and depression. *Evolution, Medicine, and Public Health, 2016*(1), 117–132.

Hagerty, M. R. (1999). Testing Maslow's hierarchy of needs: National quality-of-life across time. *Social Indicators Research, 46,* 249–271.

Hagger, M. S., Chatzisarantis, N. L. D., Alberts, H., Anggono, C. O., Batailler, C., Birt, A. R., . . . Zwienenberg, M. (2016). A multi-lab preregistered replication of the ego-depletion effect. *Perspectives on Psychological Science, 11,* 546–573.

Hahn, E., Johnson, W., and Spinath, F. M. (2013). Beyond the heritability of life satisfaction–The roles of personality and twin-specific influences. *Journal of Research in Personality, 47*(6), 757–767.

Hair, E. C., and Graziano, W. G. (2003). Self-esteem, personality, and achievement in high school: A prospective longitudinal study in Texas. *Journal of Personality, 71,* 971–994.

Hald, G. M., and Hogh-Olesen, H. (2010). Receptivity to sexual invitations from strangers of the opposite gender. *Evolution and Human Behavior, 31,* 453–458.

Hall, J. A. (1984). *Nonverbal sex differences.* Baltimore: Johns Hopkins University Press.

Hamer, D. (1997). The search for personality genes: Adventures of a molecular biologist. *Current Directions in Psychological Science, 6,* 111–114.

Hamer, D., and Copeland, P. (1994). *The science of desire: The search for the gay gene and the biology of behavior.* New York: Simon and Schuster.

Hamilton, W. D. (1964). The evolution of social behavior. *Journal of Theoretical Biology, 7,* 1–52.

Hamm, A. O., Weike, A. I., Schupp, H. T., Treig, T., Dressel, A., and Kessler, C. (2003). Affective blindsight: Intact fear conditioning to a visual cue in a cortically blind patient. *Brain, 126*(2), 267–275.

Hampshire, S. (1953). Dispositions. *Analysis, 14,* 5–11.

Hampson, S. E., Andrews, J. A., Barckley, M., and Peterson, M. (2007). Trait stability and continuity in childhood: Relating sociability and hostility to the five-factor model of personality. *Journal of Research in Personality, 41,* 507–523.

Hampson, S. E., Goldberg, L. R., Vogt, T. M., and Dubanoski, J. P. (2006). Forty years on: Teachers' assessments of children's personality traits predict self-reported health behaviors and outcomes at midlife. *Health Psychology, 25,* 57–64.

Hampson, S. E., Severson, H. H., Burns, W. J., Slovic, P., and Fisher, K. J. (2001). Risk perception, personality factors and alcohol use among adolescents. *Personality and Individual Differences, 30,* 167–181.

Handy, A. B., Freihart, B. K., and Meston, C. M. (2020). The Relationship between Subjective and Physiological Sexual Arousal in Women with and without Arousal Concerns. *Journal of Sex & Marital Therapy, 46*(5), 447–459.

Hankin, B. L., and Abramson, L. Y. (2001). Development of gender differences in depression: An elaborated cognitive vulnerability transactional stress theory. *Psychological Bulletin, 127,*(6) 773–796.

Hanna, E., Ward, L. M., Seabrook, R. C., Jerald, M., Reed, L., Giaccardi, S., and Lippman, J. R. (2017). Contributions of social comparison and self-objectification in mediating associations between Facebook use and emergent adults' psychological well-being. *Cyberpsychology, Behavior, and Social Networking, 20,* 172–179.

Hansen, C. H., Hansen, R. D., and Schantz, D. W. (1992). Repression at encoding: Discrete appraisals of emotional stimuli. *Journal of Personality and Social Psychology, 63,* 1026–1035.

Hansen, R. D., and Hansen, C. H. (1988). Repression of emotionally tagged memories: The architecture of less complex emotions. *Journal of Personality and Social Psychology, 55,* 811–818.

Hansen-Brown, A. A., and Freis, S. D. (2021). Assuming the worst: Hostile attribution bias in vulnerable narcissists. *Self and Identity, 20*(2), 152–164.

Hansson, I., Henning, G., Buratti, S., Lindwall, M., Kivi, M., Johansson, B., and Berg, A. I. (2019). The role of personality in retirement adjustment: Longitudinal evidence for the effects on life satisfaction. *Journal of Personality.*

Harden, K. P. (2021). *The genetic lottery: why DNA matters for social equality.* Princeton University Press.

Hardison, H. G., and Neimeyer, R. A. (2012). Assessment of personal constructs: Features and functions of constructivist techniques. In P. Caputi, L. L. Viney, B. M. Walker, and N. Crittenden (Eds.), *Personal construct methodology* (pp. 3–51). Hoboken, NJ: John Wiley & Sons.

Hare, R. D., Hart, S. D., and Harpur, T. J. (1991). Psychopathy and the DSM-IV criteria for antisocial personality disorder. *Journal of Abnormal Psychology Special Issue: Diagnosis, Dimensions, and DSM-IV; The Science of Classification, 100,* 391–398.

Harenski, C. L., Kim, S. H., and Hamann, S. (2009). Neuroticism and psychopathy predict brain activation during moral and nonmoral emotion regulation. *Cognitive, Affective and Behavioral Neuroscience, 9,* 1–15.

Haring, M. J., Stock, W. A., and Okun, M. A. (1984). A research synthesis of gender and social class as correlates of subjective well-being. *Human Relations, 37,* 645–657.

Harlow, H. F. (1958). The nature of love. *American Psychologist, 13,* 673–685.

Harlow, H. F., and Suomi, S. J. (1971). Production of depressive behaviors in young monkeys. *Journal of Autism and Childhood Schizophrenia, 1,* 246–255.

Harlow, H. F., and Zimmermann, R. R. (1959). Affectionate responses in the infant monkey. *Science, 130,* 421–432.

Harpending, H., and Cochran, G. (2002). In our genes. *Proceedings of the National Academy of Sciences of the United States of America, 99,* 10–12.

Harpur, T. J., and Hare, R. D. (1994). Assessment of psychopathy as a function of age. *Journal of Abnormal Psychology, 103,* 604–609.

Harrell, W. A., and Hartnagel, T. (1976). The impact of Machiavellianism and the trustfulness of the victim on laboratory theft. *Sociometry, 39,* 157–165.

Harris, J. R. (2007). *No two alike: Human nature and human individuality.* New York: Norton.

Harter, S. (1993). Causes and consequences of low self-esteem in children and adolescents. In R. Baumeister (Ed.), *Self-esteem: The puzzle of low self-regard* (pp. 87–111). New York: Plenum Press.

Hartley, E. L., Stritzke, W. G., Page, A. C., Blades, C. A., and Parentich, K. T. (2019). Neuroticism confers vulnerability in response to experimentally induced feelings of thwarted belongingness and perceived burdensomeness: Implications for suicide risk. *Journal of Personality, 87*(3), 566–578.

Hartshorne, H., and May, M. A. (1928). *Studies in the Nature of Character: Vol. 1. Studies in Deceit.* New York: Macmillan.

Haslam, C., and Montrose, V. T. (2015). Should have known better: The impact of mating experience and the desire for marriage upon attraction to the narcissistic personality. *Personality and Individual Differences, 82,* 188–192.

Hatemi, P. K., Medland, S. E., Klemmensen, R., Oskarsson, S., Littvay, L., Dawes, C. T., . . . and Christensen, K. (2014). Genetic influences on political ideologies: Twin analyses of 19 measures of political ideologies from five democracies and genome-wide findings from three populations. *Behavior Genetics, 44*(3), 282–294.

Hawes, S. W., Perlman, S. B., Byrd, A. L., Raine, A., Loeber, R., and Pardini, D. A. (2016). Chronic anger as a precursor to adult antisocial personality features: The moderating influence of cognitive control. *Journal of Abnormal Psychology, 125*(1), 64–74.

Hawkins, H. C., Lesick, T. L., and Zell, E. (2021). Implicit self-esteem following a romantic partner's success: Three replications and a meta-analysis. *Personal Relationships,* http://dx.doi.org/10.1111/pere.12408.

Hazan, C., and Shaver, P. R. (1987). Romantic love conceptualized as an attachment process. *Journal of Personality and Social Psychology, 52,* 511–524.

Hazan, C., and Shaver, P. R. (1994). Attachment as an organizational framework for research on close relationships. *Psychological Inquiry, 5,* 1–22.

He, Q., Wang, Y., Xing, Y., and Yu, Y. (2018). Dark personality, interpersonal rejection, and marital stability of Chinese couples: An actor–partner interdependence mediatio model. *Personality and Individual Differences, 134,* 232–238.

Heath, A. C., Bucholz, K. K., Dinwiddie, S. H., Madden, P. A. F., and Slutske, W. W. (1994). *Pathways from the genotype to alcoholism risk in women.* Paper presented at the annual meeting of the Behavioral Genetics Association, Barcelona, Spain.

Heaven, P. C. L., Crocker, D., Edwards, B., Preston, N., Ward, R., and Woodbridge, N. (2003). Personality and sex. *Personality and Individual Differences, 35,* 411–419.

Hebb, D. O. (1955). Drives and the CNS (conceptual nervous system). *Psychological Review, 62,* 243–259.

Heckhausen, H. (1982). The development of achievement motivation. In W. W. Hartup (Ed.), *Review of child development research* (Vol. 6, pp. 600–668). Chicago: University of Chicago Press.

Heidemeier, H., and Göritz, A. S. (2013). Perceived control in low-control circumstances: Control beliefs predict a greater decrease in life satisfaction following job loss. *Journal of Research in Personality, 47,* 52–56.

Heine, S. J., and Lehman, D. R. (1995). Cultural variation in unrealistic optimism: Does the West feel more invulnerable than the East? *Journal of Personality and Social Psychology, 68,* 595–607.

Helson, R., and Picano, J. (1990). Is the traditional role bad for women? *Journal of Personality and Social Psychology, 59,* 311–320.

Helson, R., and Stewart, A. (1994). Personality change in adulthood. In T. F. Heatherton and J. L. Weinberger (Eds.), *Can personality change?* Washington, DC: American Psychological Association.

Helson, R., and Wink, P. (1992). Personality change in women from the early 40s to the early 50s. *Psychology and Aging, 7,* 46–55.

Henderson, L., and Zimbardo, P. (2001a). Shyness as a clinical condition: The Stanford model. In W. R. Crozier and L. E. Alden (Eds.), *International Handbook of Social Anxiety: Concepts, Research and Interventions Relating to the Self and Shyness* (pp. 431–447). New York: Wiley.

Henderson, L., and Zimbardo, P. (2001b). Shyness, social anxiety, and social phobia. In S. G. Hofmann and P. M. DiBartolo (Eds.), *From Social Anxiety to Social Phobia: Multiple Perspectives* (pp. 46–85). Needham Heights, MA: Allyn and Bacon.

Henderson, N. D. (1982). Human behavioral genetics. *Annual Review of Psychology, 33,* 403–440.

Hendriks, A. A. J., Perugini, M., Angleitner, A., Ostendorf, F., Johnson, J. A., De Fruyt, F., Hrebickova, M., et al. (2003). The five-factor personality inventory: Cross-cultural generalizability across 13 countries. *European Journal of Personality, 17,* 347–373.

Hennig, K. H., and Walker, L. J. (2008). The darker side of accommodating others: Examining the interpersonal structure of maladaptive constructs. *Journal of Research in Personality, 42,* 2–21.

Henrich, J. (2015). *The secret of our success: How culture is driving human evolution, domesticating our species, and making us smarter.* Princeton, NJ: Princeton University Press.

Henrich, J., and Muthukrishna, M. (2021). The origins and psychology of human cooperation. *Annual Review of Psychology, 72,* 207–240.

Herbert, T. B., and Cohen, S. (1993). Depression and immunity: A meta-analytic review. *Psychological Bulletin, 113,* 472–486.

Herrnstein, R., and Murray, C. (1994). *The bell curve: Intelligence and class structure in American life.* New York: Free Press.

Herzog, A. R., Franks, X., Markus, H. R., and Holmberg, X. (1995). *The American self in its sociocultural variations.* Unpublished manuscript.

Hess, N., Helfrecht, C., Hagen, E., Sell, A., and Hewlett, B. (2010). Interpersonal aggression among Aka hunter-gatherers of the Central African Republic: Assessing the effects of sex, strength, and anger. *Human Nature, 21,* 330–354.

Hibbard, S., Porcerelli, J., Kamoo, R., Schwartz, M., and Abell, S. (2010). Defense and object relational maturity on Thematic Apperception Test Scales indicate levels of personality organization. *Journal of Personality Assessment, 92,* 241–253.

Higgins, E. T. (1987). Self-discrepancy: A theory relating self to affect. *Psychological Review, 94,* 319–340.

Higgins, E. T. (1996). The "self digest": Self-knowledge serving self-regulatory functions. *Journal of Personality and Social Psychology, 71*, 1062-1083.

Higgins, E. T. (1997). Beyond pleasure and pain. *American Psychologist, 52*, 1280-1300.

Higgins, E. T. (1999). Persons and situations: Unique explanatory principles or variability in general principles? In D. Cervone and Y. Shoda (Eds.), *The Coherence of Personality* (pp. 61-93). New York: Guilford Press.

Higgins, E. T. (2012). Regulatory focus theory. In P. A. M. Van Lange, A. W. Kruglanski, and T. E. Higgins (Eds.), *Handbook of theories of social psychology* (pp. 483-504). Thousand Oaks, CA: Sage.

Hilbig, B. E., Heydasch, T., and Zettler, I. (2014). To boast or not to boast: Testing the humility aspect of the Honesty-Humility factor. *Personality and Individual Differences, 69*, 12-16.

Hill, C. T., Rubin, Z., and Peplau, L. A. (1976). Breakups before marriage: The end of 103 affairs. *Journal of Social Issues, 32*, 147-168.

Hill, P. L., and Roberts, B. W. (2011). The role of adherence in the relationship between conscientiousness and perceived health. *Health Psychology, 30*, 797-804.

Hiroto, D. S., and Seligman, M. E. P. (1975). Generality of learned helplessness in man. *Journal of Personality and Social Psychology, 102*, 311-327.

Hirschfeld, L. A. (1995). Anthropology, psychology, and the meaning of social causality. In D. Sperber, D. Premack, and A. J. Premack (Eds.), *Causal cognition: A multidisciplinary debate* (pp. 313-344). Oxford, England: Clarendon Press.

Hirsh, J. B. (2015). Extraverted populations have lower savings rates. *Personality and Individual Differences, 81*, 162-168.

Hirsh, J. B., and Peterson, J. B. (2009). Extraversion, neuroticism, and the prisoner's dilemma. *Personality and Individual Differences, 46*, 254-256.

Hofer, J., Bond, M. H., and Li, M. (2010). The implicit power motive and sociosexuality in men and women: Pancultural effects of responsibility. *Journal of Personality and Social Psychology, 99*, 380-394.

Hoffman, W., Baumeister, R. F., Forster, G., and Vohs, K. E. (2012). Everyday temptations: An experience sampling study of desire, conflict, and self-control. *Journal of Personality and Social Psychology, 102*, 1318-1335.

Hoffmann, W., Vohs, K. D., and Baumeister, R. F. (2012). What people desire, feel conflicted about, and try to resist in everyday life. *Psychological Science, 23*, 582-588.

Hogan, J., and Holland, B. (2003). Using theory to evaluate personality and job performance relations. *Journal of Applied Psychology, 88*, 100-112.

Hogan, R. (1983). A socioanalytic theory of personality. In M. Page and R. Dienstbier (Eds.), *Nebraska Symposium on motivation, 1982* (pp. 55-89). Lincoln: University of Nebraska Press.

Hogan, R. (2005). In defense of personality measurement: New wine for old whiners. *Human Performance, 18*, 331-341.

Hogan, R., and Chamorro-Premuzic, T. (2015). Personality and career success. In L. Cooper and R. Larsen (Eds.), *Handbook of Personality and Social Psychology: Personality Processes and Individual Differences* (pp. 619-638). Washington, DC, American Psychological Association.

Hogan, R., and Hogan, J. (2002). The Hogan personality inventory. In B. de Raad and M. Perugini (Eds.), *Big Five Assessment* (pp. 329-346). Ashland, OH: Hogrefe & Huber Publishers.

Hokanson, J. E., Burgess, M., and Cohen, M. F. (1963). Effect of displaced aggression on systolic blood pressure. *Journal of Abnormal and Social Psychology, 67*, 214-218.

Holland, A. S., Fraley, R. C., and Roisman, G. I. (2012). Attachment styles in dating couples: Predicting relationship functioning over time. *Personal Relationships, 19*, 234-246.

Hollmann, E. (2001). *Paul Gaugin: Images from the South Seas.* New York: Prestel USA.

Holmes, D. (1990). The evidence for repression: An examination of sixty years of research. In J. Singer (Ed.), *Repression and dissociation: Implications for personality, theory, psychopathology, and health* (pp. 85-102). Chicago: University of Chicago Press.

Holmes, T. H., and Rahe, R. H. (1967). The Social Readjustment Rating scale. *Journal of Psychosomatic Research, 11*, 213-218.

Holroyd, K. A., and Coyne, J. (1987). Personality and health in the 1980s: Psychosomatic medicine revisited? *Journal of Personality, 55*, 359-375.

Holtzman, N. S., and Strube, M. J. (2010). Narcissism and attractiveness. *Journal of Research in Personality, 44*, 133-136.

Honekopp, J. (2011). Relationships between digit ratio 2D:4D and self-reported aggression and risk taking in an online study. *Personality and Individual Differences, 51*, 77-80.

Hong, R. Y., and Paunonen, S. V. (2009). Personality traits and health-risk behaviours in University students. *European Journal of Personality, 23*, 675-696.

Honkalampi, K., Järvelin-Pasanen, S., Tarvain, M. P., Saaranen, T., Vauhkonen, A., Kupari, S., Perkiö-Mäkelä, M., Rasanen, K., and Oksanen, T. (2021). Heart rate variability and chronotype—A systematic review. *Chronobiology International, 38*, 1786-1796.

Honomichl, R. D., and Donnellan, M. B. (2012). Dimensions of temperament in preschoolers predict risk taking and externalizing behaviors in adolescents. *Social Psychological and Personality Science, 3*, 14-22.

Hooper, J. L., White, V. M., Macaskill, G. T., Hill, D. J., and Clifford, C. A. (1992). Alcohol use, smoking habits and the Junior Eysenck Personality Questionnaire in adolescent Australian twins. *Acta Geneticae Medicae et Gemellologiae: Twin Research, 41*, 311-324.

Hooven, C. (2021). *T: The Story of Testosterone, the Hormone that Dominates and Divides Us.* Henry Holt and Company.

Hoover, E. (2013). Colleges seek "noncognitive" gauges of applicants. *The Chronicle of Higher Education, 56*, 1.

Hopwood, C. J., Ansell, E .B., Pincus, A. L., Wright, A. G. C., Lukowitsky, M. R., and Roche, M. J. (2011). The circumplex model of interpersonal sensitivities. *Journal of Personality, 79*, 707-739.

Hormuth, S. E. (1986). The sampling of experiences in situ. *Journal of Personality, 54*, 262-293.

Horne, J. A., and Ostberg, O. (1976). A self-assessment questionnaire to determine morningness-eveningness in human circadian rhythms. *International Journal of Chronobiology, 4*, 97-110.

Horne, J. A., and Ostberg, O. (1977). Individual differences in human circadian rhythms. *Biological Psychology, 5*, 179-190.

Horney, K. (1937). *The neurotic personality of our time.* New York: Norton.

Horney, K. (1939). *New ways in psychoanalysis.* New York: Norton.

Horney, K. (1945). *Our inner conflicts: A constructive theory of neurosis.* New York: Norton.

Horney, K. (1950). *Neurosis and human growth: The struggle toward self-realization.* New York: Norton.

Horton, R. S., and Sedikedes, C. (2009). Narcissistic responding to ego threat: When the status of the evaluator matters. *Journal of Personality, 77*, 1493-1526.

Hotard, S. R., McFatter, R. M., McWhirter, R. M., and Stegall, M. E. (1989). Interactive effects of extraversion, neuroticism, and social relationships on subjective well-being. *Journal of Personality and Social Psychology, 57*, 321-331.

Howard, A., and Bray, D. (1988). *Managerial lives in transition: Advancing age and changing times.* New York: Guilford Press.

Hoyenga, K. B., and Hoyenga, K. T. (1993). *Gender-Related Differences: Origins and Outcomes.* Boston: Allyn and Bacon.

Hsu, F. K. K. (1985). The self in cross-cultural perspective. In J. J. Marsella, G. De Vos, and F. L. K. Hsu (Eds.), *Culture and self* (pp. 24-55). London: Tavistock.

Hua, H., and Epley, C. H. (2012). Putting the "personal" into personal construct theory. *Journal of Constructivist Psychology, 25,* 269–273.

Huan, V. S., Ang, R. P., Chong, W. H., and Chye, S. (2014). The impact of shyness on problematic Internet use: The role of loneliness. *The Journal of Psychology: Interdisciplinary and Applied, 148*(6), 699–715.

Hudson, N. W., and Fraley, R. C. (2015). Volitional personality trait change: Can people choose to change their personality traits? *Journal of Personality and Social Psychology, 109*(3), 490–507.

Hudson, N. W., and Roberts, B. W. (2016). Social investment in work reliably predicts change in conscientiousness and agreeableness: A direct replication and extension of Hudson, Roberts, and Lodi-Smith (2012). *Journal of Research in Personality, 60,* 12–23.

Hudziak, J. J., van Beijsterveldt, C. E. M., Bartels, M., Rietveld, J. J. J., Rettew, D. C., Derks, E. M., and Boomsma, D. I. (2003). Individual differences in aggression: Genetic analyses by age, gender, and informant in 3-, 7-, and 10-year-old Dutch twins. *Behavior Genetics, 33,* 575–589.

Humbad, M. N., Donnellan, M. B., Iacono, W. G., McGue, M., and Burt, S. A. (2010). Is spousal similarity for personality a matter of convergence or selection? *Personality and Individual Differences, 49,* 827–830.

Hunsley, J., Lee, C. M., and Wood, J. M. (2003). Controversial and questionable assessment techniques. In S. O. Lilienfeld, S. J. Lynn, and J. M. Lohr (Eds.), *Science and Pseudoscience in Clinical Psychology* (pp. 39–76). New York: Guilford Press.

Hunt, E., and Wittmann, W. (2008). National intelligence and national prosperity. *Intelligence, 36,* 1–9.

Huprich, S. K. (2008). TAT oral dependency scale. In S. R. Jenkins (Ed.), *A handbook of clinical scoring systems for thematic apperceptive techniques* (pp. 385–398). Mahwah, NJ: Erlbaum.

Huselid, R. F., and Cooper, M. L. (1994). Gender roles as mediators of sex differences in expressions of pathology. *Journal of Abnormal Psychology, 103,* 595–603.

Hyafil, A., and Baumard, N. (2020). Evoked and Transmitted Culture models: Using bayesian methods to infer the evolution of cultural traits in history.

Hyatt, C. S., Sharpe, B. M., Owens, M. M., Listyg, B. S., Carter, N. T., Lynam, D. R., and Miller, J. D. (2021). Searching high and low for meaningful and replicable morphometric correlates of personality. *Journal of Personality and Social*

Psychology. https://doi.org/10.1037/pspp0000402

Hyde, J. S. (1986). Gender differences in aggression. In J. S. Hyde and M. C. Linn (Eds.), *The psychology of gender: Advances through meta-analysis.* Baltimore: Johns Hopkins University Press.

Hyde, J. S. (2005). The gender similarities hypothesis. *American Psychologist, 60,* 581–592.

Hyde, J. S. (2014). Gender similarities and differences. *Annual Review of Psychology, 65,* 373–398.

Hyde, J. S., and Kling, K. C. (2001). Women, motivation, and achievement. *Psychology of Women Quarterly, 25,* 364–378.

Hyde, J. S., and Mezulis, A. H. (2020). Gender differences in depression: biological, affective, cognitive, and sociocultural factors. *Harvard review of psychiatry, 28*(1), 4–13.

Hyde, J. S., and Plant, E. A. (1995). Magnitude of psychological gender differences: Another side to the story. *American Psychologist, 50,* 159–161.

Hyman, I. E., and Loftus, E. F. (2002). False childhood memories and eyewitness memory errors. In M. L. Eisen (Ed.), *Memory and suggestibility in the forensic interview* (pp. 63–84). Mahwah, NJ: Erlbaum.

Ickes, W., Snyder, M., and Garcia, S. (1997). Personality influences on the choice of situations. In R. Hogan, J. A. Johnson, and S. Briggs (Eds.), *Handbook of Personality Psychology* (pp. 165–195). San Diego: Academic Press.

Ihsan, Z., and Furnham, A. (2018). The new technologies in personality assessment: A review. *Consulting Psychology Journal: Practice and Research, 70,* 146–166.

Immelman, A. (2002). The political personality of U.S. president George W. Bush. In L. O. Valenty and O. Feldman (Eds.), *Political leadership for the new century: Personality and behavior among American leaders* (pp. 81–103). Westport, CT: Praeger.

Inglehart, R. (1990). *Culture Shift in Advanced Industrial Society.* Princeton, NJ: Princeton University Press.

Insel, P., and Roth, W. (1985). *Core concepts in health* (4th ed.). Palo Alto, CA: Mayfield.

Ip, G. W. M., and Bond, M. H. (1995). Culture, values, and the spontaneous self-concept. *Asian Journal of Psychology, 1,* 30–36.

Irwin, M. (2002). Psychoneuroimmunology of depression: Clinical implications. *Brain, Behavior, and Immunity, 16,* 1–16.

Ishihara, K., Miyake, S., Miyasita, A., and Miyata, Y. (1992). Morningness-eveningness preference and sleep habits in Japanese office workers of different ages. *Chronobiologia, 19,* 9–16.

Ishihara, K., Saitoh, T., and Miyata, Y. (1983). Short-term adjustment of oral temperature of 8-hour advanced-shift. *Japanese Psychological Research, 25,* 228–232.

Ishikawa, S. S., Raine, A., Lencz, T., Bihrle, S., and LaCasse, L. (2001). Increased height and bulk in antisocial personality disorder and its subtypes. *Psychiatry Research, 105,* 211–219.

Izard, C. E. (1977). *Human Emotions.* New York: Plenum Press.

Izuma, K., Kennedy, K., Fitzjohn, A., Sedikides, C., and Shibata, K. (2018). Neural activity in the reward-related brain regions predicts implicit self-esteem: A novel validity test of psychological measures using neuroimaging. *Journal of Personality and Social Psychology, 114,* 343–357.

Jackson, D. N. (1967). *Personality research form manual.* Goshen, NY: Research Psychologists Press.

Jackson, D. N., and Messick, S. (1967). *Problems in Human Assessment.* New York, McGraw-Hill.

Jackson, J. J., and Hill, P. L. (2019). Lifespan development of conscientiousness. In D. P. McAdams, R. L. Shiner, and J. L. Tackett (Eds.), *Handbook of personality development.* (pp. 153–170). New York: Guilford Press.

Jackson, J. J., Bogg, T., Walton, K. E., Wood, D., Harms, P. D., Lodi-Smith, J., Edmonds, G. W., and Roberts, B. W. (2009). Not all conscientiousness scales change alike: A multimethod, multisample study of age differences in the facets of conscientiousness. *Journal of Personality and Social Psychology, 96,* 446–459.

Jackson, J. J., Wood, D., Bogg, T., Walton, K. E., Harms, P. D., and Roberts, B. W. (2010). What do conscientious people do? Development and validation of the Behavioral Indicators of Conscientiousness (BIC). *Journal of Research in Personality, 44,* 501–511.

Jacoby, R., and Glauberman, N. (1995). *The bell curve debate: History, documents, opinions.* New York: Random House.

James, W. (1884). What is an emotion? *Mind, 9,* 188–205.

Jang, K. L., Dick, D. M., Wolf, H., Livesley, W. J., and Paris, J. (2005). Psychosocial adversity and emotional instability: An application of gene–environment interaction models. *European Journal of Personality, 19,* 359–372.

Jang, K. L., Livesley, W. J., Angleitner, A., Riemann, R., and Vernon, P. A. (2002). Genetic and environmental influences on the covariance of facets defining the domains of the five-factor model of personality. *Personality and Individual Differences, 33,* 83–101.

Jarnecke, A. M., and South, S. C. (2017). Behavior and molecular genetics of the Five Factor Model. In T. A. Widiger (Ed.), *The Oxford handbook of the Five Factor Model* (pp. 301–317). New York: Oxford University Press.

Jauk, E., Breyer, D., Kanske, P., and Wakabayashi, A. (2021). Narcissism in independent and interdependent cultures. *Personality and Individual Differences, 177,* 110716.

Jenkins, C. D., Zyzanski, S. J., and Rosenman, R. H. (1976). Risk of new myocardial infarction in middle age men with manifest coronary heart disease. *Circulation, 53,* 342–347.

Jenkins, S. R. (1994). Need for power and women's careers over 14 years: Structural power, job satisfaction, and motive change. *Journal of Personality and Social Psychology, 66,* 155–165.

Jensen, A. R. (2011). The theory of intelligence and its measurement. *Intelligence, 39,* 171–177.

Jensen-Campbell, L. A., Adams, R., Perry, D. G., Workman, K. A., Furdella, J. Q., and Egan, S. K. (2002). Agreeableness, extraversion, and peer relations in early adolescence: Winning friends and deflecting aggression. *Journal of Research in Personality, 36,* 224–251.

Jensen-Campbell, L. A., and Graziano, W. G. (2001). Agreeableness as a moderator of interpersonal conflict. *Journal of Personality, 69,* 323–362.

Jensen-Campbell, L. A., Gleason, K. A., Adams, R., and Malcolm, K. T. (2003). Interpersonal conflict, agreeableness, and personality development. *Journal of Personality, 71,* 1059–1085.

Jeronimus, B. F., Riese, H., Sanderman, R., and Ormel, J. (2014). Mutual reinforcement between neuroticism and life experiences: A five-wave, 16-year study to test reciprocal causation. *Journal of Personality and Social Psychology, 107,* 751–764.

Jerskey, B. A., Panizzon, M. S., Jacobson, K. C., Neale, M. C., Grant, M. D., Schultz, M., Eisen, S., et al. (2010). Marriage and divorce: A genetic perspective. *Personality and Individual Differences, 49,* 473–478.

John, O. P. (1990). The "Big Five" factor taxonomy: Dimensions of personality in the natural language and questionnaires. In L. A. Pervin (Ed.), *Handbook of personality* (pp. 66–100). New York: Guilford Press.

John, O. P., and Naumann, L. P. (2010). Surviving two critiques by Block? The resilient big five have emerged as the paradigm for personality trait psychology. *Psychological Inquiry, 21*(1), 44–49. Chicago.

Johnson, D. P., and Whisman, M. A. (2013). Gender differences in rumination: A meta-analysis. *Personality and Individual Differences, 55*(4), 367–374.

Johnson, M. K., Rowatt, W. C., and Petrini, L. (2011). A new trait on the market: Honesty-humility as a unique predictor of job performance. *Personality and Individual Differences, 50,* 857–862.

Johnson, R. E. (1970). Some correlates of extramarital coitus. *Journal of Marriage and the Family, 32,* 449–456.

Johnson, W. (2007). Genetic and environmental influences on behavior: Capturing all the interplay. *Psychological Review, 114,* 423–440.

Johnson, W., and Deary, I. J. (2011). Placing inspection time, reaction time, and perceptual speed in the broader context of cognitive ability: The VPR model in the Lothian Birth Cohort 1936, *Intelligence, 39,* 405–417.

Johnson, W., Hicks, B. M., McGue, M., and Iacono, W. G. (2007). Most of the girls are alright, but some aren't: Personality trajectory groups from ages 14–24 and some associations with outcomes. *Journal of Personality and Social Psychology, 93,* 266–284.

Johnson, W., McGue, M., and Krueger, R. F. (2005). Personality stability in late adulthood: A behavior genetic analysis. *Journal of Personality, 73,* 523–551.

Johnson, W., McGue, M., Krueger, R. F., and Bouchard, T. J., Jr. (2004). Marriage and personality: A genetic analysis. *Journal of Personality and Social Psychology, 86,* 285–294.

Johnson, W., Penke, L., and Spinath, F. M. (2011). Heritability in the era of molecular genetics: Some thoughts for understanding genetic influences on behavioural traits: Understanding heritability. *European Journal of Personality, 25,* 254–266.

Johnston, M. (1999). *Spectral evidence: The Ramona case: Incest, memory, and truth on trial in Napa Valley.* Boulder, CO: Westview Press.

Jokela, M. (2009). Personality predicts migration within and between U.S. states. *Journal of Research in Personality, 43,* 79–83.

Jokela, M., Airaksinen, J., Virtanen, M., Batty, G. D., Kivimäki, M., and Hakulinen, C. (2019). Personality, disability-free life years, and life expectancy: Individual-participant meta-analysis of 131,195 individuals from 10 cohort studies. *Journal of Personality.*

Jonason, P. K. (2018). Bright lights, big city: The Dark Triad traits and geographical preferences. *Personality and Individual Differences, 132,* 66–73.

Jonason, P. K., and Webster, G. D. (2012). A protean approach to social influence: Dark Triad personalities and social influence tactics. *Personality and Individual Differences, 52,* 521–526.

Jonason, P. K., Garcia, J. R., Webster, G. D., Li, N. P., and Fisher, H. E. (2015). Relationship deal breakers traits people avoid in potential mates. *Personality and Social Psychology Bulletin, 41*(12), 1697–1711.

Jonason, P. K., Girgis, M., and Milne-Home, J. (2017). The exploitive mating strategy of the Dark Triad traits: Tests of rape-enabling attitudes. *Archives of Sexual Behavior, 46*(3), 697–706.

Jones, A., and Crandall, R. (1986). Validation of a short index of self-actualization. *Personality and Social Psychology Bulletin, 12,* 63–73.

Jones, D. N., and Paulhus, D. L. (2010). Different provocations trigger aggression in narcissists and psychopaths. *Social Psychological and Personality Science, 1,* 12–18.

Jones, D. N., and Weiser, D. A. (2014). Differential infidelity patterns among the Dark Triad. *Personality and Individual Differences, 57,* 20–24.

Jordan, C. H., Spencer, S. J., Zanna, M. P., Hoshino-Browne, E., and Correll, J. (2003). Secure and defensive high self-esteem. *Journal of Personality and Social Psychology, 85,* 969–978.

Judge, D. S., and Hrdy, S. B. (1992). Allocation of accumulated resources among close kin: Inheritance in Sacramento, California, 1890–1984. *Ethology and Sociobiology, 13*(5), 495–522.

Judge, T., and Larsen, R. J. (2001). Dispositional sources of job satisfaction: A review and theoretical extension. *Organizational Behavior and Human Decision Processes, 86,* 67–98.

Jung, I., Lee, H., and Cho, B. (2004). Persistent psychotic disorder in an adolescent with a past history of butane gas dependence. *European Psychiatry, 19,* 519–520.

Jusepeitis, A. and Rothermund, K. (2022). No elephant in the room: The incremental validity of implicit self-esteem measures. *Journal of Personality,* http://dx.doi.org/10.1111/jopy.12705.

Jussim, L., Stevens, S. T., and Honeycutt, N. (2021). 16 The Accuracy of Stereotypes About Personality. *The Oxford Handbook of Accurate Personality Judgment,* 245.

Kagan, J. (1981). *The Second Year: The Emergence of Self-Awareness.* Cambridge, MA: Harvard University Press.

Kagan, J. (1994). *Galen's Prophecy: Temperament in Human Nature.* New York: Basic Books.

Kagan, J. (1999). Born to be shy? In R. Conlan (Ed.), *States of Mind* (pp. 29–51). New York: Wiley.

Kagan, J., and Moss, H. (1962). *Birth to maturity: A study in psychological development.* New York: Wiley.

Kagan, J., and Snidman, N. (1991). Infant predictors of inhibited and uninhibited profiles. *Psychological Science, 2,* 40–44.

Kaiser, T. (2019). Nature and evoked culture: Sex differences in personality are uniquely correlated with ecological stress. *Personality and Individual Differences, 148,* 67–72.

Kaiser, T., Del Giudice, M., and Booth, T. (2020). Global sex differences in personality: Replication with an open online dataset. *Journal of Personality, 88*(3), 415–429.

Kajonius, P. J., and Johnson, J. (2018). Sex differences in 30 facets of the five factor model of personality in the large public (N = 320,128). *Personality and Individual Differences, 129,* 126–130.

Kamakura, T., Ando, J., and Ono, Y. (2007). Genetic and environmental effects on the stability and change in self-esteem during adolescence. *Personality and Individual Differences, 42,* 181–190.

Kamble, S., Shackelford, T. K., Pham, M., and Buss, D. M. (2014). Indian mate preferences: Continuity, sex differences, and cultural change across a quarter of a century. *Personality and Individual Differences, 70,* 150–155.

Kammrath, L. K., and Scholer, A. A. (2011). The Pollyanna myth: How highly agreeable people judge positive and negative relational acts. *Personality and Social Psychology Bulletin, 37,* 1172–1184.

Kandler, C., Bleidorn, W., Spinath, F. M., and Riemann, R. (2010). Sources of cumulative continuity in personality: A longitudinal multiple-rater twin study. *Journal of Personality and Social Psychology, 98,* 995–1008.

Kaplan, H., and Hill, K. (1985). Food-sharing among Ache foragers: Tests of evolutionary hypotheses. *Current Anthropology, 26,* 223–246.

Kapogiannis, D., Sutin, A., Davatzikos, C., Costa, P. J., and Resnick, S. (2013). The five factors of personality and regional cortical variability in the Baltimore longitudinal study of aging. *Human Brain Mapping, 34*(11), 2829–2840.

Karantzas, G. C., and Simpson, J. A. (2015). Attachment and aged care. In J. A. Simpson and W. S. Rholes (Eds.), *Attachment theory and research: New directions and emerging themes* (pp. 319–345). New York: Guilford Press.

Katigbak, M. S., Church, A. T., Guanzon-Lapena, M. A., Carlota, A. J., and del Pilar, G. H. (2002). Are indigenous personality dimensions culture-specific? Philippine inventories and the five-factor model. *Journal of Personality and Social Psychology, 82*(1), 89–101.

Katz, I. M., and Campbell, J. D. (1994). Ambivalence over emotional expression and well-being: Nomothetic and idiographic tests of the stress-buffering hypothesis. *Journal of Personality and Social Psychology, 67,* 513–524.

Kaufman, S. B., Quilty, L. C., Grazioplene, R. G., Hirsh, J. B., Gray, J. R., Peterson, J. B., and DeYoung, C. G. (2016). Openness to experience and intellect differentially predict creative achievement in the arts and sciences. *Journal of Personality, 82,* 248–258.

Kavanagh, K., and Hops, H. (1994). Good girls? Bad boys? Gender and development as contexts for diagnosis and treatment. *Advances in Clinical Child Psychology, 16,* 45–79.

Kawamoto, T. (2016). Cross-sectional age differences in the HEXACO personality: Results from a Japanese sample. *Journal of Research in Personality, 62,* 1–5.

Keiser, H. N., Sackett, P. R., Kuncel, N. R., and Brothen, T. (2016). Why women perform better in college than admission scores would predict: Exploring the roles of conscientiousness and course-taking patterns. *Journal of Applied Psychology, 101,* 569–581.

Kelley, H. H. (1992). Common-sense psychology and scientific psychology. In M. R. Rosensweig and L. W. Porter (Eds.), *Annual review of psychology* (Vol. 43, pp. 1–23). Palo Alto, CA: Annual Reviews.

Kelly, E. L., and Conley, J. J. (1987). Personality and compatibility: A prospective analysis of marital stability and marital satisfaction. *Journal of Personality and Social Psychology, 52,* 27–40.

Kelly, G. A. (1955). *The psychology of personal constructs* (vols. 1 and 2). London: Routledge.

Keltikangas-Järvinen, L., Elovainio, M., Kivimäki, M., Lichtermann, D., Ekelund, J., and Leena Peltonen, L. (2003). Association between the Type 4 dopamine receptor gene polymorphism and novelty seeking. *Psychosomatic Medicine, 65,* 471–476.

Kendler, K. S., McGuire, M., Gruenberg, A. M., O'Hare, A., Spellman, M., and Walsh, D. (1993). The Roscommon Family Study III: Schizophrenia-related personality disorders in relatives. *Archives of General Psychiatry, 50,* 781–788.

Kendler, R. S., Heath, A. C., Neale, M. C., Kessler, R. C., and Eaves, L. J. (1992). A population-based twin study of alcoholism in women. *Journal of the American Medical Association, 268,* 1877–1882.

Kenrick, D. T., Griskevicius, V., Neuberg, S. L., and Schaller, M. (2010). Renovating the pyramid of needs: Contemporary extensions built upon ancient foundations. *Perspectives on Psychological Science, 5,* 292–314.

Kerkhof, G. A. (1985). Inter-individual differences in the human circadian system: A review. *Biological Psychology, 20,* 83–112.

Kernberg, O. (1975). *Borderline conditions and pathological narcissism.* New York: Jason Aronson.

Kernberg, O. F. (1984). *Severe personality disorders.* New Haven, CT: Yale University Press.

Kernis, M. H. (2006) *Self-Esteem Issues and Answers: A Sourcebook of Current Perspectives.* New York: Psychology Press.

Kernis, M. H. (2006). Measuring self-esteem in context: The importance of stability of self-esteem in psychological functioning. *Journal of Personality, 73,* 1569–1605.

Kernis, M. H. and Lakey, C. E. (2008). Secure versus fragile high self-esteem as a predictor of verbal defensiveness: Converging findings across three different markers. *Journal of Personality, 76,* 477–512.

Kernis, M. H., Grannemann, B. D., and Barclay, L. C. (1992). Stability of self-esteem: Assessment, correlates, and excuse making. *Journal of Personality, 60,* 621–643.

Kernis, M. H., Grannemann, B. D., and Mathis, L. C. (1991). Stability of self-esteem as a moderator of the relation between level of self-esteem and depression. *Journal of Personality and Social Psychology, 61,* 80–84.

Kesebir, S., Graham, J., and Oishi, S. (2010). A theory of human needs should be human-centered, not animal-centered: Commentary on Kenrick et al. (2010). *Perspectives on Psychological Science, 5,* 315–319.

Ketelaar, T. (1995). *Emotion as mental representations of fitness affordances: I. Evidence supporting the claim that the negative and positive emotions map onto fitness costs and benefits.* Paper presented at the annual meeting of the Human Behavior and Evolution Society, Santa Barbara.

Khan, S. S., Nessim, S., Gray, R., Czer, L. S., Chaux, A., and Matloff, J. (1990). Increased mortality of women in coronary artery bypass surgery: Evidence for referral bias. *Annals of Internal Medicine, 112,* 561–567.

Kihlstrom, J. F. (1999). The psychological unconscious. In L. A. Pervin and O. P. John (Eds.), *Handbook of personality: Theory and research* (pp. 424–442). New York: Guilford Press.

Kihlstrom, J. F. (2003b). Hypnosis and memory. In J. F. Byrne (Ed.), *Learning and memory* (2nd ed., pp. 240–242). Farmington Hills, MI: Macmillan.

Kihlstrom, J. F. (2013). The person-situation interaction. In D. E. Carlston (Ed.), *The Oxford Handbook of Social Cognition* (pp. 786–805). New York: Oxford University Press.

Kihlstrom, J. F., Barnhardt, T. M., and Tataryn, D. J. (1992). The psychological unconscious: Found, lost, and regained. *American Psychologist, 47,* 788–791.

Kim, E. (2002). Agitation, aggression, and disinhibition syndromes after traumatic brain injury. *NeuroRehabilitation, 17,* 297-310.

Kim, K., Smith, P. K., and Palermiti, A. (1997). Conflict in childhood and reproductive development. *Evolution and Human Behavior, 18,* 109-142.

Kim, T. D., Luo, T. Z., Pillow, J. W., and Brody, C. D. (2021, July). Inferring latent dynamics underlying neural population activity via neural differential equations. In International Conference on Machine Learning (pp. 5551-5561). PMLR.

Kim-Cohen, J., Caspi, A., Taylor, A., Williams, B., Newcombe, R., Craig, I. W., et al. (2006). MAOA, maltreatment, and gene-environment interaction predicting children's mental health: New evidence and a meta-analysis. *Molecular Psychiatry, 11,* 903-913.

Kimura, D. (2002). Sex hormones influence human cognitive pattern. *Neuroendocrinology Letters, 23*(Suppl. 4), 67-77.

King, L. A. (1995). Wishes, motives, goals, and personal memories: Relations and correlates of measures of human motivation. *Journal of Personality, 63,* 985-1007.

King, L. A., and Emmons, R. A. (1990). Conflict over emotional expression: Psychological and physical correlates. *Journal of Personality and Social Psychology, 58,* 864-877.

King, L. A., and Hicks, J. A. (2012). Positive affect and meaning in life: The intersection of hedonism and eudaimonia. In P. T. P. Wong (Ed.), *The Human Quest for Meaning: Theories, Research and Applications* (2nd ed., pp. 125-141). New York: Routledge/Taylor & Francis Group.

Kintz, B. L., Delprato, D. J., Mettee, D. R., Parsons, D. E., and Schappe, R. H. (1965). The experimenter effect. *Psychological Bulletin, 63,* 223-232.

Kipnis, D. (1971). *Character structure and impulsiveness.* New York: Academic Press.

Kirkpatrick, L. A. (2005). *Attachment, evolution, and the psychology of religion.* New York: Guilford Press.

Kjærgaard, A., Leon, G. R., and Venables, N. C. (2015). The 'right stuff' for a solo sailboat circumnavigation of the globe. *Environment and Behavior, 47*(10), 1147-1171.

Kletenik, I., et al. (2022). Network localization of unconscious visual perception in blindsight. *Annals of Neurology, 91,* 217-224.

Kling, K. C., Hyde, J. S., Showers, C. J., and Buswell, B. N. (1999). Gender differences in self-esteem: A meta-analysis. *Psychological Bulletin, 125,* 470-500.

Kling, K. C., Noftle, E. E., and Robins, R. W. (2013). Why do standardized tests underpredict women's academic performance? The role of conscientiousness. *Social Psychological and Personality Science, 4,* 600-606.

Klinger, E. (1977a). The nature of fantasy and its clinical uses. *Psychotherapy: Theory, Research, and Practice, 14,* 223-231.

Klinger, E. (1977b). *Meaning and void: Inner experience and the incentives in people's lives.* Minneapolis: University of Minnesota Press.

Klucken, T., Kruse, O., Schweckendiek, J., and Stark, R. (2015). Increased skin conductance responses and neural activity during fear conditioning are associated with a repressive coping style. *Frontiers in Behavioral Neuroscience, 9.*

Knafo, A., Iervolino, A. C., and Plomin, R. (2005). Masculine girls and feminine boys: Genetic and environmental contributions to atypical gender development in early childhood. *Journal of Personality and Social Psychology, 88,* 400-412.

Knopik, V. S., Neiderhiser, J. M., DeFries, J. C., and Plomin, R. (2022). *Behavioral Genetics,* 7th ed. Worth Publishers, Macmillan Learning.

Knutson, B., and Bhanji, J. (2006). Neural substrates for emotional traits? In T. Canli (Ed.), *Biology of personality and individual differences* (pp. 116-132). New York: Guilford Press.

Knutson, B., Wolkowitz, O. M., Cole, S. W., Chan, T., Moore, E. A., Johnson, R. C., Terpestra, J., et al. (1998). Selective alteration of personality and social behavior by serotonergic intervention. *American Journal of Psychiatry, 155,* 373-378.

Koenig, L. B., McGue, M., Krueger, R. F., and Bouchard, T. J., Jr. (2005). Genetic and environmental influences on religiousness ratings. *Journal of Personality, 73,* 471-488.

Koestner, R., and McClelland, D. C. (1990). Perspectives on competence motivation. In L. A. Pervin (Ed.), *Handbook of Personality: Theory and Research* (pp. 527-548). New York: Guilford Press.

Kofman, S. (1985). *The enigma of woman: Woman in Freud's writings.* Ithaca, NY: Cornell University Press.

Kohn, M. L., Naoi, A., Schoenbach, C., Schooler, C., and Slomczynski, K. M. (1990). Position in the class structure and psychological functioning in the United States, Japan, and Poland. *American Journal of Sociology, 95,* 964-1008.

Kohut, H. (1977). *The restoration of the self.* Madison, CT: International Universities Press.

Koole, S. L., Jager, W., van den Berg, A. E., Vlek, C. A. J., and Hofstee, W. K. B. (2001). On the social nature of personality: Effects of extraversion, agreeableness, and feedback about collective resource use on cooperation in a resource dilemma. *Personality and Social Psychology Bulletin, 27*(3), 289-301.

Koopmans, J. R., and Boomsma, D. I. (1993). Bivariate genetic analysis of the relation between alcohol and tobacco use in adolescent twins. *Psychiatric Genetics, 3,* 172.

Kopp, C. B. (1989). Regulation of distress and negative emotions: A developmental view. *Developmental Psychology, 25,* 343-354.

Kosslyn, S. M., and Rosenberg, R. S. (2004). *Psychology: The brain, the person, the world.* Boston: Allyn and Bacon.

Kosslyn, S. M., Cacioppo, J. T., Davidson, R. J., Hugdahl, K., Lovallo, W. R., Spiegel, D., and Rose, R. (2002). Bridging psychology and biology: The analysis of individuals in groups. *American Psychologist, 57,* 341-351.

Kotov, R., Gamez, W., Schmidt, F., and Watson, D. (2010). Linking "big" personality traits to anxiety, depressive, and substance use disorders: A meta-analysis. *Psychological Bulletin, 136,* 768-821.

Kotter-Gruhn, D., Wiest, M., Zurek, P. P., and Scheibe, S. (2009). What is it we are longing for? Psychological and demographic factors influencing the contents of Sehnsucht (life longings). *Journal of Research in Personality, 43,* 428-437.

Kowalski, R. M., and Brown, K. J. (1994). Psychosocial barriers to cervical cancer screening: Concerns with self-presentation and social evaluation. *Journal of Applied Social Psychology, 24,* 941-958.

Kraeplin, E. (1913). *Psychiatrie: Ein Lehrbuch* (8th ed.). Leipzig: Barth.

Krampe, H., Danbolt, L. J., Haver, A., Stålsett, G., and Schnell, T. (2021). Locus of control moderates the association of COVID-19 stress and general mental distress: Results of a Norwegian and a German-speaking cross-sectional survey. *BMC Psychiatry, 21,* Sep 6, 2021. ArtID: 437.

Krasno, J. (2015). William Jefferson Clinton: Promise, persistence, and the will to be adored. In J. Krasno, S. LaPides, J. Krasno, S. LaPides (Eds.), *Personality, political leadership, and decision making: A global perspective* (pp. 295-318). Santa Barbara, CA, US: Praeger/ABC-CLIO.

Kretschmer, E. (1925). *Physique and character.* London: Kegan Paul.

Kreuzer, M., and Gollwitzer, M. (2021). Neuroticism and satisfaction in romantic relationships: A systematic investigation of intra-and interpersonal processes with a longitudinal approach. European Journal of Personality, 08902070211001258.

Kroencke, L., Geukes, K., Utesch, T., Kuper, N., and Back, M. D. (2020). Neuroticism and emotional risk during the COVID-19 pandemic. *Journal of Research in Personality, 89.* https://doi-org.libproxy.wustl.edu/10.1016/j.jrp.2020.104038.

Krueger, J. I., Hasman, J. F., Acevedo, M., and Villano, P. (2003). Perceptions of trait typicality in gender stereotypes: Examining the role of attribution and categorization processes. *Personality and Social Psychology Bulletin, 29*(1), 108-116.

Krueger, R. F., and Markon, K. E. (2006). Reinterpreting comorbidity: A model-based approach to understanding and classifying psychopathology. *Annual Review of Clinical Psychology, 2,* 111-133.

Krueger, R. F., Markon, K. E., and Bouchard, T. J., Jr. (2003). The extended genotype: The heritability of personality accounts for the heritability of recalled family environments in twins reared apart. *Journal of Personality, 71*(5), 809-834.

Krueger, R. F., South, S., Johnson, W., and Iacono, W. (2008). The heritability of personality is not always 50%: Gene-environment interactions and correlations between personality and parenting. *Journal of Personality, 76,* 1485-1522.

Krug, S. (1981). Interpreting 16 PF profile patterns. Institute of Personality and Ability Testing, Champaign, IL.

Krupnik, R., Yovel, Y., and Assaf, Y (2021). Inner hemispheric and interhemispheric connectivity balance in the human brain. *The Journal of Neuroscience, 41,* 8351-8361.

Kuhl, J., and Kazén, M. (2008). Motivation, affect, and hemispheric asymmetry: Power versus affiliation. *Journal of Personality and Social Psychology, 95,* 456-469.

Kuhle, B. X. (2011). Did you have sex with him? Do you love her? An in vivo test of sex differences in jealous interrogations. *Personality and Individual Differences, 51,* 1044-1047.

Kuhle, B. X., Smedley, K. D., and Schmitt, D. P. (2009). Sex differences in the motivation and mitigation of jealousy-induced interrogations. *Personality and Individual Differences, 46,* 499-502.

Kurman, J. (2001). Self-enhancement: Is it restricted to individualistic cultures? *Personality and Social Psychology Bulletin, 27*(12), 1705-1716.

Kushlev, K., Dunn, E. W., and Lucas, R. E. (2015). Higher income is associated with less daily sadness but not more daily happiness. *Social Psychological and Personality Science, 6,* 483-489.

Kushlev, K., Radosic, N., and Diener, E. (2021). Subjective Well-Being and Prosociality Around the Globe: Happy People Give More of Their Time and Money to Others. *Social Psychological and Personality Science.* https://doi.org/10.1177/19485506211043379

Kvam, S., Kleppe, C. L., Nordhus, I. H., and Hovland, A. (2016). Exercise as a treatment for depression: A meta-analysis. *Journal of Affective Disorders, 202,* 57-86.

Kwapil, T. R., Wrobel, M. J., and Pope, C. A. (2002). The five-factor personality structure of dissociative experiences. *Personality and Individual Differences, 32,* 431-443.

Kwon, P., Campbell, D. G., and Williams, M. G. (2001). Sociotropy and autonomy: Preliminary evidence for construct validity using TAT narratives. *Journal of Personality Assessment Special Issue: More data on the current Rorschach controversy, 77,* 128-138.

Kyl-Heku, L., and Buss, D. M. (1996). Tactics as units of analysis in and personality psychology: An illustration using tactics of hierarchy negotiation. *Personality and Individual Differences, 21,* 497-517.

Lajunen, T. (2001). Personality and accident liability: Are extraversion, neuroticism and psychoticism related to traffic and occupational fatalities? *Personality and Individual Differences, 31,* 1365-1373.

Lalumiere, M. L., Chalmers, L. J., Quinsey, V. L., and Seto, M. C. (1996). A test of the mate deprivation hypothesis of sexual coercion. *Ethology and Sociobiology, 17,* 299-318.

Lalumiere, M. L., Harris, G. T., and Rice, M. E. (2001). Psychopathy and developmental instability. *Evolution and Human Behavior, 22,* 75-92.

Lamarche, V. M., and Seery, M. D. (2019). Come on, give it to me baby: Self-esteem, narcissism, and endorsing sexual coercion following social rejection. *Personality and Individual Differences, 149,* 315-325.

Langens, T. A. (2001). Predicting behavior change in Indian businessmen from a combination of need for achievement and self-discrepancy. *Journal of Research in Personality, 35,* 339-352.

Langevin, R., Bain, J., Wortzman, G., and Hucker, S. (1988). Sexual sadism: Brain, blood, and behavior. *Annals of the New York Academy of Science, 528,* 163-171.

Langford, P. H. (2003). A one-minute measure of the Big Five? Evaluating and abridging Shafer's (1999) Big Five markers. *Personality and Individual Differences, 35,* 1127-1140.

Langner, C. A., and Winter, D. G. (2001). The motivational basis of concessions and compromise: Archival and laboratory studies. *Journal of Personality and Social Psychology, 81,* 711-727.

Lanning, K. (1994). Dimensionality of observer ratings on the California Adult Q-set. *Journal of Personality and Social Psychology, 67*(1), 151.

Larrance, D., Pavelich, S., Storer, P., Polizzi, M., Baron, B., Sloan, S., Jordan, R., and

Reis, H. T. (1979). Competence and incompetence: Asymmetric responses to women and men on a sex-linked task. *Personality and Social Psychology Bulletin, 5, 363-366.*

Larsen, R. J. (1985). Individual differences in circadian activity rhythm and personality. *Personality and Individual Differences, 6, 305-311.*

Larsen, R. J. (1987). The stability of mood variability: A spectral analytic approach to daily mood assessments. *Journal of Personality and Social Psychology, 52,* 1195-1204.

Larsen, R. J. (1989). A process approach to personality: Utilizing time as a facet of data. In D. Buss and N. Cantor (Eds.), *Personality psychology: Recent trends and emerging directions* (pp. 177-193). New York: Springer-Verlag.

Larsen, R. J. (1992). Neuroticism and selective encoding and recall of symptoms: Evidence from a combined concurrent-retrospective study. *Journal of Personality and Social Psychology, 62,* 480-488.

Larsen, R. J. (2000a). Toward a science of mood regulation. *Psychological Inquiry, 11,* 129-141.

Larsen, R. J. (2000b). Maintaining hedonic balance. *Psychological Inquiry, 11,* 218-225.

Larsen, R. J. (2009). Affect intensity. In M. R. Leary and R. H. Hoyle (Eds.), *Handbook of Individual Differences in Social Behaviors* (pp. 241-254). New York: Guilford Press.

Larsen, R. J., and Cowan, G. S. (1988). Internal focus of attention and depression: A study of daily experience. *Motivation and Emotion, 12,* 237-249.

Larsen, R. J., and Diener, E. (1985). A multi-trait-multimethod examination of affect structure: Hedonic level and emotional intensity. *Personality and Individual Differences, 6,* 631-636.

Larsen, R. J., and Diener, E. (1987). Affect intensity as an individual difference characteristic: A review. *Journal of Research in Personality, 21,* 1-39.

Larsen, R. J., and Diener, E. (1992). Problems and promises with the circumplex model of emotion. *Review of Personality and Social Psychology, 13,* 25-59.

Larsen, R. J., and Fredrickson, B. L. (1999). Measurement issues in emotion research. In D. Kahneman, E. Diener, and N. Schwarz (Eds.), *Understanding Quality of Life: Scientific Perspectives on Enjoyment and Suffering* (pp. 40-60). New York: Sage.

Larsen, R. J., and Kasimatis, M. (1990). Individual differences in entrainment of mood to the weekly calendar. *Journal of Personality and Social Psychology, 58,* 164-171.

Larsen, R. J., and Ketelaar, T. (1989). Extraversion, neuroticism, and susceptibility to positive and negative mood induction procedures. *Personality and Individual Differences, 10,* 1221–1228.

Larsen, R. J., and Ketelaar, T. (1991). Personality and susceptibility to positive and negative emotional states. *Journal of Personality and Social Psychology, 61,* 132–140.

Larsen, R. J., and Prizmic, Z. (2004). Affect regulation. In R. Baumeister and K. Vohs (Eds.), *Handbook of Self-Regulation Research* (pp. 40–60). New York: Guilford Press.

Larsen, R. J., and Prizmic, Z. (2006). Multimethod measurement of emotion. In M. Eid and E. Diener (Eds.), *Handbook of Measurement: A Multimethod Perspective* (pp. 337–352). Washington, DC: American Psychological Association.

Larsen, R. J., and Prizmic-Larsen, Z. (1999). Marrying a culture when you marry a person. *Contemporary Psychology, 44,* 538–540.

Larsen, R. J., and Zarate, M. A. (1991). Extending reducer/augmenter theory into the emotion domain: The role of affect in regulating stimulation level. *Personality and Individual Differences, 12,* 713–723.

Larsen, R. J., Billings, D., and Cutler, S. (1996). Affect intensity and individual differences in cognitive style. *Journal of Personality, 64,* 185–208.

Larsen, R. J., Chen, B., and Zelenski, J. (2003). *Responses to punishment and reward in the emotion Stroop paradigm: Relations to BIS and BAS.* Unpublished manuscript.

Larsen, R. J., Diener, E., and Cropanzano, R. S. (1987). Cognitive operations associated with individual differences in affect intensity. *Journal of Personality and Social Psychology, 53,* 767–774.

Larsen, R. J., Diener, E., and Emmons, R. A. (1986). Affect intensity and reactions to daily life events. *Journal of Personality and Social Psychology, 51,* 803–814.

Larsen, R. J., Mercer, K. A., and Balota, D. A. (2006). Lexical characteristics of words used in emotion Stroop tasks. *Emotion, 6,* 62–72.

Lassek, W. D., and Gaulin, S. J. C. (2009). Costs and benefits of fat-free muscle mass in men: Relationship to mating success, dietary requirements, and native immunity. *Evolution and Human Behavior, 30,* 322–328.

Lassiter, G. D., Lindberg, M. J., Gonzalez-Vallejo, C., Bellezza, F. S., and Phillips, N. D. (2009). The deliberation-without-attention effect: Evidence for an artifactual interpretation. *Psychological Science, 20,* 671–675.

Laub, J. H., and Lauritsen, J. L. (1994). The precursors of criminal offending across the life course. *Federal Probation, 58,* 51–57.

Lawson, M. A., and Kakkar, H. (2021). Of pandemics, politics, and personality: The role of conscientiousness and political ideology in the sharing of fake news. *Journal of Experimental Psychology: General.* https://doi-org/10.1037/xge0001120.

Lawton, M. P., Moss, M. S., Winter, L., and Hoffman, C. (2002). Motivation in later life: Personal projects and well-being. *Psychology and Aging, 17,* 539–547.

Lazarus, R. S. (1991). *Emotion and Adaptation.* Oxford, England: Oxford University Press.

Lazarus, R. S., and Folkman, S. (1984). *Stress, appraisal and coping.* New York: Springer.

Lazarus, R. S., Kanner, A. D., and Folkman, S. (1980). Emotions: A cognitive-phenomenological analysis. In R. Plutchik and H. Kellerman (Eds.), *Theories of emotion* (pp. 189–217). New York: Academic Press.

Le Boeuf, B. J., and Reiter, J. (1988). Lifetime reproductive success in northern elephant seals. In T. H. Clutton-Brock (Ed.), *Reproductive success* (pp. 344–362). Chicago: University of Chicago Press.

Leary, M. R., and Kowalski, R. M. (1995). *Social Anxiety.* New York: Guilford Press.

Lee, B. W., and Leeson, P. C. (2015). Online gaming in the context of social anxiety. *Psychology of Addictive Behaviors, 29*(2), 473–482.

Lee, B., Kaya, C., Chen, X., Wu, J.-R., Iwanaga, K., Umucu, E., Bezyak, J., Tansey, T. N., and Chan, F. (2019). The buffering effect of character strengths on depression: The intermediary role of perceived stress and negative attributional style. *European Journal of Health Psychology, 26,* 101–109. https://doi-org.libproxy.wustl.edu/10.1027/2512-8442/a000036

Lee, C., Corte, C., Stein, K. F., Finnegan, L., McCreary, L. L., and Park, C. G. (2015). Expected problem drinker possible self: Predictor of alcohol problems and tobacco use in adolescents. *Substance Abuse, 36*(4), 434–439.

Lee, D., Kelley, K. R., and Edwards, J. K. (2006). A closer look at relationships among trait procrastination, neuroticism, and conscientiousness. *Personality and Individual Differences, 40,* 27–37.

Lee, K., and Ashton, M. C. (2008). The HEXACO personality factors in the indigenous personality lexicons of English and 11 other languages. *Journal of Personality, 76,* 1011–1054.

Lee, K., Ashton, M. C., Ogunfowora, B., Bourdage, J. S., and Shin, K. H. (2010). The personality bases of socio-political attitudes: The role of Honesty–Humility and Openness to Experience. Journal of Research in Personality, 44(1), 115–119.

Lee, K., Ogunfowora, B., and Ashton, M. C. (2005). Personality traits beyond the Big Five: Are they within the HEXACO space? *Journal of Personality, 73,* 1437–1463.

Lee-Ross, D. (2015). Personality characteristics of the self-employed: A comparison using the world values survey data set. *Journal of Management Development, 34*(9), 1094–1112.

Leeuwis, F. H., Koot, H. M., Creemers, D. M., and van Lier, P. C. (2015). Implicit and explicit self-esteem discrepancies, victimization and the development of late childhood internalizing problems. *Journal of Abnormal Child Psychology, 43*(5), 909–919.

Lee-Won, R. J., Herzog, L., and Park, S. G. (2015). Hooked on Facebook: The role of social anxiety and need for social assurance in problematic use of Facebook. *Cyberpsychology, Behavior, and Social Networking, 18*(10), 567–574.

Legare, C. H., and Souza, A. (2012). Evaluating ritual efficacy: Evidence from the supernatural. *Cognition, 124,* 1–15.

Lehmann, R., Denissen, J. J., Allemand, M., and Penke, L. (2013). Age and gender differences in motivational manifestations of the Big Five from age 16 to 60. *Developmental Psychology, 49,* 365–383.

Lei, C., Wang, Y., Shackelford, T. K., and Buss, D. M. (2011). Chinese mate preferences: Cultural evolution and continuity across a quarter century. *Personality and Individual Differences, 50,* 678–683.

Leikas, S., Lonnqvist, J., and Verkasalo, M. (2012). Persons, situations, and behaviors: Consistency and variability of different behaviors in four interpersonal situations. *Journal of Personality and Social Psychology, 103,* 1007–1022.

Leitner, J. B., Hehman, E., Deegan, M. P., and Jones, J. M. (2014). Adaptive disengagement buffers self-esteem from negative social feedback. *Personality and Social Psychology Bulletin, 40*(11), 1435–1450.

Lemay, E. P., and Dobush, S. (2015). When do personality and emotion predict destructive behavior during relationship conflict? The role of perceived commitment asymmetry. *Journal of Personality, 83*(5), 523–534.

León, F. R., Morales, O., Vértiz, H., and Burga-León, A. (2017). Universality of gender differences in 10 aspects of personality: A study of younger and older adult Peruvians. *Personality and Individual Differences, 112,* 124–127.

Leopold, D. A. (2012). Primary visual cortex: Awareness and blindsight. *Annual Review of Neuroscience, 35,* 91–109.

LeVay, S. (1991). A difference in hypothalamic structure between heterosexual and homosexual men. *Science, 253.* 1034–1037.

LeVay, S. (1993). *The sexual brain.* Cambridge, MA: MIT Press.

LeVay, S. (1996). *Queer science: The use and abuse of research into homosexuality.* Cambridge, MA: MIT Press.

Levenson, M. R. (1992). Rethinking Psychopathy. *Theory & Psychology, 2*(1), 51–71.

Levenson, M. R., Kiehl, K. A., and Fitzpatrick, C. M. (1995). Assessing psychopathic attributes in a noninstitutionalized population. *Journal of Personality and Social Psychology, 68,* 151–158.

Levenson, R. W. (1983). Personality research and psychophysiology: General considerations. *Journal of Research in Personality, 17,* 1–21.

Levenson, R. W. (2003). Autonomic specificity and emotion. In R. J. Davidson, K. R. Scherer, and H. H. Goldsmith (Eds.), *Handbook of Affective Science* (pp. 212–224). New York: Oxford University Press.

Levesque, J., Fanny, E., and Joanette, Y. (2003). Neural circuitry underlying voluntary suppression of sadness. *Biological Psychiatry, 53,* 502–510.

Levy, B. R., Slade, M. D., and Ranasinghe, P. (2009). Causal thinking after a tsunami wave: Karma beliefs, pessimistic explanatory style and health among Sri Lankan survivors. *Journal of Religion and Health, 48*(1), 38–45.

Levy, S. M. (1990). Psychosocial risk factors and cancer progression: Mediating pathways linking behavior and disease. In K. D. Craig and S. M. Weiss (Eds.), and *Health enhancement, disease prevention, and early intervention: Biobehavioral perspectives* (pp. 348–369). New York: Springer.

Levy, S. M., and Heiden. L. A. (1990). Personality and social factors in cancer outcome. In H. S. Friedman (Ed.), *Personality and disease* (pp. 254–279). New York: Wiley.

Levy, S. M., Herberman, R., Maluish, A., Achlien, B., and Lippman, M. (1985). Prognostic risk assessment in primary breast cancer by behavioral and immunological parameters. *Health Psychology, 4,* 99–113.

Lewis, D. M. (2015). Evolved individual differences: Advancing a condition-dependent model of personality. Personality and Individual Differences, 84, 63–72.

Lewis, D. M., Al-Shawaf, L., Conroy-Beam, D., Asao, K., and Buss, D. M. (2017). Evolutionary psychology: A how-to guide. *American Psychologist, 72*(4), 353.

Lewis, D. M., Conroy-Beam, D., Al-Shawaf, L., Raja, A., DeKay, T., and Buss, D. M. (2011). Friends with benefits: The evolved psychology of same-and opposite-sex friendship. *Evolutionary Psychology, 9*(4), 14747049110090040T.

Lewis, G. J., Dickie, D. A., Cox, S. R., Karama, S., Evans, A. C., Starr, J. M., . . .

Deary, I. J. (2018). Widespread associations between trait conscientiousness and thickness of brain cortical regions. *Neuroimage, 176,* 22–28.

Lewis, M., and Ramsay, D. (2004). Development of self-recognition, personal pronoun use, and pretend play during the second year. *Child Development, 75,* 1821–1831.

Li, H., Zhang, Y., Wu, C., and Mei, D. (2916). Effects of field dependence-independence and frame of reference on navigation performance using multi-dimensional electronic maps. *Personality and Individual Differences, 97,* 289–299

Li, N. P., Valentine, K. A., and Patel, L. (2011). Mate preferences in the U.S. and Singapore: A cross-cultural test of the mate preference priority model. *Personality and Individual Differences, 50,* 291–294.

Li, N. P., van Vugt, M., and Colarelli, S. M. (2018). The evolutionary mismatch hypothesis: Implications for psychological science. *Current Directions in Psychological Science, 27*(1), 38–44.

Li, P. H., Chu, L. H., Yu, M. N. (2017). Joy shared with others is more joyful: Interpersonal relationship as a mediator between optimistic explanatory style and well-being. *Chinese Journal of Guidance and Counseling, 49,* 53–77.

Lieberman, D., and Lobel, T. (2012). Kinship on the Kibbutz: Coresidence duration predicts altruism, personal sexual aversions and moral attitudes among communally reared peers. *Evolution and Human Behavior, 33*(1), 26–34.

Lilienfeld, S. O., Watts, A. L., and Smith, S. F. (2015). Successful Psychopathy: A Scientific Status Report. *Current Directions in Psychological Science, 24*(4), 298–303.

Linville, P. W. (1987). Self-complexity as a cognitive buffer against stress-related illness and depression. *Journal of Personality and Social Psychology, 52,* 663–676.

Lippa, R. (1998). Gender-related individual differences and the structure of vocational interests: The importance of the people-things dimension. *Journal of Personality and Social Psychology, 74,* 996–1009.

Liquete, E., Dekoninck, E., and Wisker, G. (2021). Exploring how degree apprentices experience their engineering identity through Life Story Interviews and the Twenty Statement Test (TST). *Design and Technology Education: an International Journal, 26*(3), 313–324.

Lishman, W. A. (1972). Selective factors in memory. Part 1: Age, sex, and personality attributes. *Psychological Medicine, 2,* 121–138.

Little, B. R. (1972a). *Person-thing orientation: A provisional manual for the T-P scale.*

Oxford, England: Oxford University, Department of Experimental Psychology.

Little, B. R. (1972b). Psychological man as scientist, humanist, and specialist. *Journal of Experimental Research in Personality, 6,* 95–118.

Little, B. R. (1999). Personality and motivation: Personal action and the cognitive revolution. In L. A. Pervin and O. P. John (Eds.), *Handbook of personality: Theory and research* (pp. 501–524). New York: Guilford Press.

Little, B. R. (2007). Prompt and circumstance: The generative contexts of personal projects analysis. In B. Little, K. Salmela-Aro, and S. D. Phillips (Eds.), *Personal project pursuit: Goals, action, and human flourishing* (pp. 3–49). Mahwah, NJ: Erlbaum.

Little, B. R. (2011). Personal projects and motivational counseling: The quality of lives reconsidered. In W. M. Cox and E. Klinger (Eds.), *Handbook of motivational counseling: Goal-based approaches to assessment and intervention with addiction and other problems* (2nd ed.). New York: Wiley-Blackwell.

Little, B. R., and Gee, T. L. (2007). The methodology of personal projects analysis: Four modules and a funnel. In B. Little, K. Salmela-Aro, and S. D. Phillips (Eds.), *Personal project pursuit: Goals, action, and human flourishing* (pp. 51–94). Mahwah, NJ: Erlbaum.

Little, B. R., Lecci, L., and Watkinson, B. (1992). Personality and personal projects: Linking Big Five and PAC units of analysis. *Journal of Personality, 60,* 501–525.

Little, B. R., Salmela-Aro, K., and Phillips, S. D. (2007). *Personal project pursuit: Goals, action, and human flourishing.* Mahwah, NJ: Erlbaum.

Little, B. R. (2020). How are you doing, really? Personal project pursuit and human flourishing. *Canadian Psychology/Psychologie canadienne, 61,* 140–150.

Little, B. R., and Balsari-Palsule, S. (2021). Fates beyond traits: The dynamics and impacts of personal project pursuit. In J. F. Raythmann (Ed.), *The handbook of personality dynamics and processes,* pp. 323–344. San Diego, CA: Elsevier Academic Press.

Lloyd, M. E. (1990). Gender factors in reviewer recommendations for manuscript publication. *Journal of Applied Behavior Analysis, 23,* 539–543.

Löckenhoff, C. E., Chan, W., McCrae, R. R., De Fruyt, F., Jussim, L., De Bolle, M., . . . and Nakazato, K. (2014). Gender stereotypes of personality: Universal and accurate? *Journal of Cross-Cultural Psychology, 45*(5), 675–694.

Löckenhoff, C. E., Chan, W., McCrae, R. R., De Fruyt, F., Jussim, L., De Bolle, M., . . . Terracciano, A. (2014). Gender stereotypes of personality: Universal and accurate? *Journal of Cross-Cultural Psychology, 45*(5), 675-694.

Loehlin, J. C. (2010). Is there an active gene-environment correlation in adolescent drinking behavior? *Behavior Genetics, 40,* 447-451.

Loehlin, J. C. (2012). The differential heritability of personality item clusters. *Behavior Genetics, 42,* 500-507.

Loehlin, J. C., and Nichols, R. C. (1976). *Heredity, environment, and personality.* Austin: University of Texas Press.

Loehlin, J. C., Neiderhiser, J. M., and Reiss, D. (2003). The behavior genetics of personality and the NEAD Study. *Journal of Research in Personality, 37,* 373-387.

Loftus, E. (2011). Intelligence gathering after post-9/11. *American Psychologist, 66,* 532-541.

Loftus, E. F. (1992). When a lie becomes memory's truth: Memory distortion after exposure to misinformation. *Current Directions in Psychological Science, 1,* 121-123.

Loftus, E. F. (1993). The reality of repressed memories. *American Psychologist, 48,* 518-537.

Loftus, E. F. (2000). Remembering what never happened. In E. Tulving (Ed.), *Memory, consciousness, and the brain: The Tallinn Conference* (pp. 106-118). Philadelphia: Psychology Press.

Loftus, E. F. (2003). Memory in Canadian Courts of Law. *Canadian Psychology, 44,* 207-212.

London, H., and Exner, J. E., Jr. (Eds.). (1978). *Dimensions of personality.* New York: Wiley.

Lönnqvist, J. E., Itkonen, J. V., Verkasalo, M., and Poutvaara, P. (2014). The five-factor model of personality and degree and transitivity of Facebook social networks. *Journal of Research in Personality, 50,* 98-101.

Lounsbury, J. W., Sundstrom, E., Loveland, James M., and Gibson, L. W. (2003). Intelligence, "Big Five" personality traits, and work drive as predictors of course grade. *Personality and Individual Differences, 35,* 1231-1239.

Low, B. (1989). Cross-cultural patterns in the training of children: An evolutionary perspective. *Journal of Comparative Psychology, 103,* 311-319.

Lowenstein, L. F. (2002). Ability and personality changes after brain injuries. *Criminal Lawyer, 120,* 5-8.

Lowry, P. E. (1997). The assessment center process; New directions. *Journal of Social Behavior and Personality, 12,* 53-62.

Lucas, R. E. (2007). Personality and the pursuit of happiness. *Social and Personality Psychology Compass, 1,* 168-182.

Lucas, R. E., and Baird, B. M. (2004). Extraversion and emotional reactivity. *Journal of Personality and Social Psychology, 86,* 473-485.

Lucas, R. E., and Diener, E. (2021). Personality and subjective well-being. In O. P. John and R. W. Robins (Eds.), *Handbook of Personality: Theory and Research* (4th ed., pp. 724-742). New York: Guilford Press.

Lucas, R. E., and Schimmack, U. (2009). Income and well-being: How big is the gap between the rich and the poor? *Journal of Research in Personality, 43,* 75-78.

Lucas, R. E., Le, K., and Dyrenforth, P. S. (2008). Explaining the extraversion/positive affect relation: Sociability cannot account for extraverts' greater happiness. *Journal of personality, 76*(3), 385-414.

Ludeke, S. G., and Carey, B. (2015). Two mechanisms of biased responding account for the association between religiousness and misrepresentation in Big Five self-reports. *Journal of Research in Personality, 57,* 43-47.

Ludtke, O., Trautwein, U., and Husemann, N. (2009). Goal and personality trait development in a transitional period: Assessing change and stability in personality development. *Personality and Social Psychology Bulletin, 35,* 428-441.

Lukaszewski, A. W. (2013). Testing an adaptationist theory of trait covariation: Relative bargaining power as a common calibrator of an interpersonal syndrome. *European Journal of Personality, 27*(4), 328-345.

Lukaszewski, A. W., and Roney, J. (2010). Kind toward whom? Mate preferences for personality traits are target-specific. *Evolution and Human Behavior, 31,* 28-38.

Lukaszewski, A. W., and Roney, J. (2011). The origins of extraversion: Joint effects of facultative calibration and genetic polymorphism. *Personality and Social Psychology Bulletin, 37,* 409-421.

Lukaszewski, A. W., Larson, C. M., Gildersleeve, K. A., Roney, J. R., and Haselton, M. G. (2014). Condition-dependent calibration of men's uncommitted mating orientation: Evidence from multiple samples. *Evolution and Human Behavior, 35*(4), 319-326.

Lukaszewski, A. W., Lewis, D. M., Durkee, P. K., Sell, A. N., Sznycer, D., and Buss, D. M. (2020). An adaptationist framework for personality science. *European Journal of Personality, 34*(6), 1151-1174.

Lund, O. C. H., Tamnes, C. K., Moestue, C., Buss, D. M., and Vollrath, M. (2006). Tactics of hierarchy negotiation. *Journal of Research in Personality, 41,* 25-44.

Luntz, B. K., and Widom, C. S. (1994). Antisocial personality disorder in abused and neglected children grown up. *American Journal of Psychiatry, 151,* 670-674.

Luo, J., Derringer, J., Briley, D. A., and Roberts, B. W. (2017). Genetic and environmental pathways underlying personality traits and perceived stress: Concurrent and longitudinal twin studies. *European Journal of Personality, 31*(6), 614-629.

Luo, S., Chen, H., Yue, G., Zhang, G., Zhaoyang, R., and Xu, D. (2008). Predicting marital satisfaction from self, partner, and couple characteristics: Is it me, you, or us? *Journal of Personality, 76,* 1231-1266.

Lykken, D. T. (1982, September). Fearlessness. *Psychology Today,* 6-10.

Lykken, D. T. (1995). *The antisocial personalities.* Hillsdale, NJ: Erlbaum.

Lynn, R. (2008). *The global bell curve: Race, IQ and inequality worldwide.* Augusta, GA: Washington Summit.

Lynn, R., and Harvey, J. (2008). The decline of the world's IQ. *Intelligence, 36,* 112-120.

Lynn, S. J., Lock, T., Loftus, E. F., Krackow, E., and Lilienfeld, S. O. (2003). The remembrance of things past: Problematic memory recovery techniques in psychotherapy. In S. O. Lilienfeld and S. J. Lynn (Eds.), *Science and pseudoscience in clinical psychology* (pp. 205-239). New York: Guilford Press.

Lyons, M. T., and Hughes, S. (2015). Malicious mouths? The Dark Triad and motivations for gossip. *Personality and Individual Differences, 78,* 1-4.

Lyubomirsky, S. (2001). Why are some people happier than others? The role of cognitive and motivational processes in well-being. *American Psychologist, 56,* 239-249.

Lyubomirsky, S. (2007). *The How of Happiness: A Scientific Approach to Getting the Life You Want.* New York: Penguin Press.

Lyubomirsky, S., King, L., and Diener, E. (2005). The benefits of frequent positive affect: Does happiness lead to success? *Psychological Bulletin, 131,* 803-855.

Ma, V., and Schoeneman, T. J. (1997). Individualism versus collectivism: A comparison of Kenyan and American self-concepts. *Basic and Applied Social Psychology, 19,* 261-273.

Ma, Y., Peng, H., Liu, H., Gu, R., Peng, X., and Wu, J. (2021). Alpha frontal asymmetry underlies individual differences in reactivity to acute psychosocial stress in males. *Psychophysiology, 58,* ArtID: e13893

Mac Giolla, E., and Kajonius, P. J. (2018). Sex differences in personality are larger in gender equal countries: Replicating and extending a surprising finding. *International Journal of Psychology.* https://doi.org/10.1002/ijop.12529.

MacDonald, G., and Leary, M. R. (2005). Why does social exclusion hurt? The relationship between social and physical pain. *Psychological Bulletin, 131,* 202-223.

MacLaren, V. V., Best, L. A., Dixon, M. J., and Harrigan, K. A. (2011). Problem gambling and the five factor model in university students. *Personality and Individual Differences, 50,* 335-338.

Macmillan, M. B. (2000). Restoring Phineas Gage: A 150th retrospective. *Journal of the History of the Neurosciences, 9,* 42-62.

Madsen, E. A., Tunney, R. J., Fieldman, G., Plotkin, H. C., Dunbar, R. I., Richardson, J. M., and McFarland, D. (2007). Kinship and altruism: A cross-cultural experimental study. *British Journal of Psychology, 98*(2), 339-359.

Malcolm, J. (1981). *Psychoanalysis: The Impossible Profession.* New York: Knopf.

Maleva, V., Westcott, K., McKellop, M., McLaughlin, R., Widman, D., and College, J. (2014). Optimism and college grades: Predicting GPA from explanatory style. *Psi Chi Journal of Psychological Research, 19*(3), 129-135.

Malone, J. C., Weston, D., and Levendosky, A. (2011). Personalities of adults with traumatic childhood separations. *Journal of Clinical Psychology, 67,* 1259-1282.

Malouff, J. M., Thorsteinsson, E. B., Schutte, N. S., Bhullar, N., and Rooke, S. E. (2010). The five-factor model of person-ality and relationship satisfaction of intimate partners: A meta-analysis. *Journal of Research in Personality, 44,* 124-127.

Maltby, J., Wood, A. M., Day, L., Kon, T. W. H., Colley, A., and Linley, P. A., (2008). Personality predictors of levels of forgiveness two and a half years after the transgression. *Journal of Research in Personality, 42,* 1088-1094.

Maner, J. K., and Shackelford, T. K. (2008). The basic cognition of jealousy: An evolutionary perspective. *European Journal of Personality, 22,* 31-36.

Mann, F. D., Engelhardt, L., Briley, D. A., Grotzinger, A. D., Patterson, M. W., Tackett, J. L., . . . and Martin, N. G. (2017). Sensation seeking and impulsive traits as personality endophenotypes for antisocial behavior: Evidence from two independent samples. *Personality and Individual Differences, 105,* 30-39.

Maranges, H. M., and Strickhouser, J. E. (2021). Does ecology or character matter? The contributions of childhood unpredictability, harshness, and temperament to life history strategies in adolescence. *Evolutionary Behavioral Sciences.*

Marangoni, C., Garcia, S., Ickes, W., and Teng, G. (1995). Empathic accuracy in a clinically relevant setting. *Journal of Personality and Social Psychology, 68,* 854-869.

Marcia, J. E. (1966). Development and validation of ego-identity status. *Journal of Personality and Social Psychology, 3,* 551-558.

Marcia, J. E. (2002). Identity and psychosocial development in adulthood. *Identity, 2,* 7-28.

Margolis, S., and Lyubomirsky, S. (2020). Experimental manipulation of extraverted and introverted behavior and its effects on well-being. *Journal of Experimental Psychology: General, 149,* 719-731.

Markett, S., Montag, C., and Reuter, M. (2018). Network neuroscience and personality. *Personality Neuroscience, 1*(E14), 1-14.

Markey, C. N., Markey, P. M., and Tinsley, B. J. (2003). Personality, puberty, and preadolescent girls' risky behaviors: Examining the predictive value of the five-factor model of personality. *Journal of Research in Personality, 37,* 405-419.

Markey, P. M., and Markey, C. N. (2007). The interpersonal meaning of sexual promiscuity. *Journal of Research in Personality, 41,* 1199-1212.

Markus, H. (1983). Self-knowledge: An expanded view. *Journal of Personality, 51,* 543-565.

Markus, H. R., and Kitayama, S. (1991). Culture and the self: Implications for cognition, emotion, and motivation. *Psychological Review, 98,* 224-253.

Markus, H. R., and Kitayama, S. (1994). A collective fear of the collective: Implications for selves and theories of selves. *Personality and Social Psychology Bulletin, 20,* 568-579.

Markus, H. R., and Kitayama, S. (1998). The cultural psychology of personality. *Journal of Cross-Cultural Psychology, 29,* 63-87.

Markus, H., and Nurius, P. (1986). Possible selves. *American Psychologist, 41,* 954-969.

Markus, H., and Nurius, P. (1987). Possible selves: The interface between motivation and the self concept. In K. Yardley and T. Honness (Eds.), *Self and Identity: Psychosocial Perspectives* (pp. 157-172). Chichester, England: Wiley.

Marschall-Lévesque, S., Castellanos-Ryan, N., Vitaro, F., and Séguin, J. R. (2014). Moderators of the association between peer and target adolescent substance use. *Addictive Behaviors, 39*(1), 48-70.

Marshall, T. C., Lefringhausen, K., and Ferenczi, N. (2015). The Big Five, self-esteem, and narcissism as predictors of the topics people write about in Facebook status updates. *Personality and Individual Differences, 85,* 35-40.

Marsland, A. L., Cohen, S., Rabin, B. S., and Manuck, S. B. (2001). Associations between stress, trait negative affect, acute immune reactivity, and antibody response in hepatitis B injection in healthy young adults. *Health Psychology, 20,* 4-11.

Martin, M., Ward, J. C., and Clark, D. M. (1983). Neuroticism and the recall of positive and negative personality

information. *Behavior Research and Therapy, 21,* 495-503.

Martins, A., and Calheiros, M. M. (2012). Construction of a self-complexity scale for adolescents. *Psychological Assessment, 24,* 973-982.

Maslow, A. H. (1968). *Toward a psychology of being* (2nd ed.). New York: Harper and Row. (Original work published 1954.)

Maslow, A. H. (1970). *Motivation and personality.* New York: Harper and Row. (Original work published 1954.)

Maslow, A. H., and Hoffman, E. (1996). *Future visions: The unpublished papers of Abraham Maslow.* Thousand Oaks, CA: Sage.

Mason, A., and Blankenship, V. (1987). Power and affiliation motivation, stress, and abuse in intimate relationships. *Journal of Personality and Social Psychology, 52,* 203-210.

Mason, J., Southwick, S., Yehuda, R., Wang, S., Riney, S., Bremner, D., Johnson, D., Lubin, H., Blake, D., and Zhou, G. (1994). Elevation of serum free triiodothyronine, total triiodothyronine, thyroxine-binding globulin, and total thyroxine levels in combat-related posttraumatic stress disorder. *Archives of General Psychiatry, 51,* 629-641.

Mason, O., Claridge, G., and Jackson, M. (1995). New scales for the assessment of schizotypy. *Personality and Individual Differences, 18,* 7-13.

Massar, K., Winters, C. L., Lenz, S., and Jonason, P. K. (2017). Green-eyed snakes: The associations between psychopathy, jealousy, and jealousy induction. *Personality and Individual Differences, 115,* 164-168.

Masson, J. M. (1984). *The assault on truth: Freud's suppression of the seduction theory.* New York: Farrar, Straus and Giroux.

Masuda, T., and Nisbett, R. E. (2001). Attending holistically versus analytically: Comparing the context sensitivity of Japanese and Americans. *Journal of Personality and Social Psychology, 81*(5), 922-934.

Matsumoto, D. (1999). Culture and self: An empirical assessment of Markus and Kitayama's theory of independent and interdependent self-construals. *Asian Journal of Social Psychology, 2,* 289-310.

Matsumoto, D. (2006). Are cultural differences in emotion regulation mediated by personality traits? *Journal of Cross-Cultural Psychology, 37*(4), 421-437.

Matsumoto, D., and Hwang, H. S. (2012). Evidence for a nonverbal expression of triumph. *Evolution and Human Behavior, 33*(5), 520-529.

Matthes, J., Wirth, W., Schemer, C., and Kissling, A. K. (2011). I see what you don't see: The role of individual differences in field dependence-independence as a predictor of product placement recall and brand liking. *Journal of Advertising, 40,* 85–89.

Matthews, G. (2000). Attention, automaticity, and affective disorder. *Behavior Modification, 24,* 69–93.

Matthews, G., and Gilliland, K. (1999). The personality theories of H. J. Eysenck and J. A. Gray: A comparative review. *Personality and Individual Differences, 26,* 583–626.

Matthews, G., Derryberry, D., and Siegle, G. J. (2000). Personality and emotion: Cognitive science perspectives. In S. E. Hampson (Ed.), *Advances in personality psychology* (Vol. 1, pp. 199–237). Philadelphia: Taylor and Francis.

Maynard Smith, J. (1982). *Evolution and the theory of games.* Cambridge, England: Cambridge University Press.

McAdams, D. P. (1990). Motives. In V. Derlega, B. Winstead, and W. Jones (Eds.), *Contemporary research in personality* (pp. 175–204). Chicago: Nelson-Hall.

McAdams, D. P. (1992). The five-factor model in personality: A critical appraisal. *Journal of personality, 60*(2), 329–361.

McAdams, D. P. (1999). Personal narratives and the life story. In L. A. Pervin and O. P. John (Eds.), *Handbook of personality: Theory and research* (2nd ed., pp. 478–500). New York: Guilford Press.

McAdams, D. P. (2008). Personal narratives and the life story. In O. John, R. Robins, and L. A. Pervin (Eds.), *Handbook of personality: Theory and research* (pp. 241–261). New York: Guilford Press.

McAdams, D. P. (2011). Narrative identity. In S. J. Schwartz, K. Luyckx, and V. L. Vignoles (Eds.), *Handbook of identity theory and research* (vols. 1 & 2, pp. 99–115). New York: Springer Science + Business Media.

McAdams, D. P. (2016). Life authorship in emerging adulthood. In J. J. Arnett, J. J. Arnett (Eds.), *The Oxford handbook of emerging adulthood* (pp. 438–446). New York: Oxford University Press.

McAdams, D. P. (2020). *The strange case of Donald J. Trump: A psychological reckoning.* Oxford University Press.

McAdams, D. P., and Bryant, F. B. (1987). Intimacy motivation and subjective mental health in a nationwide sample. *Journal of Personality, 55,* 395–413.

McAdams, D. P., and Manczak, E. (2015). Personality and the life story. In M. L. Cooper, & R. J. Larsen (Eds.), APA handbook of personality and social psychology, Vol. 4. Personality processes and individual differences (pp. 425–446). Washington DC: American Psychological Association.

McAdams, D. P., and Vaillant, G. E. (1982). Intimacy motivation and psychosocial adjustment: A longitudinal study. *Journal of Personality Assessment, 46,* 586–593.

McAdams, D. P., Hoffman, B. J., Mansfield, E. D., and Day, R. (1996). Themes of agency and communion in significant autobiographical scenes. *Journal of Personality, 64*(2), 339–377.

McCarley, N. G., and Clarskadon, T. G. (1983). Test-retest reliabilities of the scales and subscales of the Myers-Briggs Type Indicator and of criteria for clinical interpretive hypotheses involving them. *Research in Psychological Type, 6,* 24–36.

McClelland D. C. (1982). The need for power, sympathetic activation, and illness. *Motivation and Emotion, 6,* 31–41.

McClelland, D. C. (1958). Risk-taking in children with high and low need for achievement. In J. W. Atkinson (Ed.), *Motives in fantasy, action, and society* (pp. 306–327). Princeton, NJ: Van Nostrand.

McClelland, D. C. (1965). N achievement and entrepreneurship: A longitudinal study. *Journal of Personality and Social Psychology, 1,* 389–392.

McClelland, D. C. (1979). Inhibited power motivation and high blood pressure in men. *Journal of Abnormal Psychology, 88,* 182–190.

McClelland, D. C. (1985). How motives, skills, and values determine what people do. *American Psychologist, 40,* 812–825.

McClelland, D. C., Alexander, C., and Marks, E. (1982). The need for power, stress, immune function, and illness among male prisoners. *Journal of Abnormal Psychology, 91,* 61–70.

McClelland, D. C., and Jemmott, J. B. (1980). Power motivation, stress, and physical illness. *Journal of Human Stress, 6,* 6–15.

McClelland, D. C., and Pilon, D. A. (1983). Sources of adult motives in patterns of parent behavior in early childhood. *Journal of Personality and Social Psychology, 44,* 564–574.

McClelland, D. C., Koestner, R., and Weinberger, J. (1989). How do self-attributed and implicit motives differ? *Psychological Review, 96,* 690–702.

McConnell, A. R., Strain, L. M., Brown, C. M., and Rydell, R. J. (2009). The simple life: On the benefits of low self-complexity. *Personality and Social Psychology Bulletin, 35,* 823–835.

McCoul, M. D., and Haslam, N. (2001). Predicting high risk sexual behaviour in heterosexual and homosexual men: The roles of impulsivity and sensation seeking. *Personality and Individual Differences, 31,* 1303–1310.

McCrae, R. R., and Costa, P. T. (1991). Adding liebe und arbeit: The full five-factor model and well-being. *Personality and Social Psychology Bulletin, 17,* 227–232.

McCrae, R. R., and Costa, P. T., Jr. (1997). Personality trait structure as a human universal. *American Psychologist, 52,* 509–516.

McCrae, R. R., and Costa, P. T., Jr. (1999). A five-factor theory of personality. In L. A. Pervin and O. John (Eds.), *Handbook of personality: Theory and research* (2nd ed.). New York: Guilford Press.

McCrae, R. R., and Costa, P. T., Jr. (2008). The five factor theory of personality. In O. P. John, R. W. Robins, and L. A. Pervin (Eds.), *Handbook of personality* (pp. 159–181). New York: Guilford Press.

McCrae, R. R., and John, O. P. (1992). An introduction to the five-factor model and its applications. *Journal of Personality, 60,* 175–215.

McCrae, R. R., Chan, W., Jussim, L., De Fruyt, F., Löckenhoff, C. E., De Bolle, M., . . . Allik, J. (2013). The inaccuracy of national character stereotypes. *Journal of Research in Personality, 47*(6), 831–842.

McCrae, R. R., Costa, Jr, P. T., and Martin, T. A. (2005). The NEO-PI-3: A more readable revised NEO personality inventory. *Journal of Personality Assessment, 84*(3), 261–270.

McCrae, R. R., Costa, P. T., Jr., del Pilar, G. H., Rolland, J., and Parker, W. D. (1998). Cross-cultural assessment of the five-factor model: The Revised NEO Personality Inventory. *Journal of Cross-Cultural Psychology, 29,* 171–188.

McCrae, R. R., Costa, P. T., Jr., Terracciano, A., Parker, W. D., Mills, C. J., De Fruyt, F., and Mervielde, I. (2002). Personality trait development from age 12 to age 18: Longitudinal, cross-sectional, and cross-cultural analyses. *Journal of Personality and Social Psychology, 83,* 1456–1468.

McCrae, R. R., Terracciano, A., and 78 Members of the Personality Profiles of Cultures Project. (2005a). Personality profiles of cultures: Aggregate personality traits. *Journal of Personality and Social Psychology, 89,* 407–425.

McCrae, R. R., Terracciano, A., and 78 Members of the Personality Profiles of Cultures Project. (2005b). Universal features of personality traits from the observer's perspective: Data from 50 cultures. *Journal of Personality and Social Psychology, 88,* 547–561.

McCullough, M. E., Bellah, C. G., Kilpatrick, S. D., and Johnson, J. L. (2001). Vengefulness: Relationships with forgiveness, rumination, well-being, and the Big Five. *Personality and Social Psychology Bulletin, 27, 5,* 601–610.

McCullough, M. E., Emmons, R. A., Kilpatrick, S. D., and Mooney, C. N. (2003). Narcissists as "victims": The role of narcissism in the perception of transgressions. *Personality and Social Psychology Bulletin, 29*(7), 885–893.

McDaniel, M. J., Beier, M. E., Perkins, A. W., Goggin, S., and Frankel, B. (2009). An assessment of fakeability of self-report and implicit personality measures. *Journal of Research in Personality, 43,* 682–685.

McDaniel, S. R., and Zuckerman, M. (2003). The relationship of impulsive sensation seeking and gender to interest and participation in gambling activities. *Personality and Individual Differences, 35,* 1385–1400.

McGrath, R. E., and Carroll, E. J. (2012). The current status of "projective" "tests." In H. Cooper, P. M. Camic, D. L. Long, A. T. Panter, D. Rindskopf, and K. J. Sher (Eds.), *APA handbook of research methods in psychology, Vol. 1: Foundations, planning, measures, and psychometrics* (pp. 329–348). Washington, DC: American Psychological Association.

McHoskey, J. W. (2001). Machiavellianism and sexuality: On the moderating role of biological sex. *Personality and Individual Differences, 31,* 779–789.

McLoyd, V. S. (1998). Socioeconomic disadvantage and child development. *American Psychologist, 53,* 188–204.

McNaughton, N. (2020). Personality neuroscience and psychopathology: Should we start with biology and look for neural-level factors? Personality Neuroscience, 3, ArtID: e4

McNaughton, N., and Smillie, L. (2018). Some metatheoretical principles for personality neuroscience. *Personality Neuroscience, 1*(E11), 1–13.

Mead, M. (1928). *Coming of age in Samoa.* New York: Morrow.

Mead, M. (1935). *Sex and temperament in three primitive societies.* New York: Morrow.

Mealey, L. (1995). The sociobiology of sociopathy: An integrated evolutionary model. *Behavioral and Brain Sciences, 18,* 523–599.

Mecacci, L., Scaglione, M. R., and Vitrano, I. (1991). Diurnal and monthly variations of temperature and self-reported activation in relation to sex and circadian typology. *Personality and Individual Differences, 12,* 819–824.

Megargee, E. I. (1969). Influence of sex roles on the manifestation of leadership. *Journal of Applied Psychology, 53,* 377–382.

Mehl, M. R., and Pennebaker, J. W. (2003). The social dynamics of a cultural upheaval: Social interactions surrounding September 11, 2001. *Psychological Science, 14,* 579–585.

Mehl, M. R., and Wrzus, C. (2021). Ecological sampling methods for studying personality in daily life. In O. P. John and R. W. Robins (Eds), *Handbook of personality: Theory and research* (pp. 806–823). New York: Guilford Press.

Meltzer, A. L., and McNulty, J. K. (2016). Who is having more and better sex? The Big Five as predictors of sex in marriage. *Journal of Research in Personality, 63,* 62–66.

Mendle, J., Moore, S. R., Briley, D. A., and Harden, K. P. (2016). Puberty, socioeconomic status, and depression in girls evidence for gene × environment interactions. *Clinical Psychological Science, 4*(1), 3–16.

Menninger, K. (1963). *The vital balance: The life process in mental health and illness.* New York: Viking Press.

Messick, S. (1994). The matter of style: Manifestations of personality in cognition, learning, and teaching. *Educational Psychologist, 29,* 121–136.

Meston, C. M., Kilimnik, C. D., Freihart, B. K., and Buss, D. M. (2020). Why humans have sex: development and psychometric assessment of a short-form version of the YSEX? Instrument. *Journal of Sex & Marital Therapy, 46*(2), 141–159.

Miao, C., Humphrey, R. H., and Qian, S. (2017). A meta-analysis of emotional intelligence effects on job satisfaction mediated by job resources, and a test of moderators. *Personality and Individual Differences, 116,* 281–288.

Michalos, A. C. (1991). *Global Report on Student Well-Being. Vol. 1: Life Satisfaction and Happiness.* New York: Springer-Verlag.

Michel, M. and Lau, H. (2021). Is blindsight possible under signal detection theory? Comment on Phillips (2021). *Psychological Review, 128,* 585–591.

Midgley, C., Thai, S., Lockwood, P., Kovacheff, C., and Page-Gould, E. (2021). When every day is a high school reunion: Social media comparisons and self-esteem. *Journal of Personality and Social Psychology, 121,* 285–307.

Mike, A., Jackson, J. J., and Oltmanns, T. F. (2014). The conscientious retiree: The relationship between conscientiousness, retirement, and volunteering. *Journal of Research in Personality, 52,* 68–77.

Mikulincer, M., and Florian, V. (1995). Appraisal and coping with a real-life stressful situation: The contribution of attachment styles. *Personality and Social Psychology Bulletin, 69,* 1203–1215.

Mikulincer, M., Florian, V., and Weller, A. (1993). Attachment styles, coping strategies, and posttraumatic psychological distress: The impact of the Gulf War in Israel. *Journal of Personality and Social Psychology, 64,* 817–826.

Miljeteig, K., and von Soest, T. (2022, February 25). An Experience Sampling Study on the Association Between Social Media Use and Self-Esteem. *Journal of Media Psychology: Theories, Methods, and Applications.* Advance online publication.

http://dx.doi.org/10.1027/1864-1105/a000333.

Miller, A. L. (2007). Creativity and cognitive style: The relationship between field-dependence–independence, expected evaluation, and creative performance. *Psychology of Aesthetics, Creativity, and the Arts, 1,* 243–246.

Miller, G. E., and Cohen, S. (2001). Psychological interventions and the immune system: A meta-analytic review and critique. *Health Psychology, 20,* 47–63.

Miller, J. D. (2012). Five-Factor Model personality disorder prototypes: A review of their development, validity, and comparison to alternative approaches. *Journal of Personality, 80*(6), 1565–1591.

Miller, J. D., and Lynam, D. R. (2015). Understanding psychopathy using the basic elements of personality. *Social and Personality Psychology Compass, 9*(5), 223–237.

Miller, J. D., Lynam, D., Zimmerman, R. S., Logan, T. K., Leukefeld, C., and Clayton, R. (2004). The utility of the five factor model in understanding risky sexual behavior. *Personality and Individual Differences, 36,* 1611–1626.

Miller, S. L., and Maner, J. K. (2009). Sex differences in response to sexual versus emotional infidelity: The moderating role of individual differences. *Personality and Individual Differences, 46,* 287–291.

Miller, T. W. K., Smith, T. W., Turner, C. W., Guajardo, M. L., and Hallet, A. J. (1996). A meta-analytic review of research on hostility and physical health. *Psychological Bulletin, 119,* 322–348.

Millon, T. (2000a). Reflections of the future of DSM Axis II. *Journal of Personality Disorders, 14,* 30–41.

Millon, T. (2000b). Sociocultural conceptions of the borderline personality. *Psychiatric Clinics of North America Special Issue: Borderline Personality Disorder, 23,* 123–136.

Millon, T., Davis, R., Millon, C., Escovar, L., and Meagher, S. (2000). *Personality disorders: Current concepts and classical foundations.* New York: Wiley.

Minkov, M., van de Vijver, F. J., and Schachner, M. (2019). A test of a new short Big-Five tool in large probabilistic samples from 19 countries. *Personality and Individual Differences, 151,* 109519.

Mischel, W. (1968). *Personality and assessment.* New York: Wiley.

Mischel, W. (1984). Convergences and challenges in the search for consistency. *American Psychologist, 39,* 351–364.

Mischel, W. (1990). Personality dispositions revisited and revised: A view after three decades. In L. Pervin (Ed.), *Handbook of Personality: Theory and Research* (pp. 111–134). New York: Guilford Press.

Mischel, W. (2000). A cognitive-affective system theory of personality:

Reconceptualizing situations, dispositions, dynamics, and invariance in personality structure. In E. T. Higgins and A. W. Kruglanski (Eds.), *Motivational science: Social and personality perspectives* (pp. 150-176). New York: Psychology Press.

Mischel, W. (2004). Toward an integrative science of the person. *Annual Review of Psychology, 55,* 1-22.

Mischel, W., and Peake, P. K. (1982). Beyond déjà vu in the search for cross-situational consistency. *Psychological Review, 89,* 730-755.

Mischel, W., and Shoda, Y. (2010). The situated person. In B. Mesquita, L. F. Barrett, and E. R. Smith (Eds.), *The Mind in Context* (pp. 149-173). New York: Guilford.

Mischel, W., Shoda, Y., and Mendoza-Denton, R. (2002). Situation-behavior profiles as a locus of consistency in personality. *Current Directions in Psychological Science, 11,* 50-54.

Mittler, P. (1971). *The study of twins.* Harmondsworth, England: Penguin Books.

Mlacic, B., and Ostendorf, F. (2005). Taxonomy and structure of Croatian personality-descriptive adjectives. *European Journal of Personality, 19,* 117-152.

Moffitt, T. E. (2005). The new look of behavioral genetics in developmental psychopathology: Gene–environment interplay in antisocial behaviors. *Psychological Bulletin, 131,* 533-554.

Monk, T. H., Leng, V. C., Folkard, S., and Weitzman, E. D. (1983). Circadian rhythms in subjective alertness and core body temperature. *Chronobiologia, 10,* 49-55.

Montemayor, R., and Eisen, M. (1977). The development of self-conceptions from childhood to adolescence. *Developmental Psychology, 13,* 314-319.

Moon, J. H., Lee, E., Lee, J. A., Choi, T. R., and Sung, Y. (2016). The role of narcissism in self-promotion on Instagram. *Personality and Individual Differences, 101,* 22-25.

Moore, M. (1978). Discrimination or favoritism? Sex bias in book reviews. *American Psychologist, 33,* 936-938.

Moore, M., Schermer, J. A., Paunonen, S.V., and Vernon, P. A. (2010). Genetic and environmental influences on verbal and nonverbal measures of the Big Five. *Personality and Individual Differences, 48,* 884-888.

Moretti, R. J., and Rossini, E. D. (2004). The Thematic Apperception Test (TAT). In M. J. Hilsenroth and E. L. Segal (Eds.), *Comprehensive handbook of psychological assessment, Vol. 2: Personality assessment* (pp. 356-371). Hoboken, NJ: Wiley.

Morey, L. C. (1997). Personality diagnosis and personality disorders. In R. Hogan, J.

A. Johnson, and S. R. Briggs (Eds.), *Handbook of personality psychology* (pp. 919-946). San Diego: Academic Press.

Morgan, C. A., Southwick, S., Steffian, G., Hazlett, G. A., and Loftus, E. F. (2012). Misinformation can influence memory for recently experienced, highly stressful events. *International Journal of Law and Psychiatry, 36,* 11-17.

Morgan, C. D., and Murray, H. A. (1935). A method of investigating fantasies. *Archives of Neurological Psychiatry, 34,* 289-306.

Morneau-Vaillancourt, G., Dionne, G., Brendgen, M., Vitaro, F., Feng, B., Henry, J., . . . and Boivin, M. (2019). The genetic and environmental etiology of shyness through childhood. *Behavior Genetics, 49*(4), 376-385.

Morosoli, J. J., Colodro Conde, L., Barlow, F. K., and Medland, S. E. (2021). Investigating perceived heritability of mental health disorders and attitudes toward genetic testing in the United States, United Kingdom, and Australia. *American Journal of Medical Genetics Part B: Neuropsychiatric Genetics, 186*(6), 341-352.

Morris, M. L. (2016). Vocational interests in the United States: Sex, age, ethnicity, and year effects. *Journal of Counseling Psychology, 63*(5), 604-615.

Morrison, M., Epstude, K., and Roese, N. J. (2012). Life regrets and the need to belong. *Social Psychological and Personality Science, 3*(6), 675-681.

Moskowitz, D. S. (1993). Dominance and friendliness: On the interaction of gender and situation. *Journal of Personality, 61,* 387-409.

Moskowitz, D. S., Suh, E. J., and Desaulniers, J. (1994). Situational influences on gender differences in agency and communion. *Journal of Personality and Social Psychology, 66,* 753-761.

Moskowitz, J. T. (2011). Coping interventions and the regulation of positive affect. In S. Folkman (Ed.), *The Oxford handbook of stress, health, and coping* (pp. 407-427). New York: Oxford University Press.

Moskowitz, J. T., Folkman, S., Collette, L., and Vittinghoff, E. (1996). Coping and mood during AIDS-related caregiving and bereavement. *Annals of Behavioral Medicine, 18,* 49-57.

Moskowtiz, D. S., and Fournier, M. A. (2015). The interplay of persons and situations: Retrospect and prospect. In L. Cooper and R. J. Larsen (Eds.), *Handbook of Personality and Social Psychology: Personality Processes and Individual Differences.* Washington, DC: American Psychological Association.

Mota, S., Humberg, S., Krause, S., Fatfouta, R., Geukes, K., Schröder-Abé, M., and

Back, M. D. (2019). Unmasking narcissus: A competitive test of existing hypotheses on (agentic, antagonistic, neurotic, and communal) narcissism and (explicit and implicit) self-esteem across 18 samples. *Self and Identity.* doi: 10.1080/15298868.2019.1620012.

Mower, O. H. (1960). *Learning theory and behavior.* New York: Wiley.

Moya Morales, M. C., and Moya Garófano, A. (2021). Evolution of gender stereotypes in Spain: from 1985 to 2018. *Psicothema, 33, No. 1, 53-59.*

Mroczek, D. K., and Spiro, A., III. (2003). Modeling intraindividual change in personality traits: Findings from the Normative Aging Study. *Journals of Gerontology Series B-Psychological Sciences & Social Sciences, 58B,* P153-P165.

Mroczek, D. K., Spiro, A., III, and Turiano, N. A. (2009). Do health behaviors explain the effect of neuroticism on mortality? Longitudinal findings from the VA Normative Aging Study. *Journal of Research in Personality, 43,* 653-659.

Mufson, D. W., and Mufson, M. A. (1998). Predicting police officer performance using the Inwald Personality Inventory: An illustration from Appalachia. *Professional Psychology: Research and Practice, 29,* 59-62.

Mullins-Sweatt, S. N., and Lengel, G. J. (2012). Clinical utility of the Five-Factor Model of personality disorder. *Journal of Personality, 80*(6), 1615-1639.

Multon, K. D., Brown, S. D., and Lent, R. W. (1991). Relation of the self-efficacy beliefs to academic outcomes: A meta-analytic investigation. *Journal of Counseling Psychology, 38,* 30-38.

Munafo, M. R., Yalcin, B., Willis-Owen, S. A., and Flint, J. (2008). Association of the dopamine D4 receptor (DRD4) gene and approach-related personality traits: Meta-analysis and new data. *Biological Psychiatry, 63,* 197-206.

Murdock, G. P. (1980). *Theories of illness: A world survey.* Pittsburgh: University of Pittsburgh Press.

Murphy, K. R. (1995). Integrity testing. In N. Brewer and C. Wilson (Eds.), *Psychology and Policing* (pp. 205-229). Hillsdale, NJ: Erlbaum.

Murphy, M. L. M., Janicki-Deverts, D., and Cohen, S. (2018). Receiving a hug is associated with the attenuation of negative mood that occurs on days with interpersonal conflict. *PLoS ONE 13*(10): e0203522. https://doi.org/10.1371/journal.pone.0203522.

Murphy, S. M., Vallacher, R. R., Shackelford, T. K., Bjorklund, D. F., and Yunger, J. L. (2006). Relationship experience as a predictor of romantic jealousy. *Personality and Individual Differences, 40,* 761-769.

Murray, D. R., Trudeau, R., and Schaller, M. (2011). On the origins of cultural differences in conformity: Four tests of the pathogen prevalence hypothesis. *Personality and Social Psychology Bulletin, 37,* 318-329.

Murray, G., Allen, N. B., and Trinder, J. (2002). Longitudinal investigation of mood variability and neuroticism predicts variability in extended states of positive and negative affect. *Personality and Individual Differences, 33,* 1217-1228.

Murray, H. (1948). *Assessment of men: Selection of personnel for the Office of Strategic Services.* New York: Rinehart.

Murray, H. A. (1933). The effect of fear upon estimates of the maliciousness of other personalities. *Journal of Social Psychology, 4,* 310-329.

Murray, H. A. (1938). *Explorations in personality.* New York: Oxford University Press.

Murray, H. A. (1967). Autobiography (the case of Murr). In E. G. Boring and G. Lindzey (Eds.), *History of psychology in autobiography* (Vol. 5, pp. 285-310). New York: Appleton-Century-Crofts.

Murstein, B. I. (1976). *Who will marry whom? Theories and research in marital choice.* New York: Springer.

Myers, D. G. (1993). *The Pursuit of Happiness.* New York: Avon Books.

Myers, D. G. (2000). The funds, friends, and faith of happy people. *American Psychologist, 55,* 56-67.

Myers, D. G., and Diener, E. (1995). Who is happy? *Psychological Science, 6,* 10-19.

Myers, D. G., and Diener, E. (2018). The scientific pursuit of happiness. *Perspectives on Psychological Science, 13,* 218-225.

Myers, I. B., McCaulley, M. H., Quenk, N. L., and Hammer, A. L. (1998). *Manual: A guide to the development and use of the Myers-Briggs Type Indicator.* Palo Alto: Consulting Psychologists Press.

Myers, L. B. (2010). The importance of the repressive coping style: Findings from 30 years of research. *Anxiety, Stress & Coping: An International Journal, 23*(1), 3-17.

Myers, L. B., and Derakshan, N. (2015). The relationship between two types of impaired emotion processing: Repressive coping and alexithymia. *Frontiers in Psychology, 6.*

Myrseth, H., Pallesen, S., Molde, H., Johnsen, B. H., and Lorvik, I. M. (2009). Personality factors as predictors of pathological gambling. *Personality and Individual Differences, 47,* 933-937.

Na, J., and Choi, I. (2009). Culture and first-person pronouns. *Personality and Social Psychology Bulletin, 35,* 1492-1499.

Nasby, W., and Read, N. W. (1997). The life voyage of a solo circumnavigator: Integrating theoretical and methodological perspectives. *Journal of Personality, 65,* 785-1068.

Nash, M. R. (1987). What, if anything, is regressed about hypnotic age regression: A review of the empirical literature. *Psychological Bulletin, 102,* 42-52.

Nash, M. R. (1988). Hypnosis as a window on regression. *Bulletin of the Menninger Clinic, 52,* 383-403.

Nash, M. R. (1999). The psychological unconscious. In V. J. Derlega, B. A. Winstead, and W. H. Jones (Eds.), *Personality: Contemporary theory and research* (pp. 197-228). Chicago: Nelson-Hall.

Nash, M. R. (2001). The truth and the hype of hypnosis. *Scientific American* (July), 47-55.

Nathania, E., Mahdiyyah, K., Chaidir, K., Phalapi, Y., and Wiguna, T. (2019). The relationship between empathy, prosocial behavior, peer relationships, and emotional problems in elementary schoolchildren in Indonesia. *Journal of Natural Science, Biology and Medicine, 10*(3), 118-122.

Nathanson, C., Paulhus, D. L., and Williams, K. M. (2006). Personality and misconduct correlates of body modification and other cultural deviance markers. *Journal of Research in Personality, 40,* 779-802.

Neisser, U. (1998). *The rising curve: Long-term gains in IQ and related measures.* Washington, DC: American Psychological Association.

Nelson, E., Hoffman, C. L., Gerald, M. S., and Schultz, S. (2010). Digit ratio (2D:4D) and dominance rank in female rhesus macaques (*Macaca mulatta*). *Behavioral Ecology and Sociobiology, 64,* 1001-1009.

Nesse, R., and Williams, G. C. (1994). *Why we get sick.* New York: New York Times Books.

Nettle, D. (2006). The evolution of personality variation in humans and other animals. *American Psychologist, 61,* 622-631.

Nettle, D., and Liddle, B. (2008). Agreeableness is related to socio-cognitive, but not socio-perceptual, theory of mind. *European Journal of Personality, 22,* 323-335.

Newell, B. R., and Shanks, D. R. (2014). Unconscious influences on decision making: A critical review. *Behavioral and Brain Sciences, 37*(1), 1-18.

Newman, J. P. (1987). Reaction to punishment in extraverts and psychopaths: Implications for the impulsive behavior of disinhibited individuals. *Journal of Research in Personality, 21,* 464-480.

Newman, J. P., Widom, C. S., and Nathan, S. (1985). Passive avoidance and syndromes of disinhibition: Psychopathy and extraversion. *Journal of Personality and Social Psychology, 48,* 1316-1327.

Newman, L. C., and Larsen, R. J. (2011). *Taking sides: Clashing views in personality psychology.* New York: McGraw-Hill.

Newman, P. R., and Newman, B. M. (1988). Differences between childhood and

adulthood: The identity watershed. *Adolescence, 23,* 551-557.

Newton, N. J., and Stewart, A. J. (2013). The road not taken: Women's life paths and gender-linked personality traits. *Journal of Research in Personality, 47,* 306-316.

Neyer, F. J. (2006). Editorial: EJP special edition on personality change. *European Journal of Personality, 20,* 419-420.

Neyer, F. J., and Lehnart, J. (2007). Relationships matter in personality development: Evidence from an 8-year longitudinal study across young adulthood. *Journal of Personality, 75,* 535-568.

Neyer, F. J., and Voigt, D. (2004). Personality and social network effects on romantic relationships: A dyadic approach. *European Journal of Personality, 18,* 279-299.

Nicolaou, A., and Xistouri, X. (2011). Field dependence/independence cognitive style and problem posing: An investigation with sixth grade students. *Educational Psychology, 31,* 611-627.

Niederhoffer, K. G., and Pennebaker, J. W. (2002). Sharing one's story: On the benefits of writing or talking about emotional experience. In C. R. Snyder and S. J. Lopez (Eds.), *Handbook of positive psychology* (pp. 573-583). London: Oxford University Press.

Niederle, M., and Vesterlund, L. (2005). *Do women shy away from competition? Do men compete too much?* Working paper # 11474, National Bureau of Economic Research, Cambridge, MA.

Nietzsche, F. (1891/1969). *Thus spoke Zarathustra: A book for everyone and no one.* Translated with an introduction by R. J. Hollingdale. New York: Penguin Books.

Nigg, J. T., and Goldsmith, H. H. (1994). Genetics of personality disorders: Perspectives from personality and psychopathology research. *Pathological Bulletin, 115,* 346-380.

Nikčević, A. V., Marino, C., Kolubinski, D. C., Leach, D., and Spada, M. M. (2021). Modelling the contribution of the Big Five personality traits, health anxiety, and COVID-19 psychological distress to generalised anxiety and depressive symptoms during the COVID-19 pandemic. *Journal of affective disorders, 279,* 578-584.

Nisbett, R. E. (1993). Violence and U.S. regional culture. *American Psychologist, 48,* 441-449.

Nisbett, R. E., Peng, K., Choi, I., and Norenzayan, A. (2001). Culture and systems of thought: Holistic vs. analytic cognition. *Psychological Review, 108,* 291-310.

Nisbett, R., and Cohen, D. (1996). *Culture of honor.* Boulder, CO: Westview Press.

Nisiforou, E., and Laghos, A. (2016). Field dependence-independence and eye movement patterns: Investigating user differences through an eye tracking study. *Interacting with Computers, 28,* 407-420.

Niv, S., Tuvbld, C., Raine, A., Want, P., and Baker, L. A. (2012). Heritability and longitudinal stability of impulsivity in adolescence. *Behavior Genetics, 42,* 378-392.

Noftle, E. E., and Robins, R. W. (2007). Personality predictors of academic outcomes: Big Five correlates of GPA and SAT scores. *Journal of Personality and Social Psychology, 93,* 116-130.

Nolen-Hoeksema, S., Larson, J., and Grayson, C. (1999). Explaining gender differences in depressive symptoms. *Journal of Personality and Social Psychology, 77,* 1061-1072.

Noller, P. (1984). *Nonverbal communication and marital interaction.* Oxford, England: Pergamon Press.

Norbury, A., and Husain, M. (2015). Sensation-seeking: Dopaminergic modulation and risk for psychopathology. *Behavioural Brain Research, 288,* 79-93.

Norem, J. K. (1995). The power of negative thinking: Interview with psychology professor Julie Norem. *Men's Health, 10* (June), 46.

Norem, J. K. (1998). Why should we lower our defenses about defense mechanisms? *Journal of Personality Special Issue: Defense mechanisms in contemporary personality research, 66,* 895-917.

Norem, J. K. (2001). Defensive pessimism, optimism, and pessimism. In E. Change (Ed.), *Optimism and Pessimism: Implications for Theory, Research, and Practice* (pp. 77-100). Washington, DC: American Psychological Association.

Norman, W. T. (1963). Toward an adequate taxonomy of personality attributes: Replicated factor structure in peer nomination personality ratings. *Journal of Abnormal Psychology, 66,* 574-583.

Norman, W. T. (1967). *2800 personality trait descriptors: Normative operating characteristics in a university population.* Ann Arbor: Department of Psychology, University of Michigan.

Norris, C. J., Larsen, J. T., and Cacioppo, J. T. (2007). Neuroticism is associated with larger and more prolonged electrodermal responses to emotionally evocative pictures. *Psychophysiology, 44,* 823-826.

Nudelman, A. E. (1973). Bias in the Twenty-Statements Test: Administration time, incomplete protocols, and intelligence. *Psychological Reports, 33,* 524-526.

Nusbaum, E. C., and Silva, P. J. (2011). Are openness and intellect distinct aspects of Openness to Experience? A test of the O/I model. *Personality and Individual Differences, 51,* 571-574.

O'Boyle, E. H., Jr., Humphrey, R. H. et al. (2011). The relation between emotional intelligence and job performance: A meta-analysis. *Journal of Organizational Behavior, 32,* 788-818.

O'Connell, D., and Marcus, D. K. (2016). Psychopathic personality traits predict positive attitudes toward sexually predatory behaviors in college men and women. *Personality and Individual Differences, 94,* 372-376.

O'Connell, M., and Sheikh, H. (2011). "Big Five" personality dimensions and social attainment: Evidence from beyond the campus. *Personality and Individual Differences, 50,* 828-833.

O'Connor, S. L., Aston-Jones, G., and James, M. H. (2021). The sensation seeking trait confers a dormant susceptibility to addiction that is revealed by intermittent cocaine self-administration in rats. *Neuropharmacology, 195,* 108566.

O'Donnell, J. R., and Rutherford, J. (2016). *Trumped!: The inside story of the real Donald Trump—His cunning rise and spectacular fall.* Crossroad Press.

Oaten, M., Stevenson, R. J., and Case, T. I. (2009). Disgust as a disease-avoidance mechanism. *Psychological Bulletin, 135*(2), 303-321.

Oatley, K., and Johnson-Laird, P. N. (1987). Towards a cognitive theory of emotions. *Cognition and Emotion, 1,* 29-50.

Ode, S., Robinson, M. D., and Wilkowski, B. M. (2008). Can one's temper be cooled? A role for agreeableness in moderating neuroticism's influence on anger and aggression. *Journal of Research in Personality, 42,* 295-311.

Oerlemans, W. G., and Bakker, A. B. (2014). Why extraverts are happier: A day reconstruction study. *Journal of Research in Personality, 50,* 11-22.

Ofshe, R. J. (1992). Inadvertent hypnosis during interrogation: False confession due to dissociative states: Misidentified multiple personality and the satanic cult hypothesis. *International Journal of Clinical and Experimental Hypnosis, 40,* 125-156.

Oishi, S., Kushlev, K., and Benet-Martínez, V. (2021). Culture and personality: Current directions. In O. P. John and R. W. Robins (Eds.), Handbook of personality: Theory and research (pp. 686-703). The Guilford Press.

Oishi, S., Talhelm, T., and Lee, M. (2015). Personality and geography: Introverts prefer mountains. *Journal of Research in Personality, 58,* 55-68.

Olino, T. M., Durbin, C. E., Klein, D. N., Hayden, E. P., and Dyson, M. W. (2013). Gender differences in young children's temperament traits: Comparisons across observational and parent-report methods. *Journal of Personality, 81*(2), 119-129.

Oliver, M. B., and Hyde, J. S. (1993). Gender differences in sexuality: A meta-analysis. *Psychological Bulletin, 114,* 29-51.

Olson, J. (2002). *"I": The creation of a serial killer.* New York: St. Martin's Paperbacks.

Oltmanns, T. F., and Emery, R. E. (2004). *Abnormal psychology* (4th ed.). Upper Saddle River, NJ: Prentice Hall.

Olweus, D. (1978). *Bullies and whipping boys.* Washington, DC: Hemisphere.

Olweus, D. (1979). Stability of aggressive reaction patterns in males: A review. *Psychological Bulletin, 86,* 852-875.

Olweus, D. (2001). *Olweus' core program against bullying and antisocial behavior: A teacher handbook.* Research Center for Health promotion (Hemil Center). Bergen, Norway.

Ones, D. S., and Viswesvaran, C. (1998). Integrity testing in organizations. *Monographs in Organizational Behavior and Industrial Relations, 23,* 243-276.

Ones, D. S., Viswesvaran, C., and Schmidt, F. L. (2003). Personality and absenteeism: A meta-analysis of integrity tests. *European Journal of Personality, 17*(Suppl1), S19-S38.

Ong, E. Y. L., Ang, R. P., Ho, J. C. M., Lim, J. C. Y., Goh, D. H., Lee, C. S., and Chua, A. Y. K. (2011). Narcissism, extraversion and adolescents' self-presentation on Facebook. *Personality and Individual Differences, 50,* 180-185.

Oniszczenko, W., Zawadzki, B., Strelau, J., Reimann, R., Angleitner, A., and Spinath, F. M. (2003). Genetic and environmental determinants of temperament: A comprehensive study based on Polish and German samples. *European Journal of Personality, 17,* 207-220.

Oravecz, Z., Dirsmith, J., Heshmati, S., Vandekerckhove, J., and Brick, T. R. (2020). Psychological well-being and personality traits are associated with experiencing love in everyday life. *Personality and Individual Differences, 153,* 109620.

Origlio, J., and Odar Stough, C. (2022). Locus of control and pre-pandemic depressive symptoms related to psychological adjustment of college students to the covid-19 pandemic. *Journal of American College Health,* Feb 28, DOI: 10.1080/07448481.2022.2047699.

Osgood, C. E., Suci, G. J., and Tannenbaum, P. H. (1957). *The measurement of meaning.* Urbana: University of Illinois Press.

Oskis, A., Smyth, N., Flynn, M., and Clow, A. (2019). Repressors exhibit lower cortisol reactivity to group psychosocial stress. *Psychoneuroendocrinology, 103,* 33-40.

Osmon, D. C., and Jackson, R. (2002). Inspection time and IQ: Fluid or perceptual aspects of intelligence? *Intelligence, 30,* 119-128.

Ostendorf, F. (1990). *Language and personality structure: Towards the validity of the five-factor model of personality.* Regensburg, Germany: Roderer-Verlag.

Ostrov, J. M., and Godleski, S. A. (2010). Toward an integrated gender-linked model of aggression subtypes in early and middle childhood. *Psychological Review, 117,* 233–242.

Otero, M. C., Wells, J. L., Chen, K. H., Brown, C. L., Connelly, D. E., Levenson, R. W., and Fredrickson, B. L. (2020). Behavioral indices of positivity resonance associated with long-term marital satisfaction. *Emotion, 20*(7), 1225.

Otgaar, H., Howe, M. L., Dodier, O., Lilienfeld, S. O., Loftus, E. F.. Lynn, S. J., Merckelbach, H., and Patihis, L. (2021). Belief in unconscious repressed memory persists. *Perspectives on Psychological Science, 16,* 454–460

Oughton, J. M., and Reed, W. M. (1999). The influence of learner differences on the construction of hypermedia concepts: A case study. *Computers in Human Behavior, 15,* 11–50.

Owens, M.M., Hyatt, C. S., Gray, J. C., Carter, N. T., MacKillop, J., Miller, J. D., and Sweet, L. H. (2019). Cortical morphometry of the five-factor model of personality: Findings from the Human Connectome Project full sample. *Social Cognitive and Affective Neuroscience,* 14, 381–395.

Oyserman, D., and Markus, H. (1990). Possible selves in balance: Implications for delinquency. *Journal of Social Issues, 46,* 141–157.

Oyserman, D., and Saltz, E. (1993). Competence, delinquency, and attempts to attain possible selves. *Journal of Personality and Social Psychology, 65,* 360–374.

Oyserman, D., Coon, H. M., and Kemmelmeier, M. (2002a). Rethinking individualism and collectivism: Evaluation of theoretical assumptions and meta-analyses. *Psychological Bulletin, 128*(1), 3–72.

Oyserman, D., Coon, H. M., and Kemmelmeier, M. (2002b). Cultural psychology, a new look: Reply to Bond (2002), Fiske (2002), Kitayama (2002), and Miller (2002). *Psychological Bulletin, 128*(1), 110–117.

Oyserman, D., Destin, M., and Novin, S. (2015). The context-sensitive future self: Possible selves motivate in context, not otherwise. In C. Tsekeris and C. Tsekeris (Eds.), *Revisiting the Self: Social Science Perspectives* (pp. 99–114). New York: Routledge/Taylor & Francis Group.

Ozer, D. J., and Benet-Martinez, V. (2006). *Annual Review of Psychology, 57,* 401–421.

Ozer, D. J., and Buss, D. M. (1991). Two views of behavior: Agreement and disagreement in married couples. In A. Stewart, J. Healy, and D. Ozer (Eds.), *Perspectives in personality psychology* (pp. 93–108). London: Jessica Kingsley.

Palys, T. S., and Little, B. R. (1983). Perceived life satisfaction and the organization of personal project systems. *Journal of Personality and Social Psychology, 44,* 1221–1230.

Panksepp, J. (2005). Why does separation distress hurt? Comment on MacDonald and Leary (2005). *Psychological Bulletin, 131,* 224–230.

Paquet, Y., Martin-Krumm, C., Junot, A., and Gilibert, D. (2021). Explanatory style and burnout at the workplace: A cluster analysis. *L'Encéphale: Revue de psychiatrie clinique biologique et thérapeutique, 47,* 130–136 .

Paradis, C. M., Horn, L., Lazar, R. M., and Schwartz, D. W. (1994). Brain dysfunction and violent behavior in a man with a congenital subarachnoid cyst. *Hospital and Community Psychiatry, 45,* 714–716.

Paris, J. (2017). Is psychoanalysis still relevant to psychiatry? *Canadian Journal of Psychiatry, 62,* 308–312.

Park, J. H., van Leeuwen, F., and Stephen, I. D. (2012). Homeliness is in the disgust sensitivity of the beholder: Relatively unattractive faces appear especially unattractive to individuals higher in pathogen disgust. *Evolution and Human Behavior, 33*(5), 569–577.

Park, S. W., and Colvin, C. R. (2015). Narcissism and other-derogation in the absence of ego threat. *Journal of Personality, 83*(3), 334–345.

Patrick, C. J. (1994). Emotion and psychopathy: Startling new insights. *Psychophysiology, 31,* 319–330.

Patrick, C. J. (Ed.). (2005). *The handbook of psychopathy.* New York: Guilford Press.

Patrick, C. J., Bradley, M. M., and Lang, P. J. (1993). Emotion in the criminal psychopath: Startle reflex modulation. *Journal of Abnormal Psychology, 102,* 82–92.

Patrick, C. J., Cuthbert, B. N., and Lang, P. J. (1994). Emotion in the criminal psychopath: Fear image processing. *Journal of Abnormal Psychology, 103,* 523–534.

Patrick, C., Drislane, L. E., and Strickland, C. (2012). Conceptualizing psychopathy in Triarchic terms: Implications for treatment. *The International Journal of Forensic Mental Health, 11*(4), 253–266.

Patterson, C. H. (2000). *Understanding psychotherapy: Fifty years of client-centred theory and practice.* Ross-on-Wye, England: PCCS Books Ltd.

Paulhus, D. L. (1984). Two component models of socially desirable responding. *Journal of Personality and Social Psychology, 46,* 598–609.

Paulhus, D. L. (1990). Measurement and control of response bias. In J. P. Robinson, P. R. Shaver, and L. Wrightsman (Eds.), *Measures of personality and social-psychological attitudes* (pp. 17–59). San Diego, CA: Academic Press.

Paulhus, D. L., and Vazire, S. (2007). The self-report method. In R. W. Robins, R. C. Fraley, and R. F. Krueger (Eds.), *Handbook of research methods in personality psychology* (pp. 224–239). New York: Guilford.

Paulhus, D. L., and Williams, K. M. (2002). The Dark Triad of personality: Narcissism, Machiavellianism, and psychopathy. *Journal of Research in Personality, 36,* 556–563.

Paunesku, D., Walton, G. M., Romero, C., Smith, E. N., Yeager, D. S., and Dweck, C. S. (2015). Mind-set interventions are a scalable treatment for academic underachievement. *Psychological Science, 26*(6), 784–793.

Paunonen, S. V. (2002). *Design and construction of the Supernumerary Personality Inventory* (Research Bulletin 763). London, Ontario: University of Western Ontario.

Paunonen, S. V. (2003). Big Five factors of personality and replicated predictions of behavior. *Journal of Personality and Social Psychology, 84*(2), 411–424.

Paunonen, S. V., and Ashton, M. C. (1998). The structured assessment of personality across cultures. *Journal of Cross-Cultural Psychology, 29,* 150–170.

Paunonen, S. V., and Hong, R. Y. (2015). In defense of personality traits. In L. Cooper and R. J. Larsen (Eds.), *Handbook of Personality and Social Psychology: Personality Processes and Individual Differences* (pp. 233–260). Washington, DC: American Psychological Association.

Paunonen, S. V., and O'Neil, T. A. (2010). Self-reports, peer ratings, and construct validity. *European Journal of Personality, 24,* 189–206.

Pedersen, N. L. (1993). Genetic and environmental change in personality. In T. J. Bouchard and P. Proping (Eds.), *Twins as a tool of behavioral genetics* (pp. 147–162). West Sussex, England: Wiley.

Penke, L., and Asendorpf, J. B. (2008a). Beyond global sociosexual orientations: A more differentiated look at sociosexuality and its effects on courtship and romantic relationships. *Journal of Personality and Social Psychology, 95,* 1113–1135.

Penke, L., Denissen, J.J.A., and Miller, G. F. (2007). The evolutionary genetics of personality. *European Journal of Personality, 21,* 549–587.

Pennebaker, J. W. (2003a). The social, linguistic and health consequences of emotional disclosure. In J. Suls and K. A. Wallston (Eds.), *Social psychological foundations of health and illness* (pp. 288–313). Malden, MA: Blackwell.

Pennebaker, J. W. (2003b). Writing about emotional experiences as a therapeutic process. In P. Salovey and A. J. Rothman (Eds.), *Social psychology of health* (pp. 362–368). New York: Psychology Press.

Pennebaker, J. W., and Chung, C. K. (2011). Expressive writing: Connections to physical and mental health. *Oxford handbook of health psychology* (417–437). New York: Oxford University Press.

Pennebaker, J. W., and O'Heeron, R. C. (1984). Confiding in others and illness rates among spouses of suicide and accidental-death victims. *Journal of Abnormal Psychology, 93,* 473–476.

Pennebaker, J. W., Colder, M., and Sharp, L. K. (1990). Accelerating the coping process. *Journal of Personality and Social Psychology, 58,* 528–537.

Perilloux, C., Fleischman, D. S., and Buss, D. M. (2008). The daughter-guarding hypothesis: Parental influence on children's mating behavior. *Evolutionary Psychology, 6,* 217–233.

Perilloux, C., Fleischman, D. S., and Buss, D. M. (2011). Meet the parents: Parent-offspring convergence and divergence in mate preferences. *Personality and Individual Differences, 50,* 253–258.

Perry, V. G. (2008). Giving credit where credit is due: The psychology of credit ratings. *Journal of Behavioral Finance, 9,* 15–21.

Persson, B. (2020). Genotype- Environment Correlation and Its Relation to Personality—A Twin and Family Study. *Twin Research and Human Genetics, 23*(4), 228–234.$$$

Perugini, M., and Richetin, J. (2007). In the land of the blind, the one-eyed man is king. *European Journal of Personality, 21,* 977–981.

Perugini, M., Hagemeyer, B., Wrzus, C., and Back, M. D. (2021). Dual process models of personality. In J. F. Rauthmann (Ed), *The Handbook of Personality Dynamics and Processes,* pp. 551–577. New York: Elsevier Academic Press.

Petersen, J. L., and Hyde, J. S. (2010). A meta-analytic review of research on gender differences in sexuality, 1993–2007. *Psychological Bulletin, 136,* 21–38.

Peterson, B. E., Winter, D. G., and Doty, R. M. (1994). Laboratory tests of a motivational-perceptual model of conflict escalation. *Journal of Conflict Resolution, 38,* 719–748.

Peterson, C. (1991). The meaning and measurement of explanatory style. *Psychological Inquiry, 2,* 1–10.

Peterson, C. (1995). Explanatory style and health. In G. M. Buchanan and M. E. P. Seligman (Eds.), *Explanatory style* (pp. 233–246). Hillsdale, NJ: Erlbaum.

Peterson, C. (2000). The future of optimism. *American Psychologist, 55,* 44–55.

Peterson, C., and Bossio, L. M. (1991). *Health and optimism.* New York: Free Press.

Peterson, C., and Bossio, L. M. (2001). Optimism and physical well-being. In E. C. Chang (Ed.), *Optimism and pessimism:*

Implications for theory, research, and practice (pp. 127–145). Washington, DC: American Psychological Association.

Peterson, C., and Chang, E. C. (2003). Optimism and flourishing. In C. L. Keyes and J. Haidt (Eds.), *Flourishing: Positive psychology and the life well-lived* (pp. 55–79). Washington, DC: American Psychological Association.

Peterson, C., and Park, N. (2010). What happened to self-actualization? Commentary on Kenrick et al. (2010). *Perspectives on Psychological Science, 5,* 320–322.

Peterson, C., and Seligman, M. E. P. (1987). Explanatory style and illness. Special issue: Personality and physical health. *Journal of Personality, 55,* 237–265.

Peterson, C., and Seligman, M. E. P. (2003). Character strengths before and after September 11. *Psychological Science, 14,* 381–384.

Peterson, C., Maier, S. F., and Seligman, M. E. P. (1993). *Learned helplessness: A theory for the age of personal control.* New York: Oxford University Press.

Peterson, C., Schulman, P., Castellon, C., and Seligman, M. E. P. (1992). CAVE: Content analysis of verbatim explanations. In C. P. Smith (Ed.), *Motivation and personality: Handbook of thematic content analysis* (pp. 383–392). New York: Cambridge University Press.

Peterson, C., Seligman, M. E. P., and Vaillant, G. E. (1988). Pessimistic explanatory style is a risk factor for physical illness: A thirty-five-year longitudinal study. *Journal of Personality and Social Psychology, 55,* 23–27.

Peterson, C., Seligman, M. E. P., Yurko, K. H., Martin, L. R., and Friedman, H. S. (1998). Catastrophizing and untimely death. *Psychological Science, 9,* 49–52.

Peterson, J. B., Smith, K. W., and Carson, S. (2002). Openness and extraversion are associated with reduced latent inhibition: Replication and commentary. *Personality and Individual Differences, 33,* 1137–1147.

Petrie, A. (1967). *Individuality in pain and suffering.* Chicago: University of Chicago Press.

Petrill, S. A. (2002). The case for general intelligence: A behavioral genetic perspective. In R. J. Sternberg and E. L. Grigorenko (Eds.), *The general factor of intelligence: How general is it?* (pp. 281–298). Mahwah, NJ: Erlbaum.

Phillips, I., (2021). Blindsight is qualitatively degraded conscious vision. *Psychological Review, 28,* 558–584.

Pickering, A. D., Corr, P. J., and Gray, J. A. (1999). Interactions and reinforcement sensitivity theory: A theoretical analysis of Rusting and Larsen (1997). *Personality and Individual Differences, 26,* 357–365.

Pickering, A., Farmer, A., Harris, T., Redman, K., Mahmood, A., Sadler, S., and

McGuffin, P. (2003). A sib-pair study of psychoticism, life events and depression. *Personality and Individual Differences, 34,* 613–623.

Piedmont, R. L. (2001). Cracking the plaster cast: Big Five personality change during intensive outpatient counseling. *Journal of Research in Personality, 35,* 500–520.

Pietrzak, R., Laird, J. D., Stevens, D. A., and Thompson, N. S. (2002). Sex differences in human jealousy: A coordinated study of forced-choice, continuous rating-scale, and physiological responses on the same subjects. *Evolution and Human Behavior, 23,* 83–94.

Piff, P. K., Kraus, M. W., Côté, S., Cheng, B. H., and Keltner, D. (2010). Having less, giving more: The influence of social class on prosocial behavior. *Journal of Personality and Social Psychology, 99*(5), 771–784.

Pincus, J. H. (1999). Aggression, criminality, and the frontal lobes. In B. L. Miller and J. L. Cummings (Eds.), *The Human Frontal Lobes: Functions and Disorders.* (pp. 547–556). New York: Guilford Press.

Pincus, J. H. (2001). *Base Instincts: What Makes Killers Kill?* New York: Norton.

Pinker, S. (1997). *How the mind works.* New York: Norton.

Pinker, S. (2012). *The better angels of our nature: The decline of violence in history and its causes.* New York: Viking.

Pipher, M. (1994). *Reviving Ophelia: Saving the selves of adolescent girls.* New York: Ballantine Books.

Piquero, A. R., Carriaga, M. L., Diamond, B., Kazemian, L., and Farrington, D. P. (2012). Stability in aggression revisited. *Aggression and Violent Behavior, 17*(4), 365–372.

Pittenger, D. J. (2005). Cautionary comments regarding the Myers-Briggs Type Indicator. *Consulting Psychology Journal: Practice and Research, 57,* 210–221.

Plavcan, J. M. (2012). Sexual size dimorphism, canine dimorphism, and male-male competition in primates. *Human Nature, 23,* 45–67.

Plomin, R. (2002). Individual differences research in a postgenomic era. *Personality and Individual Differences, 33,* 909–920.

Plomin, R. (2019). *Blueprint: How DNA makes us who we are.* Cambridge, MA: MIT Press.

Plomin, R., and Crabbe, J. (2000). DNA. *Psychological Bulletin Special Issue: Psychology in the 21st Century, 126,* 806–828.

Plomin, R., and Davis, O. S. P. (2009). The future of genetics in psychology and psychiatry: Microarrays, genome-wide association, and non-coding RNA. *Journal of Child Psychology and Psychiatry, 50,* 63–71.

Plomin, R., and DeFries, G. E. (1985). *Origins of individual differences in infancy: The Colorado Adoption Project.* New York: Academic Press.

Plomin, R., DeFries, J. C., and Fulker, D. W. (1988). *Nature and nurture during infancy and early childhood.* New York: Cambridge University Press.

Plomin, R., DeFries, J. C., and Loehlin, J. C. (1977). Genotype-environment interaction and correlation in the analysis of human behavior. *Psychological Bulletin, 84,* 309-322.

Plomin, R., DeFries, J. C., and McClearn, G. E. (1990). *Behavioral Genetics: A Primer* (2nd ed.). New York: W. H. Freeman.

Plomin, R., DeFries, J. C., and McClearn, G. E. (2008). *Behavioral genetics.* New York: Macmillan.

Plomin, R., DeFries, J. C., Knopik, V. S., and Neiderheiser, J. (2013). *Behavioral genetics.* Basingstoke, UK: Palgrave Macmillan.

Plomin, R., DeFries, J. C., McClern, G. E., and McGuffin, P. (2001). *Behavioral genetics* (4th ed.). New York: Worth.

Plutchik, R. (1980). A general psychoevolutionary theory of emotion. In R. Plutchik and H. Kellerman (Eds.), *Emotion: Theory, Research, and Experience: Vol. 1: Theories of Emotion* (pp. 3-31). New York: Academic Press.

Pocuca, N., Hides, L., Quinn, C. A., White, M. J., Mewton, L., and Loxton, N. J. (2019). An exploratory study of the relationship between neuroticism and problematic drinking in emerging adulthood, and the moderating effect of social anxiety. *Personality and Individual Differences, 145,* 132-144.

Polderman, T. J., Kreukels, B. P., Irwig, M. S., Beach, L., Chan, Y. M., Derks, E. M., . . . and Raynor, L. (2018). The biological contributions to gender identity and gender diversity: Bringing data to the table. *Behavior Genetics, 48*(2), 95-108.

Pollock, V. E., Briere, J., Schneider, L., Knop, J., Mednick, S., and Goodwin, D. W. (1990). Childhood antecedents of antisocial behavior: Parental alcoholism and physical abusiveness. *American Journal of Psychiatry, 147,* 1290-1293.

Poropat, A. E. (2009). A meta-analysis of the five-factor model of personality and academic performance. *Psychological Bulletin, 135,* 322-338.

Post, J. M. (Ed.). (2003). *The psychological assessment of political leaders.* Ann Arbor: University of Michigan Press.

Price, M. E., Cosmides, L., and Tooby, J. (2002). Punitive sentiment as an anti-free rider psychological device. *Evolution and Human Behavior, 23,* 203-231.

Prior, H., Schwarz, A., and Güntürkün, O. (2008). Mirror-induced behavior in the magpie (*Pica pica*): Evidence of self-recognition. *Public Library of Science: Biology, 6*(8), 202. doi:10.1371/ journal. pbio.0060202.

Privado, J., Román, F. J., Saénz-Urturi, C., Burgaleta, M., and Colom, R. (2017). Gray and white matter correlates of the Big Five personality traits. *Neuroscience, 349,* 174-184.

Promislow, D. (2003). Mate choice, sexual conflict, and evolution of senescence. *Behavior Genetics, 33,* 191-201.

Prusik, M., Konopka, K., and Kocur, D. (2021). Too many shades of gray: The Dark Triad and its linkage to coercive and coaxing tactics to obtain sex and the quality of romantic relationships. *Personality and Individual Differences, 170,* 110413.

Pullmann, H., Raudsepp, L., and Allik, J. (2006). Stability and change in adolescents' personality: A longitudinal study. *European Journal of Personality, 20,* 447-459.

Pulver, C. A., and Kelly, K. R. (2008). Incremental validity of the Myers-Briggs Type Indicator in predicting academic major selection of undecided university students. *Journal of Career Assessment, 16,* 441-455.

Putwain, D. W. (2019). An examination of the self-referent executive processing model of test anxiety: Control, emotional regulation, self-handicapping, and examination performance. *European Journal of Psychology of Education, 34,* 341-358.

Quinn-Nilas, C., Kennett, D. J., and Maki, K. (2019). Examining explanatory style for failure of direct entry and transfer students using structural equation modeling. *Educational Psychology,* Feb 23, 2019, DOI: 10.1080/01443410.2019.1574340

Rafaeli-Mor, E., and Steinberg, J. (2002). Self-complexity and well-being: A review and research synthesis. *Personality and Social Psychology Review, 6,* 31-58.

Raine, A. (2002). Biosocial studies of antisocial and violent behavior in children and adults: A review. *Journal of Abnormal Child Psychology, 30,* 311-326.

Raine, A., Meloy, J. R., and Bihrle, S. (1998). Reduced prefrontal and increased subcortical brain functioning assessed using positron emission tomography in predatory and affective murderers. *Behavioral Sciences and the Law Special Issue: Impulsive Aggression, 16,* 319-332.

Ramírez-Maestre, C., Esteve, R., Serrano-Ibáñez, E. R., López-Martínez, A. E., Ruiz-Párraga, G. T., and Rivas-Moya, T. (2020). Psychometric characteristics and factorial structures of the Defensive Pessimism Questionnaire—Spanish Version (DPQ-SV). *PLoS ONE, 15.* https://doi. org/10.1371/journal.pone.0229695.

Rammsayer, T. H., and Brandler, S. (2002). On the relationship between general fluid intelligence and psychophysical indicators of temporal resolution in the brain. *Journal of Research in Personality, 36,* 507-530.

Rammstedt, B., Goldberg, L. R., and Borg, I. (2010). The measurement equivalence of Big-Five factor markers for persons with different levels of education. *Journal of Research in Personality, 44,* 53-61.

Rammstedt, B., Spinath, F. M., Richter, D., and Schupp, J. (2013). Partnership longevity and personality congruence in couples. *Personality and Individual Differences, 54*(7), 832-835.

Ramos, A. M., Griffin, A. M., Neiderhiser, J. M., and Reiss, D. (2019). Did I inherit my moral compass? Examining socialization and evocative mechanisms for virtuous character development. *Behavior Genetics, 49*(2), 175-186.

Randler, C., and Jankowski, K. S. (2014). Evidence for the validity of the Composite Scale of Morningness based on students from Germany and Poland—Relationship with sleep-wake and social schedules. *Biological Rhythm Research, 45*(4), 653-659.

Randler, C., and Kretz, S. (2011). Assortative mating in morningness-eveningness. *International Journal of Psychology, 46*(2), 91-96.

Raskin, J. D. (2001). The modern, the postmodern, and George Kelly's personal construct psychology. *American Psychologist, 56,* 368-369.

Raskin, R., and Hall, C. S. (1979). A narcissistic personality inventory. *Psychological Reports, 45,* 590.

Raskin, R., and Shaw, R. (1987). *Narcissism and the use of personal pronouns.* Unpublished manuscript.

Raskin, R., and Terry, H. (1988). A principle-components analysis of the narcissistic personality inventory and further evidence of its construct validity. *Journal of Personality and Social Psychology, 54,* 890-902.

Rattan, A., Good, C., and Dweck, C. S. (2012). "It's OK—Not everyone can be good at math": Instructors with an entity theory comfort (and demotivate) students. *Journal of Experimental Social Psychology, 48,* 731-737.

Rattan, A., Savani, K., Chugh, D., and Dweck, C. S. (2015). Leveraging mindsets to promote academic achievement: Policy recommendations. *Perspectives on Psychological Science, 10*(6), 721-726.

Rauthmann, J., and Denissen, J. J. A. (2011). I often do it vs. I like doing it: Comparing a frequency- and valency-approach to extraversion. *Personality and Individual Differences, 50,* 1283-1288.

Rawlings, D. (2003). Personality correlates of liking for "unpleasant" paintings and photographs. *Personality and Individual Differences, 34,* 395-410.

Regan, P. C., and Atkins, L. (2006). Sex differences and similarities in frequency and intensity of sexual desire. *Social Behavior and Personality, 34,* 95-102.

Reidy, D. E., Zeichner, A., Foster, J. D., and Martinez, M. A. (2008). Effects of narcissistic entitlement and exploitativeness on human physical aggression. *Personality and Individual Differences, 44,* 685-875.

Renn, K. A., and Reason, R. D. (2021). *College students in the United States: Characteristics, experiences, and outcomes.* Stylus Publishing, LLC.

Renner, W., Kandler, C., Bleidorn, W., Riemann, R., Angleitner, A., Spinath, F. M., and Menschik-Bendele, J. (2012). Human values: Genetic and environmental effects on five lexically derived domains and their facets. *Personality and Individual Differences, 52,* 89-93.

Renshon, S. A. (1998). Analyzing the psychology and performances of presidential candidates at a distance: Bob Dole and the 1996 presidential campaign. *Leadership Quarterly, 9,* 377-395.

Renshon, S. A. (2005). George W. Bush's cowboy politics: An inquiry. *Political Psychology, 26,* 585-614.

Rentzsch, K. and Schröder-Abé, M. (2022). Top down or bottom up? Evidence from the longitudinal development of global and domain-specific self-esteem in adulthood. *Journal of Personality and Social Psychology, 122,* 714-730.

Rhee, E., Uleman, J., Lee, H., and Roman, R. (1995). Spontaneous self-descriptions and ethnic identities in individualistic and collectivist cultures. *Journal of Personality and Social Psychology, 69,* 142-152.

Rheingold, H. L., and Cook, K. V. (1975). The contents of boys' and girls' rooms as an index of parents' behavior. *Child Development, 46,* 459-463.

Rhodenwalt, F., and Morf, C. (1998). On self-aggrandizement and anger: A temporal analysis of narcissism and affective reactions to success and failure. *Journal of Personality and Social Psychology, 74,* 672-685.

Richardson, A. K., and Winter, D. G. (2021). U.S. Senators' power motivation and their votes for war versus peace. *Peace and Conflict: Journal of Peace Psychology, 27,* 524-533.

Richardson, J. A., and Turner, T. E. (2000). Field dependence revisited I: Intelligence. *Educational Psychology, 20,* 255-270.

Richardson, M., and Abraham, C. (2009). Conscientiousness and achievement motivation predict performance. *European Journal of Personality, 23,* 589-605.

Ridley, M. (1999). *Genome: The autobiography of a species in 23 chapters.* New York: HarperCollins.

Rind, B., Tromovitch, P., and Bouserman, R. (1998). A meta-analytic examination of assumed properties of child sexual abuse (CSA) using college samples. *Psychological Bulletin, 124,* 22-53.

Rindermann, H. (2008). Relevance of education and intelligence at the national level for the economic welfare of people. *Intelligence, 36,* 127-142.

Ristvedt, S. L., and Trinkaus, K. M. (2005). Psychological factors related to delay in consultation for cancer symptoms. *Psycho-oncology, 14,* 339-350.

Ritts, V., and Patterson, M. L. (1996). Effects of social anxiety and action identification on impressions and thoughts in interaction. *Journal of Social and Clinical Psychology, 15,* 191-205.

Ritvo, L. B. (1990). *Darwin's influence on Freud: A tale of two sciences.* New Haven, CT: Yale University Press.

Robbins, R. and John, O. P. (1997). Accuracy and Bias in Self-Perception: Individual Differences in Self-Enhancement and the Role of Narcissism. *Journal of Personality and Social Psychology, 66,* 206-219.

Roberts, B. W., and DelVecchio, W. F. (2000). The rank-order consistency of personality traits from childhood to old age: A quantitative review of the longitudinal studies. *Psychological Bulletin, 126,* 3-25.

Roberts, B. W., Caspi, A., and Moffitt, T. E. (2001). The kids are alright: Growth and stability in personality development from adolescence to adulthood. *Journal of Personality and Social Psychology, 81*(4), 670-683.

Roberts, B. W., Caspi, A., and Moffitt, T. E. (2003). Work experiences and personality development in young adulthood. *Journal of Personality and Social Psychology, 84*(5), 582-593.

Roberts, B. W., Walton, K. R., and Viechtbauer, W. (2006). Patterns of mean-level change in personality traits across the life course: A meta-analysis of longitudinal studies. *Psychological Bulletin, 132,* 1-25.

Roberts, J. E., and Monroe, S. M. (1992). Vulnerable self-esteem and depressive symptoms: Prospective findings comparing three alternative conceptualizations. *Journal of Personality and Social Psychology, 62,* 804-812.

Roberts, W. B., and Robins, R. W. (2004). Person-environment fit and its implications for personality development: A longitudinal study. *Journal of Personality, 72,* 89-110.

Robertson, S. M. C., Short, S. D., Sawyer, L., and Sweazy, S. (2020). Randomized controlled trial assessing the efficacy of expressive writing in reducing anxiety in first-year college students: The role of linguistic features. *Psychology and Health.* https://doi.org/10.1080/08870446.2020.1827146.

Robins, R. W., and John, O. P. (1997). Self-perception, visual perspective, and narcissism: Is seeing believing? *Psychological Science, 8,* 37-42.

Robins, R. W., Caspi, A., and Moffitt, T. E. (2002). It's not just who you're with, it's who you are: Personality and relationship experiences across multiple relationships. *Journal of Personality, 70,* 925-964.

Robins, R. W., Fraley, R. C., Roberts, B. W., and Trzesniewski, K. H. (2001). A longitudinal study of personality change in young adulthood. *Journal of Personality, 69*(4), 617-640.

Rodriguez, N. N., and Lukaszewski, A. W. (2020). Functional coordination of personality strategies with physical strength and attractiveness: A multi-sample investigation at the HEXACO facet-level. *Journal of Research in Personality, 89,* 104040.

Roediger, H. L., and McDermott K. B. (1995). Creating false memories: Remembering words not presented in lists. *Journal of Experimental Psychology: Learning, Memory, and Cognition, 21,* 803-814.

Roediger, H. L., Balota, D. A., and Watson, J. M. (2001). Spreading activation and arousal of false memories. In Henry L. Roediger, III, and James S. Nairne (Eds.), *The nature of remembering: Essays in honor of Robert G. Crowder* (pp. 95-115). Washington, DC: American Psychological Association.

Roediger, H. L., McDermott, K. B., and Robinson, K. J. (1998). The role of associative processes in creating false memories. In M. A. Conway, S. E. Gathercole, and C. Cornoldi (Eds.), *Theories of memory II* (pp. 187-246). Hove, Sussex, England: Psychological Press.

Rogers, C. R. (1957). The necessary and sufficient conditions of therapeutic personality change. *Journal of Consulting Psychology, 21,* 95-103.

Rogers, C. R. (1975). Empathic: An unappreciated way of being. *The Counseling Psychologist, 5,* 2-10.

Rogers, C. R. (2002). *Carl Rogers: The quiet revolutionary, an oral history.* Roseville, CA: Penmarin Books.

Rogness, G. A., and McClure, E. B. (1996). Development and neurotransmitter-environment interactions. *Development and Psychopathology, 8,* 183-199.

Romero, C., Master, A., Paunesku, D., Dweck, C. S., and Gross, J. J. (2014). Academic and emotional functioning in middle school: The role of implicit theories. *Emotion, 14*(2), 227-234.

Romero, E., Luengo, M. T., Carrillo-de-la-Pena, T., and Otero-Lopez, J. M. (1994). The act frequency approach to the study of impulsivity. *European Journal of Personality, 8,* 119-134.

Rosch, E. (1975). Cognitive reference points. *Cognitive Psychology, 7,* 532-547.

Rose, R. J. (1995). Genes and behavior. *Annual Review of Psychology, 46,* 625–654.

Rosenzweig, S. (1986). Idiodynamics vis-à-vis psychology. *American Psychologist, 41,* 241–245.

Rosenzweig, S. (1994). *The historic expedition to America (1909): Freud, Jung, and Hall the king-maker.* St. Louis, MO: Rana House.

Rosenzweig, S. (1997). "Idiographic" vis-à-vis "idiodynamic" in the historical perspective of personality theory: Remembering Gordon Allport, 1897–1997. *Journal of the History of the Behavioral Sciences, 33,* 405–419.

Ross, K. M., Liu, S., Tomfohr, L. M., and Miller, G. E. (2013). Self-esteem variability predicts arterial stiffness trajectories in healthy adolescent females. *Health Psychology, 32*(8), 869–876.

Ross, L., Greene, D., and House, P. (1977). The false consensus effect: An egocentric bias in social perception and attribution processes. *Journal of Experimental Social Psychology, 13,* 279–301.

Ross, S. R., Canada, K. E., and Rausch, M. K. (2002). Self-handicapping and the five factor model of personality: Mediation between neuroticism and conscientiousness. *Personality and Individual Differences, 32,* 1173–1184.

Rothbart, M. K. (1981). Measurement of temperament in infancy. *Child Development, 52,* 569–578.

Rothbart, M. K. (1986). Longitudinal observation of infant temperament. *Developmental Psychology, 22,* 356–365.

Rothbart, M. K., and Hwang, J. (2005). Temperament. In A. J. Elliot and C. S. Dweck (Eds.), *Handbook of competence & motivation* (pp. 167–184). New York: Guilford.

Rotter, J. B. (1971). Generalized expectancies for interpersonal trust. *American Psychologist, 26,* 443–452.

Rotter, J. B. (1990). Internal versus external control of reinforcement: A case history of a variable. *American Psychologist, 45,* 489–493.

Rowe, D. C. (2001). *Biology and crime.* New York: Roxbury.

Rozin, P. (1996). Towards a psychology of food and eating: From motivation to module to model to marker, morality, meaning, and metaphor. *Current Directions in Psychological Science, 5*(1), 18–24.

Rozin, P. (2003). Five potential principles for understanding cultural differences in relation to individual differences. *Journal of Research in Personality, 37,* 273–283.

Rozin, P., and Nemeroff, C. (1990). The laws of sympathetic magic: A psychological analysis of similarity and contagion. In J. W. Stigler, R. A. Shweder, and G. Herdt (Eds.), Cultural psychology: Essays on comparative human

development (pp. 205–232). Cambridge University Press.

Ruch, W., Heintz, S., Gander, F., Hofmann, J., Platt, T., and Proyer, R. T. (2021). The long and winding road: a comprehensive analysis of 50 years of Eysenck instruments for the assessment of personality. *Personality and Individual Differences, 169,* 110070.

Ruchkin, V. V., Koposov, R. A., Eisemann, M., and Hagglof, B. (2002). Alcohol use in delinquent adolescents from Northern Russia: The role of personality, parental rearing and family history of alcohol abuse. *Personality and Individual Differences, 32,* 1139–1148.

Rule, A. (2000). *The stranger beside me.* New York: Norton.

Runge, J. M., Lang, J. W. B., Zettler, I., and Lievens, F. (2020). Predicting counterproductive work behavior: Do implicit motives have incremental validity beyond explicit traits? *Journal of Research in Personality, 89,* ArtID: 104019

Runyon, W. M. (1983). Idiographic goals and methods in the study of lives. *Journal of Personality, 51,* 413–437.

Russell, V. M., and McNulty, J. K. (2011). Frequent sex protects intimates from the negative implications of their neuroticism. *Social Psychological and Personality Science, 2,* 220–227.

Rusting, C. L., and Larsen, R. J. (1997). Extraversion, neuroticism, and susceptibility to positive and negative affect: A test of two theoretical models. *Personality and Individual Differences, 22,* 607–612.

Rusting, C. L., and Larsen, R. J. (1998a). Diurnal patterns of unpleasant mood: Associations with neuroticism, depression, and anxiety. *Journal of Personality, 66,* 85–103.

Rusting, C. L., and Larsen, R. J. (1998b). Personality and cognitive processing of affective information. *Personality and Social Psychology Bulletin, 24,* 200–213.

Rusting, C. L., and Larsen, R. J. (1999). Clarifying Gray's theory of personality: A response to Pickering, Corr, and Gray. *Personality and Individual Differences, 26,* 367–372.

Ryan, R. M., and Deci, E. L. (2000). Self-determination theory and the facilitation of intrinsic motivation, social development, and well-being. *American Psychologist, 55,* 68–78.

Ryff, C., Lee, Y., and Na, K. (1995). *Through the lens of culture: Psychological well-being at mid-life.* Unpublished manuscript, University of Michigan, Ann Arbor.

Sagarin, B. J. (2005). Reconsidering evolved sex differences in jealousy: Comment on Harris (2003). *Personality and Social Psychology Review, 9,* 62–75.

Sagarin, B. J., Becker, D. V., Guadagno, R. E., Nicastle, L. D., and Millevoi, A. (2003). Sex differences (and similarities)

in jealousy: The moderating influence of infidelity experience and sexual orientation. *Evolution and Human Behavior, 24,* 17–23.

Sagarin, B. J., Martin, A. L., Clutinho, S. A., and Edlund, J. E. (2009). *A meta-analysis of studies examining sex differences in jealousy using continuous measures.* Paper presented to the Evolutionary Psychology Preconference, Annual Meeting of the Society of Personality and Social Psychology, Tampa, Florida.

Sagarin, B. J., Martin, A. L., Coutinho, S. A., Edlund, J. E., Patel, L., Skowronski, J. J., and Zengel, B. (2012). Sex differences in jealousy: A meta-analytic examination. *Evolution and Human Behavior, 33,* 595–613.

Sagie, A., and Elizur, D. (1999). Achievement motive and entrepreneurial orientation: A structural analysis. *Journal of Organizational Behavior, 20,* 375–387.

Sakuta, A., and Fukushima, A. (1998). A study on abnormal findings pertaining to the brain in criminals. *International Medical Journal, 5,* 283–292.

Salgado, J. F., Moscoso, S., and Lado, M. (2003). Evidence of cross-cultural invariant of the Big Five personality dimensions in work settings. *European Journal of Personality, 17,* S67–S76.

Salovey, P., and Mayer, J. D. (1990). Emotional intelligence. *Imagination, Cognition, and Personality, 9,* 185–211.

Sam, D. L. (1994). The psychological adjustment of young immigrants in Norway. *Scandinavian Journal of Psychology, 35,* 240–253.

Samuel, D. B., and Gore, W. L. (2012). Maladaptive variants of conscientiousness and agreeableness. *Journal of Personality, 80*(6), 1669–1696.

Sandvik, E., Diener, E., and Seidlitz, L. (1993). Subjective well-being: The convergence and stability of self-report and non-self-report measures. *Journal of Personality, 61,* 317–342.

Santayana, G. (1905/1980). *Reason in common sense: The life of reason (*Vol. 1.) New York: Dover.

Sapienza, P., Zingales, L., and Maestripieri, D. (2009). Gender differences in financial risk aversion and career choices are affected by testosterone. *Proceedings of the National Academy of Science, USA, 106,* 15268–15273.

Sapolsky, R. M. (1987). Stress, social status, and reproductive physiology in free-living baboons. In D. Crews (Ed.), *Psychobiology of reproductive behavior: An evolutionary perspective.* Englewood Cliffs, NJ: Prentice Hall.

Saroglou, V. (2002). Religion and the five factors of personality: A meta-analytic review. *Personality and Individual Differences, 32,* 15–25.

Saroglou, V., and Fiasse, L. (2003). Birth order, personality, and religion: A study among young adults from a three-sibling family. *Personality and Individual Differences, 35*(1), 19-29.

Satterfield, J. H., and Schelle, A. M. (1984). Childhood brain function differences in delinquent and non-delinquent hyperactive boys. *Electroencephalography and Clinical Neurophysiology, 57,* 199-207.

Saucier, G. (2003). Factor structure of English-Language personality Type-nouns. *Journal of Personality and Social Psychology, 85*(4), 695-708.

Saucier, G. (2009). Recurrent personality dimensions in inclusive lexical studies: Indications for a Big Six structure. *Journal of Personality, 77,* 1577-1614.

Saucier, G. (2010). The structure of social effects: Personality as impact on others. *European Journal of Personality, 24,* 222-240.

Saucier, G., and Goldberg, L. R. (1996). The language of personality: Lexical perspectives on the five-factor model. In J. S. Wiggins (Ed.), *The five-factor model of personality: Theoretical perspectives* (pp. 21-50). New York: Guilford Press.

Saucier, G., and Goldberg, L. R. (1998). What is beyond the Big Five? *Journal of Personality, 66,* 495-524.

Saucier, G., and Goldberg, L. R. (2001). Lexical studies of indigenous personality factors: Premises, products, and prospects. *Journal of Personality, 69*(6), 847-879.

Saucier, G., Georgiades, S., Tsaousis, I., and Goldberg, L. R. (2005). The factor structure of Greek personality adjectives. *Journal of Personality and Social Psychology, 5,* 856-875.

Sauter, D. A., Eisner, F., Ekman, P., and Scott, S. K. (2010). Cross-cultural recognition of basic emotions through nonverbal emotional vocalizations. *Proceedings of the National Academy of Sciences, 107*(6), 2408-2412.

Scarr, S. (1968). Environmental bias in twin studies. *Eugenics Quarterly, 15,* 34-40.

Scarr, S., and Carter-Saltzman, L. (1979). Twin method: Defense of a critical assumption. *Behavior Genetics, 9,* 527-542.

Scarr, S., and McCartney, K. (1983). How children make their own environments: A theory of genotype environment effects. *Child Development, 54,* 424-435.

Scealy, M., Phillips, J. G., and Stevenson, R. (2002). Shyness and anxiety as predictors of patterns of Internet usage. *Cyber Psychology and Behavior, 5,* 507-515.

Scelza, B. A. (2014). Jealousy in a small-scale, natural fertility population: The roles of paternity, investment and love in jealous response. *Evolution and Human Behavior, 35*(2), 103-108.

Scelza, B. A., Prall, S. P., Blumenfield, T., Crittenden, A. N., Gurven, M., Kline, M., . . . and McElreath, M. (2019). Patterns of paternal investment predict cross-cultural variation in jealous response. *Nature Human Behaviour, 4,* 20-26.

Schacter, D. L. (1997). *Searching for memory: The brain, the mind, and the past.* New York: Basic Books.

Schaffhuser, K., Allemand, M., and Martin, M. (2014). Personality traits and relationship satisfaction in intimate couples: Three perspectives on personality. *European Journal of Personality, 28*(2), 120-133.

Schaller, M. (2016). The behavioral immune system. In D. M. Buss (Ed.), *The handbook of evolutionary psychology.* Hoboken, NJ: Wiley.

Schaller, M., Kenrick, D., Neel, R., and Neuberg, S. (2017). Evolution and human motivation: A fundamental motives framework. *Social and Personality Psychology Compass, 11*(6), [e12319]. https://doi.org/10.1111/spc3.12319.

Schaller, M., Murray, D. R., and Hofer, M. K. (2021). The behavioural immune system and pandemic psychology: the evolved psychology of disease-avoidance and its implications for attitudes, behaviour, and public health during epidemic outbreaks. *European Review of Social Psychology,* 1-37.

Scheier, M. F, and Carver, C. S. (1985). Optimism, coping, and health: Assessment and implications of generalized outcome expectancies. *Health Psychology, 4,* 219-247.

Scheier, M. F., and Carver, C. S. (2018). Dispositional optimism and physical health: A long look back, a quick look forward. *American Psychologist, 73,* 1082-1094.

Scheier, M. F., Matthews, K. A., Owens, J. F., Schulz, R., Bridges, M. W., Magovern, G. J., and Carver, C. S. (1999). Optimism and rehospitalization after coronary artery bypass graft surgery. *Archives of Internal Medicine, 159*(8), 829-835.

Scheier, M. F., Swanson, J. D., Barlow, M. A., Greenhouse, J. B., Wrosch, C., and Tindle, H. A. (2021). Optimism versus pessimism as predictors of physical health: A comprehensive reanalysis of dispositional optimism research. *American Psychologist, 76,* 529-548.

Schinka J. A., Letsch, E. A., and Crawford, F. C. (2002). DRD4 and novelty seeking: Results of meta-analyses. *American Journal of Medical Genetics, 114,* 643-648.

Schiraldi, G. (2007). *10 simple solutions for building self-esteem.* Oakland, CA: New Harbinger.

Schmidt, L. A., and Fox, N. A. (1995). Individual differences in young adults' shyness and sociability: Personality and health correlates. *Personality and Individual Differences, 19,* 455-462.

Schmidt, L. A., and Fox, N. A. (2002). Individual differences in childhood shyness: Origins, malleability and developmental course. In D. Cervone and W. Mischel (Eds.), *Advances in Personality Science* (pp. 83-105). New York: Guilford Press.

Schmitt, D. P. (2004). The Big Five related to risky sexual behavior across 10 world regions: Differential personality associations of sexual promiscuity and relationship infidelity. *European Journal of Personality, 18,* 301-319.

Schmitt, D. P. (2015). The evolution of culturally-variable sex differences: Men and women are not always different, but when they are . . . it appears not to result from patriarchy or sex role socialization. In *The evolution of sexuality* (pp. 221-256). Basel, Switzerland: Springer.

Schmitt, D. P., and 118 Members of the International Sexuality Description Project. (2003). Universal sex differences in the desire for sexual variety: Tests from 52 nations, 6 continents, and 13 islands. *Personality and Social Psychology, 85,* 85-104.

Schmitt, D. P., and Buss, D. M. (2000). Sexual dimensions of person description: Beyond or subsumed by the Big Five? *Journal of Research in Personality, 34,* 141-177.

Schmitt, D. P., and Buss, D. M. (2001). Human mate poaching: Tactics and temptations for infiltrating existing relationships. *Journal of Personality and Social Psychology, 80,* 894-917.

Schmitt, D. P., Jonason, P. K., Byerley, G. J., Flores, S. D., Illbeck, B. E., O'Leary, K. N., and Qudrat, A. (2012). A reexamination of sex differences in sexuality: New studies reveal old truths. *Current Directions in Psychological Science, 21,* 135-139.

Schmitt, D. P., Realo, A., Voracek, M., and Allik, J. (2008). Why can't a man be more like a woman? Sex differences in Big Five personality traits across 55 cultures. *Journal of Personality and Social Psychology, 94,* 168-182.

Schmitt, D. P., Youn, G., Bond, B., Brooks, S., Frye, H., Johnson, S., Klesman, J., et al. (2009). When will I feel love? The effects of culture, personality, and gender on the psychological tendency to love. *Journal of Research in Personality, 43,* 830-846.

Schmutte, P. S., Lee, Y. H., and Ryff, C. D. (1995). *Reflections on parenthood: A cultural perspective.* Unpublished manuscript, Madison: University of Wisconsin.

Schneider, K. (1958). *Psychopathic personalities.* London: Cassell.

Schüler, J., Sheldon, K. M., and Fröhlich, S.M. (2010). Implicit need for achievement moderates the relationship between competence need satisfaction and subsequent motivation. *Journal of Research in Personality, 44,* 1-12.

Schultheiss, O. C., and Brunstein, J. C. (2001). Assessment of implicit motives with a research version of the TAT: Picture profiles, gender differences, and relations to other personality measures. *Journal of Personality Assessment Special Issue: More Data on the Current Rorschach Controversy, 77,* 71-86.

Schultheiss, O. C., and Köllner, M. G., (2021). Implicit motives. In O. P. John and R. W. Robins (Eds), *Handbook of Personality: Theory and Research., 4th ed.,* pp. 385-410. New York: Guilford Press.

Schultheiss, O. C., and Pang, J. S. (2007). Measuring implicit motives. In R. W. Robins, R. C. Fraley, and R. Krueger (Eds.), *Handbook of research methods in personality psychology* (pp. 322-344). New York: Guilford Press.

Schultheiss, O. C., and Schultheiss, M. (2014). Implicit motive profile analysis: An if-then contingency approach to the picture-story exercise. *Social & Personality Psychology Compass, 8*(1), 1-16.

Schultheiss, O. C., Liening, S., and Schad, D. (2008). The reliability of a Picture Story Exercise measure of implicit motives: Estimates of internal consistency, retest reliability, and ipsative stability. *Journal of Research in Personality, 42,* 1560-1571.

Schultheiss, O. C., Wiemers, U. S., and Wolf, O. T. (2014). Implicit need for achievement predicts attenuated cortisol responses to difficult tasks. *Journal of Research in Personality, 48,* 84-92.

Schütz, A. and Baumeister, R. F. (2017). Positive illusions and the happy mind. In M. D. Robinson and M. Eid (Eds.). *The Happy Mind: Cognitive Contributions to Well-Being* (pp. 177-193). Cham, Switzerland: Springer International Publishing.

Schutzwohl, A. (2008). Relief over the disconfirmation of the prospect of sexual and emotional infidelity. *Personality and Individual Differences, 44,* 668-678.

Schutzwohl, A., and Koch, S. (2004). Sex differences in jealousy: The recall of cues to sexual and emotional infidelity in adaptively relevant and irrelevant context conditions. *Evolution and Human Behavior, 25,* 249-257.

Schutzwohl, A., Fuchs, A., McKibbin, W. F., and Shackelford, T. K. (2009). How willing are you to accept sexual requests from slightly unattractive to exceptionally attractive imagined requestors? *Human Nature, 20,* 282-293.

Schuyler, B. S., Kral, T. A., Jacquart, J., Burghy, C. A., Weng, H. Y., Perlman, D. M., . . . Davidson, R. J. (2014). Temporal dynamics of emotional responding: Amygdala recovery predicts emotional traits. *Social Cognitive and Affective Neuroscience, 9*(2), 176-181.

Schwartz, C. E., Wright, C. I., Shin, L. M., Kagan, J., and Rauch, S. L. (2003). Inhibited and uninhibited infants "grown up": Adult amygdalar response to novelty. *Science, 300,* 1952-1953.

Schwartz, S. H., and Rubel, T. (2005). Sex differences in value priorities: Cross-cultural and multimethod studies. *Journal of Personality and Social Psychology, 89,* 1010-1028.

Schwarzer, R., and Luszczynska, A. (2013). Stressful life events. In A. M. Nezu, C. M. Nezu, P. A. Geller, and I. B. Weiner (Eds.), *Handbook of psychology, Vol. 9: Health psychology* (2nd ed., pp. 29-56). Hoboken, NJ: John Wiley & Sons.

Schwerdtfeger, A. (2007). Individual differences in auditory, pain, and motor stimulation: The case of augmenting/reducing. *Journal of Individual Differences, 28,* 165-177.

Schwerdtfeger, A., and Baltissen, R. (1999). Augmenters vs. reducers: Cortical and autonomic reactivity in response to increasing stimulus intensity. *Zeitschrift fuer Differentielle und Diagnostische Psychologie, 20,* 247-262.

Schwerdtfeger, A., and Baltissen, R. (2002). Augmenting-reducing paradox lost? A test of Davis et al.'s (1983) hypothesis. *Personality and Individual Differences, 32,* 257-271.

Schwerdtfeger, A., Getzmann, S. and Baltissen, R. (2004). Fast reducers, slow augmenters: A psychophysiological analysis of temperament-related differences in reaction time. *International Journal of Psychophysiology, 52,* 225-237.

Schwerdtfeger, A., Heims, R., and Heer, J. (2010). Digit ratio (2D:4D) is associated with traffic violations for male frequent car drivers. *Accident Analysis and Prevention, 42,* 269-274.

Schwinger, M., Trautner, M., Pütz, N., Fabianek, S., Lemmer, G., Lauermann, F., and Wirthwein, L. (2021). Why do students use strategies that hurt their chances of academic success? A meta-analysis of antecedents of academic self-handicapping. *Journal of Educational Psychology. 114,* 576-596. https://doi.org/10.1037/edu0000706.

Scott, W. A., and Johnson, R. C. (1972). Comparative validities of direct and indirect personality tests. *Journal of Consulting and Clinical Psychology, 38,* 301-318.

Sear, R., and Mace, R. (2008). Who keeps children alive? A review of the effects of kin on child survival. *Evolution and Human Behavior, 29,* 1-18.

Seara-Cardoso, A., and Viding, E. (2015). Functional neuroscience of psychopathic personality in adults. *Journal of Personality, 83*(6), 723-737.

Sedikides, C., and Alicke, M. D. (2019). The five pillars of self-enhancement and self-protection. In R. M. Ryan (Ed.), *The Oxford handbook of human motivation* (pp. 307-319). Oxford University Press.

Segal, N. L. (1999). *Entwined lives: Twins and what they tell us about human behavior.* New York: Plume.

Segerstrom, S. C., and Sephton, S. E. (2010). Optimistic expectancies and cell-mediated immunity: the role of positive affect. *Psychological Science, 21*(3), 448-455.

Seidlitz, L., and Diener, E. (1993). Review of the satisfaction with Life Scale. *Psychological Assessment, 5,* 164-172.

Seidman, G., Roberts, A., and Zeigler-Hill, V. (2019). Narcissism and romantic relationship presentation on social media: The role of motivations and partner attractiveness. *Personality and Individual Differences, 149,* 21-30.

Selfhout, M., Burk, W., Branje, S., Denissen, J., van Aken, M., and Meeus, W. (2010). Emerging late adolescent friendship networks and Big Five personality traits: A social network approach. *Journal of Personality, 78,* 509-538.

Seligman, M. E. P. (1992). *Helplessness: On depression, development, and death.* New York: Freeman.

Seligman, M. E. P. (1994). *What you can change and what you can't.* New York: Knopf.

Seligman, M. E. P., and Csikszentmihalyi, M. (2000). Positive psychology: An introduction. *American Psychologist, 55,* 5-14.

Seligman, M. E. P., and Peterson, C. (2003). Positive clinical psychology. In L. G. Aspinwall and U. M. Staudinger (Eds.), *A psychology of human strengths: Fundamental questions and future directions for a positive psychology* (pp. 305-317). Washington, DC: American Psychological Association.

Seligman, M., and Hager, J. (1972). *Biological boundaries of learning.* New York: Appleton-Century-Crofts.

Seligman, M.E.P. (2002). Positive psychology, positive prevention, and positive therapy. In C. R. Snyder and S. J. Lopez (Eds.), *Handbook of positive psychology* (pp. 3-9). London: Oxford University Press.

Sell, A., Hone, L. S. E., and Pound, N. (2012). The importance of physical strength to human males. *Human Nature, 23,* 30-44.

Sell, A., Tooby, J., and Cosmides, L. (2009). Formidability and the logic of human anger. *Proceedings of the National Academy of Science, 106,* 15073-15078.

Selye, H. (1976). *The stress of life.* New York: McGraw-Hill.

Semenova, E., and Winter, D. G. (2020). A motivational analysis of Russian presidents, 1994-2018. *Political Psychology, 41,* 813-834

Semerci, A. (2017). Investigating the effects of personality traits on cyberbullying. *Journal of Education and Instruction, 7*(2), 211-230.

Servaas, M. N., van der Velde, J., Costafreda, S. G., Horton, P., Ormel, J., Riese, H., and Aleman, A. (2013). Neuroticism and the brain: A quantitative meta-analysis of neuroimaging studies investigating emotion processing. *Neuroscience and Biobehavioral Reviews, 37*(8), 1518–1529.

Shackelford, T. K., Buss, D. M., and Bennett, K. (2002). Forgiveness or breakup: Sex differences in responses to a partner's infidelity. *Cognition and Emotion, 16*, 299–307.

Shackelford, T. K., Goetz, A., Buss, D. M., Euler, H. A., and Hoier, S. (2005). When we hurt the ones we love: Predicting violence against women from men's mate retention. *Personal Relationships, 12*, 447–463.

Shackelford, T. K., Voracek, M., Schmitt, D. P., Buss, D. M., Weekes-Shackelford, V. A., and Michalski, R. L. (2004). Romantic jealousy in early adulthood and in later life. *Human Nature, 15*, 59–76.

Shafer, A. B. (2001). The Big Five and sexuality trait terms as predictors of relationships and sex. *Journal of Research in Personality, 35*, 313–338.

Shakeel, M. D., and Peterson, P. E.. (2022). A half century of progress in US student achievement: Agency and Flynn Effects, ethnic and SES differences. *Educational Psychology Review*, Mar 3, 2022, DOI: 10.1007/s10648-021-09657-y.

Shakur, S. (1994). *Monster: The autobiography of an L.A. gang member.* New York: Penguin.

Shatz, S. M. (2008). IQ and fertility: A cross-national study. *Intelligence, 36*, 109–111.

Shaver, P. R., and Mikulincer, M. (2010). New directions in attachment theory and research. *Journal of Social and Personal Relationships, 27*(2), 163–172.

Sheldon, K. M. and Lyubomirsky, S. (2021). Revisiting the sustainable happiness model and pie chart: Can happiness be successfully pursued? *The Journal of Positive Psychology, 16*, 145–154, DOI: 10.1080/17439760.2019.1689421.

Sheldon, K. M., and Kasser, T. (2001). Getting older, getting better? Personal strivings and psychological maturity across the life span. *Developmental Psychology, 37*, 491–501.

Shen, Y., Sun, H., Heng, C. S. and Chan, H. C. (2020). Facilitating complex product choices on e-commerce sites: An unconscious thought and circadian preference perspective. *Decision Support Systems, 137*, Oct, 2020. ArtID: 113365.

Sheppard, K. E., and Boon, S. D. (2012). Predicting appraisals of romantic revenge: The roles of honest-humility, agreeableness, and vengefulness. *Personality and Individual Differences, 52*, 128–132.

Sheppard, L. D., and Vernon, P. A. (2008). Intelligence and speed of information-processing. *Personality and Individual Differences, 44*, 535–551.

Shimotsukasa, T., Oshio, A., Tani, M., and Yamaki, M. (2019). Big Five personality traits in inmates and normal adults in Japan. *Personality and Individual Differences, 141*, 81–85.

Shiner, R. L., Masten, A. S., and Roberts, J. M. (2003). Childhood personality foreshadows adult personality and life outcomes two decades later. *Journal of Personality, 71*, 1145–1170.

Shiner, R. L., Masten, A. S., and Tellegen, A. (2002). A developmental perspective on personality in emerging adulthood: Childhood antecedents and concurrent adaptation. *Journal of Personality and Social Psychology, 83*(5), 1165–1177.

Shneidman, E. S. (1981). *Endeavors in psychology: Selections from the personology of Henry A. Murray.* New York: Harper and Row.

Shoben, E. J. (1957). Toward a concept of the normal personality. *American Psychologist, 12*, 183–189.

Shoda, Y., and Mischel, W. (1996). Toward a unified, intra-individual dynamic conception of personality. *Journal of Research in Personality, 30*, 414–428.

Shoda, Y., Mischel, W., and Wright, J. C. (1994). Intra-individual stability in the organization and patterning of behavior: Incorporating psychological situations into the idiographic analysis of personality. *Journal of Personality and Social Psychology, 67*, 674–687.

Shoda, Y., Wilson, N. L., Chen, J., Gilmore, A. K., and Smith, R. E. (2013). Cognitive-affective processing system analysis of intra-individual dynamics in collaborative therapeutic assessment: Translating basic theory and research into clinical applications. *Journal of Personality, 81*(6), 554–568.

Shoda, Y., Wilson, N. L., Whitsett, D. D., Lee-Dussud, J., and Zayas, V. (2015). The person as a cognitive-affective processing system: Quantitative ideography as an integral component of cumulative science. In M. Mikulincer, P. R. Shaver, M. L. Cooper, R. J. Larsen, M. Mikulincer, P. R. Shaver, . . . and R. J. Larsen (Eds.), *APA handbook of personality and social psychology, Vol. 4: Personality processes and individual differences* (pp. 491–513). Washington, DC, US: American Psychological Association.

Shultz, J. S. (1993). Situational and dispositional predictions of performance: A test of the hypothesized Machiavellianism X structure interaction among salespersons. *Journal of Applied Social Psychology, 23*, 478–498.

Shweder, R. A. (1991). *Thinking through cultures: Expeditions in cultural psychology.* Cambridge, MA: Harvard University Press.

Shweder, R. A., Mahapatra, M., and Miller, J. G. (1990). Culture and moral development. In J. W. Stigler, R. A. Shweder, and G. Herdt (Eds.), *Cultural psychology: Essays on comparative human development* (pp. 130–204). Cambridge, MA: Cambridge University Press.

Sibley, C. G., Osborne, D., and Duckitt, J. (2012). Personality and political orientation: Meta-analysis and test of a Threat-Constraint Model. *Journal of Research in Personality, 46*(6), 664–677.

Siegel, J. (1997). Augmenting and reducing of visual evoked potentials in high- and low-sensation seeking humans, cats, and rats. *Behavior Genetics, 27*, 557–563.

Siegel, J. M. (1986). The Multidimensional Anger Inventory. *Journal of Personality and Social Psychology, 51*, 191–200.

Siegel, J., and Driscoll, P. (1996). Recent developments in an animal model of visual evoked potential augmenting/reducing and sensation seeking behavior. *Neuropsychobiology, 34*, 130–135.

Sievertsen, H. H., Gino, F., and Piovesan, M. (2016). Cognitive fatigue influences students' performance on standardized tests. *Proceedings of the National Academy of Sciences, 113*, 2621–2624.

Sigusch, V., and Schmidt, G. (1971). Lower-class sexuality: Some emotional and social aspects in West German males and females. *Archives of Sexual Behavior, 1*, 29–44.

Sih, A., Mathot, K. J., Moirón, M., Montiglio, P. O., Wolf, M., and Dingemanse, N. J. (2015). Animal personality and state-behaviour feedbacks: A review and guide for empiricists. *Trends in Ecology & Evolution, 30*(1), 50–60.

Silverthorne, C. (2001). Leadership effectiveness and personality: A cross-cultural evaluation. *Personality and Individual Differences, 30*, 303–309.

Silvia, P. J., Nusbaum, E. C., and Beaty, R. E. (2014). Blessed are the meek? Honesty–Humility, Agreeableness, and the HEXACO structure of religious beliefs, motives, and values. *Personality and Individual Differences, 66*, 19–23.

Simonton, D. K. (1991). Emergence and realization of genius: The lives and works of 120 classical composers. *Journal of Personality and Social Psychology, 61*, 829–840.

Simpson, J. A., and Gangestad, S. W. (1991). Individual differences in sociosexuality: Evidence for convergent and discriminant validity. *Journal of Personality and Social Psychology, 60*, 870–883.

Simpson, J. A., and Rholes, W. S. (1998). *Attachment theory and close relationships.* New York: Guilford Press.

Simpson, J. A., Rholes, W. S., Orinea, M. M., and Grich, J. (2002). Working models of attachment, support giving, and support seeking in a stressful situation. *Personality and Social Psychology Bulletin, 28,* 598–608.

Singh, D., Vidaurri, M., Zambarano, R. J., and Dabbs, J. M., Jr. (1999). Behavioral, morphological, and hormonal correlates to erotic role identification among lesbian women. *Journal of Personality and Social Psychology, 76,* 1035–1049.

Singh, S. (1978). Achievement motivation and entrepreneurial success: A follow-up study. *Journal of Research in Personality, 12,* 500–503.

Six, B., and Eckes, T. (1991). A closer look at the complex structure of gender stereotypes. *Sex Roles, 24,* 64.

Skodol A. E. (2012). Personality disorders in DSM-5. *Annual Review of Clinical Psychology, 8,* 317–344.

Skondras, M., Markianos, M., Botsis, A., Bistolaki, E., and Christodoulou, G. (2004). Platelet monoamine oxidase activity and psychometric correlates in male violent offenders imprisoned for homicide or other violent acts. *European Archives of Psychiatry and Clinical Neuroscience, 254,* 380–386.

Slatcher, R. B., and Vazire, S. (2009). Effects of global and contextualized personality on relationship satisfaction. *Journal of Research in Personality, 43,* 624–633.

Smelser, N. J. (2004). Self-esteem and social problems. In A. M. Mecca, N. J. Smelser, and J. Vasconcellos (Eds.) *The Social Importance of Self-Esteem* (pp. 1–23). Berkeley, CA: University of California Press.

Smillie, L. D., and Wacker, J. (2014). Dopaminergic foundations of personality and individual differences. *Frontiers in Human Neuroscience, 8.*

Smillie, L. D., Cooper, A. J., Wilt, J., and Revelle, W. (2012). Do extraverts get more bang for the buck? Refining the affective-reactivity hypothesis of extraversion. *Journal of Personality and Social Psychology, 103,* 306–326.

Smith, C. P., and Atkinson, J. W. (1992). *Motivation and personality: Handbook of thematic content analysis.* New York: Cambridge University Press.

Smith, P., Caputi, P., and Crittenden, N. (2013). Measuring optimism in organizations: Development of a workplace explanatory style questionnaire. *Journal of Happiness Studies, 14*(2), 415–432.

Smith, R. E., and Shoda, Y. (2009). Personality as a cognitive-affective processing system. In P. J. Corr and G. Matthews (Eds.), *The Cambridge handbook of personality psychology* (pp. 473–487). New York: Cambridge University Press.

Smith, R. E., Shoda, Y., Cumming, S .P., and Smoll, F. L. (2009). Behavioral signatures at the ballpark: Intraindividual consistency of adults' situation-behavior patterns and their interpersonal consequences. *Journal of Research in Personality, 43,* 187–195.

Smith, S. F., Watts, A. L., and Lilienfeld, S. O. (2014). On the trail of the elusive successful psychopath. *The Psychologist, 15,* 340–350.

Smith, T. W. (1979). Happiness: Time trends, seasonal variations, intersurvey differences, and other mysteries. *Social Psychology Quarterly, 42,* 18–30.

Smith, T. W. (2006). Personality as risk and resilience in physical health. *Current Directions in Psychological Science, 15,* 227–231.

Smith, T. W., and Spiro, A., III. (2002). Personality, health, and aging: Prolegomenon for the next generation. *Journal of Research in Personality, 36,* 363–394.

Smith, T. W., Pope, M. K., Rhodewalt, F., and Poulton, J. L. (1989). Optimism, neuroticism, coping, and symptom reports: An alternative interpretation of the Life Orientation Test. *Journal of Personality and Social Psychology, 56,* 640–648.

Smith, T. W., Williams, P. G., and Segerstrom, S. C. (2015). Personality and physical health. In L. Cooper and R. J. Larsen (Eds.), *Handbook of personality and social psychology: Personality processes and individual differences.* Washington, DC: American Psychological Association.

Smits, I. A. M., Dolan, C. V., Vorst, H. C. M., Wicherts, J. M., and Timmerman, M. E. (2011). Cohort differences in Big Five personality factors over a period of 25 years. *Journal of Personality and Social Psychology, 100,* 1124–1138.

Snyder, J. K., Fessler, D. M. T., Tiokhin, L., Frederick, D. A., Lee, S. W., and Navarrete, C. D. (2011). Trade-offs in a dangerous world: Women's fear of crime predicts preferences for aggressive and formidable mates. *Evolution and Human Behavior, 32,* 127–137.

Snyder, M., and Cantor, N. (1998). Understanding personality and social behavior: A functionalist strategy. In D. T. Gilbert, S. T. Fiske, and G. Lindzey (Eds.), *The handbook of social psychology* (Vol. 1, 4th ed., pp. 635–679). Boston: McGraw-Hill.

Snyder, M., and Gangestad, S. (1982). Choosing social situations: Two investigations of self-monitoring processes. *Journal of Personality and Social Psychology, 43,* 123–135.

Soloff, P. H., Lis, J. A., Kelly, T., and Cornelius, J. (1994). Risk factors for suicidal behavior in borderline personality disorder. *American Journal of Psychiatry, 151,* 1316–1323.

Solomon, B. C., and Jackson, J. J. (2014). Why do personality traits predict divorce? Multiple pathways through satisfaction. *Journal of Personality and Social Psychology, 106*(6), 978–996.

Solomon, Z., Berger, R., and Ginzburg, K. (2007). Resilience of Israeli body handlers: Implications of repressive coping style. *Traumatology, 13*(4), 64–74.

Somer, O., and Goldberg, L. R. (1999). The structure of Turkish trait-descriptive adjectives. *Journal of Personality and Social Psychology, 76,* 431–450.

Sorokowski, P., Sorokowska, A., Oleszkiewicz, A., Frackowiak, T., Huk, A., and Pisanski, K. (2015). Selfie posting behaviors are associated with narcissism among men. *Personality and Individual Differences, 85,* 123–127.

Source: Scarf, M. (1996). The Mind of the Unabomber. *The New Republic,* June 10, 1996, p. 20.

South, S. C., and Krueger, R. F. (2008). An interactionist perspective on genetic and environmental contributions to personality. *Social and Personality Psychology Compass, 2,* 929–948.

South, S. C., Krueger, R. F., Elkins, I. J., Iacono, W. G., and McGue, M. (2016). Romantic relationship satisfaction moderates the etiology of adult personality. *Behavior Genetics, 46*(1), 124–142.

South, S. C., Krueger, R. F., Johnson, W., and Iacono, W. G. (2008). Adolescent personality moderates genetic and environmental influences on relationships with parents. *Journal of Personality and Social Psychology, 94,* 899–912.

South, S. C., Oltmanns, T. F., and Turkheimer, E. (2003). Personality and the derogation of others: Descriptions based on self- and peer report. *Journal of Research in Personality, 37,* 16–33.

Souza, A. L., Conroy-Beam, D., and Buss, D. M. (2016). Mate preferences in Brazil: Evolved desires and cultural evolution over three decades. *Personality and Individual Differences, 95,* 45–49.

Sowislo, J. F., and Orth, U. (2013). Does low self-esteem predict depression and anxiety? A meta-analysis of longitudinal studies. *Psychological Bulletin, 139,* 213–240.

Spangler, W. D. (1992). Validity of questionnaire and TAT measures of need for achievement: Two meta-analyses. *Psychological Bulletin, 112,* 140–154.

Spanos, N. P., and McLean, J. (1986). Hypnotically created false reports do not demonstrate pseudomemories. *British Journal of Experimental and Clinical Hypnosis, 3,* 167–171.

Specht, J., Bleidorn, W., Denissen, J. J., Hennecke, M., Hutteman, R., Kandler, C., . . . and Zimmermann, J. (2014). What drives adult personality development? A comparison of theoretical perspectives and empirical evidence. *European Journal of Personality, 28,* 216–230.

Specht, J., Egloff, B., and Schmukle, S. C. (2011). Stability and change of personality across the life course: The impact of age and major life events on mean-level and rank-order stability of the Big Five. *Journal of Personality and Social Psychology, 101,* 862–882.

Spence, J. T., Helmreich, R., and Stapp, J. (1974). The Personal Attributes Questionnaire: A measure of sex-role stereotypes and masculinity and femininity. *Journal Supplement Abstract Service Catalog of Selected Documents in Psychology, 4,* 42 (No. 617).

Spengler, M., Lüdtke, O., Martin, R., and Brunner, M. (2013). Personality is related to educational outcomes in late adolescence: Evidence from two large-scale achievement studies. *Journal of Research in Personality, 47*(5), 613–625.

Spies, R. A., and Plake, B. S. (2005). *The sixteenth mental measurements yearbook.* Lincoln, NE: Buros Institute of Mental Measurements.

Spikic, S., and Mortelmans, D. (2021). A Preliminary Meta-analysis of the Big Five Personality Traits' Effect on Marital Separation. *Journal of Divorce & Remarriage, 62*(7), 551–571.

Spilker, B., and Callaway, E. (1969). Augmenting and reducing in averaged visual evoked responses to sine wave light. *Psychophysiology, 6,* 49–57.

Spinath, F. M., and O'Connor, T. G. (2003). A behavioral genetic study of the overlap between personality and parenting. *Journal of Personality, 71*(5), 785–808.

Spinath, F. M., Wolf, H., Angleitner, A., Borkenau, P., and Riemann, R. (2002). Genetic and environmental influences on objectively assessed activity in adults. *Personality and Individual Differences, 33,* 633–645.

Spotts, E. L., Lichtenstein, P., Pedersen, N., Neiderhiser, J. M., Hansson, K., Cederblad, M., and Reiss, D. (2005). Personality and marital satisfaction: A behavioural genetic analysis. *European Journal of Personality, 19,* 205–227.

Spotts, E. L., Neiderhiser, J. M., Towers, H., Hansson, K., Lichtenstein, P., Cederblad, M., and Pedersen, N. L. (2004). Genetic and environmental influences on marital relationships. *Journal of Family Psychology, 18,* 107–119.

Srivastav, D. and Mathur, M. N. L. (2020). Helicopter parenting and adolescent development: The perspective of mental health. In L. Benedeto and M. Ingrassia (Eds.), *Parenting.* Open access, DOI: 10.5772/intechopen.93155.

Srivastava, S., John, O. P., Gosling, S. D., and Potter, J. (2003). Development of

personality in early and middle adulthood: Set like plaster or persistent change? *Journal of Personality and Social Psychology, 84*(5), 1041–1053.

Stake, J. E., Huff, L., and Zand, D. (1995). Trait self-esteem, positive and negative events, and event specific shifts in self-evaluation and affect. *Journal of Research in Personality, 29,* 223–241.

Standen, B., Firth, J., Sumich, A., and Heym, N. (2022). The neural correlates of reinforcement sensitivity theory: A systematic review of the fMRI literature. *Psychology and Neuroscience,* Feb 14, DOI: 10.137/pne0000284.

Stapleton, P., Luiz, G., and Chatwin, H. (2017). Generation validation: The role of social comparison in use of Instagram among emerging adults. *Cyberpsychology, Behavior, and Social Networking, 20,* 142–149.

Steel, P., and Ones, D. S. (2002). Personality and happiness: A national-level analysis. *Journal of Personality and Social Psychology, 83*(3), 767–781.

Steger, M. F., Hicks, B. M., Kashdan, T. B., Krueger, R. F., and Bouchard, T. J., Jr. (2007). Genetic and environmental influences on the positive traits of the values in action classification, and biometric covariance with normal personality. *Journal of Research in Personality, 41,* 524–539.

Stein, A. A. (1976). Conflict and cohesion: A review of the literature. *Journal of Conflict Resolution, 20,* 143–172.

Stein, R., and Swan, A. B. (2019). Evaluating the validity of Myers-Briggs Type Indicator theory: A teaching tool and window into intuitive psychology. *Social and Personality Psychology Compass.* E12434.

Steinberg, L., Albert, D., Cauffman, E., Banich, M., Graham, S., and Woolard, J. (2008). Age differences in sensation seeking and impulsivity as indexed by behavior and self-report: Evidence for a dual systems model. *Developmental Psychology, 44*(6), 1764–1778.

Steiner, A. W., and Coan, J. A. (2011). Prefrontal asymmetry predicts affect, but not beliefs about affect. *Biological Psychology, 88*(1), 65–71.

Steiner, M., Allemand, M., and McCullough, M. E. (2012). Do agreeableness and neuroticism explain age differences in the tendency to forgive others? *Personality and Social Psychology Bulletin, 38,* 441–453.

Stelmack, R. M. (1990). Biological basis of extraversion: Psychophysiological evidence. *Journal of Personality, 58,* 293–311.

Stelmack, R. M., and Rammsayer, T. H. (2008). Psychophysiological and biochemical correlates of personality. In G. J. Boyle, G. Matthews and D. H. Saklofske, (Eds), *The SAGE Handbook*

of Personality Theory and Assessment, Vol 1: Personality theories and models (33–55). Sage Publications, Thousand Oaks, CA

Stelmack, R. M., and Stalkas, A. (1991). Galen and the humour theory of temperament. *Personality and Individual Differences, 12,* 255–263.

Stephan, Y., Sutin, A. R., Luchetti, M., and Terracciano, A. (2019). Facets of conscientiousness and longevity: Findings from the Health and Retirement Study. *Journal of Psychosomatic Research, 116,* 1–5.

Sternberg, R. J. (1985). *Beyond IQ: A triarchic theory of human intelligence.* New York: Cambridge University Press.

Stevenson, R. J., Hodgson, D., Oaten, M. J., Moussavi, M., Langberg, R., Case, T. I., and Barouei, J. (2012). Disgust elevates core body temperature and up-regulates certain oral immune markers. *Brain, Behavior, and Immunity, 26*(7), 1160–1168.

Stewart, M. E., Donaghey, C., Deary, I. J., and Ebmeier, K. P. (2008). Suicidal thoughts in young people: Their frequency and relationships with personality factors. *Personality and Individual Differences, 44,* 809–820.

Stewart, M. E., Ebmeier, K. P., and Deary, I. J. (2005). Personality correlates of happiness and sadness: EPQ-R and TPQ compared. *Personality and Individual Differences, 38,* 1085–1096.

Stieger, S., Lewetz, D., and Swami, V. (2021). Emotional well-being under conditions of lockdown: An experience sampling study in Austria during the COVID-19 pandemic. *Journal of Happiness Studies, 22*(6), 2703–2720.

Stocker, S. (1997). Don't be shy: Advice for becoming more outgoing. *Prevention, 96.*

Stoeber, J., Otto, K., and Dalbert, C. (2009). Perfectionism and the Big Five: Conscientiousness predicts longitudinal increases in self-oriented perfectionism. *Personality and Individual Differences, 47,* 363–368.

Stopfer, J. M., Egloff, B., Nestler, S., and Back, M. D. (2013). Being popular in online social networks: How agentic, communal, and creativity traits relate to judgments of status and liking. *Journal of Research in Personality, 47*(5), 592–598.

Strauss, K., Griffin, M. A., and Parker, S. K. (2012). Future work selves: How salient hoped-for identities motivate proactive career behaviors. *Journal of Applied Psychology, 97,* 580–598.

Strelan, P. (2007). Who forgives others, themselves, and situations? The roles of narcissism, guilt, self-esteem, and agreeableness. *Personality and Individual Differences, 42,* 259–269.

Strickhouser, J. E., Zell, E., and Krizan, Z. (2017). Does personality predict health and well-being? A metasynthesis. *Health Psychology, 36,* 797–810.

Stroop, J. R. (1935). Studies of interference in serial verbal reactions. *Journal of Experimental Psychology, 18,* 643–661.

Strout, S. L., Laird, J. D., Shafer, A., and Thompson, N. S. (2005). The effect of vividness of experience on sex differences in jealousy. *Evolutionary Psychology, 3,* 263–274.

Strouts, P. H., Brase, G. L., and Dillon, H. M. (2017). Personality and evolutionary strategies: The relationships between HEXACO traits, mate value, life history strategy, and sociosexuality. *Personality and Individual Differences, 115,* 128–132.

Stucke, T. S., and Baumeister, R. F. (2006). Ego depletion and aggressive behavior: Is the inhibition of aggression a limited resource? *European Journal of Social Psychology, 36,* 1–13.

Su, R., Rounds, J., and Armstrong, P. I. (2009). Men and things, women and people: A meta-analysis of sex differences in interests. *Psychological Bulletin, 135,* 859–884.

Suls, J., and Wan, C. K. (1989). The relation between Type A behavior and chronic emotional distress: A meta-analysis. *Journal of Personality and Social Psychology, 57,* 503–512.

Suls, J., Wan, C. K., and Costa, P. T., Jr. (1996). Relationship of trait anger to resting blood pressure: A meta-analysis. *Health Psychology, 14,* 444–456.

Sun, J., Harris, K., and Vazire, S. (2020). Is well-being associated with the quantity and quality of social interactions?. *Journal of Personality and Social Psychology, 119*(6), 1478.

Sun, T., Webster, K., Shah, A., Wang, W. Y., and Johnson, M. (2021). They, them, theirs: Rewriting with gender-neutral English. *arXiv preprint arXiv:2102.06788.*

Surtees, P., Wainwright, N., Khaw, K. T., Luben, R., Brayne, C., and Day, N. (2003). Inflammatory dispositions: A population-based study of the association between hostility and peripheral leukocyte counts. *Personality and Individual Differences, 35,* 1271–1284.

Sutin, A. R., Ferrucci, L., Zonderman, A. B., and Terracciano, A. (2011). Personality and obesity across the adult life span. *Journal of Personality and Social Psychology, 101,* 579–592.

Sutton, S. K. (2002). Incentive and threat reactivity: Relations with anterior cortical activity. In D. Cervone and W. Mischel (Eds.), *Advances in Personality Science* (pp. 127–150). New York: Guilford Press.

Svartberg, K. (2021). The hierarchical structure of dog personality in a new behavioural assessment: A validation approach. *Applied Animal Behaviour Science, 238,* 105302.

Sverko, B., and Fabulic, L. (1985). Stability of morningness-eveningness: Retest changes after seven years. *Revija za Psihologiju, 15,* 71–78.

Swanbrow, D. (1989, August). The paradox of happiness. *Psychology Today,* pp. 37–39.

Swann, W. B., Langlois, J. H., and Gilbert, L. A. (Eds.). (1999). *Sexism and stereotypes in modern society: The gender science of Janet Taylor Spence.* Washington, DC: American Psychological Association.

Swann, W. R., Jr., and Selye, C. (2005). Personality psychology's comeback and its emerging symbiosis with social psychology. *Personality and Social Psychology Bulletin, 31,* 155–165.

Symons, D. (1979). *The evolution of human sexuality.* New York: Oxford.

Symons, D. (1992). On the use and misuse of Darwinism in the study of human behavior. In J. Barkow, L. Cosmides, and J. Tooby (Eds.), *The adapted mind* (pp. 137–159). New York: Oxford University Press.

Szepsenwol, O., Simpson, J. A., Griskevicius, V., and Raby, K. L. (2015). The effect of unpredictable early childhood environments on parenting in adulthood. *Journal of Personality and Social Psychology, 109*(6), 1045–1067.

Tackett, J. L., Krueger, R. F., Iacono, W. G., and McGue, M. (2008). Personality in middle childhood: A hierarchical structure and longitudinal connections with personality in late adolescence. *Journal of Research in Personality, 42,* 1456–1462.

Tamir, M., Robinson, M. D., and Solberg, E. C. (2006). You may worry, but can you recognize threats when you see them? Neuroticism, threat identifications, and negative affect. *Journal of Personality, 74,* 1481–1506.

Tamir, Y., and Nadler, A. (2007). The role of personality in social identity: Effects of field-dependence and context on reactions to threat to group distinctiveness. *Journal of Personality, 75,* 927–954.

Tate, J. C., and Shelton, B. L. (2008). Personality correlates of tattooing and body piercing in a college sample: The kids are alright. *Personality and Individual Differences, 45,* 281–285.

Tay, L., Diener, E., Lucas, R. E., and Larsen, R. J. (2019). Measuring positive emotions. In M. W. Gallagher and S. J. Lopez (Eds.), *Positive Psychological Assessment: A Handbook of Models and Measures* (2nd ed., pp. 179–202). Washington, DC: American Psychological Association.

Taylor, S. (1991). *Health psychology* (2nd ed.). New York: McGraw-Hill.

Taylor, S. E. (1989). *Positive Illusions: Self-Deception and the Healthy Mind.* New York: Basic Books.

Taylor, S. E., Kemeny, M. E., Reed, G. M., Bower, J. E., and Gruenewald, T. L. (2000). Psychological resources, positive illusions, and health. *American Psychologist, 55,* 99–109.

Teasdale, T. W., and Owen, D. R. (2008). Secular declines in cognitive test scores: A reversal of the Flynn effect. *Intelligence, 36,* 121–126.

Tedeschi, R. G., Park, C. L., and Calhoun, L. (1998). Posttraumatic growth: Conceptual issues. In R. G. Tedeschi and P. L. Crystal (Eds.), *Posttraumatic growth: Positive changes in the aftermath of crisis* (pp. 1–22). Mahwah, NJ: Erlbaum.

Telama, R., Yang, X., Viikari, J., Välimäki, I., Wanne, O., and Raitakari, O. (2005). Physical activity from childhood to adulthood: A 21-year tracking study. *American Journal of Preventive Medicine, 28*(3), 267–273.

Tellegen, A., Lykken, D. T., Bouchard, T. J., Wilcox, K., Segal, N., and Rich, S. (1988). Personality similarity in twins reared apart and together. *Journal of Personality and Social Psychology, 54,* 1031–1039.

Templer, D. I. (2008). Correlational and factor analytic support for Rushton's differential K life history theory. *Personality and Individual Differences, 45,* 440–444.

ten Brummelhuis, L. L., Calderwood, C., Rosen, C. C., and Gabriel, A. S. (2021). Is physical activity before the end of the workday a drain or a gain? Daily implications on work focus in regular exercisers. Journal of Applied Psychology, Nov 04, 2021.

Terman, L. M. (1938). *Psychological factors in marital happiness.* New York: McGraw-Hill.

Tester, N., and Campbell, A. (2007). Sporting achievement: What is the contribution of digit ratio? *Journal of Personality, 75,* 663–677.

Thalmayer, A. G., Saucier, G., Ole-Kotikash, L., and Payne, D. (2020). Personality structure in east and west Africa: Lexical studies of personality in Maa and Supyire-Senufo. *Journal of Personality and Social Psychology, 119*(5), 1132.

Theakston, J. A., Stewart, S. H., Dawson, M. Y., Knowlden-Loewen, S. A. B., and Lehman, D. R. (2004). Big Five personality domains predict drinking motives. *Personality and Individual Differences, 37,* 971–984.

Thielmann, I., and Hilbig, B. E. (2014). Trust in me, trust in you: A social projection account of the link between personality, cooperativeness, and trustworthiness expectations. *Journal of Research in Personality, 50,* 61–65.

Thielmann, I., Morten M., Benjamin E. H., and Ingo Z. "On the comparability of basic personality models: Meta-analytic correspondence, scope, and orthogonality of the Big Five and HEXACO dimensions." *European Journal of Personality* (2021): 08902070211026793.

Thomas, A. K., Bulevich, J. B., and Loftus, E. F. (2003). Exploring the role of repetition and sensory elaboration in the imagination inflation effect. *Memory and Cognition, 31,* 630–640.

Thompson, J. A., and Aukofer, C. (2011). *Why we believe in god(s): A concise guide to the science of faith.* Charlottesville, VA: Pitchstone Publishers.

Thompson, R. A. (1991). Emotional regulation and emotional development. *Educational Psychology Review, 3,* 269–307.

Thompson, R. A., Simpson, J. A., and Berlin, L. J. (2022). Taking perspective on attachment theory and research: Nine fundamental questions. *Attachment and Human Development,* DOI: 10.1080/14616734.2022.2030132.

Thorndike, E. L. (1911). *Individuality.* Boston: Houghton Mifflin.

Thornhill, R., and Gangestad, S. W. (2008). *The evolutionary biology of human female sexuality.* New York: Oxford University Press.

Thrash, T. M., and Elliot, A. J. (2002). Implicit and self-attributed achievement motives: Concordance and predictive validity. *Journal of Personality, 70,* 729–755.

Thrash, T. M., Wadsworth, L. M., Sim, Y. Y., Wan, X., and Everidge, C. E. (2019). Implicit–explicit motive concordance and moderating factors. In R. M. Ryan (Ed). *The Oxford handbook of human motivation., 2nd ed.,* pp. 187–203, New York: Oxford University Press

Tice, D. M. (1991). Esteem protection or enhancement? Self-handicapping motives and attributions differ by trait self-esteem. *Journal of Personality and Social Psychology, 60,* 711–725.

Tice, D. M. (1993). The social motivations of people with low self-esteem. In R. F. Baumeister (Ed.), *Self-Esteem: The Puzzle of Low Self-Regard* (pp. 37–53). New York: Plenum Press.

Tice, D. M., and Baumeister, R. F. (1990). Self-esteem, self-handicapping, and self-presentation: The strategy of inadequate practice. *Journal of Personality, 58,* 443–464.

Tice, D. M., and Bratslavsky, E. (2000). Giving in to feel good: The place of emotion regulation in the context of general self-control. *Psychological Inquiry, 11,* 149–159.

Tindle, H. A., Chang, Y. F., Kuller, L. H., Manson, J. E., Robinson, J. G., Rosal, M. C., Siegle, G. J., and Matthews, K. A. (2009). Optimism, cynical hostility, and incident coronary heart disease and mortality in the Women's Health Initiative. *Circulation, 120,* 656–662.

Tolea, M. I., Terracciano, A., Simonsick, E. M., Metter, E. J., Costa, P. T., Jr., and Ferrucci, L. (2012). Associations between personality traits, physical activity level, and muscle strength. *Journal of Research in Personality, 46,* 264–270.

Tolnai, L. (2021). The Power of Personality Traits in Allocation Decision-Making: A Secondary Analysis of a Laboratory Experiment. *Junior Management Science, 6*(2), 299–323.

Tomarken, A. J., Davidson, R. J., and Henriques, J. B. (1990). Resting frontal brain asymmetry predicts affective responses to films. *Journal of Personality and Social Psychology, 59,* 791–801.

Tomkins, S. S. (2008). *Affect, Imagery, Consciousness: The Complete Edition* (Vols. 1–4). New York: Springer.

Tooby, J., and Cosmides, L. (1990). On the universality of human nature and the uniqueness of the individual: The role of genetics and adaptation. *Journal of Personality, 58,* 17–68.

Tooby, J., and Cosmides, L. (1992). Psychological foundations of culture. In J. Barkow, L. Cosmides, and J. Tooby (Eds.), *The Adapted Mind* (pp. 19–136). New York: Oxford University Press.

Tooby, J., and Cosmides, L. (1996, January). Friendship and the banker's paradox: Other pathways to the evolution of adaptations for altruism. In Proceedings-British Academy (Vol. 88, pp. 119–144). Oxford University Press Inc.

Tooke, J., and Camie, L. (1991). Patterns of deception in intersexual and intrasexual mating strategies. *Ethology and Sociobiology, 12,* 345–364.

Tortoriello, G. K., Hart, W., Richardson, K., and Tullett, A. M. (2017). Do narcissists try to make romantic partners jealous on purpose? An examination of motives for deliberate jealousy-induction among subtypes of narcissism. *Personality and Individual Differences,* 114, 10–15.

Toschi, N., Riccelli, R., Indovina, I., Terracciano, A., and Passamonti, L. (2018). Functional connectome of the five-factor model of personality. *Personality Neuroscience, 1,* e2.

Toussaint, L. L., Shields, G. S., Green, E., Kennedy, K., Travers, S., and Slavich, G. M. (2018). Hostility, forgiveness, and cognitive impairment over 10 years in a national sample of American adults. *Health Psychology, 37,* 1102–1106.

Tracy, J. L., and Matsumoto, D. (2008). The spontaneous expression of pride and shame: Evidence for biologically innate nonverbal displays. *Proceedings of the National Academy of Sciences, 105*(33), 11655–11660.

Tremblay, R. E., Pihl, R. O., Vitaro, F., and Dobkin, P. L. (1994). Predicting early onset of male antisocial behavior from

preschool behavior. *Archives of General Psychiatry, 51,* 732–739.

Trinkaus, E., and Zimmerman, M. R. (1982). Trauma among the Shanidar Neanderthals. *American Journal of Physical Anthropology, 57,* 61–76.

Trivers, R. (1985). *Social evolution.* Menlo Park, CA: Benjamin/Cummings.

Trivers, R. L. (1971). The evolution of reciprocal altruism. *The Quarterly review of biology, 46*(1), 35–57.

Trivers, R. L. (1972). Parental investment and sexual selection. In B. Campbell (Ed.), *Sexual selection and the descent of man: 1871–1971* (pp. 136–179). Chicago: Aldine.

Trobst, K. K., Herbst, J. H., Masters, H. L., and Costa, P. T. (2002). Personality pathways to unsafe sex: Personality, condom use, and HIV risk behaviors. *Journal of Research in Personality, 36,* 117–133.

Trull, J. J., and McCrae, R. M. (2002). A five-factor perspective on personality disorder research. In P. T. Costa, Jr., and T. A. Widiger (Eds.), *Personality disorders and the five factor model of personality* (2nd ed., pp. 45–58). Washington, DC: American Psychological Association.

Trull, T. J. (2012). The Five-Factor Model of personality disorder and DSM-5. *Journal of Personality, 80*(6), 1697–1720.

Trull, T. J., and Widiger, T. A. (2013). Dimensional models of personality: The five-factor model and the DSM-5. *Dialogues in Clinical Neuroscience, 15,* 135–146.

Trzesniewski, K. H., Donnellan, M. B., and Robins, R. W. (2003). Stability of self-esteem across the life span. *Journal of Personality and Social Psychology, 84*(1), 205–220.

Tsai, A., Loftus, E., and Polage, D. (2000). Current directions in false-memory research. In D. F. Bjorklund (Ed.), *False-memory creation in children and adults: Theory, research, and implications* (pp. 31–44). Mahwah, NJ: Erlbaum.

Tuerlinckz, F., De Boeck, P., and Lens, W. (2002). Measuring needs with the Thematic Apperception Test: A psychometric study. *Journal of Personality and Social Psychology, 82,* 448–461.

Tupes, E. C., and Christal, R. C. (1961). *Recurrent personality factors based on trait ratings.* USAF ASD Technical Report, No. 61-97, U.S. Air Force, Lackland Air Force Base, TX.

Turiano, N. A., Chapman, B. P., Gruenewald, T. L., and Mroczek, D. K. (2015). Personality and the leading behavioral contributors of mortality. *Health Psychology, 34*(1), 51–60.

Turiano, N. A., Whiteman, S. D., Hampson, S. E., Roberts, B. W., and Mroczek, D. K. (2012). Personality and substance use in midlife: Conscientiousness as a moderator and the effects of trait change.

Journal of Research in Personality, 46, 295–305.

Turkheimer, E., Pettersson, E., and Horn, E. E. (2014). A phenotypic null hypothesis for the genetics of personality. *Annual Review of Psychology, 65,* 515–540.

Twenge, J. M. (2000). The age of anxiety? Birth cohort change in anxiety and neuroticism, 1952–1993. *Journal of Personality and Social Psychology, 79,* 1007–1021.

Twenge, J. M. (2001a). Changes in women's assertiveness in response to status and roles: A cross-temporal meta-analysis, 1931–1993. *Journal of Personality and Social Psychology, 81,* 133–145.

Twenge, J. M. (2001b). Birth cohort changes in extraversion: A cross-temporal meta-analysis, 1966–1993. *Personality and Individual Differences, 30,* 735–748.

Twenge, J. M., Konrath, S., Foster, J. D., Campbell, W. K., and Bushman, B. J. (2008). Egos inflating over time: A cross-temporal meta-analysis of the Narcissistic Personality Inventory. *Journal of Personality, 76,* 875–902.

Tybur, J. M., and de Vries, R. E. (2013). Disgust sensitivity and the HEXACO model of personality. Personality and Individual Differences, 55(6), 660–665.

Tybur, J. M., Lieberman, D., and Griskevicius, V. (2009). Microbes, mating, and morality: Individual differences in three functional domains of disgust. *Journal of Personality and Social Psychology, 97*(1), 103–122.

Tybur, J. M., Lieberman, D., Kurzban, R., and DeScioli, P. (2013). Disgust: Evolved function and structure. Psychological Review, 120, 65–84. http://dx.doi.org/10.1037/a0030778

U.S. Department of Health and Human Services, Administration on Children, Youth, and Families. (2019). *Child Maltreatment 2019.* Washington, DC: U.S. Government Printing Office.

Udry, J. R., and Chantala, K. (2004). Masculinity–femininity guides sexual union formation in adolescence. *Personality and Social Psychology Bulletin, 30,* 44–55.

Uher, R., Caspi, A., Houts, R., Sugden, K., Williams, B., Poulton, R., and Moffitt, T. E. (2011). Serotonin transporter gene moderates childhood maltreatment's effects on persistent but not single-episode depression: Replications and implications for resolving inconsistent results. *Journal of Affective Disorders, 135,* 55–65.

UNODC, U. (2014). *Global study on homicide 2013.* Vienna: United Nations Publication.

Vaidya, J. G., Gray, E. K., Gaig, J. R., Mroczek, D. K., and Watson, D. (2008). Differential stability and individual growth trajectories of Big Five and affective traits during young adulthood. *Journal of Personality, 76,* 267–304.

Vaidya, J. G., Gray, E. K., Haig, J., and Watson, D. (2002). On the temporal stability of personality: Evidence for differential stability and the role of life experiences. *Journal of Personality and Social Psychology, 83, 6,* 1469–1484.

Vaillant, G. E. (1977). *Adaptation to life.* Boston: Little Brown.

Vaillant, G. E. (1994). Ego mechanisms of defense and personality psychopathology. *Journal of Abnormal Psychology, 103,* 44–50.

Valentova, J. V., Štěrbová, Z., Bártová, K., and Varella, M. A. C. (2016). Personality of ideal and actual romantic partners among heterosexual and non-heterosexual men and women: A cross-cultural study. *Personality and Individual Differences, 101,* 160–166.

van Anders, S. M. (2012). Testosterone and sexual desire in healthy women and men. *Archives of Sexual Behavior, 41,* 1471–1484.

Van Beijsterveldt, C. E. M., Bartels, M., Hudziak, J. J., and Boomsma, D. I. (2003). Causes of stability of aggression from early childhood to adolescence: A longitudinal genetic analysis of Dutch twins. *Behavior Genetics, 33,* 591–605.

Van de Velde, S., Bracke, P., and Levecque, K. (2010). Gender differences in depression in 23 European countries. Cross-national variation in the gender gap in depression. *Social Science & Medicine, 71*(2), 305–313.

van den Berg, S. M., de Moor, M. H., McGue, M., Pettersson, E., Terracciano, A., Verweij, K. J., . . . and Hansell, N. K. (2014). Harmonization of Neuroticism and Extraversion phenotypes across inventories and cohorts in the Genetics of Personality Consortium: An application of Item Response Theory. *Behavior Genetics, 44*(4), 295–313.

van den Berg, S. M., de Moor, M. H., Verweij, K. J., Krueger, R. F., Luciano, M., Vasquez, A. A., . . . and Gordon, S. D. (2016). Meta-analysis of Genome-Wide Association Studies for Extraversion: Findings from the Genetics of Personality Consortium. *Behavior Genetics, 46*(2), 170–182.

Van der Linden, D., Figueredo, A. J., de Leeuw, R. N. H., Scholte, R. J. J., and Engels, R. C. M. E. (2012). The general factor of personality (GFP) and parental support: Testing a prediction from Life History Theory. *Evolution and Human Behavior, 33,* 537–546.

Van Eck, R. N., Fu, H., Drechsel, P. V. J. (2015). Can simulator immersion change cognitive style? Results from a cross-sectional study of field-dependence–independence in air traffic control students. *Journal of Computing in Higher Education, 27,* 196–214.

Van Iddekinge, C. H., Roth, P. L., Raymark, P. H., and Odle-Dusseau, H. N. (2012). The criterion-related validity of integrity tests: An updated meta-analysis. *Journal of Applied Psychology, 97,* 499–530.

van Scheppingen, M. A., Jackson, J. J., Specht, J., Hutteman, R., Denissen, J. J., and Bleidorn, W. (2016). Personality trait development during the transition to parenthood a test of social investment theory. *Social Psychological and Personality Science, 7*(5), 452–462.

Vando, A. (1974). The development of the R-A scale: A paper-and-pencil measure of pain tolerance. *Personality and Social Psychology Bulletin, 1,* 28–29.

Vazire, S. (2010). Who knows what about a person? The self-other knowledge asymmetry (SOKA) model. *Journal of Personality and Social Psychology, 98,* 281–300.

Vazire, S., and Gosling, S. D. (2003). The role of animal research in bridging psychology and biology. *American Psychologist, 58,* 407–408.

Vazire, S., and Mehl, M. R. (2008). Knowing me, knowing you: The accuracy and unique predictive validity of self and other ratings of daily behavior. *Journal of Personality and Social Psychology, 95,* 1207–1216.

Vazire, S., Naumann, L. P., Rentfrow, P. J., and Gosling, S. D. (2008). Portrait of a narcissist: Manifestations of narcissism in physical appearance. *Journal of Research in Personality, 42,* 1439–1447.

Veenhoven, R. (1988). The utility of happiness. *Social Indicators Research, 20,* 333–354.

Veenhoven, R. (1991a). Questions on happiness: Classical topics, modern answers, blind spots. In F. Strack and M. Argyle (Eds.), *Subjective Well-Being: An Interdisciplinary Perspective* (pp. 7–26). Oxford, England: Pergamon Press.

Veenhoven, R. (1991b). Is happiness relative? *Social Indicators Research, 24,* 1–34.

Verdon, B., and Azoulay, C. (2020). *Psychoanalysis and projective methods in personality assessment.* New York: Hogrefe Publishing.

Verduyn, P., Lee, D. S., Park, J., Shablack, H., Orvell, A., Bayer, J., . . . Kross, E. (2015). Passive Facebook usage undermines affective well-being: Experimental and longitudinal evidence. *Journal of Experimental Psychology: General, 144,* 480–488.

Verduyn, P., Ybarra, O., Résibois, M., Jonides, J., and Kross, E. (2017). Do social network sites enhance or undermine subjective well-being? A critical review. *Social Issues and Policy Review, 11,* 274–302.

Vernon, P., Villani, V. C., Vickers, L. C., and Harris, J. A. (2008). A behavioral genetic investigation of the Dark Triad and the Big 5. *Personality and Individual Differences, 44,* 445–452.

Veroff, J., Atkinson, J. W., Feld, S. C., and Gurin, G. (1960). The use of thematic apperception to assess motivation in a nationwide interview study. *Psychological Monography, 74,* 32.

Veselka, L., Schermer, J. A., and Vernon, P. A. (2012). The Dark Triad and an expanded framework of personality. *Personality and Individual Differences, 53,* 417–425.

Vidacek, S., Kaliterna, L., Radosevic-Vidacek, B., and Folkard, S. (1988). Personality differences in the phase of circadian rhythms: A comparison of morningness and extraversion. *Ergonomics, 31,* 873–888.

Vignoles, V. L., Regalia, C., Manzi, C., Golledtge, J., and Scabini, E. (2006). Beyond self-esteem: Influence of multiple motives on identity construction. *Journal of Personality and Social Psychology, 90,* 308–333.

Vining, D. (1982). On the possibility of the reemergence of a dysgenic trend with respect to intelligence in American fertility differentials. *Intelligence, 6,* 241–264.

Viswesvaran, C., and Ones, D. S. (2016). Integrity tests: A review of alternate conceptualizations and some measurement and practical issues. In U. Kumar (Ed.), *The Wiley handbook of personality assessment* (pp. 59–73). Wiley Blackwell. https://doi.org/10.1002/9781119173489.ch5.

Vohs, K. D., Schmeichel, B. J., Lohmann, S., Gronau, Q. F., Finley, Anna J., Ainsworth, S. E. et al. (2021). A multisite preregistered paradigmatic test of the ego-depletion effect. *Psychological Science, 32,* 1566–1581.

Volkert, J., Gablonski, T., and Rabung, S. (2018). Prevalence of personality disorders in the general adult population in Western countries: Systematic review and meta-analysis. *British Journal of Psychiatry, 213,* 809–715.

von Rueden, C. R., Lukaszewski, A. W., and Gurven, M. (2015). Adaptive personality calibration in a human society: Effects of embodied capital on prosocial traits. *Behavioral Ecology, 26*(4), 1071–1082.

Vrij, A., van der Steen, J., and Koppelaar, L. (1995). The effects of street noise and field independence on police officers' shooting behavior. *Journal of Applied Social Psychology, 25,* 1714–1725.

Vukasović, T., and Bratko, D. (2015). Heritability of personality: A meta-analysis of behavior genetic studies. *Psychological Bulletin, 141*(4), 769–785.

Wachtel, P. L. (1973). Psychodynamics, behavior therapy, and the implacable experimenter: An inquiry into the consistency of personality. *Journal of Abnormal Psychology, 82,* 324–334.

Wacker, J., and Smillie, L. D. (2015). Trait extraversion and dopamine function. *Social and Personality Psychology Compass, 9*(6), 225–238.

Wacker, J., Mueller, E. M., and Stemmler, G. (2012). Prenatal testosterone and personality: Increasing the specificity of trait assessment to detect consistent associations with digit ratio (2D:4D). *Journal of Research in Personality,* online first posting, digital online identifier: 10.1016/j.jrp.2012.10.007.

Wagels, L., Habel, U., Raine, A., and Clemens, B. (2022). Neuroimaging, hormonal and genetic biomarkers for pathological aggression—Success or failure? *Current Opinion in Behavioral Sciences, 43,* 101–110.

Wagner, J., Ludtke, O., and Trautwein, U. (2015). Self-esteem is mostly stable across young adulthood: Evidence from latent STARTS models. *Journal of Personality,* published online, https://doi.org/10.1111/jopy.12178.

Wagner, J., Lüdtke, O., Jonkmann, K., and Trautwein, U. (2013). Cherish yourself: Longitudinal patterns and conditions of self-esteem change in the transition to young adulthood. *Journal of Personality and Social Psychology, 104,* 148–163.

Wagstaff, G. F., Vella, M., and Perfect, T. (1992). The effect of hypnotically elicited testimony on jurors' judgments of guilt and innocence. *Journal of Social Psychology, 132,* 591–595.

Wahba, M. A., and Bridwell, L. (1973). Maslow's need hierarchy theory: A review of research. *Proceedings of the Annual Convention of the American Psychological Association (1973),* 571–572.

Wallace, H. M., and Baumeister, R. F. (2002). The performance of narcissists rises and falls with perceived opportunity for glory. *Journal of Personality and Social Psychology, 82*(5), 819–834.

Waller, N. (1994). The importance of nongenetic influences on romantic love styles. *Psychological Science, 9,* 268–274.

Walton, G. M., Paunesku, D., and Dweck, C. S. (2012). Expandable selves. In M. R. Leary and J. P. Tangney (Eds.), *Handbook of Self and Identity* (2nd ed., pp. 141–154). New York: Guilford Press.

Wang, J. L., Wang, H.-Z., Gaskin, J., and Hawk, S. (2017). The mediating roles of upward social comparison and self-esteem and the moderating role of social comparison orientation in the association between social networking site usage and subjective well-being. *Frontiers in Psychology, 8.* doi:10.3389/fpsyg.2017.00771.

Watson, D. (2000). *Mood and Temperament.* New York: Guilford Press.

Watson, D. (2003). To dream, perchance to remember: Individual differences in dream recall. *Personality and Individual Differences, 34,* 1271–1286.

Watson, D. C. (2001). Procrastination and the five-factor model: A facet level analysis. *Personality and Individual Differences, 30,* 149–158.

Watson, D., and Clark, L. A. (1984). Negative affectivity: The disposition to experience aversive emotional states. *Psychological Bulletin, 96,* 465–490.

Watson, D., and Humrichouse, J. (2006). Personality development in emerging adulthood: Integrating evidence from self-ratings and spouse ratings. *Journal of Personality and Social Psychology, 91,* 959–974.

Watson, D., and Pennebaker, J. W. (1989). Health complaints, stress, and distress: Exploring the central role of negative affectivity. *Psychological Review, 96,* 234–254.

Watson-Jones, R. E., Whitehouse, H., and Legare, C. H. (2016). In-group ostracism increases high-fidelity imitation in early childhood. *Psychological Science, 27*(1), 34–42.

Watts, B. L. (1982). Individual differences in circadian activity rhythms and their effects on roommate relationships. *Journal of Personality, 50,* 374–384.

Webster, G. D., and Crysel, L. C. (2012). "Hit Me, Maybe, One More Time": Brief measures of impulsivity and sensation seeking and their prediction of blackjack bets and sexual promiscuity. *Journal of Research in Personality, 46*(5), 591–598.

Wechsler, D. (1949). *The Wechsler Intelligence Scale for Children.* New York: Psychological Corporation.

Wehr, T. A., and Goodwin, F. K. (1981). Biological rhythms and psychiatry. In S. Arieti and H. K. Brodie (Eds.), *American Handbook of Psychiatry: Advances and New Directions* (Vol. 7). New York: Basic Books.

Weinberger, D. S., Schwartz, G. E., and Davidson, R. J. (1979). Low-anxious, high-anxious, and repressive coping styles: Psychometric patterns and behavioral and physiological responses to stress. *Journal of Abnormal Psychology, 88,* 369–380.

Weinberger, J. (2003). Freud's influence on psychology is alive and vibrant. In E. E. Smith, S. Nolen-Hoeksema, B. L. Fredrickson, G. R. Loftus, D. J. Bem, and S. Maren, *Introduction to psychology*

(p. 486). Belmont, CA: Wadsworth/ Thomson Learning.

Weinberger, J., and McClelland, D. C. (1990). Cognitive versus traditional motivational models: Irreconcilable or complementary? In E. T. Higgins and R. M. Sorrentino (Eds.), *Handbook of motivation and cognition* (Vol. 2, pp. 562–597). New York: Guilford Press.

Weinberger, J., and Westen, D. (2007). *RATS, we should have used Clinton: Subliminal priming in political campaigns.* Paper presented at the annual meeting of the International Society of Political Psychology, Portland, Oregon. *USA Online.* Retrieved February 3, 2009, from www. allacademic.com/meta/p204661_index. html.

Weinstein, A., Dorani, D., Elhadif, R., Bukovza, Y., Yarmulnik, A., and Dannon, P. (2015). Internet addiction is associated with social anxiety in young adults. *Annals of Clinical Psychiatry, 27*(1), 4–9.

Weinstock, L. M., and Whisman, M. A. (2006). Neuroticism as a common feature of the depressive and anxiety disorders: A test of the revised integrative hierarchical model in a national sample. *Journal of Abnormal Psychology, 115,* 68–74.

Weiser, E. B. (2015). # Me: Narcissism and its facets as predictors of selfie-posting frequency. *Personality and Individual Differences, 86,* 477–481.

Weiss, A., King, J. E., and Enns, R. M. (2002). Subjective well-being is heritable and genetically correlated with dominance in chimpanzees *(Pan troglodytes). Journal of Personality and Social Psychology, 83*(5), 1141–1149.

Weissberg, R. P., Kumpfer, K. L., and Seligman, M. E. P. (2003). Prevention that works for children and youth: An introduction. *American Psychologist Special Issue: Prevention that works for children and youth, 58,* 425–432.

Weller, H. G., Repman, J., Lan, W., and Rooze, G. (1995). Improving the effectiveness of learning through hypermedia-based instruction: The importance of learner characteristics. Special Issue: Hypermedia: Theory, research, and application. *Computers in Human Behavior, 11,* 451–465.

Wertsch, J., and Kanner, B. (1992). A sociocultural approach to intellectual development. In R. Sternberg and C. A. Berg (Eds.), *Intellectual development* (pp. 328–349). New York: Cambridge University Press.

Wessman, A. E., and Ricks, D. F. (1966). *Mood and Personality.* New York: Holt, Rinehart, and Winston.

Westen, D. (1990). Psychoanalytic approaches to personality. In L. A. Pervin (Ed.), *Handbook of personality: Theory and research* (pp. 21–65). New York: Guilford Press.

Westen, D. (1992). The cognitive self and the psychoanalytic self: Can we put our selves together? *Psychological Inquiry, 3,* 1–13.

Westen, D. (1998). The scientific legacy of Sigmund Freud: Toward a psychodynamically informed psychological science. *Psychological Bulletin, 124,* 333–371.

Westen, D., and Gabbard, G. O. (2002a). Developments in cognitive neuroscience: I. Conflict, compromise, and connectionism. *Journal of the American Psychoanalytic Association, 50,* 53–98.

Westen, D., and Gabbard, G. O. (2002b). Developments in cognitive neuroscience: II. Implications for theories of transference. *Journal of the American Psychoanalytic Association 50,* 99–134.

Weston, S. J., and Jackson, J. J. (2016). How do people respond to health news? The role of personality traits. *Psychology and Health, 31,* 637–654.

Wever, R. A. (1979). *The circadian system of man: Results of experiments under temporal isolation.* New York: Springer.

Whalen, P. J., Bush, G., and McNally, R. J. (1998). The emotional counting Stroop paradigm: A functional magnetic resonance imaging probe of the anterior cingulate affective division. *Biological Psychiatry, 44,* 1219–1228.

Wheeler, J. G., George, W. H., and Dahl, B. J. (2002). Sexually aggressive college males: Empathy as a moderator in the "Confluence Model" of sexual aggression. *Personality and Individual Differences, 33,* 759–775.

Wheeler, R. W., Davidson, R. J., and Tomarken, A. J. (1993). Frontal brain asymmetry and emotional reactivity: A biological substrate of affective style. *Psychophysiology, 30,* 82–89.

White, J. K., Hendrick, S. S., and Hendrick, C. (2004). Big Five personality variables and relationship constructs. *Personality and Individual Differences, 37,* 1519–1530.

White, S. J., Pascall, D. J., and Wilson, A. J. (2020). Towards a comparative approach to the structure of animal personality variation. *Behavioral Ecology, 31*(2), 340–351.

Whiting, B., and Edwards, C. P. (1988). *Children of different worlds.* Cambridge, MA: Harvard University Press.

Whorf, B. L. (1956). *Language, thought, and reality.* Cambridge, MA: MIT Press.

Whyte, S., Brooks, R. C., Chan, H. F., and Torgler, B. (2019). Do certain personality traits provide a mating market competitive advantage? Sex, offspring and the big 5. *Personality and Individual Differences, 139,* 158–169.

Wicker, F. W., Brown, G., Weihe, J. A., Hagen, A. S., and Reed, J. L. (1993). On reconsidering Maslow: An examination of the deprivation/domination proposition. *Journal of Research in Personality, 27,* 118–133.

Wickman, S. A., and Campbell, C. (2003). An analysis of how Carl Rogers enacted client-centered conversation with Gloria. *Journal of Counseling and Development, 81,* 178–184.

Widiger, T. A. (1997). Personality disorders as maladaptive variants of common personality traits: Implications for treatment. *Journal of Contemporary Psychotherapy Special Issue: Personality Disorders, 27,* 265–282.

Widiger, T. A. (2000). Personality disorders in the 21st century. *Journal of Personality Disorders, 14,* 3–16.

Widiger, T. A., and Costa, P. T. (2012). Integrating normal and abnormal personality structure: The Five-Factor Model. *Journal of Personality, 80*(6), 1471–1506.

Widiger, T. A., Costa, P. T., Jr., and McCrae, R. M. (2002a). A proposal for Axis II: Diagnosing personality disorders using the five-factor model. In P. T. Costa Jr. and T. A. Widiger (Eds.), *Personality disorders and the five-factor model of personality* (2nd ed., pp. 431–456). Washington, DC: American Psychological Association.

Widiger, T. A., Trull, T. J., Clarkin, J. F., Sanderson, C., and Costa, P. T., Jr. (2002b). A description of the *DSM-IV* personality disorders with the five-factor model of personality. In P. T. Costa Jr. and T. A. Widiger (Eds.), *Personality disorders and the five-factor model of personality* (2nd ed., pp. 89–102). Washington, DC: American Psychological Association.

Wiebe, D. J., and Smith, T. (1997). Personality and health: Progress and problems in psychosomatics. In R. Hogan, J. Johnson, and S. Briggs (Eds.), *Handbook of personality psychology* (pp. 892–918). San Diego, CA: Academic Press.

Wiederman, M. W., and Kendall, E. (1999). Evolution, gender, and sexual jealousy: Investigation with a sample from Sweden. *Evolution and Human Behavior, 20,* 121–128.

Wiggins, J. S. (1973). *Personality and prediction: Principles of personality assessment.* Menlo Park, CA: Addison-Wesley.

Wiggins, J. S. (1979). A psychological taxonomy of trait-descriptive terms: The interpersonal domain. *Journal of Personality and Social Psychology, 37,* 395–412.

Wiggins, J. S. (1996). *The five-factor model of personality: Theoretical perspectives.* New York: Guilford Press.

Wiggins, J. S. (2003). *Paradigms of personality assessment.* New York: Guilford Press.

Wilgus, J. and Wilgus, B. (2009). Face to face with Phineus Gage. *Journal of the History of the Neurosciences, 18,* 340–345.

Willerman, L. (1979). Effects of families on intellectual development. *American Psychologist, 34,* 923–929.

Willerman, L., Loehlin, J. C., and Horn, J. M. (1992). An adoption and a cross-fostering study of the Minnesota Multiphasic Personality Inventory (MMPI) Psychopathic Deviate scale. *Behavior Genetics, 22,* 515–529.

Williams, D. E., and Page, M. M. (1989). A multi-dimensional measure of Maslow's hierarchy of needs. *Journal of Research in Personality, 23,* 192–213.

Williams, J. E., and Best, D. L. (1982). *Measuring sex stereotypes: A thirty-nation study.* Beverly Hills: Sage.

Williams, J. E., and Best, D. L. (1990). *Measuring sex stereotypes: A multi-nation study.* Newbury Park, CA: Sage.

Williams, J. E., and Best, D. L. (1994). Cross-cultural views of women and men. In W. J. Lonner and R. Malpass (Eds.), *Psychology and culture* (pp. 191–196). Boston: Allyn and Bacon.

Williams, J. M. G., Mathews, A., and MacLeod, C. (1996). The emotional Stroop task and psychopathology. *Psychological Bulletin, 120,* 3–24.

Williams, L., Ashford-Smith, S., Cobban, L., Fitzsimmons, R., Sukhatme, V., and Hunter, S. C. (2019). Does your partner's personality affect your health? Actor and partner effects of the Big Five personality traits. *Personality and Individual Differences, 149,* 231–234.

Williams, P. G., O'Brien, C. D., and Colder, C. R. (2004). The effects of neuroticism and extraversion on self-assessed health and health-relevant cognition. *Personality and Individual Differences, 37,* 83–94.

Williams, W. M., and Ceci, S. J. (2015). National hiring experiments reveal 2:1 faculty preference for women on STEM tenure track. *Proceedings of the National Academy of Sciences, 112*(17), 5360–5365.

Wilmot, M. P., Haslam, N., Tian, J., and Ones, D. S. (2019). Direct and conceptual replications of the taxometric analysis of type a behavior. *Journal of Personality and Social Psychology, 116,* e12–e26. https://doi-org/10.1037/pspp0000195

Wilson, D. S., Near, D., and Miller, R. R. (1996). Machiavellianism: A synthesis of the evolutionary and psychological literatures. *Psychological Bulletin, 119,* 285–299.

Wilson, M. L., Boesch, C., Fruth, B., Furuichi, T., Gilby, I. C., Hashimoto, C., . . . and Lloyd, J. N. (2014). Lethal aggression in Pan is better explained by adaptive strategies than human impacts. *Nature, 513*(7518), 414.

Wilson, M., and Daly, M. (1985). Competitiveness, risk-taking, and violence: The young male syndrome. *Ethology and Sociobiology, 6,* 59–73.

Wilson, M., and Daly, M. (2004). Do pretty women inspire men to discount the future? *Proceedings of the Royal Society of London, B (Suppl.), 271,* S177–S179.

Wilt, J., and Revelle, W. (2017). Extraversion. In T. A. Widiger (Ed.), *The Oxford handbook of the Five Factor Model* (pp. 57–81). New York: Oxford University Press.

Winch, R. F. (1954). The theory of complementary needs in mate selection: An analytic and descriptive study. *American Sociological Review, 19,* 241–249.

Winjgaards-de Meij, L., Stroebe, M., Schut, H., Stroebe, W., van den Bout, J., van der Heijden, P., and Dijkstra, I. (2007). Neuroticism and attachment insecurity as predictors of bereavement outcome. *Journal of Research in Personality, 41,* 498–505.

Wink, P., Ciciolla, L., Dillon, M., and Tracy, A. (2007). Religiousness, spiritual seeking, and personality: Findings from a longitudinal study. *Journal of Personality, 75,* 1051–1070.

Winter, D. G. (1973). *The power motive.* New York: Free Press.

Winter, D. G. (1988). The power motive in women—and men. *Journal of Personality and Social Psychology, 54,* 510–519.

Winter, D. G. (1993). Power, affiliation, and war: Three tests of a motivational model. *Journal of Personality and Social Psychology, 65,* 532–545.

Winter, D. G. (1998). A motivational analysis of the Clinton first term and the 1996 presidential campaign. *Leadership Quarterly, 9,* 367–376.

Winter, D. G. (1999). Linking personality and "scientific" psychology: The development of empirically derived Thematic Apperception Test measures. In Gieser and M. I. Stein (Eds.), *Evocative images: The Thematic Apperception Test and the art of projection* (pp. 107–124). Washington, DC: American Psychological Association.

Winter, D. G. (2002). The motivational dimensions of leadership: Power, achievement, and affiliation. In R. E. Riggio and S. E. Murphy (Eds.), *Multiple intelligences and leadership* (pp. 119–138). Mahwah, NJ: Erlbaum.

Winter, D. G., and Barenbaum, N. B. (1985). Responsibility and the power motive in women and men. *Journal of Personality, 53,* 335–355.

Winter, D. G. (2018). What does Trump really want? *Analyses of Social Issues and Public Policy, 18,* 155–171.

Wirtz, D., Tucker, A., Briggs, C., and Schoemann, A. M. (2021). How and why social media affect subjective well-being: Multi-site use and social comparison as predictors of change across time. *Journal of Happiness Studies, 22,* 1673–1691.

Witkin, H. A. (1973). A cognitive-style perspective on evaluation and guidance. *Proceedings of the Invitational Conference on Testing Problems,* 21–27.

Witkin, H. A. (1977). Role of the field-dependent and field-independent cognitive styles in academic evolution: A longitudinal study. *Journal of Educational Psychology, 69,* 197–211.

Witkin, H. A., and Goodenough, D. R. (1977). Field dependence and interpersonal behavior. *Psychological Bulletin, 84,* 661–689.

Witkin, H. A., Dyk, R. B., Fattuson, H. F., Goodenough, D. R., and Karp, S. A. (1962). *Psychological differentiation: Studies of development.* New York: Wiley.

Witkin, H. A., Lewis, H. B., Hertzman, M., Machover, K., Meissner, P. B., and Wapner, S. (1954). *Personality through perception: An experimental and clinical study.* New York: Harper.

Witkin, H. A., Moore, C. A., Goodenough, D. R., and Cox, P. W. (1977). Field-dependent and field-independent cognitive styles and their educational implications. *Review of Educational Research, 47,* 1–64.

Woike, B. A. (1995). Most memorable experiences: Evidence for a link between implicit and explicit motives and social cognitive processes in everyday life. *Journal of Personality and Social Psychology, 68,* 1081–1091.

Wood, A. H., and Eagly, A. H. (2010). Gender. In S. Fiske, D. Gilbert, and G. Lindzey (Eds.), *Handbook of social psychology* (Vol. 1, 5th ed., pp. 629–667). New York: Wiley.

Wood, D. (2015). Testing the lexical hypothesis: Are socially important traits more densely reflected in the English lexicon? *Journal of Personality and Social Psychology, 108*(2), 317–335.

Wood, D., Nye, C. D., and Saucier, G. (2010). Identification and measurement of a more comprehensive set of person-descriptive trait markers from the English lexicon. *Journal of Research in Personality, 44,* 258–272.

Wood, J. J., McLeod, B. D., Sigman, M., Hwang, W. C., and Chu, B. C. (2003). Parenting and childhood anxiety: Theory, empirical findings, and future directions. *Journal of Child Psychology and Psychiatry and Allied Disciplines, 44,* 134–151.

Wood, J. M., Nezworski, M. T., and Stejskal, J. W. (1996). The comprehensive system for the Rorschach: A critical examination. *Psychological Science, 7,* 3–10.

Wortman, J., and Wood, D. (2011). The personality traits of liked people. *Journal of Research in Personality, 45,* 519-528.

Wright, C. I., Williams, D., Feczko, E., Barrett, L. F., Dickerson, B. C., Schwartz, C. E., and Wedig, M. M. (2006). Neuroanatomical correlates of extraversion and neuroticism. *Cerebral Cortex, 16*(12), 1809-1819.

Wright, D. B., Eaton, A. A., and Skagerberg, E. (2015). Occupational segregation and psychological gender differences: How empathizing and systemizing help explain the distribution of men and women into (some) occupations. *Journal of Research in Personality, 54,* 30-39.

Wright, L. (1988). The Type A behavior pattern and coronary artery disease. *American Psychologist, 43,* 2-14.

Wright, P. J., and Vangeel, L. (2019). Pornography, permissiveness, and sex differences: An evaluation of social learning and evolutionary explanations. *Personality and Individual Differences, 143,* 128-138.

Wrulich, M., Stadler, G., Brunner, M., Keller, U., and Martin, R. (2015). Childhood intelligence predicts premature mortality: Results from a 40-year population-based longitudinal study. *Journal of Research in Personality, 58,* 6-10.

Wrzus, C., Wagner, G. G., and Riediger, M. (2016). Personality-situation transactions from adolescence to old age. *Journal of Personality and Social Psychology, 110*(5), 782.

Wu, K. D., and Clark, L. A. (2003). Relations between personality traits and self-reports of daily behavior. *Journal of Research in Personality, 37,* 231-256.

Yarkoni, T. (2015). Neurobiological substrates of personality: A critical overview. In L. Cooper and R. J. Larsen (Eds.), *Handbook of personality and social psychology: personality processes and individual differences* (pp. 61-84). Washington, DC: American Psychological Association.

Yeh, C. (1995). *A cultural perspective on interdependence in self and morality: A Japan-U.S. comparison.* Unpublished manuscript, Department of Psychology, Stanford University, Stanford, CA.

Yik, M. S. M., and Russell, J. A. (2001). Predicting the big two of affect from the Big Five of personality. *Journal of Research in Personality, 35,* 247-277.

Young, S. M., and Pinksky, D. (2006). Narcissism and celebrity. *Journal of Research in Personality, 40,* 463-471.

Yu, D. L., and Seligman, M. E. P. (2002). Preventing depressive symptoms in Chinese children. *Prevention and Treatment, 5,* np.

Zagorsky, J. L. (2007). Do you have to be smart to be rich? The impact of IQ on wealth, income, and financial distress. *Intelligence, 35,* 489-501.

Zakriski, A. L., Wright, J. C., and Underwood, M. K. (2005). Gender similarities and differences in children's social behavior: Finding personality in contextualized patterns of adaptation. *Journal of Personality and Social Psychology, 88,* 844-855.

Zarevski, P., Bratko, D., Butkovic, A., and Lazic, A. (2002). Self-reports and peer-ratings of shyness and assertiveness. *Review of Psychology, 9,* 13-16.

Zeidner, M., Matthews, G., Roberts, R. D., and MacCann, C. (2003). Development of emotional intelligence: Towards a multi-level investment model. *Human Development, 46,* 69-96.

Zeigler-Hill, V., Myers, E. M., and Clark, C. B. (2010). Narcissism and self-esteem reactivity: The role of negative achievement events. *Journal of Research in Personality, 44,* 285-292.

Zelenski, J. M., and Larsen, R. J. (1999). Susceptibility to affect: A comparison of three personality taxonomies. *Journal of Personality, 67,* 761-791.

Zelenski, J. M., and Larsen, R. J. (2000). The distribution of emotions in everyday life: A state and trait perspective from experience sampling data. *Journal of Research in Personality, 34,* 178-197.

Zengel, B., Edlund, J. E., and Sagarin, B. J., (2013). Sex differences in jealousy in response to infidelity: Evaluation of demographic moderators in a national random sample. *Personality and Individual Differences, 54,* 47-51.

Zettler, I., and Hilbig, B. E. (2010). Honesty-humility and person-situation interaction at work. *European Journal of Personality, 24,* 569-582.

Zhao, K., Ferguson, E., and Smillie, L. D. (2016). Prosocial personality traits differentially predict egalitarianism, generosity, and reciprocity in economic games. *Frontiers in psychology, 7,* 1137.

Zhou, Y., Zhang, Z., Wang, K., Chen, S., Zhou, M., and Zhang, J. (2021). Personality and emerging adults' friend selection on social networking sites: A social network analysis perspective. *PsyCh Journal, 10*(1), 62-75.

Zhu, B., Chen, C., Loftus, E .F., He, Q., Chen, C., Lei, X., Lin, C., and Dong, Q. (2012). Brief exposure to misinformation can lead to long-term false memories.

Applied Cognitive Psychology, 26, 301-307.

Zilcha-Mano, S., Mikulincer, M., and Shaver, P. R. (2012). Pets as safe havens and secure bases: The moderating role of pet attachment orientations. *Journal of Research in Personality, 46,* 571-580.

Zimbardo, P. G. (1977). *Shyness: What it is and what to do about it.* New York: Symphony.

Zuckerman, M. (1974). The sensation seeking motive. In B. Maher (Ed.), *Progress in experimental personality research* (Vol. 7, pp. 79-148). New York: Academic Press.

Zuckerman, M. (1978). Sensation seeking. In H. London and J. E. Exner (Eds.), *Dimensions of personality* (pp. 487-559). New York: Wiley Interscience.

Zuckerman, M. (1984). Sensation seeking: A comparative approach to a human trait. *Behavioral and Brain Sciences, 7,* 413-471.

Zuckerman, M. (1991a). *Psychobiology of personality.* New York: Cambridge University Press.

Zuckerman, M. (1991b). Sensation-seeking trait. *Encyclopedia of Human Biology, 6,* 809-817.

Zuckerman, M. (2005). The neurobiology of impulsive sensation seeking: Genetics, brain physiology, biochemistry, and neurology. In C. Stough and C. Stough (Eds.), *Neurobiology of exceptionality* (pp. 31-52). New York: Kluwer Academic/Plenum Publishers.

Zuckerman, M. (2006). Biosocial bases of sensation seeking. In T. Canli (Ed.), *Biology of personality and individual differences* (pp. 37-59). New York: Guilford Press.

Zuckerman, M. and Glicksohn, J. (2016). Hans Eysenck's personality model and the constructs of sensation seeking and impulsivity. *Personality and Individual Differences,103,* 48-52.

Zuckerman, M., and Aluja, A. (2015). Measures of sensation seeking. In G. J. Boyle, D. H. Saklofske, G. Matthews, G. J. Boyle, D. H. Saklofske, and G. Matthews (Eds.), *Measures of personality and social psychological constructs* (pp. 352-380). San Diego, CA: Elsevier Academic Press.

Zuckerman, M., and Haber, M. M. (1965). Need for stimulation as a source of stress response to perceptual isolation. *Journal of Abnormal Psychology, 70,* 371-377.

Zuckerman, M., and Kuhlman, D. M. (2000). Personality and risk-taking: Common biosocial factors. *Journal of Personality, 68,* 999-1029.

Name Index

Subject Index

Note: **Boldface** page numbers indicate key terms. Italic page numbers indicate figures or tables.

A

Abilities, 77
Abnormality, **588**-589
Abnormal psychology, **588**
Academic achievement, 147-148
Acculturation, **534**
Achievement, 140
Achievement needs. *See* Need for achievement
Achievement view of intelligence, **393**
ACL, 24
Acquiescence, 39
ACT, 110
Act frequency research program, 60-61
Action tendencies, 402
Active genotype-environment correlation, 177
Activity level
 behavioral genetic research findings, 167-168
 mechanical recording devices, 31-32
 stability during childhood, 130-131
Activity measures, *131*
Act nomination, 60
Actometer, 31-32, 130
Acute stress, **568**
ADA, 112
Adaptation, **9**, 227-228
Adaptive problem, **227**, 520
Additive effects, **569**
Adjacency, **72**
Adjective Check List (ACL), 24
Adjustment domain, 14, 18, 634-635
Adoption studies, 165-166
Adult relationships, 323-327
Affect intensity, **429**-433
 AIM Questionnaire, **432**
 assessment of, 430-432
 high, 429
 low, 429
 research findings, 432-433
Affect Intensity Measure (AIM) Questionnaire, 432, **432**
Age, 592
Aggregation, **93**, 98-101
Aggression, 131-132, *132*, 477, 481
 evoked, 529-530
 Freud's basic instincts, and, 265
 sex differences, and, 239-241, 504, *504*, 505
Agreeableness, **78**, 503-505
 academic achievement, 147
 evocation of anger and upset in partners, 483

in five-factor model, 83
 marital satisfaction, 476
 marriage partner selection, 473
 mate selection, 474, 475-476
 mean level stability, 135, 136, 137
 rank order stability, 134
 sex differences, 503-505
 stability coefficients, 134
AIM Questionnaire, 432, **432**
Alarm stage, **565**
Alcoholism, 146-147
Alien, 353
Alpha press, **336**
Alpha wave, **217**
Altruism, 234-235
Ambition, 139
Ambivalently attached group, **322**
Ambivalent relationship style, **323**
American Beauty, 349, 458, 462
American Institute for Psychoanalysis, 318
Americans with Disabilities Act (ADA), 112
Amygdala, **446**
Anal stage, **284**
Analytic explanations, **536**
Androgyny, 509-514, **511**
Anger, 427, 477-480, 481-484
Anterior cingulate, **421**
Antibodies, *199*
Antisocial behavior, 175
Antisocial personality disorder, **593**-598, 619
Anxiety, **206**, 275-276, **358**
Anxious cluster of personality disorders, 610-615
Apperception, **336**-338
Approach-approach conflicts, 461
Approval Motive, The (Crowne/Marlowe), 40
Aptitude view of intelligence, 393
ARAS, **201**
Arousability, 203
Arousal level, 201
Arteriosclerosis, **582**
Ascending reticular activating system (ARAS), **201**
Asian culture, 542, 550
ASQ, 570
Assertiveness, 143
Assessment. *See* Personality assessment
Assessment of Men, The (Murray), 29
Association for Research in Personality, 626
Assortative mating, **473**
Attachment, **320**-323
Attend to information, 304
Attitudes, 169-170

Attitude traits, 72
Attraction similarity theory, **473**
Attributional style, 570-571
Attributional Style Questionnaire (ASQ), 570
Autonomic nervous system, **191**
Autonomous functioning, 175
Autonomy, 140
Autonomy *vs.* shame and doubt stage, 312
Average tendencies, **5**
Avoidantly attached group, **322**
Avoidant personality disorder, **610**-612
Avoidant relationship style, **323**

B

Balanced Inventory of Desirable Responding, 41
Balancing selection, **254**
Balkanization, **533**
Barnum statements, **104**-105
BAS, **204**, 205
Beats-per-minute (BPM), 192
Beck's cognitive theory, 424-426, 425
Behavioral activation system (BAS), **204**, 205
Behavioral genetics
 adoption studies, 165-166
 attitudes/preferences, 169-170
 biological domain, 629
 drinking/smoking, 170, 172
 family studies, 163
 goals of, 158-159
 marriage, 172-173
 methods used in, 161-166
 molecular genetics, 178-180
 personality traits, and, 167-169
 research findings, 167-173
 selective breeding, 162
 sexual orientation, 171-172
 shared *vs.* nonshared environmental influences, 173-175
 twin studies, 163-165
Behavioral inhibition system (BIS), **204**, 205, 596
Beliefs, **19**
Bell Curve, The (Herrnstein/Murray), 397
Belongingness needs, *350,* **353**
Beta press, **336**
Big Five traits. *See* Five-factor model
Biological Basis of Personality, The (Eysenck), 201
Biological domain, 14, 628-630
Bipolarity, **72**
BIS, **204**, 205, 596

Blame Externalization, 168
Blindsight, 268
Borderline personality disorder, **599**-601
BPM, 192
Brahman Indians, 531
Brain, 193-199
 connections, 197
 electrical activity, 199
 function, 194-195
 structure, 195
Brain asymmetry, 217-220
Bullying, 133
Byproducts of adaptations, **228**

C

CAH, 519
California Adult Q-Sort, 82
California Psychological Inventory (CPI), 26
 personnel selection, 113-114
 Saroka v. Dayton Hudson, 112
 workplace personality testing, 112
California Psychological Inventory Dominance scale, 30
California Q-Sort, 31
CAPS, 392-393
Cardiac reactivity, **193**
Cardiovascular activity, 192-193, *199*
Cardiovascular disease, 577-582
Carelessness, 102
Case studies, 49-51, *52*
Case study method, **49**
Castration anxiety, **285**
Casual sex, 508
Categorical approach, **403**
Categorical view, **589**
Cattell's 16 Personality Factor System. *See* 16 Personality Factor (16 PF) questionnaire
Causal attribution, **388**
CAVE, 570
Character traits, 72
Chemistry.com, 88
Chesapeake Bay retriever, 162
Children
 achievement motivation, and, 343-344
 attachment during childhood, 320-323
 temperament, and sex differences, 501-503
Child sexual abuse (CSA), 309-310
Chronic stress, **568**
Circadian rhythms, 212, *212*
Circumplex taxonomies of personality, 71-73